THE NEW INTERNATIONAL COMMENTARY
ON THE
OLD TESTAMENT

General Editors

E. J. YOUNG
(1965–1968)

R. K. HARRISON
(1968–1993)

ROBERT L. HUBBARD, JR.
(1994–)

The Book of PSALMS

NANCY DECLAISSÉ-WALFORD

ROLF A. JACOBSON

BETH LANEEL TANNER

WILLIAM B. EERDMANS PUBLISHING COMPANY
GRAND RAPIDS, MICHIGAN / CAMBRIDGE, U.K.

Published 2014 by
Wm. B. Eerdmans Publishing Co.
2140 Oak Industrial Drive N.E., Grand Rapids, Michigan 49505 /
P.O. Box 163, Cambridge CB3 9PU U.K.

Printed in the United States of America

20 19 18 17 16 15 14 7 6 5 4 3 2 1

Library of Congress Cataloging-in-Publication Data

DeClaissé-Walford, Nancy L., 1954-
The book of Psalms / Nancy DeClaissé-Walford, Rolf A. Jacobson, Beth Laneel Tanner.
pages cm. — (The New International commentary on the Old Testament)
ISBN 978-0-8028-2493-6 (cloth: alk. paper)
1. Bible. Psalms — Commentaries.
I. Jacobson, Rolf A. II. Tanner, Beth LaNeel, 1959- III. Title.

BS1430.53.D43 2014
223'.207 — dc23

2014012056

www.eerdmans.com

To:

William H. Bellinger, Jr.

Patrick D. Miller

J. J. M. Roberts

Our Teachers

Contents

TEXT AND COMMENTARY

General Editor's Preface

Long ago St. Paul wrote: "I planted, Apollos watered, but God gave the growth" (1 Cor. 3:6 NRSV). He was right: ministry indeed requires a team effort — the collective labors of many skilled hands and minds. Someone digs up the dirt and drops in seed, while others water the ground to nourish seedlings to growth. The same team effort over time has brought this commentary series to its position of prominence today. Professor E. J. Young "planted" it nearly fifty years ago, enlisting its first contributors and himself writing its first published volumes. Professor R. K. Harrison "watered" it, signing on other scholars and wisely editing everyone's finished products. As General Editor, I now tend their planting, and, true to Paul's words, through four decades God has indeed graciously "[given] the growth."

Today the New International Commentary on the Old Testament enjoys a wide readership of scholars, priests, pastors, rabbis, and other serious Bible students. Thousands of readers across the religious spectrum and in countless countries consult its volumes in their ongoing preaching, teaching, and research. They warmly welcome the publication of each new volume and eagerly await its eventual transformation from an emerging "series" into a complete commentary "set." But as humanity experiences a new century of history, an era commonly called "postmodern," what kind of commentary series is NICOT? What distinguishes it from other similarly well-established series?

Its volumes aim to publish biblical scholarship of the highest quality. Each contributor writes as an expert, both in the biblical text itself and in the relevant scholarly literature, and each commentary conveys the results of wide reading and careful, mature reflection. Ultimately, its spirit is eclectic, each contributor gleaning interpretive insights from any useful source, whatever its religious or philosophical viewpoint, and integrating them into his or her interpretation of a biblical book. The series draws on recent methodological innovations in biblical scholarship, for example, canon criticism, the so-called "new literary criticism," reader-response theories, and sensitivity to gender-based and ethnic readings. NICOT volumes also aim to be irenic in tone, summarizing and critiquing influential views with fairness while defending their own. Its list of contributors includes male and female scholars from a number of Christian faith-groups. The diversity of contributors and their freedom to draw on all relevant methodologies give the entire series an exciting and enriching variety.

What truly distinguishes this series, however, is that it speaks from within that interpretive tradition known as evangelicalism. Evangelicalism is an informal movement within Protestantism that cuts across traditional denominational lines. Its heart and soul is the conviction that the Bible is God's inspired Word, written by gifted human writers, through which God calls humanity to enjoy a loving personal relationship with its Creator and Savior. True to that tradition, NICOT volumes do not treat the Old Testament as just an ancient literary artifact on a par with the *Iliad* or *Gilgamesh.* They are not literary autopsies of ancient parchment cadavers but rigorous, reverent wrestlings with wonderfully human writings through which the living God speaks his powerful Word. NICOT delicately balances "criticism" (i.e., the use of standard critical methodologies) with humble respect, admiration, and even affection for the biblical text. As an evangelical commentary, it pays particular attention to the text's literary features, theological themes, and implications for the life of faith today.

Ultimately, NICOT aims to serve women and men of faith who desire to hear God's voice afresh through the Old Testament. With gratitude to God for two marvelous gifts — the Scriptures themselves and keen-minded scholars to explain their message — I welcome readers of all kinds to savor the good fruit of this series.

Robert L. Hubbard, Jr.

Acknowledgments

On a snowy night in 2001 at the Society of Biblical Literature Annual Meeting in Denver, Robert Hubbard and Allen Myers met with three relatively young psalm scholars to discuss the possibility of their authoring the NICOT commentary on the book of Psalms: Nancy deClaissé-Walford of the McAfee School of Theology; Rolf Jacobson, then of Augsburg College; and Beth LaNeel Tanner of New Brunswick Theological Seminary. Commentary writing can be something of a rite of passage for those of us in biblical studies. What a relief to share the task with others: none of us would have to provide translation, notes, and commentary on all 150 psalms! The euphoria quickly wore off as we each embarked on our self-assigned portions of the Psalter. What an undertaking! Years in the accomplishing.

With gratitude, we each acknowledge those who have supported and provided space, who have undertaken research and proofing work, and who have simply "been there." A myriad of students and members of the Society of Biblical Literature Book of Psalms Section have patiently and supportively listened to our lectures and presentations on the book of Psalms. We are grateful to all of them. Their questions and lively minds forced us to new horizons of interpretation that we would never have explored on our own.

From Nancy deClaissé-Walford:

I wish to express a debt of gratitude to three groups. First, for support and space, to Mercer University and to the Dean of the McAfee School of Theology, R. Alan Culpepper. In an academic environment of shrinking budgets, sabbatical leaves are coveted commodities. A sabbatical leave in the spring of 2007 allowed me to complete my portion of the commentary. Second, to Will Abney and Ben Curry, student workers who contributed valuable research and editing work. Third, and perhaps, most importantly, to those who have simply "been there." My husband Steve has been a relentlessly constant supporter of my vocation. My children, Calvin and Aaron, now adults, have always been interested in "what Mom is doing." To them, my undying love. And a final word of thanks for the wonderful collegial relationship with Rolf Jacobson and Beth Tanner that this project has fostered. It is a gift I will carry with me.

From Rolf Jacobson:

I am grateful to have the opportunity to thank the colleagues and administration at both Augsburg College and Luther Seminary. At Augsburg, I especially want to thank the scholarly writing group, who supported me and gave feedback early on during the process of writing the commentary. I am grateful to Luther Seminary for a sabbatical leave to work on the project. I am grateful to department colleagues at both Augsburg and Luther for their support and encouragement. I wish to express great gratitude to Megan Torgerson, Rachel Fuller Wrenn, and Daniel Stark — three of the best research assistants a person could ever have. Thanks also to the Wabash Center for Teaching and Learning in Theology and Religion for a study grant that helped fund early work on this commentary. Thanks also go to Beth and Nancy — for partnership, patience, and friendship. And my deepest thanks to my family, whose love means more to me than any career accomplishment: mom and dad, my first and best teachers; my sisters and brother — fellow students and great friends; and especially to my wife Amy and our children Ingrid and Gunnar, whose love sustains me. Finally, thanks be to God, who guides all our work and in whom we live, and move, and have our being.

From Beth Tanner:

I wish to add thanks to those who have guided me, especially Katharine Sakenfeld, mentor and friend who encouraged me to bring my insights as a woman to this work, and the anti-racism team at New Brunswick that showed me the importance of declaring myself as active anti-racist and to bring that perspective to my academic work. Many thanks to my colleagues at New Brunswick Theological Seminary for sabbatical support and encouragement and the Wabash Center for Teaching and Learning for providing a study grant for this work. Thanks also to all of my students who over the years have enlivened my work and taught me a great deal. Also to all members, past and present, of the SBL Book of Psalms group who have nurtured me from my graduate school days. I have a very fond place in my heart for all of you and I am proud to call you friends. Of course, many, many thanks to my family, Dan, Allison, and Nicholas, who have lived with this project along with me. I see your love for me every day, and that makes me truly blessed. Finally, to my Dad who set me on this course of academic study of religion by engaging me in theological debates at every opportunity.

Years removed from that snowy night in Denver, Nancy, Rolf, Beth, not so young anymore, are still grateful for the opportunity to participate in this undertaking. To Allen Myers and Robert Hubbard — your patience is above and beyond the call of duty. To Wm. B. Eerdmans Publishing Co. — thank you for trusting such an important volume to the three of us. To the readers of this commentary — all biblical commentary is conversation; you are invited to add your voices.

Nancy L. deClaissé-Walford
Atlanta, Georgia

Rolf A. Jacobson
St. Paul, Minnesota

Beth LaNeel Tanner
New Brunswick, New Jersey

Principal Abbreviations

AB	Anchor Bible
ABD	*Anchor Bible Dictionary,* ed. David Noel Freedman. 6 vols. New York, 1992
ABRL	Anchor Bible Reference Library
AJSL	*American Journal of Semitic Languages and Literature*
ANE	Ancient Near East(ern)
ANET	*Ancient Near Eastern Texts Relating to the Old Testament,* ed. James B. Pritchard. 3rd ed. Princeton, 1969
AnOr	Analecta orientalia
ATANT	Abhandlungen zur Theologie des Alten und Neuen Testaments
BAGD	W. Bauer, W. F. Arndt, F. W. Gingrich, and F. W. Danker, *Greek-English Lexicon of the New Testament and Early Christian Literature.* 2nd ed. Chicago, 1979
BASOR	*Bulletin of the American Schools of Oriental Research*
BDB	F. Brown, S. R. Driver, and C. A. Briggs, *A Hebrew and English Lexicon of the Old Testament.* Oxford, 1907
BeO	Bibbia e Oriente
BHQ	*Biblia Hebraica Quinta*
BHS	*Biblia Hebraica Stuttgartensia*
Bib	*Biblica*
BRL2	*Biblisches Reallexikon,* 2nd ed. Ed. Kurt Galling. Tübingen, 1977
BRS	Biblical Resource Series
BZAW	Beihefte zur Zeitschrift für die alttestamentliche Wissenschaft
CAD	*The Assyrian Dictionary of the Oriental Institute of the University of Chicago.* Chicago, 1956–
CBQ	*Catholic Biblical Quarterly*
CC	Continental Commentaries
ConBOT	Coniectanea biblica: Old Testament Series
COS	*The Context of Scripture,* ed. William W. Hallo and K. Lawson Younger, Jr. 3 vols. Leiden, 1997-2003

CTA	*Corpus des tablettes en cunéiformes alphabétiques découvertes à Ras Shamra-Ugarit de 1929 à 1939,* ed. Andrée Herdner. Paris, 1963
DDD	*Dictionary of Deities and Demons in the Bible,* ed. Karel van der Toorn, Bob Becking, and Pieter W. van der Horst. 2nd ed. Leiden and Grand Rapids, 1999
DJD	Discoveries in the Judaean Desert
ECC	Eerdmans Critical Commentary
EvQ	*Evangelical Quarterly*
ExpTim	*Expository Times*
FAT	Forschungen zum Alten Testament
FBBS	Facet Books, Biblical Series
FOTL	Forms of the Old Testament Literature
FRLANT	Forschungen zur Religion und Literatur des Alten und Neuen Testaments
GBS	Guides to Biblical Scholarship
GKC	*Gesenius' Hebrew Grammar,* ed. Emil Kautzsch, trans. A. E. Cowley. 2nd ed. Oxford, 1910
HALOT	Ludwig Koehler, Walter Baumgartner, and Johann Jakob Stamm, *The Hebrew and Aramaic Lexicon of the Old Testament.* 5 vols. Leiden, 1994-2000
HAT	Handbuch zum Alten Testament
HBT	*Horizons in Biblical Theology*
HKAT	Handkommentar zum Alten Testament
HSM	Harvard Semitic Monographs
HTR	*Harvard Theological Review*
HTS	Harvard Theological Studies
HUCA	*Hebrew Union College Annual*
Int	*Interpretation*
JBL	*Journal of Biblical Literature*
JSOT	*Journal for the Study of the Old Testament*
JSOTSup	Journal for the Study of the Old Testament: Supplement Series
JSS	*Journal of Semitic Studies*
JTS	*Journal of Theological Studies*
KAT	Kommentar zum Alten Testament
KBL	L. Koehler and W. Baumgartner, *Lexicon in Veteris Testamenti libros.* 2nd ed., Leiden, 1958
KTU	*Die keilalphabetischen Texte aus Ugarit,* ed. Manfred Dietrich, Oswald Loretz, and Joaquín Sanmartín. Neukirchen-Vluyn, 1976
LHB/OTS	Library of Hebrew Bible/Old Testament Studies
LW	Martin Luther, *Works*
LXX	Septuagint
MBS	Message of Biblical Spirituality

MT	Masoretic Text
NAB	New American Bible
NASB	New American Standard Bible
NEchtB	Neue Echter Bibel
NIB	*The New Interpreter's Bible*
NIBC	New International Biblical Commentary
NIV	New International Version
NJB	New Jerusalem Bible
NJPS	New Jewish Publication Society Version
NRSV	New Revised Standard Version
OBO	Orbis biblicus et orientalis
OBT	Overtures to Biblical Theology
OTL	Old Testament Library
OTS	Oudtestamentische Studiën
Pesh	Peshiṭta
RB	*Revue biblique*
RelSRev	*Religious Studies Review*
RevExp	*Review and Expositor*
S	Superscription
SBLDS	Society of Biblical Literature Dissertation Series
SBLMS	Society of Biblical Literature Monograph Series
SBLWAW	Society of Biblical Literature Writings from the Ancient World
SJOT	*Scandinavian Journal of the Old Testament*
SK	*Skrif en kerk*
SSN	Studia semitica neerlandica
St.	Stanza
STDJ	Studies on the Texts of the Desert of Judah
Syr	Syriac
Targ	Targum(im)
TDOT	*Theological Dictionary of the Old Testament,* ed. G. Johannes Botterweck, Helmer Ringgren, and Heinz-Josef Fabry. 17 vols. Grand Rapids, 1974–
THAT	*Theologisches Handwörterbuch zum Alten Testament,* ed. Ernst Jenni and Claus Westermann. 2 vols. Stuttgart, 1971-76
UF	*Ugarit-Forschungen*
VD	*Verbum domini*
VT	*Vetus Testamentum*
VTSup	Supplements to Vetus Testamentum
Vulg	Vulgate
WBC	Word Biblical Commentary
WMANT	Wissenschaftliche Monographien zum Alten und Neuen Testament

WTJ	*Westminster Theological Journal*
WW	*Word and World*
ZAW	*Zeitschrift für die alttestamentliche Wissenschaft*

Introduction

Martin Luther captured how central the psalms are to the life of faith, when he wrote that the Psalter

> might well be called a little Bible. In it is comprehended most beautifully and briefly everything that is in the entire Bible. It is really a fine enchiridion or handbook. In fact, I have a notion that the Holy Spirit wanted to take the trouble himself to compile a short Bible and book of examples of all Christendom or all saints, so that anyone who could not read the whole Bible would have anyway almost an entire summary of it, comprised in one little book.[1]

One of the reasons that the psalms are so beloved is that they express the full range of human emotions before God. The hymns of praise shout out the soaring joy of those who bear witness to God's faithfulness. The prayers for help give voice to the groaning pain of those who long for — but cannot find — a faithful God in their suffering. The poems of trust express the confident inner faith of those who trust, in spite of the quaking external realities all around. The songs of thanksgiving ring with the renewed song of those who have passed through a dark valley of crisis. The instructional psalms pass on the wisdom of those who have gone before to generations yet unborn. The imprecatory psalms cry out for justice against those who oppress. And the royal psalms bear witness to the mystery that God has chosen human beings as the agents through which God is at work in a broken world. Because the Psalter draws on the full range of human experiencing and emotions, William Brown has said that "the Psalter is . . . Scripture's most integrated corpus."[2]

This great diversity of emotion and perspective is the source of the

1. "Preface to the Psalter," trans. C. M. Jacobs, rev. E. T. Bachman, in *Luther's Works* (Philadelphia: Muhlenberg, 1960), p. 254.

2. *Seeing the Psalms* (Louisville: Westminster John Knox, 2002), p. 1.

Psalter's richness for believers. Because the Psalter is a collection of poetry, it does not have a plot in the same way that the narrative books of the Bible do. Nor does it have a central argument in the same way that the epistles of the New Testament do. Nor does it have a unified vision or source, as many of the prophetic books of the Old Testament do. Comprised of 150 compositions from many different authors, the Psalter more resembles a great choir of witnesses than it does a story, or letter, or collection of visions. The Psalter gives voice to the faith struggles, theological insights, and liturgical witnesses of many different people. For this reason and others, even though more than two thousand years separate us from the days when they were first written, the psalms continue to be central to the life of faith for both Christians and Jews. Near the beginning of life, people of faith memorize them as children at their mothers' feet. They sing or chant them when they come together for weekly worship. In times of trouble they recall the psalms' words of promise and hope. And to mark the end of life, they utter them solemnly when they bury their fathers.

As John Goldingay has aptly put it, the "Psalms make it possible to say things that are otherwise unsayable."[3] At times the psalms give us words to express anguish that we cannot bring ourselves to express. At other times they allow us to express the joy we feel, but to do so in a theological register. And at still other times, we do not sing them because they say or feel what we already believe or feel, but because by speaking them we can come to believe what they say, feel what they feel, and trust where they trust.

I. TITLE, TEXT, AND TRANSLATION

The English terms "Psalm" and "Psalter" are related to the Greek words *psalmoi* and *psaltērion.* The term *psalmos* is in turn a translation of Hebrew *mizmōr.* Both of these terms mean "song." The plural Greek form *psalmoi* occurs in the ancient manuscript Codex Vaticanus as the title for the book. Codex Alexendrinus employs *psaltērion,* which refers to a stringed instrument. The two terms accurately describe the contents of the book of Psalms — a set of songs that were at some point used in the worship life of ancient Israel or Judah. The Masoretic title of the collection is *tᵉhillîm,* literally, "praises," but more accurately "praise" (an abstract plural). This title does not occur in the Dead Sea Scrolls. Nor does the term, if construed narrowly, accurately describe the contents of the book, which include laments, liturgies, and instructional psalms. The redactional note at the end of Psalm 72 — *The prayers (tᵉp̱illôṯ) of*

3. *Psalms 1–41* (Grand Rapids: Baker, 2006), p. 22.

David, the son of Jesse, are ended — as well as the title that stands at the head of each of the Psalms from 120–34 — *The Songs of the Ascents (šîr hammaʿ^alôṯ)* — suggest that other Hebrew titles for collections of psalms were once used. But the term *praises (t^ehillîm)* does accurately caption the *telos* toward which both individual songs and the collection as a whole move — toward praise of the Lord. As James Limburg has written, "The two names preserved in Hebrew tradition, 'prayers' *(t^epillôṯ)* and 'songs of praise' *(t^ehillîm),* may be taken as representing two fundamental types of psalms: prayers in time of need, or laments, and songs of praise, or hymns."[4]

The quality of the Hebrew text of the psalms varies from psalm to psalm; some poems evidence little disturbance, while others show significant disturbance. Overall, the quality of the text may be said to be "fair."[5] The translation and commentary in this volume are based on the critical edition of the Hebrew text of the psalms in the *Biblia Hebraica Stuttgartensia (BHS). BHS* is based on the version of the Masoretic Text (MT) found in Codex Leningradensis (B19A or L), which is the oldest, complete extant manuscript of the Hebrew Bible. The codex is dated to about 1008 C.E., and the text claims that it was copied in Cairo from the manuscripts of the Ben Asher family of Masoretic scribes. Neither the planned Psalms volume in the *Biblia Hebraica Quinta (BHQ)* nor the new critical edition of the Hebrew Bible being prepared at the Hebrew University and to be based on the slightly older Codex Aleppo (which lacks Pss. 15:1–25:2) were yet available for our work.

It is often stated that the Masoretic Text of the Psalter contains 150 psalms — and, in fact, the Psalter presented in *BHS* does present a 150-poem lay-out. But recent research by William Yarchin has shown the matter is not so clear.[6] Yarchin has shown that both Codex Aleppo and Codex Leningrad divide the verses of the Psalter into 149 psalms. They do this by conjoining Psalms 114 and 115 into a single psalm. Yarchin has examined roughly 400 Psalter manuscripts from the medieval period — dating from Codex Aleppo (ca. 930 C.E.) to the First Rabbinic Bible (1517). Yarchin has discovered at what he calls the level of "the semantic content" — of individual words and sentences — the texts of these roughly 400 MT Psalters are stable; they share

4. James Limburg, "Psalms, Book of," *ABD* 5:523.

5. So P. Kyle McCarter, *Textual Criticism: Recovering the Text of the Hebrew Bible* (GBS; Philadelphia: Fortress, 1986), p. 92.

6. William Yarchin, "Is There an Authoritative Shape for the Book of Psalms? Profiling the Manuscripts of the Hebrew Psalter," paper presented at the 16th World Congress of Jewish Studies, Hebrew University, Jerusalem, July 2013. "Why Were the Psalms the First Bible Chapters to Be Numbered?" paper presented at the 21st Congress of the International Organization for the Study of the Old Testament in Munich, Germany, August 2013. "Was 11Q5 a True Psalter?" paper presented at the annual meeting of the Society of Biblical Literature, November 2013.

essentially the same words. But at the level of dividing the words and sentences into different psalms, these MT Psalters show great diversity. Only 84 of the Psalters (about 21 percent) divide the psalms into the configuration that is presented in *BHS*. The other 79 percent of manuscripts divide the verses of the Psalter into anywhere from 143 poems to 154 poems.[7] It is clear that from ancient days, scribes recognized that there are many different poems in the Psalter: the various superscriptions at the head of many psalms, the reference in Acts 13:33 to "the second psalm," and the line spaces between psalms in the Dead Sea psalm scrolls all indicate that ancient scribes differentiated between various psalms in the Psalter. But the delineation of the Psalter into the 150 as we have become accustomed to dividing them did not become standard until the invention of the movable-type printing press and the publication of the First and Second Rabbinic Bibles. The movable-type printing press provided the technology that stabilized the arrangement of the Psalter. The results of Yarchin's important research will have to be considered carefully by psalm scholarship — especially for those scholars who investigate the meaning and authority of the canonical "shape and shaping" of the Psalter. In this commentary, we have chosen to honor the traditional 150-psalm division, because this configuration has provided the shape of the psalter that has been standard for the last 500 years. But Yarchin's warning about assuming the authority of this division is worth pondering: "the assumption of the [now traditional 150-poem shape of the] *sefer tehillim* as the authoritative or standard shape of the Hebrew Psalter is not supported by the body of Hebrew manuscript evidence. It is rather a product of the efforts by early modern editors to create a standard text. Inasmuch as critical biblical scholarship does not restrict itself to the [now traditional shape of the Psalter], the manuscript evidence invites scholars to bring their exegetical skills to bear on psalm compositions well-attested in the manuscripts but eclipsed by the [now traditional Psalter]."[8]

Interpretation and text criticism of the MT are greatly enhanced by the discoveries that were made in the Judean Desert (known as the Dead Sea Scrolls) as well as by ancient translations of the psalms, especially the Greek translation that is popularly known as the Septuagint (but more properly called the Old Greek edition). Among the Dead Sea Scrolls, "at least thirty-nine . . . are Psalms scrolls or manuscripts containing Psalms; thirty-six were discovered at Qumran, two at Masada; and one at Nahal Ḥever."[9]

7. Yarchin notes that 33 of these MT Psalters present 150 psalms, but delineate those 150 differently than the way that we have become accustomed to dividing them. These 33 manuscripts in turn have 23 different configurations of the 150 psalms.

8. Yarchin, "Is There an Authoritative Shape for the Book of Psalms?" p. 14.

9. Peter W. Flint, *The Dead Sea Psalms Scrolls and the Book of Psalms* (STDJ 17; Leiden: Brill, 1997), p. 2.

In addition, there are other occasional witnesses to the psalms among the Dead Sea Scrolls, among the various sectarian manuscripts, *florilegia, pesherim,* etc. Although all of these psalms scrolls are significantly damaged and many are fragmentary, the scrolls yield a significant quantity of verses. The most significant scrolls, in descending order of importance, are 11QPs^{a}, 4QPs^{a}, 5/6Ḥev-Se4 Ps, 4QPs^{b}, 4QPs^{c}, and 4QPs^{e}. The critical editions of these manuscripts (particularly the *Discoveries in the Judaean Desert,* volumes IV and XI) as well as the careful cataloging work by Peter Flint are invaluable resources for interpretation, text criticism, and translation of the psalms. The critical edition of the Septuagint version of the Psalter prepared at the University of Göttingen is also invaluable.[10] The Greek version is particularly helpful because the ancient translators' preference for literal, nonidiomatic Greek makes the task of retroverting which Hebrew text the translators were reading more manageable.

Since the publication of the Second Rabbinic Bible in 1524-25, the so-called Masoretic Text as presented in *BHS* has been the standard text of the Psalter that communities of faith have read, or it has been the text upon which the vernacular translations that communities of faith have read are based.[11] For that reason, the approach to text criticism in this commentary is not to try to establish the illusive "original" text of each psalm as it came from the pen of an original scribe. Rather, the text-critical task as understood here is to establish the text of each psalm as it may have been at the beginning of the Masoretic tradition. While it is clear that for many, if not most, of the psalms the texts evolved between the time when the texts originated and the start of the Masoretic tradition, we have chosen not to reconstruct the hypothetical original texts, since those texts have not been the canonical texts of the communities of faith. As Brevard Childs wrote, at the textual level, the concern is "to describe the literature in terms of relation to the historic Jewish community rather than . . . [seeking a] reconstruction of the most original form of the book, or the most pristine form of the textual tradition."[12] For the purposes of this commentary, this Jewish community is conceived broadly as the international Yahwistic community that centered its life toward Jerusalem between the late Persian/early Hellenistic period and the start of the Christian era. In terms of establishing the texts as they may have existed at the start of the Masoretic tradition, Bruce Waltke's venerable description of

10. *Septuaginta: Psalmi cum Odis,* ed. Alfred Rahlfs (2nd ed.; Göttingen: Vandenhoeck & Ruprecht, 1967).

11. See Emanuel Tov, *Textual Criticism of the Hebrew Bible* (2nd rev. ed.; Minneapolis: Fortress, 2001), pp. 22-25.

12. *Introduction to the Old Testament as Scripture* (Philadelphia: Fortress, 1979), pp. 96-97.

the text-critical task in relation to the Old Testament is helpful, at least heuristically.[13] As Waltke wrote, "The text critic's aim will vary according to the nature of the [biblical] book. If a book had but one author, then the critic will aim to restore his original composition; if it be an edited text then he will seek to recover the final, canonical text."[14] It should be noted, however, that the task is more than merely a matter of reading Codex Leningradensis. It is clear that a certain amount of textual development has occurred since the start of the Masoretic tradition and that some of the readings and texts preserved in Codex Leningradensis are corrupt. For this reason, the effort to compare readings and to attempt textual recovery is necessary. The textual critic engages in this effort knowing that the work will never be perfect, but trusting that it is both unavoidable and, one hopes, edifying to at least some degree.

Throughout the long history of the psalms, the way the psalms have been numbered has varied. As noted earlier, Yarchin has discovered that prior to 1517 the poems of the Hebrew Psalter were configured in many different ways — from as few as 143 different psalms to as many as 154. Yarchin is currently investigating medieval Greek and Latin psalms manuscripts to learn if a similar diversity of psalm arrangement exists in those manuscript traditions. But the "standard" arrangement of the LXX Psalter numbers the psalms slightly differently than in *BHS:*

MT in *BHS*	LXX
1–8	1–8
9–10	9
11–113	10–112
114–15	113
116:1-9	114
116:10-19	115
117–46	116–45
147:1-11	146
147:12-20	147
148–50	148–50

In addition, the LXX includes Psalm 151, whose superscription introduces it as a "genuine psalm of David" *(idiographos eis dayid),* but one that is "outside the number" *(exōthen tou arithmou).* The latter phrase indicates that by the time of the Psalter's translation into Greek (most likely at least a century

13. "Aims of OT Textual Criticism," *WTJ* 51 (1989) 93-108. In terms of Waltke's five "aims" of textual critics, our approach falls closest to his fourth option, restoring the accepted text.

14. Waltke, "Aims of OT Textual Criticism," p. 107.

before the Common Era) the internal order and division of the psalms were still fluid. Within the Hebrew textual traditions, the various psalms manuscripts discovered at Qumran support the conclusion that the internal order and even the content of the Psalter were not fixed at the turn of the eras. This fluidity is especially apparent towards the end of the Psalter, indicating that the Psalter generally evolved from the front toward back, with the first part of the Psalter stabilizing earlier. Peter Flint has observed that for Psalms 1–89, no deviations in content and only two deviations in arrangement have been discovered at Qumran. "But for Psalms 90 and beyond disagreements with the Received Text are far more extensive, both in terms of the ordering of material and the presence of compositions not found in the MT-150 Psalter."[15] In this commentary, as noted above, we follow the *BHS* contents and order (although in some cases, such as Psalm 9/10, we find the LXX division persuasive and helpful).

In terms of verse numbering, for those psalms that have a superscription, the MT numbers the superscription as v. 1. In the dominant English-language tradition, since the KJV the dominant system of verse numbering has been *not* to number the superscriptions. This has created minor confusion when referring to verse numbers. In this commentary, we follow the traditional English versification, including when Hebrew forms are cited.

In keeping with the format of the NICOT series, for each psalm the commentary provides a new translation with critical notes. To the extent possible, the translations offer as literal a translation of the poetry as possible. We have preferred inclusive language for humanity where it was possible to do so without disrupting the poetry of the psalms too greatly. For the sake of gender inclusivity, some English translations (such as the NRSV) have chosen to change singular, masculine nouns and their associated pronouns into plural nouns and pronouns — thus, the "man" *('îš)* and "he" of Psalm 1 are changed into "those." In order to retain the poetic sense of the singular pronouns, we have opted for more generic terms such as "the one" — thus, *Happy is the one who does not walk in the counsel of the wicked* (1:1). For the proper name of God, YHWH, we have used "The LORD," following the centuries-long model for most English translations.

One peculiarity of this commentary is that we have opted not to translate the Hebrew term *ḥeseḏ,* but simply to transliterate *hesed* and treat it as a loanword from Hebrew to English — similar to "shalom" (from Hebrew), "aloha" (from Hawaiian), "aria" (from Italian), or "el Nino" (from Spanish). Loanwords enter a culture when there is no term or pair of terms in the borrowing language that can adequately render the meaning of an important term from the source language. That is undoubtedly the case with the He-

15. *The Dead Sea Psalms Scrolls and the Book of Psalms,* p. 141.

brew theological term *hesed.* Traditionally, a wide range of English terms have been employed in the attempt to capture the meaning of *hesed:* "mercy," "loving-kindness," "steadfast love," "faithfulness," "covenantal love," "loving faithfulness," and the like. We find that none of these words or phrases satisfactorily express the range and depth of *hesed.* While this is true of many words in many languages, we believe that for the word *hesed,* the difference in degree amounts to a difference in kind. *Hesed* includes elements of love, mercy, fidelity, and kindness. *Hesed* is a relational term that describes both the *internal character* as well as the *external actions* that are required to maintain a life-sustaining relationship. While the term is used of both humans and God, in the Psalter it is above all a theological term that describes God's essential character as well as God's characteristic ways of acting — especially God's characteristic ways of acting in electing, delivering, and sustaining the people of Israel. *Hesed* is both who the Lord is and what the Lord does. *Hesed* is an ancient term that defined for Israel who its God is. The centrality and ancient nature of the term is witnessed in the ancient, creedal fragment in Exodus 34, where the Lord passes in front of Moses and proclaims,

> The LORD, the LORD,
> a God merciful and gracious,
> slow to anger,
> and abounding in steadfast love *(hesed)* and faithfulness. (v. 6)

The centrality of the term in the Psalter is made apparent by the fact that of the 255 times the term *hesed* occurs in the Old Testament, 130 of those occurrences are in the Psalter. Gerhard von Rad wrote that the term "designates an attitude required by fellowship and includes a disposition and an attitude of solidarity . . . so it expresses . . . beneficent personal disposition plus the actions that follow."[16] The *relational nature of the term* cannot be overemphasized. It describes the duties, benefits, and commitments that one party bears to another party as a result of the relationship between them. The Lord's *hesed* is the basis on which the psalmist dares to ask for deliverance and forgiveness. The Lord's *hesed* describes how and why the Lord created and sustains the good creation. The Lord's *hesed* is that to which the hymns of praise and songs of thanksgiving bear witness. The Lord's *hesed* is what the wisdom psalms teach. And *hesed* is the most important characteristic that God desires to see embodied both in individuals and in the communities that pray the psalms.

In the text of our commentary, to serve the aims of inclusive language, we have alternated between referring to the psalmist as "he" and as "she." This alternation was done on either a paragraph-by-paragraph or section-

16. *Old Testament Theology,* trans. D. M. G. Stalker (New York: Harper & Row, 1962), 1:372 n. 6.

by-section basis. While it is likely that most of the ancient psalmists were men, we allow for the possibility that at least one of the psalmists may have been a woman.[17] In addition, this convention is consistent with the fact that throughout the centuries, both women and men have borrowed the language of the psalms to pray as their own prayers.

II. AUTHORSHIP, SUPERSCRIPTIONS, AND DATE

A. AUTHORSHIP

"The Psalms conceal their origins. It is thus an odd fact that study of the Psalms in both the premodern and modern periods paid considerable attention to their authorship and historical background."[18] John Goldingay's ironic insight is true not only for the psalms, but for much of the biblical corpus. Most of the books of the Bible are anonymous, and most originally lacked titles. But humans seem both to love a good mystery and to have a need to put a name on an anonymous work. This is true both of the Psalter in general, as well as the individual psalms.

Beginning in antiquity, communities of faith began to associate the Psalter with King David. This association most likely began because of the link between the tradition of David as a musician (1 Sam. 16:14ff.) and the nature of the psalms as songs. In the Talmud, it is stated that "David wrote the Book of Psalms, including in it the work of the elders, namely, Adam, Melchizedek, Abraham, Moses, Heman, Yeduthun, Asaph, and the three sons of Korah" (*b. Bava Batra* 14b-15a). In this tradition of interpretation of Davidic authorship, the superscriptions (particularly the superscription *lᵉḏāwiḏ*) are taken as expressing authorship (more on this issue momentarily). Throughout premodern interpretation of the psalms, David was assumed to be the author of those psalms that began with the superscription *lᵉḏāwiḏ,* and often was taken as the author of many of the psalms that lacked this superscription. The New Testament also associates David with the psalms (e.g., Mark 12:35-37; Acts 2:33-35). The Septuagint, Syriac, and Qumran Psalters indicate that this tradition was expanding very early — they include the Davidic superscription before psalms that lack it in the MT (e.g., Psalm 95).

We decided to translate the superscriptions in which a *lamedh* is prefixed to a personal name by attaching an *-ic* or *-ite* suffix to the name: thus, "Davidic," "Mosaic," "Solomonic," "Asaphite," and "Korahite." We believe

17. See Patrick D. Miller, *They Cried to the Lord* (Minneapolis: Fortress, 1994), ch. 6.

18. Goldingay, *Psalms 1–41,* p. 25.

that this solution more accurately communicates the ranges of interpretive options. We believe that it is likely that the superscription *l*^{e}*ḏāwiḏ* did not originally indicate authorship — particularly, it did not originally indicate authorship by King David. There are several reasons for this conclusion. The primary reason is the many anachronisms in the psalms that preclude the idea of Davidic authorship. The most obvious of these anachronisms are the frequent references to the temple (Pss. 23:6; 27:4; 36:8), which was built after David's time. In addition, there are many other theological, historical, and cultic anachronisms. At the most basic linguistic level, the superscription *l*^{e}*ḏāwiḏ* need not imply Davidic authorship. In Old Testament Hebrew, the name David itself does not always refer to the founder of the Judean dynasty, but can refer to the Judean people (Isa. 55:3), the Davidic dynasty (Jer. 23:5; Ezek. 37:25), or the expected future ideal Davidic king (Jer. 30:9; Hos. 3:5). The Hebrew phrase *l*^{e}*ḏāwiḏ* is translated most literally "to David" (the preposition *lamed* in its most generic sense means "to"). If the *lamed* is understood as indicating possession ("belonging to"), it is plausible to interpret it as indicating authorship. But a more likely construal of the *lamed* of possession would be as indicating that the psalm in question belonged to a group of psalms that belonged to the royal temple in Jerusalem: "belonging to the Davidic temple." For the temple as a royal possession, cf. Amos 7:13, where Amaziah asserts that the temple in Bethel was a royal possession. The use of the *lamed* in 1 Kgs. 14:11, "anyone belonging to Jeroboam who dies in the city" *(hammēṯ l*^{e}*yārāḇ*$^{e‘}$*ām bā‘îr),* as well as the common superscription found at the heads of Psalms 44–47, 49, 84–85 (*lamnaṣṣēaḥ liḇnê qōrâḥ,* "belonging to the sons of Korah") support the interpretation.[19] Alternatively, the preposition may indicate that a psalm was composed "in honor of," "dedicated to," or "inspired by" the king. In the MT, thirteen psalms of David include what scholars refer to as "historical superscriptions" — brief narratives that associate a psalm with a specific incident in David's life (although to which incident is not always clear, or else the psalms are referring to a tradition about David that was not preserved in the Bible). These are Psalms 3, 7, 18, 34, 51, 52, 54, 56, 57, 59, 60, 63, and 142. These superscriptions should not be understood as indicating the occasion on which the psalms in question were composed, but rather as a clue to the early interpretation of them.[20] The

19. For a defense of the traditional interpretation that the *lamed* implies authorship, see Bruce Waltke, "Superscripts, Postscripts, or Both," *JBL* 110 (1991) 583-96. Waltke cites Isa. 38:9 and Hab. 3:1 and quotes with approval the conclusion of J. F. A. Sawyer ("An Analysis of the Context and Meaning of the Psalm-Headings," *Transactions of the Glasgow University Oriental Society* 22 [1970] 26): "it can scarcely be doubted that the meaning of *ldwd* was 'by David.' . . ."

20. For more on this issue, see James D. Nogalski, "Reading David in the Psalter," *HBT* 23 (2001) 168-91; Melody D. Knowles, "The Flexible Rhetoric of Retelling: The Choice

approach taken in this commentary is that, for practical purposes, all of the psalms are anonymous. They are interpreted as generic poem-prayers that have been transmitted from generation to generation, so that people of *a generation yet unborn* may pray and sing them.

B. SUPERSCRIPTIONS

The issue of Davidic authorship and the meaning of *lᵉdāwiḏ* raises the more general issue of the interpretation of the psalm superscriptions. Of the 150 poems in the Psalter, only 34 lack a superscription. In the LXX, which is generally expansionistic in the superscriptions, only 17 psalms lack a superscription.[21] As already suggested, the superscriptions are not part of the texts of the psalms per se, but are later editorial additions. The superscriptions have been much debated.[22] The hymn that closes the book of Habakkuk (Hab. 3:2-19) has both an introduction ("a prayer of the prophet Habakkuk according to the Shigionoth") and a conclusion ("to the leader: with stringed instruments") and so gives some clues about the meaning and history of the superscripts. It may indicate that part or all of the various psalm superscriptions originally were postscripts rather than superscripts. Thus, the phrase "to the leader: according to the lilies" *(lamnaṣṣēaḥ ʿal šōšannîm)* in the Hebrew text of Psalm 45 may originally have been a concluding postscript to Psalm 44. And the following words — "of the Korahites. A Maskil. A love song" *(liḇnê qōraḥ maśkîl šîr yᵉḏîḏōṯ)* — may originally have been an introductory superscript for Psalm 45. The concluding editorial note to Psalm 72, "the prayers of David the son of Jesse are ended," as well as the concluding doxologies following Psalms 41, 72, 89, and 106 further support the idea that — at least originally — parts or all of the superscriptions were actually postscripts. But, that said, the superscriptions have come down to us in the final canonical form of the Psalter at the head of the various psalms, and that is where they appear in this translation and commentary.

It is further important to note that many of the terms in the superscriptions are either partially or wholly obscure. Most of the words used can be categorized as indicating (1) the subcollection to which the psalm belongs, (2) directions for the liturgical/musical performance of the psalm, (3) the psalm's genre, and (4) historical information.

---

of David in the Text of the Psalms," *CBQ* 67 (2005) 235-49; Rolf Rendtorff, "The Psalms of David: David in the Psalms," in *The Book of Psalms*, ed. Peter W. Flint and Patrick D. Miller (VTSup 99; Leiden: Brill, 2005), pp. 53-66.

21. For a discussion of the superscriptions in the LXX, see Albert Pietersma, "Septuagintal Exegesis and the Superscriptions of the Greek Psalter," in Flint and Miller, *The Book of Psalms*, pp. 443-75.

22. See Waltke, "Superscripts, Postscripts, or Both," and bibliography there.

1. Subcollection Identification (Authorship?). The most frequent type of superscription refers to the person or persons with whom a particular psalm is to be associated. As argued above, we believe that these superscriptions indicate with which subcollection of the Psalter a psalm should be associated, but many interpreters believe that this category indicates authorship. The terms that indicate the various subcollections are: *lᵉḏāwiḏ (of David* or *Davidic;* 73 Psalms), *liḇnê qōraḥ (of the sons of Korah* or *Korahitic;* Psalms 42, 44–49, 84–85, 87–88), *lišlōmōh (of Solomon* or *Solomonic;* Psalms 72, 127), *lᵉʾāsāp̱ (of Asaph* or *Asaphite;* Psalms 50, 73–83), *lᵉʾêṯān hāʾezrāḥî (of Ethan the Ezrahite;* Psalm 89), *lᵉhêmān hāʾezrāḥî (of Heman the Ezrahite;* Psalm 88, according to the MT, is also marked as belonging to the collection of the *sons of Korah,* so it might be that the Ezraites were a group of priest musicians related to the Korahites), *lᵉmōšeh (of Moses* or *Mosaic;* Psalm 90), *šîr hammaʿălôṯ (a song of ascending;* it is clearly a subcollection of psalms, but one that was apparently assembled from psalms that originally belonged to other collections, such as *Davidic* [122] and *Solomonic* [127]).
2. Directions for Liturgical/Musical Performance. Many superscriptions include terms that are not fully understood, but which probably referred in some way to the performance of the psalm in worship. The term *lamnaṣṣēaḥ (for the leader;* see note on Ps. 4:1) occurs at the head of fifty-five psalms. It may indicate a subcollection of psalms, but more likely is a reference or direction for some liturgical leader. Waltke follows Sawyer in defining the term as "to be recited by the official in charge."[23] The phrase *for the servant of the* LORD appears to modify the term in Psalm 18. Some terms may indicate the type of music or musical instruments that should accompany a psalm. For the most part, the precise meaning of the terms is unknown, so we have often opted to transliterate them. If we have used a translation, that translation is given in the parentheses: *biḡînôṯ/biḡînaṯ/ʿal nᵉḡînaṯ (with stringed instruments;* Psalms 4, 6, 54–55, 61, 67, 76; cf. 69:13 and 77:7); *ʿalmûṯ labbēn* (Psalm 9); *ʿal ʿᵃlāmôṯ* (Psalm 46); *ʿal haššᵉmînîṯ* (Psalms 6, 12); *ʾel hannᵉḥîlôṯ* (*upon the flutes;* Psalm 5); *ʿal hāggittîṯ* (Psalms 8, 81, 84); *ʿal ʾayyeleṯ haššaḥar* (Psalm 22); *ʿal šōšannîm* (Psalms 45 and 69); *ʿal māḥᵃlaṯ* (Psalms 53 and 88); *ʿal šûšan ʿēḏûṯ/ʿal šōšannîm ʿēḏûṯ* (Psalms 60 and 80); *ʿal yônaṯ ʾēlem rᵉḥōqim* (Psalm 56); *šiggāyôn* (Psalm 7; the term might refer to the genre of the poem); and *lîdûṯûn/ʿal yᵉḏûṯûn* (Psalms 39, 62, and 77). Other terms seem to indicate a particular occasion for a psalm to be used: *ḥᵃnukkaṯ habbayiṯ (for the dedication of the temple* — perhaps an early reference to commemorating Hanukkah; Psalm 30); *lᵉyôm haššabāṯ (for the day*

23. Waltke, "Postscripts, Superscripts, or Both," p. 586.

of the Sabbath; Psalm 92); *lᵉṯôḏâ (for thanksgiving;* Psalm 100); and *A prayer for an afflicted person, when faint and pouring out one's plea before the Lord* (Psalm 102). In addition, the phrase *'al tāšḥēṯ,* literally "do not destroy" and presumed to be a direction regarding the preservation of the psalm, may in fact be a liturgical direction (Psalms 57–59, 75).

3. Indication of Genre. Some terms in the superscriptions seem to indicate the poem's genre — although it should be noted that these terms do not always seem to match perfectly with the form of the following psalm (at least in terms of what modern form critics might expect). These terms include: *mizmôr (psalm;* the term appears at the head of 57 psalms, including psalms of many genres; thus it may be a generic term for a prayer-poem); *šîr (song;* the term appears at the head of 31 songs and is likely a referent to a song of praise); *tᵉp̄illâ (prayer;* Psalms 17, 86, 90, 102, 142 — a term that seems to refer to a prayer for help); *tᵉhillâ (praise;* Psalm 145); *maśkîl* (Psalms 32, 42, 44–45, 52–55, 74, 78, 88–89, 142; the meaning of the term is unknown); *miḵtām* (the term may refer to a liturgical direction or to the nature of the text — an "engraving" — rather than to a genre, but its meaning is unknown; Psalms 16, 56–60).
4. Historical Superscriptions. As noted above, thirteen psalms bear so-called historical superscriptions that relate the poems in some way to the life of David. These are Psalms 3, 7, 18, 34, 51, 52, 54, 56, 57, 59, 60, 63, and 142.

III. FORM CRITICISM AND HISTORICAL APPROACHES TO INTERPRETATION

During the past century, interpretation of the Psalter has been dominated by an interpretive approach known as form criticism. As Patrick Miller noted some years ago: "Form-critical study of the psalms has dominated, if not controlled, the way in which this part of Scripture has been handled during this century — a fact that is as evident in popular treatments of the psalms and commentaries as it is in the scholarly literature."[24] In this approach, the first task of interpretation is to understand the genre (or "form") of a poem. Once a poem is properly categorized, interpretation of its actual words flows from this categorization. The dominance of this approach can be seen in the reality that many introductory textbooks are predominantly organized around the genres of the psalms.[25]

24. *Interpreting the Psalms* (Philadelphia: Fortress, 1986), p. 3.

25. E.g., Miller, *Interpreting the Psalms;* J. Clinton McCann, *A Theological Introduction*

Form-critical approaches have many strengths. The psalms are highly conventional, with many of the poems following predictable (or at least recognizable) patterns. Based on these patterns, it is possible to group the psalms into broad categories, such as hymns of praise, songs of thanksgiving, or prayers for help and the like (see below). Form-critical interpretation pays attention to the common patterns that emerge from comparing the psalms and interprets each psalm as an example of a known type of psalm. This commentary is dependent on the insights of form criticism, but also recognizes the limits of the approach. For example, by grouping psalms into categories, form-critical approaches often pay more attention to the forest (for example, the category of "praise") than they do to the individual tree (for example, the artistry and witness of a given praise psalm). In addition, a great many of the psalms contain elements of more than one of the identified forms. Form-critical approaches have at times been confused about how to deal with these psalms. At times form critics have solved this dilemma by labeling such psalms as "mixtures" or "mixed-type psalms."[26] At other times, form critics have resorted to the unhappy alternative of simply dividing a psalm in half. Artur Weiser, for example, wrote separate commentaries on Psalms "19A" and "19B." Frustrated by the mixture of genres in one psalm, he wrote: "Why these . . . dissimilar psalms were united in one single psalm cannot any longer be established with any degree of certainty."[27] The problems of these two solutions should be obvious. Any interpretive approach that leads either to bifurcating a poem that at least at one point in history made sense to someone or to creating a "catch-all" genre such as "mixed-type" is an interpretive approach with obvious limitations.

Two broad approaches to form-critical interpretation of the Psalter have existed. In the first, the "forms" of the psalms were studied in order to "get behind" the texts of the psalms to the "life settings" that produced the forms. The pioneer of form criticism was Hermann Gunkel.[28] Gunkel believed that liturgical forms emerge from settings — that particular occasions in life

---

to the Book of Psalms (Nashville: Abingdon, 1993); Claus Westermann, *The Psalms: Structure, Content & Message* (Minneapolis: Augsburg, 1980); Bernhard W. Anderson, *Out of the Depths: The Psalms Speak for Us Today* (3rd ed.; Philadelphia: Westminster, 1983). Exceptions to this approach are Nancy deClaissé-Walford, *Introduction to the Psalms: A Song from Ancient Israel* (St. Louis: Chalice, 2004); and Alastair G. Hunter, *An Introduction to the Psalms* (London: T. & T. Clark, 2008).

26. See, e.g., Hermann Gunkel, *Introduction to Psalms: The Genres of the Religious Lyric of Israel,* completed by Joachim Begrich, trans. James D. Nogalski (Macon: Mercer University Press, 1998), pp. 306-10.

27. *The Psalms: A Commentary,* trans. Herbert Hartwell (OTL; Philadelphia: Westminster, 1962), p. 197.

28. See his *Introduction to Psalms.*

exist that include particular needs, and that liturgical "forms" evolve to meet the needs of those moments. To use a modern example, bestowing a public award such as an Oscar is a life setting that has required the evolution of the "form" of the "public, thank-you speech." If the award ceremony did not exist, the genre of the public, thank-you speech would not have developed. Regarding the psalms, Gunkel wrote, "we may dare to presume that [the Psalms] arose in the cult of Israel originally."[29] For Gunkel, a genre or "form" implies a specific life setting out of which it evolved and from which it could not be abstracted. In Gunkel's view, in order to properly understand a liturgical text, one has to imagine the cultic life setting that created it and to interpret it in that life setting. It is important to note, however, that Gunkel also believed the majority of psalms in the Psalter were not genuine literary artifacts that had been used in ancient worship; rather, they were literary creations — imitations of the "forms" that had developed in the cultic life setting. At any rate, one can see that for Gunkel, by imagining the settings that produced the ancient forms, the scholar could penetrate the mists of history and recover earlier, preliterary stages of the poems of the Psalter.

Sigmund Mowinckel developed and diverged from Gunkel's form-critical approach to the psalms. Mowinckel disagreed with Gunkel's argument that many or most of the psalms were imitations of actual worship texts. Mowinckel argued for an approach that set each of the psalms "in relation to the definite cultic act . . . to which it belonged."[30] Mowinckel identified many of the psalms within an annual New Year's "Enthronement of YHWH Festival."[31] Mowinckel's approach has been called the "cult-functional method." His views were quite persuasive for a time and spawned a series of imitators. Weiser, for example, placed many of the psalms in an annual covenant-renewal festival: "the cult of the covenant festival is to be assumed as the [life setting] of the vast majority of the individual Psalms and their categories."[32] Other similar proposals were developed.[33] Mowinckel's proposals, especially regarding the New Year's Festival, have largely lost their appeal.[34] But Mowinckel's reassertion that the texts of the psalms are actual

29. Gunkel, *Introduction to Psalms,* p. 7.

30. *The Psalms in Israel's Worship,* trans. D. R. Ap-Thomas (BRS; Grand Rapids: Eerdmans and Livonia: Dove, 2004), 1:23.

31. *Psalmenstudien II: Thronbesteigungsfest Jahwäs und der Ursprung der Eschatologie,* (Kristiania: Dybwald, 1922). He placed Pss. 47, 93, 95–100, 8, 15, 24, 29, 33, 46, 48, 50, 66A, 75, 76, 81, 82, 84, 87, 118, 132, 149, 120–34, 65, 67, and 85 in this hypothetical setting.

32. Weiser, *The Psalms,* p. 18.

33. See, e.g., the work of Aubrey Johnson, *The Cultic Prophet and Israel's Psalmody* (Cardiff: University of Wales Press, 1979).

34. Although see J. J. M. Roberts's positive reassessment of Mowinckel's proposal in "Mowinckel's Enthronement Festival: A Review," in Flint and Miller, *The Book of Psalms,*

prayer-poems and not imitations of prior cultic forms has been a contribution that is often overlooked.

Erhard Gerstenberger has been another important figure in the form-critical approach that sought to study the forms to get behind the texts to the life settings that produced the forms. Gerstenberger argued that "psalmic texts and psalmody served the needs of a religious community."[35] And further: "Form-critical work must not content itself with an analysis of linguistic patterns. . . . it must take into account customary life situations and their distinctive speech forms."[36] But unlike Mowinckel, Kraus, Johnson, and others, Gerstenberger placed most of the psalms (at least in their final forms) in postexilic, familially-based worship: in "the small, organic group of family, neighborhood, or community" and "Israel's secondary organizations" during the Persian and Hellenistic periods.[37] As for the poetic language of the Psalter, Gerstenberger maintained that this evocative, poetic language could not be abstracted "from its concrete life situations."[38] Further, "while the linguistic, poetic, and literary devices must be taken into account in form-critical analysis, they have to be evaluated in their interrelation with life situations and social settings."[39]

A second form-critical approach to the psalms did not focus on the forms as a way to get behind the poems to an original life situation that produced the forms, but rather focused more directly on the forms themselves. In this second approach, the forms assisted the interpreter to focus on the actual texts of the poem-prayers of the Psalter. Claus Westermann is representative of this broad school of thought. Westermann essentially boiled down the categories of the psalms to two broad forms: "praise and petition," which he understood as *theological* categories rather than cultic categories.[40] Westermann challenged the direction of the cult-functional approach. Focusing more on the texts of the psalms than on the cult that presumably gave birth to their forms, he asserted:

> It is high time finally to ask soberly what is regarded as cult in the Old Testament and what the Old Testament says about cult. It will then be

---

pp. 97-115. See also Hans-Joachim Kraus, *Worship in Israel,* trans. Geoffrey Buswell (Oxford: Blackwell, 1966), for a less favorable assessment.

35. *Psalms: Part 1, with an Introduction to Cultic Poetry* (FOTL 14; Grand Rapids: Eerdmans, 1988), p. 5.

36. Gerstenberger, *Psalms: Part 1,* p. 33.

37. Gerstenberger, *Psalms: Part 1,* p. 33.

38. Gerstenberger, *Psalms: Part 1,* p. 34.

39. Gerstenberger, *Psalms: Part 1,* p. 35.

40. *Praise and Lament in the Psalms,* trans. Keith R. Crim and Richard N. Soulen (Atlanta: John Knox, 1981), p. 35.

> impossible to avoid the fact that in the Old Testament there is no absolute, timeless entity called "cult," but that worship in Israel, in its indissolvable connection with the history of God's dealings with his people, developed gradually in all its various relationships . . . and that therefore the categories of the Psalms can be seen only in connection with this history.[41]

Following this line of investigation, Westermann concluded that "the life situation of the Psalms as the cult cannot really be right. For that which really, in the last analysis, occurs in the Psalms is prayer."[42] Westermann criticized Gunkel's idea that the hymn grew out of worship. Noting that two of the examples of the oldest hymns are those of Miriam (Exodus 15) and Deborah (Judges 5), Westermann concluded that these cannot "be called cultic in the strict sense" because they occur in daily life.[43] "The Song of Miriam and the Song of Deborah . . . show, rather, with unmistakable clarity what the Sitz-im-Leben of the hymn is: the experience of God's intervention in history. God has acted; he has helped his people. Now praise *must* be sung to him."[44] Similarly, Westermann maintained that "lamentation is a phenomenon characterized by three determinant elements: the one who laments, God, and the others, i.e., that circle of people among whom or against whom the one who laments stands with a complaint."[45] Westermann understood the form-critical task as paying attention to the actual texts of the psalms: what they say and to whom. For him, then, form "is primarily neither a literary nor a cultic concept. It is both of these, but only secondarily."[46] Primarily, form is a theological category.

Walter Brueggemann is another representative of this second approach to form criticism. Building both on form criticism and also on the work of Paul Ricoeur, Brueggemann understood the psalms in terms of "the life of faith": "the sequence of *orientation-disorientation-reorientation.*"[47] As should be obvious, this is a thoroughly *theological* framework. By paying attention primarily to the texts of various psalms — to what they say and to whom — Brueggemann imagined three types of theological situations in which the "forms" fit:

41. Westermann, *Praise and Lament in the Psalms,* p. 20.

42. Westermann, *Praise and Lament in the Psalms,* p. 24.

43. Westermann, *Praise and Lament in the Psalms,* p. 22. For a similar argument, see Rolf Jacobson, "The Costly Loss of Praise," *Theology Today* 57 (2000) 375-85.

44. Westermann, *Praise and Lament in the Psalms,* p. 22.

45. Westermann, *Praise and Lament in the Psalms,* p. 169.

46. Westermann, *Praise and Lament in the Psalms,* p. 35.

47. Brueggemann, "The Psalms and the Life of Faith," in *The Psalms and the Life of Faith,* ed. Patrick D. Miller (Minneapolis: Augsburg Fortress, 1995), pp. 3-32, quoting p. 9 (emphasis in original). See also his *The Message of the Psalms: A Theological Commentary* (Minneapolis: Augsburg, 1984).

1. Orientation: "The mind-set and worldview of those who enjoy a serene location of their lives. . . ."[48]
2. Disorientation: "A new distressful situation in which the old orientation has collapsed."[49]
3. Reorientation: "A quite new circumstance that speaks of newness (it is not the old revived); surprise (there was no ground in the disorientation to anticipate it); and gift (it is not done by the lamenter)."[50]

Discussion of Brueggemann's typology has often characterized him as replacing the form-critical categories. But he actually proposed his approach as "a helpful way to understand the use and function of the Psalms."[51] That is, Brueggemann's typology is an example of the second form-critical approach — one that pays primary attention to the actual texts and their forms.[52]

This second form-critical approach to the psalms also has its weakness. In spite of the attention to the actual text of the psalms, this approach tends to reduce each psalm to an example of its "type." Rather than focus on the actual cry of an individual prayer for help, for example, the approach tends to treat each prayer for help as an example of lament. Or each hymn as an example of praise. Another weakness of this second approach to form criticism (one that it shares with the first) is the basically unquestioned assumption that form and function cohere with each other. That is, it is assumed that praise language is always used to praise or that petition language is always used to petition. The example of a hymn of praise on the lips of Jonah in the second chapter of Jonah, where the prophet is in the belly of the great fish, shows that form and function need not cohere. Similarly, in the prophetic corpus of the Old Testament, the oracles of judgment against the nations take the form of announcements of punishment. But if one takes into consideration the likely difference between the fictive audience of these oracles (such as the king of Babylon in Isaiah 14) and the literal historical audience (which one might assume to be the king or people of Jerusalem), then one can again see that form and function do not automatically cohere.

The approach taken in this commentary shares more with the second form-critical approach than the first. But we try to move beyond the temp-

48. Brueggemann, "The Psalms and the Life of Faith," p. 10.

49. Brueggemann, "The Psalms and the Life of Faith," p, 11.

50. Brueggemann, "The Psalms and the Life of Faith," p, 14.

51. Brueggemann, "The Psalms and the Life of Faith," p, 9.

52. Other scholars who approach the Psalms theologically include J. L. Mays ("The Lord Reigns," in *The Lord Reigns* [Louisville: Westminster John Knox, 1994]); Brown *(Seeing the Psalms);* McCann (*A Theological Introduction to the Book of Psalms);* and Jerome Creach (*Yahweh as Refuge and the Editing of the Hebrew Psalter* [JSOTSup 217; Sheffield: Sheffield Academic, 1996]).

tation to reduce each lament to an example of the broader form and seek to interpret each psalm as a unique and particular prayer. In addition, as outlined in the section that follows, we try to be sensitive to the canonical story of the Psalter and to the evocative poetic language of each poem.

A final peculiarity to be noted about form-critical approaches to the Psalter is that when categorizing the psalms, interpreters consider both common "literary forms" of the psalms as well as the "thematic form" of each. Thus, on the one hand, among the Psalter's forms there are psalms that share common literary forms: prayers for help (also called laments), hymns of praise, songs of thanksgiving, trust psalms, entrance psalms and instructional psalms (sometimes called wisdom psalms). On the other hand, there are also psalms that share common thematic aspects, but which might differ in literary form: royal psalms, creation psalms, pilgrimage psalms, and historical psalms. This leads to the further oddity that some psalms are classified under more than one form. Psalm 2, for example, is a royal liturgy; Psalm 18, a royal song of thanksgiving; Psalm 8, a creation hymn; and Psalm 139, a creation song of thanksgiving (or sometimes a creation prayer for help). The literary forms of the Psalter include:

Prayer for Help (both of Individuals and of the Community)

The individual prayers for help are spoken by an "I," whereas the communal prayers are spoken by a "we." These psalms assume a situation of crisis, and the mode of speech is petition. The common formal traits of these poems are:

- Address to God
- Complaint, which often comes in three forms: the "I complaint" about the psalmist's self, the "You complaint" about God, and the "They complaint" about the psalmist's oppressors
- Petition, in which the psalmist requests relief and deliverance but also offers supporting reasons in order to urge God to answer
- Expressions of confidence and trust
- Promise to praise the Lord in the future

One subcategory of these prayers is the *imprecatory psalm,* in which the psalmist prays for the destruction of the oppressors. These psalms assume that the crisis was mainly caused by the oppressors. A second subcategory of the prayer for help is the *penitential psalm,* in which the psalmist prays for forgiveness. These psalms assume that the crisis was mainly caused by the psalmist him- or herself.

Psalm of Trust

These psalms also assume a situation of crisis, but the mode of speech is trust. The common formal traits of these poems are:

- A description of the crisis, usually in metaphorical terms
- Expressions of confidence and hope

Hymn of Praise

These psalms testify to the Lord by praising his character and his deeds. The common formal traits of these poems are:

- A call to praise *(Praise the Lord)*
- Reasons to praise, usually introduced by the Hebrew *kî,* "for" or "because."

Four subcategories of the hymn of praise are: the *historical psalm,* which praises the Lord's actions on Israel's behalf in history; the *creation psalm,* which praises the Lord's work of creation; and the *enthronement psalm,* which praises the Lord as the King with the phrase *The Lord reigns (YHWH mālak̲);* and the *songs of Zion,* which praise the Lord for choosing to dwell in the temple on Zion and for choosing the Davidic dynasty to be God's instruments on earth.

Song of Thanksgiving (both of the individual and the community)

The song of thanksgiving assumes that a crisis has passed and the individual or community praises God in fulfillment of an earlier promise to praise (see above, the Prayer for Help). The common formal traits of these psalms include:

- Call to praise
- Recollection of the past crisis
- Recollection of the past prayer for help
- Renewed call to praise, including the appeal for the community to join the psalmist in praising the Lord

Instructional Psalm

These psalms often include a dualistic comparison between the righteous and the wicked, the wise and the fool, or God's way and the world's way. Some formal traits that occur in these psalms are *happy are . . .* phrases (*ʾašrê;* perhaps better translated as "fortunate are . . .") and a tone of instruction. One subcategory of the instructional psalm is the *Torah psalm,* which expressly instructs regarding the Lord's Torah.

Royal Psalm

These psalms, as indicated above, are thematically related rather than related according to formal similarities. They are poems that were composed for specific events in the king's life or for other reasons related to the monarchy. The events may have included the king's coronation, marriage, or an impending military campaign. Other possibilities are prayers for the king to pray himself or to be prayed on his behalf. These psalms were retained in the canon following the end of Israel's and Judah's monarchies, and they became part of the seedbed of messanic hope — Israel's hope that one day the Lord would send the ideal Davidic king, the Messiah.

Liturgies

These psalms were composed for various liturgical purposes. They share the obvious formal characteristic that certain parts may have been spoken by a given person or persons (such as a priest, the congregation, or the king). They also share the trait that liturgical actions can be intuited. Subcategories of these psalms include: the *entrance liturgy,* in which a person or party enters the temple; the *festival psalm,* which was used at one of Israel's three great festivals (Passover, Weeks, and Booths); and the pilgrimage psalm, which may have been used by the faithful as part of their pilgrimage to the temple for one of the festivals.

A final caveat about the categorization of the forms. Many of the psalms do not perfectly fit into one of the "forms" of form criticism. The ancients were apparently not as anxious about the forms as some modern interpreters. For this reason, categorizing a psalm according to form is always a preliminary, penultimate act of interpretation. Interpreters will disagree about the form of a psalm. And they will change their minds. Labeling a psalm with one of the forms is meant as a way *into* the interpretation and understanding of a psalm. It is not meant to shut down discussion or close off interpretation.

IV. THE CANONICAL SHAPE OF THE PSALTER

Scholars have traditionally approached the book of Psalms as a collection, an anthology, of laments and hymns of ancient Israel, preserved in a somewhat random order. We pick out and use psalms — like Psalm 23 or Psalm 42 or Psalm 145 — with little or no thought to the psalms surrounding them. And why not? After all, each psalm is a self-contained unit, with a beginning, a middle, and an end. We do not need to read Psalm 22 to understand Psalm 23, or Psalm 146 to understand Psalm 145. Each psalm has an individual message.

But the canonical method of studying the biblical text has encouraged readers to reexamine the shape of the Psalter and ask questions about the possibility of a deliberate, rather than random, ordering of the psalms within the book. J. Clinton McCann, Jr., in a 1993 collection of essays titled *The Shape and Shaping of the Psalter,* states that scholars are increasingly aware that the purposeful placement of psalms within the collection seems to have given the final form of the whole Psalter a function and message greater than the sum of its parts.[53] Clues about the ordering of the psalms are evident throughout the Psalter in what may be called footprints — footprints left by the community of faith that shaped the book of Psalms into the form in which we now have it preserved in the Old Testament.

From the time of the Enlightenment to the mid-twentieth century, scholars who studied the biblical text gave the majority of their time to the disciplines of textual, source, form, and redactional criticism. As noted above, Hermann Gunkel and his student Sigmund Mowinckel devoted most of their careers to the critical study of the book of Psalms. Gunkel applied the form-critical method to the psalms, categorizing each by its *Gattung* and *Sitz im Leben.*[54] Sigmund Mowinckel built on the work of Gunkel and tried to discover where each psalm in the Psalter would have been used in the cultic worship of ancient Israel.[55] Gunkel and Mowinckel understood the psalms as individual compositions, and they wrote nothing about the shape of the Psalter as a book or a story.

The canonical approach to the text of the Old Testament was championed in the mid-twentieth century by Brevard S. Childs. In a 1976 essay titled "Reflections on the Modern Study of the Psalms," and in his 1979 *Introduction to the Old Testament as Scripture,* Childs encouraged scholars to move away from dissecting the text of the Old Testament and move toward examining the text in the form in which it was preserved for us, i.e., as a whole.[56] Childs maintained, in fact, that it was useless to attempt to understand the underlying layers of traditions which make up the biblical text. The reason is that the editors who compiled and transmitted it deliberately obscured the layers in a process Childs calls "actualization" to keep the text from "being moored in the past."[57] The only way to study and interpret the text is in the form in which we have it. The book of Psalms, therefore, should not be approached as an artifact, as the "cultic hymnbook" of ancient Israel. Childs writes:

53. J. Clinton McCann, Jr., ed., *The Shape and Shaping of the Psalter* (JSOTSup 159; Sheffield: JSOT, 1993), p. 7.

54. Hermann Gunkel, *The Psalms: A Form-Critical Introduction,* trans. Thomas M. Horner (FBBS 19; Philadelphia: Fortress, 1967).

55. Sigmund Mowinckel, *The Psalms in Israel's Worship,* trans. D. R. Ap-Thomas (2 vols.; Nashville: Abingdon, 1962; repr. BRS; Grand Rapids: Eerdmans and Livonia: Dove, 2004).

56. Brevard S. Childs, "Reflections on the Modern Study of the Psalms," in *Magnalia Dei: The Mighty Acts of God,* ed. Frank Moore Cross, Werner E. Lemke, and G. Ernest Wright (Garden City: Doubleday, 1976), pp. 377-88; and *Introduction to the Old Testament as Scripture* (Philadelphia: Fortress, 1979).

57. Childs, *Introduction to the Old Testament as Scripture,* p. 79.

> The psalms are transmitted as the sacred psalms of David, but they testify to all the common troubles and joys of ordinary human life in which all persons participate. . . . Through the mouth of David, the man, they become a personal word from God in each individual situation.[58]

James A. Sanders shared Childs's interest in studying the final form of the text of the Old Testament.[59] But he disagreed with Childs's assertion that it is useless to try to understand the underlying layers of traditions that make up a text. Sanders maintained that biblical texts are grounded in historical settings, that those settings can be discovered, and that they are important for understanding the canonical shape of the texts. But he believed that scholars have looked in the wrong places for those historical settings. Gunkel looked at the individual oral settings of the psalms, Mowinckel at the cultic settings, and Sanders at communities of faith.

Each psalm may have been composed by an individual, perhaps in an oral setting. And each psalm may have been used in ancient Israel's worship experience. But each psalm in the Psalter was remembered, valued, repeated, and passed on within the ancient Israelite community of faith. Communities found value in the texts which comprise the Old Testament, or those texts would not have been preserved. Sanders writes:

> The text cannot be attributed to any discreet genius, such as author or editor or redactor, in the past. It can only be attributed to the ancient communities which continued to find value in the received traditions and scriptures, generation after generation, passing them on for the value they had found in them.[60]

Sanders goes on to clarify that communities find value in texts when those texts provide answers to two basic existential questions: "Who are we?" and "What are we to do?"[61] The ancient Israelites repeatedly asked these questions of, and found answers to them in, their traditions — the stories and texts which they passed on orally from generation to generation. The stories and texts were authoritative for the life of the people.

At some point in the history of ancient Israel, the authoritative traditions were written down in a particular form and order and were passed from generation to generation unchanged. The Torah — Genesis, Exodus,

58. Childs, *Introduction to the Old Testament as Scripture,* p. 521.

59. James A. Sanders, *Canon and Community: A Guide to Canonical Criticism* (GBS; Philadelphia: Fortress, 1984); and *From Sacred Story to Sacred Text* (Philadelphia: Fortress, 1987).

60. Sanders, *Canon and Community,* p. 29.

61. James A. Sanders, *Torah and Canon* (Philadelphia: Fortress, 1972), p. xv.

Leviticus, Numbers, and Deuteronomy — was probably the first portion of the Old Testament to be placed in a fixed format. Next came the Prophets — Joshua, Judges, Samuel, Kings, Isaiah, Jeremiah, Ezekiel, and the Twelve — and then the Writings, which includes the book of Psalms. We know little about the process by which the traditions of ancient Israel moved from a fluid to a fixed method of transmission, but we do know that the process of fixing the text of the Old Testament was completed sometime after the turn of the Common Era.[62]

The book of Psalms appears to be one of the latest books of the Old Testament to achieve such final form. The Dead Sea discoveries and the Septuagint indicate that a number of "editions" of psalm collections circulated in the life of ancient Israel. More than thirty fragments of psalms scrolls have been discovered among the Dead Sea documents, among them two significant finds in Cave 4 and Cave 11. The fragment from Cave 4 contains portions of Psalms 6–69, which are, for the most part, in the same order as in the Old Testament book of Psalms. The fragment from Cave 11 contains thirty-nine canonical psalms with other poetry mixed in. The order of the psalms on this scroll is: 101–3, 109, 118, 104, 147, 105, 146, 148, 121–32, 119, 135–36, 145, 154 (attested elsewhere only in the Syriac Bible); a prayer for deliverance, 139, 137, 138, Sir. 51:13-30, an apostrophe to Zion, 93, 141, 133, 144, 155 (also only in the Syriac Bible), 142, 143, 149–50, a hymn to the creator, 2 Sam 23:7, a prose statement about David's compositions, 140, 134, and 151.[63]

In the Septuagint the psalms are in the same order as they are in our Old Testament, but Psalms 9 and 10 are grouped as a single psalm, as are Psalms 114 and 115. An additional psalm appears at the end of the book, and the superscriptions are longer and occur on more psalms than in the Masoretic Text.

The process by which the Psalter achieved the form in which we have it is lost in the pages of history. The superscriptions of the psalms give the reader some clues about their composition. As noted earlier, seventy-four of the psalms in our Psalter are ascribed to David; two are ascribed to Solomon; twenty-five to Korah, Asaph, Ethan, and Heman, described in 1 Chr. 15:16-19 and 2 Chr. 20:19 as musicians in David's and Solomon's courts; and one to Moses. Psalms 120–34 are identified in their superscriptions as "Songs of the Ascents," and thirty-six psalms have no superscription at all. Some psalms apparently come from early in the life of ancient Israel, such as Psalms 3 and 48, and some seem clearly to be from Israel's later life, such as Psalms 1 and 137.

62. For a full discussion of the process, see Nancy L. deClaissé-Walford, *Reading from the Beginning: The Shaping of the Hebrew Psalter* (Macon: Mercer University Press, 1997), pp. 105-18.

63. See James C. VanderKam, *The Dead Sea Scrolls Today* (2nd ed.; Grand Rapids: Eerdmans, 2010), pp. 172-76.

But why these 150 psalms, and why in this particular order? Why is Psalm 1 the first psalm in the Psalter; why is Psalm 72 placed seventy-second; and why does Psalm 150 close the Psalter? What factors influenced the ancient Israelite community to shape the book of Psalms into its final form and to order the psalms as they did? We are not the first to ask the question. The Midrash on Psalm 3 states:

> As to the exact order of David's Psalms, Scripture says elsewhere: *Man knoweth not the order thereof* (Job 28:13). R. Eleazar taught: The sections of Scripture are not arranged in their proper order. For if they were arranged in their proper order, and any man so read them, he would be able to resurrect the dead and perform other miracles. For this reason the proper order of the sections of Scripture is hidden from mortals and is known only to the Holy One, blessed be He, who said, *"Who, as I, can read and declare it, and set it in order?"* (Isa. 44:7).
>
> When R. Joshua ben Levi sought to arrange the Psalms in their proper order, a heavenly voice came forth and commanded: "Do not rouse that which slumbers!"[64]

As noted earlier, the book of Psalms preserved in the MT consists of 150 psalms, many of which appear to have been part of smaller, already-existing collections. Some of the collections that are identified within the Psalter include:

the Davidic Collections	Pss. 3–14, 51–72, 108–10, 138–45
the Korahite Collections	Pss. 42–49, 84–85, 87–88
the Elohistic Collection	Pss. 42–83
the Asaphite Collection	Pss. 73–83
the Enthronement Psalms	Pss. 93, 95–99
the Songs of the Ascents	Pss. 120–34
the Hallelujah Psalms	Pss. 111–18, 146–50

In addition to the collections of psalms within the Psalter, the Psalter itself provides some clues to its prior "shaping" process. The Psalter is divided into five books: Pss. 1–41; 42–72; 73–89; 90–106; and 107–50, each of which concludes with a doxology:

> Blessed be the LORD, the God of Israel,
> from everlasting to everlasting,
> Amen and amen. (41:13)

64. William G. Braude, *The Midrash on Psalms* (Yale Judaica Series 13; New Haven: Yale University Press, 1959), 1:49-50.

> Blessed be the LORD God, the God of Israel,
> who alone does wondrous deeds.
> Blessed be his glorious name forever;
> may his glory fill all the earth.
> Amen and amen. (72:18-19)
>
> Blessed be the LORD forever.
> Amen and amen. (89:52)
>
> Blessed be the LORD, the God of Israel,
> from everlasting to everlasting.
> And let all the people say, "Amen."
> Praise the LORD. (106:48)
>
> Let every breathing thing praise the LORD!
> Hallelujah! (150:6)

The similarities among the doxologies — especially the first four — and the fact that the word "amen" occurs only in the doxologies strongly suggest that they were purposefully shaped and added to the Psalter at about the same time, although we have no indication of when this may have been.

The five-book division of the Psalter is an early tradition. The psalms scrolls found near the Dead Sea are divided into five books, even though the individual psalms included within each book differ from those in the Old Testament book of Psalms.[65] The LXX also divides its Psalter into five books. The *Midrash Tehillim,* which contains materials that date to as early as the first century B.C.E., states in its commentary on Psalm 1:

> As Moses gave five books of laws to Israel, so David gave five Books of Psalms to Israel, the Book of Psalms entitled *Blessed is the man* (Ps. 1:1), the Book entitled *For the leader: Maschil* (Ps. 41:1), the Book, *A Psalm of Asaph* (Ps. 73:1), the Book, *A Prayer of Moses* (Ps. 90:1), and the Book, *Let the redeemed of the Lord say* (Ps. 107:2). Finally, as Moses blessed Israel with the words *Blessed art thou, O Israel* (Deut. 33:29), so David blessed Israel with the words *Blessed is the man.*[66]

Psalm types and superscriptions within the Psalter also provide clues to the present shape of the book. First, with regard to psalm types, scholars have noted a "movement" from lament psalms in the first portion of the Psalter to

65. For more information on the Dead Sea Psalm Scrolls, see James A. Sanders, ed., *The Dead Sea Psalms Scroll* (Ithaca: Cornell University Press, 1967); and Flint, *The Dead Sea Psalms Scrolls and the Book of Psalms.*

66. Braude, *The Midrash on Psalms,* p. 5.

hymnic psalms in the later portion.[67] The Psalter begins with lament. After the introductory Psalms 1 and 2, the reader encounters a string of eleven laments, broken only by the creation psalm, Psalm 8. The end of the Psalter contains the magnificent praise hymns 146–50, and in between the distribution is as follows:

- In Book One, twenty-four of the forty-one psalms (59 percent) are laments, while eight (20 percent) are hymns.
- In Book Two, twenty of the thirty-one psalms (65 percent) are laments, while six (19 percent) are hymns.
- In Book Three, eight of the seventeen psalms (47 percent) are laments, and six (35 percent) are hymns.
- In Book Four, only four of the seventeen psalms (24 percent) are laments, while five (29 percent) are hymns.
- And in Book Five, ten of the forty-four psalms (23 percent) are laments, and twenty-three (52 percent) are hymns.

Second, the superscriptions of the psalms may help us understand its shape and shaping in two ways. The number of psalms with superscriptions is significantly higher in the first three books of the Psalter than in the last two books:

- In Book One, thirty-nine of the forty-one psalms have superscriptions (95 percent).
- In Book Two, thirty of the thirty-one psalms have superscriptions (97 percent).
- In Book Three, all seventeen psalms have superscriptions (100 percent).
- In Book Four, only six of the seventeen psalms have superscriptions (35 percent).
- And in Book Five, twenty-six of the forty-four psalms have superscriptions (59 percent).

Psalms attributed to David are much greater in number in Books One, Two, and Five than in Books Three and Four.

- In Book One, thirty-nine of the forty-one psalms are attributed to David (95 percent).[68]

67. Claus Westermann was the first to write about this movement. See *Praise and Lament in the Psalms.*

68. Psalm 10 does not have a superscription, but is firmly linked to Psalm 9. See Hans-Joachim Kraus, *Psalms 1–59,* trans. Hilton C. Oswald (CC; Minneapolis: Augsburg, 1988),

- In Book Two, eighteen of the thirty-one psalms are attributed to David (58 percent).
- In Book Three, only one of the seventeen psalms is attributed to David (6 percent).
- In Book Four, two of the seventeen psalms are attributed to David (12 percent).
- And in Book Five, fourteen of the forty-four psalms are attributed to David (32 percent).

Each of these phenomena contribute to our understanding of how the communities of faith heard, preserved, and handed on the songs of ancient Israel and eventually shaped them into the book of Psalms.

A brief history of the circumstances surrounding the shaping of the Old Testament in general and the Psalter in particular may be helpful at this point. In 597 B.C.E., the army of the Babylonian Empire carried Jehoiachin, the king of Judah, and many of his subjects into exile (2 Kings 25). A decade later, the army sacked Jerusalem and destroyed the temple. The nation of Israel, ruled by a succession of Davidic kings, was at an end. In 539, Babylon fell to the Persian Empire led by Cyrus II. In the following year, Cyrus issued an edict which allowed all of the people held captive by the Babylonians to return to their homelands.[69] Sometime after 538, a number of Jewish exiles returned to Jerusalem and began the process of rebuilding the city and the temple. By 515, the temple was standing once again and functioning as the Jewish cult center (Ezra 6:15-16).

The Persian government allowed the Jews to rebuild the temple and resume their religious practices, so long as those practices did not conflict with the Persian laws. Temple and cult were restored, but the nation-state of Israel with a king of the Davidic line at its head was not. Except for a brief time of independence during the rule of the Hasmoneans (141-63 B.C.E.), the people lived continuously as vassals, first to the Persians, then the Greeks, and finally the Romans. Under the same circumstances, most of the nation-states of the ancient Near East simply disappeared from history. But ancient Israel did not. The postexilic community found a way to view their identity and to structure their existence that went beyond traditional concepts of nationhood. King and court could no longer be the focal point of national life;

---

pp. 188-89; and William Holladay, *The Psalms Through Three Thousand Years* (Minneapolis: Fortress, 1993), p. 77. Psalm 33 has solid linguistic links to Psalm 32. See Gerald H. Wilson's treatment in *The Editing of the Hebrew Psalter* (SBLDS 76; Chico: Scholars, 1985), pp. 174-75.

69. For the text of the so-called Cyrus Cylinder, see James B. Pritchard, ed., *Ancient Near Eastern Texts Relating to the Old Testament* (3rd ed.; Princeton: Princeton University Press, 1969), p. 316. The book of Ezra (1:2-4 and 6:3-5) includes two portions of the restoration policy.

temple and worship took center stage. And Yahweh, not a king of the Davidic line, reigned as sovereign over the new "religious nation" of Israel.

Postexilic Israel redefined nationhood and found a way to remain a separate and identifiable entity among the vast empires of which it found itself a part. A part of the process of redefinition involved the shaping of the Hebrew Scriptures. The people looked to their traditional and cultic literature for answers to the existential questions "Who are we?" and "What are we to do?" and then shaped the literature into a document that provided answers to the questions.

The Hebrew Bible in general and the Hebrew Psalter in particular, then, offer the hermeneutical rationale for the survival for the postexilic community. According to the Psalter, what is that hermeneutical rationale?

The Psalter begins with the story of the reign of King David in Book One, moves to the reign of Solomon in Book Two, and on to the divided kingdom and destruction of the northern kingdom by the Assyrians and the southern kingdom by the Babylonians in Book Three; Book Four recounts the struggle of the exiles in Babylon to find identity and meaning, and Book Five celebrates the return to Jerusalem and the establishment of a new Israel with God as sovereign.

The Psalter opens in Book One with words encouraging torah piety:

> Happy is the one . . .
> (whose) delight is in the instruction of the LORD,
> who meditates on his instruction day and night. (1:1-2)

It continues with words of warning to the nations and their rulers to recognize the God of Israel as king over all:

> So now, O kings, be wise!
> Be warned, O rulers of the earth!
> Serve the LORD in fear!
> In trembling kiss his feet! (2:10-11)

Readers enter the Psalter with two admonitions: diligently study and delight in the Torah and acknowledge God as sovereign.

Book One continues with thirty-nine psalms "of David." The psalms provide insight into every facet of David's life — the king, the human being, the warrior, the parent, the servant of the Lord. Most of the psalms in Book One are laments (59 percent), calling on God to act on behalf of the psalmist against enemies and oppressors. David's life was fraught with conflict and oppression, from within and without the nation-state he founded — the Philistines, Saul, David's own family (see 1 Sam. 19:11; 29:1; 31:1; 2 Sam. 3:1; 5:22; 15:6, 10; 20:1; 1 Kgs. 1:24-25).

Psalm 41, classified as an individual hymn of thanksgiving, begins with the wisdom word "content" *('ašrê)*, the same word with which Psalm 1 begins and Psalm 2 ends:

> Happy *('ašrê)* are they who consider the helpless;
> in the day of trouble, the LORD will rescue them.
> The LORD will keep them and preserve them;
> they shall be called happy *('ašrê)* in the land. (41:1-2)

Book One tells the story of the reign of David, and its *'ašre* ending reminds the reader/hearer of the dual message of the introduction to the Psalter — torah piety (Psalm 1) and God as king (Psalm 2).

Book Two of the Psalter, like Book One, also contains many laments, but not all of them are placed on David's lips. The Korahites who were, according to the book of Chronicles, temple singers during the reigns of David and Solomon, mix their voices with David in singing the laments of Book Two (Psalms 42–49).[70] Fifteen psalms of David appear in the middle of Book Two (51–65). Fourteen are laments, and eight of them are connected, in their superscriptions, to particular events in the life of David. These psalms remind readers once again that David's life was one of turmoil and strife, but they also depict a person who loved the Lord and strove to serve the Lord with fervor.

The only untitled psalm in Book Two is Psalm 71, an individual lament, which is read as the supplication of an aged person for God not to forget or forsake.[71] Verses 6 and 9 read:

> Upon you I have leaned from birth;
> from the womb of my mother you have been my protector.
> To you, my praise is constant.
> . . .
> Do not cast me off in old age;
> when my strength is finished, do not forsake me.

In its position in Book Two, one might read Psalm 71 as the words of an aged David at the end of his reign.[72]

Psalm 72 is one of only two psalms in the Psalter ascribed to Solomon.[73]

70. For a full discussion of the Korahites, see the Introduction to Book Two.

71. Many English translations of the Psalter give "titles," unrelated to the superscriptions, to psalms. Psalm 71 is titled "A Prayer for Old Age" in the King James Authorized Version and "The Prayer of an Old Man for Deliverance" in the American Standard Version (1901).

72. See 1 Kgs. 1:1–2:11.

73. The other is one of the Songs of the Ascents, Psalm 127.

Hans-Joachim Kraus describes Psalm 72 as a collection of wishes and prayers for the well-being of the king, likely used at an enthronement ceremony for a king in Jerusalem.[74] Brevard Childs suggests that the canonical placement of Psalm 72 indicates that the psalm "is 'for' Solomon, offered by David."[75]

> O God, your justice give to the king,
> and your righteousness to the son of the king.
> May he judge your people with righteousness,
> and your poor with justice. . . .
> May there be abundance of grain in the land,
> to the mountains.
> May his fruit thrive like the foliage of Lebanon;
> and they blossom from the cities as grass of the field. (72:1-2, 16)

The psalm ends with the words "The prayers of David, son of Jesse, are completed" (72:20).

Book Three opens with "A Psalm of Asaph" (Psalm 73). Like the sons of Korah, Asaph was, according to the book of Chronicles, a temple singer during the reigns of David and Solomon.[76] Fifteen of the seventeen psalms in Book Three are attributed to Asaph and the sons of Korah. Only one psalm, Psalm 86, is attributed to David. With the close of Book Two, David moves to the background. The focus is now on David's descendants, who will determine the future of ancient Israel.

Psalm 73 is, like Psalm 1, classified as a wisdom psalm. In Psalm 73, the psalm-singer looks at the world around and sees the wicked *(rᵉšāʿîm)* prospering while the righteous *(ṣaddîqîm)* suffer and questions whether conventional theology and mores still hold true in life.[77] There seemed to be no reasoned connection between righteousness and reward, wickedness and punishment. The psalmist muses:

74. H.-J. Kraus, *Psalms 60–150,* trans. Hilton C. Oswald (CC; Minneapolis, Augsburg, 1989), pp. 76-77.

75. Childs, *Introduction to the Old Testament as Scripture,* p. 516.

76. 1 Chr. 6:39 and 25:1, 2 and 2 Chr. 5:12 state that Asaph was a descendant of Levi, part of one of the great families or guilds of musicians and singers in preexilic Israel. See Harry P. Nasuti, *Tradition History and Psalms of Asaph* (SBLDS 88; Atlanta: Scholars, 1988).

77. Humankind in the ancient Near East believed in a basic moral governance of the world. Act and consequence were connected. Thus, the good prospered and the wicked perished. Sages and wisdom teachers taught that there was a fundamental order in the world which could be discerned by experience, that the gods had established the order, and that all of humanity was bound by the rules governing that order. For a detailed treatment, see *The Sage in Israel and the Ancient Near East,* ed. John G. Gammie and Leo G. Perdue (Winona Lake: Eisenbrauns, 1990).

But as for me, my feet have almost stumbled;
my steps nearly slipped.
Because I was jealous of the boastful
as I saw the well-being of the wicked;
Because there are no struggles in death,
and their bodies are fat.
The difficulties of humanity do not exist for them;
and with the human condition, they are not struck . . .
They scoff and speak with malice;
the ones in high station speak of extortion.
They set their mouths in the heavens;
as their tongues walk in the earth. (73:2-5, 8-9)

In despair, the psalm-singer enters the sanctuary of the Lord and there finds order in the seeming chaos of life.

Behold! Those who are far from you perish;
You put an end to all those who are unfaithful to you.
But as for me, it is good to be near God;
I have made the Lord God my refuge;
I will tell of all your works. (73:27-28)

Psalm 73 opens a new chapter in the Psalter's story of the life of ancient Israel. It signals a turning point. David's reign is over, and Solomon's reign will end with the nation divided into two rival kingdoms that will be in constant conflict with one another and the nations around them. Community laments and community hymns dominate Book Three of the Psalter. The voice of David, the individual, gives way to the voice of the community of faith, which is attempting to make sense of all that is going on around them.

Why, O God, have you rejected us forever?
Why does your anger smoke against the sheep of your pasture?
Remember your congregation which you acquired of old,
the tribe of your inheritance which you redeemed,
Mount Zion, where you dwell. (74:1-2)

Restore us, O God of our salvation!
Break off your anger toward us!
Will you be angry with us forever?
Will you stretch your anger from generation to generation?
Will you not turn and give us life,
so your people will rejoice in you?
Show us your *hesed,* O Lord!
Give us your salvation! (85:4-7)

Near the end of Book Three, readers/hearers encounter Psalm 88, an individual lament, but a lament like no other in the Psalter. It is almost wholly composed of only one of the five elements that are normally found in a lament psalm, the Complaint. The Invocation and Petition are brief lines within the song, and the Expressions of Trust and Praise and Adoration are missing completely. The psalm ends with the words:

Your anger has swept over me;
your dread assaults destroy me.
They surround me like waters all day;
they close in on me completely.
You cause the one who loves me
and my friend to distance themselves from me;
only darkness knows me. (88:16-18)

Psalm 88's lament is followed by a royal psalm, Psalm 89. As Psalm 88 is a lament like no other in the Psalter, Psalm 89 is a royal psalm like no other. It begins as do other royal psalms, praising God for the good provisions to the king of God's choosing.

Of the *hesed* of the Lord forever I will sing;
Generation to generation I will make known your faithfulness with my mouth;
for I will declare, "Your *hesed* is built to last;
the heavens, your faithfulness is established in them."
"I cut a covenant with my chosen;
I have sworn to David, my servant.
I will establish your descendants forever;
and build your throne for generations." (89:1-4)

But the psalm takes a sudden turn in v. 38.

But [now] you have rejected, refused,
and become very angry with your anointed.
You have renounced your covenant with your servant;
you have defiled his crown in the land. . . .
You have put an end to his splendor;
you have thrown down his crown on the ground. (89:38-39, 44)

In 722 B.C.E., the Assyrians destroyed Samaria and scattered the population of Israel. In 587, the Babylonians destroyed Jerusalem and took a major portion of Judah's population into captivity in Babylon. The nations of Israel and Judah had come to the end; Davidic kingship had come to an end; the people were exiled from their homeland. Book Three of the Psalter ends with the community of faith lamenting and asking questions of its God: "Who are we? Who will lead us? Who will help us to survive in this new world?"

Book Four opens with "A Prayer of Moses, the Man of God." It is the only psalm in the Hebrew Psalter so designated. In it, the reader/hearer encounters these words — placed in the mouth of Moses:

> Return *(šûḇ)*, LORD! How long?
> Change your mind, with regard to your servants.
> Satisfy us in the morning with your *hesed*
> so we might rejoice and be glad all our days.
> Make us glad as many days as you have afflicted us,
> as many years as we have seen evil.
> Let your work be shown to your servants
> and your splendor to their children.
> Let the splendor of the Lord, our God, be upon us;
> and the work our hands, establish it for us;
> the work of our hands, establish it. (90:13-17)

Just as Moses admonished God to "turn" and "have compassion" on the Israelites during the golden calf incident (Exod. 32:12), so now Moses asks God to once again "turn" and "have compassion." The Targum to Psalm 90, in fact, titles it "A prayer of Moses the prophet, when the people Israel sinned in the desert." Not just Psalm 90, but the whole of Book Four of the Psalter is dominated by the person of Moses. Outside of Book Four, Moses is mentioned only once in the Psalter (77:20); in Book Four, he is referred to seven times (90:S; 99:6; 103:7; 105:26; 106:16, 23, 32).[78]

The community of faith cannot return to the days of King David. They can only move forward. Moses intervenes with God on behalf of the people and then points the way forward. Enthronement psalms, which celebrate the enthronement of the Lord as king — rather than a king of the Davidic line, dominate Book Four of the Psalter.

> The LORD is king!
> He is robed in majesty, the LORD is robed;
> with strength he has girded himself. (93:1)

> For a great God is the LORD,
> and a great king over all the gods. (95:3)

> Say among the nations, the LORD is king!
> The world is firmly established; it will not be shaken.
> He will judge the people with equity. (96:10)

78. Marvin Tate describes Book Four as a "Moses Book." See *Psalms 51–100* (WBC 20; Dallas: Word, 1990), p. xxvi.

The king is strong; he loves justice!
You established equity;
justice and righteousness in Jacob
You formed.
Exalt the LORD your God;
and bow down at his footstool.
He is holy! (99:4-5)

At the end of Book Four, Psalm 105 reminds the community of faith how God provided for, protected, and sustained them throughout their history.

The LORD — he is our God;
Throughout the land are his judgments.
He has remembered his eternal covenant —
A promise he commanded for a thousand generations —
Which he cut with Abraham —
And his oath to Isaac.
And he confirmed it for Jacob as a statute,
To Israel as an eternal covenant. . . .
He sent Moses his servant
And Aaron, whom he had chosen,
Who set among them the promises of his signs
And wonders in the land of Ham. . . .
He brought out his people with silver and gold,
And none of their tribes stumbled. . . .
He gave them the lands of the nations,
And they inherited the labor of the peoples. (105:7-10, 26-27, 37, 44)

But the psalm immediately following, Psalm 106, reminds the people of their unfaithfulness to the God who protected and sustained them.

We have sinned, like our ancestors;
We have done wrong and acted wickedly. . . .
They were jealous of Moses in the camp,
Of Aaron, the holy one of God. . . .
They made a calf at Horeb;
They worshipped a formed image. . . .
They grumbled in their tents;
They did not listen to the voice of the LORD. . . .
Many times he delivered them,
But they, they willfully rebelled!
They were brought low by their sin. (106:6, 16, 19, 25, 43)

God ruled as sovereign over the Israelites before the days of Kings Saul and David (see 1 Samuel 8); God could be sovereign once again. But the message at the end of Book Four of the Psalter is: Remember the past and don't be disobedient and unfaithful in the future. Thus, Book Four of the Psalter ends very differently from Book Three. At the end of Psalm 89 are questions about why ancient Israel is suffering in its present situation. At the end of Psalm 106 is a simple petition to the Lord:

Deliver us, O Lord our God,
And gather us from the nations
So that we may testify to your holy name
And celebrate by praising you. (106:47)

In 539 B.C.E., the Persian army, under the leadership of Cyrus II, captured Babylon, the capital city of the Babylonian Empire. In 538, Cyrus issued a decree allowing captive people to return to their homelands, rebuild, and resume their religious practices. But the repatriated peoples would remain part of the vast Persian Empire and subject to Persian law. For the Israelites, it meant that they could rebuild their temple and continue their religious practices, but they could not restore the nation-state under the leadership of a king of the line of David.

Book Five of the Psalter opens with Psalm 107, a community hymn celebrating God's graciousness in delivering people from perilous circumstances. It begins with the words:

Give thanks to the Lord, for he is good,
For his *hesed* is for all time.
The ones redeemed by the Lord will thus say,
Those he has redeemed from the hand of the oppressor
And those from the lands he has gathered in,
From the east and from the west,
From the north and from the sea. (107:1-3)

Verses 33-41 outline the great beneficence that the sovereign God can bestow upon the community of faith. The people may dwell in safety, establish a town, plant a vineyard, reap a harvest, be blessed with children and cattle, be defended against the enemy, and have their future secured. Psalm 107 closes with the words:

Whoever is wise will hear these things,
And the *hesed* ones of the Lord will attend. (107:43)

Beginning with Psalm 108, David makes a dramatic reappearance in the Psalter. Psalms 108–10, 122, 124, 131, and 138–45 are "of David." David's voice returns, leading the Israelites in praise of God as sovereign. David sings:

I will give thanks to the Lord exceedingly with my mouth,
and in the midst of the multitude I will praise him.
For he stands at the right hand of the needy
in order to save from the judging ones his inmost being. (109:30-31)

All the kings of the earth will give thanks to the Lord,
for they have heard the words of your mouth.
And they will sing in the paths of the Lord,
for great is the glory of the Lord. (138:4-5)

I remember the days of old;
I muse over all of your work.
Over the doing of your hands I meditate.
I spread out my hands to you,
my inmost being like a parched land for you. (143:5-6)

In the middle of Book Five, with psalms of David forming an inclusio around them, are psalms used in various celebrations and commemorations in Jewish life:

- Psalm 113–18, the Egyptian Hallel, recited during Passover
- Psalm 119, a wisdom acrostic about torah piety, recited during the Feast of Pentecost
- Psalms 120–34, the Songs of the Ascents, recited during the Feast of Booths (Tabernacles or Sukkoth)

David leads, and the people join in to praise and give thanks to the God who created, sustained, protected, and guided them throughout their history.

The last psalm of David in Book Five, Psalm 145, is a masterful alphabetic acrostic that celebrates the kingship of God over the community of faith and over all creation. David begins the celebration in vv. 1 and 2:

I will exalt you, my God the king,
and I will bless your name for all time and beyond.
Every day I will bless you,
and I will praise your name for all time and beyond.

The community of faith joins David in v. 4:

Generation to generation will glorify your doings,
and your mighty works they will make known.

In v. 10, all creation is called upon to add its voice to the praise of God:

All of your works will give thanks to you, O Lord,
and your *hesed* ones will bless you.

The psalm ends in v. 21 with the words:

The praise of the Lord my mouth will speak,
and all flesh will bless his holy name for all time and beyond.

The Psalter ends with five doxological psalms that bring it to a climax of praise of God as sovereign:

The Lord will reign for all time,
your God, O Zion, for all generations. (146:10)

Hallelujah!
Sing to the Lord a new song,
his praise in the gathering of the *hesed* ones.
Let Israel be glad in his doings;
let the children of Zion rejoice in their king. (149:1-2)

What is the shape of the book of Psalms? It is five books that narrate the history of ancient Israel, the very history recorded in the books of Samuel, Kings, Chronicles, Ezra, Nehemiah, and a number of the prophets. Books One and Two (Psalms 1–72) chronicle the reigns of Kings David and Solomon; Book Three (Psalms 73–89) tells of the dark days of the divided kingdoms and their eventual destructions; Book Four (Psalms 90–106) recalls the years of the Babylonian exile during which the community of faith had to rethink their identity as the people of God; and Book Five (Psalms 107–50) celebrates the community of faith's restoration to the land and the sovereignty of God over them. Ancient Israel — emergent Judaism — survived in the world of which it found itself a part because it found in its past a way to make sense of the present and future.

The story of the shaping of the Psalter is the story of the shaping of survival. The Psalter was, along with the other texts that make up the Hebrew Scriptures, a constitutive document of identity for postexilic Israel. Within that collection of texts, the community of faith found a new structure for existence and identity that transcended traditional concepts of nationhood. The story of the Psalter gave the people a new rationale for existence and a new statement of national identity. With the Lord as sovereign, the people could survive as a separate and identifiable entity within the vast empires — Persian, Greek, and Roman — of which they were a part.

V. THE POETRY OF THE PSALTER

The psalms, like about a third of the Old Testament, are poetry — they are songs, prayers, liturgies, and words of instruction that take poetic form. They express their intended meanings through poetry. Two special features typical of Hebrew poetry deserve introduction here since they will aid interpretation later.

A. PARALLELISM

The basic characteristic of Hebrew poetry is known as parallelism, the juxtaposition of two or more balanced grammatical elements. But it might be useful first to say a word about poetic features from other languages that are generally not present in Hebrew. In many Western languages, including English, poetry often is characterized by end rhyme and/or meter. Neither of these is characteristic of Hebrew poetry. End rhyme is so infrequent in Hebrew poetry that instances of it can be described as the exception rather than the rule. Some scholars hold that meter was once a common characteristic of ancient Hebrew poetry.[79] The majority of scholars, however, while allowing that meter is present in Hebrew poetry, deny that meter functioned with predictable regularity in most Hebrew poetry. The pattern of syllables and stresses in Hebrew poetry is so much less regular and so much more unpredictable than it is in most Western language poetry that it cannot truly be said to be a meter. A true meter is a pattern of syllables or stresses to which poetic lines must conform. This pattern is simply not present in Hebrew poetry.[80] This is not to say that Hebrew poetry lacks a sense of rhythm. When one reads Hebrew poetry, a sense of rhythm does emerge. But this rhythm is not a set of beats or stresses to which the poetic lines conform, but rather is the simple "by-product of parallelism."[81] Because words and phrases are juxtaposed, a natural rhythm occurs — but this rhythm does not rise to the dignity of meter.

Because Hebrew poetry does not have meter, some claim that the fundamental characteristic of Hebrew poetry is the parallelism of its members, for short, simply *parallelism.* Although awareness of parallelism has existed since antiquity, the term itself was coined by Robert Lowth, a bishop of the

79. For instance, J. P. Fokkelman, *Reading Biblical Poetry: An Introductory Guide,* trans. Ineke Smit (Louisville: Westminster John Knox, 2001). See also Peter C. Craigie, *Psalms 1–50* (WBC 19; 2nd ed.; Nashville: Nelson, 2004), Introduction; Sebastian Bullough, "The Question of Metre in Psalm I," *VT* 17 (1967) 42-49; O. Loretz, "Psalmenstudien," *UF* 3 (1971) 101-3.

80. Cf. Adele Berlin, "Introduction to Hebrew Poetry," in *NIB* 4:308: "[it] seems best . . . to abandon the quest for meter in the poetry of the Bible."

81. Berlin, "Introduction to Hebrew Poetry," 4:309.

Church of England who in 1753 published a study of biblical poetry.[82] Lowth's initial theories have been challenged, reworked, and advanced in the last thirty years. Many scholars have contributed to the modern conversation, but the work of Robert Alter, James Kugel, and Adele Berlin has been particularly important.[83]

As stated above, parallelism is the juxtaposition of two or more balanced grammatical elements. At its most recognizable level, parallelism happens between phrases. Consider the opening verse of Psalm 96:

Sing to the LORD a new song;
Sing to the LORD, all the earth. (96:1)

In this example, the two phrases are said to be "in parallel" with each other. There is an obvious relationship between the two phrases — both contain the imperatival phrase *sing to the LORD*. But the two phrases are also slightly different. The first phrase describes "what" the song should be *(a new song)*, while the second prescribes "who" should sing *(all the earth)*. Different scholars use different conventions when naming these phrases, e.g., as a "verset," "half verse," or "colon." In this commentary, we have preferred the term "colon" (plural: cola). Most often in Hebrew poetry, cola appear in parallel pairs, but it is not uncommon to have three cola in parallel:

Shout to God all the earth;
Sing to the glory of his name;
set forth gloriously his praise.
(66:1-2; cf. 1:1; 64:10; 65:7; 89:19; 97:10, etc.)

The energy of Hebrew poetry is generated by the essentially endless way in which the parallel cola play off each other. Poets will pair synonyms or antonyms. They will pair question and response (or call and response). They will pair a singular noun and a plural noun, or a masculine noun and a

82. *De sacra poesi Hebraeorum* (Lectures on the Sacred Poetry of the Hebrews) (Oxford: Clarendon, 1753).

83. Alter, *The Art of Biblical Poetry* (New York: Basic Books, 2011); Kugel, *The Idea of Biblical Poetry* (Baltimore: Johns Hopkins University Press, 1998); Berlin, *The Dynamics of Biblical Parallelism* (BRS; Grand Rapids: Eerdmans, 2008). See also Luis Alonso Schökel, *A Manual of Hebrew Poetics* (Rome: Pontifico Istituto Biblico, 1988); Wilfred G. E. Watson, *Classical Hebrew Poetry* (JSOTSup 26; Sheffield: JSOT, 1984); Daniel Grossberg, *Centripetal and Centrifugal Structures in Biblical Poetry* (SBLMS 39; Atlanta: Scholars, 1989); S. E. Gillingham, *The Poems and Psalms of the Hebrew Bible* (Oxford: Oxford University Press, 1994); and M. O'Connor, *Hebrew Verse Structure* (Winona Lake: Eisenbrauns, 1980). For a review of the perspectives, cf. J. Kenneth Kuntz, "Recent Perspectives on Biblical Poetry," *RelSRev* 19 (1993) 321-27.

feminine noun. They will pair a statement with a supporting reason. They will pair an abstract concept such as "righteousness" with a concrete reality such as "earth." The variation is practically inexhaustible. The delight for the poet is in expressing something eloquently. The delight for the audience is in discovering the eloquence of the expression. Expressing something eloquently does not make it "more true" in the abstract sense. But it does make it ring with more resonance in the ear of the listener.

Even though parallelism is most recognizable at the phrase or cola level, it is misleading to limit one's understanding of parallelism to the juxtaposition between the cola. Hebrew parallelism occurs within cola, between cola, between sets of cola (a verse is a set of cola), between stanzas (a stanza is a set of verses), and between psalms (a set of stanzas). For instance, consider the opening lines of Psalm 27:

> The Lord is my light and my salvation,
>   whom shall I fear?
> The Lord is the stronghold of my life,
>   whom shall I dread? (27:1)

Notice that parallelism occurs within the first colon, where *my light* is juxtaposed with *my salvation.* This sort of parallelism within a colon is frequent in the Psalter, as two examples from Psalm 23 attest: *Your rod and your staff — they give me courage* (23:4b); *goodness and* hesed *pursue me all the days of my life* (23:6).

Parallelism also occurs between sets of cola. Notice in the example above from Ps. 27:1 that the first two cola are juxtaposed with the second two cola. Each of these "verses" has the same structure. The first colon of each has *The Lord* as the subject + an object that is modified by the pronoun *my.* The second colon of each expresses a similar question: *Whom shall I fear?* and *Whom shall I dread?* So the two "verses" (or sets of cola) are in parallel to each other.

More broadly, one can see parallelism happening between stanzas and even between psalms. In some psalms there are stanzas that are constructed in parallel fashion. In Psalm 107, the body of the psalm contains four parallel stanzas: vv. 4-9, 10-16, 17-22, 23-32. In Psalm 139, the entire psalm is made up of four very carefully balanced parallel stanzas: vv. 1-6, 7-12, 13-18, 19-24. Even between psalms — in the case of what are sometimes called "twin psalms" — parallelism occurs. For example, Psalms 111 and 112 are both alphabetic acrostic psalms of almost exactly the same length — the former focuses on theology, the latter on anthropology. Psalms 103 and 104 also parallel each other — they are the only two psalms that begin with the phrase, *Praise the Lord, O my soul.* Also, Psalms 105 and 106, which are two of the three so-called historical psalms, parallel each other: the former narrates Israel's history as the story of God's mighty acts; the latter narrates Israel's history as the story of Israel's constant disobedience. In each of these cases, the respective pair of psalms forms a literary unit in which the meaning of the whole, taken together, is greater than merely the sum of the parts.

B. EVOCATIVE LANGUAGE

Even though parallelism endows Hebrew poetry with its most recognizable feature, there is much more to Hebrew poetry than parallelism. Indeed, as William Brown has put it, "the power of Psalms lies first and foremost in its evocative use of language."[84] That is, the power of the psalms to touch people's lives flows from the way the Psalter uses metaphor, simile, hyperbole, imagery, drama, intensity, repetition, and so on. Again, as Brown writes, the Psalter is "poetry with a purpose" and "the discourse of the heart. . . ."[85] And, "it is precisely the psalmist's deployment of metaphor that enables the personal language of pathos to be felt and appropriated by readers of every generation."[86]

In this commentary, we have chosen to pay special attention to the poetry of the psalms. Without denying the power or importance of historical or form-critical approaches to the Psalter (see above, section III. Form Criticism), we recognize that because the psalms are *poetry* of faith, faithful interpretation must attend both to their theological nature (that is, to the *faith* element of the psalms) and also to their poetic nature. This is not merely to focus on the aesthetic dimensions of the poetry, but to recognize that when it comes to theological testimony, the aesthetic nature of the testimony cannot be treated as a "husk" to be discarded in search of some elusive theological kernel. The theological truth of the psalms is a truth that has "a purpose" (so Brown) — it aims to move the audience. At times this audience is God, at other times an ancient or modern human reader/hearer, and most times it is both. But in every case, the aesthetic power of the poetry is as much a part of its theological witness as its semantic content. As Patrick Miller has put it:

> Meaning and beauty, the semantic and the aesthetic, are woven together into a whole, and both should be received and responded to by the interpreter. To ignore the beauty in pursuit of the meaning is, at a minimum, to close out the possibility that the beauty in a significant fashion contributes to and enhances meaning.[87]

84. Brown, *Seeing the Psalms,* p. 2.
85. Brown, *Seeing the Psalms,* p. 2.
86. Brown, *Seeing the Psalms,* p. 3.
87. *Interpreting the Psalms,* p. 30.

But here, in our view, Miller does not go far enough. It is not simply that the evocative power of the psalms' poetry "contributes to" or "enhances" the meaning. Rather, the power of the language is inseparable from the meaning. The meaning of the psalms exists "in, with, and under" the poetic language. The psalms, like all theological witness, comprise a truth that wishes to grab hold of readers, shake them vigorously, and leave them forever changed. The truth of the psalms does not wish to be held at arm's length, considered dispassionately, and then set aside. Because this is so, the truth of the Psalter is fully bound up with how the various psalms employ the power of language. A testimony that is spoken eloquently, and thus that rings with more resonance in the ears of the hearer, is for that person "more true" than a testimony that falls flat and does not resonate at all. Therefore we must be wary of the temptation to try to extract the theological meaning from the semantic shell. We must fight against the idea that the evocative language of the Psalter only enhances, or amplifies, or contributes to meaning.[88] For that reason, in this commentary we have striven to attend carefully to the way psalms draw power from the many poetic techniques of the ancient psalmists.[89]

VI. THEMES AND THEOLOGY

As noted above, one reason for the powerful role that the Psalter has played in both synagogue and church is that it addresses such a wide span of human emotions, life experiences, and personal situations. The themes of the Psalter range from singing God's praise to crying in despair, from calling for the oppressor's destruction to confessing personal sin, from teaching about God to questioning God's ways. In many ways, the various form-critical categories express the main themes of the Psalter: *pleas for help* (including penitence for sin and curses of the oppressors), *praising testimony* (including the Lord's creation, the Lord's action in history, and God's choice of Abraham and Israel/David and Zion), *trust in the midst of crisis, thanksgiving following delivery from crisis,* and *instruction on walking in God's ways.* Various individual psalms touch various of the themes. No one psalm touches all of the Psalter themes. But as was noted above, the story of the shaping of the Psalter is the story of the shaping of survival. It is a collection of poems that charts a new structure for existence and identity for a postnational, Lord-centered community.

88. See Brown, *Seeing the Psalms,* p. 11.

89. A review of those techniques is beyond the scope of this introduction. For further reading, see Alter, *The Art of Biblical Poetry;* Kugel, *The Idea of Biblical Poetry;* Alonso Schökel, *A Manual of Hebrew Poetics;* and Watson, *Classical Hebrew Poetry.*

To answer the question "What is the theology of the Psalter?" is to endeavor on an integrating, synthetic task. Various psalms represent various theological confessions and expressions — some older, some newer; some more confident, some more questioning; some more theologically-centered in God, some more anthropologically-centered in the chosen people. When dealing with this diverse array of theological expressions, one legitimate option is to refuse to synthesize the diversity. Thus, Erhard Gerstenberger has explored how the diversity of life settings behind the Psalter's many poems contributed to the diversity of theological perspectives in the psalms.[90] Or again, Beth Tanner has argued that the synthetic task of describing the theology of the Psalter will be a frustrating task that is "transitory" and "incomplete," because "we can only find what our own context has structured and trained us to see."[91]

But other interpreters have also legitimately sought to imagine the theological mosaic that the individual songs of the Psalter create when viewed together. A sample of the current proposals illustrates the possibilities. Brueggemann has explored how the psalms bear a dialectical witness both to God's "incommensurability" and God's "mutuality."[92] Hermann Spieckermann argues that the presence of God's salvation is both the persistent theological problem that drives the Psalter's theology and the confession that answers that problem.[93]

What might be the Psalter's theological center? James Luther Mays sees the confession of the enthronement psalms that "The Lord reigns" as the center that holds together the Psalter.[94] Jerome Creach favors the metaphor of God as "refuge" as its theological center,[95] whereas William Brown has built on Creach's work to argue that the metaphors of God as "refuge" and "way" together form the dual theological centers of the Psalter.[96] In Gerald Wilson's

90. "Theologies in the Book of Psalms," in Flint and Miller, *The Book of Psalms,* pp. 603-25.

91. "Rethinking the Enterprise: What Must Be Considered in Formulating a Theology of the Psalms," in *Soundings in the Theology of the Psalms: Perspectives and Methods in Contemporary Scholarship,* ed. Rolf A. Jacobson (Minneapolis: Fortress, 2010), pp. 139-50, quoting pp. 145 and 139, respectively.

92. "The Psalms in Theological Use: On Incommensurability and Mutuality," in Flint and Miller, *The Book of Psalms,* pp. 581-602.

93. *Heilsgegenwart: Eine Theologie der Psalmen* (FRLANT 148; Gottingen: Vandenhoeck & Ruprecht, 1989).

94. *The Lord Reigns.*

95. *Yahweh as Refuge and the Editing of the Hebrew Psalter;* see his further work on this theme in *The Destiny of the Righteous in the Psalms* (St. Louis: Chalice, 2008), and in "The Destiny of the Righteous and the Theology of the Psalms," in Jacobson, *Soundings in the Theology of the Psalms,* pp. 49-61.

96. *Seeing the Psalms.*

view, however, the reign of God is the center of the Psalter's theology.[97] Thus, Wilson is not far from Mays — both working out the Reformed confession of God's sovereignty as it applies to the Psalter. J. Clinton McCann has joined the voices within this sovereignty-centered theological conversation, but has explored how this confession relates to the Psalter's approach to the issue of injustice. He concludes that "God's sovereignty is exercised ultimately as love, not force. Thus, as we move toward a theology of the Psalms, this means that, if there is a word that is as important as the word 'justice,' it is ḥesed. . . ."[98] For Rolf Jacobson, in contrast, "the dominant theological confession of the Psalter may be summed up concisely: *The Lord is faithful.*"[99]

Another synthetic approach has been to investigate the theology of collections within the psalms, such as the Psalms of Asaph or the Psalms of Ascent.[100] Or some scholars focus on certain genres of psalms, as Nancy deClaissé-Walford and Joel LeMon have done with the imprecatory psalms.[101] Whatever the approach, in this commentary we have sought to understand the theological witness of each psalm individually — but within the larger contexts of the Psalter's story and theological witness and the twenty-first century world.

In the end, what is of enduring and vital significance to the psalms is that they do testify to the character and activity of the Lord. They testify that the God who elected Abraham and David and their offspring is present and active in the world and that the Lord's character is such that the Lord's ears are open to all who cry out in pain and confusion. As such, the psalms are not simply texts about the past. They are promises about the future. Indeed, they are poems that pull us into a future that we usually cannot imagine, that is, to take our places in a community of faith that is being shaped to bear the mark and character of the Lord.

97. "Psalms and Psalter: Paradigm for Biblical Theology," in *Biblical Theology: Retrospect and Prospect,* ed. Scott J. Hafemann (Downers Grove: InterVarsity, 2002), pp. 100-110.

98. "The Single Most Important Text in the Entire Bible," in Jacobson, *Soundings in the Theology of the Psalms,* pp. 63-76, quoting p. 73.

99. " 'The Faithfulness of the Lord Endures Forever': The Theological Witness of the Psalter," in *Soundings in the Theology of the Psalms,* pp. 111-37

100. Harry P. Nasuti, *Tradition History and the Psalms of Asaph* (SBLDS 88; Atlanta: Scholars, 1988); Loren Crow, *The Songs of Ascent (120–134): Their Place in Israelite History and Religion* (SBLDS 148; Atlanta: Scholars, 1996).

101. DeClaissé-Walford, "The Theology of the Imprecatory Psalms," in Jacobson, *Soundings in the Theology of the Psalms,* pp. 77-92; LeMon, "Saying Amen to Violent Psalms: Patterns of Prayer, Belief, and Action in the Psalms," in *Soundings in the Theology of the Psalms,* pp. 93-109.

VII. ANALYSIS OF CONTENTS

The following analysis of contents presents a brief outline of the Psalter. For a fuller literary analysis of the Psalter's shape, see section IV of this introduction, "The Canonical Shape of the Psalter." This outline follows the "five books" of the Psalter as they are presented and preserved in the Masoretic tradition. The commentary in this volume corresponds to this outline — individual commentaries are provided for each psalm, and brief introductions to the five books of the Psalter are also included.

I. Book One (Psalms 1–41)
   a. Introduction (Psalms 1–2)[102]
   b. Psalms Proper (Psalms 3–41)
      i. Davidic psalms (Psalms 3:1–41:12)
   c. Closing Doxology (41:13)
II. Book Two (Psalms 42–72)
   a. Psalms Proper (Psalms 42–72)[103]
      i. Korahite Psalms (Psalms 42/43–49)
      ii. An Asaphic Psalm (Psalm 50)
      iii. Davidic Psalms (Psalms 51–71)
      iv. A Solomonic Psalm (Psalm 72)
   b. Closing Doxology (72:18-19)
   c. Editorial note: the end of the Davidic prayers (Psalm 72:20)
III. Book Three (Psalms 73–89)
   a. Psalms Proper (Psalms 73–89)
      i. Asaphic Psalms (Psalms 73–83; see also Psalm 50)
      ii. Korahite Psalms (Psalms 84–85)
      iii. A Davidic Psalm (Psalm 86)
      iv. Korahite Psalms (Psalms 87–88)
      v. An Ezraite Psalm (Psalm 89)
   b. Closing Doxology (Psalm 89:52)
IV. Book Four (Psalms 90–106)
   a. Psalms 90–106
      i. A Mosaic Psalm (90)
      ii. An Untitled Psalm (91)
      iii. A Sabbath Psalm (92)

102. Psalms 1–2 offer an introduction both to Book One and to the entire Psalter.

103. Psalms 42–82 are also often called the "Elohistic Psalter," because these psalms generally prefer the generic term for God rather than the divine name.

- iv. "The Lord Reigns" or Enthronement Psalms (Psalms 93–99; see also Psalm 47)[104]
- v. Praise Psalms (Psalms 100–106)[105]

b. Closing Doxology (Psalm 106:48)

V. Book Five (Psalms 107–50)

a. Psalms Proper (Psalms 107–46)

- i. An Untitled Psalm of Thanksgiving (Psalm 107)
- ii. Davidic Psalms (Psalms 108–10)
- iii. Twin Acrostic Psalms (Psalms 111–12)
- iv. The Egyptian Hallel (Psalms 113–18)
- v. A Torah Psalm (Psalm 119)
- vi. The Songs of the Ascents (Psalms 120–34)
- vii. Untitled Psalms (Psalms 135–37)
- viii. Davidic Psalms (Psalms 138–46)

b. Closing Doxology (Psalms 146–50)[106]

VIII. SELECT BIBLIOGRAPHY

Allen, Leslie C. *Psalms 101–150.* Rev. ed. WBC 21. Nashville: Nelson, 2002.

Alter, Robert. *The Art of Biblical Poetry.* Rev. ed. New York: Basic Books, 2011.

Anderson, Bernhard W., and Steven Bishop. *Out of the Depths: The Psalms Speak for Us Today.* 3rd ed. Louisville: Westminster John Knox, 2000.

Batto, Bernard Frank, and Kathryn L. Roberts, eds. *David and Zion: Biblical Studies in Honor of J. J. M. Roberts.* Winona Lake: Eisenbrauns, 2004.

Bellinger, William H. *Psalms: Reading and Studying the Book of Praises.* Peabody: Hendrickson, 1990.

Berlin, Adele. *The Dynamics of Biblical Parallelism.* Rev. ed. BRS. Grand Rapids: Eerdmans and Livonia: Dove, 2008.

Bouzard, Walter C., Jr. *We Have Heard with Our Ears, O God: Sources of the Communal Laments in the Psalms.* SBLDS 159. Atlanta: Scholars, 1997.

104. Psalm 94 is understood here as one of the so-called enthronement psalms, even though it lacks the phrase "The LORD reigns." See commentary.

105. These psalms include two psalms marked for particular use ("Thanksgiving," Psalm 100; "A Prayer of One Afflicted," Psalm 102), two Davidic psalms (Psalms 101 and 103), and two sets of "twin psalms" (Psalms 103–4 and 105–6; these latter two psalms are historical psalms).

106. Some scholars consider only Psalm 150 the closing doxology, but it is clear that the last five psalms are an intentional grouping — each psalm begins and ends with the imperative call: "Praise the Lord!"

Bright, John. *The Kingdom of God, the Biblical Concept and Its Meaning for the Church.* Nashville: Abingdon-Cokesbury, 1953.
Brown, William P. *Psalms.* Nashville: Abingdon, 2000.
———. *Seeing the Psalms: A Theology of Metaphor.* Louisville: Westminster John Knox, 2002.
Brown, William P., ed. *The Oxford Handbook of the Psalms.* New York: Oxford University Press, 2014.
Broyles, Craig C. *Psalms.* NIBC 11. Peabody: Hendrickson, 1995.
Brueggemann, Walter. *Israel's Praise: Doxology against Idolatry and Ideology.* Philadelphia: Fortress, 1988.
———. *The Message of the Psalms: A Theological Commentary.* Minneapolis: Augsburg, 1984.
———. *The Psalms and the Life of Faith.* Ed. Patrick D. Miller. Minneapolis: Augsburg Fortress, 1995.
Calvin, John. *Commentary on the Psalms.* Trans. James Anderson. 5 vols. Grand Rapids: Eerdmans, 1948-49.
Clifford, Richard J. *Psalms 1–72.* Nashville: Abingdon, 2002.
———. *Psalms 73–150.* Nashville: Abingdon, 2003.
Craigie, Peter C. *Psalms 1 50.* WBC 19. Waco: Word, 1983.
Craigie, Peter C., and Marvin E. Tate. *Psalms 1–50.* 2nd ed. WBC 19. Nashville: Nelson, 2005.
Craven, Toni. *The Book of Psalms.* MBS 6. Collegeville: Liturgical, 1992.
Creach, Jerome F. D. *The Destiny of the Righteous in the Psalms.* St. Louis: Chalice, 2008.
———. *Yahweh as Refuge and the Editing of the Hebrew Psalter.* JSOTSup 217. Sheffield: Sheffield Academic, 1996.
Cross, Frank Moore. *Canaanite Myth and Hebrew Epic: Essays in the History of the Religion of Israel.* Cambridge, MA: Harvard University Press, 1973.
Crow, Loren D. *The Songs of Ascents (Psalms 120–134): Their Place in Israelite History and Religion.* SBLDS 148. Atlanta: Scholars, 1996.
Dahood, Mitchell J. *Psalms I: 1–50.* AB 16. Garden City: Doubleday, 1965.
———. *Psalms II: 51–100.* AB 17. Garden City: Doubleday, 1968.
———. *Psalms III: 101–150.* AB 17A. Garden City: Doubleday, 1970.
Davidson, Robert. *The Vitality of Worship: A Commentary on the Book of Psalms.* Grand Rapids: Eerdmans, 1998.
deClaissé-Walford, Nancy L. *Introduction to the Psalms: A Song from Ancient Israel.* St. Louis: Chalice, 2004.
———. *Reading from the Beginning: The Shaping of the Hebrew Psalter.* Macon: Mercer University Press, 1997.
———. *The Shape and Shaping of the Hebrew Psalter: The Current State of Scholarship.* SBL Ancient Israel and Its Literature 20. Atlanta: Society of Biblical Literature, 2014.

Eaton, John H. *Kingship and the Psalms.* 2nd ed. Sheffield: JSOT, 1986.

Flint, Peter W. *The Dead Sea Psalms Scrolls and the Book of Psalms.* STDJ 17. Leiden: Brill, 1997.

Flint, Peter W., and Patrick D. Miller. *The Book of Psalms: Composition and Reception.* VTSup 99. Leiden: Brill, 2005.

Fokkelmann, J. P. *Major Poems of the Hebrew Bible.* 4 vols. SSN 37, 41. Assen: Van Gorcum, 1998-2004.

———. *The Psalms in Form.* Leiden: Deo, 2002.

———. *Reading Biblical Poetry: An Introductory Guide.* Trans. Ineke Smit. Louisville: Westminster John Knox, 2001.

García Martínez, Florentino, Eibert J. C. Tigchelaar, and A. S. van der Woude. *Qumran Cave 11: II, 11Q2-18, 11Q20-31.* DJD 23; Oxford: Clarendon, 1998.

Gerstenberger, Erhard S. *Psalms: Part 1, with an Introduction to Cultic Poetry.* FOTL 14. Grand Rapids: Eerdmans, 1988.

———. *Psalms: Part 2 and Lamentations.* FOTL 15. Grand Rapids: Eerdmans, 2001.

Gillingham, Susan E. *A Journey of Two Psalms: The Reception of Psalms 1 and 2 in Jewish and Christian Tradition.* Oxford: Oxford University Press, 2013.

———. *Psalms through the Centuries.* Malden: Blackwell, 2008.

Goldingay, John. *Psalms.* 3 vols. Ed. Tremper Longman III. Grand Rapids: Baker Academic, 2006-2008.

Goulder, Michael D. *The Prayers of David (Psalms 51–72).* JSOTSup 102. Sheffield: Sheffield Academic, 1990.

———. *The Psalms of Asaph and the Pentateuch.* JSOTSup 233. Sheffield: Sheffield Academic, 1996.

———. *The Psalms of the Return: Book V, Psalms 107–150.* JSOTSup 258. Sheffield: Sheffield Academic, 1998.

———. *The Psalms of the Sons of Korah.* JSOTSup 20. Sheffield: JSOT, 1982.

Gunkel, Hermann. *Die Psalmen.* HKAT 2. Göttingen: Vandenhoeck & Ruprecht, 1926.

Gunkel, Hermann, and Joachim Begrich. *Einleitung in die Psalmen: Die Gattungen der religiösen Lyrik Israels.* Göttingen: Vandenhoeck & Ruprecht, 1933.

———. *Introduction to Psalms: The Genres of the Religious Lyric of Israel.* Trans. James D. Nogalski. Macon: Mercer University Press, 1998.

Hossfeld, Frank-Lothar, and Erich Zenger. *Die Psalmen I: Psalmen 1–50.* NEchtB. Würzburg: Echter, 1993.

———. *Psalms 2: A Commentary on Psalms 51–100.* Trans. Linda M. Maloney. Ed. Klaus Baltzer. Hermeneia. Minneapolis: Fortress, 2005.

Jacobson, Rolf A. *Many Are Saying: The Function of Direct Discourse in the Hebrew Psalter.* JSOTSup 397. London: T. & T. Clark, 2004.

Jacobson, Rolf A., ed. *Soundings in the Theology of Psalms: Perspectives and Methods in Contemporary Scholarship.* Minneapolis: Fortress, 2011.

Jacobson, Rolf A., and Karl N. Jacobson. *Invitation to the Psalms: A Reader's Guide for Discovery and Engagement.* Grand Rapids: Baker, 2013.
Janowski, Bernd. *Arguing with God: A Theological Anthropology of the Psalms.* Trans. Armin Siedlicki. Louisville: Westminster John Knox, 2013.
Johnson, Aubrey R. *The Cultic Prophet and Israel's Psalmody.* Cardiff: University of Wales Press, 1979.
Keel, Othmar. *The Symbolism of the Biblical World: Ancient Near Eastern Iconography and the Book of Psalms.* Trans. Timothy Hallett. 1978; repr. Winona Lake: Eisenbrauns, 1997.
Kraus, Hans-Joachim. *Psalms 1–59.* Trans. Hilton C. Oswald. CC. Minneapolis: Augsburg, 1988.
———. *Psalms 60–150.* Trans. Hilton C. Oswald. CC. Minneapolis: Augssburg, 1989.
———. *Theology of the Psalms.* Trans. Keith Crim. Minneapolis: Augsburg, 1986.
Kugel, James L. *The Idea of Biblical Poetry: Parallelism and Its History.* Baltimore: Johns Hopkins University Press, 1998.
Limburg, James. *Psalms.* Westminster Bible Companion. Louisville: Westminster John Knox, 2000.
———. *Psalms for Sojourners.* 2nd ed. Minneapolis: Fortress, 2002.
Luther, Martin. *Works: American Edition.* Ed. Hilton C. Oswald. Vols. 10-14. Philadelphia: Fortress and St. Louis: Concordia, 1956-58.
Mays, James Luther. *The Lord Reigns: A Theological Handbook to the Psalms.* Louisville: Westminster John Knox, 1994.
———. *Psalms.* Interpretation. Louisville: John Knox, 1994.
McCann, J. Clinton, Jr. "The Book of Psalms." In *NIB* 4. Nashville: Abingdon, 1996.
———. *A Theological Introduction to the Book of Psalms: The Psalms as Torah.* Nashville: Abingdon, 1993.
McCann, J. Clinton, ed. *The Shape and Shaping of the Psalter.* JSOTSup 159. Sheffield: JSOT, 1993.
Millard, Matthias. *Die Komposition des Psalters: Ein formgeschichtlicher Ansatz.* FAT 9. Tübingen: Mohr, 1994.
Miller, Patrick D. *Interpreting the Psalms.* Philadelphia: Fortress, 1986.
———. *They Cried to the Lord: The Form and Theology of Biblical Prayer.* Minneapolis: Fortress, 1994.
Mowinckel, Sigmund. *Psalmenstudien.* 6 vols. Kristiana: Dybwad, 1921-24.
———. *The Psalms in Israel's Worship.* Trans. D. R. Ap-Thomas. BRS. Grand Rapids: Eerdmans and Livonia: Dove, 2004.
Nasuti, Harry P. *Defining the Sacred Songs: Genre, Tradition, and the Post-critical Interpretation of the Psalter.* JSOTSup 218. Sheffield Academic, 1999.
———. *Tradition History and the Psalms of Asaph.* SBLDS 88. Atlanta: Scholars, 1988.

Sanders, James A. *From Sacred Story to Sacred Text: Canon as Paradigm.* Philadelphia: Fortress, 1992.

Sarna, Nahum M. *On the Book of Psalms: Exploring the Prayers of Ancient Israel.* New York: Schocken, 1993.

Schaefer, Konrad. *Psalms.* Ed. David W. Cotter. Berit Olam. Collegeville: Liturgical, 2001.

Seybold, Klaus. *Introducing the Psalms.* Trans. R. Graeme Dunphy. Edinburgh: T. & T. Clark, 1990.

———. *Die Psalmen.* HAT 1/15. Tübingen: Mohr (Siebeck), 1996.

Strawn, Brent A., and Nancy R. Bowen, eds. *A God So Near: Essays on Old Testament Theology in Honor of Patrick D. Miller.* Winona Lake: Eisenbrauns, 2003.

Tanner, Beth LaNeel. *The Book of Psalms through the Lens of Intertextuality.* New York: Lang, 2001.

Tate, Marvin E. *Psalms 51–100.* WBC 20. Dallas: Word, 1990.

Terrien, Samuel. *The Psalms: Strophic Structure and Theological Commentary.* ECC. Grand Rapids: Eerdmans, 2003.

Ulrich, Eugene, Frank Moore Cross, et al., *Qumran Cave 4: XI, Psalms to Chronicles.* DJD 16. Oxford: Clarendon, 2000.

Waltke, Bruce K., and M. O'Connor. *Biblical Hebrew Syntax.* Winona Lake: Eisenbrauns, 1990.

Watts, James W. *Psalm and Story: Inset Hymns in Hebrew Narrative.* JSOTSup 139. Sheffield: JSOT, 1992.

Weiser, Artur. *The Psalms: A Commentary.* Trans. Herbert Hartwell. OTL. Louisville: Westminster, 1962.

Westermann, Claus. *Praise and Lament in the Psalms.* Trans. Keith R. Crim and Richard N. Soulen. Atlanta: John Knox, 1981.

———. *The Psalms: Structure, Content & Message.* Trans. Ralph D. Gehrke. Minneapolis: Augsburg, 1980.

Wilson, Gerald Henry. *The Editing of the Hebrew Psalter.* SBLDS 76. Chico: Scholars, 1985.

Rolf A. Jacobson
(Sections I-III, V-IX)

Nancy deClaissé-Walford
(Section IV)

Text and Commentary

Book One of the Psalter: Psalms 1–41

INTRODUCTION

The Introduction noted that the Psalter is divided editorially into five books (Psalms 1–41, 42–72, 73–89, 90–106, and 107–50). Each of these books ends with a doxology. In addition to the doxology at the end of Psalm 41, there are two primary editorial features that indicate that Psalms 1–41 form a distinct collection within the Psalter.

First, almost all of these psalms bear the superscription *of David*. Psalms 1 and 2 lack the superscription because they form a two-part introduction to the book and to the Psalter. Psalm 10 does not bear the superscription because it is the second half of a continuous poem that comprises Psalms 9 and 10. Other than these, Psalm 33 is the only one of these psalms that lacks a Davidic superscription. Immediately following Book One, a group of Korahite psalms occurs (Psalms 42–49). Second, these psalms are marked off as a unit by a "bookending" feature: the first and last psalms in the collection (Psalms 1 and 41) both begin with the phrase *happy are/is . . . ('ašrê)*.

The Introduction also mentioned that Book One of the Psalter, as a whole, may be read as the story of the reign of David. In addition, it was noted that — broadly speaking — the Psalter moves from prayers for help to hymns of praise. As Claus Westermann first observed, almost all of the prayers for help are contained in the first half of the Psalter, while most of the psalms of praise appear only in the second half of the Psalter.[1] Walter Brueggemann built a theological argument on Westermann's observation, arguing that the Psalter moves from "obedience to praise," from a "torah piety" that is established in Book One of the Psalter to the "unfettered" and "glad, unconditional" praise of the Psalter's climactic psalms.[2] What one finds in between the

1. *Praise and Lament in the Psalms,* p. 257.

2. "Bounded by Obedience and Praise," in *The Psalms and the Life of Faith,* ed. Patrick D. Miller (Minneapolis: Augsburg Fortress, 1995), pp. 189-213, quoting pp. 210, 193-94.

beginning and the end, according to Brueggemann, are the typical postures of "suffering and hope" that comprise the life of faith.[3] The life of faith, then, is a struggle to come to grips with God's goodness "in suffering and hope, in lament and in hymn, in candor and in gratitude."[4] What one finds in Book One of the Psalter, then, is the initial stage of that struggle-filled journey from obedience to praise. This initial stage of the journey — filled as it is with songs of lament (prayers for help) — focuses mainly on candor: on stating, as clearly as possible, the challenge that life in God's creation and life in God's community are not filled with unambiguous experiences of God's grace. Rather, there is more than a little suffering in God's world and among God's people.

The most significant feature of the canonical shape of Book One is how it begins: with Psalms 1 and 2 standing at the front of Book One as a two-part introduction not only to Book One, but indeed, to the entire Psalter. The beginning of the Psalter has often been the last place to which scholars have turned when investigating the psalms.[5] Beginnings of books are important, however. By means of a beginning, an author, or in this case an editor or editors, introduces crucial themes that will impact the rest of the book and major issues to be addressed.[6] As Patrick Miller has accurately commented, Psalms 1 and 2 "stand closely together as a single, if complex, way into the psalms that follow."[7] Psalm 1 is, significantly, an instructional psalm that teaches that the psalms are God's instruction — they are *the way* of the Lord that is to be followed by those who love the Lord and who will drink from the Lord's streams of living waters. Psalm 2 is a royal psalm that promises that the Lord has chosen David and David's heirs to be *my son.* Much has been written about this feature and what it means for interpreting Book One and the Psalter as a whole.[8] Miller's summary interpretation of it is helpful:

> Psalms 1 and 2 form an introduction that suggests, first, that one finds here a true torah piety that will show the way to go for those who love the Lord and the law, and second, that these psalms also show the way of God's rule over the larger human community.

3. Brueggemann, "Bounded by Obedience and Praise," p. 202.

4. Brueggemann, "Bounded by Obedience and Praise," p. 202.

5. J. Clinton McCann, *A Theological Introduction to the Book of Psalms* (Nashville: Abingdon, 1993), p. 25 ("seldom has it occurred to scholars to begin at the beginning").

6. See Donald Juel, *An Introduction to New Testament Literature* (Nashville: Abingdon, 1978), 82.

7. "The Beginning of the Psalter," in *The Shape and Shaping of the Psalter,* ed. J. Clinton McCann, Jr. (JSOTSup 159; Sheffield: JSOT, 1993), p. 85.

8. See, e.g., Miller, "The Beginning of the Psalter"; Nancy deClaissé-Walford, *Reading from the Beginning: The Shaping of the Hebrew Psalter* (Macon: Mercer University Press, 1997); or Hossfeld and Zenger, *Die Psalmen I,* esp. pp. 35, 45-54; and the bibliography in those sources.

Or, these two psalms function to point to two primary ways that God is working to effect God's will in the world: through God's Word (which forms a specific community of followers) and through God's messiah (who also gathers a specific community of followers around him). Thus, the two-part introduction to Book One of the Psalter is about the psalms as Torah, the psalms as promising the rule of God's messiah, and the psalms as prayers and hymns that fashion and form a certain sort of community.

One could also interpret the twofold introduction of the Psalter in a more direct way. Psalm 1 is a wisdom or instructional psalm. Why was it placed at the head of the Psalter? Perhaps simply to say that the psalms are to be read as wise instruction concerning how the Lord's people live out the life of faith. Psalm 2 is a royal psalm, which was preserved by Israel's scribes long after the Davidic kings had ceased to rule over God's people. Why was it preserved and then placed as part of the introduction to the Psalter? Perhaps simply to indicate that the Psalter is to be read as a book of prophecy concerning God's expected messiah. These two ways of reading the psalms — as wisdom and as prophecy — certainly describe much of the way in which the psalms were read both at Qumran and in the New Testament.[9]

Finally, in addition to Psalms 1 and 2 as the two-part introduction to Book One of the Psalter, scholars have also identified other subgroupings of psalms within Book One. Pierre Auffret has argued that Psalms 15–24 are a group of psalms organized chiastically, with Psalm 19 as the center of this subgroup.[10] Frank-Lothar Hossfeld and Erich Zenger have expanded this view, arguing that Book One has four subgroups: Psalms 3–14, 15–24, 25–34, and 35–41.[11] They argue that these groups are recognizable by each having distinct "corner psalms" *(Eckpsalmen)* and center psalms. The center of the first group is Psalm 8 (the only hymn in the midst of a group of prayers for help). The center of the second group is Psalm 19 (a praise/Torah psalm in the middle of royal psalms). The center of the third group is Psalm 29, a unique Yahweh-hymn in the middle of a series of prayer and thanksgiving psalms. And the center of the fourth group is Psalm 38, a prayer for help that has themes similar to its neighboring psalms). Together, these four subgroups form four pictures of the congregation of God's people, who look to the Lord for rescue and deliverance.

ROLF A. JACOBSON

9. See Donald Juel, *Messianic Exegesis* (Minneapolis: Fortress, 1988).

10. *La sagesse a bâti sa maison: Etudes de structures littéraires dans l'Ancien Testament et spécialement dans les Psaumes* (OBO 49; Fribourg: Editions Universitaires, 1982), pp. 407-549. Cited in Patrick D. Miller, *Interpreting the Psalms* (Philadelphia: Fortress, 1986), p. 14.

11. *Psalmen I,* pp. 12-13.

Psalm 1: The Way of Life

The Hebrew Psalter opens with an instructional psalm that maps the future as a choice between one of two different paths. These two paths are not characterized by their terrain or geography (cf. Matt. 7:14: "The gate is narrow and the road is hard . . ."), but by the character of the people who tread them. Down one path walk the wicked, sinners, and scoffers. Their eventual destination is judgment and unhappiness. Down the other path march the righteous, who bring with them the Torah of the Lord. Their end is happy, because they journey under the protection of the Lord.

The poem consists of four stanzas that are carefully constructed upon a basic contrast between the wicked and the righteous.[1] This contrast is exploited by means of a chiastic structure:

St. 1 The way of the wicked (v. 1)
St. 2 The Torah of the Lord (v. 2)
St. 3 The prosperity found in Torah (v. 3)
St. 4 The judgment of the wicked (vv. 4-6)

The closing verse of the psalm places an exclamation mark on the basic contrast between the ways of the wicked and the righteous, which serves as the "theological axis" around which the basic contrast swings.[2] The psalm builds on this basic contrast between the righteous and the wicked, including several related contrasts:

- between the luscious tree and the dried chaff;
- between the many wicked and the solitary righteous;
- between advice of sinners and the commandments of the Lord.

As previously noted, this psalm is an instructional psalm. Because of this classification, the suggestion has been made that the psalm should be understood as having originated in an educational setting, from whence it made its way into the cultic liturgy.[3] But any original context in which this psalm may have functioned has been obscured by one clear fact: in its *scriptural context,* the psalm introduces the book of Psalms. The placement of this wisdom psalm

1. Many commentators divide the psalm into two parts, vv. 1-3 and 4-6 (cf. e.g., Limburg, *Psalms,* pp. 2-3; Hossfeld and Zenger, *Die Psalmen I,* pp. 46-48; etc.). See also Fokkelmann (*Major Poems of the Hebrew Bible,* 2:53-54).

2. So Seybold, *Die Psalmen,* p. 6.

3. Gerstenberger, *Psalms: Part 1,* pp. 42-43. See his discussion of the genre of the psalm.

at the front of the Psalter is not an accident. Together with the second psalm, Psalm 1 functions as a two-part introduction to the Psalter. Because of this, its message of the two paths has significance beyond the mere boundaries of Psalm 1. The reader is invited to read the entire book of Psalms as a guide to life in God — a life that the psalm describes as *happy.* Likewise, because the key characteristic of the happy life is depicted as a constant meditation on God's torah, the book of Psalms itself is commended to the reader *as* torah.

1 *Happy is the one*
who does not walk[4] *in the counsel of the wicked,*
and does not stand in the way of the sinners,
and does not sit in the seat of scoffers.[5]

2 *Rather, whose delight is in the instruction*[6] *of the* LORD,
who meditates[7] *on his instruction day and night.*

3 *This one is like a tree transplanted by streams of water,*[8]
which produces its fruit in its season,
Whose leaves do not wither;
but who prospers in everything.[9]

4 *Not so the wicked!*
Rather, they are like chaff that the wind drives away.[10]

4. Syr transposes *ʿăṣaṯ* ("counsel") in v. 1b with *dereḵ* ("way") in v. 1c, which improves the correlation of the two nouns to the verbs "walk" and "stand." But this improvement is both unnecessary and is the more difficult reading; MT should be retained.

5. The word *lēṣîm* is normally translated "scoffers," overlaying the noun's basic sense of "babblers" with an additional sense of menace. Perhaps the identify of the scoffer should be understood in connection with the enemies in the psalms, who so often threaten the psalmists with their words (cf. Ps. 12:4).

6. The word *tōrâ,* often translated as "law," is properly understood as "instruction" or "teaching,"

7. The verb *hāgâ* should not be understood to imply an internalized, cognitive meditation. Hossfeld and Zenger (p. 47) even argue that the term implies "recitation." The verb also occurs in Ps 2:1 to describe the plotting voices of the nations, serving to connect Psalms 1 and 2 as a dual introduction to the Psalter.

8. The noun *peleg* denotes irrigation channels for a constant supply of water, and thus in this case "streams of water."

9. *BHS* suggests deleting this colon as a gloss (so Kraus, *Psalms 1–59,* p. 133; cf. Josh. 1:8). This is unwarranted, because the image of prosperity is necessary to set up the negative image that follows in v. 4. Furthermore, Fokkelmann's analysis of the psalm's balanced prosody relies on the inclusion of the colon.

10. LXX adds "from the face of the earth." This addition changes the nuance of the

5 *Therefore the wicked will not arise in the judgment,*[11]
nor sinners in the assembly[12] *of the righteous.*
6 *For the* L*ORD* *knows the way of the righteous,*
but the way of the wicked will perish.

1 The first of the psalm's four stanzas defines the *happy* person in terms of a contrast with the wicked.[13] The Hebrew *ʾîš* (lit., "man") is pluralized in the NRSV translation as "those" in order to avoid exclusive male language, but is rendered here as *the one,* to preserve the singular number of the noun. This is important because in the first stanza the singular *one* is contrasted with three plural nouns: the *wicked, sinners,* and *scoffers.* In two ways, the opening verse thus elegantly sets up a "one against the masses" image. On the one hand, as is often the case in the Old Testament's wisdom literature, the *one* is set up against three — *wicked, sinners,* and *scoffers.* And, on the other hand, this already mismatched equation is then multiplied because each of those three is not a single person but a group. The effect is to deepen the contrast between the way of the righteous and the way of the wicked: not only are the two ways distinguished by *who* travels down them, but by *how many* travel down. The contrast evokes the idea that the way of the righteous is the road less traveled; it is not an easy or popular choice to make. One who walks in the way of the righteous must struggle against the traffic, buffeting against the currents of peer pressure and group-think. Yet in spite of this, it is still the way of happiness.

The poem expands upon the difference between the righteous and the wicked by describing both groups in terms of the other. In the first stanza, the righteous one — although note that the word *righteous* does not occur until the third stanza — is defined at first in negative terms. He does *not* walk in the counsel of the wicked; he does *not* stand in the way of sinners; he does *not* sit in the seat of scoffers. Most English translations obscure the heavy-handed repetition in Hebrew of the word *not (lōʾ).* Further, some English translations also obscure the poetic progression evident in the three verbs of v. 1: *walk, stand,* and *sit.* This verbal progression depicts a regression from moving — to

judgment awaiting the wicked into an eschatological judgment. There is no reason to prefer this over the MT.

11. According to Craigie (*Psalms 1–50,* p. 58), "in judgment" in v. 5 means in "the *place* of judgment" (cf. Deut 25:1), meaning no place or respect in the courts. His point is that "there is not any eschatological implication of a final judgment here." However, the sense of time can be retained here — meaning "at some future time" — without implying an eschatological judgment. (But note that the LXX "from the face of the earth" in v. 4 does indeed suggest an eschatological judgment.)

12. LXX has *boulē* both here for *ʿᵃḏaṯ* and in v. 1 for *ʿᵃṣaṯ,* suggesting that it is reading *ʿᵃṣaṯ* here, but this should be understood as an error and the MT retained.

13. For the congratulatory formula "happy are . . . ," see comment in Psalm 2.

stationary — to sitting. Perhaps the idea is that sin is a temptation that one first tries out, later becomes accustomed to, and finally becomes a habit or lifestyle. Many have noted that the verbs *walk, stand,* and *sit* also call to mind the positive commandment in Deut. 6:4-9 that the person of faith is to keep the commandments of God in mind while at home and away, while coming and going.[14] Craigie has argued that the nouns *counsel, way,* and *gathering* also suggest a progression: perhaps from listening to advice, to joining on a walk, to joining in living.[15] Notice that each of these nouns requires the presence of at least one other person; these nouns continue the contrast between the singular righteous person and the plural wicked persons whose lifestyle is a temptation to be avoided.

2 In this poem, it does not suffice to define the righteous or happy life purely in terms of the negative. There is also a positive employment for the happy person: the study of the *torah* of the Lord. The translation of this word, which occurs twice in v. 2, is particularly problematic. The term can mean "law" or a collection of laws. In this context, however, it is better not to render it as "law" because of traditional negative connotations with legalism. Also, in this context, it seems not to refer to a collection of laws, nor is it a technical designation for the Pentateuch. The basic sense of the word is *instruction,* and that is the sense that best fits here.[16] In both occurrences of *tôrâ* in v. 2, the term is defined not as just any instruction, but specifically as the Lord's instruction. When this verse is contrasted with v. 1, the message is clear: the way to happiness means following not the advice of the questionable humans but rather the instruction of the Lord. The verb *hāgâ* is normally translated as "meditates," but it should be noted that the term does not imply a strictly internalized, cognitive exercise. It properly denotes a verbalized rumination, because the ancients did not read silently but out loud. The verb is used to describe the cooing of the pigeon (Isa. 38:14), the growling of the lion (Isa. 31:4), and the voice of the human (Ps. 35:28). In this context, the verb stirs up the idea of a congregation (cf. v. 5) murmuring in prayer and praise. In a poetic sense, the verb also anticipates the simile that follows in the next verse. The sound of human voices murmuring has its analogue in the soft whisper of water gurgling in a stream.

3 Like the first stanza, the second stanza opens with a succinct mention of the lone righteous one that is followed by the body of the stanza. Whereas the first stanza began with the declaration, *Happy is the one,* this stanza begins *this one is* (the Hebrew does not contain a noun, of course, but the subject of the verb *hāyâ* can only be the *one* of v. 1). What follows is one of the most striking similes in the Psalter. Here, the life grounded in the Lord's instruc-

14. E.g., see Hossfeld and Zenger, *Die Psalmen I,* p. 47.

15. Craigie, *Psalms 1–50,* p. 58.

16. See McCann, *A Theological Introduction to the Book of Psalms,* pp. 26-27.

tion is likened to a vibrant tree whose roots are sunk deep into the life-giving soil of a river bed. The sense of the verb *šāṯûl* suggests that the location is intentional — the tree has either been transplanted there or was planted as a seedling. This image is well-suited for the life characterized by study of torah. The nourishment that sustains the tree is hidden; it is internal nourishment that feeds the life of the tree, drawn up through invisible roots. Yet the life thus imparted suffices to fortify the tree against the harsh conditions of Israel's arid climate to such an extent that it never withers, but faithfully bears its fruit at harvest time. The closing colon of the stanza introduces a degree of ambiguity. It states, it *prospers in everything.* The subject of the phrase is ambiguous; it could either be the tree of v. 3 or the righteous one of v. 1. If it is the tree, then the point is that in all weather conditions the tree flourished. If it is the human, then the point is that the environment created by the wicked cannot extinguish the righteous. Like heat applied to a chemical reaction, this ambiguity serves to help the tenor and the vehicle of the simile (the righteous one and the vibrant tree, respectively) marry. The one who studies God's instruction *is* the tree transplanted near water.

4-6 This stanza begins on a sharply disjunctive note: *Not so the wicked!* The Hebrew *lōʾ ḵēn* provides a harsh transition between the second and third stanzas. As the first two stanzas began with the abrupt mention of the righteous person, this stanza also begins in a cursory fashion, but now the subject is the wicked. The agricultural simile of the second stanza is extended into the third stanza of the psalm. But in contrast to the resilient tree, which retains its leaves even through the hot winds of summer, the wicked are likened to chaff *(mōṣ),*[17] which is a helpless victim of the wind. The contrast between the two images is heightened by the lack of balance in terms of poetic length. Whereas the tree simile is indulged for four full cola, the chaff is dispensed with in just one colon. This abbreviated length implies both that the wicked lack the internal fortitude to endure difficulties and also that the time for the wicked to be judged is nigh. That judgment is specifically named in v. 5 in such a way that the contrast with the future of the righteous is highlighted. To fail in the judgment means that one is simultaneously excluded from the congregation of the righteous; to find a place in the congregation is to avoid the company and fate of sinners.

The meaning of the psalm is enhanced through a brilliant, threefold strategy of poetic delay. First, the word *righteous* occurs, having been withheld until this point. Even though the entire psalm is about the choice between *the way of the righteous* and *the way of the wicked,* the word *righteous* does not occur until the last word of v. 5. Second, the word *righteous* occurs as a *plural* noun. To this point in this short psalm, the words *wicked, sinners,* and *scoffers* have occurred a total of six times — and always in the plural — while *the one*

17. The term denotes dried and dead plant matter, usually as driven by the wind.

being addressed in the psalm is always in the singular. In v. 5 the *righteous ones* are finally named. There at last is a positive plural "community" that counterbalances the threatening community which is composed of the wicked. It is as if the solitary person of v. 1, having avoided the company of the wicked and taken refuge in the torah of the Lord, has finally found a home and community. There is a third element of poetic delay in stanza 3. God — the "proper subject" of all theology — finally is named as an actor (God is named in v. 2, not as one who acts directly, but as one whose torah is worth studying). "The only mention of a divine action in this psalm is withheld until the last verse: The Lord watches over the way of the righteous."[18] There is also a subtle poetic element in the final verse of the psalm that is particularly worthy of attention:

> For the LORD knows the way of the righteous,
> But the way of the wicked *will perish.*

The verb *yāḏaʿ* is often translated as "watch over," to convey the providential nature of God's care. But the more literal *know* is used here to convey a more intimate and internal care. The two cola of v. 6 are constructed around the parallel phrases *the way of the wicked* and *the way of the righteous.* But as Fokkelmann has observed, there is a subtle syntactic change between the first and second cola. In the first colon, *the way of the righteous* is the object of the verb. In the second, *the way of the wicked* is the subject. By means of this nuanced alteration, the poem means to say that being the author of one's own fate is to march down the path of self-destruction. The wicked are their own lords, and thus they "autonomously" move toward their own judgment.[19] Or as Mays has commented, "Their advice and path and position are their own. . . . In their very autonomy they are wrong. . . ."[20] *The way of the righteous,* by theological and grammatical contrast, is the object of God's care. The righteous are distinguished not by any action of their own, but by an action of the Lord's: God watches over them. The message of this verse, and indeed of the entire psalm, is that it is far better to give up spurious claims to subjective autonomy and become the object of the Lord's care. This is the true path to happiness and life.

Reflections

1. God's Way of Life

Perhaps there is no anthem so genuinely American as "My Way," as sung so epically by Frank Sinatra or Elvis Presley. The song expresses one of our high-

18. Broyles, *Psalms,* p. 43.
19. Fokkelmann, *Major Poems of the Hebrew Bible,* p. 53.
20. Mays, *Psalms,* pp. 42-43.

est cultural ideals — the ideal of the self-made man, the self-sufficient woman, the rugged individual. "My Way" is a paean to those who strike out on their own to break trail through the wilderness. Psalm 1 is as antithetical to that ideal as it is possible to get. Psalm 1 bears witness to the belief that the road of our own choosing leads only to our own destruction. Psalm 1 sees hope in a different path, the path defined by God's instruction. To some interpreters, the message of Psalm 1 has sounded a bit like "works righteousness." But when it is seen that the way of God's instruction is a gift for those who cannot guide themselves, then we correctly see that Psalm 1 is the opposite of works righteousness. The psalm offers the free and gracious gift of a better way. But to follow in this "way" that Psalm 1 recommends will require that we unlearn some bad habits. Chief among those bad habits is the habit of relying upon ourselves and seeking to be our own lords and masters. It will require that we relinquish our greedy grasp on what we think of as our own freedom and will. But when we do so, we will discover, as did the psalmist, that there is a better way, a way that is truly free.

2. The Tree of Life and the Streams of Water

The book of Psalms begins with a picture. Not with a prayer, or a hymn of praise, but a picture. Many commentators have noted that the picture that dominates the psalm is that of a tree.[21] In the ancient world, the tree was a symbol of divine blessing. It was a symbol of the temple where God dwelled (cf. Ezek. 41:18), it was a symbol of paradise (cf. Genesis 2), it was a symbol of God's kingly reign and of the Davidic kings who reigned as God's representatives (cf. Isa. 11:1; Zech. 6:12), and it was a symbol of Israel's worship of God rather than the idols (note that "Asherah" was both the name of a female idol and of a sacred tree; cf. Deut. 16:21). But equally important to the image of Psalm 1 is the image of the stream of water. The righteous person is not just like a tree, but one that has been *transplanted* next to a stream! In the metaphorical world of the psalm, that stream is God's instruction (Heb.: *tôrâ*). To follow the logic of the psalm, we must see that we are to identify ourselves with the tree. But that is not enough. We must identify ourselves with the tree *and* the water with God's instruction. Like a tree that quietly, invisibly, constantly receives strength and life through its roots, so are we given God's Word as a steady source of life.

ROLF A. JACOBSON

21. For the most complete analysis of the tree imagery in its ancient Near Eastern context, see Brown, *Seeing the Psalms,* pp. 55-79.

Psalm 2: Speaking of Kings

Together with Psalm 1, Psalm 2 forms a two-part introduction to the Psalter. This conclusion is reached for several reasons. First, neither psalm has a Davidic superscription. Of the forty-one psalms in Book One of the Psalter, only two other psalms lack a superscription.[1] Second, the psalms are tied together by several keywords:

- the rare verb *hāgâ,* "to murmur" (1:2 and 2:1);
- the important noun "way" (*dereḵ;* 1:1, 6; 2:12);
- and the congratulatory formula "happy are" (1:1; 2:12).

The two congratulatory formulae are especially important because they form a literary inclusio around the first two psalms, signaling the reader that the two should be read together.[2] Finally, it is worth noting that when Psalm 2 is quoted in Acts 13:33 ("as it is written in the second psalm . . ."), a variant in one manuscript reads "as it is written in the first psalm." This variant reading suggests that at least one ancient reader understood Psalms 1 and 2 to comprise one unified psalm.

Psalm 2 is a royal psalm.[3] Most commentators agree that it was most likely performed as part of the coronation ceremony of a new king in Jerusalem. On the other hand, it may have formed part of some sort of annual enthronement festival.[4] While the precise original use of the poem remains unclear, it is enough to note that the poem implies a public ceremony in which the king plays the main role.

The poem consists of four stanzas, which have an A-B-B-A structure:

St. 1 The "kings of the earth" rebel
St. 2   The divine king enthroned in heaven
St. 3   The Davidic king enthroned on Zion
St. 4 The "kings" are warned

1. Psalm 10 lacks a superscription, but Ps. 10 is actually the second half of the acrostic poem that comprises both Pss. 9 and 10. Psalm 33 also lacks a superscription.

2. This is especially true if the congratulatory formula in 2:12 was not originally part of Ps. 2 (see note on v. 12). If it was appended to the psalm, it is likely that it was appended precisely for the purpose of tying Pss. 1 and 2 together.

3. The "royal psalms" are not defined by their shared form but by the fact that they all deal with the Davidic kings. These psalms include 18, 20, 21, 45, 72, 89, 101, 110, 132, and 144. See Gunkel, *Introduction to Psalms,* pp. 99-120.

4. Kraus, e.g., imagines an annual enthronement festival after the nature of an Egyptian festival (*Psalms 1–59,* p. 126).

Each of the first three stanzas ends with a quotation, each focuses on a different character or characters, and each implies a different location. As should be obvious from the above chart, one main motif of the psalm is kingship. But a second major motif is the idea of "speech," as the preponderance of verbs of speaking suggest: "rage" (Hebrew *rāḡaš* implies speaking), "murmur," "laugh," "mock," "speak," "tell," "say," and "ask." It is with speech that the kings of the earth rebel, it is with speech that God answers their rebellion, it is with speech that the Davidic king answers their challenge, and in the end, the kings of the earth find themselves speechless before the power of God. A secondary structure complements the psalm's fourfold stanza structure. The psalm is introduced with a question (v. 1), continues with an indicative description (vv. 2-9), and closes with imperative admonitions (vv. 10-12).

1 *Why do nations rage,*
and peoples[5] *murmur*[6] *in vain?*
2 *Kings of earth take their stand,*[7]
and officials gather together,
against the LORD *and against his anointed:*[8]
3 *"Let us shatter their bonds,*[9]
and let us cast their chains from us."

4 *He who sits enthroned*[10] *in heaven laughs,*
the Lord mocks them!
5 *Then he spoke to them in anger,*
and he terrified[11] *them in his anger:*
6 *"I, yes I, have established*[12] *my king,*

5. Craigie argues (*Psalms 1–50,* p. 63) that *lᵉʾummîm* should be understood here as "warriors," because in both Hebrew and Ugaritic it can have a martial connotation. The parallel with "nations," however, argues for retaining the root sense of the word as "peoples."

6. Note that *hāgâ* occurs both here and in Psalm 1, providing a catchword link between the two psalms.

7. The sense of the verb *yāṣaḇ* in this case is to prepare for battle (cf. Jer. 46:4).

8. LXX contains the addition of *selah.*

9. 11QPsᶜ has *mwsdrwt[ymw],* "[their] regulations"; MT is retained, supported by LXX.

10. For the translation of the epithet *yôšēḇ* as "he who sits enthroned," see Shalom M. Paul, *Amos* (Hermeneia; Minneapolis: Fortress, 1991), pp. 51-52. See Pss. 9:7; 29:10; 123:1.

11. The verbs *yᵉḏabbēr* and *yᵉbahᵃlēmô* are understood as preterite forms, as is often the case following *ʾāz* (see Waltke and O'Connor, *Biblical Hebrew Syntax,* p. 465).

12. The verb *nāsaḵtî* is not from *sûḵ,* "anoint," but is related to the noun *nāsîḵ,* "leader" or "chieftain." Akkadian has a similar noun *nasiku.*

upon Zion, my holy mountain."[13]

7 *I will tell of the decree of the* LORD,
he said to me, "You are my son,
today I have begotton you.
8 *Ask of me, and I give*[14] *nations as your inheritance,*
and the ends of the earth as your possession.
9 *You shall break*[15] *them with a rod of iron,*
like a potter's vessels you shall shatter them."

10 *So now, O kings, be wise!*
Be warned, O rulers of the earth!
11 *Serve the* LORD *in fear!*
In trembling (12) kiss his feet![16]
Lest he be angry and you perish in the way,
for his anger burns quickly.

Happy are all who take refuge in him.[17]

1-3 The first stanza portrays nations and peoples, kings and officials rebelling against the universal reign of the Lord. The psalmist greets this rebellion with astonishment: "Why are they attempting this 'vain' struggle?" In this con-

13. LXX has the king speaking these words in the first person: "I have been made king by him, upon Zion his holy mountain." MT is retained here, because it suits better the speech of God in the following verses and because the report of God's speech better suits the genre of the psalm (see Gerhard von Rad, "The Royal Ritual in Judah," in *The Problem of the Hexateuch* [London: SCM, 1966], pp. 222-31; and J. J. M. Roberts, "Whose Child Is This?" *HTR* 90 [1997] 115-29).

14. LXX implies "give to you." There is no need for the intrusion, since the second person suffix is found on the direct object.

15. MT understands *t*^{e}*rōʿēm* as from *rāʿaʿ*, "to break." LXX's *poimaneis* implies *rʿh*, "to shepherd." MT is preferred in context.

16. This entire colon is problematic. Literally, the phrase might read: "Rejoice in trembling! Kiss the son." Not only is "rejoice with trembling" incoherent, but the phrase *naššᵉqû ḇar* is odd. If *bar* means "son," then why does the Aramaic word appear here when the normal Hebrew word for son, *ben,* has already occurred? Many solutions have been proposed (see Craigie, *Psalms 1–50,* p. 64, who retains MT's "kiss the son" — meaning "kiss the king"). MT is corrupt (see Kraus, *Psalms 1–59,* p. 124). Many commentators emend the text to read *birʿāḏâ naššᵉqû ḇᵉraglāyw,* "in trembling kiss his feet." The solution is not pleasing, since it requires significant revisions to MT without support from the versions.

17. The closing colon of the psalm is not properly a part of Psalm 2. Its congratulatory tone is out of sync with the admonishments that close the psalms. The line forms an inclusio with Ps. 1:1, signaling that the two psalms make up a two-part introduction to the Psalter.

text, the interrogative *why (lāmmâ)* indicates puzzlement. This is not a literal question but an exclamation of surprise.[18] The long indicative description (vv. 2-9) that follows it will eventually allow the reader to learn why this rebellion is a vain effort. But the initial survey of the rebellion seems to suggest that nations hold the advantage, because they have the advantage of greater numbers. The poetry of v. 2 elegantly sets two pair of antagonists against each other: *The kings of earth* and the *officials* (both plural nouns) stand *against the* LORD *and against his anointed* (both singular nouns). If this struggle were to be determined strictly by numbers, the kings and officials would obviously have the upper hand.

Already in the first stanza, the psalm's dominant motifs of kingship and speech are apparent. Three nouns indicate the theme of kingship: *kings (melek̲), officials (rôzēn),* and *his anointed (mᵉšîaḥ).* Likewise, the theme of speech is introduced by two verbs that connote speaking — *rage (rāgaš), murmur (hāgâ)* — and the quotation that closes the first stanza: *Let us shatter their bonds. . . .* In fact, the entire rebellion of the nations is depicted as *nothing but* speech. They do not raise sword or weapon against God, but rather only their voices.

4-6 In stanza 2, the scene shifts to heaven, where the Lord is enthroned. The dual motifs of kingship and speech are continued in this stanza. In this context, the verb *yāšab̲ — sits enthroned —* is a technical term denoting God's kingship. The Lord is far from alarmed by the revolt of the nations, which merely provokes divine scorn. The heavenly king answers the rebellious speech of the earthly kings with more speech. The Lord *laughs, mocks,* and *speaks.* And paralleling the structure of the first stanza, this stanza also closes in a quotation: *I, yes I, have established my king, upon Zion, my holy mountain.* The agency of God is underscored in several ways in v. 6. The redundant occurrence of the Hebrew pronoun *ʾᵃnî* emphasizes that the Davidic kings exist solely as a result of God's sovereign actions. God's agency is further underscored by the pronouns in *my king* and *my mountain.* These dual pronouns reflect the Old Testament tradition of God's "double election" of David and Jerusalem; in this tradition, God chose David and his descendants to be kings and Mount Zion in Jerusalem as the divine dwelling place (cf. Ps. 46:4). In terms of poetic balance, it is again worth repeating that the enthronement of the Davidic king is part of the Lord's answer to the rebellion of the kings of earth.

7-9 In the third stanza, the setting shifts back to earth, but the location is different from that in stanza 1. Stanza 2 closed by mentioning the Davidic king on Mount Zion, and that is the focus now. In fact, the change to first person verbs — *"I will tell of the decree of the* LORD*"* — implies that it is now the voice of the Davidic king that is heard. The dual themes of kingship and

18. See Waltke and O'Connor, *Biblical Hebrew Syntax,* 18.1c and 18.3c.

speech continue to be rung at the start of this stanza, as the verb *tell,* the noun *decree,* and the first person speaking voice of the king imply. Indeed, as many have pointed out,[19] the term *decree* is most likely to be understood as a technical term from royal law. "It denotes the document of legitimacy, the royal protocol that was written down at the enthronement and thereafter identified the legitimate ruler."[20]

The themes of speech and kingship continue to be developed as the king reports God's words and promises: *He said to me, "You are my son, today I have begotten you."* In the Old Testament, as in other parts of the ancient Near East, the king was considered God's son (cf. 2 Sam. 7:14). Many interpreters interpret the announcement *today I have begotten you* as a reference to God adopting the king as a son. There is no textual basis, however, for understanding the verb "begotten" *(yālaḏ)* as adoption. In the texts as we have them, the verb always means to "reproduce." Peter Craigie notes that " 'I have begotten you' is metaphorical language; it means more than simply adoption, which has legal overtones, and implies that a 'new birth' of a divine nature took place during the coronation."[21] The language emphasizes the special relationship that the king has with God. Because the relationship he has with God is now that of a "father-son" relationship, the king is in a position to ask what he will of God (cf. 1 Kgs. 3:5ff.; 2 Sam. 24:12; Ps. 21:2-4). In the quotation that ends stanza 3 of the poem, the king does not ask for anything specific from God; God merely promises that the king may ask and God will grant it. Within the promise, there is a poetic tie back to stanza 1. In vv. 1-2, *nations* and *kings of earth* rebel against God. In v. 8, the king reports that God has willed the *nations* and *ends of the earth* as the king's inheritance. This internal link underscores one link in the poem's argument, namely that a part of God's response to the rebellion of earthly powers is to install the Davidic monarch on Zion.

10-12 The final stanza of the poem continues with the established themes of the poem, yet breaks from some of the established poetic structures. The themes of kingship and speech are continued, as the *kings* and *rulers of earth* are warned to serve the Lord. But in terms of poetic structure, the fourth stanza surprises. By this point in the poem, the reader might expect a shift in the speaking voice, might expect a shift in poetic setting, might expect more explicit references to speech, and might expect the stanza to close with a quotation. The setting of the fourth stanza does indeed seem to shift back to the dispersed *kings of earth* that were encountered in stanza 1. But the stanza implies no change in speaker. Although some commentators

19. See Mowinckel, *The Psalms in Israel's Worship,* p. 55; Von Rad, "The Royal Ritual in Judah," pp. 225-26, 228.

20. Kraus, *Psalms 1–59,* pp. 129-30.

21. *Psalms 1–50,* p. 67.

have argued that stanza 4 should be understood as being spoken by a priest, there is no sound ground for thinking of a speaker other than the king who spoke stanza 3. Also, the stanza does not close in a quotation, and there are no explicit verbs of speaking.

But these changes actually are a part of the poetic structure of the psalm. In the final stanza, the verbs shift from indicative description (vv. 2-9) to imperative warning: *be wise, be warned, serve, kiss!* The disjunctive Hebrew particle *'attâ* (translated here *so now*) occurs frequently in the psalms precisely at the place where the argument of a psalm hinges. That is the case here. As for the fact that the stanza lacks both a closing quotation and verbs of speaking, that too fits the psalm's argument. The *kings* and *rulers* are depicted as rebelling against God by their speech, and so now they are in effect warned to keep silent. Many commentators have, in fact, puzzled over the strange occurrence of the verb *kiss (naššᵉqû),* especially because the Hebrew text is problematic at this point (see the note on v. 12). But when understood in terms of the poetic motif of speech, the verb fits well in this context. In the ancient world, to kiss the feet of a king (or the ground in front of the king's feet) was a symbol of humility and political obedience (see Ps. 72:9; Isa. 49:23; Mic. 7:17). The Israelite king Jehu is even depicted as kissing the ground in front of the Assyrian king Shalmaneser III on Shalmaneser's famous Black Obelisk. Thus, the poem closes by warning the *kings of earth* not to utter vain words of rebellion against the universal king of heaven and God's chosen king on Zion. Instead, those kings are adjured to employ their mouths more appropriately in an act of silent submission.

The closing colon of the poem — *Happy are all who take refuge in him* — was probably not part of the original psalm. It was most likely added to form an inclusio to Ps. 1:1, so that the reader would read the two psalms together as a unity.[22]

Reflections

1. Who Reigns?

The plot of Psalm 2 circles around a basic question: Who rules the earth? Do human princes and kings rule? Or is there a different lord of creation, one to whom the downcast might turn and to whom all might address their prayers? According to Psalm 2, the issue is never really an issue. God reigns in heaven and extends heaven's will downward into our sphere through the work of Israel. And yet, says the psalm, there are many who, to borrow the words of the poet George Herbert, do not recognize God's grandeur. These many

22. See Seybold, *Die Psalmen,* p. 33.

— whether the rulers of nations and cities, or business owners and military leaders, or maybe only the hostile neighbor down the street — are opposed both to God's will and to God's people. They seek to cast off the cords of justice and peace and live as they see fit, even though it harms others. But Psalm 2 also bears witness to the faith that God's reign, hidden and invisible though it may appear now, is the only true reality. God is active here and now, the psalm confesses, even if God's reign is not yet fully visible. As J. Clinton McCann insightfully comments,

> The power of God is not the absolute power of a dictator but the power of committed love. In worldly terms, might makes right. But on God's terms, right makes might. The righteous — those who live under God's sovereignty — will be vulnerable to the powers of the world (Ps. 3:1-2), but they will never be without help (3:8). The striking claim of Psalm 2 is that true happiness is found by those *who take refuge in* God (2:12).[23]

2. God's Son

Psalm 2 is a royal psalm, one of those psalms that originally had to do with Jerusalem's kings. In its original setting, the psalm probably was a part of a public ceremony such as a coronation or the announcement of a prince designated as the future king. In that era, the king was God's *anointed* (v. 2) and God's *son* (v. 7). But in its current setting in the Psalter, the psalm has a different function. The psalm was incorporated into the Psalter long after the institution of Israel's human kings had disappeared. According to the theological vision of the Old Testament, one of the reasons for the failure of the monarchy was that her kings never lived up to the ideals against which they were to be measured. Yet, Israel's prophets had consistently promised the advent a Davidic king who would fulfill those ideals and reign as the ideal Davidic king (cf. Isaiah 11). The New Testament associates that ideal Davidic king and the *son* and *anointed* of Psalm 2 with Jesus. At Jesus' baptism, transfiguration, and death, different voices declare him to be God's Son. Peter confessed that Jesus was the Christ (the Greek word for "anointed" or "messiah"). The book of Acts even associates Pilate and Herod, who stood in judgment over Jesus, with the kings and rulers that oppose God's will in Psalm 2. The rulers of Psalm 2 sought to cast off the chains of the Lord, in order to achieve freedom for themselves. But like Psalm 1, Psalm 2 envisions independence from God not as freedom but as bondage. True liberty consists rather of living in relationship with God and taking refuge in God and God's anointed. As the New Testament says, "if the Son makes you free, you will be free indeed" (John 8:36).

ROLF A. JACOBSON

23. McCann, "The Book of Psalms," p. 691.

Psalm 3: The "Many" and the "One"

After the two-part introduction to the Psalter that is formed by Psalms 1 and 2, Psalm 3 initiates a section of the Psalter dominated by Davidic psalms. Among Psalms 3–41, only Psalms 10 (which is correctly understood as the second half of Psalm 9/10, a unified composition) and 33 lack the Davidic superscription. This group of psalms is also characterized by a high density of prayers for help (laments); Psalms 3–7, 9–13, 16–17, 22, 25–28, 31, and 35–41 all fall into this category.[1] Thus, Book One of the Psalter is less a book of praises than a book of prayers for God's help.

Psalm 3 is such a prayer. It contains several of the usual elements of the prayer for help: the complaint (vv. 1-2), the confession of trust (vv. 3-6), and the petition (v. 7). The psalm also ends with a closing benediction (v. 8). Scholars have spilled much ink in the attempt to pinpoint a precise life setting in which this psalm may have originally been used. For example, the psalm may have been: prayed in the temple by one who takes asylum there; prayed in the temple in a juridical setting by one accused of a crime; prayed by a king prior to a battle, as part of a covenant ceremony, or as part of a new year's festival; prayed by an individual who is sick; prayed on behalf of a sick person; prepared as a performed liturgy for the use of individuals.[2] Some scholars reconstruct a history in which the prayer was used in different ways in different eras.[3] In my view, the life setting cannot be reconstructed with any confidence; the attempt to gaze three thousand years down the well of history and identify one life setting with any precision is an unpromising task. A more fruitful approach is to read the psalm as prayer/poem in its current literary setting — that is, to read Psalm 3 as one prayer/poem in a collection of psalms that is intended for communal study and use.

It should also be noted that in its current setting, the prayer is assigned to David upon the occasion of his flight from Absalom (cf. 2 Samuel 15–18). Although the psalm does bear some passing similarities to the story of David's flight from his son (most notably the presence of many enemies and the activity of those who curse the pray-er), this psalm was probably not composed by David (see Introduction). Rather, some ancient scribe noted the similarities between the sufferer of this poem and the story of David as he fled from Absalom. Having made this imaginative connection, the scribe

1. The categorization of psalms by genre is, of course, a slippery task. Some scholars would include other psalms in Book One in the above list, and many others would exclude some of the above. The point remains, however, that Book One is dominated by prayers for help.

2. See Gerstenberger's review of the literature, *Psalms: Part 1,* pp. 52-53.

3. Cf. Craigie, *Psalms 1–50,* pp. 71-75.

added the phrase "when he fled from Absalom, his son" to a superscription that already read "of David." Thus, rather than reflect authorship, this phrase evidences "the first exegetical activity" on the psalm.[4]

The Psalm consists of four stanzas, which are each two verses long and form a thematic chiasm :

St. 1 Complaint (the "many" are "rising up") (vv. 1-2)
St. 2 Confession of trust (begins with emphatic "You") (vv. 3-4)
St. 3 Confession of trust (begins with emphatic "I") (vv. 5-6)
St. 4 Petition (the one Lord is called to "rise up") (vv. 7-8)

The psalm is both a powerful prayer for help and a masterful work of art. Key literary terms and structures help the prayer build both its literary and theological impact.

A Davidic[5] psalm.[6] When he fled from Absalom, his son.

1 *LORD! How many are my foes,*
many those rising up against me,
2 *many those saying of me,*
"There is no deliverance for him in God!"[7] Selah[8]

4. So Karl-Heinz Bernhardt, *Das Problem der altorientalischen Königsideologie im Alten Testament* (VTSup 8; Leiden: Brill, 1961), p. 11, cited in Kraus, *Psalms 1–59,* p. 139.

5. Regarding "Davidic," see the Introduction.

6. The term *mizmôr* refers to a song, most likely one accompanied by instruments (cf. Kraus, *Psalms 1–59,* pp. 21-23). This meaning is derived both from etymology (*zāmar* is "to sing or praise"; in other Semitic languages, cognate nouns can refer to musical instruments) and context (cf. Sir. 49:1). The LXX translates the word as *psalmos.* The term occurs 57 times in the superscriptions of various psalms; 35 times it occurs with *lᵉdāwiḏ.* Kraus notes that in the OT, *zāmar* plus *l* "always refers to Yahweh, to whom the song . . . is addressed" (p. 22). Thus we might conclude that in context, a "psalm" is not simply a formal term (a song) but a theological term (a song to the Lord). The term does not correspond with any of the categories established by modern form criticism; it appears before prayers for help (such as Psalm 3), hymns (8), instructional psalms (15), torah psalms (19), trust psalms (23), and so on.

7. LXX implies "in his God"; Syr implies "for you in your God." Both additions should be regarded as expansions.

8. The meaning of *selâ* is uncertain, although it appears to be a liturgical direction of some sort. The term occurs 71 times in 38 psalms in the Hebrew Psalter (although 92 times in the LXX Psalter) and three times in Habakkuk 3. In light of a Persian cognate meaning "song," Koehler-Baumgartner concludes "probably a technical term added later concerning the style of music or recitation" (*HALOT,* 3:756). Cf. also Kraus, *Psalms 1–59,* pp. 27-29; Craigie, *Psalms 1–50,* pp. 76-77.

3 *But you, LORD, are a shield all around me,*
my glory and the one lifting up my head.
4 *With my voice I cry to the LORD,*
and he answers[9] *me from his holy hill.* Selah

5 *I, I lie down and I sleep,*
I get up, for the LORD sustains me.
6 *I do not fear many thousands*[10] *of people,*
who set themselves against me all around.

7 *Arise, O LORD! Deliver me, my God!*
For you strike all my enemies on the cheek,
you break the teeth of the wicked.
8 *Deliverance belongs to the LORD!*
May your blessing be upon your people. Selah

1-2 The psalm begins with a cry of address that is simultaneously a cry of pain: *LORD!* This personal address to God is far more than a mere formal opening to a prayer. As Westermann has seen, "By means of the address, contact is established which makes speaking to God possible. . . . If a person calls upon God by his name — or vice versa — something happens at that moment."[11] In this instance, what happens is that the psalmist involves God in the drama and pain of his suffering. Following this punctuated opening address, the psalmist issues a threefold outcry against the *many (rabbîm).* In the first phrase, the psalmist names who the many are; in the second, he describes what they are doing; in the third, he reports what they are saying. The tri-repetition of these phrases emphasizes the urgency of the psalmist's need. The second and third phrases also bear significance in terms of the psalm's meaning and poetic design. The second phrase says the enemies are *rising up (qûm)* against him. It is possible that this phrase might be a technical term for the rising up of hostile witnesses in a legal setting (cf. Deut. 19:16). It is better, however, to understand it as metaphorical, indicating any threat that foes or enemies may pose to a person (cf. Pss. 54:5; 86:14). In the context of this psalm, the rising up of the many enemies signals the desperation of the psalmist's crisis. The quotation of the enemies' speech in the third phrase is

9. Many commentators read the *wāw* as a simple *wāw (wᵉ-)* rather than as a *wāw*-consecutive *(wa-).* When this change is made, the verb is repointed as a preterite. This change is not necessary, because the *wāw*-consecutive can indicate habitual action, which is how the phrase is understood here (see commentary below).

10. Targum reflects the construct form *mērîḇê.*

11. Westermann, *The Psalms,* p. 36.

even more important for the meaning of the psalm, because it establishes the central theological issue of the psalm — whether God will help the psalmist. The enemies claim, *There is no deliverance for him in God.* The charge means that the enemies believe that God either *cannot* or *will not* deliver the psalmist from his troubles. That is, they are asserting that God either lacks the *power* to save the psalmist or that God has no *fidelity* to the psalmist. In either case, they interpret the psalmist's crisis as hopeless precisely because the psalmist places her hope in God, and God either cannot or will not help. As Mays has understood, "The assumption or intimation or claim that there is no help for another in God is not only an attack on a fellow human being; it is a limiting, arrogant presumption against God."[12] By thus attacking the source of the psalmist's hope, the enemies' quotation provides the theological hinge on which the psalm will later turn.

3-4 The second stanza contains the psalmist's confession of trust, a typical element of prayers for help. The first word of this stanza is *But you!,*[13] the poet's strong poetic counter to the *many* and their assertions. The psalmist confesses her ongoing faith in the Lord *(You),* and, thus, balances the *many* who threaten her with the one *you* in whom she trusts. The psalmist follows up this singular word of trust with three titles for the Lord. Poetically, these three titles counter the three phrases with the word *many* in the first stanza. The first title describes God as *a shield all around me.* The shield is a common metaphor implying protection (cf. Pss. 18:2; 28:7; 119:114, etc.). What is significant here is that, unlike a normal shield which only protects in one direction, God is seen as a *shield all around* — the perfect counterbalance to the *many* enemies overwhelming the psalmist on all sides (cf. *all around,* v. 6). The second title describes God simply as *my glory,* while the third visualizes God as the one *lifting up my head.* This is a metaphor for honor and the restoration of status and health.

In the second verse of the stanza 2, the psalmist continues to confess trust in God. *With my voice I cry to the LORD* can be heard as a repudiation of the enemies' speech. Whereas the enemies had used their voices to mock the psalmist's trust in God, the psalmist responds, not with his own mocking, but with a cry to the very One who the enemies had denied would help the psalmist. The second half of v. 4 — *and he answers me from his holy hill* — indicates the psalmist's trust that God will answer him as God has *in the past.* The psalmist here is expressing the trust that, because God has helped in the past when asked, God will do so again.

5-6 The third stanza also consists of the confession of trust. Significantly, the initial emphatic *I — I, I lie down and I sleep* — mirrors the emphatic

12. Mays, *Psalms,* p. 52.

13. The translation of *wāw* here *(wᵉʾattâ)* reflects the adversative function of the syntax.

you of the second stanza. The effect of this emphatic pronoun is both to offer a balance to the earlier emphasis on *you* and also to accentuate the psalmist's complete trust. Lying down and sleeping in the presence of threatening adversaries (cf. 23:1-5) is a remarkable demonstration of calm and trust. And this trust is based not on anything about the psalmist herself, but rather it is based outside of herself *in the Lord.* As the apodosis of v. 5 indicates, it is because the Lord *sustains* that the psalmist can sleep in peace. One major issue is how to translate the verbs in vv. 5-6. The verbs *lie down* and *arise* are in the perfect; *sleep* and *sustain* are in the imperfect. Craigie understands all the verbs as representing past completed actions ("I lay down. Then I fell asleep. I awakened, because the Lord sustains me"). He explains that the "words of trust reflect the morning after. The psalmist has already slept; God has sustained him through the night, so that now, with the confidence rooted in rest, he could look forward to another day in the presence of a God who 'sustains.'"[14] Other commentators like Clifford understand all of the imperfect verbs as representing continuing action:

> The verbs . . . can express habitual action, a future act, or in some uses, a past act. One can translate them as statements of habitual trust and hope: Whenever I cry to the Lord, he always answers me; whenever I go to bed, I always wake up safely.[15]

While each of these views smoothes over the fact that the verbs are not uniform, the second is closer to accurate. The basic sense of this confession of trust is that the psalmist is reflecting on past experience of God's protection; this reflection leads the psalmist to live in the present — to sleep now — with a trusting confidence in the Lord.

The psalmist's confession of trust reaches its climax in v. 6, as she says, *I do not fear many thousands (riḇᵉḇôṯ) who set themselves against me all around.* The Hebrew word *riḇᵉḇôṯ (many thousands)* plays on the etymological connection to the *many (rabbîm)* of vv. 1-2. The poet uses the same root here to express confidence — the *many* are no longer a source of fear, because of her trust in the Lord. With a similar poetic move, the psalmist who had earlier

14. Craigie, *Psalms 1–50,* pp. 70-74. In conjunction with this view, some commentators have tried to see the references to the "holy hill" in v. 4 and to "lying down" and "sleeping" in v. 5 as a reference to an incubation oracle performed in the temple. In this view, the psalmist is reporting that she has drunk the potion and survived to tell about it. This interpretation assumes strictly identifying the life setting of the psalm in a particular way. As already indicated, it is better to understand the poem more generically and understand the lying down and sleeping as more metaphorical — because God surrounds the psalmist like a shield, the psalmist is able to sleep, even in the presence of a dire threat.

15. Clifford, *Psalms 1–72,* p. 49.

described God as the shield that surrounds her "all around" now confidently confesses no fear of the enemies who "surround" her.

7-8 The final stanza of the psalm consists of the psalmist's plea to God and a final sentence of trust and benediction. In the opening stanza of the psalm, the sufferer had cried out that foes were *rising up (qûm)* against him and mocking, *There is no deliverance (yᵉšûʿâ) for him in God.* Now, in the petition of this prayer, the psalmist reverses two of the key terms from that stanza: *Arise (qûm), O LORD! Deliver (hôšîʿēnî) me, my God!* The force of this poetic reversal is both to express the psalmist's trust that the enemies are wrong, that God can deliver the psalmist, and also to place the future squarely on God's broad shoulders. The psalmist cannot match the power of the enemies, for he is powerless. The psalmist cannot match the numbers of the enemies, for he is alone. But the psalmist can match the unbelief of the enemies, for he has faith in his God. The psalmist asks God to *rise up* in response to those *rising up* against the sufferer, to *deliver* in response to those who claim God will not *deliver.* The motivating clause supporting his plea mentions God striking the cheeks and breaking the teeth of the wicked. On the one hand, to break the teeth means that God "shuts their mouths" — the allusion is to the arrogant speech that the enemies earlier raised against God. On the other hand, to *break the teeth* means also that God "pulls their fangs" — the allusion is also to the violence that the wicked intend for the psalmist.

In the final verse of the psalm, the poet takes one more opportunity to contradict the unbelief of the wicked with his own faith. "Deliverance" *(hayᵉšûʿâ) belongs to the LORD*!" she cries. The psalmist then closes by invoking God's blessing on the people. This final benediction shows the psalmist's identification with the righteous servants of God and further emphasizes the depravity of the wicked.

Reflections

1. Deliverance in the Lord

The central theological issue of this psalm concerns the saving activity of God. The psalmist's foes deny that God can or will help the psalmist. The psalmist contradicts this assertion by asserting trust in God's very present help. By contrasting the attitudes of the wicked with his own attitude, the psalmist nicely offers both a positive and negative lesson. On the negative side, the psalm offers a warning of the danger of arrogantly assuming that we know whom God does or does not favor. To claim such knowledge is just as heinous a crime as denying the existence of God or the ability of God to save. On the positive side, the psalm also offers encouragement to those who hope for deliverance. Against those who would deny God's agency in this world or limit God's ability to intervene on human behalf in the here and now, the psalm posits a firm faith in the power of God to deliver.

2. Trust amid trouble

The psalm also offers a strong word of assurance to those who feel surrounded by troubles and overwhelmed by worries. With its myriad poetic reversals, the poem evokes a confidence born out of a situation of trust. Though we may be surrounded by troubles, God's protection is a shield around us. Though we are assailed by many foes, the one God defeats all reasons for fear. Though throngs rise against us, God is there to rise up on our behalf. The psalm is written out of a situation in which all earthly reasons for trust have dissolved, which leads the psalmist to build his hope on an unearthly foundation — the fidelity of God. As the old hymn has it, "All other ground is sinking sand."

ROLF A. JACOBSON

Psalm 4: Room to Rest

Psalm 4 has much in common with Psalm 3 and is generally identified as a prayer for help (or "individual lament"). The language of v. 2 seems to indicate a false accusation, so many commentators identify the psalm as the prayer specifically of one who has been falsely accused. There have been many attempts to locate the psalm's original setting more precisely. Kraus, for example, has argued that this is the prayer of "an innocent person who has been persecuted and accused [and] has had his rights restored through a divine verdict in the temple," but whose persecutors refuse to acknowledge the "not guilty" verdict.[1] Another approach to the psalm is to see it as a liturgical-instructional psalm calling the community to put away false gods and worship the living God: "the psalm is not a private prayer but was probably performed for the benefit of others as well."[2] In this case, the opponents of the psalmist are the worshippers of other gods. Other interpretations abound. Dahood saw it as a prayer for rain,[3] Eaton as a royal psalm,[4] and Craigie as a psalm of trust.[5] Two aspects of the psalm are particularly important when making judgments about its genre. First, in its present context, the psalm has unmistakably been adapted for liturgical use (this is signaled by the presence of the liturgical direction *Selah*). Second, all of the attempts to fix a precise original *setting in life* for the psalm are based on exceedingly precise interpretations of individual words or phrases, most of which can be interpreted in more than one way. For example, to pursue his understanding of the psalm, Kraus argued that the psalmist's imperative demand for people to *sacrifice right sacrifices, trust in the LORD* (v. 5) refers to ritual sacrifices by which people would acknowledge the innocence of someone who had faced an accusation but been declared innocent. Thus, Kraus concluded:

> The enemies and persecutors of the petitioner should not commit sin in their protesting and slanderous efforts against Yahweh's declaration of righteousness. . . . Rather, they should now present the required [sacrifice], enter the community with the one who was declared free, and trust Yahweh . . . [which means] to agree with Yahweh's declaration of righteousness, to accept this declaration, to yield to it.[6]

1. *Psalms 1–59,* p. 146.
2. Broyles, *Psalms,* pp. 52-53.
3. *Psalms I,* pp. 23-24.
4. *Kingship and the Psalms,* pp. 29-30
5. *Psalms 1–50,* pp. 79-80.
6. *Psalms 1–59,* p. 149.

While attractive, such a precise explanation of v. 5 extends beyond what the data will allow. Moreover, the psalm is full with textual difficulties. As Gerstenberger admitted, "Textual problems abound in vv. 3, 5, 7, and the interpretation of one word may alter genre classification."[7] Craigie's warning stands as a word to the wise reader: "Thus the original thrust and context of the psalm remain uncertain and its anonymity contributes further to this uncertainty."[8]

In light of the inscrutability of the psalm's past, the approach here is to focus on its final form and canonical placement. In terms of the latter, there is reason to believe that Psalm 4 was intentionally placed next to Psalm 3. Several key words connect the two psalms: *kᵉḇôḏî* (translated as *my glory* in 3:3, *my honor* in 4:2); the pairing of *šāḵaḇ* and *yāšan* (*lie down* and *sleep,* 3:5 and 4:8); the phrase *rabbîm 'ōmrîm* (*many are saying,* 3:2 and 4:6); and the confession of trust that God hears and answers the prayer of the psalmist (3:4 and 4:3). Psalm 4, with its confident trust that *I both lie down and sleep,* is also linked to Psalm 5, which pleads, *O LORD, in the morning hear my voice* (5:3). Thus, Psalm 4 may have been understood by the editors of the Psalter as an evening prayer and Psalm 5 as a morning prayer. Whether or not the canonical placement of Psalm 4 is anything more than an arrangement based on the occurrence of key catchwords is open to debate.[9] What does seem clear is that in its final location in the Psalter, the psalm was a part of a group of prayers for help (Psalms 3–7, and indeed the larger Davidic collection of Book One of the Psalter; see the introductory comments to Psalm 3). It is also clear that in its final form, the psalm was intended for liturgical use, the goal of which surely included that the psalm be read by later generations and readers as a prayer that could be prayed by anyone in a time of need. To cite Craigie again, "the lack of precise identification of either adversaries or accusations is a part of the genius of the psalm, and that which makes it so appropriate for use by any man or woman."[10] The canonical placement and liturgical final form of the psalm also indicate that the editors of the Psalter understood that the psalmist's words of instruction in vv. 3-6 should be heeded by later generations.

The grammar of the psalm indicates that its structure is concentric. It begins and ends (vv. 1 and 6b-8) with address to God, while its middle section is addressed to humans (vv. 2-6a). The placement of the liturgical direction *Selah* suggests a three-part division (vv. 1-2, 3-4, 5-8) but the following division is to be preferred here:

7. *Psalms: Part 1,* p. 54.
8. *Psalms 1–50,* p. 79.
9. See, e.g., Hossfeld and Zenger, *Die Psalmen I,* pp. 5-15.
10. *Psalms 1–50,* p. 82.

Opening plea for help (v. 1)
  Complaint about what the community has said (v. 2)
    Words of instruction to the community (vv. 3-5)
  Complaint about what the community is saying (v. 6)
Closing confession of trust (vv. 7-8)

A key poetic device in Psalm 4 is the way in which key words or roots are repeated, often endowing the psalm with a sense either of contrast or of reversal. The following chart illustrates the sense of contrast that the repetition of these words and roots achieves:[11]

qr'	*When I call,* answer me (v. 1)	*The* L*ORD* *hears when I* call (v. 3)
ṣdq	*God of my* righteousness (v. 1)	*sacrifice* right *sacrifices* (v. 5)
šm'	*Be gracious and* hear *my prayer* (v. 1)	*The* L*ORD* hears *when I call* (v. 3)
lbb	*Speak in your* hearts (v. 4)	*You have put gladness in my* heart (v. 7)
škb	*Upon your* beds *remain silent* (v. 4)	*I both lie down and* sleep (v. 8)
bṭḥ	Trust *in the* L*ORD* (v. 5)	*You make me dwell with* trust (v. 8)

These repetitions contrast the psalmist's behavior with that of the enemies and the psalmist's request with God's deliverance. They also show that the psalmist takes his or her own advice. In short, these repetitions form a key corpus of vocabulary that embodies the message of the psalm — *The* L*ORD* hears when I call.

11. See a similar chart in Craigie, p. 79. Craigie also notes that √*rbb* repeats in v. 6 (many *are saying*) and v. 7 (*their grain and new wine* abound).

Psalm 4

For the leader.[12] *With stringed instruments.*[13] *A Davidic psalm.*

1 *When I call, answer me,*[14] *O God of my righteousness!*[15]
When in distress, you gave me room.
Be gracious and hear my prayer.
2 *O wealthy, how long will my honor suffer reproach,*[16]
will you love emptiness,
will you seek after falsehood? Selah

3 *But know that the* Lord *has set aside*[17] *the godly for himself!*
The Lord *hears*[18] *when I call to him.*
4 *Tremble, but do not sin!*
Speak in your hearts,
upon your beds remain silent.[19] Selah
5 *Sacrifice right sacrifices,*
trust in the Lord.

12. This title occurs 55 times at the start of a psalm (and also at the end of a psalm in Hab. 3:19). The word is traditionally translated as "music director," although the precise meaning of the term is uncertain (cf. *KBL,* p. 716). Etymologically, the root can mean "to be shining/eminent," "to triumph," or "to be successful/victorious." The root appears to mean "oversee" or "take charge of" in Ezra and Chronicles (always in connection with work on the temple). LXX renders with *eis to telos* ("for the end"). The sense of the word here seems to be "for/belonging to the one in charge."

13. This phrase *bingînôṯ* occurs in the superscriptions of Pss. 4, 6, 54, 61 *('al-nᵉgînat),* 67, and 76. In the passages, the word denotes a technical musical term. Elsewhere, the word means simply music or song. The related verbal root means to play music, especially on a stringed instrument (cf. Ps. 33:3).

14. The aspects of the verbs in v. 1 are a problem. *Answer, be gracious,* and *hear* are all imperatives, but *give room* is a perfect. Further, LXX reads "he answered me," suggesting that "answer" was also read as a perfect. Conversely, some commentators read "give room" as a precative perfect with imperatival force (cf. Craigie, *Psalms 1–50,* pp. 77-78). There is no reason to smooth over the differences in the aspects, however. One may retain MT with the understanding that the psalmist is recalling a past experience of salvation to support a new plea for deliverance. This is consistent with the form and syntax of many psalms.

15. Syr reads "my God and my righteousness." MT is retained.

16. The MT *(kᵉbôḏî liḵlimmâ)* is read by the LXX as *kiḇdê lēḇ lāmmâ.* MT is retained.

17. It is possible to emend "the godly for himself" *(ḥsyd lw)* to "his favor for me" *(ḥsdw ly).* The phrase then reads, "He has shown wondrous favor to me." Kraus follows this emendation based on the parallel in Ps. 31:21. But, contrary to Kraus and others, MT makes sense without emendation and is retained.

18. LXX adds the 1cs suffix to the verb.

19. The sense and translation of this verse are difficult. Craigie's solution makes the most sense. With support from Syr, LXX, and some Hebrew manuscripts, Craigie moves the conjunction from *dmw* to before *'al.*

6 *Many are saying, "Who will show us*[20] *good?"*
Lift the light of your face upon us, O LORD.[21]
7 *You have put gladness*[22] *in my heart,*
more than when their grain and new wine abound.
8 *In peace do I both lie down and sleep;*
for you alone, O LORD, make me dwell with trust.

1 The psalm opens with a plea to the *God of my righteousness* to *hear my prayer,* in which the psalmist employs four verbs. Three of the verbs are imperatives — *answer me, be gracious to me* (note that these two verbs are nearly identical, *ʿănēnî* and *ḥānnēnî,* emphasizing the psalmist's dire need), and *hear my prayer.* Each of these verbs is typical of the prayer for help, and their first person direct objects emphasize the personal nature of the psalmist's request: answer *me,* be gracious to *me,* hear *my* prayer. Each colon begins with b^e (translated as "when" in both cases), creating a sense of balance because both phrases have identical beginnings, but also a sense of contrast, because the first b^e introduces a present call for help *(answer me!),* whereas the second b^e introduces a trusting recollection of past instances of such help *(you gave me room).* The psalmist's recollection of the past help is built upon a subtle pun. The adjective *ṣār,* used here as a noun, carries the sense of "anxiety," "need" or "distress," and it is translated thusly here (cf. Ps. 32:7; 119:143). However, in a more basic sense, the word carries the metaphorical idea of "narrowness" or "tightness" (cf. Job 41:15; Isa. 5:30; 49:20). The verb *hirḥaḇtā* literally means to "create space," "give room," or "spread out," which in the psalms usually carries the notion of "rescue" (Pss. 18:19; 31:8; 66:12; 118:5). Thus, while the denotative sense of the psalmist's confession of trust is *when in distress, you* delivered *me,* a more metaphorical translation would be, "when in a tight spot, you got me out." The epithet for God — *God of my righteousness* — is also significant. The language of v. 2 suggests that the psalmist's honor or reputation has been slandered in some fashion. By addressing the Lord as the *God of* my *righteousness,* the psalmist establishes both the hope and the expectation that God will uphold the psalmist's honor in the face of the slanderous assault.

2 Verse 2 is a line of complaint that is at once typical of a prayer for help and atypical. The cry *how long* is a typical complaint, one of the basic cries

20. Some manuscripts read "me" instead of "us," but the plural is preferred.

21. The translation of this phrase is difficult. At issue is *n^{e}sâ.* Some read this as related to *nsʿ* with the sense that the phrase continues the lament of the *many.* Thus the entire verse would read: "Many are saying, 'Who will show us good? The light of your face has departed from us.'" Others read the verb as related to *nśʾ* with the sense that the phrase does not continue the lament of the many. This latter view is taken here in part because the LXX supports this reading.

22. Syriac adds a 2ms suffix.

that sufferers address to God (cf. Pss. 79:5; 89:46; 13:1; 74:10). In this case, however, the question is not addressed to God but to the wealthy members of the community. The use of this typical complaint here in this atypical fashion creates a sense of overlap between the various subjects to whom the prayer is addressed. Because the *how long* complaint is so typical of the prayer for help and because the opening verse of the psalm was addressed to God, no audience can help but hear the question as directed implicitly to God, even though God is not explicitly addressed. On the other hand, by addressing the question explicitly to the wealthy, the psalmist implies that the wealthy have impiously set themselves in God's role, displacing God as judge and lord. As many commentators have pointed out, the term *bᵉnê ʾîš,* literally "sons of man" but translated here as *wealthy,* is most likely a term for wealthy or influential members of the community (cf. 49:2; 62:9).[23] The psalmist's later confession that the gladness bestowed by God is worth more than *their grain and new wine* supports this conclusion (v. 7).

The psalmist's complaint to the wealthy is not a general complaint of suffering, but has specific content: *How long will my honor (kᵉḇôḏî) suffer reproach, will you love emptiness (rîq), will you seek after delusion (kāzāḇ)?* As noted above, one interpretation of this verse holds that the psalmist has been falsely accused. In this case, *kᵉḇôḏî* refers to the psalmist's personal reputation, and *rîq* and *kāzāḇ* refer to false accusations made against the psalmist. This is a very plausible explanation, although note that it does not explain v. 6. On the other hand, it is possible to understand *kᵉḇôḏî* as a reference to God, as it is in Ps. 3:3, and likewise to interpret *rîq* and *kāzāḇ* as references to "empty and vain things" after which the wealthy have pined. In this regard, the parallel occurrence of several of Psalm 4's key words in 62:8-9 is worth noting. Psalm 62:8 begins with an imperative calling the people to *trust* (cf. 4:5b) in God at all times. The psalm then continues: *Those of low estate are but a breath, those of high estate (bᵉnê ʾîš) are a delusion (kāzāḇ).* So we are faced with two basic alternatives for understanding Ps. 4:2; the two options might be paraphrased as the following:

> O wealthy, how long will my reputation suffer shame,
> will you love vain words and seek after lies? (cf. NRSV)

or

> O wealthy, how long will my God be mocked,
> will you love illusions and seek after delusions? (cf. NJPS)

23. Gerstenberger notes that the term may signify nobility, as does the similar term *mār awilim* in Old Babylonian (*Psalms: Part 1,* p. 55). Gerstenberger notes that when the later liturgical adaptation of the psalm is considered, the question of how to understand the phrase is murky.

Although the translation above allows for both interpretations, the second alternative seems more likely, given what follows later in the psalm. The psalm writer may be complaining about false accusations that have been brought against her, but she also may simply be adjuring those members of the community whose dreams in life are unworthy and whose goals are shallow.

3-5 The distinguishing feature of the central section of the psalm is a series of five imperatives that the psalmist directs to fellow members of the community. If we take the rhetoric of the psalm as determinative, then these imperatives are directed at the *wealthy* (the *b*ᵉ*nê 'îš*). However, if we assume a later liturgical setting for this psalm, then we should also understand the imperatives as addressing the worshipping community. The five imperatives are *know, tremble, speak, sacrifice,* and *trust.* Each of these imperatives could easily be at home in any hymn of praise (e.g., Ps. 100:3 for know/*yāḏā'*; 99:1 for tremble/*rāgaz;* 96:10 for *speak/'āmar;* 50:14 for *sacrifice/zāḇaḥ,* and 115:9 for *trust/bāṭaḥ.*) In fact, if these verses were excised from their current context and set off on their own, they would surely be identified as a hymn of praise. As they are, however, they function as words of instruction to the worshipping community. Perhaps the psalmist is exploiting the fact that the imperative verb can function both as a call to praise (cf. Psalm 100) and as an ethical admonition (cf. Psalm 75). The psalmist is adjuring the community to orient their lives more fully and more faithfully toward God in terms of both worship and morality. At stake for the psalmist is a more complete wedding of personal piety and social ethic.

The first of the three clauses of this section of the psalm employs the important verb to *know (yāḏā').* Here, as elsewhere in the Hebrew Scriptures, the word does not imply a separation of thought and action, but rather their unity (cf. Hosea 4). To know that God *has set aside the godly* is to conduct one's life in a way that is in harmony with God's gracious rule. Likewise, to *trust in the* LORD (v. 5) is not only to carry in one's heart the comforting conviction that the Lord is present to save, but carry out one's actions with a sense of responsibility to all members of the covenant community. Lest the protective presence of the Lord be forgotten, the psalm writer reminds her audience that "the LORD hears when I call to him." This again is not simply a theological witness to the belief that God answers the cries of the needy, but an ethical admonition to the community to behave in a way that does not incur God's wrath. As Deut 15:9b reminds those who contemplate breaking the law, "your neighbor might cry to the LORD against you, and you would incur guilt."

The imperative instructions of v. 4 can be difficult to interpret. The most important factor in interpretation appears to be what sort of context an interpreter assumes. If the reader assumes the psalmist is facing false accusers, then the instructions may be angry retorts aimed at silencing the accusers.

The use of the verb *tremble,* which is usually addressed to enemies of God as in Ps. 99:1, supports this interpretation, as does the reference to *beds,* which may be a reference to pagan rituals (cf. Hos. 7:14; Isa. 57:7-8).[24] If the reader assumes that the psalmist is in the company of other falsely accused people, then the instructions may be telling them not to respond "in kind" to the accusers.[25] Or again, the imperatives can be heard as advice to the worshipping community. As McCann points out, "In 1 Sam 7:10, being 'disturbed' is a state caused by the enemies. Thus v. 4 may exhort the faithful to stand firm in their identity and not be led into temptation by their opponents."[26] So how should we understand these verses? If we take the final poetic form of the psalm and its canonical placement as our clue, we must reject any proposal to limit the meaning of these verses to any one interpretation. Poetic language is often intentionally multivalent. Although the author of these verses may not have intended multiple meanings, it is certainly the case that the poetry of the psalm *as it now stands* allows for the imperatives to be heard on many levels. No "original" setting of the psalm can be constructed with total confidence, and thus no one "hearing" of the language need silence other modes of interpretation. What does seem clear is that the verses call for humans to acknowledge the lordship of Israel's God in terms of what they know and do, in terms of why they say and think, and in terms of how they worship and believe. These demands will naturally apply differently to different target populations. No single population should be insisted upon to the exclusion of others. The words of the psalm apply to the righteous and the wicked, the godly and the ungodly, accusers and the accused alike (see below).

A similar phenomenon applies to the interpretation of v. 5: *Sacrifice right sacrifices, trust in the* L*ORD*. This may be understood as the call to false accusers to recognize a not guilty verdict for one who has been accused.[27] Another way of understanding the verse is to interpret it within the context of the worship of false gods. As noted above, the reference to *beds* may be a reference to pagan fertility rites designed to entice *grain* and *wine* from the deity (v. 7). In such a context, this verse would sound the call to put away idol worship and the religious practices associated with those cults. If the focus is again on the canonical context of the psalm and its final form, once again the focus would fall on the unity between faith and morality. Within the context

24. So Broyles, *Psalms,* p. 54.

25. Limburg, *Psalms,* p. 12.

26. "The Book of Psalms," p. 697.

27. So Kraus, *Psalms 1-59,* p. 149: "The enemies and persecutors of the petitioner should not commit sin in their protesting and slanderous efforts against Yahweh's declaration or righteousness. . . . Rather, they should now present the required [sacrifice], enter the community with the one who was declared free, and trust Yahweh . . . [which means] to agree with Yahweh's declaration of righteousness, to accept this declaration, to yield to it."

of the psalm, to *sacrifice right* [or righteous] *sacrifices* and to *trust in the LORD* implies that no wedge be driven between conduct in worship and conduct in daily life. There is no trusting in God that is compatible with persecution of the neighbor or unethical practices. The same point is made in Psalm 50, Isaiah 1, Micah 6, and Amos 5.

6-8 The identity of the *many* who speak in v. 6 is, not surprisingly, once again impossible to determine. They may be the psalmist's enemies, the psalmist's fellow sufferers, worshippers of false gods, doubting members of the community, or members of the community who are neither antagonistic to nor sympathetic with the psalmist. Moreover, because of the textual difficulties in the verse, the content of what they say and where the quotation is to end is also vague (see the textual note above). Most probably, v. 6a introduces the question of to *whom* the community should turn in hope of receiving goodness. If so, the psalmist answers the question of the many with a threefold response. First, the psalmist responds by asking her own question of God born out of faith — she asks for *the light of your face.* Where should we look for good? "In God" is the psalmist's answer. Second, the psalmist answers the question by remembering the joy that God has granted her. The comparative phrase — *more than when their grain and new wine abound* — implies, once again, that different goals and values are at stake. The psalmist has instructed the community to choose wisely, to choose God rather than lies and delusions. Now, in a manner worthy of Joshua, she says in so many words, "I have chosen the Lord." Finally, the psalmist closes the psalm with a confession of trust. Earlier, the psalmist had instructed the community to be silent *upon your beds.* Syntactically, the opening phrase *in peace* and the emphatic use of the adverb *yaḥdāw* both emphasize the psalmist's security. In a similar vein, the closing phrase emphasizes that *God alone* is the source of the psalmist's security. The word *alone,* which contrasts poetically with the "abounding *grain and new wine*" of the previous verse, highlights both the psalmist's isolation from her larger culture and the sole source of her security. The psalmist had earlier adjured the community to "trust in the Lord." The psalm now closes as the psalmist confesses that her own trust is in the Lord.

Reflections

1. Belonging to God

No matter which way we read the psalm, one aspect of the psalmist's faith is clear: it is *to God* that the psalmist turns for vindication and it is *in God* that the psalmist trusts. To the extent that the language of the psalm implies an attack on the psalmist's honor, the psalmist names the Lord as *God of my righteousness,* which means roughly "the God who vindicates me." To the extent that the language of the psalm implies that others are choosing to chase after vain and delusional goals in life such as the material goods of *grain* and *new wine,* the psalmist names God as her highest joy. To the extent that the language of the psalm implies that others are worshipping false gods and trusting in their pagan fertility rites for bounty, the psalmist declares her own commitment to offer *right sacrifices* and to *trust in the LORD*. To the extent that the psalmist has been excluded from community life on some level, she notes with confidence that God has set apart the faithful for himself, and she faithfully takes her stand with them. To the extent that the psalmist experiences herself as surrounded by malicious accusers, it is the promise and presence of that God that gives her the confidence, like a Daniel in the lions' den, to lie down and sleep in tranquility. The important thing for the psalmist is that she belongs to God. As McCann has commented, "Belonging to God changes everything — values, priorities, life-style."[28]

2. "Reputation, Reputation, Reputation"

As noted above, this psalm is frequently interpreted as the desperate prayer of one who has been falsely accused. Although this interpretation should not be insisted upon to the exclusion of other ways of understanding the psalm, this view has much to offer as a way of making sense of the poetry. When we understand the psalm in this way, we are faced with issues similar to those raised by the "false witness" commandment. What that commandment seeks to protect is the reputation and honor of the neighbor. If we understand Psalm 4 as the prayer of one falsely accused, then this prayer is in part a plea to both God and community to restore a damaged reputation. Anyone who has been slandered knows the priceless value of a lost reputation. Shakespeare explored the social costs of false witness in his play *Othello.* Ironically, it is Shakespeare's character Iago, the very one who bears false witness against Othello, who best understands the value of reputation. Even while planting lies about Othello, Iago pretends that it is he who has been slandered: "Reputation, reputation, Reputation! O! I have lost my reputation. I have lost the immortal part of myself, and what remains is bestial" (*Othello* 2.3.264). The psalmist of Psalm 4 also recognizes that one's honor is part of one's humanity. False witness *dehumanizes* the neighbor. Iago also declares, "Who steals my purse steals trash. . . . But he that filches from me my good name robs me of that which not enriches him, and makes me poor indeed" (*Othello,* 3.3.155). Modern Western cultures tend to underestimate the value of social honor and the cost of social shame. The effect that our words have on our neighbors can be devastating. Thus, the New Testament speaks of a mature faith as a faith that loves the neighbor through one's words: "We must no longer be children,

28. "The Book of Psalms," p. 698.

tossed to and fro and blown about by every wind of doctrine, by people's trickery, by their craftiness in deceitful scheming. But speaking the truth in love, we must grow in every way into him who is the head, into Christ" (Eph. 4:14-15). To pick up on the above theme about "belonging to God," a bishop used to love to quote an old preacher who said, "Everyone who belongs to Jesus Christ belongs to everyone who belongs to Jesus Christ." Those who belong to God will remember that when they speak of their neighbors.

ROLF A. JACOBSON

Psalm 5: Lead Me, Guide Me

Psalm 5 is a prayer for help, similar in many ways to Psalms 3 and 4. As is the case with Psalm 4, the vast majority of commentators imagine Psalm 5 as the cry of an innocent person who has been falsely accused. In this approach, the commentators think of the psalmist seeking admission to the temple (v. 7) where he can participate in a judicial ritual in hope of being declared innocent. The conclusion that the psalmist has been falsely accused rests on the description of the wicked as *those who speak lies* (v. 6) and who have *no truth in their mouths* (v. 9). Kraus is representative of this view:

> The petitioner prays for Yahweh's intervention in the face of a threatening hostile persecution and an obvious, existing (false) accusation that is to be equated with malevolent slander. . . . In the face of threatening danger from accusing and persecuting enemies, who possibly are also present in the area of the sanctuary, the oppressed petitioner prepares a sacrifice early in the morning (v. 3). He prays for a revelation of Yahweh's help, consisting of a word of God. The cultic institution of the court of God is the context of Psalm 5.[1]

This approach to the psalm rests in large part on a particular interpretation of v. 3, which is then translated "in the morning I prepare an offering and I wait [for your answer]." The reference to *morning* is understood as a reference to a judicial decision, because the sun was seen as a symbol of justice and because in "ancient Israel court decisions were made early in the morning (2 Sam. 15:2; Jer. 21:12; Ps. 101.8), so the divine decision was awaited early in the morning. . . ."[2] An affirmation in Zephaniah also supports this interpretation: "Every morning he renders his judgment" (Zeph. 3:5). However, *morning* may also be taken simply as symbolic of a renewal of hope (see below). A key word is the verb *ʿāraḵ,* "to lay out, set in rows." In this context, where the psalmist is praying and asking God to hear a prayer (v. 2), *ʿāraḵ* means one of two things. It might mean to "prepare/lay out a sacrifice" that would accompany the prayer, as it does in Gen. 22:9, where Abraham "prepares/lays out" the wood for the sacrifice (cf. Lev. 1:8, 12, etc.). Alternatively, the verb might mean "to prepare words for a legal case," with the sense that the prayer is a verbal assertion of legal innocence (cf. Job 32:14; 33:5; 37:19). It should be noted, however, that neither of these alternatives demands the assumption that the psalmist has been falsely accused. Ancient Israelites offered prayers and sacrifices and also pled their cases before God for other reasons than having been falsely accused. Indeed, it

1. *Psalms 1–59,* p. 153.
2. Kraus, *Psalms 1–59,* p. 155.

must be pointed out that the psalmist never claims to have been accused or to be innocent — she simply asserts that the wicked speak lies. The psalmist never accuses the wicked of having harmed her in any way — she simply insists, as does the psalmist in Psalm 1, that the wicked are opposed to God's way and, by extension, to her way. The psalmist does not ask for deliverance from the enemies — she merely asks that the wicked fall prey to their own plots and plans. Although the above approach to the psalm is plausible, it is certainly not "obvious."

Broyles, among others, has charted a different interpretive course. He notes that

> a literal translation of verse 9b reveals that [the wicked people's] words are deceitful and destructive for reasons other than false accusation: "their throat is an open grave; their tongues they make smooth." . . . Here is painted the graphic picture of someone being enticed by their flattering speech and slipping on their smooth tongue into their grave-like throat. In light of this image, their words are *enticing and tempting,* not accusatory.[3]

Based on a number of parallels with the temple entrance liturgies in Psalms 15 and 24 (see below), Broyles argues that

> Psalm 5 probably belongs to the same "rite of passage" as Psalms 15 and 24. They are the voice of the priests, and Psalm 5 contains the confessional response of pilgrims. As the description of the "doer of righteousness" in Psalms 15 and 24 does not refer to a particular person or group but portrays a character profile, so the description of the wicked in Psalm 5 is probably also a character profile. Thus, the mention of the wicked in Psalm 5 may not stem from the actual circumstances of the speaker but from the entry liturgy itself. Psalm 5 was probably not a special psalm designed for individuals who fell into the particular circumstances of false accusation; rather it was a regular liturgy for all entrants into Yahweh's presence.[4]

In my view, Broyles is on the right track, but the setting in life that he offers is too precise. We cannot recover one original life setting for Psalm 5. We should not succumb to the temptation to try to isolate an original setting for it. Rather, the psalm can be broadly understood as a "prayer counterpart" to the instructional Psalm 1 and the liturgical Psalms 15 and 24. That is to say, Psalm 5 is a prayer for help that takes up similar theological themes and sociological concerns as those taken up in Psalm 1 (an instructional torah

3. Broyles, *Psalms,* p. 56. Emphasis added.
4. Broyles, *Psalms,* p. 58.

psalm) and Psalms 15 and 24 (entrance liturgies). The psalm bears significant similarities to both Psalm 1 and Psalms 15 and 24. Some significant similarities that Psalm 5 shares with Psalm 1 are: the use of the word *way (dereḵ)* to describe God's will for human life (1:6; 5:8); an impersonal description of the *wicked* as offering a tempting way of life (1:1; 5:9); the belief that the way of the wicked leads to their destruction (1:5-6; 5:10); and the belief that God's way leads to life, protection and joy (1:3-6; 5:8, 12). Some significant similarities that Psalm 5 shares with Psalms 15 and 24 are: the setting of the temple (15:1; 24:3; 5:7); the use of *gûr,* "sojourn," for those who may or may not enter the temple (15:1; 5:4); a focus on "sins of the tongue" as the cardinal sin that excludes the wicked from God's presence (15:2-4; 24:4; 5:6, 9); the phrase *doers of . . . (pōʿēl-;* 15:2; 5:5); and the promise of God's blessing (24:5; 5:12). To repeat, the point of these parallels is not to show that Psalm 5 is either an instructional psalm or an entrance liturgy. Rather, Psalm 5 is a prayer for help that takes up similar themes as Psalms 1, 15, and 24 — a concern about avoiding the temptations placed in front of us by the wicked, a recognition that God is opposed to unrighteous and wicked acts, and a concern with entering into the sphere of God's blessing, which is understood as the temple.

There are two competing structures within the psalm. On the one hand, the psalm alternates between focusing on the psalmist's relationship to God (vv. 1-3, 7-8, 11-12) and focusing on the wicked who are in opposition to God (vv. 4-6, 9-10). If this structural element is taken as decisive, the psalm has five stanzas. On the other hand, as Mays has noted, the psalm consists of "a sequence of petitions and assertions, each followed by supporting subordinate clauses attached by the conjunction 'for.'"[5] If this structural element is taken as decisive, then the psalm has three stanzas, each distinguished by a petition and a clause introduced by the Hebrew *kî,* "for." Although both structures are legitimate aspects of the psalm's structure, for the sake of the lay-out, the second structure is followed here:

St. 1 Petition: Hear my voice (vv. 1-3)
For you do not delight in wickedness (vv. 4-6)
St. 2 Petition: Make straight your way for me (vv. 7-8)
For the wicked tempt (v. 9)
St. 3 Petition: Let the wicked fall and those who love you rejoice (vv. 10-11)
For you bless the righteous (v. 12)

5. Mays, *Psalms,* p. 57. Note that there are also *kî* clauses at the end of vv. 2 and 10, but these are both subordinate elements of those verses and do not demark larger units of the psalm. In both cases, those clauses are emphatic rather than causal.

The psalm may have been placed in its present canonical location because of its reference to *morning,* as part of a pattern in Psalms 3–6 that alternates between morning and evening. Psalm 3 mentions morning (v. 5); Psalm 4 mentions evening (v. 4), Psalm 5 mentions morning again (v. 3), and Psalm 6 mentions evening again (v. 6).

For the leader.[6] *Upon*[7] *the flutes.*[8] *A Davidic psalm.*

1 *Give ear to my words O* LORD*;*
give heed to my sighing![9]
2 *Be attentive to the sound of my cry,*
my king and my God, indeed to you I pray!
3 *O* LORD*, in the morning, hear my voice,*
in the morning I prepare prayers and I wait.
4 *For you are not a God who delights in wickedness,*
evil does not sojourn with you.
5 *The boastful will not stand before your eyes,*
you hate all evildoers.
6 *You destroy those*[10] *who speak lies,*
The LORD *abhors people of bloodshed and deceit.*

7 *But I, through the abundance of your* hesed, *I will enter your house;*
I will bow down before your holy temple, in awe of you.
8 *O* LORD*, in your righteousness, lead me, on account of my foes;*
make straight before me your way.[11]

6. See note 12 on Psalm 4 superscription.

7. Reading *'al* for *'el* with some manuscripts.

8. The meaning of *hann^{e}ḥîlôṯ* is unclear; the term occurs only here. Based on parallels with other psalm superscriptions and etymology, the term is likely a musical designation. Perhaps it refers to the flutes, based on *ḥll* II, which means "to hollow out" and thus also "to play the flute" (1 Kgs. 1:40; cf. Mowinckel, *The Psalms in Israel's Worship,* 2:210). Another possibility might be to relate the word to *ḥly,* "illness," and thus have the sense that the psalm is "for illness." Two manuscripts read *hnḥlwt* (supported by Greek witnesses that have *tēs klēronomousēs,* "for the heiress," or *klērodosiōn,* "heirs," understanding the word as related to *nāḥal,* "to inherit").

9. The word *h^{a}gîḡî,* "sighing," is related to the noun *higgāyôn,* "talk," "meditation," or "musical playing" (hence worship-related prayer). Less likely, it may be a reduplicated form related to the root *hāgâ,* "murmur" (see Dahood, *Psalms 1–50,* p. 29).

10. LXX's *pantas* implies the addition of Hebrew *kōl,* "all."

11. In 4QPs^{a} the next word starts with a clear *'ālep* and then some disturbed letters. 4QPs^{s} apparently lacks *kî.* The scroll indicates space for more letters than MT contains, indicating that it had a longer text either at the end of this verse or the start of the next), as opposed to the current reading which is confirmed by 4QPs^{s}.

9 *For there is no truth in their mouths,*[12]
their inmost beings[13] *are destruction.*
Their throats are open graves,
With their tongues they flatter.

10 *O God, make them*[14] *bear guilt,*
let them fall by means of their own plans.
Through the abundance[15] *of their sins cast them out,*
Indeed, they rebel against you.
11 *But let all who take refuge in you rejoice,*
let them sing forever!
And you shelter them; may those who love your name celebrate in you.[16]
12 *For you bless the righteous, O LORD,*[17]
as[18] *with a shield, you surround us with favor.*

1-6 The first stanza begins with a manifold request for God to hear the psalmist's prayer. As occurs often elsewhere, the request consists of four verbs — three imperatives begging God to hear and one other element, in this case an indicative assurance that the psalmist is praying *to God* (cf. Pss. 4:1; 55:1; 143:1, etc.).[19] Chiasms in both vv. 1 and 2 function to "center" God in the midst of the psalmist's crying. A literal translation of the two verses would look like this:

12. Reading "their mouth" with many interpreters based on mss support, LXX, Syriac, Targums, and parallelism. But note that 4QPs^s, agreeing with MT, reads "his mouth."

13. Syriac and Arabic read "in their."

14. 4QPs^a reads "make him bear guilt."

15. Jerome and LXX imply *wkrb,* "and according to. . . ." BHS lists Qumran as agreeing with this reading, but the present author cannot find this part of Psalm 5 attested at Qumran; perhaps BHS editors confused the *bêt* and *kāp* interchange here with the one in v. 12.

16. LXX *kyrios* implies the addition of *YHWH,* "O Lord."

17. Gerstenberger (*Psalms: Part 1,* p. 59) wants to translate v. 12 with imperative force: "Please, Yahweh, bless the righteous!" However, the switch at the end of many psalms to either indicative language of trust or imperatives directed at the congregation is too well testified to allow that move.

18. 4QPs^a has *bṣnh* for MT's *kṣnh.*

19. Many commentators site the threefold nature of the call, but note that in most cases there are four verbs, three of which are positive imperatives and a fourth that is different in some way. In 55:1, the verbs are "give ear," "attend," "answer," and "do not hide"; in 143:1 they are "hear," "give ear," "answer," and "do not enter into judgment"; in 4:1 they are "answer," "be gracious," "hear," and "you gave me room."

to my words	*be attentive*
give ear	*to the sound of my cry*
O LORD	**my king and my God**
give heed	*to my sighing*
indeed to you	*I pray.*

This centering device reflects poetically a central faith commitment of all the psalms, namely, that God is present in the midst of Israel's suffering and God holds the answer to Israel's need. Whereas the first three verbs are all imperatives calling on God to hear, the fourth verb in this sequence (an imperfect) breaks the pattern as the psalmist says, *to you I pray.* The verb functions emphatically, stressing that the psalmist trusts that God can and will hear the prayer.

In vv. 1-3, the psalmist names God four times. For the first and last occurrences (vv. 1 and 3, respectively), the psalmist uses God's proper name — *YHWH.* One significant aspect of this is that at the end of the psalm the petitioner will echo God's name: *may those who love your name celebrate in you* (v. 11). In the middle references to God, both in v. 2, the psalmist calls on *my king and my God.* The reference to *my* God provides a link to Ps 4:1 *(God of my righteousness),* and like the occurrence there emphasizes the psalmist's *relationship* with God. Calling on *my God* is a typical aspect of the prayers for help and demonstrates the poet's faith that God will answer the prayer. The title *my king* is less common, occurring only here in prayers for help. Some interpreters have deduced from this title that the petitioner was the king, but that conclusion is not warranted, since God was understood as king of all of Israel, even before human monarchs arose and after they had faded away.

As noted above, v. 3 has been the fulcrum against which many commentators have leveraged their interpretations. Its language is ambiguous and does not allow for a precise isolation of some original life setting for this psalm. While *morning* may be a reference to the time of judicial decision (so Kraus, see above), it seems more likely that it is a reference to the almost universal human experience of equating the sun's rise with the rebirth of hope. See, for example, Ps 30:5: "in the morning — rejoicing!" 46:5: "God will help it in the face of the morning"; or 130:6: "My inmost being waits expectantly for the Lord, more than those watching for the morning, those watching for the morning." This last occurrence is especially significant because it pairs the concepts of "waiting" for God's action and prayer. The psalmist is the subject of two verbs in this part of stanza 1: "I pray to you" and "I wait." The verb "wait" *(ṣāp̄â)* indicates the psalmist's dependence on and trust in God. According to Ḥabakkuk, waiting in hope for God's deliverance is integral to having faith: "I will keep watch to see what he will say to me. . . . Wait for it, it will surely come . . . the righteous live by their faith" (Hab. 2:1-4; Mic. 7:7).

The second section of the first stanza consists of a *for*-clause that praises God by describing evil qualities that God will not tolerate. Contrary to the interpretation of many commentators, the language of these verses is not specific enough to conclude that the psalmist had been falsely accused, or even that the psalmist was dealing with enemies who were threatening him in any particular way. Rather, the enemies may simply represent the wicked who, as in Psalm 1, present an alternate way of life to God's *way,* which is the one that the psalmist seeks to follow. The psalmist desires to *sojourn* with God in the temple (cf. 15:1), where *evil* and *wickedness* may not sojourn (v. 4). The wicked are called *people of bloodshed and deceit,* which means not that they both harm and deceive, but rather that their deception and harm are one and the same thing — it is their deception that causes harm. It must be emphasized that this section of the psalm is not mainly about the wicked, but about how *God* views them and what actions *God* takes against wicked behavior. The verbs in this section predominantly describe God's actions rather than human actions: *you are not a God who delights in wickedness, you hate all evildoers, you destroy those who speak lies, the LORD abhors.*

7-9 At the start of the second stanza, the poet reverts to characterizing her own life and intentions. The poet emphasizes her own actions by stressing that *I . . . I will enter. . . .* She stresses her faithfulness by saying she will enter the temple (*house* and *temple*" v. 7) in order to worship God with proper *awe* (or "fear"). The *wāw* that begins v. 7 is disjunctive, demarcating vv. 7-9 from the previous verses, and thus contrasting sharply the difference between herself and the wicked. The syntax of v. 7 also scores an important theological point: by placing the prepositional phrase *through the abundance of your hesed* (v. 7) before the verb, the poet confesses that her access to the temple is based not upon her own righteousness but upon God's unmerited favor. Thus, the wicked may not sojourn in God's presence, presumably because of their sin, and yet the psalmist enters not on her own merit, but by virtue of God's free grace. The psalm gives witness to a paradox that one finds consistently throughout the Old Testament: on the one hand, human beings are responsible for their own fate, because humans choose a course contrary to God's will; yet, on the other hand, God is responsible for human fate, because God's mercy is wider than human perversity. The promise to *enter your house* is at once literal and metaphorical. The psalmist does intend to go to the temple, perhaps on a pilgrimage, but in the broader sense, the temple serves as a metaphor for the protective presence of God. The psalmist is expressing her resolution to remain in the sphere of God's protection. The temple is not so much a place as it is a symbol of the relationship that the psalmist has with the Lord.

As is the case in each of the three stanzas, the central element of this stanza is the petition. In this case, the psalmist asks God, *lead me* and *make straight before me your way.* In Pss. 23:3, 27:11, 139:24, the petitioners also ask God to "lead them" on God's "way." Here, too, the request is at the same time a petition to be guided upon God's righteous way and also a prayer for protection from the wicked. To borrow the language of Psalm 23, the "paths of righteousness" are both "safe paths" and "morally upright paths." The reason they are safe is the same reason that they are morally upright, because God has ordained those paths. It is also significant that the psalmist asks God to guide him *in your righteousness.* As with the prepositional phrase *through your steadfast love,* the poet acknowledges that walking the walk of righteousness is not a work humans achieve on their own, but is a gift that God gives to God's covenant partners.

The *for*-clause of the middle stanza again focuses on the wicked. Once again, their qualities are described in terms of their speech. Earlier, the psalmist declared that the wicked are *boastful, speak lies,* and are *people of deceit.* Now, the psalmist adds to the catalogue of their verbal sins: *there is no truth in their mouths, their throats are open graves,* and *with their tongues they flatter.* Throughout the Psalter, the wicked and the enemies are often portrayed in terms of their speech. They are people who deny God's power, mock and tempt the righteous, and delight in evil.[20] That there is *no truth in their mouths* does not necessarily imply a false accusation, but rather that the psalmist knows that the many and various things that the enemies say are not trustworthy. Their words may be smooth and the course they chart may appear easy, but their advice leads to destruction: *their throats are open graves.* In Old Testament wisdom literature, sins of the tongue are often emphasized. Likewise, the entrance liturgies (Psalms 15 and 24) concentrate on the ways in which the righteous are called to use their voices. It is easy to demean the sins of the tongue as petty, but the Old Testament is aware of the enormous harm that can be unleashed by the tongue. It is worth remembering that the reason the psalmist needs to be guided by God's righteousness is the peril that emanates from the enemies' throats. Because the psalmist is surrounded by the smooth, persuasive speech and destructive advice of the wicked, the psalmist needs the external intervention available only from God's righteousness.

10-12 The final stanza of the psalm again features a petition, this time a two-sided coin: the psalmist asks God to abandon the wicked to their own fates, and asks that the faithful be sustained in joy. The "heads side" of the petition does not ask directly that God destroy the wicked, but rather that they fall victim to their own plots: *let them fall by means of their own plans* (v. 10). This request is reminiscent of the advice that the parent gives the child in Proverbs 1. There, the parent warns the child not to join in the *way* of sinners, for the plots they set in motion in order to snare others will actually result in

20. See Rolf Jacobson, *Many Are Saying.*

their own demise: "they lie in wait — to kill themselves! And set an ambush — for their own lives" (Prov. 1:18). Psalm 5 turns that wisdom perspective into a prayer, asking God to work against evildoers so that their sins rebound on themselves. There are elegant poetic aspects to the psalmist's request. Earlier, he had confessed that he could enter into God's presence only *through the abundance (bᵉrōḇ)* of God's *hesed.* Now he asks that the wicked be cast out *through the abundance (bᵉrōḇ)* of their sins. The word for sin here (*peša'*) carries the literal meaning of rebellion, which the psalmist then exploits by adding *indeed, they rebel against you.*

In the "tails side" of the psalmist's petition, she asks, *let all who refuge in you rejoice, let them sing forever! Shelter them! May those who love your name celebrate in you* forever. The psalmist asks that God grant bountiful and everlasting joy and celebration to the righteous, who have already been given sheltering protection. The verb *shelter* is the same word (lit., "cover") as in Ps. 91:4: "He will cover you with his wings." It is also related to the word *sūkkôṯ* ("booths"/"shelters") that is associated with the Feast of Tabernacles. The psalmist uses the Hebrew prepositional phrase *bāḵ/bᵉḵā* three times in vv. 10b-11. In its first occurrence, the phrase describes the wicked, who *rebel against you.* In its second and third occurrences, it applies to the righteous, who *refuge in you* and *celebrate in you.* The phrase thus serves to support the contrast between the wicked and the righteous — the former rebel against God, while the latter shelter in God — and also serves to support the different petitions that the psalmist asks — that the wicked be handed over to their own fate, while the righteous be granted joy and protection.

Earlier in the psalm, the poet had called upon the proper name of the Lord — *YHWH.* At the end of the psalm, the poet echoes that earlier use of the name, first by asking that *those who love your name* be granted indefinite joy, and second by confessing his confidence that the *Lord (YHWH)* does indeed bless and protect *the righteous.* As Craigie notes,

> Those who love the name are those to whom it has been revealed, the chosen people, and those to whom the blessing of the name had been granted in redemption and covenant. But more than that, the name symbolized God's presence in Israel; the sanctuary was the place in which God chose to set his name (Deut 12:5), indicating both his presence and the possibility of approaching God and calling upon his name.[21]

Thus, the reference both underscores that the psalmist is one who loves God's name and trusts God's protection and also indirectly refers to the temple, in which God's name is said to reside in Deuteronomistic theology. The psalm

21. Craigie, *Psalms 1–50,* pp. 88-89.

thus ends with a strong affirmation of the earlier mentioned emphasis on the presence of God. It is in, with, and under her relationship with God that the psalmist finds complete protection, blessing, and joy. As the psalmist adds in closing, *as with a shield, you surround us with favor.* The shield mentioned here *(ṣinnâ)* is the shield that covers all of the body, not just the arm. The verb "to crown" *(ʿāṭar)* literally means to "wrap" or "surround" as well as to "crown" as with a wreath (in Psalm 5, "crown"). The translation *surround* underscores the complete sense of protection and security that God promises the faithful.

Reflections

1. God's opposition to evil

Psalm 5 bears witness to an aspect of God's will for the world that is often assumed, namely, that God is inexorably opposed to wickedness and evil. The psalm reiterates again and again that God's will is not compatible with the human tendency to harm and violate other human beings. Given the fact that religion often makes the news these days because followers of one god or another commit violence in the name of their god, the followers of Israel's God should no longer take this for granted or leave it unsaid. As the psalmist has it, God is *not a God who delights in wickedness.* Indeed, *The Lord abhors people of bloodshed and deceit.* The God of the Old Testament as a whole and Psalm 5 in particular is a *public God,* a God whose will for the world makes a concrete difference between what behaviors are allowed and what behaviors are prohibited. Psalm 5 may not be prayed by those who perpetrate evil in the name of God. Indeed, the God of Israel may not be worshipped by those who perpetrate evil for any reason.

2. A Prayer for Protection

Psalm 5 is a prayer for protection. On the one hand, it is a prayer asking that God protect the faithful from those who commit acts of evil. This much is clear. To follow God is to walk in the way of God's instruction; and to walk in the way of God's instruction is to encounter hostility at times from the wicked. As noted above, this psalm begs God to let the plots of the wicked rebound back upon them in order that the faithful might be protected from violence. As such, this psalm is typical of Israel's lament prayers for help. In those prayers, Israel seeks shelter from the one to whom they could always turn for solace. On the other hand, as Craigie has seen, this psalm is "also a prayer for protection from becoming *like*" the wicked.[22] The psalmist recognizes that the faithful are not immune to temptation, nor are the righteous so

22. Craigie, *Psalms 1–50,* p. 89.

pure as to be exempt from the human tendency to seek our best interest at the expense of others. To that extent, the prayer is a humble request for shelter from the ways of the wicked, and a request for direction, lest our human feet mislead us into walking those very ways on our own.

3. *A Song of Eschatological Hope*

Finally, this psalm bears witness to the Bible's eschatological hope in God's justice. As McCann has perceived, the psalm is aware that there are forces in the world that are opposed to God's way. "Here, as in Psalm 2 and throughout Psalms, the affirmation of God's kingship is made in the presence of the competing claims of evildoers and enemies."[23] The psalmist recognizes that the Lord alone is the true God of time and history, but also recognizes that the Lord's reign is not acknowledged by all. Thus, with the prophets Habakkuk (Hab. 2:1) and Micah (Mic. 7:7), the psalmist *waits* for the consummation of God's peaceable kingdom. But this waiting is neither a passive, quietist inaction nor a resigned, pessimistic despair. The psalmist knows whose will shall be done and awaits the coming of that kingdom.

ROLF A. JACOBSON

23. McCann, "The Book of Psalms," p. 700.

Psalm 6: The Problem and the Solution

Psalm 6 is generally identified as an individual prayer for help. Within the broad umbrella of that category, there are different ways of understanding the poem, based on which words and phrases one gives the most weight.[1] Early on, the Western church identified this as one of the seven "penitential psalms" (Psalms 6, 32, 38, 51, 102, 130, 143).[2] This identification was most likely made on the basis of vv. 1-3, which refer to God's anger. It should be noted, however, that the psalm, like some of the other penitential psalms, lacks both an explicit confession of sin and a plea for forgiveness (and it should be noted that other psalms that contain clear penitential motifs, such as Psalm 25, are not included among the seven). As Nasuti has argued, Psalm 6 was most likely understood as a penitential psalm because of the mention in v. 1 of the *anger* of God (*'ap̱* in Hebrew; *orgē* in the LXX; *ira* in the Vulgate).[3] Without question, the psalm does operate with the assumption that the crisis in which the psalmist is suffering was caused by God's anger. But again, there is no explicit reference to a consciousness of sin, only to a consciousness of God's anger, especially in vv. 1-3.

If one concentrates on vv. 7b-10, the psalm seems to be a psalm of one who is persecuted by enemies. If an interpreter makes these verses the focus, one could conceive of the psalm as a prayer for protection from enemies. But most modern commentators focus on vv. 4-7a and conclude that the psalm is the prayer of one who is desperately ill. This identification is based most specifically on the poet's request to be healed (v. 2) and her complaints that her bones are terrified (v. 2) and that she is close to death (v. 5). The precise nature of the implied disease is impossible to determine. This identification may be accepted provisionally with two very significant caveats. First, the identification of the psalm as the prayer of an ill person must not limit how the psalm is prayed, used, or interpreted today. The psalm's rich poetic language allows and even endorses the appropriation of the psalm's message in many different situations. McCann's judgment is surely correct: "In short, the psalm need not be heard exclusively as a prayer for healing from physical illness."[4] A second caveat: As Zenger has pointed out, the Psalm shares 60 percent of its language with other psalms; it is one of the most formally

1. See the helpful summary in Hossfeld and Zenger, *Die Psalmen I*, p. 67.

2. The first extant reference to the seven penitential psalms is found in the sixth-century Latin father Cassiodorus's work, *Expositio Psalmorum*. There are earlier references in the Fathers to the penitential nature of certain psalms, esp. 51. See Nasuti, *Defining the Sacred Songs*, pp. 30-56.

3. Nasuti, *Defining the Sacred Songs*, pp. 35ff. Nasuti notes that the same term occurs in Psalms 38 and 102.

4. McCann, "The Book of Psalms," p. 703.

"typical" psalms in the Psalter. The interpreter should be reminded of Gunkel's belief that many psalms were actually artistic creations that mirrored genuine cultic poems. This psalm might be such a psalm that has been, in Gunkel's words, "removed from its 'life setting.'"[5] Zenger concludes that the psalm cannot reflect any unique life situation. Rather, it was written as a prayer formula.[6]

As the text of the psalm stands, the poem can either be understood as having three or four stanzas.[7] While it has been proven that the ancient poets did indeed think in terms of stanzas, division into stanzas is at times more an art than a science.[8] It seems best to understand the poem as having three stanzas, each of which leads with an imperative or similar appeal and each of which includes, somewhere in the stanza, "reasons" that support the appeals.

St. 1 Initial petition for grace and healing (vv. 1-3)
St. 2 Repeated prayer for deliverance (vv. 4-7)
St. 3 Concluding address to foes and expression of confidence (vv. 8-10)

For the leader. With stringed instruments.[9] *ʿal haššᵉmînîṯ.*[10] *A Davidic psalm.*

1 *O Lord, in your anger, do not rebuke me,*
and in your wrath, do not discipline me.
2 *Be gracious to me, O Lord, for I am feeble,*
heal me, O Lord,[11] *for my bones are terrified.*[12]
3 *My soul is extremely terrified,*[13]
and you, O Lord, how long?

5. Gunkel, *Introduction to the Psalms,* p. 128, see pp. 123-30.

6. Hossfeld and Zenger, *Die Psalmen I,* p. 68.

7. E.g., see the differing views in McCann ("The Book of Psalms," p. 704) on the one hand, and Hossfeld and Zenger (*Die Psalmen I,* pp. 69-71) and Craigie (*Psalms 1–50,* p. 92) on the other; see also Fokkelman, *The Psalms in Form,* p. 19.

8. See Fokkelman, *Reading Biblical Poetry,* ch. 1. It should be noted that Fokkelman's commitment to counting syllables is not widely accepted and is not accepted here.

9. See note on Psalm 4 superscription.

10. The term is obscure; it literally means "eighth," which leads some to interpret it as "octave," an indication of a musical note.

11. The Vaticanus ms of LXX omits "Lord."

12. Kraus sees *niḇhᵃlû ʿᵃṣāmāy* as awkward and has proposed, on the basis of Ps. 32:3, amending to *bālû ʿᵃṣāmāy.* This is plausible, as a slip of the eye may have caused *niḇhᵃlû* to be transposed from v. 3. However, it is just as possible that the verb was used twice for rhetorical effect and the text should be maintained.

13. 4QPsᵃ reads *ʿd mʾd.*

4 Turn, O Lord*, deliver my soul!*
Save me for the sake of your hesed.
5 For in death there is no remembrance of you,[14]
in Sheol, who will praise you?
6 I am weary from my groaning;
all night I flood my bed,
With my tears, I melt my bed.
7 My eye grows dark due to vexation,
it grows weak[15] *from all my foes.*

8 Depart from me, all evildoers,
for the Lord *has heard the sound of my weeping.*
9 The Lord *has heard my request,*
The Lord *accepts my prayer.*
10 All my enemies will be shamed and terrified,
They shall turn away and be shamed in a moment.

1-3 The poem begins, quite literally, with the *Lord*. The first word of the poem is Yahweh. By beginning so, the poet not only calls on the Lord, but the psalmist names the Lord as both his problem and the One holding the antidote to his condition. As McCann has eloquently put it, the "foes are not the psalmist's main problem. Rather, the real problem is God! . . . But if God is the problem, God is also the solution."[16] The first four verbs of the poem make this clear. The first verse contains two negative appeals and the second two positive appeals: *do not rebuke me . . . do not discipline me . . . be gracious to me . . . heal me.* Together, the negative and positive appeals describe both God as the psalmist's problem and God as the solution. The poet needs both less of God's attention and more. The word *rebuke (yāḵaḥ)* carries a legal or parental connotation; it implies a rightful authority to judge and correct. The word *discipline (yāsar)* carries more of a sense of instruction than it does punishment.

A major point of interpretation is how to understand the phrases *in your anger* and *in your wrath* (v. 1). At issue is whether the interpreter should take the prepositional *bêt*s as instrumental or causal. If the former, then the sense is "do not rebuke me by means of your anger." If the latter, then the sense is

14. LXX implies *zōḵreḵā,* "no one remembers you."

15. Aquila and Symmachus read the verb as first person singular. The MT inflects the verb with a feminine subject, which would be "the eye." The Hebrew verb literally means to "advance" or move forward (cf Gen. 12:8). The Greek word that renders it means to grow old, so the sense might be here that of growing old or irrelevant.

16. McCann, "The Book of Psalms," p. 703.

"do not rebuke me because you are angry." The former interpretation would be consistent with the Old Testament view, found especially in the wisdom traditions (cf. Prov. 3:11-12; Job 5:17), that God's discipline or instruction is a source of blessing (although a difficult blessing to stomach). The absence of an explicit confession of sin also favors this interpretation. The tradition of identifying the psalm as a penitential psalm favors the latter interpretation, as does the close parallel of Ps. 38:1 (cf. 39:11). The ancient belief that sickness was caused by sin, which may be present here, also supports this view. For more on this, see "Reflections" below.

The petitions *be gracious to me* and *heal me* are appeals to the covenantal confession that God is gracious and merciful (Exod. 34:6-7; cf. Pss. 86:15; 103:8) and that God delights in healing (Exod. 15:26). The two words are often paired together (cf. Ps. 41:4). Here, they convey the sense that one cannot abstract God's favor from God's active healing or saving. The abstract concept of God's favor is known in the concrete experience of deliverance. As motivating reasons for the request to be healed, the psalmist offers only a description of her own woes: *for I am feeble . . . for my bones are terrified.* The psalmist offers neither avowals of innocence nor confessions of sins. She believes that the raw reality of her suffering is enough to bring God to action — that and the fact that she is in relationship with the Lord, whose character it is to heal and show mercy. The second of these motivating clauses is extended into a longer cry that ends in the characteristic question *how long?* The question is quite literal. For those who suffer, it is not just the physical suffering that causes anguish but also the mental suffering of not knowing how long the anguish will linger.

4-7 The second stanza begins with the plea for God to *turn* (*šûḇâ;* cf. Ps. 90:13). The word can carry the sense of repentance (Jer. 3:12), restoration (Ps. 126:4), or change (90:13). Here, where the term is paralleled with *deliver* and *save,* it seems to encompass both the second and third definitions. The psalmist is appealing for God to change course and restore him to wellness.

Again, the psalmist supplies motivating reasons to urge God's hand. The bulk of the second stanza, vv. 4b-7, is made up of these motivating clauses. The clauses include the three relational parties that are often named in prayers for help: God (you), the psalmist (I), and the enemies. With respect to God, the appeal is made based on God's internal character: *save me for the sake of your* hesed. The psalmist has faith that the most significant factor in his relationship with God is God's *hesed,* and on this basis he makes his appeal. The psalmist accentuates the relational aspect of his appeal by means of the rhetorical question, *in Sheol, who will praise you?* Sheol was understood as the place of the dead, where some believed that God was not present (although see Psalm 139). The psalmist here is not bargaining with God in the crude sense, not appealing to God's self-interest. Rather, the psalmist is stating a simple reality and placing his own hope in the divine-human relationality that remembering God and praising God describe.

With respect to herself, in the second stanza, the psalmist amplifies her lament. The psalmist's complaints about her woeful condition build in intensity, by including the poem's only tricola (v. 6) with the passionate image of a bed turned into a pool of grief, the image of a bed that dissolves because of tears. In the final clauses of the complaint, the psalmist cries, *my eye grows dark.* The eye is a metaphor for the overall health, disposition, and intentions of the person (cf. Pss. 13:3; 19:8; 25:15; 131:1, etc.). Here, the idiom indicates that the psalmist has reached the end of her resources and strength. Of the elderly Moses was said his eye had not grown dim (Deut. 34:7), indicating his vitality right until the end; the opposite is the case with the psalmist. It is worth noting that the psalmist several times uses bodily euphemisms to refer to herself: *my bones* (v. 2), *my soul* (vv. 3-4; lit., my throat), *my eye.* These referents indicate the intimately bodily nature of suffering, but they also indicate how anguish can dehumanize a sufferer, so that one's sense of self is reduced to the pain in one's bones, body, skin. The complaint section ends with an unexpected reference to the psalmist's foes. This reference is difficult to explain. The most likely explanation is that the foes are those who assume the psalmist's physical suffering is a divine punishment for some sin, and thus the sufferer experiences a double sort of pain: a physical and emotional pain on the one hand and a social and spiritual pain on the other. As Craigie has noted, "The reference to enemies may be the result of a common experience of the sick in ancient Israel; many persons believed that the sick were sinners, being judged by God, so that even a sick man's friends might become enemies. Such was apparently the experience of Job (30:1-15)."[17]

8-10 The last stanza marks a dramatic change in mood, tone, and rhetorical audience. Like the first two stanzas, this stanza begins with an imperative followed by reasons. This imperative, however, is directed at the psalmist's foes (who had only just been named in the last word of stanza 2, thus making a nice connection between the two stanzas). The mood is suddenly one of confidence that is borne of faith in the Lord's saving actions. The tone is one of triumph at having been vindicated by the Lord in the presence of those who wished the psalmist ill.

How to explain the sudden change in tone? A traditional way of explaining the change is to assume some sort of cultic intervention or ritual between vv. 7 and 8. Gerstenberger's opinion is typical of this view: The affirmation of confidence "is due to an oracle of salvation or some other sign of Yahweh's grace [delivered by a priest] that the supplicant has received during the [healing] ceremony but that would rarely be found incorporated in the

17. Craigie, *Psalms 1–50,* p. 94.

text of the prayer (cf. Pss. 12:6; 35:3; 91:3ff . . .)."[18] The fact that the first verb is in the perfect aspect — *the LORD has heard* — while the following verbs are in the imperfect — *accepts, will be ashamed and terrified, they shall turn away* — may support this interpretation. Although Craigie appears to concur with this cultic explanation, he at least offers this alternative understanding: "It may have been the case that as the psalmist progressed in prayer, he eventually reached a point where faith and confidence outstripped anguish and despair."[19] Whichever interpretation one favors, the key point is that the psalmist has faith that the Lord has moved to act on his behalf. The eyes that were dim with suffering are the eyes of faith, and in the darkness they see the hand of the Lord moving to deliver. The psalmist is firm in his conviction that his prayer has been heard, that the Lord has been present in the moment of crisis and has acted.

The closing shout of triumph that *all my enemies will be shamed* does not mean shame in the postmodern sense of internalized guilt. Rather, in the ancient context, shame was a cultural value about the exterior place of a person or persons in the social economy. The shout of triumph here is that the Lord has restored the public dignity and name of the psalmist. The psalm celebrates the characteristically evangelical manner in which the Lord reverses the conditions of the world (cf. Hannah's song in 1 Sam. 2:1-10 or Mary's song in Luke 1:46-55). The third stanza of the poem underscores this evangelical turn-around by reversing language used in the prayer. The psalmist's bones were terrified; now the enemies will be. The Lord was called on to turn; now the enemies will turn away. The psalmist earlier begged God to be gracious *(ḥnn)* and now confesses that the Lord has heard the request *(ḥnn).* The psalm's final word that the Lord will act *in a moment (rāḡaʿ)* reverses the psalmist's earlier cry of *how long?* The ending of the poem thus expresses the reversal that the psalmist had sought and has received. The reality of that reversal literally changes everything.

Reflections

1. The Problem and the Solution

As Mays has seen, the psalm is an "appeal to the grace of God against the wrath of God. It sees the Lord as the cause of death and as the giver of life."[20] In Psalm 6, the Lord is both the problem and the solution. The identification of this psalm as a penitential psalm by the Western church is consistent

18. Gerstenberger, *Psalms: Part 1,* p. 62
19. Craigie, *Psalms 1–50,* p. 94.
20. Mays, *Psalms,* p. 59.

with that basic insight. Such an identification comprehends correctly that the theological situation from which this psalm is prayed is one in which a petitioner recognizes that to be caught up in the human condition is to be caught up before God — to be caught up both in God's grace and in God's anger. The psalm thus shows that there is an indissoluble link between lament and faith. Lament is not the absence of faith or an expression of faith being tempted into despair. To lament is to speak precisely from the position of faith, from a position which recognizes that the Lord hears the cries of those who suffer and is not indifferent to them. To lament is to lay claim to God's *hesed* with the faithful expectation that the Lord will vindicate the lowly. "Just as Israel as a nation received God's love in covenant in, and after, the great deliverance from Egypt, so too each member of the covenant community could request the continuing experience of God's lovingkindness in the act of divine deliverance."[21] The reason that the psalmist cries out to God (vv. 2-3, 5-7) and the reason that the psalmist cries out in triumph to the enemies (vv. 9-10) are consistent. In the words of the psalmist: *For the Lord has heard the sound of my weeping. The Lord has heard my request, the Lord accepts my prayer.*

2. *The Anger of God*

In the commentary above, the issue of how to understand God's anger was raised. To be more specific, the question was raised as to whether to understand God's anger as instrumental or causal. If one understands God's anger as instrumental, then the notion is that the Lord is a teacher — by means of judgment, God instructs the sinners. If one understands God's anger as causal, then the notion is that God is a judge — because of crimes, God judges human sinners. One suspects that the nicety of this theological distinction might be lost on the psalmist — swimming in a bath of tears, dissolving in a bed of weeping. When one is suffering, it is usually not the time to deploy such theological distinctions, as one hopes Job's comrades learned. But such distinctions do matter for the life of faith in the long run. The concept of the anger of God is the necessary corollary to the love of God. Without God's anger, God's love is reduced to a sloppy sentimentalism. To be sure, God loves us. But because God also loves our neighbors, when our actions result in the suffering and death of our neighbors, God's love becomes indivisible from God's anger. But God's anger is in service of God's love. God's anger is not a permanent state, but one that arises from time to time when human violence against other creatures whom also God loves sparks God's anger.[22]

21. Craigie, *Psalms 1–50,* p. 93.

22. See Terence Fretheim, "Theological Reflections on the Wrath of God in the Old Testament," *HBT* 24 (2002) 1-26.

Psalm 6

God's wrath is neither random nor inexplicable. It arises for specific reasons, which the prophets, in particular, spell out. And God's wrath is certainly instrumental. That is, God is angry for the sake of the relationship God shares with the world and for the sake of the wellness of God's creation.

Rolf A. Jacobson

Psalm 7: Taking Refuge in God's Righteousness

Psalm 7 is a prayer for help. Most scholars identify the poem more narrowly as the prayer of one who has been falsely accused. The primary warrant for this assignation may be found in vv. 3-5, which is customarily labeled as an oath. In these verses, the psalmist vows that if he did *this,* then may his enemies *trample me to the ground.* The precise nature of this accusation is not knowable. Craigie has argued that the psalmist has been accused of having broken a treaty or fealty obligation, such as David was accused of having done when he was serving Saul,[1] but such a degree of specificity is not possible. Nor is the precise setting in which the prayer was spoken either known or knowable. Some scholars have argued that the psalm most likely was prayed as part of an ordeal ritual, such as that mentioned in Num. 5:12-28, and the oath in vv. 3-5 is akin to the oath mentioned there. Other scholars have posited a temple-based judicial proceeding, based in part on the idea of the temple as a sanctuary for those who have accidentally harmed another (e.g., Deut. 19:1-6) and in part on the description of the temple as the place where one who has been accused may flee to take an oath and seek judgment (1 Kgs. 8:31-32).[2] Is the psalm an actual prayer that some persecuted person once prayed, or is it a liturgy for those who have been falsely accused? There is no certainty. Gerstenberger has expressed the view that "Psalm 7 . . . as well as the other laments, does not report a single incident, for instance, of somebody being accused of theft. Rather, the complaint represents an accumulation of the agonies of generations of supplicants facing unfounded charges of various types." He adds, "I suggest that the prayer was used in regular complaint and petitionary services for an individual suffering in a legal predicament. Of course it could be recited only by and for people whose guiltlessness had been proven or could be vouched for."[3]

What is sure about the psalm is that it has a clear theological situation. The psalm is the prayer of one who seeks God in order to receive refuge, deliverance, and vindication. This should be taken as the interpretive point of departure. As Mays has written, "Taking refuge in the Lord or making the Lord one's refuge is a favorite and frequent metaphor in the psalms for the religious act of trusting one's life to the care of God in uncertain or threatening situations. . . . The prayer itself is a way of taking shelter in the providence and salvation of God."[4] Whatever historical or human situation one imagines for

1. Craigie, *Psalms 1–50,* p. 99.
2. See Kraus, *Psalms 1–59,* p. 169.
3. Gerstenberger, *Psalms: Part 1,* pp. 64, 66.
4. Mays, *Psalms,* p. 63.

this poignant poem, the theological situation that Mays outlines is the proper ground of interpretation.

The psalm is fairly long and has many textual difficulties,[5] so delineating its structure depends in part on how one resolves certain textual and translation issues (see comments below). And yet, the basic movement of the psalm is clear; it moves from a cry for help (including a protestation of innocence in the form of a vow) to a confession of trust in the Lord's righteous judgment. This structure is followed here:

St. 1 Appeal for rescue and vow of innocence (vv. 1-5)
St. 2 Appeal for vindication and justice (vv. 6-9)
St. 3 Confession of trust in God's righteousness (vv. 10-16)
Closing vow to praise (not a full stanza) (v. 17)

It is possible to subdivide each of the three stanzas into two smaller stanzas (vv. 1-2, 3-5, 6-8a, 8b-9, 10-13, 14-16); such a division would not greatly change how one understands the movement of the poem. The first stanza is set apart both by the liturgical marker *selah* and also by the repetition in vv. 1/2 and 5 of the words *rāḏap (pursuers/pursue)* and *napšî (my throat/me)*. The second stanza continues the plea for help, but the plea modulates from a cry for rescue to a cry for vindication and for judgment of those who do evil. The third stanza is notable for its linguistic shift from the second person prayer of stanza 2 to third person confession. The closing bicola is a cohortative promise to praise God.

The Davidic superscription of the psalm is evidence of the earliest interpretation of the psalm. It places the psalm in the context of David's life. The incident that the superscription describes is not attested in the Old Testament. It cannot be a reference to 2 Sam. 16:17ff. or to 2 Sam. 18:21ff. Most likely, the superscription refers to an incident about David that has been lost. What we can glean from the superscription is to be found in the words *when he sang to the LORD concerning the words of Cush the Benjaminite.* It is clear that the Benjaminites bore ill will to David and his reign. It is also likely from the psalm that the psalmist is crying to the Lord because of false words that have been spoken about the psalmist. It is also worth noting that the psalm was later associated with the Jewish Feast of Purim, a context in which the ill will and witness of an enemy play a key role.

5. See Jacob Leveen, "The Textual Problems of Psalm 7," *VT* 16 (1966) 439-45. Leveen proposes many textual emendations, many of which are plausible, but few of which are sure. The essay is a helpful guide to the textual problems of the psalm, but the text that he constructs may not be relied upon for exegesis. See also Jeffrey H. Tigay, "Psalm 7:5 and Ancient Near Eastern Treaties," *JBL* 89 (1970) 178-86.

Psalm 7

A Davidic šiggāyôn.[6] *When he sang to the* Lord *concerning the words of Cush the Benjaminite.*

1 *O* Lord *my God, in you I have taken refuge.*
Save me from all my pursuers and deliver me,
2 *Lest they*[7] *tear out my throat like a lion,*
there is no rescuer,[8] *no deliverer.*
3 *O* Lord *my God, if I have done this,*
if there is fraud on my hands,
4 *If I have repaid with evil one who did me good,*[9]
if I have tormented[10] *my foe without cause,*
5 *May my enemy pursue*[11] *me and overtake me,*
may they trample me to the ground,
and lay my honor in the dust. Selah[12]

6 *Arise, O* Lord, *in your anger!*
Lift up against the furies of my enemies.

6. The term occurs only here in the Hebrew Bible, although the presumably related term *šigyōnôṯ* occurs in Hab. 3:1. The term is likely a liturgical or musical notation, although the meaning of it has been lost. The word may be related to the Akkadian term *šigû,* meaning "dirge" or "lamentation." Kraus thinks of an "agitated lament" (*Psalms 1–59,* p. 26). If the word is related to the root *šgh,* "to stagger," then the term may refer to a staggering or ecstatic prayer or an animated musical beat. LXX translates simply as *psalmos* here and as *meta ōdēs* ("with song") in Hab. 3:1, supporting the view that it is a liturgical or musical term.

7. The Hebrew verbal forms throughout this section are 3ms, but the sense of an impersonal enemy is best rendered in English with the impersonal "they," which also better matches the plural foes in v. 1b.

8. Reading *ʾên pōrēq* with LXX and Syr. The verb *pāraq* can mean either "tear off/away" or "rescue." The versions support the sense of "rescue," as do passages such as Ps. 136:24 and Lam. 5:8; the above translation follows this line of thinking. Another possibility would be to see it as a substantive, meaning "one who devours," in some way parallel with the lion of the first colon, but the syntax does not support this approach.

9. LXX implies the plural; MT is retained.

10. The text seems to be corrupt. It has been proposed that LXX's *apopesoin* ("to fall") is reading *lāḥaṣ* ("to oppress/torment") instead of *ḥālaṣ* ("to deliver"); Pesh and Targum are said to support this reading of the Hebrew, although as Tigay has pointed out, in Syriac the root *ḥālaṣ* means "plunder" and does not mean "rescue." Tigay suggests emending *ṣôrrî* ("my enemy") to *ṣārrô* ("his enemy"), but there is no textual support for this move. HALOT suggests *ḥālaṣ* in the *piel* might mean "to despoil," a meaning otherwise unattested and not consistent with attested readings. Although LXX does not in reality support reading *lāḥaṣ* for *ḥālaṣ,* Pesh and Targum do, and this is the least objectionable solution.

11. The verbal form is a combination of the *qal* and *piel* forms, which was a scribal convention designed to offer the reader a choice. The form is jussive in meaning.

12. See comment on Ps. 3:2.

Rouse up on my behalf[13] *— you have commanded justice!*[14]
7 *The congregation of the peoples surrounds you.*
Be enthroned[15] *on high above it!*
8 *LORD, may you judge the peoples!*
Judge me, O LORD,[16] *according to my righteousness,*
and according to my integrity.
9 *May the evil of the wicked cease,*
may you establish the righteous.[17]
O examiner[18] *of thoughts and emotions,*
O righteous God!

10 *My shield is God,*[19]
O deliverer of the upright of heart.
11 *God is a righteous judge,*
God passes sentence every day.[20]
12 *Indeed,*[21] *he returns and sharpens his sword,*
he bends his bow and strings it.[22]
13 *He prepares for himself the weapons of death,*

13. LXX's "O LORD my God," reading *YHWH 'ĕlî,* is expansionistic and harmonizing; MT is retained (cf. Ps. 59:5).

14. Some commentators have trouble with the 2ms perfect *you have commanded,* treating it as the elusive precative perfect or repointing it; *mišpāṭ* is taken here as the abstract *justice* (cf. Ps. 119:137) rather than the concrete "judgment."

15. MT *šûḇâ* ("return"; so LXX) makes little sense; the context demands a repointing to *šēḇâ* ("be seated"), as in the concept of God taking the throne of judgment.

16. 11QMelch has *'l* for MT's *YHWH;* MT is retained, supported by LXX.

17. LXX reads plural, but this is not necessary. It is common in Semitic parallelism to pair a plural with a singular, with essentially synonymous sense of number.

18. It is a question whether to take the *qal* active particle here as a relative, as do most translations, or as continuing the action of the previous string of jussive-force verbs. The former alternative is followed here; although the article is missing, it is also missing in the following verses and is not necessary, especially in poetry.

19. How to take *'al 'ᵉlōhîm* is an issue, since the syntax is awkward. Perhaps originally the text was "God most high," but there is no versional support. The text as it stands is best understood as meaning that "my shield is upon God['s arm], thus *my shield is God.*

20. LXX takes *'l* as the negative particle, but this disrupts the parallelism and negates, perhaps out of apologetic motives, the sense of God as judge in this verse. Leveen has noted that LXX's *kai isxuros kai makrothymos* has no equivalent in the Hebrew text; he retrojects *gᵉḏôl kōaḥ wᵉ'ereḵ 'appayim* and then supplies *'appô* at the end of v. 12a, rendering "God is a righteous judge, mighty and slow to anger: Yet a God who is also angry every day; yea, his anger will not turn back."

21. *'im lō'* is taken as the beginning of an oath formula, not as a literal condition.

22. The Hebrew reads, lit.: "He steps on his bow and establishes it," very literally describing the action of a warrior bending the bow and making it ready for action.

he hardens his arrow tips.[23]
14 *He is in labor with sin,*
he has conceived mischief, he has given birth to deceit.
15 *He dug a pit and hollowed it out,*
he fell into the pit he was making.
16 *His own mischief turns upon his head,*
his own violence descends on his forehead.

17 *Let me praise the LORD for his righteousness,*[24]
let me sing of the name of the LORD most high.

1-5 The psalm's opening cry for deliverance (vv. 1-2) is remarkable both for the typical nature of the plea but also for its raw emotion and savage imagery. The opening cry is typical. Both the initial address *O LORD my God* (Pss. 13:3; 30:12; 35:24, etc.) and the modifying, confessing clause *in you I have taken refuge* (cf. 16:1; 25:20; 31:2; 71:1; 141:8) are so common in the psalms that they can be fairly described as formulaic. Likewise, the prayer *save me* (3:7; 6:4; 22:21; 31:16, etc.) *from all my pursuers* (35:3; 38:20; 119:150, 157), *deliver me* (22:8; 25:20; 31:2; 144:7, 11, etc.) are stock language in the Psalter. On the other hand, the brutality of the image *lest they tear out my throat like a lion* is striking. NRSV and others translate the clause "they will tear me apart," but the Hebrew is more graphic. The term rendered as "me" by the NRSV is *nap̱šî,* which can be translated as "me" or "my soul/self," but which carries the literal sense of *my throat.* It is a violent image that conveys both the desperation of the psalmist's situation and the urgent faith that drives the prayer. The psalmist's despair is underscored by her confession that *there is no rescuer, no deliverer.* By this, the psalmist means that there is no earthly power that can save her — only God has both the means and the fidelity to rescue.

Most scholars interpret vv. 3-5 as the oath of an innocent or a conditional self-cursing vow. That is, in this section of the psalm, the pray-er vows that he committed no crime to merit his enemies' wrath and vows that if he did commit a crime, he invites the punishment down upon himself. The connection between vv. 1-2 is established in two ways. First, both subsections of the psalm begin with the same address, *O LORD my God.* Second, as noted above, the use of the root *rāḏap̱ (pursuers/pursue)* and *nap̱šî (my throat/me)* in both verses ties them together as a unit. A key phrase is the beginning of the vow, *if I have done this (ʾim ʿāśîṯî zoʾṯ).* Although some have questioned the integrity of the

23. *lᵉḏōlqîm* (lit., "to burning") here refers to the act of burning the tips of arrows to make them sharp and hard.

24. Some manuscripts read "in his righteousness," which would not deliver a significantly different meaning. The Syr has a first person suffix.

text,[25] most conclude that *this* is a reference to whatever crime the psalmist has been accused of. If this reading is correct, it may be that the psalmist has been accused of having done something that she did not do, or it may be that the psalmist is being accused of having intentionally committed an act that she maintains was an accident (cf. Deuteronomy 19). There then follow three clauses that must be taken syntactically as continuing the conditional nature of the psalmist's disavowal. In the first, the psalmist says, *if there is fraud on my hands.* The term *fraud* is a rare term (Deut. 25:16; Prov. 29:27) that carries the basic sense of injustice, although the term connotes something stronger and more virulent and outrageous than merely the abstract term "injustice" can denote. Some scholars have imagined that the reference to hands indicates a hand-washing liturgy as part of the denial (cf. Deut. 21:1-8), but this is far from certain. The psalmist further denies that he has repaid with evil *one who did me good.* The term here is *šôlᵉmî,* which some have taken as a technical term to mean either "ally" (see Craigie) or "one who shares the peace of the same household as the psalmist" (see Kraus, who follows Hans Schmidt). Such a precise definition of the term overstates the conclusions at which one can arrive, but it is clear that the psalmist is denying having returned harm to one who did well by her. The last phrase in the psalmist's conditional denial is textually corrupt. As it stands, the text reads, "if I have delivered my enemy without cause," which is, in Tigay's words, "a monstrosity: it makes rescuing one's enemy . . . a sin."[26] Although the solution adopted above is by no means certain, the most promising solution is to understand that *ḥālaṣ* ("to deliver") resulted from transposing the first two letters of *lāḥaṣ* ("to oppress/torment"), thus the above translation. In the apodosis of the vow, the psalmist exposes herself to the violence of the enemy if she is found to be guilty. *May my enemy . . . overtake me . . . trample me to the ground . . . lay my honor in the dust.*

According to the logic of the psalm, the prayer for deliverance rests on the foundation of the psalmist's conditional righteousness. That is, the psalmist's assertion of innocence is not an abstract claim of absolute righteousness. Rather, it is a claim to be righteous in the matter for which he is being pursued; he is claiming innocence in a specific matter. The Old Testament knows that no human and no part of human existence can be abstracted from the broken human condition. This is a claim to be innocent of a particular crime. As Craigie has noted, "the deliverance for which the psalmist prays will only be forthcoming if indeed he is innocent, for specifically he seeks deliverance from the circumstances created by false accusations laid against him." Moreover, the psalm is also prayed upon the foundation of a relationship with

25. See Leveen, "The Textual Problems of Psalm 7," p. 440.

26. Tigay, "Psalm 7:5 and Ancient Near Eastern Treaties," p. 179.

God. The psalmist refers to God with the relational term *my God* and begs for personal deliverance. Again Craigie: "prayer for deliverance is based upon a history of relationship with God; it is possible to say 'save me' and 'deliver me' now (v. 2b[1b]), only because in the past, 'I have sought refuge in you' (v. 2a[1a])."[27]

6-9 In the second stanza, with increased urgency, the psalmist renews the plea for God to intervene. Three imperatives drive the prayer of v. 6: *arise, lift up, rouse!* These typical cries (cf. Pss. 3:7; 9:19; 10:12; 94:2; 35:23; 44:23, etc.) are pleas for God to act and do so quickly. They emphasize the urgency of the psalmist's cry. The appeal for God to rise up *in anger* balances the *furies of my enemies* — the reality of the enemies' fury requires that God respond in kind. The last phrase of v. 6 is disputed. The Hebrew *(mišpāṭ ṣiwwîṯā)* can be taken several ways, each of which can claim support from the context. NRSV ("you have appointed a judgment") takes *mišpāṭ* to mean a specific act of judging, which could mean either "you have made a decision regarding my innocence" or "you have made a decision regarding my enemies' guilt." NJPS ("you have ordained judgment") takes the term to refer to the abstract act of judgment. Both of these versions assume the verb refers to a completed action. NIV ("decree justice") renders the perfect verb as an imperative and takes the noun to mean the abstract concept of justice. The translation here, *you have commanded justice,* interprets the phrase as part of a clause urging God to act. The sense is "act quickly in regard to my just cause; it was after all you who commanded justice in the first place."

The psalmist's appeal to God as judge continues in vv. 7-8a. The psalmist holds up before God the doctrine of God as the universal judge (cf. 9:8; 96:10, etc.) in order to spur God to exercise justice in her own case. The argument is an appeal from the universal to the specific; it begs God to see the individual case as an instance of the universal battle against injustice, and thus to intercede on the psalmist's behalf.

The psalmist goes so far as to invite God's universal judgment on himself: *Judge me, O LORD, according to my righteousness, and according to my integrity.* Again, it must be emphasized that the psalmist is not claiming righteousness in the sense of spiritual perfection or theological self-justification. These verses "are not intended to be a litany of self-righteousness before God. The psalms know that there is no autonomous independent righteousness on the basis of which human beings can deal with God (130:3; 143:2). Such prayers were composed for a person who was in the right in comparison with an antagonist."[28] Job's challenge to God (Job 31) is similar. Job cried out that whatever guilt he had incurred did not rise to the level of the punishment that

27. Craigie, *Psalms 1–50,* p. 100.

28. Mays, *Psalms,* pp. 63-64.

he received (and the reader knows that Job is correct). Likewise, the psalmist does not assert an abstract theological righteousness, but rather a concrete situational righteousness. The psalmist does have an expectation that God's earthly salvation is not independent of individual guilt or innocence. The psalmist is begging God to act in a manner consistent with God's role as the *examiner of thoughts and emotions* and as judge of the peoples of the earth. If the psalmist is guilty as charged, the psalmist acknowledges that justice will require her punishment. But because she is convinced either of her innocence or that her actions were accidental, she invites God's investigation and decision.

10-16 The reader encounters a significant interpretive puzzle in vv. 10-16. The issue is whether God or the enemy is the subject of the third person masculine singular verbs in vv. 12-13; no subject is specified for those verbs. Translation of the verses depends on which subject one identifies. God is the subject of the verbs in vv. 10-11. The enemy is clearly the subject of the verbs in v. 14 — *he is in labor with sin, he has conceived mischief* — but the enemy is never explicitly named as the subject of the verbs. So, somewhere between vv. 12 and 14, the interpreter must discern where the subject of the verbs changes from God to the enemy. There are many options. NRSV: "If one does not repent, God will whet his sword. . . ." NJPS: "If one does not turn back, but whets his sword. . . ." NIV: "If he [God] does not relent, he will sharpen his sword. . . ." NJB: "[God has indignation] for those who will not repent. Let the enemy whet his sword, draw his bow and make ready. . . ." These four examples could be multiplied. To make matters worse, there are at least two corollary translation issues. How should the interpreter understand the *'im lō'* at the start of v. 12? Does it introduce a conditional clause (so NRSV and NJPS) or does it introduce an emphatic exclamation: "Indeed . . ." (so Kraus). Second, is the sense of *šûḇ* "to repent," "to relent," or "to return again"? If God is understood as the subject of all the verbs in vv. 12-13, then the psalm is fusing the images of God as judge (vv. 7-11) with God as warrior, a combination which is known to occur and thus theologically consistent with other parts of the Old Testament and indeed the Psalms (cf. Deut. 32:41-42; Ps. 38:2, etc.). If the enemy is understood as the subject of any or all of these verbs, then the imagery conveys the notion that the enemy either hardens his heart, that the enemy is sowing the seeds of his own judgment, or some combination of both. The issue is confused not only by the lack of clarity in the data but also by the fact that the images and perspectives in the surrounding poetry are fluid and lack the type of consistent, linear prose logic that might provide a clear framework within which to adjudicate the issue.

The data are not clear. Solutions must remain provisional. The interpretation followed here is that God is the subject of the verbs in vv. 12-13 and that the *'im lō'* of v. 12 is emphatic. A key reason for siding with this view is that the military imagery of vv. 12-13 can be understood as a continuation of the metaphor of God as *shield* introduced in v. 10. The overall import of this interpretation is that God's quality of righteousness extends both to God's judicial role of making the just decision and to God's providential role of actualizing that decision. Perhaps one reason that interpreters have steered away from understanding God as the subject of these verbs is that such an understanding runs counter to prevailing cultural attitudes about conceiving God as warrior or judge. Our culture prefers more domesticated metaphors for God, or metaphors that are not so troublingly linked to violence.

In Psalm 7, as in many psalms, the agency of God and the agency of the wicked are blurred — it is not precisely clear who is responsible for the pending judgment of the wicked. On the one hand, the psalm boldly confesses that God is the righteous judge, the agent responsible for the judgment of the entire world. On the other hand, the wicked are seen as the agents responsible for their own demise: *He is in labor with sin, he has conceived mischief, he has given birth to deceit. He dug a pit and hollowed it out, he fell into the pit he was making.* The psalmist draws on two metaphors to paint the picture of the wicked as the agents of their own downfall. The first has to do with conception and birth. The enemy is described as in labor with and giving birth to the evil he has conceived. The fact that this most feminine of metaphors is applied to the masculine singular enemy serves to make its poignancy all the more apparent and powerful. The idea is that the evil which was plotted against another now hatches with vengeance against the plotter. Similarly, the metaphor of the pit dug for another but which traps the digger, known from Proverbs (1:11-18), carries the same message. A sensitive reader would not be amiss in hearing an echo of the story of the pit that Joseph's brothers dug for him (Gen. 37:20-29).

17 The closing peal of praise is a word of both trust and witness. It is trust, because the psalmist voices his praise in the presence of the enemy threat, while tangible evidence of the Lord's *righteousness* is not visible. It is thus also witness, because the trust builds up the faith of others, calling the community and perhaps even the wicked and unrighteous to trust. The key word in the last verse is *his righteousness (k^{e}ṣiḏqô).* Earlier, the psalmist pleaded with God to *judge me according to my righteousness.* The psalmist also prayed, *may you establish the righteous* and confessed trust that *God is a righteous judge.* The psalmist thus ends his poem on the same note, expressing trust in the Lord's character. For the psalmist, it is the Lord's righteousness — not her own — that is the final basis of this prayer for help. Even as she insists upon her own innocence and invites investigation of her righteousness in this specific case, she trusts not in herself but in the Lord, the righteous judge and deliverer.

Reflections

1. God's Righteousness, the Basis of Prayer

As Mays has insightfully noted, "Apart from the righteousness of the Lord this prayer could not even be thought, let alone said."[29] The righteousness and fidelity of God, then, are the true bases of all prayer, but especially of any prayer in which a petitioner pleads his or her own innocence. As noted above, the psalmist's claim to innocence is not a claim of theological self-righteousness in the abstract sense, but a claim of contextual innocence in a concrete case. As also noted above, the psalmist's invitation to be examined by God is paralleled by Job's similar demand for examination (Job 31). The parallel to Job is enlightening here. As the reader of Job knows from that book's first chapter, Job is indeed innocent and righteous, and yet he suffers. Just as Job argues that any sin that he may have committed certainly does not match the magnitude of the suffering that he endured, so also the psalmist of Psalm 7 seems to be facing punishment that is "out of scale." As McCann has seen, "Neither the Book of Job nor Psalm 7 is about self righteousness. Rather, both are fundamentally about the righteousness of God. Like Job, the psalmist rests the case with God, trusting God to be a 'righteous judge.'"[30] Thus, even as the psalmist maintains her own righteousness in regard to the concrete issue at hand, she submits her case to the Judge whose righteousness is her one sure refuge. To put this in another way, we pray not because of who we are or what we are; we pray because of whose we are and what God is.

2. God and the Wicked

The so-called "double wish" of the psalms — in which the psalmist prays both for delivery from enemies and for the destruction of those enemies — troubles modern sensibilities. Perhaps we are right to be so troubled, since people of faith have so often justified violence by appealing to such biblical passages. But there is another side to this. Western religious tradition has focused so intently on the guilt of sin that we often have been blind to the victims of sin. That is, we confess our sins and our guilt, but turn a blind eye to the victims of our sin. But sin can never be disconnected from its victims. When we understand this, then the double wish of the psalms might not only strike us as less troubling, it might strike us as necessary. After all, when an oppressor has his boot on a victim's neck, is there any way to deliver the sufferer without removing the oppressor? Is there any way to remove the threat posed by the oppressor without removing the oppressor? For the psalmist, harried and harassed by pursuers, the hope of deliverance cannot be abstracted from the

29. Mays, *Psalms,* p. 64.
30. McCann, "The Book of Psalms," p. 709.

pursuers, and thus to ask for deliverance is to ask for deliverance from the pursuers and thus to ask for the removal of the pursuers. One question that must be asked by everyone who prays such a psalm now is this: Are there people today who could be praying this psalm with me as the enemy? Are there victims of my own sins who could cry to the righteous judge for recompense? And if so, to whom should I turn? From what should I turn away?

The psalmist has faith that the deliverance from the enemies — and thus the judgment of the enemies — is both impending and inevitable. And for the psalmist, there are two agents who both share responsibility for the enemies' judgment: God and the enemy. Paradoxically, God's righteousness and the enemies' unrighteousness bind both parties to the impending judgment of the wicked. God's characteristic quality of righteousness binds God to the reality of delivering the innocent and thus of punishing the wicked. But the enemy is fully the agent of his or her own demise. When the enemy plotted evil against another, the enemy initiated the sequence of events that will eventually result in his own judgment. Paradoxically then, the enemy is fully the agent of his own destruction, but so is the Lord.

Rolf A. Jacobson

Psalm 8: A Natural Question

Psalm 8 is a hymn of praise, the first such in the Psalter. The poet stands on the earth and looks toward the heavens. Limburg has described this as "a psalm for stargazers,"[1] and indeed, it is that. But even more, this is a psalm for soul searchers. Overcome by the vast expanse of creation, the psalmist is led to ask the searching internal question about the purpose of human existence: *What are human beings that you remember them? Or mortal persons that you attend them?* Yet, having at first been turned inward by a sense of awe at the external, the psalmist then turns back outward: *You have made them to rule over the works of your hands, you have set everything under their feet.* The bank vault of human worth, according to this psalm, is not located in our own existence, but rather in the twin sources of the God who created us and the creation over which that God has directed us to exercise responsibility: We are valuable because God values us and because God has commanded us to value creation!

The poem consists of two stanzas that are enclosed in a poetic inclusio. The first stanza starts with a focus on the *glory* of God in creation and ends with a question about the value of humanity. The second stanza answers this question by affirming that God has crowned humanity with *glory* and ends with a discussion of the various creatures over whom humans have been given responsibility. The entire psalm is thus a chiasm constructed around the question in v. 4:

St. 1	Praise to God *in all the earth* (v. 1a)
	God's *glory* in creation — the question of human worth (vv. 1b-4)
St. 2	Answer: crowned with *glory* — responsible for creation (vv. 5-8)
	Praise to God *in all the earth* (v. 9)

The main poetic theme of this poem is without a doubt creation, but a secondary theme within the poem is royalty. God is celebrated as creator of all the earth and heavens, but in terms that are usually reserved for royalty. God here is king of creation. Human beings are celebrated as the royalty of God's creation, who have been commanded by God to govern nature in the same responsible way that kings are commanded to govern nations. This is a psalm that weds reflection on creation with devotion to God and a concern for the royal responsibility humans bear for the earth. When the Apollo 11 spacecraft journeyed to the moon in 1969, the leaders of the nations of earth were each invited to compose a message to be included on a small disk that was to be left on that heavenly body. Pope Paul VI — who was devoted to God, felt

1. Limburg, *Psalms,* p. 24.

responsible for creation, and was the political leader of the Vatican — sent along the text of Psalm 8. How appropriate![2]

For the leader.[3] *According to the gittith.*[4] *A Davidic psalm.*

1 *O LORD, our lord, how magnificent is your name in all the earth!*
You have placed[5] *your glory above the heavens,*
2 *from the mouths of babes and infants.*
You have established might because of your foes,
to put an end to enemy and avenger.[6]
3 *When I see*[7] *your heavens,*[8] *the works*[9] *of your fingers,*
moon and stars, which you established,
4 *What are human beings that you remember them?*
Or mortal persons that you attend them?[10]

2. NASA News Release No. 69-83F; cited in Limburg, *Psalms,* p. 24.

3. See note 12 on Psalm 4 superscription.

4. The meaning of "Gittith" *(gittîṯ)* is unknown. The term occurs here as well as in the superscriptions of Pss. 81:1 and 84:1. It is most likely a musical term, referring to a melody, instrument, or perhaps a ritual action (cf. Mowinckel, *The Psalms in Israel's Worship,* 2:215).

5. The MT, lit. "which give" is impossible both in terms of grammar and sense. The text is corrupt. LXX reads *hoti epērthē,* perhaps reading the Hebrew verb *tnh* ("recount, sing"). Other versions (Symmachus, Vulg, Syr, Targ) understand the verb as "give," from *nāṯan.* Thus, "the earth, which put your glory upon the heavens" (?) or "your name . . . which put your glory. . . ." HALOT summarizes the many attempts at reconciling this problem (pp. 1760-61); see also H. Alberto Soggin, "Textkritische Untersuchung von Ps VIII, vv. 2-3 und 6," *VT* 21 (1971) 565-71; Frank Crüsemann, *Studien zur Formgeschichte von Hymnus und Danklied in Israel* (WMANT 32; Neukirchen: Neukirchener, 1969), p. 289; Kraus, p. 178; Craigie, pp. 104-5). Based on the parallel in v. 2, *you have established,* the translation *you have placed/set* is used here (but notice that the translation "sing" would fit better with *from the mouths of* . . .). The above translation is a conjecture.

6. The textual problems that begin in v. 2 continue in v. 3 and are multiplied by the confusion of the previous verse. The versions offer no help. Again, many solutions have been proposed (cf. Craigie, p. 105; Jacob Leveen, *VT* 21 [1971] 48-58). Working from the end of v. 2 backward, it is obvious that *to put an end to enemy and avenger* forms the close of a colon. It also seems clear that *babes and infants* forms a poetic parallel to *enemy and avenger.* The versification of MT is broken up, and the above translation is based on the two sets of parallelisms *(you have placed . . . you have established; babes and infants . . . enemy and avenger).* Again, note the hypothetical nature of the translation.

7. Syr reads a third person plural verb. MT's first person singular is preferred, supported by other ancient versions.

8. LXX omits the 2ms suffix. MT is retained.

9. Both here and in v. 6, there is mss support for the singular "work." The plural is both better attested and fits better with the grammatical referents.

10. The Hebrew reads, lit.: "What is man that you remember him? The son of man that you attend him?" The above translation reflects a desire to use inclusive language.

5 *You have made them but a little lower than heavenly beings,*[11]
you have crowned them with honor and glory.
6 *You have made them to rule over the works of your hands,*
you have set everything under their feet.
7 *All sheep*[12] *and oxen,*
even the beasts of the field.
8 *Birds of the heavens and fish of the sea,*
whatever passes the paths of the seas.

9 *O LORD, our lord, how magnificent is your name in all the earth!*

1a Most of the Psalter's hymns begin with an imperative call to a congregation to praise God.[13] Psalm 8 begins differently — with an exclamation of praise spoken directly to God. The first word out of the psalmist's mouth is *LORD*. No other hymn begins in this fashion. To begin a psalm with God's name is a characteristic way for a prayer for help to begin; this connection is appropriate, for as a prayer for help begins with a passionate cry for help, this psalm begins with a similarly passionate cry of praise.[14] The import of this nuance is that Psalm 8 is not just a poem *about God.* Psalm 8 is a poem *about God and us* and *about our relationship with God.* The opening exclamation prepares the ground for the rest of the psalm by foreshadowing later themes. The Lord is called *our lord.* The title *lord"* (Heb. *ʾᵃḏōn*) is a royal title.[15] When applied to God, it refers to God's transcendent power and nature (cf. Pss. 135:5-12; 147:5; Neh. 10:29). In this verse, the title evokes God's infinite superiority to humans but also foreshadows the psalm's idea that humans are God's royal representatives amid creation. The suffix *our lord* also underscores the relationship between humanity and God that is at the heart of this psalm and indeed the heart of the Psalter as a whole. The verse ends with a rhetorical exclamation that is preceded by the interrogative pronoun *mâ: How magnificent is your name in all the earth!* The use of the pronoun is repeated in the psalm's central question: *What (mâ) are human beings that you remember them?* And perhaps most importantly, the theme of creation is introduced here by the prepositional phrase *in all the earth.*

1b-4 The exclamation of praise with which the psalm opens begs the

11. This line reads, lit., "a little less/lower than gods *(ʾᵉlōhîm).*" The concept here is of the divine counsel of angelic beings who surround the one God of Israel (see Isaiah 6 and 1 Kings 22).

12. *Reading ṣʾnh* for *ṣōneh.*

13. Gunkel, *Introduction to Psalms,* pp. 23-41.

14. Cf. these hymns: Pss. 29, 33, 65, 66, 89:5ff., 100, 103, 105, 107, 111, 113, 117, 134–36, 145–50; also cf. these prayers for help: Pss. 3, 6, 7, etc.

15. See Sarna, *On the Book of Psalms,* p. 52.

question: What sort of ecstatic event or experience has caused the psalmist to cry out in praise? The answer is given in the first full stanza of the psalm. As v. 3 indicates, the psalmist has wandered outdoors at night, gazed up at the heavenly wonders, and been moved to praise the Creator. It is worth stressing that throughout the entire poem, the Creator is addressed directly and intimately: *your name, you have established, your heavens, you remember them,* and so on. The vast expanse of the firmament impresses the psalmist deeply, but it does not overawe to the point where the personal dimension of faith is squelched. This hymn is a prayer to God, not merely a poem about God. This aspect of the psalm is even more striking when considered in light of the psalmist's ancient Near Eastern context. Many in Israel and among her neighbors worshipped the heavenly bodies as divine bodies. In this pagan conception, the heavenly orbs were endowed with sentience, power, and identity. Here, they are merely objects that testify to their Creator's glory — indeed, the psalmist belittles them by calling them *the works of your fingers.*

The first stanza of the poem continues to borrow concepts that are at home in the royal courts. In spite of the textual problem with v. 1b, it is clear that the poet describes *your glory above the heavens.* The term *glory (hôḏ)* is again a royal term, often used of both God and human royalty. The conception here is of God as Creator king. The creation motif of the psalm thoroughly permeates this stanza, as vv. 1b and 3 indicate. But v. 2bc may also reflect the creation motif, as Nahum Sarna has argued.[16] The *enemy and avenger* in v. 2c are best explained as a reference to the foes that God overcomes in the process of creation. As is well known, the mythic concept of creation as a conflict was commonly held among Israel's neighbors. Within the Old Testament, vestiges of this mythic idea are found. In Ps. 74:13-14a, 16-17, for example, the psalmist writes:

> You split, by your might, the sea;[17]
>   you broke the heads of the sea-monster on the waters.
> You shattered the heads of Leviathan;
> . . .
> Yours is the day, also yours is the night;
>   You fixed the light and the sun.
> You set the boundaries of the earth;
>   summer and winter, You formed them.

It is particularly enlightening that both Psalms 8 and 74 refer to God's *might* (*ʿōz;* cf. Isa. 51:9; Ps. 89:11). The term is part of the vocabulary of the creation

16. Sarna, *On the Book of Psalms,* pp. 53-61.

17. "The sea" in this case is best understood as Yamm (a pagan sea deity representing chaos), as the parallel with "sea-monster" indicates.

conflict myth, lending support to the view that the phrase *you have established might because of your foes, to put an end to enemy and avenger* is another reference to the act of creation.

The first stanza swells to its finale with the question that is posed in v. 4: *What are human beings that you remember them?* This daunting question, which was inspired by the psalmist's sudden awareness of God's glory that is revealed in creation, is the axis on which the poem pivots. The interrogative pronoun *mâ (what)* that occurs in the first and last lines of the psalm, occurs here in the middle of the psalm. The result is a poetic echo between the start, middle, and end of the psalm. In the first and last lines of the poem the word carries a sense of awe; in v. 4 the term is tinted with scorn. The psalmist does not ask, "*Who* are human beings?" even though "who" is the normal pronoun for animate beings.[18] Rather, the poet uses *mâ, the pronoun normally reserved for inanimate* objects. The resulting connotation is derisive: *What are measly human beings . . . ?* If the psalm ended here, the implication would be that in light of God's infinite glory, it is only with a scornful wonder that this world can see finite human beings.

5-8 The second stanza provides the answer to the disdainful question with which the first stanza closed. Far from being insignificant, human beings are *but a little lower than heavenly beings.* Indeed, the king of creation has made humanity into royalty who are to govern creation responsibly. What is notable about the start of the second stanza is that even though the topic is the worth of human beings, the poet stresses the actions of God. In each of the four lines that comprise vv. 5-6, the subject of the verbs is God: *You have made, you have crowned, you have made them to rule,* and *you have set.* What gives human beings dignity and value is not anything that humans have done for themselves, but rather something that God has done for them. Our worth comes to us from outside of ourselves *(extra nos).* That which God confers upon us is the key to our status, not that which comes from inside of us.

Just as the first stanza celebrated God using royal terminology as king of creation, the second half of the psalm honors humans as those whom God has *crowned* with royal responsibility. The second stanza begins with the assertion that God has made human beings *but a little lower than heavenly beings.* This phrase plays on the ancient Near Eastern concept of the heavenly luminaries as divine beings. As mentioned earlier, many among Israel's neighbors and indeed among Israel worshipped sun, moon, and stars as deities. In the first stanza, the psalmist spoke of these as the work of God's *fingers,* that is, mere objects. The psalmist, who stands far down on the earth and looks up at the distant heavens, playfully asserts that human beings are, in fact, just a little

18. Waltke and O'Connor, *Biblical Hebrew Syntax,* pp. 315-27.

lower than the true heavenly beings (meaning angelic beings such as seraphim and cherubim). The next phrase ups the ante even more: *You have crowned them with honor and glory. You have made them to rule over the works of your hands.* The verbs *crowned (ʿāṭar)* and *made to rule (māšal)* are royal terms, and the English translation preserves this royal sense. But the terms *glory (kāḇôḏ)* and *honor (hāḏār)* and the phrase *set under their feet* also carry royal connotations. For example, Ps. 21:5 describes the Davidic king: "His glory *(kāḇôḏ)* is great through your help; splendor and majesty *(hāḏār)* you bestow on him."[19] Both art and text throughout the ancient world indicate that the phrase "to place under the feet" was understood as symbolic of the authority given to kings. In Ps 110:1, for example, God says to the king: "Sit at my right hand until I make your enemies your footstool."[20] The conclusion to be drawn from this is that in the second stanza of the psalm, the concept of royalty is extended from God the creator king to humanity in general, who are anointed as the royalty responsible for creation.

The second stanza closes with four balanced cola that specify the subjects over which royal humanity is to exercise dominion: sheep and oxen, beasts of the field, birds and fish, and the mysterious creatures in the deeps of the sea. The order of this list is not haphazard, but is part of a careful poetic strategy in the psalm. This poetic strategy plays on the ideas of vertical and horizontal dimensions. Throughout the first six verses of the poem, the poet has subtly woven in a motif of vertical descent:

v. 1b *above the heavens*
↓
v. 3 *heavens . . . moon and stars*
↓
v. 5a *but a little lower than heavenly beings*
↓
v. 5b *crowned them* (a reference to the head)
↓
v. 6a *hands*
↓
v. 6b *feet*

Having descended to earth, the psalmist now changes directions and describes a horizontal vector that moves outward from human society:

19. This example could be multiplied many times over. Note also that "splendor" in Ps. 21:5 is the same word as "splendor" in v. 1b.

20. For a discussion of the visual art in relation to this concept, see Keel, *The Symbolism of the Biblical World,* pp. 243-68.

sheep and oxen → beasts of the field → birds → fish → whatever passes the paths of the seas

The first animals, *sheep and oxen,* are the domesticated animals that share space in the midst of human society. The trajectory described then proceeds outward until it ends in the sea, which in the ancient Near East was conceived as the place of chaos, least hospitable to human society. But that is all the more reason to marvel at the assertion made here in Psalm 8! The *fish of the sea* and even those mysterious creatures that pass in the depths of the sea are realms of human responsibility! God has placed even these wild and unknown creatures under our care.

Notice that the psalm does not answer the question asked in v. 4 by merely *telling* that God does care for humans. Rather, the psalm *shows* that God values humans to the extent that God grants them a responsible role in creation. Any person who has been around small children may be able to relate to the message here. Children do not want only to be helped and provided for. Children want to help, to contribute, to be valuable to the household. They want to do things themselves. The powerful message of this psalm is that God does not merely care about human beings, but values them so much that they are given a role in God's economy.

9 The closing verse of the psalm is identical to the first, creating what is known technically as an inclusio or envelope structure around the psalm. An inclusio functions to stamp a particular rhetorical meaning on a poem.[21] When it is repeated at the end of the poem, the opening line sounds both largely the same and slightly different at the same time. It sounds the same in the sense that the ideas of the phrase have not changed and are being repeated and so reemphasized. On the other hand, because of the poetry that has intervened, the phrase sounds a little different — perhaps more sad, or more poignant, or more joyful. In the case of Psalm 8, the body of the poem has been about the twin concepts of creation and the royal caretaking role that humans have been assigned by God. Thus, when the psalmist ends this poem with the cry, *how magnificent is your name,* the psalm's audience now understands *why* the psalmist says that God is majestic. God is majestic because of God's work as creator and because God values humans for their role as caretakers. A second way in which the enveloping phrase sounds a little different at the end of the psalm has to do with the clause *in all the earth.* When the audience

21. Some scholars see the function of an inclusio as primarily to signal the limits of the poem (e.g., Wilfred G. E. Watson, *Classical Hebrew Poetry* [JSOTSup 26; Sheffield: JSOT, 1984], pp. 282-87; Luis Alonso Schökel, *A Manual of Hebrew Poetics* [Rome: Pontificio istituto biblico, 1988], pp. 75-83). This view is overly wooden and fails to account for the artistic impact of the poetry. Perhaps the best way to define the rhetorical impact of an inclusio is to say that it functions emphatically. Exactly what is emphasized depends on context.

first hears this phrase at the start of the psalm, the audience is likely to hear it as a typical universal call for praise, such as occurs in Ps. 148:3 ("Praise the LORD, moon; praise him, all you shining stars!") or 148:7, 11 ("Praise the LORD from the earth. . . . Kings of the earth and all peoples . . .). However, because the intervening verses of Psalm 8 have dealt precisely with matters of heaven and earth, when the final verse is spoken the audience may hear *in all the earth* with new ears.

Reflections

1. The Responsibility of Royalty

As noted above, the psalm casts human beings in royal terms, depicting them as the crown of God's good creation. But the sense of being royalty is not that human beings have the right to do whatever they want with creation, like toddlers who wreak havoc and destroy because they know no better. Rather, to be royalty in the Old Testament means to be called to a higher standard of responsibility. The message of this psalm is that we human beings, in the words of Limburg, are called to the "responsibility of royalty."[22] God has placed all things under our feet not so that we may walk all over them, but so that we might tend and care for them, as Adam was instructed to do in the garden. The laws that govern royal behavior in Deut. 17:14-20 make it clear that the king was given *authority* and *responsibility* in equal measures. The authority was for the sake of the responsibility and not for the purpose of self-aggrandizement. The king was to be a responsible servant, never "exalting himself above other members of the community. . . ." That same burden of responsibility rests upon humanity as a whole. The care of God's creation is our collective vocation.

2. Midway between Heaven and Earth

Psalm 8 is rich in both theology and anthropology. It speaks eloquently of God's roles as creator and keeper of the universe, but it also speaks passionately about the identity, calling, and nature of human beings. On one side of the equation, the psalm pictures the identity of human beings as *but a little lower than heavenly beings*. Through the use of the royal imagery that is applied to both God and human beings, the psalm suggests that humans share some part of God's nature. Like the famed "image of God" phrase in Gen. 1:26, the psalm asserts that we are like God in some ways. On the other side of the equation, again similar to Genesis 1 where humans and most animals are created on the same day, the psalm asserts that we share much with the rest

22. *Psalms*, p. 26.

of creation. This is the central paradox at the heart of human identity. We are of creation, of small account, bearing the dust of the earth in our bodies and the nature of the animals in our very beings. Yet we are of heaven, carrying our maker's mark on our souls and sharing in the likeness and image of God. Caught up in the glories of this paradox, the psalmist can find no other words equal to the situation than these: *O Lord, our lord, how magnificent is your name in all the earth!*

Rolf A. Jacobson

Psalm 9/10: The Power and Presence of God

Psalms 9 and 10 comprise one lengthy acrostic psalm and are to be read as a unit. Although some scholars dispute it, this judgment is made for several reasons. First, taken together, the two psalms form an extended alphabetic acrostic psalm. For the most part, the first word of every second verse of the psalm begins with consecutive letters of the Hebrew alphabet. If the psalms were treated individually, each would form half an acrostic. Second, Psalm 10 lacks a superscription, which is almost unknown in the first book of the Psalter. Third, the Septuagint and Vulgate, along with some Hebrew manuscripts, treat the psalms as one unit. Fourth, certain idiosyncratic vocabulary (such as *ʿ^{a}nāyîm//ʿ^{a}nāwîm* [vv. 9:12, 18; 10:12, 17]; or *ʾ^{e}nôš* [vv. 9:20, 21; 10:18]; *l^{e}ʿittôṯ baṣṣārâ* [9:9; 10:1]) and themes (such as God judging in favor of the afflicted, or remembering and forgetting) tie the psalms together. Fifth, the occurrence of *selah* at the end of Psalm 9 is a liturgical direction that occurs within poems, not after them.

Alphabetic acrostic poems are well known both within the Psalter and Hebrew Bible (Psalms 25, 34, 37, 111, 112, 119, 145; the four poems of Lamentations 1–4; Prov. 31:10-31; Nah. 1:2-8)[1] as well as in Israel's noncanonical writings (Sir. 51:13-30) and among Israel's neighbors. Psalm 9/10 may be said to be an imperfect acrostic at best. As Gerstenberger has noted, "With twenty-one letters to the alphabet the poem needed at least forty-two lines. The stichoi opening with *d, m, n, s, ṣ* are entirely missing, or rather, unrecognizable. Other lines are irregular in length."[2] Moreover, the *pê* stanza is out of order, the *kāp* stanza is only one verse long, and the *hê* stanza is disputed. If one assumes that at one point the psalm was a completely regular acrostic with each stanza containing two verses[3] — an assumption which is by no means secure — then one must admit that the poem has been corrupted, especially in 9:7-10 and 10:3-11.

The acrostic nature of the psalm obscures identification of both genre and setting. Perhaps the alphabetic acrostic indicates that the poem is more of a literarily composed prayer than a cultically performed prayer. Gerstenberger disputes this: "Acrostic poems certainly can be used in rituals, especially if they are the handiwork of skilled, literary singers or clergymen."[4] He thinks of the psalm in a synagogal setting as the prayer of an afflicted

1. Many more partial alphabetic acrostics, "alphabetizing acrostics," and nonalphabetic acrostics have been proposed. See, e.g., David Noel Freedman, "Acrostic Poems in the Hebrew Bible: Alphabetic and Otherwise," *CBQ* 48 (1986) 408-31.

2. Gerstenberger, *Psalms: Part 1,* p. 72.

3. Gerstenberger, *Psalms: Part 1,* p. 73.

4. Gerstenberger, *Psalms: Part 1,* p. 75.

person or community. Many elements of a typical prayer for help, such as complaints about the enemies, petitions for deliverance, and vows of praise and trust, are present. But the constraints of the alphabetic acrostic pattern certainly control and perhaps obscure what one might expect of the normal flow and movement of a prayer for help (if such a flow actually exists). But the general themes of the psalm — trust and praise in the Lord's judgment and justice along with pleas for God's intervention for the oppressed — do seem to encompass themes traditionally associated with the prayer for help. The purpose of alphabetic acrostics is debated. As many have pointed out, acrostic devices aid in memorization and recitation. But memorization is a means, not an end. To what end does the memorized poem point? Perhaps the purpose of the psalm is instruction in prayer and praise. More likely, the purpose is a prayer for help. The structure of the psalm is provided by the alphabetic acrostic, but the individual stanzas seem to fall into roughly defined larger sections, each of which can be understood to correspond loosely to a larger prayer-for-help structure: 9:1-12 is a section of praise analogous to the vows of praise and trust in more compact lament psalms; 9:13-20 is a section of petition, with motivating clauses and trust; 10:1-11 is a section of complaint that focuses on the threat and impiety of the wicked; 10:12-18 is a closing section of petition and trust. In the commentary below, the verses assigned to each letter of the acrostic will be called stanzas, but it should be noted that this designation borders on doing violence to the concept of a stanza.

For the leader. According to mûṯ labbēn.[5] *A Davidic psalm.*

'Ālep 9:1 *I will praise the LORD with all my heart,*
I will recount all your wondrous deeds.
2 *I will rejoice and I will exalt in you,*
I will sing of your most high name.
Bêt 3 *When my enemies turn away,*
they stumble and perish before you.
4 *For you have established my right and my decision,*
you are seated[6] *upon the throne, judging righteously.*[7]

5. The Hebrew phrase, which is unknown, perhaps describes the tune to which the psalm was to be performed. The phrase *'almûṯ labbēn* should probably be redivided *'al mûṯ labbēn* (with some mss; cf. LXX; Ps. 48:14), yet the meaning still is unclear. The phrase literally means "according to a death for/of the son." It is even more likely that the text originally read (*'al 'almôṯ,* "according to *the almoth,*" as in the superscription to Psalm 46).

6. 11QPs[a] has *wšbth* for MT's *yšbt* and *špṭth* for *šwpṭ,* implying imperatival forms.

7. Syriac and Targum reflect *ṣaddîq,* "the righteous."

Gîmel 5 *You rebuke the nations, you destroy[8] the wicked,*
you blot out their name forever and ever.
6 *The enemy[9] are finished — ruins[10] forever,*
you have uprooted their cities, their very memory perished.
7 *[11]But the LORD is enthroned forever,*
he has established his throne for judgment.
8 *And he judges the world in righteousness,*
he decides for the peoples with uprightness.
Wāw 9 *May the LORD be a haven for the oppressed,*
a haven in times of trouble.
10 *And may they trust in you, may they know your name,*
for you do not abandon those who see you, O LORD.
Zayin 11 *Sing praise to the LORD, O dweller of Zion!*
Declare his deeds among the peoples!
12 *For the One who calls to account for bloodshed remembers them,*
he does not forget the cries of the afflicted.[12]
Ḥêt 13 *Be gracious to me,[13] O LORD, see[14] my suffering at the hands of those who hate me,*
O you who lift me from the gates of death!
14 *In order that I might recount all of your praises,*
in the gates of daughter Zion, let me rejoice in your deliverance.
Ṭêt 15 *The nations have sunk in the pit they made,*
their own foot is caught in the net that they hid.
16 *The LORD is known! He has done justice!*

8. LXX, "and the wicked perish," reflects *w*^{e}*ʾābaḏ*.

9. Syriac reads the plural "enemies," thus harmonizing subject and verb, but the singular noun can be understood as collective thus requiring the plural verb.

10. LXX understands *ḥorāḇôṯ* as related to *ḥereḇ* ("sword") rather than *ḥorbâ* ("ruin").

11. This verse should begin with either a *dālet* or a *hê* to keep the acrostic pattern of the psalm intact. Instead, it begins with a *wāw.* The acrostic pattern of this psalm is not as regular as one expects. But efforts to restore the pattern are not to be trusted. Nevertheless, many (including *Biblia Hebraica,* 4th ed.) transfer the last word of v. 6 *(hēmmâ)* to the start of v. 7; but then what does it mean? One solution is to emend the word to *hinnēh* ("behold"; see Craigie) while another solution is to repoint to *hōmâ* ("impassioned"; cf. LXX). But this does not work with the syntax of the next word, *wYHWH.*

12. The Qere *(ʿ*^{a}*nāwîm)* and kethib *(ʿ*^{a}*nîyîm)* offer different forms for essentially the same word.

13. The form *(ḥan*^{e}*nēnî)* is odd, the only time the form appears. In spite of this oddness, the intent is clearly ms imperative with 1cs suffix.

14. Some mss read *hānēnî* ("he was gracious to me"); Aquila reads *rāʾâ* ("he saw"). These moves see the verse as a continuation of the causal phrase introduced by *kî* in v. 12.

The wicked one is struck down by the work
of his own hand! ḥiggāyôn.[15] Selah

Yôd 17 *The wicked will return to Sheol,*
all nations who forget God.

Kāp 18 *For the needy will not be forgotten forever,*
nor the hope of the poor perish forever.

19 *Arise, O LORD! Do not allow mortals to prevail!*
Let the nations be judged before your face.

20 *Set a teaching*[16] *before them, O LORD!*
Let the nations know that they are mortals. Selah

Lāmed 10:1 *Why, O LORD, do you stand at a distance?*
Why do you hide at times of trouble?

2 *In arrogance, the wicked persecutes the afflicted,*
may they be seized by the plot they have conceived.

3 [17]*For the wicked praises the desires of his soul,*
the grasping one curses[18] *and rejects the LORD.*

4 *According to the the pride of his nose, the wicked thinks, "He*
will not call to account.
There is no God," are all his thoughts.

5 *His paths*[19] *are sure at all times,*
your judgments are far above him,
he scoffs at all his enemies.

6 *He says in his heart, "I shall not stumble,*
from generation to generation there will be no evil."[20]

15. The meaning of *ḥiggāyôn* is unknown.

16. Many commentators emend MT's *môrâ* ("teaching") to *môrāʾ* ("fear"), following versions such as Aquila and Theodotion. The more difficult MT stands. Another possibility would be to understand *môrâ* as "razor" with the sense of the psalmist asking for the enemies' heads to be shaved in shame.

17. The text of the psalm is problematic, especially from this point on. The expected *mêm* stanza is missing, as are the expected *nûn* and *sāmek* stanzas in following verses. LXX and other witnesses suggest that MT's consonantal text *ky hll* might originally have been *mhll* ("he is praised," thus LXX's passive form), thus restoring the expected chiastic structure, but even though LXX supports the change, it is ruled out as a harmonization with an expected pattern.

18. MT is lit. *bērēḵ* ("to bless"), but the use of *brk* to mean "curse" is a well-known euphemism; see Job 1. LXX and Syr reflect the passive form, perhaps misunderstanding the euphemism.

19. Qere reflects the plural form, matching the subject to the verb; Kethib reflects singular, which is allowable because the singular can carry the collective sense.

20. LXX's *aneu kakou* most likely reflects a consonantal text such as *blʾ rʿ* rather than MT's *lʾ brʿ*. This text is preferable, but the translation rendered is not significantly different.

Pê[21] 7 *A curse fills his mouth — deceit and injury,*
sin and trouble are under his tongue.
8 *He sits in ambush of villagers,*[22]
from hiding places he slays[23] *the innocent.*
ʿAyin *His eyes lie in hiding for the unfortunate,*[24]
9 *he lies in wait like a lion in a thicket.*
He lies in wait to seize the afflicted,
he seizes the afflicted when he pulls in his net.

10 *He stoops,*[25] *he bows down,*
and the unfortunate[26] *fall to his might.*[27]
11 *He says in his heart, "God has forgotten.*
He has hidden his face, he will never see."
Qôp 12 *Arise, O* LORD *God,*[28] *lift up your hand,*
do not forget the afflicted.[29]
13 *Why should the wicked scoff at God,*
and say in his heart, "God will not call to account"?[30]
Rêš 14 *But you do see! Indeed, you do notice trouble and grief,*
to take it in your hand.
The unfortunate commit themselves to you,
you, yes you are the helper of the orphan!
Šîn 15 *Break the arm of the wicked and the evil,*

21. The word "oath" *(ʾālâ)* is actually the first word of v. 7; the second word is "his mouth" *(pîhû);* thus the acrostic structure is imperfect. Some repoint *ʾālâ* and place it at the end of the previous line.

22. LXX's *meta plousiōn* likely reflects *bʿšrym* ("with the rich"). The parallelism suggests retaining MT.

23. LXX implies the infinitive construct *lhrg.*

24. The Hebrew *ḥēlkâ* and *hēlkaʾîm* occur only here and in v. 10 in the Old Testament. The Qere offers a variant reading for the term in v. 10. The meaning of the term is ambiguous. The most sound interpretation is to understand both of the words as forms of the same word meaning "unlucky ones" or "unfortunate."

25. MT as it stands makes little sense: "He is crushed, he bends down and he falls in his might. . . ." LXX's *kypsei* normally renders the root *qāḏaḏ.* The Kethib reflects a *wāw*-consecutive form of *dāḵâ* ("to be crushed," and thus to be bowed down?) while the Qere reflects the imperfect form. Craigie believes that the verse is corrupt and suggests restoring *ṣaḏîq,* thus "The righteous is crushed," thereby restoring the missing *ṣādê* line of the acrostic.

26. The Kethib is *ḥēlkāʾîm* (see note on 10:8); the Qere, *ḥyl kʾym* ("hapless host").

27. Reading with LXX's *katakyrieusai, beʿāḥsmô.*

28. Some LXX versions (R, L, A) and Syr add "my" God.

29. See note on 9:12.

30. Reading with LXX and Syr a 3ms form, making the phrase part of the direct discourse rather than indirect discourse ("he says in his heart that you do not call to account").

call to account his wickedness.[31]
16 *The Lord is king*[32] *forever and ever,*
the nations will perish from his land.
Tāw 17 *The desires of the afflicted, O Lord, you hear.*[33]
You make firm their hearts, you make ready your ear.
18 *To do justice for the orphan and the oppressed,*
so that the mortals of earth may not terrorize any more.

9:1-12 — Praise and Trust

1-2 ***(ʾĀlep)*** The poem begins with a statement of praise to the Lord. This is most likely dictated by the alphabetic acrostic nature of the psalm, since by definition an *ʾālep*-stanza necessitates a word that begins with *ʾālep.* So, while not the only option (cf. Ps. 25:1; 37:1), the series of first person imperfect verbs that begins Psalm 9/10 works well: *I will praise, I will recount, I will rejoice, I will exalt, I will sing.* Later, the psalm includes notable descriptions of the suffering of the oppressed and the evils of the wicked, pleas for God's intervention, and trust in God's intervention. All of the material that follows is framed by the initial word of praise. As Craigie has written, the "intention to praise God issues not only from the knowledge and remembrance of such works in the past, but from anticipation of God's deliverance from a specific situation and from a current experience."[34] That is, the thrust of the first two verses is about more than just one moment of praise; it is about having praise serve as the feature that defines the rest of the prayer. It might not be too much to say that the opening verses of the psalm are about having praise serve as the feature that defines all of life. The psalmist's praise is self-emptying; he praises with all his heart. The psalmist praises God for *nip̱lᵉʾôṯêḵā (your wondrous deeds),* a form that occurs only in the psalms (26:7; 71:17; 75:1; 106:7; 145:5); the term is a reference to the characteristic acts of deliverance, such as the exodus, in which God reveals the divine character. The psalmist also praises God's name, the covenantal gift that God bestowed upon Israel as part of one of God's wondrous deeds. The name itself is the revelation of God's character. Thus the psalmist praises both the deeds and word by which God has revealed divine faithfulness and mercy.

3-4 ***(Bêt)*** The praise of God grows more concrete. The psalmist praises

31. The text seems corrupt. It makes little sense as is: "you will call his wickedness to account, you will not find it out." Some versions of LXX (Aquila and Symmachus) and Syriac reflect a 3ms niphal, "his wickedness will be called to account."

32. LXX implies something like *mālaḵ,* which is more expected: "The Lord reigns," as in many other psalms.

33. LXX implies a 3ms form: *yišmaʿ* ("he hears").

34. Craigie, *Psalms 1–50,* p. 118.

God for the deliverance from her enemies that she expects to receive at God's hands. As in many psalms, the identity of the enemies is obscure. What is important about the enemies is not who they are, but *before whom* the threat they pose evaporates: they will turn away and *stumble and perish before you.* The psalmist employs the metaphor of God as judge: *you have established my right and my decision, you are seated upon the throne, judging righteously.* But this should not be narrowly construed to think of a juridical setting for the psalm or to conceive narrowly of the psalmist's enemies as legal accusers. In the ancient Near East, serving as judge was one of the roles played by royalty. Here, as elsewhere in the psalms, God as judge is a common metaphor that signifies God's saving power and fidelity (see Psalm 7). The point here is that God's preferential option for the psalmist, like that of a judge who decides in favor of a petitioner, will result in the psalmist's deliverance from threat, like a verdict that turns away accusers.

5-6 *(Gîmel)* Earlier, the psalmist had praised God's name. Now, the psalmist confesses that God will turn away the threat of the nations and wipe out their names forever. In vv. 3-4, the scope of the psalmist's praise was on the individual level. Here, it is on the international level. Again, one should not narrowly construe the reference to the nations by conceiving of a national setting or international incident behind the psalm. The point is rather that as God delivers the chosen people in the face of threats from the nations, so that the people are preserved and the nations are forgotten, so is God's mercy present in the deliverance that the psalmist expects to receive. As Kraus notes, "The [*gwym*] are the embodiment of a foreign power that lives outside of the covenant and the divine order."[35] Thus, they pose a fundamental threat to the people and are often synonymous with the wicked, as they are here. To have one's name wiped out is a cultural threat that does not translate very well into our milieu (cf. Exod. 17:14). The force is that if memory of one's existence is completely expunged, one may as well never have existed. The metaphor of the enemy city destroyed and in ruins was a powerful symbol in the ancient Near East. The city was far more than simply an urban location and cultural center; it was a metaphor for identity of the people themselves and for the people's relationship with their god.[36] When the poet says *The enemy are finished — ruins forever, you have uprooted their cities,* the poet is confessing not simply a military defeat for the enemies, but a military, religious, and societal calamity for the enemies of God.

35. Kraus, *Psalms 1–59,* p. 195.

36. See the work of F. W. Dobbs-Allsopp on the city-lament genre of the ancient Near East, specifically his *Weep, O Daughter Zion: A Study of the City-Lament Genre in the Hebrew Bible* (BeO 44; Rome: Pontifico Istituto Biblico, 1993) and *Lamentations* (Interpretation; Louisville: Westminster John Knox, 2002).

7-8 ***(Dālet? Hê?)*** The content of the psalm indicates that a new stanza of the acrostic starts in v. 7, because the metaphor shifts back to God as judge. As referenced in the notes to the translation, in order to keep up the acrostic pattern, the verse should strictly start with a *dālet;* many translators move the last words of v. 6 to the start of v. 7, so that the verse at least starts with a *hê,* thus partially restoring the presumably corrupted acrostic text. In any case, the poem both returns to the judge metaphor and retains the international focus. God *judges the world in righteousness . . . decides for the peoples with uprightness.* The conception here, as in v. 4, is of God enthroned on the heavenly seat of judgment. God's judgment is an act of righteousness and uprightness; it is not done out of vengeance or pique. In fact, without judgment there is no righteousness, because the quality of righteousness demands acts of justice/ judgment (the same word in Hebrew, it also occurs in v. 4 where it is translated as *right*). The phrase God *decides for the peoples* is ambiguous and can be taken either positively or negatively — that God decides for the punishment of violent people or that God decides in favor of defending innocent people, although the latter is the more likely meaning.

9-10 ***(Wāw)*** The poet now switches to a new metaphor: God as *haven (miśgāḇ).*[37] Whereas the metaphor of judge gives a personal profile to God's saving power, the metaphor of refuge lends spatial profile. The refuge is the place of safety for the oppressed, or provision for the needy, and of joy for the sorrowing. There is also a temporal sense to the metaphor, as the poem notes, *a haven in times of trouble.* The metaphors of judge and refuge are both part of the larger metaphor of God as king, but God as a king who operates differently than any earthly king (cf. Deut. 17:14-20), because God's sanctuary and protection are explicitly for the needy, for those who have been figuratively crushed by the realities of fallen human community. The needy are those with few or no resources of their own to call upon and no social capital that would allow them to trust in human systems. But God's preferential option for the needy is so characteristic of God's ways that the needy may *trust in you.* Note again that the psalmist pleads that they *may know your name,* that is, that they may know the character of God in personal experiences of God's deliverance.

11-12 ***(Zayin)*** The psalmist returns to the theme of praise, but this time calls others to join in the chorus. The call to praise is a common element of the song of thanksgiving, in which the person who has experienced God's deliverance calls upon others to join in thankful response. Here, the call functions analogously to a vow of trust, because the psalmist calls upon others to praise the Lord in expectant trust that the Lord will deliver the needy — including the psalmist and perhaps the psalmist's community — in the near future.

37. See Creach, *Yahweh as Refuge and the Editing of the Hebrew Psalter;* Brown, *Seeing the Psalms.*

The Lord's epithet here is *dweller of Zion,* the one whose presence is known most fully on Mount Zion. But the *dweller of Zion* is to be praised among the peoples. This polarity between God's revelation locally on Zion and the knowledge going out internationally to the people is known in such passages as Isa. 2:1-4//Mic. 4:1-3, where the metaphor of judge also plays a strong role. The connection between praise of God and mission is inescapable here. Praise is not for God's personal benefit, but for the sake of God's mission to the nations. God is also termed *the One who calls to account for bloodshed* here. The epithet most likely means that God the Creator acts in the role similar to that of the "avenger of blood," who was the community member set aside to punish those guilty of violence (cf. Numbers 35). One purpose that this role served was to interrupt the cycle of violence by limiting the responsibility and right of individuals to retaliate for bloodshed. But that is not the only purpose. The psalm depicts God, who *does not forget the cries of the afflicted,* in this role. Thus, a second purpose of God as *the One who calls to account for bloodshed* is to provide justice for the victims of injustice.

9:13-20 — Petition, Motivation, and Trust

13-14 *(Ḥêt)* Broadly speaking, the poem now switches to a section comprised of petitions with motivating clauses and statements of trust. The section begins with the first of several pleas for help: *be gracious to me, O LORD, see my suffering.* The plea to *be gracious* is typical (4:1; 6:2; 31:9, etc.); it is a plea for God's merciful intervention. The plea for God to *see (rᵉʾēh) my suffering* is less typical, but see Pss. 25:18, 19; 119:153, 159. The verb "to see" does not merely indicate visual perceptivity, but also God's understanding and God's active intervention. For God to see is for God both to know and to take action. This plea is especially important in light of the poet's later complaints that the enemies assert that the Lord *will never see* (10:11) and *God will not call to account* (10:13). The psalmist prays for God to do precisely what the enemies confess that God cannot and will not do: take notice and take action. What is more, the psalmist desires that God see her suffering at the hands of oppressors and connects her petition back to her promise to praise. Here, says the psalmist, God's deliverance serves the purpose of praise. And as noted above, praise serves the purpose of God's mission. The reference to God as the one *who lift(s) me from the gate of death* is not a reference to life after death, but to deliverance from a near death situation. The poet offers a lovely contrast by means of a play on words. God is the one who *lift(s) me from the gates of death,* while the psalmist praises God *in the gates of daughter Zion.* The reference to *daughter Zion,* the female personification of the city, is a deeply loaded metaphor.[38] As noted above, the reference to the city is more than a geographical reference; it is a metaphor that portrays the city as a woman who embodies what it is for the people to be Israel, to be God's people. It lends the city personality; it gives the city a cast of humanity. As F. W. Dobbs-Allsopp has written concerning the personification of Jerusalem as daughter Zion in Lamentations, the personification "ups the emotional ante — Jerusalem as city is something more than the sum of all its walls, buildings, gates, and roads. . . ."[39] As *daughter Zion,* the city is a fellow member of God's family; it is the familial place in which the deliverance of God is experienced, and thus in which the praise of God should take place. It is the place in which we know who the Lord is and who we are. Who is the Lord? The Lord is the one who rescues the suffering from the courts of death. Who is the psalmist? She is a fellow daughter who has been brought into the familial courts of God and joyfully sings praise.

15-16 ***(Ṭêt)*** The psalmist continues the contrast between the poor and needy and the nations and the wicked. As mentioned above, the nations are those who are outside of the covenant and thus a danger to God's people; the nations are those whose cities are to be rendered to mere ruins. The needy, on the other hand, are those whom the Lord will deliver, who will be given a place in *daughter Zion* to sing praise. The psalmist here employs a metaphor of the nations being caught in their own trap — falling into a pit that they dug for others and catching their feet in a net that they had hidden for others. These metaphors are not uncommon in the Old Testament (cf. Ps. 7:15-16; Prov. 1:16-19). At the level of plain meaning, they indicate that the malevolent will of those who seek to harm others will in the end boomerang back on themselves. At the level of theological meaning, these metaphors say something about the way in which God's justice, righteousness, and law operate within God's creation. On the one hand, these passages suggest that God has woven a measure of retributive justice into the very fabric of creation. That is, that the laws of God are at times self-enforcing, so that when a person habitually breaks God's law — digging a pit or setting a trap for a neighbor, in the words of Psalm 9 — the law-breaking behavior itself is the punishment for the law, since it is destructive for the one who manifests the behavior. Thus, at least to a small extent, the law does not always need an external enforcer, since the law is its own enforcer. On the other hand, the metaphor suggests that God's justice and righteousness are both qualities of God's character and also qualities of God's creation. The poet confesses, *The LORD is known! He has done justice! The wicked one is struck down by the work of his own hand!* Thus, the Lord's justice and righ-

38. See Dobbs-Allsopp, *Weep, O Daughter Zion.*

39. Dobbs-Allsopp, *Lamentations,* p. 52.

teousness are made known and manifested by the reciprocal retribution built into creation.

17-20 ***(Yôd, Kāp)***[40] Vv. 17-18 straddle the *yôd* and *kāp* sections, but fit together to form a unity. The verses are tied together thematically and structurally. Thematically, both verses voice trust in the future — "negative" trust that the wicked will be defeated and "positive" trust that the needy will be delivered. Structurally, the two verses form a chiasm, which hinges on the word *forget* — the nations who forget God will perish, whereas *the needy will not be forgotten.* The themes of forgetting and remembering are central theological elements of the psalm. Theologically, the psalm employs a paradox that explores the sticky problem of theological agency. On the one hand, the wicked are the agents of their own destruction, since they *forget God.* On the other hand, the righteous are not the agents of their own deliverance; rather, God is the agent of their deliverance, since God remembers them and does not forget them. The phrase *the needy will not be forgotten forever* is poetically ambiguous. Does it imply that the needy are being momentarily forgotten by God? Psalm 13:1 is consistent with such an interpretation. Or does it imply that God's remembrance of the needy and power is permanent? The last phrase of v. 18 supports this interpretation.

The second two verses of the *kāp* stanza are a unit. In these verses, the poet appeals to God to *arise . . . let the nations to judged* and to *set a teaching before them . . . let the nations know that they are mortals.* The verbal structure of the verses is ABAB. The first colon of each verse leads with an imperative verb *(arise/set),* and the second colon of each verse leads with a jussive verb that essentially has imperatival force. The cry for God to arise is typical language in the psalms (3:7; 7:6; 17:13, etc.), which is a plea for God to act decisively and immediately. In the nominal structure, the verses use an inclusio structure, with the first and last clauses both containing the Hebrew word *ʾᵉnôš,* translated here as *mortal.* In the first phrase, the psalmist begs God to defeat mortals, whereas in the last phrase, God is implored to teach them that they are only mortals. There is a poetic contrast here between the finitude characteristic of humanity and of human wickedness and the *forever*-ness (twice in v. 18, *lāneṣaḥ* and *lāʿaḏ*) of God and the needy, on whose behalf God acts. The detail that God is implored to *teach* is worth noting. The concept of teaching does not merely imply an abstract noetic idea of instruction, but a concrete, experiential embodiment of instruction — the request here is not just for God to impart knowledge to the wicked, but to provide an unmistakable experience of judgment, an experience so concrete that the wicked will

40. The next element of the alphabetic acrostic is only one verse long and is followed by a section that is three verses long. No attempt should be made to restore the presumed regular acrostic pattern, however, since such attempts are always too speculative.

have no choice but to acknowledge that God is immortal and infinite and they are mortal and finite (cf. Jer. 31:33-34).

10:1-11 — Complaint Regarding the Enemy

10:1-2 ***(Lāmed)***[41] A new section of the psalm begins with a "why-question" typical of prayers for help: *Why, O Lord, do you stand at a distance?* (cf. Pss. 22:1; 88:14, etc.). The poet continues the spatial poetic theme introduced in 9:13-14, in which the psalmist espoused trust that she would praise *in the gates of daughter Zion,* by means of a spatial metaphor, complaining that God is standing far away. This spatial metaphor paints a picture of the psalmist as isolated — literally — from God. Inasmuch as the complaint also recalls the taunt that the wicked often level at those who suffer, "Where is your God?" (cf. 115:2; 79:10), the metaphor effectively ups the emotional ante of the complaint. In the second colon, the poet continues with the spatial metaphor, but amplifies it by adding a temporal quality to the complaint: *Why do you hide* at times of trouble? The psalmist's sense of isolation is thus augmented by adding the note that God is staying distant at a particularly inopportune moment. That moment is defined by the psalmist as a moment in which the wicked have acted against the afflicted *in arrogance; arrogance (ga'ᵃwâ)* is the state of mind in which people imagine that they will not be held accountable for their actions, and therefore that they are free to oppress and act wickedly (cf. 10:4; Isa. 9:8-9). The psalmist speaks for those who have no recourse against such earthly oppression and begs God to act.

10:3-11 ***(Lāmed continued, Mêm?, Nûn?, Sāmek?, 'Ayin?, Pê?)*** In the following verses, the psalmist expresses an extended "they-complaint" against the wicked. As is noted above, the acrostic structure deteriorates, but this section of the psalm builds on the question that is posed in 10:1. The leading motif of this part of the psalm is the enemy's mouth. If one assumes that the structure of having two verses per stanza continues — thus vv. 3-4, 5-6, 7-8a, 8b-9, 10-11 — it is worth noting that three of these five stanzas (3-4, 5-6, 10-11) close with a quotation of what the enemy says, while a fourth stanza speaks of the enemy's mouth directly: *a curse fills his mouth — deceit and injury* (v. 7).

The first of these five stanzas speaks specifically of the infamy that the wicked one achieves with her mouth. She *praises* her own desires, but *curses and rejects the Lord*. Then the psalmist directly quotes the wicked one's pride-

41. As noted above, the alphabetic acrostic is particularly disturbed in 10:3-8, in which one might have expected to encounter verses starting with *mêm, nûn,* and *sāmek,* but these are missing and the *pê* stanza is out of order. The approach here is not to try to restore the acrostic, but to treat the received psalm as the only established text to be interpreted.

ful words: *He will not call to account. There is no God.* The description here is of one who trusts fully in herself, imagining herself as a fully independent lord, immune to God. The second of the stanzas continues this description, suggesting that the wicked one thinks of herself also as one who is immune to interference or threats from enemies. Again, this stanza closes with a direct discourse citation of the enemy's thoughts, which illustrate again the enemy's belief that she has nothing to fear: *I shall not stumble, from generation to generation there will be no evil.* The boast *I shall not stumble* is a case of a phrase that can be either positive or negative in the psalms. If one makes this boast based on his own capacities and virtues, the boast is understood as an impious trust in one's self, as is the case here (cf. also 30:6). However, if one makes the boast based on the providence of the Lord, the phrase is understood as a pious trust in the Lord (cf. 16:8; 62:2, 6).

In v. 6, the words that the wicked speaks *in his heart* are reported. The poem continues this bodily imagery in the next two stanzas, which are the *pê* and *ʿayin* stanzas (but note that they occur in the reverse order from which one would expect). In these two stanzas, the poem employs the poetic device of synecdoche, portraying the wicked person via the efficient metaphors of the mouth and the eye. The *pê* stanza metaphorically portrays the enemy's mouth: *his mouth — a curse fills his mouth — deceit and injury* (v. 7). A parallel in Job 31:30, "I have not let my mouth sin by asking for their lives with a curse," may indicate that the enemy has taken a vow to do the psalmist harm; *ʾālâ* refers most often to an oath, but perhaps to a false accusation that is directed against another. The pair of words *deceit and injury* also occurs in Ps. 55:11. The *ʿayin* stanza portrays the wicked via *his eyes — his eyes lie in hiding for the unfortunate* (v. 9b). Poetically, these two uses of synecdoche reduce the wicked to the mouth and eyes, which he uses to do violence. The latter metaphor creates an especially powerful impact, because the image of the eyes spying for victims from the cover of a secret ambush is particularly chilling. The object of the wicked one's violence is described as *innocent, unfortunate,* and *afflicted.* These terms underscore the predatory violence of the wicked by portraying the victims as vulnerable and/or undeserving.

The final stanza of this section of the psalm continues themes already established — that the wicked prey on the innocent and consider themselves immune to God, whom they view as powerless. In this stanza, the psalmist also continues poetic references to body parts: the wicked *says in his heart* that God *has hidden his face.* As with the first two stanzas of this section of the psalm, this one closes with a direct discourse citation of the words of the wicked: *God has forgotten. He has hidden his face, he will never see"* (v. 11). The force of this quotation, like that of the first citation in v. 4 and of one yet to come in v. 13, is the belief of the wicked that God does not have the effective power to save and help the psalmist and effective power to judge or stop the wicked. This theological issue can be said to name the central theological issue of the psalm. As is typical when the voices of the enemy are quoted in a prayer for help, the direct discourse occurs at the end of the complaint section and functions as the culmination of the complaint. As shall be seen in a moment, the quoted language of the wicked also provides the psalmist with the language that will become the pivot point in the argument that the poet sets before God.[42]

10:12-18 — Petition and Trust

10:12-13 ***(Qôp)*** The last section of the psalm is best characterized as renewed petition with trust. The renewed petition bears marked similarities to the earlier section of petition in the psalm. The first words of this stanza — *Arise, O Lord!* — repeat the imperative cry from earlier in the psalm (9:19), thus renewing the call for help. Similarly, just as the psalmist had previously pictured the wicked via his mouth, eyes, and heart, now the psalmist calls on God to *lift up your hand,* the hand serving as a metaphor for the active manifestation of God's power and presence. There is something else new in this section of petition also, namely, that the psalmist now uses the scandalous words of the enemy that had been quoted earlier in the prayer and reserves those words. Earlier, the psalmist had quoted the wicked as saying *God has forgotten* (10:11); now the psalmist turns that around: *do not forget the afflicted!* Lest this subtle reversal of the enemies' scoffing language be missed, the psalmist restates her complaint in the form of a question: *Why should the wicked scoff at God, and say in his heart, "God will not call to account"?*

10:14 ***(Rêš)*** At the beginning of the *rêš* stanza, the psalmist again reverses the impious, mocking language of the wicked, this time in a passionate outburst of trust. Earlier the wicked had been quoted as saying that God *will never see.* Now, the pray-er cries out, *But you do see!* As mentioned above, the concept of seeing here is a metaphor for the active power and presence of God. The enemies perceive themselves as free to pursue wickedness because they do not fear an active divine power or presence. The psalmist emphatically (the *kî* in this syntax functions emphatically) asserts the opposite: *indeed, you do notice trouble and grief, to take it in your hand.* Again, as throughout this section of the psalm, the poetic references to body parts provide power and poignancy to the psalmist's prayer. Here, the psalmist's trust in God's sight and the power of God's hand both bear witness to an active trust in God's ability to intervene and save. But the psalmist's trust is more than simply about God's power; it is also about God's character. The

42. See Jacobson, *Many Are Saying,* pp. 27-30.

psalmist bears witness of a faithful God, who takes notice of *trouble and grief* (the terms *ʿāmāl* and *kaʿas* are morally ambiguous, but in this context it is very likely that they refer to the woes of the innocent; cf. Jer. 20:18; Ps. 6:7), who is worthy of the trust of the unfortunate, who is the helper of the orphan.

10:15-16 *(Šîn)* The poet continues the plea for action, the poetic references to body parts, and the reversal of the wicked's language: *Break the arm of the wicked and the evil, call to account* (cf. 10:4, 13) *his wickedness.* Just as God's hand is symbolic of God's active power and presence, the request to *break the arm of the wicked* should not be understood literally, but rather as a request to put an end to the power of the wicked. This impassioned plea is paired again with a statement of trust: *The LORD is king forever and ever, the nations will perish from his land.* As Mays notes, the metaphorical statement that *the LORD is king* "is both royal and pastoral." That is, the metaphor makes claims about who God is and about what this means for the world. "It comprehends Yhwh's work of leading and guiding and providing a place of support."[43] The detail that God is king *forever and ever* should not be overlooked or dismissed. The fact that the triumph of the wicked is temporary, in comparison with the eternal victory of the Lord, is precisely that which undergirds the psalmist's confidence.

10:17-18 *(Tāw)* The psalm closes with a final expression of confidence: *The desires of the afflicted, O LORD, you hear.* As one might expect, the poetic references to the body feature prominently: *You make firm their hearts, you make ready your ear.* Throughout the psalm, a pressing issue has been that the wicked oppress the innocent. The psalm ends with the affirmation that God judges the wicked for the very purpose of protecting the innocent — there is no separation between the two actions.

Reflections

1. The Power and Presence of God

The central theological problematic named in Psalm 9/10 has to do with the power and presence of God, or the lack thereof. On the one hand, the wicked person denies both God's presence and God's active power. The wicked are quoted several times expressing this view: *"He will not call to account. There is no God"* (10:4); *"God has forgotten. He has hidden his face, he will never see"* (10:11); and *"God will not call to account"* (10:13). As Craigie notes, this view can be called "*practical or theoretical* atheism. . . . The functional atheist is not concerned so much with the theoretical question as to the existence of

43. Mays, *The Lord Reigns,* p. 18.

God; rather, he lives and behaves *as if* God did not exist."[44] The threat that practical atheists pose to both community and to powerless individuals is so much in the content of their beliefs (except to the extent that their beliefs result in actions) as in the actions that they take. Because they live their lives without "the fear of God," they feel free to oppress the widow, the orphan, and the weak.

The psalmist, on the other hand, both affirms God's active power and calls on God to rise up and make that power known. As noted in the comments above, the psalmist reverses this language in the climactic petition/trust section of the psalm: *Do not forget the afflicted* (10:12); *But you do see!* (10:14); and *Call to account his wickedness* (10:15). Specifically, the psalmist calls for God to see the oppression of the wicked, which in turn causes the suffering of the innocent. Contrary to the practical atheism of the wicked, the psalmist is a practical theist. The psalmist has more than merely an abstract intellectual faith in God. The psalmist lives out this faith in the concrete choices of daily life, in decisions to pray in the face of suffering, to stand firm in faith in the face of evil, and to refuse to join forces with oppression. Note especially that to keep faith in God means two things simultaneously. It means both to continue to trust in God's faithfulness in spite of the presence of oppression, and it means to struggle against oppression, to refuse to throw in one's lot with those who oppress the poor.

2. Embodying the Word

As was noted in the commentary, a major poetic element of the last section of the psalm has to do with images of the body: mouth, eyes, heart, face, hand, arm, and even nose (the Hebrew word *ʾap̱* that is translated as *anger* literally means "nose"). At times, the metaphorical use of these bodily images soars to the height of synecdoche, in which the wicked persons are portrayed by means of nothing other than their body parts: *a curse fills his mouth* (10:7); *his eyes lie in hiding for the unfortunate* (10:8). It is not pushing the use of this metaphor too far to suggest that we all embody our faith, or lack thereof. According to legend, Saint Francis is said to have taught, "Preach the gospel at all times; if necessary use words." Psalm 9/10 seems to be saying something akin, namely, that the everyday choices that a person makes and actions that a person takes proclaim our inner beliefs, even if we do not use words. In short: we embody our faith in God, or lack thereof.

ROLF A. JACOBSON

44. Craigie, *Psalms 1–50,* p. 126.

Psalm 11: What Can the Righteous Do?

Psalm 11 is generally described as a psalm of trust.[1] The psalm answers the question — whether rhetorical or literal — *If the foundations are torn down, what can the righteous do?* (v. 3). The psalm does not just offer an answer to this question, the psalm *is* the answer. That is, the psalm does not just give advice in answer to the question by, for example, saying, "The righteous can trust in the Lord." Rather, the psalm is itself a radical and countercultural expression of trust in the face of chaos. In this sense, the psalm then is the very answer to the question it reports.

As is usually the case with the interpretation of the psalms, some commentators are confident that they can identity the original life setting for which or in which the psalm was composed. And yet, even those commentators who share such confidence do not agree on this identification. For example, Kraus imagines that "the petitioner has found refuge from persecuting enemies in the temple area. At the sanctuary he obviously meets those people who recommended a different way to him, namely, not the way of refuge with Yahweh but that of flight to the hills."[2] Or again, Gerstenberger posits a cultic setting in which a dispute between parties is adjudicated and the accused party has the opportunity to refute the charge, although he notes that there is no specific evidence in the OT for such a ceremony: "The cultic situation, however, is important: the supplicant is given a chance to refute all allegations as well as the supposedly friendly counsel that recommends alienation from human society."[3] Craigie notes, "It is possible, though not certain, that the psalm's initial setting was in the context of the temple (see v. 4), though it need not be found in the context of formal worship."[4] A second question is, how many voices are there in the psalm? Is the entire psalm spoken by one person? Or should one understand a supplicant speaking in vv. 1-3 and then a priest or some other cultic functionary answering in vv. 4-7? Other possibilities have been posited.

The reality is that efforts to identify a precise historical setting or "original" speakers will remain speculative. It is better to remain open on such questions, and instead to understand that Psalm 11 is a poem, and that the interpreter must play with the possibilities of what imagined settings and voices might fit the psalm. Above all, it is crucial not to lose sight of the bigger theological issue that the psalm names: trust in the midst of threat.

1. Kraus sees it as a prayer song (*Psalms 1–59,* p. 201). Gerstenberger considers it unique and coins it a "psalm of contest, or a disputing prayer" (*Psalms: Part 1,* pp. 78-79).

2. Kraus, *Psalms 1–59,* p. 201.

3. Gerstenberger, *Psalms: Part 1,* p. 79.

4. Craigie, *Psalms 1–50,* p. 132.

The psalm has two stanzas: vv. 1-3, 4-7. Each stanza begins with poetic play involving the name of the Lord and the preposition *b* (v. 1: *byhwh ḥsyty;* v. 4: *yhwh bhykl*) and each stanza ends with a causal clause introduced by the particle *kî* and in which the word "righteous" occurs prominently.

St. 1 Statement of trust followed by faithless advice: (vv. 1-3)
For the wicked have bent the bow . . . what can the righteous do?
St. 2 Statement of trust in response to the faithless advice: (vv. 4-7)
For the LORD is righteous, he loves righteous deeds.

To the leader.[5] *Davidic.*

1 *In the LORD, I have taken refuge,*
how can you say to my soul,
"Flee like a bird to a mountain.[6]
2 *For the wicked have bent the bow,*
they have fixed[7] *arrows*[8] *upon the string,*
to shoot from darkness at the upright of heart.[9]
3 *If the foundations are torn down,*[10]
what can the righteous do?"

4 *The LORD is in his holy sanctuary,*
the LORD — in heaven is his throne.
His eyes see,
his pupils examine humanity.
5 *The LORD tests the righteous and the wicked;*
and the lover of violence, his soul hates.[11]

5. See note 12 on the superscription to Psalm 4.

6. The MT consonants are *nwdw hrkm ṣpwr.* The first word seems to be a plural imperative, but both the object *ṣippôr (bird)* and the antecedent *l^enap̄šî (my soul/me)* are singular. LXX, Syr, and Qere reflect a singular verb, thus *nwdy.* LXX's "flee to the mountain like a bird," may reflect a redivision of the consonantal text: *hr kmw.* Thus, the text is read here as: *nwdy hr kmw ṣpwr.*

7. 4QCatena A has *wykynu,* with no change in meaning.

8. Reading the plural, *ḥiṣîm,* with LXX and 4QCatena A, in place of MT's *ḥiṣṣām.*

9. Following Fokkelmann's division of the first two verses into tricola; *The Psalms in Form,* p. 24.

10. LXX "what you have made" reflects a repointing of MT's *haššāṯôt* to *haššattôṯ* and a repointing of MT's *yĕhārēsûn* to *yeher^esûn.*

11. The verse has a couple of minor problems. The phrase *yhwh ṣdyq ybḥn wrš' w'hb ḥms šn'h npšw* might be divided as "The Lord tests the righteous, but the wicked and the one loving violence — his soul hates" (so Craigie, *Psalms 1–50,* p. 131; NIV; NJPS), or "Yahweh tests the righteous and the wicked . . ." (so Kraus, (*Psalms 1–59,* p. 200; NRSV). LXX supports

6 *He causes coal,*[12] *fire, and brimstone to rain down upon the wicked,*
and a scorching wind shall be the portion of their cup.
7 *For the LORD is righteous, he loves righteous deeds,*
the upright shall behold his face.

1-3 The first stanza names a dire threat to the psalmist's faith and life. This naming of a threat is a characteristic part of every psalm of trust, similar though not identical to the complaint sections of individual prayers for help. In Psalm 23, for example, the psalmist acknowledges the real danger in "the valley of the shadow of death" (v. 4, KJV). In Psalm 27, the petitioner says, "if an army encamps against me . . . if battle arises against me" (v. 3). In Psalm 46, the worship leader sings, "when the earth changes itself, when mountains quake in the heart of the seas" (v. 2b). Each of these psalms, like Psalm 11, is a psalm of trust. In a sense, this naming the real threats of life is what provides the real power and drama to the psalms of trust. This is so, because without genuine threats and causes for fear, the psalm's avowals of trust and lack of fear are just so much vapor and hot air. Can one imagine Psalm 23's statement "I fear no evil" ringing with the same power, had not the threats posed by enemies been named? In Psalm 11, the introductory declaration of trust — *In the LORD, I have taken refuge* (cf. 7:1; 16:1; 25:20; 31:1) — dramatically stands over against those who advise the psalmist to flee from the threat of the wicked. Note that the psalmist faces a dual threat — first, there is the physical threat posed by the wicked; second, there is the spiritual threat posed by advice from (perhaps well-meaning) advisors.

Rhetorically, the first stanza consists of a question inside of another question. Another way of saying the same thing would be to say that the first stanza consists of an unfaith statement inside of a faith statement. First, the faith statement: *In the LORD, I have taken refuge, how can you say to my soul . . . ?* (v. 1a). Some interpreters take the phrase *I have taken refuge* to mean that the psalmist has literally sought asylum in the temple, perhaps by ritually grabbing the horns of the altar, as did Joab, when he feared Solomon's wrath (1 Kgs. 2:28). The phrase occurs so often in the Psalter and the concept of refuge is so frequent, however, that it is better to understand the phrase as referring to the spiritual act of placing trust in the Lord in the face of danger. The point is not that the psalmist sought protection in the temple, but that the psalmist sought the Lord's protection. Having sought such protection,

---

the latter, "The Lord tries the righteous and the ungodly, and the one loving unrighteousness hates his own." Yet, this reading does not make sense of MT's *šn'h npšw,* which requires a feminine subject for "to hate."

12. Hebrew *paḥîm* ("trapping nets") should be read as related to the root *pḥm,* thus "coals."

the psalmist then poses a rhetorical question to unnamed bystanders: *how can you say to my soul . . . ?* This question is in truth the second half of the statement of faith. The psalmist neither anticipates nor desires an answer to the question. Rather, by asking the question, the psalmist states her faith in God and rejects the advice to flee.

There is some dispute as to how one should understand vv. 1b-3 of the psalm. Aside from a few significant textual problems that affect the interpretation of the psalm and are addressed in the footnotes to the translation, the key issue is how long the quotation of the speech directed at the psalmist continues. In Hebrew poetry, quotations (more precisely called direct discourse) are normally marked only at the beginning — by means of a verb of speaking. The close of quotations is not marked. That is the case here. The verb of speaking *tō'mᵉrû (you say)* marks the start of the direct discourse, but the ending is unmarked.[13] There are three basic views. The first view is represented by Gerstenberger, who concludes that only v. 1b is quoted speech, while vv. 2-3 are the speech of the psalmist himself.[14] Craigie represents the second view; they see the quoted speech covering vv. 1b-2, while v. 3 is the speech of the psalmist.[15] The view taken here follows the majority of interpreters and understands that the entirety of vv. 1b-3 consists of the speech of an unnamed group (*tō'mᵉrû, you say,* is plural) that advises the psalmist to flee from the wicked. There are two primary reasons for this. First, the occurrence of *kî* at the start of vv. 2 and v. 3 militates toward this conclusion; after the psalmist is urged to flee in v. 1b, the causal clause in v. 2 only makes sense if the same speaking voice continues. Because v. 3 also starts with *kî* it makes further sense that this verse should be understood as part of the quotation. Second, the question at the end of v. 3, *What can the righteous do?,* does not make sense as the speech of the psalmist, who has just asked, *how can you say to my soul, "Flee. . . ."* Thus, the psalmist returns question for question, faith and trust for unfaith and mistrust.

The image of the fleeing bird (cf. Ps. 102:6-7; Prov. 27:8) evokes a sense of both homelessness and isolation. It captures both the sense of powerlessness that the righteous can feel in the face of evil and the temptation to relinquish the public square to those who feel no scruples about using violence to control society.

4-7 The second stanza counters the threat that was named in the first stanza by confessing trust in the Lord. Presented with the powerless situation in which the righteous sit, the psalm does not try to argue that there are

13. For a lengthy discussion of the issues of delineating direct discourse, see Jacobson, *Many Are Saying,* pp. 19-26.

14. Gerstenberger, *Psalms: Part 1,* p. 77.

15. Craigie, *Psalms 1–50,* p. 131.

indeed steps the righteous can take or earthly options available to confront evildoers. Rather, the psalm confesses faith in the Lord. It does so in four terse phrases: *The LORD is in his holy sanctuary* (v. 4a); The LORD's *eyes see* (v. 4b); *The LORD tests the righteous and the wicked* (v. 5); *The LORD is righteous* (v. 7). The first phrase is not so much about the Lord's location, but about the Lord's fidelity and power (cf. Ps. 115:3). To confess that the Lord is *in his holy sanctuary* (which means that God actively reigns in the heavenly council) is to confess that there is one who possesses both the power and character to counter the wicked. The second phrase names God as an active force on earth. The wicked often are quoted as saying, "God does not see" (cf. 10:11). To assert that God does see is to confess God as a relevant, active power in the present situation. God's power is neither abstract nor limited to the past or future. As Goldingay comments, "The psalms know that Yhwh is involved in life now, and they often testify to that involvement; Psalm 11 is declaring a conviction about this. If Yhwh's activity belonged only to the future, the scornful response to the advisers (vv. 1-2) would hardly make sense."[16] The third phrase draws on the important metaphor of God as judge in order to confess that the presence of God leads to a more just and equitable world. God possesses the wisdom to discern both righteousness and wickedness. And God possesses the character to embrace righteousness *(The upright shall behold his face)* and to reject wickedness *(the lover of violence, his soul hates).* As Mays notes, "When there is no action for the righteous to take that has promise of succeeding in the face of the power and danger of wickedness, they can testify to the righteous judge of all, in whose hands rests the estimate and outcome of every life."[17] The fourth phrase sums up and concludes the matter by confessing the Lord's character. If human righteousness has to do with the internal character of a human being, then to declare God as righteous is to make a statement about God's character.

The metaphor that *a scorching wind shall be the portion of their cup* (cf. 23:5; 75:8; 116:13) may be an echo of a drink ordeal (Num. 5:23-28). If so, "here it is a matter of standing metaphors, the specific original sacral connection of which has faded away."[18] Conversely, the cup may also simply offer an image of one's fate, as Ps. 16:5 and Matt. 20:22 indicate. Either way, the image communicates the trust that in the imbalanced equation between the sufferer and the evildoers, God is the factor that will even all the sums.

16. Goldingay, *Psalms 1–41,* p. 194.
17. Mays, *Psalms,* p. 76.
18. Kraus, *Psalms 1–59,* p. 204.

Reflections

God Is the Master of Fate

In his infamous ode to the individual, "Invictus," William Ernest Henley wrote, "It matters not how straight the gate,/how charged with punishment the scroll,/I am the master of my fate:/I am the captain of my soul."[19] Psalm 11 utterly rejects this worldview and offers in its place an older, more true confession: "God is the master of my fate; God is the captain of my soul." When there is no earthly recourse in the face of evil, the psalm reminds that there is always a heavenly recourse. And so those on earth may turn and take refuge in the Lord. To take refuge in the Lord is not a passive move, but an active one. To take refuge in the Lord is to embrace one of the persistent paradoxes of the life of faith: to relinquish control over one's future can be an aggressive action. Although the circumstances of this life often put us in the place of the exiled sparrow — homeless and vulnerable — God, who has been our dwelling place in all generations, is a refuge, shelter, and home to which we can flee in the day of trouble.

The act of taking refuge in God is not purely an eschatological trust. True, the faith does make claims that stretch beyond the curved-in horizons of earth. As St. Paul has it, it is not for this life only that we have hope. But neither is faith solely bent on the next life, the new creation. The Bible confesses that God sees and reaches into the here and now — even when it does not seem to be the case. What can the righteous do in the face of evil? The righteous can confess trust in God's righteousness and embrace the hope that the righteous will see God's face. The new creation has already broken into the now — can you perceive it?

ROLF A. JACOBSON

19. Henley, *A Book of Verses* (3rd ed.; New York: Scribner & Welford, 1906).

Psalm 12: Now Shall I Arise!

Psalm 12 is about words. It begins with the words of the wicked and the considerable violence that they achieve by means of their speech. In the middle, the words of God are spoken, which counter the words of the wicked. The poem closes with the assurance that the word of God is trustworthy.

The genre of the poem is debated. There are two general sets of options. On the one hand, some scholars understand the poem as a prayer for help (either of the community or of an individual).[1] Others see the psalm as a liturgy, spoken by a cultic prophet on behalf of the needs of others.[2] Gerstenberger has it both ways: "Early Jewish communities have remodeled an old individual complaint to accommodate it to congregational services for the poor and oppressed (cf. Nehemiah 5)."[3] It is possible that the psalm is a later literary-theological composition that only mimicks the form of an actual cultic prayer, and therefore one should not think of a life setting at all for this psalm. But there are no late linguistic or orthographic features in the psalm that might indicate that the psalm is a later literary composition. It seems best to assume that it is an actual prayer or liturgy from Israel's cult. LXX understands the psalm as a prayer for help, as the first person pronouns that LXX adds in vv. 1 and 7 indicate: "save me" (*sōson me,* v. 1) and "you shall keep us and preserve us" (*phylaxeis hēmas kai diatērēseis hēmas,* v. 7). The view taken here is that the MT preserves an older tradition than does the LXX, and the psalm is best understood as a liturgy of intercession and promise. Similar to Hab. 1:1–2:5, in which the prophet alternately performs a lament on behalf of the people and then announces God's response, Psalm 12 is a liturgy in which the speaker first pleads for deliverance and complains on behalf of an oppressed community (vv. 1-4), then announces God's response (v. 5) and speaks words of assurance (vv. 6-8). The lack of the first person anywhere in the psalm other than in the speech of God in v. 5 and the key placement of the God quotation at the center of the psalm support this conclusion. Such God quotations (often referred to by the problematic term "oracles of salvation"[4]) are not found in individual prayers for help.

A precise setting in life cannot be determined. One can imagine the liturgy being performed on behalf of a group (or even an individual) that has approached the temple in need or on behalf of the community in a time of crisis. No original setting can be reconstructed with any confidence. The interpretation here leaves the question open, assuming only that the liturgy

1. So Mays, Clifford, Limburg, McCann et al.
2. So Kraus, Jeremias, Goldingay et al.
3. *Psalms: Part 1,* p. 83.
4. See Jacobson, *Many Are Saying,* pp. 91-98.

is performed by a community leader on behalf of a group of people in crisis. The psalm has three parts (vv. 1-4, 5, 6-8). In the first part, the liturgist cries out on behalf of another or others. In the second, a community leader speaks on behalf of God. In the third part, the liturgist announces assurance that God's word is trustworthy.

To the leader. ʾal haššᵉmînîṯ.[5] *A Davidic psalm.*

1 *Save,*[6] *O Lord, for the faithful have ceased,*
for the trustworthy have disappeared[7] *from among humanity.*
2 *Everyone speaks falsely to the neighbor,*
with slick lips and duplicitous heart do they speak.
3 *May the Lord cut off all slick lips,*
every tongue speaking arrogance.[8]
4 *Those that say, "With our tongue we will prevail,*
our lips belong to us, who can be our master?"

5 *"Because of the devastation of the poor and the groans of the needy,*
now shall I arise!" says the Lord.
"I will place in safety a witness[9] *on their behalf."*

6 *The promises of the Lord are pure promises,*
silver refined in a furnace on the earth,[10] *purified seven times.*

5. See footnote 10 on Psalm 6 superscription.

6. LXX adds an expansionistic 1cs suffix: "save me." The addition would turn the poem into an individual prayer for help.

7. The geminate verb *pāsas* occurs only here in the Old Testament. It is most simple to assume this is a mistake for *sûp̱* ("to cease") since geminates and hollow verbs were often confused and the parallelism suggests such a meaning. LXX's *ōligōthēsan,* which is used to translate a variety of Hebrew terms with the similar meaning of "to end/cease," supports this.

8. Lit., "great things." This is a case in which the plural indicates an abstract concept. In this context, "grandiosity" or the preferred *arrogance* is communicated (cf. Ps 131:1, in which the term is used similarly and in contrast to that psalmist's humility).

9. The translation of *yāp̱îaḥ* is disputed. Patrick Miller ("*yāp̱îaḥ* in Psalm XII 6," VT 29 [1979] 495-500) has argued convincingly that the term means "witness" on the basis of Ugaritic *ypḥ* (see also Dennis Pardee, "*ypḥ* 'Witness' in Hebrew and Ugaritic," VT 28 [1978] 204-13; J. G. Janzen, "Another look at Psalm xii 6," VT 54 [2004] 157-64). Note also that 11QPsc has . . . *qym ʾšy* . . . , likely reflecting *ṣᵉḏāqîm ʾāwîṯ:* ". . . to the righteous. 'I have set. . . .' "

10. The phrase *baʿᵃlîl lāʾāreṣ* is awkward. Many solutions have been tried, often involving various emendations of *lāʾāreṣ.* Such emendations are plausible, but hardly necessary. Although the syntax is awkward, the meaning is fairly clear. Furnaces for refining metal sat in or on the ground (see Keel, *The Symbolism of the Biblical World,* p. 185); this is a reference to such a refining furnace. 11QPsc has the partial *ʿyl lʾrḥs;* while XHev/Se4 reads the same as MT.

7 *You, O Lord, will keep them,*
you will protect him[11] *from this generation forever.*
8 *The wicked walk to and fro, all around,*
because worthlessness is exalted among humanity.

1-4 The psalm begins with the slightly awkward appeal, *Save.* While it is not uncommon for a prayer to lead off with a verb — *Keep me* (16:1), *Hear a legitimate cause* (17:1), *Judge me* (26:1) — the only direct parallel is found in 69:1: "Save me." As the four examples just provided demonstrate, one expects an object after the initial verb, but the Hebrew lacks such an object (which the LXX supplies; see note 9). The reason that there is no object is that the poem is not the prayer of an individual. Rather, the psalmist cries out on behalf of others: *Save, O LORD.*

The reason that God's deliverance is requested is no *faithful (ḥāsîd)* or *trustworthy ('ĕmûnîm)* person can be found. These two roots often occur in parallel in their adjectival forms, which normally apply to God's character (61:7; 69:13; 85:11, etc.). In their nominal forms (cf. 31:23), the terms refer to those people whose character and actions are consistent with God's covenantal expectations. The *faithful* and *trustworthy* protect the widow, the orphan, and the weak. In this case, because no such person can be found *among humanity* to step forward on behalf of the one who is suffering, the psalmist intercedes on the sufferer's behalf and pleads with God to save. The faithful are absent, but the wicked are not. As is so very often the case in the psalms, the wicked are described primarily by means of the violence they commit with their mouths. They *speak falsely;* the term *šāwᵉ'* signifies emptiness, worthlessness, or vanity. The false witness commandment uses the same language in Deuteronomy's formulation, "you shall not answer as a false witness *('ēḏ šāwᵉ')*" (Deut. 5:20). The term may or may not signify that the psalmist has been falsely accused, as vv. 2-4 do not seem to imply a false accusation has been made. Indeed, the quotation in v. 4 lends specific content to the adjective *šāwᵉ'*, suggesting that the wicked's sin is that they imagine themselves as their own masters: *who can be our master?* It is characteristic of the wicked that they refuse to acknowledge the Lord's reign or the claims of God's law on themselves. In this same vein, the psalm describes the wicked as *speaking arrogance* (*gᵉḏōlôṯ* in this case carries the sense of "things too grand" and thus arrogance). Thus, arrogance is the diagnostic sin of the wicked.

In the quotation, they are fictively described as claiming that their tongues will prevail, and the wicked are even metaphorically represented

11. LXX has 1cp suffixes on both verbs. But as noted, LXX treats the psalm as an individual prayer for help rather than as a liturgy of promise. The change of suffixes is required for LXX's understanding of the genre.

by the synecdoche of the tongue. Behind this metaphor is the Hebrew conception of the complete unity of thought and action. Their tongues assert their own false independence, and thus their rebellion against God and God's ways. The Hebrew phrase that is translated as *duplicitous heart* reads, literally, "with a heart and a heart." This idiom, otherwise unknown, can be taken as the opposite of the Hebrew "one heart" (*lēḇ 'eḥāḏ;* Jer. 32:39; Ezek. 11:19; cf. Deut. 25:13 for a similar syntactical construction), which signifies the unity of a human will with God's will. In Hebrew, the heart was the organ of thinking and willing (rather than emoting). The translation *duplicitous* nicely conveys both the repetition in the syntax as well as the sense of a human will set in opposition to God's will. The point is not that the wicked are two-faced (that they say one thing but do another), but rather that what they say and do is fundamentally opposed to God's will.

For a poor person or persons caught in the net of such oppressors, the psalmist prays for God's effective help.

5 The speech of God is the center of the psalm. As noted above, the response of God here bears certain similarities to the response of God in Hab. 1:5-11 and especially 2:2-5. God speaks a promise pregnant with hope and rescue: *Now shall I arise!* In many prayers for help, the psalmists beg, *Arise, O LORD!* (*qûmâ YHWH;* Pss. 3:7; 7:6; 9:19, etc.). Although such a plea is not present in Psalm 12, God's promise, *now shall I arise,* announces God's clear intention to answer the intercession favorably and respond to the need of the sufferer. The *now ('attâ)* of the response signals both that God's help will be immediate and that God's help will be the determinative event in the sufferer's drama. God's help will not merely even the contest between the sufferer and those who oppress; it will end the contest in the sufferer's favor. The syntax of the God quotation accents the reason why God chooses to become involved in the matter — *because of the devastation of the poor and the groans of the needy.* It is neither the righteousness of the intercessor, nor of the sufferer, nor the intercession itself that provides the grounds for God's response. Rather, it is the suffering of the poor that motivates God's response. Similar to the exodus story, in which "God heard their groaning *(na'ᵃqāṯām)*" and was moved to deliver the people, in Psalm 12 God hears *the groans (mē'anqaṯ) of the needy* and is moved to action. As Clifford has noted, the terms "poor" and "needy" are commonly paired in the psalms. Together, the terms "designate economic poverty as well as the powerless state that comes from lack of resources."[12]

The interpretation of v. 5c is much debated, with the term *yāp̄îaḥ* proving a particular point of disagreement. As seen in the translation notes above, the view taken here is that *yāp̄îaḥ* is a noun that is related to *pwḥ* II, "bear witness" (rather than *pwḥ* I, "breathe") and that means *a witness.* As Miller

12. Clifford, *Psalms 1–72,* p. 83.

has explained, "The problem of the psalmist is the action of the wicked... specifically in regard to what they say, what they do with their tongue." The testimony that the witness would provide "on behalf of the poor may have been in juridical proceedings, or it may have been as a witness to transactions or contracts.... Yahweh will protect whoever will stand as witness to transactions either written or oral and thus preserve the right or justice of the" poor.[13]

6-8 The final stanza of the psalm continues to build on the key rhetorical theme of the poem: words. The stanza consists of the psalmist's assurance that the words of the Lord are trustworthy. The term translated *promises* means, literally, "words" *('imᵃrôṯ),* although in the Psalter the term often carries the meaning of promise, as it does here. The syntax of the verbless clause — *'imᵃrôṯ YHWH 'imᵃrôṯ ṭᵉshōrôṯ* — repeats the word *promises* and pairs *the* LORD with *pure,* subtly communicating that God's words are trustworthy precisely because God's character is itself pure. The image of silver being *refined (ṣārûp̱)* is a common image for being tested, as Ps. 66:10 attests: "you have tested us *(ṣérāp̱tānû),* O God, you refined us as silver is refined *(kiṣᵉrāp̱).*" The point is that God's word has been tested and has achieved a standard — *seven times* indicates both perfection and unsurpassed purification — a standard that no human speech or word could hope to attain. Within the overall scope of the psalm, the implication is that the words of the oppressors have been tested and found to be empty, arrogant, and violent. They are the opposite of God's refined word — they are dross. But God's words, which promise deliverance for the poor and oppressed, are pure silver.

The psalm continues with a trusting statement of assurance about God's deliverance. This statement is directed at God: *You, O* LORD, *will keep them, you will protect him from this generation forever.* The pronominal suffixes have bothered interpreters, both modern and ancient — the LXX has 1cp pronouns, a reading which most modern versions adopt; Syr has 1cs pronouns. Some readers are thrown by the Hebrew text's switch from the 3mp *them* to 3ms *him.* But this variation, which is simply for the purpose of poetic parallelism, is very common (cf. Isa. 28:6; 32:1). Even within the psalm, *the faithful* in v. 1 is singular while *the trustworthy* is plural, and the *poor* and *needy* of v. 5 are plural, but the pronoun translated here as *on their behalf (lô)* is singular. In both v. 5c and 8b, the singular pronominal suffix carries a collective sense, referring to the plural group on whose behalf the psalmist intercedes. The psalmist expresses confidence that God will *keep them (tišmᵉrēm),* a familiar image for God's protecting care (cf. Ps. 121:3-8). *This generation,* which refers to the oppressors described in vv. 2-4, gives a sense that the threat from evildoers is not a momentary threat, but an enduring one. Likewise, *forever* promises that God's care will be equally enduring. The closing verse

13. Miller, "*yāpîaḥ* in Psalm XII 6," p. 499.

further underscores the enduring nature of the threat that the wicked pose. The hithpael form *yiṯhallāḵûn* suggests continuous, reiterative action, thus the translation *walk to and fro.* This looming threat is further heightened by the description of the wicked *all around.* Why is the threat so constant? Because fallen human beings inherently value the wrong things: *Because worthlessness is exalted among humanity.* Humans value that which can be described as *worthlessness (zūllûṯ),* that which contributes nothing to society, but only tears down. All of *humanity (liḇ*ᵉ*nê ʾāḏām)* shares this problem. The occurrence of the term *b*ᵉ*nê ʾāḏām* as the last words of both v. 1 and v. 8 rounds off the poem with a fitting inclusion — the poem starts with a complaint that the faithful have disappeared from humanity and ends with the statement that humanity values only that which is worthless.

Reflections

Denying Reality

The human condition seems to come with an incredible temptation to deny reality. The problem with denying reality is not merely that one embraces a delusion in place of that which is true. The problem is also that in the course of denying reality, one almost inevitably does violence to others. The sin of the wicked in Psalm 12 is that in some way they are denying reality. Perhaps they are doing so by falsely accusing the poor. Perhaps they are reneging on a contract or claiming falsely that the poor have not fulfilled their end of a contract. Perhaps they have committed a crime against the poor and simply deny it. Each of these are examples of how denying reality can harm the neighbor. But behind each of these little denials, according to the psalms as a whole and Psalm 12 in particular, is a greater denial — the denial of the Lord's reign. A denial in which the sinner sets up oneself as one's own lord, as the arrogant do in Psalm 12: *Our lips belong to us, who can be our master?* In order to set up the self as lord, one has to deny God's will and God's reign, just as the fool does in Psalm 14.

But though denial of reality is a universal temptation, it is also a rather flimsy foundation on which to base one's life. The chemically dependent person who denies his or her addiction still has the addiction. The problem is still there; denial will not make it go away. The remedy to denial is the truth. And when a person or persons will not hear the truth, it does not make the truth less true or relevant. In Psalm 12, the truth is in God's hands, or even better, in God's word. The denial of God's reign by the oppressors, which leads them to imagine that they can get away with other denials of reality that harm the neighbor, is a flimsy foundation on which to build a case. Against this delusion, God speaks a word that is at once judgment for the oppressor and redemption for the oppressed: *Now shall I arise!* It is only a small phrase. Two words in Hebrew, three in English. But those brief words contain the power to unmask the delusion behind which we live, to reveal the fake wizard behind the curtain who seeks to manipulate and control. Those brief words contain the truth that sets us free — both from our own denial of reality and from those who would oppress us. As Martin Luther wrote, "One little word subdues."

ROLF A. JACOBSON

Psalm 13: Waiting on the Lord

Psalm 13 is used by many form critics as the prime example of the type of psalm known either as a "prayer for help" or an "individual lament."[1] As is the case with most of this type of psalm, the prayer is spoken from a situation of severe crisis, but the specific nature of that crisis is unclear. The original crisis may have been a physical, emotional, social, or economic crisis. But two things are clear. First, the psalmist definitely understands her crisis as a *spiritual and theological* crisis — this is about her relationship with God. Second, the psalm is now available to any believer for reuse in a variety of life situations. Perhaps references to the particular crisis from which this psalm was originally composed were later intentionally obscured in order to make this psalm usable by later sufferers undergoing a variety of crises.

The psalm includes many of the hallmark elements of the prayer for help: the complaint (vv. 1-2), the request for help (vv. 3-4), the affirmation of trust (v. 5), and the vow to praise (v. 6). The structure of the psalm — three stanzas with parallel structures — is quite clear:

St. 1 Complaint in the midst of crisis (vv. 1-2)
St. 2 Request for deliverance from crisis (vv. 3-4)
St. 3 Ongoing faith in the midst of crisis (vv. 5-6)[2]

One important issue that scholars have debated about psalms such as this one has to do with the relationship between the complaint and request elements, on the one hand, and the affirmation-of-trust and vow-to-praise elements, on the other hand. For more on this issue, see below in the commentary.

To the leader. A Davidic psalm.

1 *How long, O Lord, will you constantly forget me?!*
How long will you hide your face[3] *from me?!*
2 *How long must I bear pain*[4] *in my soul,*

1. See, e.g., Westermann, *The Psalms,* pp. 53-59, or Gerstenberger, *Psalms: Part 1,* pp. 83-86.

2. Following the convention in English Bibles of numbering MT v. 6c as v. 6 in English.

3. 4QCatena A lacks the sign of the definite direct object *ʾt.*

4. The translation of the Hebrew *ʿēṣôṯ,* lit., "counsels" or "advice" (based on *ʿṣh* I) presents a difficulty. It has been suggested to amend the text to read *ʿṣbt* ("pain") or *ʿṣbwt* ("hardship"). Kraus notes that the sense of "sorrows" is documented in Prov. 27:9 and Sir. 30:21 (*Psalms 1–59,* p. 212). HALOT lists an *ʿṣh* II with the meaning of "rebellion," but notes that in no instance of the proposed *ʿṣh* II is this meaning absolutely necessary, so this solution is questionable. Craigie (*Psalms 1–50,* p. 140) concludes that "the simplest and most satisfactory solution is to retain [*ʿṣwt*] and translate 'pain.' "

and grief in my heart all day?![5]
How long will my enemy be exalted over me?!

3 *Look! Answer me, O LORD my God!*
Illumine my eyes, lest I sleep the sleep of death![6]
4 *Lest my enemy say, "I have prevailed over him."*[7]
My adversaries rejoice because I am shaken.

5 *But I — in your* hesed *have I trusted,*
and my heart rejoices in your deliverance!
I will sing to the LORD for he has done well for me.[8]

1-2 The first stanza of the psalm contains the psalmist's complaint. As many have noted, the complaint has three elements. First, there is a *theological* element — the "you complaint" against God (v. 1). Second, there is a *personal* element — the "I complaint" about the self (v. 2a). Third, there is a *social* element — the "they complaint" against the enemies (v. 2b). But this division is a bit arbitrary and artificial. The "you complaint" and "they complaint" both contain "I" elements *(hide your face from me, my enemy be exalted over me).* The important point to notice is that personal, social, and theological elements are seamlessly interwoven. From the psalmist's perspective, the relationships that make up his existence cannot be atomized or compartmentalized into separate headings. Rather, the psalmist's problems with his enemies and with his own self are also God's problems. As McCann has aptly stated, "For the psalmist, every experience of the self or the other is also an experience of God."[9] On the basis of this holistic and organic understanding of all of life as being caught up in God, the psalmist cries out to God for deliverance.

The intensity of the crisis from which this prayer is uttered is signaled by the fourfold repetition of the cry, *How long?!* Within this fourfold repetition, there is a staircase effect, by which the volume of the psalmist's cry, as it were, is increased. The simple repetition of the cry *How long* creates

5. The Gk Codex Alexandrinus and Lucianic recensions add "and night," but this is most likely a reflexive addition based on the common couplet "day and night."

6. Lit., "I sleep death." Dahood and others emend the text, which is unnecessary, since the intransitive verb may take an object in a complementary sense (see Waltke and O'Connor, *Biblical Hebrew Syntax,* pp. 161-75).

7. BHS suggests that LXX *(pros auton)* may be reading *yklth lw.* But there is no need for this revision, because pronominal suffixes can carry the sense of "datival accusatives" (see Waltke and O'Connor, p. 169).

8. LXX adds "and I will make psalms to the name of the Lord most high." This harmonizing expansion (cf. Ps. 17:7) is rejected.

9. McCann, "The Book of Psalms," p. 726.

this intensification.[10] Yet the repetition also introduces variety — each *How long* introduces a different complaint, and these complaints mount upon the others to intensify the psalmist's cry. In the opening cry, the psalmist accuses God of having *forgotten me.* The suggestion is that God is guilty of a *passive* sin of omission — God has neglected the psalmist. Yet in the second phrase, the accusation against God is intensified. God is accused here of an *active* sin of commission — *How long will you hide your face from me?!* God has not simply neglected the psalmist but has intentionally withdrawn protection and salvation from him. As Robert Alter notes, the third phrase "translates the general condition of abandonment into the inward experience of the speaker. . . ."[11] The verbal phrasing here also helps to build up the emotion, as the psalmist stretches out the length of the complaint; the first two phrases are five and six words long in Hebrew, respectively. The psalmist stretches out the third phrase to eight words, suggesting that the psalmist's suffering grows worse the longer it continues. In the final phrase of the complaint, the sense of crisis is again increased by the addition of *enemy* to the equation. The psalmist has not simply been abandoned by God, but has been abandoned into the hands of a contrary power. Some scholars understand the enemy in this psalm as death in the abstract sense.[12] While this is a valid way to interpret the psalm today, as the references to plural *adversaries* suggest, it is preferable to understand the enemies as human beings who are opposed to the psalmist and his God. The psalmist's outrage is inflamed by his belief that God has abandoned him into the hands of those who are opposed to God.

3-4 In the second stanza of the poem, the pray-er parallels the structure of the first stanza in two ways. First, there is repetition. This time, however, rather than repeating one phrase *(How long?!),* the psalmist repeats a grammatical form, using three imperative verbs: *look!, answer!,* and *illumine!* Second, the psalmist mirrors the structure of the two stanzas by matching the content of the request to the content of the complaint. The complaint stanza opened with the "you complaint." The request stanza matches this as the psalmist demands, *Look! Answer me, O LORD my God!* Not only is God the focus of the request, just as God was the focus of the complaint in stanza one, but the request to *look* matches the complaint that God had hidden God's *face.* The first stanza continued with the "I complaint"; the second stanza continues with what we might call an "I request": *Illumine my eyes, lest I sleep the sleep of death!* Finally, whereas the "they complaint" closed the first stanza, the second stanza closes with a motivational clause in which the psalmist mentions the enemies: *Lest my enemy say, "I have prevailed over him,"*

10. See Alter, *The Art of Biblical Poetry,* pp. 63-66.
11. Alter, *The Art of Biblical Poetry,* p. 65.
12. See, e.g., Craigie, *Psalms 1–50,* pp. 141-42.

my adversaries rejoice because I am shaken. The mirrored structure might be illustrated in this way:

Stanza 1		*Stanza 2*
"You complaint"	→	"You request"
"I complaint"	→	"I request"
"They complaint"	→	"They request"

It is also worth noting that whereas the first stanza intensified the outcry as has been described, the second stanza follows its own course of development. Each of the three sections of the second stanza contains two parts. The first section is two parts request — *look!* and *answer!* The second section is one part request — *illumine* — and one part motivational clause — *lest I sleep the sleep of death.* The third section is two parts motivational clause — *Lest my enemy say . . . lest my adversaries rejoice.*

The overall mirroring of the complaint and request sections of the psalm once again emphasizes the psalmist's conviction that all of her problems are theological problems. Commenting on vv. 1-2 of the psalm, Kraus concluded that "The real distress in which the petitioner of the psalm utters his groans is the separation from God, that is, his experiencing of the wrath of God."[13] This observation can be extended. Just as the psalmist's real distress is separation from God, her real hope and real trust are the conviction that God also holds the answer to her prayer. If it is true that the psalmist understands that God stands at the center of her crisis, then it is just as true that she sees God as the one who can deliver her from her crisis.

5-6 In the closing stanza of the psalm, the psalmist leaves both the enemies and the situation of crisis behind. In some sense, a corner is turned at the start of v. 5. As the Hebrew grammar indicates with the *wāw* at the start of v. 5, and as most English translations show by rendering the *wāw* as "but," a transition occurs. The psalmist moves now to trust in God's fidelity and praise for God's mercy. The precise reason of this transition from lament to praise is debated. Some scholars imagine that after some supplicant had prayed vv. 1-4, a priest would have arisen to announce that the psalmist's prayer had been heard or to pronounce an actual oracle from the Lord. In this view, the closing stanza of the psalm is a word of praise in response to the priest's message.[14] (See, for example, in 1 Samuel 1 how Hannah first prays for help, then receives a favorable oracle from the priest, and then sings forth in praise.) Another view holds that the praise of vv. 5-6 was a later addition, added only after the psalmist's crisis had passed: "It is a long wait after verse 4, a wait in

13. Kraus, *Psalms 1–59,* p. 213.

14. See Joachim Begrich, "Das priesterliche Heilsorakel," *ZAW* 52 (1934) 81-92.

the darkness of death. . . . Then — we do not know how long the wait was — things are changed."[15] Still another view holds that neither deliverance nor priestly oracle occurs between vv. 4 and 5. Rather, the situation of crisis still remains, but in his heart, the psalmist has come to believe that his prayer has been heard by God. And the simple conviction that God has heard the prayer leads the psalmist to change his lament to a song of praise. "It should be noted that the grief over which the suppliant is lamenting . . . still remains. During the praying of these Psalms no miracle has occurred, but something else has occurred. God has heard and inclined himself to the one praying; God has had mercy on him."[16] It is neither possible nor desirable to still the voices of this debate by imposing one of the above views at the expense of silencing the other views. It is unlikely that we will ever be able to know for sure which, if any, of these interpretations is most faithful to how the psalm was originally written or used. However, one thing is abundantly clear: the psalm, in its current and final form, ends on this note of trust and praise. The closing of the psalm has a sense of looking backward at yesterday, of living with eyes wide open in the now of today, and of gazing ahead hopefully to tomorrow. Looking backwards, the psalmist acknowledges, *in your* hesed *I have trusted.* Of today, she confesses, *my heart rejoices in your salvation.* And of tomorrow, she adds her vow that she *will sing to the LORD*. It is that sort of three-dimensional theological perspective that Psalm 13 engenders in those who pray it still.

Reflections

1. A Model for Prayer

Psalm 13 is a model for prayer. For many in the Western world, the idea of crying out to God in a way that includes accusation and blame is inconsistent with faith. But this has not always been the case, and that notion certainly is not faithful to the biblical model of prayer, especially as embodied in Psalm 13. Psalm 13 teaches not only that we can take all of our burdens to the Lord in prayer, but also that when our very relationship to God seems to be part of the problem we can take even that to God in prayer. That was the case for Jeremiah, who experienced God's call to prophesy as a burden, and so Jeremiah made accusations against God in the strongest possible language (Jer. 20:7-18). That was also the case for Job, who experienced God's delay in ending his suffering as a burden, and likewise made complaints with the choicest of words (see especially Job 3). And that was the case for the psalmist

15. Brueggemann, *The Message of the Psalms,* pp. 59-60.
16. Westermann, *Praise and Lament in the Psalms,* p. 79.

in Psalm 13, who failed to understand why God had turned away and ignored his suffering. But this tradition of lament has not been totally lost in the West. Parts of both Judaism and Christianity preserved it. One of the places where this tradition has been most faithfully preserved is in the African American spirituals. In songs such as "Nobody Knows the Trouble I've Seen," the slaves of the American South did a better job of interpreting the biblical tradition than did the culture that enslaved them. Another place where the prayer for help has been preserved in Western Christianity is in the "Kyrie" section of the liturgical tradition. As the body of Christ gathers, it cries "Lord, have mercy" — acknowledging that all is not right in the world and God's mercy is desperately needed. As Brueggemann has convincingly argued, the lament accusation is not antithetical to a covenant relationship with God, but rather, in a true covenant relationship, the believer *needs* to have the freedom to take up such accusations. "Where there is lament, the believer is able to take initiative with God and so develop over against God the ego-strength that is necessary for responsible faith. But where the capacity to initiate lament is absent . . . [t]he outcome is a 'False Self,' bad faith that is based in fear and guilt and lived out as resentful or self-deceptive works of righteousness. The absence of lament makes a religion of coercive obedience the only possibility."[17] Thus, lament and accusation are not the opposite of faith but part and parcel of it.

2. *The Question of Theodicy*

The theology of Psalm 13 presents some problems to modern people of faith. At the heart of the matter is the deep conviction that God is not removed from suffering, but is intimately bound up with suffering — God is involved both with sufferers and also with the answer to suffering. Some modern interpreters struggle with this way of understanding the world, especially because it can lead to the conclusion that God causes suffering. This may take the form of a sufferer who wonders what he has done to be punished by God, or it may take the form of a sufferer who despairs because he feels abandoned by God. On the other hand, the psalm faces head-on the brute facts about injustice and suffering in the world. It confronts God with the psalmist's experience that things are not right in God's creation. The psalm knows that the way things are is not the way things are supposed to be. The psalm refuses to take a fatalistic or stoic approach to suffering. It confronts God as covenantal partner and demands that God refuse to stay hidden behind the veil of heaven. To this extent, accusing God is the psalmist's way of refusing to despair. It is the psalmist's way of clinging to the promise of salvation.

Rolf A. Jacobson

17. Brueggemann, *The Psalms and the Life of Faith,* pp. 103-4.

Psalm 14: Not a Stop-Gap God

Psalm 14 is been variously classified as a lament, as a prophetic liturgy, or as a psalm of trust, but it is best understood as a poem of instruction. The psalm, which betrays evidence of having been influenced by Israel's wisdom tradition (especially the contrast between the "fool" and those with "insight"), instructs the community of faith about the fool and the fate that awaits those who reject the Lord's will. The instruction it offers is neither about why one should follow the Lord nor how one can follow, but is more of a word of hope which teaches that those who reject God's ways will not triumph in the end. As Goldingay has written, "it constitutes more a kind of statement of faith encouraging people to believe that scoundrels will not win out than a direct attempt to encourage them to be people of insight rather than scoundrels."[1]

The poem features staccato-short lines, with a predominant 3:2 meter, like that of the Hebrew dirge or *qinah* (cf. 2 Sam. 1:19-27; Jer. 9:17-19; Amos 5:1-3).[2] If the song is intended to echo the style of a *qinah,* then it fictively mourns the funeral of the fool who opposes the will of God.

A key question in the interpretation of the psalm revolves around v. 4a, in which the psalm refers to *my people.* Should one understand the speaker as God or simply as the psalmist expressing concern over the suffering of *my people?* One's interpretation of the structure of the psalm hinges on how one resolves that question. Here, the view is that the voice speaking v. 4 is the same as the one speaking in the rest of the psalm — a priest or teacher who feels responsibility for the community. The psalm is understood as having two stanzas — vv. 1-3, 4-7.[3]

Psalms 14 and 53 are nearly identical. Questions regarding the genetic relationship between the two poems and how to resolve the slight textual differences between them are generally unhelpful. The approach taken in this commentary is that the two psalms should be treated as individual, albeit nearly identical, psalms. For that reason, we make no attempt to harmonize the texts of the two psalms or to generate an ur-text that may have existed behind the two. There are two primary differences between the psalms. First, Psalm 14 uses the divine name *YHWH* in vv. 2, 6, and 7, whereas as Psalm 53 employs the more generic *ʾᵉlōhîm* (which is characteristic of the Elohistic

1. Goldingay, *Psalms 1–41,* p. 211.

2. So S. E. Gillingham, *The Poems and Psalms of the Hebrew Bible* (Oxford: Oxford University Press, 1994), p. 65. Kraus, *Psalms 1–59,* sees the meter as more complicated, but agrees that at least vv. 1-2, 4b-6 have the 3:2 meter (p. 220).

3. An alternative understanding of the structure would be to see v. 4 as a separate keystone element, holding together two stanzas: vv. 1-3, 4, 5-7 (thus NRSV).

Psalter). Second, in v. 14:5//53:5, there is a more substantial difference, in which 53:5 reads, *Then they shall be overcome with terror, as has not been; because God will scatter the bones [plans?] of the one encamped against you; he will put them to shame, for God rejected them.* (See the commentary on Psalm 53.)

To the leader. Davidic.

1 *A fool says in the heart, "There is no God."*
They have become corrupt,[4] *they commit abominations;*
there is no one who does good.
2 *The LORD looks down from heaven,*
upon humanity,
To see if there is anyone who has insight,
who seeks God.
3 *Every one has turned aside,*
altogether they have been corrupted.
There is no one who does good;
there is not even one![5]

4 *Do all those who do evil not know,*
those who eat my people?
They eat bread,
they do not call on the LORD.[6]
5 *There they shall be greatly terrified,*
for God is among the generation of the righteous.
6 *The discernment of the poor, you would put to shame,*
but the LORD is their refuge.

4. The verb *hišᵉḥîtû* is a denominative use of the hiphil, "they have become corrupt." In spite of the fact that no object is present, it is also possible that a transitive use is intended, "they corrupt [everything]."

5. LXX includes a lengthy segment that is missing in the Hebrew of both Psalms 14 and 53, but which is present in Rom. 3:13-18. Because the Romans passage seems to have been composed from Pss. 5:9; 140:3; 10:7; Isa. 59:7-8; and Ps. 36:1, one suspects that the extra segment in the LXX is a harmonizing addition from the hands of early Christians.

6. The syntax of the phrase is odd. Gk *brōsei artou* seems to reflect *ʾōḵel,* which does not substantially alter the syntax or help the awkwardness. The general sense is that they have eaten bread in the past and similarly hunger to devour God's people. The last phrase is especially awkward. Does the phrase define who they are (those who do not call on the Lord) or does it define their sin (they do not call on the Lord). The *atnaḥ* divides the verse after the word *bread,* but this later syntactical marker is in this case incorrect. The consistently short phrases throughout the psalm argue for dividing the verse as above.

7 O that the Lord might send
Israel's rescue from Zion!
When the Lord utterly restores his people,
Jacob will rejoice, Israel will be glad.

1-3 It is almost a truism that the first thing that must be said about Psalm 14 is that the phrase *"There is no God"* represents practical rather than theoretical atheism. The point is that in the ancient Near East there was nothing akin to today's atheistic conception that there is no spiritual realm, that no God or gods exist. This view can be seen in various translations of Ps. 14:1, such as that of NJPS, "God does not care," or Goldingay, "God is not here."[7] But far from weakening the psalm's assertion that only a fool takes this position, when one understands that the psalm is targeting practical atheism the psalm packs an even bigger punch. This is so because the psalm's accusatory finger points not only at nonbelievers, but also at every believer whose daily life is shaped by anything less than total conformity to God's will. The attitude that the fool of Psalm 14 expresses toward God is similar to the attitude that the wicked display so often throughout the Psalter (cf. 10:4, 11, 13; 64:5; 94:7; 3:2; 71:11, etc.), namely, that God is not an active presence or power in the world. And that therefore God and God's will are irrelevant when reflecting on one's own behavior, actions, or direction in life.

Psalm 14 identifies this as the belief of the *fool.* A fool is not one who lacks raw intelligence, but rather one who "decides and acts on the basis of the wrong assumption."[8] The fool's mistaken assumption is that God is not an active presence in the world. The psalm is colored by Israel's wisdom tradition, although it should be noted that the word for fool used here is not the normal word that Proverbs uses *(k^e^sîl),* but *nāḇāl* — one who lacks the discipline of self-control (cf. Prov. 30:21-23). The ironically named Nabal in 1 Samuel 25 is a literary type for understanding who the fool is. One feature of the wisdom tradition is a tendency to contrast behaviors and beliefs by means of dualistic comparisons. Although the psalm does not use the most common Hebrew word for one who is wise *(ḥāḵām),* it nevertheless does contrast the fool with one having *insight,* a term which is indeed often translated as one having wisdom (*maśkîl;* cf. Prov. 14:35; 17:2; etc.). The one having insight, unlike the fool, *seeks God.* This is not far from the similar statement in Proverbs that the one having wisdom fears God. To seek God can mean to go to the temple in search of a sign or oracle (cf. Exod. 18:15; 1 Sam. 9:9; Pss. 24:6; 34:4), but more generally in the psalms to seek God is to place God first in one's life and

7. Goldingay, *Psalms 1–41,* p. 212. See also Klaus Seybold's *"Gott is nicht da!"* (*Die Psalmen* [HAT 1/15; Tübingen: Mohr (Siebeck), 1996], p. 65).

8. Mays, *Psalms,* p. 81.

to trust in and rely upon God above all other things (cf. 9:10; 69:32; 105:4). This latter, more general meaning is intended here.

Two poetic flourishes in the first stanza are worth considering. First, the psalm refutes the fool's assertion that God is not an active presence in the world by immediately asserting that God actively watches over the earth and keeps track of human behavior. Second, there is a poetic repetition built upon the Hebrew particle *ʾên*. The fool says, *ʾên ʾᵉlōhîm — There is no God.* But the psalm asserts in both vv. 1b and 3b that, in fact, *ʾên ʿōśēh ṭôḇ — There is no one who does good.* And then the psalm repeats the particle one more time, just for good measure: *ʾên gam ʾeḥāḏ — There is not even one!* This poetic turn of phrase neatly refutes the fool's assumption about the nature of reality.

It is important to recognize that the Old Testament refuses to accept the split between mind and body, between belief and action, which is characteristic of our modern world. For this reason, one who is a fool is not known by one's intellectual processes, but by what one does and does not do. The fool does not do good. The fool turns aside from God's ways and embraces the corruption of creation.

4-7 The second stanza begins with the rhetorical question, *Do all those who do evil not know?* The psalm knows, in fact, that the evil-doers do not know. What do they not know? That *the LORD looks down from heaven . . . to see if there is anyone who has insight.* Once again, the unity of thought and action is presupposed in the Old Testament mind. To know (Hebrew *yāḏaʿ*) is not merely to grant intellectual assent to an idea, but to embody that idea in one's being. To know God's will, for example, is to do God's will (cf. Hos. 4:1-2, 6). The very fact that the wicked do evil deeds shows that they do not know any better. It shows that they do not know the Lord.

The poem further illustrates who the wicked are by employing a harrowing metaphor. The wicked *eat my people.* The prophet Micah also employs the metaphor of devouring God's people in a judgment speech against the rulers of Israel, "who eat the flesh of my people, flay their skin off them, break their bones in pieces, and chop them up like meat in a kettle, like fish in a caldron" (Mic. 3:3). The broader context of Micah helps define the predatory behavior that Psalm 14 condemns by means of the metaphor. What is condemned is the behavior of political and religious leaders who publish glad tidings even though the poor have nothing to eat (3:5) or who fail to establish justice for the lowly (3:9). Such people may have eaten bread, but the fact that they also devour God's people shows that they have not learned the lesson of Deut. 8:3: "one does not live by bread alone, but by every word that comes from the mouth of the LORD."

Psalm 14 now turns to a word that is at the same time both a promise of deliverance and threat of judgment. This promise is the flip of the so-called double wish of the psalms, in which a petitioner asks for rescue from and punishment of the wicked. As Westermann has noted, "part of the afflicted person's supplication for rescue from misery (and a necessary concomitant) was the petition against the enemies. If God heard this petition, then God's hearkening had two sides: if God intervened for the righteous, this was at the same time an intervention against the enemies."[9] Psalm 14 announces precisely such an intervention against those who *would put to shame* the *discernment of the poor.* The Hebrew phrase *ʿᵃṣaṯ ʿānî* is normally translated "counsels of the poor." But *ʿᵃṣaṯ* here does not mean counsels in the sense of plans or advice, which would make little sense. Nor is HALOT's attempt to understand the syntax as "plans against the poor" convincing. Rather, the sense is *discernment,* as is the case in Deut. 32:28, since the opposite of the fool's lack of knowledge is the discernment of those who have insight — namely, *the poor,* which in this case refers to God's suffering people as a whole. The word *šām* can carry a temporal sense — "then" (cf. Pss. 53:5; 66:6; 132:17) — with the idea being that the psalm is announcing God's impending judgment against those who oppress the discerning poor. But the normal sense of the word is a locative sense — *there.* That is the meaning preferable here, especially in light of the exclamation in v. 7: *O that the Lord might send Israel's rescue from Zion! There* refers to Zion, from where God's help will arise. The restoration *(šûḇ šᵉḇûaṯ)* of God's people may refer to the return from exile, but can also refer to a more general restoration of stability and prosperity to the people. Whenever such restorations occur, the psalm literally concludes, the people will *rejoice* and *be glad* (cf. 118:24).

Reflections

1. God of the Oppressed

There is a certain interpretive danger posed by this psalm — the danger that the psalm could be misinterpreted by a smug, self-congratulatory faith community as warrant for concluding that unbelievers are nonreflective, intellectually dishonest people. In truth, both the vice of intellectual dishonesty and the virtue of cerebral reflection are equally distributed throughout all of humanity — among both believers and unbelievers. The psalm does not teach that atheists are all intellectually bankrupt, but rather that those who do not make God a central factor in their everyday lives are making a mistake. And as noted above, people who confess faith in God are often as guilty as anyone else of going about every day without factoring God into the moment-by-moment nitty-gritty of life. And, as the psalm bears witness, one of the tragedies of this false assumption is that it can lead to the suffering of the neighbor.

9. Westermann, *The Psalms,* p. 66.

Regarding this interpretive danger, Mays has insightfully commented that the "psalm could be taken as the self-serving lament over the evil of the world by those who polish their own piety in contrast; but the lament is authentic and bears the hurt of those who suffer from things as they are."[10] People of faith who read this psalm need to remember that its accusation is aimed as much inside the community of faith as it is at those who are outside.

2. *Godlessness in Everyday Life*

The psalm's witness about the danger of failing to connect the dots between God and everyday life was relevant in its ancient context and is even more relevant today. The biblical standard of the first commandment requires that God be at the center of daily life. As Dietrich Bonhoeffer wrote from a prison cell: "God is no stop-gap; he must be recognized at the centre of life, not when we are at the end of our resources; it is his will to be recognized in life, and not only when death comes; in health and vigour, and not only in suffering; in our activities, and not only in sin."[11] But the modern world, in its very intellectual assumptions, has made this impossible:

> God as a working hypothesis in morals, politics, or science, has been surmounted and abolished; and the same thing has happened in philosophy and religion. . . .
>
> And we cannot be honest unless we recognize that we have to live in the world *etsi dues non daretur.* And this is just what we do recognize — before God! God himself compels us to recognize it. So our coming of age leads us to a true recognition of our situation before God. God would have us know that we must live as men who manage our lives without him. The God who is with us is the God who forsakes us (Mark 15:34). The God who lets us live in the world without the working hypothesis of God is the God before whom we stand continually. Before God and with God we live without God. God lets himself be pushed out of the world on to the cross. He is weak and powerless in the world, and that is precisely the way, the only way, in which he is with us and helps us. Matt. 8:17 makes it quite clear that Christ helps us, not by virtue of his omnipotence, but by virtue of his weakness and suffering.[12]

ROLF A. JACOBSON

10. Mays, *Psalms,* p. 81.

11. *Letters and Papers from Prison,* trans. Reginald H. Fuller (London: SCM, 1953), p. 312.

12. Bonhoeffer, *Letters and Papers from Prison,* pp. 360-61.

Psalm 15: In the Presence of God

The majority view of scholars is that Psalm 15 is an entrance liturgy. Some scholars prefer to understand the psalm as a literary poem describing the ethical requirement for entering in the Lord's presence, which was based on the genre of the entrance liturgy (such as Mic. 6:6-8 or Isa. 33:14b-16). For the historian, perhaps the distinction between these two interpretive options is crucial. For the theological interpreter, however, the distinction is practically moot. Whether this is a genuine liturgy or a literary imitation of such, the witness of the poem does not change much. Even if one comes down firmly on the side that the psalm is a genuine liturgy — and this does seem most likely — the exact setting in which the psalm was used still cannot be unearthed. Mowinckel thinks of the enthronement festival.[1] Kraus imagines that "participants in the worship stand at the portals of the [Jerusalem temple] worship area and ask the question: 'O Yahweh, who may sojourn in your tent, who may dwell on your holy hill?' From the inside a priestly speaker answers them with the declaration of the conditions of entrance. . . ."[2] But who were the worshippers? The laity did not go inside the temple, so were they Levites in worship procession (Psalm 24)? Were they pilgrims arriving at the temple to fulfill the commands of Exod. 23:14-19? Were they fugitives who had come to seek asylum in the sanctuary (Exod. 21:12-14)? Were they God-fearers who approached in order to consult a priest about God's will (cf. Zech. 7:1-14; Hag. 2:1-9)? Were they worshippers who had passed through a time of crisis and now had come to fulfill the vows of praise that they had uttered when they were in despair (cf. Pss. 40:1-10; 118:19-27)? Or was the worship setting not the temple, but some later synagogue, as Gerstenberger would have it? "The total lack of any ritual requirement virtually excludes" the possibility that this is a genuine liturgy between pilgrim and priest at the temple, so he imagines a later "nonsacrificial, 'ethical' worship of the early Jewish community."[3] In a similar vein, who was the "liturgist" of the liturgy? A Levitical priest (Psalm 24)? Or a choir (118:3)? A prophet (cf. Mic. 6:6-8; Isa. 33:14b-16)? A later synagogal leader? Did the liturgist speak v. 1 and the petitioners/choir answer with vv. 2-5b, or the opposite?

We must admit that the original setting and use of this psalm have been buried and, like Moses, the burial site is unknown. But the psalm still speaks a clear and intelligible message about what is required of those who would enter into God's presence. When read against the background of the penta-

1. *The Psalms in Israel's Worship*, 1:179-80, 86.

2. *Psalms 1–59*, p. 227.

3. *Psalms: Part 1*, p. 88.

teuchal law, the most striking part of its witness (as we shall see) is that the requirements are strictly ethical, with no cultic overtones whatsoever.

The structure of the psalm is clear: 1) Question (v. 1); 2) Response (vv. 2-5b); 3) Promise (v. 5c). (This threefold structure can also be seen in the entrance liturgies in Isa. 33:14b-16 and Ps. 24:3-6.)

A Davidic psalm.

1 *LORD, who may sojourn in your tent?*
Who may dwell on your holy mountain?

2 *The one who walks in integrity,*
who does what is right,
who speaks truth from the heart.
3 *The one who does not slander with the tongue,*
who does not do the neighbor harm,
who does not taunt a neighbor.
4 *In whose eyes the evildoer is despised and rejected,*[4]
who honors those who fear the LORD,
who makes a vow and does not recant.
5 *Who does not earn money through usury,*
or take a bribe against the innocent.

The one who does these things will never be moved.

1 The opening, double question of the psalm inquires regarding who may enter into God's presence. The references to *your tent* (*bᵉʾoholeḵā;* cf. 61:4; 91:10) and *your holy mountain* (*har qoḏšeḵā;* cf. 2:6; 43:3; 48:1; Isa 11:9; 56:7) positively identify the location as the temple. The concept of the *tent* as God's abode predated the temple, reflecting the tradition of the ark being kept in the tabernacle, but the term continued in use even after the more permanent temple was built. The reference to the mountain (cf. 48:1) — Zion in Jerusalem — assures that the psalm has the temple complex in mind.

Interpreters should take care not to overread meaning into the verbs *gûr (sojourn)* and *šāḵan (dwell)*. The petitioner is not asking to dwell perma-

4. The verse is corrupt. We read *lᵉhāraʿ* here, with LXX's *ponēreuomenos,* assuming that the occurrence later in the verse has been misplaced, since it makes little sense there ("he has sworn to do harm). The verse might literally be rendered, "he is despised in his eyes and he is rejected." But in whose eyes? In God's eyes? This reading (cf. Gerstenberg, *Psalms: Part 1,* p. 87) is syntactically awkward. In the psalmist's own eyes? The idea of the *odium sui* is both anachronistic and awkward in the context, which focuses on how one treats the neighbor. The LXX reading is preferred.

nently in the temple — nobody dwelt permanently in the temple, although the practice may have been known at other sanctuaries (cf. 1 Sam. 3:1-9). And Kraus states too much when he maintains that the words "refer to the conception that the participant in worship who has been admitted to the sanctuary is under the protection of God."[5] The words do not indicate that a person was seeking asylum in the temple. Rather, they reflect the belief that God's presence transforms a space from profane to sacred, and that this change has ramifications concerning who may enter that space. This concept is reflected in the story of God's appearances to Moses (Exod. 3:1-6) and Isaiah (Isa. 6:1-6), as well as Isaiah's reference to God's presence as "the devouring fire" and "everlasting flames" (Isa. 33:14) and a number of theophanic references in the psalms (cf. Pss. 18, 68, 144, etc.). But the closest parallels to Psalm 15 are probably Psalm 24, another entrance liturgy, as well as Psalms 51, 81, and 95 — three liturgical-festival psalms that feature moral exhortation in the midst of the mutual comings of the people into God's presence and God into the people's presence (cf. 51:15-18; 81:9; 95:9).

2-5b The answer that the psalm voices to the question of who may enter into God's presence is somewhat surprising in the light of both the biblical and ancient Near Eastern contexts.[6] What is unusual — or at least slightly surprising — is that the psalm focuses exclusively on the moral requirements to the complete exclusion of cultic, physical, or sacrificial requirements. In Deut. 23:1-6 and Lev. 21:17-21, by comparison, the emphasis is on physical requirements and exclusions. Here — as also in Isa. 33:14b-16; Ps. 24:1-3; and Mic. 6:6-8 — the requirements are described in strictly ethical terms. Purity here is transformed from a ritually-based requirement to an ethically-based one.

Many interpreters make a great deal out of an analysis of the text that recognizes ten different stipulations in the psalm.[7] According to this analysis, there are ten balanced, short phrases: three positive requirements (v. 2; the verbs are all participles), three negative requirements (v. 3; the verbs are all negated perfects), two positive requirements (v. 4; the verbs are niphal imperfects), two negative requirements (v. 5; the verbs are negated perfect). There are three problems with this analysis. First, it obscures the fact that the

5. Kraus, *Psalms 1–59,* p. 228.

6. There are many examples of requirements for a person to enter a temple from Israel's neighbors. E.g., a parallel from the Egyptian temple of Edfu states: "and everyone who may enter through this door: that he avoid entering with impurity" (see Gerstenberger, *Psalms: Part 1,* p. 88). Or again, among the examples cited by Kraus: "Who enters here should be clean, and he should cleanse himself the way he cleanses himself for the temple of the great god" (*Psalms 1–59,* p. 227; see more examples there).

7. See, e.g., Craigie and Tate (*Psalms 1-50,* p. 150), Broyles (*Psalms,* pp. 91-92), or Mowinckel (*The Psalms in Israel's Worship,* 1:179-80).

second half of v. 4b includes includes a negative: . . . *does not recant.* Second, this way of numbering the phrases is internally inconsistent, because in vv. 2, 3 and 5 it counts each colon as an independent phrase, but in v. 4 it combines four cola into two phrases. Third, this way of numbering the restrictions does not take into account the parallelism of the poetry. If the question of v. 1 is considered a dual question rather than two questions, should not the same logic govern how one enumerates the parallel phrases of vv. 2-5? The psalm should not be considered a Decalogue of any kind. This does not lessen the significance of the psalm's moral witness; rather, it insists that the psalm's witness be heard in its own right, instead of being drowned out by a comparison to the Decalogue.

The overall theme of the psalm's ethical witness is that Israel's Lord refuses to isolate God's relationship with you from your relationship with your neighbor. To put this another way, when the Lord extends an invitation for a person to enter the sacred space, God insists that one's neighbors are also invited. The first two requirements are holistic terms that encompass the entire life of one who obediently follows the Lord's way. The term *tāmîm,* translated *integrity,* literally means something like "all encompassing."[8] It suggests that a life lived in the Lord's sphere of influence is completely dominated and saturated by God's will. To cleanse one's hands ritually before entering the temple is not enough. All of life must become part of one's relationship with God. The second phrase, *does what is right* or "does righteousness" *(pō'ēl ṣeḏeq)* is an active description of one whose life conforms with God's will. To perform *ṣeḏeq* is to match one's deeds to God's will. In Isa. 1:21 the term describes God's will for how the people as a whole should conduct themselves. In Isa. 11:5 the term describes the reign that the ideal Davidic king would inaugurate.

The next phrases revolve around the weal and ill that a person can achieve via speech. To speak *truth from the heart* (*bilᵉḇāḇô;* cf. the fool in 14:1) does not refer in this case to one's interior thoughts, but refers to a person whose speech is both pure and a pure reflection of one's internal character. The phrase carries a double meaning. Those who enter God's presence are both sincere in how they speak and are peaceful in what they say. The next three phrases all posit negative restrictions, especially in terms of a person's speech. God's people do not *slander* or *taunt a neighbor.* The Hebrew idiom *ḥerpâ lō' nāśā' 'al qᵉrōḇô,* literally, "a taunt he does not lift against his neighbor," refers to uttering a *ḥerpâ* against someone. Our culture does not have a word that can adequately convey the power of *ḥerpâ,* which is often translated as "taunt" or "reproach." The Hebrew term is far weightier than that communicated by the English "taunt" or "reproach." It carries a sense of social shame and rejection that is highly odious. To utter a *ḥerpâ* against the neighbor is to

8. See McCann, *A Theological Introduction to the Book of Psalms,* p. 28.

compromise a person's participation in society and thus to rob one of access to the basic structures of communal life.

The syntax of v. 4 is awkward, and the text is likely corrupt (see translation note 6). The sense of the first two phrases is that the person who enters God's presence is expected to reject those behaviors that God rejects and embrace those behaviors that God embraces. While this may strike modern readers as a self-righteous attitude, there is nevertheless a very serious value being named here. If a society ignores, tolerates, or actively embraces violent and oppressive behaviors, that society is in effect sanctioning oppression. The society that turns a deaf ear to battered women, for instance, is a society that in effect licenses the abuse of women. Because life in God's community is about the welfare of the neighbor, one cannot simply look to one's own person and house. One bears a constant and all-encompassing duty to the neighbor. The restrictions in v. 4c regarding not *recanting on a vow* and v. 5b against *taking a bribe* further sharpen the psalm's emphasis on sins of the tongue. The law against taking of bribes was among Israel's most important proscriptions (Deut. 27:25). Taking bribes and bearing false testimony in public juridical situations went hand in hand, as the legislation in the Pentateuch attests (see Exod. 23:6-8). Understood more broadly, the psalm's overall insistence on speaking uprightly and avoiding crimes of the tongue go to the requirements for creating a trustworthy world. The world God is fashioning is at its foundations trustworthy. Speech is irenic, filled with integrity, and promises are kept. The command against *usury* in v. 5a is not a general command against taking interest, but against predatory interest, which was a widely attested problem in the ancient Near East. Interest rates of 33 and 50 percent are attested. Against this background, the biblical commands regarding loans can be seen as laws working to create a trustworthy world. These laws specify that lenders must lend to those in need, that loans were forgiven every seven years (Deuteronomy 15), that in exchange for a loan only a pledge could be received, and that items taken in pledge could not include items essential for life and could not be kept overnight (Deut. 24:6-13).

5c The last line of the psalm utters a promise regarding those who do *these things.* Goldingay has argued that the last line of the psalm is not a promise; he translates the phrase as "one who does these things, never faltering." "The last line rather emphasizes the need to stand firm in doing 'these things.' . . ."[9] But the occurrences of *môṭ* in Pss. 112:6 and 125:1 argue strongly for considering this a promise, as do the parallel promises that occur in the entrance liturgies of Isa. 33:14b-16 and Ps. 24:1-3. The promise, as is the case with many of the promises in the psalms (cf. Psalm 91), appears overly general and, in fact, too encompassing. Will those who do this really never suffer any

9. Goldingay, *Psalms 1–41*, p. 223.

ill? Surely the remainder of the Psalter argues against such an interpretation. Nor would the psalmists have understood the promise in that sense. Rather, the promise is that those who walk in the integrity of God's law found their lives on the most sound bedrock and foundation possible. Suffering and death come for all, but for those who live in God's presence, the shadows of earth become thin.

Reflections

The Presence of God

Psalm 15 is an entrance liturgy to the temple. In Israel's faith, the temple was the abode of God (Ps. 46:4), the place where God's name was made to dwell (Deut. 16:6). The temple was the intersection between heaven and earth, where the two realms overlapped and shared space. God was seen as dwelling in heaven (Pss. 115:3; 14:2) as well as being present throughout creation (139:7-12), but God's spirit was seen as being specially revealed and available in the temple. Seen against this background, the disturbing and transforming aspect of the witness of Psalm 15 is the liturgy's insistence that all of life is lived within the sphere of God's will. The requirement to enter into the one, holy space of God is that one live everywhere in a manner consistent with the welfare of the neighbor — whom the Lord loves just as much as the Lord loves you. People of all cultures and times are aware that when one enters into the presence of a powerful lord or leader, one pays a special attention to decorum. One dresses well, cleans up, and watches one's manners. The surprise, then, is that fussing with such issues of decorum is practically irrelevant when it comes to God's presence. What God demands is that one treats the neighbor with the utmost respect, not that one give a lip-service respect to the temple compound. In the New Testament, Jesus says nothing new, then, when he teaches, "when you are offering your gift at the altar, if you remember that your brother or sister has something against you, leave your gift there before the altar and go; first be reconciled to your brother or sister, and then come and offer your gift" (Matt. 5:23-24). The New Testament, in fact, insists that every believer is a temple of the Holy Spirit (1 Cor. 6:19). God's presence is realized wherever two or three gather in Christ's name. How should these two or three behave, given that merely by gathering together they are in the presence of God? By walking in integrity, doing what is right, speaking truth from the heart. . . .

ROLF A. JACOBSON

Psalm 16: You Are My Lord

Psalm 16 is a song of trust and confession of faith. Although the opening phrase is reminiscent of the appeals that often begin prayers for help, the appeal functions here as a confession of trust rather than as a literal appeal.[1] The sense of trust and confession continues through the poem, especially in vv. 4 (in which the psalmist rejects false ways), 5-6 (in which the psalmist testifies to blessings received), and 10-11 (in which the psalmist expresses confidence in God's continued guidance). The identity of the psalmist is widely debated, but based on a number of terms that are closely related to the Levitical priesthood (see below), the interpretation here views the psalmist as a priest.[2] Although some scholars prefer to understand the psalmist more generally (seeing the references to sacrificial elements as representing the gifts of the pilgrim one supposes),[3] the comparatively higher literacy rate among priests is a further argument in support of interpreting the psalmist as a priest. No firm setting can be established. The opening confession of the Lord as refuge (cf. 7:1; 11:1; 25:20; 31:1; 71:1; 141:8; 144:2) is a general confession of faith rather than a specific appeal for asylum. The interpretation of the speaker as a priest as well as the references to both rituals (v. 4) and God's presence (v. 11) lead one to identify the psalm with the temple (or at least with a cultic site; Gary Rendsburg's view that the psalm has northern origins would rule out a narrow identification with the temple[4]).

The structure of the psalm is fairly straightforward, being built upon short stanzas mainly of two verses each:

St. 1 Opening statement of faith in the Lord (vv. 1-2)
St. 2 Description of those with whom the psalmist does and does not identify (vv. 3-4)
St. 3 Testimony of blessing (vv. 5-6)
St. 4 Hymnlike section of praise (vv. 7-8)
St. 5 Closing stanza of trust (vv. 9-11)

1. So also Clifford (*Psalms 1–72*, p. 97) and Goldingay (*Psalms 1–41*, p. 227).

2. See Raymond Jacques Tournay, "A propos de Psaume 16,1-4," *RB* 108 (2001) 21-25; Kraus, *Psalms 1–59*, p. 235.

3. See, e.g., Goldingay, *Psalms 1–41*, pp. 226-34; compare with Clifford.

4. *Linguistic Evidence for the Northern Origin of Selected Psalms* (SBLMS 43; Atlanta: Scholars, 1990), pp. 29-33).

Psalm 16

A Davidic miktam.[5]

1 *Keep me, O God, for I take refuge in you.*
2 *I say*[6] *to the* Lord, *"You are my lord,*
my welfare indeed[7] *is in you."*

3 *Regarding the holy ones, those who are in the land.*
They are my mighty ones, all my delight is in them.[8]
4 *They have multiplied*[9] *their sorrows, they have hurried after another (god).*[10]
I will not pour out their drink offerings of blood,
and I will not take their names upon my lips.

5. The meaning of the term *mik̠tām,* which appears in the superscriptions of Pss 16, 56, 57, 58, 59, and 60, is unknown. The LXX renders the term with *stēlographia* ("inscription"). This translation may reflect a reading of *mik̠tāb̠* ("inscription" or "written document"; cf. Exod. 32:16; 2 Chr. 21:12). This interpretation is somewhat supported by the Aramaic *mik̠tāb̠* ("writing utensil"). Although this is the most likely solution, others exist. Another option is to relate the term to a root *ktm* (Jer. 2:22), which may mean "ink" or "dye" (HALOT cites Arabic *katam* as a plant used to dye hair, and there is Akkadian *katāmu,* "to cover/conceal"), thus rendering something such as "an inking [article of writing]" or, alternatively in some scholars' view, "an atonement psalm" (but this seems unlikely). Equally unlikely is the idea relating the term to the root *ket̠em* ("gold") and thus "a golden psalm." The psalms to which the term is affixed also offer little clue as to what it may have meant. Pss. 56–60 share some traits (they seem to be prayers for help). The occurrence of the term in Psalm 16's superscription does not support the interpretation that it is a term identifying the psalm's genre.

6. Reading *ʾāmartî* with LXX and Syr, in place of MT's *ʾāmart,* "you (2fs) say."

7. *bal* can either be a negative particle or an intensifying particle, "indeed" (cf. Prov. 19:23). Here the intensifying function is used (with Craigie, *Psalms 1–50,* p. 155).

8. The verse is problematic and many reconstructions have been proposed, without a consensus being reached. LXX "For the saints who are in his land, he has magnified all his pleasure in them." The opening plural noun *liqᵉd̠ôšîm* is taken as parallel to *lYHWH* in v. 2; the psalmist speaks to the Lord and then about the holy in the land. LXX's suggestion of a 3ms suffix is declined. The plural construct form *wᵉʾaddîrê* makes little sense. LXX reads a verbal form, as Goldingay suggests, conflating the verse with Isa 42:21 (*Psalms 1–41,* p. 226). The least intrusive solution is to point the ending as a 1cs suffix *(-ay),* "my mighty ones" (see Craigie, *Psalms 1–50,* p. 155).

9. It may be that we should relate *ʿaṣṣᵉb̠ôt̠ām* to *ʿṣb* ("false god"), rather than to *ʿṣb* ("hurt"), in which case the translation would be "They multiply their idols, they hurry after [them]."

10. The meaning of *māhārû* is uncertain. Cf. Arabic *maharu,* "to give a dowry," a meaning similar to which is reflected in Exod. 22:16. Some interpreters try to make the sense here "to acquire another (god)," but admit that this reading challenges the lexicography. The basic meaning of *māhār* is "to hasten"; *ʾaḥēr* can carry the sense of "after" (thus LXX) or "another (god?)" (cf. Isa. 42:8). In context, the phrase is clearly describing undesirable, even harmful, behavior, such as hastening after foreign gods. That sense is preferred.

5 *O Lord, my assigned portion and my cup,*
you hold my lot.
6 *The boundaries have fallen for me pleasantly.*[11]
Indeed, my inheritance is pleasing.
7 *I bless the Lord, who counsels me;*
even at night my conscience chastens me.
8 *I keep the Lord before me continually,*
because he is at my right hand, I shall not be moved.

9 *Therefore, my heart is glad and my glory rejoices,*
even my body dwells securely.
10 *For you will not abandon my soul to Sheol,*
you will not allow your faithful one to see the pit.
11 *You show me the path of life.*
In your presence there is complete gladness,
everlasting pleasures at your right hand.

1-2 As noted above, the opening appeal functions here as a confession of trust in God's providential guidance, rather than as an appeal for God to intervene. The request *keep me (šām*ᵉ*rēnî)* does not reflect a specific life situation or speaker, but rather indicates God's more general protecting guidance (cf. Pss. 17:8; 121:3-8; 140:4; 141:9; Gen. 28:15, etc.). Paradoxically, when paired with the concept of God as refuge (cf. 7:1; 11:1; 25:20; 31:1; 61:4; 71:1; 141:8; 144:2, etc.), the image of God as keeper projects the promise of God's guiding and protecting power extending far beyond the temple compound. Because one's refuge is the omnipresent God (rather than a literal, physical fortress or stronghold), the shadow of God's protection extends over one no matter where the road of life leads (121:3-8; 139:7-12). The twin concepts of keeping and refuge, furthermore, suggest the looming presence of a genuine threat to the psalmist and/or her community. This looming threat is a characteristic element of the psalm of trust — it is precisely the presence of the threat that makes a confession of trust meaningful (see the dark valley of Psalm 23, the encamped armies of Psalm 27, or the tumultuous sea of Psalm 46).

The confession *I say to the Lord, "You are my lord"* (cf. 31:14; 140:6; cf. 142:5) is an emphatic confession of faith, which goes one step beyond the common confession, "You are my God/lord" (cf. 22:10; 25:5; 43:2; 63:1; 86:2, 5, 15; 118:28). The emphatic element especially sets off the psalmist's confession as opposed to those who surround the psalmist, who do not share

11. The plural form here indicates the abstract concept, lit., "with pleasantness," thus *pleasantly.*

in this confession.[12] This emphatic confession of faith is further accented in the second phrase of v. 2, *my welfare indeed is in you.* The Hebrew particle *bal* is interpreted here as a positive emphatic. Others interpret the particle in its negative sense and translate the phrase *bal ʿālêḵā* as "not apart from you," and thus "with you alone." Either way, the psalmist is clearly confessing that she trusts and finds goodness in God alone. As Kraus has aptly commented, "we are to notice and to consider how emphatically the formulation 'with you alone' corresponds to the exclusive demand of the First Commandment."[13] That is, the psalmist not only trusts in the Lord, she trusts in the Lord alone. She spurns the culturally attractive sin of syncretism — worshipping not only the Lord on the Sabbath, but Baal, Asherah, and El on their holy days.

3-4 The interpretation of vv. 3-4 is disputed and, we shall have to admit, even the translation of these verses is less than clear. In v. 3, the primary question revolves around how one should construe the identity of *the holy ones (līqᵉḏôšîm)* and *mighty ones* (*ʾaddîrê,* as the consonantal text of MT is revocalized here). Some modern scholars, such as Clifford and Seybold, follow an older tradition of identifying them as heavenly beings who rebel against the Lord's counsel: "it is more likely that the holy and mighty ones are gods (as in Ps 89:7 and 1 Sam 4:8) whom the pray-er rejects (as in NAB and NJPS)."[14] But *qᵉḏôšîm* seems to carry the positive connotation of those in good favor with the Lord, even where it applies to heavenly beings. And the phrase *all my delight is in them* is difficult to reconcile with the notion of heavenly beings who rebel against God's will. It is most likely that the *holy ones* and *mighty ones* refer to the company of faithful Yahweh-worshippers with whom the psalmist is in community. Thus, in v. 3 the psalmist names those people with whom a relationship is affirmed, while in v. 4 the psalmist names those people with whom affinity is rejected.

The translation and interpretation of v. 4 are even more disputed than those of v. 3 (see translation notes). The syntax of v. 4a is difficult and likely is disturbed. As the text stands, v. 4 is a tricola, which is slightly out of the pattern for the psalm, so one wonders whether a colon dropped out — especially given that vv. 4b and 4c would form a tightly constructed bicolon — *I will not pour out their drink offerings of blood, And I will not take their names upon my lips.* But vv. 1-2 and v. 11, respectively, are tricola, so the disturbance is not glaring. Overall, the interpretation offered here is that in v. 4 the psalmist describes either those who worship other gods in addition to the Lord (syncretists) or those who worship other gods exclusively. Such people *have multiplied their sorrows,* because the petty and tyrannical gods that they worship

12. Cf. Jacobson, *Many Are Saying,* p. 68.

13. *Psalms 1–59,* p. 236.

14. Clifford, *Psalms 1–72,* p. 97; Seybold, *Die Psalmen,* p. 71.

require disturbing and even violent ritual practices. This is probably what is meant by the *drink offerings of blood* that the psalmist refuses to *pour out.* As Psalm 106 describes, "They worshipped their idols [*ʿăṣabbêhem;* cf. translation note above]. . . . They sacrificed their sons, and their daughters to demons; they shed [poured out] innocent blood" (vv. 36-38). The psalmist refuses to take the names of false gods on his lips and refuses to associate with those who engage in bloody worship practices. (On child sacrifice in Israel, see also Lev. 20:3; 2 Kgs. 16:3; 21:6; Isa. 66:3.) Perhaps the psalmist is distinguishing himself from other priests who are willing to blend worship of the Lord with that of other gods. More likely, the psalmist is completely disassociating himself from those other gods and their worshippers. In spite of the translation difficulties in these verses, the overall impression of the passage is clear. As Clifford writes, "The textually damaged verse 3 is not a major hindrance to understanding the poem. Verses 1-2 and 4 are comprehensible without it: The poet is choosing the Lord and rejecting other gods."[15]

5-6 The next four verses comprise a stanza of trust and a stanza of praise, both of which function as the psalmist's confession of faith. In the trust-filled vv. 5-6, the psalmist piles up a series of technical terms that draw one to conclude that the psalmist is a Levitical priest: *portion, lot, boundaries,* and *inheritance* describe the distribution of the land among God's people. The tribe of Levi, notably, was given no land as its *inheritance;* the tithes and offerings of the land (Lev. 6:16-18) and the Lord (Num. 18:20) are described as their *portion* (on the distribution of the land, see also Josh. 13:14, 33; 14:4). The term *cup* symbolizes the abundance of God's gifts (cf. Ps. 23:5) and also indicates Israel's ritual thanksgiving celebrations (cf. Ps 116:13). The term makes one think of the ritual duties of a priest, as does the reference in v. 4 to the psalmist refusing to *pour out their drink offerings of blood.*

The psalmist's confession of faith is difficult to hear, because of the intervening centuries, which insulate our ears against hearing the psalmist's voice. Today, land is just one more commodity that is traded. In the ancient world, however, land was the means of generating wealth and the means of sustaining life. To be born into a landless class or caste might have been experienced as something far from a blessing. Ironically and powerfully, then, the psalmist, who has inherited no land and thus no literal boundaries, is able to confess, *The boundaries have fallen for me pleasantly.* The reason the psalmist can confess this as a blessing is that the Lord, the very God of Israel, is the psalmist's portion and inheritance. The relationship that the psalmist has with God is the psalmist's all — the portion, cup, lot, boundary, and inheritance.

7-8 The psalmist continues his confession of faith with a brief stanza of praise. Specifically, the psalmist praises God for God's *counsel.* Some have

15. Clifford, *Psalms 1–72,* p. 96.

interpreted the term *counsel (yāʿaṣ)* here as referring to a priestly oracle that the singer of the psalm has received in response to seeking asylum in the temple.[16] But the term can refer either to the plots or plans that one makes (cf. Ps. 83:3-5) or to advice or counsel that one offers (32:8). The psalm later references the *path of life* (*ʾōraḥ ḥayyîm,* v. 11), which in Prov. 5:6 and 15:24 refers to the ways in which the wise live and represents the opposite of the path to Sheol. It is best to understand the *counsel* of Psalm 16 as referring to advice or even laws about how to live. The psalmist praises God because of the experience of having been guided through life by God's good and gracious law. Without this counsel, the psalmist might have wandered blindly down the path to destruction. The concepts of *counsel* and *conscience* go hand-in-hand. By *my conscience (kilyôṯāy),* literally "my kidneys," is meant the organ of emotion or feeling. In modern culture, guilt has so often bordered on the narcissistic that the value of discipline and being aware of one's flaws is obscured. God's counsel is efficacious when the conscience becomes aware of shortcomings and the sinner is driven to repent by seeking forgiveness and seeking renewal (cf. Deut. 8:5-6).

The assurance that a person *shall not be moved (bal ʾemmôṭ)* is a statement of confidence that can reflect either positive or negative spiritual orientation, depending on whether the individual is basing this confidence on God (cf. 15:5) or on the self (cf. 30:6). Here, the positive connotation is intended, because the psalmist trusts in the external grace of the Lord, who is *before me continually* and *is at my right hand.*

9-11 The psalm crescendos in a fitting stanza of trust. V. 9 sums up the psalmist's embodiment of the Lord's salvation. *Heart* and *body* (or "flesh," *bāśār*) combine to represent the totality of the psalmist's life. God's deliverance is not merely an intellectual matter for the mind, or a spiritual matter for faith, but a reality in which the entirety of the self partakes. The terms *is glad (gîl)* and *rejoice (śāmaḥ)* form a regular pair (cf. also 31:7; 118:24; note that *śāmaḥ* also occurs in v. 11). Perhaps the pairing here indicates that the psalmist is singing or intends to sing a formal song of thanksgiving in response to an experience of God's deliverance. The confession in v. 10 is the negative counterpart to what was confessed in vv. 7-8. God, stated positively, gives the psalmist the counsel and guidance so that the psalmist is secure. God, stated negatively, does not allow the psalmist to go down to Sheol or *see the pit.*

The psalm ends with a tricolon, just as it opened with one. As mentioned above, the phrase *path of life* may indicate communion with God in the temple. In support of this, the reference to God's *presence* in v. 11b can be taken as a reference to God's dwelling in the temple. However, the *path of life*

16. Cf. Kraus, *Psalms 1–59,* p. 238; Joachim Begrich, "Das priesterliche Heilsorakel," *ZAW* 52 (1934) 81-92.

also occurs in Prov. 2:9; 5:6; 10:17; 12:28; and 15:24, so the direct connection with the temple is not necessary. Rather, the role of the priest as a teacher of the people (cf. Hos. 4:4-10) is in mind here. The priest is only able to show the path of life to others because God has first shown and guided the priest along the path to begin with.

Reflections

My Portion and Cup

The countercultural confession of faith and trust that is found in Psalm 16 resonates deeply, precisely because the values that it expresses are so profoundly dissonant with our culture. For one who has been bequeathed no tangible *inheritance* and been born into no *boundaries* to confess, nevertheless, that *my inheritance is pleasing* and *the boundaries have fallen for me pleasantly* is astonishing, both for the psalm's rejection of the primary cultural values of wealth and self-sufficiency and in its embrace of the lordship of God and acceptance of God's promises of guidance and care. The psalmist here grasps firmly onto God's promises in a way that King Ahaz in Isaiah 7 could not. In that case, the king wanted the promise of assurance from God without the costly necessity of relinquishing personal independence or the insurance policy of relying on the help of Babylon.

The psalmist of Psalm 16, moreover, rejects the syncretistic and worldly values of the gods of Canaan, whose rituals included, according to the Old Testament, such horrendous practices as child sacrifice. To be sure, both the Christian and Jewish faiths that have inherited the promises of the Old Testament have themselves been guilty of horrendous crimes in the name of faith and the name of God. This has been especially the case in the Christian tradition, which has often found itself deeply entangled with political and military leadership. Moreover, there are few or no — thanks be to God — religions today that would actively promote harm to children as a part of ritual adherence (although child abuse in the name of faith is still a global problem, including for Christians). So in order to confess with Psalm 16 that *I will not pour out their drink offerings of blood,* the modern disciple needs to be able to confess this not merely over against the extinct worship cults of Canaan, but also over against the still extant violent ideologies that constantly spring up in the name of the Lord and in the name of Jesus. Psalm 16 teaches us that to confess that *"You are my LORD"* one also must be ready to say to anyone who would do violence in the name of keeping God, "No, I will not pour out your drink offerings of blood."

ROLF A. JACOBSON

Psalm 17: The Embodiment of a Legitimate Prayer

Psalm 17 is a prayer for help, as the term *t^e^pillâ (a prayer)* in the superscription indicates. The term encompasses individual prayers for help (as is the case here) and communal prayers for help (as in Psalm 80, *t^e^pillaṯ ʿammeḵā* [v. 4]). As Gerstenberger notes, the term "comes close to being a technical term for 'psalm of complaint and petition.'"[1] The threefold convergence in this psalm of a strong assertion of innocence by the psalmist (vv. 3-5), a complaint against the enemies (vv. 9-14), and hints that the psalmist may be seeking asylum in the temple (indicated by the metaphorical language for God's presence such as *your face* [vv. 2, 15] and *shadow of your wings* [v. 8]) have led some to define this poem as the prayer of one who has been falsely accused.[2] In this light, the terms *try, test,* and *visit* in v. 3 are often taken to indicate that an overnight ritual ordeal may have accompanied the psalm (cf. Num. 5:11-31). Kraus, for example, sees the situation of the psalm as that of an individual who, "persecuted and surrounded by enemies . . . [and] seeking protection accordingly awaits the verdict of Yahweh in the cultic institution of the divine dispensation of judgment."[3] While this argument is plausible, the psalm's interpretation should not be limited to such a setting. As Kraus notes, it is especially striking that "in the collection of the Psalms no actual rituals are transmitted. Research oriented toward the cultus has a limitation here which precisely then should not be exceeded or forgotten when in a synthetic process conclusions are drawn and issues are reconstructed."[4] Moreover, metaphors that symbolize God's protection (*wings, face, eyes,* etc.) or that symbolize threat and rescue (night and morning, vv. 3, 15) are too universal to be narrowly associated with the temple. That is to say, these metaphors can be said to have been derived from the temple, but they can also be said to have been derived from the experiences of daily life. The poem is most fruitfully interpreted as the prayer of any desperate individual who desires protection from imminent persecution.

The structure of the psalm is debated, but one detects in the psalm's developing argument a threefold movement that reinforces the central plea of the psalm. The psalm has three sections of plea (vv. 1-2, 6-9, 13-14), each of which is supported by a characteristic element of a prayer for help: a protestation of innocence supports the first plea (vv. 3-5), a complaint against the enemy supports the second plea (vv. 10-12), and a succinct declaration of trust supports the final plea (v. 15).

1. Gerstenberger, *Psalms: Part 1,* p. 93.
2. See references in Gerstenberger, *Psalms: Part 1,* pp. 94-95.
3. Kraus, *Psalms 1–59,* p. 245.
4. Kraus, *Psalms 1–59,* p. 246.

St. 1 First plea (vv. 1-2)
St. 2 Support in the form a protestation of innocence (vv. 3-5)
St. 3 Second plea (vv. 6-9)
St. 4 Support in the form of a complaint against the enemies (vv. 10-12)
St. 5 Third plea (vv. 13-14)
St. 6 Support in the form of a declaration of trust (v. 15)

Three poetic features of the psalm are worth noting. First, a set of terms that occur at the start and end of the poem provide a strong "bookending" feature, which serves poetically to complete the move from petition to trust: *your face* (vv. 2, 15; *millᵉp̄ānêḵā* and *pānêḵā*), *legitimate cause* and *righteousness* (vv. 1, 15; both translate *ṣeḏeq*), and *see* (vv. 2, 15; *ḥāzâ*). Second, three times in the psalm (one time in each major section of the poem) the petitioner employs the emphatic construction *ʾᵃnî* + 1st person verb, translated below as *I, yes I* . . . (vv. 4, 6, 15). The first instance underscores the psalmist's innocence, the second the urgency of the psalmist's plea, and the third the integrity of the psalmist's hope. Third, the poem is notable for its "running references to parts of the body" — lips, face, eyes, heart, mouth, feet, ear, right hand, bellies, etc.[5]

A Davidic prayer.

1 *Hear, O Lord, a legitimate cause,*[6]
attend to[7] *my cry.*
Give ear to my prayer,
not spoken with deceitful lips.
2 *May a decision about me come forth from before your face,*
may your eyes[8] *see that which is right.*

3 *You try my heart, you visit at night;*
you test me, you do not find a thing wrong.

5. Goldingay, *Psalms 1–41,* p. 237.

6. LXX *kyrie tēs dikaiosynēs mou,* is reading *YHWH ṣdqy;* cf. Ps. 4:1. Kraus notes that "MT is unusual and hardly original" (*Psalms 1–59,* p. 244); it may be that the psalm is ancient and that the text preserves the unusual use of the tetragrammaton in construct, such as the venerable "Lord of hosts" or "Lord of multitudes" (Num. 10:36). The parallelism suggests that the term stands as an absolute and means a plea for a judgment announcing vindication.

7. 4QCatena A supplies, unnecessarily, *l-*.

8. LXX *ophthalmoi mou* is reading a 1cs suffix, "my eyes," in parallel with *krima mou,* "decision about me."

I have resolved: nothing wrong will come from my mouth.[9]
4 *Regarding the deeds of humanity, by the word of your lips*
I, yes I, have kept from the paths of the violent!
5 *My steps grasp your paths,*
my feet have not slipped.

6 *I, yes I, call on you, for you answer me, O God;*
incline your ear to me, hear my word!
7 *Show forth*[10] *your deeds of* hesed,
you who rescue those seeking shelter
from[11] *those who rebel against your right hand.*
8 *Keep me as the apple of your eye,*
hide me in the shadow of your wings,
9 *from the wicked who despoil*[12] *me,*
my mortal enemies, who encircle me.

10 *Their hearts are closed,*
with their mouths they speak arrogantly.
11 *They have cast me out,*[13] *now they surround me;*
they set their eyes to cast me to the ground,
12 *Like a lion longing to tear,*
like a young lion lurking in ambush.

13 *Rise up, O Lord, confront them, throw them down!*
Rescue me from the wicked by your sword,
14 *from mortals,*[14] *by the power of your hand, O Lord,*
from mortals, whose lifespan and portion[15] *are in this life.*[16]

9. In vv. 3-5 there is some disagreement about the division into poetic lines (cf. *BHS,* Goldingay [*Psalms 1–41,* pp. 235-36], Kraus [*Psalms 1–59,* p. 243], but the stichography above mostly follows the MT, which is not as difficult as some suggest (cf. Craigie [*Psalms 1–50,* p. 159]).

10. Following the Cairo ms of MT, with other witnesses.

11. 8QPs seems to have a haplography, *mt-* for MT's *mmtqwmmym.*

12. 11QPs^{c} has *drš-* ("seek") in place of MT's root *šdd;* LXX supports MT.

13. Reading with LXX *ekballontes me* and 11QPs^{c} *gršny.* MT *ʾaššurênû ʿattâ s*^{e}*ḇāḇûnî* ("our steps now they surround me") is corrupt. The Qere, "they surround us," offers little in the way of a solution. A widely followed proposal is to repoint as *ʾiššě*^{e}*rûnî.*

14. 11QPs^{c} has *mmwt[ym]myd[h]* ("from those dead by your hand"?), while LXX has *echthrōn tēs cheiros sou.*

15. 11QPs^{c} has *bhyyh[m]* ("in their life"); LXX has *diamerison autous en tē zōē autōn* ("scatter them in their life").

16. As Craigie and others note ([*Psalms 1–50,* p. 161), the verse is difficult and may be corrupt. The above translation assumes the text is coherent, with the double occurrence of

But your treasured ones,[17] *may their bellies be filled,*
may their children be satisfied,
and may they have extra for their young.

15 *I, yes I, will see your face in righteousness,*
when I awake, I shall be satisfied with seeing your likeness.

1-2 The first plea section of the psalm is notable because, as is not infrequently the case in the psalms, it is a cry to be heard: *attend to my cry. Give ear to my prayer.* Similar to Ps. 4:1, the petitioner casts her plea as a *legitimate cause.* The Hebrew *ṣeḏeq* is translated here as *legitimate* because this word best represents the sense of the psalmist's claim — that her prayer should be heard because her outcry (her complaint? her request?) has merit. She has two other reasons for confidence. Her first reason for confidence is that the prayer is *not spoken with deceitful lips.* The metaphor of the lips or mouth is often used as a synecdoche. The reason this is such a prevalent synecdoche is that, given that God cannot be seen or touched, the relationship between God and human rests that much more firmly on the word and on speech. The psalmist lies neither to God nor to others (in contrast to the enemies, who are perhaps offering false accusations about her). Her second reason for confidence is that God's *eyes see that which is right (mêšārîm).* This phrase is a miniature confession of trust in this psalm. The psalmist trusts that the Lord has the wisdom to be able to discern guilt and innocence, has the active power to be able to set it right, and has the character to do so. There is thus a twofold basis for the psalmist's appeal — a belief in her own innocence and a trust in God's fidelity.

3-5 The second stanza of the psalm can be described as an argument in support of the opening plea to be heard. In this section, the psalmist vigorously asserts his innocence. Broadly speaking, as Goldingay notes, the poems of the Psalter "commonly assume that a person who prays needs to be able to say they are doing so from a life lived God's way."[18] As has been noted in the case of other psalms in which vigorous protestations of innocence are offered, the psalmist is not asserting a universal, theological guiltlessness with respect to his relationship with God. If the psalmist is falsely accused, the point is that he believes himself innocent of the charges. Or if the psalm-

---

mīmᵉṯîm indicating parallel phrases that modify the appeal of v. 13. V. 14b presents difficulties; *mēḥeleḏ ḥelqām* is understood by LXX as "divide [remove?] them from this earth," assuming the second term is a verb. The first term more often means "lifespan" than "world" (cf. 39:5; 89:47; Job 10:12; 11:17).

17. Reading with the Kethib; the singular form with plural verbs is no problem, as also in vv. 11-13.

18. Goldingay, *Psalms 1–41,* p. 239.

ist is suffering from some more generic crisis such as an illness, the point the psalmist is making is that he, like Job, has not done anything to deserve the present suffering.

The intensity of the assertion of innocence is underscored by the threefold verbs *you try, you visit,* and *you test.* This sequence emphasizes the thoroughness of God's searching gaze (cf. Psalm 139). The psalmist has vowed that *nothing wrong will come from my mouth.* Thus, he draws a picture of one whose prayer and practice are a house undivided — the same mouth with which he prays for help is a mouth that has kept faith with God and neighbor. The psalmist shifts metaphors to that of the path. As in Psalm 1 and many other places in the psalms,[19] the metaphor for the life of discipleship is that of the road less traveled. The psalmist balances the earlier threefold pattern that was used for God's verbs of searching with a threefold claim that he has kept to God's way: *I have kept from the paths of the violent! My steps grasp your paths, my feet have not slipped.*

6-9 The third stanza consists of a renewed appeal, which builds in a staircase fashion upon the initial appeal — at first picking up the earlier appeal to be heard *(answer me, O God; incline your ear to me, hear my word)* and then sharpening the appeal by asking for *deeds of* hesed. These acts of *hesed* that the psalmist requests *(ḥ^{a}sāḏêḵā)* are the paradigmatic actions of God, the gracious actions that only God can do and that reveal God's faithful character. These acts include such things as rescue from crisis and healing of disease — as the psalmist expands here, *you rescue those seeking shelter from those who rebel against your right hand.* In the nation's history, the exodus was the supreme act of *hesed.* In essence, the psalmist is begging God to be God — to be faithful, to show grace in deeds of mercy.

The second section of appeal culminates with two elegant metaphorical petitions — *Keep me as the apple of your eye, hide me in the shadow of your wings.* In Deut. 32:10-11, the nation of Israel is referred to "as the apple of [God's] eye" (v. 10) and God is described as protecting Israel, as an eagle who "hovers over its young" (v. 11). This parallel is striking. It shows that in this psalm of individual prayer, the supplicant is begging God to show an individual the same gracious attention as God has shown the nation. As Goldingay sums it up, the poet "asks that Israel's story become the suppliant's story, asks for a personal exodus deliverance as someone who relies on Yhwh."[20] The phrase *apple of your eye* (see also Prov. 7:2) indicates one who is specially treasured and cared for. In stanza 2, the psalmist had asserted, *I have kept (šāmar) from the paths of the violent.* The language is picked up again here, with the request to *keep (šāmar) me as the apple. . . .* The image of the *shadow*

19. See Brown, *Seeing the Psalms,* pp. 31-54.

20. Goldingay, *Psalms 1–41,* p. 241.

of your wings[21] (cf. Pss. 36:7; 57:1; 63:7; 91:1) indicates the sort of temporary shelter in which one can find safety in the midst of a sudden, intense crisis.

10-12 The fourth stanza of the poem supports the appeal of stanza 3; the two stanzas are also tied together closely by poetic features. In the third stanza, the psalmist requested deliverance from *those who rebel against your right hand.* This appeal is supported by the extended complaint against the enemy that is found in stanza 4. It is striking to contrast the bodily metaphors used to depict the enemy threat with the earlier bodily language used to portray the psalmist's innocence. The psalmist *does not speak with* deceitful lips, *has a* heart *that can stand up to God's searching gaze, has no sin* come from my mouth, *and* feet [that] have not slipped. The *enemies,* by contrast: have *hearts [that] are closed, with their mouths they speak arrogantly, they set their eyes to cast me to the ground.*[22] The poetic connections are completed as each stanza closes with an image drawn from the source domain of the animal kingdom. In stanza 3, the psalmist appeals for God to *hide me in the shadow of your wings.* In stanza 4, the animal imagery is threatening, and the enemies are portrayed as an inhuman threat: as the *lion lurking in ambush* and *longing to tear.*

13-14 According to the alternating logic of the poem, the fifth stanza switches back to a section of appeal — and just as the appeal of the third stanza is more intense than that of the first stanza, so the appeal of the fifth stanza is more intense than that of the third. The third stanza appeals for rescue from the enemies. The fifth stanza appeals for the enemies' downfall: *confront them, throw them down!* The appeal for God to *rise up* is a typical prayer in the Psalter (cf. 3:7; 7:6; 9:19; 10:12, etc.). It is an appeal for God to act decisively, to be moved to action on the basis of what God has heard in the appeal. Twice in v. 14 the psalmist asks God for rescue *from mortals (mīmᵉṯîm).* As Goldingay points out, the terms "could simply mean 'human beings' but likely suggests their wretchedness (cf. Isa. 41:14). . . . It hints that it should not be too much for Yhwh to rescue me from them."[23] The last verse of the stanza is difficult to interpret, but as understood here, the motif of the contrasting bodily metaphors continues. God has *the power of your hand,* with which God should be able to deliver God's treasured ones and grant them full *bellies.* The closing prayer is an appeal for the children of the psalmist's community to be cared for. If this approach is correct (and it allows the second half of v. 14 as is;

21. The term *wings* may refer to the image of the outstretched arms of the cherubim on the ark of the covenant in the temple (1 Kgs. 6:24ff.; cf. also Ps. 18:10). But the image is also used more broadly to signify God's delivering and protecting actions (cf. Exod. 19:4; Deut. 32:11). Even if the immediate source for the metaphor was the imagery of the temple, the temple in turn drew from nature as the source of the metaphor.

22. The phrase *mortal enemy* also literally references the bodily, since *mortal* here renders the Hebrew *nep̱eš,* which literally means "throat."

23. Goldingay, *Psalms 1–41,* p. 243.

other approaches require the verse to be disrupted[24]), it may be a sign that the psalm may not be best understood as the prayer of an isolated individual who has been falsely accused, but as that of a leader interceding on behalf of a threatened community.

15 The psalm ends with an abbreviated expression of trust. A common feature of prayers for help, this expression of confidence supports the third section of appeal. Two aspects of the statement of confidence are notable. First, as noted above, the references to awaking *to see your face* and *your likeness* may be hints that the petitioner is facing an overnight trial in the temple. But poetically speaking, the morning is the time of deliverance and hope (cf. Pss. 30:5; 5:3, etc.), and to *awake* (*qîṣ;* 3:5; 73:20) is to have the veil of fear lifted and to see God's purpose unfold. Second, the psalm ends with the third occurrence of the emphatic construction *ʾănî* + 1st person verb — in this case, the expression of trust *I, yes I, will see your face.* The psalmist, having prayed himself as it were almost into an exhausted sleep, closes his eyes in the trusting confidence that the new day will dawn with hope — because all tomorrows are in the hands of the Lord.

Reflections

An Embodied Prayer

As noted above, one of the striking poetic aspects of this psalm is the thoroughgoing fashion in which images of the body carry the drama of the prayer. The sequenced and repeated references to lips, face, eyes, heart, mouth, feet, ear, right hand, bellies, and so on dramatically score the point that the psalmist is, quite literally, in a tough place. The psalmist is being forced to embody a crisis. The references also score the point that the crisis has been brought about by the embodied violence that the enemies pose. That is to say, because the enemies have chosen to embody threatening behaviors — expressed here metaphorically as having closed hearts, arrogant mouths, and eyes set on violence — because of these embodied actions, the psalmist is in danger. Even more to the point, the psalmist's prayer is that God's answer to this prayer would be embodied in the form of granting the psalmist a new situation — one in which the psalmist sees God's face. This reference evokes the Aaronic blessing, in which the light of God's face cast upon the worshipper is also the favor of God. As such, this prayer reminds us that the incarnation is not only an action that God took once, but that God's grace comes to us again and

24. Goldingay, e.g., interprets the remarks about children as wishing harm on the children of the enemies (cf. Job 21:17-19), with the idea being that the enemies' children's bellies will be filled with the harm that the enemies intend for others (*Psalms 1–41,* p. 243).

again in the flesh. Indeed, God's grace must come to us again and again in the flesh, precisely because we are flesh. And precisely because others who are flesh often pose dire threats to our bodily existence. And the good news is that God does indeed visit us repeatedly with blessing, deliverance, and love. As Martin Luther writes in the *Small Catechism,* "God . . . still preserves my body and soul: my eyes, ears, and all limbs and senses. . . . God daily and abundantly provides shoes and clothing, food and drink, and all property — along with the necessities and nourishment for this body and life."

Rolf A. Jacobson

Psalm 18: My God, My Rock

Psalm 18 is a royal song of thanksgiving.[1] This classification is evident both from the psalm's content and from the fact that the psalm (or a nearly identical poem) occurs in 2 Samuel 22. The poem is introduced, both in 2 Sam. 22:1 and in the superscription to Psalm 18, as a royal song of thanksgiving: *Of David, who spoke the words of this song to the LORD, on the day the LORD delivered him from the palm of all his enemies and from the hand of Saul.* Significant studies comparing the two texts have been written, most notably an important article by Frank Moore Cross and David Noel Freedman.[2] It seems likely either that the two poems share a common *Vorlage* or that Psalm 18 is directly dependent on 2 Samuel 22. But the approach in this commentary is to interpret the text of Psalm 18 in its canonical shape, rather than try to get behind the text of the two poems and establish the textual history of the poem.[3] For this reason, the text of the poem in 2 Samuel 22 is used very sparingly in textual criticism here. Comparison of the two texts is valuable for many reasons, such as the fact such a comparison has proven valuable in advancing the study of Hebrew linguistics and textual criticism,[4] but such a comparison is not the intent of this commentary. The text of Psalm 18 is generally viewed as the later of the two texts, since Psalm 18 often employs "full" spellings where 2 Samuel 22 has "defective" spellings.[5] Generally, the morphology of Psalm 18 is viewed as being later.[6]

The narrative context of the poem in 2 Samuel 22 is instructive, because there the psalm is the first of two final songs that cap the long saga of David's life. That is, in its narrative context the psalm is not a song of thanksgiving for any one instance of divine delivery, but is a song of thanks for a lifetime lived under the canopy of divine salvation. Thus, interpretation of the psalm should not presume that distress, deliverance, or theophany that are related

1. For a different understanding of the genre, see Gerstenberger (*Psalms: Part 1*, p. 100), who sees the psalm, as is typical in his approach, as a messianic hymn of hope that is set in postexilic early Judaism.

2. "A Royal Song of Thanksgiving: II Samuel = Psalm 18," *JBL* 72 (1953) 15-34.

3. By the "canonical shape," I mean the text of the poem at the protomasoretic point of development, as best we can establish it.

4. Cross and Freedman, "A Royal Song of Thanksgiving," pp. 15 and 17.

5. James Barr, *The Variable Spellings of the Hebrew Bible* (Schweich Lectures 1986; Oxford: Oxford University Press, 1989), p. 171. There are 23 instances of longer spellings of the same word in Ps. 18 versus 2 Sam. 22. Meanwhile, there are 8 instances of longer spellings of the same words in 2 Sam. 22 versus Ps. 18, but Barr says most of these can be attributed to dialectic differences.

6. Emanuel Tov, *Textual Criticism of the Hebrew Bible* (2nd rev. ed.; Minneapolis: Fortress, 2001), p. 224.

in the psalm refer to any one experience, but rather to a longer experiential arc — to a life, like David's, in which there were both highs and lows. As McCann has sensitively noted, both in its narrative context in 2 Samuel as well as in its canonical context in the Psalter, the psalm "proclaims the reign of God amid circumstances that suggest God does *not* reign. . . ."[7] The psalm's song of thanks is thus profoundly countercultural. In this respect, a link between this psalm and a similar song of hope at the end of Habakkuk is worth noting (Ps. 18:33 and Hab. 3:19bc are similar). This connection reinforces McCann's insight. Like the psalm in Habakkuk, Psalm 18 should be interpreted not only as a psalm of thanks for when times are good and all seems bright, but also as a song of hope for when times are hopeless and all seems dark. Like the song in Habakkuk, Psalm 18 teaches that the faithful are to rejoice in the Lord not only when times are good, but also when "rottenness enters": "Though the fig tree does not blossom, and no fruit is on the vines; though the produce of the olive fails and the fields yield no food; though the flock is cut off from the fold and there is no herd in the stalls, yet I will rejoice in the LORD" (Hab. 3:17-18a).

As McCann notes, the "structure of Psalm 18 is complicated enough that some scholars contend that it should be viewed as two separate psalms (1) vv. 1-30 and (2) vv. 31-50; however there is a unifying plot."[8] This plot, as McCann points out, is familiar from other individual psalms of thanksgiving: opening praise, description of the distress, description of the rescue, and renewed praise of God.[9] Although the psalm may have had a complicated textual history, it is treated here as a unified royal song of thanksgiving. The structure is:

Narrative Superscription

vv. 1-3	Opening announcement of praise
vv. 4-6	The distress
vv. 7-15	The theophany
vv. 16-19	The rescue
vv. 20-24	The king's righteousness
vv. 25-30	The Lord's faithfulness
vv. 31-36	Praise
vv. 37-45	The rescue, revisited
vv. 46-50	Concluding praise

7. "The Book of Psalms," p. 747.

8. "The Book of Psalms," p. 747.

9. McCann, "The Book of Psalms," understands the structure slightly differently: "Out of his distress, the king calls upon God (vv. 1-6), and God comes down to rescue him (vv. 16-19), an action that is introduced as a dramatic theophany (vv. 7-15). The praise that is expected following the account of deliverance is postponed until vv. 31-50, being preceded by descriptions of the king's righteousness (vv. 20-24) and God's faithfulness (vv. 25-30)."

For the leader. For the servant of the Lord. Davidic. The one who spoke the words of this song to the Lord, on the day the Lord delivered him from the palm of all his enemies and from the hand of Saul.[10] *He said:*

1 *I love you,*[11] *O Lord, my strength.*
2 *The Lord is my cliff, my fortress, my deliverer;*
My God, my rock, in whom I take refuge;
My shield, and the horn of my salvation, my stronghold.
3 *In praise,*[12] *I call*[13] *to the Lord;*
For from my enemies[14] *I was saved.*

4 *The cords of death wrapped me up,*
The torrents of destruction overwhelmed me.
5 *The cords of Sheol surrounded me,*
The snares of death approached to me.
6 *In my distress, I called upon the Lord,*
And to my God I cried.
He heard my voice from his sanctuary,[15]
And my cry to him reached his ears.

7 *Then the earth rumbled and quaked,*
the foundations of the mountains quaked
and rumbled because he was angry.
8 *Smoke came from his nose,*
Devouring fire from his mouth;[16]
glowing charcoals blazed forth from him.[17]
9 *He spread apart the heavens, and came down;*

10. Perhaps this word should be read as "Sheol" (cf. v. 5); in Hebrew the consonantal text for the words Saul and Sheol are identical. See Dahood, *Psalms I,* p. 104.

11. 11QPs[c] has *rḥm-* in place of MT's *'rḥmk,* probably indicating a perfect form *(rḥmtykh)* for MT's imperfect. Alternatively, if the root is emended slightly to *rwm,* one would have the more familiar "I exult." But the textual witnesses all support retaining MT.

12. Reading a *piel* participle, with LXX's *ainōn* in place of MT's pual participle; the syntactical function is verbal coordination, to communicate the sense that the *call* here is not for help but in praise.

13. 11QPs[c] has the cohortative *'qr'h* ("let me call").

14. 11QPs[c] and 2 Sam. 22:4 have what most likely is an orthographic variant, reading *wm'yby* in place of MT's *wmn 'yby.*

15. LXX *ek naou hagiou autou* suggests adding *qāḏôš* ("from his holy sanctuary").

16. LXX *apo prosōpou autou* suggests *mpny* ("from his face").

17. LXX has *autois ho theos,* "God [was angry] at them."

and darkness was underneath his feet.
10 *Then he rode on a cherub and flew;*
he soared upon wings of wind.
11 *He made darkness his enclosing veil,*
his shelter was a darkness of rain clouds of the sky.
12 *Clouds advanced from the brightness before him;*
hailstones and coals of fire.
13 *Then the Lord thundered from the heavens,*
while the Most High gave his voice.
14 *Then he sent out his arrows, and scattered them;*
He multiplied[18] *lightning bolts and routed them.*
15 *Then the channels of the sea were seen,*
and the foundations[19] *of the world were uncovered,*[20]
by your rebuke, O Lord,
from a blast of your nostrils' breath.

16 *He reached from on high and*[21] *seized me,*
he drew me from great waters.
17 *He delivered me from the power of my enemies,*[22]
from those who hated me and were stronger than me.
18 *They confronted me in the day of my calamity;*
but the Lord was a support for me.
19 *He brought me out to a broad place;*
he delivered me, because he delighted in me.

20 *The Lord dealt with me according to my righteousness;*
according to the purity of my hands he restored to me.
21 *Surely I have kept the ways of the Lord,*
and have not been guilty before my God.
22 *Surely all his ordinances were before me,*
while I have not turned away from his statutes.
23 *I was blameless before him,*
and I kept myself from guilt.

18. Reading with LXX *eplēthynen.*

19. 11QPs^c may have the masculine form *[mwsd]y* for MT's feminine form *mwsdwt* with no change in meaning; alternatively, since only the *yôd* is extant, an entirely different word may be postulated, but not enough remains to supply a different word.

20. 11QPs^c has *yšl-,* most likely indicating *yšlḥ,* but the meaning of the variant cannot be interpreted; 4QPs^c supports MT.

21. Reading *wyqḥny* with 11QPs^c and LXX; note that 4QPs^c supports MT.

22. Reading the plural *'ōyḇê* with LXX *echthrōn mou dynatōn,* but retaining the singular *'āz* and reading as a construct.

24 *Therefore the Lord has restored me according to my righteousness,*
according to the purity of my hands in his sight.

25 *With the faithful, you deal faithfully;*
With the blameless, you act blamelessly;
26 *With the pure, you act purely;*
but with the crooked, you act shrewdly.
27 *Surely, you deliver a needy people,*
but haughty eyes you bring down.
28 *Surely, you make my lamp burn;*
You, O Lord my God, light up my darkness.
29 *With you, I can rush*[23] *a wall,*
and with my God I leap over a wall.
30 *The true God, his way is perfect;*
the word of the Lord is pure;
he is a shield for all who take refuge in him.

31 *Who is God except the Lord?*
And who is a rock except our God?
32 *The true God, who girds me with strength,*
And makes my way perfect.
33 *He makes my feet like the feet of a doe,*
and causes me to stand upon the heights.[24]
34 *He trains my hands for war,*
so that my arms can bend a bow of bronze.
35 *You give me the shield of your salvation,*
and your right hand supports me;
your response[25] *exults me.*
36 *You broaden the path beneath me;*[26]
and my ankles do not twist.

23. LXX *rysthēsomai* implies a passive form of *rāḏap;* 2 Sam. 22:30 has *'ārûṣ,* a variant in spelling, but the same Hebrew root, "run" — which is also supported by the LXX there.

24. MT's 1cs suffix ("my height") is anomalous and not supported by the versions; reading the plural with LXX.

25. The Hebrew term *ʿᵃnāwâ* is difficult. The form is rare and the root *'nh,* to which the word is likely related, has several radically diverging meanings — making the interpretation difficult. LXX translates with *paideia,* meaning "correction" or "instruction." 4QSam[a] has "help/support" here. Perhaps *'nh* was understood to mean "answer" — a reference to a priestly oracle of salvation? — and was interpreted by the LXX translator as "teaching."

26. 4QSam[a] lacks *taḥᵉtāy* ("beneath me"), apparently a haplography.

37 *I pursued my enemies and overtook them;*
and I did not return until they were finished.
38 *I smote them so that they could not arise,*
they fell[27] *under my feet.*
39 *For you girded me with strength for the battle;*
you brought low my adversaries under me.
40 *You gave me the back of my enemies,*
and those who hated me I silenced.[28]
41 *They cried for help, but there was no one to save them;*
to the Lord, *but he did not answer them.*
42 *I ground them like dust in the wind;*[29]
I empty them out like the mire of the streets.
43 *You delivered me from the disputes of people;*
you set me as head of the nations;
people whom I had not known serve me.
44 *As soon as they hear me they obey me;*
foreigners submit to me.
45 *Foreigners lose courage,*
And come trembling out of their strongholds.

46 *As the* Lord *lives, praised be my rock!*[30]
And may the God of my salvation be exalted —
47 *The God who has given me retribution,*
He has subdued[31] *peoples under me;*
48 *My deliverer — who delivered me from my enemies,*
Yes, you exalted me above my foes;
From the violent man delivered me.
49 *Therefore I extol you among the nations, O* Lord;
I sing praises to your name.
50 *He multiplies deliverance for his king,*
and shows hesed *to his anointed one,*
to David and to his seed forever.

27. In 11QPs[d] the editors' reconstruction of the variant *ypwlw* for MT's *yplw* is too tentative to emend the text; MT is retained.

28. LXX has *exōlethreusas,* implying both the Lord as subject and perhaps that it is reading the verb *kāraṯ*. MT's more unexpected reading is retained.

29. "Dust in the wind" translates *'al pᵉnê ruaḥ,* lit., "upon the face of wind." 4QSam[a] has "dust on the face of the path"; 2 Sam. 22:43 has "earth."

30. LXX's *theou mou* ("my God") is likely a harmonization with the second half of the verse.

31. LXX's *hypotaxas* implies a participial form, but this is a harmonization with the participial form in the first half of the verse.

1-3 The psalm begins, as do other songs of thanksgiving (cf. 30:1), with an opening declaration of praise. The declaration *I love you, O LORD* is unique as an opening word of praise. The verb *(rāḥam)* is related to the noun that is usually translated as "mercy" *(reḥem)*. It is used elsewhere in the Psalter to describe God's parental love for his human children (102:14; 103:13), but here describes the king almost as a child who returns the parental love of God. The stanza then piles up a series of metaphors for the Lord. For the psalmist God is *my strength, my cliff, my fortress, my deliverer, my rock, my shield, and the horn of my salvation, my stronghold.* The series is striking for three reasons. First, all of the images are martial — in harmony with the king's responsibility to lead the defense of the people. Second, each of the images includes the first person pronoun *my* — emphasizing the relationship between God and king. Third, the series of eight images for God is unique in the Psalter for its length — by piling up such a long list of metaphors, the psalmist speaks with great intensity about the help that has been received over a long lifetime of faith. The final phrase of the stanza succinctly sums up the reason for the song: *In praise, I call to the LORD; for from my enemies I was saved.* The song is a response to God's saving help. The traditional translation — "I call upon the LORD, who is worthy to be praised, so shall I be saved from my enemies" (NRSV) — changes the phrase into a request for help, thereby missing the basic import of the verse and of the entire psalm.

4-6 The second stanza of the psalm describes the situation of distress from which the psalmist was rescued. The psalmist employs stock metaphorical language that draws on the mythological imagery of the chaos conflict: *cords of death, torrents* (lit., "streams"; cf. 124:4) *of destruction, cords of Sheol, snares of death.* Note that each of the four nouns that are in construct (e.g., *cords of . . .*) are plural. If the psalm is read against the canonical background of David's life, the images could refer to any number of events. And that is the point — that the psalm is not looking back on any one event, but on the entire range and variety of distresses that a person or a people have been through. Each such distress is a microcosm of the cosmic battle with chaos — *death, destruction* (the term is *belîya'al,* lit., "worthless thing" or "vile matter," but elsewhere it may refer to a false god — see commentary on 101:3), *Sheol,* and *death* (*māweṯ,* also a name of the Canaanite god of death). This stanza, like the first stanza, concludes with a summary description of the help that was received: *In my distress, I called upon the LORD. . . . He heard my voice from his sanctuary.*

7-15 The Lord's response to the psalmist's cry is then described in two parts — a report of the coming of God (the theophany; vv. 7-15) and a report of the help received. The report of the theophany again draws on stock mythological language — God's coming is like the arrival of a towering, threatening thunderstorm (cf. Psalm 29). God is pictured as arriving on a thunderhead, which is mythologically depicted as God's chariot (vv. 9-14). Images of an earthquake may also be behind the description (vv. 7-8) along with images of flash flooding (v. 15). The modern reader of the psalm should not miss the terrifying nature of the description. Those who have been caught in an earthquake, been caught in the open when the leading edge of a thunderstorm comes through, or witnessed the power of a raging flood may be able to relate to the terror the poetry is trying to evoke: *the earth rumbled and quaked, the foundations of the mountains quaked, he sent out his arrows* (presumably the image is of lightning), *the channels of the sea were seen, and the foundations of the world were uncovered.* Contrary to 1 Kings 19, this is not the gentle advent of God in "the still, small voice." Here, God *is* in the earthquake, *is* in the thunderstorm, *is* in the flood. The Lord's arrival is impossible to ignore, and the Lord comes to *rebuke* (v. 15).

16-19 The description of the deliverance continues to draw on the mythological language of the chaos conflict: *he drew me from great waters* and *brought me out to a broad place.* The psalmist describes the distress generically as *the day of my calamity.* The word for *calamity* occurs only here in the Psalter. It refers to an unmitigated disaster, such as those that Job experienced (Job 21:17, 30; 31:23) or the fall of Jerusalem (Jer. 18:17). In such situations of ultimate distress, a human being is utterly overmatched by both human foes *(those who hated me and were stronger than me)* and natural threats *(great waters).* With no human hand to lend aid, the *LORD was a support.* The metaphor of the *broad place* to evoke security, safety, and blessing is also a familiar image (cf. Ps. 4:1; 16:6; 31:8) — it is the opposite of the threatening image in which a sufferer is beset by enemies on every side (cf. 22:16-18). Rescue came from God, according to the king, *because he delighted in me.*

20-24 The next section, in which the poem describes the king's righteousness, can be understood as an aside in which the king expands on the phrase *he delighted in me.* The king has just stated that the reason God delivered him is that God *delighted* in him. What follows is a thick description of why God has delighted in the king. It is because of *my righteousness; the purity of my hands;* how *I have kept the ways of the LORD, and have not been guilty; I have not turned away from his statutes; was blameless;* and *kept myself from guilt. Therefore,* the psalmist confesses, *the LORD has restored me according to my righteousness, according to the purity of my hands.* The reader should note both the poetic inclusion that sets off this section of the poem from the rest of the composition — *according to my righteousness, according to the purity of my hands* occurs in both v. 20 and v. 24. The reader should also note the language and concepts that are characteristic of Deuteronomistic theology, such as *turn from* (*sûr;* v. 22; cf. Josh. 1:7), *ordinances* and *statutes* (*mišpāṭ* and *ḥuqqōṯ;* v. 22; cf. 1 Kgs. 2:3), and especially the metaphor of the king as walking in the *way* of God or of his ancestors as a characteristic metaphor for his fidelity or infidelity (cf. 1 Kgs. 11:33, 38; 15:34; 16:19, etc.). As is well known, the reign and character of the kings in the Deuteronomistic History are evaluated according to which *way* they walked in — whether following the way of David, or of another ancestral king such as Jeroboam (1 Kgs. 16:26), or Asa (1 Kgs. 22:43), or the "kings of Israel" (2 Kgs. 8:18), and so on. The presence of such language here certainly does not fit with an early date for the composition of the psalm, which has led some to question whether the stanza is a later interpolation.[32] The language here mirrors quite closely the language of the law of the king in Deut. 17:19-20. The language here is hyperbolic — no king, especially David, was ever completely *pure* or *righteous.* And when the Deuteronomistic History evaluates the kings of Israel and Judah, most are found terribly wanting. The chiastic structure of the section, as McCann has pointed out, focuses attention on v. 22, which describes the Lord's *ordinances* and *statutes* as the source of the king's righteousness — this focus places the emphasis on God's agency through the law.[33] And even though no human being can ever measure up perfectly to the law — especially those human beings who are entrusted with monarchical power! — the power of the law to shape a righteous society is nevertheless affirmed.

25-30 The next section of the psalm praises the Lord's faithfulness. In spite of a living in a world in which enemies and haters (v. 17) oppress those who rely on God, the psalm confesses trust in the Lord's fidelity: *you deliver a needy people.* As the leader of the people who depend on God, the king confesses a personal dependence on God. Drawing on the stock metaphor of light and darkness, the psalmist confesses *you make my lamp burn; you, O LORD my God, light up my darkness.* Once again, the active and present agency of God through God's word is underscored: *the word of the LORD is pure.* That active word enables the king to live up to the steep vocational responsibilities that he bears — the responsibilities of placing himself in danger while leading battle are specifically mentioned. God is the king's *shield* and *with you, I can rush a wall, and with my God I can leap over a wall.* In all of this, the emphasis is not on the king, but on the fidelity of the Lord, who is faithful with the *faithful,* blameless toward the *blameless,* and *pure* toward the *pure.* With those who are *crooked,* however, the Lord acts in judgment.

31-36 Beginning with v. 31, the psalm turns to the long-expected praise. The praise begins with a typical rhetorical question that functions as praise: *Who is God except the LORD? And who is a rock except our God?* (cf. 73:25; 94:16; 113:5). The praise extols not a disembodied, distant God, but the Lord

32. See Hossfeld and Zenger (*Die Psalmen I,* pp. 118-22), who are very confident of their ability to judge what verses and phrases were added to a given psalm and when.

33. McCann, "The Book of Psalms," p. 748.

who is known in Israel's history and in the personal experience of the king. The themes of preservation in battle *(girds me with strength, trains my hands for war, bow of bronze, you give me the shield of your salvation)* as well as of the secure place of rescue *(makes my feet like the feet of a doe, causes me to stand upon the heights, you broaden the path beneath me)* again carry the weight of the psalm's testimony of faith. The praise here is not of the Lord generically, but of the Lord as the one who has equipped the king for success in his vocation.

37-45 The psalm then revisits the theme of the rescues that the Lord had granted the psalmist — here, the poem combines the earlier theme of divine rescue (vv. 16-19) with the just-introduced theme of the Lord as the one who had equipped the psalmist for success. Equipped by the Lord with strength and martial puissance, the psalmist now attributes the victories that he had gained over his foes to the faithfulness of the Lord. Because the Lord had girded the king *with strength for the battle,* the king was able to pursue his enemies and be victorious. The king then, in hyperbolic language that was typical of the royal propaganda of the ancient Near East, describes who completely vanquished his enemies — *ground them like dust in the wind* and emptied them *like the mire of the streets* (the earthy image of a slop pail being emptied into the gutter may be at work here). The hyperbolic language here must be interpreted in context. For example, shortly before 1200 B.C.E. the Egyptian Pharaoh Merneptah erected a victory monument in which he boasted that he had destroyed Israel — "Israel is laid waste, his seed is not."

46-50 The psalm's final stanza is dedicated to praise, as is typical of songs of thanksgiving. This closing stanza repeats key thematic vocabulary from the psalm's opening sentences — *my rock, my salvation, my deliverer.* The stanza begins with the oath, *as the LORD lives,* which is familiar in the historical narratives, but occurs only here in the Psalter. The king's praise is specifically of the Lord's *name* and is to be heard *among the nations.* This vocabulary evokes memories of the promise that the descendants of Abraham, the only nation to which the proper name of the Lord was revealed, were blessed not for their own sake, but to be a blessing to the nations.

The closing words confess the enduring fidelity of the Lord. The psalm closes by proclaiming the faith that the Lord will continue to be faithful in the future — just as he proved faithful throughout the long, up-and-down saga of David's life, and just as the Lord proved faithful to Israel throughout the long, up-and-down history of the people. If the theological interpretation of such scholars as Gerstenberger and McCann is correct, the closing phrase conveys a messianic hope. In spite of the failure of the Davidic monarchy, the people continued to have faith that the Lord would prove faithful to the promises made to David (cf. 2 Sam. 7:1-16).

Reflections

1. The Song of a King

Psalm 18 may be read as a royal song of thanksgiving by a Judean king, in the days before the exile. This reading emerges when the psalm is read in light of the narrative superscription: *Of David, who spoke the words of this song to the* LORD*, on the day the* LORD *delivered him from the palm of all his enemies and from the hand of Saul.* Limburg has helpfully termed such superscriptions "the earliest commentary" on the psalms.[34] He comments that the "editors who placed the same psalm near the end of the second book of Samuel (chap. 22) are suggesting that the psalm expresses David's thanks to God after a lifetime of deliverances, some of which are recorded in the books of Samuel. That setting of the psalm suggests that it be viewed as words of thanks from the old king to the God who had been faithful to him for a lifetime, since his deliverance from the hand of Goliath."[35] Read in that light, the psalm is the faith testimony of an aged elder. Praise is often described as the spontaneous reaction to an experience of divine deliverance.[36] This psalm, however, is far from spontaneous. Its praise is carefully measured, well considered — the mature fruit of an old vine. This psalm preserves the wisdom that comes from one who has run the marathon of faith and is nearing the finish line. It teaches that the long life of faith has many ups and downs, but that one may trust that there is a guiding hand — *The* LORD*, my rock, my fortress, my deliverer, my shield, the horn of my salvation, my stronghold.* The promise of the psalm is that God is faithful. Or, to use the psalm's own words: *The true God, his way is perfect; the word of the* LORD *is pure; he is a shield for all who take refuge in him* (v. 30).

2. A Word of Messianic Hope

The psalm may also be read as a divine promise that was preserved by a displaced, wandering people. Gerstenberger and McCann have especially made the case that the psalm should be read in a postexilic context, when God's people no longer had their own land, nation, or king. While the poem certainly dates back to monarchical times, the fact that it was preserved in the Psalter by postexilic editors shows, in the words of McCann, that "the intent of Psalm 18 [was] to keep hope alive."[37] Israel and Judah had experienced their human monarchs as wanting — their kings certainly never lived up to the law of the king in Deuteronomy 17 or to the king's hyperbolic description

34. *Psalms*, p. 55.
35. *Psalms*, p. 55.
36. See, e.g., Brueggemann, *Israel's Praise.*
37. "The Book of Psalms," p. 749.

of his righteousness in Ps. 18:20-24. Israel and Judah were then deprived of their own king and were subject to the tyrannies of a series of foreign kings. And yet, in spite of the failure of both these internal and external kings, God's people clung to the promise of God to David that a descendant of David would forever reign as king of the people. The psalm preserves that promise in its closing verse: The Lord *shows* hesed *to his anointed one, to David and to his seed forever.* Christians confess that the Lord proved faithful to this promise when Jesus, the seed of David, was born to a peasant girl named Mary.

ROLF A. JACOBSON

Psalm 19: Tune My Heart to Sing Your Praise

Psalm 19 has been variously described both as a "problem child of the Psalter"[1] and as "the greatest poem in the Psalter and one of the greatest lyrics in the world."[2] Either of these judgments is valid, depending on what approach one takes to interpreting a psalm.

Psalm 19 creates problems for those readers whose approach to interpretation requires that they fix a genre label on every psalm in order to understand it. This is so because Psalm 19 appears to have been constructed out of either two or three different parts, each of which was most likely written by a different author in a different era. There are several convincing grounds for this conclusion. In vv. 1-6, the focus is on creation, the genre is similar to a hymn,[3] the poetry is flexible and playful, and the more generic name for God *('el)* is used. In vv. 7-10, the focus is on *torah* (perhaps better translated as "instruction"), the genre is that of a psalm of instruction or torah psalm, the poetry becomes rigid and formal, and the proper name for God *(YHWH)* is used six times (always in a construct chain). In vv. 11-14, the focus shifts to the *servant* who speaks the psalm, the genre becomes a prayer, the poetry becomes less stylized and more conversational, and the proper name for God *(YHWH)* is used, but this time only once (and not in a construct chain, but as the addressee of the prayer). Because of the psalm's fragmented nature, some older Psalms commentaries treated the psalm in two parts — vv. 1-6, the "creation hymn," and vv. 7-14, the "torah hymn." The Revised Common Lectionary follows this bifurcating approach, dividing the psalm and then assigning the two parts to different seasons in different years.[4] Weiser went so far as to write, "Why these . . . dissimilar psalms were united in one single psalm cannot any longer be established with any degree of certainty."[5]

Against this older, fragmenting approach, more recent interpretation has almost universally focused on the poetic unity of the psalm. While acknowledging that the psalm most likely arose in two or three stages over a span of years, the newer approach focuses on interpreting the psalm in its current form as an understandable unity. To this end, it is important to

1. Mays, *The Lord Reigns,* p. 128.

2. C. S. Lewis, *Reflections on the Psalms* (New York: Harcourt, Brace, 1986), p. 63.

3. Even to classify 19:1-6 as a hymn is tenuous, because these verses include neither an imperative "call to praise" nor any self-evident "reasons to praise," which are the usual symptoms of the hymnic genre. But 19:1-6 fits the genre of the hymn more closely than it does any other genre. See Gerstenberger, *Psalms: Part 1,* 100-103.

4. Vv. 1-6 are appointed for the festival of St. Andrew, while vv. 7-14 are assigned for 3 Lent B.

5. *The Psalms,* p. 197.

note that the theme of speech provides a clear unifying presence within the psalm. When this unifying theme is seen, the structure of the psalm can be described:

vv. 1-6	Creation's Speech — praise for God
vv. 7-10	Torah's Speech — instruction of humanity
vv. 11-14	Servant's Speech — prayer to God

A second theme also helps unify the psalm — the theme of creation or nature. The first part of the psalm describes creation's praise of God, the second part describes the torah of the Lord as better than any joy that creation can offer, and the third part uses the natural metaphor of the rock to describe God. In addition to these two themes, other key vocabulary also serves to unify the psalm. The same Hebrew term *('ōmer)* occurs in both vv. 2-4 (three times, translated here as *word* and *speech*) and in v. 14 *(words)*. The Hebrew root *tmm* ("to be whole, blameless, perfect") occurs in v. 7 and v. 13. The motif of light occurs in each part of the psalm — the sun gives light (vv. 4-6), and the torah *enlightens* (v. 8) and *illumines* (v. 11).

In short, although Psalm 19 arose in stages, in its present form it is a unified poem and deserves to be interpreted as such.[6] In terms of the genre of the present psalm, one should not try too mightily to force a restrictive label onto it. Perhaps the best one can do is to describe Psalm 19 as an instructional torah psalm. As McCann has accurately written, "Psalm 19 intends to teach."[7] What does it teach? It teaches that the Creator can be known *about* through creation, but the torah is the only way that one can *know* the personal God of Israel. And once one knows this God through torah, one can pray to God in a relational way.

To the leader. A Davidic psalm.

1 *The heavens are recounting the glory of God,*
and the firmament is declaring the work[8] *of his hands.*

6. As Miller has recognized, creating new composite compositions was an accepted artistic approach in ancient Israel: "Such literary creations . . . are clearly present in the Psalter. Indeed one can identify obvious use of certain psalms in the composition of other psalms, for example, in the relationships between Psalms 18 and 144 or Psalms 15 and 135 (the latter pair drawing on a number of psalm texts as well as other Old Testament material), the identity of Psalm 70 with Ps. 40:14-18[13-17], and the composition of Psalm 108 out of Pss. 57:8-12[7-11] and 60:7-14[5-12], as well as 1 Chronicles 16 out of Pss. 105:1-15; 96:1-13; and 106:1, 47-48" (*Interpreting the Psalms,* p. 12).

7. McCann, "The Book of Psalms," p. 751.

8. Some Hebrew manuscripts and some versions (Symmachus, Targum, and Vulgate)

2 *Day to day pours forth speech,*
night to night declares knowledge.
3 *There is no speech, there are no words,*
neither is their voice heard.
4 *Yet to all the earth their voice*[9] *goes forth,*
and their words to the end of the world.

For the sun, he has set a tent in the heavens,[10]
5 *and it goes forth — like a bridegroom from his wedding chamber,*
it rejoices — like a strong man running a course.
6 *From the end of the heavens it goes forth,*
along its circuit to[11] *the end.*[12]
There is nothing hidden from its heat.

7 *The torah*[13] *of the LORD is perfect, refreshing the soul.*
The decrees of the LORD are established, making wise the simple.
8 *The precepts of the LORD are upright, rejoicing the heart.*
The commandment of the LORD is clear, enlightening the eyes.
9 *The fear*[14] *of the LORD is pure, enduring forever.*

---

read "works," which matches the plural form of *heavens* in the first colon of the verse. This harmonizing variant should be rejected.

9. Joining many scholars, MT's *qawwām* (lit., "their line") is emended to *qôlām.* Arguing against this emendation are both the fact that the *wāw* and *lāmed* are not easily confused visually and also that many scholars have been able to make sense of the text as it is (e.g., Brown, *Seeing the Psalms,* pp. 82-103; 237 n 2). Arguing in favor of the emendation is that LXX (with Symmachus and Syriac) clearly is reading *qôlām,* the *lāmed* mostly likely was omitted and not confused with the *wāw* (see the plene spelling in v. 3), and "their line" makes no sense in parallel with *their words* in the second half of the verse. Kraus retains the sense of "sound" by assuming that *qaw* is an onomatopoetic word, as in Isa. 28:10.

10. Lit., "in them," but the meaning is clearly *in the heavens.* The correction to "in the sea" misses the poetic point that the first four verses speak of the speech of the *heavens, the firmament, day,* and *night,* while vv. 5-6 focus on the sun — and the *sun* dwells in the heavens and its orbit defines day and night.

11. Several Hebrew manuscripts (supported by LXX) emend *'al* to *'aḏ.* Alternatively, *'al* may be translated "to" rather than the rigid "upon" (see Waltke and O'Connor, *Biblical Hebrew Syntax,* p. 217; cf. Exod. 20:26).

12. MT reads *qṣwtm* ("their end"). LXX and Syriac suggest *qṣwtw* ("its end"). Although MT is preferred, we render it "the end" for the sake of a smooth translation.

13. 11QPs[c] has the plural, *[tôr]ôṯ.*

14. It has been suggested that *yr't (fear)* should be replaced by something such as *'mrt* ("word") or *mr't* ("edict"; so Dahood, *Psalms I*), which is visually similar but fits better in the list of synonyms for "words" in vv. 7-10. There is no textual support among the versions for this change, although some cite Ps. 119:38 in support of the change. *Fear* is the more difficult

The ordinances of the LORD are truth; they are righteous altogether.
10 *They are more desirable than gold, more than much fine gold;*
they are sweeter than honey, drippings from the honeycomb.

11 *Moreover,*[15] *your servant is illumined by them,*
in keeping them there is much reward.
12 *Omissions! Who can detect them?*
Cleanse me of hidden errors!
13 *Moreover, hold back the insolent*[16] *from your servant,*
do not let them rule me,
then I shall be perfect,[17] *innocent of much transgression.*

14 *May the words of my mouth and the meditation of my heart*
be acceptable to you, O LORD, my rock and my redeemer.

1-4 The first section of the psalm consists of two separate stanzas. Verses 1-4 deal with the speech of the heavens; vv. 5-6 revolve around the sun. Many commentators have noted that vv. 1-6 focus on creation. But the focus is not on creation qua creation, but rather on the *speech* with which creation lauds her Creator. Verses 1-4 are replete with references to speech: *recount, declare, pour forth* (Heb. *yabbîaʿ* means, lit., "to gush forth," but in the Old Testament it almost exclusively refers to the act of speaking; cf. Pss. 78:2; 119:171; 145:7; Prov. 10:32, etc.), *speech, knowledge, words,* and *voice* (if the textual emendation in v. 4 is correct). The dense occurrence of so many explicit references to speech firmly establishes speech as the main poetic theme of the psalm.

The first four verses of this poem explore a fundamental paradox. God's creation resounds with a *speech* that human beings can neither hear nor understand. *There is no speech, nor are there words, neither is their voice heard.* In these verses, the poet personifies creation, yet stresses that even personified in poetry, creation remains a fundamentally different sort of creature than human beings. Via personification, the poet endows nature with voice, speech, and even knowledge. *Knowledge (dāʿaṯ)* in this context implies not just any knowledge, but *knowledge of God* (cf. Hos. 4:1ff.). Likewise, creation is given a tongue not for the purpose of praising God. Indeed, the idea of nature prais-

---

reading, although not so difficult as to indicate a corrupt text. Lacking textual support, the emendation should not be made.

15. LXX and Syriac may be read to suggest moving *gam* before the verb, perhaps in line with the use of the particle in prose (cf. Gen. 31:15; Num 16:13). In this case, the intensifying effect of this particle is clear without this emendation; thus it is translated "moreover."

16. LXX has *allotriōn* ("strangers"), perhaps reading *zrym* for MT's *zdym.*

17. The verb *'ytm* is from the root *tmm* ("to be whole or perfect"). Note that the same root occurs in v. 7a, *The torah of the LORD is perfect.*

ing God is not foreign to the Psalter. Psalm 148:3-10, for example, implores sun, moon, heavens, waters, and the like to praise God. Both in Psalm 148 and here in Psalm 19, the call to praise God is a tacit polemic against Israel's polytheistic neighbors.[18] Whereas Israel's neighbors worshipped sun, moon, stars, and so on as divine beings, the poems of the Psalter stress that the Creator is one God and these natural phenomena are merely creatures whose true end is to praise the one God. But even as the poet personifies creation, this personification is playfully limited. The voice and tongue of nature may speak, but not in words that human beings can discern. Similar to the poet of Psalm 8, this poet understands that humanity holds a special role within the divine ecology. But whereas in Psalm 8 that role is described in *royal* terms as exercising *dominion,* here that role is described in *priestly* terms as consisting of torah obedience (see the comment on vv. 11-14 below).

The poetry of the first four verses is both artistically and theologically intricate. Verse 1 is a chiasm that is difficult to translate smoothly into English. Literally:

> The-heavens (subject) <u>are-recounting</u> (verb) *the-glory-of-God* (object)
> *and-the-work-of-his-hands* (object) <u>is-declaring</u> (verb) the-firmament (subject).

There is theological balance in the two cola of the verse. Because God dwells in the heavens, it is appropriate that the heavens praise God's glory. The *work of his hands* refers to the moon and stars (cf. Ps. 8:3). Because the *firmament (rāqîaʿ)* was considered a level beneath the heavens in which the moon and stars dwelt (cf. Gen. 1:6-8; 14-19), it is appropriate that the firmament praises the *work of his hands.* Verses 2-3 both employ repetition in their opening cola *(day to day . . . night to night* and *there is no . . . there are no)* and both reserve the verb and object *(declares knowledge* and *their voice* [is not] *heard)* for their second cola. Though the two verses have similar structure, they have dissimilar meaning. Verse 2 emphasizes that creation speaks a message about God and passes on knowledge of God; v. 3 denies that the message can be interpreted. Thus the similar structure of these two verses underscores their dissimilar theological message essentially by making the two verses "like" and "unlike" at the same time.

5-6 In the second stanza — still a part of section 1 of the psalm — the focus narrows in upon the *sun.* Although this shift may seem slightly abrupt, the poet has laid the ground for it by referring to *day* and *night* in v. 2. The sun's coming and going measure the beginning and end of both day and night. The same Hebrew word — *going out (yāṣāʾ)* — occurs in vv. 5-6 of stanza 2 and in

18. See Sarna, *On the Book of Psalms,* pp. 69-96.

v. 4 of stanza 1, where it is an allusion to the sun. The sun is said to have a tent *in the heavens.* The Hebrew reads, literally, "in them," but because this clearly refers to the heavens, the above translation makes this reference explicit. In addition, these two stanzas are tied together through repetition of key words. The repetition of *yāṣā'* has already been noted. *The heavens (šāmayim)* occurs in vv. 1 and 6, and *end (qāṣeh)* occurs in v. 4 and twice in v. 6.

In the ancient Near East, the sun was worshipped as the god of justice. Both iconographic and literary data from Israel's neighbors establish the fact that the poet of Psalm 19 was playing off of this idea.[19] A Sumerian hymn calls the sun-god the "hero who goes out" (here, the Hebrew word often translated "hero" is translated as *strong man* in v. 5), an Akkadian/Sumerian bilingual hymn refers to the sun-god as a "warrior" who enters his bed chamber with his wife, and the sun-god was often called "bridegroom" in Akkadian.[20] Such examples could be multiplied literally many times over, but these few examples should serve to make the point that the polytheistic idea of the sun as a god does lie behind this psalm. But in terms of understanding Psalm 19, the question to ask is: "What point is the psalm writer scoring by using this imagery?" In Psalm 19, the answer is that the poet employs this familiar imagery in order to continue the polemic against creation worship, especially worship of the sun. This psalm stresses that the sun is not a god but something created *by God.* It is God who set it in the heavens. The sun runs the circuit that God has appointed for it. The sun is said to *rejoice (śûś).* This verb often refers (cf. Ps. 68:3; 119:14) to the songs of praise directed to God. In this case, it is an allusion to the praise that creation gives to its Creator.

Of particular importance for understanding Psalm 19 is the ancient concept of the sun as the god of justice. This concept serves two purposes in Psalm 19. First, it paves the way for the transition to the second and third sections of the psalm. The concept of judgment that is introduced here prepares the audience for the transition to torah/laws (vv. 7-10) and the abrupt request to be cleansed of *hidden* sins (v. 12). It also prepares the audience for the prayer in v. 13 for protection from the *insolent.* As the god of justice, the sun-god was seen not only as the one who judges sinners but the one who could provide protection. In this Israelite psalm, those functions are obviously transferred to the one God of Israel.

Second, the concept of the sun as the god of justice supplies the nec-

19. Although many scholars have investigated the ANE background to this psalm, two scholars who have presented the research particularly clearly are Brown, *Seeing the Psalms,* pp. 81-104; and Sarna, *On the Book of Psalms,* pp. 69-96.

20. Cf. O. Schroeder, "Zu Psalm 19," *ZAW* 34 (1914) 70 (cited in Kraus, *Psalms 1–59,* p. 272); cf. Benjamin R. Foster, *Before the Muses* (Bethesda: CDL, 1993), 2:660; cf. Gunkel, *Die Psalmen,* p. 75.

essary background to understand the closing image of the second stanza: *From the end of the heavens it goes forth, along its circuit to the end. There is nothing hidden from its heat.* The image here is that the sun's rays, which can be understood to symbolize its efficaciousness, reach every corner of the earth. Indeed, *nothing is hidden* from it (note the repetition of *There is no . . .* in v. 3 and here in v. 6). The Hebrew word *ḥammāṯô,* translated here as *heat,* is a double entendre. The Hebrew root *ḥmt* can mean both "heat" and "wrath." There is no reason to choose between the two meanings; the poetry allows for both at the same time. To the extent that the audience thinks of the sun's heat, the sense of a devouring thirst comes to mind. To the extent that the audience thinks of the sun as a god of judgment, the sense of divine wrath comes to mind. Likewise, the two occurrences of the noun *end (qāṣeh)* in vv. 4 and 6 carry a complementary double entendre. The basic sense of *qāṣeh* is spatial, meaning the "edge" of the earth. But the root also can carry a temporal sense, meaning "expiration." These two double entendres borrowed from the metaphor of the sun work together to provide a stunning poetic climax to the second stanza. The passage suggests both that the heat of the sun reaches the *end* of the earth and also that divine judgment reaches even to the *end* of life.

7-10 The tone and theme of the psalm modulate at v. 7. The focus shifts to the *torah of the LORD*. Whereas the name for God in v. 1 is *God (ʾēl),* the name beginning in v. 7 is *the LORD (YHWH).* Each of the first six lines of the second section of the psalm begins with a synonym for the law of the Lord. These synonyms — *torah, decrees, precepts, commandment, fear,*[21] and *ordinances* — are a reference to the word of God available to Israel in the statutes and laws of the Pentateuch. Torah is understood here not strictly as law in the legal sense, but as instruction for right living. These six synonyms establish the primary continuity between this section of the psalm and the rest of the psalm: a continuity based on the theme of *word* or *speech.* This section teaches that while creation may utter a voiceless praise of God's glory, the Lord has given to human beings a concrete *word* that humans can access by studying the Scriptures of Israel.

The poetry also changes dramatically beginning in v. 7, becoming extremely regular — one might dare to say it becomes formulaic. The first six cola of this section share a symmetrical structure, with only minor variations:[22]

Noun + YHWH + adjective + participle + noun

21. As noted above, some commentators prefer to alter the word *fear* to "word," which would make for a more harmonious fit in this list of synonyms.

22. In v. 7b, the adjective is replaced by a *niphal* verb (*neʾᵉmānâ,* "to be made steadfast, to be confirmed"); in v. 9b, the adjective is replaced by an abstract noun *(truth)* and the normal participle + noun pattern is replaced by a finite verb + adverb *(ṣādqû yaḥdāw, they are righteous altogether).*

Although the sudden change in the mood and style of poetry in v. 7 has given many readers pause, there are strong threads of continuity connecting the first section of the poem (vv. 1-6) and the second section (vv. 7-10). As mentioned above, the strongest thread is the theme of words or speech. A second unifying feature is a set of words and phrases that correspond to concepts in vv. 4-7. The first section of the poem spoke of the *circuit* of the sun; v. 7 echoes this by asserting that *the torah of the LORD is perfect.* (The Hebrew root *tmm* has the basic sense of "all-encompassing"; thus the word provides a resonance with the image of the sun's circuit.) The first section of the poem ended with the image of all creation suffering thirst beneath the sun's glaring *heat* in v. 6; v. 7 echoes this by claiming that the instruction of the Lord *refreshes the soul.* The word translated as "refresh" (*šûḇ)* here in the *hiphil* stem means to restore. But *šûḇ* is also the normal word for "repent"; thus v. 7 continues the series of double entendres that play with the "natural" and "moral" senses of various words. The poetic sense of this double entendre is that the word of God as found in the torah both metaphorically refreshes the thirst brought about by the scorching judgment of God and also restores one's relationship with God by providing for a means of repentance (see below). There are other connections with the first part of the psalm. The sun *rejoices* as it circles the earth (v. 5); the *precepts of the LORD* cause the heart to *rejoice* (v. 8; note that the Hebrew words for rejoice are not the same in these two instances). The sun by definition shines in the heavens and is an immortal part of God's creation; the *commandment of the LORD enlightens* (v. 8), and the *fear of the LORD endures forever* (v. 9). The last of these six cola — *the ordinances of the LORD are truth, they are righteous altogether* — breaks the pattern of adjective + participle + noun. By breaking the pattern, it provides a fitting poetic climax to these verses. The final claim that *they are righteous altogether* accords with the image of the sun as an image of judgment. In the face of judgment, God's word provides a refuge of perfect righteousness for humanity.

The second section of the psalm closes with a summary verse (v. 10) that echoes the creation theme of vv. 1-6 by affirming that the word of the Lord is more to be desired than anything in creation. This verse also plays off the image of the sun because both *gold* and *honey*[23] share the golden hue of the sun.

11-14 The final section of the psalm is again marked by shifts in poetic style and focus. The focus of this section shifts to the author of the psalm, who

23. Sarna (*On the Book of Psalms,* pp. 90-91) argues that "honey" *(dᵉḇaš; nōp̱eṯ)* most likely does not refer to bee's honey, since there is no evidence of apiculture in biblical Palestine. Yet the reference could refer to wild bee's honey. If it does not refer to bee's honey, it is most likely to refer to syrup made from grapes or dates. Even if this is the case, the color would still be golden, and thus the point made here is still established (cf. *HALOT,* 1:212-13; 2:713-14).

self-identifies as *your servant* and who now speaks conversationally to the Lord in prayer. But even as this focus shifts, the poetic theme of the psalm — speech — continues. What we have now is the speech of the psalmist, who has been moved by the abstract speech of creation and the concrete word of God to utter a personal prayer to the Lord of heaven and earth. In addition to this thematic connection with the rest of the psalm, there are other connections. Whereas the second section closed by affirming that the instruction of God is more desirable than *much (rāḇ) fine gold,* v. 11 affirms that in keeping God's law there is *much (rāḇ) reward* and v. 12 affirms that God's protection makes one innocent of *much (rāḇ) transgression.* The Hebrew root *tmm* that occurs in v. 7 reappears toward the end of v. 13. The theme of sun/light is echoed at the start of v. 11 by the psalmist's confession that *your servant is illumined* (*zāhar*[24]) by God's laws. Finally, the closing petition that the poet's *words ('imrê)* be acceptable to God *my rock* recalls both the psalm's primary theme of speech and the psalm's secondary theme of nature/creation.

Poetically, this third section of the psalm has its own style, yet also connects with the earlier sections via both key words and themes. The new style of this section is unlike that of either earlier section, mirroring neither the rigid structural formality of vv. 7-10 nor the artistic play of vv. 1-6. But there is a noteworthy style here. The third section can be divided into three pair of couplets. Each of the first two pair of couplets begins with the emphatic particle *gam (moreover);* each includes the self-identification *your servant ('aḇdeḵâ),* the adjective *much (rāḇ),* and the Hebrew root for *innocent (nāqâ);* and each couplet includes an imperative petition. Note the poetic structure indicated by these key words:

11	*gam . . . 'aḇdᵉḵâ . . .*	*rāḇ*	
12	*nqh*		[imperative petition]
13a	*gam . . . 'aḇdᵉḵâ . . .*		[imperative petition]
13b	*nqh*	*rāḇ*	

The first pair of couplets (vv. 11-12) discusses both the rewards and risks found in the instruction of God. As McCann observes, the phrase *much reward* does not imply that God's torah "represents a mechanistic system of reward and punishment for obedience and disobedience. . . . The prosperity or reward consists of connection to the true source of life: God."[25] Through Israel's torah, the Creator of heaven and earth becomes personally available to any pray-er. The risk located in the commandments of God consists of the in-

24. The word is likely yet another double entendre. The root can mean either "warned" (as translated by NRSV) or "illumined."

25. McCann, "The Book of Psalms," p. 752.

ability to obey them perfectly. This danger is acknowledged in other parts of the Old Testament, such as Eccl. 7:20: "there is no one righteous person on earth who does good and never sins." In addition, there are the twin dangers of mistakenly transgressing a law either because one was unaware of the true impact of one's actions (intending one thing but doing another) or because one was unaware of the law (unintentionally breaking a rule). Leviticus 4:2ff. and Num. 15:22-26 speak of such "unintentional sins" and the sacrificial process by which one is cleansed of them. The psalmist implores God to *cleanse me of hidden errors!*

The second pair of couplets (v. 13) may be understood in two different ways. On the one hand, it may be understood as a request for protection from false accusers. The psalmist appeals for God to *hold back the insolent (zēḏîm).* Although *zēḏîm* is not a technical term for "false accusers," the word often refers to those who speak falsely, as it does in Jer. 43:2; Mal. 3:13-15; Ps. 119:69, 78. If this interpretation is taken, the psalmist's vow that *then I shall be perfect, innocent of much transgression* might be paraphrased "then I shall be acquitted of any guilt." On the other hand, *zēḏîm* may refer to a person who opposes God and therefore opposes the psalmist because the psalmist obeys God's laws; this sense of *zēḏîm* is supported by its usages in Ps. 119:21, 51, 85, 122; and Prov. 21:24. If this second interpretation is taken, then the vow in v. 13b might be paraphrased, "then I will be completely fine,[26] innocent of their transgression." If this second interpretation is taken, then the psalmist's point is that obeying God's law may bring the reward of a relationship with God, but it also may bring suffering from a world that is determined to oppose God's way.

The closing petition of the psalm, similar to the closing petition in Ps. 104:34-35, is a request that God receive the entire psalm as an acceptable sacrifice. As mentioned above, the vocabulary here and at other places in the psalm is priestly vocabulary. The root *tmm,* which the psalmist uses to describe the torah in v. 7 and himself in v. 13, can mean "complete" or "unblemished." In the cultic statutes of the Pentateuch, the root frequently prescribes that only an animal "without blemish" may be sacrificed. Likewise, the word *rāṣôn (acceptable)* is priestly language. It can refer to the person or persons offering a sacrifice, as in Exod. 28:38, or it can refer to the offering that is presented, as in Lev. 19:5. No sharp distinction should be made between these two uses. The point of a sacrifice is to bring the one presenting it into a right relationship with the deity. Thus it is both the sacrifice and the sacrificer who need to be acceptable. The point in Psalm 19 is that the poet now presents her words and thus her life as a living sacrifice (cf. Rom. 12:1-2) to God, *my rock and my redeemer.*

The final word of the psalm, *gō'ēl,* translated here as *redeemer,* is lan-

26. The Hebrew root *tmm* carries the basic sense of "to be complete, finished."

guage borrowed from the realm of kinship law. The *gō'ēl* refers to the next-of-kin who bears the responsibility to "buy back" or "redeem" a relative who had fallen into slavery (Lev. 25:48-49) or the responsibility to execute vengeance against someone who has murdered a kinsman (Num. 35:16-28). The poet closes this psalm by referring to God as a family member. Yet God is not just any family member. God is the family member who bears the responsibility to rescue the psalmist when the waters of life run too deep or to execute justice on the psalmist's behalf when justice is beyond the psalmist's grasp.

Reflections

1. God Hidden and Revealed

Psalm 19 is dominated by the metaphor of "speech." It speaks of the unintelligible praise of creation, the tangible, life-giving instruction of God, and the humble prayer of the psalmist. One question that the psalm begs is whether there is a connection between these three types of speech — is there revelation in nature or only in God's word? What is the connection between the two? As Mays writes, "The question is, and theologians usually raise it in connection with the psalm, whether the psalm speaks of 'natural revelation.' Is this voice of the universe that can be seen but not heard visible to all? Do and can all hear the music of the spheres praising God? Does one have to know of the creator first to perceive God's praise in the creation?"[27] Perhaps a clue to this is found in the way the names of God change in the psalm. In the first half, where nature's voice is described, God is called only *El,* the generic reference to God. In the second half, where the torah's words are described, the proper name *Yahweh* is used. Perhaps the point is that one can know a god vaguely, impersonally through nature, but to know God personally, then the direct revelation of the word is required. Just imagine, after all, what kind of a god Israel would have worshipped if all they knew of God they had had to deduce from earthquakes and floods; predators and prey; sun, rain and seasons. In creation, the Creator comes to us hidden, wearing nature as a mask. In the word, the Lord (Yahweh) comes to us personally. Here, we meet a God who is gracious and merciful, slow to anger, abounding in steadfast love, showing faithfulness to the thousandth generation.

2. Hidden Sins

One of the concerns of the psalm is with hidden sins, those incorrect things that we either do or fail to do, but of which we are unaware. As the old saying goes, "ignorance is no excuse." It may be troubling to imagine that there is a

27. Mays, *Psalms,* p. 98.

need to be forgiven for things that we are not aware that we are even doing. Does that not go against many of our ethical assumptions, where we often presume that one's intentions are the most important factor? If it is true that we bear guilt for actions of which we are unaware, then, as Jesus' disciples wondered, "Who then can be saved?" (Luke 18:26). Israel's Scriptures were aware of the fragility of human awareness and allowed for ways to address guilt that accrued because of it (cf. Lev. 4:2ff. and Num. 15:22-26). But perhaps no sentence of Scripture addresses this issue as poignantly as the words of Jesus from the cross: "Father, forgive them for they know not what they do" (Luke 23:34). Christ's request, a faithful extension of Psalm 19, is both prayer and promise for all who pray Psalm 19.

ROLF A. JACOBSON

Psalm 20: Intercession for the Day of Trouble

Psalm 20 is an intercessory prayer on behalf of one who is facing *the day of distress.* The day of distress is a generic term that can mean any time of crisis, with the added caveat that the crisis is too great for the individual or community to face without the saving help of another (see Pss. 50:15; Prov. 24:10, 25:19; Obad. 12, 14; Nah. 1:7). The siege of Jerusalem by Sennacherib is singled out as a day of trouble for the nation (2 Kgs. 19:3//Isa. 37:3). Internal evidence indicates that the psalm was composed as an intercession for a king (*his anointed,* v. 6) prior either to a battle or to entering into a covenant of military alliance (v. 7).[1] But the prayer, especially vv. 1-5 and 9, may be appropriately prayed in secondary usage on behalf of any sufferer who sits in need of intercession. The psalm was most likely composed and performed in the Jerusalem temple (see the references to the name of God, vv. 1, 5, 7, and to *the sanctuary, Zion,* and offerings, vv. 1-3).

The structure of the psalm is rather straightforward. It is made up of two stanzas, each of which begins with four verses (of eight cola) and is capped with a closing verse of petition:

St. 1 Intercession on behalf of one facing the day of trouble (vv. 1-4)
Closing cohortative petition (v. 5)
St. 2 Expression of confidence (vv. 6-8)
Closing petition to God as king (v. 9)

The psalm is tied together poetically by the inclusio formed by the opening intercession *answer you in the day of distress* (*ya'ankâ YHWH b^e^yôm ṣārâ;* v. 1) and the closing petition *answer us on the day of our calling* (*ya'^a^nēnû b^e^yôm qār'ēnû;* v. 9).

For the leader. A Davidic psalm.

1 *May the* L*ORD* *answer you in the day of distress,*
may the name of the God of Jacob protect you.
2 *May he send you help from the sanctuary,*[2]
and support you from Zion.

1. It is plausible that the psalm may have been performed either at some festival occasion (Weiser, Eaton) or ritually repeated before some military crisis, but it is most likely a prayer of intercession immediately before a battle (see Mowinckel, *The Psalms in Israel's Worship,* 1:245).

2. Syr and Targum have a 3ms suffix.

3 *May he remember the entirety of your offering,*[3]
and may he accept your burnt offering.[4] Selah[5]
4 *May he*[6] *grant you the wish of your heart,*
and may he fulfill your every plan.
5 *May we shout for you over your deliverance,*
and may we unfurl banners[7] *in the name of our God.*
May the Lord *fulfill all your plans.*

6 *Now I know that the* Lord *will deliver his anointed.*
He will answer him from his heavenly sanctuary,
with a mighty[8] *victory by his right hand.*

7 *Some trust in the chariot and some in horses,*
but we praise[9] *the name of the* Lord *our God.*
8 *They, yes they will collapse and fall!*
but we shall arise and stand together.
9 *O* Lord, *Grant deliverance.*
O King, answer us on the day of our calling.

1-5 The opening stanza is slightly strange in the Psalter, because rather than consisting of a petition directed to God from one who suffers, it is made up of an intercessory petition by some unnamed speaker(s) directed rhetorically to the king, and thus only implicitly directed to God. The first four verses of the stanza include eight cola, each of which has one jussive verb. These verbs express the intercessory wishes of the pray-er: May God *answer, protect, send help, support, remember, accept, grant wishes,* and *fulfill.* Altogether, this sequence of intercessions most likely hints at a ritual worship service in which a king approached the temple prior to a battle, offered sacrifices, asked for the Lord's blessing upon his *plan,* and then awaited the message. As mentioned above, the *day of distress* can refer to any crisis that is too great for an

3. Some Hebrew mss from the Cairo Geniza have the plural, "all your offerings" (so NRSV).

4. Some mss, Syr, Targum, and Arabic have the plural, "your burnt offerings" (NRSV "sacrifices").

5. Syr omits.

6. Some mss, Syr, Arabic include *YHWH.*

7. LXX (*megalynthēsometha,* "to declare great") has likely transposed the interior consonants on the rare verb *ndgl* (*unfurl banners;* cf Song 6:4, 10), reading *ngdl.*

8. MT's plural *big*ᵉ*ḇûrôṯ* is problematic, as the singular form attested in multiple mss, Aquila, Jerome, Symmachus, and Syriac indicates.

9. LXX again has *megalynthēsometha* ("to declare great"). But the hiphil of *zkr* in this case means to cause to be remembered in the sense of to give praise.

individual or a community to face alone, but in this case almost surely refers to a military crisis — either to an impending battle or to an impending military alliance. The references to God's name in vv. 1, 5, and 7 are reminiscent of the so-called Deuteronomistic "name theology,"[10] which strove to avoid the implication that the Lord literally resided in the temple (cf. Psalm 46) and substituted the language that God's name resided there. God's name, therefore, is not merely a referent for God, but is God himself. When the psalmist prays that *the name of the God of Jacob protect you,* it is a prayer for God's direct saving help, not some talismanic understanding. Likewise, to *praise the name of the Lord our God* (v. 7) is to praise God, not some aspect or appellative of God. The temple does not denote God's literal home, but a contact point between the heavenly and earthly realms, a central point to which the needy may go to seek God's help and from which the saving help of the Lord was to emanate outward.

Regarding the concept of offering a sacrifice before battle, 1 Sam. 7:8-9 shows that the concept was that the sacrifice as a ritual joining of a prayer to a gift was a way to entreat the Lord's favor: "The people of Israel said to Samuel, 'Do not cease to cry out to the Lord our God for us, and pray that he may save us from the hand of the Philistines.' So Samuel took a suckling lamb and offered it as a whole burnt offering *('ôlâ)* to the Lord; Samuel cried out to the Lord for Israel, and the Lord answered *('ānâ)* him" (see also 1 Sam. 13:9-12). Thus, here the king most likely offered a *burnt offering ('ôlâ)* in hope of getting a favorable answer *('ānâ)* from the Lord. The *minḥâ* offering (v. 3a) is a tribute or gift offering, by which an individual indicates his loyalty to a god (1 Kgs. 18:29, 36) or to a greater human lord (Judg. 3:15-18). Here, the offering underscores both that the human king is loyal to the divine King and also that the crisis is so deep that the human king is dependent on the divine King for help.

The anonymous supplicant further begs that the Lord *fulfill your every plan ('ēṣâ).* In Isa 30:1, the prophet excoriates those leaders "who carry out a plan *('ēṣâ),* but not mine; make an alliance, but against my will." Similarly, in Isa. 29:15 and 36:5 the term *'ēṣâ* refers to plans for military allegiance or action. The prophet was apparently condemning the king, most likely Hezekiah, for failing to seek the Lord's will through a prophet (see 1 Kings 22) before entering into a military alliance (in this case with Egypt). If Psalm 20 is read in that light, it is plausible that the king had approached the temple, revealed a plan for a battle or strategic alliance, and that a prophetic/priestly figure prayed for God's favorable response.

The first stanza ends with a slight modulation in tone. The string of

10. See Tryggve N. D. Mettinger, *The Dethronement of Sabaoth: Studies in the Shem and Kabod Theologies,* trans. Frederick H. Cryer (ConBOT 18; Lund: Gleerup, 1982).

eight jussive verbs is broken. By means of two cohortative verbs — *may we shout . . . may we unfurl banners* — the anonymous liturgist announces the hope that after God has given answer to the king's petitions, the news will be worth celebrating.

6-9 The turning point of the psalm comes in v. 6: *Now I know.* It is often the case in the psalms that the word *now ('attâ)* signals the turning point in the rhetoric of a poem. In 39:7, it signals the psalmist's existential turn to God in desperate prayer. In 2:10, it signals the poem's turn from description to warning. And perhaps most poignantly, in 12:5 it signals the intention of God to arise in power on behalf of the poor and needy. Here, it signals that the liturgist of the psalm has changed footing — from that of hopeful intercessor to that of confident proclaimer of good news. The next word — *I know (yāḏa'tî)* — continues the change of mood. In Pss. 56:9 and 41:11, the term expresses trust in God. It is this confidence in God that is the basis for the turn in Psalm 20. The complete phrase, *now I know ('attâ yāḏa'tî),* signals the unveiling of an earth-shattering revelation. In Gen. 22:12, God learns based on Abraham's willingness to sacrifice Isaac, that Abraham truly fears God. In Exod. 18:11, Jethro learns, based on the exodus, that "the LORD is greater than all gods." Frustratingly, we do not know precisely what has transpired for the psalmist. Was there a vision? Perhaps a favorable omen? Was the ritual sacrifice successfully completed, signaling that the king's petition and offering were accepted? We cannot know. But what is clear is this — the psalmist has been moved from hopeful prayer for the Lord's saving help to confident proclamation about the Lord's saving help. The king has received his favorable *answer ('ānâ).* God's help, moreover, will come from God's *heavenly sanctuary.* As mentioned above, the temple was understood as a point of contact between the heavenly and earthly realms.

The military nature of the crisis that originally occasioned the psalm is made clear by the imagery of vv. 6-7. The *chariot* and the *horse* were the most fearsome military instruments of the day. As such, they could either be the cause of fear if one was opposed to them or of confidence if one was supported by them. Israel was neither to fear horse and chariot (Deut. 20:1) nor were they to trust in them (Ps. 20:7). Rather, they were to fear and trust the Lord, whose salvation does not come by means of the horse or chariot (Hos. 1:7). Deliverance belongs to the Lord, who defeated horse and chariot at the Red Sea. This psalm, which announces the present unfolding of the Lord's deliverance, warns against trusting in the means of God's saving help and points the king past those means — which *will collapse and fall* — to *the name of the LORD our God.*

The second stanza, like the first, closes with a slight modulation in tone — while vv. 6-8 contained mostly imperfect verbs expressing the psalmist's confidence, v. 9 brings the psalm to a close with a final petition. As noted above, the language of this petition — *Answer us on the day of our calling* — echoes the language of v. 1 and thus rounds off the prayer-poem nicely. The translation of the verse is disputed. Most versions render something like, "O LORD, deliver the king. Answer us on the day of our calling" (cf. NRSV, NIV, etc.). NJPS, following the verse division of MT, reads the word *hammeleḵ* with the second colon of the verse.[11] That reading, which is followed here, underscores the dependence of the earthly king on God, whose help is the one necessary thing in order to face the day of trouble.

Reflections

1. An Intercessory Prayer for Anyone in Need

On the surface, a modern reader may wonder what to do with an ancient prayer for an Israelite king. Such an ancient, royal psalm may seem so foreign that the average person of faith may be tempted to treat it as a historical artifact rather than a living word of Scripture. But, in fact, the psalm may be read and indeed prayed, almost in total, by any modern person as an intercessory prayer on behalf of any neighbor in need. If one focuses on vv. 1-5a, 7, and 9, the psalm can speak to the needs of a neighbor facing almost any crisis. In this light, it is striking that this prayer for help betrays not even the slightest hint of lament or complaint. Unlike the more common personal prayers for help that are spoken by an individual facing crisis, this prayer is remarkable for the fact that there are no complaints against God, about the self, or against the enemy. Perhaps the reason for this is that the singer of the psalm is not himself or herself facing the crisis (or is not the primary person facing the crisis). Instead, the speaker lifts his or her voice on behalf of another who is facing the day of trouble. As such, the prayer lacks the personal touch of the complaint. In its place, the rhetoric of the poem moves the speaker into a solidarity of prayer with the individual in crisis. The prayer starts out as a wish that God would *answer you in the day of distress.* By the end, the *you* has become *us* and the *day of distress* has become the *day of our calling.* The singer has joined his or her life and voice to that of the suffering and has entered into the solidarity of hope with the one facing crisis.

2. The End Breaking In on the Middle

One of the strange poetic features of this psalm is that the poem moves "forward" from petition to trust, but then moves "backward" from trust to renewed petition. The poem ends with a petition, even though the psalmist has

11. See *Mikra'ot Gedelot Haketer* (Ramat Gan: Bar-Ilan University Press, 1992–), 7:64. See also Mays, *Psalms,* p. 102.

just voiced soaring words of confident trust in vv. 6-8. Is this change a prayerful form of spiritual backsliding? No. Is this renewed petition a sign that the confident trust of vv. 6-8 is a sham? Again, no. Rather, the renewed petition is a hint of what it means to live a life of faith. As noted above, the psalmist has received some revelation, some good news that moves him or her from petition to trust. In short, the psalmist has received a promise. And what else is the life of faith other than the living out of life in light of having received the promise of God. A former colleague of mine at Luther Seminary, Mary Hinkle Shore, refers to the way that the biblical narrative keeps having "the end of the story break in on the middle." And, as she says, when the end of the story breaks in on the middle, then the question becomes, "How do I live now?" The psalmist has heard a promise about the end: God's kingdom will prevail; *he will answer . . . from his heavenly sanctuary.* And what now? The psalmist lives in the already-and-not-yet moment of having received and believed that promise. Thus, the psalmist at the same time expresses confidence that *the Lord will deliver,* even as the psalmist continues to pray *Grant deliverance.*

Rolf A. Jacobson

Psalm 21: Blessings

Psalm 21 is a royal psalm — a psalm that arose in close conjunction with the institution of the monarchy. The poem contains words addressed to God on behalf of the king (vv. 1-6), a declaration about the king's fidelity (v. 7), and words addressed to the king about God (vv. 8-12). But after this initially clear identification, the psalm's sharp profile begins to lose definition. With this psalm, as with so many others, how one interprets the poem will in large part rest on how one imagines the psalm may have been performed. How one imagines the life setting in which the poem was employed will, to a large extent, shape how one translates, explains, and contextualizes its ancient words. Many scholars, such as Craigie, imagine it "is probable that the liturgy was associated with some ceremony pertaining to the anniversary or renewal of a king's coronation in the Davidic tradition."[1] Others imagine the psalm in the setting of an actual coronation.[2] Kraus wonders about a "royal Zion festival."[3] Mowinckel thinks of a liturgy or prayer for "before the king marches to war."[4] Dahood thinks of a prayer "of thanksgiving [after a battle in gratitude] for the royal victory prayed for in the preceding psalm."[5] The interpretation of v. 3b *(you set a gold crown upon his head)* is key. The phrase might indicate the ritual coronation of a king, or the ritual recoronation of the monarch, or might simply be a metaphorical allusion to the divine authorization of the king's rule. While pinning the psalm down to one reconstructed life setting can serve to focus interpretive options, the approach taken here is that the psalm cannot be assigned to any one life setting. The interpreter is better served by taking an approach that reads the poem with a range of possibilities in mind. Reading with such a range of possibilities in mind will, admittedly, not allow one to narrow interpretive options. But this is not necessarily negative; the approach can be more theologically generative and may open up the interpreter's imagination to theological possibilities.

The psalm's structure is finely balanced, with two major stanzas, each of which consists of six couplets and each of which is followed by a singular verse.

St. 1 Address to the Lord on behalf of the king[6] (vv. 1-6)
Summary affirmation about the king's trust (v. 7)

1. *Psalms 1–50,* p. 190. Similarly, Gerstenberger, *Psalms: Part 1,* p. 107.
2. Weiser; Seybold, *Die Psalmen,* p. 92.
3. *Psalms 1–59,* p. 285.
4. *The Psalms in Israel's Worship,* 1:69.
5. *Psalms 1–50,* p. 131. So also Hossfeld and Zenger, *Psalm 1–50,* p. 139.
6. Notice that stanza 1 is finely balanced, with two halves (vv. 1-3, 4-6), each of which begins with two verses of imperfect declarative praise, followed by a third verse that begins with *for (kî).*

St. 2 Address to the king about the Lord's blessings (vv. 8-12)
Summary praise to God (v. 13)

The artistic craft of the poem is also evident in such poetic flourishes as the inclusio formed by the repetition of *O LORD, in your strength* (*YHWH b'zk;* vv. 1, 13) and the way each major stanza culminates with a reference to the Hebrew term *pāneh* (*your presence* in v. 6 [cf. also v. 9]; *their faces* in v. 12 — the poetic turnabout contrasting the revelation of God's presence on behalf of the king with the fleeing presence of the threatening enemies).

For the leader. A Davidic psalm.

1 *O LORD, in your strength the king rejoices,*
and in your deliverance how[7] *greatly he exults.*[8]
2 *The wish of his heart you have given to him,*
and the desire of his lips you have not withheld. Selah[9]
3 *For you greet him with blessings of that which is good,*
you set a gold crown upon his head.
4 *He has asked of you life — you have given it to him —*
length of days for ever and ever.
5 *His glory is great in your deliverance,*
splendor and majesty do you bestow upon him.
6 *For you give him blessings forever,*[10]
you gladden him with the joy of your presence.

7 *For the king trusts in the LORD,*
and on the hesed *of the Almighty he shall not stumble.*

8 *Your hand will find out all your enemies,*
your right hand will find those who hate you.[11]
9 *You set them ablaze like a fiery furnace,*
at the time when you find favor.
In his anger the LORD[12] *destroys them*
and fire devours them.
10 *You will destroy their fruit from the earth,*

7. LXX and Syr omit *how.*

8. Reading *yāḡel* Qere in some mss (see *Mikra'ot Gedelot Haketer* [Ramat Gan: Bar-Ilan University Press, 1992–], 7:64), as opposed to Kethib *yāḡêl.*

9. Omitted in Syr.

10. LXX has a dittography from v. 4, reading *'ôlām wā'eḏ.*

11. LXX and Targum have "all who hate you."

12. Here reading the Lord as the subject of the second colon.

and their seed from amongst humanity.
11 *For they have directed evil against you,*
they have devised a scheme,[13] *but they shall not succeed.*
12 *For you will make them show their backs,*[14]
when you aim your bows[15] *at their faces.*

13 *Be exalted, O LORD, in your strength!*
Let us sing and let us rejoice in your might!

1-6 The opening stanza can be described as intercessory praise (if there is such a thing) of the Lord on behalf of the king. An anonymous speaker praises the Lord for God's wide range of actions on behalf of the king. This broad range of actions can be summed up in two general categories — God's acts of *deliverance* (vv. 1, 5) and God's acts of *blessing* (vv. 3, 6).[16] That is, God's gracious actions have two characteristic modes. The first is the mode of *deliverance.* In this mode, God proves salvific in granting rescue of enemies; God proves merciful in granting forgiveness of sins; and God proves powerful in granting rescue from exile or imprisonment. It is worth noting that the king's *glory, splendor,* and *majesty* — royal attributes that many mortals might covet — are divinely bestowed: they come from God's deliverance. The second is the mode of *blessing.* In this mode, God provides the bounties of harvest, God multiplies wealth and prosperity, God renews both the earth and the human family through fertility, and God rules the chaotic creation through law and order.[17] God's acts of deliverance are, by definition, occasional — they arise to meet a particular crisis and change the stream of history. God's acts of blessing are, by definition, ongoing — they move along with the current and are cyclical.

The psalm employs two primary metaphors for God's agency — God's *strength (ʿōz)* and God's *presence (pāneh).* It would be tempting to suggest that the psalm matches these two metaphors up in a complementary fashion with the two modes of God's actions: God's strength is made known in deliverance, God's presence is made known in blessing. Such a complementary pairing of the two sets of concepts is supported by the pairing of strength/deliverance in v. 1 and blessings/presence in v. 6.

13. LXX reads plural *(mᵉzimmôṯ).*

14. Lit., "you will set their shoulders."

15. Lit., "bow strings."

16. See Claus Westermann, *Elements of Old Testament Theology,* trans. Douglas W. Stott (Atlanta: John Knox, 1982).

17. As Kraus points out, the Lord's blessings denote "the 'enhancement of life' in a comprehensive sense (F. Horst, *EvTh* 7 [1947], 29); it is promised to the house of David (2 Sam. 7:29). The symbol of the powerful blessings coming from God and showered on the royal life is the golden crown"; *Psalms 1–59,* p. 286.

In v. 2, the reference to granting the king's requests is striking. If the psalm is imagined as a coronation liturgy, a comparison to Solomon's request to be granted wisdom (1 Kings 3) at his own coronation is attractive (cf. Pss. 2:7ff.; 20:4). Upon assuming the throne, the tone and color of the king's prayers change — to ask for guidance in governing and blessings on his reign. In a broader cultural context, throughout the ancient Near East the king played a priestly role on behalf of the nation. He was the chief intercessor for the people in times of crisis. In this light, if the psalm is imagined as a prayer before some national crisis, comparison to Hezekiah's prayer in response to Sennacherib's invasion (Isa. 37:14-20) or David's prayer in response to the census plague (2 Sam. 24:10ff.) is attractive.

The request for *life* in v. 4 may be a request for a long reign at the occasion of a coronation (serving as a king was not always the safest vocation, as the widows of any number of Israelite kings could have attested) or maybe a request for the preservation of life prior to some crisis. The request that *length of days for ever and ever* be granted is neither a request for eternal life nor a literal request for an immortal earthly existence. Rather, it is a formulaic and hyperbolic request for long life. In the ancient Near East, to pray for long life for the king was a stock petition (cf. 1 Kgs. 3:11) — and this blessing was not just for the king but for the nation. Short royal reigns are often symptomatic of nation turmoil, and the common folk were just as likely to suffer in such times as were the nobility. Thus, the prayer that the monarch live long is at least equally a prayer in the people's own interest.

7 The first of two summary verses occurs in v. 7. In this verse, the psalm declares the king's trust in the Lord's *hesed.* Craigie's description of the import of v. 7 cannot be improved upon: "The language of the declaration is the language of covenant, especially notable in the words [*bṭḥ,* trust] and [*ḥsd, hesed*], and these two words sum up, in a sense, the entire theology of the psalm. There are two partners to the covenant, God and Israel (represented by the king); God's fundamental character in the covenant relationship is *lovingkindness* [*ḥsd*], and the king's response was to be one of *trust* [*bṭḥ*]."[18]

8-12 The chief interpretive difficulty with the second stanza of the poem is in discerning who is meant by the *you* of vv. 6-12. There are two options: the *you* might be the Lord, in which case the genre of this part of the poem might be considered something like imprecatory trust (if such a thing exists). Or, the *you* might be the king, in which case the genre of this part of the poem might be called something like an oracle of assurance. The verse where the two interpretations meet the fork in the road is v. 9. In *Biblia Hebraica Stuttgartensia,*[19] which is based on Codex Leningrad, the word *YHWH* is taken as

18. *Psalms 1–50,* p. 192.

19. Ed. R Kittel, 4th ed. (Stuttgart: Deutsche Bibelstiftung, 1967/77).

a vocative: *You set them ablaze like a fiery furnace/at the time of your presence, O LORD* [*l^{eʿ}ēṯ pānêḵâ YHWH*]/. . . In *Mikra'ot Gedelot Haketer,* which is based on Codex Aleppo, *YHWH* is taken as the subject of the succeeding phrase: *You set them ablaze like a fiery furnace/at the time of your presence./In his anger the LORD destroys them* [*YHWH b^{eʾ}appô y^{e}ḇall^{eʿ}ēm*]. The interpretation that makes the best sense is that throughout this stanza, the *you* is the king. The enemies direct their evil scheme (v. 11) against the king, who in turn aims his bows (lit., "when you prepare/establish your [bow]strings") at them in self-defense.[20] The strange phrase *l^{eʿ}ēṯ pānêḵâ* (lit., "for/to the time of your face") means "at the time when you are shown favor by God," as the usage of *pānêḵâ* in Ps. 45:12 supports.

The section is, in essence, an extended poetic promise to the king that though under attack, he will be sustained by the presence and protection of God. One cannot help but think of the prophet Isaiah's promise to King Ahaz (Isaiah 7) in this regard. Given that the enemies are portrayed as the ones who initiate the violent confrontation through their evil schemes and intentions, most readers can accommodate themselves to the reality that the ancient king would have seen no choice other than to defend himself and his people in a like matter. So Goldingay: "Yhwh does not take initiative in attacking people; Yhwh is responding to attack."[21]

But the most difficult section of this stanza for modern readers is doubtless the promise that the king *will destroy their fruit from the earth, and their seed from amongst humanity* (v. 10). The *fruit* and *seed* are references to the enemies' children. The notion that the leader of God's people would (with God's apparent sanction) desire the end of the enemies' bloodline is horrific. It should be noted that this sort of language is hyperbolic. The Egyptian Pharaoh Merneptah, for instance, boasted in a victory monument that "Israel is laid waste, his seed no longer exists." But Israel was, of course, not completely eliminated. The metaphor does not literally mean the genocidal annihilation of the enemies' progeny, but is a metaphor that reflects the complete defeat of the enemies' violent scheme and the subjugation of the enemies' military capacity.

13 The psalm closes with a summary word of praise, which functions in a similar manner to v. 7. Whereas v. 7 is a statement about the king's trust, the single verse of praise in v. 13 summarizes the Lord's power — and by extension, offers assurance of the trustworthiness of the promises made on behalf of the Lord in vv. 8-12. The imperative term *be exalted* is a characteristic word

20. The idea of the *you* aiming a bow at enemies best fits with the interpretation that the *you* is the king. It should be noted, however, that the notion that the *you* sets the enemies ablaze in a fiery furnace does fit well with images of God's actions (cf. Ps. 11:6).

21. *Psalms 1–41,* p. 317.

of praise that can serve as a refrain (57:5, 11) or as the climax of a poem (as is the case here). There is also at least a hint of petition in the term. That is, this is praise that is also functioning as plea: "Be exalted in strength, so that we can sing and rejoice" (as it were).

Reflections

Blessed to Be a Blessing

When reflecting on Psalm 21's promises to the king, one might be misled by the mistaken notion that the king received blessings from God for his own sake. And, indeed, the biblical narrative often suggests that the ancient kings did indeed often seek their own advantage in God's blessings. But as the Deuteronomic law makes clear and as Clifford has aptly stated, the king's "task was to protect and rule the people justly so their prosperity would show forth the grandeur of their God."[22] Or, as Goldingay extrapolates, "The idea of Yhwh's making (the verb is *sit* as in v. 3b) the king an abundant blessing is that Yhwh turns him into such an embodiment of multiple blessing that he becomes a standard whereby people seek blessing for themselves (cf. the idea of 'being a blessing' in Gen. 12:2; Isa. 19:24; Zech. 8:13)."[23] The king, then, is merely the channel through which God blesses the people. Indeed, there is a close relationship between the Psalter's theology of kingship and the related Old Testament concept that the chosen people's blessedness was not for themselves, but for the sake of the larger world (cf. Gen. 12:1-3). As Mays puts it, "the theological purpose of Psalm 21 is to subordinate the human king to the divine king. Everything the king is, has, and does comes from God."[24] Thus, in terms of the various personal offices that the modern person of faith assumes — whether it is faith community leader, family leader, business leader, community leader, etc. — the psalm directs us to remember that leadership is a gift and a trust that comes from God. And the blessings that come with leadership do not exist for the advantage of the leader, but for the sake of the community and for the sake of the world. The kings of Israel and Judah never learned this lesson. And the leaders of today seem to do no better. One is reminded of the old saw that people get elected to Congress in order to do good, but end up doing well. So perhaps Jesus' warning is still apt: From those to whom much has been given, much is expected.

ROLF A. JACOBSON

22. *Psalms 1–71,* p. 120.

23. *Psalms* (Baker Commentary on the Old Testament Wisdom and Psalms; Grand Rapids: Baker, 2006), p. 315.

24. *Psalms,* p. 103.

Psalm 22: Desperate Cries and Recounting God's Ways

Psalm 22 opens with a line that echoes all the way to the cross (Mark 15:34 and Matt. 27:46), making it possibly the most well-known prayer for help in the entire psalter. In addition, the connections to the Gospels do not stop with v. 1a. Several other verses appear in the New Testament accounts of Jesus' death: v. 7 in Mark 15:29; v. 8 in Matt. 27:43; and v. 18 in Mark 15:24; Matt. 27:35; Luke 23:34; and John 19:23-24. This use speaks to the powerful legacy of this psalm. The psalm is clearly important to the New Testament writers, but it is also a powerful message in its own right.

The psalm itself is complex. The first twenty verses are part of a prayer for help, with v. 21 serving as a transition to the prayer of trust in vv. 22-31. These are the major sections, but there are multiple stanzas giving the psalm this structure:

vv. 1-2 Cry for help
    vv. 3-5 Declaration of confidence based on the ancestors' trust
vv. 6-8 Description of distress
    vv. 9-11 Declaration of confidence based on God's past protection
vv. 12-18 Description of distress and the acts of the enemies
    vv. 19-21a Plea to God for rescue
v. 21b Declaration of God's intervention
    vv. 22-25 Assurance of being heard expressed in the congregation
vv. 26-31 Sharing of a meal in the house of the Lord[1]

The first twenty-one verses have an alternating structure. The prayer moves from a cry lifted to God into a section of trust. There is no transition between these sections explaining the change in expression, leaving the hearer/reader to decide how the move is made. This structure, then, is disjointed, possibly reflecting the emotional turmoil that a faithful one undergoes as she tries to make sense of suffering and pain and even attacks from others with a belief in a powerful and loving God. After v. 21, the psalm moves into pure praise and declarations of God's great acts.

The psalm also has some of the most significant textual problems in the entire psalter, with v. 18 and vv. 29-31 having so many problems that any translation is tentative. The general topic of these sections can be discerned, but the specific language and metaphors are impossible to state with any certainty. The superscription is probably a musical instruction along with the simple *"A psalm for David."*

1. Most scholars use a similar division. Craigie divides v. 21 into three lines but notes that the verse is a transition as noted here (*Psalms 1–50,* p. 195). Kraus also sees the division at 21a-21b (*Psalms 1–59,* p. 298).

To the leader. On aylet-hasahar.[2] *A Davidic psalm.*

1 *My God, My God,*[3] *why have you forsaken me;*
and why are you so far from saving me,
from my roaring[4] *words?*[5]

2 *O my God, I cry by day and you do not answer;*
and by night, there is no rest[6] *for me.*

3 *But you are holy,*[7]
sitting[8] *on the praises of Israel.*[9]
4 *In you, our ancestors*[10] *trusted;*
they trusted and[11] *you delivered them.*
5 *To you they cried out and they were rescued;*
in you they trusted and they were not ashamed.[12]

6 *But I am a worm and not a human;*[13]
the scorn of humanity and the despised of the people.[14]

2. The meaning of this phrase is unknown. Some try to translate into a song title, "The Deer of the Dawn" (NRSV). The LXX has a similar, possibly corrupt "For the end, concerning a morning aid." NJPS leaves it untranslated as above because any translation is uncertain.

3. LXX adds "attend to me."

4. The NRSV and NIV "words of my groaning" is weak; *šᵉʾāg̱â* means to roar like a lion or to scream.

5. The grammar of this verse is problematic. The *lāmah (why)* appears to govern all three subsequent phrases as in the NRSV and NIV. The LXX reads, "the account of my transgressions is distant from my salvation."

6. Lit., "no rest or repose for me." This is not a verbless clause, but it is added here for clarity in English.

7. It is also possible to read this as a title, "Holy One."

8. Most translations use "enthroned" here, and that may be the sense, but the word is a common one in Hebrew that means either "to sit" or "to dwell."

9. This line is problematic. The LXX reads, "But you, the praise of Israel, dwell in a sanctuary," reading holy as sanctuary. NIV reads, "you are the praise of Israel." The above stays as close to the MT as possible.

10. Lit., "our fathers."

11. XHev/Se4 is missing the connecting *wāw* that is present in the MT and LXX; Flint, *The Dead Sea Psalms Scrolls and the Book of Psalms,* p. 88.

12. Kraus (*Psalms 1–59,* p. 290) and Craigie (*Psalms 1–50,* p. 194), also NIV, translate *bôšû* as "disappointed" (BDB, p. 101) but shame seems to fit the context better here.

13. Lit., "a man."

14. Both of these phrases are in the construct form, which suggests they are descriptive terms instead of acts of other humans as reflected in the NRSV.

7 *All those who see me, they mock me;*
they sneer at me[15] *and they shake their heads.*[16]
8 *"Trust in the LORD,*[17] *let him deliver;*
let him snatch this one up for he takes delight in this one."[18]

9 *Because you brought*[19] *me from the belly;*
my reason to trust[20] *upon my mother's breast.*
10 *Upon you I was cast from the womb;*
from my mother's belly, my God you have been.
11 *Do not be far from me*
for distress is near;
there is no one who will help!

12 *Many bulls surround me;*
mighty ones of Bashan encircle me.
13 *They set free their mouths upon me;*
lions devouring and roaring.
14 *Like water, I am poured out;*
all my bones are disjointed;
my heart has become like wax,
melted[21] *within my chest.*
15 *My strength is dried up like a ceramic shard;*

15. Craigie notes that this literal phrase "separating the lips" means to sneer (*Psalms 1–50,* p. 196).

16. "Head" is singular in the MT with a 3mpl verb.

17. The verb here is problematic. The MT has *gol* ("to roll"). LXX reads "hope." NRSV uses "commit your cause." Adding a direct object is unnecessary since the line is understandable without it. NIV and Craigie (p. 194) use "he trusted," reading the 3ms verb instead of the imperative as suggested in the *BHS* apparatus from a Targum manuscript. Another Targum manuscript retains the imperative form for "trust" (*BHS,* p. 1104). There is no clear solution to this problem, but an imperative seems to make the most sense. I have adopted the Targum reading, but the choice is tentative.

18. MT "him" for "this one."

19. Meaning of this word is uncertain. In the context, "took or brought" is a good general option.

20. NIV adds "in you." The LXX reads not the *hiphil* participle of *bṭḥ* but a noun "my hope," but the MT is understandable as it is. The *hiphil* participle can mean "the one who caused another to trust," as above.

21. 4QPs^f has a variant of *nms* that appears to be a *niphal* of either *mwš* ("remove") or *mšš* ("touch"; Ulrich, Cross, et al., *Qumran Cave 4: XI,* p. 88). Neither of these words has any other occurrences in the *niphal,* and since the MT and LXX agree here, there is no reason to alter the MT.

my tongue sticks[22] *to the top of my mouth;*[23]
you set me down[24] *in the*[25] *dust of death.*
16 *For dogs, they surround me;*
the congregation of evil ones,

they circle me like a lion, my hands and feet.[26]

22. 4QPs^f contains a variant *mdbš,* but this verb is unknown in Hebrew, although the noun means "honey" (Ulrich, Cross, et al., *Qumran Cave 4: XI,* p. 88).

23. This word appears only here, so meaning is uncertain.

24. Although part of broken text, 4QPs^f appears to use the participle here (*šwpṭ* and then broken text) matching the participle in the line above it (Ulrich, Cross, et al., *Qumran Cave 4: XI,* p. 88).

25. 4QPs^f has a variant reading instead of the MT's *wlʿpr,* where the *wāw* and the preposition are definitely not attached to "dust" (Ulrich, Cross, et al., *Qumran Cave 4: XI,* p. 88).

26. There are no less than ten monographs and countless attempts in commentaries to untangle the meaning of 22:16 (for this complex history, see James Linville, "Psalm 22:17B: A New Guess," *JBL* 124 [2005] 733-44). It is not possible to give a full rehearsal of all of the arguments here, so only the most likely are offered. It is important to remember, however, that any translation is tentative. First, the ancient sources are divided. The MT reads, "like a lion my hands and my feet," and seems nonsensical. The Targum adds an additional verb, *nktyn* ("they gnaw"), a meaning preserved in the NJPS.

While not completely readable, 4QPs^f probably has the first two letters *kr* (Ulrich, Cross, et al., *Qumran Cave 4: XI,* p. 88). This may be reflected in the LXX and Syr, which derive from a Hebrew noun *kārâ* ("to dig"). But these may have been influenced by the role of Psalm 22 in Jesus' crucifixion reading as a piercing of hands and feet (Kristin Swenson, "Psalm 22:17: Circling Around the Problem Again," *JBL* 123 [2004] 638). However, recent readings of the 5/6ḪevPsalms by Peter Flint reflects the LXX with *k'rw,* a 3cpl verb (James H. Charlesworth, *Miscellaneous Texts from the Judaean Desert* [DJD 38; Oxford: Clarendon, 2000], pp. 133-66). Based on this evidence, this reading must be seriously considered. However as noted by Brent A. Strawn, the fragment (col. XI, frg. 9) is very faded, and *y* and *w* are quite similar. In addition, he notes that the LXX may not be following the same Hebrew *Vorlage* as the MT ("Psalm 22:17b: More Guessing," *JBL* 119 [2000] 447-48). This line of possibilities is reflected in the NIV's "they have pierced my hands and my feet."

J. J. M. Roberts suggests that *kārâ* also be understood as a verb, but from Akkadian and Syriac cognates with a meaning of "be short or shriveled"; thus the NRSV's reading of "my hands and feet have shriveled" ("A New Root for an Old Crux, Psalms 22:17c," *VT* 23 [1973] 252).

The translation above is not superior to those listed, but offers another possibility, following Swenson, who suggests this is a two-line verse where the break is misplaced ("Psalm 22:17," p. 642). This preserves the text as it is, although the above translation is altered from Swenson's reading for it preserves the exact order of the MT. Her reading, however, is not without its critics; see Linville, "Psalm 22:17B," pp. 738-39. Swenson's "Like a lion, they circumscribe my hands and feet" reads better in English, but in a translation that is so uncertain, I believe the order of the text should be maintained if for no other reason than to remind us of its difficulties.

17 *I can recount all my feelings;*
they[27] *watch and they stare at me.*
18 *They divide my robes among themselves;*
and upon my garments they cast lots.
19 *But you, O* LORD, *do not be far away;*
O my strength![28] *Come quickly to my aid!*
20 *Snatch me*[29] *from the sword;*
from the hand of the dog, my only life![30]
21 *Save me from the mouth of the lion;*

from the horns of the ox you answered me!
22 *I will recount your name to my siblings;*[31]
in the midst of the assembly, I will praise you!
23 *Those fearing the* LORD, *praise him!*
All descendants[32] *of Jacob, honor him!*
Stand in awe, all the descendants of Israel!
24 *Because he did not despise,*
and he did not disdain the affliction of the afflicted;
he did not hide his face from the one;[33]
when the one cried out to him he heard.
25 *From you is my praise*[34] *in the great assembly;*
my vow I will fulfill before those fearing him.

27. Both the 3mpl personal pronoun and the 3mpl verb appear here for emphasis.

28. The word appears only here, so *HALOT*'s "helper" is tentative. Craigie notes that based on the Ugaritic the term means "might or strength," and this is certainly possible, but the meaning of the word is unclear (*Psalms 1–50,* p. 197).

29. Lit., my *nep̱eš,* this word has a wide range of meaning: "soul, living being, self." It is the essence of what makes a sack of bones alive.

30. This word is clear in Hebrew, but the context is difficult. It probably points to the idea "of my only life" (also 35:17). It usually refers to an only child or son (Genesis 22). The idea here may be to call on God to realize the precious resource God has made as a motivation for God to act.

31. Lit., "my brothers."

32. Singular in the MT.

33. LXX uses the 1cs suffix here and in the next line. The NRSV adopts this reading. The decision is a difficult one. The third person fits with the call to praise of v. 25, but not with the declaration of individual praise that follows. Most scholars read the MT as it is without the change adopted by the NRSV (Kraus, *Psalms 1–59,* p. 491; Terrien, *The Psalms,* 225; Craigie, *Psalms 1–50,* p. 195).

34. Most modern translations add the verb "come" to this line, but this is a verbless clause that is understandable without the addition.

26 *The afflicted will eat and be satisfied;*
they praise the LORD, those who seek him;
may your hearts live forever!
27 *They remember and they return unto the LORD, all the ends of the earth;*
they bow down before him,[35] *all the families of the nations,*
28 *for to the LORD is kingship;*
he rules in the nations.
29 *All the robust ones*[36] *of the earth will feast and worship;*[37]
before him all the ones going down to dust will bow down;
they[38] *who cannot be revived.*[39]
30 *May my descendants serve him;*[40]
may they[41] *tell about the LORD to the generation.*[42]

35. MT has the 2ms suffix, but the LXX, Syr, and Jerome have the 3ms suffix, which is probably the correct one considering the context.

36. *Dišnê* can have the meaning of "fat," but both in Isa. 30:23 and Ps. 92:13 it has the meaning of "alive, vital, healthy." This can be understood as a contrast to *the ones going down to dust* (i.e., dying) in the next line. Many emend to *yᵉšēnê* ("those who sleep"; Craigie, *Psalms 1–50,* p. 197, among others).

37. Usually translated as "bow down," it also means to bow down in worship. It is a different root from the one used in the next line.

38. The MT has *nap̱šô* ("his life force"). The suffixes for 3ms and 3mpl are easily confused, and the plural "they" more clearly fits the context and is the only change actually needed in this verse.

39. This verse is extremely corrupt, as the number of different translations demonstrates. The NRSV and NJPS both emend the text extensively while noting that the Hebrew is uncertain. Likewise, each scholar emends this verse in a variety of ways. The plethora of translations and reasons for them are beyond the scope of this discussion. The MT critical apparatus alone has eleven suggested changes to vv. 29-30. The NIV translates the verse very close to the MT, and even though it is difficult to make sense of it, this may be the best option. The MT is readable, and the general sense of the section can be discerned using the text as it stands, as here.

40. Reading the jussive verb with Dahood (*Psalms I,* p. 138), also reading a 1cs suffix as in the LXX and suggested in the *BHS* critical apparatus (p. 1105). "Seed" is singular here but is understood as plural in most instances (see Gen. 15:3).

41. MT has 3ms, which fits with the singular "seed" but is understood as plural in most instances, so here it should be understood as a collective plural.

42. There are two possible understandings. One is that the direct article indicates "that," so the descendants are to tell to *that,* i.e., their own, *generation.* The other possibility is that like the verse above, the singular noun may also represent the plural, so they are to recount to the generation*s.* This verse is as corrupt as the one preceding it, and multiple emendations are suggested.

31 *May they come*[43] *and declare his righteousness*
to a people yet to be born;
for he[44] *has done it.*[45]

1-5 The first two verses are wrenching. The urgency of the words and the intimacy between the parties jump off the page. The cry is to *My God,* and there is no formal address or introduction. Instead there are questions of why. Why has God abandoned? Often God has promised not to *ʿāzaḇ ("forsake"*; e.g., Deut 31:6, 8; Pss. 9:10; 37:28, 33; 94:14). Even if parents do, God will hold fast (27:10). The cries do not stop there, however. The questions continue: why is God so far away from saving and from these *roaring words?* "Roaring words" is not an elegant phrase, but is an exact translation of the Hebrew. This is not groaning or complaining or whining. These words are expressed in the raspy scream of one in deep distress. The next verse tells that this is not a temporary issue. Indeed, the pain has lasted too long already.

Verses 3-5 are an abrupt about-face. First, God's lofty position compounds the distance from the one crying out. God is *sitting* or enthroned on Israel's *praises.* Does that mean there is no room for cries of abandonment? Or is this a title of honor offered as a sincere act of praise? The next two verses rely on the verb "trust," which appears three times. The ancestors *trusted* and were heard and *were not ashamed.* Is the purpose of this section sarcastic, as suggested by McCann?[46] Or is this truly an about-face with memories of God's acts for the people in the past a basis to trust now, as argued by Limburg?[47] Miller notes, I think rightly, it is both. Crying out in pain and expressing trust are not incompatible.[48] Faith and trust ebb and surge in life, and the appearance of contrasting situations causes a clash in the one suffering. I know what I feel *and* I know what I believe. The prayer clearly demonstrates the emotional roller coaster of the suffering of a faithful one.

6-11 Praise is put aside, and now the suffering is described, but as noted by Miller, the transition here is clearer. The last line of the section above ended with *they* (the ancestors) *were not ashamed* (v. 5). Verses 6-8 tell of the

43. Most follow the LXX here and read *yāḇōʾû* as modifying *generation* in the verse above. This is not a participle but a regular verb which cannot modify the noun. There is no compelling reason to follow the LXX here. It should be noted that all of the translations of vv. 29-31 are problematic and very tentative.

44. LXX has "the LORD" here.

45. Lit., *kî ʿāśâ* without a direct object. A suffix could be missing, and it could read as "he did it" with a 3ms suffix or "he made them" with a 3mpl suffix.

46. McCann, "The Book of Psalms," p. 762.

47. Limburg, *Psalms,* p. 69.

48. Miller, *Interpreting the Psalms,* p. 102.

shame that the suffering one bears.[49] One wonders why the one praying feels so ashamed and is mocked (v. 7). But the truth be told, one does not have to look far to understand. President Roosevelt hid his polio because he knew people would equate paralysis with weakness. AIDS patients suffer from terrible shame as they must face not only their disease, but the questions of how they got it. Many suffer the depression and hurt that comes from not being "normal" in a culture where health and vitality are prized. The problem, of course, does not have to be sickness. Those who have been imprisoned or suffer from addictions or mental illness find the doors closed to full participation in society. Indeed, even the loss of a marriage or relationship leaves one feeling as if he or she has failed and is looked down on by the world. Biblical examples also abound. Job's friends were determined to equate his suffering with his sin in a failed attempt to prove that good people thrive and bad ones suffer. Lepers were sent away instead of being offered human comfort and aid. And of course, Jesus, an innocent man, was mocked by the ones who had a parade for him just a few days before (Mark 15:29; Matt. 27:39). These words reflect all of the times sufferers have been told or looked at in a way that implies they are responsible for their current condition.

The next section is another reflection on God's acts in the past, not for the ancestors, but for the one praying (vv. 9-10). *Trust* appears here again as God is named as this one's *reason to trust* since birth. God is seen as a faithful presence always. This declaration gives way to a plea for God to be near to the suffering one (v. 11).

12-21a The last plea above was that there was no one to help. Verses 12-13 explain just how alone the one praying is as the enemies are portrayed as encircling animals, first the large *bulls of Bashan*[50] and second as a pack of *lions.* From the image one can picture the threat of having no exit as large and menacing wild animals inch closer. In the ancient Near East, these images of bulls and lions represent images of power and strength, indicating these are no ordinary enemies but are menacing and powerful enemies that would discourage others from getting involved.[51]

The next two verses (14-15) describe in detail the physicality of fear.[52] The point where you feel as if your body has become like water flowing away,

49. Miller, *Interpreting the Psalms,* p. 104.

50. Bashan is a northern region known for great mountains (Psalm 68) and large bulls.

51. Keel, *The Symbolism of the Biblical World,* p. 86. Keel also notes that lions can represent demons, but the dual reference here to the bulls and the lions probably says more about the power, political or physical, of the threats, especially in light of v. 21, where the *horns* of oxen are specifically mentioned.

52. Others see the problem as sickness (Kraus, *Psalms 1–59,* p. 297) or the nearness of death (McCann, "The Book of Psalms," p. 763), but this does not have to be the case. Miller notes it can also represent the anguish of suffering (*Interpreting the Psalms,* p. 105).

joints become harder to hold in place, joined with that hollow feeling in the chest as finally the mouth dries up. This is the way fear impacts not just the brain but the whole self. The last line of v. 15 states, *you set me down in the dust of death.* Who is the "you" here? The last "you" was God in vv. 9-11, and most commentators read it as God here also, and this may very well be the case.[53] This would then echo the problem with God that began the prayer. The enemies are vexing, but the center of this one's distress is the feeling of separation from God to the point that here God is seen as actively participating in this one's suffering. Finally however, the "you" is undetermined. It is probably God, but without a clear indication all the possibilities remain open.

Verses 16-17a are a reprise of 12-15. The animals are *dogs,* and here they are clearly equated with not just enemies, but a *congregation (ʿᵃḏaṯ) of evil ones.* The word *congregation* is significant here because it names the evil ones, not as distant, but as ones that share a cultic community.

The next line may be one of the most debated in all of Scripture as noted in the translation, and any suggestion must be offered tentatively. Clifford notes that the problem with the LXX and Dead Sea reading of "pierced" is that this verse is not quoted in the NT stories of Jesus' crucifixion, which would be expected considering the other appearances of this psalm in those texts.[54] My translation reflects a suggestion offered by Swenson that follows the MT closely and provides a parallel with v. 12, where the congregation of evil ones is like a pack of animals, dogs or lions that threaten.[55]

Like the above section, this one moves from the circling of enemies to the feelings of the one surrounded. Commentators note that this means the one praying has been stripped so that this one's bones are showing.[56] But the Hebrew word *ʿeṣem* can have a much broader meaning, such as the seat of emotions or even the whole self.[57] In addition, the verb is clearly in a *piel* form here that usually indicates a "recounting or telling," so it is just as possible that the line is *I can recount all my feelings,* which is roughly the equivalent of "recounting one's life or taking stock," just like the phrase "my life flashed before my eyes" in our vernacular — another reaction of a person in an extremely fearful or stressful situation. This is followed by a further reaction of the enemies (vv. 17b-18), who seem to think their work is done; first they watch the suffering, then divide up the last of the suffering one's belongings.

This long section gives way to a final plea. The plea is the same as it has

53. Craigie, *Psalms 1–50,* p. 200; Kraus, *Psalms 1–59,* p. 297, among others.
54. Clifford, *Psalms 1–72,* p. 126.
55. Swenson, "Psalm 22:17," p. 642.
56. Kraus, *Psalms 1–59,* p. 297; Clifford, *Psalms 1–72,* p. 126.
57. *HALOT,* p. 869.

been throughout (v. 1, and even the same verb as in vv. 11 and 19): *do not be far away.* The rest of the plea has urgency, as God is asked to *come quickly, snatch me,* and *save me.* The enemies are again portrayed as dogs and lions. God needs to arrive quickly to save, since this one only has one life and it is threatened (vv. 20-21a).

21b-31 Occasionally in the prayers for help, God's help arrives while the person is still crying out, as is the case here. Verse 21 begins with an imperative verb, *save me,* and ends with a perfect verb meaning *you answered me.*[58] The turn is unexpected and seems small compared to the lengthy emotional cries. God answered and the matter is settled; pain gives way to rejoicing. The cries of rescue are completed as the enemies disappear from the picture. We wish to know what happened. How was the problem managed, and did the enemies get what they deserve? But the prayers for help never narrate God's dealings with the enemies, only the relationship with this one and God. It seems too abrupt; but it is what it is. The whole psalm pivots on this one word (at least in Hebrew), *ʿᵃnîṯānî* ("you answered me")

At v. 22, this one is no longer alone but is now praising God in the assembly and inviting others to do the same (v. 23). Being surrounded by menacing enemies is exchanged for being surrounded by the worshipping community. Verse 24 gives the reason why such praise is due. A new chapter has been added to vv. 3-5 and 9-11. Another reason why God keeps God's promises is that even in the lowest moments when the feelings of fear and shame surround, God did not abandon. This may be the most powerful verse in the whole psalm. For those times when we feel rejected and shamed and all alone, here is the hope of tomorrow. God does *not despise* or *disdain.* The next verse is a traditional one in prayers for help. This one will complete the story by praising God and fulfilling vows among the congregation. God's act of deliverance is to be added to the community's great story so that all can benefit from the event. In the concluding verse (v. 26), the afflicted become the ones who sit at the table and *eat* and are *satisfied.* The theme here is much like the Beatitudes in Luke where "the kingdom of God belongs to the poor and those who are hungry will be fed" (Luke 6:20-21).

The psalm could have easily ended at v. 26 with the life of the afflicted one restored. The remaining verses remind us that even God's act to the afflicted one has world-wide impact. Just as in the enthronement psalms, the nations come to the Lord, not because of sheer power or force, but they stream to God because of God's justice and equity among the peoples (Psalms 96, 97, 98). God is the God of the universe *because* God is the God of the one

58. Some modern translations ignore the perfect verb, reading "save me" (NIV), but Kraus rightly notes," the certainty of being heard is definitely expressed. The verbal form [*ʿny-tny*] closes the lament and forms a transition to the song of thanksgiving" (*Psalms 1–59,* 292).

alone and shamed. The same equity shown to this one will be the way God will rule the world.

The last three verses are very problematic textually, and any exact translation is tentative. What is clear here is that all will praise God because of this, and all of God's acts go even beyond the nations that one can see in the present. Both the healthy and robust ones will praise along with those nearing the grave (v. 29), and beyond all of them, the story will grow and go on to new *generations,* to those yet unborn.

Given the scope of Psalm 22, it is no surprise that it was seen by the New Testament writers as applicable to the death of Jesus. The cry of the one who loves the Lord, who is afflicted and shamed and surrounded by enemies, is still heard by God, and God's act of deliverance of this one has world-wide, earth-shattering consequences. What we should not do with this prayer is leave it there at the cross, for the cry of the afflicted one could also be Israel crying out for deliverance from the Egyptians, for here too God acted decisively against the powerful to liberate the afflicted, or it could be the African slaves who cried out to God in their misery. God has an ear for the ones who are suffering hurt and sorrow and shame. God had that ear before the advent of Christ. Jesus had that ear during his ministry and has it today. Jesus' love still transforms the world, one suffering person at a time.

Beth Tanner

Psalm 23: You Are with Me

Has any psalm occasioned the spilling of more ink than Psalm 23? The psalm may be the most-beloved, most-sung, most-prayed, and most-studied poem in the Psalter. A review of the secondary literature for this psalm alone could fill an entire volume.[1] Miller observes that "the very familiarity of the psalm presents a challenge to bring it alive so that even, if not especially, those who know it well may not pass it by too quickly."[2] The majority of scholars have approached the poem as a psalm of trust, as Gerstenberger summarily states: "Every reader of Psalm 23 will agree that the motif of trust is predominant in the psalm."[3] Beyond applying that broad label, however, little further consensus exists about the psalm's form and setting. Gerstenberger, for example, argues that "the extremely personal tone of the Psalm 23 excludes its royal and national use (against Eaton; Merrill). . . . we may think of a worship service for an individual person held within the small circle of family or clan."[4] Tanner disagrees, arguing that the psalm is "indeed royal" since "every image can be understood under the rubric of Yahweh as king" and therefore that "the images evoked provide a picture of Yahweh as the great Shepherd-King and the psalmist as a vassal to that king."[5]

Given that a definitive, original social or liturgical life setting is unrecoverable, we should instead think of the theological setting of the psalm. The best clue for imaging its theological setting comes from the witness the psalm offers to dual, dueling presences: the Lord and the valley of deep darkness. As with many psalms of trust, a striking feature is the psalm's tacit acknowledgment of the presence of danger. In Psalm 27, the threat of enemies is named. In Psalm 46, the threats of raging chaos and roaring nations are named. Here, the threatening presence of *the darkest valley* is named. But the fear-evoking

1. Some of the more helpful recent essays devoted to understanding Psalm 23 include: Beth L. Tanner, "King Yahweh as the Good Shepherd: Taking Another Look at the Image of God in Psalm 23," in *David and Zion: Biblical Studies in Honor of J. J. M. Roberts,* ed. Bernard F. Batto and Kathryn L. Roberts (Winona Lake: Eisenbrauns, 2004), pp. 267-84; Nancy deClaissé-Walford, "An Intertextual Reading of Psalms 22, 23, and 24," in Flint and Miller, *The Book of Psalms,* pp. 139-52; Patrick Miller, "'The Lord is my shepherd, I shall not want': Psalm 23," in *Interpreting the Psalms,* pp. 112-19; Dennis Pardee, "Structure and Meaning in Hebrew Poetry: The Example of Psalm 23," *Maarav* 5-6 (1990) 239-80; Mark S. Smith, "Setting and Rhetoric in Psalm 23," *JSOT* 41 (1988) 61-66; Andrew E. Arterbury and William H. Bellinger, Jr., "'Returning' to the Hospitality of the Lord: A Reconsideration of Psalm 23,5-6," *Bib* 86 (2005) 387-95.

2. Miller, *Interpreting the Psalms,* p. 112.

3. *Psalms: Part 1,* p. 115; see also Gunkel (*Introduction to Psalms,* p. 190); Westermann, *The Psalms,* p. 69; Miller, *Interpreting the Psalms,* p. 112, etc.

4. *Psalms: Part 1,* p. 115.

5. "King Yahweh as the Good Shepherd," p. 270, 283.

danger of that presence is more than balanced by the courage-providing, fear-removing presence of the Lord. This is the true setting of the psalm: the existential space of being in the presence of something that is terrifying, a space in which every reflective human being finds himself or herself at some point, and a space in which, according to the witness of the poem, the Lord can also be found.

There are two structural developments in the psalm. Most commentators focus on the change in metaphor from the Lord as shepherd (vv. 1-4) to that of the Lord as banquet host (vv. 5-6). This provides an understanding of the structure that looks like this:

St. 1 The Lord as Shepherd (vv. 1-4)
St. 2 The Lord as Host (vv. 5-6)

But an equally important development takes places in v. 4c, where the poem changes from speaking about the Lord in the third person to speaking to the Lord in prayer. This change is important because of the rhetorical location where it happens (in *the darkest valley*) and also because of what is said: *you are with me.* As Limburg has noted, these words are "the center of this psalm."[6] This provides an understanding of the structure:

Speech about the Lord (vv. 1-4b)
    Speech to the Lord (vv. 4c-5)
Speech about the Lord (v. 6)

These two views of the poem's structure are not mutually exclusive, but complement each other and illustrate two different movements at work within the poem.

A Davidic psalm.

1 *The LORD is my shepherd, I do not lack;*
2 *he provides rest for me in green pastures.*
He leads me to peaceful waters.
3 *He restores my life.*
He leads me along the paths of righteousness,
for the sake of his name.
4 *Even if I walk through the darkest valley,*[7]
I fear no evil.

6. *Psalms*, p. 74.

7. LXX's *en mesō skias thanaton* suggests a possible *bên ṣalmôṯ*. MT stands.

For you are with me;
your rod and your staff —
they give me courage.

5 *You set a table for me,*
in the presence of my enemies.
You anoint my head with oil,
my cup[8] *is abundant.*
6 *Indeed, goodness and* hesed[9]
pursue me all the days of my life.
And I will return[10] *to the house of the* LORD,
for the length of my days.

1-4 The poem begins with an almost creedal statement: *The Lord is my shepherd.* As many commentators have noted, within Israel and throughout the ancient Near East, the shepherd was a royal metaphor.[11] Kings were portrayed as shepherds (cf. 1 Kgs. 22:17; Jer. 23:1-4; Ezek. 34:1-10), and to portray God as shepherd is to portray God as a royal figure (cf. Ezek. 34:10-16). Tanner goes so far as to assert that shepherd is "a title that is synonomous with 'king.'"[12] In the psalms (as well as throughout the Old Testament) the metaphor is normally communal, describing God's relationship with the entire people: "O Shepherd of Israel, hear us!" (Ps. 80:1); "we are his people and the sheep of his pasture" (100:3). In this case, the normally communal image is rendered intensely personal: *The Lord is my shepherd.* This transposition is one of the reasons for the power and popularity of Psalm 23 — and indeed, for the power and popularity of the Psalter. Here we see the personal dimension of Israel's faith and the individual application of Israel's creeds. The God who created heavens and earth, sea and dry land, who shepherded Israel out of bondage in

8. LXX reads "your cup."

9. LXX has only "and your mercy pursues."

10. MT's *I will return* (from Hebrew *šûḇ*) is often changed in light of LXX (*katoikein,* reflecting Hebrew *yāšaḇ*), thus "I will dwell." But MT should stand. It should be noted that the sense is not greatly altered, because a verb of motion (such as *šûḇ*) plus the preposition *b-* gives the sense of move to a place in order to remain there permanently (cf. Ronald J. Williams, *Hebrew Syntax: An Outline* (3rd ed.; Toronto: University of Toronto Pres, 2007), p. 46; with appreciation to my colleague Mark Throntveit for pointing this out). This reading need not imply a pilgrimage vow (against Kraus, *Psalms 1–59,* p. 304).

11. For the ancient Near Eastern context, see, e.g., "The Laws of Hammurabi," epilogue, where Hammurabi claims that Marduk had entrusted the "shepherding" of the people to him and offers a blessing that a future king "may shepherd his people in justice"; Martha T. Roth, *Law Collections from Mesopotamia and Asia Minor* (2nd ed.; SBLWAW 6; Atlanta: Scholars, 1997), pp. 133, 136.

12. Tanner, "King Yahweh as the Good Shepherd," p. 272.

Egypt — this grand, cosmic Lord also cares for and shepherds the individual. As Miller aptly summarizes, Psalm 23 "is the song of trust of someone who knows in the midst of the vicissitudes of her or his personal life and over the course of years that he or she has been carried in the bosom of God, sheltered from harm, and given rest."[13]

The rest of stanza 1 can be interpreted as poetic commentary on the opening, creedlike statement, *The Lord is my shepherd.* After the initial statement, a series of terse phrases unpack the shepherd metaphor by charting the protecting, providing, pathfinding presence of the Lord. The unqualified statement, *I do not lack (lōʾ ʾeḥsār),* with no direct object, is a remarkable assertion of trust. Given the sheep-shepherd metaphor, the term may imply something such as "I do not lack any necessity," as the parallel in 34:10 suggests: "Young lions can go without and be hungry, but those who seek the LORD lack *(lōʾ yaḥsᵉrû)* for nothing good." The verb *yarbîṣēnî* (translated here as *he provides rest for me*) is difficult to render smoothly into English. Many translations try to capture the causative nature of the *hiphil* with something such as "he makes me lie down" (NRSV). Such a translation is too wooden and depicts God's power in a highly reductive fashion as one who forces something upon the psalmist. The term rather denotes the active agency of the shepherd in seeking out an environment in which the sheep may thrive (the *green pastures*), as the NIV's translation of the *hiphil* occurrence of *rbṣ* in Ezek. 34:15 indicates: "I will have them lie down. . . ." The image of the green pasture as the ideal environment is stock language from the ancient Near East, as Hammurabi's boast in the epilogue of his law code indicates: "I have sought for them peaceful places. . . . I made the people of all settlements lie in safe pastures."[14] Tanner also points out that the image of the shepherd providing *peaceful waters* for the flock is stock language with royal overtones, as the description of Marduk as the one "who provides grazing and drinking places" demonstrates.[15]

The word translated *peaceful (mᵉnuḥôṯ)* is related to the important theological concept of *rest,* which most English language readers may not fully appreciate. *Rest* means more than mere bodily repose. *Rest* connotes protection from enemies, the environment in which life might thrive, and indeed, the lifting of any threat of divine punishment (see Genesis 6-9 and the story of Noah, whose name derives from the word *nûaḥ,* or "rest," as well as the book of Judges, in which God grants "rest" during the reigns of faithful judges). The confession *he restores (šûḇ) my life* sums up the restorative power of life-giving water, but also hints at a double meaning: *šûḇ* carries the

13. Miller, *Interpreting the Psalms,* p. 113.

14. "Law Codes of Hammurabi," Roth, p. 133.

15. Tanner, "King Yahweh as the Good Shepherd," p. 274, quoting *ANET,* p. 69.

overtones of repentance as well as the simple meaning to restore. The sense of returning to God in repentance for the purpose of being restored is hinted at here (cf. Jer. 50:6, 19).

The image of the shepherd leading the sheep implies not only that a desirable destination is reached, but also that the journey itself is safe. The psalmist's trust in protection and guidance while the journey is underway is expressed in the phrase *he leads me along the paths of righteousness.* The metaphor of God's leading is prominent in Scripture, reaching its most poetically powerful expression in Psalm 121 (cf. also 40:11). The image of the *paths of righteousness (maʿgᵉlê ṣedeq)* is a double entendre. The phrase occurs only here, although "paths of uprightness" (Prov. 4:11; cf. Isa. 26:7) and "good path" (Prov. 2:9) fall within the same semantic range. The basic sense of the phrase is "safe pathways"; perhaps even "easy roadways" would fit. But the phrase includes ethical and theological overtones, implying that the pathways in which the Lord leads have to do with obedience to the will and law of God: "Keep straight the path of your feet. . . . Do not swerve to the right or to the left; turn your foot away from evil" (Prov. 4:26-27). The warning against turning neither "to the right or to the left" is especially reminiscent of the formulaic Deuteronomistic warning regarding obeying God's law (cf. Deut. 5:32; 17:11, 20; 28:14) — a formula applied most notably to King Josiah, the model of Deuteronomistic obedience (2 Kgs. 22:2).[16] Thus, the reader should understand the character of the Lord's leading here primarily as a leading that is mediating via the instructing guidance of Scripture (cf. "All the paths of the LORD are *hesed* and truth," Ps. 25:10).

The interpretation of the final clause — *for the sake of his name* — is difficult. Does the phrase describe God's motive for leading? If so, what role does God's name play in this motivation? Does it describe the follower's motivation for following God's paths? The parallel request in 31:3, "for your name's sake, lead me and guide me," suggests that the phrase here describes God's motivation. As Goldingay states, "Yhwh is a God characterized by faithfulness. . . . In a sense, that is the meaning of the name 'Yhwh.' So acting in faithfulness demonstrates that the name is a true reflection of the character."[17] This interpretation is borne out by the hymnic interpretation of the Lord's name given in Exod. 34:6: "The LORD, the LORD, a God merciful and gracious, slow to anger, and abounding in steadfast love." The name often functions as a virtual double for the Lord's presence, as in Ps. 20:1: "The name of the God of Jacob protect you." Thus, to reduce the meaning of *for the sake of his name* merely to God's motivation is inadequate. This is about far more than mere motiva-

16. This data offers support for Tanner's argument that the persona of Psalm 23 should be understood as a Judean king.

17. Goldingay, *Psalms 1–41,* p. 350.

tion; it is about God's character. God's very nature is to be faithful. God has promised — through the sheer act of giving God's name to Israel — to guide and protect those who bear God's name. Thus, *for the sake of his name* is a claim on God's promise and on God's character. It is a statement expressing the psalmist's trust that God is completely committed to maintaining the relationship that God has established.

Perhaps the most basic of theological promises is the assurance "I am with you." This is the promise God offered Jacob (Gen. 28:15). It is the word of assurance God proclaimed to the young Jeremiah (Jer. 1:8, 19), which he in turn passed on to the people of Judah (15:20; 30:11; 42:11; 46:28). It is the promise that the Lord spoke to the exiles through the anonymous prophet known as Second Isaiah (Isa. 41:10; 43:5). It is the heart of the message that Haggai announced to those who had returned from exile (Hag. 1:13; 2:4). And it was the promise that fueled the early church for perseverance and mission (Matt. 28:20; Col. 2:5; Acts 18:10). According to some scholars, this promise formed the basis of the so-called oracle of salvation, in which a priest spoke a word of assurance to a supplicant in distress.[18] To be sure, as the above litany of texts bears witness, the promise plays a central role in the rhetoric of many prophets. But as the presence of the formula outside of prophetic texts also bears witness, this is because of the raw power of the promise of God's presence and because of the ubiquitous human experience of crisis (that is, of *the darkest valley*). In Psalm 23, the familiar phrase of assurance is transformed into a word of trusting prayer, spoken to God: *you are with me.* It is noteworthy that it is precisely in the middle of the crisis *(the darkest valley)* that the psalm shifts from creedal affirmations about God to trusting prayer to God. It is in moments of crisis that the Lord moves from an abstract concept (a *he* about whom one has memorized doctrinal statements) to a living God with whom one has a relationship (a *you* in whom one trusts, to whom one speaks, on whom one can rely).

The Lord's presence in moments of crisis is both a profound assurance and also a profound warning for how we theologically construct God's presence. As a promise, it is the good news that there is no place in which the Lord's presence cannot manifest itself to dispel fear *(I fear no evil)* and to deliver those who suffer (cf. Psalm 139; Rom. 8:31ff.) As a warning about theological constructions of God's presence, it is an element that critiques and subverts the dominant cultural theology of glory, which can only understand God's presence in the good moments. The psalm asserts that, yes, the

18. See Joachim Begrich, "Das priesterliche Heilsorakel," *ZAW* 52 (1934) 81-92. But see also the questions of Edgar W. Conrad, "Second Isaiah and the Priestly Oracle of Salvation," *ZAW* 93 (1981) 234-46. Gerstenberger falls in line with the oracle-of-salvation view (*Psalms: Part 1,* p. 115).

Lord is present in the *green pastures, peaceful waters,* and along the *paths of righteousness.* But the Lord is also present "under the sign of the opposite" — in *the darkest valley.* The metaphor of the *rod and staff* is an image of the shepherd's effective power to save the sheep from threat. The verb translated here as *give me courage (nḥm)* is normally translated as "comfort." But comfort is not a strong enough word. It does not convey the power of the emotion that the psalmist is able to feel because of God's presence. The concept of *courage* gives a better sense of the emotion.

5-6 In the second half of the poem, the basic metaphor changes to that of banquet host. The basic interpretive challenge is to discern what type of banquet table the poem imagines. Is this simply a metaphor for provision, such as that alluded to in Ps. 78:19, where the grumbling people question whether God can spread a table in the wilderness? Is this a table of hospitality, such as the one that the unaware Abraham spread while entertaining angels (Gen. 18:1-8)? Is this a feast of thanksgiving, such as one might celebrate after a harvest or some other experience of God's blessing (Deut. 12:17-19; 14:22-29)? Is the meal a ritual meal in response to the "oracle of salvation" that the psalmist has heard from a priest? Should we think of a royal context, such as that mentioned in 2 Sam. 9:7-13 and alluded to in Prov. 25:6-7, in which rival courtiers are the "enemies" who seek to disgrace the psalmist? Or should we imagine an eschatological feast in which God's provision for the poor and needy is manifest (cf. Isaiah 55)? The many possibilities prevent isolating any singular setting in life for the metaphor. What is undeniable is that the Lord is a hospitable host, who provides plenteous nourishment *(my cup is abundant)* and honor *(you anoint my head with oil)* for the psalmist in the face of hostile foes.

The necessity of understanding this *theological setting* is emphasized by the anthropomorphic description of the Lord's *goodness and* hesed, which *pursue* the psalmist with relentless grace. Traditional translations render the Hebrew *rāḏap̄* with "follow," but this domesticated language fails to communicate the tenacity of God's purpose that the term denotes. Normally in the psalms, it is the enemies who pursue the psalmist in order to inflict bodily harm (cf. 7:5; 31:15; 35:3; 71:11; 109:16, etc.). Here, the divine attributes of *goodness (ṭôḇ)* and *hesed* are pictured as incarnate forces, which will not rest until they have tracked down and provided a safe harbor for the endangered psalmist.

The final couplet of the psalm is debated. As noted in the translation, a basic issue is whether to understand the first verb as related to Hebrew *šûḇ* (return) or *yāšaḇ* (dwell). But as noted above, and as Goldingay rightly sees, "it finally makes little difference which we follow"[19] because either way one

19. *Psalms 1–41,* p. 353.

ends up at *the house of the LORD*. To *return* does not necessarily imply a pilgrimage, not does "to dwell" there imply anything like a priestly vocation or seeking after asylum. The point of the metaphor is that the destination that one reaches after being led along *the paths of righteousness,* the destination one reaches at the end of *the days of my life,* the destination toward which one is shepherded and indeed toward which one is harried by God's pursuing *goodness* and *hesed* is none other than God's very self. God is the psalmist's destination.

Reflections

1. The Lord Is My Shepherd

Theologically, it is important to note that the use of the shepherd metaphor contains within it a powerfully subversive element — subversive of both human kings and of misguided human appropriations of the divine sovereignty. In terms of subverting human royalty, the metaphor is a powerful polemic arguing that the vocation of the king is to protect, guide, care for, and even give one's life for the people who have been entrusted to the king. Thus, prophets such as Jeremiah (ch. 23) and Ezekiel (ch. 34) employed the metaphor so powerfully in criticizing the wayward, curved-in-on-themselves kings of Judah. Precisely because it was the human kings of Israel and Judah inevitably bent to the temptation to use their royal office to serve their own needs, the metaphor of a vocation that exists to protect and serve another was the perfect foil within which the prophets could couch their criticisms of the royalty — "you shepherds of Israel who have been feeding yourselves! Should not shepherds feed the sheep?" (Ezek. 34:2). Thus, even though the psalm contains much royal imagery, as Tanner argues so strongly, the imagery contains within it a built-in critique of all human privilege and power. Similarly, when applied to God talk, the metaphor is a potent corrective to naïve and unnuanced notions of God's sovereignty. The task of the shepherd is to be faithful in protecting the sheep. The task of God is to be faithful in tending God's flock. God's power does not render God immune to criticism or deaf to lament. Rather, God's sovereignty is a servant type of sovereignty that the world cannot understand. Some theological expressions of God's sovereignty are too quick to assert God's right to punish, because God is God (and, of course, the person who has asserted this divine right almost always has perfect knowledge of whom God is punishing and for what reason). The shepherd metaphor is a helpful corrective against these types of arguments. It is a helpful corrective against views that see law as unchallengeable simply because it is God's law, or the types of argument that would assert that "acts of God" are just simply because they are ascribed to God. Thus, when the New

Testament names the one who lays down his life for the sheep (rather than taking up sword to defend himself) as the Good Shepherd (see John 10), the New Testament is faithfully confessing the incarnation in Jesus of the same divine shepherd whom the ancient psalmist trusted.

2. *You Are with Me*

At the heart of Psalm 23 is an elegant and enduring statement of faith: "You are with me." This simple word of trust is the faithful response to God's most basic promise: "I am with you." It is between those two dynamics — the divine promise, "I am with you," and the response of faith, "You are with me" — that the currents of the life of faith ebb and flow. The first pastor I served with lost his oldest daughter to a sudden death when she was thirty-four. He told me, "You never get over it. And you don't want to. And through it all, one promise was most important: God is with us." The pastor's words speak to the experience of millions of faithful throughout the millennia who have been comforted by the promise of God's presence in the darkest moments of life. Psalm 23 gives us the words to speak that faith out loud. *Even if I walk through the darkest valley, I fear no evil. For you are with me.*

Rolf A. Jacobson

Psalm 24: Mutual Advents

Psalm 24 is an entrance liturgy. It is very likely that the liturgy was designed to accompany a procession into the temple. Many see the procession as involving the ark of the covenant. Cross could confidently state that the "psalm is an antiphonal liturgy used in the autumn festival. The portion of the psalm in vv. 7-10 had its origin in the procession of the Ark to the sanctuary at its founding, celebrated annually in the cult of Solomon and perhaps even of David. On this there can be little disagreement."[1] But of course there is disagreement. Gerstenberger judges that "because of the advanced stage of community formation reflected in vv. 3-6, a preexilic date hardly seems feasible for this psalm. This relative dating would exclude the idea of a procession with the ark, although vv. 7-10 might reach back into the old times of the monarchy."[2] Or again, the psalm may be a liturgy of thanks following a military victory, as the ark is returned to the temple (having accompanied the army into battle). As Craigie writes, "the original liturgical usage of the passage, is that of the return of the Ark from war. In battle, the Ark symbolized God's presence; in victory, the return of the Ark symbolized the victorious return of the warrior God to his people (Num 10:36)."[3] These examples could be multiplied. The unity of the psalm is often questioned, so that Seybold and others can easily assert the composite character of the poem.[4] However, even if the psalm is a composite composition, the unity of the poem is clear. The theme of entrance unifies the poem. The poem has holistic integrity and should not be dissected.

The implied theological life setting of the psalm is the mutual advent of God and humans entering into each other's spheres. The poem describes the contrasting natures of the identity of the God who enters into human space and the nature of those humans who are able to meet the advent of this God. The poem is similar, but not identical, to other entrance liturgies such as Psalm 15 (a liturgy of human entrance into the temple), 118:19-29 (a liturgy of thanksgiving of one who comes to fulfill a vow of praise), or Isa. 26:2-6 (a communal entrance liturgy). Psalm 24 is about the advent of human beings into the presence of God and the mutual advent of the *King of glory* into the presence of *those seeking the face of God.*

The psalm bears a three-part structure:

1. *Canaanite Myth and Hebrew Epic,* p. 93; cf. Mowinckel, *The Psalms in Israel's Worship,* 1:6, 142, who sees the psalm used in a New Year's festival in conjunction with the autumn harvest, at which the enthronement of the Lord was also celebrated.

2. Gerstenberger, *Psalms: Part 1,* pp. 118-19.

3. *Psalms 1–50,* p. 213.

4. Seybold, *Die Psalmen,* p. 104.

St. 1 Declaration of the Lord as creator of all (vv. 1-2)
St. 2 Liturgy of the entrance of humans into God's sphere (vv. 3-6)
St. 3 Liturgy of the entrance of the Lord into the human sphere (vv. 7-10)

The ending of the liturgical poem both completes the rhetorical movement of God into the human space and provides a fitting theological bookend to v. 1. The *King of Glory* of vv. 8-10 is the same Lord who first established his kingship by creating and founding the world (v. 1).

A Davidic psalm.

1 *The earth is the LORD's and all that is in it,*
the world and those[5] *who dwell in it.*
2 *For*[6] *it was he who founded it upon the waters,*
and upon the rivers he established it.

3 *Who ascends the mountain of the LORD?*
And stands in his holy place?
4 *The clean of hand and pure of heart,*
who do not take up my life[7] *falsely,*
and do not swear deceitfully.
5 *These will take a blessing from the LORD,*
and vindication from the God of their deliverance.
6 *This is the generation of those who seek him,*[8]
of those seeking the face of the God of Jacob.[9] Selah

7 *Lift up your heads, O gates!*
And be lifted up, O eternal doors,
so the King of Glory may enter!
8 *Who is this*[10] *King of Glory?*
The LORD, strong and mighty.

5. LXX and Syr ("all those dwelling") suggest something such as *kōl yōšᵉbê.*

6. LXX, Symmachus, and Theodotion omit *kî.*

7. Reading with MT and other versions (so NJPS), supported by the parallel construction in Exod. 20:7. LXX (Alexandrinus) and Coptic, which have "his soul" *(npšw),* which is probably a harmonization, making sense of the idiom "does not lift up his soul" as a negative action by the subject (cf. Job 34:19; Ps. 15:3; Ezek. 18:6, 15)

8. Reading with Qere and LXX "those who seek him" against Kethib *(dōršô).*

9. Reading with LXX "the face of the God of Jacob" *(pny 'lhy y'qb);* the text is corrupt.

10. LXX's addition of *hû' (tis estin outos)* harmonizes with v. 10.

The LORD, mighty in battle.
9 *Lift up your heads, O gates!*
And be lifted[11] *up, O eternal doors,*
so the King of Glory may enter.
10 *Who is he, this King of Glory?*
The LORD of hosts.
He is the King of Glory. Selah[12]

1-2 The opening verses begin the movement of the poem by asserting that the earth belongs to the Lord, because it was created by the Lord. The rhetorical point scored is that the earthly sphere — into which the Lord moves in this psalm — is already the Lord's by virtue of the fact that he created it. The Lord's coming is not the hostile act of an invader conquering that which properly belongs to another. Rather, the Lord comes precisely as the proper lord of earth. The verses contain two poetic pairs: *the earth . . . and all that is in it* and *the world and those who dwell in it.* What is significant about the earth/world is precisely that they form the environment for life. The earth[13] is the ecology that contains life — *all that is in it (mᵉlôʾāh)* refers to all the nonhuman animal and plant life that fill the earth (note that *ʾereṣ ûmᵉlôʾāh* ["earth and all that is in it"] forms a known pair in Hebrew [Jer. 8:16; 47:2]). *Those who dwell in it* refers to the human residents of the earth.

The second verse refers to the primitive cosmological view that the earth was founded on the chaotic waters that were hostile to life (cf. Gen. 1:1-13, etc.). The Lord's act of creation was to transform a nonplace that was inhospitable to life (cf. Pss. 46:2-3; 65:7) into a place that is hospitable to life. God performs this transformation by imposing order onto chaos. The metaphor here is that God *founded* and *established* the earth on *the waters (ʿal yammîm)* and *the rivers (ʿal nᵉhārôṯ).* The metaphor cuts two ways. On the one hand, chaos remains an active element in creation. God has limited the reach of chaos ("thus far shall you come, and no farther," Job 38:11), but chaos and randomness remain present. On the other hand, creation is secure, because of the Lord's ongoing providence and stewardship of creation.[14] Thus,

11. Reading *hinnāśʾû* with v. 7 and LXX *eparthētē.* MT's *śᵉʾû* would need a direct object such as *your heads* in v. 7; it is likely a mistake taken from the first word of vv. 7 and 9.

12. LXX omits.

13. As Kraus and most translations note, *ʾereṣ* here "tends toward the idea of a universal area" rather than merely the promised land (*Psalms 1–59,* p. 313).

14. The insight of Mays here is at least worth noting: "The declaration that the LORD is owner is an intentional denial that anyone else is. In Israel's culture the denial was directed against any deity, such as Marduk, for whom similar claims of sovereign possession were made in Babylon. It relativized the claims of human rulers and entrepreneurs whose ownership of parts of the world always tended to absolutize itself" (*Psalms,* 120).

the creation into which God is entering in the psalm needs God's presence, because only God can hold chaos at bay and secure the environment for life.

3-6 In the second stanza, the focus of the liturgy zooms in from a cosmic frame of reference to a local, Jerusalem, frame of reference. The stanza asks and answers a question that is at once starkly simple and infinitely complex: Who may process (*ʿālâ* refers to the ritual procession; see the definition of the "psalms of ascent") from the profane space of the world into the holy space of God's temple? The *mountain of the* LORD *(har YHWH)* is the Temple Mount, and *his holy place (bimqôm qoḏšô)* refers to the temple. In terms of the poetic rhetoric of the psalm, we might put the question like this: What does the advent of the Creator mean for those human beings who dwell in God's presence? Does the coming of the Holy One change anything in the profane realm? Does the Lord's coming require any changes on the part of mortals?

The answer is a resounding yes. As with Psalm 15, the surprise is that the transformations required of humans in order to enter into the holy space are not ritual (becoming ritually pure) but moral (becoming *clean of hand and pure of heart*). As Mays notes, "The adjectives 'clean' and 'pure' do not belong to the Old Testament vocabulary of ritual purification; they are ethical terms."[15] Throughout the Old Testament, Israel is understood as a people blessed in order to bless others (Gen. 12:1-3), a priestly nation set apart for and by the Lord (Exod. 19:5-6). As such, they are the people to whom God's name has been revealed and indeed who bear the name of the Lord (cf. Jer. 14:9; Dan. 9:19). The requirements that the people *do not take up my life falsely (lōʾ nāśāʾ laššāwᵉʾ nap̱šî)* and do *not swear deceitfully* should be understood in light of this theological understanding and in light of the Decalogue prohibition against taking up the name of the Lord falsely *(lōʾ tiśśāʾ ʾeṯ šem YHWH ʾᵉlōhêḵā laššāwᵉʾ*, Exod. 20:7). This is about how one bears the name of the Lord (here: bears the *life* of the Lord) as a representative of the Lord's people. To interpret this prohibition within the dominant poetic motif of the psalm, when God and human beings enter into each other's realms, the human being actually becomes the bearer of God's name and thus of God's presence. As such, the human being is required to comport himself or herself in a manner consistent with the Holy One's nature — that is, to be clean and pure. And this cleanliness and purity is not for one's own sake, but for the neighbor. Precisely because the one who bear's God's *life (nap̱šî)* represents God, one must be *pure* and *clean* in one's dealing with the neighbor.

If the first half of this second stanza (vv. 3-4) is about law (what is required of humans when entering into God's presence), the second half (vv. 5-6) is about promise (what is bestowed on humans when they enter into God's presence). If entering into God's sphere requires one to leave something

15. *Psalms,* p. 121.

at the altar, as it were, one also leaves the altar with something sacred: *a blessing from the LORD*. The connection between what one leaves behind and what one leaves with is reinforced by the verb *nāśā'*, which is used in both halves of the second stanza. One does *not take (nāśā') up my life falsely,* and when one leaves one *will take (nāśā') a blessing from the LORD*. Thus, there is a promise to balance the law. And like the law, the blessing is bestowed not for the sake of the individual per se, but for the sake of the neighbor. The stanza ends with the assertion that this way of life, taking up law and taking away gospel, both for the sake of the neighbor, is the way of God's people — the way of *the generation of those who seek him, of those seeking the face of the God of Jacob.* As Kraus notes, "The 'true Israel' consists of human beings who subordinate daily life to the demands of the [*tôrâ*]."[16]

7-10 If the second stanza maps the coming of mortals into God's sphere, the final stanza returns the favor by heralding the coming of *the King of Glory* into the human realm. The stanza is a tightly composed antiphon, in which vv. 7 and 9 announce the coming of *the King of Glory* and vv. 8 and 10 name the identity of the king as the Lord. It is impossible to reconstruct where these processional verses were originally performed or who spoke which lines. Interpreters have to be satisfied with imagining different possible historical settings for the psalm and concentrating on the theological witness of the psalm to the entrance/return of God.

The psalm's key word *lift (nāśā'),* which occurred twice in stanza 2, now appears four more times in stanza 3, in the twice-repeated call of vv. 7 and 9. But how to interpret the metaphor of gates lifting up their heads is a challenge. J. J. M. Roberts notes that "ancient Palestinian gates had no parts that moved up and down" and concludes that the imperative "to lift up their heads . . . is a secondary metaphor, borrowed from another setting."[17] Roberts identifies an Ugaritic parallel as the setting from which the metaphor is borrowed. The council of gods has learned that Yamm (sea) has claimed kingship among the gods. The gods sit with heads hanging in dejection.

> They lowered their heads onto their knees and onto their royal seats.
> Baal rebuked them then, "Why do you lower, O gods, your heads?"[18]

A few lines later, Baal exhorts them, "Lift up, O gods, your heads!" In this case, the idiom "to lift the head" seems to be a call to take courage. The id-

16. *Psalms 1–59,* p. 314.

17. "The King of Glory," in *The Bible and the Ancient Near East* (Winona Lake: Eisenbrauns, 2002), pp. 104-5.

18. KTU 1.2.23-24; using a slightly emended version of Mark S. Smith's text in *The Ugaritic Baal Cycle.* Vol. 1: *Introduction with Text, Translation and Commentary of KTU 1.1–1.2* (VTSup 55; Leiden: Brill, 1994). My translation.

iom of lifting a part of one's body can mean anything from expressing pride to demanding recognition to asking for help.[19] In Ps. 25:1 *nāśā'* + *yhwh* is an expression of trust, while in 83:2 *nāśā'* + *rōš* connotes an arrogant assertion of autonomy, and in 121:1 *nāśā'* + *'ayin* connotes the need for guidance. In 24:7-10 the metaphor seems to connote an acknowledgement of the Lord's kingship. Perhaps having returned from victory in battle, the gates of the temple figuratively play the role of creation (including the full mortal and immortal realms) acknowledging the Lord's claim on universal kingship.[20]

This reverent and faithful attitude, metaphorically commanded of the temple gates, is the proper stance of all life toward the Lord. As the antiphonal response makes clear, the confession that is required when the Lord enters human space is to acknowledge that the Lord is king. As with all confessions of faith, this confession is simultaneously an anathema: as Roberts notes, to confess the Lord as king is to deny all other claims to sovereignty. "The king of glory is Yahweh. That is, he is not Baal or El as the Canaanites might claim. He is not Dagan as the Philistines say. Or Chemosh of the Moabites or Milcom of the Ammonites. The real king of glory is Yahweh."[21]

But this begs another question, who is *the LORD*? What is this Lord's nature and character? There are manifold answers regarding this in the Psalter, but in this psalm, the answer is carried by the series of epithets: *strong and mighty, mighty in battle, the LORD of hosts,* and of course the main title in this stanza, *the King of Glory.* All together, this series of epithets conjures the image of the Lord as divine warrior-king.[22] The sum of this metaphor is of the Holy One who has the power and presence to deliver creation from the threats of chaos and, moreover, of the one who has the power to grant *vindication* and *deliverance* to those who seek him (vv. 5-6). The warrior-king metaphor echoes the claims of vv. 1-2 of the psalm, because throughout the psalms (cf. Psalms 29, 89) the Lord's kingship is established precisely through the act of creation (i.e., of founding creation on the waters of chaos).

19. Thorkild Jacobsen, *The Harps That Once . . . Sumerian Poetry in Translation* (New Haven: Yale University Press, 1987), p. 388.

20. My colleague Brent Strawn, in a personal communication, argued that the metaphor is more literal and connotes the need of the temple to expand (lift its ceiling and lintels) in order to accommodate the grandeur of the Lord. So also Keel, *The Symbolism of the Biblical World,* pp. 171-72.

21. "The King of Glory," pp. 104-5.

22. The best treatment of this theme remains Patrick D. Miller, Jr., *The Divine Warrior in Early Israel* (HSM 5; Cambridge, MA: Harvard University Press, 1973).

Reflections

Where God Meets Us

Psalm 24 is about *who* in two senses. It is about who the *King of Glory* is and about who may stand in this Holy One's presence. The psalm says that the Lord is the Holy One. It says that only those who have clean hands, pure hearts, who know no falsehood, and who never speak ill or deceitfully may enter the Holy One's space. Thus, as Psalm 24 plots the mutual vectors of the King of Glory and those who seek him, like a computer-animated projection of an asteroid shooting toward earth, the poem heralds the tidings of an inevitable conflict. We are the immovable object, we cannot meet the requirements to enter God's presence. And God is the irresistible force, strong and mighty, mighty in battle, the *King of Glory.*

What happens upon the advent of one whose presence cannot be borne but who also cannot be resisted? Every Western movie ever filmed knows the answer. Someone — either the stranger or the townfolk — will have to die. According to the New Testament witness, when the *King of Glory* came, they tried to kill him. At his birth, King Herod took the first shot. Further on, the good townfolk of Nazareth tried to throw him off a cliff. Still later, some of his coreligionists tried to stone him. And of course in the end, a conspiracy of the ruling elite nailed him. The New Testament maintains that it was necessary that Christ, the Son of God, die. What made it necessary? Because when the King of Glory, who is *strong and mighty* and thus cannot be resisted and who will not compromise with us, who is not satisfied to remain at a reasonable, rational distance, who will not negotiate with Satan, or Pharaoh, or any other power that would share lordship over us, when this one comes, someone has to die.

But the New Testament witness regarding the *King of Glory* is deeper and more complex than the plot of any Western. According to the New Testament, the One who came from eternity had the power, authority, even sovereignty — and he gave it up. Rather than kill, he chose to be killed. "You who were once estranged and hostile in mind . . . he has now reconciled in the body of his flesh through death" (Col. 1:21-22). And in his death, moreover, death itself dies, so that we need not die in the same way. "We have been buried with him by baptism into death . . . we have been united with him in a death like his, and we will certainly be united with him in a resurrection like his" (Rom. 6:4-5). Who is the *King of Glory?* Jesus Christ, who did not count sovereignty or equality with God a thing to be exploited, but emptied himself into a manger, being born in human likeness, in human form.

ROLF A. JACOBSON

Psalm 25: Remember, Forgive, and Teach Me

Psalm 25 is a prayer of confidence in God's great acts in a person's life. Some scholars have identified it as a prayer for help,[1] but it does not have the urgency of that type of prayer. In addition, it covers a host of topics, including the absence of God (vv. 3, 16-18, 21), the threat of enemies (vv. 2, 19-20), personal sin (vv. 7, 11, 18), God's instruction and teaching (vv. 4-6, 8-10, 12-14), and pleas for God's intervention (vv. 1-3, 15-20). This list indicates that the prayer is not reacting to a single happening but is more of a reflection on the events that have shaped the life of the one praying. This broad scope of topics is also suggested by its form. Psalm 25 is one of the nine acrostic psalms in the book of Psalms.[2] It literally covers everything from *'ālep* to *tāw*.

It is possible that because the prayer is an acrostic, it should not be divided into stanzas and instead be thought of as a whole piece. However, thematically the psalm does fall into divisible themes or sections. Scholars quibble about some of the specifics, but most agree on the major divisions:

vv. 1-3	God save me from my enemies and I will not be shamed
vv. 4-7	Teach me and forgive me
vv. 8-11	God is the teacher and forgives me
vv. 12-14	God teaches those God loves
vv. 15-18	God saves me and forgives me
vv. 19-21	God save me from my enemies and I am will not be shamed
v. 22	Do likewise for Israel

Möller and McCann both suggest that there is a center to the psalm,[3] and this is possible, but the multiple interlacing themes makes the selection of only one as a central theme difficult.

1. Craigie, *Psalms 1–50*, p. 217; Gerstenberger, *Psalms: Part 1*, p. 122.

2. An acrostic poem is where each verse begins with a successive letter of the Hebrew alphabet. The acrostic psalms are 9, 10, 25, 34, 37, 111, 112, 119, and 145. As noted in the translation, there are some problems with the acrostic pattern in this psalm, notably in vv. 2 and 18.

3. Hans Möller suggests a chasitic structure with v. 11 at the center; "Strophenbau der Psalmen," *ZAW* 50 (1932) 246-50. Though the structure is compelling, it is difficult to justify. This is not a penitential psalm historically, and the psalm asks as much for instruction and God's salvation from others as it does forgiveness, making the selection of v. 11 as the center problematic. McCann focuses on the repetition of words around vv. 10-11 and the attributes of God in those verses ("The Book of Psalms," p. 777). This is also possible, but the repetition is not in a completely regular pattern and the section of vv. 8-11 can be seen as a restating of vv. 4-7.

Psalm 25

Davidic.

ʾĀlep 1 *To you, O* Lord*, I lift my soul;*[4]
O my God,
Bêt 2 *in you I trust,*[5]
do not let me be put to shame;
do not let my enemies triumph over me.
Gîmel 3 *Moreover, do not let all those waiting on you be shamed;*
let those who act vainly faithlessly be put to shame.[6]

Dālet 4 *Your ways, O* Lord*, cause me to know;*
your paths, teach to me.
Hê 5 *Lead me in your truth and*[7] *teach me*
for you are the God of my salvation;
Wāw *you I wait for all the day.*
Zayin 6 *Remember your mercy, O* Lord*;*
your hesed *for they have been from old.*
Ḥêt 7 *The sins of my youth and my transgressions, do not remember;*
according to your hesed, *YOU*[8] *remember me,*
on account of your goodness, O Lord*!*[9]

Ṭêt 8 *Good and upright is the* Lord*;*
therefore, you instruct sinners in the way.

4. *Napšî* should be understood as "self" and is often translated in the psalms as "me" or "I." Here because of the additional 1cs verb, the noun should be translated but still understood as the self as in the whole self instead of the dual understanding of soul and body in Greek dualism.

5. This is an acrostic poem, which means every verse begins with a subsequent letter of the Hebrew alphabet. Verse 2 then should begin with *b*^{e}*ḵā*. To do this, the BHS apparatus suggests emending v. 1 to read "For you, I have waited (adding *qiwwiṯî*) O Lord; I will lift my soul to (adding *ʾel* from v. 2) my God." This is possible but unnecessary. It is just as possible that the versification was such to allow for the above structure. It is not elegant, but it does preserve the acrostic without adding to the text.

6. The BHS apparatus suggests that the side by side appearance of *yēḇōšû* is dittography. This is not necessary however. Craigie notes this is the same pattern as in vv. 20-21 in reverse, making it part of the pattern of this prayer (*Psalms 1–50,* p. 216).

7. 11QPs^{c} omits the *wāw;* Florentino García Martínez, Eibert Tigchelaar, and A. S. van der Woude, *Qumran Cave 11: II, 11Q2-18, 11Q20-31* (DJD 23; Oxford: Clarendon, 1998), p. 60.

8. Lit., "You remember to me-you," expressing emphasis. The capitalization here and elsewhere aims to convey this in written translation.

9. Craigie, following the BHS critical apparatus, moves the cola from v. 7 to v. 5, but there is no compelling reason for this change. The MT is clear here, and the LXX follows same.

Yôd	9	*He leads the afflicted in justice;* *and teaches the afflicted his way.*
Kāp	10	*All the paths of the* LORD *are* hesed *and truth;* *to those preserving his covenant and decrees.*
Lāmed	11	*For the sake of your name, O* LORD*;* *forgive my iniquities for they are many.*[10]
Mêm	12	*Who is the one that fears the* LORD*?* *He will instruct that one*[11] *in the path he*[12] *should choose.*
Nûn	13	*That one*[13] *in goodness will remain;* *and his offspring will possess the land.*
Sāmek	14	*The counsel of the* LORD *is to the one fearing him;* *and his covenant is made known to that one.*[14]
ʿAyin	15	*My eyes are continually upon the* LORD*,* *for GOD*[15] *will lift out my foot from the snare.*
Pê	16	*Turn to me and be gracious to me,* *for lonely and afflicted I am.*
Ṣādê	17	*The troubles of my heart have expanded;*[16] *from my troubles, deliver me!*
[?]	18	*Look upon*[17] *my affliction and my distress;* *and lift away all my sins.*

10. The MT is singular here (see NRSV); however, the adjective *raḇ* usually indicates quantity, not intensity, thus the adjustment here to better fit the Hebrew meaning. The word *gāḏôl* is usually used when the meaning is intensity.

11. MT has the 3ms direct object marker.

12. MT has the 3ms verb, but the subject is indefinite. Some read the *he* here as the one(s) instructed (NRSV), while others see it as God (NIV).

13. MT has *napšô,* which is not exclusively "soul" but the whole self (see v. 1).

14. This *hiphil* infinitive 3mpl is odd, since the line above was in the singular. Many translations read the plural in both lines, but this is difficult in the context of the preceding verse.

15. There is a double emphasis of "he" here (the pronoun plus the 3ms verb).

16. The change suggested by the critical apparatus and shown in the NRSV to change the verb to 3ms is not necessary, as noted above.

17. Because this is an acrostic poem, the first word of the line should begin with *qôp.* The word that begins vv. 18 and 19 is the same in both the MT and the LXX, so the error is from the earliest manuscripts. The critical apparatus suggests the verb here should be from *qšb* ("listen to"), and this is possible. Other scholars have suggested other words beginning with *qôp.* Since the word is unknown and there are no traces in other manuscripts, it is best to leave it as it is, noting that the word is not correct.

Rêš 19 *Look upon my enemies for they are many;*
and with violent hatred they hate me.
Šîn 20 *Guard my life,*[18] *and snatch me up;*
do not let me be put to shame for I seek refuge in you.
Tāw 21 *May integrity and uprightness preserve me,*
for I wait for you.

22 *Redeem Israel, O God, from all its troubles.*[19]

1-3 The prayer begins as a typical prayer for help with petitions to God, and the problem here appears to be the shame of the one praying and the success of the enemies. In fact, the theme of shame predominates this section. Here it appears that the vindication of the one praying and her community is predicated on God's answering this prayer. A dichotomy is set up: if God answers, the one praying and her community are vindicated and the enemies are the ones shamed. The community's reputation depends on God's action. The poem then opens with the questions that we carry about God and God's actions in our world. We, too, can wish for God to appear and settle some matter and vindicate our years of faith with one definitive show of presence.

4-7 What does God's teaching have to do with vindication from shame? Poetry is work, and this prayer forces hearers and now readers to work to make sense of the connection. This section could easily be the start of a separate, different prayer with the only connection being the *waiting (qwh)* of vv. 3 and 5. Is God's teaching a way to extricate one's self from the feeling of shame? The pleas are clear, and God is being called upon to teach a way or path in life.

But the puzzle does not stop there. Verses 6 and 7 are a plea for God to remember God's great *hesed* and *not to remember* the sins of the one praying. Somehow God's lessons are related to God's forgiveness and a person's shame. One is tempted here to accuse those preserving this prayer of mixing up texts into a mashed-up whole. But the psalm is an acrostic, which gives it a very specific and rigid structure. The meaning must somehow be comprehensive, just as the form is. The whole will need to be seen in order to understand the individual parts.

8-11 This section shares seven words with the previous one *(way, path, teach, lead, truth, hesed,* and *goodness/good)* and the teaching theme continues. In addition, these words are about God and not the condition of the one praying. Verses 8-10 tell of God's great acts as a teacher. Verses 4-6 ask for God to teach and remember, and here is confirmation that God has and continues

18. Lit., *napšî,* which is not exclusively "soul" but the whole self or life (see v. 1).

19. This verse is not part of the acrostic structure and is possibly a later addition or a summary of the prayer.

to do just that for God's people. Verse 8 declares that God instructs sinners in God's *way,* followed by God's leading and teaching of the *afflicted (ʿᵃnāwîm).*[20] "Afflicted" literally means to be "bowed down," and that yields a plethora of possible meanings. Certainly, those with sin or those who are ashamed often take this posture. Yet v. 10 asserts that God's paths are available to *those preserving his covenant and decrees.* The combination is striking and explains our human condition. We can be sinners and afflicted and still preserve, in the sense of knowing, God's instructions and receive teaching and leading. Life is not an "or" but an "and." We are both faithful and sinners; we are both taught by God and bowed down and afflicted by our and others' actions. We can preserve the sense of God's covenant and decrees for others and still feel our shortcomings.

Verse 11 ends this section much as v. 7 ended the last one. But what is asked is different. Verse 7 asked that God *not remember* the *sins* and *transgressions* of the past but *remember* the one praying. Here God is asked to *forgive,* not for the sake of the one praying, but because God is God. The *iniquities are many,* and the word choice (sing.) probably does not introduce another form of transgression here but collectively incorporates all of the available words in Hebrew for acts against God. At this point in the prayer, it would seem that the problem is specifically the personal sin of the one praying.

12-14 This section has the effect of an assurance of pardon. God will respond and offer *instruction* and *counsel* to the one who *fears the LORD.* That one is *in goodness,* or good standing, and the *offspring* will be blessed with the *land* of promise. This is the status of the one forgiven. The prayer could end here: sins forgiven, life restored to goodness. All is as it should be. The themes of shame and sin and God's teaching and God's forgiveness have been reviewed.

15-21 The place of peace offered above does not last long. These verses return to description of the pain and troubles of the one praying. Verse 17 states that the *troubles have expanded* and the one praying is again in need of God's intervention and, yes, even God's forgiveness. Did time pass, or is the one praying not assured by the assurance? The poetry does not give any clear indication, and certainly most humans have been in both places, so the reader or hearer must determine the understanding from within her own framework. What is clear is that, no matter the conclusion, the one praying does not stop calling out to God. The prayer may seem to end with the one praying in the same place as when the prayer began, but there have been a cry to God and an assurance of God's promises. Indeed, it is the cyclic nature of our lives.

20. The combination with *sinners* of v. 8 is probably what leads the NRSV and NIV to use "humble" here. "Humble" has a very different meaning than "afflicted" and seems an unnecessary change.

God does not save us once and for all, but comes to us continually as we go through the ups and downs of life.

22 The final verse of the prayer may have been added by an editor; it offers assurance that, just as God acts over and over for the individual, so God will also act for the whole of God's people.

The acrostic structure of the poem points to a comprehensive understanding of the multiple messages. From beginning to end, God is there when we are afraid of enemies, or shamed in any way, or when we have sinned against God. The well of God's support and comfort never runs dry. The structure can indicate that this is a relationship for the long haul; on God we can depend time and time again. The psalm, then, is not a prayer for help itself but a comprehensive prayer that confirms the other prayers for help. God will restore and give new life from the very beginning until the very end.

BETH TANNER

Psalm 26: Prepare to Appear

Psalm 26 continues the frank discussion with God begun in Psalm 25. Also, the genre of this psalm is as much in dispute as with Psalm 25. Some scholars have seen it as a prayer for help of one wrongly accused[1] or for suffering from illness.[2] Others see it as a song for a specific ritual setting, either of the temple entrance of a worshipper[3] or a priest preparing to ascend the altar.[4] Any of these is a possible ancient setting, given the flexibility of poetry. Psalm 26 read in the context of Psalm 25 can be seen as a continuation of the conversation with God. First was the concern of sinfulness and enemies and shame (Psalm 25), followed here by the confident request that God judge and examine the one praying. It is a prayer that reflects the absolute opposite of shame. It almost seems narcissistic, especially if read through the lens of a Reformed theology. But this same confidence is also seen in the enthronement psalms (Pss. 93, 96–99), where there is a strong theme of celebrating God's judgment, and in Psalm 1, where the one praying declares the ways he has followed God. The prayer expresses one's confidence in the relationship with God. God can judge and examine, because ultimately this one depends on God's *hesed.*

The psalm can be divided into three stanzas with an *inclusio* in vv. 1-3 and 11-12.[5] The center section which I have left undivided is often split into three sections (vv. 4-5, 6-8, and 9-10). But as Bellinger notes, these verses blend together[6] and may be considered as a single section. The psalm, thus, begins with a declaration to God with a matching confirmation at the end, while the middle declares the type of life the one praying has chosen.

Davidic.

1 *Judge me, O LORD,*
for I, in my integrity, I have walked,
in the LORD, I trusted and I will not stumble.
2 *Examine me, O LORD and try me,*

1. Kraus, *Psalms 1–59,* p. 326; and William H. Bellinger, Jr., "Psalm XXVI: A Test of Method," *VT* 43 (1993) 460.

2. Hermann Gunkel, *Die Psalmen* (5th ed.; Göttingen: Vandenhoeck & Ruprecht, 1968), p. 109.

3. Ernst Vogt, "Psalm 26, ein Pilgergebet," *Bib* 43 (1962) 328-37.

4. Paul G. Mosca, "Psalm 26: Poetic Structure and the Form-Critical Task," *CBQ* 47 (1985) 230-34.

5. Also noted by Mosca, "Psalm 26," p. 228; and Bellinger, "Psalm XXVI," p. 454.

6. "Psalm XXVI," p. 454.

refine[7] *my inward parts*[8] *and my heart*
3 *for your* hesed *is before my eyes,*
and I walk constantly in your truth.

4 *I did not sit with ones focused on emptiness,*[9]
and with ones who hide[10] *I did not go.*
5 *I hate the assembly of evil ones,*
and with the wicked I do not sit.
6 *I will wash my hands in innocence,*
and I will go around your altar, O LORD,
7 *proclaiming*[11] *in a voice of thanksgiving,*
and recounting all your wonderful deeds.
8 *O* LORD, *I love the dwelling place*[12] *of your house,*
the place of the tabernacle of your glory.
9 *Do not gather me*[13] *up with the sinners;*
and my life with the bloodthirsty ones,
10 *in whose hands is wicked behavior,*
and their right hands are full of bribes.

11 *But I, in my integrity, I shall walk,*
redeem me and grace[14] *me.*[15]

7. Reading the Qere *ṣārpâ* as the *qal* imperative.

8. Lit., "kidneys," traditionally interpreted as "my mind" (NRSV, NIV, NJPS), but this may be too much of a Western interpretation. The point here is the deepest parts of the person.

9. Lit., "men of emptiness or worthlessness." The term seems to convey the meaning that these ones *chose* to focus on emptiness or worthless things. The NRSV's "worthless" runs the risk of being interpreted as something these ones are. Instead the meaning is more about what these ones chose to do.

10. The understanding of "hypocrites" (NIV, NRSV) is pushing the meaning of this word too far. The word means "to be secret" or "to hide," but the meaning is not necessarily pejorative. This English meaning may come from the LXX, which has a word meaning "illegal" or "contrary to law." The word is probably parallel to *emptiness* of the first coda.

11. The Hebrew word choice is unusual. It is a *hiphil* infinitive construct of *šāmaʿ*, meaning, lit., "causing to hear" instead of the more common "singing" or "shouting."

12. The LXX reads "the beauty of your house," but the change is not necessary since the MT is readable as it stands and 4QPs[r] has the same *mʿwn* (Ulrich, Cross, et al., *Qumran Cave 4: XI,* p. 151).

13. Lit., "my *nep̄eš*," this word has a wide range of meaning: "soul, living being, self." It is the essence of what makes a sack of bones alive.

14. Terrien notes that the *qal* imperative is stronger than "be gracious to me." "Grace me" is more the meaning; *The Psalms,* p. 259.

15. 4QPs[r] appears to read *hḥyny,* a *hiphil* imperative with a 1cs suffix as in Isa. 38:16: "give me life" or "let me live" (Ulrich, Cross, et al., *Qumran Cave 4: XI,* p. 152).

12 *My foot stands in uprightness;*[16]
in the great assembly,[17] *I will bless the* LORD.

1-3 The prayer begins with a plea for God to judge the one praying. The NRSV and NIV's "vindicate" probably assumes that the genre is a prayer for help of one wrongly accused. The Hebrew word *šopṭēnî,* however, is usually rendered as "judge," and this fits with what follows in v. 2. From a modern perspective, it seems a strange way to begin a prayer, for we carry a heavy dose of fear when contemplating God's judgment. But the prayers of the psalms do not exhibit that fear. This one is asking God to judge in the same way that one might ask a friend to look over the character and actions of another to determine what kind of person she is. The second Hebrew line translates into awkward English, but the translation stresses the threefold use of *I.* This one is sure of her integrity because of trust in God. Again, this is a foreign concept to modern ears; our integrity is based on whom we trust, not on what we do. Verse 2 asks (actually, demands [the verbs are imperatives]) for God to *examine, try,* and even *refine* the speaker's deepest *parts.* Even if one walks in *integrity,* there is still more that God can *refine,* indicating that this is a lifelong project. Verse 3 again emphasizes that it is because of God's *hesed* and *truth* that this one would dare to ask God for such a test. Life lived with God is not about sinlessness but about faithfulness and belief in God's great gifts.

4-10 This lengthy middle section moves from what this one does not do, to the things he enjoys most in life, to a plea that may seem out of place.

Verses 4 and 5 focus on the type of people this one does not associate with as a rule (see Psalm 1 for a similar understanding). Verse 4 may seem inelegant, but most English translations reach too far in attempts to smooth it out. The first line uses the same term as the commandment in Exod. 20:7 (*šāwᵉʾ*, "emptiness"), which literally means "You shall not lift the name of the LORD your God *to emptiness*" (italics mine). This one does not associate with those who ignore God's commandments and use God's name for empty purposes. The typical translation of Heb. *naʿᵃlāmîm* (lit., "hiding themselves") in the second line as "hypocrites" also goes too far. These ones *hide* away, but the purpose of their acts is not clear. Verse 5 offers two more examples of persons this one does not associate with *(evil ones, the wicked),* even if they are in the *assembly.*

Verses 6 to 8 turn from what is not done to what is done. What is repre-

16. NRSV has "level ground," but the noun also means "uprightness," and that more clearly portrays the metaphorical nature of the phrase.

17. This is an unusual form of the word with a *mêm* suffix and in plural form that appears only here and in Ps. 68:27. This may indicate either the various groups or assemblies together or is an honorific plural. The latter is the choice above (NIV, NRSV).

sented here is the practice of one entering the temple. Some scholars argue that this section of the psalm indicates its use as part of the entrance ritual at the temple. Certainly, a religious ritual is described here, but the ritual here is not a concurrent act. It is an act that the righteous one performs, and it is used as a contrast to what others do. It seems to serve as an example, the difference between the one praying and the wicked. In the context of the whole prayer, it indicates, further, the way this one chooses to live and what this one chooses to love. In some ways, one is drawn to see parallels here with Job as he stands in his integrity and performs the required rituals, not out of duty, but with a glad heart.

Verses 9 to 10 seem to reverse the idea of this one's integrity before God *(Do not gather me up with the sinners),* but there are other texts that reflect the fear of offenses unknown to the one doing them (e.g., Job 1:5; Ps. 19:11-13). This petition could also be another way of claiming uprightness, i.e., by making sure that this one is excluded when God cleans house of the evil ones.

11-12 These two verses form a type of *inclusio* with vv. 1-3. This one is not like the other ones, but is faithful to God and God's promises. The pleas to *redeem* and *be gracious* are not based on the person's actions, but presuppose that one's relationship with God allows for such pleas, and it is for this reason that the one will stand and *bless the LORD* among God's people.

Limburg writes, "Some have been uncomfortable with the seemingly self-righteous 'What a good boy am I' tone of the declaration of innocence in verses 4-7 of this psalm. . . . [But] here is one desperate for vindication (v. 1), fearing that life itself might be swept away."[18] We have all faced times when our integrity is on the line. This is a psalm for those times: "Weigh my life in the balance; see what I have done and what I have chosen not to do! Put me to the test and see how I act. Check me out, God, and see if my motives are pure. Lord, my motives come from the heart and not for show" (v. 2). To face God and ask God to judge can seem a frightening place, especially for one who is well aware of the sins and missteps that are a part of life. The point here is not to prove oneself, but to demonstrate one's trust in God's power of *hesed* and grace. In times when our integrity is on the line, it is comforting to stand before God, depend on God's relationship with each of us before we go out and face the not-so-forgiving world.

BETH TANNER

18. *Psalms,* p. 84.

Psalm 27: Trust in the Day of Trouble

Psalm 27 begins with stolid words of trust (vv. 1-6). Halfway through, it modulates into desperate words of petition (vv. 7-12). It then closes with renewed trust and a verse of admonition to *hope in the LORD* (vv. 13-14). Because the psalm's segments are so disjointed, scholars from an earlier generation divided it into separate poems.[1] It is possible, perhaps even probable, that two or more originally separate prayers, which originated in two radically different situations, have been joined together here. The approach taken here is to treat the psalm as a coherent unit because of the reality that the psalm was passed down through tradition as a unit. This reality indicates that the poem made sense to someone in its current form (if perhaps only to a scribe who — hypothetically — combined earlier fragments together to fashion a hybrid psalm). And, indeed, it must be admitted that it is very possible that the psalm was always a unit, as many scholars argue. Gerstenberger, for instance, approaches the psalm having imagined that "the contingencies of ritual procedure . . . are responsible for alternating 'moods' in one and the same psalm. . . ."[2]

But the decision to treat the psalm as a unit begs the question of genre. Basically, how one labels the genre of the psalm will depend on how one decides to relate the two halves of the psalm to each other. Does the trust expressed in vv. 1-6 express the psalmist's faith before the cry of vv. 7-12? Or concurrent with the plea of vv. 7-12? Or even after that plea? As Gerstenberger helpfully notes,

> The interpretation of the Hebrew tenses . . . does have an impact on form-critical analysis. The English pattern of distinguishing past, present, and future does not coincide with the Hebrew perfect and imperfect, and much less so in poetic language. I generally follow Michel's suggestion that the perfect tense in the Psalms indicates a self-sufficient, strong, dominant action regardless of tense, while the imperfect tense is dependent, subordinate, and likewise indeterminate in time.[3]

Gerstenberger pays further witness to the complexity of the problem, however, when he backtracks in a slightly circular move: "The problem of tenses, in any case, can best be dealt with on the basis of form-critical analyses and context."[4] The position taken here is that the psalmist is in a situation of need. The trust that is expressed at the beginning and end of the psalm is genuine,

1. See Gunkel, *Introduction to Psalms,* p. 121; Weiser, *The Psalms.*

2. *Psalms: Part 1,* p. 125.

3. *Psalms: Part 1,* pp. 124-25.

4. *Psalms: Part 1,* p. 125.

but it also rhetorically fuels the pleas that dominate the center of the psalm. It should be remembered that the trust psalms, no less than the prayers for help, assume the presence of threatening dangers — the darkest valley of Psalm 23 or the raging seas and nations of Psalm 46. Thus, trust and plea are compatible with one another. They are two complementary responses to crisis.

Can anything more definite be said about the psalmist or his situation? It depends on how one interprets language such as the following:

> *When evildoers draw near to me* (v. 2)
> *If an army encamps against me. . . . If battle arises against me* (v. 3)
> *One thing I have asked . . . that I might dwell in the house of the LORD* (v. 4)
> *He hides me in the hiding place of his tent* (v. 5)
> *Even my father and my mother have abandoned me* (v. 10)

Is any of this language literal? Is any of it metaphorical? If one assumes the poem's integrity, as is done here, it seems almost impossible to imagine a situation in which all of it together can be understood literally.[5] While some would imagine this as a royal prayer prior to battle, it seems just as plausible to imagine the battle imagery as metaphorical, since it occurs once and then is not taken up again. The approach here is to interpret all of the language metaphorically, at least in the sense that images that might originate with a literal use by one supplicant (a soldier who prays for success in battle or a sick person who prays for health) can later be used metaphorically by another supplicant (a frightened person who prays for "victory" or a depressed person who prays "to be made whole").

The psalm's structure is:

St. 1 Trust in the Lord (vv. 1-6)
  Trust in the midst of threat (vv. 1-3)
  Shelter in the midst of threat (vv. 4-6)
St. 2 Plea to the Lord (vv. 7-12)
  The prayer of one who seeks the Lord (vv. 7-9)
  The prayer of one abandoned and lost (vv. 10-12)
St. 3 Trust in the Lord (vv. 13-14)

5 Admittedly, this is circular logic. But there you have it. Assuming the poetic integrity of the poem (rather than assuming separate historical life settings behind the two halves of the poem) leads in turn to a poetic approach to the language of the psalm (rather than a strictly historical approach of using the language to identify a specific life setting).

Davidic.[6]

1 *The LORD is my light and my salvation,*
whom shall I fear?
The LORD is the stronghold of my life,
whom shall I dread?
2 *When evildoers draw near to me,*
to consume my flesh,
My foes and my enemies against me,
they[7] *stumble and they fall!*
3 *If an army encamps against me,*
my heart will not fear.
If battle arises against me,
even in this, I will trust!

4 *One thing I have asked of the LORD,*
this I still seek.
That I might dwell in the house of the LORD,
all the days of my life.
To behold the wonder of the LORD,
and to inquire in his sanctuary.
5 *For he conceals me in a shelter,*
in the day of trouble.[8]
He hides me in the hiding place of his tent,
he raises me high on a rock.
6 *And now, my head is raised up,*[9]
above my enemies, all around me.[10]
And I offer sacrifices in his tent,
sacrifices of festal shouting.[11]
I sing and I make music to the LORD.

6. LXX adds *pro tou christhēnai,* suggesting *lᵉmmišḥâ* (before the anointing [of David? Of any king?]).

7. Following LXX and Syr, reading *hēmmâ* as part of the phrase.

8. LXX adds 1cs suffix.

9. LXX's *hypsōsen* normally renders the *hiphil* form *(yārîm),* with the implied subject being the Lord. The meaning is not dramatically altered, since *my head* as the subject implies that the Lord was the one raising up the head.

10. LXX *ekyklōsa* is reading something like *sabbôṯî* ("I went around"; cf. Eccl. 7:25) in place of *sᵉḇîḇôṯay* and as part of the next line; this reading may have resulted from the changed understanding of *yrwm.*

11. Hebrew *ziḇḥê ṯᵉrûʿâ* is an odd phrase, attested only here. The *tᵉrûʿâ* is the sound of the trumpet on the festal day (Lev. 25:9) or the sound of shouting in triumph (Josh. 6:5, 20).

7 *O LORD, hear the sound of my voice when I cry,*
be gracious to me and answer me.
8 *To you my heart said,*[12]
"Seek my face."
Your face, O LORD, I do seek,
9 *do not hide your face from me!*
Do not turn from your servant in anger,
O You who have been my help!
Do not forsake me and do not abandon me,
O God of my deliverance!

10 *Even my father and my mother have abandoned me,*
but the LORD will gather me in.
11 *Teach me, O LORD, your way,*
and guide me along a sure path because of my enemies.
12 *Do not give me over to the will of my foes,*
for false witnesses have risen against me,
a violent witness.[13]

13 *Indeed*[14] *I believe that I shall see*
the goodness of the LORD in the land of the living.
14 *Hope in the LORD!*
Be strong and let your heart be confident.
Hope in the LORD!

1-3 The psalm begins with soaring words of trust. The confession of the Lord as *my light ('ôrî)* is unique to this psalm, although it is a frequent metaphor for God's presence and purpose (cf. Ps. 36:9; 43:3; John 1:4-9). The word is employed here as part of a pun — Because the Lord is *my light ('ôrî),* the psalmist asks, [*whom shall*] *I fear? ('îrā').* The pun underscores the basic causal link in the psalm — because of faith in the Lord, the psalmist can face any crisis without being paralyzed by fear. The dual confession — *Whom shall I fear? Whom shall I dread?* — should not be interpreted in some heroic sense to mean that the psalmist feels absolutely no fear or sees no cause for fear. The

12. MT is corrupt; Jacob Leveen's solution is too confused ("Textual Problems in the Psalms," *VT* 21 [1971] 54). LXX is followed here.

13. The term *wîpēaḥ* was traditionally taken to mean "breathing" and understood as an adjective. Ugaritic studies, however, uncovered a root *yph* meaning "witness," which fits far better with the sense and poetry of the psalm. See Patrick D. Miller, Jr., "*yāpîaḥ* in Psalm XII 6," *VT* 29 (1979) 495-500; Dennis Pardee, "*yph 'Witness'* in Hebrew and Ugaritic," *VT* 28 (1978) 204-13; J. Gerald Janzen, "Another Look at Psalm xii 6," *VT* 54 (2004) 157-64.

14. Hebrew *lûlē'* is taken to indicate a vow.

psalmist is acutely aware of the dangers that threaten him *(evildoers . . . foes . . . enemies . . . an army . . . battle).* One must imagine that this awareness in turn results in at least some degree of fear and dread. Paradoxically, it is the very presence of this fear that causes the psalmist to confess the Lord as light. This confession in turn leads to the statement of courage: *whom shall I fear?* The two verbs — *fear* and *dread* — are in the imperfect aspect, which here connotes ongoing confidence. The sense is that the trust that the psalmist developed when seas were smoother, is a trust that is ongoing in spite of the fact that he has now hit rougher waters. The psalmist's trust is further emphasized by the affirmations that crown v. 3: *My heart will not fear. . . . Even in this, I will trust!* The sense of the psalmist's faith as ongoing in the midst of trial, as persevering in spite of danger, is again communicated by the choice of the imperfect *(will not fear; yîrā')* and participial forms *(will trust; bôṭēaḥ).*

The ensuing metaphors for both God and the threatening danger are drawn from a martial domain. The Lord is *stronghold,* while the crisis is described using the language of *evildoers, foes, enemies, army, battle* who *draw near* (which occurs with a military meaning in 1 Kgs. 20:29), *encamp, arise.* The language may have originated on the lips of an ancient king or military leader prior to battle,[15] but just as likely the language originated as a powerful metaphor for anyone facing the *day of trouble* (v. 5). No matter the origin, the language may serve as the prayer of anyone who feels besieged by life — by illness, conflict at home or work, stress, or depression, and so on.

4-6 The confident theme of trust is interrupted briefly in v. 4, as the poem modulates briefly into a promise (often called a vow). Such promises are frequent themes in songs of trust (cf. 23:6; 16:8; 52:8-9), as well as in prayers for help (cf. 13:6). The vows underscore a fundamental unity in the psalmist's life — the trust of her heart is mirrored by the actions of her body. Her actions of trusting that God is there for her and committed to her are one with her actions of being committed to God and seeking God. Based on the perfect form of the word *asked (šā'altî),* Kraus, Goldingay, and others understand v. 4 to be a looking "back to a prayer offered in the midst of danger" à la Psalm 30, "the appeal which the petitioner in his distress uttered while still far away from the sanctuary."[16] But the perfect *šā'altî* is followed by an imperfect and three infinitive constructs *('abaqqēš; šibtî; laḥazôt; lebaqqēr).* It is better to understand this verbal sequence as reflecting that the psalmist's past desire is still her desire: "I once asked to and it is still my desire to seek God." The series of phrases indicates that the psalmist continually seeks

15. See Craigie, *Psalms 1–50,* pp. 232-33. But Gerstenberger: "The military language is metaphoric throughout; there is no need to invent an army leader or king as the original supplicant . . ." (*Psalms: Part 1,* p. 126).

16. Goldingay, *Psalms 1–41,* p. 393; Kraus, *Psalms 1–59,* p. 334.

God's presence. The phrases cascade, one on top of the other, like a relentless wave, until the psalmist names her persistent commitment: to *seek* God, to *dwell* with God, to *behold* God's *wonder,* to *inquire* in the sanctuary. It may be that the language of seeking and inquiring in the temple suggests that the psalmist sought an oracle from a priest.[17] Or it may be that the language reflects an afflicted psalmist who sought asylum in the temple.[18] The Hebrew term translated here as *inquire* does not generally mean to request an oracle, although its use in 2 Kgs. 16:15 supports the sense of inquiring through sacrifice (and note the reference to such sacrifices in v. 6). But as Hossfeld points out, the rhetorical use of the term here is a way for the supplicant to announce her continuing trust.[19] The sense here is not of a present request for an oracle, but rather to underscore that the psalmist inquires the Lord's will precisely because the Lord is the only trustworthy source of guidance and wisdom (cf. Isa. 30:1).

In the relationship between God and psalmist, the divine attribute that corresponds to the psalmist's trust is the Lord's fidelity. In this case, the Lord's fidelity is demonstrated by the Lord's protection of the psalmist. Verse 5 paints a vivid image of the Lord's protection with the serial metaphors of *shelter (sukkâ), hiding place (sēṯer),* and *rock (ṣûr).* The common terms *hiding place* and *rock* are paired here with the unique word *shelter,* which is used only here in the Psalter as a metaphor for God's protecting grace. It is the term from which the Jewish festival of Sukkoth (or Booths) draws its name, a reference to the protective shelters in which the people stayed during the Wilderness years, as they wandered under God's protection. The Lord's *tent ('ōhel)* is a frequent metaphor for the temple, but also a metaphor for God's protecting presence. Both senses are meant here. The power of these metaphors for God's protection is amplified by pairing them with the phrase *in the day of trouble* (cf. 41:1; Jer. 17:17; 51:2). This phrase refers to any time of crisis or desperate danger. The metaphors of protection are followed by the image of the psalmist's head being *raised up, above my enemies.* The metaphor draws on the ancient cultural values of honor and shame. By protecting the psalmist from enemy threats, the Lord bestows honor on her and, by extension, diminishes those who would wish to bring her down. In response, the psalmist again reiterates her constant and ongoing trust in the Lord, by *offering sacrifices* and *singing* for joy. The *festal shout* is a visceral, almost primal, expression of joy. It is the shout of battle (1 Sam. 4:5) and the trumpet blast of the festival worship (Lev. 23:24; 25:9). The psalmist's ongoing singing and

17. Craigie, e.g., who imagines the speaker as the king, has the king seeking an oracle before battle (*Psalms 1–50,* p. 232).

18. So Seybold, *Die Psalmen,* pp. 115-16.

19. *Die Psalmen I,* p. 174.

melody making (a regular poetic pair in Hebrew) suggest a soul that is both dedicated and confident.

7-9 The tone and energy of the poem change dramatically starting with v. 7. As noted above, however, this need not suggest that a completely separate prayer was appended to a previously existing psalm. Rather, it should be noted that in the midst of crisis, prayers for help and poems of trust are two complementary prayerful actions. It is dangerous to make too much of the causal sequence, but if the poem is taken as a rhetorical unit, one is tempted to say the trust element that begins this psalm functions rhetorically to fuel the prayer element that follows. The raw cry of v. 7 is characteristic of so many petitions in the psalms: first, there is the simple request to gain a hearing, to be acknowledged (7a). Then there is the characteristic appeal for the Lord to *be gracious* and to *answer* (*ḥānnēnî waʿănēnî;* 7b). The text of v. 8 is difficult, but the sense is that in this prayer, the psalmist is pleading for a mutual seeking — the psalmist longs for God to *seek* the psalmist's *face.* At the very same time, the psalmist earnestly and passionately *seeks* God and the restoration that only God can provide. The despair of the psalmist's current crisis is cast in stark relief by the psalmist's plea, *do not hide your face from me!* The mutual seeking for which the psalmist longs is a picture of a restored relationship — the opposite of the "hidden face" motif. The stanza, in fact, ends with four negative appeals: *do not hide, turn from, forsake, abandon.* These four appeals are offset with two affirmations of who God is in relation to the psalmist: *my help* and *my deliverance.* The relational aspect of these appellatives for God should be stressed. The sufferer does not merely confess God as an abstract helper or deliverer, but *my helper* and *my deliverer.* The psalmist takes her stand of faith with, as it were, one foot standing firmly on God's internal character (as deliverer and helper) and one foot standing on God's external relational commitment (to the psalmist).

10-12 The previous stanza ended with the psalmist's appeal, *do not abandon me.* This stanza picks up where that one left off, but amplifies the imperative appeal into a powerful complaint: *Even my father and my mother have abandoned me.* Yet even this complaint, which so forcefully communicates the psalmist's desperate relational isolation, leads the psalmist back to trust: *the LORD will gather me in.* The word translated as *gather ('āsap̱)* is a relational term that is used for the gathering and welcoming of one into a family in 2 Sam. 11:27 and Josh. 2:18; here, the Lord is depicted as the one who welcomes precisely the one whom even the family has abandoned! In the next line, the Lord is asked to continue to play a familial role. In Prov. 4:3-4, the student of wisdom confesses that his father "taught me" *(yārâ),* and in 6:22 the father's commandments and mother's words are said to "lead" *(nāḥâ).* In Ps. 27:11, the psalmist asks God to *teach me (yārâ)* and *guide me (nāḥâ)* — to play the relational role that the psalmist's parents have, at least metaphorically, abandoned. The psalmist's relational isolation and danger are further depicted via the images of enemies who lurk along the road and false witnesses who raise charges in court and by the psalmist's plea not to be given over to them.

13-14 The psalm's closing stanza expresses trust by means of both a statement of confidence and a communal exhortation. The statement of confidence — *Indeed I believe that I shall see the goodness of the* LORD *in the land of the living* — sums up the psalmist's trust. The verb to *believe ('mn)* expresses the paradigmatic relational reliance that is required of God's servants (see Gen. 15:6; Exod. 14:31; Isa. 7:9). The *goodness of the* LORD (*ṭôḇ YHWH;* Pss. 34:9; 100:5; 135:3; 145:9; Jer. 31:12) is a summary statement that encompasses the entire range of gracious actions that a follower can expect from the Lord — from the bounties of harvest, to rescue from dangers, to forgiveness of sins, to healing. The psalmist's communal exhortation transposes the psalmist's interior trust into an exterior witness. The psalmist bids those who hear her testimony to be *strong* and *confident.* These two verbs *(ḥzq* and *'mṣ)* are paired together frequently in the Old Testament, most poignantly in Joshua 1 (vv. 6, 9, and 18), where they describe a wide range of qualities that Joshua is to embody — from boldness in leading God's people, to diligence in keeping the commandments, to confidence in trusting God's promises. All together, Joshua 1 provides something of a thick description of what the psalmist means when she calls on Israel to hope and trust in the Lord. To trust in God is to look to God for the good in life — to wait for good things from God, to hope for God's deliverance. Connecting this with the first commandment, to trust in God means to wait for and hope in God *and in God alone.*

Reflections

1. Whom Shall I Fear?

If the reader will forgive a deeply personal reflection, it may well have been Ps. 27:1 that first inspired the present writer's fascination with the psalms. When I was fifteen years old, I was diagnosed with bone cancer. The cancer led to the amputation of both of my legs and about ten lung surgeries to check the cancer's spreading threat. Throughout that lengthy *day of trouble* (v. 5), which lasted over three years, there was a great deal indeed to *fear* and *dread.* There was the frightful prospect of death — the cancer that *consumed my flesh* (v. 2). Even more, there was the terrifying prospect of life — of spending *all the days of my life* with a disability. Would I find a career? Purpose? Love? In those dark years, this psalm became a favorite word of Scripture. Not because it denied the fears of life, but because through its powerful metaphors (war, enemies, abandonment by family, etc.) it sketched in an authentic way a picture of the terrific challenges of life. And then, looking those dangers in the eye, the psalm expresses trust in the Lord. For that reason, this psalm has spoken so well for many of God's suffering people in so many and various circumstances. And, indeed, it still speaks for those who suffer. It speaks words of fear. And words of trust. The two are not as far removed from one another as one might imagine. *The LORD is my light and my salvation, whom shall I fear?*

2. Nobody Loves Me but My Mother

The African American spirituals and blues tradition is one place that the biblical practice of lament was preserved. B. B. King, perhaps the greatest blues man of all, sang this same sentiment: "Nobody loves me but my mother, and she could be jivin' too." In one version of the song, King then asked, "What I wanna know now, is what we gonna do?" The ancient psalmist already had an answer: *Even my father and mother have abandoned me, but the LORD will gather me in.* The psalms know the betrayals and abandonments we can face in our lives. But the psalms also know the persistent faithfulness and loyalty of the Lord, who has promised to gather in all who *hope in the LORD.*

ROLF A. JACOBSON

Psalm 28: Silence, Hearing, and Song

Psalm 28 is at once an urgent prayer of one who is surrounded by a hostile community consisting of those who should be neighbors (v. 3) and at the same time the heartfelt song of one who has experienced divine deliverance (v. 6). As Clifford notes, certain aspects of the poem do not fit the anticipated pattern of a prayer for help. Specifically: "The statement 'Blessed be the Lord' (v. 6) does not occur elsewhere as anticipated thanksgiving, and the statements associated with the thanksgiving are so confident that it is difficult to regard them merely as anticipated."[1] Similarly, the reference to the *anointed* in v. 8 and the corporate appeal in v. 9 complicate the task of genre identification. The psalm, in other words, contains elements from more than one genre.

The approach followed here is that the psalm is an appeal for help (vv. 1-4), followed by an oracle of salvation (v. 5), followed by a song of thanks (vv. 6-9).[2] This identification is problematic, however, because the poem is missing the normal framework of a song of thanksgiving (such as one sees in the first verses of Psalms 30 and 40). Furthermore, the approach is problematic because it forces the interpreter to assume either that different voices speak different parts of the psalm, that time has passed between vv. 5 and 6, or both.

It should be noted, therefore, that the psalm's interpretation depends greatly upon what an interpreter is expecting to find in a genre and also upon which elements of the psalm the interpreter privileges. If one emphasizes the first half of the psalm, it is a prayer for help.[3] If one emphasizes the last four verses, it is a song of thanksgiving.[4] If one emphasizes the prayer for the enemies' destruction (v. 4) or the reference to *mᵉšîḥô (his anointed one),* it can be counted among either the imprecatory psalms or royal psalms,[5] respectively. Similarly, one's interpretation will be affected by whether one imagines the entire song to be spoken in a single moment by a single speaker or whether one posits multiple speakers with time having elapsed between, for example, vv. 5 and 6. All of which is a reminder that genre identification is as much a constructive interpretive act as it is a descriptive interpretive act.[6]

From a theological perspective, the psalm is a poem that alternates between polarities. First, there is the polarity of sounds. The psalmist lives a

1. *Psalms 1–72,* p. 150. Clifford writes that "it is reasonable to conclude . . . the psalmist is undergoing a legal ordeal and asking for a divine judgment as to innocence or guilt."

2. See, e.g., Hossfeld and Zenger, *Psalmen 1–50,* p. 176; Seybold, *Die Psalmen,* p. 118; Craigie, *Psalms 1–50,* p. 237. Perhaps vv. 8-9 are also to be considered the words of the priest (so Craigie et al.).

3. So, e.g., Gerstenberger, *Psalms: Part 1,* p. 128.

4. So, e.g., Clifford, *Psalms 1–72,* p. 150; see also Kraus, *Psalms 1–59,* p. 339.

5. See Mays, *Psalms,* p. 135.

6. See Nasuti, *Defining the Sacred Songs,* esp. chs. 1-2.

life caught up between being heard and not being heard, God being deaf and God being silent, and God hearing. Second, there is the polarity of work. The psalmist lives in a world caught between the works, deeds, and conduct of those who fashion evil, and the work and deeds of God, who fashions deliverance. In this sense, the psalm is both about learning to live in the midst of these polarities and also about learning to discern the work and voice of God.

The structure of the psalm:

St 1 *Hear the sound of my plea* (v. 2; vv. 1-5)
  Cry for deliverance (vv. 1-4)
  Announcement of deliverance (v. 5)
St. 2 *He has heard the sound of my plea* (v. 6; vv. 6-9)
  Individual thanksgiving for deliverance (vv. 6-7)
  Corporate thanksgiving and petition (vv. 8-9)

Davidic.

1 *To you, O LORD, I cry;*
my rock,[7] *do not be deaf to me.*
For if you are silent to me,
then I will be like those who descend to the pit.
2 *Hear*[8] *the sound of my plea,*
when I cry to you,
When I lift up my hand,
toward your inner sanctuary.
3 *Do not drag me*[9] *away with the wicked ones,*
with those who do evil,[10]
Who speak peace to their neighbors,
but evil is in their hearts.
4 *Give to them according to their work,*[11]
according to the wickedness of their conduct,
Give to them according to the deeds of their hands,
return to them their dues.[12]

7. LXX *theos mou* suggests it is reading *ʾēlî.*

8. Lucian and Jerome add "O Lord," most likely a harmonization with 27:7.

9. LXX adds "my soul," suggesting *ʾal timšak̠ nap̠šî.*

10. LXX *mē synapolesēs me* suggests the addition of something like *ʾal teʾabb*^{e}*d̠ennî.*

11. LXX and other ancient witnesses read this as a plural *(k*^{e}*ma*^{ʿa}*śê),* most likely harmonizing with the succeeding verse.

12. Syr omits the entire second half of the verse, but its presence in other ancient versions indicates that this is most likely haplography.

5 *Because they do not perceive the works*[13] *of the* LORD,
or the labor[14] *of his hands,*
He will break them[15] *and will not rebuild them.*

6 *Blessed be the* LORD,
for he has heard the sound of my plea!
7 *The* LORD *is my strength and my shield;*
in him my heart trusts.
I have been helped[16] *and my heart*[17] *exalts,*
and with my song[18] *I praise him.*

8 *The* LORD *is the strength of his people;*[19]
he is a refuge of deliverance for his anointed one.
9 *Deliver your people and bless your inheritance!*
Shepherd them and carry them forever!

1-4 The psalm is launched with a cry to be heard. The Hebrew word order, which begins with *ʾēlêḵā YHWH (to you, O* LORD*)*, emphasizes the identity of the One who is called to hear — the identity of the only One whose hearing matters. The psalmist brings the cry to be heard to the Lord, because the Lord is the only One who *can* deliver. The fact that the Lord is the only sure deliverer is scored elegantly by pairing the metaphor of God as *my rock* with the metaphor of the psalmist's fate apart from God as *the pit.* The cry to be heard is emphasized by a series of verbs and nouns — *I cry (ʾeqrāʾ), do not be deaf (ʾal teḥᵉraš), if you are silent* (*pen teḥᵉšeh*[20]), hear the sound of my *plea (šᵉmaʿ qôl taḥᵃnûnay).* The motivating clause, *then I will be like those who descend to the pit* (cf. 30:3), does not seek to bargain with God, but seeks to name the desperate reality of his situation — help must come from the Lord or the psalmist shall die.

13. Some ancient mss and Aquila read the singular form, most likely harmonizing with the previous verse.

14. LXX, Targum, and some mss read the plural, most likely harmonizing with the previous verse.

15. LXX has 2ms verbs, suggesting *tehersēm wᵉlōʾ tiḇnēm.*

16. Syr omits.

17. LXX *sarx mou* may suggest it was reading *bᵉśārî* (LXX 62:2), but the term more often translates *libbî.*

18. LXX *kai ek thelēmatos mou* may suggest *ḥēp̱eṣ,* thus "and in my pleasure." MT is retained.

19. Reading *lᵉʿammô* with LXX and Syr.

20. The particle *pen* functions in a telic sense here to name the psalmist's fear that if God does not hear (but instead remains silent), the psalmist will perish.

The metaphor of God as *rock* may depend on the image of the temple as built upon Mount Zion, but because the metaphor is ancient (cf. Deut. 32:4), it is more likely that it stems from the enduring nature and securing power of stone. The specific reference to the psalmist's gesture of raising her hands to the *inner sanctuary* (*d*ᵉ*ḇîr* is literally the innermost chamber of the temple known as the holy of holies; occurring only here in the Psalter), therefore, evokes the concept of God's presence. The elusive original psalmist may have been present at the temple or may have turned in the direction of the temple to beg for God, who had promised to be present there, to extend the power of the divine presence in deliverance. The psalmist embodies this sense of presence by lifting her hand — an incarnational action signifying, as it were, the absence of God when she is in need but also the desire and faith in the nearness of God. The dialectic of presence-versus-absence is then amplified with the psalmist's plea, *do not drag me away ('al timš*ᵉ*ḵēnî).*[21]

Desiring the power that comes forth from God's presence, the psalmist fears the power that is present in the community of hostile humans. Verses 3-4 describe that community as characterized by a fundamental disjunction between words, intentions, and deeds. The evildoers speak words of *peace* (v. 3), but their intentions *(evil is in their hearts)* and their *deeds* belie the false words of peace. A key motif of this section of the psalm is the *work* of the wicked — the psalm employs three near synonyms for work — *pō'al* (translated here as *work*), *ma'*ᵃ*lāl (conduct),* and *ma'*ᵃ*śēh (labor).* All together, these three terms mount the strong rhetorical argument that the wicked are more accountable for the rough work of their hands *(y*ᵉ*ḏêhem)* than the smooth speech of their tongues. Thus the psalmist's plea that their evil work be returned to them in due proportion to what they have dealt others. As McCann notes, "The prayer that the wicked get what they deserve is not a matter of personal revenge but a matter of divine justice. . . . In effect, the behavior of the wicked sows the seeds of its own destruction."[22]

5 The announcement of v. 5 answers the plea of vv. 1-4. The psalm makes the connection between the plea and the answer by taking up the terms *work (pō'al), labor (ma'*ᵃ*śeh),* and *hand (yaḏ),* which had just been used of the wicked, and now using them of God — *the works (pō'al) of the* LORD and *the labor (ma'*ᵃ*śēh) of his hands (yāḏâw).* This is the third time in the psalm that the term *hand* has been employed, and all three occurrences aptly chart the difference between the three relational entities of the prayer. The psalmist raises his hands to God in prayer (v. 2), the wicked raise their hands against

21. As Clifford notes, " 'Drag away' is conjectural for an uncertain word, which may also mean 'count, reckon' " (*Psalms 1–72,* p. 151). But the occurrences of the term (cf. Ps. 10:9; Gen. 37:28; Job 24:22, etc.) seem clearly to support a violent physical action, thus "drag away."

22. McCann, "The Book of Psalms," p. 789.

their neighbors to work violence (v. 4), and they do so because they are not able to discern the work of God's hands (v. 5). The work of God's hands is to be a refuge and deliverance for the needy who call for and trust in God's help (vv. 7-8). As often the case in the Psalter, the psalm asserts that the sin of the wicked is sown in their inability to see, discern, or acknowledge that the Lord is an active, saving presence on the earth (cf. Pss. 10:3-13; 14//53; 73:1-11). Thus, a major difference between the wicked and the psalmist is that because they trust their eyes, which tell them that God's power is not real, the wicked do violence. The psalmist has no more proof of God's power than the wicked have, but nevertheless trusts in God's presence — with the twin results that the psalmist waits upon God and does not do violence to the neighbor. Verse 5 ends with the announcement that, because the wicked do not discern God's work (and this leads them to do violence), God will break and not rebuild them.

As noted above, the interpretation followed here is to imagine this verse being spoken by a different voice from that which prayed the petition in vv. 1-4 — perhaps a priestly, prophetic, or judicial figure presiding at the sanctuary. As Craigie notes, "These words are distinguished from the preceding part of the liturgy partly by their declarative substance and partly by the change in the form of address."[23] In this interpretation, v. 5a is understood as causally introducing the reason why God *will break them and will not rebuild them,* and the conjunction *kî* is translated as *because.* It is possible, however, to understand the speaker as a continuation of the voice of vv. 1-4, with 5a functioning as a motivating clause, which supports the request of 4d, with *kî* being translated as *for: Return to them their dues, for they do not perceive. . . .* In this reading, the plaintiff voice continues, and the statement of v. 5c *(he will break them)* is understood as a simple statement of anticipatory trust, similar to those found in many prayers for help. In both readings, the theological affirmation is made that the promise of the Lord's presence on earth may be trusted (contrary to the beliefs, actions, and expectations of the wicked). This promise, and faith in this promise, are at the center of the psalm.

6-7 The song modulates suddenly into the key of praise. Even though such shifts are frequent features of prayers for help, the exclamation, *blessed be the* LORD *(bārûḵ YHWH),* is a typical call for praise in the Psalter's hymns (124:6; 135:21; 144:1). Psalm 28:6 is the first occurrence of the phrase in the Psalter. When the phrase does occur in prayers for help, it does so in those poems that do not have a mere mention of trust or praise, but which seem to transform fully into songs of thanksgiving (cf. 31:21). When the phrase occurs in narrative passages, it is a response to some event or message of good news, such as deliverance from an enemy, the birth of a child, the death of an

23. *Psalms 1–50,* p. 239.

enemy, or the receiving of a favorable word from God (cf. Exod. 18:10; Ruth 4:14; 1 Sam. 25:39; 1 Kgs. 8:15). In the case of Psalm 28, the petitioner has experienced God's deliverance in the form of the promise of v. 5. For one with faith, having received God's promise is the same as having already received the thing that was promised — in this case, deliverance from enemies.

In v. 2, the petitioner had begged God to *hear the sound of my plea (š^{e}maʿ qôl taḥ^{a}nûnay).* The reason for the psalmist's tears being transformed into shouts of joy is, as he exclaims, God *has heard the sound of my plea (šāmaʿ qôl taḥ^{a}nûnāy).* This rhetorical reversal in the poetry bears witness to the existential reversal that the psalmist has received at the word of God. This reversal is further expressed poetically by the shift from words and images of mournful prayer (*I cry, I lift up my hand,* etc.) to words and images of music-filled praise *(my heart exalts, with my song I praise).* As noted above, the motif completes a movement in the psalm from the original position in which the psalmist cried out, because God was *silent* and did not hear, to the new position in which the psalm sings forth, because God has heard. The psalm itself, of course, is a voiced prayer and song. The rather literal transition in this sung prayer from the place of not-being-heard to the place of being-heard is one of the major developments in the poem — a development that expresses a fundamental dialectical tension of the life of faith. Verse 7's metaphors of God as *strength* and *shield* are stock images in the Psalter (cf. 59:17; 118:14; 33:20; 59:11; 84:11, etc.). They emphasize God's commitment to protect those who are vulnerable, on the one hand, and God's effective power to do so, on the other. They are powerful symbolic representations of the psalmist's contention that *my heart trusts.*

8-9 The closing verses of the psalm can be plausibly imagined either on the lips of the petitioner or on the lips of the liturgical figure who spoke (we presume) the promise of v. 5. Although the latter interpretive trail is followed here, the point is largely the same either way — v. 8 transforms the personal faith of the psalmist (v. 7) into a normative word of instruction, and v. 9 reframes the prayer of/for the individual into a prayer for the entire community. In the first phrase, the liturgist takes up the vocabulary that the psalmist had used in v. 7 *(ʿōz* and *māg̱ēn* become *ʿōz* and *māʿôz)* and pronounces them as a reality not just for the individual who has experienced deliverance, but for the people as a whole. As noted above, some have interpreted the announcement that God *is a refuge of deliverance* (this phrase occurs only here) *for his anointed one* as a clue that the petitioner of the psalm should be understood as the king and thus the psalm should be counted among the royal psalms. While such an identification is promising, perhaps even likely, the more enduring point is that the welfare of the individual and the welfare of the community go hand-in-hand. The *anointed one,* presumably the king, is to live a life of trust in the Lord as his *refuge of deliverance,* not simply for his own sake but for the sake of the people whom he shepherds. Earlier in the poem, it was precisely the wicked and evil-doers' failure to *perceive the works of the LORD* that led them to treat their neighbors with violence. In adjuring the king to look to the Lord for deliverance, the psalm strikes what is simultaneously a spiritual and an ethical chord. One cannot but help think of King Ahaz in Isaiah 7, whose refusal to trust in the prophet's promise was a spiritual failing, which in turn led to the suffering of his people.

The psalm ends with a petition for God's deliverance, blessing, and ongoing guidance. God's *inheritance* is a reference both to the land and the people of Israel. The people are those who inherit God's promise and blessing, a theme that begins in Gen. 12:1-3 and continues through the entire Old Testament. The theme of the inheritance of the blessing runs throughout Genesis, with the blessing being passed on to the next generation — sometimes with more than a little drama involved. Although the book of Genesis ends with the promise of the land at risk, because Israel has been chased off by a famine, the promise of the land is always the horizon toward which the people are journeying. It is the inheritance for the *people* who are themselves God's *inheritance*. But to remain God's inheritance, the people require God's ongoing blessing *(bārēḵ)*, shepherding (meaning "royal leadership," because the metaphor of the shepherd is always a royal metaphor; *rᵉʿēm*), and guidance (the Hebrew term translated *carry* is literally "to lift," *nāśaʾ*, symbolic of the shepherd's duty to carry home the lost or injured sheep. Such ongoing providence is exactly what Israel experienced from God in the wilderness, throughout the monarchy, through the exile, and into Israel's unknown, but sure, future.

Reflections

Trusting the Promise

The heart of this psalm is the promise of v. 5: *Because they do not perceive the works of the LORD, or the labor of his hands, he will break them and will not rebuild them.* The promise is issued to the psalmist from one whose identity is not precisely clear in the psalm, but who speaks authoritatively on God's behalf words that assure the psalmist that her enemies shall be defeated, and thus that her deliverance is assured. Her response is to trust the promise and to sing praise in witness to the reality of her trust. Although imagining the ancient context of this psalm may be difficult for modern readers, the life of faith today is much the same as for the ancient petitioner, for whom the only lifeline to hold onto was the spider-web-thin thread of a promise. To live the life of faith is to trust now and live today as if all that has been promised — eternal life, forgiveness of sins, meaningfulness, purpose, the reward for faith, and so on — has already been realized. In fact, to live the life of faith is nothing else than to be so gripped by God's promises that we live as if the promises have already been kept. As McCann writes, "the perspective is eschatological. The psalmist and the people already experience the benefits of God's reign . . . yet not completely. As is always the case, the reign of God is proclaimed amid circumstances and powers that seem to deny it."[24] Thus, the psalm's prayer for deliverance is both a prayer for God to save the individual from a hostile community and a call for the righteous community to be rescued and guided. And, because of this, the psalm bears witness to the vocation of the community as a whole to follow God and struggle against oppression. New Testament scholar and pastor Elisabeth Johnson extends the logic of this line of thinking in what she has written concerning Rom. 8:22-27: "Because we are joint heirs with Christ, we can expect to share in both his sufferings and his glory (8:17)." She continues, "there is no exemption from suffering for believers. Being children of God indwelled by the Spirit does not remove us from the suffering of creation but draws us ever more deeply into solidarity with our suffering world. As joint heirs with Christ, we can expect to share in his sufferings (8:17) on behalf of a world in bondage. As the Spirit of Christ dwells within us, at odds with the powers of sin and death, we experience conflict and suffering, yet we are not driven to despair. The Spirit groans with us and intercedes for us, giving us hope in the promise of redemption."[25]

Rolf A. Jacobson

24. "The Book of Psalms," p. 790.

25. "Romans 8:22-27: Commentary on the Second Reading for May 31, 2009," www.workingpreacher.org.

Psalm 29: Ascribe to the Lord

It is often posited that Psalm 29 is an Israelite hymn that was adapted from an older, Canaanite hymn to Baal — that this older hymn was "only slightly modified" for use by Yahweh worshippers.[1] Yet, as is always the case in scholarship, support for this hypothesis is not universal.[2] Craigie suggests a middle ground: "it is clear that there are sufficient parallels and similarities to require a Canaanite background to be taken into account in developing the interpretation of the psalm, but it is not clear that those parallels and similarities require one to posit a Canaanite/Phoenician original of Ps 29."[3] That is to say, the question of how this psalm originated both cannot be solved and is rather uninteresting. But thematically it is clear that this Israelite poem borrows from its Canaanite environment. The themes that it borrows — God's voice as the sound of thunder, God's advent as the arrival of the storm, God as king over the powers of chaos — it also baptizes: the God who so speaks, who so comes, and who is so enthroned is the Lord (the psalm makes this point emphatically — it uses the name of the Lord eighteen times). In this sense, the poem's use of these themes is like the church's use of the pagan tree as a symbol of the Christmas festival of the incarnation or the church's use of the pagan name Easter for its festival of the resurrection. In that sense, as McCann has noted, "Psalm 29 is fundamentally polemical, for it clearly attributes all power to Yahweh (Lord), who is enthroned in v. 9 with the exclamation, 'Glory!' "[4]

A public worship setting for the use of this hymn is implied by the text. The LXX's superscription associates the psalm with the fall Festival of Tabernacles, which was the most important festival of the year during the Old Testament period. As such, it may be considered a festival psalm. It has also been numbered among the enthronement psalms — those psalms that celebrate the Lord as king with the ritual shout, "The Lord has become king!" *(YHWH mālāḵ* or *mālāḵ YHWH).*[5] Craigie's identification of the psalm as a

1. Cross, *Canaanite Myth and Hebrew Epic,* p. 152. See also Theodore Herzl Gaster, "The Earliest Known Miracle-Play?" *Folklore* 44 (1933) 379-90; H. L. Ginsberg, "A Phoenician Hymn in the Psalter," *XIX Congressor Internzionale degli Orientalis* (Rome, 1935) 472-76; Cross, "Notes on a Canaanite Psalm in the Old Testament," *BASOR* 117 (1950) 19-21.

2. Such as B. Margulis, "The Canaanite Origin of Psalm 29 Reconsidered," *Bib* 51 (1970) 332-48; Peter C. Craigie, "Psalm XXIX in the Hebrew Poetic Tradition," *VT* 22 (1972) 143-51.

3. *Psalms 1–50,* p. 245.

4. McCann, "The Book of Psalms," p. 792.

5. See McCann, "The Book of Psalms," p. 792; for more on the enthronement psalms and the translation of *mālāḵ YHWH,* see Mowinckel, *Psalmenstudien* and *The Psalms in Israel's Worship,* 1:106-29.

"hymn of victory" is particularly attractive.[6] Craigie cites significant parallels between Psalm 29 and earlier Israelite victory hymns, such as Exodus 15 and Judges 5 and concludes that whereas those hymns were associated with particular military victories, "Ps 29 reflects a slightly later period . . . it is a *general* victory hymn, though it was probably devised for use in the specific celebration of victories over Canaanite enemies. . . . The initial setting for its use would have been in a victory celebration undertaken on the return of the army from battle or military campaign." The notion of a general victory hymn should be pressed beyond what Craigie imagined, however. The hymn should be understood to reflect the cultic witness of the community during the period after which Israel had emerged from beneath her Canaanite oppressors. In this setting, the witness of the psalm is that the Lord had proven victorious over both cosmic and earthly foes, and the Lord would continue to bless and protect his people (thus the indicative translation of the verbs in v. 11).

The structure of the psalm is straightforward, although some scholars divide the main body of the poem into two or more stanzas:[7]

Introduction	Call to praise (vv. 1-2)
Body	Advent of God's glory in the storm (vv. 3-9)
Conclusion	Announcement of God's reign and promise of blessing (vv. 10-11)

A Davidic Psalm.[8]

1 *Ascribe to the* Lord, *sons of God!*[9]
Ascribe to the Lord, *glory and strength!*
2 *Ascribe to the* Lord *the glory of his name!*
Bow down to the Lord *in his holy courts!*[10]

3 *The voice of the* Lord *is over the waters,*
the God of glory thunders,

6. *Psalms 1–50,* pp. 245-46.

7. E.g., see Fokkelman, *The Psalms in Form,* p. 40.

8. LXX adds *exodiou skēnēs* ("upon leaving the tent"), perhaps indicating *b^{e}ḥs'ēṯ 'ōhel,* but most likely reflecting later usage of the psalm during the Festival of Tabernacles.

9. LXX has *enenkate tō kyriō houious kriōn,* possibly reflecting *hāḇû lYHWH b^{e}nê 'ēlîm,* but this reading does not fit the context and reflects an apologetic agenda.

10. Reading with LXX *en aulē hagia autou,* reflecting *b^{e}ḥaṣraṯ qoḏšô;* MT's *b^{e}ḥaḏraṯ qōḏeš* ("in holy attire"; so Craigie, *Psalms 1–50,* p. 242; or "at 'his' holy appearance"; so Kraus, *Psalms 1–72,* p. 344) is problematic. The normal recourse to render MT as "in holy splendor" (so NRSV) or "in the splendor of his holiness" (so NIV) is awkward.

the Lord is over the mighty waters!
4 *The voice of the Lord is strength,*[11]
the voice of the Lord is majesty.
5 *The voice of the Lord breaks cedars,*
the Lord shatters the cedars of Lebanon.
6 *He makes*[12] *Lebanon skip like a calf,*
and Sirion like the son of a wild ox.
7 *The voice of the Lord cuts with spears of fire.*[13]
8 *The voice of the Lord shakes the wilderness,*
the Lord shakes the wilderness of Kadesh.
9 *The voice of the Lord causes oak trees*[14] *to shake,*
and strips the forest bare.
And in his temple, all say, "Glory!"[15]

10 *The Lord is seated above the flood,*
the Lord is seated as king forever!
11 *The Lord gives strength to his people!*
The Lord blesses his people with peace!

1-2 The key word in the two introductory verses is *hāḇû,* translated by most versions as "ascribe" in this context. The term is related to the root *yāhaḇ,* which most simply means "to give." The term occurs in its imperative form in the context of hymns with the sense of "acknowledge" or "ascribe" (Ps. 96:7-8; 1 Chr. 16:28; Deut. 32:3). As the parallels in Psalm 96 and Deuteronomy 32 indicate, the sense of the Hebrew term is certainly stronger than the English word "ascribe" can accurately capture. In Deuteronomy 32, to "ascribe greatness to the Lord" is parallel to the poet's proclamation of "the name of the

11. Reading a *bēṯ* of identity (R. J. Williams, *Hebrew Syntax* [2nd ed.; Toronto: University of Toronto Press, 1976], p. 45), similar but not identical to Dahood: "an emphasizing particle, a kind of exponential strengthening of the substantive" (*Psalms I,* p. 177).

12. The 3mp suffix is read not as a suffix, but as an enclitic *mem* (with Craigie, *Psalms 1–50,* p. 243).

13. The suggestion of reading *ḥṣb* as related to Arabic *ḥḍb* ("to rake [fire]") is not helpful. The much better attested sense of the root as "hewing stone" and thus as "cutting" resonates poetically with the image of lightning as a spear (*lehāḇâ* occurs in 1 Sam. 17:7 in reference to Goliath's spear).

14. Reading *'êlôṯ,* with NRSV, NIV, and others; in parallel with the succeeding verse.

15. Goldingay (*Psalms 1-41,* p. 412) argues that v. 9c belongs in the final stanza of the psalm, that *kullô* refers to the "palace," which is not the earthly temple but the heavenly abode, and thus the psalm ends: "And in his palace each one in it is saying: 'In honor Yhwh took his seat. . . .' " It would fall outside of the rhythm of the psalm to have the closing stanza begin with the *wāw* or for that stanza to include five cola. In addition, Goldingay must stretch to supply the word "in," which is not present in the Hebrew text.

LORD." And in Psalm 96, the call to ascribe to the Lord the glory and strength "of his name" is paralleled by the universal call to bring offerings, worship, and tremble. In other words, to ascribe *glory and strength* to the name of the Lord is to acknowledge that glory and strength belong only *to the Lord and to none other.* The threefold use of the imperative *hābû* here is the syntactical throwing down the polemical gauntlet to any who would withhold from the Lord that which rightly is due to him — and only to him.

There are both a personal and corporate element to this polemic. In the personal sense, each individual self is likely to guard jealously whatever meager *glory and strength* he or she has been able to earn. After struggling in the marketplace of human honor and shame to gain a small share of glory or honor, the worshipper is immediately enjoined to turn it over to the Lord. This call to literally give it over to God is both law and gospel. It is law in the sense that to name the Lord alone as the rightful lord is to admit the frailty and fraud of all human efforts at self-justification. But it is gospel in the sense that with the admission of truth come both a freedom that can come only from uttering the truth and the relational gifts that come when one tethers one's self to the true Lord.

There is likewise a corporate element to the polemic (similar to that in Psalm 96), as can be seen in the rhetorical call for the *sons of God* (see note on v. 1 above) to ascribe honor to the Lord. The *sons of God* are residents of the Lord's heavenly court — beings at once eternal but less than God.[16] Rhetorically, by enjoining this imagined heavenly choir to acknowledge the Lord's glory, the implied earthly congregation is acknowledging the vanity of all the things to which we cling with trust and love in place of God — whether those things are the literal gods that the ancients worshipped in place of or alongside of the Lord or whether those things are the material goods and abstractions that many modern people cling to in place of the Lord. Thus, all of the external things to which we cling to grant ourselves security or identity are to be regarded as rubbish compared to the *glory* of the Lord.

3-9 Two literary features of the middle section of the psalm offer clues to the meaning of the poem. The first is the sevenfold repetition of the key phrase *the voice of the* LORD *(qôl YHWH).* Perhaps in imitation of the rebounding sound of the thunderstorm which the poem describes, the phrase echoes seven times in this section. This repetition rather clearly establishes the connection the psalm is making between the metaphor of the storm and the voice of the living God.

16. Goldingay's comment here is helpful: "As well as being subordinate to Yhwh, they are metaphysically different from Yhwh, who is the sole God with no possible beginning and no possible end"; *Psalms 1–41,* p. 416.

The second literary feature of the middle section is the inclusio that is formed by the word *glory (kāḇôḏ).* In v. 3, the term is used in construct in an adjectival sense to describe a quality that belongs to God — *the God of glory ('ēl hakkāḇôḏ).* The implication is that glory is a quality that belongs to God . . . and God alone. The very last word of this section of the psalm, in v. 9, is again *glory (kāḇôḏ),* but this time the word is the liturgical response that is placed on the lips of those who worship in the temple: *And in his temple, all say, "Glory!"* The inclusio here does more than neatly tie off the loose rhetorical threads of the stanza. Rather, it signals the *telos* of the coming of the Lord. God comes in order to reveal God's glory to God's creatures. And those creatures, having experienced the manifestation of the Lord, are to recognize both the reality and the meaning of God's appearance. The exclamation *"Glory!"* is both a recognition that God has come — that the *God of glory* is now present — and at the same time a recognition that true glory (and thus true worship, obedience, and discipleship) belongs to God alone.

The combination of these two literary features makes for a highly interesting poetic witness. It is ironic that *the voice of the LORD* is mentioned seven times, but unlike other psalms (cf. Psalms 50, 81, or 82), no words of God are quoted — God never actually speaks. Rather, humans are the only ones who speak, and they say only one word, *glory.* In Deut. 5:25 and 18:16, the phrase *voice of the LORD* refers to God's revelation of the law,[17] while in Mic. 6:9 and Isa. 66:6 it refers to announcements of God's prophetic words. In Psalm 29, by contrast, the phrase is less about content than about an impression that is left — the impression of the Lord's strength, might, and glory. The reason that the phrase here is less about the content of the revelation and more about the impression is the tie between the *voice of the LORD* and the metaphor of the thunderstorm. Especially for the ancient imagination, the thunderstorm was a powerful metaphor for God's coming, because it tidily combined both natural and supernatural connotations. In Canaanite mythology, Baal was the god of the thunderstorm. He bears the epithet "rider of the clouds" in Ugaritic literature and is pictured wielding thunder in one hand and lightning in the other in Canaanite art. In the Baal Cycle, he does battle with Yam ("Sea"), so it is instructive that Psalm 29 declares *the voice of the LORD is over the waters . . . over the mighty waters.* Thus, the metaphor of the thunderstorm was symbolically potent precisely because it was a natural phenomenon rife with such supernatural connotations. As the thunderstorm is employed by this psalm, the storm is pictured as the embodiment and arrival of pure power — a voice

17. Although note that the revelation at Sinai is described as being accompanied by "the fire, the cloud, and the thick darkness" (Deut. 5:22), so there is ambiguity. It may be that the phrase *voice of the LORD* would have connoted both speech and something like thunder to the ancient imagination.

that is nothing other than *strength* and *majesty;* a voice that *shatters* trees, causes the very earth to *shake, strips the forest bare,* and terrifies animals. The storm rolls in from the sea and impresses its power across the entirety of the land — from *Lebanon* and *Sirion* in the north, to *the wilderness of Kadesh* in the south, and everything in between . . . especially the *temple,* the epicenter of the earth, the closest point of contact between heaven and earth.

10-11 The closing two verses provide a suitable culmination to the movement of the psalm. The poem started out in the heavenly realm, with the *sons of God* being bid to acknowledge the Lord's *glory* and moved to earth — following the path of an inland-moving storm — where those who have gathered for worship in God's earthly temple also acknowledge the Lord's *glory.* The final stanza, as it were, then summarizes the meaning of the earthly and heavenly acknowledgement of God's glory — the Lord reigns as king (the Hebrew *yāšāḇ* here, as in 2:4, carries the technical sense of "to be enthroned as king") in both the heavenly realm *(above the flood)* and in the earthly realm (the Lord is the king of a particular people, *his people*). The reign of the Lord is thus both universal in space as well as in time — *the LORD is seated as king forever.*

In the closing couplet of the psalm, a further consequence of the arrival of this heavenly king is revealed. An attribute of the Lord, which only the Lord possesses, namely *strength* (*ʿōz,* v. 1), is imparted to his people (*The LORD gives strength to his people,* v. 11). The use of the lexeme *ʿōz* here both forms an inclusio (vv. 1 and 11) that nicely rounds off the psalm and, more importantly, extrapolates on the meaning of God's theophany. The significance of God's coming is that God comes both to be known and to impart something to the people that only God can impart. That God comes to be known is evident in the psalm's witness that, at God's coming, the people in the temple acknowledge God's nature by responding with the chant, *"Glory!"* That God comes to impart a unique gift to the people is evident in the detail that precisely that quality *(strength)* that even the supernatural *sons of God* have to acknowledge belongs properly only to God is, in the end, bestowed upon God's people in a free and gracious gift. The nature of God's strength, moreover, is qualified by the closing line: *The LORD blesses his people with peace!* The strength of God is given not for the purpose of warfare or conquering power, but paradoxically God's strength quells the warring madness of the children of Adam and Eve. Psalm 46 promises that the Lord breaks the bow and shatters the spear. Similarly, Psalm 29 promises that God's strength is made known when God blesses the people with *peace.* McCann writes, "Thus *shalom* — peace, well-being, security — does not begin with our efforts but with our openness to God's claim upon us and the ways God has gifted us."[18] And maybe even better, the

18. "The Book of Psalms," p. 793.

search for true strength and peace is not a search in which we can ever hope to be successful. Rather, true strength and peace were forged in the moment that decided to bridge the gap between divine infinity and human finitude.

Reflections

The Metaphor of the Thunderstorm

Psalm 29 is devoted (not to say dominated) by its exploration of the thunderstorm as a metaphor for God's advent or manifestation on earth. As already noted, the meaning of God's coming, according to the witness of Psalm 29, is that the Lord comes both to establish a relationship with the people (they acknowledge his *glory*) and to bestow a gift through his coming (the Lord shares the divine *strength* with his people). But what more can be said about the metaphor of the storm? It is commonplace now to assert about metaphors that they are both true and untrue at the same time, that they generate because they suggest both similarity and dissimilarity at once. As Jeffrey Osowski writes, "A metaphor, then, is both true and untrue in its relationship to a concept or set of concepts in a theory."[19] Another way to say this is that metaphors bear witness to a truth about some subject precisely by asserting something that is, on the grossly literal level, false about the subject. The psalmists name the Lord as rock, light, shepherd, fortress, and so on. These metaphors are powerful witnesses about God, in fact, because of and not in spite of the gap between the truth of the statements and the nontruth of the statements. As Sallie McFague writes, "metaphor creates the new, it does not embellish the old, and it accomplishes this through seeing similarity in dissimilars. This process, in essence, is the poet's genius — the combining of old words in new ways to create new meanings."[20] Applying this to Psalm 29, the point that is scored is that God's coming is both like and unlike the coming of the thunderstorm, that to compare God's coming to that of the storm is both true and untrue at once. The Lord is not literally in the thunderstorm, nor is God's revelation located in natural phenomena. But there are similarities (as well as differences) between the advent of the Lord and the power and arrival of the storm. The point is not to make two lists — one of similarities/truths and another of dissimilarities/untruths. Rather, the point is that the metaphor unsettles. It pokes holes in tidy theological boxes; it disturbs comfortable

19. "Ensembles of Metaphor in the Psychology of William James," in *Creative People at Work,* ed. Doris B. Wallace and Howard E. Gruber (New York: Oxford University Press, 1989), p. 142.

20. *Speaking in Parables: A Study in Metaphor and Theology* (Philadelphia: Fortress, 1975), p. 50.

conceptions of God. Especially in respect to the metaphor of the thunderstorm — which as the psalm says, breaks trees, shakes the wilderness, and strips bare the forest — the disturbing and disruptive force of the metaphor may be its most potent feature.

Rolf A. Jacobson

Psalm 30: From Mourning to Morning

Psalm 30 is a classic example of a type of praise psalm known as the psalm of thanksgiving (called by Westermann a psalm of narrative or declarative praise).[1] The psalm reflects a situation in which a sufferer has passed through a dark period of crisis and now finds herself in the bright light of safety. She credits the Lord for this salvation and thus returns praise for her deliverance. One may emphasize the "thanksgiving" aspect of this psalm; this is correct in the sense that the praise with which the psalmist lauds God is a *grateful response* to her rescue from crisis. Or one may emphasize the "praise" aspect of this psalm; this is also correct in the sense that the psalm's primary emphasis is a grateful response *to God.* In addition, one may emphasize the faith aspect of this psalm, because the praise that the psalmist offers God in response to deliverance is a *confession of faith* in God's continuing presence and power.

Even though the psalm is the prayer of an individual, a corporate setting is implied. Having passed through crisis, the psalmist rises up before the congregation and calls others to join in his praise of God. As with most thanksgiving psalms and prayers for help, the precise nature of the original crisis that occasioned the psalm has been (intentionally?) obscured. Many commentators identify the crisis generically as an illness, but even this general identification cannot be made with confidence. The language that the psalm uses to describe the crisis and rescue — *you healed me, you raised up my soul, you restored my life,* and so on — may be understood just as readily in a poetic rather than a literal sense. The generic language allows believers in every generation to pray and sing this psalm anew, using it to reflect on the myriad crises that humans pass through in life and using it to deflect toward God any credit for having "made it." Evidence that such reuse of this psalm is appropriate is present in the superscription of the psalm. The phrase *a song of dedication (ḥᵃnukkâ) of the temple* was mostly likely inserted into the superscription that originally read *a Davidic psalm.*[2] The insertion suggests that this song of an individual was later recontextualized by the community with the *I* of the psalm being understood as a corporate identity. But what was the new context? To what does the *dedication of the temple* refer? Ancient Israelite and Jewish writings suggest two possibilities. The first possibility is the dedication of the second temple after the exile ca. 515 B.C.E., as described in Ezra 6. The second possibility is the rededication of the temple in 165 B.C.E. under Judas Maccabeus following its profanation

1. See Gunkel, *Introduction to Psalms,* pp. 199-221; Westermann, *The Psalms,* pp. 71-80.

2. See Sarna, *On the Book of Psalms,* pp. 148-49.

ca. 167, as described in 1 Maccabees 4. The second possibility seems more likely for two reasons. First, the Talmud (*b. Sop.* 18.3) assigns Psalm 30 to be read during the Festival of Hanukkah, which is the annual celebration of the 165 event. Second, if the superscription of Psalm 92 ("a song for the day of Sabbath") is used as a clue, then it is likely that the heading of Psalm 30 implies an instruction to use the psalm at a regularly repeated temple occasion, which fits Hanukkah and its annual commemoration of the 165 event better than it does the 515 rededication of the temple. The Talmud also prescribes that the psalm be used by pilgrims at the presentation of firstfruits (*Bik.* 3.4).

The poem has five stanzas, through which the psalm moves in a rational progression:

St. 1 Introductory praise from the individual (vv. 1-3)
St. 2 Call for the community to join in praise (with reasons for praise) (vv. 4-5)
St. 3 Recollection of the time of crisis (vv. 6-8)
St. 4 Quotation of a prayer for help prayed during the crisis (vv. 9-10)
St. 5 Concluding praise from the individual (vv. 11-12)

There are two key motifs that provide the mortar from which the psalm is built. The first building block is poetic — a series of contrasting polarities that build on the basic comparison in the psalm between the previous distress and the present deliverance that the psalmist has experienced.[3] These poetic polarities, which are explored more in the commentary below, include: distress/deliverance; anger/favor; I cried/you healed; night/day; I went down/you raised up; moment/lifetime; mourning/dancing; sackcloth/rejoicing; sing/be silent. The second building block is thematic — the theme of praise. This theme may seem obvious, and the skeptical reader may grouse that of course praise is a theme because this is a praise psalm. But in Psalm 30, praise functions both formally — this is a psalm *of praise* — and also thematically — this is a psalm *about praise.*

A psalm. A song of dedication of the temple. Davidic.

1 *I will exalt you, O LORD, for you have drawn me up,*
and you have not let my enemies rejoice over me.
2 *O LORD, my God, I cried to you,*
and you healed me.

3. See Mays, *Psalms,* pp. 139-40.

3 *O LORD, you raised up my soul from Sheol,*
you restored my life from those gone down[4] *to the pit.*

4 *Sing to the LORD, his faithful ones!*
And give thanks to his holy name.[5]
5 *For his anger*[6] *is for a moment,*
his favor for a lifetime.
Weeping may sleep over for an evening,
but in the morning — rejoicing!

6 *But as for me, I said in my complacency,*
"I shall never be moved."
7 *O LORD, in your favor, you had established me as a strong mountain.*[7]
You hid your face, I was dismayed.
8 *To you, O LORD, I cried,*
and to[8] *my lord*[9] *I made supplication.*

9 *"What profit is there in my blood?*
In my going down to the pit?
Will the dust praise you?
Will it declare your faithfulness?
10 *Hear, O LORD, and be gracious to me!*[10]
O LORD, be a helper for me!"

4. The Qere reflects the infinitive construct form *miyyārdî* in place of the Kethib's participial form *mîyôrᵉḏê*. As Craigie (*Psalms 1–50,* p. 251) argues, the Kethib is preferable, because the normal form of the infinitive construct occurs in v. 9, which makes Qere's alternate form of the infinitive construct unlikely here.

5. Hebrew *zēḵer* means literally "mention," "remembrance," or "vow." The sense here is to give thanks to the mention of God's holy name. LXX woodenly translates "to the remembrance of his holiness."

6. LXX and Syr read "For anger is in his wrath, but life in his favor." LXX most likely confuses *regaʿ* with the root *rāḡaz*. The second part of the clause remains problematic (see commentary below).

7. MT is corrupt ("you made-to-stand strength for my mountains"). LXX has "my beauty," likely reading *lhdry* for MT *lhrry* ("as my strong mountain"). Craigie regards the problematic MT consonants as a plural construct, but this fails to explain the singular adjective ("strong"). The easiest solution is to eliminate the suffix on mountain and read "as a strong mountain."

8. Syr and Targum read "to you."

9. Reading with 4QPsʳ, *YHWH* here in place of MT's *ʾᵃdōnāy*, while LXX and Targum reflect "my God" *(ʾᵉlōhay)*.

10. 4QPsʳ, supported by LXX, has *wyḥnny* ("he was merciful to me"), apparently understanding the quotation that begins in v. 9 as ending at the end of v. 9.

11 *You have turned my mourning into dancing,*
you have taken off my sackcloth and clothed me with rejoicing,
12 *So that my soul*[11] *will sing praises to you and not be silent,*
O LORD my God, I will give thanks to you forever.

1-3 The psalm erupts immediately in an ecstatic outburst of praise. The psalmist, who has passed through the dark veil of distress into the new light of deliverance, unleashes pent-up words of praise to God. The praise in these verses confesses the psalmist's glad belief that it was God — not herself — who was responsible for her deliverance. Note that every line in vv. 1-3 is a personal confession of praise directly to God: *I will exalt* you . . . you *have drawn me up* . . . you *have not let my enemies rejoice* . . . *I cried to* you *and* you *healed me* . . . you *raised up* . . . you *restored my life*. . . . It is the relationship between the psalmist and the cosmic God who is also a personal *you* that is the driving force of Psalm 30.

This first stanza of the psalm introduces the poetic theme of praise. The verb *rûm* in the hiphil *(exult)* is a typical verb of praise. But so is the verb *śāmaḥ* — you have not let my enemies *rejoice* over me. The word appears frequently in the psalms, where we learn that one normally "rejoices" *(śāmaḥ)* in God and God's deeds. The occurrence in Ps. 16:9-10 is particularly apt for comparison:

Therefore, my heart is glad and my glory *rejoices;*
even my body dwells securely.
For you will not abandon my soul to Sheol,
you will not allow your faithful one to see the pit.

In 30:1, by contrast, the enemies rejoice not in God's salvation, but in the psalmist's distress. Thus the issue, as the psalmist subtly casts it, is whether one's praise is correct praise (as is her own) or incorrect praise (as is her enemies').

The second poetic feature, that of polarities, also is introduced in the first stanza of the poem. The vertical polarity of "go down"/"raise up" occurs in both v. 1 and v. 3, forming an inclusio around v. 2, which contains the psalmist's central praise: *I cried to you, and you healed me.* The word *exalt* *(ʾᵃrômimkâ)* means literally to "raise up" or "lift up" and is part of this rhetorical play. The psalmist playfully "raises up God" because God has *raised up* the psalmist. The term translated here as *drawn up* is a picturesque word that is normally used for drawing water from a well (Exod. 2:16; Prov. 20:5). In the context of Psalm 30, the word provides a particularly fitting poetic image for

11. Translating *kābôd* as "my soul" as in Ps. 7:5 (where the term occurs in parallel with "my life/soul"); adding suffix as reflected in LXX reading.

deliverance from danger because the psalmist describes how he was almost like *those gone down to the pit.* The *pit (bôr)* literally means a well or a cistern where water was collected. Perhaps the modern idiom of "going down the drain" would be a more faithful translation. Yet it should also be noted that it was common practice to imprison criminals in these cisterns (cf. Gen. 40:15; 41:14; Jer. 37:16), and since some prisoners surely died in these cisterns, the language here is more than just poetic — for the ancient Israelite, the phrase *those gone down to the pit* might have evoked the names and faces of those who had met such a fate. The word *bôr* came to imply the land of the dead, perhaps because the idea of the pit provided a fitting image of the entry into Sheol, the land of the dead (cf. Isa. 14:19).[12] In terms of the poetry of this stanza, it is crucial to note that the metaphorical polarity of going *down to the pit*/being *drawn up* mirrors the more realistic polarity of being in distress/experiencing deliverance at God's hand.

4-5 The poetic theme of praise continues in the second stanza of the psalm, which is a call by the psalmist for the community to join him in praising God for his deliverance. Once again, the issue is the correct praise of God. The psalmist's enemies rejoice in his suffering, which amounts to inappropriate praise, whereas the psalmist enjoins the community to praise God for his salvation, which would amount to appropriate praise of God. If this stanza were isolated from its context, scholars would classify it as a hymn. The stanza exemplifies the two major form-critical aspects of a hymn: an imperative call to praise (v. 4) and reasons for praise (introduced by *for* [*kî*], v. 5). For two reasons, the psalmist's call for the community to join him in praise for his deliverance is more than simply an invitation to celebrate his personal good fortune. The first reason is a theological issue involving the community's ability to discern God at work in its midst. As the psalmist indicates in v. 1 when he says, *you have not let my enemies rejoice over me,* what is at stake is a communal recognition of how God works. By delivering the psalmist from distress, God has deprived some members of the community of reasons for rejoicing. The enemies who would rejoice at another's downfall should not be understood as sadists who enjoy the pain of others. Rather, they should be understood as akin to Job's counselors, people who concluded that the psalmist's suffering was the result of some sin, and thus they assumed that he "deserved" his fate. By delivering him, God has deprived them of this conclusion. By inviting the community to join him in his praise of God, the psalmist puts before them the opportunity to give witness to God at work in a different way. The second reason is a communal reason involving the acceptance of the psalmist back into the community's full life. The previous period of distress marked a period of alienation for the

12. Cf. Keel, *The Symbolism of the Biblical World,* pp. 69-72.

psalmist. By joining him in praise, not only does the community acknowledge God's actions on his behalf, but also it acknowledges the psalmist as a full member of the community. As Gerstenberger comments, the "subtle message to the participants of the ceremony could be 'I am restored; accept me back into your community!' "[13] Note also how this restorative element of the call to praise mirrors the Pentateuch's prescription for the restitution of members to the congregation (cf. Leviticus 13–14).

The psalmist's "reasons for praise" consist of a creedal-like confession of faith. Having passed through crisis, the psalmist has learned that God's "anger is for a moment, his favor for a lifetime. Weeping may sleep over for an evening, but in the morning — rejoicing!" The building blocks of this confession of faith are another set of poetic polarities: *anger/favor, moment/lifetime, evening/morning, weeping/rejoicing.* These four polarities echo and reinforce the psalm's main polarity of the previous distress versus the present deliverance. The poet beautifully orchestrates these four polarities into a triumphant poetic confession of faith. God's anger, the cause of our weeping, is momentary, like an evening past; God's favor, the cause of our rejoicing, is for a lifetime. The text translated here as God's *anger is for a moment, his favor for a lifetime* is difficult to translate. A literal and wooden translation would read: "For a moment in his anger, life (or lifetime) in his favor." NRSV and many commentators follow a translation similar to the one above. NJPS, supported by some commentators, translates it as "For He is angry but a moment, and when He is pleased there is life." The crux arises over how to translate *ḥayyîm.* The Hebrew plural often expresses abstraction, and that is clearly the case here.[14] The question is whether the abstraction here should be understood as "lifetime" (NRSV) or as "life" (NJPS). The broader context of the psalm cannot solve the issue, since either translation makes sense in context. The contrasting of *regaʿ* ("a moment") with *ḥayyîm* and the next phrase that compares the weeping of one evening with the rejoicing of the next morning weigh slightly in favor translating *ḥayyîm* as *a lifetime.*[15] The important thing to note is that the psalmist is grounding the call for the congregation to praise in the confession that God's favor is longer and stronger than God's anger — God's favor suffices both to give life and to last a lifetime. The psalmist elegantly closes the call to praise by imagining weeping as a guest who "spends the night" (*lîn,* the only verb in this verse) *for an evening.* And even more elegantly, the psalmist describes the deliverance of God as the joy that comes with sunrise. By depicting weeping as a guest through the use of the verb *lîn,* the psalmist

13. Gerstenberger, *Psalms: Part 1,* p. 135.

14. See Waltke and O'Connor, *Biblical Hebrew Syntax,* pp. 122-24.

15. But note that if LXX and Syr are correct that the text originally read *rgz* ("anger"), then the parallelism supports "life."

also implies that the joy of the Lord's saving help remains for the long run — it does not just stay for the night, it moves in permanently.

6-8 In the third and fourth stanzas of the psalm, the psalmist turns the focus again to his personal story, but not in an introspective fashion. The setting is still corporate. The psalmist refers to his own experience in order to offer a lesson to the community. In the third stanza, the psalmist looks back to a period of pride that led to downfall. In the fourth stanza, the psalmist rehearses part of a prayer for help that he spoke during his distress. The third stanza begins with an emphatic quotation that represents his attitude prior to the time of crisis: *But as for me, I said in my complacency, "I shall never be moved."* The phrase *I shall never be moved* does not in itself imply a sin, as occurs in the Old Testament both as an appropriate expression of praise that exhibits faith in God's providence (cf. Pss. 16:8; 62:2; 96:10; 121:3) and also as an inappropriate expression of pride that exhibits trust in one's own self-mastery (cf. Ps. 10:6). In terms of this psalm's use of the thematic issue of praise, what is at stake is whether the psalmist's earlier attitude was characterized as appropriate praise of God or inappropriate trust in self. As the prepositional phrase *in my complacency* indicates, the psalmist clearly views her earlier attitude as flawed because it was based on personal pride. The word translated here as *complacency* is *šalwî;* the form occurs only here, but is related to *šalwâ,* which clearly means negligent self-confidence in a text such as Prov. 1:32: "the *complacency* of fools destroys them." The psalmist quotes his earlier speech — *I shall never be moved* — here both to indicate that this attitude was a sin (i.e., he is confessing his sin) and also to indicate that he no longer holds this attitude (i.e., he has repented and changed his attitude).

The psalmist continues by addressing God directly — the ancient audience and the modern reader both overhear this personal conversation between believer and Lord. In v. 5, the psalmist had confessed that God's *favor (rāṣôn)* lasts longer than God's *anger.* Here, the psalmist recalls that *in your favor" (rāṣôn)* God had *established* him. The word *you established (heʿᵉmaḏtâ)* is another play on the vertical "go down"/"draw up" metaphor of the psalm — *you established* means literally "you caused me to stand." The psalmist's point is that he had incorrectly conceived of his prosperity as the result of his own merit rather than as a result of God's undeserved favor. Thus, when God turned away from the psalmist, he had no leg left to stand on. In the Old Testament, God's *face* is a metaphor for God's favor and protection.[16] In this context, the metaphor evokes a hostile action on God's part in which God withdrew *favor* and protection. It is difficult for the modern reader to grasp how aggressive this metaphor must have felt to the ancient believer. The psalmist's crisis was not simply the result of divine oversight, but an active

16. Cf. Brown, *Seeing the Psalms,* pp. 172-75.

and intentional withdrawal of protection that led to a period of distress for the psalmist. This is an instance of what Martin Luther called God's "alien work" (see below).

The stanza ends by pointing the way out of despair and distress. The psalmist remembers that in distress, he cried to the Lord *my God* (v. 2). The first person pronominal suffix is significant. The psalmist did not conceive of his relationship with God as ended, but sought redemption and deliverance from the very one who seemed the problem. To cry out in lament is not the lack of faith, but precisely the opposite — it is a form of faith appropriate for life in the pit.

9-10 As mentioned above, the fourth stanza consists of the quotation of an older prayer for help that the psalmist prayed from the pit. Verse 9 consists of a motive clause that supports the petition itself (v. 10) by giving reasons why God should answer the psalmist's plea. Many commentators have wondered why the psalmist chooses to cite the motive clause from the older prayer. Why cite this particular part of the lament? While it is impossible to know the ancient author's intent, it is possible to note how this older motive clause fits into the present psalm's poetic rhetoric. First, note that the theme of "going down"/"being drawn up" is again mentioned: *What profit is there. . . . in my* going down *to the pit?*[17] Second, it is helpful to see that the motive clause again has to do with the issue of praise: *Will the dust* praise you? *Will it* declare *your faithfulness?* So while we cannot fix on why the ancient author chose to quote this part of the earlier prayer, we can appreciate how the quotation from the earlier prayer fits perfectly with the poetics and rhetoric of the current psalm of praise. Some modern readers are uncomfortable with the content of the motive clause, being disturbed by what sounds like bargaining with God for a positive answer to prayer. Offering God reasons for a prayer to be answered, however, is not the same as bargaining. The older prayer was an appeal to God's *faithfulness.* By offering supporting reasons for the prayer to be answered, the psalmist strengthens the appeal to God's fidelity — God should answer the prayer precisely because the psalmist will praise God for God's fidelity, something that the *dust* cannot do. The reference to *dust,* of course, is an allusion to the eventual fate of all mortals, to return to the dust from which we were originally created ("For you are dust, and to dust you shall return"; Gen. 3:19).

The psalmist also has a pedagogical purpose in quoting the earlier prayer. The psalmist intends that her audience — her ancient community and by extension all modern readers — learn from her experience that *life* when properly lived is a life of praise for God. Since for the ancients, death was the

17. It should be noted that the word translated as *pit* here *(šāḥaṯ)* is a different word than that used in v. 3.

place and time when praise stopped, her near-death experience brought her to the precipice of that place where praise ceases. Having been called back from that silent land, she now wishes to fill every corner of this life with praise of the God who is faithful. As Mays writes, "The psalmist has made the loss of praise the very basis of his supplication and thereby dared to make one of the most important statements in the Bible about the theological value of praise. At issue is there being someone to proclaim the faithfulness of the Lord. Praise has a theological basis as well as an anthropological one. Praise is the way the faithfulness of the Lord becomes word and is heard in the Lord's world (v. 9)."[18]

The last verse of the fourth stanza quotes the petition from the earlier lament. This plea is a standard request similar to those found in numerous individual prayers for help. In this context, perhaps the cry to God to *hear* should be emphasized, because God's hearing is in itself an act that shows both God's faithfulness and God's power.

11-12 In the final stanza of the psalm, the poet returns to the present moment and celebrates the reversal that God has accomplished for him. Similar to how the psalm opened, the speech here is praise speech directed to God. The poetic theme of polarities continues, as the psalmist employs three tight phrases to compare the distress of the past with the joy of the present. In the first phrase, the psalmist contrasts *mourning (mispēḏ)* with *dancing.* The term *mispēḏ* goes beyond an internal, reflective state of mourning; it implies external, ritual acts of mourning. The *mispēḏ* is the dirge sung over the dead.[19] In this context, *my mourning* either means that mourning that friends and loved ones would do over the psalmist or — more poetically — the psalmist might be likening his previous prayer to a dirge he sang for himself. The basic sense of the root *spd* is to beat one's breast, as one might do in grief. Thus, "to mourn" is to give physical expression — a dance, if you will — to grief. The psalmist confesses that God has changed this "mourning dance" into a "dance of praise." (Note that Eccl. 3:4 pairs these same two words: "A time to mourn, and a time to dance.") In the second phrase, the psalmist contrasts *sackcloth* with *rejoicing.* The psalmist here replaces the concrete image of the sackcloth — clothing that a mourner would wear to symbolize humility, repentance, or sorrow — with the abstract concept of rejoicing. In the third phrase, the psalmist contrasts the silence that would have been his fate had God allowed him to die with the praise that he has been left to *sing.* It should be stressed that the positive words in all three of these phrases — *dancing (māḥôl), rejoicing (śimḥâ),* and *sing (zāmar)* — all are terms borrowed from

18. *Psalms,* p. 141.

19. See Sarna, *On the Book of Psalms,* p. 148 n. 53; H. L. Ginsberg, *Koheleth* (Jerusalem: Newman, 1961), p. 73.

the vocabulary of *praise.* The final line of the psalm is itself a word of praise and the psalmist's promise to praise God for all his days. Thus the psalm ends by sounding again the keynote of praise that is so central to the psalm's poetry and meaning. In v. 4, the psalmist had bid the community to *sing (zāmar)* and *give thanks (yāḏâ)* to God. The psalmist repeats those two key words at the end of the psalm, demonstrating his willingness both to take his own advice and live out his promise to God.

Reflections

1. The Nature of God

Psalm 30 posits the fundamental thesis that the God of Israel is a God who delivers. For this reason, God is worthy of praise. The psalm springs to life from a background of suffering and distress. But the psalmist desires that we focus not merely on the distress from which she has emerged, but on the living God who brought her out of the depths of mourning into the fresh breath of morning. The psalmist bears witness to the faith that in, with, and under the tangible reality of her deliverance from a stout time of trial there was an even more tangible reality at work — God. Readers who take the testimony of Psalm 30 seriously will have to come to grips not only with the psalmist's proclamation that this God exists, but also with Psalm 30's claim about the fundamental nature of this God. If the poet speaks truth, then God's nature is to be a God who saves, one who intervenes in order to spark a basic reversal in the affairs of God's people. The psalmist explores reversal marvelously in the many polarities described above. But perhaps the phrase that best captures how the psalmist sees God at work is this: The God of Israel is a God who turns *mourning into dancing.* That is good news indeed.

2. A Life of Praise

In addition to being a psalm of praise, Psalm 30 is a psalm about praise. The psalm calls the faithful not just to one isolated act of praise, but to a complete life of praise. The psalm enjoins us to lead a life that celebrates and bears joyful witness to the reversals and Easters that only Israel's God can fashion. At the individual level, to live such a life of praise is to commit one's self fully into the care of the God who is praised. As Brueggemann has commented, the idea of thanking/praising God here "means a confessional acknowledgement of who it is that has given new life. Thanks is more than being grateful. It is a confessional statement, in some sense relying upon and committing one's self to the other. To thank is to make commitment."[20] At the communal level, to live as

20. Brueggemann, *The Message of the Psalms,* p. 127.

a people of praise means that we are always willing to accept those stunning reversals in the lives of sinners and sufferers as gifts from God's hand. The psalmist had passed through an experience that was at once an experience of personal suffering and public marginalization. To live as a people of praise means that we live ready to welcome into our communities sufferers such as the poet of Psalm 30, sinners such as David, and doubters such as Thomas.

3. The Alien Work of God

Perhaps the most difficult theological issue raised by Psalm 30 is its testimony not that only the deliverance came from God's hand, but also that the initial distress was authored by God. Does God work this way? Does God "bring low" in order to "raise up" again? Borrowing language from Isa. 28:21 (in which Isaiah announced God's judgment of Judah and cried, "strange is his work! . . . alien is his work!"), Martin Luther referred to this type of divine activity as God's "alien work." Luther wrote, "God's 'alien' works are these: to judge, to condemn, and to punish those who are impenitent and do not believe. God is compelled to resort to such 'alien' works and to call them His own because of our pride. By manifesting these works He aims to humble us that we might regard Him as our Lord and obey His will."[21] As Luther emphasized, God's alien work exists only for the purpose of accomplishing God's proper work, which is to save, bless, and be gracious: "It is as if he were saying: 'Although He is the God of life and salvation and this is His proper work, yet, in order to accomplish this, He kills and destroys. These works are alien to Him, but through them He accomplishes His proper work. For He kills our will that His may be established in us. He subdues the flesh and its lusts that the spirit and its desires may come to life."[22]

ROLF A. JACOBSON

21. *LW,* 13:135.
22. *LW,* 14:335.

Psalm 31: Protect Me from Those Wishing Me Harm

Psalm 31 is a prayer for help that like Psalm 30 has an irregular literary structure with two sections (vv. 1-8 and 9-24), each with cries for aid, expressions of trust, and thanksgiving. Poetically, the prayer seems to conclude in v. 8, only to start all over again with v. 9.[1] What does this double structure indicate? Were the trust and thanksgiving premature, or does this prayer represent two different episodes in a person's life when God came to this one's aid? The prayer itself gives no hint as to which way it should be understood, so ultimately it is up to the individual hearing or reading this piece to decide for herself. This gives the poem the ability to be understood differently in a variety of situations. Its structure is divisible into two large sections with smaller stanzas:[2]

- vv. 1-8 — First prayer for help
  - vv. 1-6 — Pleas to God for aid
  - vv. 7-8 — Trust and thanksgiving
- vv. 9-24 — Second prayer for help
  - vv. 9-13 — Pleas to God for aid and deliverance
  - vv. 14-18 — Trust and petitions for salvation
  - vv. 19-24 — Thanksgiving

While there are a few lines with translation difficulties, overall the reading is clear. There are, however, several differences between the MT and the LXX that may indicate two early versions of this psalm.[3] 5/6Ḥev agrees with the MT.[4]

1. Kraus notes this double structure is seen in Pss. 18, 30, and 102; *Psalms 1–59,* p. 360.

2. Gerstenberger notes that Ps. 31 "shows neither logical nor literary order," *Psalms: Part 1,* p. 137. This lack of discernable order makes the division of the psalm difficult. Gerstenberger uses a complex structure: vv. 1-2, 3-6, 7-8, 9-13, 14-18, 19-20, 21, 22, 23-24. Craigie sees only two sections: a prayer in vv. 2-18 that is chiastic in form with additional thanksgiving in vv. 19-24; *Psalms 1–50,* 2nd ed., p. 259. Kraus sees the divisions close to the structure above; *Psalms 1–59,* p. 360.

3. Also noted by Gerstenberger, *Psalms: Part 1,* p. 137.

4. Peter W. Flint, "5/6ḤevPsalms," in James H. Charlesworth et al., *Miscellaneous Texts from the Judean Desert* (DJD 38; Oxford: Clarendon, 2000), pp. 141-72.

Psalm 31

To the leader. A Davidic psalm[5]

1 *In you, O* Lord, *I sought refuge;*
do not let me be shamed forever;[6]
in your righteousness, deliver me![7]
2 *Bend your ear to me,*
rescue me quickly!
Be for me a rock of refuge,
a fortified dwelling to save me,
3 *for my cave*[8] *and fortification, you are;*
so for your name's sake, lead me and guide me.
4 *Bring me out from the net,*
which they hid for me;
for you are my refuge.
5 *Into your hand, I entrust my life;*[9]
you have ransomed me,[10] *O* Lord, *God of truth.*
6 *I hated*[11] *the ones who keep to worthless nothingness;*
and I, upon the Lord, *I trusted.*

7 *Let me rejoice and be glad in your* hesed,
for you have seen my affliction;
you knew[12] *the anguish of my inner self,*[13]
8 *and you did not deliver me into the hand of the enemy;*
you placed my feet in a broad place.

5. The LXX adds "in extreme fear or agitation."

6. Most English translations read some form of an adverb, "let me never be put to shame" (NIV), but the intensive verbal forms are not used here. Instead, it is the preposition, *lᵉʿôlām,* indicating a period of time "until forever."

7. LXX adds "and rescue me."

8. This word is a synonym of "rock" and probably means more like a crag or cleft in the rock. Since it is used without modifiers here, *cave* gives the modern reader the same understanding as the ancient "crag" or "cleft."

9. Lit., *rūḥî* has a multitude of meanings: "wind, breath, life." The translation of "spirit" should be avoided because in Hebrew culture the spirit was not separable from the physical body.

10. Some modern translations read *pāḏîṯâ* as an imperative, indicating this is still part of the pleas to God. The form here, however, is clearly a *qal* perfect, indicating that God has indeed acted on behalf of the one praying.

11. LXX and Syr read "You hated."

12. LXX reads "You have delivered."

13. Lit., *napšî* has a wide range of meaning: "soul, living being, self." It is the essence of what makes a sack of bones alive.

9 *Be gracious to me, O LORD,*
for there is distress for me;[14]
my eyes and my inner self and my belly waste away with grief.[15]
10 *For my life is spent in sorrow;*
my years in groaning;
my strength fails on account of my iniquity;[16]
and my bones waste away,
11 *because of all my foes I have become a disgrace;*
and to my neighbors more so;[17]
and a dread to my friends;
the ones seeing me in the street flee from me!
12 *I am forgotten in their hearts,*[18] *like the dead;*[19]
I have become like a smashed pot,
13 *for I hear the gossip of the multitude,*
terror from all around!
They conspire together against me;
they consider taking my life.[20]

14 *But I, in you, I trust, O LORD;*
I say, "You are my God."
15 *My times are in your hand;*
rescue me from the hand of my enemies,
and the ones pursuing me.

14. The modern translation of "I am in distress" is not indicated via the Hebrew syntax, where the distress is the main noun with *lî* as the dependent preposition.

15. Most translations separate "eye" as the subject of the 3fs verb, and this is possible. However as noted by Waltke and O'Connor, the *wāw* can be attached to all of the nouns in a series or simply the last in the series (*Biblical Hebrew Syntax,* p. 648). The singular verb is not uncommon with multiple subjects if they are related, especially since the person is considered a unified whole without the division of body and soul.

16. Most read with Symmachus as "distress" or "misery," but there is no compelling reason to read against the MT here, especially since the manuscript from Naḥal Ḥever also reads "iniquity"; Flint, "5/6ḤevPsalms," p. 165.

17. Many emend the text here, noting that *mᵉʾōḏ* makes little sense even though both LXX and 5/6Ḥev read the same as MT. Kraus, following Briggs, suggests a change to *māḏôn* ("feud"); *Psalms 1-59*. However, Waltke and O'Connor note that *mᵉʾōḏ* also expresses degree as above (*Biblical Hebrew Syntax,* p. 215).

18. *Lēḇ* is singular here, but in the context of all the groups in v. 11 it is clearly meant to be understood as a plural.

19. Most commentators substitute "mind" here, arguing the ancient Near Eastern understanding of "heart" was the place of thought, but that is unnecessary. In modern culture, we also remember the dead "in our hearts" instead of "our minds."

20. See note 13 above.

16 *Let your face shine on your servant;*
save me in your hesed.
17 *O LORD, do not let me be shamed*
for I cried out to you.
Let the wicked be shamed,
let them be silent in Sheol.
18 *Let the lying lips be stilled,*
the ones speaking against the righteous arrogantly,
with pride and contempt.
19 *How abundant is your goodness*
which you have stored up for those who fear you,
(which) you have prepared for those taking refuge in you,
in front of the children of humanity.
20 *You hide them in the shelter of your face;*
from the plots of humans you hide them,[21]
from tongues of strife.
21 *Blessed be the LORD,*
for he has wondrously shown his hesed *to me;*
as an entrenched city![22]
22 *In my alarm, I, I said, "I am cut off from your eyes";*
yet you heard the sounds of my pleas to you,
when I cried to you!
23 *Love the LORD, all his loving*[23] *ones!*
The faithful ones the LORD preserves;[24]
but is repaying upon those who are excessively proud.
24 *Be strong, let your hearts be strengthened,*
all those waiting for the LORD.

1-6 The opening of the prayer centers on rescue. In this section are the key words *refuge, deliver, rescue, rock of refuge, fortified dwelling, save, cave,* and *fortification.* God is seen as a place of safety in troubled times, and God is called upon to *save* and *rescue,* not because of the one praying, but because of God's own character *in your righteousness* (v. 1) and *for your name's sake* (v. 3). Verse

21. LXX adds "in the tabernacle."

22. The meaning here is uncertain. The BHS critical apparatus is followed by most; it emends the text to "in the time of oppression" (Kraus, *Psalms 1–59,* p. 359). The NJPS, however, reads this as an epithet for God; this is possible based on the large number of references in this psalm to God as a refuge or protection. In this case, the phrase would have to be read as a city that withstood a siege.

23. As has been noted with the abstract noun, there is no adequate English equivalent for *ḥ^{a}sîḏāyw.* "Loving ones" is one of several inadequate options.

24. LXX reads "the LORD seeks truth."

4 introduces a new metaphor — a *net* — but God is still the place of protection. This portrayal of God is very physical, a place of safety both in the wilderness (*cave* and *rock of refuge*) and in the midst of human turmoil (*fortified dwelling* and *fortification*). Verse 5 continues the theme of trust in God, for this one has placed her very life into God's hands because God has *ransomed* in the past. Verse 6 goes further, confirming that this one does not place her trust in humans but in God. God will rescue this one now because God has done so in the past, and this one knows not to trust in human powers but only in God.

The first line of v. 5 has had a life beyond this psalm that demonstrates how psalmic passages are reused (and with a different meaning) in different cultures. Here the line affirms trust in God and in God's ability to protect the life of the one offering prayer. In Hebrew thought, the word *rûaḥ* means, literally, "wind" or "breath." Used in Greek culture, the line is given a different meaning in Luke 23:46, when Jesus speaks from the cross, "Father, into your hands I commend my spirit," and in Acts 7:59 at the stoning of Stephen. Spirit in these Greek texts is something that lives on after physical death and is not the same as the breath of life; indeed, it is the very thing that transcends physical life.[25] Craigie notes the change: "The psalmist prayed for life, for deliverance from death, and that is the psalm's fundamental and legitimate sense. But in the context of resurrection faith, the psalm may also be used as a prayer in death, expressing trust and commitment to life lying beyond the grave."[26] What does not change about the meaning of the line is that no matter what, God is the one to whom one entrusts oneself. The poetic flexibility allows for multiple meanings that expand this prayer from what was originally intended.

7-8 The first refrain of thanksgiving is a fitting rejoinder to vv. 1-6. God has seen this one's affliction and torment and responded by providing another safe place *(broad place)* that echoes the places of safety requested in vv. 1-6.

9-13 It is no surprise that some have wondered if vv. 9-24 were at some point separate from vv. 1-8. The prayer returns to pleas to God, but the vocabulary and the condition expressed are different. The pleas are more urgent, more descriptive, and the one praying seems to be in dire distress, a distress present for a long period of time (v. 10). The trust expressed earlier is soon eclipsed by great sorrow. The pain is both mental and physical, and it has no nexus: it is caused both by *iniquity* (v. 10) and by *foes* (v. 11). This is a common idea that both the actions of the one praying and the actions of others have contributed to the present pain. Verses 12 and 13 speak of alienation and terror. The one praying has certainly reached a place of terror, as some forget him and others begin to *gossip* and *conspire.*

25. In Greek, the word *pneuma* can also mean breath or life, but also and especially in the NT, it refers to the noncorporeal part of a human; *BAGD.*

26. Craigie, *Psalms 1–50,* p. 263.

14-18 *But I, in you, I trust, O LORD* comes without warning or introduction and reminds those listening of the first eight verses of the prayer. Verses 14-16 speak in the same confident voice as the earlier piece and even return to the themes of *trust* and *rescue.* The additional element here is that there are petitions for God to act against the enemies. The shame should be on them and not the one offering the prayer (v. 17). They and their lies should be silenced.

19-24 These final verses turn to thanksgiving and praise. First, God is praised for providing a *refuge* and for hiding those who fear God *in the shelter of your face.* God's *refuge* is not just a place of hiding, but is the very *face* of God. It is better than safety (v. 20). God is to be blessed for offering *hesed* and presence (v. 21). The final line of this verse is difficult. In both the NIV and NRSV, the one praying either is in that city or is like a city besieged. The NJPS reads it as an epithet for God, "a veritable bastion," describing how God has acted. This rendering seems more likely, based on the ways that God has been called a refuge throughout the piece, but ultimately the meaning of the line is unclear.

Verse 22 recalls a time when the one praying was separated from God and *cried out* in fear. God hears and restores, which is why all those *loving* and *faithful* to God should rejoice (v. 23). The psalm ends with an assurance to all listening that indeed God hears God's people when they call.

Psalm 31 seems to conclude at v. 8, only to offer another set of cries for aid that are more desperate than the first, followed again by declarations of trust that again come without explanation. It is no wonder that Gerstenberger concludes that Psalm 31 "shows neither logical not literary order." But instead of assuming that those that kept and edited this psalm did not see its lack of logical order, could it be that the psalm only looks confused to a post-Enlightenment Western audience? Is there something we can learn from this psalm? As much as we want to believe otherwise, our lives do not unfold in logical order. Things happen that we do not expect, and faith and doubt are part of that cycle. We can believe one moment and know that our lives, both physical and spiritual, belong in God's faithful hands and the next second feel alone and full of doubt and hurt. This psalm tells about this reality in our lives. Is this two different occurrences of doubt, or did this one falter just as she was about to place all her trust in God? It depends. Just as a line of this psalm was reimagined for a different context and even a different understanding in the New Testament, the one reading this psalm will be the one to make sense of its twists and turns. Poetry is meant to engage our memories and our imagination and in that transform our relationship with God, so the meaning of this psalm is to examine the thin line between faith and doubt that we all share as we strive to better understand and embrace our relationship with God.

BETH TANNER

Psalm 32: Celebrating Forgiveness

Psalm 32 bursts on the scene with a surprising declaration: *Happy is the one whose transgression is lifted.* Technically, it is a thanksgiving song, but it is really a celebration of the forgiveness and restoration that only God can provide. As a liturgical piece, it goes beyond the assurance of pardon into a celebration of restoration. The prayer also has a clear flow:[1]

vv. 1-2 — The moments after forgiveness is granted
vv. 3-5 — A remembrance of the weight of unconfessed sin and its release
vv. 6-7 — An invitation for all to celebrate in the moment
vv. 8-9 — The importance of teaching others
vv. 10-11 — Another final call for all to rejoice

Textually, the prayer has a few very problematic lines where the exact understanding is difficult to discern. The overall meaning, however, is clear.

A Davidic maskil.[2]

1 *Happy is the one whose transgression is lifted;*
whose sins are covered.
2 *Happy is the human to whom the* Lord *imputes no iniquity;*
and in whose breath[3] *there is no deceit.*
3 *When I kept silent, my bones wore out,*
from my roaring[4] *all day long,*
4 *for day and night, your hand was heavy upon me;*
my tongue is turned like a summer drought.[5] Selah

1. Most scholars use the same divisions, although some see v. 11 as a separate stanza of concluding praise (Kraus, *Psalms 1–59,* p. 370; Craigie and Tate, *Psalms 1–50,* pp. 267-68; Gerstenberger, *Psalms: Part 1,* p. 140).

2. The precise meaning of *maśkîl* is unknown. *HALOT* lists "cult song" (following Kittel) and "wisdom song performed to music" (following Mowinckel). The root has the meaning of "to instruct" (see 32:8), indicating the possibility of being associated with teaching and perhaps wisdom. The difference between this designation and that of *mizmôr* is unknown.

3. Lit., *rûḥô,* which has a multitude of meanings: "wind, breath, life." The translation of "spirit" should be avoided, because in Hebrew culture the spirit was not separable from the physical body. LXX reads "mouth" and Syr "heart."

4. NRSV and NIV's "groaning" is not strong enough. NJPS rightly translates "my anguished roaring." The Hebrew does not mean quiet moaning but a full-throated scream.

5. Meaning of this phrase is uncertain. MT reads *šaddî.* This word appears only twice and probably means a buttery cake (*HALOT,* p. 536), but this makes little sense

5 *Then my sin I made known to you;*
my iniquity I did not cover.
I said, "Let me confess against myself,[6]
my transgression to the LORD,"
and you, you lifted the iniquity of my sin. Selah
6 *Therefore, all the loving ones shall pray to you,*
at a time of distress;[7]
for the flood of many waters, they shall not reach him.
7 *You are a hiding place for me;*
from distress you protect me;
with glad cries of deliverance you surround me. Selah
8 *I will instruct you and I will teach you in the way that you should go;*
I will advise with my eye upon you.
9 *Do not be like a horse or a mule*
without knowledge of bit and bridle;
his ornament to curb;
not coming near you.[8]
10 *Many are the sorrows of the wicked;*
but to the one who trusts in the LORD,
hesed *surrounds him.*
11 *Be glad in the LORD,*
Rejoice O righteous ones;
And shout for joy all you upright of heart!

---

here. LXX "I became miserable with a thorn was fastened in me" does not aid the reading. Most interpreters suggest emending the word to *šuddî tongue* as above, but any translation here is tentative.

6. Modern translations omit *ʿălê,* which is probably a misspelled "against my self."

7. This line is unclear, as the plethora of possibilities attest. The translation above emends the last two words from *mᵉṣōʾ raq* to *māṣâoq (distress),* as do NRSV and Craigie, *Psalms 1–50,* p. 264. The other common possibility, given by D. Eberhard Baumann, "Struktur-Unterschungen im Psalter I, *ZAW* 61 (1945/48) 140, is "while you may be found," followed by NIV. LXX also reads a different line: "in a fitting time." Any translation of this line is tentative.

8. This verse is very problematic, as the host of translations demonstrates. The verse is probably corrupt, and no solution is superior to the other. There are two problems. First is the meaning of *ʿeḏyô* ("his ornament") in MT and "cheeks" in LXX. Mowinckel (*Psalmenstudien,* 1:52-53) suggested this Hebrew word can also mean "strength," as noted by Kraus's "whose strength only bit and bridle tame" (*Psalms 1–59,* p. 367), reflected in NRSV and NJPS. Craigie, following A. A. Macintosh ("A Third Root עדה in Biblical Hebrew?" *VT* 24 [1974] 454-73), believes the root means "gallop" (*Psalms 1–50,* p. 265). The second issue is the syntax of the verse, and any translation requires the addition of helping particles. The translation above is as close to the Hebrew as possible, and even if the exact phrasing is elusive, the general meaning of the verse can still be discerned.

1-2 The prayer opens with dual beatitudes, *Happy is the one. Happy* is not an adequate definition in modern English, for "happiness" has been significantly diminished by our consumer-driven culture. The Hebrew root means "to go straight" or "march forward" and indicates not a condition, but a way of life. In other psalms, this happiness comes from life choices and training, but here we learn that is not the entire formula, for one's "happiness" is also completely dependent on God's forgiving grace. First, the passive voice of v. 1 makes it clear that this is God's action and not human. God forgives and God *covers.* Second, God restores this one back to a state of grace, so this one is restored to full humanity (v. 2).

3-5 These verses speak of how unconfessed sin feels. The ancients were much more likely to equate emotion and its physical response, but we all know that we too can feel our sins physically as well as mentally. Verse 3 characterizes the turmoil when one keeps her sins to herself as the *roaring* that goes on in her mind. The phrase *my bones wore out* probably refers to something like the NRSV's "my body wasted away." The burden of sin actually hurts and can feel like a *heavy* pressing *hand* (v. 4). The last line in v. 4 is difficult to translate, but we all know that dry mouth which comes with the adrenaline rush of panic, hurt, and guilt.

Verse 5 describes the release from our torture. The balance of the verse is interesting. There are four lines describing how the person confesses, with three words for *sin.* Just as above, these lines describe the difficulty of coming to that place of confession. The human is laid bare, making known the sin and confession against his own self-interest. The weight of vv. 3-5c is relived in one scant line where *you* appears twice as a pronoun and as part of the verb stressing this is God's action. It has taken eight lines to describe the weight of sin and the path to confession, and here it is reversed with four words describing God's act.

6-7 Limburg points out the importance of the first word, translated as *therefore:* "Therefore, because the Lord forgives sins, such forgiveness results in true happiness."[9] An individual act of forgiveness is a reason for all of those who love God to be confident and celebrate that, even if the *waters* of sin press hard, God will not allow these ones to drown. Verse 7 returns to the individual, and like v. 6 it uses images that are often reserved for the enemies, demonstrating that sometimes the enemy is not others but indeed ourselves.

8-9 Scholars debate who is speaking here. Some, like Kraus, argue that it is God.[10] The argument is twofold. First, it is common form for an oracle to follow thanksgiving, and second, the *I* and singular *you* language exclude the "they" from vv. 6-7 from being the focus here. However, psalms often change

9. *Psalms,* p. 104.
10. *Psalms 1–59,* p. 371; also Limburg, *Psalms,* p. 104.

from the plural to singular person and back again without explanation. Second, Psalm 51 makes the same move, going from confession and forgiveness to teaching (51:13-15). A response to forgiveness is warning others so they will not follow the same path. Ultimately here, however, one could understand the teacher as either God or the one praying, for the central focus is the act of teaching, not necessarily the identity of the teacher. Verse 8 reminds that there are paths that will lead away from sin, and much can be learned from seeking that path.

Verse 9 has a host of problems that make an exact translation impossible. What is clear is that, whatever the metaphors are here, the lesson is the same as in v. 8, and this time it is in the form of a proverb. A trained animal has to learn to accept *bit and bridle* so animal and human can work together; without it the animal can run unrestrained, and often that animal will run into trouble. We too must learn the path to "happiness" through responsibility and learning from others.

10-11 It is possible that v. 10 is also a proverb like v. 9 and should belong with what comes immediately before. But it also summarizes the entire situation expressed here in the poetry. The weight of the *wicked* is great as sin presses them down. The true happiness of vv. 1-2 can only be found in the Lord who forgives and restores God's own. Just as in Psalm 1, this psalm makes a way of life outside of trust in God the foolish choice. Really, would you rather drag around all of your *sorrows* or be *surrounded* at all times by God's *hesed?* There hardly seems to be a choice at all.

The psalm ends in the celebration of all of God's people. We should be *glad* because God has redeemed us, not only at that one point of decision when we first become aware of God's gift of salvation, but also each and every day as we confess and begin again as new and transformed creatures of God.

This psalm celebrates what is the very heart of the Christian tradition, God's grace and forgiveness that allows for us to know true happiness. Yet amazingly, we rarely take the time to celebrate this pivotal act of daily grace. Psalm 32 gives us just that opportunity to *be glad* and *rejoice* and *shout,* for God does reckon us *righteous!*

Beth Tanner

Psalm 33: The *Hesed* of the Lord Fills the Earth

Psalm 33 is a hymn of praise, with a special emphasis on the Lord as creator. The poem has twenty-two lines, but unlike its neighbor, Psalm 34, it is not an acrostic poem.[1] The psalm's emphasis on creation is unique, as Diane Jacobson notes, because it "alone among all of the psalms, speaks of God's creation by word."[2] Jacobson succinctly describes the psalm's dual rhetorical force: "The Lord is praised for a justly ordered world while (the audience, the readers, the supplicants) are instructed, comforted, encouraged, and finally given grounds to appeal to God's steadfast love."[3]

The structure of the psalm is debated. It is clear that vv. 1-3 offer the characteristic "call to praise" that is indicative of a hymn, that vv. 4-19 comprise the normal "reasons for praise" (introduced by the characteristic *kî;* cf. vv. 4, 9), and that vv. 20-22 are a concluding prayer of confidence. But interpreters differ as to how (or if) the main body should be divided into smaller sections, or what the rhetorical flow of that main body is. If one traces a series of changes in content (e.g., the shift of focus at v. 18 from the trustworthiness of God to a focus on the instability of human efforts) and in syntactic signals (e.g., the renewed call in v. 8 followed by a second "reason for praise" section introduced by a second *kî*), then a balanced, six-part structure emerges. There are four, four-verse-long stanzas, bracketed by a three-verse-long introductory call to praise and a three-verse-long concluding prayer.

Introduction	Threefold call to praise (vv. 1-3)
St. 1	The trustworthiness of God's creation (vv. 4-7)
St. 2	The trustworthiness of God's plans (vv. 8-11)
St. 3	The trustworthiness of God's discernment (vv. 12-15)
St. 4	The untrustworthiness of human agency (vv. 16-19)
Conclusion	Renewed prayer of hope in God's fidelity (vv. 20-22)

1. But see William Wallace Martin, "The Thirty-Third Psalm as an Alphabetical Psalm," *AJSL* 41 (1924-25) 248-52. And Kraus, who follows G.-W. H. Bickell in identifying it as an "acrostic song" because it has as many lines as there are consonants in the Hebrew alphabet (*Psalms 1–59,* p. 374). This correspondence, however, should not be overinterpreted.

2. "Psalm 33 and the Creation Rhetoric of a Torah Psalm," in *My Words Are Lovely,* ed. Robert L. Foster and David M. Howard, Jr. (LHB/OTS 467; New York: T. & T. Clark, 2008), pp. 107-20; quotation, p. 107.

3. "Psalm 33 and the Creation Rhetoric of a Torah Psalm," pp. 107-8.

Psalm 33

1 [4]*Rejoice, O righteous ones, in the* L*ORD*,
to[5] *the upright praise is fitting.*
2 *Praise the* L*ORD with the lyre,*
with the ten-stringed harp play to him.
3 *Sing to him*[6] *a new song,*
play very well, with shouts.

4 *For the word of the* L*ORD is upright,*
and his every deed is done in faithfulness.
5 *The one who loves*[7] *righteousness and justice,*
the hesed *of the* L*ORD fills the earth.*
6 *By the word of the* L*ORD, the heavens were made,*
and by the spirit of his mouth, all of their hosts.
7 *The one who gathers the waters of the sea like a wall,*[8]
who sets up the deeps in vaults.[9]

8 *Let all the earth revere*[10] *the* L*ORD*,
all the inhabitants of the world be in awe of him.
9 *For he spoke, and it is;*[11]
he commanded, and it endures.
10 *The* L*ORD confounds the purposes of nations,*

4. LXX *tō dauid* suggests *ldwd.* 4QPsq has *ldwyd šyr mzmr* ("To David, a song, a psalm . . ."). Both are expansionistic, as is characteristic of psalm superscriptions in those documents.

5. Syr suggests *w*^{e}*layšārîm.*

6. Targum's replacement of *lô* with *lYHWH* is expansionistic.

7. Most commentators and translators understand the participles (cf. vv. 7, 15) to carry a verbal sense with a present tense meaning, thus "he gathers" (see Goldingay, *Psalms 1–41,* p. 462). But the rhetoric of the psalm prefers a nominal understanding of the participles, since the focus is on the Lord's character (see also Kraus, *Psalms 1–59,* p. 373).

8. Hebrew *kannēḏ* (*like a wall* or "like a dam") was seen as a problem by some. LXX has *hōs askon,* reflecting *k*^{e}*nō'ḏ* ("like a wineskin"); so also Targum. But the parallels in Exod. 15:8, Ps. 78:13; and Josh. 3:13, 16 show that the image of the waters dammed up behind a wall was a stock metaphor in Israelite poetry and should be retained.

9. 4QPsq expands the verse, perhaps in a gloss (see Flint, *The Dead Sea Psalms Scrolls and the Book of Psalms,* p. 88; Ulrich, Cross, et al., *Qumran Cave 4: XI,* p. 147). This addition reads: *šm hmym [nḥsbw kmw] nwd* ("there the waters [stood up like] a dam"). This expansion is either a gloss, as Flint suspects, or it may retain a variant of the clause.

10. 4QPsq has *yr'w,* which reflects a variant orthography. It is likely that MT's orthography reflects a later stage in the development of the tradition than Qumran.

11. 4QPsq has *whyh,* importing a *wāw*-consecutive form. MT is retained as the aspects function differently in poetry.

he forbids the plans of peoples.[12]
11 *But the purposes of the* LORD *endure forever.*
The plans of his heart, for each generation.

12 *Happy is the nation whose God is the* LORD,[13]
the people whom he chose as his inheritance.
13 *From heaven the* LORD *looks down,*
he sees all the children of humanity.
14 *From his dwelling place he regards*
all who dwell on the earth.[14]
15 *The one who forms the hearts of all,*
the one who discerns all of their deeds.

16 *There is no king who is saved by the greatness of his army,*
[15]*a warrior is not delivered by the greatness of his strength.*
17 *The horse is a vanity when it comes to salvation,*
by the greatness of its strength, it cannot provide escape.
18 *Indeed the eye*[16] *of the* LORD *is on those who fear him,*
on those who hope in his hesed,
19 *To deliver their lives from death,*
to sustain them through famine.

20 *Our souls wait for the* LORD,
he is our help and our shield.
21 *For our heart rejoices in him,*
for we trust in his holy name.
22 *May your* hesed *be upon us, O* LORD,
just as we hope in you.

1-3 The opening call covers two aspects of proper praise of the Lord: Who is to praise and what shape that praise should take. Those called to praise, in this case, are the *righteous (ṣaddîqîm)* and the *upright (yᵉšārîm)*. The terms

12. LXX includes an entire extra line: *kai athetei boulas archontōn* ("and he rejects the plots of princes"). This near duplicate of v. 10b most likely retains a variant of that clause. Note that 4QPsᵃ supports MT.

13. 4QPsᑫ has *whyh ʾlwhw* rather than MT's *YHWH ʾlhyw*. MT is the more difficult text and in spite of its awkwardness is retained. The anachronistic form *whyh* in 4QPsᵃ is a later correction (see note on v. 9).

14. 4QPsᑫ has [*tb*]*l* for MT's *ʾrṣ*, a synonym that does not change the meaning of the verse and is likely a harmonization with v. 8. LXX supports MT.

15. 4QPsᑫ adds *w-*.

16. LXX reflects *ʿyny* (pl.), but 4QPsᑫ supports retaining MT.

are often mistakenly understood to be merely moral — that the *righteous/ upright* are those who do right and refrain from doing evil. The terms do indeed carry moral significance, but in the Psalter at least, before they are moral terms they are relational terms — the righteous and upright are, first and foremost, those who rely on God. The righteous are those who are so aware of their own frailty, finitude, and fallibleness, that they are driven into the arms of mercy, to be totally reliant on a relationship with the Lord. As Creach has persuasively shown, "the righteous are distinguished from the wicked mainly by their confession of helplessness . . . and therefore they 'seek refuge' in the Lord."[17] The moral dimension of these terms issues from and is dependent upon the relational aspect — because men and women are drawn into relationship with the Lord, upon whom they can rely absolutely, they are also challenged (Goldingay says the terms "implicitly challenge people to live up to their name"[18]) to live in right relationship with each other (as poems such as Psalm 15 and 24 explore).

The opening verses also address what shape praise of God should take. First, regular praise of God is communal. The verbs are plural imperatives and the setting implied for the psalm is without doubt a public gathering. This implies that the testimony (see Reflections, below) is a community vocation. When the individual comes to join the larger group for public worship, the individual acknowledges implicitly that he or she is not the sole author of his or her identity — that identity comes from belonging to a group. But the group, in turn, by praising God, acknowledges that it is neither transcendent nor independent. The group, too, receives identity from a higher power — from its relationship with the Lord.

Second, praise of God is a musical expression of witness. Two musical instruments are mentioned: The *kinnôr* is the *lyre,* a stringed instrument attached to a resonating sound chamber.[19] The *nēḇel ʿāśôr* is the *ten-stringed harp,* a wooden (1 Kgs. 10:12) stringed instrument also with a sound chamber (implied by the root meaning of *nēḇel,* which is "jar").[20] Although only two instruments are mentioned, they stand as representatives for all musical instruments — both those common in antiquity as well as those employed today.[21]

17. *The Destiny of the Righteous in the Psalms,* p. 29. Clifford makes a similar point, basing the identity of the righteous in their election: "'You righteous' and 'the upright' refer to Israelites made holy by God's choosing them and bringing them into the sanctuary; their righteousness derives from the holiness of the place on which they stand. As God is righteous and upright (vv. 4-5; cf. Ps 119:137), so are those invited into the Temple precincts" (*Psalms 1–72,* p. 170).

18. *Psalms 1–41,* p. 465.

19. See *BRL2,* pp. 390-91. See Keel, *The Symbolism of the Biblical World,* p. 349.

20. *BRL2,* pp. 390-91.

21. Cf. Craigie, *Psalms 1-50,* p. 272.

Moreover, the playing of music for praise should be done well. The phrase *hêṭîḇû naggēn* means to play skillfully. A *new song* is elsewhere a technical term for the song of thanksgiving, which is praise composed in response to some particular action of God (cf. Psalm 40). Zenger has argued that here the term does not imply a brand new composition, but implies a *renewed* witness in response to God's constantly renewed turning in mercy toward Israel and the world.[22] That is not to say that new hymns are not always called for — indeed, this psalm was obviously once a new hymn itself. Rather, it is to say that the gracious action of God to which this psalm was composed to give testimony is the constantly renewing creative activity of God — and thus the *new song* is the constantly new and renewed sung testimony of God's people. Finally, it should be noted that praise is to be joyful. The *tᵉrûʿâ (shouts)* refer to ecstatic shouts that could either herald alarm and war (Jer. 4:19; Amos 1:14, etc.) or celebration and joy (Lev. 25:9; Job 8:21).[23]

4-7 The second stanza marks the shift from the imperative, introductory call to praise, to the body of the psalm, which answers the question, "Why praise the Lord?" In this hymn, the emphasis is upon praise as the faithful response to God's once-and-ongoing creative activity. "Verses 4-5 . . . begin to build the internal logic of Ps 33 by detailing the character of God's word and work."[24] The precise meaning of the phrase *word of the LORD* is debated. But as Jacobson notes, a "vast array of prophetic, legal, and wisdom/Torah traditions stand behind this phrase."[25] The phrase connotes images of Scripture for most modern people of faith. But here the term implies some independent, metaphysical reality that both is God's will and does God's will. That is, as Isa. 55:10-11 also suggests, *the word of the LORD* is both a nearly tangible expression of the divine purpose and at the same time the very agent that ensures that the divine purpose (God's *every deed, kol maʿᵃśēhû*) is achieved. This is what the psalm means when it says the word is *upright (yāšār)* — that it does what it is intended to do, just as the morally upright are those who do what God has commanded.

The psalm then introduces the most basic and powerful theological confession of the Psalter — that the Lord is faithful. Here, as is common in the psalms (cf. Psalm 136), the fidelity of the Lord is apparent, for those with eyes to see, in the trustworthy and wise ordering of creation. As is also the case in Genesis 1, which resonates so strongly with Psalm 33, God's creative work is

22. Hossfeld and Zenger, *Die Psalmen I,* p. 208. The eschatological dimension that many German scholars such as Zenger and Kraus see behind this term is, in my view, unlikely. See Craigie (*Psalms 1-50,* p. 272) or Kraus (*Psalms 1-59,* p. 375) for alternative views.

23. It may be that the term is a clue that the psalm was originally composed, then, for the New Year's Festival, at which the act of creation was cultically reenacted.

24. Jacobson, "Psalm 33 and the Creation Rhetoric of a Torah Psalm," p. 109.

25. "Psalm 33 and the Creation Rhetoric of a Torah Psalm," p. 109.

described as occurring when God speaks a word that in turn orders creation in a truthful and trustworthy manner. The *heavens* are set up above and the limits are set on the always threatening waters of chaos, which are *gathered* into one place *(the sea)* where they are carefully guarded by a damming wall. It is this gathering and limiting of the disruptive and rebellious forces of chaos that is the first step in creating a trustworthy world — a world that is filled with the *hesed* of the Lord. As Mays insightfully concludes, the statement that *the* hesed of the LORD *fills the earth* is "the pivot point on which the psalm turns. The rest of the psalm will expound its meaning."[26]

8-11 God's ongoing work of creating a trustworthy world extends to creating a people who will *revere* him and, as a result, become a people of order — conforming their lives to his word and plans. The internal logic of the psalm makes this rhetorical claim by taking the indicative declaration of the previous stanza that *the* hesed *of the LORD* fills the earth *('āreṣ)* and extending it now to a jussive call for *all the earth ('āreṣ)* to *revere the LORD*. The rhetoric of vv. 4-7 was that the Lord fashioned the earth in a trustworthy manner. Now the rhetoric in vv. 8-11 follows that the inhabitants of that earth should conform themselves to the Lord's will, because God's word is both a once and an ongoing reality — *he spoke, and it is; he commanded, and it endures*. The imperfect forms *wayyehî* and *wayya'ᵃmōḏ* are often misunderstood. NRSV and NIV both have "and it came to be . . . and it stood firm." NJPS has "and it was . . . and it endured." But the syntax and rhetoric of the psalm point to the incomplete and ongoing nature of God's work: *it is* and *it endures*. The stanza bears further witness to the ongoing effectiveness of God's word and will in the form of God's providence within history. The Lord frustrates the *purposes ('ᵃṣaṯ)* and *plans (maḥšᵉḇôṯ)* of the nations, but his own *purposes* and *plans endure*. The rhetorical play of the poem is particularly powerful when one contrasts the fashion in which the poet balances the endings of the two stanzas. In the previous stanza, the disruptive and rebellious waters of chaos are portrayed as gathered up, limited, controlled. At the end of the current stanza, the disruptive and rebellious plans and purposes of the nations are described as frustrated and undone. The contrasting images, when juxtaposed in the imagination, suggest a God whose work is to be active in history, bottling up and containing the transient and temporal threats of the nations. All the while, God is establishing *forever* and *for each*

26. *Psalms*, p. 149. But note then how Mays then immediately, in his characteristically Reformed manner, subsumes the category of God's fidelity underneath the category of God's sovereignty: "The Lord is God over all, the sole sovereign of every sphere of reality. . . ." It never occurs to Mays to wonder if God's fidelity has not, in fact, caused God to relinquish some aspects of his sovereignty, that out of faithfulness to creation, God may have withdrawn some of his sovereignty in order to faithfully allow freedom.

generation a faithful and trustworthy world. To borrow a colloquialism from Mays, the Lord puts both the powers of chaos and the rebellious factors of the nations "in their place."[27]

12-15 In the third main stanza of the psalm, the rhetoric turns to the one chosen nation — *Happy is the nation whose God is the LORD.* Again, the relationship between God and people is stressed, rather than any particular quality of the people. The nation is not even named! It is not called Israel, merely *the nation whose God is the LORD.* The point scored, again, is that it is the relationship with God that defines the people — the people do not author their own identity. They are those who have been *chosen (bāḥar).* The word *inheritance (naḥ^{a}lâ)* also bears significant theological weight. Although the word can refer simply to property or possessions, the sense here is that of promise. To have an *inheritance* is to have a share in something, to be a part of someone or something. In 1 Kgs. 12:16, the seceding northern tribes explain that they have "no inheritance in the son of Jesse." In Ezek. 36:12, Ezekiel speaks metaphorically to the mountains of Israel promising them that they shall be the "inheritance" of "my people Israel." Here, the sense is that the people have a future and an identity, because they have a share in and are a part of the Lord.

The metaphor of the psalm then modulates from the mouth of the Lord to the eye of the Lord.[28] The Lord *looks down, sees, regards,* and *discerns . . . all the children of humanity, all who dwell on the earth, the hearts of all,* and *all their deeds.* This fourfold confession of God's ability to know and see that which happens both on the earth and in the human heart is characteristic of the faithful in the psalms. The wicked (those who are independent of the Lord) are those who say, "God does not see" (Pss. 94:7; 10:11), or doubt that God can "hear" (59:7). The righteous (those who rely on the Lord) in turn faithfully confess that "you do see" (10:14) and the like. In Psalm 33, the characteristic confession of trust in God's knowledge and discernment is emphatic — it is repeated, with staccato confidence, in four parallel statements. Altogether, the four statements emphatically underscore the thoroughgoing, universal, and complete nature of the Lord's seeing and knowing.[29] The connection between God's ongoing providential knowledge and God's creative activity should also not be missed — *the one who discerns (hammēḇîn,* 3ms participle) is no other than *the one who forms (hayyōṣēr,* 3ms participle).

27. *Psalms,* p. 150.

28. Although as Craigie notes, the "eye of the Lord" is not explicitly mentioned (*Psalms 1–50,* p. 274).

29. It should be noted, however, that the emphasis of this knowing is on the present moment. This text is not a witness to God's omniscience extending into the future but is rather a radical confession that God knows everything that a human does or thinks in the present moment.

There is a seamless connection between God's creative activity (which is, after all, ongoing) and God's providential or guiding activity (which is by nature ongoing).

16-19 In the fourth and final stanza of the body of the psalm, the theme changes to "what saves," or perhaps better, "in whom can one trust?" As in the past stanzas, the poet's strategy is to bring out both what is old and what is new in answering the questions. In terms of the new, the poet introduces the theme of "what saves" by deriding traditional metaphors of military strength. In terms of the old, the poet continues the pattern of the previous two stanzas, by drawing on the metaphor of the previous stanza — in this case, the *eye of the LORD.*

The theme of what saves is introduced with the stark declaration: *There is no king who is saved by the greatness of his army.* The force here is dual — both that armies and military might cannot save, so trust not in their empty promises, and that kings themselves, mortal men, cannot save. The king, as the "son of God" (cf. Ps. 2:7), was seen as the both the political and spiritual leader. Thus the king is cast as the leader who in turn needs a leader, the king who in turn needs a lord — the Lord. The term *saved (yāšaʿ)* does not refer to spiritual, eschatological salvation, but to deliverance from earthly threats. That term, along with two synonyms, occurs a total of five times in this stanza (*yāšaʿ, saved/salvation,* vv. 16, 17; *nāṣal, delivered/deliver,* vv. 16, 19; *mālaṭ, provide escape,* v. 17). The chorus of terms used for those who cannot provide salvation/deliverance/escape are thoroughly military in nature — the *king,* the *army (ḥāyil* simply means strength, but the term here certainly connotes military strength, as it does in Exod. 14:4; 2 Kgs. 11:15, etc.), the *warrior (gibbôr),* and the *horse* (in ancient Israel, the horse was not used for agriculture or transportation, but for the military, especially for pulling the chariot; thus the horse was a favorite symbol for military power and for the vanity of trusting in that power; 1 Kgs. 10:28-29; Ps. 20:7; 147:10; Amos 2:15). The rhetoric is elegant — no matter the *greatness* of a king's army or a warrior's strength, they are *vanity (šeqer)* — they cannot save. In sum, the first two verses of this stanza make the point: deliverance cannot come from military strength. Military strength is here a metaphor for all human power and earthly efforts. It stands as the symbol for all of the earthly sources of comfort — wealth, security, family, career, home, etc. — in which the mortal will is bound to trust.

The last two verses of the stanza draw back in the metaphor of the previous stanza — *the eye of the LORD* — in order to confess Israel's faith that although there is no earthly object worthy of trust, there is a heavenly object of worship who is more than a mere *object.* The Lord is an active *subject,* whose eye is upon those who rely on him and who can deliver — from *death* or from *famine* (this pair of terms most likely suggests threats brought on by human agents — death by military violence — and by natural agents — natural famine that threatens life). As was the case earlier in the psalm, the term that comprises the Lord's gracious activity is *hesed* — that untranslatable Hebrew term that we have opted to transliterate in this commentary. The term connotes God's faithfulness, mercy, grace, and love. Thus, what the human who relies on God is to do is to *hope* in God's *hesed.*

20-22 The conclusion of the poem again introduces a new theme — rejoicing in God — even as it continues the military metaphor of the previous stanza. The previous stanza confessed that king, warrior, army, and horse are not to be trusted for deliverance. The psalm's conclusion confesses that the Lord is *our help and our shield.* The conclusion of the poem has to do with hoping and waiting. This concluding prayer of confidence picks up the rhetorical thread of hoping from the previous stanza and then amplifies it by employing multiple words that are steeped in this theme: *wait (ḥāḵâ), trust (bāṭaḥ),* and *hope (yāḥal)* — one verb for each of the last three verses in the poem. These terms — *wait, trust, hope* — are often misunderstood as passive terms, as activities that one does instead of engaging in more fruitful or active activities. This is partially accurate, since hoping, trusting, and waiting are indeed what one learns to do only when one realizes that one's own efforts have either been exhausted or are completely meaningless. But to hope, to trust, and to wait, in the Old Testament, are not empty, passive activities — at least not if one means that there is not specific content or urgency to them. To wait is not just to do nothing. To hope is not merely to close one's eyes and accept what comes next. They are aggressive verbs in the theological sense that to hope in the Lord's *hesed* is actively to place one's identity and future in God's hands. To wait on the Lord is to look confidently to God for deliverance and to expect that deliverance.

Reflections

The Fidelity of God

As Mays has stated, "The psalm as a whole expresses . . . the theological vision of reality that belongs to the worshiping community."[30] And as Craigie notes, the hymn bears witness to "the essence of biblical theology."[31] The central theological confession of that theology is that the Lord is faithful — in the words of the psalm, *the* hesed *of the LORD fills the earth* (v. 5; cf. vv. 18, 22). The centrality of that confession is witnessed in the ancient covenantal hymn of Exodus 34, where the Lord passes in front of Moses and proclaims,

30. *Psalms,* p. 151.
31. *Psalms 1–50,* p. 275.

The LORD, the LORD,
a God merciful and gracious,
slow to anger,
and abounding in steadfast love *(hesed)* and faithfulness.
(v. 6; cf. Jonah 4:2, etc.)

The centrality of this confession to the Psalter's theology is further witnessed by the fact that of the 255 times the term *hesed* occurs in the Old Testament, 130 of those occurrences are in the Psalter. The term, as noted in the Introduction, is notoriously difficult to translate, because English has no single term that does justice to its richness. Even two words together — such as "steadfast love," or "loving kindness," or "covenant loyalty" — cannot plumb its depths. The venerable Gerhard von Rad noted concerning the term that it "designates an attitude required by fellowship and includes a disposition and an attitude of solidarity . . . so it expresses . . . beneficent personal disposition plus the actions that follow."[32] That is, it is a *relational term.* It describes the duties, benefits, and commitments that one party bears to another party as a result of the relationship between them. Philip Melanchthon famously asserted that "to know Christ is to know his benefits rather than his natures. . . ."[33] Similarly, the Psalter bears witness that to know the Lord is to know of the benefits of being in relationship with the Lord, rather than to know the Lord's natures. In Psalm 33, the emphasis is first of all upon the relationship that the Lord forges with all humanity through the act of creation (vv. 6-7, 9, 15) and also upon the special relationship that God forged with Israel through the election of the chosen people (v. 12).

The psalm goes on further to offer praise testimony to the faithfulness of God both to all of creation and to Israel. In terms of creation, God's faithfulness is made known in God's continuing acts of creating and of making creation into an orderly, trustworthy environment in which human life can thrive. As a colleague of mine says, "Consider the law of gravity — works every time!" God's trustworthiness is seen in the orderliness and consistency of nature, in the limiting of chaos and disorder. In terms of the human sphere, God's trustworthiness is made known in the election of the chosen people and in God's continuing providential watching over the people who revere him, rejoice in him, hope in his *hesed,* and trust in his holy name. God's fidelity to this relationship that God initiated — even when fidelity to the relationship required God to relinquish some of his sovereignty — is the central theological confession of the psalm and of the Psalter. Karl Barth is said to

32. *Old Testament Theology,* trans. D. M. G. Stalker (New York: Harper & Row, 1962), 1:372 n. 6.

33. In *Melanchthon and Bucer,* ed. Wilhelm Pauck (Library of Christian Classics 19; Philadelphia: Westminster, 1969), pp. 21-22.

have enjoyed quoting the answer that Frederick the Great received from his personal physician when he asked for proof of the existence of God: "The Jews!"[34] They are at once the people whom God has chosen and upon whom the name of the Lord has been placed, and also those who strive to conform their lives to God's will.

ROLF A. JACOBSON

34. In Joseph L. Mangina, *Karl Barth: Theologian of Christian Witness* (Louisville: Westminster John Knox, 2004), p. 82.

Psalm 34: The Nearness of a Personal God

Psalm 34 is one of the alphabetic acrostic psalms of the Psalter. The first word of each verse, excluding v. 22, begins with a successive letter of the Hebrew alphabet — the letter *wāw* is missing (unless one assumes that the second half of v. 5 is the *wāw* verse, but this would mean both the *hê* and the *wāw* verses are only one clause long); as in other acrostics, *śîn* and *šîn* are considered one letter, not two. But can any further definition be given to the psalm? The psalm seems to contain the characteristic marks of the individual song of thanksgiving: the individual's announcement of praise (vv. 1-2; cf. Ps. 30:1-3); a call for the community to join in the praise (v. 3; cf. 30:4); a report of the crisis and of God's help (vv. 4-6; cf. 30:6-10); exhortation and testimony to the gathered community regarding the Lord (vv. 7-21; cf. 30:5, 11). However, two points should be made. First, the emphasis is decidedly on the exhortation and testimony to the community. If this psalm is understood as a song of thanksgiving, it is a song of thanksgiving that majors in community exhortation and instruction. Second, the acrostic structure strongly suggests that this poem is a theological composition that mimics the form of the individual song of thanksgiving. Rather than a prayer composed by one who has freshly passed through crisis, it is more likely a poem composed on behalf of a community — written in order to instruct the community on how to move in and out of such crises.

The superscription of the psalm has been the source of some mild confusion. The phrase *When he acted insane before Abimelech, who drove him out, so he left* apparently refers to the account in 1 Sam. 21:10-15 of how David acted insane when in the presence of Achish, the king of Gath. It is possible that the superscription may refer to some now lost tradition, which the psalmist's community knew, in which David appears before a king named Abimelech. Or perhaps the name Abimelech has been substituted, in error, for Achish.[1] Craigie argued that "It is more plausible to assume that 'Abimelech' (literally, 'my father is king') was an official title for Philistine kings, just as *Pharaoh* was an official title for Egyptian kings."[2] The main point, however, is for modern readers to take the incident in David's life as an interpretive key as to how to read and use this psalm. It is a psalm of thanks to God and instruction for God's people, which is appropriately used in times when God's deliverance has been experienced.

1. So, e.g., Kraus, *Psalms 1–59,* p. 383.
2. *Psalms 1–50,* p. 278.

Psalm 34

Davidic. When he acted insane[3] *before Abimelech, who drove him out, so he left.*

ʾĀlep 1 *I will bless the* Lord *in every time,*
his praise shall continually be in my mouth.
Bêt 2 *My soul boasts in the* Lord,
let the needy hear and rejoice!
Gîmel 3 *Magnify the* Lord *with me,*
let us exalt his name together.
Dālet 4 *I sought the* Lord, *and he answered me,*
he delivered me from all my fears.
Hê 5 *Look*[4] *to him and be radiant;*
[Wāw?] *your faces will not be put to shame.*
Zayin 6 *This poor one cried out, and the* Lord *heard;*
and he delivered this one from every trouble.
Ḥêt 7 *The angel of the* Lord *encamps*
around those who fear him, and he delivers them.
Ṭêt 8 *Taste and see the goodness of the* Lord,
happy is the one[5] *who takes refuge in him.*
Yôd 9 *Fear the* Lord, *O his holy ones,*
for there is no insufficiency for those who fear him!
Kāp 10 *Young lions*[6] *can go without and be hungry,*
but those who seek the Lord *lack for nothing good.*
Lāmed 11 *Come, children, hear me!*
I will teach you the fear of the Lord.
Mêm 12 *Whoever is a person who desires life,*

3. The Hebrew phrase *b*^{e}*šannôṯô ʾeṯ ṭaʿmô* (lit., "when he altered his judgment") is an idiom meaning to pretend madness.

4. Reading, with LXX and Vulg, imperatival forms and a 2mp suffix in the second clause ("look to him . . . be made radiant . . . your faces"). In order to retain MT, the sense of *ʾal* must be taken as unconditional — which is possible but unlikely (see Wilhelm Gesenius, *Gesenius' Hebrew Grammar,* ed. E. Kautzsch, trans. A. E. Cowley [2nd ed.; Oxford: Clarendon, 1910], pp. 479-80). In addition, LXX's first word in the verse, *proselthate,* normally translates *nāgaš,* leading some to wonder if the verse originally began *g*^{e}*šû.* The acrostic structure, unbroken elsewhere in the psalm, would demand a form such as *haggîšû,* of course.

5. Hebrew *geḇer* denotes a male (see Prov. 30:19; Jer. 30:6; Deut. 22:5), but in the context of the psalm, which offers promises about the Lord's refuge, an inclusive language term better carries the sense that this promise is offered for all.

6. LXX's *plousioi* ("the rich") suggests something such as Hebrew *k*^{e}*ḇēḏîm.* But as J. J. M. Roberts has shown, the term *lions* is not odd here and should be retained ("The Young Lions of Psalm 34:11," in *The Bible and the Ancient Near East* [Winona Lake: Eisenbrauns, 2002], pp. 262-65).

who loves daily[7] *to see good —*
Nûn 13 *Keep your tongue from evil,*
and your lips from speaking deceit.
Sāmek 14 *Turn from evil and do good,*
seek peace and pursue it.
ʿAyin 15 *The eyes of the* LORD *are attentive to the righteous,*
and his ears to their cries.
Pê 16 *The face of the* LORD *is against those who do evil,*
to cut off their memory from the earth.
Ṣādê 17 *The righteous*[8] *cry out, and the* LORD *hears;*
from all their troubles, he delivers them.[9]
Qôp 18 *The* LORD *is near to those with shattered hearts,*
and those with crushed spirits, he saves.
Rêš 19 *Many are the afflictions of the righteous one,*
but the LORD *delivers them from all.*
Šîn 20 *He is the keeper of all this one's bones,*
not one of them will be shattered!
Tāw 21 *Evil itself will kill the wicked,*[10]
those who hate the righteous shall be held guilty.
22 *The* LORD *redeems the life of his servants,*
all those who seek refuge in him shall not be held guilty.

1-3 The opening verses are similar in form to the opening announcement of praise found at the start of other songs of thanksgiving. This feature of the song of thanksgiving, in turn, parallels one that is found in many individual prayers for help, where the psalmists (usually toward the end of their prayers) vow to praise the Lord once the Lord has delivered them from their crisis. For example, in Psalm 26, the psalmist vows, "in the great assembly, I will bless the LORD *(ʾaḇārēḵ YHWH)*" (v. 12). Here, using precise language, the psalm begins with the announcement that she has come to *bless the* LORD *(ʾaḇārăḵâ ʾeṯ YHWH)*. The qualification that this praise will happen *in every time* does not indicate that the psalm is a general hymn, but rather, having passed through crisis, the psalmist now will make praising the Lord a consistent way of life. According to Clifford, the phrase *boasts in the* LORD means "to acknowledge triumphing with God's help and to attribute victory to God."[11] The chief point

7. Understanding the use of the plural *(yāmîm)* to signify repetition (see Waltke and O'Connor, *Biblical Hebrew Syntax,* pp. 121-22).

8. Reading with LXX (and other ancient versions), *hoi dikaioi.*

9. Syr lacks "and from all their troubles."

10. LXX has *thanatos hamartōlōn* ("the death of sinners"), suggesting *môṯ haḥăṭāʾîm,* which is unlikely as it breaks the acrostic structure.

11. *Psalms 1–72,* p. 174.

is that the psalmist is neither taking credit for her own vindication, nor is she "bragging" that she somehow has God more on her side than others do.[12] Rather, the sense is that this boast is a nonboast, because she is boasting about her own inability to save herself, which is why she sought refuge in the Lord (v. 8). The second phrase of v. 2, *Let the needy hear and rejoice,* carries a double sense. The needy can rejoice precisely because, although they, like the psalmist, may not be capable of saving themselves in crisis, they have a relationship with the Lord, who shows mercy to the needy. But there is a second sense, too. By rejoicing with the psalmist, they accept her back into the community. The term *rejoice (śāmaḥ)* occurs frequently in songs of thanksgiving (30:1; 32:11; 40:16; 66:6; 92:4; 118:24) — so often, in fact, that the presence of the term could almost be considered a diagnostic clue to the form of the psalm. The occurrence in 40:16 makes clear that when the community joins the psalmist in rejoicing, they are both acknowledging that it was the Lord who saved the psalmist and acknowledging that the psalmist is legitimately part of the worshipping community. Thus, praise is a way of rehabilitating the reputation of one who may have fallen under a cloud of doubt when she was in crisis. In a word, to join one in praise is to *welcome* her. This is precisely what the psalmist bids the community to do in v. 3 — *magnify the LORD with me.* To magnify (lit., to "make great," *giddēl*) should be understood in the relational sense — to praise God is to acknowledge that God is greater than one's self. Praise does not make God greater, but it acknowledges that God is greater than I.

4-6 The next verses are similar to the section in many songs of thanksgiving in which the psalmist reports on the time of crisis and how God delivered. These descriptions of those times usually lack specificity, relying mainly on poetic metaphors — they are the times of going "down to the pit" (30:3), of "roaring all day long" and being dried up as by the "summer drought" (32:3-4), or of being stuck in the "wet clay" (40:2). It is likely that the reason for the lack of specificity is that these poems are then made more readily available for reuse by people going through most any crisis. Here, the metaphor is spare. The poet describes himself as having been a *poor one* (lit., "this poor man") who faces *fears* and *trouble.* In the midst of these, he reports, he *sought the LORD*. It is possible that to seek the Lord *(dāraš YHWH)* is a technical term for making a visit to the temple or some other sanctuary to seek help from God (see Amos 5:6; 1 Chr. 21:30, etc.).[13] But here, it is more plausible to interpret

12. As Craigie notes, "to boast, in itself an unpleasant human characteristic by virtue of its self-centeredness, is here transformed by the object of the boasting, external to the self" (*Psalms 1–50,* p. 279).

13. As Roberts notes, "The Hebrew expression drš yhwh, 'to seek Yahweh,' can sometimes be used as an almost exact cultural equivalent of the Akkadian berû bīrī, 'to observe omens' . . ." ("The Young Lions of Psalm 34:11," p. 265).

the term to refer more generally to the act of pleading for help and seeking refuge in the Lord.

On the basis of the psalmist's personal experience with God — *This poor one cried out, and the LORD heard; and he delivered this one from every trouble* — the psalmist confesses Israel's characteristic faith in the fidelity of the Lord and offers a promise as part of the testimony: *Look to him and be radiant.* The metaphor of looking at God and having a *radiant* face *(nāhar)* is also found in Isa. 60:5, where the synonym *rā'â (see)* replaces Psalm 34's *nāḇaṭ (look).* The promise implicit in the metaphor here is that those who look to God for good things will in turn quite literally embody God's gracious actions in their own beings. Rather thans setting one's face like flint when things go poorly (Isa. 50:7), those who rely on God will have no need of poker-faced stoicism — they will be freed to wear joy openly on their faces.

7-10 In the next verses of the poem, the rhetoric of the psalm turns to another image for the proper human response to God — the *fear* of the Lord. This phrase is often misunderstood. It can be viewed as the paradoxical awareness that one is fragile, mortal, and sinfulness, on the one hand, and that the Lord is rock-solid, immortal, and gracious, on the other. To fear the Lord is therefore simultaneously both to tremble in dread anticipation and to tremble in joyous anticipation. The psalm's use of the participial form to describe God's people — *those who fear him (lîrē'āyw;* cf. Pss. 115:11; 118:4) — suggests that this dual awareness is properly not a one-time mental acknowledgement, but a way of life. For those who take up this way of life, the psalm again offers a promise. Using the metaphor of the Lord as an army *encamping* in a protective fashion around those who fear the Lord, the psalm promises that God will similarly deliver others, just as the Lord has delivered the psalmist. The *angel of the LORD* is often a military image for God's power to be on the side of those whom God elects (Josh. 5:13-15). As Mays has written, "It is not enough simply to be the needy who cry to the LORD when they are in trouble. It is the God-fearers who have already made the LORD the basis and guide for the conduct of life around whom the angel of the LORD sets up a protecting camp."[14] The psalm goes on to promise specifically that *there is no insufficiency for those who fear him!* This verse should not be misunderstood. In the broader context of the Psalter, which contains many cries of pain from those of God's people who are suffering either at the hands of enemies or because they are mortal and finite creatures, the verse does not imply an absolute promise that no harm or ill can befall God's people. Indeed, later in this poem, the psalmist acknowledges that *many are the afflictions of the righteous one* (v. 19). The point is that God is the only sure source of grace and blessing. Those other people and forces that make promises cannot be trusted, as can the Lord, in whom there is no insufficiency.

14. *Psalms,* p. 153.

The psalmist's imperative in v. 8 to *taste and see the goodness of the LORD* is probably a reference to sacrificial meals that worshippers would share as part of the thanksgiving ritual (cf. Deut. 14:23-29; Lev. 7:12-15; Num. 15:2-5). In thanksgiving to the Lord for deliverance from a crisis, the God-fearer offers a thank offering, which is then shared with the community. By partaking in the meal with the celebrant (similar to the act of praising God; see vv. 2-3), the community both shares in the act of thankful sacrifice and also welcomes the individual back into good standing in the community. The act of sacrifice is a theological witness to *the goodness of the LORD*. The confession that *goodness (ṭôḇ)* is a part of the fiber of God's character is among the central theological confessions of the Psalter (cf. 23:6; 25:7-8; 27:13, etc.). Here, the poetry of the psalm invites people to experience God's goodness sensually — by tasting, smelling, and consuming the gifts of creation. The poem also witnesses relationally to *the goodness of the LORD*, since the concrete experience of God's goodness is found both in those fruits of creation as well as in the psalmist's experience of deliverance.

In v. 10, as Roberts has clearly shown, *lions* are an apt metaphor for those who neither *fear* nor *seek the LORD*. Frequently in the Psalter, the lion symbolizes those who prey on the helpless (cf. 10:9; 35:17; 57:4; 58:6, etc.). Far from fearing or revering, the lion is the cause of fear. Perhaps for these reasons, in the ancient Near East, the lion was a powerful symbol for the self-confident fool who disregarded both the deity and communications from the deity. Lions are portrayed in ancient Near Eastern literature as impiously refusing to offer sacrifices to appease the god's anger and as refusing to attend to divine omens.[15] Here, the psalm testifies that even those who believe themselves to be as self-sufficient and fearless as lions have reason to fear the Lord. As Roberts concludes, "the poor starving lion of Ps 34:11 is only the pious man's pictorial response to the skeptic's image of the surfeited, steak-gorging lion."[16] The term *those who seek the LORD* means, then, those who look to God continuously for good and who trust in God alone. It also refers to the practice of revering communications from the Lord and honoring God's messages.

11-14 The rhetoric of the poem now modulates into the key of instruction. The vocabulary here is clearly representative of Israel's wisdom traditions: the invitation for the children (lit., "sons," *bānîm;* cf. Prov. 5:7; 6:1, 7:1, etc.) to *come* (cf. Prov. 7:18; 9:5, etc.). A child "comes" or "goes" in wisdom to the one from whom there is a lesson to be learned — whether it is the ant (Prov. 6:6) or one whom the Lord has delivered, such as in Psalm 34. The phrase *fear of the LORD*, as discussed above, is also characteristically sapiential.

15. See references in Roberts, "The Young Lions of Psalm 34:11," pp. 263-64.
16. "The Young Lions of Psalm 34:11," p. 265.

It is a summary term for the proper attitude of one with whom God has established a right relationship. That this attitude can be taught *(ʾalammedkem)* is a fundamental conviction of the Psalter. Those who gathered for worship did so not only to experience the divine presence and blessings, but to be schooled by elders and fellow community members.

The invitation to come (v. 11) extends into the following three verses, which form an extended syntactical unit. Verse 12 introduces a conditional protasis (*whoever desires life* and goodness). The following two verses continue with the proscriptive apodosis (they should *turn from evil and do good*). Again, the wisdom character of the vocabulary stands out. The concern for the tongue and speech — *keep your tongue from evil, and your lips from speaking deceit* — is especially noteworthy. Israel was extremely sensitive to the evil that humans can wreak with false witness and loose lips (cf. Psalm 15). The plural nominal forms in v. 12 do not indicate number, but abstraction. The first, *ḥayyîm* (lit., "lives"), indicates *life,* or better, "fullness of life." The second, *yāmîm* (lit., "days"), indicates repetition, thus one who loves to experience good things on a *daily* basis. The expressed desire *to see good* hearkens back both to the earlier references to the character of God *(the goodness of the LORD)* and the promise that those who seek the Lord will *lack for nothing good,* and also forward to the v. 14's prescriptive warning to *turn from evil and do good.* This warning shows the additional influence of Israel's prophetic theology, as the clear parallel in Amos 5:15 demonstrates ("hate evil, love good"). There is a threefold connection here between the character of the Lord (goodness), the character of the behavior of those whom the Lord has claimed (they are to do good), and the promise that the Lord holds in store for the same (they will see good). But a warning: this connection cannot be reduced to a formula (do good and you will see good). The world that God has created and freed is far too complicated for such reductive formulas. Verse 14 goes on to define the seeking of good more precisely — it means to *pursue* the welfare of the community. Welfare or *peace (šālôm)* is a communal, relational term. To pursue *šālôm* is to turn away from pursuing only one's self-interest and instead to seek the welfare of others, especially the welfare of the most vulnerable. It is also striking that in the Psalter, the wicked and the unrighteous are those who *pursue (bāqaš)* false gods (4:2) and the vulnerable to take advantage of them (cf. 35:3; 37:32), while God's community is enjoined to seek God (24:6; 27:4) and the welfare of others (34:14).

15-22 In the psalm's concluding section, the rhetoric returns to a descriptive style, with the content alternating between descriptions of the Lord and of the righteous. A final summary statement describes the deeds and fate of the unrighteous.

The statements about the Lord (vv. 15-16, 18, 19b-20) describe the Lord's relational orientation toward both those who are dependent upon him and those who defy him. In these verses, those who are dependent on the Lord are called *the righteous* (*ṣaddîq;* vv. 15, 19, 21, plus the restored occurrence in v. 17). Before the term *righteous* is a moral term, it is a relational term. The righteous are those who are dependent on the Lord (in Psalm 34 that notion is present in the phrase *the fear of the Lord*), *take refuge* in the Lord (v. 8), and *seek* the Lord (v. 10).

The promise (and threat) of the psalm is powerfully portrayed in a series of sensual, anthropomorphic metaphors regarding the *eyes, ears,* and *face* of the Lord (vv. 15-16). It is striking that the three clauses in which these bodily metaphors occur are all verbless clauses. The relational commitment of the Lord to those who depend upon him is communicated through prepositions. That the eyes and ears of the Lord are attuned to the needs of the righteous in a redemptive way is communicated by the Hebrew preposition *'el,* which here connotes a positive relationship. That the face of the Lord is turned *against* the wicked in a judgmental way is communicated by adversative use of the Hebrew preposition *b-,* which here connotes negative relationship. The metaphor, therefore, signals more than merely that God is aware in a sentient way of what transpires on earth. It promises that God is responsive to the suffering of the needy.

The psalm continues the poetic theme of bodily metaphors, as it intensifies the description of God's elected but suffering people. They are those *with shattered hearts* (the *piel* form of *šāḇar* carries the intensive sense of "completely broken") and *with crushed spirits* (the term *spirit* here translates *rûaḥ,* which does not denote a disembodied soul, but the living breath of a human body). The psalm goes on to promise that the Lord is *the keeper of all this one's bones* (lit., "He is the keeper of all his bones"). The final verse of the acrostic portion of the psalm (v. 21) seems to give more shape to this promise. The verse promises that *evil itself will kill the wicked.* It is interesting that the subject of the verb is evil, rather than the Lord. The sense here is that the very crimes or evil deeds that the wicked plot against the righteous will boomerang back against them. The righteous do not need to return harm for harm, because, as the metaphor in Proverbs 1 has it, they will be caught in their own net: "they lie in wait — to kill themselves! And set an ambush — for their own lives!" (Prov. 1:18). This is not to say that the Lord does not exercise some agency in the judgment of evil or in the frustration of evil plans. Rather, it suggests that the Lord works in a less-than-wooden way as an agent of redemption who brings about retribution. Perhaps part of God's design in creation has been to build into the fabric of creation certain factors that tend toward (but do not guarantee) the outcome that the evil a person does often comes back against one's self. All of this, as the psalm says, the Lord has done in order to save those in need — *the Lord delivers them from all* (v. 19).

The psalm closes with a summary verse, which falls outside of the acrostic structure, but which faithfully sums up the promises of the psalm: Whereas the previous verse promised that *those who hate the righteous shall be held guilty (ʾāšam),* the closing verse announces that *all those who seek refuge in him shall not be held guilty (ʾāšam).* The reflexive sense of judgment and deliverance here is the promissory side of the familiar "double wish" in the prayers for help of the Psalter. Because the psalmist can imagine no other way to be saved than have the threatening agent forcibly removed, the psalmist begs for deliverance to come in the form of the destruction of those who threaten violence. The psalm promises that deliverance (not being held guilty) will come in the form of the guilty being held accountable. When that bright morning arrives, says the psalm, it will mean the redemption of God's servants.

Reflections

1. Instruction for Thanksgiving

This poem seems to be a marriage of a psalm of thanksgiving and an instructional psalm. It is wise to understand Psalm 34 as a psalm of instruction in how to give thanks after deliverance from a time of trial. The psalm teaches that one should sing praises to the Lord as one leaves the house of suffering. When we sing such praise, as McCann has seen, our voices lift into song a new "mode of existence" that is desperately lacking in the world. It is a mode of existence in which the Lord is named, and because the Lord is named, the activity of the Lord is able to be experienced: "The Psalms tell us both who God is and what God does, and thus who we are and what we are to do."[17] Then, according to the psalm, we are to teach others to know God, by telling others our stories. In the psalm, the poet tells his own story — or at least poetically tells the story of an idealizing type of person — of how he cried out to the Lord and how the Lord saved him. Although we live in a world today that is obsessed with self-narrative, we often shut down our stories. Or we tailor them so as not to tell our stories in such a way that the Lord can be seen, heard, and felt walking next to us. The psalm teaches us to tell our stories in such a way that others will see the Lord taking a closer walk with us and learn that *the LORD is near* (v. 18).

2. "The Anatomy of a Personal God"

Brown has written eloquently about how the psalms map out the anatomy of a personal God.[18] He writes of God's "sensitivity to human need. . . . Without God's 'ears' attuned to both the cry of the afflicted and praise from the

17. *A Theological Introduction to the Book of Psalms,* p. 55.
18. *Seeing the Psalms,* pp. 167-95.

delivered, the psalmist is literally without a prayer."[19] Brown's insight can be pushed further. The psalm is all about embodiment. On the one hand, the psalm employs a series of robust anatomical metaphors: eyes, ears, face, heart, breath, bones. Some of the metaphors are used of God, in order both to proclaim both God's sensitivity to human suffering, but also to bear witness to God's commitment and ability to save and deliver. On the other hand, the psalm uses a series of participles to describe God, those who rely on God, and those who oppose God. Without trying to be exhaustive, these participles announce that God is the one who keeps our bones (v. 20). The righteous are those who take refuge in him, who fear him, who seek him, who desire life, who love daily to see good, and so forth, while the wicked are those who hate the righteous. This dual poetic strategy points to the reality that at some level, as embodied creatures, we are what we do. Certain actions may begin at one moment or another as a singular action, but through repetition and through repeated practice, those actions become our identity. Living in bodies made up of eyes, ears, face, breath, and bones, we become what we do. The psalm points us towards those practices in which we might become those who seek God, seek good, pursue peace, and fear the Lord.

ROLF A. JACOBSON

19. *Seeing the Psalms,* p. 171.

Psalm 35: Fight for Me, Save Me

Psalm 35 is a complex poem that begins with images of war, but as this prayer develops, it is clear that the enemies are not foreign powers, but those close to home. The psalm is lengthy and has a major break after v. 18. Indeed, it is possible that these are two earlier prayers placed together. But even if that is the case, the prayer as it now stands gives a unique perspective on suffering and hurt and as such is a complex prayer for help. As noted, the psalm has two major parts, with further divisions within those parts:[1]

- Part 1 (vv. 1-18)
  - Petition to God for aid (vv. 1-3)
  - Petitions against the enemies (vv. 4-8)
  - Expressions of trust in God (vv. 9-10)
  - The acts of the enemies (vv. 11-16)
    - Plea to God (v. 17)
    - Promise of thanks to God (v. 18)
- Part 2 (vv. 19-28)
  - Petition against and acts of the enemies (vv. 19-21)
  - Petitions to God for action (vv. 22-26)
    - Call to praise (v. 27)
    - Thanksgiving (v. 28)

Textually, the problems multiply. The text is corrupt in several places, and in addition, the syntax and the metaphors portrayed are difficult to understand. Overall, the meaning of the psalm can be discerned, but individual lines cannot be translated with certainty.

Davidic.[2]

1 *Fight,*[3] *O LORD, those who fight me;*
do battle with those who do battle with me.
2 *Take up small and large shields;*[4]

1. Because the psalm is complex, there is little agreement on its division into stanzas. Craigie argues for a three-part structure of vv. 1-10, 11-18, and 19-28 (Craigie and Tate, *Psalms 1–50,* p. 287) as does Terrien, but his structure is different: vv. 1-10, 11-22, and 23-28 (*The Psalms,* p. 309). Kraus has a five-part structure (*Psalms 1–59,* p. 391), and Gerstenberger a seven-part (*Psalms: Part 1,* pp. 149-50). A three-part structure is certainly possible, but more than that seems too cumbersome.

2. LXX adds "a psalm."

3. The LXX reads "Judge."

4. Reading these two words in parallel as in Jer. 46:3; Ezek. 23:24; 38:4; 39:9.

rise up to help me![5]
3 *Unsheathe spear and javelin;*[6]
say to me,[7] *"I am your salvation."*

4 *Let them be ashamed and humiliated, the ones seeking my life;*[8]
let them be turned back and disgraced, the ones devising evil against me.
5 *Let them be like chaff before the wind;*
with the messenger of the LORD pushing (it).[9]
6 *Let their path be dark and slippery,*
with the messenger of the LORD pursuing them,
7 *for without cause they hid a net for me;*[10]
without cause they dug a pit for me.[11]
8 *Let devastation come upon him without him knowing;*[12]
and let the net that he hid capture him;
in devastation,[13] *let him fall in it.*

9 *But I*[14] *will rejoice in the LORD;*
and I will exult in his salvation.

5. The syntax is difficult here. Kraus notes this construction should not be read as a preposition, noun, 1cs suffix but as an indication of motion toward a goal (*Psalms 1–59,* p. 391).

6. The meaning of this word is uncertain. It is possibly from a verbal root meaning "to shut." Both Dahood and Craigie give evidence of the meaning being an implement of war: Dahood's "javelin" is followed by most (*Psalms I,* p. 210). Craigie, following Akkadian, understands it as a double-edged battle-ax (*Psalms 1–50,* p. 391). Either way, it is a parallel to the spear.

7. Lit., "to my *nep̱eš*"; this word has a wide range of meaning: "soul, living being, self." It is the essence of what makes a sack of bones alive.

8. Lit., "my *nep̱eš.*" For this word, see above.

9. Many, including the *BHS* critical apparatus, emend the last word with a 3mpl suffix so it reads "pushing them." But the MT makes sense as it is, and in the context, it would make more sense that the messenger is pushing the wind, which is the instrument dislodging the enemies.

10. This verse is problematic in MT, reading "for without cause they hid to me a pit a net without cause they dug to me." Most suggest a simple transposition of the words *pit* and *net.*

11. Lit., "my *nep̱eš.*" For this word's wide range of meanings, see above.

12. LXX reads 3mpl here, and this is followed by several modern translations (NRSV, NIV, NJPS).

13. Syr reads "a pit" (Hebrew equivalent *baššûḥâ,* which some translations adopt [NIV]). 4QPsq does not have the complete line, but based on its existing fragment, the *bêt* is probably missing (Ulrich, Cross, et al., *Qumran Cave 4: XI,* p. 148), making the reading of "into the pit" more improbable.

14. Lit., "my *nep̱eš.*" For this word, see above.

10 *All my bones say, "O LORD, who is like you?"*
You snatch the oppressed from those stronger than them;
the oppressed and the needy from those that rob them.[15]

11 *Wicked witnesses arise;*
and I do not know (what) they ask me.[16]
12 *They repay me evil instead of good;*
it is hurtful to me.[17]
13 *But I, in their sickness, put on sackcloth;*
I humbled myself[18] *with fasting;*
my prayer returned to my bosom,[19]
14 *like (they were) a friend or a brother;*
I walked to and fro like mourning a mother, dark and downcast.[20]
15 *But at my stumbling, they rejoiced and*[21] *gathered;*
they gathered against me;
attackers[22] *I did not know;*
they tear and are not silent.[23]
16 *They tempted me, they maliciously mocked me;*[24]

15. MT has a 3ms "him" in both lines; *them* substituted for clarity.

16. Modern translations try to smooth these lines out in a variety of ways, but all expand the text. This translation is an accurate reflection of MT and LXX.

17. Lit., "my *nep̱eš*." See above.

18. Lit., "my *nep̱eš*."

19. This is a direct translation of the MT. Others try to make sense of this line: "When my prayers returned to me unanswered" (NIV) or "I prayed with my head bowed on my bosom" (NRSV). Any of these are possible, but the meaning can be seen with the MT text without emendation.

20. LXX reads "to grieve and be downcast." Modern translations try to smooth this line out, often following LXX.

21. 4QPsª omits the *wāw;* Ulrich, Cross, et al., *Qumran Cave 4: XI,* p. 13.

22. This word is problematic. LXX reads "and plagues," which is not helpful. Craigie notes that instead of the MT's *nêḵîm,* one should read the 4QPsq's *ḥkyt* ("oppressors") (*Psalms 1–50,* p. 285; also Ulrich, Cross, et al., *Qumran Cave 4: XI,* p. 148). Whether "smiting ones" or "oppressors," a general term such as *attackers* is probably best.

23. Another problematic line rendered above as in MT. LXX reads "they tore apart and they did not repent," which is possible in the context. The enemies are often spoken of as ignoring God and God's ways. Craigie (*Psalms 1–50,* p. 285) notes that Dahood (*Psalms I,* p. 214) followed by others have argued for Ugaritic cognates meaning "slander"; this is adopted by the NIV, but the evidence is not compelling. Others substitute some form of stopping or ceasing for "they are not silent," but the Hebrew metaphor should be preserved whenever possible.

24. MT reads "like the profanest of mockers of a cake," which is obviously corrupt. The LXX reads "They tempted me, they sneered at me scornfully." The critical apparatus suggests reading LXX here. But most translations accept only the second of the two verbs. Above, the

grinding[25] at me with their[26] teeth.

17 O LORD, how long will you look?
Return me[27] from their ravages;[28]
from the lions, my life.[29]
18 I will give thanks in a large congregation;
among a mighty people, I will praise you.

19 Let them not rejoice over me,[30] lying enemies;
or those hating me without cause pinch their eyes,
20 for no peace do they speak;[31]
against[32] the quiet ones of the land, words of deceit they devise.
21 They open wide their mouth against me;
they say, "Aha, Aha, our own eyes have seen!"

22 You have seen, O LORD; do not be silent;
O LORD, do not be far from me!
23 Arise, wake up to my justice;
My God, My Lord to my dispute!
24 Judge me according to your righteousness, O LORD my God;
do not let them rejoice over me.
25 Do not let them say in their hearts,
"Aha, our pleasure!"[33]
Do not let them say, "We have swallowed him up!"
26 Let them be ashamed and disgraced, all of them together,
all those who rejoice at my misery;

---

complete line of LXX is used, for there seems little justification for accepting only half of the reading.

25. MT form is an infinitive absolute. LXX and 4QPsᵃ have a 3mpl verb, "they gnashed" (Ulrich, Cross, et al., *Qumran Cave 4: XI,* p. 12). Either way, the meaning is still the same.

26. 4QPsᵃ does not have the 3mpl pronoun suffix (Ulrich, Cross, et al., *Qumran Cave 4: XI,* p. 12).

27. Lit., "my *nep̄eš.*"

28. Reading with MT. The critical apparatus suggests emendation to *miššᵊʾăḡîm* ("those that roar"), but this change is unnecessary since the MT is understandable.

29. Lit., *yᵉḥîḏāṯî* ("my only").

30. MT reads *lî,* which does not have the sense of *over.* However, it is clear that the enemies are not rejoicing to this one, but that it is meant as a statement of mocking.

31. LXX "To me they spoke peacefully."

32. 4QPsᵃ reads *w'l* ("and to") instead of the MT "against" (Ulrich, Cross, et al., *Qumran Cave 4: XI,* p. 12). LXX has yet another reading: "but imagined deceits in their anger."

33. MT reads *nap̄šēnû* ("our souls"). The meaning is an idiom but the "just what we wanted" of modern translations seems expansionary.

let them be clothed with shame and insult,
all those making themselves great against me.

27 Let those shout and rejoice who delight in my righteousness;
and let them say continually, "Great is the Lord,
the one delighting in the well-being[34] *of his servants."*
28 My tongue will declare your righteousness;
all the day, your praises.

1-3 The pleas begin with military imagery.[35] God is called upon to *fight* and *do battle* with others on this one's behalf. God is asked to arm up, to prepare, to get ready all of the standard implements of war. This emphasis has caused scholars to suppose that this prayer is made by the king.[36] But this is not necessary, for many engaged in battle other than the king, and everyone from ancient to modern folks knows that sometimes many life situations can feel as if one is at war. What will be clear soon is that this is not a foreign enemy. Indeed, the enemy will be compared with family members (v. 14). The one praying feels as if he is engaged in a *battle;* with whom and why is still to be determined.

4-8 The psalmist pleas that God give way to wishes for the punishment of the enemies. One would expect that the military language and imagery would continue, but that is not the case. The wishes are not for their weapons to be turned against them. The wishes are for them to know shame and humiliation, to be driven away *like chaff,* and to be captured in their own traps. We learn more here also, for the one praying claims she is attacked *without cause* (vv. 7-8). The enemies then are seen as ones who attack without reason.

Verses 5-6 are unique in all of psalmic literature. The evil ones are compared with *chaff* in Ps. 1:4, but the request that the *messenger* (NRSV "angel") *of the Lord* appear to offer protection to the one praying is unique. The *messenger of the Lord,* in most Hebrew Bible texts, is that one sent to convey the word of God to a person or people.[37] Here and in the previous psalm (34:7), this messenger is seen as protective of God's people. The messenger acts in the same way that God does. Why does the messenger appear in these two psalms? One cannot be sure. It could simply be poetic license to use all of the

34. Lit., *šᵉlôm.*

35. LXX, however, begins by asking God "to judge." It is not clear if this is a change that protects God by exchanging "judge" for "fight" or if this is meant to harmonize the end and the beginning of the psalm (vv. 24-25). It is also possible that the LXX was using a different form of this psalm.

36. E.g., Craigie, *Psalms 1–50,* p. 286.

37. As in Genesis 16 and the appearance to Hagar and to Abraham on the mountain (Genesis 22), or to Moses at the burning bush (Exod. 3:2).

images available, or it could be that these psalms draw on the same tradition from some specific place or group of people. It may be impossible to know. It does, however, recall the military imagery of vv. 1-3 of God as the great commander over both humans and the "hosts" and reinforces God's great power as one that controls great powers.[38]

9-10 Wishes for destruction are followed without explanation by praise and thanksgiving. This expression of trust has several purposes. First, it contrasts the acts of the one praying and the enemies who harm without cause. Second, it serves as an additional reason or motivation for God to save the one who has trust in God's grace and power. Finally, it is the way humans under stress react. We too can flip from wishes against those hurting us to trust in God and back again. We, like the one praying, are confronted with that dual reality: life is difficult and painful, and God loves us and wants us to be happy and whole. God acts for those who are in the most need (v. 10). It is often hard, if not impossible, to reconcile these two truths.

11-16 Again the topic switches without warning. This section describes both the acts of the enemies and the one praying, without any of the trust described above. This section is an example in contrasts. The enemies' acts are described in vv. 11-12 and 15-16, with this one's actions as the contrast (vv. 13-14). This section is complicated by textual problems in several of the lines. What is finally clear here is that the enemies are definitely not fighting a war. They do, however, gather together to threaten and do harm (vv. 15-16). They laugh and mock and repay good with bad. The contrast is that the one praying prays for them, offering prayers and adopting a stance of mourning on their behalf. She acts like a good friend supporting them in their time of trouble (vv. 13-14), but when she stumbles they rejoice.

17-18 Verse 17 is a plea again for God to act. God seems just to be looking on, and this one needs action! It is as if her very life is at stake. Verse 18 notes that if God acts, then this one will offer thanksgiving and praise among the people. This may seem a bit like empty promises, but like the declaration of trust, it looks forward to another time when the current difficulties have been resolved.

19-21 Part 2 opens with wishes for the enemies, and this time the wishes are, frankly, for them to shut up! These ones use words like weapons and *rejoice* and *pinch their eyes* against this one. This idiom is probably in parallel with *rejoice;* others have suggested it is a malicious winking,[39] but it could also be the crinkling of the eyes in raucous laughing and taunting. Verse 20 notes that it is not just the one praying that these mock. They are against

38. As in the messenger of the Lord striking down the Assyrians in 2 Kgs. 19:35 and Isa. 37:36.

39. Craigie, *Psalms 1–50,* p. 283, and both NRSV and NIV.

shalom and *the quiet ones of the land.* In other words, it would seem they have contempt for the very things that God values. These ones are a threat to the very fabric of God's kingdom values.

22-26 Again God is called on to act, but not necessarily against the enemies. Verses 22-23 tell of this one's frustration at God's long silence. Here instead of a warrior, God is called upon to act as judge: *do not be silent, arise, wake up to my justice!* Other translations often substitute "my defense," but that presumes our judicial system. This section demonstrates that in ancient times God's coming to judge the world was seen as a good thing, and indeed the way to vindication for God's people. This one asks for his actions to be weighed against those of the others: *judge me according to your righteousness* is the cry. Test me and my actions; do not let them *rejoice* and let them win. Verse 26 returns to the requests of v. 4, and this forms a strong connection between the two parts of the psalm. This one still wishes for the enemies to know shame and disgrace for their gloating over this one.

27-28 Again the psalm turns without warning from a call for the enemies to get their just deserts to a call for those who believe in the one praying to *rejoice* at her vindication. Has time passed, or has God intervened between vv. 26 and 27? We simply do not know. What is clear, however, is that this crisis has passed. This one can stand and call for the people to praise God, and in v. 28, this one declares God's praise. Life has returned to a better place.

This prayer is both brave and dangerous. It is brave for it calls on God to suit up and do battle with the powers that harm. It is brave because it dares to ask God to come and judge all who are involved in the conflict. It is, of course, dangerous for the same reasons, for often these words can be translated into our own human actions for God so we are the ones waging war and standing in judgment of others for God. The equation does not work that way. What it does teach us is how to be brave before God, to stand up and ask for God's aid and even God's justice for both us and the other parties involved in conflict.

Beth Tanner

Psalm 36: In Your Light, We See Light

Psalm 36 is an elegant composition that pits two contrasting forces against each other: the character of the wicked and the character of God. In this way, the psalm is both similar to and different from Psalm 1. In Psalm 1, the way of the wicked is contrasted with the way of the righteous. In Psalm 36, the character of the wicked is actually contrasted with the character of the Lord. The main force of the psalm's witness is precisely that God's character and God's actions cannot be separated — that God is faithful is known in God's deliverance and in the blessings of God's bountiful creation; that God's creation is bountiful and God's deliverance is known are signs of God's gracious character.

It is not helpful or possible to assign any precise genre to the psalm, although many suggestions have been offered.[1] Verses 1-4 sound like a wisdom psalm (cf. Prov. 6:12-15), vv. 5-9 resemble a praise hymn, and vv. 10-12 close the psalm with a petition for help. Dahood's wry observation should be kept in mind: "The coexistence of three literary types within a poem of thirteen verses points up the limitations of the form-critical approach to the Psalter."[2] Nevertheless, when the psalm's overall rhetorical impact is considered, the psalm seems to function very much like a prayer for help. Three elements that are often found in prayers for help are (1) a complaint about enemies, (2) a confession of trust in God, and (3) a petition for help. In Psalm 36, complaint about enemies is replaced in vv. 1-4 by a description of the corrupt character of *the wicked one,* who represents the incarnation of wickedness and temptation. (In the NRSV, the masculine singular "wicked one" is pluralized into "they" for the sake of inclusivity; in the translation below, the third-person masculine singular pronouns have been rendered as *who* or *whose.*) The expression of trust is replaced by a hymn that praises God's character (vv. 5-9). The petition in vv. 10-12 is typical of petitions in prayers for help.

The poem consists of four stanzas. The middle two stanzas praise God's character, especially God's characteristic *hesed.* The first stanza, as already noted, consists of a didactic description of *the wicked one.* The last stanza balances the first stanza by closing the psalm with a plea for protection from the wicked.

1. Some of the possibilities that have been offered are: a prayer for help, an entrance liturgy, a liturgy of lament, a didactic wisdom poem, a mixed-type psalm, and so on. Some scholars of an earlier generation were content to question the poem's unity and divide it into subpsalms.

2. Dahood, *Psalms I,* p. 218.

St. 1 Description of the wicked (vv. 1-4)
St. 2 Praise of God's character (vv. 5-6)
St. 3 Praise of God's *hesed* in particular (vv. 7-9)
St. 4 Petition for deliverance from the wicked (vv. 10-12)

The Lord's *hesed* furnishes the unifying theme of the poem. The term *hesed* is lacking in stanza 1, precisely because the wicked rejects the *dread of God.* In stanza 2, the psalmist praises God for God's *hesed, faithfulness, righteousness,* and *judgments.* In stanza 3, the psalmist intensifies this praise by focusing more tightly on God's *hesed.* In the final stanza's plea, the psalmist begs for the Lord to *extend your* hesed *to those who know you,* and thus protect them from evil-doers.

For the leader. For the servant of the LORD. Davidic.

1 *Transgression whispers*[3] *to the wicked one deep in the heart:*[4]
before whose eyes there is no dread of God;
2 *Who is self-deceptive, in whose eyes is the belief*
that personal sin cannot be found out and hated;
3 *The words of whose mouth are sin and deceit;*
who has ceased to act wisely or to do good;
4 *Who plots sin while in bed,*

3. The opening words of the psalm are undoubtedly corrupt. MT's *n'm pš'* ("an oracle of transgression") could be taken as a heading for the entire psalm, but such a construction is otherwise unknown in Biblical Hebrew. Many proposals have been offered (see Craigie, *Psalms 1-50,* p. 200; and Kraus, *Psalms 1-59,* p. 396 for summaries). Because the word *n'm* is normally followed by the name or description of a person (as in Num. 24:4, "an oracle of one who hears the words of God"), one possibility is to repoint the word "sin" *(peša')* as "sinner" *(pōšea');* the root *pš'* is attested in the *qal* active participle (see Isa. 1:28). With this emendation, the rest of the line could be left as is (see the next note). This would render a translation of "an oracle of a sinner to the wicked, deep in my heart." However, this would make sense but would theologically be anachronistic; the ancient Israelites did not apply words such as "sinner" to those in good standing in the community. Further, this translation would not make sense in light of vv. 1b-4. The translation above takes *pš'* as the subject and reads a verbal form of *n'm,* otherwise unattested in Hebrew, but related to Arabic *na'ama* ("to whisper, growl, sigh"), akin to Akkadian *umma* — a reading somewhat supported by LXX, although LXX reads "sinner" instead of "sin." Hossfeld offers an artistic interpretation that retains the MT. In his view, the opening verses are the words of a personified "Sin" that are spoken to "my heart." It may well be that some part of the opening of the psalm has been lost. If so, it cannot be recovered.

4. MT's *libbî* makes no sense here; read *libbô* with Syr, a few mss, and partially supported by LXX *(en heautō).*

who stands in the way[5] *that is not good,*
who does not reject evil.

5 *O* Lord, *your* hesed *is in the heavens,*[6]
your faithfulness reaches to the clouds.
6 *Your righteousness is like the mountains of God,*
your judgments like the great deep.
You save both human and animal, O Lord*!*

7 *How precious is your* hesed, *O God,*
and the children of humanity shelter in the shadow of your wings.
8 *They feast on the abundance of your house,*
and from the river of your delights you give them drink.
9 *For with you is the spring of life,*
in your light we see light.

10 *Extend your* hesed *to those who know you,*
and your righteousness to the upright of heart.
11 *Let not the foot of the arrogant step on me,*
and let not the hand of the wicked drive me out.
12 *There*[7] *evil-doers fall,*
they are pushed down and are not able to arise.

1-4 The first stanza paints a portrait of a type of individual that every faithful follower of God encounters somewhere along life's path: *the wicked one . . . before whose eyes there is no dread of God.* The Hebrew text of the psalm in this stanza is corrupt at several points (see the notes on the translation). The most serious of these corruptions is found in v. 1; it affects how one un-

5. 4QPs^a reads *yty'ṣ kwl drk* rather than MT's *ytyṣb ʿl drk.* LXX's *parestē pasē* supports MT's *ytyṣb* but 4QPs^a's *kwl.* The parallelism of the verbs supports 4QPs^a, but the parallelism of the syntax of the end of the verse supports retaining MT. What we have here are three different texts, and it is not possible to hypothesize an "original" text with any significant confidence. We retain MT because that has been the accepted text for centuries. At any rate, the sense of the verse is similar in all three readings.

6. A few mss read the more expected *baššāmayim* rather than MT's odd *b^{e}haššāmayim,* but the sense remains the same. 4QPs^a reads *mhšmym* ("from the heavens"). Seybold cites some mss as reading "like the heavens" *(k* rather than *b)* and prefers this reading.

7. Commentators find *šām* problematic in this context and often emend to *šām^{e}mû* (see Kraus, *Psalms 1-59,* p. 397; Craigie, *Psalms 1-50,* p. 200). The word is slightly awkward, but on analogy of Ps. 73:17, the word is treated here as a reference to the temple, mentioned in v. 8, where the wicked meet their punishment. As Clifford points out, in psalms "about Zion, 'there' occurs often, always in reference to the holy mountain, for example, Pss 48:6; 76:3," etc. (*Psalms 1-72,* p. 186).

derstands the first stanza of the psalm. The first phrase of the psalm reads, literally, "an oracle of sin" *(n^e'um peša')*. But this literal translation makes no sense syntactically, because the word *n^e'um* is normally followed by the name of a God (usually the Lord) or a person (such as Balaam in Num. 24:3 or David in 2 Sam. 23:1) or by a description of a person, such as "the oracle of one who hears the words of God" (Num. 24:4). In spite of many suggestions, the original text cannot be recovered. The translation above — *transgression whispers to the wicked one deep in the heart* — offers a provisional solution, yet the interpreter should not leverage too much of an interpretation on it, especially not on the first two words. In spite of the lack of clarity of the exact wording, the sense of the first line emerges clearly: the wicked harbor a place for sin in their hearts. That is, their interior lives provide an environment in which sin thrives.

Indeed, the sense of the entire first stanza is quite clear: it is a description of the wicked, who lack the proper interior quality of having the fear of God. This basic lack, in turn, leads *the wicked one* to manifest behaviors that are evil. The most important characteristic of the wicked one is that rather than fearing the Lord, this one is completely self-governed: *before whose eyes there is no dread of God; who is self-deceptive, in whose eyes is the belief that personal sin cannot be found out and hated* (vv. 1b-2). The notion here is that because the wicked person does not fear God, she deceives herself into thinking her sin will not be *found out.*

In most individual lament psalms, the enemy poses a threat that is both urgent and lethal. For instance, only one psalm earlier, in Psalm 35, the psalmist complains of those who "fight against me" and "seek my life" (vv. 1, 4). Here in Psalm 36, the danger that the wicked poses is less urgent, although no less insistent. The danger here is that the wicked is a looming, ever-present threat and a temptation for the righteous (as Psalm 73 indicates) to succumb and become like the wicked. *The wicked one* here is the incarnation of the temptation to live life by setting up the self as the autonomous standard, to live life according to "what seems good to me." The psalm portrays the wicked's failings both negatively and positively — that is, the psalm portrays both the virtues that the wicked lacks and the vices that the wicked does not lack. What virtue does the wicked one lack? The *dread of God.* This phrase is obviously a synonym for the well-known "fear of God" of the wisdom tradition (cf. Proverbs 1). And as many have noted, the first stanza of this poem is rife with wisdom elements. The lack of the *dread of God* leads the wicked one to become *self-deceptive.* The Hebrew here reads, literally: "he smoothes things out for himself in his own eyes." The meaning is that because the wicked lacks fear of God and thus lacks the wisdom received from God, he or she is vulnerable to self deception, or, as the poem itself says, the wicked *has ceased to act wisely or to do good.* To *act wisely* is to have the practical capacity to live in such a way that brings peace both to one's self and one's neighbors. The wicked lacks the practical insight to live in this way in community.

What vice does the wicked have? In a word, the wicked rebels against God. The word translated *transgression* here carries the basic sense of rebellion. The wicked stands intentionally in the tradition of Adam and Eve, rejecting the prescribed way of God's torah (see Psalm 1) in favor of *the way that is not good.* The wicked stands in rebellion against God and God's way. The wicked sets herself up as her own authority. She *does not reject evil.* Verse 4 offers a glimpse of the complete depravity of the wicked, who is so perverse that even abed, her mind restlessly stretches forth to comprehend what harm she can do in the future (cf. Mic. 2:1).

5-6 The marvelous surprise at the heart of Psalm 36 is that the character of the wicked is contrasted with the character of the Lord. It is normal in instructional psalms to contrast the ways and character of the wicked with the ways and character of the righteous (see Psalms 1, 37, 73, etc.). Psalm 36, however, contrasts the character of the wicked with the character of the Lord! One can say that rather than merely describing the behavior of the righteous, the psalmist *embodies* the behavior of the righteous. In Psalm 37, for example, the psalmist advises that the righteous "trust in the LORD," "enjoy the LORD," and so on. In Psalm 36, one can say that the psalmist delights in the Lord: *O LORD, your* hesed *is in the heavens, your faithfulness reaches to the clouds!* Just as the wicked is the incarnation of temptation and rebellion, the psalmist here is the incarnation of trust, praise, and righteousness. In prayers for help, there is often an expression of trust in God. The hymnic praise in vv. 5-9 functions analogously to that trusting element; the psalmist expresses trust by praising. Perhaps the reason for this is that the need for an expression of trust arises out of the dire threat that the enemy poses. Because Psalm 36 lacks such a dire threat, the two stanzas of praise express that trust in a more fitting fashion.

Poetically, this stanza of praise is a masterpiece. In Hebrew, the stanza both begins and ends with a vocative use of the name *Yahweh.* The Lord literally — and figuratively — surrounds the psalmist's praise. The stanza consists of five lines or cola. Throughout these five lines, the poet interweaves references to God's character with references to God's creation, in which God meets us and through which God's character is made known. The first four lines share a common structure:

a characteristic of God + "your" suffix + a reference to creation

In these four lines, the psalmist praises *your* hesed, *your faithfulness, your righteousness,* and *your judgments.* The second masculine singular suffix — *your* — indicates the covenantal relationship between the one who praises and the one who is praised. Together, the four words encompass the fidelity that defines God's character (cf. Ps. 89:14). These words are covenantal boundary markers; they delineate the holy ground over which the Lord rules and within which the Lord's people can know safety. The four references to creation form a descending pattern: *in the heavens . . . to the clouds . . . like the mountains . . . like the great deep.* As McCann has described the poetry: "To be noted is that each attribute of God in vv. 5-6 is described in cosmic terms that are arranged in descending order according to the ancient view — 'heavens' above all, 'clouds' above the earth, 'mighty mountains' as the highest earthly point, and 'the great deep' below the earth. In short, God's character is built into the very structure of the universe."[8] Those who know the Lord are able to discern the grace of God in creation. The references to creation also ground — literally! — God's character in the vast creation (as opposed to the wicked one, who is finite and mortal). The poetic force contrasts the boundless reign of God's faithfulness; the heavens and earth cannot contain God's faithfulness. There is also a mythological polemic at work. The Hebrew reads, literally: "your righteousness is like the mountains of El *('ēl),* your judgments like the great Deep *(tᵉhôm).*" It is hard to imagine that in these words an ancient Israelite would not have heard echoing references to two of the deities that were worshipped in surrounding cultures: El, the chief god of the pagan pantheon, and Tiamat, the pagan goddess of chaos. The poet weaves in overtones of these mythological deities here to make even more emphatic the universal faithfulness and loyalty of the Lord. There is poetic multivalency at work here. The Lord's faithfulness is known both in the Lord's sovereignty over the metaphysical realm and in the Lord's faithful immanence within the created order.

In the fifth line of this stanza, the psalmist abruptly changes the pattern away from the rigid structure of the first four lines. The Lord is suddenly named as the subject of the verb, and the object of the Lord's care is both humans and animals: *You save both human and animal, O LORD!* The syntactical shift deftly creates a poetic climax to this stanza. The word *save (yšʿ)* is another of those characteristically covenantal terms; in this case, the word, which is often translated as "deliver," describes God's ongoing care for all of creation, for *both human and animal.*

7-9 Whereas in the second stanza, the poet praised God's *hesed,* faithfulness, righteousness, judgments, and saving power, in the third stanza of the psalm, the focus of the poet's praise narrows in on the key covenantal *hesed* of the Lord. In the second stanza, the poet spoke of God's character against the backdrop of creation; in the third stanza, the poet relocates the praise of God to a new location: the temple. The third stanza is filled with mythological, metaphorical, and literal references to the temple. The *shelter of your*

8. "The Book of Psalms," p. 823.

wings is a delightfully ambiguous poetic term. It provides a smooth transition from the realm of creation, which was sounded in the second stanza, to the new temple venue, because the phrase is at once an image of nature — the mother bird protecting her brood (cf. Ps. 91:1-4) — and also an image of the outstretched wings of the cherubim, which were in the temple (cf. 1 Kgs. 6:23-35). The reference to *your house* is an explicit reference to the temple. *The river of your delight* and *spring of life* (cf. Ps. 46:4; Ezekiel 47) refer to mythological conceptions of the temple as the new garden of Eden and the mythological conception of a river issuing from the throne of God (Rev. 22:1). The reference to *your light* is both a metaphor borrowed from the realm of creation and one that has ties directly to the temple. Some scholars have suggested that the phrase is a truncated form of the formula "the light of your face" (cf. Pss. 4:6; 44:3; 89:15). It may also be a reference to ritual processional lamps (cf. 118:27). The point here is that in the third stanza the poet offers praise for the Lord's *hesed,* specifically for the *hesed* that is made known and available to humanity in and through the temple. The temple is the place where heaven and earth intersect. As Clifford has put it, "the Temple, like any ancient Near Eastern temple, had cosmic significance. The temple represents the god's heavenly palace. . . . The Temple is the place where the Lord's steadfast love is experienced directly."[9]

The exact significance of the references to the temple cannot be determined. Some scholars have understood the psalm as a psalm of asylum, in which a petitioner approaches the temple in order to receive protection.[10] Others have seen the psalm as a liturgy of entrance to the temple or simply as an instructional poem. Likewise, it is unclear whether references to drinking of *your delight* and eating *the abundance* (lit., "fat") *of your house* are to be taken figuratively or as pertaining to the portions of sacrifices that were eaten either by the worshippers or by the priests (cf. Leviticus 3, 7). To pin the meaning of the poem's metaphorical witness down to one "life situation" seems both unwise and impossible. The poem witnesses to the fidelity of the Lord, to the protection that the Lord promises, and also to the blessings with which the Lord showers the creation.

Like the previous stanza, this stanza ends with a slight syntactical change, which brings the stanza to a fitting culmination. The disjunctive particle *kî* introduces the final clause: *For with you is the spring of life, in your light we see light.* As already mentioned, the phrase surely draws on mythological

9. *Psalms 1–72,* p. 184.

10. So, e.g., Kraus: "The persecuted petitioner flees to the sanctuary and seeks refuge in Yahweh's protective area, which is indicated by means of the image of the outstretched wings of the cherubim. In the sanctuary, however, the one who seeks protection has access to the fullness of the blessings of God's presence." *Psalms 1-59,* p. 399.

images of the temple and is grounded thoroughly in temple theology. The precise meaning of the final phrase has puzzled interpreters. Does it signify protection? Revelation? Blessing? Guidance? Salvation/Deliverance? All of these, and more! The variety of interpretation is fitting, because the metaphor of light as applied to God is surely too rich and textured to stand for reductionistic interpretations. As Brown has written, "most generally, light signifies flourishing life. . . . To ascribe light to God is to acknowledge the fullness of life that God imparts to creation."[11] But the light of God also guides (Ps. 119:105), reveals sins (90:8), brings victory (44:3), and so on. In Psalm 36, the astonishing connection is made between human knowledge (perception) and God's light. The psalm says that it is *in your light* that *we see light.* The inference here is that true perception requires a light that is beyond our own ability to kindle. It comes only from God.

10-12 The poem closes with an appeal to God: *Extend your* hesed *to those who know you.* God's *hesed* is the poetic bind that ties the psalm together as a unity. *Hesed* is not mentioned in the first stanza, which is fitting, because the wicked lack fear of God and thus both lack access to God's *hesed* and lack *hesed* themselves. God's *hesed* is the backbone and focus of the psalmist's praise in stanzas 2 and 3. And now, in the last stanza, the psalmist appeals to God that divine *hesed* might extend to *those who know you.* The term *those who know you (yōḏʿêḵā)* implies people who have a relationship with God. The term also implies more than simply intellectual or mental acknowledgement of the relationship; it implies a relationship that is experienced firsthand and lived out in daily life, with mutual obligations (cf. 100:3; Hos. 4:1, 14). The plea to *extend your* hesed implies that God's *hesed* both be extended to all of God's covenantal partners and be extended fully to those same.

The closing stanza mirrors the first stanza of the poem in that it picks up the theme of *the wicked.* Whereas the first stanza was mostly a distanced description of the wicked's character, the last stanza is an example of the so-called "double wish" of the Psalter: the psalmist prays deliverance from the wicked and for judgment on the wicked. "The meditation on the character of the wicked . . . is also converted into a prayer, for the wicked not only cut themselves off from God's lovingkindness, but may also be a constant and powerful threat to the survival of the righteous."[12] The picture of the foot treading on the downtrodden is a stock image for defeat (cf. Ps. 110:1). The closing petition of the psalm is often debated. Some interpreters have found the reference to *there* awkward and out of place and have suggested textual alterations. However, the term makes perfect sense both as a reference to the

11. *Seeing the Psalms,* pp. 197-98.
12. Craigie, *Psalms 1–50,* p. 293.

temple (cf. 69:35; 87:4-6) and in the context of a plea for the Lord to judge the wicked (cf. 14:5//53:5). The reference in this case is to the temple, which is the intersection between the heavenly and earthly spheres and thus the location at which both the righteous know God's deliverance and the wicked know God's judgment.

Reflections

The Character of God

As Clifford has seen, "Pervading the poem is an implicit contrast between the 'self-ruled' individual and the God-ruled cosmos."[13] The key rhetorical feature of the psalm is that it contrasts the character of the wicked with the character of God. In this Psalm, the wicked is not described so much as a violent threat to the righteous individual or to the community of the righteous (although such a threat lurks in the background), but the wicked one is pictured as the incarnation of the temptation to live life by setting up the self as the autonomous standard, to live life according to "what seems good to me." Thus, the wicked individual of Psalm 36 is portrayed as a perfect prototype of the modern American myth of the rugged individual, whose autonomous self generates the standards by which life is lived. In our day, William Ernest Henley's wretched poem "Invictus" has become the clichéd anthem of this autonomous individualism: "I am the master of my fate: I am the captain of my soul."[14]

Sounding as a discordant melody over against this myth of autonomous individuality, Psalm 36 offers the promise of a different standard for life. The standard of a relationship with God, in whose character every fragile and finite human being has access to *hesed,* faithfulness, righteousness, and salvation. The key theological point of the psalm is the character of God. McCann has captured the pulse of the poem: "The psalmist can be confident in praying for God's steadfast love and righteousness, because the psalmist trusts that God's love is the fundamental reality in the universe."[15] According to the psalm, even human knowledge and perception depend upon a relationship with God and the blessings that are offered in the relationship. The autonomous individual in our culture has been taught to say, "I call them as I see them." Psalm 36 teaches us to confess, *In your light we see light.* C. S. Lewis's famous dictum, which is inscribed on his memorial, is an apt commentary on this truth: "I believe in Christianity as

13. *Psalms 1–72,* p. 182.
14. Henley, *A Book of Verses* (3rd ed.; New York: Scribner and Welford, 1906), p. 56.
15. "The Book of Psalms," p. 824.

I believe that the Sun has risen, not only because I see it but because by it I see everything else."[16]

The psalm understands that life — indeed "fullness of life" — is not something that the individual generates for himself or herself. It is a gift that comes from only one source: the Lord. The poetry and theology of the psalm all point to this confession. Mays sums it up beautifully: "Life as existence, as full and good living, as community, as restoration — life in every sense is the gift of the Lord. The source of life is 'with him.' . . . Wherever there is life, there is a receiving from the source."[17]

Rolf A. Jacobson

16. From "Is Theology Poetry?" an address delivered to the Oxford Socratic Club. Cites in Holly Ordway, "A Report from the C. S. Lewis Memorial Service," christianthought.hby.edu/2013/12/5/a-report-from-the-CS-Lewis-memorial-service.

17. *Psalms,* p. 157.

Psalm 37: Advice for the Upright

Psalm 37 stands in the wisdom tradition and sounds more like the book of Proverbs than the book of Psalms. Craigie notes, "The psalm stands firmly within the tradition of Wisdom and should be interpreted as an *instructional poem*."[1] This psalm offers advice for the way one is to live, often contrasting the LORD's way with the way of the wicked. Like other wisdom literature, it offers comfort, stressing that the ways of the wicked do not lead to happiness and prosperity, but to death and destruction. It reminds those hearing it to hold fast even in the face of a world where the wicked seem to do better than the faithful. The psalm is also of the acrostic type with all of the letters of the Hebrew alphabet in order, usually every other line, and literally covers everything from *ʾālep* to *tāw*.

This proverb-type psalm is difficult to divide into clear stanzas because the subject remains the same throughout, and the acrostic form may mean that it is meant either to be seen as a complete whole or with a letter-by-letter division, but that would mean a twenty-two-part division that is quite cumbersome. Scholars most often divide the psalm into five sections, but the content of these five sections varies. It is possible to divide it in this way:

vv. 1-11	Do not worry about the wicked
vv. 12-15	The wicked and their fate
vv. 16-26	Better are the righteous
vv. 27-33	Advice for the righteous
vv. 34-40	God will help the righteous

The psalm is complicated by some textual difficulties and a grammar structure using a great number of imperatives, participles, and verbless clauses.

Davidic.

ʾĀlep 1 *Do not let your anger burn concerning the evil ones,*
nor be jealous of those who do wrong,
2 *for like grass quickly they wither,*
and green plants, they droop.
Bêt 3 *Trust in the LORD and do good;*
dwell in the land and shepherd faithfulness.[2]

1. *Psalms 1–50,* p. 296.

2. Many modern translations inexplicitly read "enjoy security" or "safe passage." The verb here is an imperative meaning "shepherd" or "protect," not a passive construction. Just like *dwell* before it, this verb implies action on the part of the human.

4 *Enjoy[3] yourself in the LORD,*
and he will give you the petitions of your heart.
Gîmel 5 *Commit[4] your way to the LORD;*
trust in him and he will act.[5]
6 *He will cause your righteousness to go forth like the light,*
and your justice like the noon-day.
Dālet 7 *Be silent[6] before the LORD;*
wait[7] upon him;
do not let your anger burn over the one prospering in his way,
the one planning schemes.[8]
Hê 8 *Be released from anger, and forsake rage;*
do not let your anger burn, surely it (leads)[9] to evil
9 *for the evil ones will be cut off;*
but those waiting for the LORD, they will inherit the land.
Wāw 10 *Yet a little while, and the wicked will be no more;*
you can search out at his[10] place, but this one does not exist.
11 *The oppressed[11] will inherit the land;*
they will enjoy peace in overabundance.[12]

Zayin 12 *The wicked one schemes against the righteous one*
and gnashes his teeth against him.

3. The form of this verb is a *hithpael* imperative that implies enjoying one's self, and this probably accounts for the word "delight" appearing so often in modern translations. However, this is not the word for delight in Hebrew.

4. Most translations use *commit,* from the emendation suggested in the critical apparatus and LXX, just as in 22:8.

5. Lit., *ya'aśeh* ("he will do or make").

6. The root does mean "to be silent," but most use the sense of LXX "to subjugate" as "be still."

7. *BHS* reads "to writhe or dance," and it is possible to use this here, but it seems in conflict with the "be silent" of the first line. The critical apparatus suggests emending to *hōḥēl* ("to wait") based on LXX and Targum. Because of the problems with the two verbal roots here, any translation is tentative.

8. The verb is, lit., "making." Modern translations tend to read "evil devices" here, but this word is used both of God and of humans in positive and negative ways, so "evil devices" seems to go too far. The point here may not indicate evil in the human but that God should be trusted above all humans, whether their schemes are for good or ill.

9. This is a verbless clause ("surely to evil") that requires some form of helping verb.

10. Every attempt is made to translate with inclusive language for humans, but there are some places where this is not possible.

11. This is a difficult word to represent with one English word. It means the "poor," "afflicted," and possibly "the meek." Kraus notes, "The 'poor' are those whose troubles drive them to rely on Yahweh alone" (*Theology of the Psalms,* p. 152).

12. The preposition here is *'al,* which implies something over or on top of abundance.

13 *The LORD laughs at the wicked one,*[13]
for he sees that the wicked one's[14] *day will come.*

Ḥêt 14 *The wicked ones draw a sword and bend bows*
to fell the oppressed and the needy,
to kill those whose having straight paths.
15 *Their swords will enter their own hearts,*
and their bows will be broken.

Ṭêt 16 *Better is the little of the righteous*
than the abundance of many wicked ones,[15]
17 *for the strength*[16] *of the wicked ones is broken,*
and the LORD is supporting the righteous.

Yôd 18 *The LORD knows the days of the perfect ones,*[17]
and their inheritance will last forever.
19 *They will not be shamed in evil times;*
in the days of famine, they will be filled.

Kāp 20 *But the wicked perish,*
and the enemies of the LORD are like the splendor of the pastures;
they vanish, in smoke, they vanish.

Lāmed 21 *The wicked borrow and cannot repay;*
but the righteous are generous and giving,
22 *for the one (God)*[18] *blesses will inherit the land,*
the one (God) curses will be cut off.

Mêm 23 *From the LORD, the steps of this one are established;*
and his path is God's delight,
24 *for this one may fall, but will not be overpowered,*[19]
because the LORD holds this one's hand.

13. MT uses the 3ms pronoun here; *the wicked one* is substituted for clarity.

14. The 3ms pronominal suffix is in MT.

15. Reading with the MT without emendation. Other translators follow the LXX, Jerome, and Syr, changing *rabbîm* modifying *the wicked* to *rāḇ* ("abundant wealth"); Craigie, *Psalms 1–50*, p. 294, and Kraus, *Psalms 1–59*, p. 402. There is no clear indication that wealth is the only possibility here.

16. Can also mean "arms"; this meaning is reflected in most modern translations, but there is no compelling reason to see this as a physical body part when it is most often translated as "strength," and *strength* maintains the metaphorical language of the prayer.

17. Reading *perfect* here instead of "blameless," simply because this is what the Hebrew means. It is a good point of reflection in this prayer, since it is such a foreign concept in modernity.

18. Added for clarity. Hebrew reads "He who he blesses."

19. Most modern translations read "though he stumble, he will not fall" (NIV). But, the first verb is from the root *npl* ("to fall") instead of *kšl* ("to stumble"), and the second is

Nûn 25 *I have been young and now I am old,*
and I have not seen a righteous one deserted,
nor this one's child seeking bread.[20]
26 *All day, this one is gracious and is lending;*
this one's offspring are a blessing.

Sāmek 27 *Turn aside from evil and do good;*
and reside forever,
28 *for the LORD loves justice,*
and will not forsake his faithful ones.
'Ayin *They will be kept forever,*[21]
but the offspring of the wicked will be cut off.
29 *The righteous will inherit the land,*[22]
and they will dwell forever.
Pê 30 *The mouth of the righteous one utters wisdom;*
and this one's tongue speaks justice.
31 *The instruction of God*[23] *is in this one's heart;*
and this one's steps do not waver.
Ṣādê 32 *The wicked one watches the righteous one,*
seeking to kill the one.
33 *The LORD will not abandon this one to the wicked one's*[24] *hand,*
nor let this one be condemned when he is judged.[25]

---

from the root *ṭwl,* which means "to hurl" or in the case of Job 41:9, "to be overpowered." The NIV and NRSV translations do not seem to capture adequately the meaning of the verse.

20. NRSV and NIV "begging" is a bit overstated. The word is from the root *bqš* ("seeking").

21. This is the line scholars believe should start with an *'ayin.* Craigie suggests that a word has dropped out and should be read *'awālîm lᵉʿōlām* ("forever to forever"). This is the best and least intrusive option; *Psalms 1–50,* p. 296. Both Craigie and Kraus (*Psalms 1–59,* p. 402) also emend the verb to match LXX, thus changing the subject to the wicked: "the wicked are destroyed forever." This change is unnecessary, however. The subject has changed several times from the righteous to the wicked in parallel lines of the same verse. NJPS simply skips the *'ayin* designation in the acrostic and maintains the line as it appears in the MT.

22. Considering the every-other-verse acrostic pattern of the psalm, this line should begin with a word beginning with *'ayin.* Instead, it begins with *sāmek.* Most scholars emend the third line of v. 28 instead, assuming that the versification is in error. The versification error probably occurred at 20-21, the only place where consecutive verses are part of the acrostic pattern.

23. Lit., "his God."

24. Lit., "his hand." Modern translations that preserve the pronoun as either "his" or "their" are confusing here. It is clear from the context that the "he" here is *the wicked one.* Also there is no need to substitute "power" for *hand* as NRSV and NIV.

25. NRSV and NIV "when they are brought to trial" assumes a context that is not

Qôp 34 *Wait for the LORD, keep to God's way,*[26]
and God will raise you up to inherit the land;
when the wicked are cut off you will see.
Rêš 35 *I have seen a powerful*[27] *wicked one,*
a rich citizen showing himself off.[28]
36 *Then the wicked one*[29] *passed and did not exist anymore;*
I searched for that one, he could not be found.
Šîn 37 *Guard the perfect and observe the upright,*
for the end of this one is peace.
38 *But sinners will be exterminated all together;*
the end of the wicked ones is cut off.
Tāw 39 *The salvation of the righteous ones is from the LORD;*
God is their refuge in times of trouble.
40 *The LORD helps them and rescues them,*
rescues them from the wicked ones,
and saves them for they take refuge in God.

1-11 The psalm opens offering comfort and encouragement. The NRSV and NIV's "do not fret" is weak, for the command is to "not let your anger burn" over the wicked who are transient. Verses 3-6 speak of how to live an alternate life, placing trust in God and believing in God's promises. It is a life lived in trust of God instead of anger about the wicked. Verses 7-8 return to the theme of anger, again stressing it will lead down the wrong path. *Waiting upon* the Lord is a better choice than *letting your anger burn* against the wicked and their schemes. Craigie notes, "because such anger is futile, bringing only grief,

clear here. It could be a human trial or it could be the judgment of God. The open language of the poem should be maintained whenever possible; Kraus agrees (*Psalms 1–59,* p. 402).

26. Lit., "his way."

27. This verse is corrupt, as the plethora of translations indicates. The LXX appears to be reading a different line than MT. MT reads *ʿārîṣ,* meaning "awe" or "terror-inspiring." LXX has a different but possible emendation to *ʿallîz* ("raised on high"). *Powerful* is a more general term that still retains the meaning of both MT and LXX.

28. This line is very problematic. Many follow LXX, "and towering like a cedar of Lebanon" (NRSV), but the Greek is suspicious because the last word of the first line and the first word of the second are the same word, although not the same form, suggesting a possible transcription error, but certainly the reading is possible. I have chosen to try to make sense of MT as it is. The verb means "to expose" or "uncover," so it is possible to be understood as showing one's self. The last two words are as reflected here, lit., "a citizen, luxuriant." The adjective is usually used as a definition for foliage, but if the metaphor is taken seriously, this reading is possible. Despite the differences in translations, the general meaning of the verse is still clear. This *wicked one* appears to be *showing off* and doing well.

29. The switch to 1cs in NRSV here has no textual reference and is puzzling.

and because. . . the evil will eventually be cut off."[30] Verses 9 and 11 tell that it is the faithful ones who will *inherit the land,* while v. 10 stresses that the wicked will simply *not exist.* Using the Hebrew particle on nonexistence, *ʾên,* the wicked are simply out of existence, gone. It is *the oppressed* that will *inherit the land* and have *shalom* in great abundance (v. 11). As with all of the wisdom or instructional poetry, being wicked seems like the stupidest choice one can make.[31] You may choose to trust in God and inherit the land or forsake God, trust yourself, and disappear!

12-15 The matter is not settled, however, as these verses turn to the acts of the wicked ones and their threats against the others. But even here, God has the upper hand and will turn their *schemes* and *swords* and *bows.* They will be felled by their weapons, be those real implements of harm or metaphors for their schemes and their lives. The Hebrew text itself does fluctuate here between the singular *wicked one* and *wicked ones* as it does several other places in the psalm. This is not uncommon in ancient poetry; most modern translations smooth it out by making all references plural, but this is unnecessary. There are often singular and plural threats in our world, and there is no reason to smooth out those realities.

16-26 Beginning with *better is the little of the righteous,* these eleven verses lay out this argument. Using parallel and contrasting lines, the good and the wicked are described, and again the purpose is both to show the way to live life and to encourage the righteous not to be fooled, because the wicked will get what is due them. Verse 18 is especially compelling for modern folks to contemplate, "the LORD knows the days of the perfect ones." The Hebrew word *tāmîm* often means a sacrificial animal without blemish, hence the common modern translation of "blameless," but this meaning is not exactly correct. "Blameless" implies this is a moral state, but the sense of the word is different, such as "created or made perfect." A sheep with a blemish cannot be transformed into a blemish-free one. In a sense then, when we follow God, we are the perfect creatures that God made us to be. It is not about a moral choice but a life choice that allows one to be a *perfect one.* Again, by the time one arrives at v. 26, it is clear that *the little of the righteous* is indeed the better way. This *little* and *abundance* contrast should not be reduced to a monetary measure (v. 16). Since it is these very ones that give generously in v. 21, it is a contrast in ways of life, from where our satisfaction stems, where our hearts are.

27-33 Again this section begins with a command, *turn aside from evil,* with the explanation of why. Again it is because the ones firm in the Lord will be the ones that finally prosper and *inherit the land.* As in the previous

30. *Psalms 1–50,* p. 297.
31. See, e.g., Psalm 1.

sections, the wicked are not just going about their life in ignorance of God and the righteous ones. The wicked actively seek the lives of others (v. 32). The threat is real, but so too is God's protection of God's own (v. 33).

34-40 The command here is one of the hardest: to *wait for the Lord* and *keep to God's way.* The wicked are to be *cut off,* but the waiting seems forever, as many of the prayers for help stress. At v. 35, this one offers some first-hand testimony about the wicked (see also v. 25) and their fate. As the psalm concludes, again the contrast between the faithful and the wicked appears to be no choice at all, for the *end* of *the perfect* is *peace* (v. 37) and the end of the wicked is *cut off.* God saves those ones that belong to God (vv. 39-40). The instruction is clear. The wicked may prosper for a moment, but the righteous, perfect ones prosper forever and live in peace. Anyone that would choose a different path is foolish indeed.

This psalm requires little translation in today's world. We too need the encouragement in a world where it is now clear that many, many bankers, con artists, and mortgage brokers feed off the dreams and hope of those who have less resources and education. Greed is now an American value that is blessed and coveted. The lives of the righteous seem pitiful and stupid in comparison. The psalm offers a pair of glasses with a longer vision that offers us a way to see the world though kingdom eyes. There are values that last and make for peace and those that are transitory and destroy, even if at the time the latter look tempting.

Beth Tanner

Psalm 38: I Am in Need, Please Come!

Psalm 38 has been traditionally understood as an individual prayer for help by someone who is ill.[1] Certainly this is possible, but it is not the only possibility. These authors assume that the wounds and pain here have a physical cause. But the psalms are poetry, and as such the images are just as likely to be metaphorical, describing in graphic physical terms what suffering and sorrow feel like in the soul and body of one who is in extreme emotional pain. If the problem is left more open to interpretation, then this may be an in-depth description of how guilt from sin can affect a person both mentally and physically.[2]

Psalm 38 has also been traditionally known as one of the penitential psalms. This group of psalms (6, 32, 38, 51, 102, 130, 143) has been regarded by the church as a distinct genre, even though only two of them speak specifically of confession and forgiveness (Psalms 32 and 51). In his comprehensive study of penitential psalms, Nasuti observes that in the medieval period these seven psalms were closely associated with the popular penitential system of the time.[3] This designation then was a liturgical and not an academic or genre-related one. What is interesting, however, is that the church read and understood this psalm as one where sin, instead of sickness, is the central issue.

The psalm can be divided into six unequal stanzas.[4]

Pleas for help (vv. 1-2)
Description of suffering (vv. 3-8)
Wishes lifted to God (vv. 9-10)
Description of alienation from the community (vv. 11-14)
Wishes lifted to God (vv. 15-20)
Final plea for help (vv. 21-22)

The MT text is without major problems, but both the LXX and 4QPs[a] have variations on the MT, especially in the latter part of the psalm.

1. Craigie (*Psalms 1–50,* p. 300), Terrien (*The Psalms,* p. 323), and Gerstenberger (*Psalms: Part 1,* p. 160) all title this psalm as one voiced by a sick person.

2. McCann, while still holding that in ancient times this was a psalm of sickness, concurs with the disassociation now: "Actually, the nature of the imagery and its extent discourage an individualistic or biographical interpretation of Psalm 38" ("The Book of Psalms," p. 833).

3. *Defining the Sacred Songs,* p. 39.

4. Scholars do not agree on how to divide this psalm. Most set v. 1 apart from v. 2, but this sets the plea apart from the reason. Fokkelman concurs that vv. 1 and 2 belong together (*Reading Biblical Poetry,* p. 214). Terrien argues for a chiastic structure with vv. 13-15, but the connections seem forced (*The Psalms,* p. 324). Fokkelman uses some additional smaller divisions for this psalm, but overall it is the same as above (*Reading Biblical Poetry,* p. 214).

A Davidic psalm. Lehazkir.[5]

1 *O Lord, do not in your anger punish me,*
nor in your wrath discipline me;
2 *for your arrows have pierced into me;*
and your hand came down heavy upon me.

3 *There is no soundness in my flesh because of your indignation;*
there is no peace in my bones because of my sin,
4 *for my iniquities are higher*[6] *than my head,*
like a heavy burden that weighs upon me.
5 *My wounds reek and*[7] *fester,*
because of my folly.
6 *I am bowed down, I am exceedingly stooped down;*
all day, I walk about dark,
7 *for my loins are filled with burning,*
and there is no soundness in my flesh.
8 *I am faint and exceedingly crushed;*
I roar because of my groaning heart.

9 *Lord, in front of you are all my desires;*
my sighing from you is not hidden.
10 *My heart pounds, my strength deserts me;*
and as for the light in my eyes, it also is no longer in me.

11 *The ones who love me and my friend from my affliction stand far off,*[8]
and my neighbors stand at a distance.
12 *Those seeking me*[9] *set traps;*[10]

5. Meaning uncertain. The root appears to be *zkr* ("to remember"). Weiser notes that "for a memorial" comes from Luther's translation, while others think it may mean "the offering of incense" (*Psalms,* p. 324). LXX adds an additional "for the Sabbath."

6. Lit., "pass over" my head, but the intent seems to be one of measurement.

7. LXX and 4QPs[a] add "and" between the two verbs, which is missing in MT (Ulrich, Cross, et al., *Qumran Cave 4: XI,* p. 12).

8. 4QPs[a] reads not "from before my affliction" but "my friends and those knowing me" (Ulrich, Cross, et al., *Qumran Cave 4: XI,* p. 15). Unfortunately, these are the only words preserved, so it is impossible to know if *wmywd* (rest of word lost) replaces the verb *yʿmdw* or is added to the line from MT. Likewise, LXX reads "drew near to me and stood," reflecting not the noun "my affliction" but the 3cpl verb *ngʿw* ("to reach"). With three divergent sources, it is best to read MT, but this is a tentative determination.

9. Lit., "to my *nepeš*"; this word has a wide range of meaning: "soul, living being, self." It is the essence of what makes a sack of bones alive.

10. LXX has "They pressed hard upon me that sought my soul."

those intent on my harm speak destruction,
and deceit all the day they utter.
13 *But I, like the deaf, did not hear,*
and like the mute, did not open my mouth.
14 *Truly, like one that does not hear;*
and there is no argument in his mouth,

15 *for you,* LORD, *I wait,*
You will answer, O Lord, my God.[11]
16 *For I say, "Lest they rejoice over me when my foot slips;*
over me they exalt!"[12]
17 *For I am prepared for limping;*[13]
and sorrow is before me continually,
18 *for my iniquity,*[14] *I declare;*
I am distressed because of my sin.
19 *Those who are my enemies without cause*[15] *are mighty;*
and many are those hating me with lies.[16]
20 *Those repaying me evil instead of good*
are my adversaries because I pursue good.[17]

11. 4QPsa reads "O Lord, you, you will answer me for my God [missing]," but the reconstruction does seem to allow room for additional words (Ulrich, Cross, et al., *Qumran Cave 4: XI,* p. 15). LXX follows the MT.

12. Lit., "to make great," a 3mpl *hiphil* perfect form. 4QPsa replaces the perfect verb with an imperfect 3mpl, which matches the imperfect *rejoice* (Ulrich, Cross, et al., *Qumran Cave 4: XI,* p. 15).

13. This translation is as close to MT as possible. LXX reads "for I am prepared for plagues." Both the NRSV and NIV smooth out this translation to "I am ready to fall" and NJPS "I am on the verge of collapse," but these do not carry the meaning well. MT reads, lit., "to limp, it is established," and with the second line this seems to carry the connotation that this is something the person will carry for some time.

14. 4QPsa reads *kh ʿwnty* ("thus, my iniquities [missing]") (Ulrich, Cross, et al., *Qumran Cave 4: XI,* p. 15). LXX reads the singular form like MT.

15. Reading with 4QPsa, *ḥnm* ("without cause") instead of MT and LXX's *ḥyym* ("alive" or "vigorous") (Ulrich, Cross, et al., *Qumran Cave 4: XI,* p. 15).

16. 4QPsa appears to have a 1cs suffix on *šqr,* but "my lies" makes little sense. However, *wāw* and *yôd* are easily confused, and it is possible to read "their lies" (Ulrich, Cross, et al., *Qumran Cave 4: XI,* p.ts15).

17. 4QPsa reads *yššny tht dbr twb*, possibly meaning "he plundered me instead of speaking good"; this is not overly helpful in understanding the meaning of MT. LXX is similar to MT for the first two lines ("the ones rendering evil instead of good for I pursue righteousness") but has an additional line that is nonsensical.

21 Do not forsake me, O Lord, my God;[18]
do not be far from me.
22 Come quickly to help me,[19] *Lord of my salvation!*

1-2 The psalm opens with a dual plea to God with the reason for the plea. The problem is clearly God's *anger.*[20] The problem, then, appears not to be sickness, but sin and guilt. Indeed, to argue for sickness here is a dangerous theology that implies that God punishes sin with sickness. This theology was put on trial in the book of Job and found wanting by the very canon of Scripture.

3-8 The next line may be the reason for the diagnosis of sickness here. The NIV uses the word "health" for *mᵉṯōm,* but this word is from a root that means "completeness"; it also appears in Isa. 1:6, where the context, like this one, is definitely sin and not health. This section speaks not of a physical ailment, but of how sin and guilt feel. Verse 4 begins this description; it is *a heavy burden.* Verses 5-8 continue to tell about the physical effects of sin. It is a festering wound because of this one's *folly,* which in both Ps. 69:5 and Prov. 24:9 are directly equated with sin. This one feels low and *dark* (v. 6). The burden of sin burns inside, and the whole body feels the strain (v. 7). The insides feel *faint,* and spirit is *crushed* (v. 8); even if quiet on the outside, the mind *roars* over the torment in this one's *heart* (v. 8). Gerstenberger notes, "Events that happened in the past are burdening the supplicant now."[21]

9-10 Here are wishes for restoration. The prayer turns to say that despite all of these feelings of guilt and sin, there is still a relationship with God, and God knows both the *desires* (v. 9) and the hurt of this one (v. 10). Why is there no confession here as in Psalm 51? Why is there not an unburdening of all of the guilt and pain? I am not sure, but I also know that as humans, sometimes we are just not ready to confess and be made whole — be it because of stubbornness or a sense that we have not suffered enough for our deeds. Even if there is no confession, these verses confirm that there still exists a relationship with God.

11-14 Sin does not only impact the relationship between the one and God, but the community also. Verse 11 could be taken as *friends* and *neighbors* shunning the sick. But we also shun the guilty. Just ask a church member who has been indicted or the one people perceive as breaking up the marriage how their relationship with the community has changed. This alienation only adds

18. 4QPsᵃ either omits *YHWH* or transposes it. The only readable part of the line reads "Do not forsake me, O God [missing]" (Ulrich, Cross, et al., *Qumran Cave 4: XI,* p. 15).

19. 4QPsᵃ is slightly different: "Come quickly (defectively written *ḥyšh* as in Ps. 71:12) to me to help me, Lord of my salvation" (Ulrich, Cross, et al., *Qumran Cave 4: XI,* p. 15).

20. Scholars note the similarity of this verse to the opening petition of Ps. 6; Craigie, *Psalms 1–50,* p. 302.

21. *Psalms: Part 1,* p. 162.

to the sorrow and guilt. Do they deserve this treatment? Maybe the point of the poem is to remind us how it feels to be shunned for our sins. Verses 13 and 14 are clear textually but are not easy to understand. It seems as if this one does not strike back at the ones who have turned their backs. One tries to ignore the slights and chatter, but it only adds to the misery.

15-20 These verses return to the conversation with God. The section is difficult to understand, especially the last verse. It begins with the hope that waiting on God is the best course and that the others are looking on to celebrate the fall of the one praying (v. 16). Verses 17 and 18 appear to be a confession of sorts. Verse 17 is difficult to understand, as a host of emendations testify. It probably indicates that the one praying is aware that God's forgiveness will not set all right and that this one will still have to atone for her actions. Verse 18 is the confession, for there is a declaration of *iniquity* and an understanding of the price of guilt. Verse 19 declares that there are now *enemies* that will continue to assume the worst, possibly thwarting the *good* acts of the past and the future because of this sin (v. 20).

21-22 The prayer ends with more pleas for God not to *forsake* or *be far* and to *come quickly,* ending with the declaration *Lord of my salvation.*

The one praying here is bowed down by her own actions. The truth is laid out: both God and the community are impacted by this one's acts. My guess is that we have all been there. We know the physical burden of guilt. We know how difficult it is to ask God for forgiveness when we feel terrible. We also know that our acts not only impact the community but have the power to create enemies that will last long after the act. The psalm ends with the only way forward, to cling to God as the *Lord of salvation* as one must chart the path through the aftermath of sin.

BETH TANNER

Psalm 39: From Silence to Speech to Silence

This psalm combines various forms in order to create a unique poetic composition. The uniqueness of the final form led Gerstenberger to label it "an enigmatic piece," Mays to call it "a strange prayer," and Alter to wonder about the psalmist's "world of radical ambiguities."[1] Yet, for all the consternation, the poem is an elegant composition. It is part prayer for help, but it draws on some conventions of the song of thanksgiving and borrows from the lexicon of sapiential instruction. As Craigie notes, it is an individual lament "containing a mixture of sad reflection and prayer."[2] But as Goldingay qualifies, although "it uses the form of personal reflection on experience, this is a means of offering a theological meditation. Its form may involve more 'biographical stylization' than an indication that the psalm is a transcript of an actual [historical incident]."[3] The best way to understand the poem is as a pained cry for help, which draws on the style of thanksgiving and the vocabulary of wisdom in order to launch a passionate theological witness that is both *spoken to God and against God.*

The unique poetry of the psalm has led to confusion about how to understand its structure both at the micro- and macro-levels. According to the tradition followed in the *Biblia Hebraica Stuttgartensia,* this psalm makes frequent use of tricola (cf. vv. 2, 3, 4, 5, 6, 11, 12), and this interpretation is plausible.[4] The structure must be treated as tentative, but there are two main sets of clues to follow. First, the psalm has a type of refrain found at the ends of vv. 5 and 11: *Surely every person is futile,* which both times is followed by the enigmatic liturgical marker *selah.*[5] In addition, the psalm's rhetoric is marked by frequent first person singular *qal* "verbs of speaking": *I said (ʾāmartî;* v. 1a), *I spoke (dibbartî;* v. 3c), *I was silent (neʾᵉlamtî;* v. 9a). Navigating between these two formal clues, the psalm can be seen to have five largely regular stanzas:

St. 1 The psalmist's silence (vv. 1-3b)
St. 2 The psalmist speaks out (vv. 3c-5) — first refrain and *selah.*
St. 3 The psalmist's meditation (vv. 6-8)

1. Gerstenberger, *Psalms: Part 1,* p. 165; Mays, *Psalms,* p. 165; Alter, *Art of Biblical Poetry,* p. 69.

2. *Psalms 1–50,* p. 307.

3. *Psalms 1–41,* p. 555.

4. For examples of other structures, see Fokkelman, who divides the poem into seven stanzas (*The Psalms in Form,* p. 51) or Goldingay, who sees three main sections (*Psalms 1–41,* pp. 554-55).

5. Following only this clue, one might divide the psalm into three sections: vv. 1-5, 6-11, 13-14.

St. 4 The psalmist's renewed speech (vv. 9-11) — second refrain and *selah*
St. 5 The psalmist's prayer (vv. 12-13)

The dominant poetic theme of the psalm is speech and silence. The psalm's structure and poetic development parallel Psalm 30. In both poems, the psalmist's journey is narrated by the use of three speech acts — the quotation of two older speech acts (vv. 1 and 4 in this psalm) and then a new speech act (in this case, especially vv. 12-13). It is the poetic interplay between acts of speech, reports of silence, and a crescendo cry of pain which lends great power to this artistic prayer.

For the leader. For Jeduthun.[6] *A Davidic psalm.*

1 *I said, "Let me watch over my ways,*[7]
to keep from sinning with my tongue.
Let me fit[8] *a muzzle on my mouth,*
as long as the wicked is before me."
2 *Although I was utterly silent,*
I made myself keep quiet[9]*; it did no good.*[10]
My pain increased,
3 *My heart grew hot within me.*
As I pondered, a fire burned.

I spoke with my tongue:
4 *"Make me to know my end, O LORD,*
the span of my days and what I am,
I would know how I can forbear."[11]

6. Vocalizing here with the Qere; Kethib has *lîḏîṯûn. Jeduthun* (or Jedithun) is an attested Hebrew name, associated with Levitical service, especially with the sons of Asaph (cf. Pss. 77:1; 62:1; 1 Chr. 9:16; 16:38; Neh. 11:17, etc.). He may have been *the leader,* or some other ancient priestly figure. Gerstenberger (*Psalms: Part 1,* p. 165) suggests that the term may refer to a melody or liturgical element, but more likely it is a reference to an ancient person. Either way, its significance is unclear.

7. Kraus's suggestion of amending *ways* to "words" in order to align with the parallel *tongue* is both unnecessary and harmonizing (*Psalms 1–59,* pp. 415-16).

8. Reading with LXX, in which *ethemēn* appears to be reading *'āśîmâ*. MT's second *'ešmᵉrâ* is a dittography.

9. The *hiphil* form of *ḥšh* can be understood as intensive: "I forced myself to keep quiet"; cf. Isa. 42:14.

10. Understanding a comparative *mêm* in *miṭṭôḇ* to carry a causal sense.

11. The term *ḥāḏēl* does not mean "transient" as HALOT and most translations indi-

5 *Indeed, you have made my days but a handbreadth,*
my forbearance is as nothing before you.
Surely every person is futile.[12] Selah[13]

6 *Surely, a person walks about in shadow,*
surely one ambles about[14] *futilely,*
A person heaps up, but does not know who will gather them in.
7 *And now, my lord, what should I wait*[15] *for?*
My hope? It is in you!
8 *Deliver me from all my transgressions,*
do not inflict me with the taunt of the fool,

9 *I was silent, I did not open my mouth;*
for you have done this.[16]
10 *Remove your slap from me!*
Under the hostility[17] *of your hand I am perishing.*
11 *As a rebuke for sin, you discipline a person;*
You melt what one desires, like a moth.
Surely every person is futile. Selah[18]

---

cate. Rather, following Clifford (*Psalms 1–72,* p. 199), it is a term meaning "to abandon," thus "to cease from my affliction," thus "forbear."

12. Reading *'aḵ heḇel kol 'āḏām* in parallel refrain in v. 11. The first *kol* is a dittography that is the result of an eye skip and thus omitted. The verb *niṣṣāḇ* is to be omitted, with LXX. It is possible that the word was placed here, at a date later than when the LXX translators worked, as a textual comment indicating that some scribe knew that the first *kol* was a dittography, but to "let it stand" — similar to the marginal correction in Exod. 1:5 that "Joseph was in Egypt."

13. Syr omits.

14. Given the singular forms in the preceding and succeeding clauses, the plural form is a problem. Craigie proposes amending to *yhmywn,* with the sense of "wealth" (*Psalms 1–50,* p. 307), whereas Kraus chooses *hmôn* or *hônîm,* translating "Only for nothing does one heap up 'blows' " (*Psalms 1–59,* p. 415). The parallel in v. 11 is little help. LXX's *tarassō* renders such a wide variety of Hebrew roots that one can appeal to it only with hesitancy. But in Gen. 19:16, it renders *mhh,* vocalized here as *yiṯmahmâ,* meaning a slow, ambling walk, which is attractive here in parallel with *yiṯhalleḵ.*

15. LXX *hypomonē mou* suggests the nominal form *tiqwāṯî;* this should probably be understood as harmonizing the forms with the second clause of the verse. MT is retained.

16. LXX *ho poiēsas me* understands the phrase to refer to God as creator: "you made me" (cf. Job 35:10: *'ᵉlôah 'ōśî*), but such a theological concept is foreign here.

17. The meaning of *tigraṯ yāḏḵâ* is debated, because the former word is a *hapax legomenon.* LXX has *ischyas tēs cheiros* ("the strength of your hands"; the plural form can be disregarded), but likely the translators also were confused, so not much help is provided. Akkadian *tagriātu* ("hostilities") is related to the root *garû,* while Hebrew has the root *gārâ* ("to stir up strife"). This is the most attractive approach, thus *hostility.*

18. Syr omits.

12 *Hear my prayer, O LORD!*
And give ear to my cry!
Do not be deaf to my tears!
For I am a stranger, staying with you;
a clanless visitor, like all my ancestors.
13 *Look away from me, that I may smile,*
before I walk away and am no more.

1-3b The poet launches her prayer with the paradoxical declaration, which one may paraphrase, "I said, 'I will keep silent.'" The seemingly inconsistent idea of one declaring aloud the intention to keep silent is made possible because in Hebrew, even more than in English, the verb of speaking, *'āmar,* can refer to one's internal thoughts. Notice that the speech that is then reported is addressed to herself: *Let me watch over my ways.* This is not speech addressed to God, but the report of a decision that the sufferer had made in the past. In the reported speech, the psalmist reports that she had two reasons for remaining silent — one a "resulting reason" and one a "causal reason." The "resulting reason" was that she was suffering at the hands of some unnamed persecutor. In the closing phrase, the poet vows to keep silent *as long as the wicked is before me (rāšā' lᵉnegdî).* This is the only reference in this psalm to the enemy. It is not clear what should be made of this reference, but one can understand the phrase primarily as a metaphorical reference to her perception that her suffering was the result of someone else's actions, not of her own. She was suffering at the hands of others — at least originally, she did not bring her own suffering on herself. At least from her perspective, she did not. The "causal reason" she decided to remain silent was that she wanted *to keep from sinning with my tongue.* She was afraid that if, in her anger, she spoke out against God and against her enemy, it would be a sin. The strength of her resolution to keep silent is underscored by the visceral metaphor that she determined to *fit a muzzle on my mouth.* The metaphor is a poignant symbol both of the psalmist's determination not to speak, not to offend God, but also of the psalmist's urgent and compelling need to speak. Only someone who does not believe that one will be able to resist the temptation to speak will need to *fix a muzzle* over one's mouth. As for why she believed that what she might say could be a sin of the tongue, see below.

The psalmist then reports that her decision to remain silent *did no good.* The integrity of the psalmist in keeping silent is underscored in the emphatic statement *ne'ᵉlamtî ḏûmiyyâ heḥᵉšêṯî,* lit., "I was dumb, silence, I made myself be silent." It took a tremendous act of will, but the psalmist succeeded in not speaking out and, one is led to conclude, in not sinning against God. But *it did no good.* Instead of the silence resulting in her situation getting better, her situation in fact grew worse: *My pain increased. My heart grew hot within me.*

As I pondered, a fire burned. The image of suffering as heat — of fire in one's flesh or of one's bones melting — is familiar imagery in the psalms (cf. 22:14). The language invokes the steadily banking crisis and declining strength of one being afflicted by a fever. And all of this, the psalmist reports, occurred while *I pondered* — which should be understood as another term meaning "while I kept silent."

In terms of the argument of the psalm, it should be noted here that the poem borrows a rhetorical structure from the song of thanksgiving. It is typical of the psalm of thanksgiving that the psalmist reports a past crisis and also quotes a bit of the prayer that the sufferer had cried out during the crisis. Thus, in 30:8-9, the psalmist remembers crying out, "I cried . . . 'What profit is there in my blood?'" In 31:22, "In my alarm, I, I said, 'I am cut off from your eyes.'" And in 32:5, the psalmist says, "I said, 'Let me confess against myself, my transgression to the LORD.'" What is particularly striking about Psalm 39, however, is that rather than serving to facilitate the rhetorical movement from lament to praise and thanksgiving, here the psalmist is stoking the furnace of her anger. She is banking up a fire of burning outrage.

3c-5 Similar to Job, who remained silent for a spell before erupting into speech, the psalmist bursts forth in anger in stanza 2. The one who had vowed not to sin *with my tongue (bilšônî)* now says, *I spoke with my tongue (dibbartî bilšônî).* The repetition of the term *bilšônî* suggests that there was an element of risk in the psalmist's new speech act. It explicitly draws the connection between the new speech act and the previous vow to remain silent, showing that at least in the psalmist's understanding, his new speech act was a violation of the earlier vow. But was the new speech act a sin? It is possible to interpret the repetition of the term *bilšônî* as indication that the psalmist understood the violation of the vow to remain silent as sinful in some way. And in a different context, I argued for that approach.[19]

But in spite of the fact that the psalmist later asks that God *deliver me from all my transgressions* (v. 8), I now take a different approach. Although almost all commentators interpret the quoted prayer in v. 4 as a reference

19. "[T]he psalmist viewed his second self quotation as sinful. This interpretation is supported by the fact that later in the psalm, the psalmist speaks of his sufferings as the result of sin (v. 11a) and he asks for forgiveness (v. 8a). It is difficult to understand what might have been sinful about a request to 'know my end.' Perhaps the psalmist's demand to know 'my end' was a demand for forbidden knowledge of the future, which is reserved only for God. Or perhaps the demand 'make me know' [*hôdîʿēnî*] was in itself sinful. Job also confronted God with the demand to know ([*hôdîʿēnî*]; Job 10:2; 13:23). God threw that demand back in Job's face (38:3; 40:7), and in the end Job confessed that 'I uttered that which I did not understand, things too marvelous for me, which I did not know, [when I said] . . . cause me to know [*hôdîʿēnî*]' (42:3b-4). If Job is an adequate parallel, perhaps the psalmist's sin was simply his demand to know"; *Many Are Saying,* pp 64-65.

to the fleeting nature of life, Clifford has presented a compelling alternative. The quoted prayer in v. 4 is not a sapiential reflection on the brevity of existence, but a request for God to disclose the length of the psalmist's current punishment — literally, to make known "how long" the current crisis would last. In the ancient world, both in Israel and among her neighbors, the belief was held that God's discipline was often imposed for a set period, or "term" (Isa. 40:2). Thus, in Jer. 25:11-12, the prophet announced that the exile would last for seventy years before God would bring the people home. Similarly, in Ps. 74:9, during a time of national crisis, the psalmist laments that "there is none among us who knows how long!" — that is, who can announce on behalf of God how long the crisis would last. The quoted prayer, *"Make me to know my end, O LORD, The span of my days and what I am, I would know* how fleeting I am," reflects an urgent request to know how long a personal crisis would last. This is indicated by several factors. The word *end (qiṣṣî)* refers to a precise term or day of death; it is not a reference to brevity. Similarly, *span of my days* refers to the definite number, not to the general shortness.[20] The psalmist is not piously asking for God to instruct him regarding how short life is, but is asking for that which cannot be known. Clifford paraphrases: "Lord, let me know my term (of affliction),/what the measure of my days is (that is, the predetermined length of my affliction)./May I know how to cease (from my affliction)."[21]

The urgency of this request is then reinforced by the psalmist's acknowledgement that yes, life is indeed brief: *you have made my days but a handbreadth. . . . Surely every person is futile.* Within the rhetoric of the psalm, this borrowing from Israel's wisdom tradition, which acknowledges that life is brief, serves both to heighten the urgency of the psalmist's request to know how long the crisis would last and also to turn up the volume on the psalmist's lament against God.

What should not be lost here is the mounting force of the psalmist's witness against God. It was pointed out above that in this psalm, the sufferer borrows the formal patterns of "theological witness" from the song of thanksgiving. But instead of giving testimony to the gathered community and inviting the community to praise God, here the psalmist bears witness against God, in the hopes that the testimony would move God to act graciously toward the psalmist. That is the context in which the rhetoric about God in v. 5 should be understood. The vocabulary and perspective portrayed here are well known in Israel's wisdom traditions. In a sapiential context, such as Psalm 90, the language can function as instruction for human beings: that they may gain wise hearts (90:12) or learn to fear the Lord. But here, the audience is God. The

20. So Clifford, *Psalms 1–72,* p. 199.

21. *Psalms 1–72,* pp. 199-200.

effect is to throw the burden of the knowledge back upon God. The psalm's argument is beginning to take shape. The psalmist is building an argument for the Lord to act, based precisely on the belief that humans do not know their end, precisely because *you have made my days but a handbreadth.* The psalmist sums up this argument with the phrase of the refrain: *surely every person is futile. Futile* here translates the well-known Hebrew term *heḇel,* which is notoriously difficult to render. The term literally means "vapor" or "breath" and thus is a powerful metaphor for the insubstantiality of human life and effort. It is traditionally translated as "vanity," but futility comes closer to its meaning in this context.

6-8 The third stanza picks up where the previous stanza left off, but advances the argument. Whereas the previous stanza spoke of the brevity of human life, now the focus is on the meaningless of human effort. In the first two clauses, the metaphor of walking in shadow and ambling slowly without purpose is employed. The verb *hālaḵ* in the *hithpiel* means "walk back and forth." It is often translated as to go about "to and fro" (cf. Job 1:7). The metaphor is a rather poignant symbol of the futility of human effort. Rather like Sisyphus in Greek mythology — whose eternal fate was to roll a large rock daily up a hill, only to watch it roll back down to the bottom — the metaphor of walking meaninglessly through life captures the psalmist's sense of futility (again the Hebrew here is *heḇel*). To that metaphor, the psalmist adds the image of a harvester who is able to accomplish the backbreaking, initial work of *heaping* the produce into piles, but does not last long enough to *gather* it into the storehouse.

After this series of dismal images of futility, the psalmist has reached the turning point of his argument. As is often the case in the psalms, the turning point is signaled by the disjunctive particle *w*^{eʿ}*attâ* — *and now.* Having established the initial grounds of the argument, the psalmist turns to her plea. She introduces this plea with a rhetorical question: *my lord, what should I wait for?* Even in the way the psalmist asks the question, she tips her answer, because she addresses the question to *my lord.* The word for "lord" here is not the personal name of Israel's God but is the more generic *ʾ*^{a}*ḏōnāy.* But sort of like a heavy counterweight, which once released smoothly lifts the other side of the balance by naming God in the question, the equation is set up so that God, and only God, can be the answer: *My hope? It is in you!* The two terms for *hope, qāwâ and tôḥeleṯ,* technically refer to "waiting" and "expecting," which can be understood as two of the components of hope. To hope is first of all to wait, in the full sense of waiting. That is, to wait is to be stuck in the present moment without something or someone that one desires. But to wait is also to linger in the expectation that the something or someone will show up. This is the sense of *qāwâ,* especially as it is used in the Psalter. To expect, by comparison, is to imagine the future. It has to do with one's imagination about what the anticipated future will be like (cf. Job 41:9; Prov. 10:28). The psalmist's confession here names the reality that only God can deliver the psalmist's preferred future but is also an accusation that the waiting has lasted too long.

The plea proper occurs in v. 8, and its vocabulary is typical of those prayers for help that are known as the penitential psalms — 6, 32, 38, 51, 102, 130, 143. Even though Psalm 39 is not considered one of the penitential psalms, the theme of sin and forgiveness is actually more readily present here than in some of those psalms, such as Psalm 6. The psalmist asks, *Deliver me from all my transgressions.* What does it mean to be delivered from sins? Here, it means to be spared the rightful consequences of one's actions. In a word, it means to be forgiven. And to ask for forgiveness is an appeal to the character of the forgiving one. Thus in 119:170, the psalmist there prays, "My prayer enters into your presence; according to your promise deliver me." The psalmist here appeals, then, for forgiveness, and this appeal is based on her hope in the character of God. Precisely what the psalmist's sins were is not stated in the psalm. As mentioned above, the outburst in v. 4, by means of which the psalmist violated her vow to keep silent, should not be interpreted as sinful. The psalmist neither asserts her innocence (as do many other psalmists) nor confesses her sins (as do many other psalmists). It is possible that the psalmist was unaware of what her sins were, but she was aware that everyone has "hidden errors " (19:12) or "unintentional sins" (Lev. 4:2).

The closing phrase about being spared *the taunt of the fool* refers to the frequent taunt *(ḥerpâ)* in the psalms of the wicked and the enemy. Often, that taunt is something to the effect that God has no effective power to save the psalmist (cf. 10:1-11) or that God has rejected the psalmist (cf. 3:2; 71:11). Either, or both, of those possibilities is in play here. But given the psalmist's reference to her sin, it is more likely that the taunt she is referring to may have been something to the effect of others rejoicing in the punishment that they assumed the psalmist was receiving at God's hands.[22]

9-11 In the fourth stanza, having now quoted both his earlier vow to keep silent (v. 1) and then his later outburst of speech (v. 4), the psalmist returns to the theme of silence. The psalmist narrates a new period of silence, which will again burst forth in speech. Most likely the psalmist is renewing the attack on God, reminding God that his initial orientation towards the crisis he is in was to remain silent, accepting the Lord's discipline, because he believed that *you have done this.*

The psalmist then renews the appeal: *Remove your slap from me! Under the hostility of your hand I am perishing.* The metaphor here may make many

22. For more on the taunt, see my discussion of the issue in *Many Are Saying,* pp. 40-48.

modern Westerners uncomfortable, because it is the metaphor of corporal punishment. The psalmist is experiencing whatever crisis that he is in — and it is not clear whether it is a health, legal, military, or economic crisis — as a rebuke from God. The word translated here as *your slap* is *nigʿeḵā,* which might be most colloquially translated as "your spanking." Although such a rendering is too trivial for a formal translation, it faithfully conveys the Old Testament notion that God's anger is for the sake of discipline. The psalmist says explicitly that by punishment, *you discipline a person.* God's anger exists only in order to bring about changed behavior by those who persecute others and violate God's will. In that sense, God's anger exists only to quench itself. God's *hostility (tigrâ)* here refers to God's change of mood. Hostility here technically means the start of a fight or a disciplinary action. God's mood changes here from looking favorably on the psalmist to looking with anger on the psalmist. The psalmist is aware that this change of mood was something that he caused himself. It is occurring *as a rebuke for sin.* I have chosen to retain what for English readers might seem an awkward metaphor — the metaphor of the melting *moth,* instead of smoothing over the metaphor as do those translations that say something such as "consuming like a moth what he treasures" (NJPS). The word *melt* better retains the poetic connections with the earlier references to fire and heat, and conveys the sense of slowly being dissipated, rather than conveying the sense of being consumed in an instant.

The stanza closes with the second occurrence of the refrain: *Surely every person is futile.* This repetition, coming as it does as the final word of this stanza and as the final word before the psalmist turns to his closing plea for help, sums up the psalmist's angry, desperate argument. Under God's stare, the sinner melts, because all people are *futile* — lit., "vapor" *(heḇel).* As was stated above, in another context this observation might be intended to introduce an instruction on the beginning of wisdom. But here, directed at God, it is the rhetoric of anger — anger with a faithful Lord, whose fidelity seems to have evaporated, like human breath dissipating on a cold day.

12-13 At the heart of the psalm's final stanza stands the powerful metaphor of the *stranger (gēr)* and *clanless visitor (tôšāḇ).* Older translations of these terms include "sojourner," "alien," "resident alien," and "passing guest." The English language has no equivalent term, because the norms of modern social customs are different than those of the ancient world. Israel was a kinship society, in which one's security within the society was dependent upon a network of extended family relationships. The term *gēr* and its synonym *tôšaḇ* refer to "anyone outside the kin group or solidarity unit and, therefore, defenseless."[23] In a remarkable metaphor, which functions both as mournful

23. Philip J. King and Lawrence E. Stager, *Life in Biblical Israel* (Louisville: Westminster John Knox, 2001), p. 61.

complaint and poignant plea, the psalmist asserts both his kinlessness among humanity, but also his relationship with God. Having, at least metaphorically, no solidarity group on which to rely, the psalmist claims a place in God's family. Somewhat paradoxically, the psalmist sees this claim as a sort of family tradition — he is a *clanless visitor, like all my ancestors* (lit., like all my fathers).

The final plea of the psalm turns to the use of bodily metaphors: *Hear, give ear, do not be deaf, look away.* Each of these four verbs is paired with some personal reference to the psalmist: hear → *my prayer;* give ear → *my cry;* do not be deaf → *my tears* (meaning the sound of my weeping); look away → *from me.* This tightly balanced poetry bears witness to the deeply personal, theological dimensions of the psalmist's suffering. Just as "to have a god is nothing else than to trust and believe him with our whole heart,"[24] so also to have a God while in crisis is to demand that God enter into the crisis "with me" — the "with me" here is signaled so clearly by the four personal clauses. The last of these four clauses is longer than the others: *that I may smile, before I walk away and am no more.* This clause ends the psalm on a plaintive note, without the expected word of trust, ending instead with a final "but if not . . . ," which trails off into a final silence that awaits God's answer. Thus, the psalm ends where it began, in a silence that waits for an answering word from God.

Reflections

1. From Silence to Speech to Silence

The powerful poetic trajectory of the psalm — from silence, to speech, to silence, to speech, to silence — is in itself a testimony to the tensions and vicissitudes of the life of faith. On the one hand, as McCann has seen, the movement from silence to speech that is twice narrated in the psalm is a theological witness to the reality that a mature faith is one in which the individual can take the initiative with God and say, "enough is enough." God does not require meek submission of those with whom he is in relationship. As Brueggemann has famously written, "The Psalm evidences courage and ego strength before Yahweh which permits an act of hope, expectant imperatives, and an insistence that things be changed before it is too late."[25] As McCann concludes, "the very existence of the psalmist as a speech-partner with God belies the apparent insignificance of humanity."[26] The psalmist's act of speaking out so aggressively against God bears witness to the psalmist's faith — the

24. Luther, *Large Catechism,* trans. Robert H. Fischer (Philadelphia: Fortress, 1959), p. 9.

25. "The Costly Loss of Lament," *JSOT* 36 (1986) 66.

26. "The Book of Psalms," p. 839.

faith that God will remain faithful in spite of the psalmist's assertiveness and the faith that deliverance belongs to the Lord. "Any being that has the courage to tell God, 'Look away' (v. 13), cannot be entirely insignificant, even if life is fleeting."[27] And the fact that the psalmist concludes this prayer-poem by so artistically trailing off into silence bears witness to the psalmist's living hope that as long as the Lord reigns, the human silence that is brought about by suffering will never be the last word. Paul's word that "In [Christ] every one of God's promises is a 'Yes'" (2 Cor. 1:20) is a fitting New Testament commentary on the psalmist's hope.

2. A Clanless Visitor, like All My Ancestors

Ripped from a native homeland, oppressed by slavemasters, at times having families torn asunder by the slave trade, the voices of African Americans rose in lamentation:

> Sometimes I feel like a motherless child.
> Sometimes I feel like a motherless child.
> O my Lord, sometimes I feel like a motherless child.
> Then I get down on my knees and pray.

That spiritual may be the most faithful paraphrase of this psalm's message available in the English language. The psalm closes with the metaphor of the sufferer as a displaced stranger, lacking a family or other solidarity group upon which to rely. But this isolation, this exile into the spiritual space of the stranger, is not the last word. The isolation drives the supplicant to pray — Deliver me, do not inflict me, remove your slap from me, hear my prayer, give ear to my cry, do not be deaf to my tears. *For I am a clanless visitor, like all my ancestors.* Implicit in the prayer is a promise. For those with no other group, no other support, the Lord himself is family. And the people who bear the Lord's name are called to be family to all who are displaced.

ROLF A. JACOBSON

27. "The Book of Psalms," p. 839.

Psalm 40: From Praise to Prayer

Psalm 40 is a composition that seems to be half individual song of thanksgiving (vv. 1-11 or 1-12, depending on whose interpretation is followed) and half individual prayer for help (vv. 12-17 or 13-17).[1] The fact that the words that comprise 40:13-17 appear in nearly identical form as Psalm 70, an independent prayer for help, seems to confirm the two-part structure of the psalm. As Gerstenberger writes, "In Psalm 40, the text is used as an appendix to a thanksgiving hymn. All psalmic texts being communal and liturgical in essence, we should not be taken by surprise with doubled transmissions and varying uses."[2] But recognizing the two distinct halves of this poem does not mean that the two do not form a coherent whole. Kraus can be taken as representative of an older approach that sought to drive a wedge between the two halves: "Psalm 40 separates into two different songs that in form and theme clearly diverge. Psalm 40A (vv. 1-11) . . . [and] Psalm 40B (vv. 12-17)." Kraus continues: "The question arises whether the two sections of Psalm 40, which have been characterized as two different psalms, can in some way — if not in a formal way, then at least by content — be related to each other. Basically, of course, nothing would prevent our understanding the phases of pleading and thanking as complementary. . . . We have to begin with the assumption that two different psalms have been joined into one in Psalm 40 — for what reason cannot be ascertained." Kraus postulates that a scribal error is to blame for a poem that is in his opinion rather ill-formed: "think of a seamless transition from one element to the other in copying."[3] In his commentary, Kraus comments only on Psalm 40A, reserving comment on the so-called Psalm 40B to his treatment of Psalm 70.

That approach is rejected here, as it is by most recent commentators. Gerstenberger speaks for the newer consensus: "the division of the text depends on a rather dubious literary and biographical interpretation. Under liturgical considerations the sequence of praise and thanksgiving followed by lament is quite feasible in the Psalms, as evident from Psalms 9/10, 27, 44, and 89."[4] Because the approach here is to treat the psalm as a unity,

1. Gunkel went so far as to cite 40:1-12 as one of the twenty "complete thanksgiving songs preserved" in the Psalter (*Introduction to Psalms,* 199). Strangely, he does not cite 40:13-17 as an "individual complaint song," but given that he classifies Psalm 70, which parallels vv. 13-17, as such a song (p. 121), one can assume that he indeed classified 40:13-17 as such.

2. *Psalms: Part 2,* 55.

3. *Psalms 1–59,* 423-24.

4. *Psalms: Part 1,* 169. See also McCann ("The Book of Psalms," p. 842), who cites many linguistic connections between the two halves of the psalm; Weiser (*Psalms,* 334), who sees the first half as representing the "past . . . to which he now clings in the face of a new calamity"; and Brueggemann (*The Message of the Psalms,* 131), who wrings from the

the question of which text is earlier or whether one text borrowed from the other is irrelevant.

Because the thanksgiving section of the psalm actually has two movements, the psalm is understood as having three main sections:

Section 1 The Waiting (vv. 1-3)
One stanza (vv. 1-3)
Section 2 The New Song (vv. 4-11)
Three stanzas (vv. 4-5, 6-8, 9-11)
Section 3 The Renewed Prayer (vv. 12-17)
Three stanzas (vv. 12-13, 14-16, 17)

Rather than attempting to posit or reconstruct a hypothetical original life setting for this prayer,[5] a theological life setting will suffice. This is the song of one who has experienced divine deliverance from crisis in the past and now prays a renewed prayer in the midst of a renewed crisis.

For the leader. A Davidic psalm.

1 *I waited and waited for the LORD,*
he turned and heard my cry.
2 *He lifted me up from the desolate[6] pit,*
out of the wet clay.
He set my feet upon a rock,
making my steps sure.
3 *He put a new song into my mouth,*
a song of praise to our God.
Many will see and fear,
they will trust in the LORD.

4 *Happy is the one who places[7]*
one's trust in the LORD,

---

unexpected turn from praise to lament the lesson that "the move from disorientation to new orientation is not a single, straight line, irreversible and unambiguous. Life moves in and out."

5. Gunkel (*Introduction to Psalms,* 199-201) reconstructs a life setting and ritual for the entire genre; Gerstenberger (*Psalms: Part 1,* 173) less grandiosely places the "liturgy" in the context of an "early Jewish local congregation" where it was "destined to reconcile the supplicant with his God, to heal him and better his conditions, and to grant to him support and rehabilitation from the community."

6. Relating the *hapax legomenon šā'ôn* to the root *š'h* I ("to be desolate"; cf. Isa. 6:11).

7. LXX *to onoma* is reading *šēm:* "Happy is the one whose trust is in the name of the Lord."

and does not turn toward idols,[8]
and those who swerve after a lie.
5 *Many are your wonders — you,*
O LORD my God,[9] *have done them!*
And your plans regarding us,[10]
one cannot arrange them before you.
If I were to announce and speak them,
they would be too many to number.

6 *You do not delight in sacrifice and offering,*
you have opened for me my ears,[11]
you have not asked for burnt offering or sin offering.
7 *Then I said, "Now*[12] *I have come,*
in this scroll is recorded what happened to me."
8 *I delight to do that which is acceptable to you, my God;*
your teaching is deep within me.

9 *I have brought good news of righteousness,*
in the great congregation!
My lips, I have not withheld!
O LORD, you know it!
10 *I did not hide your righteousness in the midst of my heart,*
I have spoken of your truth and your deliverance,
I did not conceal your hesed,
and your faithfulness from the great congregation.
11 *You, O LORD, you have not withheld your mercy from me!*
Your hesed *and your faithfulness continually preserve me.*

8. LXX *(mataiotētas)* clearly understands the term as a generic for "false gods" (cf. LXX Ps. 30:7//MT 31:7[6]). Most translators and commentators relate the term to "arrogance" (cf. Aramaic *rahᵃḇā*), but it is dubious that this meaning is attested in Hebrew.

9. Syr apparently is reading *-ênû* ("our God"). This is a harmonization with the next phrase.

10. LXX omits "to us." But Syr's harmonization with this phrase suggests retaining it.

11. Heb. 10:5 quotes this verse and has *sōma de katērtisō,* perhaps indicating a variant tradition in LXX, but all extant LXX mss have *ōtia de katērtisō,* so this is unlikely. The metaphor here is a bit stilted, thus LXX renders the odd Hebrew word "dug" *(kārâ)* with *katartizō* ("to mend"), perhaps meaning that LXX was reading *kālal.* But MT is retained, since the array of terms that *katartizō* translates is too wide to provide any control. Likely LXX did not know how to handle the Hebrew idiom

12. Often in Biblical Hebrew, *hinnēh* plus a verb (esp. of motion) indicates a change in perspective or character, hence *hinnēh* is rendered here as *now* rather than "behold," which is certainly a misleading translation.

12 *But crises surround me,*
they are without number!
My sins have caught up with me,
and I cannot see.
They number more than the hairs of my head,
and my heart has abandoned me.
13 [13]*Be pleased, O Lord, to deliver me!*
O Lord, make haste to help me!

14 *May they be altogether ashamed and embarrassed —*
those who seek to carry away my life!
May they be turned back and humiliated —
those who delight in my distress!
15 *May they be astonished*[14] *on account*[15] *of their shame —*
those who say, "Aha, aha!"
16 *May they exult and rejoice in you*[16] *—*
all those who seek you!
May they continually say, "Great is the Lord!" —
those who love your salvation!

17 *But I am poor and needy,*
may my Lord take thought for me!
You are my help and my deliverer,
O my God, do not be slow!

1-3 In the opening section of the psalm, as is typical in songs of thanksgiving, the psalmist recalls a time of crisis and the divine help that delivered the psalmist from the crisis (cf. 30:2-3, 6-12). It should not be missed here that the audience to which the psalmist addresses his words is other humans. This is not yet speech to God (prayer), but speech about God (testimony). This, too, is typical of the song of thanksgiving.[17]

Looking back on such a time, the psalmist recalls, *I waited and waited*

13. Vv. 13-17, by and large, are repeated as Ps. 70, as part of the so-called Elohistic Psalter. There are some textual differences, but no attempt should be made to harmonize the two texts. Although the two clearly have some sort of genetic relationship, they now stand as independent poems.

14. LXX *komisasthōsan* may have been reading a *hiphil* form of *yāšaḇ* (70:3 has *yāšûḇû* ["may they flee"]), meaning "may they receive," although this is unlikely since *komizein* never translates *yāšaḇ* in LXX.

15. LXX *parachrēma* suggests either *piṯʾōm* or *l*^{e}*peṯaʿ*, but MT is retained.

16. LXX suggests adding *YHWH.*

17. Note the consistent use of the 3rd person verbs in vv. 1-3. Because of this pattern,

for the LORD. Many versions translate the emphatic phrase with which the psalm opens, *qawwōh qiwwîṯî,* as "I waited patiently." But *qāwâ* denotes an expectant longing for God to act, rather than a patient endurance. This is indicated clearly in 130:5-6: "I wait expectantly. My inmost being (waits expectantly) for the LORD, more than those watching for the morning, those watching for the morning." The emphatic repetition of *qāwâ* only makes the translation "patiently" more inappropriate. The psalmist is recalling a desperate, impatient waiting for the Lord to deliver him from an intolerable situation. Thus, *I waited and waited.*

This abrupt opening announcement of the song immediately transitions into a more gentle melody. The psalmist reports, *he turned and heard my cry.* The verbs employed in this report, *turn (nāṭâ)* and *heard (šāma'),* are typical pleas found in prayers for help (cf. 27:9; 31:2; 4:1; 17:1). By using verbs typical of the petitions in prayers for help, the psalmist is connecting the dots for his listeners — he cried to the Lord in distress, the Lord heard the cry and delivered him, and now he has come to praise God in grateful response.

The poet's report of deliverance is rounded out and expanded through the use of two metaphors. The first metaphor draws upon vocabulary and imagery for the place of the dead. The *bôr šā'ôn (desolate pit)* and *ṭîṭ hayyāwēn (wet clay)* both refer poetically to the place of the dead, a place of separation from God (cf. 30:3; 69:2, etc.). The image, which was characteristic not only within Israel but also among Israel's neighbors, evokes the image of a body being buried. That is, it is an image for one who was near to death (near to being buried) but was saved. The counterpart of this image is the image of having one's feet set *upon a rock, making my steps secure.* Both the image of being set upon a rock or some other firm foundation (26:12; 27:5; 31:8, etc.) and the image of not stumbling/have sure steps (121:3; 30:6) are stock images for security, deliverance, and safety. These images also naturally evoke the frequent metaphor of God as the psalmists' rock of refuge (18:2; 31:3, etc.). Thus, the metaphor powerfully communicates the experience of delivery from a near death experience, while also offering compelling and thankful testimony that the rescue came from God.

The singer closes the opening stanza of the song with a statement of confidence. The psalmist is confident that many of the faithful will respond to the thankful testimony in faith. They will *see, fear,* and put their *trust in the LORD.* The statement of confidence is a reminder that the purpose of thanksgiving and praise is testimony. Praise and thanks are not primarily for God, but for the neighbor. A slightly mixed metaphor may confuse the reader. Given the testimony, one expects "many will hear" in place of the poem's *many will see.*

---

the opening phrase is translated *I waited and waited for the LORD,* rather than "O LORD, I waited intently," even though *YHWH* does not have a preposition before it.

But Hebrew *they will see (yir'û)* plays poetically off of *they will fear (yîrā'û).* In addition, it calls attention not only to the psalmist's song, but to the psalmist's entire life as testimony to God's salvific intervention.

4-5 It is customary in a song of thanksgiving for the singer to offer a word of "renewed" praise of God (cf. 30:4-5). The praise character of these sections is often so generic that if one were to excise these sections from the thanksgiving psalms in which they occur and treat them as separate poems, they would likely be characterized as hymns. Verses 4-5 are such a renewed section of praise. This praise picks up where the previous stanza left off by declaring the benefit of placing one's *trust in the LORD* rather than in other objects of faith. Whereas in v. 3, *trust* occurs in a verbal form *(yiḇṭᵉḥô),* here a nominal form occurs *(miḇṭaḥô).* Thus, trust is portrayed both as an action that one may take or not take (v. 3c) and as an attribute with which one does or does not do something. In both cases, the relational aspect of trust is emphasized. To trust, or to place one's trust, is to commit one's self relationally to another. The psalm, consistent with the witness of the entire Psalter, bears witness that the only worthy object of trust is *the LORD.* To place one's trust or faith in any other object is to serve *a lie (kāzāḇ).* NRSV and NIV both translate this term as "false gods" (cf. 4:2). Indeed, "false god" is the main sense of *kāzāḇ* here, as the parallel term *rᵉhāḇîm*[18] (lit., "Rahabs") indicates. But the underlying theological polemic should not be missed. The reason the false gods are false is that they are lies. They have not the fidelity that is necessary to sustain a trust relationship. Thus, the one taking the happy path in life not only cleaves to the Lord, but also does not *turn* or *swerve (pānâ, śûṭ)* toward other objects of faith (compare this with the frequent Deuteronomistic standard that the faithful leader should follow in David's footsteps, turning neither to the right or to the left; e.g. 2 Kgs. 22:2).

An integral part of praise is to speak not only *about* God, but *to* God (see below in "Reflections"). The psalmist now turns in praise to the Lord: *Many are your wonders.* The term *wonders (niplᵉ'ōṯêḵā)* is a standard praise term that encompasses all of God's faithful and salvific deeds, from the rescue of an individual (31:21), to the founding election of Israel and rescue at the Red Sea (77:12-20), to the gift of the law (78:4-5), to God's providential protection and guidance of the nation throughout its history (78:11, 31), to the stilling of storms and feeding of the hungry (107:8, 15, 21, 24, 31), to creation itself (96:5; 136:4-5). By employing the term here, the psalmist casts her own rescue at God's hands as part of the ongoing salvation history of God's faithful intervention. At the same time, she also characterizes her rescue as consistent

18. The plural, nominal form of *rahaḇ* ("arrogance") occurs only here. Normally, the singular refers to the mythological Rahab (cf. 87:4; 89:10), which is often a symbol for Egypt (Isa. 30:7).

with God's basic character as a faithful Lord. Throughout the Psalter, not only is the Lord cast as one who does wonders, the Lord is cast as the only one who does wonders (72:18, etc.). This testimony is consistent with the previous verse, which declared the Lord as the only fitting object of trust. The psalmist goes on to praise God for *your plans (maḥšᵉḇōṯêḵā) regarding us,* which as Clifford notes, is to be understood as God's "intentions."[19] The sense here is similar to Jeremiah's well-known promise, "I know the plans *(hammaḥᵃšāḇōṯ)* that I am planning for you . . . plans for peace and not for harm" (29:11; my translation). The psalmist confesses that the future that God intends for the people is to be so full of wondrous, redemptive actions that *they would be too many to number.* And precisely because they cannot all be spoken or numbered, there is even more urgency to the telling of the psalmist's own particular experience of God's wondrous love. The point is not because there are so many that one need not recount them, but rather this one particular experience of God's redemption needs to be told as an example of the numberless other wondrous deeds of the Lord.

6-8 In the third stanza, the psalmist turns his eye to the present moment, to the praise that he has come to offer in response to God's redemption. It is customary in prayers for help that the psalmist will promise to praise God once God has delivered the psalmist from the crisis (cf. 13:6). Even though these verses do not mention such an earlier promise explicitly, the verses implicitly acknowledge that the psalmist considered the reporting-out-in-praise of his experience of delivery as a sacred obligation to which he was bound.

The psalmist begins with a negative, describing what God does not require of him in terms of fulfilling the promise to praise: *You do not delight in sacrifice and offering. . . . You have not asked for burnt offering or sin offering.* The psalmist uses four different terms for various sacrifices that the Lord has not required. *Zeḇaḥ* most likely refers to food that is eaten in a communal meal, the purpose of which is to rehabilitate a sufferer back into the community by means of sharing food together (cf. Lev. 7:11-18; 3:1-17). *Minḥâ* likely refers to a "gift" or "loyalty" offering that is symbolically given to the one whom the worshipper acknowledges as his lord (cf. Judg. 3:15-18, where Ehud delivers the *minḥâ* to Eglon, thus signaling political loyalty). *'Ōlâ* refers to the highest form of offering, the whole *burnt offering* in which an entire animal is consumed by fire either as a sacrifice to atone for some personal or national sin (Lev. 16:23-24); it also serves to honor God in the highest form possible. *Hᵃṭā'â,* which means, lit., "sin," refers to a sacrifice to make up for a sin either moral or ritual, either known or unknown, either intentional or unintentional (Lev. 4:1–6:30). These four terms, taken together, refer to the liturgical pattern that when a worshipper came to the sanctuary to offer thanksgiving, such

19. *Psalms 1–72,* p. 205.

an act normally included a report of the deliverance, renewed praise of the Lord, and a sacrifice of some sort (the type of sacrifice differing based on the circumstances of the worshipper). The point here is that no sacrifice can meet the threshold of what God truly desires from us. For what God does desire, see vv. 9-11, or compare Pss. 50:10-23 and 51:16-17.

The interpretation of v. 7 is a crux. There are three interrelated issues. First, what is the *scroll* that is referred to? Second, given that Biblical Hebrew contained no punctuation markers, where should we understand the quotation that is initiated by the words, *I said,* to end? Third, how should v. 7 be translated? Many translations offer something such as the NRSV has:

> Then I said, "Here I am;
>   in the scroll of the book it is written of me.
> I delight to do your will, O my God;
>   your law is within my heart." (vv. 7-8)

Patrick Miller neatly sums up the interpretive options: "*Scroll of the book* is interpreted variously. If the song is by a king, this could refer to the 'law of the king' in Deut 17.14-20. More likely, it is the heavenly record of human deeds of good or ill [cf. Exod. 32:32; Ps. 69:28; 139:16], though some have assumed it referred to the written record of this song of thanksgiving, offered in place of a sacrifice."[20] The interpretation that is followed here is Miller's third option. The reasons for this view are offered more fully in a longer investigation of all such quotations in the Psalter.[21] For here, it must suffice to point out that shorter quotations are preferred, especially since other common markers of the end of the quotation are missing in this context. One may further note that if the quotation were to extend through v. 8 or further, then the quotation would be shifted from direct discourse *(Now I have come)* to indirect discourse ("it is written about me that I delight . . .") — such a shift destroys the logic of a quotation and would be singular in the Psalter. The Hebrew phrase *bimᵉgillaṯ sēp̄er kaṯûḇ ʿālāy* — "in the roll of the writing it is written of me" — allows for several interpretations, but in the context of having just announced that God does not desire sacrifice, one expects the psalmist to offer something in place of the missing sacrifice. The notion of a scroll recounting

20. "Annotated Notes to the Psalms," in *The HarperCollins Study Bible: Revised Edition,* ed. Wayne Meeks (San Francisco: HarperSanFrancisco, 2006), p. 766. Craigie is the example of one who takes the first route of interpretation (*Psalms 1–50,* 315). One further comment is necessary. If one is convinced that the best understanding of the scroll here is the idea of a book in heaven, based on the parallels cited it is better to understand that the book records the events of one's life or the characteristics of one's heart, rather than an account of one's deeds.

21. Jacobson, *Many Are Saying;* see esp. 19-26 and 66-67.

the psalmist's praise fits this expectation the best. Furthermore, examples of worshippers presenting written accounts of their narratives in place of sacrifices is attested in both the ancient Near East and Asia Minor.[22] Thus, the final translation as rendered above describes the worshippers' arrival to present a scroll, in which is detailed the narrative of the Lord's rescue of the person.

Earlier, the psalmist had claimed that God does not *delight (ḥāp̄aṣ) in sacrifice, offering,* whole *burnt offering,* or *sin offering.* In an elegant play on words, the psalmist now says, *I delight (ḥāp̄aṣ) to do that which is acceptable to you.* The term *rāṣōn* ("acceptable") normally refers to sacrifices in which the actions of the worshipper meet or exceed God's minimum threshold, and thus are pleasing to and accepted by God. But the point is that the Lord does not delight in such actions, and moreover the psalmist delights in doing what God truly does find *acceptable.* And what God delights in is a life that conforms itself to God's *teaching (tôrâ;* see comment on Ps. 1:2) — a life so conformed to God's teaching that the *torah* is alive *deep within (bᵉṯôḵ mēʿāy)* a person.

9-11 In some ways, Psalm 40 is like a two-movement symphony, with each movement having its own texture, mood, and voice. If so, vv. 9-11 present the culmination of the first movement of the symphony, in which the voice is praise, the mood is joy, and the texture is firm. In vv. 9-11, the psalmist reports with joy that she has kept the obligation to offer a praise witness to what God had done. As above, the actions of the Lord are reported using technical theological terminology. The psalmist characterizes her praise as *good news (bśr)* of God's *righteousness (ṣedeq), your righteousness (ṣedeq), your* hesed, *your faithfulness (ʾemeṯ),* and *your mercy (reḥem).* Taken together, these words describe the very character of the faithful Lord whom Israel had encountered over and over again throughout her history. In choosing such words, the psalmist again aligns her experience of God with the basic "gospel" (the English rendering of Hebrew *bśr* and Greek *euangelion)* of the Old Testament: the Lord's great deeds of salvation for the nation, such as the redemption from exile (cf. Isa. 40:9; 41:27; 52:7).

But there is one more striking aspect to the psalmist's praise. Other psalmists characterize praise of the Lord as "fitting" (33:1; 147:1). This psalmist casts praise as that which the neighbor cannot live without. She claims that to withhold praise of the Lord *in the great congregation* (v. 9) is to conceal knowledge of God's very character *from the great congregation* (v. 10). To withhold praise does not damage God, but it does damage God's mission, in the sense that to withhold praise is to withhold saving knowledge from the neighbor who needs it. It is to withhold God's *righteousness, faithfulness, mercy,* and *hesed* from the neighbor.

12-13 Beginning with v. 12, a second movement of the psalm begins. If

22. See, e.g., Kraus, *Psalms 1–59,* 426.

the first movement was joyful, solid praise, this movement might be characterized as frightened, tentative petition. As a rhetorical whole, the psalm can be said to move from praise to petition. The psalmist began by recalling an old crisis and recounting how the Lord *set my feet upon a rock.* Then the psalmist renewed his by praise by recounting how he kept the obligation to return praise to the Lord. Now, entering a new time in which *crises surround me,* the psalmist renews both complaint and petition. In terms of the complaint, as Goldingay notes, the "verbs suggest the activity of a powerful army pursuing, catching up, and then surrounding, in such a way that the one attacked cannot see."[23] But rather than an army, the psalmist is pursued by his own *sins (ʿᵃwōnōṯay).* In place of the usual complaint that God has abandoned the psalmist (cf. 22:1; 71:11), he says *my heart has abandoned me.* The heart, of course, is the center of the will in the Hebrew imagination, not the center of emotions. So the confession here is that the psalmist has lost the ability to will that which is acceptable to God. And in place of the frequent question about whether God can or does see (cf. 10:11), and in a shocking reversal of the psalmist's earlier confidence that *many will see and fear* (v. 3), the psalmist now acknowledges that *I cannot see.* To see, in this and other psalms, is to trust God. So the sum of this rhetoric is a surprising poetic reversal. The psalmist announces that he has been betrayed by his own character. His character has failed him in a threefold way — he has sinned in act (by failing to do that which is acceptable), will (by failing to desire that which is acceptable), and faith (by failing to trust as is acceptable).

This new and desperate situation leads the psalmist to a new petition: *Be pleased, O LORD, to deliver me!* The term *be pleased (rāṣah)* makes a striking connection with something the psalmist said earlier. In v. 8 the psalmist had said, *I delight to do that which is acceptable (rāṣôn) to you, my God.* The two terms, *rāṣah* and *rāṣôn,* are related. As noted above, the term often refers to sacrifices in which the actions of the worshipper meet or exceed God's minimum threshold and thus are pleasing to and accepted by God. The rhetorical force here is that what is most pleasing to God — namely, the deliverance of God's beloved — can only come from God. The urgency of the psalmist's new crisis is underscored in the cry *make haste to help me!*

14-16 The psalmist's crisis, as is frequently the case in prayers for help, has a communal dimension as well as a personal and theological dimension. Earlier, the psalmist had described how when she had experienced God's help, she had not withheld the *good news* of that help *from the great congregation.* But in the new crisis, she now describes her renewed isolation from the community. This description comes in the form of the so-called negative

23. *Psalms 1–41,* p. 576. Although note that the progression is actually reversed: the psalmist is *surrounded* first, then *caught.*

wish that those in the community who oppress her or who have turned on her may *be altogether ashamed and embarrassed.* Although Craigie notes that the congregation might refer to the entire nation, it is more fitting to imagine a particular community, an actual group in which the now suffering psalmist is experiencing the opposite of hospitality. Earlier, the psalmist had noted that God does not *delight (ḥāp̱ēṣ) in sacrifice,* and that the psalmist herself *delights (ḥāp̱ēṣ)* in doing that which is *acceptable* to God. Now, the psalmist complains about those who *delight (ḥāp̱ēṣ)* in her *distress.* Perhaps "the enemies" here are not those who actively will evil or commit crimes against their neighbors, but rather simply those who enjoy seeing others brought down. The German term *Schadenfreude* — taking joy in another's suffering — captures this sense. The emptiness of this emotion is depicted by the fact that there is no linguistic content to the enemies' gloating: *Those who say, 'Aha, aha!'"* Rather, all they can muster is a nonrational exclamation of joy at another's sorrow.

The psalmist prays, in contrast, that God would in turn bring these people down. The verbs — *be ashamed, be embarrassed, be turned back and humiliated* — speak of the restoration of a proper social order — a societal order in which the foundations of good order and care of the suffering neighbor are reestablished by God's intervention; a societal order in which those who suffer may find a community of fellow sufferers who also seek after God. The verbs in v. 16 — *exult in, rejoice in, seek* — describe the righteous in the Psalter, those who are dependent on God. Such a community, the psalmist reminds both God and the reader of this psalm, always delights when they can praise God for the *salvation* (v. 16) of one who has cried to the Lord for help.

17 As the psalmist acknowledges in v. 17, the longed-for help is at this point merely a hope, not a reality. This psalm ends with hope and petition, which is a knife that cuts both ways. Negatively, the psalm ends with the sufferer still suffering — *But I am poor and needy.* Positively, the psalm ends with the hoping one still hoping — *You are my help and deliverer, O my God, do not be slow!*

Reflections

1. Praise as Relational Talk

One of the questions that is often asked concerning praise is "Why does God need our praise?" The question is both right and wrong. First, it is right because God does need our praise, but not in the way in which this question usually presumes. As noted above, God needs our praise for the sake of God's mission. Praise is, first and foremost, testimony to others — to the world, to the neighbor, to the great congregation — about what God has done. Therefore, praise is the cup of cold water that the faithful person has no right to withhold from a neighbor who is thirsty for God. The point here is that God does not need our praise for God's self, but for God's mission. Praise spoken for the benefit of the neighbor is usually in the third person: *He lifted me up; He set my feet upon a rock; He put a new song into my mouth.* Second, the question is wrong because it is not God who needs our praise, but we who need to praise God. Praise spoken out of our own need to praise is usually in the second person: *You, O LORD, you have not withheld your mercy from me!* Many modern people chafe under the burdens of this sort of praise, because they assume such praise must exist in order to massage God's ego. One thinks here of the parody of this view of praise in the famous scene from Monty Python's *The Meaning of Life,* in which the liturgist leads a litany:

> Liturgist: "Let us praise God. O Lord!"
> Congregation: "O Lord!"
> Liturgist: "O you are so big."
> Congregation: "O you are so big."
> Liturgist: "So absolutely huge."
> Congregation: "So absolutely huge."
> Liturgist: "Gosh, we're all really impressed down here. . . ."

And so on. And such parodies are welcome because they help to undermine the mistaken notion that the purpose of praise is to feed God's supposedly hungry ego. But the second person form of praise, *You, O LORD,* is important because it offers a grammar for the believer-Lord relationship. In praise, the believer acknowledges to the Lord that we are not the lords of our own lives, that the good things we have are not solely or even primarily the results of our own strength or effort, and that we are in need of guidance, mercy, grace, and love that can only come from God. In this sense, praise translates the first commandment, "You shall have no other gods," into the grammar of relational speech.

2. From Praise to Petition

Within psalms' scholarship, it is usually noted that many psalms and indeed the Psalter as a whole move from prayer to praise. Westermann wrote, "The first half of the Psalter is comprised predominantly of Psalms of lament, the second predominantly of Psalms of praise."[24] Similarly, Brueggemann speaks of an "authoritative shape and structure of torah faith," a shape that moves in a "staggering drama . . . from innocent obedience to unencumbered doxology." But as Brueggemann also notes, this movement takes place in fits and starts, "by way of the suffering voiced in the complaints and the hope sounded in the

24. "The Formation of the Psalter," in *Praise and Lament in the Psalms,* 257.

hymns."[25] In this context, it should be noted that Psalm 40 bears witness to the fact that the life of faith is not an unbroken, linear trajectory from petition to praise. It is not a pious, uninterrupted climbing of Jacob's ladder. The life of faith does move from petition to praise, but Psalm 40 reminds us that it also moves from praise to petition. Those who praise God with feet set on secure rocks today may cry to the Lord from the watery depths tomorrow. And, indeed, the Psalter knows that every man and woman who walks the earth today will one day cry out to the Lord for rescue from the grave. The closing words of this poem are a fitting reminder that this movement, too, is part of the life of faith: *I am poor and needy, may my LORD take thought for me!*

ROLF A. JACOBSON

25. "Bounded by Obedience and Praise," in *The Psalms and the Life of Faith,* 190, 210-11.

Psalm 41: A Plea for Communion

Psalm 41 is the final psalm of the first book of the Psalter. Two aspects of the psalm call for comment in this regard. The first is its opening word *'ašrê,* translated here as *happy* (other options include "blessed" and "good fortune"). The editorial choice to place a psalm that begins with this term as the last psalm in Book One creates a bookend effect, since Psalm 1 begins with the same term. At the very least, this bookend effect serves to signal that Psalms 1–41 are a coherent collection. Risking slightly more, an interpreter can argue that the fact that the first and last psalms of Book One begin with this term signals that the entirety of Book One is to be prayed and studied as a means to living the *happy* (or blessed, or fortunate) life (see Introduction, "The Canonical Shape of the Psalter"). The second feature of this psalm that deserves comment is the closing verse of doxology: *Blessed be the LORD God of Israel, from everlasting to everlasting. Amen and amen.* Each of the five books of the Psalter ends with such a doxology (cf. 72:18-19; 89:52; 106:48; 150:6). With the exception of Psalm 150, these doxological phrases are generally not considered by scholars to be parts of the psalms that they conclude, but are considered editorial additions to these psalms (but see below). These doxologies signal that, as a whole, the Psalter is a book of praise — hence its Hebrew name *tᵉhillîm (Praises).* Thus, Book One of the Psalter, and the Psalter as a whole, is both a book of instruction in the godly way of life as well as a worship book, a book of praise.

As an individual poem, the classification of Psalm 41 is debated (as is so often the case).[1] Some see it as a song of thanks, others as a prayer for help.[2] The basic issue is how one performs the psalm, or how one imagines the psalm to have been performed/prayed in antiquity. McCann summarizes the issue: "What is unclear . . . is whether the complaint [in vv. 5-9] describes the psalmist's current situation or whether the psalmist is rehearsing what he or she had said during a past situation of distress."[3] The text may be interpreted as an individual song of thanksgiving, in which case the psalmist is understood as reporting a past situation of distress. Or, the psalm may be understood as a prayer for help, in which case the psalmist is viewed as reporting a current crisis. Or, similar to Psalm 40, the psalmist may be drawing on an existing song of thanks (cf. 40:1-11) in order to offer a renewed prayer for help (cf. 40:12-17). The entire matter is further complicated by the strong possibility that Psalm 41 is a composite poem, in which both vv. 1-3 and 13 were added by some later

1. See, e.g., Craigie, *Psalms 1–41,* p. 319; McCann, "The Book of Psalms," pp. 846-47.

2. For the former option, see McCann or Mays; for the latter option, see Gerstenberger, Kraus, or Craigie.

3. "The Book of Psalms," p. 846.

hand to an existing poem.[4] When one considers the canonical shape of the text, these (possible) additions function in the same way that praise usually functions in a song of thanksgiving — as both praise to God (v. 13) and as testimony to the community (vv. 1-3). As Goldingay states, "its didactic tone is merely an enhanced form of something implicit in the nature of testimony itself with its concern for the congregation to learn from a testimony."[5] The approach taken here is that the psalm is to be read as a unity, in spite of the likelihood that it developed over time. In that regard, when the commentary below refers to "the psalmist" it is referring to an implied voice of an implied poet. Similarly, the approach here is that the poem is most promisingly understood as a song of thanksgiving. It should be noted, however, that this does not dismiss the legitimacy of the readings offered by those who take a different approach.

The structure of the psalm is:

St. 1 Beatitude concerning those who are considerate (vv. 1-3)
St. 2 The recollection of a past prayer for help (vv. 4-10)
St. 3 Concluding praise (vv. 11-13)

For the leader. A Davidic psalm.

1 *Happy are they*[6] *who consider the helpless;*[7]
in the day of trouble, the LORD *will rescue them.*
2 *The* LORD *will keep them and preserve them,*
they shall be called happy[8] *in the land,*
you will not give[9] *them over to the desire*[10] *of their enemies.*
3 *The* LORD *will support them on the sickbed;*
you have transformed[11] *the entirety of their bed, in the midst of their disease.*

4. See Hossfeld and Zenger, *Psalms 1–50,* pp. 257-60.

5. *Psalms 1–41,* p. 581; Goldingay also cites Weiser, with approval.

6. To avoid the 3ms pronoun, which is constant in the psalm, the 3cp "they" and "their" is used. This runs against the general practice in this commentary, which is to use "the one," but it is too clunky in Ps. 41.

7. LXX *kai penēta* suggests *w^{e}ʾānî* or *w^{e}ʾeḇyôn* ("and needy" or "and poor"), but this is rejected as expansionistic and harmonizing (cf. 40:17; 72:13, etc.).

8. Reading a pual with the Kethib, rather than reading an active form with Qere, LXX, and others.

9. Reading 2ms with MT and Targ rather than emending to read with LXX's 3ms *(paradōē).* But the psalm, as is common in Hebrew poetry, often alternates its parallel phrase between third and second person.

10. LXX has *eis cheiras,* suggesting *b^{e}yaḏ* ("into the hand"). But MT is retained, with support of Targ, with the meaning *desire.*

11. Some LXX versions read 3ms, but 2ms is again retained.

4 *I, I said, "O LORD, be gracious to me;*
heal my life, for I have sinned against you."
5 *My enemies talk of trouble for me,*
"When will he die and his name perish?"
6 *And if they*[12] *come to see me, they speak falsehood,*
their hearts collect trouble within, they go outside and speak it.
7 *United against me, those who hate me murmur together,*
they think troubled thoughts about me:
8 *"A deadly disease*[13] *has been poured out on him;*
once he sleeps, he will not rise again."
9 *Even the friend of my good health, whom I trusted,*
who ate my bread, has turned his back on me.[14]
10 *But you, O LORD, be gracious to me;*
raise me up that I might repay them.

11 *In this I will know that you delight in me,*
that my enemy does not shout triumphantly over me.
12 *As for me, in my integrity you support me;*
you establish me in your presence forever.
13 *Blessed be the LORD God of Israel,*
from everlasting to everlasting.
Amen and amen.

1-3 As Clifford has seen, "The opening declaration is actually the *conclusion* derived from the profound experiences described in the psalm."[15] The opening verses testify that the blessed, or fortunate, or *happy* life is the one in which the prosperous person gives thought to those in need. This is testimony that can only be made after the fact of a crisis, because the content of the testimony is so counterintuitive. Similar in nature to Jesus' countercultural beatitudes in Matthew 5, the witness here is to a blessing or happiness that

12. Consistent with the translation strategy for this psalm, the 3ms pronoun for the enemy is rendered by the 3cp "they."

13. Understanding *dbr* to relate to *deḇer* ("plague") rather than *dāḇār* ("word" or "thing"), although it must be granted that the parallel in Ps. 101:3 argues against this. But note that the normally rigidly consistent LXX renders *pragma* ("deed") in 101:3 but *logon* here, suggesting at least that the phrase was not understood as a perfect parallel.

14. Goldingay argues that *ʿāqēḇ* must mean "cheater" here rather than "heel." The *hiphil* of *gdl*, more literally "has become great," could be understood as "he has become great against me as a cheater," thus "has become my great betrayer." The normal "he has lifted against me the heel," however, makes better sense and seems to be a metaphor for denial rather than betrayal. The closest metaphor in English is to turn one's back on a friend.

15. *Psalms 1–72*, p. 210.

is not available to the eyes of the world. The term *śāḵal* refers to a practical wisdom or the prosperity or knowledge that is gained from observing daily life (cf. Isa. 44:18; Jer. 10:21; Ps. 94:8; 119:99; Prov. 19:14). As such, *the helpless* (which is a better translation than "poor," since in the context of the psalm the term seems to encompass more than economic distress) are not usually studied for the positive lessons one can gain from them. The term also has overtones of "being successful" or "prosperous" (cf. Josh. 1:8; Isa. 52:13, etc.). But as the LXX translation *syniōn* ("to understand") indicates, in this context the term connotes the act of considering, or even being considerate toward. Thus, there is a double entendre at work in the poetry; the world conceives of good fortune as the practical consideration and exploitation of material reality. God's view of good fortune consists of those who take consideration of the helpless.

The psalm makes promises to those who follow this countercultural path of blessing. Like Psalm 121, it promises that *the LORD will keep them and preserve them.* Like Psalm 1, which promises that the righteous will prosper in everything but warns that the wicked cannot endure the judgment (meaning any time of crisis), this psalm promises rescue *in the day of trouble.* Like Psalms 16 and 27, which promise blessings "in the land," this psalm promises happiness *in the land* — which means that the considerate will find not only a place, but a community (which is a major theme of this psalm). Like Psalms 18 and 20, which show confidence in the Lord's sustaining support, this psalm promises healing and support. As is the case with all of the promissory and benedictory sections of the psalms, these promises do not betray a naïve faith on the psalmist's part that God's elect are immune from the realities of life in a fallen world. Rather, the promises indicate something about the basic character of God and thus bear witness to something about the characteristic way that the Lord acts. As such, these promises teach the faithful to perceive in each individual experience of God's saving grace an inbreaking of the eschatological victory, a foretaste of the feast to come.

4-10 In the middle section of the poem, the psalmist recollects an older time of crisis in which she prayed for rescue. These verses are marked off as a section by the identical petitions of vv. 4a and 10a: *O LORD, be gracious to me (YHWH ḥonnēnî).* The first time this petition occurs, the psalmist emphasizes herself — *I, I said (ʾᵃnî ʾāmartî)* — and thus the human aspect of the divine-human relationship. The second time, the psalmist emphasizes the Lord — *But you, O LORD (wᵉʾattâ YHWH)* — and thus the divine aspect of the relationship. The cry for help, *be gracious to me,* is among the most basic pleas in the Psalter (cf. 4:1; 6:2; 31:9; 51:1; 56:1; 57:1; 86:3; 119:29, 58). The basic sense of the root *ḥānan* is "to be gracious/merciful." Its imperative form here and elsewhere in the Psalter brings to mind Israel's creedal declaration that the Lord is "a God merciful and gracious" (*raḥûm wᵉḥannûn;* Exod. 34:6; cf. Num.

14:18; Neh. 9:17; Pss. 86:15; 145:8; Joel 2:13; Jonah 4:2; Nah. 1:3). As such, the petition is an appeal to the basic character of God — because graciousness is basic to who God is and how God works in the world, the psalmist is bold enough to ask for a manifestation of grace. What the psalmist asks for is, first of all, healing: *Heal my life, for I have sinned against you.* As a secondary benefit of the healing, the psalmist expects to receive honor from the Lord in a community in the midst of which she is experiencing great shame. Something must be said both about the connection the psalm makes between sin and illness, as well as the matter of the enemies and the experience of shame.

First, the relationship between sin and illness is a very complicated matter. All that can be said of the sufferer of Psalm 41 is that he assumes that his suffering is the result of his own actions. Moreover, he turns to God for help with the full expectation that God can and will offer aid. For more on this matter, see the Reflections below.

The second matter that deserves comment is that of the enemies, and of the public shame that the psalmist is experiencing in their midst. In many and various ways, the psalmist asserts that the suffering he is experiencing is exacerbated by those around him. When the text of the psalm is examined closely, it seems as if the sin of the enemies is a sin of omission rather than of commission. It seems that rather than acting as active agents of evil, the enemies have simply turned their backs on the psalmist by giving up hope for his recovery and by expecting his demise. They *talk of trouble for me (yōʾmᵉrû raʿ lî)* and *they think troubled thoughts about me (yaḥšᵉḇû rāʿâ lî),* meaning not necessarily that they plot evil against the psalmist, as many commentators assume, but rather simply that they assume the worst. As McCann has noted, "The enemies clearly do not show any awareness of the beatitude of v. 1a."[16] The content of what they say bears this interpretation out. They say, *"When will he die and his name perish?"* They expect him to die. The perishing one's name is a metaphor that refers to a man dying without a son who can carry on his name. Matters of property and inheritance may be at stake, so those who await his death may be experiencing a certain amount of *Schadenfreude* as they anticipate the material wealth that they may gain if the psalmist dies. They also say, *"A deadly disease has been poured out on him; once he sleeps, he will not arise."* Again, there does not seem to be active malice among the enemies, but a comfortable acceptance of the psalmist's fate. Most painful of all, for the psalmist, is the fact *the friend of my good health* (meaning the person who was happy to stand by me when I was healthy) *has turned his back on me* (see translation notes above for this rendering). The psalmist employs a pun here that works on two levels. The *friend of good health* is the *ʾîš šêlômî,* lit., "man of my health." It means both "close friend" and "friend while I was

16. "The Book of Psalms," p. 847.

healthy." Thus the first level of the pun is that the supposed good friend, *who ate my bread (laḥmî),* was only faithful when the psalmist did not truly need anything from a friend. The second level of the pun can be seen in v. 10b, where the psalmist pleads, *Raise me up that I might repay them.* The term *repay them* is *ʾašallᵉmâ lāhem,* which plays off of both *my bread* and "man of my health." At one level, the psalmist is asking quite literally for a restoration to health so that the enemies might get what they deserve, which, in terms of not receiving the psalmist's inheritance, would be nothing. At another level, the psalmist is hinting that in her own return to health, she would be the "good friend" to them that they have not proven to be for her.

11-13 The poem's final stanza functions similarly to the closing sections of other songs of thanksgiving (cf. 31:21-24). In such sections, having rehearsed the time of crisis, the psalmist offers a concluding word of praise for the deliverance that she has received from the Lord. The interpretation followed here is that the verbs in vv. 11-12 reflect a situation in which the crisis has passed and the psalmist has experienced healing. The psalmist has interpreted this healing (Hebrew *bᵉzōʾṯ* is taken to refer to the healing[17]) as a sign that *you delight in me (ḥāp̄aṣtā bî).* As elsewhere in the Psalter, the *ḥāp̄aṣ (delight)* of the Lord is manifested in the act of delivering the needy (cf. 18:19; 22:8; 37:23, etc.). Similarly, that the Lord *supports (tāmaḵ)* and *establishes (nāṣaḇ)* the psalmist is a sign that the Lord has acted decisively on the psalmist's behalf. The reason that the Lord has acted so is the psalmist's *integrity (tummî).* This integrity should not be taken to refer to an abstract self-righteousness on the psalmist's part, but as an assertion of innocence regarding a particular accusation. The psalmist's health has been restored to integrity, and thus the assumption of some that the psalmist has deserved her suffering has been refuted by God's intervention. Similarly, the psalmist's assertion of integrity is a claim to depend fully on the Lord for help and to be in steadfast relationship with the Lord. This commitment is made explicit in the psalmist's trust that the Lord has not simply healed her, but has established her *in your presence forever.*

The closing doxology, marking the end of both the psalm and Book One of the Psalter, connects the dots between the enduring relationship that the psalmist claims with God *(in your presence forever)* and the universal reign of the Lord *(from everlasting to everlasting).* Thus the psalmist's praise both

17. Craigie interprets *this* as referring to an antecedent priestly oracle of salvation, and if the psalm is understood as a liturgy for help this is a realistic view. In fact, given that both types of poems culminate in trust and praise, there may not be as much difference between the two types of psalms as is often assumed. Rather, the main difference seems to be in the life setting that the interpreter assumes for the poem. It is no less likely that *this* refers to an actual experience of recovery as to the promise of one.

emerges from her enduring relationship with the Lord and also bears witness that the experience of deliverance that she has received from the Lord is characteristic of the Lord's eternal reign.

Reflections

1. The Connection between Illness and Sin

The psalms, both here and elsewhere, can make a connection between illness and sin (cf. Psalms 6, 38, and perhaps 51). When this connection is considered, people of faith are often either too quick to dismiss it or too quick to assume it. When people are too quick to assume it, like Jesus' disciples in John 9, they move from the observation that someone is ill to the assumption that the person must have sinned, and thus the person must deserve the suffering that they are experiencing. Even modern agnostics or atheists prove themselves capable of making this assumption when they assume that a person's poor health is automatically the result of poor lifestyle choices. In my own life, when I was diagnosed with cancer as a teenager, a well-meaning but misguided neighbor remarked to my mother that it was a shame she had not been feeding her family the proper, high-antioxidant diet, or her son would not have developed cancer. Besides being incredibly unhelpful, this comment was simply wrong — the type of cancer I had is not lifestyle dependent. On the other hand, when people are too quick to dismiss the connection between personal behavior and illness, they can ignore the pastoral needs of a person who may, in fact, be suffering due to their own choices. It is certainly a fact that one cannot generalize from the reality that a person is ill to a conclusion that the person brought it upon oneself. But it is also sometimes the case that some instances of suffering *are* brought about by poor choices that a person has knowingly engaged in. Many examples come to mind. If a pastoral caregiver is too quick to assure a person that they have done nothing wrong so as to be in the situation they are in, but the sufferer knows full well that their own choices have contributed to their crisis, the caregiver both loses credibility and also ignores the needs of the sufferer. The key witness of the psalm here is that the Lord is a refuge to which the suffering, the helpless, and the sick may turn in any event — whether the sufferer is completely innocent of wrongdoing, completely culpable, or (as in most cases) somewhere in between.

2. The Role of the Community in Suffering

The lion's share of the psalm (vv. 5-11) is devoted to the complaint that describes the faithless community in which the psalmist is drowning. Even the most individual suffering has a communal element. When a person loses a job, or marriage, or health, or family member, or wealth, or anything else, he or she usually experiences some degree of social shame. No matter how painful the personal suffering is, the communal shame always makes that suffering worse. In some cases, this shame can actually cause more acute suffering than the original crisis. A deep irony dwells at the heart of Psalm 41. On the one hand, it is a song that sings the lament of a person for whom the congregation has not acted as community. In this regard, the song lends painful voice to all those who have been unable to find even one neighbor who is willing to share their burdens with them, attend them on their sickbeds, or refuse to take joy in their sufferings. On the other hand, Psalm 41 is an instructional psalm that teaches the people of God that the way of happiness and blessedness is found precisely in the act of being considerate to the helpless. Psalm 41 is a poem intended to shape a particular community — one that knows how to welcome and stand with those who are suffering.

Rolf A. Jacobson

Book Two of the Psalter: Psalms 42–72

INTRODUCTION

Book Two of the Psalter consists of Psalms 42–72. Psalm 42 marks the beginning of what is commonly known as the Elohistic Psalter (Psalms 42–83), so named because of its somewhat distinct use of the divine name. In the Hebrew Psalter, the name most frequently used for God is the tetragrammaton YHWH (translated in English Bibles as "LORD"). But in Psalms 42–83, the name used most frequently is Elohim (*ʾelōhîm,* translated in English Bibles as "God").[1] The difference in the preferred name for God in these psalms suggests that the Elohistic Psalter was a discrete collection of psalms that was incorporated into the Hebrew Psalter.

One of the major questions in psalm study today concerns the origins and transmission of the Elohistic Psalter. Textual evidence indicates a sharing of material between the psalms included in the Elohistic Psalter and psalms found elsewhere in the Psalter. Examples include:

- Psalm 53, "a Maskil of David,"[2] is almost identical to Psalm 14. The only difference between them is that wherever the name YHWH (LORD) occurs in Psalm 14 (vss. 2, 4, 6, and 7), the reader finds Elohim in Psalm 53.

1. John Day maintains that in Pss. 1–41, YHWH occurs 278 times and Elohim occurs 15; in Pss. 42–83, YHWH occurs 43 times and Elohim 200; in Pss. 84–150, YHWH occurs 370 times and Elohim 13; *Psalms* (Old Testament Guides 14; Sheffield: Sheffield Academic, 1995), p. 113. According to James D. Nogalski, in Pss. 1–41 and 84–150, YHWH occurs 650 times, while Elohim occurs 120 [*sic?*]; in Pss. 42–83, YHWH appears 45 times and Elohim 245; "From Psalm to Psalms to Psalter," in *An Introduction to Wisdom Literature and the Psalms,* ed. H. Wayne Ballard, Jr., and W. Dennis Tucker, Jr. (Macon: Mercer University Press, 2000), p. 45. Gerald Wilson maintains that in Psalms 42–83, Elohim occurs 197 times and in Pss. 1–41 and 84–150, only 19 times; *The Editing of the Hebrew Psalter,* pp. 196-97.

2. For an explanation of the term "Maskil," see the commentary for Ps. 42.

- Psalm 70, a psalm "of David," parallels vv. 13-17 of Psalm 40, also "of David." But unlike Psalm 53, where the only divine name used is Elohim, Psalm 70 uses Elohim only in the first line of each poetic bicola. Compare, for example, Ps. 40:13 with 70:1:

  Be pleased, O LORD, to deliver me.
  O LORD, make haste to help me. (40:13)

  Elohim, deliver me!
  LORD, as my help, hurry! (70:1)

  In addition, where Elohim appears in the second line of the poetic bicola in Psalm 40, in Psalm 70 it occurs as YHWH (LORD). Compare Psalm 40:17 with 70:5:

  But I am poor and needy, may my Lord take thought for me!
  You are my help and my deliverer; O my Elohim, do not be slow! (40:17)

  But I am oppressed and needy; Elohim, hurry to me!
  You are my helper and my deliverer! LORD, do not delay! (70:5)

- Psalms 57:7-11 and 60:5-12 are taken from Psalm 108, or Psalm 108 is made up of Pss 57:7-11 and 60:5-12. Interestingly, the divine names used in Psalms 57 and 60 occur exactly as they do in Psalm 108.

Thus we observe that in the Elohistic Psalter (Psalms 42–83), in many instances the name Elohim occurs instead of YHWH; in some instances the name YHWH occurs instead of Elohim; and in other instances, no difference exists between the psalm(s) within the Elohistic Psalter and the duplicate psalm(s) outside it. The origins and shaping history of the Elohistic Psalter are unclear to modern students of the Hebrew Psalter. While many scholars understand the Elohistic Psalter as the product of a postexilic editing (by a community that no longer found it acceptable to vocalize the personal name of the deity), others maintain that it is simply impossible to state with certainty its origins. Theories abound, but no single one is compelling. We can simply observe the phenomenon of the use of the divine name in Psalms 42–83 and continue to wonder.[3]

3. For two good treatments of the Elohistic Psalter, see Laura Joffe, "The Elohistic Psalter: What, How, and Why?" *SJOT* 15 (2001) 142-66; and Frank-Lothar Hossfeld and Erich Zenger, "The So-Called Elohistic Psalter: A New Solution for an Old Problem," in

Like Book One, Book Two consists mainly of laments (twenty out of thirty-one psalms or 65 percent), but unlike Book One, not all of them are ascribed to David.[4] In Book Two, only eighteen psalms are attributed to David (58 percent). Instead, the Korahites (Psalms 42–49) and Asaphites (Psalm 50) mix their voices with David in singing the psalms. According to 1 Chronicles, the Korahites were temple keepers and temple singers during the reigns of David and Solomon (1 Chr. 6:31-37; 9:19).[5] The Korahites are listed in Num. 26:58 as one of the five major levitical families, but in the book of Chronicles, they generally appear as a subgroup of the Kohathites (1 Chr. 6:22, 31-37; 9:19).

Numbers 16 relates a dramatic incident in which Korah, along with Dathan and Abiram, question Moses' and Aaron's authority over the people of Israel. This narrative appears to have served as the rationale for separating the levitical priests into two groups — those who could trace their lineage directly through Aaron — and through Zadok, according to Ezek. 44:10-16 — and those who were descendants of Levi through other sons. The Aaronic priests performed the major sacrificial and cultic duties at the Jerusalem temple, while the Korahites were doorkeepers and singers and performed the more menial chores.[6]

Book Two opens with a collection of Psalms of the Sons of Korah (Psalms 42–49), and the Korahites, in fact, sing the first community lament of the Psalter:

> Yet you have rejected and you reproach us;
> you do not go forth with our armies.
> You cause us to turn back from an oppressor,
> and the ones who hate us have plundered for themselves.
> You give us like a flock of sheep as food,
> and among the nations you have scattered us. (44:9-11)

Psalm 50 is a psalm of Asaph. Asaph was, according to 1 Chr. 6:31-48, the eponymous ancestor of a guild of singers and musicians who, along with the Korahites, served at the temple in Jerusalem during the reigns of David and Solomon. We read that after Solomon had completed the work

A God So Near, ed. Brent A. Strawn and Nancy R. Bowen (Winona Lake: Eisenbrauns, 2003), pp. 35-51.

4. In Book One, thirty-nine psalms, all but the introductory Pss. 1 and 2, are attributed to David.

5. For a full discussion of the Korahites, see Michael Goulder, *The Psalms of the Sons of Korah* (JSOTSup 20; Sheffield: JSOT, 1982).

6. See Exod. 6:18-21; 1 Chr. 6:22-24, 31-38. In each of these, the Korahites are listed in third position, always after the Kohathites.

on the temple and the ark of the covenant had been put in its place in the holy of holies:

> When the priests came out of the holy place (for all the priests who were present had sanctified themselves without regard to their divisions), and all the levitical singers, Asaph, Heman, and Jeduthun, their sons and kindred, arrayed in fine linen, with cymbals, harps, and lyres, stood east of the altar with one hundred twenty priests blowing trumpets, then the trumpeters and singers made themselves heard in unison in praise and thanksgiving to the LORD. (2 Chr. 5:11-13)

Fifteen psalms of David appear in the middle of Book Two (Psalms 51–65). Fourteen of them are laments. Eight are connected, in their superscriptions, with particular events in the life of David. These psalms remind readers once again that David's life was one of turmoil and strife; but they also depict for readers a king who loved the Lord and strove to serve the Lord with great fervor. In Psalm 63, when David "was in the wilderness of Judah," we read these words:

> O God, you are my God, I seek you;
> my soul thirsts for you;
> my flesh faints for you;
> like a dry and weary land with no water.
> So I envisioned you in the sanctuary;
> beholding your power and glory;
> for your *hesed* is better than life;
> my lips shall praise you.
> So I will bless you all my life;
> and in your name, I will lift up my hands. (63:1-4)

Many scholars dismiss most of the psalmic superscriptions, particularly those that link the psalms to specific events in the life of David, as late additions that offer little in the way of helping readers to understand the psalms. Brevard Childs, for example, maintains that the most important factor in the formation of these superscriptions appears to be not precise references in the psalms to events in David's life, but "general parallels between the situations described in the psalms and some incidents in the life of David." He writes further, "The psalms are transmitted as the sacred psalms of David, but they testify to all the common troubles and joys of ordinary human life in which all persons participate."[7] Thus the psalms need not be read in light of the stories

7. *Introduction to the Old Testament as Scripture* (Philadelphia: Fortress, 1979), pp. 520-22.

about David to which they refer. As late additions, the superscriptions may be ignored in our modern context of interpretation.

Not all scholars agree.[8] James Sanders maintains that the editors of the Psalter purposefully drew attention to very specific events in the life of David, situations with which they expected their readers to be familiar:

> Does not such editorial work indicate the intense interest of redactors in date lines and historical contexts? They seem to be saying fairly clearly, if the reader wants to understand the full import for his or her (later) situation of what Scripture is saying, he or she had best consider the original historical context in which this passage scored its point.[9]

Therefore, according to Sanders, the superscriptions *do* matter, especially in the case of the thirteen psalms that refer to specific events in the life of David. The superscriptions call readers to go back and review the stories and think about the characters and emotions, the actions and the outcomes. Then, when readers return to the psalms, they are able to ask themselves, "How do the psalms express the emotions and outcomes of the characters and events of those stories?" The contexts of the superscriptions provide initial "hooks" on which readers can "hang" the psalms and ponder on their words as they attempt to appropriate their messages into their own lives.

The only untitled psalm in Book Two is Psalm 71, an individual lament, which may be read as the supplication of an aged person that God not forget or forsake:

> God, you have taught me from my youth;
>   and still I proclaim your wonders.
> Even until old age and gray hair,
>   O God, do not forsake me,
>   until I can declare your strength,
>   to all generations to come, your power. . . .
> Though you caused me to see great troubles and calamities;
>   you revive me again;
>   from the depths of the earth you will again bring me back.
>
> (71:17-18, 20)

Book Two ends with Psalm 72, a psalm "of Solomon." It is classified as a royal psalm, and its words call on God to bestow upon the new king all of the attributes required to make the king successful in his reign. Childs suggests that

8. See James D. Nogalski, "Reading David in the Psalter: A Study in Liturgical Hermeneutics," *HBT* 23 (2001) 168-91.

9. "Canonical Context and Canonical Criticism," in *From Sacred Story to Sacred Text* (Philadelphia: Fortress, 1987), p. 170.

the placement of Psalm 72 within the story of the Psalter indicates strongly that the psalm "is 'for' Solomon, offered by David."[10]

> May he live as long as the sun;
> as long as the moon, through all generations.
> May he descend like rain upon mown grass;
> like showers that water the earth.
> May righteousness flourish in his days;
> and much well-being until the moon is no more. . . .
> May the kings of Tarshish and the islands return tribute;
> and kings of Sheba and Seba present gifts.
> May all the kings fall down before him;
> may all the nations serve him. (72:5-7, 10-11)

Book Two of the Psalter closes with the usual doxology:

> Blessed be the LORD God, the God of Israel,
> who alone does wondrous deeds.
> Blessed be his glorious name forever;
> May his glory fill all the earth. Amen and Amen.
> (72:18-19; cf. 41:13; 89:52; 106:48)

Book Two is a moving and poignant segment of the story of the Psalter. It opens with King David in the background and the temple singers at the forefront. David steps forward again in Psalms 51–65 and 68–70, but the reader is constantly reminded of the humanness of the great king (Psalm 51 — Bathsheba, 56 — the Philistines, 57 — hiding from Saul). The book concludes with abrupt finality, ending the celebration of David's kingship that has dominated the first two books of the Psalter:

> The prayers of David, son of Jesse, are completed. (72:20)

David, the psalm-singer of ancient Israel, will move to the background of the Psalter in Books Three and Four. Only one psalm in Book Three is attributed to David (Psalm 86) and only two in Book Four (Psalms 101 and 103). Other voices will dominate as the Psalter moves through the story of the life of ancient Israel.

10. *Introduction to the Old Testament as Scripture,* p. 516. See the Introduction to this commentary for a discussion of the possible meanings for l^e in the psalmic superscriptions.

Psalm 42: Where Is Your God?

Psalm 42 opens Book Two of the Psalter. Its superscription identifies it as "a Maskil according to the Korahites." Thirteen psalms in the Hebrew Psalter (Psalms 32, 42, 44, 45, 52–55, 74, 78, 88, 89, and 142) are designated as *maśkîl.* The Hebrew root of the word is *śāḵal,* and in the verbal stem in which we find it in the Psalter, the word means "to have insight, to teach." Scholars believe that the *maśkîl* is meant to be an artistic or teaching song.

Psalm 42 is the first of twelve psalms in the Psalter which are attributed to the Korahites (Psalms 42–49, 84–85, and 87–88), and it begins what is called the Elohistic Psalter. For a discussion of the Korahites and the Elohistic Psalter, see the Introduction to Book Two.

The Psalm is classified as an individual lament and may be divided into four stanzas:

Words of Lament (vv. 1-4)
Refrain (v. 5)
Words of Lament (vv. 6-10)
Refrain (v. 11)

For the leader. A Korahite[1] *maskil.*[2]

1 *Just as a deer ever longs for running brooks of water,*
Thus my inmost being ever longs for you, O God.
2 *My inmost being thirsts for God, for the living God.*
When will I come and see[3] *the face of God?*
3 *My tear has been bread to me by day and by night,*
While they say to me[4] *all day, "Where is your God?"*
4 *These things I remember*
and I pour out my inmost being on my behalf,

1. There are two collections of the Korahite *(bᵉnê-qōraḥ)* psalms. The first is in Book Two (Pss. 42–49) and the second in Book Three (Pss. 84–85, 87–88). The name appears in the Hebrew Bible in several contexts (Exod. 6:21-24; 1 Chr. 6:7; 2 Chr. 20:19). It is impossible to state which or any of these traditions are associated with this psalm. For a more complete explanation, see Tate, *Psalms 51–100,* p. 351.

2. See note 2 on Psalm 32 superscription.

3. MT renders the verb in the *niphal* stem, "I will be seen (by)." Some suggest that the use of the *niphal* is an emendation reflecting an exilic/postexilic belief that no human can see God's face and live (Exod. 33:20). A number of manuscripts render the verb in the *qal* stem, providing the translation given above.

4. MT has *beʾᵉmōr* ("while saying"), but the editors of *BHS,* based on a few manuscripts, suggest an emendation to *bᵉʾomrām,* which harmonizes with v. 10.

How I would pass over with the crowd,[5]
And I would lead them up to the house of God
With a sound of rejoicing and thanks,
a crowd keeping festival.

5 *How you are bowed down, O my inmost being,*
And how you have been disquieted because of me.
Wait for God, for yet I will praise him,
the help of my countenance and my God.[6]

6 *My inmost being is bowed down because of me.*
Therefore I will remember you
From the land of the Jordan and Hermon,
From the mountain of Mizar.
7 *Deep is calling to deep at the sound of your waterfalls.*
All of your breakers and waves have passed over me.
8 *By day the* LORD *will command his* hesed,
And in the night, its song[7] *is with me,*
A prayer[8] *to the living God.*[9]
9 *I say to God, my rock,*
"Why have you forgotten me?
Why must I go about mourning,
While the enemy presses in?"
10 *With a crushing of my bones,*
My oppressors have scorned me
While they say to me all day, "Where is your God?"

5. The meaning of the Hebrew *(bassāḵ ʾeddaddēm)* is uncertain. LXX translates the phrase as "into a dwelling place of glory" in order to parallel the next phrase, "up to the house of God," leading the editors of *BHS* to suggest an emendation to *b^{e}sōḵ ʾaddîr* ("into a tent of glory").

6. In MT, this phrase is *y^{e}šûʿôṯ pānāyw* ("the helps of his countenance"), and *ʾ^{e}lōhāy* ("my God") begins v. 6. Manuscript evidence suggests emending "helps" (*y^{e}šûʿôṯ* pl.) to "help" (*y^{e}šûʿaṯ* sg.) and harmonizing the phrase with v. 11 and the same phrase in 43:5. Changing 42:5 to conform to the other two refrains requires, then, emending the consonantal text, making the first word of v. 6 the last word of v. 5 and changing the word divisions. Thus the consonantal text *yšwʿwt pnyw ʾilhm* would become *yšwʿt pny wʾlhm.*

7. The Qere of MT changes the pronoun suffix on *song* from 3fs *šîrâ,* referencing *ḥeseḏ,* to 3ms *šîrô,* referencing God.

8. A few manuscripts render this word as *t^{e}hillâ* ("hymn").

9. MT includes a 1cs pronoun suffix on *ḥay,* but many manuscripts omit the suffix.

11 *How you are bowed down, O my inmost being,*
And how you have been disquieted because of me.
Wait for God, for yet I will praise him,
the help of my countenance and my God.[10]

1-4 Verses 1-4 use powerful water imagery to express the psalmist's need for God and the feeling of being removed from the Lord's presence.[11] The verses are nostalgic, lamenting that life is no longer as it used to be. Thus the psalmist thirsts for running brooks of water, cries tears, pours out the inmost being, and asks, *When will I come and see the face of God?* (v. 2). And the psalmist remembers: *How I would pass over with the crowd, and I would lead them up to the house of God with a sound of rejoicing and thanks, a crowd keeping festival* (v. 4).

The books of Psalms and Chronicles suggest that worship at the temple in Jerusalem was a dynamic and awe-inspiring experience. In Psalm 150, worshippers are instructed to praise God with trumpet, harp, lyre, and tambourine and with dancing, strings, pipe, and clanging, clashing cymbals. 2 Chr. 29:20-36 tells us that during the reign of King Hezekiah, the people worshiped at the temple with blood sacrifices — seventy bulls, one hundred rams, and two hundred lambs; with singing and musical instruments — cymbals, trumpets, and "the instruments of King David"; and with thank and drink offerings.

Because Psalm 42 appears to be a cry of sorrow from a person who can no longer worship God at the temple — and indeed, according to v. 4, lead the worshippers to the temple — many suggest that it was composed while Israel was in exile in Babylon in the sixth century B.C.E. For indeed, at that time, the people were far away from the temple and felt removed from the presence of God.

As if these feelings aren't enough, the psalmist is also taunted by people all around who ask, *"Where is your God?"* (v. 3). The psalmist feels God's absence all the more because the question of the people constantly reminds the psalmist that God is not "here," is not present.

5 The psalmist's *inmost being (nep̄eš)* is sunk down with the weight and enormity of the despair. But in the midst of the lament, the psalmist speaks to the inmost being: *How you are bowed down, O my inmost being, and how you have been disquieted because of me. Wait for God, for yet I will praise him, the help of my countenance and my God* (vv. 5, 11).

10. See note 6.

11. For an excellent treatment of water imagery in the book of Psalms, see Brown, *Seeing the Psalms,* pp. 105-34.

Because the psalmist is in dialogue with the self — the *inmost being* — Psalm 42 is often likened to a third-millennium B.C.E. Egyptian tale called "The Dispute between a Man and His Ba." Miriam Lichtheim summarizes the tale:

> A man who suffers from life longs for death. Angered by his complaints, his *ba* — [inmost being] — threatens to leave him. This threat fills the man with horror, for to be abandoned by his *ba* would mean total annihilation, instead of the resurrection and immortal bliss that he envisages. He therefore implores his *ba* to remain with him, and not to oppose him in his longing for death.[12]

In a similar way in Psalm 42, the psalmist persuades the inmost being not to despair, since the psalmist is convinced that the Lord is still a source of help.

According to v. 4, the psalmist remembers *these things,* but the psalmist is far away from home, from the temple, and from the presence of God. The psalmist, however, carries the memory of what has been left behind and can picture that past. Because of the strong memories, the psalmist calls the *inmost being* to *wait* (v. 5). The Hebrew root which we translate as *wait* is *yāḥal.* Its basic connotation is "expectation," perhaps in a painful circumstance.[13] And so the psalmist calls the being to remember and *wait for God* — i.e., to be expectant — for the psalmist will again *praise* God. God will again be present and the psalm-singer will have an answer for people when they ask, *"Where is your God?"*

The affirmation *yet I will praise* shows that the psalmist still trusts that God will come through. God will again be present, and our singer will be able to worship with the congregation of the faithful. The psalmist is confident, confident enough to speak words of trust not just once (v. 5), but twice (vv. 5 and 11). In fact, the psalm ends with these words of assurance.

6-10 As in vv. 1-4, vv. 6-10 use water imagery to express the psalmist's feelings. Here, however, the sought-for *running brooks* of water and the singer's *tears* are supplanted by the *deep,* by *waterfalls,* by *breakers,* and by *waves.* The sought-after water has become an overwhelming flood. The psalmist *remembers* — brings to mind — God's presence in the powerful headwaters of the Jordan River: *My inmost being is bowed down because of me. Therefore I will remember you from the land of the Jordan and Hermon, from the mountain of Mizar. Deep is calling to deep at the sound of your waterfalls. All of your breakers and waves have passed over me* (vv. 6-7).

12. For the full text of the story, see Lichtheim, *Ancient Egyptian Literature* (Berkeley: University of California Press, 1973), 1:163-69; and *ANET,* pp. 405-7.

13. See Christoph Barth, *"yāḥal," in TDOT,* 6:49-55.

The psalmist accuses God: *Why have you forgotten me? Why must I go about mourning, while the enemy presses in?* (v. 9). The psalmist remembers God (vv. 4, 6), but accuses God of forgetting. And so the enemy *presses in.* The word translated *enemy* is *'ôyēḇ*. Used some seventy-five times in the Psalter, it can refer both to personal enemies (3:7; 43:2; 102:8) and enemies of the larger community (21:8; 89:22; 110:1, 2). As in most of the Psalter, the enemy in Psalm 42 is not specified, but is an unnamed foe, a constant force pressing in upon the psalmist. And so the psalm-singer laments the feelings that accompany the perceived absence of God and the taunt of the ones oppressing: *With a crushing of my bones, my oppressors have scorned me while they say to me all day, "Where is your God?"* (v. 10). *Oppressors* translates the Hebrew word *ṣôr^e rîm,* a word often used in synonymous parallelism with *'ôyēḇ (enemy;* 27:2; 74:10; 89:22-23). The psalmist laments that enemies are pressing in, oppressors are crushing the psalmist's bones, and that they continually question, *"Where is your God?"*

11 But before the feelings of despair suffocate and drown the psalmist, the psalmist calls the *inmost being* back from its musing, reflecting the psalmist's confidence and hope that God is present, even in apparently difficult circumstances. Despite all, the singer of Psalm 42 remembers and waits, and so has hope: *Wait for God, for yet I will praise him, the help of my countenance and my God.*

The ancient Israelites had waited many times in their history for God to appear and deliver them. In Egypt, they waited for deliverance from slavery. In the wilderness, they waited to go into the promised land. In exile in Babylon, they waited to return to Jerusalem and to the presence of God.

When we find ourselves in circumstances where God seems to be absent, when our very beings feel as though the weight of the world is upon them, may we be able to speak the assuring words, "Wait for God . . . for I will again praise him."

NANCY DECLAISSÉ-WALFORD

Psalm 43: Judge Me and Plead My Case

Most scholars maintain that since Psalm 43 has the same refrain as Psalm 42 (42:5, 11; and 43:5) and because Psalm 43 has no superscription (which makes it one of only two psalms in Book Two without a superscription[1]), Psalms 42 and 43 belong together as a unit.[2] Although a large number of Hebrew manuscripts join them into a single psalm, the Masoretic Text, the Septuagint, and the Vulgate present them separately. And, interestingly, the Septuagint and the Vulgate give Psalm 43 its own superscription: "A Psalm of David."

The common refrains in Psalms 42 and 43 certainly provide justification for considering the two psalms as a single unit, but a significant difference between them provides a compelling argument for regarding them as distinct compositions. In Psalm 42 the psalmist is speaking to the inmost being, the *nepeš,* but in Psalm 43 the psalmist is speaking to God. Therefore, we should consider the possibility that the common refrains may have prompted the collectors of the Korahite songs to place these similar psalms side by side, but not necessarily that they were at one time a single psalm. Psalm 43 is classified as an individual lament, with the same basic structure as Psalm 42:

Words of lament (vv. 1-4)
Refrain (v. 5)

1 *Judge me, O God, and plead my case*
against a people without hesed*;*
From a person of deceit and dishonesty
may you deliver me.
2 *For you are the God of my strength;*
Why have you rejected me?
Why must I continually walk about mourning,
while the enemy presses in?
3 *Send your light and your faithfulness;*
they will guide me.
They will bring me to the mountain of your holiness
and to your sanctuaries.
4 *And I will come to the altar of God,*

1. The other is Ps. 71.

2. See, e.g., Kraus, *Psalms 1–59,* pp. 435-42; Craigie, *Psalms 1–50,* pp. 176-77; Hossfeld and Zenger, *Psalms 1–50,* p. 265; and McCann, "The Book of Psalms," pp. 850-63.

to the God of the gladness of my rejoicing.[3]
And I will praise you with a harp,
O God my God.

5 *How you are bowed down, O my inmost being,*
And how you have been disquieted because of me.
Wait for God, for yet I will praise him,
the help of my countenance and my God.

1-4 The words of the lament in verses 1-4 are spoken by the psalmist directly to God: *Judge me . . . plead my case . . . you are the God of my strength . . . send your light and your faithfulness.* The psalmist cites the *hesed* (v. 1) of the Lord as the rationale for claiming a right to God's judgment. The word *hesed* occurs some 245 times in the Hebrew Bible, 127 times in the Psalter.[4] One Jewish scholar defines *hesed* as "a free-flowing love that knows no bounds."[5]

Hesed is most closely connected in the Hebrew Bible with the covenant relationship between God and the children of Israel. In Genesis 15, God covenants with Abram, saying: "To your descendants I give this land, from the river of Egypt to the great river, the river Euphrates" (Gen. 15:18). Genesis 17 records these words of God to Abram: "I will establish my covenant between me and you, and your offspring after you throughout their generations, for an everlasting covenant, to be God to you and to your offspring after you. And I will give to you, and to your offspring after you, the land where you

3. The editors of *BHS* suggest emending *śimḥaṯ* ("gladness of") to *śimḥāṯî* ("my gladness"); rendering *gîlî (my rejoicing) as 'āg̱îlâ* ("I will rejoice") and moving it to the following bicola. Thus the two bicola would be translated:

And I will come to the altar of God,
to the God of my gladness.
I will rejoice and I will praise you with a harp,
O God my God.

LXX renders the two lines as:

And I will come to the altar of God,
to God, the one making glad the youthfulness of me.
I will praise you with a harp,
O God my God.

Neither emended translation, however, is wholly compelling.

4. For recent discussions of *ḥeseḏ,* see Katharine Dobb Sakenfeld, *Faithfulness in Action: Loyalty in Biblical Perspective* (OBT 16, Philadelphia: Fortress, 1985), and Gordon R. Clark, *The Word* Hesed *in the Hebrew Bible* (JSOTSup 157; Sheffield: JSOT, 1993).

5. Arthur Green, *These Are the Words: A Vocabulary of Jewish Spiritual Life* (Woodstock: Jewish Lights, 1999), p. 152.

are now an alien, all the land of Canaan, for a perpetual holding; and I will be their God" (Gen. 17:7-8). In Exodus 19, God says to the children of Israel: "If you obey my voice and keep my covenant, you shall be my treasured possession out of all the peoples. Indeed, the whole earth is mine, but you shall be for me a priestly kingdom and a holy nation" (Exod. 19:5-6). In each instance, God calls the Israelites into a special relationship centered around a covenant.

Hesed is often used in parallel thought construction with the Hebrew word *ʾemeṯ,* which is translated as *faithfulness.* In Psalm 43, for example, the psalmist declares that the people have no *hesed* (v. 1) and asks God to send light and *ʾemeṯ* (v. 3). In Exodus 34, God speaks to Moses words of self-description from the top of Mount Sinai: "The LORD, the LORD, a God merciful and gracious, slow to anger, and abounding in *hesed* (covenant love) and *ʾemeṯ* (faithfulness), keeping *hesed* for the thousandth generation" (Exod. 34:6-7).

In v. 2, the psalmist is confronted with a people who have no knowledge of *hesed,* this special relationship between God and people, and asks questions of God that parallel the questions voiced by the psalmist in Psalm 42.

> "Why have you rejected me?" (43:2) = "Why have you forgotten me?" (42:9)
>
> "Why must I continually walk about mourning?" (43:2) = "Why must I go about mourning?" (42:9)

But in vv. 3 and 4, the psalmist quickly moves to the petition to God and the anticipated results of the granting of that petition: *Send your light and your faithfulness (ʾemeṯ)* because: *They will bring me to the mountain . . . and I will come to the altar. . . . And I will praise you. . . . Light and faithfulness* are not commonly paired in the poetic structure of the Hebrew Psalter. Perhaps the psalmist asks for *light* so that the path to the mountain of God's holiness and to the sanctuary will be clear and for *faithfulness* so that the psalmist is not distracted from following the path. Only then will the psalmist be able to *come to the altar,* encounter the God of the *gladness of rejoicing,* and *praise* God *with a harp.* In contrast to Psalm 42, where the psalmist speaks only of a nostalgic remembrance of the sanctuary of God, the singer of Psalm 43 expresses a sense of confidence that if God will indeed send light and faithfulness, then the psalmist will be able to come to the altar and praise God with the harp.

5 In the final verse of the psalm, the psalmist (as does the singer of Psalm 42) calls the *inmost being* to *wait for God.* But, in keeping with the contrast already drawn in vv. 3-4, in the closing verse of Psalm 43 the psalmist's words seem not so much to draw the inmost being back from the brink of despair as they gently remind the inmost being of the words of confidence that the psalmist has uttered in vv. 3 and 4: *Send your light and your faithfulness. They will guide me. . . . And I will come to the altar of God . . . And I will praise you.*

In our own struggles with those who do not honor the *hesed* of God, Psalm 43 offers us words with which to demand *light* and *faithfulness* from God. And it provides words of assurance that we may *come to the altar* and *praise* the God of our deliverance.

NANCY DECLAISSÉ-WALFORD

Psalm 44: O God, Why Do You Hide Your Face?

Psalm 44 is the first of eleven community laments in the Hebrew Psalter.[1] The voice of the individual, which the reader has encountered repeatedly in the Psalter (e.g., Psalms 3, 7, 22, 31, 42), is supplanted in Psalm 44 by the voice of the community. The words of the psalm suggest that the people have gathered together in a sanctuary or in the temple in Jerusalem to cry out to God about a situation of grave danger — a military attack, political persecution, or some unjust action against them. The speakers of Psalm 44 alternate between the gathered people and a leader in their midst who praise God for God's goodness and recount God's provisions to the ancestors of Israel; move on to declare their innocence to God in the face of the current circumstances; call God to account for what is happening — that is, accuse God of not remembering the covenant with them; and finally offer a concluding prayer to God. The psalm's main sections and its speakers may be outlined as follows:

- Words of Praise and Recounting God's Provisions (vv. 1-8)
  - the people (vv. 1-3)
  - the leader (v. 4)
  - the people (v. 5)
  - the leader (v. 6)
  - the people (vv. 7-8)
- The Declaration of Innocence and Calling God to Account (vv. 9-22)
  - the people (vv. 9-14)
  - the leader (vv. 15-16)
  - the people (vv. 17-22)
- Concluding Petition: people and leader together (vv. 23-26)

Psalm 44 is unique among the community laments of the Psalter because in it the gathered congregation declares its absolute innocence before the Lord and claims that its suffering and shame are undeserved. In vv. 20 and 21, the people confront God with a question: *If we had forgotten the name of our God (ʾᵉlōhîm), and we had spread the palms of our hands to a foreign god (ʾēl), would God not spy this out? For God knows the hidden things of the heart.*

The book of Job and Psalm 73 wrestle with the issue of unjust suffering at an individual level. Psalm 44 wrestles with it at a community level. Why would God punish the innocent? The people engage in inward scrutiny: Have we betrayed God? Have we worshipped other gods? Does our God have a reason to turn away from us? The answers to the questions are a persistent "No."

1. The others are Pss. 60, 74, 79, 80, 83, 85, 90, 94, 123, and 137.

God's faithful people suffer even though they have done nothing to deserve suffering. They cannot reconcile their life experiences with their understanding of who God is and how God acts. Thus we read the lament of a community of people who find themselves in circumstances beyond their understanding, people accusing God of violating the covenant promises.

Humankind in the ancient Near East believed in a basic moral governance of the world. Act and consequence were connected in daily life. The good person prospered and the wicked one perished. Sages and wisdom teachers argued that there was a fundamental order in the world which could be discerned by experience, that the gods had established the order, and that all of humankind was bound by the rules governing that order.[2] But the singers of Psalm 44 see no connection between their actions and their suffering and shame. And so they bring their questions to God.

Rabbinic tradition links Psalm 44 to the time of the persecutions of the Greek Emperor Antiochus IV Epiphanes, who ruled Palestine between 168 and 164 B.C.E. Antiochus banned circumcision, observance of the sabbath and holy days, and the reading of the Torah. In addition, he converted the Jerusalem temple into a pagan sanctuary. The books of 1 and 2 Maccabees relate the story of the Jewish revolt against these policies. In 1 Macc. 2:19-22, the Maccabean leader Mattathias says:

> Even if all the nations that live under the rule of the king obey him, and have chosen to obey his commandments, every one of them abandoning the religion of their ancestors, I and my sons and my brothers will continue to live by the covenant of our ancestors. Far be it from us to desert the law and the ordinances. We will not obey the king's words by turning aside from our religion to the right hand or to the left.

Thus began the Maccabean revolt against the oppressive rule of Antiochus IV. The Babylonian Talmud tractate *b. Soṭah* 48a states that v. 23a of Psalm 44 was, at the time of the Maccabees, sung daily by the Levites: "Awaken! Why do you sleep, my Lord?"

In reality, a number of times of oppression in the life of ancient Israel would fit the message of Psalm 44: the Assyrian attack on Jerusalem in 701 B.C.E., the destruction of the temple by the Babylonians in 587, the subsequent exile of the ancient Israelites that lasted until 538. Abraham Heschel, a twentieth-century Jewish theologian, dedicated his seminal work on the

2. For detailed treatments, see James L. Crenshaw, *Old Testament Wisdom* (Atlanta: John Knox, 1981); Roland E. Murphy, *The Tree of Life* (2nd ed.; Grand Rapids: Eerdmans, 1996); and John G. Gammie and Leo G. Perdue, eds., *The Sage in Israel and the Ancient Near East* (Winona Lake: Eisenbrauns, 1990).

Hebrew Prophets[3] to the martyrs of the Holocaust of 1939-1945, and quoted from Psalm 44 in the dedication:

> All of this has come to us, but we have not forgotten you;
> we have not acted falsely with your covenant.
> We have not drawn back our heart,
> nor did our steps turn away from your way.
> But you have crushed us in a place of sea monsters. . . . (vv. 17-19)

Indeed, Psalm 44 is a psalm for all times of unjust suffering by the people of God.

For the leader. A Korahite[4] maskil.[5]

1 *O God, with our ears we have heard.*
Our ancestors have recounted to us
the works which you accomplished in their days,
in the days of the beginnings.
2 *You,[6] with your own hand, you have driven out nations,*
but you planted them.
You have broken peoples,
but you have sent them forth.
3 *For not with their swords did they take possession of a land,*
and their power will not deliver them.
But with your right hand and your power and the light of your face,
because you delight in them.
4 *You are indeed my king, O God.[7]*
Command[8] the deliverances of Jacob.
5 *With you our oppressors we will beat down;*
with your name we will crush the ones who rise up against us.
6 *For not in my bow will I trust,*
and my sword will not deliver me.
7 *For you have delivered us from our oppressors,*
and the ones who hate us you have put to shame.
8 *In God we have celebrated all day long,*
and your name for all time we will praise. Selah

3. Abraham J. Heschel, *The Prophets* (New York: Harper, 1962).

4. See note 1 on Psalm 42 superscription.

5. See note 2 on Psalm 32 superscription.

6. *'attâ (you):* emphatic in the Hebrew. LXX and Syr omit this word.

7. *'ĕlōhîm (God).* LXX renders this phrase as "my God." Aquila translates it "O God of me."

8. LXX and Syr translate this imperative verb as a participle, "who commands."

9 *Yet you have rejected and you reproach us;*
you do not go forth with our armies.
10 *You cause us to turn back from an oppressor,*[9]
and the ones who hate us have plundered for themselves.
11 *You give us like a flock of sheep as food,*
and among the nations you have scattered us.
12 *You sell your people for nothing,*
and you make no profit on their purchase.
13 *You make us an object of scorn to our neighbors,*
a mockery and an object of ridicule to those around us.
14 *You make us a proverb among the nations,*
a shaking of the head among the peoples.[10]
15 *All day long my reproach is in front of me,*
and the shame of my face has covered me,
16 *because of the noise of the one despising and the one reviling,*
because of the face of the one abhorring and the one being revengeful.
17 *All of this has come to us, and we have not forgotten you;*
we have not acted falsely with your covenant.
18 *We have not drawn back our heart,*
nor did our steps turn from your way.
19 *But you have crushed us in a place of a sea monster,*[11]
and you have covered us over with a shadow of death.
20 *If we had forgotten the name of our God,*
and we had spread the palms of our hands to a foreign god,
21 *would not God spy this out?*
For God knows the hidden things of the heart.
22 *But because of you we are slain every day;*
we are reckoned as a flock of sheep for slaughter.

23 *Awaken! Why do you sleep, my Lord?*[12]
Rise! Do not reject forever.

9. *Minnî ṣār* (from an oppressor). LXX renders this phrase as "from our oppressors." The Syriac version omits it altogether.

10. MT renders this phrase as *bal-ʾummîm.* Many manuscripts omit the *maqqēp̱,* rendering the phrase *balʾummîm* ("among the peoples").

11. The English translations render this word *(tannîm)* as "jackals" by understanding the word as the plural of the root *tan;* but *sea monster* — a singular noun — is preferable in this context, since in many instances in the Psalter, the sea is viewed as a place of chaos. See, e.g., 46:2-3; 65:7; 74:14; 89:9; and 148:7. See also Brown, "The Voice of Many Waters: From Chaos to Community," in *Seeing the Psalms,* pp. 105-34.

12. Many manuscripts render this word *(ʾᵃḏōnāy)* as *YHWH* ("O LORD").

24 Why do you hide your face,
and forget our affliction and our oppression?
25 For our being has sunk down to the dust,
our inmost part has clung to the earth.
26 Arise,[13] *be a help for us,*
and redeem us because of your hesed.

1-3 In vv. 1-3, the people praise God and recount God's work among them in the past — specifically during the settlement in the land of promise under the leadership of Joshua. The people know of the work of God because their *ancestors* told the stories and handed them on generation after generation, from grandparent to parent to child. The stories emphasize the power of God; they remind the people of God's provisions for them over the centuries. The people speak to God: *You, with your own hand, you have driven out nations.* Craigie writes:

> It was the essence of the Hebrew faith that the past could always be appropriated for the present, that the people in faith could look in the present moment for the continuation of those mighty acts of God in the past which had been so pregnant with future implications.[14]

The God who provided for and protected the children of Israel in the past could be called to remember and to act. In Exodus, God said to the children of Israel: "If you obey my voice and keep my covenant, you shall be my treasured possession out of all the peoples" (Exod. 19:5). And over and over again in the pages of the Old Testament, we read that God delivered and protected the Israelites from enemies and oppressors (Exodus 14; Numbers 31; Judges 7–8; 1 Samuel 7).

4-6 The voice of the people gives way to the singular voice of a leader, who sings "You are indeed my king." Many scholars understand the first person voice in Psalm 44 to be that of the king and thus place the psalm in the time of the Israelite monarchy. The singular voice, however, could be that of any trusted leader of the people — king, military commander, prophet, postexilic governor — who continues the words of confidence in the Lord begun by the people. The voice reaffirms that God, not any earthly leader, is the source of deliverance and strength.

7-8 In v. 7, the communal voice returns to state the sure knowledge that the Lord has *delivered* and protected the people from *oppressors* and those *who hate* them from the time of their ancestors until present times. In v. 8, the people recall that they have always *celebrated* God and that they will *praise*

13. LXX adds "O Lord."
14. Craigie, *Psalms 1–50,* p. 333.

God's *name for all time.* The stories of the past are trustworthy and give the people confidence that they can call upon God to remember the covenant promises once again.

9-14 With the brief Hebrew word *'ap̄ (yet)* at the beginning of v. 9, the tone of the psalm changes. Verses 10-14 all begin with the Hebrew letter *tāw,* pronounced as the English consonant "t," giving the verses what Clifford calls "a staccato effect."[15] The terse harshness of the sound "t" acoustically emphasizes the harshness of the people's indictment of the Lord that is recorded in these verses.

The people accuse God of rejecting and reproaching them. In the past the Lord *delivered* them from oppressors and *put to shame* the ones who hated them (v. 7). Now the people *turn back* from the oppressor and are *plundered* by those who hate them (v. 10). The people are given over *like a flock of sheep* for *food* (v. 11) and are sold, but with *no profit* to God (v. 12). They are being made by God *an object of scorn, a mockery, an object of ridicule, a proverb,* and *a shaking of the head* (vv. 13-14). In short, among non-Israelites, "Israel" is the butt of cynical jokes and biting mockery, the spark for disdainful head-shaking. When it was needed most, God's power failed to show, and God sold his people, his *flock of sheep,* for nothing (vv. 11-12).

The Hebrew word translated as *proverb* in 44:14 is *māšāl.*[16] Why is *māšāl* included in a list of words that includes *object of scorn, mockery,* and *object of ridicule?* The basic verbal meaning of *māšāl* is "to be like," and it is used to describe various types of discourse in the Hebrew Bible. The book of Proverbs has the superscription "The proverbs of Solomon." Job's speeches are called "proverbs" (Job 27:1; 29:1). The word is used to designate certain prophetic speeches: Balaam's oracles in Num. 23:7, 18; Ezekiel's words in Ezek. 17:2; 24:3.

But *māšāl* is also used to describe words of derision spoken about the people of Israel as punishment from God. In 1 Kgs. 9:7, Solomon warns the people that if they turn away from following God, Israel will become a *māšāl* and an object of ridicule among the nations. Moses issues a similar warning to the people in Deut. 28:37. In Num. 21:27 and Isa. 28:14, people who compose and sing taunt songs are called *mōšᵉlîm.*

---

15. Clifford, *Psalms 1–72,* p. 220.

16. NRSV translates MT *māšāl* as "byword," which means a common saying by which a person or thing is identified as the embodiment of a particular quality, usually not very flattering. In modern use, a byword for dachshund is "sausage dog"; a byword for lawyer is "ambulance chaser"; a byword for a big car or an SUV is "gas guzzler."

15-16 The voice of the individual leader returns, reiterating and personalizing the accusations of the people. The leader speaks of the reproach that is *in front of me, the shame of my face,* because of the sight and sound of those who relentlessly oppress the psalmist.

17-22 The accusations of the people against the Lord continue, as they remind the Lord that they *have not forgotten* or *acted falsely.* Nevertheless, God has *crushed* them *in a place of a sea monster.* While most translations and commentaries follow the Syriac and LXX and translate the Hebrew word *tannîm* as "jackals," the plural of the root *tan,* the word may also come from the root *tannîm* (pl. *tannînîm*), which means *sea monster.* In ancient Israelite thought the sea is a source of chaos, an image that fits well in the context of v. 19, where, in the first line, the singers complain to God that they are being *crushed* in the sea (suffocated and drowned) and in the second line that they are being *covered over* (suffocated) *with a shadow of death.* For a detailed treatment of the sea as a symbol of chaos, see especially the commentary for Psalm 46.

And the singers ask, *If we had forgotten the name of our God* (if the people had turned away from the Lord), *and we had spread the palms of our hands to a foreign god* (upraised palms were symbols of prayer and worship), *would God not spy this out* (would the Lord not have known and said something to them)? The people admit of no guilt in any of these matters. Instead they say, *Because of* you *we are slain every day; we are reckoned as a flock of sheep for slaughter.* The people call God to accountability and responsibility to uphold God's end of the covenant relationship.

23-26 In the last four verses of Psalm 44, the people cry out to the Lord. The accusations continue, but they are coupled with pleas for assistance: *Awaken! . . . Rise! . . . Do not reject forever. . . . Arise! . . . redeem us.* In other words, remember, O God, that you promised to be our God if we would be your people (Exodus 19); rise up and redeem us just as our grandparents and parents told us that you did so many times in the past. In the words *Awaken, Rise, Arise!* we observe a reference to the "sleeping deity," a depiction found in other texts in the ancient Near East.[17] The words of Psalm 44 seemingly stand in sharp contrast to those of Psalm 121, which state that God "will not slumber" (121:3).[18]

But, ultimately, why? Why should the Lord *awaken* and *rise up* and *redeem?* In the last line of v. 26, the psalm-singer reminds the Lord of the ultimate reason for redeeming the children of Israel — the covenant and God's covenant love, God's *hesed.*[19]

17. See Bernard F. Batto, "The Sleeping God: An Ancient Near Eastern Motif of Divine Sovereignty," *Bib* 68 (1987) 153-77.

18. We also observe "bad shepherd" imagery in vv. 11, 19, and 22.

19. See the commentary on *hesed* in Psalm 43 and in the Introduction.

Psalm 44 gives the reader a wonderful glimpse into a liturgy of ancient Israelite worship. People and leader gather at the temple or sanctuary and alternate their voices as they cry out to the Lord, protesting their innocence in the face of grave danger and demanding that the Lord act on their behalf. *Arise, be a help, redeem . . . because of your* hesed." They base their plea on the bold, blunt accusation that God has, for absolutely no reason, withheld his power, failed to rescue them, and did not even inform them of their wrongs because (so they claim) there were none. Theologically, their song appeals to God's character and voices the common experience of believers of God's mysterious ways.

Every person will have an experience of feeling unjustly punished at some point in life. And every believer will question God concerning justice at some point in life. The words of Psalm 44 affirm that God invites believers to cry out, ask questions, reflect on our own faithfulness, and call God to account for what is happening in our lives. And, while answers may elude us, we may affirm, along with the psalmist, that God's *hesed* is the compelling reason for us to be confident that, in the end, God will *redeem us* and *be a help for us.*

NANCY DECLAISSÉ-WALFORD

Psalm 45: I Will Cause Your Name to Be Remembered

Psalm 45 is classified as a "royal psalm."[1] It most likely was composed as a wedding song for the marriage of a king of Judah or Israel. The words of v. 12, *a princess of Tyre,* suggest to some that the psalm dates to the time of Solomon, who married an Egyptian bride (1 Kgs. 3:1); some connect it to the union of Jehoram and Athaliah (2 Kgs. 8:18). But the marriage of Ahab to the Sidonian princess Jezebel (1 Kgs. 16:31) is the most common association for Psalm 45. Because of the corrupt nature of the text of the psalm, scholars generally agree that while it was composed for a specific wedding in Judah or Israel, it was passed on from generation to generation and used over and over in subsequent wedding ceremonies in the kingdoms. We may say, then, that Psalm 45 was a part of the fabric of wedding celebrations in many periods in the life of ancient Israel.

A vexing problem for modern readers of Psalm 45 is how to understand and appropriate the poem in a modern context. Is the psalm not, after all, indisputably about the marriage of an Israelite king? What possible relevance can it have for our modern situations? Early interpreters struggled with the same questions. The Aramaic Targum of Psalm 45 understood the psalm messianically. Its comment on v. 2 reads, "Thy beauty, O King Messiah, is greater than that of the children of humanity."

The Aramaic Targum comes from as early as the period of the second Jerusalem temple (after 515 B.C.E.), at a point when the Hebrew of the Jewish Scriptures ceased to be a spoken language. The Targum translates the Jewish Scriptures into Aramaic, the *lingua franca* of the Persian Empire, and adds commentary to help hearers more fully understand the meaning of the text. We may have evidence of a "targumic" rendition of Scripture in Nehemiah 8. In this text, the people gather in Jerusalem and Ezra reads from "the book of the law of Moses." In Neh. 8:7-8, we are told that members of the Levites "helped the people to understand the law . . . so they read from the book, from the law of God, with interpretation. They gave the sense, so that the people understood the reading."

In support of the Targumic interpretation, the writer of the New Testament book of Hebrews quotes Ps. 45:6 and 7 in the book's opening words about the Son whom God sent to reveal Godself to humankind (Heb. 1:8-9).

The words of Psalm 45, which were words addressed to a royal groom and bride, may also be understood as words addressed to the church as the

1. The other royal psalms in the Psalter are Pss. 2, 18, 20, 21, 72, 89, 101, 110, 132, and 144.

bride of Christ. The Hebrew Bible certainly provides many analogies of the relationship between God and the Israelites as that of husband and wife (see Hosea 1-3; Jeremiah 2; Ezekiel 16 and 23; and Isa. 62:1-5). The Christian Scriptures continue the analogy (see Matt. 9:15; John 3:29; Eph. 5:22-33; Rev. 19:7-9).

The two interpretations of Psalm 45 discussed above — messianic and the church and Christ — are what C. S. Lewis calls "second meaning in the psalms."[2] But is this the only way in which the modern reader may understand and appropriate the words of Psalm 45? Two other options are available to us. First, the words of Psalm 45 convey to the reader the power and majesty of the earthly ruler, but an earthly ruler whom God alone has chosen as a representative of God on the earth. Thus the psalm can be read as a reflection of God's powerful reign over this world we inhabit. Second, the words of Psalm 45 may simply reflect, as does the Song of Songs, the sensuous joy of sexuality, a God-given gift to humankind.[3]

However one may interpret it, though, Psalm 45 in its basic form is words addressed to a royal groom and bride as they prepare for a celebration of marriage. The psalm begins with the words of a poet, the composer of the psalm; moves on to praise the royal groom and the bride; and closes with the words of the poet once again. Thus, we may outline its structure in the following way:

The Poet Speaks (v. 1)
The Praise of the Groom (vv. 2-8)
The Praise of the Bride (vv. 9-16)
Concluding Words of the Poet (v. 17)

An interesting element of the structure of Psalm 45 is the repetition of two phrases in vv. 2 and 17: *'al kēn (therefore)* and *lᵉʿôlām (for all time)*. The repetition of phrases at the beginning and end of a literary unit is called an "inclusio," and often indicates that the composer feels that, within the words of that literary unit, all that is necessary to say about a particular subject has been said. Therefore, we may read Psalm 45 as the "last word" on the beauty of the royal couple and their subsequent marriage.

2. *Reflections on the Psalms* (New York: Harcourt, Brace, 1958), pp. 101-15.

3. Nancy R. Bowen, "A Fairy Tale Wedding? A Feminist Intertextual Reading of Psalm 45," in *A God So Near,* ed. Brent A. Strawn and Bowen (Winona Lake: Eisenbrauns, 2003), p. 71, insists that Psalm 45 reflects a gendered society in which a woman's sexuality belonged exclusively to her husband and abuse of that sexuality was commonplace. She therefore can find no place for it in the "liturgical, devotional, pastoral, or theological-homiletical dimensions" of contemporary faith communities. She concludes, "Psalm 45 is a song we might *sing in memoriam,* in memory of the damage done to women and men by this fairy tale world."

Psalm 45

For the leader. Upon Shashanim. *A Korahite*[4] *maskil.*[5] *A love song.*

1 *My heart has poured forth a good word;*
I am speaking my compositions to the king,
my tongue is the writing instrument of a ready scribe.

2 *You are more beautiful than any other mortal being;*
Favor has been poured out upon your lips;
therefore God has blessed you for all time.
3 *Put your sword upon your*[6] *hip, O mighty one,*
in your splendor and your glory.
4 *And in your glory succeed;*[7]
Ride upon the word of truth
and the gentleness of righteousness,[8]
and your right hand will show you fearful things.
5 *Your arrows are sharpened;*
peoples will fall under you
in the midst of the enemies of the king.
6 *Your throne, O God, is for all time and beyond,*
a scepter of honesty is the scepter of your kingdom.
7 *You loved righteousness, and you hated wickedness;*
therefore God your God has anointed you with the oil of gladness
instead of your companions:
8 *Myrrh and aloes and cassia, all of your garments;*
From palaces of ivory musical instruments have made you glad.

9 *Daughters of kings*[9] *are among your precious ones,*
stationed as a consort at your right hand,
with the gold of Ophir.
10 *Hear, O daughter, and see and incline your ear;*
and forget your people and the house of your father.

4. See note 1 on Psalm 42 superscription.

5. See note 2 on Psalm 32 superscription.

6. MT does not include the second person possessive pronoun. A number of translations, however, include the pronoun.

7. The editors of *BHS* point out that the text is corrupt and suggest reading "adorn your loins," and ending v. 3 after this phrase.

8. A number of translations add the conjunction to *righteousness,* rendering the line as "Ride upon the word of truth and humility and righteousness." The general consensus is that vv. 3 and 4 have been significantly corrupted in the transmission process.

9. Syr renders this phrase in the singular, "the daughter of the king." The context seems to favor this reading.

11 *The king will desire your beauty,*
for he is your lord; bow down to him.
12 *Then a princess of Tyre with a gift,*
the wealthy of the people will seek your favor.
13 *All dignity is a daughter of a king within,*
inwoven gold is her clothing.
14 *In embroidered clothes she is brought to the king,*
maidens, her companions, after her,
being brought in to her.[10]
15 *They are led with gladness and exultation;*
they enter into the palace of the king.
16 *In the place of your ancestors will be your sons;*
you will place them as princes in all of the earth.

17 *I will cause your name to be remembered in all generations.*
Therefore people will praise you for all time and beyond.

1 The composer/poet speaks introductory words in the opening verse of the psalm. Psalm 45 provides the only instance in the Hebrew Psalter of a poet being self-consciously present in a composition. The words *I am speaking my compositions* and *my tongue is the writing instrument* remind the modern reader of the originally oral nature of psalm composition. Therefore, perhaps our best method of studying and appropriating the psalm may be "to hear" it rather than "to read" it.

2-8 In these verses, the poet offers words of praise to the groom, who is most likely a king or king-to-be of Israel. Descriptive words dominate in the verses, eulogizing the ideal king — *beauty, favor, blessedness, splendor, glory, truth, righteousness,* and *honesty.* The ideal king is just and honorable (vv. 2, 6, 7), mighty in battle (vv. 3-5), and sensually pleasing (vv. 7-8). In v. 6, the psalmist sings, *Your throne, O God (ʾᵉlōhîm), is for all time and beyond,* apparently in reference to the groom-king. Since Psalm 45 is unique in using such language to refer to the human king, a number of commentators insist that the words are addressed to the Lord, who is the ultimate keeper of the throne of ancient Israel. The deification of the human king was a pervasive concept in the cultures of the ancient Near East. In Israel these ideas were adapted into a concept of the king being the "son of God," an earthly representative of the Lord, chosen by the Lord to rule over the people Israel. In Ps. 2:7, for example, the psalmist declares: "I will tell of the decree of the LORD; he said to me, 'You are my son, today I have begotton you.'" In the highly poetic

10. MT has "to you," but two Hebrew manuscripts render "to her." Context supports the emendation.

language of Psalm 45, the psalm-singer addresses the groom-king with a hyperbolic appellation that reflects the ancient Near Eastern culture of which Israel was indisputably a part.

9-15 In vv. 9-15, the poet turns attention to the bride-queen, first giving words of advice to the future wife of the monarch (vv. 10-12) and then offering an eloquent description of how she will look as she is being led to the chamber of the groom-king, outfitted in *inwoven gold* and fine embroidery (vv. 13-15).

16-17 The first person voice of the poet returns, stating confidently that the royal couple will have progeny through whom their rule will be extended *in all the earth* through many *generations.* The psalm ends in v. 17 with a vow from the psalmist: *I will cause your name to be remembered in all generations.* How? As it was recited over and over as a part of the fabric of wedding ceremonies in ancient Judah and as it is recited over and over as part of the Hebrew Psalter, the psalm becomes the living witness to the groom-king and bride-queen and fulfills the vow of the psalmist as each new generation hears the words of praise for the royal couple.

Psalm 45 thus celebrates a new beginning in the lives of the royal bride and groom and affirms the beauty of sexuality. It also celebrates the reign of God over the earth and affirms God's intimate connectedness with the daily living of human beings as they celebrate joys and commemorate movements through life. God rejoices over the *oil* (v. 7), the *myrrh and aloes and cassia* (v. 8), and the *embroidered clothes* (v. 14) of human joyfulness in equal measure to God's concern for justice and equity for all people. Generation to generation, God celebrates with humanity in their moments of utter joy and jubilation — a small glimpse, perhaps, into a future of dwelling endlessly in God's presence.

NANCY DECLAISSÉ-WALFORD

Psalm 46: The Lord of Hosts Is with Us

Psalm 45's celebration of a royal marriage is followed by three psalms that focus on God's reign over the earth from the city of Jerusalem. The first, Psalm 46, is a community hymn which is more specifically classified as a "psalm of confidence" or a "song of Zion."[1] While the psalm never specifically mentions the city of Jerusalem or uses the word "Zion," its content and structure suggest that it was sung liturgically by the community of Israelites — perhaps at a time of threat to the security of Jerusalem sometime in the preexilic period — as a confirmation that God was enthroned in Jerusalem and would protect the people of God from all threats. It is also, interestingly, the text which inspired Martin Luther to write the magnificent hymn "A Mighty Fortress Is Our God." The psalm consists of three stanzas:

St. 1 God, a Shelter and Refuge (vv. 1-3)
St. 2 The City of God (vv. 4-7)
St. 3 Behold the Works of the Lord (vv. 8-11)

In the second and third stanzas, the reader encounters a refrain (in vv. 7 and 11): *The LORD of hosts is with us; a fortress for us is the God of Jacob.* The first stanza (vv. 1-3) does not contain this refrain, but the well-formed structure of the psalm leads some scholars to believe that the refrain should be included there and suggest inserting it after v. 3. On the other hand, the omitted refrain may be a rhetorical device that moves the reader/hearer from the opening verses of the psalm into the heart of the psalm's message in vv. 4-5: *The city of God, the righteous dwelling of the Most High. God is in its midst.* And thus we may say that the theme and focus of Psalm 46 is God's ability to protect and safeguard the stronghold of Israel's faith, the city of Jerusalem, Zion.

For the leader. Korahitic.[2] *Upon* ʾalāmôṯ.[3] *A song.*

1 *God is to us a shelter and a refuge,*
a helper against distress, found to be strong.
2 *Therefore, we will not fear when the earth changes itself,*
and when mountains quake in the heart of the seas.
3 *Its waters sound; they foam;*
mountains tremble with its majesty.[4] Selah

1. The other songs of Zion are Pss. 48, 76, 87, and possibly 84 and 122.
2. See note 1 on Psalm 42 superscription.
3. For a discussion of *ʾalāmôṯ,* see the Introduction.
4. Commentators suggest inserting the refrain found in vv. 7 and 11 here.

4 *There is a river whose streams are joyous, the city of God,*
the righteous dwelling of the Most High.
5 *God is in its midst; it will not be quaked;*
God will help it in the face of the morning.
6 *The nations have sounded; kingdoms have quaked.*
He has given his voice; the land, the earth, will not tremble.
7 *The LORD of hosts is with us,*
a fortress for us is the God of Jacob. Selah

8 *Come, behold the works of the LORD*
who has brought desolation upon the earth,
9 *Causing wars to cease as far as the end of the earth.*
A bow he will break and he will cut through the spear.
The war chariots he will burn in the fire.
10 *Stand still, and know that I am God,*
I will be exalted among the nations,
I will be exalted in the earth.
11 *The LORD of hosts is with us;*
a fortress for us is the God of Jacob. Selah

1-3 The focus of the first stanza is God. The psalmist characterizes God as a "well-proven" *shelter, a refuge,* and *a helper against distress.* God as *refuge (ʿōz)* is a common designation for God in the Hebrew Bible, used some ninety-four times, forty-four times in the Psalter. God will provide protection and stability even if *the earth changes,* the *mountains quake in the heart of the seas,* and the *waters foam.*

The words concerning the earth changing and mountains quaking are most likely the depiction of an earthquake, a common but unsettling phenomenon for the inhabitants of ancient Syria and Palestine. Water, described as raging and foaming, is a common metaphor for chaos in the poetry of the Hebrew Bible and the ancient Near East.[5] We recall the Babylonian creation epic *Enuma Elish,* in which the god Marduk pits his prowess against Tiamat, the goddess of the seas, and her army of sea monsters:

> Then Tiamat and Marduk, wisest of gods, joined issue.
> They strove in single combat, locked in battle.
> The lord [Marduk] spread out his net to enfold her,
> he let loose the Evil Wind, which followed behind, in her face.
> When Tiamat opened her mouth to consume him,

5. For an excellent treatment of water imagery in the book of Psalms, see Brown, *Seeing the Psalms,* pp. 105-34.

he drove in the Evil Wind that she could not close her lips. . . .
He released the arrow, it tore her belly,
it cut through her insides, splitting the heart.
Having thus subdued her, he extinguished her life.
He cast down her carcass to stand on it.

Marduk takes the corpse of Tiamat and fashions it into the heavens and the earth.

He split her like a shellfish into two parts:
half of her he set up and ceiled it as sky. . . .
He crossed the heavens and surveyed the regions. . . .
He constructed stations for the great gods,
fixing their astral likenesses as the Images. . . .
He determined the year by designating the zones:
And had established the precincts of night and day,
He formed the clouds and filled them with water. . . .
The raising of winds, the bringing of rain and cold,
Putting her head into position he formed the mountains,
Opening the deep which was in flood,
He caused to flow from her eyes the Euphrates and Tigris,
Stopping her nostrils he left . . . ,
He formed at her udder the lofty mountains,
Therein he drilled springs for the wells to carry off the water.
Thus he created heaven and earth . . . ,
their bounds . . . established.

Marduk then constructs a city in which to dwell:

I will build a house, it will be my luxurious abode.
I will found therein its temple,
I will establish my sovereignty . . .
I will call [its] name [Babylon], the House of the Great Gods,
I shall build it with the skill of craftsmen.[6]

Marduk is depicted in *Enuma Elish* as the one who conquers Tiamat, the goddess of the sea, and her chaotic group of sea monsters; as the one who forms and fashions the heavens and the earth; as the one who reigns supreme over the gods and over the city of Babylon; and as the final word of authority in matters pertaining to Babylon. In the same way, according to Psalm 46,

6. Bill T. Arnold and Bryan E. Beyer, eds., *Readings from the Ancient Near East* (Grand Rapids: Baker, 2002), p. 41. See also *ANET*, pp. 60-72, 501-3; and Benjamin R. Foster, "Epic of Creation *(Enuma Elish)*," in *COS*, 1:390-402.

the Lord, the God of Jerusalem, conquers the watery chaos and rules from the throne in Jerusalem.[7]

4-7 The scene changes subtly, but dramatically, in vv. 4-7. These verses focus on the city of God. The noisy and foaming waters of v. 3 are transformed in v. 4 to a river and its streams that make *the city of God* joyful. God dwells in the *midst* of the city, and the quaking and the trembling of the mountains have ceased. Even though the nations are agitated and quake, God's voice has sounded and *the earth will not tremble.* All of the geographic elements and many of the verbs used in vv. 1-3 *(quake, tremble, sound)* are present in vv. 4-7, but in the latter verses the chaotic elements have been transformed to peaceful symbols of the presence of God.

The water imagery used in Psalm 46 may be compared with that used in Psalm 42. In Psalm 42, the singer begins with calm images of water — running brooks and tears — and moves to chaotic images — waterfalls and breakers and waves. In Psalm 46, the imagery moves in the opposite direction, from chaos — mountains quaking in the heart of the seas and waters foaming — to calm — a river with streams. In each instance, the presence of God signals calm and order, while God's absence or distance from the psalmist elicits images of chaos.

The second stanza of Psalm 46 ends with the refrain, *The LORD of hosts is with us; a fortress for us is the God of Jacob* (v. 7). The phrase *the LORD of hosts (YHWH ṣᵉḇāʾôṯ)* is used some 285 times in the Hebrew Bible, but only fifteen times in the Psalter.[8] The word translated *hosts (ṣᵉḇāʾôṯ)* is often connected with military undertakings, in both the human and cosmic realms. Many understand the phrase *the LORD of hosts* as descriptive of the God who commands the heavenly army; others view it as an epithet for the God who rules over a heavenly council (see, e.g., Job 1:6). Whatever its meaning, the phrase most likely has its origin in the cultic life of Jerusalem and refers to the God who sits enthroned upon the cherubim in the inner sanctuary of the temple. Zion, the city of God, is the place from which God will command peace and security for all the earth.

8-11 The last stanza is a call in the imperative voice to *Come, behold the works of the LORD* (v. 8). The God who instills trust in the midst of the fear of earthquakes, who sits enthroned in Jerusalem, the city of God — this God will cause wars to cease by breaking bows, cutting through spears, and burning war chariots.

Yahweh as warrior is a powerful metaphor that occurs in many of the psalms in the Psalter.[9] Examples include:

7. See also Pss. 29:3-4; 65:7; 89:9-10; 95:5.

8. Also Pss. 24:10; 48:8; 59:5; 69:6; 80:4, 7, 14, 19; 84:1, 3, 8, 12; 89:8.

9. According to Marc Zvi Brettler, the image of "YHWH as warrior" occurs in 75

Arise, O Lord, in your anger!
Lift up against the furies of my enemies. (Ps. 7:6)

Some trust in the chariot and some in horses,
but we praise the name of the Lord our God. (Ps. 20:7)

With God, we will do valiantly;
he, he treads on our foes. (Ps. 60:12)

For surely your enemies, O Lord,
surely your enemies, O Lord, will perish;
all evildoers will be scattered. (Ps. 92:9)

If I walk in the midst of oppression,
you cause me to live in spite of the anger of my enemies.
You send forth your hand and your hand delivers me. (Ps. 138:7)

The image of God as warrior provided the ancient Israelites with a powerful picture of protection and defense in the midst of the chaos of the natural and political world in which they lived.

In v. 10, God speaks and admonishes, in the same imperative voice we heard in v. 8, to *stand still, and know that I am God.* Stop the tumult and the warfare; stop for a moment and consider the God of the Israelites. And in v. 11, we are reminded, *The Lord of hosts is with us; a fortress for us is the God of Jacob.* The Lord of hosts *will* bring peace to the ends of the earth.

A wonderful legendary story exists about Psalm 46. According to the tale, the translators of the King James Version, who worked in 1604-11 C.E., were determined to arrive at the best possible English translation of the biblical text. When they considered the translation of the poetic material of the Old Testament, especially the book of Psalms, they felt the best choice for a translator was none other than England's own poet and playwright of the time, William Shakespeare. And so they prevailed upon him to work with them in rendering the psalms into good English. Shakespeare agreed and undertook the task. One by one the psalms were transformed from their enigmatic Hebrew and Latin predecessors to the lively English of Shakespeare's day. Serendipitously, Shakespeare arrived at the translation of Psalm 46 on the day of his forty-sixth birthday. Not one to let a good opportunity pass by, Shakespeare decided to "leave his mark" on the Psalter to mark the occasion. The words cooperated, and when readers examine the King James translation of Psalm 46, they discover an interesting phenomenon. The forty-

---

percent of the psalms in the Psalter; "Images of YHWH the Warrior in Psalms," *Semeia* 61 (1993) 136.

sixth word from the beginning of the text of Psalm 46 is "shake": ("though the mountains shake," v. 3); the forty-sixth word from the end of the text of Psalm 46 is "spear": ("he cutteth the spear in sunder," v. 9) — an enduring tribute to the forty-sixth birthday of England's great poet laureate. Thus, according to the legend, Shakespeare, the master English poet of the sixteenth and seventeenth centuries, lent his immeasurable talent to the English Bible translation that was the standard for the English Protestant church for over three hundred years.

In the midst of our tumultuous, chaotic modern world, Psalm 46 reminds us that God can calm the raging seas and the trembling mountains and turn them to rivers of life and calm dwelling places. All that is required of us is that we *stand still* and acknowledge the God who is *with us.*

NANCY DECLAISSÉ-WALFORD

Psalm 47: Clap Hands and Shout to God

Psalm 47 is classified as an enthronement psalm, a psalm that celebrates the enthronement of the Lord as king in the midst of the people. It is an anomaly in the Psalter, since it is the only enthronement psalm that occurs outside of Book Four (Psalms 90-106).[1] In Christian tradition, Psalm 47 is read on Ascension Day (or the following Sunday), the fortieth day after Easter, the day on which Jesus was taken up into heaven (Acts 1:1-11).

Sigmund Mowinckel maintains that the *Gattung* described as an "enthronement" psalm was used in preexilic Israel during the annual New Year's festival (Rosh Hashanah), which is celebrated just prior to the Feast of Tabernacles (Booths or Sukkoth), the fall harvest festival.[2] He writes:

> (The enthronement psalms) salute Yahweh as the king, who has just ascended his royal throne to wield his royal power. The situation envisaged in the poet's imagination, is Yahweh's ascent to the throne and the acclamation of Yahweh as king; the psalm is meant as the song of praise which is to meet Yahweh on his 'epiphany', his appearance as the new, victorious king.[3]

We have no clear evidence in the biblical text of the celebration of such a festival, although some have cited the story of David bringing the ark of the covenant into Jerusalem in 2 Samuel 6 as a description of the rite:

> David and all the house of Israel brought up the ark of the LORD with shouting, and with the sound of the trumpet. . . . They brought in the ark of the LORD, and set it in its place, inside the tent that David had pitched for it; and David offered burnt offerings and offerings of well-being before the LORD. When David had finished . . . he blessed the people in the name of the LORD of hosts, and distributed food among all the people. (2 Sam. 6:15-19)

In Babylon in the second millennium B.C.E., the god Marduk was enthroned at each New Year festival as king over the land and as victor over all the forces that challenged his rule. The epic story known as *Enuma Elish* was most likely composed to support and justify Marduk's position as high god within the Babylonian pantheon. Evidence indicates that it was read on the fourth day of the New Year festival. The first portion of the epic is a history of the gods of Babylon. It begins:

1. The other enthronement psalms are Pss. 93, 95, 96, 97, 98, and 99.

2. For a full description of the New Year Festival and the Feast of Tabernacles, see Mowinckel, *The Psalms in Israel's Worship,* 1:106-92; and Kraus, *Psalms 60–150,* pp. 232-33.

3. *The Psalms in Israel's Worship,* 1:106.

When on high *(Enuma Elish)* the heaven had not been named,
firm ground below had not been called by name,
there was nothing but primordial Apsu, their begetter,
and Mummu-Tiamat, she who bore them all,
their waters commingling as a single body;
no reed hut had been matted, nor marsh land had appeared,
when no gods whatever had been brought into being,
uncalled by name, their destinies undetermined —
then it was that the gods were formed within them.[4]

Soon the godly realm was well-populated and the noise from the younger gods disturbed the elder gods, Tiamat and Apsu. They plotted to destroy the younger gods, but Apsu was prevented from doing so by the god Ea, who killed Apsu. Left on her own, Tiamat created an army of sea monsters to assist her in carrying out the task of destroying the noisy younger gods. Ea was not able to defeat Tiamat as he had Apsu, so the gods appealed to Marduk, Ea's son, to take on the task.

Marduk agreed to go to battle against Tiamat on one condition. If he was successful, the gods would acclaim him as king. The story continues in *Enuma Elish:*

Forth came Marduk, the wisest of gods, your son,
his heart having prompted him to set out to face Tiamat.
He opened his mouth, saying unto me:
"If I indeed, as your avenger,
am to vanquish Tiamat and save your lives,
set up the assembly, proclaim supreme my destiny!
When in Ubshukinna jointly you sit down rejoicing,
let my word, instead of you, determine the fates.
What I may bring into being shall be unalterable;
neither shall the command of my lips be recalled nor changed!"

The young gods agreed to Marduk's request:

Joyfully they did homage: "Marduk is king!"
They conferred on him scepter, throne, and vestment;
They gave him matchless weapons that ward off the foes:
"Go and cut off the life of Tiamat.
May the winds bear her blood to places undisclosed."

4. For a full text of *Enuma Elish,* see Bill T. Arnold and Bryan E. Beyer, eds., *Readings from the Ancient Near East* (Grand Rapids: Baker, 2002), pp. 31-50; *ANET,* pp. 60-72, 501-3; and Benjamin R. Foster, "Epic of Creation *(Enuma Elish),*" in *COS,* 1:390-402.

Thus Marduk set out to destroy Tiamat and her sea monsters. He was, of course, successful. After the battle, he took the corpse of Tiamat and fashioned it into the heavens and the earth. Humankind was created from the blood of a lesser god named Kingu, who had acted as Tiamat's second-in-command in the battle against the younger gods. Babylon was built as the city of Marduk, and the gods celebrated the kingship of Marduk.

> "His name shall be 'king of the gods of heaven and underworld,' trust in him!"
> When they had given the sovereignty to Marduk,
> They declared for him good fortune and success:
> "Henceforth you will be the patron of our sanctuaries,
> Whatever you command we will do."

Marduk is depicted in *Enuma Elish* as the one who conquers Tiamat, the goddess of the sea, and her chaotic group of sea monsters; as the one who forms and fashions the heavens and the earth; as the one who reigns supreme over the gods and over the city of Babylon; and as the final word of authority in matters pertaining to Babylon.

The enthronement psalms depict Yahweh, the God of the Israelites, in much the same way as *Enuma Elish* depicts Marduk. Yahweh is the great king over all the earth who sits upon the holy throne; all people will gather and sing praises.

An interesting feature of Psalm 47 is its location in the midst of a collection of six nonlament psalms at the beginning of Book Two. Since Book Two consists mainly of laments (twenty out of its thirty-one psalms are laments), readers must pay attention to the grouping of which Psalm 47 is a part. The sequence of psalms is: Psalm 45: royal; Psalm 46: a song of Zion; Psalm 47: enthronement; Psalm 48: a song of Zion; Psalm 49: wisdom; and Psalm 50: community hymn of thanks. Psalm 45 celebrates a royal wedding; Psalms 46, 47, and 48 focus on God's reign over the earth from the city of Jerusalem. Psalm 49, a wisdom psalm, emphasizes that human life is transitory and that true wisdom comes only from God; and Psalm 50 again celebrates God's reign from Jerusalem. With Psalm 51, Book Two returns to its characteristic lamenting. Book Two, whose focus is the Davidic dynasty, reminds readers that though the Davidic dynasty is ruling over Israel, the true king of the people is Yahweh, who rules from the temple in Jerusalem.

Psalm 47 is a simple hymn with two well-defined stanzas, each beginning with a call to revere the Lord and followed by a rationale for giving reverence, a rationale introduced with the Hebrew causal particle *kî*, meaning "for, because." The psalm ends with a concluding rationale for revering the Lord, also introduced by the particle *kî*.

St. 1 (vv. 1-5)
Clap hands and shout to God (v. 1)
kî . . . (vv. 2-5)
St. 2 (vv. 6-9a)
Sing praises to God (v. 6)
kî . . . (vv. 7-9a)
Concluding rationale, *kî* . . . (v. 9b)

For the leader. A Korahite[5] *psalm.*

1 *All peoples, clap hands;*
shout to God with a sound of rejoicing.
2 *For the* LORD *Most High is to be reverenced,*
a great king over all the earth.
3 *He will subdue peoples under us,*
and nations under our feet.
4 *He will choose for us our possession,*
the splendor of Jacob whom he has loved. Selah
5 *God has ascended with a shout,*
the LORD *with the sound of a trumpet.*

6 *Sing praises to God, sing praises.*
Sing praises to our king, sing praises.
7 *For the king of all the earth is God.*
Sing praises with a maskil.
8 *God rules over nations,*
God sits upon his holy throne.
9 *Princes of peoples have gathered,*
with[6] *the people of the God of Abraham.*

For to God belong the shields[7] *of the earth,*
God is exalted exceedingly.

1-5 God is mentioned eleven times in the ten short verses of Psalm 47, beginning with the "call to worship" in v. 1: *Shout to God.* The call is given, not just to the people of Israel, but to *all peoples (kol hā'ammîm).*

5. See note 1 on Psalm 42 superscription.

6. The LXX adds *meta.* Thus we may restore the Hebrew text to *'im 'am,* adding the word *with* to the English translation.

7. LXX and Syr manuscripts suggest that *māginnê,* should be emended to *signê* ("governors"), but there is no compelling reason to emend the MT.

In vv. 2-5, the worshippers are told why they should *shout. "Because (kî) the LORD Most High is . . . a great king over all the earth* (v. 2). The appellation *Most High* is a term often used to describe the God of Israel when people other than the Israelites alone are being addressed.[8] Thus, from the outset, the psalm celebrates the enthronement of *the LORD Most High* as a *great king* over *all peoples.*

And yet the center of the first stanza declares that God *will choose for us our possession, the splendor of Jacob whom he has loved* (v. 4). God is *king over all the earth,* and all peoples are to reverence God, but God has chosen a special people for a *possession, the splendor of Jacob.*

Verses 1 and 5 use the same words to admonish the people to acclaim God as king: *shout (rûaʿ)* and *sound (qôl).* The repeated use of the words forms an inclusio around the first stanza of the psalm. Verse 1's *sound of rejoicing* is complemented in v. 5 with the *sound of a* shofar, the *trumpet* blown repeatedly at the New Year's festival. In modern Jewish life, the sound of *shofar* at the New Year's festival serves to remind the faithful of many things, including acclaiming God as king and recalling the giving of the torah at Mount Sinai. In Exod. 19:16-19, we read:

> On the morning of the third day there was thunder and lightning, with a thick cloud over the mountain, and a very loud trumpet *(shofar)* blast. Everyone in the camp trembled. . . . Mount Sinai was covered with smoke, because the LORD descended on it in fire. The smoke billowed up from it like smoke from a furnace, the whole mountain trembled violently, and the sound of the trumpet grew louder and louder. Then Moses spoke and the voice of God answered him. (NIV)

The acoustic component of the theophany at Mount Sinai is reenacted annually as a reminder to the people of the powerful presence of their God as king over all the earth.

6-9a The opening verse of the second stanza admonishes people to *sing praises* by repeating the phrase four times: *Sing praises to God, sing praises. Sing praises to our king, sing praises.* Verses 7-9a begin with the word "because *(kî),*" the same word the reader encounters in vv. 2-5, and provide the rationale for why worshippers should *sing praises. They are to sing praises* because God is *the king of all the earth; God rules over nations; God sits upon his holy throne; princes of many peoples have gathered* at the throne along with *the people of the God of Abraham.*

9b For the third time in the psalm, the psalmist uses the causal particle *because (kî).* Ultimately, when all is said and done, the reason that all peoples should *clap hands, shout to God,* and *sing praises* is that God rules over

8. See, e.g., Gen. 14:18-22; Num. 24:16; Isa. 14:14.

the earth. *To God belong the shields of the earth,* the weapons and symbols of power and rule; God alone is exalted above the earth.

Christians brought up in more traditional, rather staid worship environments often find the ideas of "clapping hands," "shouting," and "singing praises" too boisterous for the context of the formal worship of God. But in situations of utter joy and thankfulness, the raucous "joyful noise" to God is not only appropriate, but the only response that fully expresses the heartfelt gratitude of communities of faith.

NANCY DECLAISSÉ-WALFORD

Psalm 48: Walk around Zion

Psalm 48 is a community hymn, which is more specifically classified as a song of Zion. It is the fourth in a group of six psalms that interrupt, for a brief time, the lamenting which dominates Book Two of the Psalter:[1] Psalm 45 is a royal psalm, Psalm 46 a song of Zion, Psalm 47 an enthronement psalm, Psalm 48 another song of Zion, Psalm 49 a wisdom psalm, and Psalm 50 a community hymn. With Psalm 51, the reader is returned to the familiar lamenting of Book Two.

Psalm 48 is the climax of four psalms in Book Two that celebrate God's reign over the earth. Psalm 45's words of confidence that God has indeed anointed the king who reigns in Jerusalem (45:6-7) are followed by Psalm 46's assertion that the city of God will stand firm since God is in its midst (46:4-5) and Psalm 47's celebration of God as a great king over all the earth (47:2, 7-9). The singers of Psalm 48 call on hearers to survey Zion and marvel at the great city of God.

Psalm 47 may have been used in preexilic Israel during the annual New Year's festival (Rosh Hashanah), and some scholars speculate that Psalm 48 was sung as a part of the liturgy of the Feast of Tabernacles.[2] Tabernacles was one of the major festivals in ancient Israelite life in which pilgrims came to Jerusalem from outlying villages in order to commemorate the provisions of God during the time of the wilderness wanderings. Readers can imagine themselves standing at the foot of the holy mountain in Jerusalem, being invited to "walk around Zion," observe the great city, and celebrate the God who rules over them. The structure of Psalm 48 may be outlined as follows:

A Celebration of the Glories of Mount Zion (vv. 1-3)
A Celebration of the Invincibility of Zion (vv. 4-8)
The Celebration of the Congregation (v. 9-11)
An Invitation to Walk around Zion (vv. 12-14)

A song. A Korahite[3] psalm.

1 *Great is the LORD and to be praised greatly,*
in the city of our God,[4] the mountain of his holiness.
2 *Beautiful of height,*
the object of the joy of all the earth,

1. In Book Two, twenty of the thirty-one psalms (65 percent) are laments.

2. See Mowinckel, *The Psalms in Israel's Worship,* 1:106-92.

3. See note 1 on Psalm 42 superscription.

4. The editors of *BHS* suggest moving the *soph pasuq* ("end of sentence") here, and making *the mountain of his holiness* part of the following bicola, but there is no compelling evidence for such an emendation.

is the mountain of Zion, in the recesses of Zaphon,
the city of the great king.
3 *God is in its citadels;*
it is known as a protective fortress.

4 *For behold kings have come together;*
they have crossed over with one another.
5 *They saw, thus they were astonished;*
they were frightened, thus they fled.
6 *A trembling terror seized them there,*
a trembling like labor pains.
7 *With a wind of the east*
you will shatter the ships of Tarshish.
8 *Just as we heard, thus we have seen*
in the city of the Lord *of hosts, in the city of our God.*
God will establish her beyond all time. Selah

9 *We have considered, O God, your* hesed
in the midst of your temple.
10 *Like your name, O God,*
thus is your praise over the ends of the earth.
With righteousness your right hand is filled.
11 *The mountain of Zion will be glad,*
the daughters of Judah will rejoice,
because of your judgments, O Lord.[5]

12 *Walk around Zion and go around her;*
count her towers.
13 *Consider her strength;*
walk through her citadels,
in order that you may recount
to a generation after.
14 *For this God*
is our God for all time and beyond.
He will lead us unto death.[6]

5. The LXX and Syr add *YHWH,* forming an inclusio with "O God" in v. 10.

6. This phrase, *ʿal mûṯ,* is placed on a separate line at the end of Psalm 48. *Unto death* seems awkward here. The LXX translates the phrase as *eis tous aiōnas* ("for all ages"), perhaps on the model of the many psalms which end with the word *l^{e}ʿōlām* ("for all time"). A number of manuscripts remove the *maqqēp̱,* rendering a single word. A change in vowel pointing renders the word the same as the musical notation encountered in Psalm 46's superscrip-

1-3 The first verse of Psalm 48 sets the tone and theme of the whole psalm. The first colon of the verse proclaims, *Great is the LORD,* and the second colon speaks about *the city of our God.* The Lord is great; therefore the city is holy. God's presence imbues the city with a special character. The city does not inform who God is; God informs what the city will be. Verse 2 goes on to describe the magnificent city of God's dwelling: *beautiful of height, the object of the joy of all the earth.*

A key to understanding Psalm 48 is v. 2, in which the psalm-singer describes the mountain of Zion as *the recesses of Zaphon. Zaphon (ṣāp̱ôn)* is the usual Hebrew word for "north." It is identified in Ugaritic and various other Canaanite myths as the dwelling place of the storm god Baal-Zaphon and as an assembly place for the gods. Its location is the modern-day Jebel-el Aqra at the mouth of the Orontes River, 25 miles north of Ugarit.

In the Baal Cycle of stories from Ugarit, Baal sends a message to Anat, goddess of war, bidding her to come to him:

> in the midst of my mountain, the divine Zaphon,
> in the sanctuary, in the mountain of my inheritance,
> in the pleasant place, in the hill I have conquered.[7]

The concept of the god dwelling on a far mountain is common throughout the ancient Near East. In one of Isaiah's oracles against the king of Babylon, we read: "You said in your heart, 'I will ascend to heaven; I will raise my throne above the stars of God; I will sit on the mount of assembly in the recesses of Zaphon'" (Isa. 14:13).

The Israelites also conceived of their God, Yahweh, as dwelling on a mountain. For them, the mountain was Zion, the city of Jerusalem. In Psalm 48, however, the psalm-singers equate Mount Zion with Mount Zaphon: *Beautiful of height, the object of the joy of all the earth, is the mountain of Zion, in the recesses of Zaphon, the city of the great king* (v. 2). Craigie writes, "The psalmist affirms, in effect, that the aspirations of all peoples for a place on earth where God's presence could be experienced were fulfilled in Mount Zion, the true Zaphon."[8] The mountain dwelling place of the high god has been appropriated by Yahweh, the God of the Israelites. God, not Baal, is the high God. Jerusalem, the new Zaphon, is the holy mountain.

Verse 2 closes with the words *the city of the great king,* which appears at first glance to be a repetition of the words found at the beginning of v. 1:

---

tion, *ʿalāmôṯ*. Do we have a final musical notation at the end of the Psalm 48 or perhaps one displaced from the beginning of Psalm 49?

7. *KTU* 1.3, lines 28-29. See Bill T. Arnold and Bryan E. Beyer, eds., *Readings from the Ancient Near East* (Grand Rapids: Baker, 2002), pp. 50-62.

8. *Psalms 1–50,* p. 353.

great is the LORD . . . in the city of our God. A closer examination of the Hebrew words reveals that two different words are used to express God's greatness. In v. 1, the Hebrew adjective is *gāḏôl,* the usual word for "great or big." In v. 2, however, the Hebrew adjective is *rāḇ. Rāḇ* is used frequently in Ugaritic and other ancient Near Eastern texts as a descriptive word for the king, but the word is used only here in the biblical text to refer to God's greatness. As with the reference to *Zaphon,* the description of God as the *rāḇ* king emphasizes God's position as the high God of all gods.

The words of v. 3 praise Zion as a *protective fortress* because God is *in its citadels.* The descriptive words change from those extolling the beauty and joy of Jerusalem to words celebrating its invincibility. As the reader learns in vv. 4-8, the change in focus is because *kings have come together.*

4-8 Verses 4-8 describe an act of war: *kings come together;* they *cross over;* they are *frightened;* they flee; they are destroyed. Do the words describe an actual battle in which ancient Israel was involved? Some maintain that these words recount Sennacherib's invasion of Judah and the siege of Jerusalem in 701 B.C.E.[9] Should the words be understood eschatologically? Medieval Jewish commentators saw in these verses a vision of the time when the Messiah would conquer and rule the world. Or are vv. 4-8 a nonliteral literary device, depicting a chaotic assault on God's ultimate reign over the world and demonstrating God's ability to withstand any challenge?

Perhaps the best answer to these questions is "yes." "Yes," vv. 4-8 are an appropriate description of Sennacherib's siege; "yes," vv. 4-8 reflect the hope of the coming Messiah; and "yes," these verses remind hearers that God will reign despite all assaults on the world.

Verse 6 uses a vivid metaphor to describe the reaction of the invading kings upon "seeing" the city of the LORD of hosts (v. 5), with its statement that *trembling terror seized them . . . like labor pains.* The all-consuming pain and the high risk of death in the birthing process are used often in the biblical text as a metaphor for the reaction of a people to an enemy invasion. In Jer. 6:24, for example, the prophet speaks concerning the enemy of Jerusalem who is about to invade:

> We have heard news of them,
>   our hands fall helpless;
> anguish has taken hold of us,
>   pain as of a woman in labor.

Isaiah writes this about the inhabitants of Babylon:

9. See 2 Kings 18-19.

Therefore all hands will be feeble,
and every human heart will melt,
and they will be dismayed.
Pangs and agony will seize them;
they will be in anguish like a woman in labor. (Isa. 13:7-8)

Verse 7 employs a metaphor for God's reaction to the invading kings. *With a wind of the east* God will *shatter the ships of Tarshish.* The term "east wind" seems to be a general name for any devastating wind that occurred on the seas in the ancient Near East. In Exod. 14:21, the story of the parting of the Reed Sea, we read that "the LORD drove the sea back by a strong east wind." Jeremiah 18:17 states: "Like the wind from the east, I will scatter them before the enemy."

Tarshish is the point of origin for the ships that will be shattered. The word "Tarshish" first occurs in the biblical text in Gen. 10:4, part of the so-called Table of Nations. Tarshish is listed as one of the peoples of the coastlands, a descendant of Japheth. When Jonah fled from God, he set sail on a ship going to Tarshish (Jonah 1:3). We cannot know its exact location or if indeed it ever had a specific location. The name, rather, indicates a sea-faring place, far from the homeland of the ancient Israelites.[10]

When the psalm-singers described Zion as *in the recesses of Zaphon* (v. 2), they were stating that Yahweh, the God of the Israelites, not Baal-Zaphon, the storm-god, was the high god. In v. 7, when God sends *a wind of the east* to *shatter the ships of Tarshish,* the psalm-singers reiterate Yahweh's status as high god, with all the power and ability of the great storm-god Baal-Zaphon. And they emphasize Yahweh's ability to command the great force of chaos, the sea.[11]

Verse 8 is a transitional verse which moves the singers from the battle scene to a direct address to Yahweh in vv. 9-11.

9-11 In vv. 9-11, the psalm-singers shift from third person descriptions of God, the ruler of the city of Zion, to a direct address to God. They celebrate a number of attributes of God in these three verses, most prominently: *your hesed,*[12] your *righteousness (ṣeḏeq),* and *your judgments (mišpāṭîm).* The God who is victorious over the enemy kings rules with equity and justice.

The term *daughters of Judah* in v. 11 references the villages and towns that surrounded Jerusalem and were dependent upon the city for protection and economic viability.[13] The whole area was under the care and rule of the great king, Yahweh.

10. For other biblical references to Tarshish, see 1 Kgs. 10:22; Isa. 23:1, 6, 10, 14; Ezek. 27:12, 25.

11. See the commentary for Psalm 46.

12. For a discussion of *hesed,* see the commentary for Psalm 43.

13. See Num. 21:25; Josh. 17:16.

12-14 The people are called to embark on a processional around the city and to *count (sāp̱ar)* the *towers, consider* (lit., "place your heart upon"; *šîṯû libbᵉḵem)* the city's *strength,* and *walk through her citadels.* In the ancient Near East a city with strong and impregnable walls was a symbol of military strength and protective ability.

The purpose of the processional is found in v. 13: *in order that you may recount (sāp̱ar) to a generation after.* The God who established Zion *in the recesses of Zaphon,* who destroyed enemy kings with *a wind from the east,* who ruled with *hesed* and *righteousness* and *judgment, is our God for all time and beyond.*

The God who dwelt on Zion in ancient Israel will transcend place and time to be the God of all times and all places, even *unto death.* The Midrash on Psalm 48 states:

> The sons of Korah said: *Great is the Lord, and greatly to be praised, in the city of our God, His holy mountain.* Does this mean that our God is great only in His city? No — the sons of Korah really meant: "Great is the Lord because of what He has done in His city and in His sanctuary."[14]

Psalm 48 celebrates the safety and peace of Zion as a sanctuary in which God has made God's dwelling place. Zion has become symbolic in Judaeo-Christian language of the presence of God among humanity. Entering a sanctuary, a place in which we are aware of the presence of God more than in other places we enter in our daily lives, can evoke in us many of the same words and ideas as the singers of Psalm 48. Each of us needs a place of refuge, a place to feel secure in the presence of God. For there we gain strength to face a world in which God's presence is sometimes difficult to find.

NANCY DECLAISSÉ-WALFORD

14. William G. Braude, *The Midrash on Psalms* (New Haven: Yale University Press, 1959), 1:460.

Psalm 49: Like the Beasts That Cease to Be

Psalm 49 is the last Korahite psalm in Book Two. Classified as a wisdom Psalm, its didactic, instructive qualities recall for the reader/hearer the content of Psalm 1 and Proverbs 1–9. It is possible that compositions such as these originated in educational settings in ancient Israel and were incorporated into the cultic material out of which the Hebrew Bible was formed.[1]

Despite the common didactic, instructive qualities of Psalm 49, Psalm 1, and Proverbs 1–9, however, Psalm 49's subject matter is markedly different. Psalm 1 and Proverbs 1–9 deal with right living — *tôrâ* instruction and fear of the Lord; Psalm 49 deals with the issue of death in the context of human wealth and power. The psalmist explores an answer to a riddle posed in vv. 5 and 6: *Why should I fear in the days of trouble, when the iniquity of my deceivers surrounds me, those who trust in their wealth, and in the abundance of their riches boast?*

The singer of Psalm 49, like the singer of Psalm 44, recognized that sages and wisdom teachers in the ancient Near East argued for a basic moral order in the world. If people were righteous, good fortune befell them. If they were wicked, destruction was their fate. The singer of Psalm 49 does not question the basic order. Rather, the psalmist asks whether the deceivers (from the Hebrew root *'āqaḇ* ("defraud, sneak up on") who trust in their wealth and boast in their riches should be feared.

Psalm 49 is a tightly woven literary unit; in v. 4 the psalmist promises that the listener will hear "a proverb" and "a riddle." The riddle is found in vv. 5-6 and the proverb is rehearsed in the repeated refrain of vv. 12 and 20. We may outline the form of Psalm 49 as follows:

Introductory Words (vv. 1-6)
    A Call to All Peoples to Hear (vv. 1-2)
    The Format, "A Riddle" (vv. 3-4)
    The Content of "The Riddle" (vv. 5-6)
First Response to the Riddle (vv. 7-12)
    Meditation on Boasting in Riches (vv. 7-11)
    Refrain (v. 12)
Summary Interlude (vv. 13-15)[2]

1. For two good treatments of education in Ancient Israel, see James L. Crenshaw, *Education in Ancient Israel: Across the Deadening Silence* (ABRL; New York: Doubleday, 1998); and Philip R. Davies, *Scribes and Schools: The Canonization of the Hebrew Scriptures* (Louisville: Westminster John Knox, 1998).

2. I understand vv. 13-15 as a separate strophe, along with Terrien, *The Psalms,* p. 390. Terrien, however, does not place vv. 13-15 at the structural center of the psalm.

Second Response to the Riddle (vv. 16-20)
- Admonition to Hearers (vv. 16-19)
- Refrain (v. 20)

In this structure, vv. 13-15 are the center of Psalm 49 and provide the answer to the riddle posed in v. 5: *Why should I fear?* The answer given is, "You should not fear because, *Like sheep, to Sheol they are appointed*" (v. 14).

The word *Sheol (š^{e}ʾôl)* occurs some sixty-five times in the Hebrew Bible. It comes from the root *šʾl* ("to be extinguished"). The text identifies it as the abode of the dead and generally locates it in the depths of the earth (Gen. 37:35; 1 Kgs. 2:6; Ps. 86:13; Prov. 9:18; Isa. 38:10). The image the word *Sheol* conjures up for the modern reader is that of a shadowy, dark existence, cut off from the presence of God — similar to the idea of "hell." But the idea of Sheol is very different from the idea of hell.

In ancient Israelite thought, Sheol was the place to which all who died went — regardless of whether they were righteous or wicked. In Gen. 37:35, Jacob states that he will go down to Sheol to be with Joseph; Pss. 6:5 and 18:5 use "Sheol" as a poetic parallel for "death."

Sheol is also depicted negatively. In Isa. 38:10, King Hezekiah, who had been mortally ill, states: "I said: In the noontide of my days I must depart; I am consigned to the gates of Sheol for the rest of my years." The singer of Psalm 88 says: "for my soul is saturated with distress, my life draws near to Sheol. I am thought of as one of those going down to the Pit" (vv. 3-4). The psalm-singer goes on to enunciate another reason for the negative view of Sheol: "With the dead, I am set free, like the one slain, ones lying in a grave, whom you do not remember anymore; who is cut off from your hand" (v. 5).

God is not in Sheol. God is the god of the living. In the ancient Israelite view, life was the time in which one served God. Life was the time to be righteous and just, the time in which to find joy and purpose. Death marked the end of the presence of God, the end of joy and purpose. The singer of Psalm 6 states: "Turn, O LORD, deliver my soul! Save me for the sake of your *hesed.* For in death there is no remembrance of you; in Sheol, who will praise you?" (vv. 4-5).

Death, and the inevitable descent into Sheol, marked the end of the possibilities of life. Sheol was the opposite of life, the opposite of living in the presence of God, with all the benefits that it brings. To be rescued from Sheol meant that the person would be alive and would still have available the goodness of life lived in the presence of God. The singer of Psalm 16 says: "Therefore, my heart is glad and my soul rejoices, even my body dwells securely. For you will not abandon my soul to Sheol, you will not allow your faithful one to see the pit" (vv. 9-10).

The words of Ps. 49:15 praise God for rescuing the psalmist from the *iniquity of my deceivers* (v. 5), for allowing the psalmist to continue in life: *But God will rescue my inmost being from the hand of Sheol, for he will take me.*

Psalm 49 is fraught with textual problems. In the translation below, the MT has been followed as far as is possible. In those instances where the MT is largely incomprehensible, this translation will follow the majority voice of the textual emendations.

For the leader. A Korahite psalm.

1 *Hear this, all the peoples.*
Give an ear, all inhabitants of the world,
2 *also the humble and the mighty,*[3]
together with the rich and the poor.
3 *My mouth will speak wisdoms,*
and the meditation of my heart insights.
4 *I will incline my ear to a proverb,*
I will reveal my riddle with a harp.
5 *Why should I fear in the days of trouble,*
when the iniquity of my deceivers surrounds me,
6 *those who trust in their wealth,*
and in the abundance of their riches boast?

7 *Alas! A person cannot in any way redeem,*
cannot give to God their own ransom.
8 *For the redemption money of the inmost being is costly,*
and one will give it up for all time.
9 *And then that one would live always,*
would not see the pit.
10 *For a person can see that wise ones will die;*
all together the foolish and the stupid will perish,
and they will leave to others their wealth.
11 *Their grave*[4] *is their home for all time,*
their dwelling places for all generations,

3. The Hebrew translated here as *humble* and *mighty* is *bᵉnê ʾāḏām* and *bᵉnê ʾîš* ("children of humanity" and "children of a man"). The phrases are idioms, indicating "all folk" and "special folk." See Ps. 62:9 for the same use of the phrases.

4. MT has *qirbām* ("their inward thought"). LXX, Syr, and Targumim have *qiḇrām* ("their grave"). In addition, the Midrash on Psalm 49 states, "Do not read *kirbam*, 'their inward thought,' but *kibram*, 'their grave.'" See William G. Braude, *The Midrash on Psalms* (New Haven: Yale University Press, 1959), 1:466.

though they have given their names to the lands.
12 *And a human being with such wealth cannot have insight;*[5]
that one is like the beasts that cease to be.

13 *Such is their path, their folly,*
and their end[6] *is that in their own portion they take pleasure.*
Selah
14 *Like sheep, to Sheol they are appointed.*
Death is their shepherd.
For the upright shall subdue them in the morning,
and their form will waste away;
Sheol will be a dwelling place for them.[7]
15 *But God will rescue my inmost being from the hand of Sheol,*
for he will take me. Selah

16 *Do not fear if a person should become rich,*
when the wealth of that one's house becomes great.
17 *For in the time of death, that one will not take it all;*
wealth will not go down with the person.
18 *Though in life, a person may bless their own inmost being,*
because others will praise you when your inmost being does well,
19 *That one will go to the generation of their ancestors,*
for all time not seeing the light.[8]
20 *A human being with such wealth cannot have insight;*
that one is like the beasts that cease to be.

1-2 Psalm 49 begins with a call to all people to listen. The choice of words in the second line of the bicola is unusual and gives hearers a clue about the content of the message they are about to hear. The psalmist calls *all inhabitants of the world (kôl yōšᵉḇê ḥāleḏ)* to *give an ear (haʾᵃzînû).* The word *ḥāleḏ* does mean "world," but "world" in a very specific sense. The word that hearers

5. MT has *yālîn* ("lodge, abide"). LXX harmonizes the words of this verse with v. 20, rendering the verb as *yāḇîn* ("understand, have insight"). In addition, transcriptions from the DSS indicate that 4QPsᶜ also renders the verb in this bicola as *yāḇîn.* See Ulrich, Cross, et al., *Qumran Cave 4: XI,* pp. 56-57. Therefore, the emendation to the MT seems justified.

6. MT has *ʾaḥᵃrêhem* ("after them"). Targ renders the word as *ʾaḥᵃrîṯām* ("their end"). Based on the context, the emendation seems justified.

7. The text of v. 14 is very corrupt in MT. This translation has attempted to maintain the MT wherever possible, but has made emendations where the text is incomprehensible. See the critical apparatus of *BHS* for a full discussion of the suggested emendations.

8. The two verbs in v. 19 are problematic. The first *(tāḇôʾ)* is 2ms. The second *(yirʾû)* is 3mp. The notes for *BHS* suggest emending both verbs to 3ms forms.

would most likely expect here, *'ereṣ,* references more the physical land of habitation. *Ḥāleḏ,* in its basic meaning, has to do with life, with lifetime, with the space and time in which human beings live.[9] Thus a better translation for this phrase might be "all of the inhabitants of this life."

In v. 2, the psalm-singer identifies "all of the inhabitants of this life." They encompass the entire realm of humanity, *the humble and the mighty, together with the rich and the poor. Humble* translates the Hebrew words *b^enê 'āḏām,* a phrase that means, lit., "children of all humanity." The word *'āḏām* is the designation given to the first human whom God created from the ground, the *'^adāmâ,* in Gen. 2:7. "Mighty" translates *b^enê 'îs* and means, lit., "children of an individual person." A better, although less poetic translation, of the two phrases might be "all human beings, regardless of their status in life, including those who occupy special positions within their societies."

3-4 After calling all the inhabitants of this life to listen, the psalmist enunciates the content of the message. The psalmist will *speak wisdoms* and *insights,* will ponder upon a *proverb,* and *reveal a riddle — with a harp! Wisdom* (from the root *ḥāḵām*) and *insight* (from the root *bîn*) have to do with right conduct and proper discernment in living life. The wisdom and insight will be revealed in the words of a *proverb (māšāl)* and a *riddle (ḥîḏâ).* The basic meaning of *māšāl* is "to be like." It is usually translated in the LXX as *parabolē.* A proverb in its basic form contrasts and compares two seemingly unrelated phenomena to show their relationship with each another. In Prov. 10:26, for instance, we read: "Like vinegar to the teeth, and smoke to the eyes, so are the lazy to their employers." *Ḥîdâ (riddle)* is translated in the LXX as *problēma* and is used to designate a perplexing saying or question.[10]

5-6 The perplexing question, the *riddle,* promised in v. 4 is expounded in vv. 5-6. It begins, *Why should I fear in the days of trouble?* For the psalmist the *days of trouble* are *when the iniquity of deceivers surrounds. Iniquity* translates the Hebrew *'āwōn.* The word occurs some thirty-one times in the Psalter and is used to refer to hurtful acts or deeds by human against human. *'Āwōn* may be related to the Arabic root *'āwāh* ("be bent or twisted"). Terrien translates the word in v. 5 as "the twisted words," a suggestion that fits well with the theme of the psalm, that is, speaking wisdoms and propounding proverbs and riddles.[11]

Verse 6 states that the *iniquity* or "twisted words" of the psalmist's deceivers involves them *trusting in their wealth* and *boasting in their riches.* The

9. The noun occurs only five times in the biblical text, in the books of Psalms and Job. See, e.g., Pss. 39:5; 89:47.

10. See, e.g., the use of the word in Judg. 14:12-14; Prov. 1:6; Ezek. 17:2.

11. *The Psalms,* pp. 386-88.

arrogance and taunting of the rich is a common wisdom theme.[12] The riddle of Psalm 49 asks, "Should I fear the words and deeds of the oppressive wealthy folks which confront me each day?"

7-11 Verses 7-9 state that the fate of all human beings is the same and that no one can *redeem* (from the root *pāḏâ*) or *ransom* (from *kāp̱ar*) their being from that fate. The language used in these verses is most likely based on the Israelite tradition of the redemption of the firstborn, which the book of Exodus describes as originating in the event of Passover:

> You shall set apart to the LORD all that first opens the womb. All the firstborn of your livestock that are males shall be the LORD's. . . . Every firstborn male among your children you shall redeem [*pādâ*]. When in the future your child asks you, "What does this mean?" you shall answer, . . . "When Pharaoh stubbornly refused to let us go, the LORD killed all the firstborn in the land of Egypt, from human firstborn to the firstborn of animals. Therefore I sacrifice to the LORD every male that first opens the womb, but every firstborn of my sons I redeem [*pādâ*]." (Exod. 13:12-15)

Even the wealthy do not have enough riches to pay the ransom to redeem themselves from the inevitable fate of all humanity — death, *the pit* (v. 9).

Verses 10-11 remind hearers of the age-old saying "death is the great leveler." All will die, whether wise or foolish, whether poor or rich, even those who have had lands named after them. Their wealth will remain on the earth; others will inherit it.

12 Verse 12 is the first refrain of Psalm 49. It, along with the identical v. 20, constitutes the words of the *proverb* which the psalmist promised in v. 4. The first line of the proverb states that *a human being with such wealth cannot have insight.* The word translated *human being* here is the Hebrew *'āḏām,* the same term used in v. 2 to describe *the humble,* the children of the ground whom God created in Gen. 2:7. This human being has *wealth (yāqār* — things that are "splendid, precious, prized, highly valued"), but does not have *insight (bîn* — "discern, decide between").[13] This person, in fact, is *like* (from the root *māšal,* from which we derive the word "proverb") *the beasts.* Therefore we may translate this phrase, "This human being is a proverb like the beasts that cease to be." The beasts die; the human being with wealth will die.

13-15 In vv. 13-15, the hearer arrives at the answer to the riddle posed in vv. 5-6. The riddle, "Why should I fear in the days of trouble, when the iniquity (or, 'twisted word') of my deceivers surrounds me?" is answered simply, *to Sheol they are appointed . . . but God will redeem my inmost being from the hand of Sheol.* In the end, the boastful rich will have to make do by taking

12. See, e.g., Ps. 73.

13. Proverbs 3:15 says, "She (wisdom) is more precious *(yāqār)* than jewels. . . ."

pleasure *in their own portion.* The Hebrew words here echo the words of the riddle in v. 5. *Portion* translates Hebrew *peh,* which means, lit., "mouth." In v. 5, the deceivers utter "twisted words," and in the end, they will have to take pleasure in their own "mouths."

The *upright* (from the Hebrew root *yāšar,* which means "straight, level") will *subdue them* (the "twisted") *in the morning, and their form will waste away.* And God will redeem (see vv. 7-8) the *inmost being (nep̱eš*] of the psalmist from Sheol.[14] The psalmist is not being promised eternal life after death, as some commentators suggest, but life in this life.[15] When all has been said and done, God will shield the psalmist from the oppression of those who boast in their wealth and allow the psalmist to live peacefully in the presence of God.

16-19 The riddle has been answered. Therefore, *Do not fear.* The next four verses of Psalm 49 admonish hearers to heed the words of the psalm's first fifteen verses, and move forward through life with confidence in the power of their God.

20 Verse 20 reiterates the words of v. 12, closing the psalm with proverbial words of remembering. The words echo those of the preacher, Qoheleth:

> All go to one place; all are from the dust, and all turn to dust again. Who knows whether the human spirit goes upward and the spirit of animals goes downward to the earth? (Eccl. 3:20-21)

and:

> The end of the matter; all has been heard. Fear God, and keep his commandments; for that is the whole duty of everyone. (Eccl. 12:13)

In its position in Book Two of the Psalter, might the words of Psalm 49 be words of admonition to King Solomon? Book One focuses on David. In Book Two, David moves to the background as his son and successor, Solomon, assumes control of the kingdom. Solomon was a great king, known far and wide for his wisdom and his riches (1 Kings 3–10). But Solomon was not without his flaws. We read in 1 Kings 11:

> King Solomon loved many foreign women . . . when Solomon was old, his wives turned away his heart after other gods; and his heart was not true to the LORD his God . . . then the LORD was angry with Solomon,

14. God rescuing from "death" is a common metaphor in the Psalter. See, e.g., Pss. 9:13, 18:16 17; 56:13.

15. For a good discussion of the phrase "God will take me," see J. David Pleins, "Death and Endurance: Reassessing the Literary Structure and Theology of Psalm 49," *JSOT* 69 (1996) 19-27.

> because his heart had turned away from the LORD, the God of Israel. (1 Kgs. 11:1, 4, 9)

Indeed, Solomon could boast in his riches and could claim great wisdom. But, in the end, he turned away from God and did not find favor in God's eyes. As the proverb goes: *A human being with such wealth cannot have insight . . .* (Ps. 49:12).

Psalm 49 reminds the hearer that wealth and position and boasting do not give one position in the realm of God. Craigie writes, "The wisdom teacher in Ps 49 eliminates two possible kinds of human fear: the fear of foes in times of trial (v. 5) and the fear that the wealthy have some kind of advantage in the face of death (v. 17)."[16] The reverence of the Lord is the path to wisdom and meaning in life, the message echoed by Jesus in Luke 12: "Do not keep striving for what you are to eat and what you are to drink, and do not keep worrying . . . instead, strive for [God's] kingdom, and these things will be given to you as well" (Luke 12:29, 31).

NANCY DECLAISSÉ-WALFORD

16. *Psalms 1–50*, p. 361.

Psalm 50: Listen, My People, and Let Me Speak

Psalm 50, a community hymn, is the first psalm of Asaph in the Hebrew Psalter.[1] Because of its references in vv. 5 and 16 to the *covenant (bᵉrîṯ)* and because of the alternation of voices within the psalm between first plural and first singular, many understand it as a liturgy that was used as part of a covenant renewal ceremony in ancient Israel, perhaps during the Feast of Tabernacles.[2]

The form and tone of the psalm, however, raise some questions about its *raison d'etre.*[3] The psalm urges hearers to a proper faithfulness to their God, and major portions of it are identified as words spoken by God to the people (vv. 5, 7-15, 16b-23). Gerstenberger reads Psalm 50 as an example of levitical, priestly preaching — as a sermon.[4] Kraus corroborates: "In the 'great festival psalms' priestly (Levitical) speakers take the floor. They actualize the commandments of God in a speech of judgment."[5] But Terrien makes the following observation:

> . . . [I]t is not a hymn, a complaint, a supplication, or a sapiential meditation. Is it a prophetic oracle that could not be included in the prophetic books on account of its anonymity? Its inclusion in a book of sacred songs seems to indicate that it was originally a cultic sequence used during a festive celebration, perhaps a liturgy for covenant renewal.[6]

Whether a cultic liturgy or a levitical sermon, Psalm 50 contains words of admonition and instruction to the community of faith. The psalm may be divided into four distinct parts, outlined as follows:

Introduction (vv. 1-6)
Words about Right Sacrifice (vv. 7-15)
Words about Right Living (vv. 16-22)
Conclusion (v. 23)

1. For information about Asaph, see the Introduction to Book Two.

2. Pss. 81 and 95 may have been used similarly.

3. For a history of the discussion about the *Gattung* of Psalm 50, see Stephen Breck Reid, "Psalm 50: Prophetic Speech and God's Performative Utterances," in *Prophets and Paradigms* (JSOTSup 229; Sheffield: Sheffield Academic, 1996), pp. 217-30.

4. *Psalms: Part 1,* p. 207.

5. *Psalms 1–59,* p. 490.

6. *The Psalms,* p. 396.

An Asaphic[7] psalm.

1 *God, God the LORD*
has spoken and summoned the earth
from the rising of the sun until its setting.
2 *From Zion the perfection of beauty*
God is shining forth;
3 *Our God enters and will not keep silence.*
A fire in his presence is devouring;
And around him it rages exceedingly.
4 *He summons the heavens from above,*
and the earth to judge his people.
5 *"Gather to me, my* hesed *ones,*
the ones who keep my covenant by offering up a sacrifice."
6 *The heavens make known his righteousness,*
for God is the one judging. Selah

7 *"Listen, my people, and let me speak,*
O Israel, and I will testify against you.
God, your God, am I.
8 *Not because of your sacrifices will I rebuke,*
nor your burnt offerings which are in front of me continually.
9 *I will not take from your house a bull,*
from your sheepfold he-goats.
10 *For every living being of the forest belongs to me,*
the beasts on a thousand hills.
11 *I know every bird of the mountains,*[8]
and what moves and lives in the fields is mine.
12 *If I hungered, I would not tell you,*
for to me belong the inhabited world and its fullness.

7. This is the first of twelve psalms with the inscription "for Asaph" (Pss. 50, 73–83). Early scholars associated these psalms with one of the Levites appointed by David as a chief musician (1 Chr. 15:17-19; 16:5). In Ezra, there is a group called "the sons of Asaph" (Ezra 3:10). Tate notes that the "psalms of Asaph" should be understood as sponsorship instead of authorship (*Psalms 51–100,* p. 228). Harry Nasuti has done extensive work on this collection and concludes that the Asaphites were a historical group that functioned in the cult and in the life of Israel from pre- through postexilic times with a definite Ephraimite *traditio* (*Tradition History and the Psalms of Asaph* [SBLDS 88; Atlanta: Scholars, 1988]). Goulder disagrees and sees the collection as coming from Israel between 732 and 722 B.C.E. and argues that the psalms are a liturgically ordered group for an autumn festival *(The Psalms of Asaph and the Pentateuch).* Either way, this is a discrete collection, even if scholars are unsure of the psalms' original purpose.

8. LXX, Syr, and Targ translate the word as "the heavens" *(šāmayim).*

13 *Do I eat the flesh of bulls,*
or the blood of goats do I drink?
14 *Sacrifice to God thank offering,*
and fulfill to Elyon your vows.
15 *Cry out to me in a day of distress;*
I will deliver you and you will honor me."

16 *But to the wicked, God has said,*
"What is this that you make known my decrees,
and carry my covenant on your lips?
17 *For you, you have hated correction,*
and you cast off my words behind you.
18 *If you saw a thief, you would run*[9] *with him,*
and with adulterers would be your portion.
19 *Your mouth you send forth for evil,*
and your tongue contrives falsehood.
20 *The shame of*[10] *your brother you speak;*
to the son of your mother you give scorn.
21 *These things you have done, and I have kept quiet;*
you imagine that I am like you.
I will rebuke you and I will draw up for battle before your eyes.
22 *Discern please, this, you who forget God,*
lest I tear in pieces and there will be no escape.

23 *The one who sacrifices with thanks will honor me;*
and to the one who lays down a right path
I will reveal the salvation of God."

1-6 In words of introduction, the psalm-singer tells the worshippers that *God, God the Lord* has *summoned* all of creation to the event that is about to transpire. The appellation *God, God the Lord* employs three names for God — *'ēl,* the traditional name for the Canaanite high god; *'ᵉlōhîm,* a common name for God in the Hebrew Bible; and *YHWH,* the personal name for the God of the Israelites.[11] The phrase could also be translated, "God of gods, the Lord," emphasizing *YHWH* as God over all. Verses 2 and 3 invoke images of the Mount Sinai theophany of Exod. 19:16-19: the noise, the fiery light, the

9. MT has *wattirĕṣ,* translated "you would take pleasure." LXX, Syr, and Targ suggest emending to *wattārāṣ* ("you would run")

10. MT has *tēšēḇ bᵉ* ("you will dwell with"). The editors of *BHS* suggest emending the word to *bōšeṯ bᵉ (the shame of).*

11. See Exod. 3:13-15.

all-consuming *presence.* Indeed, the reader will find that it is because of the Sinai covenant with the people of Israel that the Lord is calling the people to account in Psalm 50. In v. 4, God calls the *heavens* and *earth* — the products of God's creative handiwork — to be arbiters.[12]

And then God speaks. *Gather to me, my* hesed *ones.* For a full explanation of *hesed,* see the commentary for Psalm 43. In its context in Psalm 50, the word conveys the idea of "those who participate in the covenant relationship that God has established with Israel." A further definition of *my* hesed *ones* comes in the second bicolon of v. 5 — *the ones who keep my covenant by offering up a sacrifice.* The word *keep* translates the Hebrew root word *kāraṯ,* which means, lit., "cut" and describes the practice of covenant-making ceremonies in the ancient Near East. Thus a better translation for this phrase is "the ones who cut my covenant." God, the *one judging* (v. 6), summons the people to account for their breach of the covenant.

In the ancient Near East, the act of making a covenant with someone was a solemn and serious ceremony. We have glimpses of the ceremony in two biblical passages, Genesis 15 and Jer. 34:18-20, and there are records of similar covenant ceremonies from the Mari texts (eighteenth century B.C.E.) and from Qatna (fifteenth century B.C.E.). In Genesis 15, God commanded Abram to bring a number of animals to an altar, cut them in two, and lay them "each half over against the other" (15:10). When the sun had gone down, "a smoking fire pot and a flaming torch" passed between the carcasses of the animals, and God said to Abram, "To your descendants I give this land, from the river of Egypt to the great river, the river Euphrates" (15:17-18). In Jeremiah 34, the prophet says that the fate of those who do not keep the covenant will be "like the calf when they cut it in two and passed between its parts" (34:18). At Mari, the phrase "to kill an ass" was equivalent to "to make a covenant." A common element in the covenant ceremony was the recitation of words such as: "As this beast is cut up, may the gods do to me and more, if I do not fulfill the stipulations of this covenant."[13]

Thus we surmise that covenant-making in the ancient Near East involved the slaughter and placement of animal halves on either side of an altar and a ceremony in which each participant in the covenant walked between the slain carcasses and declared their intent to observe the stipulations of the covenant. If any of the participants violated the stipulations, then they swore they would receive the same fate as the slain animals. The verb used in the Hebrew Bible to describe covenant-making — *kāraṯ,* to cut — is thus appropriate and descriptive.

---

12. For similar images, see Isa. 1:2; Deut. 32:1; Mic. 6:1-2.
13. For examples of this kind of vow, see Ruth 1:17; 1 Kgs. 19:2.

7-15 God begins the judgment with the words *Listen, my people.* Such a phrase is unusual in the Psalter, but appears frequently in the prophetic literature. In Hos. 5:1; Joel 1:2; Mic. 6:9; and Isa. 44:1; 48:12, God calls on the people to "listen" to words of indictment. The indictment in Psalm 50 involves the attitude in which worshippers approach the sacrificial ceremony. God says, *Not because of your sacrifices will I rebuke you.* Sacrifice is a necessary part of the human-God relationship — at least for humanity. Humankind needs a costly act of reparation — one in which life, which only God can give, is given back to the creator — in order to fully participate in a relationship with God. Unlike other gods in the ancient Near East, the God of Israel does not accept sacrifice to appease an incessant appetite but to lead worshippers to a true understanding of the costliness of their relationship with God.

In vv. 14 and 15, God admonishes worshippers, in the imperative voice, to do three things: (1) *sacrifice to God thank offerings;* (2) *fulfill to Elyon your vows;* and (3) *cry out to God in a day of distress. Thank offerings* showed gratitude to God for release from trouble, affliction, or death (Lev. 7:11-18) and appear to have been more pleasing to God than animal sacrifice (Ps. 69:30-31). The phrase translated *fulfill to Elyon your vows* means, lit., "send to the God Most High your vows." Rather than sending sacrifices, God requests the worshipper to send consecrated promises.

The recipient of the promises is identified as *Elyon* — "God Most High," an appellation used to describe the Canaanite high god as well as the God of the Israelites. The title may be used in the context of Psalm 50 to remind worshippers that the God of the Israelites is above all gods and is, indeed, the god of all creation. Worshippers should, then, "cry out" to God *in a day of distress.* And if worshippers do this, then God will *deliver* them and they will *honor* God.

16-22 Verse 16's designation *but to the wicked* contrasts with v. 7's *my people.* Both are singular nouns in Hebrew, although in English translation *wicked* conveys the idea of an individual person, while *people* conveys the idea of a group. In v. 16 and in v. 7, the psalmist is using "collective" noun forms. *Wicked* refers to all those who do not keep the stipulations of the covenant they made with their God. *People* refers to all of the covenant-makers. While all of the people have participated in the covenant-making ceremony, only some actually follow its stipulations. Others give lip service to its strictures. God questions the rights of those who do not keep the stipulations to quote the decrees associated with the covenant. And God accuses them of acts which directly contradict the words of the Decalogue (Exod. 20:1-17): "you run with thieves; you cavort with adulterers; you slander others, even your own brother" (Ps. 50:18-20).

God has *kept quiet* up to this point — perhaps in hopes that humanity would come around — but now God must speak and judge those who have forgotten God. Just as a lion will eventually *tear in pieces* its prey, so God will punish those who do not honor the covenant.

23 Verse 23, the concluding comments to the gathered worshippers, reiterates the words of v. 14. God admonishes the people to *sacrifice with thanks* in order to *honor* the God Most High. And to the one who lays down a right path, God will *reveal salvation.*

The God of Israel, the Most High God, speaks forth from the beauty and terror of creation to admonish worshippers to approach God with honesty, sincerity, and integrity. Sacrifice, while important, is not enough. Sacrifice with proper attitude is the acceptable offering to God. God does not need sacrifice; humanity does. God is the creator and sustainer of all living things; humanity is the recipient and caretaker. Sacrifice is an act of worship and thanks to God, not a way to even the score. Sacrifice is an acknowledgement of humanity's place within the created order. When humankind approaches the altar of the Most High God, God will look at the *inmost being (nep̄eš)* and render judgment. Acts of worship, whatever forms they take, must be carried out in honesty, sincerity, and integrity. In the words of the prophet Jeremiah:

> Thus says the LORD of hosts, the God of Israel: Amend your ways and your doings, and let me dwell with you in this place. Do not trust in these deceptive words: "This is the temple of the LORD, the temple of the LORD, the temple of the LORD." For if you truly amend your ways and your doings . . . then I will dwell with you in this place. (Jer. 7:3-5, 7)

NANCY DECLAISSÉ-WALFORD

Psalm 51: When Nathan Entered Unto David

Psalm 51 is the first psalm in Book Two of the Psalter attributed, in its superscription, to David. An individual lament, it begins a series of fifteen psalms of David, eight of which are located, in their superscriptions, in specific events in the life of David.[1] Psalm 51's superscription is: *To the leader. A Davidic psalm, when the prophet Nathan entered to him, just as he had entered to Bathsheba.* The superscription places the psalm in a historical time frame, in the context of a particular event in the life of King David.

David, in residence in Jerusalem while his armies are battling the Ammonites, spies Bathsheba, the wife of one of his military generals, bathing on her rooftop. He sends for her, has intercourse with her, and then conspires to have her husband, Uriah, killed in battle (2 Samuel 11). When Nathan confronts David with the implications of what he has done with Bathsheba, David's only words are, "I have sinned against the LORD" (2 Sam. 12:13). Might we read Psalm 51 as the rest of David's words: David's confession of sin and his plea for forgiveness? They are indeed appropriate.

But does the superscription limit the message and meaning of the psalm? Patrick Miller writes about Psalm 51:

> The superscription does not force one to confine the power of those words to that occasion alone, but it does illustrate with power where such words of passionate self-condemnation and extreme plea for transformation and cleansing are appropriate. The setting of that psalm against the context of the taking of Bathsheba by David is certainly not without justification in the light of what one actually encounters in the psalm.[2]

Placing Psalm 51 in the context of Nathan's meeting with David does not limit our application of its words to that event alone. That is, Psalm 51's superscription does not anchor it to the past, but instead provides a beginning point for reading the psalm, a point of reference for the faithful to reflect on their own acts of unfaithfulness to God. The timeless quality of Psalm 51 is demonstrated in its inclusion as one of the seven penitential psalms of the Lenten season, the lectionary reading for Ash Wednesday.[3]

1. The Psalter contains thirteen psalms that have superscriptions locating them in specific events in David's life: Pss. 3, 7, 18, 34, 51, 52, 54, 56, 57, 59, 60, 63, 142. For a discussion of the importance of the historical superscriptions, see the comments in the Introduction to Book Two.

2. *Interpreting the Psalms,* p. 53.

3. The other penitential psalms are Pss. 6, 32, 38, 102, 130, 143. See the concluding remarks in the commentary for Ps. 130.

PSALM 51

Psalm 51 is classified as an individual lament, but it lacks many of the elements that are characteristic of the lament.[4] It has no complaint against an enemy and no plea to God to act against the enemy. It is a straightforward confession of transgression against God and humanity with a plea for restoration and promises of proper action in the future. Nevertheless, "lament" is an apt description of the psalm. We may analyze its structure in the following way:

Introductory Words — a Plea for Mercy (vv. 1-2)
Words of Confession (vv. 3-6)
The Plea Resumed (vv. 7-12)
The Vow (vv. 13-15)
Concluding Words — the Nature of Sacrifice (vv. 16-17)
A Prayer for Zion (vv. 18-19)

To the leader. A Davidic psalm, when Nathan the prophet entered to him just as he had entered to Bathsheba.

1 *Have mercy upon me, O God,*
according to your hesed;
according to the greatness of your compassion,
blot out my transgressions.
2 *Thoroughly wash me from my guilt,*
and from my sin make me clean.
3 *For my transgressions indeed I, I know,*
and my sin is in front of me continually.
4 *Against you, you alone I have sinned,*
and what is evil in your eyes I have done.
Because you are righteous in your speaking,
so you are pure in your judging.
5 *Behold, in guilt I was born,*
and in sin my mother conceived me.
6 *Behold, you delight in truth in the inmost parts,*
and in what is secret you make wisdom known to me.
7 *Purify me from sin with hyssop, and I will be pure.*
Wash me and I will be whiter than snow.
8 *Cause me to hear joy and gladness;*
May the bones rejoice which you have crushed.
9 *Hide your face from my sins,*
and all of my iniquities blot out.

4. For a discussion of the elements of a lament in the Hebrew Psalter, see the Introduction.

10 *A pure heart create in me, O God,*
and a spirit of hesed *restore within me.*
11 *Do not cast me away from your presence,*
and the spirit of your holiness do not take from me.
12 *Restore to me the joy of your deliverance,*
and let a spirit of willingness support me.
13 *Then I will teach transgressors your ways,*
and sinners will return to you.
14 *Free me from bloodshed, O God,*
O God of my deliverance,
and my tongue will exult in your righteousness.
15 *O Lord, open my lips,*
and my mouth will declare your praise.
16 *For you do not take pleasure in sacrifice;*
and if I gave[5] *a burnt offering, you would not receive it.*
17 *The sacrifices of God are a spirit being broken;*
a heart being broken and crushed, O God, you will not despise.
18 *Do well in your kindness to Zion;*
build the walls of Jerusalem.
19 *Then you will take pleasure in sacrifices of righteousness,*
in burnt offerings and whole offerings.
Then bulls will be offered on your altar.

1-2 The psalmist begins with a series of pleas in the imperative voice: *have mercy, blot out, wash, make clean,* introducing language about cleansing that will run throughout the psalm. The psalmist's imperatival pleas are grounded in the essential character of God's being: *according to your* hesed and *the greatness of your compassion (raḥ^{a}mîm)* (v. 1).[6] The psalmist seeks cleansing from *my transgressions (peša‘), my guilt (‘āwōn),* and *my sin (ḥaṭṭā’ṯ).* The three are the words used most often in the biblical text to describe acts against God and humanity, and they are often found in parallel construction in Hebrew poetry. In Psalm 51, the words occur in vv. 1, 2, 5, 7, 9, and 13. While each word has a basic root meaning — *pāša‘* means "go against, to rebel," *‘āwâ* means "bend, twist," and *ḥāṭā’* means "miss a mark or goal," attempting to define each as a particular kind of action or attitude is not productive. Psalm 51 opens, then, with a piling up of pleas for cleansing and of words describing the past action of the psalmist.

3-6 Words of confession occur in the next section of the psalm. The psalmist begins with an emphatic acknowledgement (with the use of the

5. The *’aṯnāḥ* should be transposed from *w$^{e’}$ettēnâ* to *zeḇaḥ* for the sake of meter.
6. See Exod. 34:6-7.

personal pronouns "I" and "you") of culpability and of the gravity of the situation. Verse 3a is translated literally as *For my transgressions (pᵉšāʿîm) I, I* know. And in v. 4a we find *Against you, you alone I have sinned* (from the root *ḥāṭāʾ*). The specific sin of the psalmist is not enumerated; there appears to be no need to rehearse the details. It is an issue between the psalmist and God.

Is the psalmist not guilty of committing harm against humanity as well as committing harm against God? The obvious answer is "yes." And yet the words of the psalm are addressed to God alone. In other places in the Old Testament, sins against human beings are considered to be sins against God. In Gen. 39:9, Joseph says to Potiphar's wife when she attempts to get him to lie with her: "He (Potiphar) is not greater in this house than I am, nor has he kept back anything from me except yourself, because you are his wife. How could I do this great evil *(rāʿâ),* and sin (from the root *ḥāṭāʾ*) against God?" When Nathan confronts David with his sin in 2 Samuel 12, David replies in v. 13, "I have sinned *(ḥāṭāʾ)* against the LORD."

Verse 5 of Psalm 51 is perhaps one of the most misinterpreted verses in the Psalter. The psalmist, in the depths of remorse for the sin committed, declares that *guilt (ʿāwôn)* and *sin (ḥēṭᵉʾ)* were parts of the psalmist's very conception and birth. Many have understood the words to reflect the concept of "original sin," a depraved nature that is intrinsic to every human being, passed on to us by the first human pair. A more plausible interpretation, however, is that the psalmist is expressing in these words the all-pervasive quality of the guilt which accompanies the wrong-doing.

In the final verse of the confession (v. 6) the psalmist affirms that rather than dealing in transgression, guilt, and sin, God *delights in truth (ʾemeṯ)* and bestows *wisdom (ḥoḵmâ).*

7-12 In v. 7, the psalmist returns to the plea that began in vv. 1-2. The themes introduced in the introductory plea are taken up and expanded on. Verbs request God to cleanse: *purify me* and *I will be pure. Wash me* and *I will be white.*

Beginning in v. 8 and continuing in vv. 10-12, the psalmist moves a step beyond the immediate sinful situation and introduces restoration into the plea to God. In a beautifully alliterative cola in v. 8a, the psalmist seeks the sounds of *joy and gladness (tašmîʿēnî śāśôn wᵉśimḥâ).* The psalmist continues, asking for rejoicing, *a pure heart,* a spirit of steadfastness, a spirit of *holiness,* the joy of *deliverance,* and *a spirit of willingness* in order to move past the present painful situation.

13-15 If restoration is possible, then, vows the psalmist, *I will teach transgressors (pōšᵉʿîm) your ways, and sinners (ḥaṭṭāʾîm) will return to you.* With *tongue, lips,* and *mouth,* the psalmist will teach those who have committed offenses against God and humanity out of the depths of the psalmist's own despair.

16-17 In these verses of Psalm 51, the psalmist reflects on the nature of *sacrifice.* Sacrifices are not offered by humanity to appease God. Sacrifices are necessary because humanity needs symbols, acts with which to come before God to restore right relationships.[7] But the symbol is not the sole element of the sacrificial system. Proper sacrifice requires proper attitude; in the case of the singer of Psalm 51, the attitude is *a spirit being broken* and *a heart being broken and crushed.* The word translated *broken* is from the Hebrew root *šāḇar* and includes the ideas of "contrite, sorry, and humble."

In Leviticus 1–7, God gives to the people of Israel instructions concerning the sacrificial system. An important element of that system is outlined in Lev. 6:2-7. The text tells us that if a person defrauds, robs, or swears falsely against a neighbor, the first thing that person must do upon realizing what they have done is to restore that which was taken to its rightful owner, along with an additional 20 percent of its value. Then, and only then, must the person go to the priest and present a guilt offering. Verses 16-17 of Psalm 51 are not a polemic against the sacrificial system. They are a polemic against sacrifice of material goods without sacrifice of spirit and heart. In the same way that sin cannot be forgiven without a *broken spirit and heart,* so proper sacrifice cannot be offered without a proper attitude.

18-19 The concluding verses of the psalm are a prayer for the city of Jerusalem. Many view the verses as a late addition to the psalm, and thus dismiss their worth to the overall message of the psalm. But Jerusalem, the city of David, the center of YHWH worship in ancient Israel, was a symbol that far surpassed its size or importance in the ancient Near East. It was the cultic center, the only place where proper sacrifice could be offered. If God "caused goodness *(hêṭîbâ)*" for Jerusalem, then it would be well for David and for the people of Israel. And unless that were the case, could the psalmist ever experience true *mercy, compassion* and *hesed*? Rather than viewing vv. 18-19 as a late addition, we may read them as a fitting conclusion, a resolution, to a situation of abject contrition.

Psalm 51 moves the hearer from the words of a penitential plea, *Have mercy upon me, O God* (v. 1), to words of bold confidence, *Then you will take pleasure in sacrifices of righteousness* (v. 19). The movement involves pleas, confessions, vows, reflections, and statements of confidence. The psalmist has lived through the dark night of the soul and emerged on the other side, ready to teach others the ways of God.

As one of my colleagues once remarked, David sinned big and repented big, and the biblical text remembers him as "a man after God's own heart." The words of Psalm 51 are indeed fitting for the great king of ancient Israel and for worshippers in the twenty-first century. Our sins and transgressions

7. See the commentary for Ps. 50:7-15.

may not be as public and blatant as David's in Psalm 51, but we all fall short of living in the *hesed* and compassion of the Lord. When God's *hesed* is restored within us, then we may enter worship with joy and gladness and teach those who have transgressed and sinned, just as we have transgressed and sinned, the good ways of the Lord.

Nancy deClaissé-Walford

Psalm 52: A Lesson on Life's Direction

Psalm 52 does exactly what the one crying out in Psalm 51 promises, "to teach transgressors your ways" (51:13). The psalm teaches not by lecture or proverb, but by offering two contrasting ways of life. By offering this contrast, the psalm leads the audience to see that indeed there is only one way to live, and that is to *trust in the steadfast love* (hesed) *of God forever and ever* (v. 9).

Structurally, the center of the psalm is v. 5:

The way of the one who is against God (vv. 1-4)
    God's future verdict on the way of vv. 1-4 (v. 5)
The way of the righteous (vv. 6-9)

In MT, v. 5 (Hebrew v. 7) is indented slightly from the rest of the psalm. By this visual technique, the psalm's structure places the two ways of life on different sides of God's verdict. The structure may be clear, but the "story" of the psalm does not conform to these divisions. The first four verses describe a way of life, but do so via a challenge to the *Mighty One.*[1] Verse 5 describes God's action, and this may be the reason why this verse is set apart. The action of God is clearly a response to the actions of the one in vv. 1-4. On the other side of the division, the subject changes to *the righteous* and will remain so to the end of the psalm (vv. 6-9). But unlike the single image of the way of the *Mighty One,* the psalm gives a more complex picture of *the righteous.* Verses 6-7 complete the story line begun at v. 1 as *the righteous* respond to the happenings of vv. 1-5. Verses 8-9 offer a "new story." It depicts a life lived as righteous. Without being explicit, the psalm leaves the audience with the clear word that the way of vv. 8-9 is the only logical way of life. It is the only *forever* (vv. 5 and 9) that any thinking person would choose.

To the leader. A Davidic maskil for when Doeg the Edomite came and announced to Saul, saying to him, "David has come to the house of Ahimelech."[2]

1. The address has prompted several scholars to read the genre of this psalm as a prophetic judgment speech (Kraus, *Psalms 1–59,* p. 510; and Tate, *Psalms 51–100,* p. 35). Certainly, vv. 1-4 have much in common with prophetic speech, but the contrasting ways of life (vv. 1-4 and vv. 6-9) also exhibit wisdom characteristics as in Ps. 1. Hossfeld argues the psalm is neither prophetic or wisdom but a prayer for help (*Psalms 2,* p. 28).

2. The superscription added by editors refers to the events depicted in 1 Sam. 21:1-8 and 22:1-22.

1 *Why do you boast in evil, Mighty One?*
violence all the day?[3]
2 *You are devising destruction;*
your tongue is like a sharp razor,
worker of treachery.
3 *You love evil more than good,*
lying more than speaking righteousness. Selah[4]
4 *You love all the words that devour,*
O tongue of treachery.

5 *But God will pull you down forever;*
will snatch you and tear you from your[5] *tent;*
will uproot you from the land of the living.[6] Selah

6 *The righteous will see and fear;*
and[7] *at this one will laugh, saying,*[8]
7 *"Behold, the one who did not set God as his*[9] *refuge,*
but trusted in the abundance of his riches,
growing strong by destruction."
8 *But I am like a flourishing olive tree in the house of God.*
I trust in the steadfast love of God forever and ever.

3. This colon is quite problematic. MT reads "the steadfast love of God all the day." Syr transposes and repoints the MT to "against the godly." LXX reads "violence all the day." The original meaning of the text is difficult to discern as the plethora of translations indicates. However, MT appears to interject a disconnected or misplaced line. The Syr. version interjects a direct object of the one's actions that is not consistent with the rest of vv. 1-4. Considering the context, LXX retains the focus of the first stanza and would then be the better choice (Clifford concurs; *Psalms 1–72,* p. 255). Hossfeld, however, argues to retain the MT as it is, thus opening the psalm with the two contrasting ways of life, and this is also a good solution (*Psalms 2,* p. 26). Any choice here is tentative.

4. *Selah* is probably misplaced here. V. 4 clearly continues the thought of v. 3, even using the same verb to begin.

5. MT reads "a tent," but the implication of *your* seems clear.

6. 4QPs^c reads *hḥyym,* retaining the article inside the construct; Ulrich, Cross, et al., *Qumran Cave 4: XI,* p. 58.

7. 4QPs^c omits the *wāw;* Ulrich, Cross, et al., *Qumran Cave 4: XI,* p. 58.

8. LXX adds *saying.* This may not be necessary, but aids in comprehending the meaning. Syr. follows a different tradition: "and the righteous saw and rejoiced and trusted in the LORD."

9. My translation has made every attempt to use inclusive terms for humans. However, the pronouns here are crucial to the reading of the psalm. The person's own riches are set over and against trusting in the Lord and making God *his* own personal refuge. The same applies to the following two cola.

9 *I*[10] *will give thanks forever because of what you have done;*
I will proclaim[11] *your name that is good,*
in the presence of your loyal ones.

1-4 The psalm opens with a question. *Why* is often directed to God in the psalms,[12] but here the question is addressed to a *Mighty One.* The term usually refers to a hero or great warrior, indeed someone who would be held in high esteem in the community.[13] This one may be mighty but is hardly held in high esteem. As the story unfolds further, the audience learns that this *Mighty One* uses her own words as another warrior would use weapons: *tongue like a sharp razor* (v. 2) and *words that devour* (v. 4). Words are not the weapons of a foreign invader; words are the weapons of someone closer whose love of lying slashes the community as surely as a sword. Verses 3 and 4 reveal even more. The *Mighty One* is accused of loving *evil,* loving *lying,* and loving *words that devour* more than what is good and righteous. What is at stake is not just speech, but the object of the heart's affection. Instead of loving God with all her heart, this one loves evil and words that harm. The whole of the stanza is presented as a question, but also details a way of life that destroys as surely as a weapon. The question of *why* places this way of life in question from the beginning, while the following seven lines demonstrate the depth of the *Mighty One's* commitment to this very way.

5 Verse 5 changes the subject to God. The one speaking this psalm may wonder about the actions of the Mighty One, but there is no doubt where these actions, this way of life, will lead. God's verdict is sure. The verbs describe removal from the community in which the one is rooted. *God will pull you down, snatch you, tear you,* and *uproot you.* The 2ms suffix on the end of each of these verbs is redundant to make the point clearly. God will remove this Mighty One from his *tent* and *the land of the living.* This way leads to oblivion.

6-9 The final stanza changes the subject to the *righteous* ones, but as noted above, it does so in two different ways. Verses 6-7 continue the story line of the poem. *The righteous will see* the verdict of God. The downfall of the Mighty One now becomes not just judgment, but a lesson. Not only do the righteous *see,* they will *fear.* It is not that the righteous are afraid of God in the way we are afraid of a terrorist bomb. They have a deep respect for the

10. 4QPs^c adds a beginning *wāw;* Ulrich, Cross, et al., *Qumran Cave 4: XI,* p. 58.

11. The usual translation of *qāwâ* is "to wait or hope for." Tate rightly argues that the thrust of the psalm has centered on speech, so the meaning here can be understood as speaking or proclaiming hope; see also 19:4 (*Psalms 51–100,* p. 34).

12. E.g., Pss 3:1; 35:17, etc.

13. Gen. 10:8; Pss. 19:5; 33:16, etc.; *gibbôr* is often paired with *ḥayil* ("warrior of valor"; Judg. 6:12; 11:1, etc.); but it can mean the might of the enemy as in Judg. 5:13, 23.

way God has structured human life and the accountability that is part of that structure. The righteous, after seeing and responding to God, react to the way of the Mighty One. Indeed, in what may seem like a cold act, they *laugh* (v. 6), just as God does in Psalms 2:4; 37:13; 59:8 and as Personified Wisdom does in Prov. 1:26. The effect is chilling, but just as in these other instances, the audience learns here that the reason for the laughter is that the Mighty One has trusted in the things he has acquired, instead of placing trust in God. The one could speak arrogantly because he believed that he needed nothing from the community or from God. However, what the righteous know is that his *tent* (v. 5) is set on unstable sand.

The psalm could easily end here, the story told, and indeed at some time in the life of this poem it may have,[14] but instead of being a psalm exclusively of judgment, it continues to teach by providing a contrast to the life portrayed in vv. 1-4. From the hurtful and self-centered life of the Mighty One, the words of vv. 8-9 rush in like a fresh breeze. This is the way of bounty and *trust* and praise. This way could not be more different. The poem brings another change as well. The speaker and the narrator become one with the introduction of "I" language. This way is personal. The speaker is no longer an observer, but a full participant. The words move beyond description and become confession. These words do not *devour* (v. 4) but lift hope (v. 8) and praise (v. 9) in the presence of the community. Unlike the way of destruction, this way allows one to flourish like an *olive tree in the house of God* (v. 8). Theologically, this psalm shares much in common with Psalm 1. Both depict two divergent ways of life. The one is a way of sin and judgment, and the other is a way that brings delight and praise. Both psalms even use the imagery of the righteous one being like a tree planted deeply in a secure place (1:3 and 52:8) provided by God. Instead of depending on human resources, both clearly make God's way of life the only one that any sane person would choose. Other texts may question God as to why the wicked prosper, but in these two psalms the verdict on a selfish life is clear. This is clearly a choice between abundant life or alienation and death (52:5).

The words of Psalm 52 can teach today in the same way they did in ancient Israel. We all know the damage of words. In a media-saturated world, lying words still cut like a razor. Indeed, we are surrounded by a culture that encourages us to be out only for ourselves and believes that our only protection is the wealth and possessions we amass behind gates that lock out the rest of the world. Words of advertisers and terrorists reduce our lives and diminish our delight. Abusive words by one we love and trust can do as much damage as a fist or knife. We know just as these ancient ones do that this way

14. Gerstenberger observes that vv. 1-7 is an older complaint form that is later adapted as communal instruction; *Psalms: Part 1,* p. 217.

leads only to alienation and death. Any sane person would not choose this way to live, but instead grow slowly and surely as a great tree that flourishes in the house of God.

Beth Tanner

Psalm 53: A Lesson of Hope

Psalm 53 is a twin of Psalm 14, but it is not an identical twin. When compared side-by-side, two differences are apparent. The first is that Psalm 53 uses the term *Elohim* instead of the divine name. This is a characteristic of the Elohistic Psalter and demonstrates that the psalm was used in two different collections probably from two different geographical areas.[1] The second difference is that the lines 5b, c, d, and e deviate significantly from Psalm 14's 5b, 6a, and 6b.[2] These differences confirm that psalms were adapted for different circumstances and for use in different communities,[3] and as such, they should be treated separately, instead of one as a redacted or corrupted version of the other.[4]

For such a brief psalm, there is a great amount of debate concerning both its genre and its structure. Some scholars have argued that the psalm is a prophetic message,[5] while others see it in the wisdom tradition.[6] Robert A. Bennett has noted that the psalm contains wisdom, prophetic, and hymnic material.[7] Certainly the psalm does have elements of each of these traditions, and its genre is ultimately determined by what the reader determines is the purpose or meaning of the poem. Is it meant to teach the *fool* to follow a different path, or is it meant as a prophetic condemnation of Israel's enemies? While both are possible, I see it as another lesson continuing the connection with Psalms 51 and 52 as a second way to *teach transgressors your ways* (51:13). These two psalms demonstrate that in exilic and postexilic communities, prophetic material was both predictive in its reading of human nature and pedagogical in reflecting what sin had cost the previous generations.

The first two stanzas present the same theological message as Psalm 52, the fate of the ones who are against God. Psalm 52, however, ends with an alternative view of life lived in God's kingdom (vv. 8-9), while Psalm 53 moves to a wish for the future restoration of Israel. The psalm can be divided as follows:

1. For more on the Elohistic psalter, see the Introduction to Book Two.

2. Ps. 53 is one colon longer than Ps. 14 in Hebrew manuscripts. Ps. 14, however, is one verse longer because of the different numbering in this section of the poem.

3. Kraus, (*Psalms 1–59,* p. 220), Weiser, (*Psalms,* p. 164), Mays, (*Psalms,* p. 80), and Gerstenberger (*Psalms: Part 1,* p. 218) also point out these two psalms confirm the existence of multiple versions of psalms. Also, the LXX text roughly follows Ps. 53 in vv. 5-6, but some editions of LXX have an expansion between vv. 2 and 3 that is quoted in Rom. 3:10-18. This further confirms that psalms were adapted for different uses. For a complete discussion of this Greek addition, see Craigie, *Psalms 1–50,* pp. 146-47.

4. Older commentaries present Ps. 53 in the discussion of Ps. 14 and treat it as a redaction of same (e.g., Weiser, *Psalms,* pp. 164-66).

5. Kraus, *Psalms 1–59,* p. 220; Tate, *Psalms 51–100,* p. 41, following Gunkel, *Introduction to Psalms,* pp. 232-34.

6. E.g., Craigie, via Ps. 14; *Psalms 1–50,* p. 145.

7. "Wisdom Motifs in Psalm 14=53: *nābāl* and 'ēṣāh," *BASOR* 220 (1975) 15.

The acts of fools (vv. 1-4)
God's verdict (v. 5)
A wish for restoration (v. 6)

To the leader according to Mahalath.[8] *A Davidic maskil.*[9]

1 *A fool says in his heart, "There is no God."*
They are corrupt and they commit injustice;[10]
there are none doing good.
2 *God looks down from heaven upon humankind*
to see if there are any who act prudently,
seeking God.
3 *All of them are disloyal;*[11]
they are perverse all alike.
There are none doing good;
there is not even one.
4 *Will these workers of iniquity not know,*[12]
the ones who eat up my people as they eat bread,
and do not call[13] *upon God?*

5 *Then,*[14] *they will be overcome with terror,*[15]
as has not been;[16]

8. This word appears in the title here and in Ps. 88, but not in the title of Ps. 14. The exact meaning of the Hebrew is unknown. It probably refers to the name of a tune, or possibly an instrument.

9. See note 2 on Psalm 32 inscription.

10. The Hebrew is more forceful than what is easily conveyed in English. The verb *tā'aḇ* means "to act abominably" along with the direct object *'āwel,* which means "injustice" or "unrighteousness." The direct object here is also different from Ps. 14's "abominable deeds."

11. Both MT and 4QPs[a] (Ulrich, Cross, et al., *Qumran Cave 4: XI,* p. 18) have *sāḡ,* meaning "to withdraw" or possibly even "be disloyal" (*HALOT,* p. 744); LXX as well as Ps. 14 read the more common word *sār* ("to turn aside").

12. Many translations read "Have they no knowledge" (NRSV). However, the Hebrew clearly uses an active verb here, indicating that knowing is an act.

13. 4QPs[a] has the 3ms form "he did not call; Ulrich, Cross, et al., *Qumran Cave 4: XI,* p. 18.

14. *Šām* usually means "there," but there is no geographic reference. It has a temporal meaning here (Waltke and O'Connor, *Biblical Hebrew Syntax,* p. 658), instructing the audience to read the perfect verbs here in the future, but to understand that since the perfect tense indicates a completed action, the fate of these wicked ones is inevitable.

15. MT reads, lit., "They terror a terror." This verb and noun construct is used for emphasis to indicate an extreme situation much like the function of an infinitive absolute (Waltke and O'Connor, *Biblical Heberew Syntax,* p. 167).

16. Lit., "there is not terror," leading to a variety of English translations. The one above

because God will scatter the bones of the one encamped against you;
they will put them to shame,[17]
for God rejected them.

6 *Would God give*[18] *salvation for Israel from Zion!*[19]
When God restores the captives[20] *of his people*
Jacob will rejoice;
Israel will be glad.

1-4 Psalm 52 introduced a "Mighty One" who was going to fall because of her arrogance. Psalm 53 tells of the *fool,* but the result will be the same.[21] The subsequent description of the *fool* tells not of the simple-minded, but of the malicious (doing abominable deeds, v. 1; going astray and acting *perverse,* v. 3; *eating up people* like *bread,* v. 4). The fool "is someone who, within a particular sphere of influence, counts for nothing, has nothing to offer, gives no help, commands no respect."[22]

This stanza is also dominated by the Hebrew word *'ên,* which appears four times. The word has a range of meanings,[23] but here functions both grammatically and theologically as a particle of nonexistence. *The fool says, "there is no God"* (v. 1), meaning that God does not exist.[24] But the truth is revealed in the next three uses: "good does not exist in them," meaning fools (vv. 1 and 3), and "there does not exist good in *even one*" (v. 3). They may think God is

reads the MT without change and assumes this continues the temporal statement above (see Tate, *Psalms 51–100,* p. 40). The "terror" from the second line is not rendered in English, but is implied.

17. The verb form is a 2ms *hiphil* without a direct object. NIV reads it as "you put them to shame," but this is odd since the cola before and after are in the 3ms form. The *hiphil* can also mean that the subject is put to shame: "They are put to shame," as in Pss. 44:7; 119:31; Jer 2:26.

18. MT 3ms "he would give."

19. 4QPsª has "in the day of Zion"; Ulrich, Cross, et al., *Qumran Cave 4: XI,* p. 18.

20. Often translated as "fortunes," but the exact meaning is unclear. The problem is that the etymology of the word is not certain. It could be from the root *šbh* ("take captive"), with a meaning of "captives," or it could be from the root *šwb* ("to turn back"), with a meaning of "restore back" (*HALOT,* p. 1385). Here the word appears to have the meaning of *captives.*

21. Reading Pss. 52 and 53 together makes the title "Mighty One" even more ironic since this is the same as the "way" of the *fool.*

22. *HALOT,* p. 663.

23. *'Ên* can serve as a particle of negation in a verbless clause (Exod. 5:11), but it also refers to the nonexistence of a person (Gen. 11:30; Num. 27:9); *HALOT,* p. 42.

24. Craigie notes rightly that this is not atheism as we know it, but a *practical* atheism, meaning it is not a philosophical statement, but "he [the fool] lives and behaves *as if* God did not exist" (*Psalms 1–50,* p. 126). See his lengthy treatment of this topic (pp. 126-28).

not capable of action, but indeed, they are not capable of any good. This is further demonstrated by v. 2, which should be taken as referring to the foolish ones of v. 1, not all of humankind.[25] God *looks down from heaven* seeking to find prudent ones, but finds *not even one* that seeks after God. The meaning is clear; a fool is neither prudent nor does he seek God. The stanza ends with their most malicious action: they *eat up my people as they eat bread,* with the nonchalant attitude that just as one eats bread with a meal, so they devour others.

5 Just as in Psalm 52, the end of the fool is not in doubt; these ones will be destroyed. God will cause great *terror* and *scatter their bones.* Interestingly, this act by God is much like the one in the preceding psalm.[26] God will remove *(scatter)* the fools. This section is where the difference with Psalm 14 is the most significant. Where Psalm 14 refers to those who are not righteous and confound the poor, a probable reference to abuses within the community,[27] Psalm 53 calls for God to act against those *encamped against* Israel, an obvious reference to an outside force. The *fool* is often seen as an insider, here defined as an outsider. If this poetic rendering refers to a specific event or group of persons is unknown. The more important point is that those who have not believed in God will be destroyed.

6 Again just as in Psalm 52, the psalm moves from one story line to another. This final image, in the form of a wish, is hard to reconcile with what has come before. Verse 5 spoke of destruction of the enemy. This final verse expresses the hope that v. 5 will quickly come to pass. The psalm is certain about God's action, but is uncertain of the timing of that act. This is a lesson in hope. In both Psalms 52 and 53 God's verdict seems clear, but here the audience learns that sometimes one must wait for that verdict. The three names *Zion, Jacob,* and *Israel* not only make this psalm a national one, but also serve as the final contrast to the *fool* who does not *know* God, for these are the names for *my people* (v. 4) — the ones who know their God.

Psalm 52 teaches that there is one clear way to live one's life. Psalm 53, through another negative example, demonstrates the same, but with a different ending. Psalm 53 teaches that although we may be confident in who controls the world, that reality is not always seen immediately. We all know how hard it can be to keep the faith. It does often seem that the wicked are

25. V. 4 speaks of *my people* and v. 5 of those *encamped against you,* indicating that there are those that are not like the fools. Indeed, the prayer of the psalm is that Israel be delivered from such as these.

26. Ps. 52:5: "[God] will snatch you and tear you from your tent; will uproot you from the land of the living." In Ps. 53 however, the evil one is part of the Israelite community.

27. Ps. 14:5 reads: "They shall be greatly terrified, for God is among the generation of the righteous. The discernment of the poor, you would put to shame, but the LORD is their refuge."

the ones prospering. This psalm describes, not their glory and riches, but the real way the wicked obtain their desires (vv. 1, 3, 4). Their way is not attractive because it is horribly destructive. The psalm's lesson of hope is one for today's world as well. God invites us to look at the hard realities of a corrupt life and to be confident in God's ultimate control of the world. We are called to hope, just as we were taught to pray "thy kingdom come, thy will be done on earth as it is in heaven."

Beth Tanner

Psalm 54: Leveling the Field

Psalm 54 is a prayer for help by an individual. It is the opening prayer of a thematic grouping of prayers (Psalms 54–59 and 61–63) that express a deep confidence in God's protection and vindication. These psalms all express great trust even as the enemies in these prayers grow more and more menacing.

The literary structure is one of poetic narrative, moving from problem to solution.

A cry to God for rescue from the enemies (vv. 1-3)
An expression of confidence in God's aid (vv. 4-5)
A thanksgiving offering and a confession (vv. 6-7)

The superscription to the psalm places it with a particular account on David's life, specifically 1 Sam. 23:15-29. While hiding, David is betrayed by a group of Ziphites who report his whereabouts to Saul. The superscription is added by a later editor, but can aid the modern interpreter to see in what situations the psalm might have been prayed.

To the leader. With stringed instruments. A Davidic maskil[1] *when the Ziphites came and said to Saul, "Is not David hiding among us?"*

1 *O God, by your name, save me!*
And by your might defend me.[2]
2 *O God, hear my prayer;*
incline your ear to the words of my mouth,
3 *for estranged ones*[3] *have risen up against me,*
fierce ones seek my life.[4]

1. See note 2 on Psalm 32 superscription.

2. The context of the psalm infers that the meaning "defend" or "vindicate" be used for the Hebrew word *dîn,* instead of "to judge." The meaning here is not just to *defend* someone, but to judge them and find them worthy of that defense. God is called upon to serve both as the defense attorney and the judge.

3. The word *zār* is debated. Tate, *Psalms 51–100,* uses "stranger" (p. 44), as does NIV. Kraus, *Psalms 1–59,* emends to "presumptive people" (p. 513), and several Hebrew manuscripts, the Targum, and NRSV read "insolent ones." Within the context, all three words could be correct. *Zār* can mean a foreign enemy (Hos. 7:9, 8:7; Isa. 1:7; 25:2, 5) or an estranged one (Isa. 1:4; Ps. 69:8) or one not belonging to your tribe (Num. 1:51; 18:4). If the editor-added superscription is considered, the incident (1 Sam. 23:15-29) involves ones in Judea, but not of David's family. This group betrays David to Saul, and this gives credence to the use of "estranged ones" instead of the "insolent," but without that context, the meaning could be any of the three.

4. Lit., "my *nep̱eš,*" this word has a wide range of meaning: "soul, living being, self." It is the essence of what makes a sack of bones alive.

They do not set God before them. Selah

4 *Surely, God is helping me;*[5]
the Lord is the one who upholds my life.[6]
5 *He will cause evil to be returned*[7] *to my enemies.*
In your faithfulness, put an end to them.[8]

6 *I will give a sacrifice to you with an offering;*
I will give thanks to your name, O LORD,
for it is good.
7 *For he has delivered me from every trouble,*
and my eyes have looked (in triumph)[9] *on my enemy.*

1-3 The psalm opens with a call to God for help. These first two verses give no indication of the exact trouble. The plea is for God to act: to *save,* to *defend,* to *hear.* The opening focuses squarely on God and God's action. First, God is called on to save *by your name.* This is a call to God's reputation and character.[10] Second, God is called to "judge" or *defend.* This may seem like a contradiction, but the understanding here is that just as God will act on behalf of God's reputation, so God will also act to set the world right as a judge. God will weigh the situation and set it right.

5. Most scholars translate *ʾᵉlōhîm ʿōzēr lî* as "God is my help" (Tate, *Psalms 51–100;* Kraus, *Psalms 1–59;* NIV; NRSV), but the construction is not one of a possessive suffix on a noun as it is in Ps. 121:1 and 2, but a participle followed by a 1cs suffixed preposition. The participle can also function as a continuing form of the verb. The LXX also uses a regular verb here *boēthei.*

6. The *b* preposition is not to be read as "God is with or among those who uphold my life." This is a *bêt* of identity *(bêt essentiae)* and indicates the capacity in which the subject acts (Waltke and O'Connor, *Biblical Hebrew Syntax,* p. 198).

7. Reading the Qere (as do LXX and Syr.) as a 3ms *hiphil* verb with God as the subject, since God is the subject of the second colon. Others read with the Kethib and the Targum as a *qal* 3ms with "evil" as the subject (Tate, *Psalms 51–100,* p. 44; NIV).

8. *HALOT* notes that cognate languages allow that this word could mean "put an end to" or "destroy," or it could mean "to silence." The second meaning is possible, but as noted in *HALOT,* in the psalms the first meaning seems to be what the poet intends (p. 1036).

9. The Hebrew reads "my eye has looked on my enemy." The singular is common in Hebrew, but the plural is the normal English rendering. The *in triumph* is added by most commentators to demonstrate explicitly the essence of "looking at enemies" in the context of the poem (see also Tate, *Psalms 51–100,* p. 45; and Johnson, *The Cultic Prophet and Israel's Psalmody,* p. 190).

10. God swears by God's self, i.e., God's own name, as in Gen. 22:16; Ps. 89:35; Isa. 45:23; Jer. 22:5; 49:13. Kraus, likewise, notes that the name depicts God's presence among the people (*Psalms 1–59,* p. 515).

The final plea is for God to hear the *prayer* of the one in need. Notice that the plea to *hear* is last in the sequence and is linked grammatically to the psalmist's current problem. It calls not on the universal characteristics of v. 1, but for immediate aid in the present situation. As in most of the cries for help, the exact problem is not specified. The one praying is threatened, but by exactly whom is not clear. Indeed, translators disagree on the meaning of the word *zārîm*. Either "estranged" or "strangers," on one hand, or "insolent," on the other, are both possible. As noted, I selected *estranged* because it seemed to fit with what the editor who wrote the later superscription would have read. What is certain here, however, is that these enemies stand both against the one in need (v. 3) and against God (*they do not set God before them,* v. 3). The last line of v. 3 provides a type of *inclusio* with the first colon of the poem. God should act not just on behalf of the one, but also should act for the sake of God's self.

4-5 The one praying may be besieged by *enemies,* but she is also confident in God's aid. There is no reason given for the confidence, and that omission makes the statement all the more powerful. The enemies may *seek my life* (v. 3), but the one speaking is also sure that *the Lord upholds my life* (v. 4). The one praying knows this as surely as she knows anything. The contrast confronts the audience and calls them to decide if they can affirm the same statement. Is the hearer of this psalm as confident in God's deliverance as the one praying obviously is? Verse 5 switches from a statement of confidence about God's support to a confidence in how God will dispose of the enemy. Read in isolation, this verse could be understood as an act of revenge seeking, but in the context of v. 1 where God is asked not only to save, but to judge, it is an act of trust in God's way. Indeed, v. 5 states the flip-side of the golden rule. The one praying wishes that all of the harm the enemies have caused will be visited back onto them *(cause evil to be returned to my enemies).* The second line of the verse should be interpreted within the context of the first. God is faithful and thus will *put an end to them.* In other words, God will set the world right, even if that involves destruction of the ones who *do not set God before them* (v. 3).

6-7 The psalm ends in confidence. The one praying is so sure that God will *save* that she tells of what will occur when the threat is over. Verse 6 tells of how the one delivered will bring an *offering* and sing praises. The verse carries a double meaning, for the phrase *it is good* can be referring to God's name (connecting it to v. 1) but can also be referring to the whole situation. Many psalms confirm that giving praises to God in the temple is the way life should be (Psalms 15, 24, 27). Both God's *name* and offering praise in the temple are the essence of good. Verse 7 makes it clear that God's rescue is based on this and *every trouble* the one praying has experienced. Like above, it carries a double meaning. It can be read as a statement of what will occur when God delivers the one praying, and at one and the same time, it says that this is not the only time that God has been called on to save. This one is confident here because he has seen God's actions in the past.

The last line seems harsh to the modern reader, but one can never accuse the psalms of being less than honest; the one injured *looks (in triumph)* on the enemies. I am not willing to go as far as Weiser does in claiming that human vindictiveness is the final note of this psalm and thus these words will have to endure their own judgment.[11] However, the psalm does end with a note of triumph for the one vindicated by God. If God's purpose as judge is taken seriously as one of the guiding metaphors for this psalm, then this little story with its ending functions in the same way as the words of Jesus: "All who exalt themselves will be humbled, and all who humble themselves will be exalted" (Matt. 23:12).

In a world of violence and cruelty, it is hard to be confident that God will make it right. This psalm invites each reader to affirm its words and to share in the confidence of the one praying. The psalm opens with cries lifted to God's character — the power of God's name and the belief that God will judge the world and make it right. The psalm ends with more confidence that God will do exactly as God has done in the past. The last line, which may be unsettling, reminds us of God's care of the least of the world and how Jesus promises to lift the lowly and humble the haughty. There are many powers in this world that try to thwart the purposes of God's kingdom of justice, and those same powers have taught Christians to be docile and polite because Jesus loved his enemies. Yet Christians throughout the centuries have risen up against those powers for the very sake of God's kingdom. Justice may be delayed, but justice is the end result. Those who live to harm others will eventually have to face up to how they have chosen to live their lives.

BETH TANNER

11. *The Psalms,* p. 417.

Psalm 55: But I Will Trust in God

Psalm 55 is a prayer for help from an individual. The prayer's most unique feature is its abrupt changes in thought that give an uneven, disjointed, and complex structure and place the hearer of the psalm within the emotional roller coaster that is suffering.[1]

Cry to God (vv. 1-3)
Description of the impact of the enemies (vv. 4-5)
Wish of the one praying for escape (vv. 6-8)
Result of the acts of the enemies on the city (vv. 9-11)
Description of a betrayal by a close friend (vv. 12-14)
Wish for the end of the enemies (v. 15)
Confession of God's faithfulness (vv. 16-19)
Description of the acts of the betraying friend (vv. 20-21)
Words of encouragement to others (v. 22)
Belief in God's actions (v. 23)

In addition to the complex structure, the psalm's text is very problematic. It contains five words that appear only here, another four words where the Hebrew root is uncertain, and ten lines where the syntax or meaning of the phrase is difficult to impossible to determine, accounting for the great variety in English translations.

To the leader. With stringed instruments. A Davidic maskil.[2]

1 *Give ear to my prayer O God;*
and do not hide yourself from my supplication.
2 *Pay attention to me and answer me;*
I am troubled[3] *with my complaint;*
and I am driven wild,[4]
3 *by the voice of the enemy;*

1. Instead of seeing the chaotic structure as a literary device, Gunkel and Kraus (*Psalms 1–59,* p. 519) argue the psalm is two psalms (vv. 1-19 and 20-23). Others such as Weiser (*The Psalms,* p. 419) read the chaotic form as noted here.

2. See note 2 on Psalm 32 superscription.

3. The root of *'ārîḏ* is uncertain. Many older sources see it from the root *rwd* ("to wander restlessly"; *BDB,* p. 923). Kraus suggests it is from *'bd* ("to perish"; p. 518). Tate suggests that LXX indicates the root *r''* ("to be in a bad way"; *Psalms 51–100,* p. 51). *HALOT* suggests the root is *rdd* ("to be downtrodden," following the Vulgate; p. 1190). NIV and NRSV use "troubled." This is a good solution, since there is no clear root and "troubled" is a general term.

4. The root of *'āhîmâ* is uncertain. The cohortative form of *hwm* does not fit the context ("May I be discomforted"). LXX has a word meaning "troubled." *HALOT* reads it as a

by the stares[5] of the wicked,
for they bring[6] trouble upon me,
and in anger they are hostile toward me.

4 *My heart twists in my chest,*
and the terrors of death fall upon me.
5 *Fear and trembling come upon me,*
and horror overwhelms me.

6 *I cry, "Who would give me wings like the dove,*
so I could fly away and be at rest?
7 *Surely I would flee far away,*
I would lodge in the wilderness. Selah
8 *I would hurry to a shelter for myself*
from the rushing wind and tempest."

9 *Confuse (them), O Lord;[7]*
confound their speech,[8]
for I see violence and strife in the city;
10 *day and night they go around it, upon its walls,*
and iniquity and toil are in the midst of it.

11 *Destruction is in its midst,*
and oppression and treachery do not depart from the marketplace.

---

possible *niphal* of *hmm* ("to be beside oneself"; pp. 242, 251), as does Hossfeld (*Psalms 2,* p. 51). Again a general term is the best solution.

5. The root of *ʿāqat̠* is uncertain and appears only here. BDB argues it may be from Aramaic root *ʿwq* ("to press"; p. 734). *HALOT* notes that the Syr root means "pain" and the Ugaritic means "eyeball" (p. 873), which accounts for the NIV's "stares of the wicked." *Stares* seems a better choice with the parallel of voice in v. 3a, but this is a tentative choice. Hossfeld translates it as "shouts" (*Psalms 2,* p. 50).

6. The root of *yāmîṭû* is uncertain. BDB lists it as a *hiphil* of the root *mwṭ* meaning "to drop or fall" (p. 557). Kraus prefers the LXX reading from *nṭh* ("to stretch or extend"; p. 518). *HALOT* argues it is probably from *ʾwṭ* ("to scream or threaten doom"; p. 816). NRSV and NIV's "bring" substitutes a general word for the more specific options.

7. This colon contains multiple difficulties. First, *blʿ* means both "to swallow or engulf" (i.e., "destroy"; Isa. 49:19; Ps. 21:9; 35:25) and "to confound or confuse" (Isa. 3:12; 19:3; 28:7). Most translations choose *confuse,* seeing a parallel to the second colon (NIV, NRSV, NJPS). Also, there is no direct object in the first line. Some, then, combine the first and second lines into one (NRSV: "Confuse, O LORD, confound their speech") despite a large spatial gap in the Hebrew manuscript. It is quite possible that, based on these difficulties, the line should be left untranslated, but adding a direct object is also possible as above.

8. Lit., "divide their tongues."

12 *Because it is not an enemy who taunts me, I could bear that;*
it is not one who hates me greatly;[9]
I could hide myself from him.
13 *But it is you, my equal,*[10] *my close friend!*
14 *Together we shared pleasant counsel in the house of God,*[11]
as we walked in the crowd.[12]

15 *Let death come upon them with surprise;*[13]
let them go down to Sheol alive,
for evil is in their home,[14] *inside them.*

16 *But upon God, I call;*
and the LORD *saves*[15] *me.*
17 *Evening and morning and at noon,*
I complain and moan,
and he hears my voice.
18 *He ransomed*[16] *my life unharmed*[17]

9. The exact translation is problematic. The verb *gāḏal* means "to grow or become great." It is used in the *hiphil* form here as in Pss. 35:26 and 38:16 and seems to indicate some type of magnification of the participle *one who hates me.* Modern translations vary greatly.

10. Lit., "a man of my own value," commonly thought to mean an *equal.*

11. The exact translation of this verse is problematic. The meaning of the first verb, *māṯōq* ("to be sweet"), is paired with *counsel. HALOT* suggests it means "keep close company" but the word is used in that way only here (p. 655).

12. The word *regeš* appears only here. The fem. noun is in 64:2; the verb form appears in three texts. *HALOT* notes a related Syr word meaning "noise or commotion" (p. 1189), which accounts for the English translation "throng." Kraus, following Gunkel, reads the line as completely corrupt and emends this line adding it to the beginning of v. 15, but this change is not adopted by most (*Psalms 1–59,* p. 519).

13. Reading the Qere "Let come suddenly death" instead of the Kethib "desolations of death."

14. Lit., "their sojourning place" in Job 18:19; Ps. 119:54; Ezek. 20:38. The word implies a *home* or place of residence.

15. The tense of the verbs in vv. 16-17 is difficult to determine. Four imperfect verbs are followed by a *wāw*-consecutive. This structure, according to Waltke and O'Connor, indicates a present situation with the subsequent *wāw*-consecutive representing a sequential or explanatory event (*Biblical Hebrew Syntax,* p. 559). Tate reads the section as a future event (*Psalms 51–100,* p. 50) as does NRSV.

16. The Hebrew text uses the perfect form in v. 18, further complicating the problem of tense in this section. Most continue the tense adopted in v. 16. However, based on the epithet used for God in v. 19, it is possible to read the line as expressing that the past is evidence that God will also act in the present situation. This reading preserves the MT text as it is.

17. Lit., "he will ransom in *šālôm* my *nep̱eš,*" meaning that my very life will be protected, not just from harm, but will be restored to complete wholeness and happiness.

from the battle around me,
for many times it happened.[18]
19 *God, the one enthroned from old,*
will hear and humble them,[19] Selah
because they do not change,
and they do not fear God.

20 *He stretched out his hands against those at peace with him;*[20]
he violated his covenant.
21 *His mouth was as smooth as butter,*[21]
but threats were in his heart.
His words were softer than oil,
but they were drawn swords.[22]

22 *Cast your burden*[23] *upon the LORD,*
and he will sustain you;
he will not let the righteous fall.

23 *You, O God, will throw them down into the lowest pit;*
the ones of blood and treachery,
they will not live out half their days,
but I will trust in you.

1-3 The psalm begins as most prayers for help, with imperative cries to God (vv. 1-2). This fourfold plea sets a stage of urgency: *give ear, do not hide, pay attention, answer me.* The one praying is desperate for response from God. This is followed by the explanation of the trouble and why this one needs God's aid so urgently. This one is crying out because of her enemies.

18. Translations vary greatly for these two cola. NRSV reads, "from the battle that I wage, for many are arrayed against me." *Many* here does not necessarily mean persons, and interpreted as a measure of quantity or time, the verse continues the thought from above.

19. Most follow LXX here, which reflects the *piel* ("to *humble them*").

20. Many translations read the *he* here as the *friend* of v. 13 (NRSV, NIV, NJPS). LXX, however, reads the *he* without the referent to the friend: "He reached out his hand in retribution." The "he" could be the friend or another.

21. This word appears only here. BDB and *HALOT* suspect the word means cream or a dairy product, thus deriving a meaning for this line that is equivalent to the English idiom "butter would melt in his mouth."

22. This word also appears only here. It is thought to mean a dagger or sword (*HALOT,* p. 989).

23. This word also appears only here and is thought to derive from "that which is given" (*HALOT,* p. 393), here meaning something negative (Tate, "lot in life"; NIV "cares"; NRSV "burden").

4-5 The next section turns from the acts of the enemies to the way the one praying is feeling. The torment is not only emotional; it is physical. *My heart twists in my chest* in v. 4 begins a physical description to which anyone suffering emotional hurt can relate: the feeling in the chest, the *terror* and *trembling* that feel overwhelming.

6-8 After the feeling of panic, the one praying wishes he could take flight away from troubles and hide in the safety of a *lodge in the wilderness* (v. 7). This one longs for *rest* (v. 6), for *shelter* from the storm (v. 8). Interestingly, to flee away to a safe place in the wilderness is the same wish that God expresses in Jer. 9:1-2. Both texts express in very physical terms the wish of those experiencing great suffering. Read together, they show that the suffering human and the suffering God both long for an escape from their plight.

9-11 Verse 9 begins a new topic. The sufferer moves from thought of escape to the realities of the city streets. The purpose of this section may be to intensify the desire to flee, for not only is the person physically afraid, but the city is unsafe because of enemies. Verse 10 suggests that the violence extends from the city *walls* to the very *midst* or middle, and this destruction is constant (*day and night,* v. 10). Verse 11 echoes the same image: the city is corrupt throughout, and that is especially true of the *marketplace.* There is no place or no time where this one can escape unless one runs far away. The very city that shelters is now the threat.

12-14 Another new topic, and one begins to feel the bouncing of topic to topic that characterizes the shape of this psalm. Up to this point, the enemies were described with plural nouns and their actions were violent. The enemies lurked in the public places of the city. This betrayal is by one who shared the closest of confidences. Verses 13-14 stress the intimate relationship of these two, an *equal,* a *close friend.* The word translated as *close friend* comes from the Hebrew root *yd'* ("to know") and indicates the most intimate of relationships. Verse 14 reinforces that image. These two shared conversation *in the house of God,* and even in the midst of a *crowd* they were *together.* Is this former friend part of the enemies from above, or has a new threat been introduced? The poem does not answer that question, and the audience is left to wonder. For the moment, readers do not know how this relates to what has come before it.

15 The next step adds to the mystery. The prayer returns to the plural as a wish for the destruction of the enemies. Focus on the friend has not removed the pain of the assault of the many. This verse ties together the first fifteen verses of the psalm. We still do not know if these enemies are related to the friend, but here all of them are put in the same light. This wish may seem as vindictive, but who has not wished for the *death* of the ones who have hurt us? The psalms reflect our real thoughts and our real sorrow. We do wish for others to feel the same pain that they have inflicted on us.[24]

16-19 Just when the psalm has poured forth in disjointed stanzas all of the pain in the praying one's life, this section offers a literary oasis that is equivalent to the *lodge* of vv. 6-8. As noted with the translation, it is very difficult to know the correct verb tense here. I have rendered it as close to the MT text as possible, but the translation of v. 18 remains tentative.[25] I read it as what we often find in the midst of chaotic pain — trust in God. Even in the midst of distress, there is assurance. This one can call upon God and God *saves* (v. 16) and God *hears* (v. 17), and he knows this because God has done it before, *many times* (v. 18).[26] The epithet for God in v. 19 reinforces the feeling that this is the security the one praying needs. After all, God is *the one enthroned from old.* I can be confident in God today because God has been the Ruler of the world forever. Verse 19 further declares that God will *hear* and deal with the ones causing the hurt, for they have no reverence for God.

20-21 But this assurance is often short-lived, and soon the one praying returns to the present pain. Most translations see the *he* of this stanza to refer back to the former *friend* of vv. 12-14. This does not preclude that the friend was included among those in v. 15. Again the story told is one to which all can relate. His words seemed friendly, but in his heart was deceit. This structure fits well with the chaotic nature of a tortured soul as emotions cause a chaotic speech where thoughts have less order than in calmer times. There are two stories here, and it will take time for the one in pain to tell the full tale. This prayer illustrates the way we as humans process our sorrow.

22 The one praying now offers advice directly to the audience, but not about being betrayed by a friend. Again an abrupt shift in thinking takes the audience by surprise. The speaker is now back to assurance and the certainty that God will *sustain* and *not let the righteous fall.* One wonders if the assurance is really for the audience, or is it another way of convincing the soul that God's promises are sure? It is the heart of what the person crying out to God is depending on — it is a wish expressed as an affirmation.

23 This last verse directly on the heels of the previous one serves as a final plea to God. Couched as a statement of truth but within the context of this prayer, it is a statement of hope. I know, God, what you will do to those

24. Dahood notes that this shift from a singular to plural enemies "is characteristic of impassioned style" (*Psalms I,* p. 35).

25. Others such as Kraus have a very different translation of vv. 18b-19, where Kraus argues that a second psalm begins: "'For archers are approaching to me,' there have come to me 'Ishmael and Jalam' and the inhabitants of the east 'all together,' who do not exchange and do not fear God" (*Psalms 1–59,* p. 518).

26. Miller notes, "Frequently, the expressions of confidence point to God's salvation and may refer to such deliverances experienced in the past" (*They Cried to the Lord,* p. 127).

who are against you. I *trust in you* to do it. The psalm ends, then, not with complete resolution, but with the hope that the one who cries to God can trust God to "hear and answer" (vv. 1-2).

This psalm eloquently reflects the emotional roller coaster of one in pain. The twists and turns allow the audience to enter into that emotional territory. Its feeling of besiegement from within and without is one everyone has unfortunately experienced. Yet within the midst of being surrounded on all sides, the oasis is not found in that wished-for wilderness lodge, but in the confidence and security that the one suffering has God to deliver and to save. In that sense, it is both a prayer for help and a psalm of trust. Indeed, the confident trust is a theme in this small section of psalms (Psalms 54–59 and 61–63). Even in the midst of suffering and betrayal by human enemies and friends, the one praying knows that he can depend on God. Thousands of years later, we can still relate to the roller-coaster emotions of betrayal and fear and know, as this prayer claims, that we too can call upon *God, the one enthroned from old,* to come to our aid.

BETH TANNER

Psalm 56: Who Can Do Me Harm?

Psalm 56 is an individual prayer for help, but that cry is embedded in a prayer that speaks of great trust in God's care as do Psalms 54–59 and 61–63. Indeed, there are more lines focusing on trust in God than on cries for help here. The situation is described using several military terms (vv. 1, 2 6), leading some scholars to see this prayer as a national lamentation.[1] The military language may also be the reason an editor connected this psalm with David's problem with the Philistine king in Gath (1 Sam 21:10–22:1). The exact trouble, however, is not specified and thus could apply to any circumstance where the person praying feels surrounded and pursued by those wishing harm.

The text of the psalm is quite problematic, leading to a wide range of English translations, especially in vv. 5-7 and 10-13. The poetic structure is typical of prayers for help, with the exception of an additional declaration of trust in vv. 3-4.

Cry to God for rescue from enemies (vv. 1-2)
Declaration of trust (vv. 3-4)
Description of the acts of the enemies (vv. 5-6)
Petition for God to act against the enemies (vv. 7-9)
Declaration of trust (vv. 10-11)
Offering of thanksgiving for deliverance (vv. 12-13)

To the leader. According to yonath-elem-rachoqim.[2] *A Davidic miktam*[3] *when the Philistines seized him in Gath.*

1 *Be gracious to me, O God,*
for people pursue[4] *me;*

1. Mowinckel, *The Psalms in Israel's Worship,* p. 219. This view is supported by the additional superscription in LXX ("For the people removed from the sanctuary") and the alternative superscription in Targ ("For the congregation of Israel, which is compared to a silent dove at the time when they are far from their cities, and turn again and praise the Lord of the world").

2. The meaning of this phrase is uncertain. MT reads "according to a dove of speechlessness," but many amend *'ēlem* to *'ēlîm,* reading "the dove on distant large oaks or Terebinths." LXX reads "concerning the people removed far from the sanctuary," seeing "the dove" as representing the people of Israel. These interpretations are possible, but it is just as possible that this term indicates a tune to which the psalm is sung that is lost to the modern reader.

3. See note 5 on Psalm 16 superscription.

4. The meaning of the root is unclear. According to BDB, it means either "pant" or "crush, trample on" (p. 983). *HALOT* believes in the case of this psalm it means "to be a nuisance, pester" (p. 1375). In the military context of this prayer, "pester" does not seem strong enough; the NIV's "pursue" seems more appropriate. The same word in used in v. 2.

all day warriors[5] *oppress me.*
2 *My enemies pursue (me) all day,*
for many are fighting against me, O Most High.[6]

3 *When*[7] *I am afraid, I will trust you.*
4 *In God, whose word I praise;*[8]
in God, I trust; I am not afraid.
What can flesh do to me?

5 *All day, they hurt my cause;*[9]
all their plans are against me for evil.
6 *They stir up strife,*[10] *they hide;*[11]
they watch my steps,
for they lie in wait for me.[12]

5. The word is an active participle from the verb "to fight."

6. The word *mārôm* is problematic. Some translations (e.g., NIV) read it as "many are attacking me *in their pride.*" *HALOT* suggests to read *rômmēnî,* thus making it an imperative plea, "Raise me up" (p. 633). As noted by Tate and several English translations, this word is used in Ps. 92:8 as a designation for God. Tate translates the word as a vocative and places it as the beginning of v. 3 (*Psalms 51–100,* p. 64) to make the lines more equal. A vocative seems to be the best fit, but it does not necessarily need to begin v. 3.

7. MT and 4QPs[a] read *yôm,* which the critical apparatus suggests be emended to *b*[e]*yôm,* but DJD suggests there is no room for a *bêt* in the manuscript (Ulrich, Cross, et al., *Qumran Cave 4: XI,* p. 18) or that it is dittography from the line above. With the DSS evidence, dittography seems the best solution.

8. MT reads "in God I praise his word." The line is repeated in v. 10 without the 3ms suffix. The line is problematic, and various solutions have been offered. Kraus notes that this line along with the end of the previous verse is corrupt; he does not translate it here, but does in v. 10 (*Psalms 1–59,* p. 525). Tate translates it as "By God's help, I will be able to praise his word" (*Psalms 51–100,* p. 67). It is possible that, based on the surrounding text, "his word" is a gloss or addition and it should read "In God, I praise; In God, I trust; I am not afraid. What can flesh do to me?" But any translation is tentative.

9. The root *ʿṣb* means either "to hurt" or "grieve" or "to shape." The cognate in Syr and Arabic means to "bind" or "wrap (a wound)" (*HALOT,* p. 864). "They twist my words" of NIV and Tate (*Psalms 51–100,* p. 65) seems to stretch the meaning too far. *HALOT* follows Gunkel and Kraus, who suggest emendation to *yiddāḇrû yiwwāʿ*[a]*ṣû* ("They confer and plan together"), but there is no compelling reason to emend the text here. *Dāḇār* has a wide range of meanings including "business," "matter," "cause," or "event."

10. The Hebrew root *gwr* means to "cause strife" or "attack." Tate, following Gunkel, emends the root to *gdd* ("to conspire"), but there is no compelling reason to make this change (*Psalms 51–100,* p. 65).

11. May be read as the *hiphil* (Kethib) "to spy" or the *qal* (Qere) "hide, lie in wait."

12. Lit., "they lie in wait for *napšî,*" but *nepeš* should not be reduced to "my soul" as many modern translations do. It means the whole self.

7 *For (their) iniquity, will they be delivered?*[13]
In anger, cast down the peoples, O God!
8 *You have kept count of my restless nights,*[14]
put my tears in your bottle;
are they not in your record?
9 *Then my enemies will be turned back*
on the day when I call.
This I know because God is for me.

10 *In God, whose word I praise;*[15]
[in the LORD, whose word I praise.][16]
11 *In God I trust; I am not afraid.*
What can humanity do to me?

12 *I will keep my vows to you, O God;*[17]
I will complete a thanksgiving offering to you
13 *because you snatched me*[18] *from death.*
Have you not kept my foot from stumbling?[19]

13. This is Tate's solution, reading the text as in the MT (*Psalms 51–100,* p. 67). The line reads, lit., "for iniquity, rescue for them." BHS suggests emending the *'āwen* to *'ayin,* as does the LXX, to a noun meaning "nothingness": "On no account will you save them." Others emend *palleṭ* to *palas* ("to weight out/recompense"), thus the NRSV reading of "so repay them for their crime." Tate offers a good and readable solution without changing the text that also fits with the series of rhetorical questions in this prayer.

14. The root is uncertain. BDB lists the root as *nwd* ("to wander aimlessly" [sic 59:9], p. 627). *HALOT* lists the root as *ndd* ("restlessness" or "sleepless nights"; p. 672), which seems to fit better with the verb "to count."

15. There is no suffix on *dāḇār* in either line (see v. 4). Johnson prefers to leave the text as it is ("I thank God for a 'Word' "), assuming that "the word" is a prophetic message (*The Cultic Prophet and Israel's Psalmody,* p. 337). Likewise, Westermann argues that "word" means a salvation oracle (*THAT,* 1:496); also Mays (*Psalms,* p. 208). However, there is no indication of a specific message or oracle given to the one in distress here or that this line should be different from v. 4.

16. This line may be a gloss or addition in an attempt to insert the theophoric name to the Elohistic Psalter. The line is not present in the Syr. For more information on the Elohistic Psalter, see Introduction to Book Two of the Psalter.

17. Lit., "upon me, O God, your vows." Waltke and O'Connor note "your vows" is equivalent to "vows made to you" (*Biblical Hebrew Syntax,* p. 141).

18. Lit., *napšî.*

19. MT uses an interrogative *he,* so it clearly intends this line to be a question. LXX does not reflect a question, and many modern translations follow this reading. MT is understandable as it stands and should be read as such, especially in light of the other rhetorical questions in this psalm.

So I may walk before God
in the light of life.

1-2 This psalm begins with the common petition *be gracious to me* (Psalms 4:1; 6:2; 26:11; 27:7; 51:1; 86:16) and then turns immediately to why God's favor is needed. The need is expressed in military terms. Active participles of *lḥm* ("wage war") appear in vv. 1 and 2. The verb form of *š'p* also appears twice and has the sense of *pursue.* The one praying senses that he is at war with his enemies. However, within the metaphorical world of prayer, these enemies could be real soldiers or it could be any other situation where the one praying feels war is being waged against her. What is clear is its action is ongoing (*all day,* vv. 1 and 2).

3-4 Verse 3 begins with *I am afraid,*[20] a typical response to the situation described above. The phrase is emphatic in the MT,[21] but is directly followed with *I will trust you.* The one praying expresses his fear, but that fear is immediately countered with his trust in God. Verse 4 is repeated at v. 10 with slight variations, forming an *inclusio* of trust for the body of the prayer. This confession ends with the prayer's first rhetorical question, and it stands in direct opposition to the situation in vv. 1-2; in contrast to being surrounded by enemies, the one praying now asks *What can flesh do to me?* The question ends this section and serves to draw the audience into the situation and wonder "what indeed can flesh do?"

5-6 One might think that with this declaration of trust the situation is handled, but the prayer returns to a description of the acts of enemies. This section is tied to the beginning petition by the *all day* (vv. 1 and 2 and the beginning of v. 5). The introduction described acts of war. Here the acts of the enemy are portrayed as premeditated ("making plans," "hiding," and "lying in wait"). The description in vv. 5-6 appears less like attacking soldiers and more like enemies within one's own community who lie in wait for the one praying. The one praying has to worry about the *many fighting against me* (v. 2), but also the surprise attack from those who *watch my steps* and *lie in wait* (v. 6).

7-9 Description gives way to petition. The first line of v. 7 is difficult to read, but Tate's translation posing a rhetorical question preserves the text of the MT and fits well with the other four rhetorical questions in the psalm (vv. 4, 8, 11, and 13), and again the audience is drawn in to respond to the question posed. The petition itself is only one line in length, asking God to *cast down* the peoples. The choice of the plural has caused many commentators to claim

20. MT begins with the word "day," but *BHS* and many commentators see this as a dittography from the verse above and omit it from the translation.

21. Indicated by the redundant independent personal pronoun.

that this psalm is directed against foreign powers,[22] but as noted above, vv. 1b-2 and 5-6 seem to present two different groups of enemies. The movement from a specific enemy to enemies in general is not uncommon (see Psalm 55), and it is just as possible that the plural represents both groups.

Verse 8 explains the reason why God should act, for God has *kept count* of the suffering of the one praying. The verse expresses the belief in God's intimate relationship with her, for God not only knows but can count the physical signs of prolonged suffering (*restless nights* and *tears*). Another rhetorical question aids in the framing of the prayer and again calls on active participation from the audience.

Verse 9 could be read as a statement of trust, but its placement here right after the question to God means it also serves as motivation for God to act. *My enemies will be turned back* because I know God and I am confident that *God is for me* (v. 9). The verse does state boldly the one praying's trust in God, but also works to "remind" God to act as a result of that relationship.

10-11 These verses are the thematic conclusion to the body of the prayer, being almost identical with v. 4. Like v. 4, it is God's *word* that is praised. The exact meaning of this focus is unknown, but it is possible that it refers to the promises of God in which the one praying's trust is grounded.[23] God is often called on to act in response to previous promises made (Gen. 15:2-3; Exod. 32:13). The one praying trusts that God is as good as the promises God makes. Indeed, God is known as keeping the promises made to humanity, so to *praise* God's *word* is to praise the very attribute that the one praying is depending on for his deliverance.

12-13 Secure in the promises of God, the one praying can make his own confident promises. The resolution of the situation is grateful thanksgiving, and the one praying is confident that he will be able to fulfill "his words" because God will fulfill "God's words."[24] The psalm ends with another rhetorical question: *Have you not kept my foot from stumbling?* The question is directed to God as the other questions have been, but again serves to draw the audience into the conversation. The one praying can walk before God, not because of any attribute of his own, but only because of God's protection. *The light of life* is a gift from the God whom he trusts, not one of human invention.

The uniqueness of this psalm is in its use of the five rhetorical questions, questions that are as relevant to the modern audience as to the ancient one.

22. See Johnson, *The Cultic Prophet and Israel's Psalmody,* p. 334. Tate notes that this plural form is also used in a collective sense in Gen. 17:14; Exod. 30:33, 38; Lev. 7:20, 21, etc. (*Psalms 51–100,* p. 70).

23. Tate notes that these may be promises in a general sense or may indicate a specific oracle of salvation (*Psalms 51–100,* p. 69).

24. The giving of a thanksgiving sacrifice is a common response to God's deliverance from trouble (Pss. 7:17; 51:15-17; 54:6-7; 61:8; 69:30-31).

The questions serve to offer a different perspective on immediate troubles and move anyone listening from a human to an eternal perspective. *What can flesh* (v. 4) or *humanity* (v. 11) *do to me?"* makes the audience think beyond the temporal, for the answer from a temporal perspective is that humanity can do a great deal of damage and indeed even take our human life! But from an eternal perspective, there is nothing they can really do because *God is for me* (v. 9). Likewise the question in v. 7 has both a temporal and eternal answer. From a temporal perspective, it does appear that the enemies are thriving; but in God's eternal book, they will be *cast down* (v. 7) because God *counts* the sorrows of the righteous (v. 8). The final question in v. 13 completes the picture and shatters the last vestige of temporal perspective, for it forces the audience to realize that it is God, not their human ability, that has protected them and allowed them to live as long as they have. Trust in God is placed in direct opposition to the enemies and self-sufficiency of the present. Trust in God is the very grounding that gives a way to turn from a temporal to an eternal perspective.

Today the enemies surrounding us may not be "warriors" in a real sense, but the onslaught of those temporal worries and influences is certainly a constant reality that in this modern too-fast world is difficult to escape. The onslaught is sometimes an open confrontation as in war, but we also know that the troubles of this world also lie in wait for us as we journey through life. The psalm can also remind us that for some in our world, the images of war are as real today as they were thousands of years ago. For them, the temporal world is a world fraught with danger, and their only path to the future is a belief in God and God's deliverance. Today, as in ancient times, trust in God is the surest way to live in the present and "not be afraid."

Beth Tanner

Psalm 57: Even Now My Heart Is Steadfast

Psalm 57 is a prayer for help by an individual. However, like Psalms 54–59 and 61–63, the confident trust in God offered in this psalm is the dominant feature. Indeed, this trust surrounds the problem with the enemies and is one of the structuring components of the psalm. Another feature is the repeating petition in vv. 5 and 11 and the unique character of that petition. These two features give Psalm 57 a literary structure where the problem with the enemies is literally surrounded by confident statements of trust.[1]

Opening cry to God (v. 1)
Declaration of trust in God (vv. 2-3)
Acts of the enemies (v. 4)
Petition for God to act (v. 5)
Acts of the enemies (v. 6)
Declaration of trust in God (vv. 7-8)
Offering of thanksgiving (vv. 9-10)
Repeat of the petition for God to act (v. 11)

Psalm 57 shares its last five verses with Psalm 108:1-5 (with some variations), and v. 10 is almost identical to Ps. 36:5. This demonstrates that there were common phrases or stanzas which the composers of the prayers used in a variety of settings.[2]

Like the preceding psalm, Psalm 57 is given a superscription by an editor that associates it with an event in the life of David when he fled from Saul into a cave (1 Sam. 22:1; 24:3). The association may have been made because of v. 1, where the one praying sought *refuge* and remained *in the shadow of (God's) wings* until the danger passed. This added circumstance is not meant to indicate who composed the prayer, but to give the audience an example of a situation when this prayer could be prayed.

To the leader. Al-tasheth.[3] *A Davidic miktam*[4] *when he was fleeing from Saul in the cave.*

1. Terrien notes that this structure makes the psalm architecturally symmetrical (*The Psalms*, p. 434).

2. Gerstenberger notes that this process of using phrases and stanzas in several different settings is a characteristic of ancient liturgy composition (*Psalms: Part 1*, p. 231).

3. Translated lit., "Do not destroy." The exact meaning of the phrase is unknown. Most translators believe it indicates the name of the tune (Kraus, *Psalms 1–59*, pp. 30, 529). Adele Berlin and Marc Zvi Brettler note that this notation is found in Pss. 57, 58, 59, and 75 and probably indicates a "mini-collection" (*The Jewish Study Bible* [Oxford: Oxford University Press, 2004], p. 1344).

4. See note 5 on Psalm 16 superscription.

1 *Be gracious to me, O God; be gracious to me,*
for in you I[5] *seek refuge;*
in the shadow of your wings, I will seek refuge,
until the danger passes by.

2 *I call to God Most High,*
to God who avenges[6] *me.*
3 *He will send from heaven and he will save me;*
he will put to shame those who trample me; Selah
God will send his hesed *and his faithfulness.*

4 *I*[7] *lie down in the midst of lions;*
these devouring ones[8] *are the children of humanity;*[9]
their teeth are spears and arrows,
their tongues sharp swords.

5 *Rise up upon the heavens, O God;*
let your glory be over all the earth.

6 *They prepared a net for my steps;*
I was bowed down.[10]
they dug a pit before me,
(but) they fell into its midst. Selah

5. *Napšî,* which should not be reduced to "my soul" as many modern translations reflect. It means, lit., "my whole self."

6. The verb in MT is from the root *gmr.* BDB (p. 170) argues this word means "bring to an end, complete," thus NRSV "to God who fulfills his purpose for me." NJPS follows LXX, which reads the root as *gml* ("to deal bountifully with"), thus "to God who is good to me." *HALOT* (p. 197) argues that Dahood correctly identified this word as being from Akkadian *gamāru* ("requite, avenge"). Within the context, "avenge" seems the best choice.

7. Lit., *napšî.*

8. The primary meaning of this root is "to burn." *HALOT* offers a second meaning of "devour," and this seems more appropriate in the context of lions (p. 521). The word is in the form of a participle.

9. Most translators read the participle as the verb of the clause, indicating that the devourers are eating humans (Tate, *Psalms 51–100,* p. 73; NRSV; NJPS). NIV divides these two words, placing devouring in the first clause and "humans" as the noun for the next sentence, "men whose teeth are . . ." The grammar in MT is unclear. It could be read as a dependent clause (as NRSV) or as a verbless sentence, "the devouring ones are children of humanity" (also see Gerstenberger, *Psalms: Part 1,* p. 231). Reading it as a verbless clause, the human enemies are like lions, as in Pss. 7:2; 10:9; 17:12; 22:13, 21; 35:17.

10. Lit., "my *nepeš* is bowed down."

7 *My heart is steadfast, O God;*
my heart is steadfast;
I will sing and make music.
8 *Awake, O my honor;*[11] *awake, O harp and lyre!*
I will awake the dawn.

9 *I will give thanks to you among the peoples, my Lord;*
I will sing praises to you among the peoples,[12]
10 *for your* hesed *is as great as the heavens;*
your faithfulness is (as great as) the clouds.

11 *Rise up upon the heavens, O God;*
let your glory be over all the earth.

1 Psalm 57 opens with a double plea using the same imperative as Psalm 56.[13] The reason for the plea in Psalm 56 is that the enemies are threatening. What is sought here is *refuge,* a place of safety from the dangers of the world. Hebrew *ḥāsâ* ("refuge") appears first as a perfect verb, indicating that the very act of taking refuge happens the moment the sentence is uttered,[14] while the second occurrence is in imperfect form, telling that the situation is ongoing until *the danger passes by.* Instead of running from the arms of the enemy as many prayers of help express, here the one praying is running toward God *(in the shadow of your wings),* where this one will be and remain safe. Some have seen in this verse a possible reference to the refuge of the temple and the wings of the cherubim that guard the ark (see Pss. 17:8; 32:7; 63:7).[15] This is certainly a possible context, but that does not mean that the image is limited to this context alone, especially since the editor of the superscription associates this psalm with a cave in the wilderness.

2-3 The addressee changes from God to the audience as the one pray-

11. *K^{e}ḇôḏî* is often changed to *k^{e}ḇēḏî* ("liver"), following Gunkel (*Introduction to Psalms,* p. 27), hence NRSV "my soul." LXX reflects the MT reading, and there is no compelling reason to alter MT.

12. MT is problematic (the same pointing appears in 44:14; 108:3; 149:7) but instead of *b^{e}ʾummîm* ("not peoples"), it should probably be pointed *balʾummîm* ("among the peoples").

13. Both NRSV and NIV break this connection by using "be gracious" in Ps. 56 and "be merciful" in Ps. 57. Gerstenberger notes that this double plea is rare in the psalms (*Psalms: Part 1,* p. 230).

14. Waltke and O'Connor refer to this as an "instantaneous perfective," meaning that the situation is occurring at the very same time as the sentence is uttered (*Biblical Hebrew Syntax,* p. 488).

15. E.g., Kraus (*Psalms 1–59,* p. 530).

ing declares her trust in God. These lines declare that the one praying is certain of God's action on her behalf: "God will *avenge,* come *from heaven,* and *save me* and *put to shame those who trample me.*" The *Selah* may seem misplaced at first, but it serves to both put a definitive end on the preceding declaration as it also sets the last line in the verse apart as the climax of this section: *God will send his* hesed *and his faithfulness* — an expression that will be repeated in slightly different form in v. 10. God's *hesed* and *faithfulness* are often paired in the psalter (25:10; 40:10; 61:7; 85:10; 89:14; 115:1; 138:2) and usually serve a restorative or protective function. The pair, then, fits well within the context of one seeking refuge, where one is in need of both restoration and protection.

4-6 This center section of the psalm describes the acts of the enemies, with an interruption in v. 5 of a petition. This form is unusual and sets the acts of the enemies in the middle surrounded by confident statements of trust (vv. 2-3 and 7-8). The first description of the acts of the enemies is fierce as they are compared with a pack of *lions.* The one praying is surrounded by this pack, who turn out to be not actual lions but humans whose *teeth* and *tongues* are just as dangerous. The syntax of the second colon is problematic, as indicated in the translation notes. But either way the line is read, it is clear that the danger is not being eaten, but harmed by the teeth and tongues that are as destructive as the work of a pride of lions.[16]

Verse 5 interrupts this description and calls on God to *rise up and let your glory be over all the earth.* This same statement will end the psalm. The petition is unusual, as Gerstenberger notes: "In an individual complaint one expects a direct plea for help, not the solicitation of a grand theophany."[17] Why a theophany instead of a plea for aid? A theophany is always associated with God's sovereignty as king of the world.[18] As Kraus states, "[YHWH] as king and judge should now step forward and implement his wonderful power."[19] The one praying is calling for God with all the power of the king, judge, and divine warrior to come and address the situation.

After this great cry, v. 6 seems a letdown as it returns to a description of the enemies and the distress of the one praying *(I was bowed down),* but something has changed. First notice that all of the verbs here are in the perfect form, indicating a situation that is finished or completed. In addition, the last two lines note that the very trap that the enemies set for the one praying is

16. The tongue or mouth of the enemy is often set against the one praying, and in 52:2, it is a weapon, as it is here.

17. *Psalms: Part 1,* p. 231.

18. E.g., Weiser, *Psalms,* p. 427; Kraus, *Psalms 1–59,* p. 531; Tate, *Psalms 51–100,* p. 79; Terrien, *The Psalms,* p. 436.

19. *Psalms 1–59,* p. 531.

the same *pit* those enemies fall into themselves. The addition of *Selah* here accentuates the point that the enemies are done, finished. Their very own traps did them in.

7-8 The one praying's trust turns here to song, and just as the opening of the psalm had the dual cry *be gracious to me,* the dual cry here is one of confidence and trust: *my heart is steadfast.* This trust then turns to singing praise. The one praying cries to the whole world in expanding declarations: awake, O my honor;[20] then *awake* to the instruments of praise *(harp and lyre);* then *awake* to the cycles of creation *(dawn).* The one praying is now leading the chorus that rings through the heavens.

9-10 Trust gives way to thanksgiving, and the one praying *will give thanks* and *sing praises among the peoples.* Thanksgiving among others is a common response to God's saving actions. The reason for this offering of praise and thanks is the very attributes that the one praying was confident that God would send in v. 3. God's *hesed* and *faithfulness* are declared in creational terms and are *as great as the heavens* and *the clouds.* This connection to creation may have a dual meaning, with *great* (v. 10) meaning both the size of these attributes and the fact that they are as sure and constant as the sky and clouds.

11 The psalm ends with a repeat of the petition of v. 5.[21] Some argue this is a later addition or is to be a response from the congregation.[22] This may be the case, but it also serves as a final affirmation of God's reign and the way in which God sets the world right. In v. 5, this refrain functioned as plea, but here the plea has been transformed to an affirmation of God's protection of the one in need.

Today as in the time of the ancient Israelites, we can relate to the need for *refuge,* for a place of safety within the stress and strain of life. The one praying here appears to be one of the righteous ones. The overwhelming trust in God's *hesed* and *faithfulness* tells of a life lived learning hard lessons. The one praying knows that there is no such thing as depending on human power to protect and guard in times of trouble. These hard learnings have brought her to a place where she confesses by acclamations of trust that only God can offer refuge. She has learned so much about the world that she does not even cry for retribution against the enemies, but only for God to act, to *rise up* and be God.

We are daily bombarded by fear. The news tells of murder, rape, and

20. *My honor* is not simply one's self, but as Weiser states, it is the condition when one is filled with praise for God (*The Psalms,* p. 428). The *honor,* it would appear, comes from turning one's whole self to praise for God.

21. Except in v. 11, *heavens* is missing the definite article.

22. As argued by Tate, *Psalms 51–100,* p. 80.

slaughter until it seems an unsafe proposition to ever set foot outside our own door. The advertisements are constantly offering us a cream or pill to ward off death, or a home security system to protect what belongs to us, or a car that will protect us from all ills; but all of these are fallacies. Our trust belongs in God and only God. Refuge will not be found in the security humans create, but in trust in God to care for us when we are threatened. Trust in God and praise of that confident refuge is the only antidote to our fear-driven culture.

Beth Tanner

Psalm 58: How the Mighty Will Fall

Psalm 58 is an individual prayer for help, and the central problem is the acts of evil ones who attack the one praying.[1] It also expresses deep trust in God to act (vv. 10-11), like Psalms 54–59 and 61–63. This psalm, however, adds the additional element of a series of seven wishes or imprecations that tell the audience exactly what the one praying wishes would happen to the *Mighty Ones* described in vv. 1-5. The literary structure is straightforward and moves the audience through three perspectives of the situation.

Description of the enemies (vv. 1-5)
  Rhetorical address to the "Mighty Ones" (vv. 1-2)
  Description of the nature of the enemies (vv. 3-5)
Demand for God to act (vv. 6-9)
Rejoicing of the righteous (vv. 10-11)

The Hebrew text is problematic and most probably corrupt, especially vv. 7-9, where any translation made must be a tentative one.

To the leader. Al-tasheth.[2] *A Davidic miktam.*[3]

1 *Indeed, Mighty Ones,*[4] *do you speak in righteousness?*
  Do you judge uprightly, O humans?[5]

1. Several scholars have argued that the psalm is not a prayer for help, but a prophetic judgement speech (Jörg Jeremias, *Kultprophetie und Gerichtsverkündigung in der späten Königszeit Israels* [WMANT 35; Neukirchen: Neukirchener, 1970], pp. 120-25; Tate, *Psalms 51–100,* p. 84). There certainly are features of a judgment speech here, but the *Mighty Ones* are addressed only in vv. 1-2 and the wish is made by a human to God, not a human giving the words of God to others as would be expected in a prophetic speech.

2. See note 3 on Psalm 57 inscription.

3. See note 5 on Psalm 16 inscription.

4. MT has *ʾēlem* ("silence" or "muteness") and could be read as "Indeed do you speak righteousness (in) silence?" Many translators emend to *ʾēlîm* ("Mighty Ones") in reference to gods as in Ps. 82:1 (*HALOT,* p. 57; Mowinckel, *The Psalms in Israel's Worship,* 1:148; Kraus, *Psalms 1–59,* p. 534; Tate, *Psalms 51–100,* p. 83), hence NRSV "you gods." LXX and Jerome read *ʾulām* ("truly"). MT is readable but does not fit the context. *Mighty Ones* can refer to gods (Ps. 82) or mighty human leaders (Exod. 21:6; 22:7, 8, where the NIV translates *ʾᵉlōhîm* as "judges") and seems to be the best choice.

5. Most translators read *humans* (lit., "sons of man") as the direct object of the verb *you judge* (Kraus, *Psalms 1–59,* p. 533; Tate, *Psalms 51–100,* p. 83; NRSV, NIV). The grammar is not clear; it may be a vocative and is read as such in LXX. If this is the case, then the first line begins with a vocative (after the question) and the second line ends with a vocative, creating a typical Hebrew chiastic pattern. Based on the content of the psalm, there is no

2 *No, in your[6] hearts, you work out wrongs;*
(and) on the earth, you deal out[7] the violence of your hands.

3 *The wicked are strangers from the womb;*
they wander about from birth, speaking lies.[8]
4 *They have venom like the venom of a snake;*
like the unhearing cobra that has stopped its ears,[9]
5 *so it does not listen to the voice of the charmers,*
or the expert caster of spells.

6 *O God, shatter their teeth in their mouths;*
tear out the fangs[10] of the young lions, O LORD.
7 *Let them disappear[11] like water running away;*
let them shoot arrows that fail.[12]

---

reason to believe that these Mighty Ones are any other than humans (Gerstenberger agrees, *Psalms: Part 1,* p. 233).

6. MT does not have the possessive suffix, but Syr. adds the 2mpl suffix to smooth the translation and to match the suffix ending on *hands* in the second line.

7. The meaning of the root is uncertain. BDB lists it as "to weigh" or "make level" (p. 814). *HALOT* argues it has the meaning of "to clear" or "make a way" (p. 935). The above is the best translation while preserving as much of the grammatical structure of MT as possible.

8. The last two words are in construct form that could be read "speaking a lie" or "ones who speak a lie." Several translations read the construct as the subject of the sentence "the liars go astray from the womb" (NJPS) or "wayward liars from the womb" (Tate, *Psalms 51–100,* p. 82). Instead of the participle, the LXX has a 3pl verb, "they speak lies." The phrase "speaking a lie" seems to fit better since *the wicked* from the first line can easily be understood as the subject here. The singular "lie" is altered to a plural for a smoother English reading.

9. Lit., "his ear."

10. The root of this word is uncertain. *BHS* (p. 1139) suggests several manuscripts have *tlʿ* ("jaw teeth"), as in Job 29:17; Joel 1:6; Prov. 30:14. *HALOT* states it is from a hypothetical root *ltʿ* ("jaw-bone"; p. 595).

11. The root of this word is uncertain. It is either a *niphal* imperfect verb or a jussive. The root appears to be *mʾs* ("to be rejected"), but "to be rejected like water" makes little sense. *HALOT* (p. 541) suggests it is from the root *mss* and means "to transgress," but again this makes little sense. BDB (p. 549) suggests the secondary meaning is "to flow" or "run," as in Job 7:5, and most translations adopt this.

12. This line is problematic. Many follow Gunkel, who suggested emending to *kᵉmô ḥāṣîr hadderek̲* and thus read the line as "like grass withered on the pathway" (Kraus, *Psalms 1–59,* p. 534; Weiser, *The Psalms,* p. 429; *HALOT,* p, 344; NRSV). LXX reads the "he" here to be God: "he will bend his bow until they fail," as does Terrien (*The Psalms,* p. 438). Any reading is uncertain, but it is possible to read this line without emending MT. First, a change from plural enemies to a singular enemy is common in the curse sections of the psalter, as shown by Dahood and others (*Psalms II,* pp. 34-35). Second, there is an idiom in Hebrew "to tread his arrow" in the sense of bending the bow (Jer. 51:3; Pss. 11:2; 37:14, etc.), so these two

8 *Let them be like the snail*[13] *that melts as it moves along,*
like an aborted fetus that never sees the sun.
9 *Before their pots*[14] *can discern thorns,*
whether green or blazing,
may he sweep them[15] *away.*[16]

10 *The righteous will rejoice when they see*[17] *vindication.*
They will bathe their feet in the blood of the wicked.
11 *Then humans*[18] *will say, "Surely there is a reward for the righteous.*
Surely, there is a God who is judging the earth."

1-2 The prayer begins not with an address or cry to God. Instead, it asks two rhetorical and probably sarcastic questions of the *Mighty Ones.* As noted above, there is debate as to who these beings are. They may be gods, as reflected in the NRSV translation. The structure of the verse, however, suggests that the vocative *Mighty Ones* is a parallel term to the closing vocative, *O humans.*[19] It would seem that these Mighty Ones are claiming to *speak* with *righteousness* and to *judge uprightly;* but to the one praying nothing could be further from the truth. Indeed, v. 2 proclaims that these Mighty Ones devise harm *in their hearts* and then bring it to fruition in the land. Their evil,

words do not need to be emended as others do. Tate notes that the final section can mean either "as if they were headless," understanding *mll* as "to be cut off," or "as if they faded" in the sense of not reaching their target (*Psalms 51–100,* p. 83).

13. This word appears only here, so the meaning is uncertain.

14. MT has "your thorns." The *BHS* apparatus suggests the change to *their* to match the rest of the verse. The verse is very corrupt and possibly should be left untranslated.

15. MT has "may he sweep him away." This makes little sense, so the *BHS* apparatus suggests a change to the 3mpl *them.*

16. This entire verse is problematic and probably corrupt, so any reading is uncertain. Dahood refused even to offer a translation (*Psalms II,* p. 56). The LXX reading is also corrupt: "Before your thorns feel the white thorn, he will swallow you up as living, as in his wrath." Kraus determined the verse to be "Before your thorns grow for the shrub, like thorny bush, like weeds he blows them away" (cf. Kraus, *Psalms 1–59,* p. 533). There is no good solution and the above translation follows MT as closely as possible. What is clear is the first word and the last. "May he sweep them (him) away" indicates confidence that God will deal decisively with these enemies.

17. MT has "he will see," which could indicate *righteous* be read as a collective plural, as argued by Gerstenberger (*Psalms: Part 1,* p. 234). *They* is used for a smooth English translation here and in the next colon.

18. V. 11 also remains in the masculine singular.

19. In addition, Ps. 52 begins in a parallel way, asking a rhetorical question of the "Mighty One" (using *gibbôr*) and moving to a statement about the premeditative nature of the Mighty One's evil in v. 2. This psalm is part of a small group and is thus read in the same way.

it seems, is premeditated and well executed. This charge of injustice in the community occurs often in the psalms and the prophetic literature and is problematic, not only to the one suffering, but also to the community and to God.[20] These enemies are ones with power over the community in which the one praying lives, so he had no earthly place to turn.

3-5 Questions turn to declaration in vv. 3-5, and these descriptions have no direct connection to what is learned about the Mighty Ones in the preceding stanza. The *wicked* are described, not by their acts (as in vv. 1-2) but by the condition of their hearts. and these wicked ones were corrupt *from their birth.* The two verbs of v. 3 mean "to be a *stranger*" and "to *wander about*," respectively, as if the prayer is saying that these ones were never part of the covenant community. This could indicate that these ones are foreign-imposed rulers; but it may just as well be a hyperbole to reiterate that the wicked are not part of God's kingdom, even while claiming they are. Verse 4 turns to a different image: not only are they as dangerous as a poisonous *snake,* but they refuse to *listen* to anyone (v. 5a), even the most skilled orator (v. 5b), and so cannot be moved by anyone.

6-9 The audience is ill prepared for the next section. Many prayers have much longer and more painful descriptions of the enemies and their acts, but the time for descriptions is over abruptly. The one praying turns now to God and tells God in very forceful terms exactly what he wishes for God to do to these enemies. What follows is seven imprecations or curses. This section is the centerpiece of the psalm. As noted above, these Mighty Ones are powerful leaders in the community, so that the one praying sees no recourse except from God and pours out her pain in the form of imprecations against these ones. Verse 6 is a wish that their power be diminished just as a lion who loses his *teeth.* Terrien has noted that this verse is set apart by the two vocatives (God and LORD) that begin and end the verse.[21] Interestingly, this chiasm reminds us of the same structure in v. 1, so that v. 6 becomes a poetic response to v. 1. If God removes the rulers' power, then they will be like toothless beasts. But the one praying is not finished. The next four imprecations alternate first with wishes for the Mighty Ones to disappear (v. 7a, like *water,* and v. 8a, like a *snail* that *melts* into its own slime[22]) with wishes for them to become powerless and ineffective (v. 7b, shooting *arrows that fail,* and v. 8b, *like an aborted fetus*). Unfortunately, v. 9 is so problematic that the image is impossible to understand. What is clear about the verse, however, is that the metaphor is meant as an image of God sweeping the Mighty Ones away, possible as in a fire or flood.

20. E.g., Pss. 10:8-9; 12:5; 26:10; 53:4; Amos 5:7; 6:12; Isa. 1:23; 5:23; Micah 3:11.

21. *The Psalms,* p. 440.

22. As in v. 9, the meaning of the Hebrew is uncertain here.

This entire section then creates a rhetorical whole. Verse 6 begins the imprecations with a wish for the evil ones' power to be destroyed, which corresponds to the wishes of vv. 7b and 8b. Verse 9 wishes for these ones to be swept away, just as do vv. 7a and 8a. In addition, the chiastic structure of v. 6 makes a poetic parallel with the acts of these Mighty Ones.

10-11 Verse 10 offers the audience another surprise. From imprecation the prayer moves to rejoicing without explanation. This gap that occurs in many of the prayers for help has caused scholars to provide a reason for the dramatic turn in the psalm, but here the poem offers no reason. Does this continue the wish that this will be the end point of God's action against the wicked? Does this mean that time has jumped forward and the Mighty Ones have indeed fallen? The psalm leaves the audience to ponder this great change in circumstance.

What is certain is that this stanza uses the same forceful imagery as does the rest of the psalm. It is vindication for the suffering *righteous.* The words are harsh, and it is here that we get some idea of the depth of the suffering by the one praying. The one praying cannot imagine any end to the situation other than "bathing his feet *in the blood of the wicked.*" The image is harsh, but not unique in ancient literature.[23] The injustice is so pervasive that other options have ceased to be possible. But the true resolution of the situation lies in v. 11, not in v. 10 and its gruesome imagery. The true resolution is a world where God is *judging the earth,* or in other words, where God is the king, judge, and ruler of all so that justice is administered fairly — the very opposite of the condition of v. 1. A world where everyone will know that the *reward for the righteous* is not bathing *their feet in the blood of the wicked* but is the "fruit" of a righteous way of life.[24] The bloodbath signals the end of the old regime (as it does in Ezekiel 37 and the book of Revelation) in v. 10 and the beginning of a new age of God's justice in v. 11. This psalm could be labeled by some as un-Christian because of its harsh wishes (vv. 7-9) and its gloating literally in *the blood of the wicked* (v. 10). Its words are hard to hear, and its wishes certainly do not reflect an attitude of "love your enemies." Instead, it reflects the reality of human systems that are so polluted that there is nowhere to turn for justice. The pain is so real that the least of the society wishes for the destruction and violent deaths of their oppressors. The prayer truthfully tells what happens in a system of massive injustice when even the most patient and loving persons can express violent wishes when inhumanity and treachery are all that they see. In this psalm, the audience, if it can release its judgmental reading, can

23. There are other biblical texts with similar images: 1 Kgs. 22:37-38; Ps. 68:23; Isa. 63:3-6; Ezek. 39:17-20; Rev. 14:20, as well as ANE texts such as *KTU* 1.3.II.20-23, 27-29.

24. The word that means *reward* in this verse is also the word for "fruit," as in the fruit of a righteous life.

look for a moment through the eyes of persons forced to reside in such systems — to see into the wounded soul of a refugee, or a Palestinian, or any citizen who knows that the justice system is so perverted that justice will never be achieved for him. These psalms can teach all to see through the eyes of the least of all societies and to hear their cry lifted to God for the destruction (vv. 6, 7b, 8b) and the disappearance (vv. 7a, 8a, 9) of these oppressive and unjust systems. From this perspective, the audience can hear anew the call to God to end oppression and bring forth a kingdom of justice.

Beth Tanner

Psalm 59: Be My High Fortress

Psalm 59 is an individual prayer for help, and it also continues the theme of Psalms 54–59 and 61-63 of complete trust in God to protect and preserve. The literary structure is one of seconding[1] in both the metaphorical description of the enemies (vv. 6-7 and 14-15) and of trust in God (vv. 8-10 and 16-17).

Cry to God for rescue from enemies (vv. 1-5)
Metaphorical description of the enemies (vv. 6-7)
Statement of trust in God's power and aid (vv. 8-10)
Wish for the end of the enemies (vv. 11-13)
Second and similar metaphorical description of the enemies (vv. 14-15)
Similar statement of trust in God's power and aid[2] (vv. 16-17)

Like Psalms 54, 56, and 57, this psalm is given a superscription by a later editor that associates it with an event in the life of David, probably 1 Sam. 19:11-17. The actual circumstance for which the psalm was voiced is unknown, but the Samuel text does reflect a time when one would call out to God for deliverance. Indeed, the men *watching the house* could easily look like the *prowling dogs* of Ps. 59:6 and 14. Also in response to the enemy "watching the house," the one praying "watches" for God's rescue (v. 9). The mention of *nations* could mean that this is a psalm to be prayed in times of national distress, as argued by several scholars.[3] But it is just as likely that these two sections are a paraphrase of stock confessions about God in any situation (vv. 4b-5 and 8-9). Zenger notes that the combination of both personal and communal prayer is a structuring element to bridge the personal prayers of Psalms 52–58 with the communal prayer in Psalm 60.[4]

1. Seconding is different from repetition. The two sets of sections have much in common and even share some lines in common. However, each also adds lines so that the meaning of each section is unique. Kraus disagrees, arguing that these are not repetitions or refrains at all, but "variants," which he disregards (*Psalms 1–59,* p. 543).

2. This structure is also followed by Carroll Stuhlmueller (*Psalms 1* [Old Testament Message 21; Wilmington: Glazier, 1983], p. 275) and Tate (*Psalms 51–100,* p. 96). Others use slightly different, but similar divisions.

3. Such as Mowinckel, *The Psalms in Israel's Worship,* 1:226; Dahood, *Psalms II,* p. 70; and Eaton, *Kingship and the Psalms,* p. 47.

4. Hossfeld and Zenger, *Psalms 2,* p. 85.

To the leader. Al-tasheth.[5] *A Davidic miktam*[6] *when Saul sent (men)*
and they watched the house in order to kill him.

1 *Deliver me from my enemies, O my God;*
raise me up higher than those who arise up against me!
2 *Deliver me from workers of iniquity;*
from the bloodthirsty save me!
3 *for indeed they lie in wait for me;*[7]
fierce ones stir up strife[8] *against me,*
for no transgression or sin of mine, LORD.
4 *Without any iniquity on my part,*
they run and they prepare.
Rouse yourself to meet me and see;
5 *for you are* LORD, *God of hosts, God of Israel.*
Awake to visit all the nations;
do not show mercy on any iniquitous deceivers.[9] Selah

6 *They return in the evening;*
they howl like dogs
as they prowl around the city.
7 *See! They are bellowing*[10] *from*[11] *their mouths,*
swords[12] *from their lips,*
for who is listening?

5. See note 3 on Psalm 57 superscription.

6. See note 5 on Psalm 16 superscription.

7. Lit., *l*^{e}*nap̱šî,* but it should not be reduced to "my soul" as many modern translations do. In Hebrew, it refers to the whole self or "me."

8. Reading with MT. Some scholars emend *yāgûrû* to *yāgôddû* ("to plot or conspire"; *HALOT,* p. 177; NIV), but there is no compelling reason to make this change.

9. The phrase *bōg*^{e}*ḏê 'āwen* appears only here and is difficult to read as a construct. Tate suggests the construct here has been confused with the similar phrase *workers of iniquity* in v. 2 (*Psalms 51–100,* p. 93). He notes that LXX uses "workers of iniquity" in both verses. This is certainly possible. However, the MT is awkward but still readable and is preserved in some form in most current translations.

10. Gunkel (*Introduction to Psalms,* p. 254), Kraus (*Psalms 1–59,* pp. 542-43), and Tate (*Psalms 51–100,* p. 93) prefer the word "foam" or "slather," arguing that the phrase is referring to actual dogs. The more common usage is "gushing or pouring forth" as in Ps. 19:2.

11. The preposition *b* is not usually translated as *from.* However, Waltke and O'Connor note that this preposition can indicate a motion of through (*Biblical Hebrew Syntax,* p. 198). The bellowing is "through" the mouth. The more typical English rendering would be *from.*

12. *HALOT* suggests that *swords* be emended to "insults" (p. 665), but the change is unnecessary. Some modern translations substitute "sharp words" (NJPS, NRSV) so the metaphor is clear. Ps. 57:4 reflects the same metaphor: "their tongues (are) sharp swords."

8 *But You, O LORD, laugh at them;*
you mock all the nations!
9 *O my Strength,*[13] *I will watch for you;*[14]
for you, O God, are my high fortress.[15]
10 *My loving God*[16] *will meet me;*
God will let me look (in triumph)[17] *on my enemies.*

11 *Do not kill them,*
or my people will forget.
Make them wander about[18] *by your power;*
bring them down, O Lord, our Shield.[19]
12 *For the sin of their mouths, the words of their lips,*
let them be trapped in their arrogance;

13. MT reads "his strength." Many suggest a change to the 1st person suffix as above (LXX, Targ, NIV, NJPS, NRSV). *HALOT* suggests that the pointing should be *'uzzî* and read as "my refuge" (p. 806), as does Kraus (*Psalms 1–59,* p. 538). Either emendation is possible, but the phrase "my Strength" is repeated in v. 17, making it the preferred emendation here.

14. RSV follows Syr and emends the root of the verb to *zmr,* matching the line in v. 17. This reading is possible and would provide an inclusio for vv. 8-17. Most scholars, however, adopt the more difficult reading of MT as above (NIV, NJPS, NRSV; Tate, *Psalms 51–100,* p. 94; Weiser, *The Psalms,* p. 432).

15. This word appears often in the psalms as "fortress" or "refuge." I have selected *high fortress* in this psalm because of the wordplay with the piel verb in v. 1 that is from the same root. The prayer is for God to lift the faithful "up high," indeed, *higher* than the ones rising up against her!

16. MT is corrupt, using the 3ms suffix in the Qere. The Kethib alters this phrase to match the one in v. 17, as above. Other scholars emend the text from a construct to a noun-noun construction, reading "My God will come to meet me with his *hesed*" (Tate, *Psalms 51–100,* p. 94; Terrien, *The Psalms,* p. 442). Either reading requires emendation, but the first preserves the Kethib reading of MT.

17. The *in triumph* is added by most commentators to explain the meaning of "looking on the enemies" (see Tate, *Psalms 51–100,* p. 45).

18. The root of this verb has two meanings: a) "to stagger" or "totter"; and b) "to wander." Translations and scholars are divided between the two meanings. "Totter" is used in NRSV, Tate (*Psalms 51–100,* p. 92), and Dahood (*Psalms II,* p. 66), while "wander" or "scatter" is preferred by NJPS and NIV, Kraus (*Psalms 1–59,* p. 539), and Terrien (*Psalms,* p. 442). *HALOT* suggests using "totter" here but "wander" in v. 15 (p. 681). LXX indicates "scatter" or "wander" via *diaskorpizō.* Either translation is possible, but based on the usage of the same word in vv. 11 and 15, it would seem more likely that the MT intended for the same meaning to be used in each verse.

19. MT reads *our shield* as above. LXX and Syr read "my shield," but there is no compelling reason to read "my" here. Tate notes the *shield* here is a metaphor of God's protection as in Pss. 3:3; 18:2; 28:7; 33:20; 84:9 (*Psalms 51–100,* p. 94).

for[20] *the curses and lying they declare,*
13 *consume them*[21] *in your anger;*
consume them until they are no more.
Then they will know to the ends of the earth,
God is ruling over Jacob. Selah

14 *They return in the evening;*
they howl like dogs,
as they prowl around the city.
15 *See! They wander around for food*
and if they are not satisfied, they growl.

16 *(But) I will sing of your power;*
I will shout in the morning of your hesed,
for you are a high fortress to me
and a refuge in the day of my distress.
17 *O my Strength, I sing praises unto you,*
for God is a high fortress,
my loving God.

1-5 The prayer opens with a series of petitions; two times the one praying cries to be *delivered* from his *enemies* (vv. 1a and 2a). The two echoing petitions are just as fervent. *Raise me higher* and *save me* (vv. 1b and 2b) add to the urgency of the situation. At v. 3, the pleas give way to specific reasons why the one praying needs deliverance. It is the enemies and their actions that are the cause of trouble, and the descriptions of these acts escalate. In v. 1a, they are simply *enemies,* but the prayer progresses to *those who rise up* (v. 1b), to *workers of iniquity* (v. 2a), to *the bloodthirsty* (v. 2b), to those who *lie in wait* (v. 3a), to *fierce ones* who *stir up strife* (v. 3b), and finally to the problematic *iniquitous deceivers* (v. 5b). Verse 4 also intensifies the situation by declaring the innocence of the one praying.

Another petition to God begins in v. 4c. This time the cry is for God to "wake up" or *rouse yourself.* This is a term used in Ps. 44:23 and Isa. 51:9 as a passionate call for God to act. The one praying calls on God to wake up and show up and *see* for God's self what the enemies are doing. This demand

20. This line uses both a conjunction and the preposition *min.* This construction sets it apart from the rest of the verse and seems to indicate this phrase should be attached to the proceeding line. In this case, the preposition should not be translated literally, but as an indication of its difference from what came above.

21. The two imperatives here do not have direct objects, but most translations add *them* for clarification (NIV, NJPS, NIV, Tate, Terrien).

again adds to the urgency, but it also demonstrates the powerful relationship between the one praying and God. The one praying is in need and dares to expect God to show up and remedy the situation. This is a brave one, as she calls not on a personal God, but none other than the God of Israel *(LORD, God of hosts, God of Israel)* and of the whole world *(awake to visit all the nations)* in v. 5. Tate notes that the effect here is to call on the God who judges all nations to come to the aid of the one lifting the prayer.[22] The point of the poetry is probably not to suggest these are foreign enemies, as Dahood and others have argued, but to call on the great God of the *whole world* to "wake and see" and then act on behalf of the one suffering.

6-7 The refrain returns to the characterization of the enemies, this time as a pack of marauding dogs. The comparison of the enemies to threatening animals is not uncommon in the psalms.[23] The metaphor also reinforces the idea of the "many" dogs against the solitary one. These "dogs," however, use speech as their destructive power (v. 7)[24] and think that they are powers unto themselves.[25]

8-10 These verses provide a direct contrast to the above. These *dogs* may think their power is great, but God *laughs,* and this laughter is reminiscent of God's laughter against the powers of this world in Ps. 2:4.[26] The entire section is a confession of trust in God's power (*O my Strength,* v. 9; and *God will let me look in triumph on my enemies,* v. 10), and in God's presence (*I will watch for you,* v. 9; and *My loving God will meet me,* v. 10), and in God's protection (*my high fortress,* v. 9). These are the attributes that the one praying is depending on. These same attributes will be "seconded" in vv. 16-17 as praise.

11-13 Trust in God results in wishes for the fate of the enemy. These wishes can seem harsh to the modern reader. But the psalms are honest prayers lifted to God that reflect the thoughts of one persecuted. In the first two verses here, the one praying wants God to make an example of these enemies. They will serve as living examples, not only of God's *power,* but of the one praying's vindication. Verse 12 declares that the enemies' end is completely justified because of their own acts (contra the one praying's innocence in v. 3). This declaration of the acts of the enemies is the justification for their

22. *Psalms 51–100,* p. 97.

23. E.g., the enemy as a lion or wild beast (Pss. 7:2; 10:9; 17:12; 22:13; 57:4); dog as enemy appears also in 22:16.

24. See a parallel using lions and speech acts in 57:4.

25. As do the enemies in 64:6.

26. While not an exact parallel, the two verbs here and in 2:4 are the same. As noted concerning v. 5, this lends more credence to the idea that this does not necessarily indicate that the enemies are foreign nations. The phrase may indeed be one known in Israel as a definition of YHWH's power in all situations, foreign and domestic.

downfall (v. 11) and their destruction (v. 13). Verse 13's cry for the destruction of the enemies seems to contradict v. 11's wish for their public downfall, but the wish of v. 11 is on behalf of the one praying and her community, whereas v. 13 will show God's power to the world *(ends of the earth).* The one praying wishes that God's dealing with the enemies will not only have community ramifications, but worldwide ones.

14-15 These verses return to the theme of the enemies as *dogs.* This revisitation[27] reminds God and the audience once again why the wishes of vv. 11-13 are justified and God's intervention is needed. The focus on the evening's *prowl* heightens the sense of danger. One can hear the threat because, if they have not found enough prey (i.e., the one praying), they continue to *prowl* and *growl* as they hunt.[28]

16-17 This final section *sings, shouts,* and *praises* the attributes the one praying needed for deliverance in vv. 8-10. Interestingly, the violence wished in vv. 11-13 is not praised or even mentioned. Any talk of the enemies has been replaced with song. While these two related sections do not use the duplicate phrasing of vv. 6-7 and 14-15, the word repetition is striking: *strength* in vv. 9 and 17; *high fortress* in vv. 9, 16, and 17; *hesed* in vv. 10 (see note 16), 16, and 17 (Hebrew). The final word on the matter then is not retribution to the enemies but the *hesed* that preserved the life of the one praying. This gush of praise also creates a gap for the hearers to traverse. There is no indication of change in the circumstances or mind of the one praying. Hearers must discern for themselves how this one went from petition and fear to praise and assurance.

This psalm ends this cycle of six psalms that have the form of prayers for help but also demonstrate a strong trust in God to save and protect the one praying. Over and over these psalms declare that God will deliver the righteous one in need. These prayers can seem naive and fanciful in today's world. Deliverance seems far away, and all accounts seem to demonstrate that the wicked are succeeding on the backs of the righteous. These psalms reflect the same perspective as the famous text, Heb. 11:1: "Now faith is the assurance of things hoped for, the conviction of things not seen." They inspire hope to persevere in the world and to continue to believe. But more than that, Psalm

27. The revisitation is very clear here. Verses 14 and 6 and the opening imperative of vv. 15 and 7 are identical. The variation is what the one praying is urging the audience to *see.*

28. Tate argues that it is possible to read this section, not as threatening, but as one that answers vv. 6-7 by declaring that the "power" of the dogs has been vanquished, and so they do not find prey and "whine" in complaint. This is a possible reading that might even account for the "seconding" structure. Yet, the major repetition theme in this psalm is one of *refuge* or *high fortress* that suggests, despite the wishes, that the chief metaphor of the psalm is protection, not destruction (*Psalms 51–100,* p. 98).

59 declares loudly that we can tell God how we truly feel the enemies should be treated, but at the end of the day we are to praise God for protection, instead of taking retribution into our own hands. The one praying trusts that God will appear as the Creator and King of the world to provide justice for all.

Beth Tanner

Psalm 60: We Will Do Valiantly

Psalm 60 is a communal or national prayer for help. The prayer is lifted by the people who see their plight as directly related to God's rejection of them and appears to be associated with a national military defeat (v. 10). The structure of the psalm is such that the speech of God (vv. 6-8) forms its center. The psalm's text is problematic, and Tate asserts that "all interpretation is tentative."[1]

A description of God's rejection (vv. 1-3)
    A description of God's salvation (vv. 4-5)
        God's declaration of power (vv. 6-8)
    A second description of God's rejection (vv. 9-11)
Cry for deliverance and assurance of trust (v. 12)

Like Psalms 54 and 56-59, this psalm was given a superscription (vv. 1-2 in Hebrew) that associates it with events in David's life. This superscription is different from the others, for it seems to refer to multiple events. In addition, it refers to events when David and Israel's army were successful,[2] whereas the prayer is clearly about a defeat. Superscriptions were added by a later editor and usually indicate a situation in which the prayer might be prayed. The reason for this particular superscription is unclear. It may serve to demonstrate that God has not abandoned Israel, or it may serve to glorify David despite the situation the psalm represents. Psalm 60 also sits inside a group of psalms that are prayers for help and that also demonstrate complete trust in God (Psalms 54–59 and 61–63). This placement may serve to demonstrate God's care even in the midst of crisis.

1. *Psalms 51–100*, p. 103

2. The reference to the Edomites is found in 2 Sam. 8:13-14; 1 Chr. 18:12-13. The other two place names are probably from 2 Samuel 8, referring to a Mesopotamian city (Aram-naharaim) and an Aramean state (Aram-ṣobah).

To the leader.[3] *On* shushan eduth.[4] *A Davidic miktam*[5] *for teaching*[6] *when he fought Aram-naharaim and Aram-ṣobah and Joab returned and killed twelve thousand Edomites in the Valley of Salt.*[7]

1 *O God, you have rejected us, you have broken us;*[8]
you have been angry, return to us!
2 *You have caused the earth to shake, you have torn it open;*[9]
heal its cracks for it is swaying.
3 *You have caused your people to see*[10] *hard times;*
you have caused us to drink wine that left us staggering.[11]

4 *For those who fear you, you set a banner;*
to assembly under from the face of the bow;[12] Selah
5 *that*[13] *your beloved ones may be delivered.*

3. This section of the superscription is missing in LXX.

4. See Ps. 45. Meaning of this Hebrew phrase is unknown. Some translate it as "lily of the covenant or testimony," but it may be the name of a tune or musical instruction that is lost to modern readers. LXX has a variant: "for those that will be changed."

5. See note 5 on Psalm 16 superscription.

6. The meaning of the phrase *for teaching* is unknown. Mowinckel suggested that it be understood as meaning "to goad" and as a call to warfare (*The Psalms in Israel's Worship,* 2:217). It could also have a liturgical meaning.

7. LXX has a different superscription: "when he burned Mesopotamia of Syria and Syria Sobel and Joab returned and smote twelve thousand in the Valley of Salt."

8. This verb means either "to breach" as in a city wall or to "break out" with the preposition "against." The direct object here is contained in the verbal construct without a preposition, so *you have broken us* is a unique but accurate representation of the Hebrew. Zenger concurs (*Psalms 2,* p. 93).

9. The verb *pāṣam* appears only here, so its meaning is uncertain.

10. NRSV and NJPS translate this as "you have made your people suffer hard things," but this seems to lose the sense of MT which is a *hiphil* of "to see."

11. Lit., "you caused us to drink 'wine of reeling.'" Many modern translations translate "you have given us wine to drink," but the intent of the *hiphil* is not just that humans were given the wine but that they had to partake. The "wine of reeling" appears to be a metaphor for God's wrath as in Isa. 51:22. The concept, although not the exact metaphor, is detailed in Jer. 25:15-16.

12. Meaning of MT is uncertain. The line above is as close as possible to MT. This reading does move the phrase *For those who fear you* to before the verb. This verse is quite problematic and has yielded a whole host of English interpretations. LXX is clearer: "that they might flee *(phygō)* from the bow."

13. The preposition, *lᵉmaʿan,* makes this line dependent on the verse above. However, both NRSV and NIV (contra NJPS) read the first line of v. 5 as dependent on the second and reverse the order of the lines in MT. My reading preserves the MT order. The reading is not without problems, for the preposition comes immediately after *Selah,* which usually indicates the close of a section. Tate concurs with the reading (*Psalms 51–100,* p. 102).

Save (us) by your right hand and answer us![14]

6 *God has spoken in his holiness;*[15]
"I will triumph (and)[16] *I will divide Shechem,*
and I will measure out the valley of Succoth.
7 *Gilead is mine, and Manasseh is mine;*
Ephraim is my helmet;[17]
Judah is my scepter.
8 *Moab is my wash pot;*
over Edom, I cast my shoe;
because of me, Philistia shouts!"[18]

9 *Who will bear me up to the fortified city?*
Who will lead me to Edom?
10 *Is it not you, God, who have rejected us?*
God, you do not go out with our armies.
11 *Give us help from foes,*
for the deliverance of humans is nothing.
12 *With God, we will do valiantly;*
he, he treads on our foes.

1-3 The prayer opens with a declaration of how God had deserted the *people,* followed by a plea for restoration. Verse 2 repeats the same pattern. However, God is now taking direct action against the land of promise, and the plea is for God to mend what God has broken. Verse 3 tells of God's acts against the people. They are desperate and *staggering.*

4-5 Verse 4 continues the pattern of vv. 2-3, beginning with a 2ms verb.

14. Reading with the Kethib instead of the 1cs of the Qere. The Kethib matches the plural of the preceding line.

15. Or "God has spoken from his holy place (i.e., his sanctuary)." Either understanding of this word is possible, but it appears from the context that it is the word given that is important. If God speaks from a specific holy place or speaks from his own holiness, the message is still the same. Tate translates: "God made a holy promise" (*Psalms 51–100,* p. 100).

16. NIV and NRSV read the first 1cs verb as a preposition, "with exultation." MT and LXX read the line as two distinct verbs, as above. Zenger concurs (*Psalms 2,* p. 93).

17. Lit., "a stronghold or refuge of my head."

18. The parallel passage in Ps. 108:9 is clearer: "over Philistia I will shout with joy," and NIV and NRSV adopt as "I shout in triumph." However, the Hebrew here is readable as it is. The preposition *'al* can have a meaning of introducing a norm (Waltke and O'Conner, *Biblical Hebrew Syntax,* p. 218), as these verses indicate. The verb here is a *hithpoel* imperative indicating the subject is Philistia (see also NJPS). LXX has a different verb and *binyan:* "the Philistines are subjected to me."

The grammatical form is the same, but the message has changed from God against to God for. In addition, the text is problematic here, making translation difficult. However, the gap is striking and generates a great amount of scholarly comment on its meaning. It could be a plea, as suggested by McCann,[19] or it could be a statement of hope in the future, as suggested by Terrien.[20] Both of these fit with the lament genre. What is clear is that for all or for a remnant (Isaiah 10), this abandonment by God is only temporary. God has set forth a place of protection *(banner)* so that the ones who *fear* God can *be delivered.*

6-8 The center of the psalm is spoken by God, possibly in response to the declaration and pleas of vv. 1-5. If the first two sections stand in tension with each other, the center of the psalm settles the question. Scholars debate if someone in charge speaks these words for God or if God, God's self, is speaking here. Either way, the section declares that both southern Israel *(Judah)* and northern (*Gilead, Manasseh,* and *Ephraim*) and the Transjordan (*Shechem* and *Succoth*) belong to God. Indeed, God sees all of Israel as God's *helmet* and *scepter.* This is divine warrior royal language. Israel is God's alone to divide up as God will.

Verse 8 is very difficult, and any translation is questionable. However, what is clear is the names of the three countries that surround Israel — *Moab, Edom,* and *Philistia* — and that the territory they claim also belongs to God. This may reflect a historical reality at some time during Israel's past, but more likely it reflects the idea that God is always in control of other nations, whether they acknowledge God or not (Isa. 45:1-8).

9-11 The word of God is not enough to settle all of the fears, for the prayer returns to questioning God. Israel may be fighting Edom (v. 9), but it is God that is still seen as the problem. This may reflect the lessons of the past where Israel was defeated when God was not with them (Num. 14:42-45; Judg. 2:11-15). The cries of concern are followed by a final plea for *help* (v. 11), and the reason given is that humans cannot save. Again this could reflect a very real situation in Israel's life (Isaiah 7) or be a statement of God's continuing presence.

12 Verse 12 creates the final gap of the prayer declaring that indeed Israel will do well because God will handle all of the *foes* they face.

The prayer as a whole demonstrates the tension within which God and Israel live. It is a bold and faithful relationship where Israel can accuse God of deserting them and God can answer by declaring God's power as Creator and King of all of the world, both within and outside of the borders of Israel. The prayer pulls the hearer this way and then that in the endless tug-of-war

19. "The Book of Psalms," p. 916.
20. *The Psalms,* p. 448.

between God and God's people. It speaks of doubt and hope. It speaks of how Israel is to cry out to God, even when God seems to be absent. It speaks of a time of crisis when all seems lost for God's people. It speaks of a people defeated and powerless looking to the only one who can come to their aid.

Looked at in a historical sense, the prayer seems to be of a people who lived long ago and of their relationship with God, but that relationship is what the whole of the Bible is about. We too as a nation have known times of darkness and fear, and our answer has been to rely on our own military power for a solution. This has often led to disaster for us and for others across the world. This prayer demands, just as Isaiah demanded of Ahaz, that we place our trust in God instead of human power. It may seem foolish in the face of terrorism, but how else are we to live? We can choose to fear others, or we can rally as those who fear and love God and depend on God for all of our tomorrows.

BETH TANNER

Psalm 61: In the Shelter of God's Wings

Psalm 61 is often classified as a prayer for help, and it certainly begins as one in vv. 1-3. Yet on the whole, the psalm speaks more about the safety found in God's care than in the trouble that caused that distress. This psalm then is also part of the psalms of trust that surround Psalm 60, and all of these psalms tell of great trust in God in times of struggle (Psalms 54–59, 61–63). This psalm clearly moves from a place of cries lifted in fear to petitions given from within the safety of God's *wings*.[1]

Cry to God (vv. 1-2b)
Petitions for aid (vv. 2c-5)
Wishes for the king (vv. 6-7)
Final petition (v. 8)[2]

To the leader. With stringed instruments. Davidic.

1 *Hear my cry, O God;*
pay attention to my prayer.
2 *From the end of the earth, to you I cry*
when my heart is faint;

lead me to a rock that is higher than I[3]
3 *for you have been a refuge to me,*
a tower of strength in the presence of the enemy.
4 *Let me live in your tent forever;*
let me find refuge in the shelter of your wings. Selah
5 *For you, O God, heard my vow;*
you gave me the inheritance[4] *of those fearing your name.*

6 *Add days upon days to the king,*
his years from generation to generation.[5]

1. Likewise, Weiser (*The Psalms,* p. 443) and Kraus (*Psalms 60–150,* p. 8) characterize this psalm as one of thanksgiving.

2. Gerstenberger uses a similar division (*Psalms: Part 2,* p. 3).

3. Some translations read with LXX and Syr as "lift me up and set me on a rock," but there is no reason to change the Hebrew text here.

4. Some read *'ᵃrešeṯ* ("grant the request") instead of *yᵉruššaṯ* ("You gave the inheritance") (NJPS; Dahood, *Psalms II,* p. 86), but this is unnecessary since inheritance or heritage can be understood metaphorically as a family, a people, a land, or even life itself.

5. Difficult to translate into English: lit., "years as generation to generation," meaning enduring forever (Pss. 10:6; 45:17).

7 *May he dwell forever in the presence of God;*
Appoint hesed *and faithfulness to guard him!*[6]

8 *Then let me sing praise*[7] *forever to your name,*
to fulfill my vow day after day.

1-2b The prayer begins with a plea for God to hear and pay attention, much like Psalms 5, 17, 55, and 64. This beginning seems to imply that the prayer is lifted by someone who is in urgent need of God's aid. The prayer gives no indication of what the problem might be, and the petition is brief, ending at v. 2. This cry *from the end of the earth* could be either a physical/geographical reality or a poetic rendering of how far the one praying feels he is removed from God. In addition, the one praying is not only removed from God, but is *faint* of *heart* and fading fast.[8] These words set us the readers at that far-away place where we understand the feeling of distance from God from our own memories of similar times in our lives.

2c-5 The next section contains a series of petitions or requests. The person praying first wishes to be led by God and protected (v. 2c). This is the needed response by God to the distance and pain expressed at the beginning. The petition in Ps. 59:1 also requests to be lifted up to a place of safety, thus connecting this psalm to what has come before while at the same time the image of rock and tower of strength connects to the following Psalm 62. Each of these images *(rock, refuge, tent,* and *shelter of your wings)* are metaphors that represent God's temple or dwelling place, so the petitions in vv. 2c-4 move the one praying from a distant place to the very center of God's dwelling on earth. We too go for the metaphorical ride from the edges to the very heart and *shelter* of God's *wings,* and we too are confident in this movement, for v. 3 reminds that God will be here now because God has been a *refuge* before. I can trust God to act for me now, for God has acted for me in the past. The trust here is trust borne out over time.

Verse 5 is more difficult to understand. What is clear here is that God has

6. Meaning uncertain. The line contains two verbs: *man* ("appoint") and *yinṣ*^{e}*ruhû* ("guard him"). The question is how to read the verbs. Most translations read the second verb as an infinitive, as above. *BHS* critical notes suggest the first verb may be dittography, thus "Steadfast love and faithfulness watch over him" as a statement instead of a plea.

7. Most translations switch the cohortative to the future "I will" here (NRSV) while reading the other cohortatives as "Let me" (v. 4). Waltke and O'Conner remind that, "where the speaker cannot effect a desire without the consent of the one addressed, it connotes request" (*Biblical Heberew Syntax,* p. 573). There is no reason to change the form here, except to fit the standard prayer for help form.

8. The words from the root *'ṭp* demonstrate serious distress and proximity to death (Pss. 102 superscription; 107:5; Lam. 2:11).

indeed heard the one in distress and has provided for his needs. *Inheritance* almost always refers to the land that God promised. This image combined with the images of *tent, refuge,* and *shelter of your wings*[9] may indicate the one praying is depending on the same gifts God gave those brought forth from Egypt. In other words, the metaphors can work together to provide an image from one of Israel's oldest confessions of God from the exodus and wilderness, but at the same time also represent the temple as the place where God dwells. But the images are certainly not limited to the exodus and the temple, for these images can be a remembering of God's protection for a modern audience who would use other referents for these words.

6-7 This section offers wishes for the life and the well-being of *the king,* like other royal psalms such as Psalm 72. Scholars have suggested that this section is a later addition. Psalm 61 does not have a historical superscription that links it to events in the life of King David, but nearby psalms do (Psalms 54, 56, 57, 59, 60, 63), and it is possible that this is another way of connecting this prayer to David. The prayer then claims God's protection from old, and now that *the enemy* (v. 3) is finished, the king and the people can live forever in God's tent. Others such as Tate suggest this section was added to provide a Messianic hope in the midst of the post-exilic community when there was no king.[10] Either or even both of these interpretations are possible since prayers for one situation can be reused in another situation. Indeed, this is the reason why the psalms can and are part of the church's life today. Ultimately, this prayer is demonstrating that God can and does provide aid in all periods of Israel's life.

8 The verb in this line is clearly in the cohortative form and as such expresses not a future happening but a final wish. Not only does the one praying wish for safety for himself and long and abundant life for the king; now he asks God to be allowed to *sing* to God and *fulfill* the vows or promises made for all of the days of his life.

The whole of the psalm moves from cries of pain and loneliness to wishes and petitions for abundant life and praise. In light of the eternity expressed in vv. 7-8, the cries of pain take on a temporariness not heard earlier in the psalm, not only for the one praying but for the king and by extension the whole of Israel. Even in a world where kings do not govern us anymore, we still know that our happiness and our safety are wrapped up in the community, the country, and the country's leaders. Limburg notes, "Here there is absolutely no separation between the responsibilities of those in the temple

9. *Tent* can reflect the way that God tabernacled with the people in the wilderness, where God was their own *refuge. The shelter of your wings* can be seen as the top of the ark of the covenant that was God's presence in Israel's early life.

10. *Psalms 51–100,* p. 115.

and those in the state house."[11] For one to be at peace with only praise on his lips, one must be part of a people that also lives in peace and safety. This prayer reminds even a modern hearer that we are all in this world together and for God to secure one, God must also secure all.

BETH TANNER

11. *Psalms,* p. 203.

Psalm 62: Testimony of Trust

Psalm 62 is a testimony addressed to God's people in vv. 1-10 with an address to God in vv. 11-12. It also shares themes of God as rock and refuge with Psalms 59 and 61, connecting it to this larger section of trust that began at Psalm 54.[1] It declares trust alone in God in three sections and uncovers the way humans act in two additional sections, giving it a chiastic structure with trust as the beginning, middle, and end.

Trust in God (vv. 1-2)
    Actions of the enemies (vv. 3-4)
        Trust in God (vv. 5-8)
    Attributes of humans (vv. 9-10)
Trust in God (vv. 11-12)

Some of the text is quite problematic, and translations vary greatly, especially in vv. 3-9.

To the leader. For Jeduthun.[2] *A Davidic psalm.*

1 *For God alone,*[3] *I*[4] *wait calmly;*[5]
    From him is my salvation.
2 *He alone is my rock and my salvation,*
    my high fortress, I will not be severely shaken.[6]

3 *How long will you assault*[7] *a person?*

1. Except Ps. 60, as noted earlier.
2. See note 6 on Psalm 39 superscription.
3. *'Aḵ* can mean "surely" but can also mean "only," thus the translation here of *alone.* A sixfold repetition in a psalm is significant, especially when it begins a verse (vv. 1, 2, 4, 5, 6, 9). Note neither NRSV nor NIV reflects this important structuring element. Tate does, using the interjection "Yes" (*Psalms 51–100,* p. 117).
4. Lit., *nap̱šî,* but the meaning of this word should not be reduced to "my soul" as many modern translations do. In Hebrew, it refers to the whole self or "me."
5. Most read as a participle from the root *dmh,* meaning "be silent" or "still" (*HALOT,* p. 225). Tate rightly translates as "calmly" (*Psalms 51–100,* p. 117).
6. Identical to v. 6 with the exception of the last word, *rabbâ.* The *BHS* critical apparatus suggests deleting this word, as do NIV, NRSV, and NJPS. However, there is no compelling reason to omit the word, especially since it is retained in LXX; Terrien concurs (*The Psalms,* p. 456) as does Zenger (*Psalms 2,* p. 110).
7. Root uncertain. BDB notes it is from *hwt,* meaning "shout at" or "threaten" (p. 223), as does LXX. *HALOT* argues the root is *htt,* meaning "to overwhelm with reproofs (p. 257)." Either root implies a threat to the person, be it verbal or physical, hence the selection of *assault.*

Will you batter this one,[8] *all of you,*
like a crooked stone wall or a collapsing wall?[9]
4 *Alone, they counsel together to bring down my dignity;*[10]
they take pleasure in lies;
they bless with their mouths,[11]
but inside they curse. Selah

5 *For God alone, I wait calmly;*
from him is my hope.
6 *He alone is my rock and my salvation,*
my high fortress, I will not be shaken.[12]
7 *Upon God is my salvation and my honor;*
my mighty rock, my refuge is in God.[13]
8 *Trust in him at all times,*[14] *O people;*
pour out your hearts before him;
God is a refuge to us. Selah

9 *Alone, humans are a puff of air;*
mortals are a deception.[15]
On the scales, they go up;

8. This word is problematic. MT reads 2mp pual, meaning "to be killed," but that makes little sense in the context. Tate suggest reading a piel which means "to kill" and notes the more general terms "to attack" or "batter" are possible (*Psalms 51–100,* p. 118).

9. The meaning of these two lines is uncertain because the subject here is uncertain. It can be read as above assuming the leaning wall and tottering fence is the one being attacked (as it is in NRSV, NIV, and NJPS). Others read it as a verbless clause making a description of the enemies (Dahood, *Psalms II,* p. 89).

10. MT is questionable. Hebrew *śᵉʾēṯ* does mean "to be elevated" but can also mean "majesty" of both God (Hab. 1:7) and people (Gen. 49:3). In addition, LXX and Syr read "my honor or dignity." Kraus and others emend the text, making the subject the enemies, using Ps. 73:18 *maššûʾôṯ* ("deceptions"; *Psalms 61–150,* p. 12). The better choice, I believe, is to go with the ancient sources, which all use a word meaning "honor" or *dignity.*

11. MT "with his mouth."

12. Vv. 5-6 present a dilemma for interpreters. Should this section be read as a duplicate of vv. 1-2, as represented in NRSV and Kraus (*Psalms 60–150,* p. 11) with the exception of exchange of *salvation* in v. 1b with *hope* in v. 5b? Or should it be read as it appears in the MT with an imperative in v. 5 instead of the regular verb of v. 1 and with the omission of *rabbâ* in v. 6b? An answer is difficult to discern, as the plethora of translations in commentaries testifies. The decision here is to read with the MT with the above differences reflected in the translation.

13. As Tate notes, the last line of the verse is one long construct chain, but this term is very difficult to put into sensible English, so the helping word *is* is added to most translations.

14. LXX reads "all the congregation of the people": *ʿᵃḏaṯ* instead of *ʿēṯ.*

15. Many modern translations add class distinctions to *bᵉnê ʾāḏām* ("lower") and *bᵉnê ʾîš* ("highborn"), as in KJV, NIV and NRSV. There is no compelling reason for these addi-

yet they are together a puff of air.

10 *Do not trust in extortion;*
and do not take pride in robbery;
if power[16] *increases do not set your heart on it.*

11 *First God spoke,*
two things I heard;[17]
that to God is strength,
12 *and to you, my Lord, is* hesed,
for YOU[18] *repay to each one according to one's works.*

1-2 The psalm begins as a testimony to others which recalls times when the one praying had been *severely shaken* by life. She has learned to wait in peace and believe in her *salvation,* for God is her protection (*rock* and *high fortress*).

3-4 At v. 3, the psalm moves from descriptions of God's protection to questions about humans. The gap is unsettling, for the subject of the *you* is unclear. However, since the Hebrew designates the masculine plural "you," it would be immediately obvious to the ancient hearer that the *you* here is not God. The verse is further complicated by translation difficulties, and several of the images are uncertain. What is clear, however, is that the *you* here is threatening the one praying. These are rhetorical questions meant to shed light on the actions of the enemies. Verse 4 moves from questions to descriptions, and the descriptions here are typical of prayers for help. Again a translation issue clouds the understanding of this verse. I have chosen to follow the LXX and see the object of the enemies's *counsel* as the one's *dignity.* I believe this best matches the reflections of vv. 1-8, which center on the one praying instead of some unknown "one of prominence." Verse 4 continues to describe the enemies as ones who say one thing and do another and *take pleasure* in deception.

5-8 This section is the center of the psalm and returns its focus to the relationship between God and the one praying. Verses 5 and 6 are almost identical to vv. 1-2, but with three significant differences. First, the verb form has changed to an imperative, and this change alters the tenor of the verse from testimony to exclamation. Second, the word in the second line changes

---

tions, especially since LXX uses the same phrase for humans in both lines. Zenger concurs (*Psalms 2,* p. 110).

16. This word can be translated as "might," "wealth," or "power." Several modern translations chose "wealth" here (NIV, NRSV), but there is no compelling reason to do so. *Extortion* and *robbery* are just as related to *power* as they are to wealth.

17. This is probably an ancient saying: "one thing . . . two things," as in Prov. 6:16-19 (Tate, *Psalms 51–100,* p. 119). It is made easier here for modern readers to understand.

18. The capitalization here is to indicate the emphasis of the double *you* in the Hebrew that cannot be easily communicated in English.

from *salvation* to *hope,* and finally the word *severely* in v. 2 is omitted in v. 6.[19] In this reading then, the testimony of vv. 1-2 has been transformed to a cry of distress precipitated by the arrival of the enemies in vv. 3-4. The confession of ordinary times has become the exclamation of stressful times. This exhortation is further intensified by the next two verses. Verse 7 reuses the images from other verses; *salvation* of vv. 1, 2 and 6; *honor* here is a synonym of *dignity* in v. 4; *mighty rock* is an expansion of *rock* in vv. 2 and 6; and *refuge* is a synonym of *high fortress* in vv. 2 and 6. This verse then serves as a type of crescendo of vv. 1-7, reminding the hearer that these words for God are true in all times of life.[20]

Exclamation of the one praying expands in v. 8 to the exhortation of others. What the one praying knows, she now invites the congregation to believe also. You can *trust* this God and *pour out your hearts* because God is the place of safety.

9-10 From the actions of the enemies in vv. 3-4, the prayer now returns to the topic of humans, but this time the humans and their acts are only *a puff of air.* The images used here are much like the wisdom sayings of Ecclesiastes and Proverbs. Modern translations have used Babylonian and Egyptian sources to translate the *humans* in v. 9 in terms of class differentiations, and this may be correct, but it is unnecessary to understand the point.[21] Indeed, if the sixfold repetition of *'aḵ* is translated as *alone,* the contrast between what God does alone (vv. 1, 2, 5 6) and what humans do alone (vv. 4 and 9) is sharp. Humans without God are simply *a puff of air.* However, God alone is one's salvation and refuge. Verse 10 continues in the wisdom tradition, exhorting all not to trust in crime and *power* and wealth (*ḥayil* means both), but remain steadfast in God alone.

11-12 God spoke, and this one understood two things that summarize all that God is, for God is both strong and gives steadfast or unconditional love. Both are required for the one praying to be safe, and both are required for God to judge each. The psalm ends with a belief that God has the power and the love to even up the ways of the world.

This psalm has three structures making it quite complex. The first is the chiastic structure that makes trust in God the beginning, end, and center of the prayer. In addition, there is also a progression of trust in God from an opening declaration, to the arrival of enemies, to an exclamation of trust in

19. Translations vary greatly here, and as noted in the translation many smooth out vv. 5-6 to more closely match vv. 1-2. E.g., in NRSV, only the change of a single word from v. 2 is discernable.

20. This may be why several scholars see vv. 1-7 as a single section (Kraus, *Psalms 60–150,* p. 14; McCann, "The Book of Psalms," p. 922.

21. Tate, *Psalms 51–100,* p. 119.

light of the enemies, to the declaration of uselessness of humans, and finally to a testimony of trust directed at all in the congregation. The psalm also has a third structure that shows how *God alone* acts (vv. 1, 2, 5, and 6) and how *humans* act *alone* (vv. 4 and 9). All three structures work together to reinforce the message of trust in God at all times in life.

Trust in God is the tripart message of the psalm and also provides a complex and interwoven structure on which the words are formed. The prayer asks us to see the ways that trust in God and our own faith is woven into the structures of our lives, invoking memory. The psalm also encourages those listening to understand the difference between God's eternal kingdom and the temporal human one. In this, it provides all who hear it with a reorientation of their lives. Finally, the psalm teaches about the mystery of God, for God *alone* does great things, but when humans are left to their own devices the result is fleeting and often harmful.

BETH TANNER

Psalm 63: My Soul Is Satisfied

Psalm 63 moves beyond the previous ones (Psalms 54–59 and 61–62) in theme. The fear expressed has completely disappeared, and this psalm is one of complete trust and confidence in God. The one praying is firmly rooted in God's world and confident of God's power and love. The psalm is divided into three sections:

> Expressions of longing and trust (vv. 1-4)
> Description of life lived with God (vv. 5-8)
> Description of the fate of the enemies (vv. 9-11)[1]

The psalm has a superscription added by a later editor indicating this prayer might have been prayed in a situation such as David experienced in the wilderness when he was running from King Saul or when he escaped from his son Absalom. Yet since many of the psalms connected to David's life on the run are prayers for help, this prayer could also indicate the times David spent in the wilderness in happier circumstances, such as when he is portrayed as tending the sheep for his father.

A Davidic psalm when he was in the wilderness of Judah.

1 *O God, you are my God, I seek you;*
my soul[2] *thirsts for you;*
my flesh faints for you,
like[3] *a dry and weary land with no water.*
2 *So I envisioned you in the sanctuary,*
beholding your power and glory;
3 *for your* hesed *is better than life;*
my lips shall praise you.
4 *So I will bless you all my life;*
and in your name,[4] *I will lift up my hands.*

1. It should be noted that some scholars saw significant problems in the arrangement of this psalm and went as far as to rearrange the verses so it fits the standard lament formula (Gunkel, *Die Psalmen,* p. 266). This change seems unnecessary, since the poem is understandable in its present form. This is especially true if this psalm is a conclusion to this section where trust in God is more powerful than fear of humans.

2. The translation *my soul* fits well poetically; however, the term refers to the whole self and should be so understood.

3. Several manuscripts have *ḳ*^{e} here, probably as a correction of MT. However, Waltke and O'Conner note that *b*^{e} can be translated as "like" when it is describing the manner in which a thing functions (*Biblical Hebrew Syntax,* p. 198).

4. NRSV follows Syr, which adds the additional verb *yērā'u* but changes the person

5 *My soul will be satisfied with a rich feast;*[5]
with joyful lips my mouth will give praise.
6 *When upon my bed, I remember you;*
in the night,[6] *I meditate on you;*
7 *for you are a help to me;*
and in the shelter of your wings I sing for joy.
8 *My soul clings to you;*
your right hand upholds me.

9 *Those seeking to destroy my life,*
they will go down into the depths of the earth.
10 *They will be given over*[7] *to the sword*
and become food for jackals.

11 *The king will rejoice in God;*
everyone who swears by him will rejoice,
for the mouths of those speaking lies will be shut.

1-4 The psalm opens with a longing for God that is compared to one seeking *water* in a parched land. The metaphor equates spiritual longing with a physical sense so hearers can feel the longing for God. The one praying provides the solution to the longing, not by changing his geographic setting, but by activating his memory. This one remembers God *in the sanctuary* and the characteristics of the King God: *power and glory* and *hesed.* Remembering, then, gives way to praise for the remainder of the stanza. The mouth that began dry and dusty is now full of praise and blessing for God.

5-7 The next section switches from seeking God to envisioning how one embraced by God can look forward to life lived to its fullest. Verse 5 again provides a metaphor of physical sense so that, just as one can know the feeling after a particularly delicious meal, that is how the soul feels when it is full of praise and thanksgiving to God. The emptiness of v. 1 is again filled with a richness of bounty. Verse 6 moves from the table to the *bed.* Sleep is a time when a human is the most vulnerable to surprise attack and injury. It is also subject to nightmares and terror. In Ps. 6:6, the bed is a place drenched with tears. But here, the one praying can remember and meditate on God in the

---

of the verb to 1cs to match the rest of the verses. This change is not necessary and is simply an expansion of MT.

5. Lit., "fat and fatness," indicating a rich feast of rare foods (Ps. 36:8; Job 36:16).

6. Hebrew "the watches of the night," referring to the time when guards stand watch over the sleeping city. *Night* makes more sense in a modern context.

7. MT has a *hiphil* verb, but LXX and Syr use the passive *hophal* form that is adopted by most translations.

shelter of God's *wings* and find rest. The image of God's *wings* can also reflect the wings over the ark of the covenant, recalling the image of the *sanctuary* from v. 2. This one is content with God as his help, both day and night.

9-11 This final section reminds all that the trust this one places in God is not part of an unrealistic and perfected world. The enemies are still in full view, but as in Psalm 1 they are little threat. They will *go down into the depths* and *become food for jackals.* This is a particularly shameful end, reserved for enemies of God (2 Kgs. 9:30-37). The confidence that the one has placed in God is seen in vindication as the ones who sought to destroy are indeed destroyed.

Verse 11 calls on others, not as in the previous psalm where others are called on to praise (62:8), but as if their adoration of God is the next step. Indeed, *the king* and *everyone* will open their mouths in praise, while those *speaking lies* will find their *mouths shut.* This verse serves as a final contrast between those who trust in God and those who do not.

This psalm encourages the ones hearing to use memory to bring God closer. We all know of these times when God seems far away and we thirst for presence. Memory aids us in realizing our blessings by remembering not only God's presence but God's power and *hesed.* In this, the prayer offers a refuge from current troubles and encourages us to trust in God today because of God's aid in our past. Just like the one praying, our current circumstance may not be altered, but confidence can come in remembering who God is to us.

Beth Tanner

Psalm 64: They Will Tell of the Works of God

Psalm 64 moves from a cry for aid to a call to praise. The first six verses of the psalm stress the aloneness of the one against the many who threaten with their poison words and who believe that no one, including God, can stop them. The prayer abruptly changes at v. 7 as God interrupts the wicked and dispatches them quickly. The psalm ends with a call to praise for all who *take refuge* in the Lord. This prayer then moves from a place of danger and fear to a place of refuge and praise.

The poem consists of four stanzas:[1]

St. 1 Cry to God for aid (vv. 1-2)
St. 2 Description of the acts of the evil ones (vv. 3-6)
St. 3 God's action and humanity's response (vv. 7-9)
St. 4 Call to the righteous to praise (v. 10)

These stanzas move from a call to God (vv. 1-2), to *fear* of the evil ones (vv. 3-6), to a place where the one praying is part of a congregation that *fears* the Lord because of God's deeds (vv. 8-9), to a final call for the righteous to sing of God's protection (v. 10). The psalm is a prayer for help imploring God to come to the aid of the one praying.[2]

The text of the psalm is quite problematic, especially vv. 6-9, where translations vary greatly, depending on the emendations selected. The translation below preserves as much of the MT reading as possible.

To the leader. A Davidic psalm.

1 *Hear my voice, O God, in my complaint;*
from the dread enemy, guard my life.
2 *Hide me from the council*[3] *of the evil ones,*
from the throng of workers of iniquity[4]

1. A four-stanza division is not adopted by most scholars, except Gerstenberger (*Psalms: Part 2,* p. 17). They argue for a three-stanza division: vv. 1-2, 3-6, 7-10 (see Kraus, *Psalms 60–150,* p. 4; Tate, *Psalms 51–100,* pp. 133-34) or 1-2, 3-8, 9-10 (Weiser, *The Psalms,* pp. 438-39). While they may be correct, v. 10 has different vocabulary, notably the name of God and different verb forms, suggesting the last verse is a later addition to the psalm.

2. Mowinckel sees this psalm as a "protective psalm," one that implies imminent danger, but not the physical harm of individual laments (*The Psalms in Israel's Worship,* 1:219-20).

3. Several scholars translate this word to indicate a "secret plot" (NRSV; Limburg, *Psalms,* p. 210), but *sōḏ* is not the act of making a plot, but a gathering of a company of persons.

4. As in the first line, the phrase is often translated as indicating a plotting against

3 *Who sharpen their tongues like a sword;*
who aim their bitter arrows of words,[5]
4 *shooting from hiding places at the blameless;*
suddenly they shoot and they are not afraid.
5 *They strengthen themselves for an evil purpose;*
they talk of hiding snares;
they say, "Who will see us?"[6]
6 *They can search out wrongs;*
but[7] *we have thought out a well-planned plot,*[8]
and the inward person and the heart are deep.[9]

7 *God will shoot them with an arrow;*
suddenly, there will be wounds.
8 *God causes them to stumble upon their tongues;*[10]

---

someone, "from the scheming of evildoers (NRSV)," but this phrase indicates a gathering of persons, not the actions of that company. This act of gathering heightens the suspense of the opening. The audience watches as the evil ones gather, waiting to see what action will happen next.

5. MT reads, lit., "They tread bitter arrows of word," as a construct chain. The phrase "they tread their arrow" is difficult to understand. Several translators argue that this phrase is describing the act of stringing a bow (BDB, p. 202; J. A. Emerton, "The Translation of Psalm LXIV.4," *JTS* 27 [1976] 391-92). In the context of the stanza, it would seem most likely this should be read as parallel to the first line, with both indicating preparation for an attack of words that cut like weapons.

6. Lit., "who will see them" but this makes little sense in the context. This line and the following verse are corrupt, and any translation is tentative. However, if the enemies are indeed speaking here, it would be easy for a *nun* to be missed due to a copyist's error, reading *lāmô* instead of *lānû*.

7. In MT, there is no indication of the preposition *but,* causing some to change the text (NRSV: "Who can see us? Who can search out our crimes?"). These changes, however, require a change of both the last preposition of v. 5 and the addition of a question marker at the beginning of v. 6. The addition of "but" is always possible in poetic texts because particles are often omitted, and this reading results in the least amount of change to MT.

8. The words of MT are clear, but the meaning is difficult. The participle and noun come from the same root and the noun appears only here, *ḥēp̄eś mᵉḥuppāś* ("a searched-for plot"). In other words, they thought long and hard about what they planned to do. These words are also from the same root as the verb used in the first line, so the problem may be the result of a copyist's error.

9. MT reads "and the inner man and heart are deep." This would seem to have something to do with the searching out of the mind in the line above, possibly that it is quite difficult to find the secret places where evil plots are hidden in the human heart.

10. The text of v. 8 is also difficult. It reads, lit., "They cause him to stumble, upon them, their tongue." The central question is who is the subject of the *hiphil* verb. It is read here as a 3ms verb without a suffix *(yakšîlûhô),* "He caused them to stumble upon their tongues,"

all who see them will flee.[11]
9 *Everyone will fear;*
and they will tell of works of God;
and God's works they will ponder.

10 *Let the righteous rejoice in the* LORD
and take refuge in him;
let all the upright in heart glory.

1-2 The poem opens with an imperative cry to God: *Hear me! Guard me! Hide me!* The rush of words lends urgency to the situation. This opening also sets both the one praying and God against the enemies and points to the unequal distribution by using three terms for the gathering of the enemies *(dread enemy, council of the evil ones, throng of workers of iniquity).* Not only are there many enemies, but they are gathering together against the one.[12] The one praying is clearly outnumbered and in need of aid. This urgency invites all who hear the psalm to remember times when they too felt the same urgency and the same sense of being the one against the many.

3-6 This stanza focuses on the acts of the enemies. They use words as their instrument, but they use them like weapons of war (*sword* and *arrows*).[13] The violent imagery continues the dichotomy of the opening. The enemies hide and ambush. The many hide and *shoot suddenly.* The one here is completely exposed and vulnerable as the enemies attack from hidden places. Verses 4 and 6 tell of the arrogance of the enemies. They do not fear

retaining the same subject, God, as the line above (Gerstenberger also adopts this reading; *Psalms: Part 2,* p. 19; also Zenger, *Psalms 2,* p. 129). The other option is that the subject of the verb is 3mpl and the verbal suffix is also 3mpl. The subject, then, is their tongues, reading "Their tongues cause them to stumble," with "upon them" being an untranslated repetition (NRSV and Tate adopt this reading; *Psalms 51–100,* p. 136).

11. Although the root is clear (both BDB [p. 626] and *HALOT* [p. 672] agree the verb is from *ndd* ["to run or flee"]) and this word fits well with the context of the psalm that is focused on running, hiding, and attacking, most scholars see it from the root *nwd* ("to shake or move the head in disgust" (NRSV, NIV; Tate, *Psalms 51–100,* p. 132, among others). This change is unnecessary.

12. Several translations, including NRSV, translate v. 2 as the motive of the evil ones, reading "hide me from the secret plots of the wicked, from the scheming of evildoers." This translation, while understandable, goes beyond the Hebrew meaning that juxtaposes the *me* of the petitioner against the *council* and the *throng* of the others.

13. Kraus, Schaefer, and Tate all comment on the possibility of these words as weapons being associated with magic spells and sorcerers. This reading in its ancient context is certainly possible. However, a modern reader does not have to make this association to understand the psalm. Persons from all cultures are well aware of the damage words can do when used against another as a weapon.

and are determined in their course. This description also sets them clearly against God. *They are not afraid* (v. 4), but the just *fear* God (v. 9). Their plots and schemes are hidden deep in their hearts, yet Ps. 92:5 declares it is God's thoughts that are deep *('mq)*. The more one knows the world of the psalms, the more arrogant these ones appear as they act as God acts.

The poem then records their arrogant speech (v. 6). They tell themselves that their secret traps cannot be seen or prevented, even if others *search* for them. Their hiding of traps, however, offers a parallel to what they have hidden *deep* inside themselves. The arrogant ones believe that others can *search* for their evil, just as they do for their traps, for their minds are so *deep* that no one can prove their *wrongs*. Even with the problematic text here, it is clear that the schemes of the evil ones are being described.

7-9 Just when all seems to be lost, God appears. In the last stanza, the enemies were sure that they were like God and unassailable. God is portrayed here using the same methods of warfare as the evil ones to show God's power and strength. The enemies may attack the blameless *suddenly,* but God's attack will be just as stealthy and sudden. It took ten lines to describe the scheming of the enemies, but God dispatches them in only three. They thought they were so smart that they had hidden well both their *snares* and their thoughts, but God's sudden ambush demonstrates they are not smarter than God. Indeed, their little plans do not even require effort on the part of God. The psalm argues that the enemies get exactly what they planned for the lone one. It was an unfair and unbalanced fight, but God is always on the side of the one threatened and outnumbered. The image of God using *arrows* to wound the wicked may not be the parallel that we would use in the twenty-first century, but the psalm is not a statement about violence. The parallel is meant to convey that "you get what you give." This lesson is the opposite of the Golden Rule, and God did to them as they planned to do to a weaker party. God is a God, not of vengeance, but of justice, and in God's kingdom, everyone — and I mean everyone — gets what they deserve!

The remainder of the stanza does not deal with the enemies at all. They have disappeared with the phrase *all who see them will flee.* The tables have turned. The psalm began with the lone believer surrounded by the many. The enemies are now scattered, and the believer joins the congregation of the ones who *fear God.* Instead of using words as arrows, this congregation will *tell* of the works of God. Instead of devising well thought out plots, they will *ponder* the *works* of God (v. 9).

10 The last verse does not continue the themes of the psalm as the above structure has done.[14] In addition, *Elohim* is the name used for God in

14. Note that in vv. 7-9 the verses begin with an unusual series of *wāw*-consecutives. V. 10, however, begins with an imperfect verb that most read as an exhortation.

vv. 1 and 7, but here the divine name is used. Finally the generic *all* and *they* of vv. 8-9 take on the titles *righteous* and *upright.* For these reasons, I suggest this verse is a later addition.[15] Yet while it may be a further reflection, it is certainly a fitting ending of the psalm. After *all* tell and ponder the works of God, *the righteous rejoice* and *take refuge* in God. The psalm began with a cry for help and ends with the assurance of God providing a "hiding place" of God's own. A *hiding place,* not of enemies and their threat, but a hiding place of *refuge* and safety — one that the reader is not to fear, but to rejoice in its safety from the evils of the world.

One of the most pressing theological questions today is "why do the evil ones prosper?" If one looks around, it certainly seems as if the bad ones are winning, be that on the streets or in the hedge fund industry. Yet the picture of God arriving with arrows is not exactly comforting either. This psalm attempts to put the question in the long view of time. God acts and gives back exactly what the evil ones have done to others. In that, it is not a psalm of vengeance but one of balance, where those who hurt others get their acts brought back to them. God comes to set the world right, and for Christians this is the good news of the second coming. God comes not to destroy ruthlessly, but to set the world back in balance. This is the hope to which we cling when we see the suffering of the righteous at the hands of evil ones.

BETH TANNER

15. Likewise, Gerstenberger sees this last verse as possibly a redaction (*Psalms: Part 2*, p. 17).

Psalm 65: God's Great Gifts

Psalm 65 provides the reader with three scenes that tell of God's goodness and power. These scenes are discrete, with no indication of how the audience is to connect them. As Tate notes, it is how one understands the connection of these scenes that is central to understanding this poem.[1] The psalm is, then, much like a play with three acts. Most scholars argue that this piece is a thanksgiving psalm in hymnic style, and thus God's acts are either in the past or are currently unfolding.[2]

Acts of forgiveness (vv. 1-4)
Acts of power (vv. 5-8)
Acts of grace (vv. 9-13)

To the leader. A Davidic psalm. A song.[3]

1 *To you praise is due,*[4] *O God, in Zion;*
to you a vow is performed.[5]
2 *O Hearer of prayers,*
to you all flesh comes.
3 *When words of iniquity*[6] *overpower us,*
our transgressions you forgive.
4 *Happy is the one you choose and bring near,*
the one who lives in your courts.
We are satisfied with the goodness of your house,
of your holy temple.

1. *Psalms 51–100,* p. 138.

2. Mowinckel, *The Psalms in Israel's Worship,* 1:119-20; Weiser, *The Psalms,* p. 461; Gerstenberger, *Psalms: Part 2,* p. 23. Kraus sees it as a hymn, but will not call it one of thanksgiving (*Psalms 60–150,* p. 28).

3. LXX has an additional superscription: "Of Jeremiah and Ezekiel, under the rule of deportation, as they were about to march forth." The meaning of this additional note is unclear (Gerstenberger, *Psalms: Part 2,* p. 21, Kraus, *Psalms 60–150,* p. 28).

4. MT reads "To you, silence *(dumiyyâ)* is praise." This is a possible reading, but unlikely in a hymn of praise where sound is the central act. Most follow LXX, which uses *prepō* ("it is fitting or proper"), as does Syr.

5. Some Greek manuscripts add "in Jerusalem."

6. Hebrew *dab̲ar* has a multitude of meanings: "words, things, matter." Many translations use the general term "deeds" (NRSV, NIV). The meaning *words* has been retained here because the psalm is focused on hearing and speaking (vv. 2, 5, 13).

5 *With awesome acts you answer us in righteousness,*
God of our salvation,
the trusted one of all the ends of the earth
and the farthest seas.
6 *Establishing the mountains by your strength,*[7]
you are girded with might,
7 *silencing the roaring seas, the roaring waves*
and the turmoil of peoples.
8 *Those who dwell at the corners of the earth fear your signs;*
the sources of the morning and the evening shout for joy.

9 *You visit the earth and water it;*
you greatly enrich it.
The river of God is filled with water;
you secure their grain by establishing its course,[8]
10 *causing the furrows to drink, descending into its ridges,*
softening it with showers;
you bless its growth.
11 *You crowned the year with your goodness;*
and your tracks are overflowing with abundance.
12 *Pastures of the wilderness overflow;*[9]
the hills gird themselves with rejoicing.
13 *The meadows are clothed with flocks;*
the valleys are decked with grain;
they shout and they sing for joy!

1-4 The first vignette is a study in contrasts. First is the contrast between form and content of vv. 1-2. The content of the first two verses gives the impression that this will be a song of Zion where the greatness of God and God's universal rule are the central metaphors.[10] But the form is odd for a hymn. Instead of

7. MT has a 3ms suffix, which is problematic; several Greek manuscripts and Jerome have a 2ms suffix, which is more appropriate.

8. MT is difficult to understand: "you established their grain, you established her." The next phase in v. 11 uses two infinitive absolute verbs that further clarify this phrase by adding to or explaining the situation represented by the verb "establish" (see Waltke and O'Conner, *Biblical Hebrew Syntax,* pp. 588-89). The grain is "established" by the process of watering.

9. The *BHS* critical notes suggest the verb *yārîʿû* ("shout for joy") in place of *yirʿăp̱û* ("overflow"). However, the line is clear and readable in MT, and no change is warranted (as noted by Tate, *Psalms 51–100,* p. 138).

10. E.g., see Pss. 48 or 76, where God is praised, Zion is a place of worship, and the psalm has a universal quality that extends beyond the borders of Jerusalem or Israel to other countries and to all of creation.

beginning with the expected imperative call to praise or sing,[11] the psalm's first two lines begin with the preposition *to you,* and the typical imperative form is replaced with passive verb constructions. While the passage is hymnic in content, an unfamiliar style serves to disorient.

This disorientation continues as v. 3 also offers a twist. Unlike the other songs of Zion, the center of this stanza is not God's care or blessing from Zion, but is God's forgiveness and restoration. God is praised and vows are brought because God *forgives.* This is an attribute cried for in the penitential psalms (Psalms 6, 32, 38, 51, 102, 130, 143), but is not praised as an attribute of the God of Zion except in this psalm. Unexpected form gives way to unexpected content.

The last verse of the stanza offers a final twist. Often referred to as a beatitude,[12] *ʾašrê* or *happy* is a word that usually represents an exemplary and good person.[13] But here it is clear that wholeness of life stems from God's forgiveness. Satisfaction comes from the goodness of God's house, where one is restored to happiness.

5-8 The second stanza introduces a global perspective to God's activities. It takes the images of the first stanza and expands them to the ends of the earth. The stanza begins by celebrating God's *awesome* (from the root for "fear") *acts* and uses the epithet *God of our salvation* and could be understood relating to the act of forgiveness above. But as the stanza progresses, the sense is that God's *awesome acts* are expanded from those of the first scene. God is the controller of the world and the container of chaos. The one who forgives is the one who plants *the mountains* and the one who through *might* controls the *seas* and the *peoples.* If the first stanza represents the personal God of grace, this stanza focuses on the power of the divine warrior and controller of creation.[14] This is a God who chooses to dwell in Zion, but that is hardly the scope of God's reach.

9-13 God forgives; God keeps the creation in order; and in this final stanza, God provides the necessities of physical life. This final scene is pastoral,[15] and the humans disappear, reaping only derivative rewards from God's

11. Gunkel notes this is the most common "introduction" for a hymn (*Introduction to Psalms,* p. 23).

12. Tate, *Psalms 60–150,* p. 141; Gerstenberger, *Psalms: Part 2,* p. 22.

13. Gerstenberger, *Psalms: Part 2,* p. 22.

14. Most commentators have noted that the terms used in this section reflect ancient Near Eastern mythical motifs of God as the conqueror and controller of chaos, most fully seen in Ps. 74 (see Kraus, *Psalms 60–150,* p. 30; Tate, *Psalms 51–100,* pp. 142-43).

15. V. 11 shares a rare vocabulary set with Ps. 23: *and your tracks* (the same word as "right paths," 23:3) *are overflowing* ("my cup overflows," 23:5) *with abundance* or fatness ("you anoint my head with fatness," 23:5). While establishing literary dependence is not possible, the shared vocabulary is striking.

blessing of the creation. The humans are called to praise because the great God of Zion offers forgiveness (vv. 1-4). In contrast, the creation *shouts* and *sings for joy* because God is the giver of rain and *grain* and *goodness.*

The three stanzas function to teach those listening that God provides all things needed for life, and at the same time it also offers praise to God who reigns as the Supreme Monarch. The writers of the psalms certainly knew of and used the theme from their neighbors. Loren Fisher notes that the theme of Creator-King in the Ugarit myths included temple-building, the ordering of chaos, and the ongoing care of the created order.[16] The combination of themes is the same in this psalm. Together the stanzas work at expanding the vision of God's greatness and goodness. God's reign is not only within the confines of Zion. Here one finds forgiveness and contentment and a home, but one should not stop there. Forgiveness, the act praised by the humans, is placed in its proper context. The direction of the poem suggests that forgiveness and contentment in Zion is the first step in seeing beyond one's self and beyond the walls of Zion. God's work extends well beyond human restoration. God's work is greater than what any of us can see with earthly sight. The poem serves to open up the horizons to other people and other lands. All of God's kingdom should be in sight from Zion.

This prayer can function in the same way today. We as people of an industrial world are even farther removed from creation than our ancestors. God can be seen as serving only the human world. This prayer praises God for all of God's great gifts and reminds all to lift their heads and look around and see all that God does to maintain the delicate balance of life. It invites all to praise God for what is seen and unseen.

BETH TANNER

16. "Creation at Ugarit and in the Old Testament," *VT* 15 (1965) 320.

Psalm 66: The Mystery of Grace

Psalm 66 opens exactly where Psalm 65 ends, with shouts of praise lifted to God. This call to praise continues for the next twelve verses, extolling God's works, power, and teaching. The second section of the psalm focuses on one who brings sacrifices to God and shares the story of God's goodness with the congregation. Just as in Psalm 65, these two sections are discrete and call upon the hearer to struggle to understand their combined meaning.

The psalm is clearly divided into two major sections with several stanzas in each:

- Section 1 (vv. 1-12)
    - Praise to the God of all (vv. 1-4)
    - Praise to the God of the waters (vv. 5-7)
    - Praise to the God of guidance (vv. 8-12)
- Section 2 (vv. 13-20)
    - Bringing sacrifices to God (vv. 13-15)
    - Telling of God's goodness (v. 16-20)

Scholars focusing on why the two seemingly different psalms are joined fall into two camps. A first group is interested in "how" and "where" psalms were used in religious life. They see this psalm as indicating something about how Israel worshipped.[1] Other scholars focus not on what the psalm can teach us about how Israel worshipped, but what we can learn from the psalm about the relationship between God, the community, and the individual.[2] How Israel worshipped is certainly an interesting question, but is also one that is difficult to know based on these poetic texts. It is important to note that these ancient people left us prayers and poems that describe God and their relationship with God and not a manual for worship. It would appear then that the enduring legacy of the psalms is not in describing worship, but in describing God.

1. Kraus argues that these psalms are part of a festal reenactment where worshippers at Gilgal actually cross the Jordan River celebrating both the crossing of the Sea and the passage into the land (*Psalms 60–150*, p. 36). Others, providing slightly different details, see it as a temple celebration where vv. 1-12 offer a choral introduction for the individual thanksgiving and sacrifice. The psalm, then, demonstrates how Israel worshipped God (Weiser, *The Psalms*, pp. 468-69; Gerstenberger, *Psalms: Part 2*, p. 30; Mays, *Psalms*, p. 221).

2. Limburg, e.g., argues that this psalm aids in reflecting the relationship between "they" (the world), "we" (Israel), "I" (the individual); *Psalms*, p. 218.

To the leader. A song. A psalm.

1 *Shout to God all the earth;*
2 *sing to the glory of his name;*
set forth gloriously his praise.[3]
3 *Say to God, "How awesome are your works!*
So massive is your power that your enemies must kneel[4] *before you."*
4 *All the earth bows down before you;*
and sings praises to you,
sings praises to your name. Selah

5 *Come and see the works of God,*[5]
awesome deeds all around[6] *humankind.*
6 *He turned the sea to dry land;*
they crossed the river on foot.
There we rejoiced in him,
7 *the one who rules in might forever,*
whose eyes keep watch on the nations.
The rebellious ones shall not rise up against him.[7] Selah

8 *Bless our God, O peoples,*
and let the sound of his praise be heard!

3. MT reads, lit., "set/establish glory his praise." It is possible that the pointing is incorrect and the last two nouns should be in construct, reading "Set the glory of his praise," as is indicated by Syr and Targ. This is also consistent with the construct at the end of the first line. Many translations also add "to him" (NRSV: "Give to him glorious praise"). Instead of reading a construct or adding an additional preposition, this translation reads *kāḇōḏ* as adverbial, preserving the line in MT, also Tate (*Psalms 51–100,* p. 144) and Hossfeld (*Psalms 2,* p. 143).

4. The meaning of the root *kḥš* is uncertain in this context. It normally means "to deceive" or "to grow lean." In two texts, however, it seems to mean "to fend obedience" (see Pss. 18:44; 81:15; *HALOT,* p. 470). Like above, Hossfeld translates "bow down" (*Psalms 2,* p. 143).

5. Both NRSV and NIV inexplicitly read "Come and see what God has done," but the Hebrew text clearly uses a construct form here, "works of God."

6. The preposition *ʿal* is difficult to translate here. It most often has a spatial meaning "over," or "around," as translated here. However, Waltke and O'Connor note it can also have the meaning of "on behalf of" (*Biblical Hebrew Syntax,* p. 217), and this meaning is also possible here.

7. The last verb is read either as the *hiphil* jussive of *rwm* (Kethib: "let the rebellious not exalt or raise themselves") or as the *qal* (Qere: "The rebellious ones shall not rise up against him"). The *qal* is used here because this line is part of a series of statements that began in line 5b in which God is the subject.

9 *Who has kept us*[8] *among the living,*
and does not let our feet[9] *slip;*
10 *because you have tested us, O God,*
you refined us as silver is refined.
11 *You brought us into the net;*[10]
you set burdens[11] *on our backs.*
12 *You let people ride over our heads;*
we went through fire and through water;
then you brought us out into plenty.[12]

13 *I come to your house with burnt offerings;*
to you I will fulfill my vow,
14 *that my lips uttered*
and my mouth spoke in my distress.
15 *Burnt offerings of fatlings I will offer to you,*
with the aroma of the sacrifice of rams;
I will offer bulls and goats. Selah

16 *Come and hear all of you who fear God,*
and I will recount what he has done for me.[13]
17 *Unto him, I cried out with my mouth,*

8. Lit., *nap̱šēnû* ("our soul"). The dual meaning of a soul separate from a body should be avoided in Hebrew. *Us* is a more appropriate conveyance of the Hebrew meaning. Also, MT has the singular "our soul," although multiple manuscripts have the plural "our souls." There is no way to convey this meaning in English, for it implies metaphorically a shared sense of life within the community.

9. MT has the singular "foot," while multiple manuscripts have *feet.*

10. The exact root of *m^{e}ṣûḏâ* is unclear. It may derive from *ṣûḏ,* a root meaning "to hunt," and seems to indicate an implement of hunting, or the root may be *ṣûr,* indicating a stronghold or fortress. The content of this section of the poem indicates that the word is probably supposed to mean something bad, hence the selection of *net* (also NRSV), but NIV's "prison" or Hossfeld's "stronghold" (*Psalms 2,* p. 143) is also possible, and any translation is tentative.

11. This word appears only here, so its meaning is unknown. Tate (*Psalms 51–100,* p. 145) and Kraus (*Psalms 60–150,* p. 34) use "affliction," whereas Weiser uses "oppression" (*The Psalms,* p. 467). Both NRSV and NIV use *burden,* which this translation retains because of its more general meaning.

12. MT has *lār^{e}wāyâ* ("to be satisfied or sated"), as in Ps. 23:5. LXX, Syr, Jerome, and Targ use *lār^{e}wāḥâ* ("a spacious place or place of relief"). MT can be read without the change to a geographic place as these other texts do. Tate reads "abundance" instead of "plenty" (*Psalms 51–100,* p. 146).

13. Lit., *nap̱šî* ("my soul"), but in Hebrew it does not mean only soul but the whole individual.

and extolled him with my tongue.[14]
18 *If I found*[15] *iniquity in my heart,*
my Lord would not have heard me.
19 *But indeed God heard me;*
he has paid attention to the voice of my prayer.
20 *Blessed be God*
who did not turn away from my prayers,
or remove his hesed *from me.*

1-4 The poem opens with pure praise and celebration. Plural imperatives in vv. 1-2 and 4[16] frame this section. Verse 3, the center of the chiasm, indicates the content of the praise. God is to be praised for God's great *works* and for a *power* so *massive* that the *enemies must kneel.* These awesome works and great power are not given specific content here, but what is clear is that friend and foe alike will see and know the acts of this God.[17] Like many psalms, this one also divides the world into two ways: one praising his *name* and one kneeling reluctantly before this great God.

5-7 Verse 5 is a call to experience these great deeds of God praised above. Verse 6 details a water crossing, but does it have a specific historical referent?[18] Certainly the exodus sea crossing comes to mind for those familiar with Israel's great confession. This connection is even more pronounced by the change in person. The second line of v. 6 is in the third person *they.* However, the last line reorients the audience to become part of the experience: *There we rejoiced in him.* This is the same change of perspective that occurs in the exodus confessions that commemorate the event.[19] Certainly this is

14. Lit., "and he was extolled under my tongue." Tate states this is an idiom meaning "on the tip of my tongue" (*Psalms 51–100,* p. 146).

15. MT has *rā'îṯî* ("I saw"). NRSV and NIV go too far in using "cherish" here. *Found* reflects the understanding of "seeing" without going as far as to indicate intent or premeditation as does "cherish."

16. V. 4 uses imperfect forms that are read as imperatives (Waltke and O'Conner, *Biblical Hebrew Syntax,* p. 577).

17. In the movement of the stanzas, then, Ps. 66 moves in an opposite direction from Ps. 65, which opened with God's works in Zion and moved to God's universal reign. Here, the move is opposite and has the effect of placing the praise of God in 65:13 and 66:1-4 as the center of these two psalms.

18. The adverb *there* and the cohortative verb are seen as further evidence of a historical reference. Kraus argues this represents an actual "festal situation" where the crossing of the Jordan symbolically represents both the exodus escape and the crossing of the Jordan (*Psalms 60–150,* 36). This may indeed be a clue to Israel's cultic worship, but it may also simply be a poetic rendering with many meanings. Any direct link to how Israel worshipped is speculative.

19. Such as Deut 6:20-21: "When your children ask. . . . We were Pharaoh's slaves in

not the only understanding of the verse, but it is by far the clearest of the connections and the one that would come to mind for an audience where the exodus is part of their confession.[20]

Verse 7 introduces a slightly different motif and returns the mind of the audience from a particular event and a particular people to God's universal rule. No matter what else the exodus may represent, it is part of God's control of the whole earth and the whole of time (*forever,* v. 7a). The last line of the stanza reminds the audience of the two types of people again. You may *come* and *see* and *rejoice,* or you can choose another path that is bound to fail.

8-12 The next section again calls for *praise* (v. 8), followed by the reasons for praise. The call to *bless* is universal, but the remainder of the stanza is in the particular, using all first person plural pronouns. The reason to *bless* is different from above, here focusing on salvation in the form of guidance and correction. One who is listening can certainly hear echoes of the wilderness wandering. God *kept us among the living* with the dramatic rescue at the sea and also with the gifts of manna and water.[21] In addition, the testing of v. 10 is clearly reminiscent of how the Israelites *tested* God at Massah (Exod. 17:7; Deut 6:16; 33:8; Ps. 95:8-9). Salvation here is announced as being more than a miraculous deliverance, but involves God's guidance and correction. Certainly, the wilderness episode centers on these two issues. God provided guidance in a physical way via the cloud and the pillar of fire, but also in the form of the giving of the torah at Sinai. Correction was also needed as this group of slaves struggled to become a holy people and priests to the world (Exod. 19:5-6). In the stanza before, the audience was brought through the waters; here they are brought through the hard lessons learned by the wilderness generation. The movement of the poem is such that we take the journey with them. But the calls to *praise* and *bless* are more complex, making these events not just for Israel, but the whole world. The world is eavesdropping on Israel's formation into God's people. Just as the "they"

Egypt . . . (and) the LORD brought us out of Egypt with a mighty hand. . . ." To make this confession is to make the exodus experience part of our own story of salvation. Hossfeld notes, "This is an example of the solidary culture of memory in the Bible, which cuts across all times" (*Psalms 2,* p. 145).

20. Dahood argues this represents the exodus crossing (*Psalms 51–100,* p. 120); Gerstenberger sees the verse as representing the Jordan crossing in Josh. 3:1-5:1 via shared vocabulary (*Psalms: Part II,* p. 26). Schaefer thinks it is a fusing of the beginning and end of the wilderness journeys (*Psalms,* p. 160). Certainly all of these readings are possible and open the psalm to a greater vista of God's awesome deeds.

21. Several scholars agree that this is reflective of the wilderness narratives but not clearly dependent on this experience alone (e.g. McCann, "The Book of Psalms," p. 938). Others, such as Mays, focus more on the phrase *refined us as silver is refined,* seeing this as a close parallel to similar phrases in prophetic texts such as Isa. 48:10; Jer. 9:7 (*Psalms,* p. 223).

became "we" in the section above, here the world praises and so becomes a part of this central confession. Israel's story has become a reality for the world. The two ways of the other sections have disappeared; all are praising God for God's works.

13-15 At v. 13, the whole poem shifts: from "God" to "I"; from wilderness to temple; from voiced praise to acts of sacrifice. As noted above, scholars such as Westermann see this as a second psalm added to vv. 1-12, and this may indeed be the case in the distant past of this psalm. But as the psalm stands here, it is one complete piece with a hugh poetic gap. A poetic gap is a device where the audience must make the connection. One stumbles to form a connection between this act and the previous section with a different subject (God) and a different action (voiced praise). Just as the audience was drawn in by turning "their" narrative into "our" praise, here the audience is drawn in by being forced to connect the sections. The question of how to connect the gap will continue long into this second section and possibly leave the audience puzzling long after the prayer's last word is uttered.

But this is not the only surprise for the audience. Verse 13 opens with the one bringing a sacrifice in payment for a fulfilled *vow* made to God during a time of crisis.[22] The audience knows nothing of the crisis that brings the person before the throne of God. They are left to wonder what vow and what situation have brought the person to this place. Another issue is added in v. 15 in the extreme amount of sacrifice used for the fulfillment of this vow. This is not a minor sacrifice. Indeed, it is overkill. The act is extreme, over the top, maybe even wasteful.[23] This entire stanza serves to disorient the audience and move them to a different physical place (the temple), where we are eavesdropping on another's vow repayment and where the connections to the first twelve verses remain in question.

16-20 The act of sacrifice given to God is only part of the process. The final stanza reflects that along with sacrifice comes testimony. Using the Hebrew word for "recounting or telling a story," the one praying proclaims *what he (God) has done for me.* This proclamation is given to *all of you who fear God.* This certainly implies the worshipping community, but in the context of the

22. This act of vow fulfillment is seen in other poetic texts (Pss. 22:25; 56:12; 61:8; 116:18; Jonah 2:9).

23. Several have suggested that the amount of sacrifice tells that the person is possibly the king or a representative of the people (Mowinckel, *The Psalms in Israel's Worship,* 2:28; Tate, *Psalms 51–100,* p. 150; Gerstenberger, *Psalms: Part 2,* p. 29). Gerstenberger further argues that this must be a communal sacrifice. This is certainly possible, but the first person singular language here makes it problematic. It is also plausible that just as the "enemies kneeling" of v. 3 is metaphorical hyperbole, this may also tell less about the individual's or Israel's worship process than it makes a poetic statement about personal distress and/or the greatness of God.

psalm, it is possible that this relates both to the followers of God and also all of the peoples who have seen God's wonders and deeds.

Verse 18 provides another bump for one reading this psalm. Does the psalm state that one must be "pure of heart" for God to listen to their cries?[24] Although a common theme in prayers for help, this phrase again gives the audience pause. The gap invites one to reimagine what the relationship is between the condition of one's self and the hearing of cries by God. No easy formula resolves this tension. Psalms of innocence and individual righteousness stand with psalms where the sin of the human heart is central (i.e., Psalm 51); psalms of accusation concerning God's lack of attention (Psalm 44) are contained in the same book with psalms of great confidence in God's guidance (Psalm 23); and psalms of praise and thanks stand directly beside psalms of excruciating sorrow and pain (Psalms 22 and 23). This psalm, which speaks clearly of painful periods of testing by God (vv. 8-12), here speaks of a concept that one must be clear from iniquity for God to pay attention.

The psalm, then, moves from the cosmic to the particular. In its final form, although we may learn something about how thanksgiving is offered to God in the temple, what is most evident is this psalm is a word picture that reflects the mytho-poetic reality of thanksgiving. The sacrifice of one person is played out in the midst of the courtyard of the throne of God, so that this very personal thanksgiving to God is given in the midst of the congregation of the faithful, but also given to the great King of the Universe. We also see the complex relationship between God and humanity. We know that none is completely innocent of transgression (Ps. 51:3-5), but yet a child of the covenant community can stand before God with a "clean heart." Such is the mystery of grace.

We live in a world of instant and often easy answers. Yet at the same time, we are aware of how very complex our relationships are. Rarely can a relationship be seen as simplistic and clear, and if that is our relationship with humans, should we expect our relationship with God to be any less complex? We miss out on so much of our relationship with God because we do not spend enough time meditating on how we can have a personal relationship with the Creator and King of the Universe. We see God's grace as mechanical instead of a mystery where one can be both sinner and saint and yet always loved by God. Some psalms serve to shake up our worldview, and this is one of them. It forces the audience to make connections that are difficult and possibly even contradictory. It teaches ones who have ears to hear to embrace the mystery and puzzle over God's rule in the world.

BETH TANNER

24. Certainly this is a common declaration in the prayers for help (e.g., Pss. 7:3-5; 17:3-5; 26:1-12), but there are also the so-called penitential psalms (Pss. 6, 32, 38, 51, 102, 130, 143) that call upon God to redeem from one's own acts of sin against God.

Psalm 67: A Prayer of Blessing

This brief psalm is in the form of a prayer for blessing echoing the priestly benediction of Num. 6:22-27. The psalm begins in the first person, requesting God's blessing upon us so that God's ways will be known and subsequently be a reason for praises to be lifted by all the nations and peoples of the earth (vv. 3, 4, 5 and 7). While the psalm is free of textual problems, scholars disagree on how the verbs in vv. 3-7 should be translated. Some translations see all of the verbs until v. 6 as being in the jussive form, and thus the entire psalm is a prayer-wish (NRSV).[1] Others read vv. 3-6 as future tense verbs instead of wishes (NJPS) so the psalm is more of a prayer of thanksgiving. In addition, as noted by Clifford, how the verbs are read is directly related to how one understands the genre of the psalm.[2] Tate notes there is no easy way to resolve the issue.[3] Mays says both ways of reading are possible and even correct in their own right.[4] This psalm clearly illustrates the problem of translating Hebrew into English, since either translation is possible. Indeed, in the ancient world the poem could function as either without a change in its written text. This may be an example of a poem that was both a prayer-wish and a prayer of thanksgiving, depending on the circumstance in which it was read.

This small psalm has a chiastic structure:

A Request for blessing and the global result (vv. 1-2)
  B Refrain (v. 3)
    C The confession of God's care of the nations of the earth (v. 4)
  B′ Refrain (v. 5)
A′ Another global result of the blessing (vv. 6-7)

To the leader. With stringed instruments. A psalm. A song.

1 *May God be gracious to us and bless us;*
may he make his face to shine among us,
2 *that your way*[5] *shall be known on the earth,*

1. This reading favors putting the psalm in the category of a prayer song, as do Tate (*Psalms 51–100,* p. 153), Kraus (*Psalms 60–150,* p. 40), and others. Earlier scholars, such as Gunkel, saw the psalm as a hymn of harvest thanksgiving (*Die Psalmen,* p. 45).

2. *Psalms 1–72,* p. 311. If read as a series of jussives, the psalm is a prayer. If read as a series of imperfects in either the present or future, the psalm is a descriptive thanksgiving hymn.

3. *Psalms 51–100,* p. 155. For the most complete discussion of this issue, see Hossfeld and Zenger, *Psalms 2,* pp. 150-53.

4. *Psalms,* 224.

5. Several manuscripts reflect the plural "your ways," while others and Syr use "his

your salvation to all the nations. Selah

3 *Let the peoples praise you, O God;*
let the peoples praise you, all of them.

4 *Let the nations rejoice and shout,*
because you will judge the peoples with equity,
and all the nations in the earth you will guide. Selah

5 *Let the peoples praise you,*[6] *O God;*
let the peoples praise you, all of them.

6 *The earth gives its harvest;*
God, our God has blessed us.
7 *God has blessed us;*[7]
let all the ends of the earth fear him.

1-2 The psalm opens with a plea for God's action in the form of offering grace and blessing. The request as noted by many is reminiscent of the great blessing of Aaron in Numbers 6, but here it is a request of the people instead of a priestly pronouncement. This request comes directly on the heels of the blessing of God in the last verse of Psalm 66, connecting these psalms.[8] Verse 2 is dependent on v. 1 and offers the reason why God is to bless Israel — not for their own benefit, but so God's way and salvation *be known* by the *nations.* God's action toward Israel is not for its benefit alone, but God's independent action toward the one will be seen by the whole. Just as Psalms 65 and 66 have stressed, God's grace given to an individual or to Israel is done for the benefit of the whole world.

3 Verse 3 is identical to v. 5 and reflects the result of knowing the ways of God: all the people will lift praise to God. Just as God's promise to Abram in Gen. 12:3 ("and in you all the families of the earth shall be blessed"), here the people are to praise God because of God's blessing shining on the *us* of

way" or "his ways." The difference between plural and singular may simply reflect a disagreement as to the grammatical form of the collective plural (Tate, *Psalms 51–100,* p. 154). The person and number of the pronoun are more problematic. "He" would be the better choice for a subordinate clause to line 1b, but most English translations reflect the more difficult 2ms reading (NRSV, NIV, NJPS).

6. 4QPs[a] adds a *wāw* at the beginning of this line (Ulrich, Cross, et al., *Qumran Cave 4: XI,* p. 19).

7. 4QPs[a] has a 3mpl verb with a 2ms suffix: "Let them bless you, O God" (Ulrich, Cross, et al., *Qumran Cave 4: XI,* p. 19).

8. Schaefer, *Psalms,* p. 162.

v. 1. These verses form a frame around the center of the psalm, a frame of praise spoken in hundreds of languages of all the peoples. This same praise is reflected in the narrative of the Pentecost in Acts 2:1-13.

4 Verse 4 forms the center of the chiastic structure. It is also highlighted by virtue of its three lines. The heart of the matter is that God *will judge* all *with equity,*[9] and *all the nations* will be guided by God.[10] God will treat all the people just as God treats Abraham's family. God's justice is not contained by national borders or by religion or by race. God's justice and guidance are intended for all. God's judgment is the reason for praise, for God comes, not to destroy but to set the world right and bring all into God's kingdom.

6-7 The conclusion of the psalm opens with assurance. God wishes to bless all of the nations, but humans are a fickle lot and blessing to all is often thwarted by the greed of some. Yet even in the midst of being unable to see God's promise of blessing and justice within the people, there is one sure sign. God sets the gift of the earth and its abundance. The message, then, is that the result of God's blessing is already seen throughout all the earth in the bounty of the *harvest,* further stressing that the knowing of God is already unfolding as the world continues to wait for God's full reign in all of the earth (v. 4).[11]

As a whole, this chastic structure seeks to send the same message as God's guidance of Cyrus in Isa. 45:1-5. The blessing is a reality on behalf of God's people, even if the foreign ones do not "know" that it is God who guides the world. Yet the very basis of life, the *harvest,* is the sign of God's graciousness and blessing of all of humanity. The culmination will be the justice and salvation of the whole world. In the end, then, the psalm's content matches its possible dual character as both a prayer of thanksgiving and a prayer-wish. For God is already providing and blessing the earth and the creation, but the full form of this blessing is yet to be seen. Its meaning is both/and here, and so there is no reason to decide between the two forms. It is the English language that limits our ability to see this piece in its full meaning and complexity. John Lennon scandalized good folks when he wrote, "imagine there's no countries . . . and no religion too."[12] Lennon is speaking out against the world where national interest and religious interest favor one group over the rest of the world. He was longing for a world where these things do not cause division and war. The world he wishes for is the very same world reflected in this

9. See, e.g., Pss. 9:8; 96:13; 98:9; 99:4; Isa. 11:4.

10. See, e.g., Isa. 45:1-5.

11. Unlike the argument by Weiser and others, who contend that it is this verse that provides the context for the psalm and that it is a harvest-thanksgiving festival (*The Psalms,* p. 472). This completion of the chiasm simply affirms that the blessing requested is already in evidence. Instead of a special circumstance, this is the status quo of God's blessing of the earth as God's on-going creation ("be fruitful and multiply").

12. John Lennon, Blackwood Music, Inc., 1971.

prayer-wish — a world where justice is administered with equity and all are blessed. Christianity seems to often be about who is right and who is wrong. This psalm is a wish for all of those issues to be put aside so that all can be blessed by God. It challenges us to live a different life and to focus on a world without the artificial things that divide us from each other.

BETH TANNER

Psalm 68: From Beginning to End, the Same

No matter how one divides Psalm 68 or how one chooses to understand its unity or lack thereof, one thing is certain: its theme is one of unflinching praise for the powerful Warrior God of Israel. Its images are some of the most ancient in the Bible,[1] and many of its words and phrases are so difficult that any translation is a tentative one where no one reading is superior to the multiple others that have been proposed.[2] Further, scholars find it impossible to assign the psalm to a genre or to agree if the images presented are depictions of actual historical happenings or are mythic battles between the gods.

In structure, the psalm is cyclic, beginning and ending with the same proclamations (praise of *the Rider,* vv. 4 and 33), and both of these proclamations are centered in sections that declare God's *power* and *might* over all the world. Yet in the center, there is movement. God moves from the sanctuaries of old (*Sinai,* v. 8, and *Bashan,* v. 15) via a great *procession* (vv. 24-27) to the *temple* in *Jerusalem* (v. 29). The psalm, then, in effect declares that God may have made the historic move from the older sanctuaries to Jerusalem, but this is still the same God and the works of old can be relied upon for securing Israel's future.[3] Using this rubric of a poetic portrayal of God's movement with Israel, the psalm has three major sections. The large center section is further divided into three smaller sections:[4]

1. Its poetry shares much in common with other ancient pieces such as Exodus 15, Judges 5, and Deuteronomy 33.

2. Tate notes that fifteen words or phrases appear only here and thirty-five other words are uncommon (*Psalms 51–100,* p. 172). Hossfeld adds, "the number of odd expressions and seldom seen syntactical constructions is far above the quantity to be expected in poetic texts" (*Psalms 2,* p. 160).

3. This movement, which may very well represent the process of the conquest and the period until the taking of Jerusalem by David, is one of the reasons for giving this psalm an early date (Weiser, *The Psalms,* p. 483). Others give some sections an early date, but note that some sections carry the mark of a later period (Kraus, *Psalms 60–150,* p. 51; Gerstenberger, *Psalms: Part 2,* p. 44).

4. This method of dividing this psalm is not reflected in the greater scholarly community. Many scholars use a complicated twelve-section division (Kraus, *Psalms 60–150,* p. 48; John Gray, "A Cantata of the Autumn Festival: Psalm LXVIII," *JSS* 22 (1977) 21-24; Gerstenberger, *Psalms: Part 2,* pp. 35-44), although each varies as to exact divisions. J. P. Fokkelmann also uses three divisions that are different than above and based on very different criteria ("The Structure of Psalm lxviii," in *In Quest of the Past,* ed. A. S. van der Woude [OTS 26; Leiden: Brill, 1990], 72-83). Recently, Terrien has offered an eleven-part chiastic structure that is intriguing (*The Psalms,* p. 490). The approach here is to assume that it is the book of Psalms that is the primary context (as opposed to the cult) and that poetic subject, movement, and juxtaposition are the main criteria for the division of sections.

God without geography (vv. 1-6)
God travels with the people who become Israel (vv. 7-27)
    God in the wilderness (vv. 7-10)
    God in conquest and procession to the mountain (vv. 11-23)
    God in festal procession to Jerusalem (vv. 24-27)
God of Israel and the world (vv. 28-35)

To the leader. A Davidic psalm. A song.

1 *God rises up, his enemies scatter,*
and the ones hating him flee from before him.
2 *As smoke is blown away, they are blown away;*[5]
as wax is melted from before the fire,
the wicked perish before God.
3 *The righteous rejoice; they exult before God,*
and they shout with joy.
4 *Sing to God! Make music to his name!*
Prepare the way for the Rider in the Clouds.[6]
Yah is his name!
Exult before him!
5 *Father of Orphans and Defender of the Widows;*
God is in his holy abode.
6 *God who gives the forsaken ones*[7] *a home,*
who brings out prisoners with singing;[8]
but the rebellious dwell in a parched land.

7 *God in your going forth before your people,*
in your marching through the wilderness, Selah[9]

5. *BHS* reads *ḥindōp̱* without a direct object referent. The verb can be read as either a 2ms *qal* imperfect plus an assumed direct object (NIV) or a 3fs *niphal* imperfect (NRSV). Either form is readable. The line here follows the MT without the addition of a direct object.

6. The meaning of *lārōḵēḇ bāʿᵃrāḇôṯ* ("Rider of the West [or 'Deserts']") appears to derive from the Ugaritic phrase *rkbʿ rpt* ("Rider in the Clouds") as an epithet for Baal (Aqht 1:1:43-44; Baal 2:3:10, 17). The more ancient "Rider in the Clouds" is used.

7. In the singular form, this word normally means an only child (Gen. 22:2, 12, 16) but can also mean an isolated one (Pss. 25:16; 35:17). It appears in the plural form only here.

8. *Kôšārôṯ* appears only here. BDB suggests the word is from a root meaning "succeed" or "prosper" (NRSV; Kraus, *Psalms 60–150*, p. 44). Gordon identified a Ugaritic cognate, *kṯrt*, indicating both "a birthgoddess " or "female jubilantes" (*Ugaritic Textbook* [AnOr 38, Rome: Pontificium Institutum Biblicum, 1965], 19:1335). The above translation reflects this meaning of the word (also NIV). But either translation is tentative.

9. Normally the term *Selah* indicates the close of a major section (see Introduction),

8 *the earth shakes and the heavens overflow with rain*[10] *before God,*
the One of Sinai, (from) before the God of Israel.
9 *A generous rain you caused to fall, O God;*
when your inheritance languishes, you restore it.[11]
10 *Your people*[12] *dwell in it;*
in your goodness, you provide for the poor, O God.

11 *My Lord gives a command*
and the women bearing tidings are many;[13]
12 *"Kings of the armies flee, they flee;*
at the entrance of the house,[14] *the booty is divided.*
13 *Even though you dwell between sheepfolds,*[15]
there are wings of the dove covered with silver,
its pinions in green-gold.

---

but here it appears to be misplaced (see NJPS; Tate, *Psalms 51–100,* p. 176; Gray, "A Cantata of the Autumn Festival," p. 21).

10. The verb *nāṭap̱* means "to drip" (Cant. 4:11; 5:5, 13; Prov. 5:3, etc.) and does not fit the context. Gray argues the verb is from the root *ṭwp,* "to overflow" ("Cantata," p. 11). This suggestion seems to make the most sense in this context.

11. The verb *kûn* usually means "to set or establish"; only here does it have the sense of "to revive" (BDB, p. 465; *HALOT,* p. 465). The LXX follows the same sense of "revive."

12. *Ḥayyâh* usually means a "wild animal," and LXX uses this reading, rendering it as "your creatures." William F. Albright ("A Catalogue of Early Hebrew Lyric Poems [Psalm LXVIII]," *HUCA* 23 [1950-51] 21) and Gray ("Cantata," p. 22) note Egyptian, Arabic, and Ugaritic cognates meaning "tribe" or "family" extended to the more common "people."

13. Vv. 11 and 12 are notoriously difficult to translate, as the great variation among translations demonstrates. Gray changes the feminine plural participle to masculine, reading "which shatters a mighty army" (Gray, "A Cantata of the Autumn Festival," p. 22), making the entire section about God's rout of the enemy. Others struggle with the feminine subject and the masculine referent ("many") and change it to "the company of those who bore the tidings" (NRSV). The translation above reflects the tradition in the NJPS which reads these verses as the words of the women singers that God has sent forth (also Hossfeld, *Psalms 2,* p. 158). This tradition is certainly reflected in other contexts and seems to make the most sense here (Exod. 15:20-21; Judg. 5:29-30).

14. *Ûnᵉwaṯ bayiṯ* is a problematic phrase and appears only here. The root of the first word is uncertain. If it is from the root *nwh,* it means a pasture or meadow (2 Sam. 7:8). Kraus understands it this way to mean a front yard or courtyard (*Psalms 60–150,* p. 46). Another possibility is to read it from the root *n'h* ("beauty"), referring to the women (Tate, *Psalms 51–100,* p. 165). Given the context, it makes sense that it denotes a place, but even this is uncertain.

15. The meaning of this word is dubious. The best translation relies on a similar phrase in Judg. 5:16 meaning "sheepfolds." Tate suggests that the meaning should be based on the idea that those that did not participate in the battle still profited from booty (*Psalms 51–100,* p. 179), although he substitutes "saddlebags" for "sheepfolds." It is possible that this entire verse should be left untranslated because of multiple problems.

14 *When the Almighty scattered kings there,*
it snowed on Zalmon;[16]
15 *The mountain of God is*[17] *the mountain of Bashan.*
The mountain of peaks is the mountain of Bashan.
16 *Why, mountains of peaks, do you look with envy*[18] *on*
the mountain God desired for his dwelling;
where the LORD will dwell forever?
17 *God's chariots are myriads upon myriads,*
thousands upon thousands.[19]
The Lord came[20] *from Sinai with the holy ones.*[21]
18 *You ascended to the heights;*
you took captives;
you received gifts from humanity,
even the stubborn ones dwelling there,[22] *LORD God.*
19 *Blessed be the Lord,*

16. This is another problematic verse. The first line has an infinitive construct followed by "kings in her," but the "her" has no referent. The verse is read either indicating a specific time and location (NRSV; Kraus, *Psalms 60–150,* p. 44; Tate, *Psalms 51–100,* p. 165) or as a comparative; the scattering is somehow like the snow (NIV, NJPS). A third possibility is that the two lines demonstrate God's power as the warrior and the creator. None of these choices is superior to the other, and any translation is tentative.

17. 11QPs^d appears to contain an extra word, *zah* ("here"). Only the first letter is visible, and the text is very fragmentary. This would help clarify the situation, for the DSS reads this as declaring a specific place for God on this mountain (Florentino García Martínez, Eibert Tigchelaar, and A. S. van der Woude, *Qumran Cave 11: II, 11Q2-18, 11Q20-31* [DJD 23; Oxford: Clarendon, 1998], p. 72).

18. The root *rṣd* appears only here, but has Akkadian and Arabic cognates that provide a fairly certain meaning.

19. *Šin'ān* appears only here and may be related to the root *šnh* ("a repetition"), as reflected here. Albright has argued the word is related to the Ugaritic *ṯnn* (a class of warrior; "Catalogue," p. 25; also see Patrick D. Miller, *The Divine Warrior in Early Israel* [HSM 5; Cambridge, MA: Harvard University Press, 1973], p. 109). This may indeed be the reading here, but it does not add much to the general idea that God is leading forth the hosts to do battle.

20. Reading *bā'* ("he came") instead of *bām* ("among them"), as do NIV and NRSV. This reading continues the idea of God moving to the sanctuary as a sign of victory (cf. *CTA* 1.4.7.29-35).

21. Reading with Miller. He notes the parallel between this phrase and Deut. 33:2. Miller reads *qōḏeš* as a collective plural, meaning that this final colon is still a reflection of the march of God and God's army (*Divine Warrior,* p. 109).

22. MT reads "stubborn ones living LORD God." Kraus omits the troublesome section (*Psalms 60–150,* p. 44). Others offer some type of translation as above, but all indicate their translation is tentative. What the interpreter must focus on is the general idea of the phrase — that of a celebration of God's victory and the bringing of gifts — even if the specific phrase is problematic.

Day-to-day he bears burdens for us;
God is our salvation. Selah[23]
20 *God is for us, a God of salvation!*[24]
Through the Lord *God is escape from death.*[25]
21 *When God shatters the heads of his enemies,*
the hairy skull of the one who walks in his guilt.
22 *The Lord speaks from Bashan,*
'I will bring back, I will bring from the depths of the sea,'[26]
23 *so that you may splash*[27] *your feet in blood,*
and the tongue of your dogs may have their portion from the enemies."

24 *They have seen your processions, O God,*
the processions of my God, my King with the holy ones.
25 *Singers are in front, minstrels after,*
in the middle young women playing timbrels.
26 *In the congregation,*[28] *they bless God;*
the Lord *is the fountain of Israel.*[29]
27 *There Benjamin, the least one, is leading;*
Princes of Judah are gathered,[30]
Princes of Zebulun, Princes of Naphtali.

23. As above, this ending marker seems misplaced.

24. The plural appears only here and probably has the same meaning as the singular.

25. Another difficult sentence syntactically. Lit., "to the death outsides." *HALOT* (p. 1706) notes this final word can mean the exits from a walled city (Ezek. 48:30), hence the above translation.

26. MT lacks a direct object for both of the *hiphil* verbs, leading to a variety of emendations to this line. Most English translations simply add the direct object "them," as in NRSV, but it is unclear if the "them" relates to God's people or the enemies. However, in the context of the next verse, it would appear that God is returning the enemies so that the people can participate in the victory. This type of victory banquet is reflected in *KTU* 1.3.II.20-23, 27-29, where Anat and her soldiers fill themselves with the blood and gore of the bodies of the enemies.

27. The verb in MT means "to shatter" or "break into pieces." Most emend the text to *ṭirḥaṣ* ("to bathe"; *HALOT,* p. 1220) or read an Arabic cognate that means "to churn or agitate" (Dahood, *Psalms II,* p. 146).

28. The word *maqḥēl* appears only here, but comes from *qhl* ("to assemble"), so the sense seems to be clear. The plural ending may indicate either the various groups in the procession or possibly the congregations of the tribes (v. 27).

29. The syntax of this verbless clause is debated. Some emend *fountain* to *mimmiqerāʾê* ("convocation"; NIV; Kraus, *Psalms 60–150*). Others (NRSV) read it as a description of God.

30. Meaning of *rigᵉmâ* is dubious. If from the root *rgm,* it means "to kill by stoning," extended to "a heap of stones" (i.e., gathered together). If from Akk. *rigmu,* it means a noisy throng. Either way it indicates some form of people gathered for a purpose.

28 *Command, O God, your strength!*
Show your strength, O God,[31]
which you displayed to us,
29 *from your temple above Jerusalem.*
To you, kings bring gifts.
30 *Rebuke the living one of the reed,*
herds of the mighty with calf-peoples,
trampling pieces of silver;[32]
scatter peoples who inwardly delight.[33]
31 *Let them bring goods*[34] *from Egypt;*
let Ethiopia hurry to stretch out[35] *his hands to God.*

32 *Kingdoms of the earth, sing to God,*
make music (to) my Lord, Selah
33 *to the Rider in the Uppermost of the Ancient Heavens.*
Lo, he gives with his voice, mighty voice.
34 *Yield strength*[36] *to God,*
over Israel is his majesty;
and his power in the clouds.
35 *Fearsome is God from his holy places;*
El of Israel, he gives power and strength to the people.
Blessed be God!

31. MT reads "Your God commanded your strength." Most suggest repointing the 3ms perfect verb to an imperative with an additional change of *ʾᵉlōhêḵā* to *ʾᵉlōhîm* (Dahood, *Psalms II,* p. 32; Gray, "Cantata," p. 24; Kraus, *Psalms 60–150,* p. 45) as above.

32. There are as many translations of this line as there are translators. The only word of certain origin is the last one, *silver.* Many try to change the line to reflect the idea of bringing tribute to relate it to the surrounding images, e.g., "they submit themselves with pieces of silver" (Tate, *Psalms 51–100,* p. 161). The line is presented here without emendation since no reading is certain. It should probably be left untranslated.

33. There is no direct object for the verb. Most commentators add "in war" (Kraus, *Psalms 60–150,* p. 45; Tate, *Psalms 51–100,* p. 161; Gray, "Cantata," p. 25).

34. The word *ḥašmannîm* appears only here. There are a variety of interpretations: "envoys" (NIV), "bronze" (NRSV), "cloth" (Albright, "Catalogue," p. 61). In the context, Hossfeld's choice of the generic "goods" seems to capture the general meaning (*Psalms 2,* p. 160).

35. The verb usually has the meaning of "to run," but in the *hiphil* can imply "to hasten toward" (*HALOT,* p. 1208), extended here to *stretch.*

36. The verb is a 2mpl imperative usually translated as the command "Give." Yet the idea of giving strength to God is odd. Most translations use "Ascribe," but that does not reflect the meaning of the verb here. Tate extends "Give" to "Yield" and in the context seems to make the most sense (*Psalms 51–100,* p. 170).

1-6 This section begins with a declarative stanza (vv. 1-3)[37] and is followed by a stanza that calls for praise to God (vv. 4-6). Verse 1 is reminiscent of Num. 10:35, a declaration of Moses as the ark moves forth in the wilderness. This opening, then, sets the stanza within Israel's ancient past. The association with the ark in the context of the enemies of God clearly recalls the early battles in Israel's history, and just as with those battles, the outcome of the wicked against God is never a question. All this God has to do is *rise up* and the *enemies* are *blown, melt,* and *perish* (v. 2).

Next (vv. 4-6), the righteous are called to praise this great God. The epithets used have clear ties to the Divine Warrior/King motif. The *Rider in the Clouds* is an epithet for Baal, but is used here of Israel's God. Indeed, the title may have a double meaning here since the phrase in Hebrew can also mean "Rider in the Wilderness," further stressing this first period of Israel's travels with God. In addition, God is praised because of God's protection for the weakest of society. Indeed, God has been given the titles of *Father of Orphans and Defender of the Widows.* This theme of the Divine Warrior is always closely associated with God's justice and support for the least of society.[38]

This first section sets the stage for what is to come. It reflects the beginning of Israel's story where God acted as the divine warrior against God's enemies (the Pharaoh and his armies) for the sake of the weakest of the society.[39] It uses the epithet of another ancient god to declare which God is indeed the chief God of the pantheon (see comments on Psalm 82). It declares God's power over all other enemies and gods known. It demonstrates that God alone is the one who defeats the enemies and provides the *forsaken ones* with *a home.* This was and remains one of the oldest and most enduring declarations of this God. This is who God shows God's self to be in the exodus, wilderness, and conquest narratives.

7-10 Declaration gives way to procession. The words that are proclaimed as the ark begins its trip are brought to fruition in v. 7 as God marches *through the wilderness.* Just as nature responds to the command of God during the plagues and in the original wilderness journey, here the creation responds to God's movement. The part of the creation that is highlighted is *rain,* as both a fearsome force (v. 8) and a life-giving force (v. 9). This theme also declares that it is the God of Sinai who is the controller of the storm and the fructify-

37. NRSV and NIV translate this opening section as "May God rise up." However, following Kraus (*Psalms 61–150,* p. 43) and others, the prayer is not a future wish but is instead reflective of a long history with God.

38. See, e.g., Amos 1:3–2:6; Hos. 5:8-15; or Ps. 96.

39. This connection to the exodus appears in several verses. First, the use of *Yah is his name!* (v. 4) is reminiscent of the refrain in Exod. 15. Also in v. 6, God *brings out the prisoners. Bring out* is from the root *yṣ'.* This verb is often used in the *hiphil* form in the confessions of Israel concerning the exodus event (e.g., Deut. 5:6, 15; 6:12).

ing rain, attributes that in Canaanite mythology are attributed to Baal. These verses also reflect the theophany for which the people were commanded to *prepare* in v. 4. In terms very much like Judg. 5:4-5, God's movement is described as one that *shakes the heavens* and that causes the clouds to pour.

11-23 This section has a great many translation difficulties that result in the variety of English translations. At v. 11, the scene shifts. The battle is already done. The scene opens with God commanding *the women* to sing of God's victory over the enemies.[40]

The victory song begins at v. 12, but its ending is disputed.[41] If it is indeed a song of victory lifted by the women, instead of an announcement of the end of the battle, the scope of the song should continue through v. 23. Gerstenberger and others may indeed be correct that this section represents several victory song fragments strung together.[42] But even if that is the case, taken as a whole this song presents the major themes of ancient Near Eastern victory songs.

12-16 There are a multitude of translation problems in this small section, but it appears to be a report of *kings fleeing* before God and then the division of the *booty* that was left when the battle is done. The booty was so great that even those that did not participate in the battle were able to divide the spoil at home and away from the battle scene (v. 12).

Victory songs often contain not only a declaration of victory, but a coming of the divine warrior to his new *mountain* temple.[43] This is the content of vv. 14-16. *Shaddai,* another ancient name for God, appears in v. 14 *(the Almighty),* and the scattering of the kings is associated with snow, another form of God's control over nature and water. Verse 15 continues to proclaim that once the kings are scattered, God settles into a home on *the mountain.* Scholars have offered a whole host of geographical places for the names *Zalmon* and *Bashan,* but the point of the passage seems to be God's taking of the mountain, not the exact location of the mountain conquered. Verse 16 declares that the warrior king has settled, and thus the battle is ended: *the* L*ORD will dwell forever.*

17-20 This section is another stanza that tells of the march of God. Some of the terms are different, but it covers the same themes: v. 17 tells of

40. As noted for the translation, this section's interpretation is heavily debated. But in light of historical evidence that it was women who were primarily responsible for singing songs of victory, at least in the earlier periods of Israel's history, the translation presented seems plausible. (See Eunice Blanchard Poethig, "The Victory Song Tradition of the Women of Israel" [Diss., Union Theological Seminary, 1985].)

41. Some commentators do not see this as a quotation of a song at all (Kraus, *Psalms 60–150,* p. 52; McCann, "The Book of Psalms," p. 945).

42. *Psalms: Part 2,* p. 39.

43. As noted by Cross, *Canaanite Myth,* p. 156.

God's great army leaving *Sinai;* in v. 18 God *ascends* an unnamed mount, and *gifts* or "booty" are brought. Cross has noted the similarity of this section to Judg. 5:4-5 and Deut. 33:26-29.[44] The section ends with accolades lifted to God (vv. 19-20) for the victory and subsequent *salvation.* The great God is *blessed,* not for the destruction of the enemies, but for providing security for the people.[45]

21-23 Depending on the translator, this section can have very divergent meanings. As presented here, it represents yet another statement about the victory of the warrior God: that of the victory banquet. *CTA* 3.2 records such a banquet. The images are gruesome because the centerpiece of the banquet is bathing in the blood of the enemies.[46] This is certainly the most gruesome image in the psalm, but it clearly reflects the traditions of the greater ancient Near East. The point of the text is to demonstrate God's power over all of the enemies with the image of being able to "eat" or literally consume those that oppose the warrior/king.

24-27 This section clearly describes a *procession* of the *King.* The warrior has taken the throne, and now a procession moves from the mountains of legend to God's home in Jerusalem. This second procession tells Israel's story from God's perspective. The historical reality of the conquest might be one of battles and losses and a two-hundred-year struggle for the land, but here it is portrayed as God's great procession from one mountain to another. The singers and music makers are in the procession along with the tribes. Scholars have devoted a great deal of speculation to the tribes listed here. They probably have no specific historical reference but are meant to portray part of the great procession. *Benjamin* is called *the least one,* reminding all that the King God's responsibility remains with the least of the society, as in v. 5. Just as in the procession of the warrior, the people *bless God* (v. 26). The Lord of all now has a particular place and a particular people. Mowinckel and Kraus argue that this section reflects the yearly cultic procession of the enthronement festival. This may be the case, but there is no definitive proof of such a procession.[47]

28-31 This psalm of description turns now to petition. If one of the

44. *Canaanite Myth and Hebrew Epic,* p. 157.

45. Likewise, Baal is praised for the giving of security after his taking of the throne, but it is in the language of rain that provides the security of food (Cross, *Canaanite Myth and Hebrew Epic,* p. 151). God's defining narratives are different than Baal's, and here the security is in the form of *salvation* and *escape from death* (exodus).

46. The text reads, in part, "The goddess comes to her palace. Yet she is not yet sated with her fighting. . . . She arranges seats for the warriors; Arranges tables for the soldiers; She plunges her knees indeed in the blood of soldiers; her hips in the gore of the warriors; until she has had her fill of fighting in the house" (*CTA* 3.2).

47. Mowinckel, *The Psalms in Israel's Worship,* 1:155; Kraus, *Psalms 60–150,* p. 55.

poem's purposes is to fuse the ancient acts of God with the acts of God in Jerusalem, then it is here that the fusion is complete. The people (or possibly the priests) implore God to show the same *strength* and power now as in the myths of old. It is *Jerusalem* that is now the base of power, and interestingly, *kings bring gifts* and come here to acknowledge God (vv. 29 and 31). In days of old, the *gifts* were booty taken in the midst of battle. Now God's reign has become a reality, and battle is no longer the rule of the day. Verse 30, as noted above, is a notoriously difficult verse to translate and understand, but whatever translation is used, it is clear that part of God's function as king is to judge those who still rebel against the great God of all.

32-35 These ending verses are then like the beginning, but the *Rider* has elevated from the clouds (or wilderness) to the highest part of *the ancient heavens* (v. 33). God has won the victory over all who oppose God's rule. God rests in God's place, *power* has been yielded to God (v. 34), and God's power and might are obvious to all. God has transformed the titles of the lesser gods; Baal's "Rider in the Clouds" has now become the Lord's *Rider in the Uppermost of the Ancient Heavens,* and El, the chief god of the Canaanite pantheon, is now known as *El of Israel,* an epithet for the Lord. The psalm is declaring that it is the Lord, the God of Israel, who controlled the ancient sanctuaries and has now moved to rule over God's holy place and God's holy people and also the rest of the world.

As noted in the title, the psalm begins and ends with the same proclamation. The great God of the myths is indeed the Lord of Israel. In the center section, the psalm describes poetically how the move from the old sanctuaries to Jerusalem is to be envisioned. If indeed there is a historical event behind the procession in vv. 24-27, it would seem to be David's procession with the ark into Jerusalem instead of the conquest, since the battle is won before this great procession begins, and this would also serve as an opportunity to show that God had indeed moved from the older sanctuaries and now resides in Jerusalem. This was an important understanding during the Davidic/Solomonic monarchy.

The psalm also deals with the reality of the myths of other peoples and their gods. The development in the psalm tells of the violent defeat of these peoples and the taking of their gods and making these sacred names into epithets for Israel's God. This is dangerous theology in the wrong hands. The psalm can seem to authenticate violence and the destruction of another people's culture by the ones with the most powerful God. The victory celebration seems gruesome and paints a horrible picture of God, but the psalms reflect the people's words about their God and tell of their and our own warring nature. Their ancient images are not different from the words of a victor in today's wars. We too can revel in the defeat of persons we consider enemies. But to read the psalm this way is to follow the way of the wicked ones. This mytho-poetic telling of Israel's story of conquest never places the battle in the hands of the humans. Those that become Israel are completely dependent on God and do not take violence into their own human hands. Further, the purpose of God's acts of power is first for the least of the society (v. 5) and second so that all can settle into a kingdom of peace, where kings do not flee from before God (vv. 12, 14) but come to bow before the throne of God (v. 31). God is blessed by the people, not for the destruction of the enemies, but as *a God of salvation* (v. 20). The psalm declares the broken, violent, oppressive nature of humanity, but offers the hope that even if violence must be met with violence, it is not done for revenge, but for the establishment of God's kingdom and God's justice for all the world.

This psalm with its defense of the powerless ones holds a special place in the African-American church tradition. Cheryl Townsend Gilkes explains: "The believing communities of Africans in the United States selected, repeated, and popularized among themselves Psalm 68 as well as other texts that their oppressors neglected or discarded. The Afrocentric biblical tradition extended the 'life' of these texts."[48] The church came to understand v. 31 as including them specifically in the great cloud of witnesses that come to find and praise God. With the mention of *Egypt* and *Ethiopia,* they were part of the tradition that they had been excluded from by slavery and racism. A second line of this psalm in v. 5 was expanded so that "father to the fatherless and mother to the motherless" became a well-known way of describing God in these communities, for it "connects a personal God who cares about the individual's circumstance with a powerful liberating God."[49] In this, it reflects the central meaning of the great warrior God as the one who cares for those who struggle in a system where they have no voice. This use shows all the way to understand the violent images in the psalm, for it was the reality from which African-American faith arose amid slavery and the violence of racism in this country.

Beth Tanner

48. "'Mother to the Motherless, Father to the Fatherless': Power, Gender, and Community in an Afrocentric Biblical Tradition," *Semeia* 47 (1989) 70.

49. Gilkes, "'Mother to the Motherless,'" p. 60.

Psalm 69: The Complexity of Relationships

This is one of the longest prayers for help in the book of Psalms. Its petitions are complex, covering multiple themes. The prayer opens with a proclamation of personal trouble (vv. 2-3), followed quickly by cries about the enemies (v. 4). Next is a declaration of one's own sin (vv. 5-6). The prayer also addresses problems with God's inaction (vv. 3, 13-15) and also the suffering perceived as caused by God (v. 26) Another element is an expression of suffering because of dedication to God, a Suffering Servant motif (vv. 7-12). In and of themselves, none of these motifs are unusual in prayers for help. What is unusual is that all appear in one prayer. This psalm shows just how complicated life can be and that one can suffer because of God's action and/or inaction and that the enemies can threaten because of personal pain, sin, or because of the person's faithfulness — or in this case, all of the above at the same time. The remainder of the psalm is typical for a prayer. It offers petitions for God's action followed by the praise that testifies to the promise of being heard.

The psalm has a large section with a thematic *inclusio* (vv. 1-29) that describes the problems interspersed with pleas to God. The final section moves from pain and plea to vows of praise to God first from the individual (vv. 30-33) and then from the community (vv. 34-36). The prayer can be seen as ten stanzas long:[1]

vv. 1	Plea to God
vv. 2-4	Introductory description of distress
vv. 5-6	Personal confession and second plea
vv. 7-12	Second description of distress
vv. 13-18	Third set of pleas
vv. 19-21	Third description of distress
vv. 22-28	Petitions of actions against the enemies
v. 29	Final plea to God for relief of personal distress
vv. 30-33	Vow of praise of the individual
vv. 34-36	Vow of praise of the community

1. Scholars are divided into two camps on how to divide this poem. The first group uses either structural or thematic divisions with slight verse-to-verse variations (Weiser, *The Psalms,* p. 494; Kraus, *Psalms 60–150,* p. 60; Limburg, *Psalms,* 228). The second group's work is based on an article by Leslie Allen that sees a distinctive repetition of themes in vv. 1-29: "The Value of Rhetorical Criticism in Psalm 69," *JBL* 105 (1986) 577-98. Allen's work is very complex, but he also notes the break at v. 29. The divisions here are based thematically, but take into account Allen's observations.

The text has some difficulties but for the most part is readable. Its form is one of a prayer for help. A large section of this psalm is found in 4QPsa and, as is shown below, has some significant differences from the MT.

To the leader. According to Shoshanim.[2] *Davidic.*

1 *Save me, O God,*
because the water has come to my neck.[3]

2 *I have sunk in deep mire,*[4]
and[5] *there is no foothold.*
I have come into deep waters,
and[6] *the flood washes over me.*
3 *I grow weary in my crying;*
my throat is parched;
my eyes are failing,[7]
waiting for my God.[8]
4 *More in number than the hairs of my head*
are those who hate me without cause;
mighty are those who would destroy me, my lying enemies.
What[9] *I did not steal, now must I restore?*

5 *God, you know my folly;*[10]
my errors from you are not hidden.

2. Often translated as "lilies," but the meaning is uncertain. It is possibly a musical notation.

3. MT does not have the 1cs suffix, but LXX does, and most translations follow LXX. The word *nep̱eš* can mean either "self," "life," or "neck."

4. 4QPs[a] reads "between an abyss," probably confusing *byn* ("between") for *bîwēn* ("in mire"); Ulrich, Cross, et al., *Qumran Cave 4: XI,* p. 20.

5. 4QPs[a] is missing the *wāw;* Ulrich, Cross, et al., *Qumran Cave 4: XI,* p. 20.

6. 4QPs[a] is missing the *wāw;* Ulrich, Cross, et al., *Qumran Cave 4: XI,* p. 20.

7. 4QPs[a] reads "my teeth fail," if indeed *klw* is from the verb *klh* and is not the noun *kly* with a 3ms suffix. Either way, the meaning in 4QPs[a] is uncertain; Ulrich, Cross, et al., *Qumran Cave 4: XI,* p. 20.

8. 4QPs[a] reads "in anguish for the God of Isr[ael]"; Ulrich, Cross, et al., *Qumran Cave 4: XI,* p. 20.

9. *ʾašer* most often introduces a subordinate clause. There are instances, however, when the word is substantive in form; see Gen. 7:23; 31:1; 43:16; Num. 22:6; Ezek. 23:28 (Waltke, O'Connor, *Biblical Hebrew Syntax,* pp. 334-35).

10. 4QPs[a] reads "you, you know not my wreath or crown." This meaning here is uncertain; Ulrich, Cross, et al., *Qumran Cave 4: XI,* p. 20.

6 *Let them not be put to shame through me;*[11]
those who wait for you, my Lord, LORD of Hosts.
Let them not be dishonored through me,[12]
those who seek you, God of Israel.

7 *For your sake, I carry reproach;*
shame has covered my face.
8 *A stranger I am*[13] *to my brothers;*
and[14] *an alien to the sons of my mother,*
9 *because the zeal of your house has consumed me;*
and the reproach of those who reproach you has fallen on me.
10 *Even as I myself wept in fasting,*[15]
my soul has become the cause of reproach to me.[16]
11 *I made my clothing sackcloth;*
I became[17] *for them a byword.*
12 *The ones who sit at the gate talk about me;*
and songs of drunkards are about me.

13 *As for me, my prayer is to you,*[18] *LORD,*
for a time of favor.[19]

11. 4QPs^a lacks "through me"; Ulrich, Cross, et al., *Qumran Cave 4: XI,* p. 20.

12. 4QPs^a lacks "through me"; Ulrich, Cross, et al., *Qumran Cave 4: XI,* p. 20.

13. 4QPs^a reads "who has become a stranger"; Ulrich, Cross, et al., *Qumran Cave 4: XI,* p. 20.

14. 4QPs^a is missing the *wāw;* Ulrich, Cross, et al., *Qumran Cave 4: XI,* p. 20.

15. MT reads "I wept in fasting my self *(napšî).*" LXX reading of "bowed down" instead of "wept" is used in some translations (NRSV "humbled"). 4QPs^a reads "and surely in fasting was my self" as a verbless clause (Ulrich, Cross, et al., *Qumran Cave 4: XI,* p. 20). Others read "fast" as a second verb (NJPS, NIV). All of these suggestions are possible, but the MT is readable, if awkward.

16. In MT, the verb form is 3fs, so the referent is unclear. The only possible referent is the feminine *nepeš.* A 3ms verb appears in some LXX and Syr manuscripts. The 4QPs^a may aid in clarifying the situation. The form of the verb is also 3fs. This follows the MT exactly, making the reading of "She (meaning 'my soul') is a reproach to me" all the more probable (Ulrich, Cross, et al., *Qumran Cave 4: XI,* p. 20).

17. 4QPs^a also has the 2fs form of the verb here, and the manuscript is clear and readable. So it appears that the scroll continues the understanding of her referring to "soul" as in v. 10; Ulrich, Cross, et al., *Qumran Cave 4: XI,* p. 20.

18. 4QPs^a reads "and (for) me what (is) my prayer" as a verbless clause; Ulrich, Cross, et al., *Qumran Cave 4: XI,* p. 20.

19. Following Tate (*Psalms 51–100,* p. 187); MT is difficult. 4QPs^a has "now" instead of *time,* with a meaning of "now (is) acceptable" as a verbless clause (Ulrich, Cross, et al., *Qumran Cave 4: XI,* p. 20). NRSV and NIV suggest that the prayer be heard at an acceptable time, but based on the context, Tate's reading makes more sense.

O God, in the abundance of your hesed,
answer me with your faithful salvation.
14 *Rescue me from the mire,*
that I may not sink.[20]
Let me be delivered[21] *from those hating me,*
and[22] *from deep waters.*
15 *Do not let the flood waters sweep me away,*
or do not let the deep swallow[23] *me,*
or do not let the mouth[24] *of the pit close upon me.*
16 *Answer me,* Lord,[25] *because your* hesed *is good,*[26]
according to your motherly compassion,[27] *turn to me.*
17 *Do not hide your face from your servant*
because of my distress, quickly answer me.
18 *Draw near to*[28] *me, redeem me!*[29]
On account of my enemies, ransom me!

19 *You, you know my reproach and my shame and my humiliation;*
all my foes are before you.
20 *Reproach has broken my heart and I am sick.*[30]
I anticipated sympathy,[31] *but there was none;*

20. 4QPsª adds an additional line: "do not let the one who seizes me take me"; Ulrich, Cross, et al., *Qumran Cave 4: XI,* p. 20.

21. 4QPsª has a 2ms imperative, "deliver me," instead of the MT "let me be delivered"; Ulrich, Cross, et al., *Qumran Cave 4: XI,* p. 20.

22. 4QPsª omits the *wāw;* Ulrich, Cross, et al., *Qumran Cave 4: XI,* p. 20.

23. 4QPsª substitutes *ṭṭbʿny* ("sink me"); Ulrich, Cross, et al., *Qumran Cave 4: XI,* p. 20.

24. 4QPsª adds a 1cs suffix, "my mouth," so the line reads "or the pit close my mouth upon me," which is awkward; Ulrich, Cross, et al., *Qumran Cave 4: XI,* p. 20.

25. 4QPsª is missing the vocative; Ulrich, Cross, et al., *Qumran Cave 4: XI,* p. 20.

26. 4QPsª exchanges the *kî* of MT for the preposition *kᵉ* ("according to the goodness of your *hesed*)"; Ulrich, Cross, et al., *Qumran Cave 4: XI,* p. 20.

27. The Hebrew word *raḥᵃmêm* is often translated as "compassion" or "mercy," but this does not quite capture the Hebrew meaning of the word. From the word "womb," it indicates a particular type of mercy or compassion: that of a mother for a child.

28. 4QPsª has *ʿl* instead of the MT's *ʾel;* Ulrich, Cross, et al., *Qumran Cave 4: XI,* p. 20.

29. Both pronouns refer to *nep̱eš,* which indicates more than "soul," rather the whole self.

30. This verb appears only here and is in the *qal* cohortative form. BDB, 633, states the meaning as "to be sick." LXX indicates the Hebrew should be a *qal* fem. participle of *ʾnš,* hence the NRSV's "despair," but the fem. meaning is unclear so it is best to stick with the BDB reading.

31. This infinitive is from the root *nwd* ("to wander or move aimlessly"). It can be used as a verb to express grief in lamentation (Jer. 16:5) or as here to express sympathy. *Sympathy* seems a better choice than the more traditional "pity."

and comforters, but I found none.
21 *They put poison in my food,*
and for my thirst they caused me to drink vinegar.

22 *May their table before them become a snare,*
their sacrificial feasts[32] *a trap.*
23 *Let their eyes be darkened so they cannot see,*
and their loins constantly tremble.
24 *Pour out upon them your indignation;*
and let your fierce anger overtake them.
25 *Let their settlement be a desolation;*
in their tents let there be no dwellers,
26 *because the one you have struck,*[33] *they persecute;*
the pain of your wounded, they recount.
27 *Add iniquity upon their iniquity;*
do not let them come into your righteousness.[34]
28 *Let them be blotted out of the book of life;*
with the righteous, let them not be enrolled.

29 *I am afflicted and in pain;*
may your salvation, O God, protect me.

30 *I will praise the name of God with a song;*
I will magnify him with thanksgiving.
31 *Let this please the* LORD
more than an ox, a bull, horns, and hoofs.[35]
32 *Let the oppressed see and rejoice;*[36]

32. The phrase *lišlômîm* is uncertain. Some scholars stay with some form of *shalom,* making the second line "a snare for their allies" (Tate, *Psalms 51–100,* p. 188; NRSV). Others follow the pointing in the Targum and read as *w^ešalmêhem* ("sacrificial feasts"; Kraus, *Psalms 60–150,* p. 58); this is a good solution (see Amos 5).

33. MT is awkward, reading "because you whom you persecute they reproach." The LXX reads "the one you smite they reproach."

34. The translation is a literal one from MT. The meaning appears to be as reflected by Limburg, "may they have no acquittal from you" (*Psalms,* p. 229).

35. This translation follows the succession of nouns in MT. Three of the four have an attached *min* preposition, and the other noun may reflect a textual error. However, this seems to be a succession of nouns as in vv. 19 and 22, although most read the last two as referring only to the bull.

36. The verb *rāʾû* is in a *qal* perfect form that is problematic. Several Greek manuscripts suggest the form should be imperfect (NRSV, NJPS, NIV reflect this form) as in this translation. Others have suggested that it should be read as an imperative "Behold!" (Kraus, *Psalms 60–150,* p. 58; Tate, *Psalms 51–100,* p. 188).

those seeking God, let their heart be revived[37]
33 *because the* LORD *hears the needy;*
he does not despise his captives.

34 *Let the heavens and the earth praise him,*
the seas and all that move in them,
35 *because God will save Zion*
and will rebuild the cities of Judah;
and they will dwell there and possess it.
36 *The children of his servants shall inherit it;*
and those who love his name,
they will dwell in it.

1 While most scholars see v. 1 as part of the complaint over personal distress, there is enough similarity between vv. 1 and 29 to argue for a thematic *inclusio.* Both verses contain a cognate of the word "salvation."[38] Both verses also speak of the dire situation. Verse 1 pleads for God to save, for "the water has come to my neck." The trouble is characterized by the metaphor of deep water, but what is at stake is not just a wet neck — it is the very life of the one praying. Likewise, v. 29 summarizes the distress presented in the whole of vv. 1-29: "I am afflicted and in pain."

2-4 The plea to God gives way to a more explicit description of the problem. The image of being trapped is intensified in v. 2. The waters are deep and swift, and there is no way to pull one's self out.[39] While this may be a metaphor for death, the actual situation, like most of the psalms, is not specified, giving the interpreter the opportunity to understand the metaphor in relation to one's own life. But it is not just entrapment. There is also great sorrow (v. 3). One would think that this distress would be enough, but the enemies have gathered and demand payment even in the face of confessed innocence (v. 4). The feeling here is one of extreme distress and sorrow compounded by the taunts of the hateful enemies. Trapped, barely keeping one's head above the water, while others threaten and taunt, tell of one at the very edge of life and sanity.

5-6 The abrupt change of this section is disorienting. Now the concern is one of personal acts against God. Why the switch? One possible reason is

37. MT has a *wāw,* separating *those seeking God* from the verb. Most readings omit the "and."

38. Used as an imperative in v. 1 and as a noun in v. 29. Most scholars make this connection, even if they do not separate these two verses as a type of *inclusio* (see, e.g., Allen, "The Value of Rhetorical Criticism," p. 579, and others).

39. As in Pss. 40:2; 88:6; 124:4; Lam. 3:53; Jonah 2:6.

the confession is an additional way to assure God will hear and come to help. "God, others will see me and be shamed also." It could be an additional motivation. Another reason is to contrast the suffering of the one who is willing to confess with the enemies who lie. It also declares complete dependence on God, not only to save the one suffering, but to save the others in the community who are observing all of this turmoil (v. 6). Finally, this one, even in great distress, could be thinking beyond self. The poem does not give an indication, so all of these meanings are possible.

7-12 The prayer moves back to the current situation. Verses 2-4 described suffering in physical terms, but here the pain is emotional. The images are ones of shame, reproach, and alienation. In addition, this shame is borne because of faithfulness to God: *For your sake, I carry reproach* and *because the zeal of your house has consumed me.* A host of commentators have speculated just what *the zeal of your house has consumed me* may be referring to in this context.[40] The reference may indeed be to the temple and its care or rebuilding, but as Tate rightly noted, " 'the house of God' does not mean just a building but extended to the whole household of God."[41]

As the section continues, the prayer further explains the humiliation. Scholars have noted the striking resemblance here to others who have suffered, namely Job, Jeremiah, the unnamed servant of Isa. 52:13–53:12, and the one in Lamentations 3.[42] Each verse further describes the alienation: home (v. 8), temple (v. 9), religious ritual (vv. 10-11), and the city gate (v. 12). It has gotten so bad that she is the subject of the songs made up by drunken revelers (v. 12)! The enemies are in all the spheres of life. There is nowhere to turn for comfort. This section paints a painful picture of the broken community, for it tells that good can appear evil (v. 9); suffering can imply God's punishment (v. 11); the one can be more faithful than the whole (v. 12); and one can be faithful and suffer for that faith (vv. 7-9). This section demonstrates how hard it can be when there is no one to aid and shame is almost too much to bear. The aloneness is palatable. Everyone — family, friends, and the community — all have either deserted this one or actively make fun of her. This one's commitment to God has cost everything.

13-18 The prayer returns to pleas for God's aid. The pleas are again urgent: *answer me, rescue me, do not let the flood waters sweep me away, turn to me, do not hide your face, ransom me.* Verse 13 opens with a plea for God to hear and *answer* this one's prayer, speaking of both God's *hesed* and *faithful*

40. Kraus (*Psalms 60–150,* p. 62) and Limburg (*Psalms,* p. 231) suggest it may be one trying to rebuild the temple after its destruction in 586 D.C.E., while Tate suggests it may be a king who built and/or tended the temple (*Psalms 51–100,* p. 196).

41. Tate, *Psalms 51–100,* p. 196.

42. Mays makes the connection between this psalm and Lamentations; *Psalms,* p. 232.

salvation. Next, the lines turn from hearing to active rescue. Verses 14-15, like v. 2, use the imagery of being trapped, not only in water but in deep rapids, where each second feels like forever as one struggles to survive. Like v. 13, verses 16-18 continue the pleas, but instead of focusing on distress, they focus on the very attributes of God that both individuals and the community depend on for salvation.[43] Verse 16 adds God's *motherly compassion.* The effect here is to move again and again from the feelings of great human distress at the point of death to the comforting peace of God's care. The section itself offers for the hearer or reader the very feeling of being tossed on the waves, finding a small patch of peaceful water, and then being tossed once again. Here all who hear this psalm can literally feel the turmoil of the soul.

19-21 Plea gives way again to descriptions of suffering. The descriptions here are more intimate than in vv. 7-12. The shame now is in the heart, and there is nowhere to turn (v. 20). The hearers can feel the pain that is so real it causes sickness. As for the enemies, they have turned from talk to evil action so that even food and drink are suspect. The word used for *food* here is no ordinary one, but one that indicates the food (and drink) brought to the sick bed (as in 2 Sam. 13:5, 7, 10), presumably because the person is too ill or too upset to prepare food for himself.[44] Before was the imagery of the person caught in the raging waters, here the image is calmer and even more threatening. There is no one to comfort, there is no sympathy anywhere and even the food brought as a seemingly good act of compassion is bitter and poison.

22-28 In this final plea section, the words turn to wishes against the enemies. The one in pain now wishes the same pain on those who caused the suffering, with some striking parallels: the suffering one's food and drink are threatened (v. 21) and the request is for the enemies' table to be a trap (v. 22); the feelings of pain are physical (vv. 2-3), and the wish is that *their loins constantly tremble* (v. 23); shame and humiliation that are heaped on the victim (vv. 9-12) should be repaid with the same (vv. 24-26). The desire for the enemies to be paid back is a typical element in prayers for help and is also typical of one suffering at the hands of others. We have all wished that our hurt and pain and shame be given back fullfold to the ones causing such sorrow.

There is, however, an unusual element in v. 26. The enemies are taunting and abusing the one that God *(you)* has *struck.* God, it appears, has caused this one's pain and suffering. This may be the hardest concept for a modern audience and begs the question, why would God do such a thing, or is the purpose of God's wounding of the one praying a sign of sin? The psalm gives

43. The attributes listed here for God are ones that Israel has depended on again and again. They are all listed in Exod. 34:6-7, a central confession about who God is to the people.

44. Kraus argues that this word indicates a "bread of comfort" for one in great sorrow, using the verb usage in 2 Sam. 3:35 and Lam. 4:10 (*Psalms 60–150,* p. 63).

no indication that this is the case. Indeed, this belief may be one of the reasons the enemies have acted the way they have, as illustrated by the friends of Job. The acts of God are not lamented; they are simply stated. The complaint is not against God here but against the enemies who further persecute and tell of the victim's pain.

So how is a modern interpreter to understand this verse? In the ancient world, God was seen as the source of everything. If a person suffered, or was ill or injured, God was the ultimate cause, just as God also brought the good things in life; but do not mistake these happenings in life as being either reward or punishment via some moral map. It is a difficult theological understanding and one that even today remains a mystery. The mystery is presented here, not to be answered, but accepted — a gap that gives pause and causes the hearers to search their relationship with God and others for understanding of this great mystery.

29 As a reminder of v. 1, this finale of the section takes the interpreter back to the beginning of the psalm. The petitions against the enemies give way to one last plea for God's salvation and protection.

30-33 As is typical of most prayers for help, the psalm changes from one of petition to vows or promises of thanksgiving. The weeping and sackcloth of vv. 10-11 are replaced with *song* and acts of *thanksgiving* (vv. 30-31). The community also reappears (vv. 32-33). Those that were disillusioned in v. 6 now see a very different reality. The day of mourning has been replaced by rejoicing. But as with most prayers for help, there is no clear indication how this happened. The gap must be bridged by hearers who must look to their own lives for answers — possibly filling the gap by remembering the acts of God in their own lives.

34-36 The final three verses place the prayers of the psalm in the cosmic realm. Not only is the individual praising God as an example to his community, but now *the heavens and the earth* and *the seas* join into the act of praise. Yet notice that the reason for the great praise is not the salvation or rescue or redemption of this individual, but the saving of *Zion* and the rebuilding of *Judah*. Just as Job is given an answer by God of cosmic proportions (Job 40:6–41:34), this psalm ends with God's care for all of God's kingdom. The psalm's ending transcends the suffering of the human and even the oppression of the community and moves to a description where all live in harmony in the kingdom of God.

With the complex web that the one suffering is experiencing, it is no surprise that parts of this prayer were used by the gospel writers to describe Jesus' ministry and suffering (Mark 15:36; Matt. 27:34, 48; Luke 23:36; John 19:29-30). Jesus knows all about the complex relationship between God and humans and humans with other humans. He came to save the world, but that very same world betrayed and crucified him. Yet, he would still offer them salvation. His enemies were those he created and he loved. He suffered as part of a divine mystery, but his suffering was not punishment from God for sin. This prayer and Jesus' ministry, death, and resurrection all proclaim that God's kingdom does not operate on a strict system of punishment and reward. We too live in this complex web of relationships where we depend on God's mercy. The answers are not simple to questions of suffering and sin and retribution. We, like Job, will not get some of the answers we seek. This prayer encourages us to see how complicated these relationships are and to learn to praise in the midst of the mystery, even when we do not completely understand.

Beth Tanner

Psalm 70: Hurry, God, My Helper!

The brief form of this psalm speaks to its function, a plea for God to hurry to the aid of the one suffering. This prayer ends as it begins with a plea for God to get to it! This ending is unusual because most of the prayers for help end with a vow of thanksgiving (see Introduction). Indeed, even the ancient copyists may have been surprised by the psalm's length and form because several Hebrew manuscripts combine Psalm 70 and 71 into one longer psalm.[1] But the puzzle of this text does not end here. The words of Psalm 70 appear in a slightly altered form as part of Psalm 40 (40:13-17).[2] It is impossible to determine which of the two pieces is the original, but since the final form of the psalter preserves both, the more important issue is to look at this psalm as a complete piece. In its place here, it adds a sense of urgency, standing between two lengthy laments that each have concluding vows of praise. It indicates that on occasion, the resolution of a problem is not clearly apparent: one must indeed wait upon the Lord.

The structure of the psalm is clear, with a plea at the beginning and end and an uneven chiastic structure.[3]

Plea to hurry (v. 1)
    The world as it is (vv. 2-3)
        The world as it should be (v. 4)
    The world as it is (v. 5a)
Plea to hurry (v. 5b)

1. See the critical apparatus in *BHS,* p. 1151. The MT of Ps. 71 does not contain a superscription, so it would be simple to combine the two psalms. The LXX psalm does have a superscription, meaning in that tradition these were understood as separate psalms. There are literary and thematic links between the two psalms (McCann, "The Book of Psalms," p. 955), but these links are not significantly higher in number or connection than other side-by-side psalms.

2. This dual placement has produced a great amount of scholarly interest, mostly around the question of which of the two texts is the "original." Craigie (*Psalms 1–50,* p. 314) and Eaton (*Kingship and the Psalms,* pp. 42-43) argue that it is Ps. 40 that is the original, based on shared vocabulary and Ps. 40's similarity to Pss. 9–10, 27, and 89. Others such as Kraus (*Psalms 60–150,* p. 67), Gerstenberger (*Psalms: Part 2,* p. 55), and Mays (*Psalms,* p. 233) argue that Ps. 70 is probably the original, based on its completeness here and the difference in the first lines of the psalm. While a definitive decision is impossible, it seems probable, based on the above arguments, that Ps. 70 is an independent composition.

3. Schaefer develops this chiastic structure into a complex ten-part structure on each side of v. 4 (*Psalms,* p. 169).

To the leader. Davidic. Lahazir.[4]

1 *God deliver me!*[5]
LORD, as my help, hurry!

2 *Let them be put to shame and disgraced,*
those who seek my life.
Let them be turned back and humiliated,
those who desire my misery.
3 *Let them turn away because of their shame,*
the ones who say, "Aha, Aha!"[6]

4 *May they be glad and rejoice,*
all those seeking you![7]
May they constantly say, "God is great,"
those loving your salvation.

5 *But I am oppressed and needy.*

God hurry to me!
You are my helper and my deliverer!
LORD, do not delay!

1 and 5b-d The psalm begins and ends in the same way, using much of the same vocabulary (*helper or help*[8] and *hurry*[9] and *deliver*[10]). This twofold plea (v. 1) and threefold plea (v. 5) frame the brief prayer. The mood set is one of great urgency which at the end remains unresolved.

2-3 This next section describes the current situation. It provides both

4. See note 5 on Psalm 38 superscription.

5. The first line is problematic, having only a *hiphil* infinitive construct. Several read the line from Ps. 40:13 instead, adding the imperative of *rṣh* ("be pleased to deliver me"; NRSV; Kraus, *Psalms 60–150,* p. 66; Limburg, *Psalms,* p. 232). Others assume that the final imperative *hurry* serves as the main verb of both lines (NJPS; NIV; Tate, *Psalms 51–100,* p. 202). However, as noted by Dahood (*Psalms II,* p. 168), both of these options are unnecessary. *lᵉhaṣṣîlēnî* is probably a *hiphil* imperative with a 1cs suffix and an emphatic *lāmed* (Waltke, O'Connor, *Biblical Hebrew Syntax,* pp. 211-12) as in Ps. 31:2; 71:3; Isa. 38:20.

6. Preserving the verse order in MT. Most modern translations reverse the lines (NRSV, NIV, NJPS).

7. Also preserving the MT line order.

8. Both from the same root, *'zr.*

9. Both from the same root. *ḥuš.*

10. The term "deliver" is from two different roots, *nṣl* (v. 1) and *plṭ* (v. 5), that have the same meaning.

a plea for God to act against the enemies (vv. 2a, c, and 3a) and a description of the acts of those enemies (vv. 2b, 2d, 3b). Just as in Psalm 69, the issue is one of shame and disgrace. The wishes of the one praying are for those who are the tormenters to be exposed for who they are. Let them know the same shame that the one now feels.

4 This verse stands in direct contrast to the description of the enemies and is disorienting at first, since the two verbs are in the third masculine plural just as in vv. 2-3. It takes a few moments to distinguish that the *they* here is different from the *they* above. This may be part of the point. Sometimes it is hard to tell our enemies from our friends, at least until they open their mouths and speak, as the change in speech from vv. 3 to 4 demonstrates. This is the way people should be speaking, instead of the ways of the enemies.

5 Just as quickly as the psalm turned to a glimpse of how the world should look, it returns to the current situation. It is unclear if the glimpse of praise in v. 4 is intended as a ray of hope, or as a contrast to show how awful the actions of the enemies are, or an offer of additional motivation for God. Indeed, the poem can function as all three at the same time. Verse 5 opens with the reason that God should act, because the one praying is *oppressed and needy*. Both words are used throughout the Hebrew Bible to depict the least of the society.[11]

As noted at the beginning, the psalm is almost a staccato of images: help, enemies, a glimpse of the kingdom, the current condition, help. There is no guide as to how to read the gaps. It is as if the prayer was lifted in such a hurry that there is no time to explain in more detail. One can almost imagine that the fuller form in Psalm 40 ("I waited intently for the LORD, he turned and heard my cry") will have to wait for another day when the situation is less urgent. Here there is no resolution, for sometimes real life is exactly that way. We cry out for answers, we cry out for God to hurry, and all we hear back is a deafening silence. Sometimes the wait can seem forever, and we feel as if God has gone away. Doubt in these times is seen by some as a lack of faith in the heart of the victim or even as sin. Yet here, the Bible confirms that aloneness and the absence of answer or resolution. This psalm speaks as loudly or even louder that its counterpart, Psalm 40, which tells of patient waiting. Here we are left, not with reassurance, but with scary silence, and we all know that some days are like that.

BETH TANNER

11. See, e.g., Deut. 15:11; 24:14; Prov. 31:20. These words are used together to indicate the lowest members of society, usually in economic terms (see Ps. 72) but also as a metaphor for all of those who cannot fully participate in the kingdom of God.

Psalm 71: Teaching about Managing Doubt

Several Hebrew manuscripts read Psalms 70 and 71 together.[1] The two psalms certainly share a common genre, both are prayers for help, and also share some similar ideas, but the central focus as well as the mood created by the two pieces is vastly different. Psalm 70 is brief and pointed. In contrast, Ps. 71 takes its time in arriving at the descriptions of distress (vv. 9-13) and contains more lines that praise God than those of petition to God.[2] The mood, then, is not one of urgency but is reflective of a lifetime lived trusting in God's faithfulness.

The psalm is divided into four stanzas, but the transitions from one stanza to the next are not distinct.[3]

Opening petitions and declarations about God (vv. 1-8)[4]
Description of distress (vv. 9-11)
Petition and motivation (vv. 12-18)
Praise and motivation (vv. 19-24)

1 *In you, LORD, I have taken refuge;*
let me not endure shame forever.

1. Wilson covers this topic extensively and notes that the combination occurred in many ancient Hebrew manuscripts because of Psalm 71's lack of a superscription (*The Editing of the Hebrew Psalter,* p. 131). In LXX, the psalms are not combined, and 71 has an added superscription ("By David, a Psalm sung by the sons of Jonadab, and the first that were taken captive"), giving support to Wilson's argument. Interestingly, in the 4QPs[a] scroll from Qumran, Ps. 71 follows Ps. 38 with "virtually no interval suggesting these were considered a single psalm"; Eugene Ulrich, Cross, et al., *Qumran Cave 4: XI,* p. 15). This combination with Ps. 38 suggests yet another tradition in ancient literature.

2. E.g., Ps. 69 is much more strident in its descriptions of the physical and emotional pain. This has led to scholars to hesitate to categorize this psalm as a lament or prayer for help (Tate, *Psalms 51–100,* p. 211; Mowinckel, *The Psalms in Israel's Worship,* 1:220).

3. This "softer" transition is seen in the ways that scholars divide this psalm. Some divide the psalm into smaller sections; see, e.g., Gerstenberger, who divides the psalm into seven stanzas but admits that clear divisions are difficult (*Psalms: Part 2,* pp. 58-59), or Clifford, who bases the stanza divisions on word count (*Psalms 1–72,* p. 328). Hossfeld divides it differently based on "the movement of the text" in five sections: vv. 1-3, 4-8, 9-16, 17-21, 22-24 (*Psalms 2,* p. 194).

4. Many scholars divide this large section into two stanzas, usually between vv. 4 and 5 (Tate, *Psalms 51–100,* p. 211; McCann, "The Book of Psalms," p. 959; Schaefer, *Psalms,* p. 171), but this division is problematic, since it ends the first stanza at v. 4, separating the petitions from their motivational clause marked by *kî* at the beginning of v. 5. Hossfeld's solution of a division between vv. 3 and 4 is also possible and alleviates this problem as well (*Psalms 2,* p. 192).

2 *In your righteousness, rescue me and*[5] *deliver me;*
incline your ear to me and[6] *save me.*
3 *Be to me a rock of shelter*[7] *to go to continually;*[8]
give a command to save me,[9]
because you are my rock and my fortress.
4 *My God, deliver me from the hand of the wicked,*
from the palm of the unjust and the ruthless;[10]
5 *for you are my hope, O Lord God,*
my trust from my youth.
6 *Upon you I have leaned from birth;*
from the womb of my mother you have been my protector.[11]
To you, my praise is constant.
7 *I have been an example to many;*
and you have been my strong refuge.
8 *My mouth is filled with your praise,*
all the day with your glory.

9 *Do not cast me off in old age;*
when my strength is finished, do not forsake me.
10 *For my enemies talk about me;*
the ones waiting for me consult together,

5. In 4QPsª, the *wāw* is missing (Ulrich, Cross, et al., *Qumran Cave 4: XI,* p. 15).

6. In 4QPsª, the *wāw* is missing (Ulrich, Cross, et al., *Qumran Cave 4: XI,* p. 15).

7. Most scholars and major translations emend *mā'ôn* ("habitation or dwelling") to *mā'ôz* ("refuge"; NRSV, NIV; Tate, *Psalms 51–100,* p. 207; Weiser, *The Psalms,* p. 495), but there is no compelling reason for the change since the MT is readable as it is, as in NJPS "sheltering rock." 4QPsª has the same word as the MT (Ulrich, Cross, et al., *Qumran Cave 4: XI,* p. 15).

8. This line is often changed from *lāḇô' tāmîḏ* ("to go to continually") to the LXX's "house of protection" (NRSV; Weiser, *The Psalms,* p. 495). But as noted by Tate, the line is readable and adds the idea of a place of permanent refuge (*Psalms 51–100,* p. 209; NIV). 4QPsª follows a different tradition, and the last part of the line is missing. It reads "heart, lion [missing]" (Ulrich, Cross, et al., *Qumran Cave 4: XI,* p. 15).

9. Following NIV. Other translations leave out *ṣiwwîṯā* altogether, reading "a strong fortress to save me" (NRSV). There is no need for removal of this word since MT is readable as it stands. Hossfeld also preserves this word (*Psalms 2,* p. 192).

10. The meaning of *ḥômēṣ* is questionable, appearing only here and as a noun in Isa. 1:17. In 4QPsª, the noun is used just as in Isa. 1:17 (Ulrich, Cross, et al., *Qumran Cave 4: XI,* p. 15).

11. The meaning of the word in MT is uncertain. It may mean "to sever," thus to cut the umbilical cord (*HALOT,* p. 186). Some change to *gāḥî* as in Ps. 22, meaning "to burst forth" (NRSV). However, the LXX, Targum, and 4QPSª reflect a participle of *'ōzî* meaning "protector," as noted by Kraus, *Psalms 60–150,* p. 70.

11 *saying, "God has forsaken him!*
Chase him and[12] *seize him! For there is no one to rescue him."*[13]

12 *God, do not be far from me!*
My God, hurry to help me!
13 *Let my adversaries be put to shame, finished!*[14]
May those seeking my harm be covered with reproach and humiliation.
14 *And I will continue to hope;*
I will add to all of your praises.[15]
15 *My mouth will tell of your righteousness,*
all day of your salvation;
although I do not know the measure.[16]
16 *I will come telling of the mighty deeds of the sovereign* LORD.[17]
I will commemorate[18] *your righteousness, yours alone.*
17 *God, you have taught me from my youth;*
and still I proclaim your wonders.
18 *Even until old age and gray hair,*
O God, do not forsake me,
until I can declare your strength,
to all generations to come, your power.

19 *Your righteousness, O God, to the heights;*
you have done great things;

12. In 4QPs[a], the *wāw* is missing (Ulrich, Cross, et al., *Qumran Cave 4: XI,* p. 15).

13. Every attempt is made in this commentary to use inclusive language for humans. Here is a case where the pronoun is central to the meaning of the text and cannot be changed.

14. MT has no conjunction between the two verbs, leading to a multitude of translations. Both LXX and 4QPs[a] have a *wāw* connecting the two verbs. However, MT is readable and no change is necessary.

15. Some (NRSV, NIV) read the verb as a repetition ("I will praise you more and more"), but the line's syntax indicates the one is adding to *all of your praises;* also Tate, *Psalms 51–100,* p. 210.

16. This word appears only here. The LXX manuscripts are divided. Some translate it as "writings" and others as "occupation." Most scholars adopt some form of "number" or "measure" (Kraus, *Psalms 60–150,* p. 70; Weiser, *The Psalms,* p. 498; NIV, NRSV). Tate translates as "scribal art" (*Psalms 51–100,* p. 210). Any translation here is tentative.

17. This line is problematic, reading, lit., "I come in might of the Lord LORD." Most commentators adopt a reading much like above: "I would come [with an account of your] mighty deeds" (Tate, *Psalms 51–100,* p. 208; "I come with praise of Your mighty acts" (NJPS, NRSV).

18. The verb *zāḵar* generally means "to remember," but it is clear here that the act of remembering is not a private one. I am following Tate's "commemorate" (*Psalms 51–100,* p. 208) which seems more appropriate than the NRSV's "praise."

O God, who is like you?
20 *Though you caused me*[19] *to see great troubles and calamities;*
you revive me again;
from the depths of the earth you will again bring me back.
21 *You will increase my honor*
and comfort me again.
22 *Then I will praise you with a harp,*
your faithfulness, O my God!
I will sing to you with a lute,
O Holy One of Israel.
23 *My lips will shout for joy;*
I will sing to you,
me[20] *whom you have ransomed.*
24 *All day, my tongue will tell of your righteousness;*
for they have been put to shame,
those who seek my harm have been disgraced.

1-8 From the opening word, this psalm is different from the surrounding ones. Instead of an imperative plea to God as in Psalms 69 and 70, the psalm opens with an address to God, followed by a perfect verb. This syntactical change announces that this psalm is something unique,[21] but not completely unfamiliar. This opening confirmation then gives way to a series of imperative cries (*rescue me, deliver me, incline your ear, save me,* v. 2; again, *deliver me,* v. 4), but these imperatives are interspersed with assurance (vv. 1a and 3). This is different from the hurried imperatives of many prayers for help and sets the tone for the rest of the psalm. This structure also sets it apart as distinctive from the hurried lines of Psalm 70.

The pleas of vv. 2 and 4 give way to a testimony of lifelong relationship. Each line except v. 7a contains the word *you,* telling over and over of a life of faith. God is this one's *hope* and *trust* and has been so since birth (v. 6). The poem stresses how this one has always had God as a constant (v. 3) place of safety (vv. 3 and 7), and the response is to be an *example* (v. 7)[22] and to *praise*

19. Reading the Qere over the Kethib with a 1cpl direct object.

20. MT reads *napšî,* but this should not be reduced to "soul" since in Hebrew it represents the whole self.

21. As noted above, this psalm has no superscription, and this has led to supposed confusion between Pss. 70 and 71, but the use of the perfect verb form at the beginning of the psalm may indeed be the mark of a new poem.

22. This verse is often read as if this one is presenting a negative example (see NRSV, where the conjunction *wāw* that begins the second line is read as "but." The word *mōpēṯ,* however, does not always have a negative meaning. Thus, the meaning of this verse is ambiguous; this one could be a negative example or a positive one. What is certain is that the

(v. 8). This section reminds all of God's sustaining grace, but as the next section opens, it also serves as a reminder for God to act again as God has acted in the past.

9-11 Testimony gives way to petition, and the petition continues the theme of vv. 5-9: "God, you have been there for a lifetime, so *do not cast me off* now" (v. 9). The remainder of the stanza is why God's intervention is needed. The description of distress centers on the *enemies* and the trouble they cause. In vv. 10 and 11 the enemies are plotting and verbally attacking. Their actions have caused doubt as they cry *"God has forsaken him!"* (v. 11). The poetic words tell a human truth. A few sentences of accusation and hurt can challenge a lifetime of relationship. The enemies have caused doubt to spring up. God has been faithful throughout life, but what if this time, God has turned and there is no *rescue*? The tension hangs as the words of faith stand against the words of the enemies.

12-18 The two pleas in vv. 12-13 are thematically and physically the center of this psalm. Tate and others have noted how the psalm is connected tightly in its presentation of "shame."[23] In v. 1, the first plea asks that I *not endure shame forever;* in v. 13, the request is for the enemies to be the ones *put to shame;* and in v. 24, *my tongue will tell of your righteousness* because those speaking wrongly have, indeed, *been put to shame.* The turning of *shame* from the one praying to the enemies indicates that God has set the world right.

Schaefer and McCann have noted that after the pleas in vv. 12 and 13, the psalm moves back to praise of God,[24] and that praise parallels vv. 2-9. Verses 14-18 reflect that the one praying *will continue to hope* (v. 14 as in v. 5), *will add* to God's *praises* (v. 14 as in vv. 6, 8), *will tell* of God's *righteousness* and *salvation* (v. 15 as in v. 2), was faithful *from youth* (v. 17 as in v. 5), will tell that God did not *forsake in old age* (v. 18 as in v. 9).[25] It appears that the relationship laid out in the early part of the psalm will continue after the threat of the enemies has passed. Everything will return as it was, except now there is a bit more to tell as noted in this section. *I will add to all of your praises* (v. 14). *I will commemorate your righteousness* (v. 16). In the description section, it was the "talk" of the enemies that dominated; here harmful speech is replaced with grateful and praise-filled speech.

The poem uses a great number of terms for God and most identify a

---

verse should be interpreted as neutrally as possible so the reader-interpreter can see the ambiguity inherent in the phrase. Mays notes the ambiguity but then falls on the side of this as a negative (*Psalms,* p. 235).

23. *Psalms 51–100,* p. 214.

24. Schaefer, *Psalms,* pp. 170-71; McCann, "The Book of Psalms," p. 958.

25. V. 9 is actually a plea to God. V. 18 answers the cry of v. 9.

place of safety or aid *(refuge, rock, protector),* especially in the first section of the psalm. In the latter portion of the psalm, the primary image emerges as God's *righteousness.* This trait is mentioned in v. 2 and also appears four more times in the last two sections (vv. 15, 16, 19 and 24). It is clear that it is this *righteousness* that the one praying is most dependent on for the future. The faithful relies on the "righteous" ways of God to "set right" all that is wrong in the world.

The division between the final two sections is not clear, especially since time is stressed by the fourfold use of *'aḏ* in vv. 17-19. The poetic phrasing and word repetition form the ideas of longevity and continuity in the mind of the reader: i.e. all my life (v. 6) I have proclaimed your wonders and now *until* I am old, *do not forsake me, until* I can tell *generations* to follow you (v. 18) because your *righteousness* reaches *to the heights.* The poetry offers the long view of God's kingdom and the lives of people who see their lives as part of that kingdom.

19-24 The psalm ends much as it began, with more praise than petition. It seems as if the one praying's faith and belief in God never faltered, except for a moment upon hearing the words of the enemies. But those words and the doubts they brought are finally silenced under the speech acts of vv. 12-18, and in this final section praise speech turns to song speech (vv. 22-23). Yet v. 20 reminds the reader that this is no artificial piety. There has been struggle, not only with enemies, but also with God. But those *great troubles and calamities* (v. 20) like the enemies seem to pale in comparison with the ways God has and will care for those faithful ones: reviving and bringing back from death (v. 20); increasing *honor* and providing *comfort* (v. 21); and ransoming the one's life (v. 23). After all of the praise of God, the psalm seems to end with a sour note as the psalm seems to imply that the one praying will tell of God only because the enemies have been taken care of. But this verse neatly ends the psalm as it began. The human one trusts in God's *righteousness,* and so he can again *sing* of God's greatness because those who planted seeds of doubt have not prevailed.

The poetry of the psalm teaches how to manage a time of doubt. The enemies are troublesome and the pleas are strident, but the overall tone of the prayer is one of trust through one's whole of life. The psalm invites all who enter its poetic words to take a long view when trouble surrounds. In this way, Psalm 71 is the exact opposite of the hurried words and pleading ending of Psalm 70.

Today's world travels at warp speed, and the long view of life is rarely the norm when one is struggling with accusations and fears of God's absence. The prayer's message can teach us, just as it did an ancient audience, to take the long view of God's path in our lives, to look from birth to the age of gray hair and see where God has been a refuge and protector. It also praises God's righteousness, a righteousness that will not act out of unjust anger or vengeance, but out of a desire to set the world right, this day and all the days of our lives. It is a lesson in patience and in realigning one's life as part of God's great eternal righteous kingdom.

BETH TANNER

Psalm 72: Responsibilities in the Kingdom of God

Psalm 72 stands at a major juncture in the Psalter at the end of Book Two, but it does much more than provide part of the Psalter's structure. Psalm 72 stands as a prayer of joining: from monarch to monarch, from past to present to future, from king to every person.

Psalm 72 is, first and foremost, a royal psalm.[1] It is concerned with the human king of Israel. Most scholars recognize this psalm as a coronation hymn.[2] The psalm presents the job description of the king in hymnic form. This use as a coronation hymn is further confirmed by the superscription and the last line of the psalm. The superscription is the only one dedicated to Solomon. The last line states that *the prayers of David, son of Jesse, are completed.* This implies that the editors that shaped the book of Psalms understood this as the point of transition from one monarch to the next. In addition, the theme of the prayer, one of wishes and blessings for a just kingdom, is a theme of other ancient Near Eastern poems about monarchs.[3] The psalm, then, is universal. This king with the guidance of the Lord God is to be what the other kings could not be, and, as such, the whole world is to recognize his reign as one of justice and righteousness.

The psalm also brings together the spheres of human time. During the monarchy, the hymn was part of the celebration of a human king. It offered direct guidance for a physical historical period of time. But the psalm also recalls the people's past. That the king is to be a blessing to the nations recalls the promise God made to Abraham (Gen. 12:1-3). The tie to Abraham is a reminder that all of Israel is to act in the ways of this prayer. The king is only a representative of the people, and as such the prayer is also a prayer for all. In addition, placing the psalm as the last prayer of David connects each monarch's reign to that of David. The king stands in a long tradition of God and God's people and is accountable to that tradition. Finally, it is worth noting that this psalm's view of kingship is highly idealized. The realities of this small country as portrayed in 1 and 2 Kings, 1 and 2 Chronicles, and the prophetic books tell a very different story of how Israel's kings acted. The wishes here are, in reality, just that — wishes. The psalm, then, has an eschatological el-

1. The royal psalms do not share a similar genre, but are united via their thematic content of being about human kings, presumably of the Davidic line. The royal psalms include 2, 18, 20, 21, 45, 72, 89, 101, 110, 132, and 144. See Gunkel, *Introduction to Psalms,* pp. 99-120. Others have suggested a greater circle of royal psalms (Eaton, *Kingship and the Psalms*), but most scholars do not move beyond Gunkel's proposal.

2. Kraus, *Psalms 60–150,* p. 76; Tate, *Psalms 51–100,* p. 222.

3. E.g., the Code of Hammurabi, king of Babylon (1728-1686 B.C.E.), states, "to promote the welfare of the people . . . to cause justice to prevail in the land, . . . to destroy the wicked and the evil, that the strong might not oppress the weak" (*ANET,* p. 164).

ement. It anticipates the future hope when a "real" king is crowned; a future hope for after the exile when there is no human king, but only a messianic dream of God's kingdom; a future hope that in Christian theology is fulfilled in Jesus, who becomes understood as the king of Psalm 72. Finally, the prayer becomes a prayer for the church, because the church is to be the sign of God's reign in the world. Thus, because it speaks of how leaders are to act in God's kingdom, this psalm forges a link not only within the psalter itself, but also with the whole of Judeo-Christian theology.

One remark concerning the psalm and language: This commentary consistently uses inclusive language for humanity, but a central theme in Psalm 72 concerns the singular person who stands responsible to God. To grasp what I believe is the complete and full meaning of the psalm today, "she" or even "you" could also be a substitute in personal reflection or in preaching and teaching this text. The *he* in the preserved words of the poem is no doubt the king, but now the *he* is anyone who chooses to live as part of God's kingdom.

The Psalm is divided into five stanzas, without vv. 18-20 because it is a later editorial addition.[4]

Opening petitions to God for the king (vv. 1-4)
Wishes for long life and internal security (vv. 5-7)
Wishes for international recognition (vv. 8-11)
The acts of the king that will bring forth vv. 5-11 (vv. 12-14)
More wishes for the king's reign (vv. 15-17)
Editorial addition to close Book Two (vv. 18-20)

Solomonic.

1 *O God, your justice*[5] *give to the king,*
and your righteousness to the son of the king.
2 *May he judge your people with righteousness,*
and your poor with justice.
3 *May the mountains bring well-being*[6] *for the people*

4. There is little consensus on stanza division. Terrien sees six stanzas *(The Psalms),* while Gerstenberger argues for four stanzas *(Psalms: Part 2).* Kraus, *Psalms 60–150;* Limburg, *Psalms;* and Clifford, *Psalms 1–72* use a five-stanza format (plus vv. 18-20). I concur, on the basis that the *kî* clauses of vv. 12-14 govern all of the wishes in vv. 5-11.

5. MT has a plural noun ("your justices"), and several scholars used this reading to indicate "statutes" (Weiser, *The Psalms,* p. 500) or "ordinances" (Zenger, *Psalms 2,* p. 201) in a technical sense. Kraus retains the plural as "judgments" (*Psalms 61–150,* p. 74). Both LXX and Syr use the singular form. The singular form is retained since, as noted by Tate, the word is meant to be read in parallel with the singular *your righteousness* (*Psalms 51–100,* p. 220).

6. *Šālôm* has a broad meaning of "peace," "well-being," "completeness," or "con-

and the hills righteousness.[7]
4 *May he judge*[8] *the poor of the people;*
may he save the children of the needy
and crush the one who oppresses.

5 *May he live*[9] *as long as the sun,*
as long as the moon, through all generations.
6 *May he descend*[10] *like rain upon mown grass,*
like showers that water[11] *the earth.*
7 *May righteousness flourish in his days*
and much well-being until the moon is no more.

8 *May he have dominion from sea to sea*
and from the river to the ends of the earth.
9 *Before him, may foes*[12] *bow down*
and his enemies lick the dust!
10 *May the kings of Tarshish and the islands return tribute*
and kings of Sheba and Seba present gifts.
11 *May all the kings fall down before him;*
may all the nations serve him,

---

tentment." Both "peace" and "prosperity" (NRSV, NIV) have too narrow a sense in the modern usage of English. *Shalom* is much more than just the absence of war, and likewise, "prosperity" in modern cultural usage indicates monetary success instead of a completeness of life.

7. MT has *biṣᵉḏāqâ,* as reflected in NRSV, but the preposition is missing in multiple manuscripts. The preposition is most likely an addition via dittography.

8. Most translate *yišpōṭ* as "may he defend," but the word is from the root meaning "to judge" in the verb and "justice" as a noun. One point of this psalm is that the king is to *judge the poor* fairly, i.e., make sure they get fair treatment in legal issues. This is one way that the king saves or delivers these ones.

9. *Yîrā'ûḵā* ("May they fear you") in MT is obviously corrupt. Most follow the LXX, which has emended the root to *w ya'riyk* ("to prolong or continue").

10. Many scholars change the readable *BHS* text to "He is like rain" (NIV, NRSV; Kraus, *Psalms 60–150,* p. 74; Tate, *Psalms 51–100,* p. 219; Zenger, *Psalms 2,* p. 201), but there is no compelling reason to do so (Weiser, *The Psalms,* p. 500; Terrien, *The Psalms,* p. 516).

11. The word appears only here, but it means "drops" in Aramaic and "heavy rain" in Syr (*HALOT,* p. 283).

12. MT has *ṣîyîm,* which may mean "Desert Tribes or Peoples" as per NIV, NJPS; Zenger, *Psalms 2,* p. 202. This would fit well with vv. 10-11, but not with v. 9b. The LXX has "Ethiopians." Other scholars emend the text to *ṣārāyw* ("his foes"; Weiser, *The Psalms,* p. 500; Kraus, *Psalms 60–150,* p. 75; Tate, *Psalms 51–100,* p. 219; NRSV). Any of these readings is possible, but with the meaning of the word being questionable, the emendation to a more general term seems the better choice.

12 *because*[13] *he rescues the needy crying for help*
and the poor and the one with no helper.
13 *He looks with compassion upon the lowly and the needy*
and the lives[14] *of the needy he saves.*
14 *From oppression*[15] *and violence he redeems their lives*[16]
and their blood is precious in his sight.

15 *Long may he live!*[17]
may the gold of Sheba be given to him;
may prayer be lifted for him continually;
all the day may blessing be made for him.
16 *May there be abundance*[18] *of grain in the land,*
to the mountaintops.
May his fruit thrive[19] *like the foliage of Lebanon*
and they blossom from the cities[20] *as grass of the field.*

13. The syntax is heavily debated here. Some scholars continue the future wish into this section "because he *will* rescue . . ." (Tate, *Psalms 51–100,* p. 291; Terrien, *The Psalms,* p. 517). Others use a present tense to imply the honor given is conditional: "for he delivers the needy" (NRSV, NJPS; Kraus, *Psalms 61–150,* p. 75; Weiser, *The Psalms,* p. 501). Interestingly, LXX uses the aorist middle indicative form so that the king has *delivered* the needy already. This puts in doubt that, at least by the time of LXX, this is seen as a coronation hymn. The *kî* usually has a meaning "because" or "for" or "if," implying a condition, and that sense is preserved here.

14. Lit., *nap̄šōṯ,* but this term should not be reduced to "souls," for it means the whole self or life.

15. The meaning of *tōḵ* is questionable. It appears only a few times in the Hebrew Bible, and most are in the psalms (10:7; 55:11). There is an Akkadian cognate, *takāku* ("to press or oppress"; *HALOT,* p. 1729).

16. Lit., *nap̄šām.*

17. MT reads "May he live!" but the exclamation probably has the same sense as in v. 5, to wish long life to the king.

18. *Pissaṯ* appears only here. The meaning is derived from the surrounding verses and is "abundance" in most translations. What is apparent from the context is that the word indicates a situation of plenty. Zenger concurs (Zenger, *Psalms 2,* p. 204).

19. The meaning of the verb is unclear. One meaning is to shake violently as in an earthquake. Some translations use "wave" (NIV, NRSV; Zenger, *Psalms 2,* p. 202). *HALOT* lists a second meaning as "to be abundant" (p. 1272), and others adopt this meaning (NJPS; Tate, *Psalms 51–100,* p. 220).

20. The problems of the above lines continue here. The subject of the verb *blossom* is not specified. The situation is complicated by what follows: "from a city" *(mēʿîr).* There are two usual options: emend to the plural "cities" (NRSV; Tate, *Psalms 51–100,* p. 220) or to "its sheaf" (*BHS,* p. 1153). The above translation uses the clearer *cities* but does not add "people" or "humans" in place of the generic "they" of the verb. This leaves the possibility that the produce is what is blossoming in the cities, indicating the greatness of the prosperity.

17 *May his name endure forever,*
continue as long as the sun.[21]
All nations will be blessed through him,
and they call him happy.

18 *Blessed be the LORD God, the God of Israel,*
who alone does wondrous deeds.
19 *Blessed be his glorious name forever;*
May his glory fill all the earth. Amen and Amen.
20 *The prayers of David, son of Jesse, are completed.*

1-4 The psalm opens with petitions to God that set v. 1 apart from all the others that follow.[22] The petitions are simple but weighty, asking God to give God's *justice* and *righteousness* to the king. Everything that follows is dependent on these two petitions. If this is the vision of God's kingdom, then it is God's justice and righteousness that form the core values. Mays notes, "They (justice and righteousness) are not just one item in a list but the foundation on which the other possibilities rest."[23] Justice and righteousness are *given* by God. They are not human attributes but Creator-bestowed gifts.

Vv. 2-4 turn to specific functions of the king, with an intervening thought in v. 3. Verse 2 is concerned with how the king is to *judge* the people. Kraus notes that this is one of the central functions of the king, equating him with the chief elder of the land.[24] He is the highest judge and responsible for the righteous function of the court system.

Verse 3 abruptly changes the subject from the king to the creation. Now it is wished that *the mountains bring well-being* or *shalom* and *righteousness.* The king will return as the subject in v. 4 and remain so until v. 16, so why the intrusion? The traditional answer is that the rule of a good king will also impact nature (i.e., in a good king's rule nature will produce),[25] but the acts of nature in v. 3 are not dependent on the acts of the king.[26] Instead of the good rule of the king causing a good response by nature, the structure of the poem

21. The verb appears only here and appears to be related to the noun meaning "progeny" (Gen. 21:23; Job 18:19; Isa. 14:22). It is thus possible that the colon reads something like "May his name increase or multiply as long as the sun (Tate, *Psalms 51–100,* p. 20).

22. Roland Murphy has made this same argument based on the grammatical structure of this verse; *A Study of Psalm 72(71)* (Washington: Catholic University of America Press, 1948), pp. 6-14.

23. *Psalms,* p. 237.

24. *Psalms 60–150,* p. 77.

25. Kraus, *Psalms 60–150,* pp. 77-78.

26. Note in contrast that vv. 8-11 are dependent on the king's acts of justice and righteousness as a series of conditional clauses in vv. 12-14.

apparently is stressing that the king and the creation are to work in tandem for the good of the world. As in v. 1, the grammatical structure reminds the audience that *shalom* and *righteousness* belong to God and can flow through human rule or God's creation.

While vv. 2 and 4 concern the work of the king, the real focus here is on the ones for whom the king is to work. The terms *poor* and *needy* have a wide range of meaning in Hebrew, including "ones that are economically disadvantaged."[27] But as Kraus and others note, the *poor* and *needy* are commonly the ones oppressed by others.[28] They are suffering from "trouble" of all kinds, e.g., unfair court practices,[29] malicious gossip, or shaming from the community.[30] The king, then, is to be concerned with the welfare of the whole community, especially those who are marginalized.

5-7 The wishes turn from the work of the king to the king himself. Long life is associated with the vision of God's kingdom (Isa. 65:17-25), and, as noted above, the wishes of the king extend to the people. The king's good reign is to be like the life-giving *showers* that provide food. Notice that the *shalom* and *righteousness* of v. 3 appear here again as entities that are independent of human action. The king is simply to provide the environment where the benchmarks of God's kingdom can grow.

8-11 Verses 8-11 push the circle further, for the king is to have worldwide impact. Even the rulers at the ends of the earth are to come and acknowledge God's kingdom and come to Jerusalem with *gifts.*[31] Verse 11 stresses the extent of this adoration: kings are to *fall down before him,* and *all the nations* are to *serve him.* The final verb is especially important, for it is always a key word for Israel. Hebrew *'āḇaḏ* means both to "serve" and "worship." It is a key word in the Exodus narrative. Israel goes from being "slaves" of the bad reign of Pharaoh to being "servants/worshippers" in God's kingdom. In the poem here, all the world, through Israel and its king, will become servants in the kingdom of God.

12-14 This stanza opens with a conjunction, *because,* an unusual beginning that sets this section off from those that surround it. Verse 1 contains petitions to God, and vv. 2-11 express wishes for the king and the kingdom, and indeed for the world. Verses 12-14 tell what must happen for these wishes to become reality. The king has responsibilities as well. He must act as God's

27. As in Deut. 24:14; Ezek. 16:49; 22:29. *'ebyōn* seems to be the more specific of the two words meaning primarily being economically poor (G. Johannes Botterweck, "*'eḇyôn,*" *TDOT,* 1:30).

28. *Theology of the Psalms,* pp. 150-54.

29. As in Amos 5:10, 12.

30. As in Ps. 10:2, 9; 14:6.

31. Kraus notes the nations listed in v. 10 are the most remote and most exotic known at the time (*Psalms 60–150,* p. 79) and encompass both the Mediterranean nations and Africa.

image in the world. Indeed, his actions must be God-like. He is to *rescue,* have *compassion, save,* and *redeem* those who are the most oppressed in the society (as in v. 4).[32] According to Kraus, these are acts that in the rest of the psalter are reserved for the Lord God.[33] The king and by extension, then, all of Israel, and finally all of the servants in the kingdom, are to act as God acts. It is only when vv. 12-14 become the norm for the world that the wishes of vv. 5-11 will be fulfilled.

15-17 This stanza returns to the wishes for the king and the kingdom. Verses 15-16 have much in common with vv. 5-7 but also add references to the lifting of *prayers* and *blessings* for the king. At v. 16, the creation reappears, and its *abundance* is an added wish. Verse 16 has the two most problematic lines of the psalm, and their exact meaning is unclear. Whatever the specific reference, clearly the overall meaning of the verse is the desire that the human kingdom and the kingdom of creation are both blessed and bountiful.

Verse 17 connects the reign of the king to two key concepts. First, as many scholars note, the idea that "all nations will be blessed through him" is virtually the same statement made by God to Abraham in Gen. 12:1-3. The king and the audience are reminded that this has been God's plan all along. The end of David's reign marked the end of the warfare, and now it is time for the kingdom of God to become the standard for all of God's people — not by might but with God's justice and righteousness. Here at the end of the "conquest," another way of governance is envisioned. In addition, the last word of Psalm 72 prior to the doxological closing is a *piel* form of the root *'šr, and they call him happy. Happy,* of course, is the first word of Psalm 1, also a derivation of the same root. This verbal *inclusio* of Psalms 1–72 ties the first two books together. This frame also encircles all of the cries for help and all of the praise in those books. All of the doubt and abandonment and the saving grace and presence of God give this word *happy* deep and abiding meaning. The audience can learn what it means to be *happy* from reading these two books, and only the poetry of praise and pain can teach such lessons.

18-20 These last verses have long been noted to be a hymnic addition to Psalm 72. It was Wilson who demonstrated that this doxology was placed here as part of the editorial shaping of the Psalter into five books.[34] This transition, however, is greater than just a move from one book to another. The psalm's superscription and the last words in v. 20 serve to place these two books with the story in 1 and 2 Samuel, where we meet and hear of David and Israel's be-

32. These are the imperative pleas of the prayers for help in the Psalter. This again demonstrates that while the situation may be one of economic injustice, it is certainly not the only situation that the king is to attend to for the sake of those in the kingdom.

33. *Psalms 60–150,* p. 79.

34. *The Editing of the Hebrew Psalter,* pp. 139-45.

ginning. The last *prayer of David* is for the next monarch, indeed, a coronation hymn. It sets the psalter within a particular history of a particular people. But it also sets this particular history within the scope of the world and, indeed, within the cosmic scope of all that exists. Psalm 72 places the king and Israel in the same position as Abraham. God may have selected a particular people, but the mission of the kingdom is to show forth God's justice and righteousness and to be a blessing to all nations.

Knowing that Psalm 72 is a coronation hymn, modern readers may be tempted to look at it as merely an interesting piece of history. But this hymn offers so much more. It defines the kingdom of God, be that kingdom the historical one of ancient Israel or the kingdom of God for which we pray, "thy kingdom come." This prayer teaches us what righteous leadership is to be. The lesson is as relevant today as it was three thousand years ago. In God's kingdom, God's ways of justice and righteousness are to be the norms. In this way, we can avoid the traps of power and position that tempt humans to take the power into their own hands and to govern for some and ignore others. This is the way that God intends the world to be; it was true in Abraham's time, in the time of the kings, and in the world today. It is the kingdom to which we all press forward and the place in which our future hope is vested.

Beth Tanner

Book Three of the Psalter: Psalms 73–89

INTRODUCTION

As noted in the previous discussion of Psalm 72, Book Two ends on a high note. This coronation hymn speaks of the hope that the people have for the monarchy and for the country under a monarchy. It also makes clear that the gifts of righteousness and justice are gifts from God and that the king is simply to be a human administrator of God's greater kingdom.

ASAPH PSALMS (73–83)

This high note is not lived out, however, in Book Three. Psalm 73 opens the collection of eleven Asaph psalms.[1] This further confirms that something different is happening in Book Three. Indeed, all but one of the Asaph psalms appear here.[2] In addition, while individual prayers dominated the earlier book, in this small collection, community concerns are the focus.[3] Michael Goulder notes that this section taken as a whole "is marked by a sense of dire crisis; the community is on the verge of the unthinkable."[4] Something has definitely changed.

Who is this Asaph? The name "Asaph" appears as a Levite musician in

1. These superscriptions, however, are not uniform: Pss. 73, 79, and 82 share an identical superscription, "A Psalm for Asaph"; Pss. 74 and 78 share "A *Maskil* for Asaph." The others in the collection, however, are unique. Five of them begin with "To the leader" followed by a distinct term that is probably a musical direction (Pss. 75, 76, 77, 80, 81). The last in the collection breaks these patterns with "A Song. A Psalm for Asaph" (Ps. 83).

2. Ps. 50 is the exception.

3. Pss. 74, 75, 76, 78, 79, 80, 81, 83 are focused on the community voice instead of the individual.

4. "Asaph's History of Israel (Elohist Press, Bethel, 625 BCE)," *JSOT* 65 (1995) 74.

1 Chr. 15:17-19 and 16:4-5, and in Ezra 3:10 a group of musicians are known as "the sons of Asaph." So the name Asaph is associated with the music of the temple. Unfortunately, this is all that is known about this Asaph. It is impossible to connect the verses in 1 Chronicles and Ezra with this psalm collection. Asaph may indicate a family name, a specific group, or simply be a marker such as a musical notation. Some scholars have focused on when and where this collection was written. Goulder has argued that, since these psalms focus on Israel's origins, this collection comes from the northern kingdom of Israel.[5] Harry Nasuti disagrees, believing instead that the Asaphites were a historical group that functioned in the cultic life of Israel from pre- through postexilic times with a definite Ephraimite *traditio.*[6] There are clues that point to both, but neither can be stated with Goulder's and Nasuti's certainty. What is clear is that this is a collection with a specific theme or theological message.

What is that specific message? Walter Houston argues that "themes of the narratives enshrined in the Pentateuch, Joshua, and Judges are relatively rare in the Psalter as a whole and extremely rare in those headed 'of David,' but relatively common in the psalms of Asaph."[7] Goulder noted that the tone of these texts is one of distress. The period of history of Israel and Judah after the death of Solomon and the clear division into two kingdoms with two kings would be such a time of uncertainty. The two countries struggled with each other, with surrounding nations, and later with the larger distant countries that would dominate Judah and Israel's life from 700 B.C.E. onward. Early in this period appears to be one of the most prosperous times the two countries ever knew, but after the rise of the Assyrians, times grew more and more uncertain, wars raged, and the destruction was widespread. The turmoil evident in Book Two may indeed be a reflection of that period. It would also make sense that, at this time of crisis, the people would look back to other times of uncertainty (e.g., the exodus, wilderness, and settlement of the land, the exile, the Persian hegemony, the Greek conquests, etc.) when God offered salvation and guidance.

Another feature of these prayers is that they voice God's frustration with the people, first as a narrative in Psalm 78 and then in God's own words in Psalm 81. Then Psalm 82 offers a unique look at God's work that is outside of the human realm. This psalm affirms that God has duties other than tending to the humans. The collection reminds us that God, too, has a story to tell about the people. These last psalms in the book tell that God's kingdom is much larger and concerns much more than humans and their plans.

5. "Asaph's History of Israel," pp. 77ff.

6. *Tradition History and the Psalms of Asaph* (SBLDS 88; Atlanta: Scholars, 1988).

7. "David, Asaph and the Mighty Works of God: Theme and Genre in the Psalms Collections," *JSOT* 68 (1995) 111.

PSALMS 84–89

The superscriptions change in this section, but the back and forth of the relationship does not. Four of the psalms (84, 85, 87, and 88) are Korah psalms that form a bridge between Books Two and Three (Psalms 42, 44–49, 84–85, 87–88), and like the Asaph psalms they fluctuate between songs of praise and prayers for help. The songs of praise are unique, however, in their focus on Jerusalem and Zion, and this places the end of Book Three in a particular place. The last two psalms are prayers for help, but these two pieces are particularly haunting in that they are cries to God that end without resolution. Both accuse God of not responding to an individual (Psalm 88) and the community (Psalm 89) and demand an answer, but no such answer arrives. J. Clinton McCann notes, "The effect of the final form is to suggest that Book Three has been decisively shaped by the experience of exile and dispersion."[8] This may be the case, but this ending does not have to have a specific historical referent. Book Three represents every time when the world and its violence make no sense, times when we do not understand why God does not simply fix it. Book Three is a poetic rendering of theodicy, and its themes fit as well today as they did in its ancient context.

BETH TANNER

8. "Books I-III and the Editorial Purpose of the Hebrew Psalter," in *The Shape and Shaping of the Psalter* (JSOTSup 159; Sheffield: JSOT, 1993), p. 98.

Psalm 73: Why Do the Wicked Prosper?

Psalm 72 strikes a high note. It is flush with the hopes and dreams for the future. In contrast, Psalm 73 opens Book Three on a note of confusion and doubt. Life with God will not be lived in an idyllic world, at least for the moment, but in a world where the values espoused in the previous psalm do not always meet with the realities of life.

Psalm 73 refuses easy evaluation. After years of study, scholars cannot determine the genre for this psalm, fluctuating between several possibilities: didactic or wisdom,[1] a lament,[2] and/or first person narration or testimony.[3] Genre may be difficult to determine, but the poetic movement of the psalm is not. At first glance, it appears that it begins and ends in the same place.[4] However, the confident promise of v. 1 is questioned and undermined in vv. 2-16, and then at v. 17, a type of reimagining occurs. It is not surprising that several scholars equate this psalm with the book of Job.[5] It also has much in common with the questions lifted in the book of Ecclesiastes. The psalm, in essence, presents a hypothesis and questions that hypothesis, coming finally to a resolution.

The psalm is also unusually symmetrical in its form. The Hebrew word *'aḵ* provides the three major divisions for the psalm at vv. 1, 13, and 18. McCann has pointed out that vv. 1-12 explain the problem in twelve lines; vv. 13-17 serve as the turning point; followed by the solution to the problem also in twelve lines.[6] The psalm may speak of confusion and doubt, but it does so in a very orderly way.

1. Kraus places this form as secondary to first person narration (*Psalms 60–150,* p. 85). Many now refer to this psalm as wisdomlike (see Tate, *Psalms 51–100,* p. 231; McCann, "The Book of Psalms," p. 968; Terrien, *The Psalms,* p. 526). Zenger notes that this psalm displays "a new form of Wisdom theology . . . of theologized wisdom" (*Psalms 2,* p. 224).

2. Westermann argues that Ps. 73 is a poem of transition exhibiting elements of individual lament, a song of confidence, and also has a didactic aspect (*Praise and Lament in the Psalms,* p. 80).

3. This view is favored by James L. Crenshaw (*The Psalms: An Introduction* [Grand Rapids: Eerdmans, 2001], p. 111).

4. Several scholars argue for an *inclusio* or frame between the beginning and the end of the psalm: vv. 1 and 28 (Tate, *Psalms 51–100,* p. 231; Schaefer, *Psalms,* p. 177); vv. 1-2 and 28 (Clifford, *Psalms 73–150,* p. 16); vv. 1-2 and 27-28 (Weiser, *The Psalms,* p. 505); vv. 1-3 and 27-28 (Crenshaw, *The Psalms,* p. 99). The difference in the frame depends on two factors: 1) how the scholar translates v. 1b and if the subject of the frame is God (vv. 1 and 28) and 2) if the frame contains both praise of God and a comment about the two pictures of humanity painted in the psalm.

5. See, e.g., Weiser, *The Psalms,* p. 507.

6. "The Book of Psalms," p. 968.

Surely God is good! (v. 1)
    My problem (vv. 2-3)
    The wicked are well off (vv. 4-12)
Surely I have been good for nothing (vv. 13-16)
    Until I came into God's presence (v. 17)
Surely I see the fate of the wicked (vv. 18-20)
    My problem resolved (vv. 21-27)
God is good! (v. 28)

An Asaphic psalm.[7]

1 *Surely God is good to Israel,*[8]
to those who are pure in heart!

2 *But as for me, my feet have almost stumbled,*
my steps nearly slipped.
3 *Because I was jealous of the boastful*
as I saw the well-being of the wicked;

4 *Because there are no struggles in death,*
and their bodies are fat.[9]

7. This is the first of eleven continuous psalms with the superscription *Asaphic* (Pss. 73–83; also Ps. 50). Early scholars associated these psalms with one of the Levites appointed by David as a chief musician (1 Chr. 15:17-19; 16:5). In Ezra, there is a group called "the sons of Asaph" (Ezra 3:10). Tate notes that the "psalms of Asaph" should be understood as sponsorship instead of authorship (*Psalms 51–100,* p. 228). Harry Nasuti has done extensive work on this collection and concludes that the Asaphites were a historical group that functioned in the cult and in the life of Israel from pre- through postexilic times with a definite Ephraimite *traditio (Tradition History and the Psalms of Asaph* [SBLDS 88; Atlanta: Scholars, 1988]). Goulder disagrees and sees the collection as coming from Israel between 732 and 722 B.C.E. and the psalms as a liturgically ordered group for an autumn festival (*The Psalms of Asaph and the Pentateuch* [JSOTSup 233; Sheffield: Sheffield Academic, 1996]). Either way, this is a discrete collection, even if scholars are unsure of their original purpose.

8. Following the proposed change in the *BHS* critical apparatus, some scholars emend *lᵉyiśrāʾēl* ("to Israel") to *layyāšār ʾēl* ("to the upright El"; NRSV; James Crenshaw, *A Whirlpool of Torment: Israelite Traditions of God as an Oppressive Presence* [OBT 12; Fortress, 1984], p. 99; Kraus, *Psalms 60–150,* p. 82; Gerstenberger, *Psalms: Part 2,* p. 71; Patrick Miller, "Psalm 73 as a Canonical Marker," *JSOT* 72 [1996] 46 n. 6). Others read as in the MT (NIV; NJPS; Goulder, *The Psalms of Asaph and the Pentateuch,* p. 52; Weiser, *The Psalms,* p. 505; Terrien, *Psalms,* 523; Tate, *Psalms 51–100,* 226; Brueggemann, *The Psalms and the Life of Faith,* p. 206; Hossfeld and Zenger, *Psalms 2,* p. 221). LXX follows MT: "How good is God to Israel, to the upright in heart." There is no compelling reason to change, especially since MT and LXX agree.

9. This verse is problematic. MT reads, "There are no struggles or bonds in their death,

5 *The difficulties of humanity do not exist for them;*
and with the human condition,[10] *they are not struck.*
6 *Therefore their necklace is pride,*
and violence covers them as a garment.
7 *Their eyes bulge out with fatness,*[11]
their hearts overflow with delusions.[12]
8 *They scoff*[13] *and speak with malice;*
the ones in high station[14] *speak of extortion.*
9 *They set their mouths in*[15] *the heavens;*
as their tongues walk in the earth.
10 *Therefore his people turn to them,*[16]

---

and fat are their bodies." Most commentators follow the suggestion in the *BHS* critical apparatus to divide *lᵉmôṯām* ("in their death") into *lāmô* ("to them") to complete the first line and *tām* ("be complete") to begin the second (NRSV, NIV, NJPS; Weiser, *The Psalms,* p. 505; Dahood, *Psalms II,* p. 189; Kraus, *Psalms 60–150,* p. 82; Terrien, *The Psalms,* p. 523). There remains the possibility that this line does indicate that their deaths are without struggle, as in LXX, and thus it is retained.

10. The word in MT is *ʾāḏam* ("humanity"), but in the context *the human condition* seems to communicate better the meaning of the phrase (also Kraus, *Psalms 61–150,* p. 82; Tate, *Psalms 51–100,* p. 227, and others).

11. Reading with MT. There are many proposed changes to this line. LXX and Syr suggest a change from "their eyes" to "their iniquity" (see Kraus, *Psalms 61–150,* p. 82; Weiser, *The Psalms,* p. 505; NIV). The MT reading is used here with the understanding that this is an ancient metaphor, as in v. 4, indicating that these ones are *fat,* meaning wealthy and/or lazy (also Tate, *Psalms 51–100,* p. 228; Terrien, *The Psalms,* p. 523; Brueggemann, *The Psalms and the Life of Faith,* p. 207).

12. This word's meaning is problematic. It most often means "carved figure" (cf. *HALOT,* p. 641). It appears in combination with *heart,* here and in Prov. 18:11. BDB offers a meaning here of "conceit" (p. 967), whereas *HALOT* suggests "delusion" (p. 641). Either meaning is possible and indicates a bad intention.

13. This word appears only here. *HALOT* reports a Syriac cognate meaning "to mock" (p. 559). LXX has "takes counsel" instead of *scoff,* and this is certainly possible based on the dubious definition of the Hebrew word.

14. In many translations, this word is read as a participle and used as an adverb, as in NRSV, "loftily they threaten oppression." But the word can also be a noun, and if it is considered a collective plural as in "the ones of high station," it further stresses that the ones being described are ones of position and power.

15. NRSV "against heaven" goes too far for this preposition. This is probably a statement about the extent of their power, not of their character (also Tate, *Psalms 51–100,* p. 228).

16. The two lines of this verse are the most problematic of the psalm. Some such as C. A. Briggs have eliminated the verse as a gloss (see Tate, *Psalms 51–100,* p. 228). MT reads "therefore his people turn (or return) hither." As expected, this line has produced a whole host of translations, but most indicate that his (meaning God's) people have turned to the ones of vv. 3-9 (contra Crenshaw: "Therefore the people return hither; *A Whirlpool of Torment,* p. 100).

and the waters of abundance are drained by them.[17]
11 *They say, "How can God know?*
Is there knowledge with the Most High?"
12 *Behold, these are the evil ones,*
at ease forever as they increase in power.[18]

13 *Surely in vain I kept my heart clean,*
and I washed my hands in innocence,
14 *but I have been struck all day,*
and my rebuke[19] *was every morning.*
15 *If I said, "I will speak thus,"*
I would have betrayed a generation of your children.
16 *But when I tried to understand this,*
it was a wearisome task to my eyes.[20]

17 *Until I came to the sanctuary of God,*
then I perceived their final destiny.

18 *Surely, you will set them on slippery ground;*
you will cause them to fall in ruins.[21]
19 *How suddenly they are destroyed;*
they are swept away by terrors.

17. Again the uncertainty of the MT has led to a whole host of translations. MT has, lit., "and waters of fullness will be drained by them." The translation of this line depends on what each interpreter adopted for line 1. The above follows the MT and assumes this is an ancient metaphor for what the arrogant are really doing.

18. Often translated as "prosperity" (Tate, *Psalms 51–100,* p. 227), "wealth" (Terrien, *The Psalms,* p. 524; NIV, NJPS), "riches" (Weiser, *The Psalms,* p. 505; NRSV). But these translations may be under the influence of seeing this as a "wisdom" psalm. The Hebrew word *ḥāyil* has a much broader meaning, and in the context of the description of the ones, the term *power* seems more likely than "wealth" (also Kraus, *Psalms 61–150,* p. 83; Hossfeld and Zenger, *Psalms 2,* p. 222).

19. Most translations read *tôḵaḥaṯ* as a verbal form, "was chastened every morning," per Kraus, who notes that the verbal form provides better parallelism (*Psalms 60–150,* p. 84). However, it is also possible that the verb of the first line is to govern the second as above, retaining the MT text without emendation, as reflected in LXX and Tate (*Psalms 51–100,* p. 227).

20. Many scholars change the phrase *my eyes* to better fit the context: Dahood, "my mind" (*Psalms II,* p. 187).

21. There is not a consensus on the root of the word *maššû'â.* If it is from *š'h,* it has the meaning of "wasteland" or "desolate place" (Zeph. 1:15; Job 30:3; 38:27; *HALOT,* p. 643), as reflected in "ruins." If it is from the root *nš',* it has the meaning of "deception" (*HALOT,* p. 643). Scholars are split on the translation of the word. The translation used here is *ruins* because it is a better fit in the context of vv. 18-19.

20 *Like a dream when one awakes,*
O Lord, on awakening,[22] *you will despise their images.*[23]
21 *For my heart was embittered;*
and in my inward parts I was pierced.[24]
22 *I was stupid and I did not know;*
I was a beast before you.
23 *But I am continually with you,*
you hold my right hand.
24 *With your counsel, you guide me,*
and afterward you receive me with honor.[25]
25 *Whom do I have in heaven but you?*
I do not desire anything on earth except for you.
26 *My flesh may fail and my heart;*
but God is the rock[26] *of my heart and my portion forever.*
27 *Behold! Those who are far from you perish;*
you put an end to all those who are unfaithful to you.

28 *But as for me, it is good to be near God;*
I have made the Lord God my refuge;
I will tell[27] *of all your works.*

22. MT reads "in the city," and this reading is possible but problematic. Most make the change suggested in *BHS* (p. 1155) and read the word from the root *'wr* as a *hiphil* infinitive construct *(on awakening).*

23. *Ṣelem* is commonly translated "phantoms" (NIV, NRSV; Kraus, *Psalms 60–150,* p. 83; Weiser, *The Psalms,* p. 507; Crenshaw, *A Whirlpool of Torment,* p. 106). Crenshaw comments that the use of "phantoms" indicates that these wicked ones are nothing more than characters in a dream (p. 106). However, if the word *images* is retained as in the MT, the poem may be interjecting a pun on Gen. 1:27, where humans are made in God's image — i.e., these wicked wealthy are the anti-image. Possibly in addition, *images* can mean "images of other gods." This could be a reference to their lifestyle and a further indication of their uttering disregard for the Lord God (v. 11). See the suggestion of another double meaning in v. 7.

24. The root verb of this word means "to sharpen." It appears only here in the *hithpoel.* Tate notes that this metaphor indicates deep, internal anguish (*Psalms 51–100,* p. 230).

25. The word *kāḇôḏ* has many meanings: "glory," "importance," or "honor." The Hebrew words here are clear, but the meaning is problematic. Some Christian scholars have argued that it should indicate the "glory" that one receives in heaven, but there is no indication of this in the context. For a good discussion on this topic, see Tate, *Psalms 51–100,* pp. 236-37.

26. Most modern translations read *ṣûr* as "strength" (NRSV, NIV), but this is not what "rock" means. This word most often refers to a place of refuge or God as a constant place of security. "Strength" is stretching the meaning too far. *Rock* is preserved here as the ancient metaphor.

27. This last verb of the psalm is in a *piel* infinitive construct form that is difficult to translate into English. Grammatically, it is interesting that the psalm ends with a verb form that has a continuing or continuous sense.

1 As noted by Crenshaw, the psalm begins with a statement that has the force of a creed.[28] However, exactly to whom God is good is a matter of debate. Many twentieth-century commentators have rejected the reading from the MT of "Surely God is good to Israel" in favor of "Surely El is good to the upright; God to the pure in heart."[29] Terrien notes that the change is based on a belief that "to Israel" was a later reading of the unpointed, unspaced text.[30] Tate also notes that the respacing provides better parallelism between "the upright" of v. 1a and *the pure in heart* of v. 1b.[31] Certainly, "the upright" would make more sense if one reads the psalm as a didactic or wisdom piece, but *Israel* makes more sense if it is seen as a type of creedal statement, as argued by Crenshaw. In the final analysis, I agree with those who do not alter the text from the MT, primarily because there is no ancient textual evidence for doing so.

2-3 These verses offer a human contrast to the goodness of God. First, v. 2 presents a picture of a misstep in the path, followed by an even more significant danger. The word for *steps* (v. 2b) is related to the word *ʾašer*[32] that begins the Psalter. Using the metaphorical understanding of this word, the line could read "my happiness nearly slipped." It is another way of saying that my way of life, and my underpinning, almost slipped away.[33] Verse 3 gives the reason for the stumble: *jealousy* of the lives of the *wicked.*

4-12 In v. 4, the psalm presents a very different *because.*[34] In v. 3 the word implies that the problem was in the heart of the one praying; here the *because* elaborates on exactly the content of the *well-being* or *shalom* of the wicked. Verses 4 and 5 imply that the *struggles* of humans do not exist for these ones. It is not that these wicked ones are rich or powerful enough to buy their way out of trouble; but, using the Hebrew particle of nonexistence,[35] the poet writes that these *difficulties,* very human limitations (v. 5), and even the *struggle* of *death* (v. 4) simply do not exist for these wicked ones.

Verses 6-7 turn to the results of these wicked ones' altered human state. Granted some of the metaphors are difficult to understand, but even without a complete understanding of the specifics, the general direction is not hard

28. *A Whirlpool of Torment,* p. 98.

29. See, e.g., NRSV.

30. *The Psalms,* p. 527.

31. *Psalms 51–100,* p. 229.

32. Also as noted by Terrien, *The Psalms,* p. 527.

33. For more information on *ʾašer,* see Ps. 1. This is a rare word for "step," appearing only seven times in the Hebrew Bible. BDB notes that it appears only in poetic texts (p. 81), where the meaning seems as much metaphorical as literal.

34. Both vv. 3 and 4 begin with *kî,* whicih usually introduces a causal statement.

35. Hebrew *ʾên* can be used as a simple negation of a verbless clause but often denotes the fact that something or someone does not exist (e.g., Exod. 9:14; Jer. 6:14).

to grasp. These persons are utterly corrupt. They wear *pride* and *violence* like prized jewels and clothing (v. 6). *Their eyes* and *their hearts overflow* with riches and *delusions* (v. 7).[36] This is a complete opposite of v. 1, where the *heart* is *pure.*

Verses 8-11 move from describing the wicked ones to a description of their speech. Verses 9 and 10 are difficult to understand for the modern reader. P. A. H. de Boer notes that the meaning of v. 9 can be understood from other texts as a metaphor indicating that their words reach everywhere.[37] They are powerful people whose words matter to a great number of persons, and certainly v. 10 continues that thought. People are turning and listening to these wicked ones, who think they know more than God (v. 11). Verse 10b is again difficult to interpret, especially since it is unclear if the *they* are the people speaking or the ones listening. It could be read that *the waters of abundance* represent the ill-gained prosperity and those listening are drinking it up.[38] But a better reading would be that *waters of abundance* could also represent the good gifts of God that are being destroyed by the greedy and self-interested wicked ones.[39]

Verse 12 summarizes the entire section. The wicked *at ease* is a summation of vv. 4-5. The second concept is their power; *ḥāyil* is a word used for Israel's kings and warriors. It denotes an important person in the society with all of the "blessings" that go along with power and position. The power of the wicked occupies the concerns of vv. 6-11. The word picture tells of the wicked's seeming easy existence and their ability to lead others down the path of destruction.

13-16 In the face of seeing the lives of the wicked, the one praying wonders why she is one of the *pure in heart* of v. 1. The certainty of that statement has been turned on its head: keeping a pure heart seems to be a futile effort. These two statements of "truth" demonstrate the deep conflict, for not only do the wicked prosper, but the *pure in heart* suffer (v. 14). Indeed, v. 5 asserts that the wicked *are not struck (ngʿ)* by the human condition, and in contrast here, the one praying is *struck all day* long. Using the same word further

36. As noted in the translation, there are certain problems in understanding this verse. As translated above. the lines seem to imply that both *their eyes* and *their hearts* are corrupted; possibly the bulging eyes are meant to be a physical sign of the inward leaning of their hearts.

37. Isa. 13:13; 51:6; Jer. 4:28; 31:37; Joel 2:10; Pss. 36:5; 108:5; de Boer, "The Meaning of Psalm LXXIII 9," *VT* 18 (1968) 260-64.

38. As argued by Tate (*Psalms 51–100,* p. 229) and McCann ("The Book of Psalms," p. 969).

39. This second reading would seem to make the most sense, since it does not require a shifting of the subject away from the wicked ones for this line. If the other reading is accepted, then the subject of v. 10b is different than 10a and 11-12.

demonstrates how different the situations are for the two groups. However, vv. 15-16 demonstrate that the faithful one will not become completely disillusioned with God's promises, for she is still not willing to speak against God as the wicked ones did in v. 11. She may indeed harbor the same questions in her own heart, but will keep silent. Yet even this act of hers (v. 16) she cannot *understand.* As this long "problem" section comes to an end, her frustration is evident, for it seems she is no closer to understanding the "whys" and "hows" than she was in v. 2. What the audience has learned, however, is that unlike the wicked, she is unwilling to foist her doubts and pain on others. She chooses silence for the sake of the community.[40] This one, even in doubt, is different from the others.

17 Brueggemann states that the psalm, and in a way the whole psalter, pivots on this verse.[41] But the "how" and "why" of the change are as enigmatic as the earlier dilemma. The word *perceived* often means to "discern" or "understand," yet the prayer does not use the same word as in vv. 11 and 16.[42] This implies that whatever was the process of "discerning" as he entered the *sanctuary of God,* it was different from the process of his thoughts before. This poetic gap forces the audience to "fill in their own blanks" about the change of mind. Each must decide for oneself how she might make the same transition.

18-20 *Surely* appears again and returns to an understanding, in line with v. 1. It is the wicked that will "slip" and "fall," contra v. 2. These words are spoken directly to God. The observations of the problem were fully within the physically observable world. The entry into the sanctuary marks the change in perception.[43] It is as if he can now see another reality that reaches far beyond his "eyes."[44] He now sees that God will tend to the wicked, even if not in this time and place. It is only in the temple where the earth and heaven meet that

40. Also making a similar observation: McCann, "The Book of Psalms," p. 969; Mays, *Psalms,* p. 242; Limburg, *Psalms,* p. 248.

41. *The Psalms and the Life of Faith,* p. 207.

42. Vv. 11 and 16 use forms of *yd'* ("to know"), but v. 17 uses a form of *byn* ("to discern"). This change in pattern is noticeable in a psalm that has used so much repetition in its structure.

43. Like Tate, I read v. 18 as a series of models: *you* will *set* and *you* will *cause them to fall* (*Psalms 51–100,* p. 227). Most major translations and scholars place these verses in the present tense (NRSV "you set them"). Unfortunately, English forces the translation into either a future or present tense that Hebrew does not. The future tense was selected here because it seems that God will set it right, but there is no evidence that this is a reality in the world at the moment.

44. McCann argues that the direct address to God begins in v. 15: *I would have betrayed a generation of* your *children* ("The Book of Psalms," p. 969). This is possible, but it may be that the statement in v. 15 is more reflective than it is direct address. Either way, the change is not complete until here.

a new vista is opened. These things that were so troubling are nothing more substantial than a *dream.*[45]

21-27 With the solution foreseen, the prayer returns to penitence (vv. 21-22). The doubts and "embitterment" have led finally to a new understanding of God and the kingdom. Penitence turns to confession. But the confession in v. 23 is in an altered form. The well-known phrase is "God is with me (or us)," Emmanuel. Here the prayer turns the phrase on its head: *but I am continually with you.* McCann notes that this is a reversal of v. 22, *a beast before you.*[46] This may certainly be the case, but it may also be a reflection that despite all the doubts expressed, the one now realizes that even during periods of doubt, the purpose was not rejection but renewed "discernment." The one is and always will be "with God." In v. 24, it seems that this whole process of questioning and doubting results not in shame or sin, but *honor.*[47] God does not punish, but *afterward receives with honor.* Verses 24-25 reiterate the relationship. One may have doubts, but there is no other option than to trust in God and God's promises. It may seem that the voice of the wicked reaches both heaven and earth (v. 9), but it is only God that the one needs and desires *in heaven* and *on earth* (v. 25). Even in floundering again (*heart* and *flesh may fail,* v. 26), God will be there as a *rock* and a *portion.*

Verse 27 opens with the same word as does the summation of the life of the wicked (v. 12), and here is the final reversal. For now the wicked may seem at ease and all-powerful, but life lived without God guarantees another end.

28 The psalm ends with a "revised" creed. God is *good* to Israel (v. 1), and so *it is good to be near God.* The psalm has been the words of one who *was embittered* (v. 21), but now and continually the one's words will be to tell of the *works* of the Lord.

Psalm 73 opens Book Three of the psalter, and scholars have noted that it shares a great amount of vocabulary with Psalm 1 and is concerned primarily with the dichotomy between the "pure in heart" and the wicked.[48] As noted clearly by Brueggemann, this psalm challenges and then ultimately

45. This verse is another one that is difficult to understand. But relating the brevity of human existence to a *dream* (Ps. 90:5), this translation retains the word *images* instead of "phantoms" because by using the more common meaning there is another possible implication, that their *images* are indeed other "gods." God will deal with these lesser "images" in Ps. 82.

46. "The Book of Psalms," p. 969.

47. It is easy to see why so many have associated this psalm with the book of Job, for the same result ends each. What seems like sin to others, results in an altered state of understanding of both God and humans. In the end, Job is honored by God instead of chastised.

48. McCann, "The Book of Psalms," p. 968; Brueggemann, *The Psalms and the Life of Faith,* p. 206.

accepts the premise of Psalm 1.[49] Its placement then is key. Books 1 and 2 end with Psalm 72 and the statement that the "prayers of David" are ended and the superscription to Solomon places it at a very historical juncture. Solomon will be the first king to inherit the throne by way of birth. Israel, equated earlier with geography, is now those who are "pure in heart," and they will hold their collective breath to see if Psalm 72 can become a reality.[50] Historically, we know that it did not, and according to 2 Kings, each successive king has more traits of the wicked ones than of the human king described in Psalm 72. Psalm 73 opens a collection and a book that on the whole will stand beside a specific period in Israel's history and will end with the painful questions of the exile as a haunting end to Psalm 89.

Psalm 73, then, teaches a theological and philosophical lesson about a very concrete historical period of Israel's history, and there is much to be learned from the lesson. However, the prayer also teaches a valuable lesson about the way religion is practiced in our time and place. For some reason, Christian faith is often understood as a religion of blind faith. This idea can be traced to our culture in part from the "war" that raged between a historically critical understanding of the Bible and a "blind faith" perspective on the Bible. In this second perspective, doubt either in God or in the way the stories in the Bible tell of historical reality is seen as sin and something to be discouraged at all cost. This perspective is alive and well in many Christian communities despite prayers such as this one that demonstrate the growth and change that can happen in times of doubt and questioning. We, like our ancient sisters and brothers, see a world that does not seem to reflect God's values and God's kingdom, and this leads us to wonder about God and about God's ways in the world. If this conflict is not resolved, our faith becomes stuck and cannot grow further. This prayer goes into those places of doubt and, like the books of Job and Ecclesiastes, finds a path through these times to another level of faith. It is a guide for the times when we have similar questions and encourages us to keep looking for truth in the midst of an imperfect world.

BETH TANNER

49. *The Psalms and the Life of Faith,* p. 206.

50. Miller and Brueggemann go so far as to call this a royal psalm, noting its shared vocabulary with other royal psalms ("Psalm 73 as a Canonical Marker," pp. 46-50). This is certainly possible, but since it does not clearly denote the human king as the speaker, it is not certain. There is no doubt, however, that the placement of the psalm at the beginning of Book Three reflects the "historical realities" of the monarchical period of Israel's history.

Psalm 74: Great God and King, Where Have You Gone?

Psalm 74 is a prayer of the community that sounds a harsh note after the restored confidence at the end of Psalm 73. The arrogant ones here are clearly foreign invaders who not only mock God (vv. 4, 10, 18, 23) but have destroyed the temple (vv. 4-8). The plight of the people is dire, and God seems nowhere to be found. The psalm returns again and again to the concern that all that Israel has come to depend on for stability is gone and there is no "sign" pointing to a new way. It appears as if the vision at the close of Book Two (Psalm 72) is now a distant memory.

Interestingly however, the psalm does not focus on the plight of the community.[1] Instead, after initial questions to God in v. 1, the psalm is an extended plea for God to act, with five reasons for doing so. These reasons are used to motivate God, much in the same way that Moses tries to motivate God *not* to act in Exodus 32. The psalm, then, while a cry for help, is shaped as an argument that will motivate God to reappear and set this horrible event right.[2]

Questions to God (v. 1)
Remember God's long relationship with Israel (vv. 2-3)
The devastation done by the enemy to God's sanctuary (vv. 4-8)
The taunting words of the enemy (vv. 9-11)
God's great cosmic power (vv. 12-17)
Remember your covenant and arise (v. 18-23)

The psalm ends without resolution. God does not reappear, nor is there a renewed understanding as in Psalm 73. The psalm leaves the audience right where they started, with the questions of *why* and *how long* still on their lips. The psalm is a lesson in prayers of motivation that must wait for action and resolution. Hope is based on God's acts in the distant past (vv. 12-17) as the community awaits God's acts in the present.

1. Westermann notes that this "reporting" style of the situation is indicative of "community prayers for help" and is quite different from the lament of the individual that describes an individual's suffering in great detail (*Praise and Lament in the Psalms,* p. 173).

2. Scholars generally agree on these divisions, esp. of vv. 12-17 and 18-23. Differences center mostly on the division of the early part of the psalm. Some scholars see only three stanzas: 1-11, 12-17, 18-23 (Mays, *Psalms,* p. 244; McCann, "The Book of Psalms," pp. 973-74; Limburg, *Psalms,* p. 250). Tate sees v. 9 ending the second stanza and the cry of "How long" in v. 10 opening the third stanza as a linking mechanism (*Psalms 51–100,* p. 246).

An Asaphic maskil.[3]

1 *Why, O God, have you rejected us forever?*[4]
Why does your anger smoke against the sheep of your pasture?

2 *Remember your congregation which you acquired of old,*
the tribe of your inheritance which you redeemed,
Mount Zion, where you dwell.
3 *Lift up your steps to an enduring ruin,*
all that the enemy has destroyed in the sanctuary.

4 *Your foes have roared in the midst of your meeting place;*
they set up their signs as signs.[5]
5 *At the entrance, they cut*[6]
the wooden trellis with axes;
6 *and then,*[7] *all its carved wood*
with hatchets and hammers[8] *they hacked down.*
7 *They burned your sanctuary with fire to the ground;*
they defiled your name's dwelling place;
8 *and they said in their hearts, "We will subdue them completely."*
They burned all the meeting places of El in the land.

9 *Our signs we cannot see;*
there is no prophet any longer,
and there is none among us who knows how long!
10 *How long, O God, is the foe to mock?*
Is the enemy to scorn your name forever?

3. See note 2 on Psalm 32 superscription.

4. In MT there is no direct object for the verb, but it is assumed by most (NIV, NRSV, NJPS; Kraus, *Psalms 60–150*, p. 94; Weiser, *The Psalms*, p. 517; Terrien, *The Psalms*, p. 535).

5. Peter R. Ackroyd ("נצח — εἰς τέλος," *ExpTim* 80 [1968] 126) and Kraus (*Psalms 60–150*, p. 95) argue that the dual use of "sign" is probably dittography. This is possible, but it is also possible that the phrase indicates the replacement of the old *signs* for the ones of the enemy.

6. The meaning of this line is uncertain in MT. The *BHS* critical apparatus suggests several changes, but scholars are deeply divided on which changes should be made, and none of the arguments are ultimately convincing. Reflected above is the NRSV translation since it is the result of two small emendations to the text, changing *yiwwāḏa‘* to *yigdᵉʿû* and *kᵉmēḇî’* to *kᵉmāḇō’*, but any translation of this line is tentative at best.

7. Reading *wᵉʿāttâ* ("and then") with the Qere, reflecting a temporal condition. MT has *wᵉʿēṯ* ("and a time"), which is problematic.

8. The meaning of both words is questionable and they appear to be loanwords, but this is far from certain (*HALOT*, pp. 472, 502).

11 *Why do you turn back your hand?*[9]
And why do you turn back your right hand,
from the midst of your bosom completely?[10]

12 *God is my king from old,*
working salvation in the midst of the earth.
13 *You, you*[11] *split, by your might, the sea;*
you broke the heads of the sea-monster[12] *on the waters.*
14 *You, you shattered the heads of Leviathan;*
you gave him (as) food to the people in the ships.[13]
15 *You, you cleaved open spring and brook;*
you, you dried up ever-flowing rivers.
16 *Yours is the day, also yours is the night;*
You, you fixed the light[14] *and the sun.*

9. NJPS, NIV, NRSV all use "hold back your hand," while many scholars read this word as some form of drawing or pulling back (Kraus, *Psalms 60–150,* p. 95; Tate, *Psalms 51–100,* p. 240; Weiser, *The Psalms,* p. 517; Terrien, *The Psalms,* p. 536; Dahood, *Psalms II,* p. 198). The modern translations are puzzling. The Hebrew word *šûḇ* indicates an active state of movement. God does not withhold; God actively "turns around" God's hand.

10. The line is difficult, as seen in the great variety of translations. This translation preserves as much of MT as possible, reading the Qere *hêqᵉḵā* ("your bosom") instead of the Kethib *hôqᵉḵā* ("your statute"). This is followed by most commentators. While the exact wording is problematic, the line seems to be a parallel to v. 11a as represented here, but the translation is tentative.

11. This begins a series of emphatic statements where the 2ms subject is both part of the Hebrew verb and an "extra" personal pronoun. What is reflected in the translation is exactly what the Hebrew says. I have preserved this emphatic subject in this hymnic piece since there is no way to indicate this grammatical structure smoothly in English.

12. MT has the plural. Waltke and O'Connor note that this pluralization is an intensive form (*Biblical Hebrew Syntax,* p. 122).

13. This line is problematic. MT reads "He gave him food to the people, *lᵉṣîyim.*" Most understand this as meaning "he gave them as food to the people" but the last phrase is problematic. *BHS* suggests reading *lᵉʿamlᵉṣê yām* ("he gave them as food to the sharks"), but few follow this change. *HALOT* suggests a meaning of "animals of the desert," hence NRSV "creatures of the wilderness," but this meaning is uncertain (p. 1020). LXX uses "Ethiopians." However, *ṣî* can also can mean "ship" (Isa. 33:21 [singular]; Num. 24:24 and Ezek. 30:9 [plural]). So it is just as plausible that the line reads "for the people, for the ships," with an understanding that the monster of the sea is fed to the people who are at sea in ships. Any translation is uncertain.

14. MT has the singular *māʾôr.* Dahood (*Psalms II,* p. 207) and Tate (*Psalms 51–100,* 244) argue that this means the moon (also NIV). Others assume the plural "luminaries" (NRSV); "stars" (Weiser, *The Psalms,* p. 517); "lights" (Kraus, *Psalms 61–150,* p. 95). Changing to the word "moon" seems unwarranted since there is clearly a Hebrew word that means moon *(yārēaḥ)* that often appears with "sun" (Josh. 10:12, 13; Ps. 72:5; 89:36-37;

17 *You, you set the boundaries of the earth;*
summer and winter, You, you formed them.

18 *Remember this!*
An enemy mocks, O LORD*!*
Foolish people scorn your name.
19 *Do not give over the life*[15] *of your dove to the wild animal;*
the life of your poor do not forget forever!
20 *Have regard for the covenant,*
because the dark places of the earth are full,
the habitations of violence.[16]
21 *Do not let the downtrodden turn away in shame.*[17]
Let the poor and needy praise your name.
22 *Arise, O God, argue your dispute;*
remember the mocking from the foolish all the day.
23 *Do not forget the voice of your foes,*
nor your adversaries going up constantly.

1 The psalm begins with two questions that define the problem. The first question asks about God's rejection, and while the same verb appears in several psalms, here it is feared that this rejection will become *forever.* This abandonment seems permanent, and the subsequent pleas for action will try to reverse the course. The second question has in its background God's promises in covenantal and royal theology. The people are called *the sheep of your pasture,* a phrase often used in describing the subjects of a king.[18] It reminds God that the king-shepherd's purpose is to care for the *sheep.* The people are

121:6; Isa. 60:19). The translation above reflects MT, since there seems to be no compelling reason for changing it other than a modern sense of poetic balance.

15. *Nepeš* has a wide range of meanings but should be understood not as a separate soul, but as the whole self.

16. This translation follows MT, where the mpl *dark places of the earth* is the subject of the 3cpl verb and the *habitations of violence* is a modifier of the subject (also NRSV).

17. NIV uses "retreat in disgrace," and NRSV has "be put to shame." Tate (*Psalms,* pp. 51-100, 241) emends the text to "sit," following the Syr, representing the idea of mourning. The verb, however, is from the root *šûḇ* ("to turn") and may be a reminder of the question of v. 11: "why do you turn your hand away?"

18. God as a shepherd appears in a variety of texts, either by the specific title *rōʿeh* (Gen. 49:24; Isa. 40:11; Jer. 31:10: Ezek. 34:15; Pss. 23:1; 28:9; 80:1) or by an image of the people as sheep (Isa. 5:17; 49:9; Jer. 50:19; Ezek. 34:2-24; Zeph. 3:13; Pss. 79:13; 95:7; 100:3). A multitude of ancient Near Eastern texts also use the title of "shepherd" for the gods in the context of their function as king. The Sumerian god Enlil is referred to as "God Enlil, faithful Shepherd, Master of all countries, [faithful] Shepherd, . . . The lord who drew the outline of his land" (*ANET,* p. 337). Marduk is also referred to as a shepherd of humans: "Most exalted

merely poor sheep in need of the protection and guidance of the great King, which makes the abandonment all the more offensive.

2-3 The psalm changes from questions to imperative pleas. The solution to God's being angry is for God to *remember,* just as Moses implores God to "remember" when God's anger burned against the people at Sinai (Exod. 32:13). What God is called to remember is also significant. The *congregation of old* and *the tribe of your inheritance*[19] recall another type of "forever"; the forever of the relationship of God and the people. Other words in v. 2 also remind God of this long relationship. The Hebrew verb *acquire* is used with heaven and earth (Gen. 14:19, 22) and the people (Exod. 15:16; Isa. 11:11). *Redeem* means literally "to buy back from slavery," recalling the slavery of the people in Egypt. These terms of acquisition serve to "remind" God of the length of the relationship. The final line brings these *old* ties to the present, for now it is on *Zion* that God *dwells.* The plea in v. 3 is for God to hurry back to Zion, to what is left of God's *sanctuary.*

4-8 These verses, even if somewhat problematic textually, depict the destruction of the temple. This section has generated a great amount of scholarly debate as to the historical event behind this description, but poetry is notoriously difficult to pin to a single event since its meaning is expressed in imagery and metaphor.[20] What is clear is that the enemy has entered the temple and destroyed it, first with weapons (vv. 5-6) and then setting it on *fire* (v. 7). The place where the Lord lives has been *defiled.* Indeed, the enemy is so confident of victory that they set up the memorial markers of victory before they act instead of after (v. 4). This section is in the form of a description, but in the context of the questions in v. 1, it is clear that this description is also motivation. The awfulness of the act is laid out for God to hear as a reason to *lift up your steps* (v. 3) and return and

---

be the Son, our avenger; Let his sovereignty be surpassing, having no rival. May he shepherd the black-headed ones, his creatures" (*ANET,* p. 69).

19. Several of the themes of v. 2 especially and this psalm in general appear in Isa. 63:15-19. It too is a plea for God to act after a catastrophic loss of land and power. *Tribes of your inheritance* appears in Isa. 63:17; Jer. 10:16. In Isaiah, it is also part of a plea for God to act, but in Jeremiah, it is given as a statement of God's creative work. Inheritance implies that this tribe was "bought" at some point in the distant past and that it is precious since the inheritance is guarded as the legitimate connection to the ancestors and is a deed from God. See Numbers 36 or 1 Kings 21 for an understanding of the importance of the *inheritance* in theological terms.

20. The dating argument centers on two historical periods. An obvious connection is to the destruction of the temple in 586 B.C.E. (e.g., Hossfeld and Zenger, *Psalms 2,* p. 243). But others have argued, based on the plural *all the meeting places of El in the land* (v. 8) as well as the similarity of v. 9 to 1 Macc. 4:46; 9:27; 14:41, that it should be dated to the Maccabean era. For a complete explanation of the issues involved, see J. J. M. Roberts, "Of Signs, Prophets, and Time Limits: A Note on Psalm 74:9," *CBQ* 39 (1977) 474-81.

deal with those who would defile the house that shows forth God's power, strength, and universal rule.

9-11 At v. 9, the poem turns from the enemies' acts to the heart of the theological crisis. The status quo ways of meeting God are destroyed along with the temple, and if that is not bad enough, even the prophetic voices offer no aid. The prophets are either silent or untrustworthy. No one can say *how long,* if ever, it will be before God reappears.[21] The dual use of *how long* at the end of v. 9 and the beginning of v. 10 returns the audience to the initial cry of *Why have you rejected us?* There are no prophets to answer the question, so in v. 10 the *How long* is directed to God. But as in v. 1, it is not just a simple question; it is also motivation. The motivation in this section is related, not to the people or the destroyed temple, but God's reputation. The question in v. 10 asks God how long the enemies will *mock* and *scorn,* not the people, but God. This section appeals to God's character and world-wide reputation, again just as Moses did when God was going to destroy the people previously (Exod 32:12). If God will not act on behalf of the sheep, or on behalf of the temple, maybe God will respond to the enemy's mocking of God and God's power. The meaning of v. 11 is difficult, but it seems to continue the question of "how long." God's power as the divine warrior is often paralleled with the strength of God's *right hand.*[22] The question here is why has God *turned back* that powerful hand.

12-17 The psalm changes direction abruptly at v. 12. These verses are hymnic in form and may indeed be an older hymn inserted into the psalm by the writer or a later editor.[23] The situation to this point has been complete and utter chaos. The hymn section praises God's mastery over chaos in the ancient past and serves as a further motivation to come and conquer chaos again. Further, this section uses the creation myth of the invaders in vv. 4-8 to declare the God of Israel as the one and only legitimate *king* over the gods

21. This is another verse that has received a great amount of scholarly attention. Arguments center on if the *sign* is a physical one as in v. 4, or if it is a prophetic sign. Roberts argues convincingly for this to be understood as directly associated with a prophetic sign ("Of Signs, Prophets, and Time Limits," pp. 475-77). Other arguments center again on dating, arguing that it must be a "late" psalm since there are *no prophets.* The issue is as above. Poetic writing is not necessarily historical accurate. It has no need or responsibility to report how it really was, only how it really felt to those crying to God. For a full description of the scholarly debate, see Roberts, "Of Signs," pp. 474-81.

22. E.g., Exod. 15:6, 12.

23. This section seems to be a complete hymn stanza, and if vv. 12-17 are removed, then vv. 10-11 and 18 follow the same pattern as vv. 1-2: questions followed by the imperative *Remember!* An additional element is this section's sevenfold use of the emphatic *You* (seven is considered a complete number in Hebrew thought). This use of the emphatic "you" appears only in this section. If it was written by the same hand as the rest of the poem, the emphatic "you" would probably have been used throughout the piece.

and the people. This is clearly theological *chutzpah* that claims in the midst of a ruined temple that it is the Lord of Israel who stands in the place of Marduk.[24] This section is clearly associated with God's kingship (v. 12) and tells of a time when God defeated all the other gods. The sevenfold use of the emphatic double "you" stresses that it is the Lord God that is the center of this section. This hymn, which alone would be confessional in nature, serves here as a call to action. If God could defeat the gods of the enemy then, God should rise up and do the same again.

18-23 This last section of the psalm is composed of seven pleas for God to act. These pleas both reiterate the previous calls to action and introduce additional ones. The section opens as does the first plea of the psalm with *remember.* However, the reason to remember is not the people of God but the taunting and scorn of the invaders, using much of the same vocabulary as v. 10, providing a frame around the hymn that calls for God to hear and subsequently act against these enemies as alluded to in the cosmic hymn inset. God is called to act for God's sake.

Verses 19-21, although problematic textually, return to pleading for action on behalf of Israel. Verse 19 pleas for their lives, using both *nep̱eš* and *ḥayyāṯ.* It places the very lives of God's *poor* in the hands of God, surrounded by verbs that are in the negative (*do not give over* and *do not forget*), implying that all God has to do is act as God has done in the past, just as the hymnic section implies. Verse 20 calls on God to *have regard for the covenant.* This reference probably does not refer to any covenant specifically, but is an appeal to the promises God has always made to this particular people. In Exodus 32, Moses reminds God of God's sworn promise to the ancestors, and it is this reason that appears to cause "God to change God's mind" and not destroy the people. The call for God to honor the covenant, then, has served as a powerful tool of persuasion in the past. Unfortunately, the remainder of v. 20 is difficult to translate and uses unfamiliar metaphors, but the use of the word *ḥāmās (violence)* makes the threat clear, even if the exact metaphors are not. Verse 21 returns to the plight of the people and presents God with one more call: do not let your people be shamed, instead *let the poor and needy* praise *your name* (contra vv. 7, 10, 18, where the enemy mocks God's name).

The final verses call on God to act within God's responsibility as Judge, using the images of a court dispute. God is called to *arise* and *argue* the *dis-*

24. The allusions in this section are clearly connected to the claims in the *Enuma Elish* (*ANET,* pp. 60-72) where Marduk kills Tiamat, the sea-goddess (v. 13a), and her chaotic sea-monsters (vv. 13b-14b) and then fashions heaven and earth (vv. 15-17). Further, Marduk then becomes king over all of the other gods and over Babylon. This seems to be the clearest connection with a true "date" for this psalm. It is clear that the "myth" circumvented here is Babylon's, increasing the possibility that the enemies are indeed Babylonian.

pute. God judges the peoples of the world (Ps. 7:6), the other gods (Ps. 82:1), and Israel (Isa. 3:13-14) as a function of being the King. The psalm ends on this note, this final call to action. The previous psalm moved from doubt to confidence and ended with the psalmist "telling continually of God's works." Psalm 74 ends with the *voice of the foes going up constantly.* This psalm teaches that sometimes the resolution must be trusted even in the face of God's absence.

The king in Psalm 72 seems to be forgotten as chaos ensues and Israel reaches back to its divine king, warrior, and judge. No human can set this destruction right. These threats are too real and too awful. Book Three is beginning just as it will end, with the country lost and with cries to God.

In summary, this psalm is overtly a cry to God to return to the people and to God's ruined house. Yet underlying these pleas is a confidence that these pleas will ultimately be successful. Many of the pleas are based on God's action in the past, possibly shaped on the arguments presented in Exodus 32. The hymn testifies to both a theological confidence in God's power and in God's "remembering" of the "forever" promised by God in the covenants of old. Israel cannot depend on its own fickle nature, but is confident in God keeping God's promises, even if this promise keeping is not seen in the present.

This psalm is a cry of the people of faith when it seems that all is lost and hope is fading. Yet in this prayer for God to act there are also great faith in God's acts in the past and a belief that God will again come to their aid in the future. In this way, this prayer teaches us to maintain our past, not for the sake of a historical record, but as a means of faith in the present and future. The stories of our ancestors can shape our faith in the present.

Psalm 74 ends without a resolution to the problem of God's absence, and this too teaches a lesson: to continue the conversation, even in periods of perceived absence by God. This lesson is set in stone in a memorial for the Hauptsynagoge (Main Synagogue) in Munich, which was destroyed during the *Kristallnacht* pogrom, November 10, 1938. The center of the memorial uses Psalm 74:18 and reminds all that the questions of this prayer are still part of our own theological struggle.

BETH TANNER

Psalm 75: An Answer to Where God Has Gone

Psalm 75 is a fitting follow-up for Psalm 74, for it provides the answer to the cries for God to act. The prayer opens with the congregation giving thanks for God's great acts. The form of the prayer is debated among scholars, and how one understands the form will ultimately impact the message of this poem. What is clear is that v. 1 stands alone as the voice of the people. Most scholars believe that at v. 2 the speaker changes to God.[1] What is less clear is when God's speech ends. Many see it extending to vv. 5 or 6.[2] However, there are several clues that indicate the speech of God is contained in vv. 2-3, with another speaker adding vv. 4-9 (see below).[3] The final puzzle of the psalm is the identity of the speaker in v. 10. Scholars are divided between the speaker as God or an official. However, additional clues point toward God having the last word in this multivoiced poem. This change of speaker is not unusual in Hebrew poetry, but it can be puzzling to a modern reader who has no warning or guide in how to read and understand the changes of person in this prayer. This prayer then is not in the style of a monologue, but is in a conversational style and was probably part of an ancient liturgy.

Praise from the congregation (v. 1)
Pronouncement by God (vv. 2-3)
Words about the boastful (vv. 4-9)
The final word by God (v. 10)

For the leader. Al-tasheth.[4] *An Asaphic psalm.*[5] *A song.*

1 *We give thanks to you, O God, we give thanks,*
and those calling on your name[6] *recount your*

1. Tate, *Psalms 51–100,* p. 258; Clifford, *Psalms 73–150,* p. 27; Limburg, *Psalms,* p. 254; Schaefer, *Psalms,* p, 185; Mays, *Psalms,* p. 248; Gerstenberger, *Psalms: Part 2,* p. 82.

2. Tate, *Psalms 51–100,* p. 258; Clifford, *Psalms 73–150,* p. 27; Limburg, *Psalms,* p. 254; Schaefer, *Psalms,* p. 185; also NRSV and NIV break the psalm between vv. 5 and 6.

3. Hossfeld concurs, *Psalms 2,* p. 253.

4. See note 3 on Psalm 57 superscription.

5. See note 7 on Psalm 73 superscription.

6. MT reads "and near your name, they recount." LXX and Syr read "and we call on your name. One will tell of your deeds." The *BHS* critical notes suggest *wᵉqōr'ê bišmeḵā sippᵉrû.* Dahood argues that *wᵉqārôḇ* be read as an epithet for God: "O Near One" (*Psalms II,* p. 210). John Kselman has offered a complex reading of this line via a *Janus* parallelism. He argues that *šmk* actually does double duty without changing the text. Thus the lines read, "For near is *your name/your heavens* recount your wonders; "Janus Parallelism in Psalm 75:2," *JBL* 121 (2002) 531-32. But he does not account for this spelling of "your heavens." While

extraordinary deeds.[7]

2 *At an appointed time, I choose,*
I, myself,[8] *will judge with equity.*
3 *When the earth and all its inhabitants sway,*[9]
I, myself,[10] *steady its pillars.* Selah.

4 *I said to the boastful, "Do not boast";*
and to the wicked, "Do not lift up your horn.[11]
5 *Do not lift up your horn on high,*
or speak with an outstretched neck."
6 *Indeed*[12] *not from east, nor from west,*
nor from the wilderness is there lifting up.[13]
7 *Indeed God is the one judging;*
one he causes to be lowered and another he causes to be lifted up.
8 *Indeed there is a cup in the hand of the LORD,*
with wine fermenting, a full mixture.

---

any translation is tentative, it is read above as *BHS* suggests, instead of current translations (NIV, NRSV, NJPS).

7. The change from the 3mpl of MT to the 3ms of the critical apparatus is puzzling. It does not reflect the same change as LXX, but emends the text unnecessarily. With the changes used in the first part of the verse, any additional change is unnecessary. As noted by Tate, however, the subject of *recount* could also be "your wondrous deeds" (*Psalms 51–100,* p. 256), but this would also require a switch of subject.

8. The use of an additional 1cs pronoun indicates an emphatic emphasis on *I* (God).

9. Traditionally this verb was thought to mean "to melt" (BDB, p. 556). More recent studies, however, have identified the meaning as "to wave, sway backwards and forwards" (*HALOT,* p. 555).

10. The use of an additional 1cs personal pronoun indicates an emphatic emphasis on "I" (God).

11. MT reads "do not lift up a horn," as does LXX. But in the next line "your (mpl) horn" is used. Most scholars use "your" in v. 5 also.

12. Vv. 6, 7, and 8 all begin with the preposition *kî.* The preposition can be translated as a dependent clause using "for" or "because," or a temporal "when" or as an emphatic as above. It is difficult to determine exactly which meaning should be applied in these verses, but since it seems to be a structuring element, they should be translated with the same word in each case; contra NRSV, NIV, Tate, *Psalms 51–100,* p. 255; Kraus, *Psalms 60–150,* p. 102, and with Weiser, *The Psalms,* p. 520.

13. The problem here is that the plural form of *wilderness* and the *hiphil* infinitive construct of "to lift" are identical in form. Some scholars argue that the word is "mountains" to complete the geographical references (Dahood, *Psalms II,* p. 209; Weiser, *The Psalms,* p. 520). However, most read it as the *hiphil* infinitive construct since the word "to lift up" is central to this section of the psalm (Tate, *Psalms 51–100,* p. 257; Kraus, *Psalms 60–150,* p. 102; Hossfeld and Zenger, *Psalms 2,* p. 253; also NIV, NRSV, NJPS).

He will pour from it,
(and) surely its dregs they will drain.
All the wicked of the earth will drink.
9 *I, myself, will praise*[14] *forever;*
I will make music to the God of Jacob.

10 *All the horns of the wicked, I will cut off;*
but the horns of the righteous will be lifted up.

1 The first verse of the psalm has all the hallmarks of a community hymn of thanksgiving, with a shout of praise that an audience would expect to set the theme for the entire poem. Like a modern prayer of confession or opening collect, the words may vary but the form is so well known that everyone knows what should come next, and what should follow are the reasons for this praise and thanksgiving.[15] This opening verse makes it clear that this is a psalm of celebratory worship within a community.

2-3 The words of God interrupt the usual pattern in the form of an announcement, but the audience will have to deduce these are the words of God from the context, for the speaker is identified only as *I.*[16] Kraus notes that while the pattern is disorienting, it has theological purpose and the lack of introduction indicates that God will speak as God will and not on a schedule.[17]

The opening line tells the listener of *an appointed time* and place or an assembly, for the Hebrew word carries all of these meanings at once. It announces that the speaker will choose to "call" an event of great importance, possibly even a festival. The line announces the purpose of the event. The grammar makes the subject emphatic, placing the focus not on the action but the subject. *I will judge with equity.* It is still possible that the *I* of v. 2 is an elder or king, since both are given the responsibility of "judging" Israel.[18] Verse 3, however, clarifies the situation, for no mortal could manage to *steady* the

14. Following NRSV. The word in Hebrew usually means "to declare," but there is no direct object and "I will declare forever" is awkward in English. Tate adds "extraordinary deeds," taking the direct object from v. 1 (*Psalms 51–100,* p. 255). This is too much a departure from the MT, so *praise* is a better choice.

15. As noted by Westermann, *Praise and Lament in the Psalms,* p. 123.

16. Many scholars add here that the voice is one of an official or even a cultic prophet speaking for God (Tate, *Psalms 51–100,* p. 258; Mays, *Psalms,* p. 248; Clifford, *Psalms 73–150,* p. 27). This may well be the case in the setting of worship, but as with the prophets, the human person is not nearly as important as the words spoken.

17. Kraus, *Psalms 61–150,* p. 104.

18. Exod. 18:13-26 tells of elders appointed to "judge" Israel. Samuel calls a gathering at Mizpah for the purpose of judging Israel (1 Sam. 7:5-6). Psalm 72 attributes "judging" the people to the king. Certainly an official could declare this type of appointed time.

pillars of the earth. The image of connecting God's justice with God as Creator is a common one; indeed, it is one of the hallmarks of God as the Ruler of the Universe.[19] The first line of v. 3 is the chaos of humanity. But God's judgment/justice[20] will bring not more chaos but a stabilizing of the foundations of the world. Modern understanding of God's judgment is mainly pejorative. This psalm proclaims that "God's judgment" belongs in the place of praise-filled worship.[21] It is, indeed, good news for the servants of God.

4-9 The announcement of a time of judging that will bring stability is followed by preparation for that time. As noted above, many scholars think that God's words continue at least through v. 4, but there are several textual clues that show that this is the response to that announcement. First, this argument ignores the word *Selah* at the end of v. 4 which usually indicates the end of a section. Second, v. 4 opens with *I said,* and that is unusual in the middle of a speech section. In addition, when "I said" appears in the psalms, fourteen times it refers to the one praying[22] and only once does it refer to God.[23] These grammatical markers suggest that v. 4 opens a separate section. In addition, there are theological issues which also indicate a change of speaker here. An appointment with God always involves preparation, and that preparation usually involves warnings as in Exod. 19:9-15. The speaker here is probably a priest or official. A similar time of preparation is called by the king of Nineveh in Jonah 3:6-9.[24] This section is also tightly woven with a play on the words "lifting" and "lowering." The boastful are to stop boasting. The most common weapon of the wicked in the psalms is their own tongues. Speech is often malicious in the personal prayers for help or it appears as proof that the humans think they know more than God. The speech here could be either, setting oneself over others in the community or over God. Verses 4b and 5a use the metaphor of *lifting up your horn.* The horn, especially the lifting of the horn, is a symbol of dignity, power, and strength.[25] Yet in

19. God as king is often tied to God's administration of justice (e.g., Pss 82 and 99).

20. The word here is a form of *špṭ,* which means at one and the same time both judgment and justice. God's judging of the world is not vengeful but is meant to establish justice for all.

21. See also the enthronement psalms, esp. Pss. 96 and 98.

22. Pss. 30:6; 31:14; 32:5; 38:16; 40:7, 10; 41:4; 73:15; 89:2; 94:18; 116:11; 119:57; 140:6; 142:5.

23. This is probably an editorial addition; see Ps. 82.

24. Gerstenberger calls this section "Exhortation" and possibly a type of homiletical venture (*Psalms: Part 2,* p. 83). Jensen sees it as an exhortation based on God's oracle (p. 421). Jensen, however, connects the "boastful" and "wicked" to those same ones in Ps. 74 ("Psalm 75: Poetic Context and Structure," *CBQ* 63 [2001] 421), but this seems doubtful since this is addressed to the worshipping community and the ones in Ps. 74 are obviously outside invaders. It would seem more likely that this is a warning for the people to prepare to meet God.

25. 1 Sam. 2:1, 10; Lam. 2:17; Pss. 89:17, 24; 92:10; 112:9.

all other examples, it is God that causes a person's horn to be lifted. Here the admonishment concerns lifting one's own horn. The admonishment is to cease from "blowing your own horn." The final line reiterates this warning to the arrogant. The exact understanding may allude us, but it is obvious that it is related to the three lines above it. What is clear is that what is being warned against are specific types of behavior.

The next three verses explain why such behavior should be stopped. Verse 6a may refer back to vv. 4b-5a, implying that earthly things cannot *lift up* your horn. Indeed, this meaning could be a statement much like Isaiah gave to Ahaz about trusting foreign powers instead of God (Isaiah 7). Verse 7 returns to the announcement: it is God who judges and God who "lifts up" or brings down. Verse 8 continues the theme of judging/justice with a different metaphor. The *cup* of God's wrath is used in the prophets to indicate an approaching judgment.[26] The metaphor here is more visual, painting a picture of the foaming cup, possibly a representation of God's wrath, that will be completely emptied on the wicked.

Verse 9 offers a different way of life. Verses 4-8 may be the way of the wicked, "but as for me I will praise or declare forever and sing to the God of Jacob." The voice is made for praise instead of slander. There are two ways to live, and both will meet God at the appointed time — one with praise and the other with wicked intent.

10 As in some of the other sections, there is debate about the speaker in v. 10. It does not seem that the same speaker would speak so arrogantly, especially since the section above made clear that it is only God that raises up and lowers humans and there is no ancient textual evidence to change "I" to "he," as Kraus does,[27] or to argue that the speaker for the whole of this section is the king or some other official who will act for God and thus *cut off the horns of the wicked.*[28] It seems more probable that God has the last word here, confirming the praise of the people for God's great acts. The only reasonable alternative is that God again speaks a final summarizing word that affirms the announced preparations and consequences.

Psalm 74 spoke of a catastrophic situation where enemies were invading and God was not to be found. Psalm 75 provides an answer and thus completes the crisis of the previous psalm. If Book Three is indeed a reflection of the events of the divided monarchy, Israel and Judah both underwent a series

26. Isa. 51:17; Jer. 25:12; 49:12; 51:7; Ezek. 23:31-33; as here the drinking down to the dregs is often part of the saying.

27. Kraus, *Psalms 60–150,* p. 103.

28. This is offered by Eaton (*Kingship and the Psalms,* p. 56), but it is far from certain, especially since "holy war" usually involves initiation from God, not the king. While possible, it seems a stretch to attribute this to the king. Indeed, this may be an editorial addition that clearly makes the connection with Ps. 73 (esp. vv. 17-20 and 28).

of attacks from each other and from Assyria and finally from Babylon. The dark night of destruction would lift for a time, but the threat of destruction was never far away. Interestingly, this also reflects the early period of Israel where God would give them victory and the people would "do what was right in their own eyes" and be captured by others (Joshua and Judges). The pattern in Book Three is familiar and reminds all that God's return must be to a people who are faithful. God will not return to a sinful Israel, but only to one seeking true relationship.

This poem confirms, like Psalm 73, that there are two ways of life: one lived with God and one lived against God. This is as true today as it was to our ancient ancestors. What should be stressed here is that it is up to God to be the judge and to bring justice to the world. God's judgment is not a time of revenge nor a time for the ones who have chosen to dread. Indeed, the purpose is to lift the weak and lower the arrogant. This justice will still the tottering earth.

Beth Tanner

Psalm 76: God Is Supreme

Psalm 76 is a song of victory to the Lord, and as such many of its metaphors are military ones. Several scholars have attempted to tie this prayer to a historical battle, but a direct connection remains unproven. Likewise, even while the psalm has much in common with ancient poems such as Exodus 15 and Judges 5, there is nothing in its lines that would confirm a date of origin. The psalm, another one from the Asaph collection, fits well into this section of recurring community distress.[1] Here, as in periods of Israel's early history, God is seen as providing a victory for God's united people (v. 1). All is well again as God triumphs and is set as the king and judge of the world (v. 9).

The psalm is very focused with one subject, and each line reflects that main subject. In that, the psalm could be a unified piece, but there are ancient indicators of stanzas, and these give clear and logical dividing lines:[2]

vv. 1-3
vv. 4-9
vv. 10-12

For the leader. With stringed instruments.[3] *An Asaphic psalm.*[4] *A song.*

1 *In Judah, God is known;*[5]
in Israel, his name is great.
2 *His lair is set in Salem*
and his den in Zion.
3 *There he broke the flaming arrows of the bow,*[6]
shield and sword and war.[7] Selah.

1. Zenger notes this psalm shares many similarities with Pss. 46 and 48 and characterizes it as part of the Zion tradition (*Psalms 2,* p. 261).

2. Most scholars use these ancient stanza markers (Gerstenberger, *Psalms: Part 2;* Tate, *Psalms 51–100,* p. 263).

3. See note 13 on Psalm 4 superscription.

4. See note 7 on Psalm 73 superscription.

5. Tate notes that it is possible that these are both verbless clauses, with *nôḏāʿ* being an epithet for God, "The Renowned One is great in Israel" (*Psalms 51–100,* p. 260).

6. Many translations change this to "flashing arrows" (NIV, NRSV). The meaning of the first word is uncertain, but probably means a *flaming arrow* (*HALOT,* p. 1298).

7. Many argue that, based on this list, *milḥāmâ* must mean "weapons of war" (NIV; NRSV; Kraus, *Psalms 60–150,* p. 107; Tate, *Psalms 51–100,* p. 261). NJPS removes the *wāw,* making the phrase a construct "sword of war." But these changes are not necessary, and the line is readable in MT.

4 *You are shining forth,*[8]
more majestic than the everlasting mountains.[9]
5 *The strong of heart are despoiled;*[10]
they sleep their sleep.
All the men of valor are unable to find their hands.[11]
6 *At your rebuke, O God of Jacob,*
both chariot and horse lay sleeping.
7 *You! You are fearsome!*
and who can stand before you when you are angry?
8 *From the heavens you caused your justice to be heard;*
the earth was afraid and was still.
9 *When God rose to judge,*
to save all the poor of the land. Selah.

10 *For the anger of humans praises you;*
the remnant of the anger you will gird.[12]
11 *Make vows and fulfill them to the* Lord, *your God;*
let all the ones around him bear gifts to the Fearsome One,
12 *the one cutting off the breath of the princes,*
the Fearsome One to the kings of the earth.

1-3 Verse 1 focuses on the country and declares Judah and Israel for God's own. Being *known* means more than acknowledgment. In Hebrew it is a way of expressing intimate relationship. In contrast, the second line declares God's

8. The *niphal* participle appears only here. Tate (*Psalms 51–100,* p. 261) reads it as an epithet, "Resplendent One." Kraus (*Psalms 60–150,* p. 108) argues that it should be understood as from the root *yr'* and should be translated as "'Fearful' you are" (also Weiser, *The Psalms,* p. 524). LXX reflects MT, using "You shine forth." There is no compelling reason to alter the MT reading.

9. This line is problematic. *Ṭārep̱* ("prey") is thought by most to be a copyist error of another word for prey, *'aḏ* (Gen. 49:27; Isa. 33:23). The word *'aḏ* also means "forever," and this word is reflected in LXX and Syr as "everlasting mountains." Both readings are possible, and scholars and translations are divided, but *everlasting* seems to be the better choice since it has other ancient witnesses.

10. The *hithpoel* form of the verb appears only here, and in addition, it is corrupt: probably a transposition of *'ālep* for *yôd.* If *yôd* is used, the 3cpl form matches the subject. The other issue is if the *hithpael* form here is reflexive or passive. Within the context, the passive seems to be the only reasonable solution.

11. Following MT. Many translations use "lift their hands" (NRSV, NIV), but the text is clear and should be retained. Zenger concurs (*Psalms 2,* p. 259).

12. This verse is notoriously difficult and should probably be left untranslated. There are as many translations as there are translators. Since none of the many suggestions are more preferable than others, the above follows the MT without change.

name is great. In this way, this verse reflects both the intimate relationship between God and Israel and the clear reality that God is the supreme one in that relationship. Verse 2 turns to the place of God's home, which is located in *Salem* (Jeru*salem*) and *Zion.* In addition, the use of the words *lair* and *den* for God's home adds the metaphor of God as the lion, and that would make Israel and Judah part of God's protected territory.[13] Verse 3 seems out of place to a modern reader, but in its ancient context it declares that God's home is now a place of peace where the instruments of war have been destroyed.[14] This opening stanza declares that God is in control of the land of God's people and now the time of peace will begin.

4-9 The center section is a song to the Divine Warrior. It begins by declaring the majesty of God. There is some question about the translation of the *mountains* here, but no matter which words are used, God is seen as shining and majestic. Verses 5-6 describe how God was victorious over the enemy. The images may be a bit difficult to understand, but the overall message is clear. The most powerful of the warriors have been destroyed and now *sleep the sleep* of death.[15] After this victory, God is declared *fearsome.*[16] God then comes forth to *judge* the earth. This is also a common theme in the Divine Warrior texts. God judges the earth for the sake of *the poor of the land.*

10-12 Verse 10 could belong either to the second stanza or the third. But since v. 9 ends with the *Selah* marker, v. 10 is placed with the last stanza. Unfortunately, the verse is either corrupt or has an ancient meaning that is lost to the modern reader. Kraus follows Hans Schmidt and through some complex emendations changes the verse to "Indeed, fierce 'Edom' shall praise you, what is left of 'Hamath' 'shall celebrate you,'" arguing that as in other psalms after victory the Divine Warrior is then also praised by other nations.[17] The change is logical but hard to substantiate from the text of the MT. It is probably best to assume that the verse contributes to the theme of the sovereignty of God without understanding the exact metaphors used. The psalm ends with performing of *vows* and the bringing of *gifts* to the Lord, who has *cut off* all of the enemies.

A victory hymn such as this one can seem out of place and even offensive to modern ears. We have learned through countless wars the cost of destroying others. In addition, many believe that the Christian way is one of

13. The image of God as a lion appears several times in the prophetic texts (e.g., Amos 1:2; 3:8; Hos. 5:14; Isa. 31:4; 38:13; Jer. 4:7; 5:6; 25:30; 49:19).

14. As in Ps. 46.

15. The victory of the Divine Warrior here is much like Exod. 15:1-18.

16. Several modern translations use "awesome," and this is also a meaning for this word. However, within the context of the Divine Warrior *fearsome* is exactly what is meant. This warrior is someone to be afraid of unless one submits to God's rule.

17. Kraus, *Psalms 60–150,* p. 108.

tolerance and peace. One thing this psalm can do is force us to contemplate its words and images. They can lead us to truth-telling about our world, for we have almost never lived as tolerant and peaceful people. My mother is eighty-five years old, and in her lifetime this country has engaged in six wars, justified or not, and thousands upon thousands have died. This psalm praises not the human war machinery, but praises God's ability to bring war to an end (v. 3), declares that God is stronger than the most fierce of human fighters (vv. 5-7), and announces that God judges not by some arbitrary moral scale but to lift up *the poor of the land* (v. 9). In other words, nothing could be further from our modern war strategy than what is declared in this poem. It declares that kingdom beyond all of our human destruction and the place where all are cared for. The psalm declares that we are to put our trust in God and not in human war for our security. Yes, there are psalms that praise the Divine Warrior, yet in those psalms what is praised is not revenge or war for profit, but a kingdom where God is supreme and all who still wish to hurt and destroy others will be vanquished.

Beth Tanner

Psalm 77: I Remember the Deeds of the Lord

Psalm 77 is a prayer of movement, but the transitions from one stage to the next are not always clear. The prayer begins as a prayer for help, then moves to the distress of remembering, then to questions, then back to contemplation. But slowly the thoughts here are transformed from ones of pain to ones of wonder, and finally these thoughts give way to a hymn to the God of creation. Because some of the transitions are not clear, the division of the prayer into stanzas is different, depending on the interpreter.[1] Here using both the ancient stanza markers and thematic ones, the psalm can be divided into five stanzas:

St. 1 Cry to God (vv. 1-3)
St. 2 Description of distress (vv. 4-6)
St. 3 Questions to God (vv. 7-9)
St. 4 Reasoning through the problem (vv. 10-15)
St. 5 Hymn to the Creator God (vv. 16-20)

These stanzas move from despair to a hymn to God's greatness.

For the leader. According to Jeduthun.[2] *An Asaphic psalm.*[3]

1 *My voice unto God;*
I will cry out my voice unto God,
and he will give ear to me.
2 *In the day of my distress, I seek the Lord;*
at night, my hand is stretched out[4] *without wearying;*
I[5] *refuse to be comforted.*
3 *I remember God and I groan;*
I contemplate and my breath grows faint. Selah

4 *You keep my eyelids open;*[6]
I am disturbed and cannot speak.

1. Divisions range from three (McCann, "The Book of Psalms," p. 983) to six (Gerstenberger, *Psalms: Part 2,* p. 88).

2. See note 6 on Psalm 39 superscription.

3. See note 7 on Psalm 73 superscription.

4. *Ngr* means "to stretch out" only here. Usually it means "to pour out" or "be spilled," and this may represent the extent to which this one is reaching for God.

5. MT has *napšî,* which is often translated as "soul," but it has more of a meaning of self or the whole person than the more restrictive soul.

6. Lit., "you grasp the eyelids of my eyes," but it probably means that the person is kept from sleep.

5 *I contemplate the days past,*
years of long ago.
6 *I remember my songs*[7] *in the night;*
with my heart, I contemplate;
and I search[8] *my own self.*[9]

7 *Will the Lord reject forever*[10]
and never give favor again?
8 *Has his* hesed *ceased forever?*
Will his word[11] *fail for generation after generation?*
9 *Has God forgotten to be gracious?*
Has he in anger shut up his motherly compassion? Selah

10 *And I say, "My sickness is this,*[12]
the changing of the right hand of the Most High."
11 *I remember*[13] *the deeds of Yah;*
yes,[14] *I remember your wonders of old.*
12 *I reflect on all your work,*
and I contemplate your deeds.
13 *O God, your path is holy;*
what god is as great as God?[15]
14 *You are the God doing wonders;*
you made known your strength among the peoples.

7. *N^{e}gînāṯî* means, lit., "music," but *songs* makes the image clearer.

8. This line is problematic. The 1cs verb *contemplate* is followed by a 3ms piel verb and a feminine noun. Either the person or the number of the verb must be adjusted. Several ancient manuscripts including Syr adjust to 1cs, and based on the lines above, this change makes the most sense. Modern translations choose one or the other of these options.

9. *Rûḥî* does not mean "spirit" as a separate part of a person (see NRSV). Indeed, it can also mean "breath" and should probably be understood as parallel to *heart,* like "I search myself."

10. Many translations add "us," but the addition is unnecessary.

11. Many translations use "promises" for *'ōmer,* but God's *word* vanishing has even a more critical sense than promise. It implies that God has ceased to speak either a good or bad word; the conversation is over.

12. This line is problematic, as the plethora of English translations indicates. *Ḥallôṯî* appears as a *qal* only here and is obviously corrupt. The best suggestion is to read it as a *piel* infinitive with a 1cs suffix from the root *ḥlh,* meaning "to be sick" (Kraus, *Psalms 60–150,* p. 113).

13. Reading the Qere as a *qal* 1cs instead of the Kethib, *hiphil* 1cs.

14. *Kî* can have an emphatic function (Waltke and O'Connor, *Biblical Hebrew Syntax,* p. 665).

15. Many translations read "our God" following LXX, Syr, and Targ, but the change is unnecessary.

15 *You redeemed your people with a strong arm;*[16]
the descendants of Jacob and Joseph. Selah

16 *The waters saw you, O God;*
the waters saw you and they danced;
the very deep quaked.
17 *The clouds poured out water;*
the clouds gave voice;
your arrows shot back and forth.
18 *The voice of your thunder was in the whirlwind;*
your lightning bolts lit up the world;
the earth quaked and shook.
19 *Your path through the sea,*
your way through the great sea,
though your footprints were unknown.
20 *You led your people like a flock,*
through the hand of Moses and Aaron.

1-3 Most modern translations smooth out the jagged grammar of the opening verse, but a literal translation of the Hebrew better exemplifies the distress. Coherent speech has given way to sounds lifted to God. Yet even in distress, this is a prayer that is confident that God will hear (v. 1c). In the next two verses, the state of this one is further illuminated. In v. 2, the *seeking* of God and the *stretching out* of the arms in petition go on and on, even when there is no comfort. Verse 3 adds the mental anguish when memory is painful and contemplation brings a physical faintness. The physical feelings of distress are ones that all who have suffered understand.[17]

This first section also introduces a central theme for the first sixteen verses, that of thinking or contemplating. Ten times synonyms for thinking will be used. The process of thinking will tie these verses together, both causing the problem and providing the solution.

4-6 The next section continues to describe the distress of suffering. Verse 4 again states the inability to *speak* and adds the inability to sleep. Verse 5 returns to thinking as the *past* is recalled. Verse 6 is another verse that is

16. MT does not have the 2ms suffix on *arm,* but other ancient manuscripts do (LXX, Syr, Targum). However, MT is understandable as it is.

17. As translated here, the psalm indicates that the pain is concurrent with the words. Unfortunately, the Hebrew language is not so clear, and the verbs could be translated either as concurrent or in the past tense. Reading the verbs here in the past tense, some scholars have identified this psalm as one of "thanksgiving," as John Gray does in "The Kingship of God in the Prophets and Psalms," *VT* 11 (1961) 9. However, the language of suffering is so intense here it would seem to be a concurrent happening.

smoothed out in modern translations, but in the Hebrew there is no direct object for the contemplation and the seeking. Just like the inability to speak coherently, the ability to think clearly and logically is impossible. The heart contemplates and seeks something within but exactly what is unknown. The lack of objects reflects the state of mind.

7-9 The next stanza finally reports the what, and the what is painful to read. A series of rhetorical questions replace the descriptions of physical pain with the pain thinking brings. The attributes that have disappeared are comprehensive of all of the gifts God offers the human: *favor* and *hesed,* graciousness and *motherly compassion.*[18] These attributes are what has been the foundation of the relationship with God, and it seems as if all of them are no longer apparent. Even God's *word* has disappeared from the generations. To further increase the pain, this abandonment may continue even onto those yet unborn (v. 8). Notice also that the problem is God. There are no enemies threatening as in so many of the prayers for help. God and God alone is the problem that weighs heavily here.

10-15 The division of these six verses is heavily debated, and that division impacts exactly how this prayer is finally to be understood. Many see a break between vv. 10 and 11, arguing that this is where the cries end and the praise begins.[19] However, the whole of vv. 10-15 can also be seen as a more nuanced transition.[20] Verse 10 begins just as vv. 1-9 do. The sickness is not a physical problem, but that God seems to have turned away. The verse is difficult, but the *right hand* of God is usually something that protects.[21] Here the right hand has "changed." We would probably say "turned," but nevertheless, the problem seems to be the same. Verse 11 begins with the same word as vv. 3 and 6, so one hearing this prayer would expect another description of distress. The first line leaves the reader in suspense, still expecting distress. Verses 11b and 12 continue the tension as God's works of old are recalled, but the purpose for these recollections remains unstated.

Finally, the turn arrives at v. 13, when it is clear that this period of contemplation has produced new thoughts of God's greatness and *strength* and redemption. Something has changed but what exactly has changed is not told. It is up to the one who hears to decide how this time thoughts brought praise instead of depression and fear. Walter Brueggemann notes that this psalm is dominated by *I* until v. 13, where there is a transformation to *You*

18. See Exod. 34:6, where three of the four appear. This is what Israel has confessed about their God and how God acts toward them.

19. See, e.g., McCann, "The Book of Psalms," p. 984; or Gerstenberger, *Psalms: Part 2,* p. 89.

20. Kraus, *Psalms 60–150,* p. 115; Hossfeld and Zenger, *Psalms 2,* p. 275.

21. E.g., Pss. 17:7; 18:35; 20:6; 44:3; 63:8; 73:23.

that remains until the end of the work. This transition represents for him a movement from the "preoccupation with self to a submission to and reliance upon God."[22] Here the poetry invites all who listen to decide how one can make such a change in their thinking.

16-20 The recalling of God's great wonders gives way without warning to a hymn where creation dances at the sight of their God. The psalm as a whole moves from despair and a fear of God's abandonment to a new kind of thinking, remembering instead God's great acts and wonders. This remembering becomes a song where a giant thunderstorm is seen as a great symphony and light show to the Creator, used to tell of God's greatness (vv. 16-19). The song ends with a final verse of praise for the one who led the people in the wilderness.

This psalm can seem chaotic, and the ending ode to God by the creation seems out of place. But what this psalm reminds us is that everything, a lone person searching for God, questioning absence, and coming to a new understanding of God, is part of life lived as a creature of the Creator. Just as the creation responds in its way, humans respond in theirs. Doubt can give way to telling of God's great acts in the past. But moreover, the song remembers that God calls on creation as the method of liberating the people. God's gift and control of the creation is a blessing that always surrounds us. When life feels chaotic, God's control of the universe holds firm. So with a change in perspective, my own situation in the world seems different, not because anything external has changed but because I have changed. This distinction makes Psalm 77 unique, for it is not concerned with external enemies or even the sin of the one crying to God. It speaks instead of a theological crisis and how these crises are often sorted out, not with direct answers to human questions but with a remembering and thus an altered understanding of humans and God. This lesson is as applicable today as it was to our ancient ancestors.

Book Three narrates a time of uncertainty, and this prayer certainly fits within that rubric. This one looks back on God's great acts in the past and wonders why God refuses to act in the present. Times of crises create these thoughts. Who has not read the miracles in the Bible and wondered the same thing? Times of crises push each of us through the process in this psalm. The situation may not change, so our thinking about God and humans and the way the universe works needs to change. Transformation is often not dramatic but comes in the night when one tosses and turns, trying to discern one's place in the universe and what it means to belong to God.

BETH TANNER

22. "Psalm 77: The 'Turn' from Self to God," *Journal for Preachers* 6 (1983) 8.

Psalm 78: A Teachable History

Psalm 78 is a unique piece of literature. It could be understood as a historical psalm like Psalms 105, 106, and 136; however, it should not be understood as simply a recitation of historical happenings. It is shaped in a particular way to teach a particular lesson: that of the cost of disobedience to the Lord and what that faithlessness has cost Israel.[1] The lesson is clear, but what is not clear to scholars is when this particular psalm was written and used. The issue of the psalm's date has taken up the bulk of the articles written on the psalm, and dating opinions range from the tenth century during the period of David and Solomon, to the period of Josiah's reforms, to the exilic and postexilic periods.[2] The issue of when the psalm appeared in Israel is yet unresolved. It is certainly possible that this poem was used and reused in the life of the community, making all of the these dates possible.

Since the psalm tells a specific history, it has a unity or flow that has made it difficult to divide into clear stanzas. It does have some duplication of ideas, but for the most part, the psalm is one continuous text. Richard Clifford, using rhetorical analysis, has developed a useful stanza division:[3]

- A three-part introduction (vv. 1-11)
- First recital: wilderness events (vv. 12-39)
  - God's acts (vv. 12-16)
  - Rebellion (vv. 17-20)
  - God's response (vv. 21-31)
  - God's grace (vv. 32-39)
- Second recital: Egypt and Jerusalem (vv. 40-72)
  - God's acts (vv. 40-55)
  - Rebellion (vv. 56-58)
  - God's response (vv. 59-64)
  - God's grace (vv. 65-72)

1. Anthony Campbell notes it is this very perspective that separates this psalm from the other historical ones; "Psalm 78: A Contribution to the Theology of Tenth Century Israel," *CBQ* 41 (1979) 62.

2. Campbell argues for a tenth-century date. Weiser argues that the psalm was written after the fall of the northern kingdom in 722 B.C.E. (*The Psalms,* p. 540). Kraus sees it as part of Deuteronomic influence (*Psalms 61–150,* p. 124). Adele Berlin argues that the psalm should be dated post-586 ("Psalms and the Literature of Exile," in Flint and Miller, *The Book of Psalms,* p. 78).

3. Clifford, *Psalms 73–150,* p. 43. The stanza division here is altered some from Clifford's.

An Asaphic[4] *maskil.*[5]

1 *Give ear, my people, to my teaching;*
incline your ears to the words of my mouth.
2 *I will open my mouth in a parable;*
I will pour out a riddle of old.
3 *What we have heard and known,*
that our fathers recounted to us,
4 *We will not hide them*[6] *from their children,*
telling to future generations
the praises of the LORD,
his strength and his wonders that he has done.
5 *He set up statutes for Jacob,*
and teachings he established in Israel,
which he commanded our ancestors
to make known to their children.
6 *So the next generation might know them,*
the children yet to be born,
and they rise up and recount [the story] to their children;
7 *then*[7] *they would set their confidence in God*
and not forget the deeds of God
and keep his commandments
8 *and not be like their ancestors,*
a stubborn and rebellious generation,
a generation that did not steady its heart
and their spirit was not faithful to God.
9 *The Ephraimites armed*[8] *with shooting bows*
were turned back on the day of battle;
10 *they did not keep the covenant,*
and they refused to walk according to his teaching;
11 *they forgot his deeds and his wonders that he had shown them.*

4. See note 7 on Psalm 73 superscription.

5. See note 2 on Psalm 32 superscription.

6. The direct object is missing in MT, and modern translations add it without a note. MT reads "we will not hide from their children," and this is puzzling since until now the words are directed to the second person "you."

7. Unlike v. 6, the marker here is a simple *wāw* that follows markings in MT indicating the end of a section. Most modern translations assume the *lᵉmaʿan* governs both verses, with or without a period at the end of v. 6.

8. Multiple Hebrew manuscripts transpose the MT's *nôšqê* to *nôqšê.* 11QPs[d] supports MT; Ulrich, Cross, et al., *Qumran Cave 4: XI,* p.74.

12 *Before their ancestors he did wonders,*[9]
in the land of Egypt, the fields of Zoan;
13 *he split the sea and caused them to pass through;*
and he caused the waters to stand like a heap.
14 *He led them by a cloud in the day*
and all the night by a fiery light;
15 *he split rocks in the wilderness;*
and he caused them to drink abundantly as from the deep;
16 *he caused streams to flow from a rocky crag;*
and he caused waters to come down like a river.

17 *They continued to sin against him,*
to rebel against the Most High in the desert;
18 *they tested God in their heart,*
asking for the food they wanted;[10]
19 *they spoke against God, saying,*
"Is God able to set a table in the wilderness?
20 *True! He struck a rock,*
and water gushed out and streams overflowed;
but is he able to give bread,
or can he provide meat?"

21 *When the* Lord *heard, he was angry,*
and fire was kindled against Jacob,
and his anger rose against Israel
22 *because they did not have faith in God;*
they did not trust in his salvation.
23 *He commanded the clouds above,*
and he opened the doors of heaven,
24 *and he rained on them manna to eat;*
the grain of heaven he gave to them.
25 *Humans ate the bread of valiant ones;*[11]
food he sent to them in abundance;
26 *he set an east wind in the heavens;*
and he led the south wind by his strength;
27 *and he rained meat down on them like dust,*

9. *Pele',* lit., "a wonder," as a singular noun. It is a plural participle in v. 11 above. The plural is used here also.

10. *Napšām,* lit., "their soul," but can also mean passion or desire (Ezek. 24:25) or a craving (Hos. 4:8).

11. Most modern translations follow LXX and substitute "angels" here, but this is misleading and interjects a later theological construct into the Hebrew culture.

flying birds like the sand of the seas,
28 *making them fall inside his camp,*[12]
surrounding his dwelling place.[13]
29 *They ate and were well satisfied,*
for he gave them what they wanted.
30 *Before their desire was satisfied,*
with food still in their mouths,
31 *the anger of God came up against them;*
he killed their nobles;[14]
he brought down the young men of Israel.

32 *Despite all of this, they sinned again;*
they did not believe in his wonders;
33 *so he made their days vanish like a breath,*
their years in terror.
34 *If he killed them, they sought him;*
and they would turn back and look earnestly for God;
35 *they remembered because God was their rock,*
and God Most High, their redeemer.
36 *But they deceived him with their mouths;*
and with their tongues they lied to him;
37 *their heart was not steadfast on him;*
and they were not faithful to his covenant.
38 *But he is compassionate,*
covering iniquity and does not destroy,
often turning back his anger and not raising up all his wrath;
39 *he remembered that they were flesh,*
a breath passing and not returning.

40 *How often they grieved him in the wilderness,*
and they caused him pain in the desert.
41 *They turned back and they tested God;*
they pained the Holy One of Israel;
42 *they did not remember his hand,*[15]
the day he ransomed them from the foe,

12. Many modern translations follow LXX and use "their camp," but the change is unnecessary since it could easily be considered God's camp.

13. As above, the camp can belong to God since it is God that is leading them.

14. Lit., "in their fatness." Fatness has a positive meaning of nobility or strength, as indicated in a related Arabic word.

15. NIV and NRSV read as "power." The Hebrew word is clearly *yaḏô,* or "hand." God's hand does represent God's power, but the change is unnecessary.

43 when he set his signs in Egypt,
his wonders in the field of Zoan.
44 He turned their rivers to blood;
they could not drink of their streams.
45 He sent among them a swarm, and it devoured them,
and frogs, they ruined them.
46 He gave their produce to the grasshopper,
their toil to the locusts.
47 He killed their vines with hail,
their sycamore trees with frost.[16]
48 He gave over their cattle to hail,
their flocks to thunder bolts.
49 He sent his burning anger among them,
fury and indignation and distress,
a band of destroying messengers.[17]
50 He leveled a path for his anger;
he did not spare them from death;
he delivered the living to the plague.
51 He smote all the firstborn of Egypt,
the firstfruits of their vigor in the tents of Ham.
52 He led out his people like sheep
and drove them in the wilderness like a flock.
53 He led them to safety
so they were not in dread;
and the sea overwhelmed their enemies.
54 He brought them to his holy territory,
this mountain his right hand had gotten.
55 He drove out nations before them;
and he apportioned territory as a possession
and settled the tribes of Israel in their tents.

56 They tested and they rebelled against God Most High,
and his decrees they did not guard.
57 They turned away and acted faithlessly like their ancestors;
they failed like a treacherous bow.
58 They angered him with their high places;
and with their idols they made him jealous.

16. This word appears only here, so its meaning is uncertain. LXX uses "frost," whereas *HALOT* suggests "devastating flood" (p. 334).

17. Many modern translations follow the LXX's "angels," but this change from *messengers* is unnecessary and introduces a later theological construct to the Hebrew text.

59 God heard and he was angry;
he completely rejected Israel.
60 He forsook his dwelling place at Shiloh,
a tent where he dwelled with humans.
61 He gave his power to captivity
and his splendor to the hand of the foe.
62 He delivered his people to the sword;
and he was angry with his inheritance.
63 Fire devoured their young men;
their maidens were not praised;
64 their priests fell by the sword;
their widows did not lament them.

65 The Lord awoke as from sleep,
like a strong man from the stupor of wine.
66 He smote his adversaries from behind;
he gave them everlasting reproach.
67 He rejected the tent of Joseph;
and the tribe of Ephraim he did not choose.
68 He chose the tribe of Judah,
Mount Zion which he loves.
69 He built his sanctuary like high places;
like the earth he established forever.
70 He chose David his servant;
and he took him from the sheepfolds;
71 from after the nursing ewes he brought him,
to shepherd Jacob his people
and Israel his inheritance;
72 and he shepherded them with his upright heart;
with skillful hands he led them.

1-11 The three-part opening sets the stage for what is to follow. Verses 1-4 state the purpose: to tell future generations of God's *strength and wonders* (v. 4). This is important to remember, because some of the lines of this poem are fierce and tell truths about human disobedience that make it hard to remember this is a song of praise to the Lord. The second introduction opens at v. 5 and is much like vv. 1-4, stressing that this story should be told to each *generation* so they too *would set their confidence in God.* The last "because" appears in v. 8. Until now, the reasons for the story were all positive. Verse 8 reminds that this lesson is also a warning, to learn from the ancestors not only what to do, but what not to do. Verses 9-11 tell the same story as v. 8, but here the acts of the ancestors are more specific. The *Ephraimites* were a northern tribe known for their fierceness in *battle.*[18] This incident does not match any battle recorded in the Bible, but the point is not historical accuracy, but that they did not keep the covenant (v. 10). The introduction ends with the complete failure of the Israelites; their heart is not steady (v. 8) and *they did not keep the covenant* (v. 10).[19]

12-39 Richard Clifford has noted a type of flow through the two major sections of history-telling that make helpful subdivisions. He notes that the sections begin with God's gracious acts (vv. 12-16), then move to rebellion (vv. 17-20); and divine anger and punishment (vv. 21-31), followed by a type of summary (vv. 32-39).[20]

Verses 12-16 give a poetic summary of the crossing of the sea and some of the wilderness period. The section is tied directly to the introduction by the use of *wonders* (vv. 11 and 12). The verbs used make the point clear: all appear in the *hiphil* except for three ("did in" v. 12; and "split" in vv. 13 and 15). God is the cause of the acts of creation in control of the waters and of the humans in God's leading through the wilderness.

Verses 17-20 report the people's response to these wonders; *they continued to sin against him* (v. 17). These lines tell a similar story to Exod. 16:1-3; 17:1-7 and Num. 11:1-15; 20:2-13. Even after seeing some of God's wonders with their own eyes, they still do not believe that God can *set a table in the wilderness* (v. 19). Indeed, the people even taunt God (v. 20).

Verses 21-31 describe God's response to the disobedience of the people. At first, the poem is confusing. Verse 21 describes God's anger, and v. 22 gives the reason for that anger. After this introduction, one expects that God speaking to the *clouds* and the *heavens* will not bode well for the unfaithful ones. Verse 23 builds suspense as we wait to see what God is going to do. Verses 24-29 come as a surprise. God's response in anger is to give the people exactly what they asked for in the first place. Verses 30-31 take the hearers in a surprising direction. Much like the story in Numbers 11, God gave them what they asked for as part of the lesson.[21] Verse 31 is clearly God's action against the unfaithful ones. Out of context, it can seem harsh. Verses 33-39 further place God's actions in context. Despite food from heaven and destruction of some, God's chosen ones still did not believe. Even God's wrath does not convince this people, and here it is important to remember what came before, for first

18. Tate, *Psalms 51–100,* p. 289.

19. Notice that the community shares a collective *heart.* This speaks to the way the ancient people thought of themselves — not as autonomous humans, but as a community of people.

20. Richard Clifford, "In Zion and David a New Beginning: An Interpretation of Psalm 78," in *Traditions in Transformation. Turning Points in Biblical Faith,* ed. Baruch Halpern and Jon D. Levenson (Winona Lake: Eisenbrauns, 1981), pp. 121-41.

21. Clifford has made a similar observation; "In Zion and David," p. 133.

there was God's care and provision that the people mocked (v. 20). Verse 34 notes God's problem with the people. God could offer them all good things and they would turn away, ignore the gifts, or doubt God's continuing power to provide. But if God *killed them, they sought him* (v. 34). God is caught up in the matter and has found that destruction is what keeps the people close — certainly a puzzlement for a God who is gracious. But even then, the people quickly *turn back* away (vv. 36-38). Finally, God's problem must be fixed in God's own heart (vv. 38-39).

40-42 These verses could certainly be seen as a continuation of the description of God's dilemma, and indeed they are, but they can also serve as an introduction to the next section where the people again turn away from God. Indeed if Clifford is right, the whole story will be repeated again with the escape from Egypt and the taking of the land as the examples.

43-55 The poem here begins in *Egypt,* with God's *signs* and *wonders,* and tells of the plagues sent on Egypt. Because this list of plagues does not match the ones in the exodus account, there has been a great deal of scholarly attention given to it, especially to bolster dating arguments. Tate sums it up correctly: "It is much more probable that the plague traditions were relatively fluid and malleable enough to be fashioned in different ways for different contexts. The exact details of the plagues were not a matter of great concern. What mattered most was the impact of the account."[22] The impact here is to stress again what God had done to save the Israelites from their captors and to demonstrate that God's weapon is the creation. This tells all listening that God is truly the Creator, for creation obeys God's command.

52-55 This section summarizes the postexodus leading of the people. It skips what vv. 12-16 covered of God's care in the wilderness. Here the people are *led out* (vv. 52-53) and led into a new territory (vv. 54-55).

56-58 In familiar pattern, the people's response to God's gift is ingratitude. The verses are a parallel to vv. 17-20. Again they *tested* and *rebelled against* God. This time their disobedience comes from their worship of other gods (v. 58). The people have found a new way to grieve God.

59-64 Just as in the first recital, vv. 59-64 give God's response to the people. Unlike the first time, there is no suspense. Here God is so fed up that God chooses to leave (vv. 59-60), and this results in the destruction of the people (vv. 61-64). Israel, without God, cannot stand up to its enemies.

65-72 The end of the psalm can be seen as a parallel to the way the relationship continues as in vv. 33-39, but the mix of historical happenings is interesting. If the poem followed the history, one would expect either the story of Judges or Saul's campaign against the Philistines. However, the poem skips to the selection of *David* as king and *Zion* as God's sanctuary. The poem

22. Tate, *Psalms 51–100,* p. 293.

may skip some history, but it ends with the establishment of the nation. The psalm began as *praises* to God (v. 4), and it is time to remember that beginning. This poem ultimately is not about the divisions and issues between the northern tribes *(Ephraim)* and the southern tribes *(Judah),* but it reflects the frustrated and tortured way that God's grace and love went on, even in the face of constant disobedience from the ones God chose to love. It is about God working out why the people will not accept God's gifts to them in the wilderness and of the land and love God with all their hearts and follow the covenant. It is about God trying to figure out why the people only return when God destroys (vv. 30-31, 60-64). It is about God finding a way to have relationship with a humanity that *grieves* and *causes God pain* (v. 40). Psalm 78 is not one of the penitential psalms, but maybe it should be, because it tells of God's great passion for humans, even when those humans turn away. It also tells the sad story of human determination to ignore the good gifts of God and to remember God only when the way becomes hard or violent.

The lesson set in Book Three offers another reflection piece, just as Psalm 77 did. Here, instead of seeing it from the struggles of the humans, it shows the long, long struggle that God has had with humanity. It takes the learnings of Psalm 77 and pushes them even further. To begin really to understand, one must see both parties in the relationship. One must understand God's frustration and God's efforts to love and offer grace. One must contemplate why the people of God turn away from God's great gifts and only respond to God's anger. A more nuanced and complex theology is created in Book Three as these poems are contemplated.

This message of history is as relevant today as it was for the ancient Israelites. We could easily substitute our history of warfare and our desire to claim the good things in the world as of our own making. We too pain God with what we do and what we do not do. We too need to learn from the actions of our ancestors so that we can be faithful to God and choose to be a thankful people and not turn aside. We too need to see the relationship from the side of God to understand the life-long relationship we share with God and to understand as this psalm teaches that God is involved and wrapped up in a very real way in this relationship with us.

BETH TANNER

Psalm 79: Help Us, God of Our Salvation

Psalm 79 is a community cry for help. The cry comes from a national disaster brought on by other nations. Verse 1 certainly gives the impression that the national crisis is the destruction in 586 B.C.E., but there are several incidents where Jerusalem is threatened both before and after the destruction of the temple. The central point is the conversation with God about the disaster, not necessarily the exact nature of the threat. There is no doubt, however, that the threat is grave, as vv. 2 and 3 indicate. Schaefer also notes the speed of this downturn: "Psalm 78:68-69 ends with the sanctuary in Jerusalem and David's election, and Ps 79:1-3 opens with the devastation of Jerusalem."[1]

The form of the poem is interesting. Tate notes that many of the verses in the psalm appear in other pieces as well.[2] This fact demonstrates that Israel had a language of prayer that could be used in different constructions to address a multitude of circumstances. This may be one of the reasons why the psalm is divided in several different ways. Most scholars divide it into three sections, with some making the first section end at v. 4,[3] while others argue that the first division is between vv. 5 and 6.[4] This division hinges on whether the questions to God in v. 5 close the first section or open the second. Either is possible, but there is a cycle of petitions in the second section, and as will be shown below, v. 5 probably opens this section.

Description of the distress (vv. 1-4)
Pleas and petitions to God (vv. 5-12)
Vow of praise (v. 13)

An Asaphic psalm.[5]

1 *O God, the nations have come into your inheritance;*
they have defiled your holy temple;
they have laid Jerusalem in ruins.

1. Schaefer, *Psalms,* p. 194.

2. V. 1, see Jer. 26:18 and Mic. 3:12; v. 4, see Ps. 44:14; v. 5, see Pss. 6:3; 13:1; 89:46; vv. 6-7, see Jer. 10:25; v. 8c, see Pss. 116:6; 142:6; v. 9d, see Pss. 23:3; 25:11; 31:3; 54:1; 106:8; 109:21; 143:11; v. 10ab, see Pss. 115:2; 42:3; Joel 2:17; v. 11a, see Ps. 102:20; v. 11c, see 1 Sam. 26:16; v. 12, see Pss. 89:51-52; 44:13; Gen. 4:24; Lev. 26:18 (*Psalms 51–100,* pp. 299-300).

3. Kraus, *Psalms 60–150,* p. 133; Gerstenberger, *Psalms: Part II,* p. 100; Hossfeld and Zenger, *Psalms 2,* p. 303.

4. Tate, *Psalms 51–100,* p. 300; McCann, "The Book of Psalms," p. 995.

5. See note 7 on Psalm 73 superscription.

2 *They gave the corpses of your servants*[6]
as food for the birds of the heavens,
the flesh of your devoted ones to the wild animals of the land.
3 *They poured out their blood like water*
all around Jerusalem;
and there was no one to bury them.
4 *We have become a reproach to our neighbors,*
of scorn and derision to those around us.

5 *How long, O LORD?*
Will you be angry forever?
Will your indignation[7] *burn forever?*
6 *Pour out your wrath on the nations*
that do not know you,
and the kingdoms that do not call upon your name,
7 *for they devoured*[8] *Jacob*
and destroyed his habitation.
8 *Do not remember against us our former iniquities;*
let your motherly compassion come quickly to meet us,
for we are very low.
9 *Help us, God of our salvation,*
for the glory of your name.
Deliver us and forgive our sins,
for your name's sake.
10 *Why do the nations say, "Where is your God?"*
Let it be known among the nations to our eyes
the retribution of the outpouring of blood of your servant.
11 *Let the cries of the prisoners*[9] *come before you;*
by your great arm
spare the ones condemned to death.[10]
12 *Return to our neighbors sevenfold into their bosoms*

6. MT has the singular "corpse of your servant," but LXX uses the plural. MT is probably indicating a collective plural for Israel.

7. Many modern translations use "jealousy." This is an acceptable word for the Hebrew. However, in our culture the word has become pejorative and thus is often misunderstood. NJPS also uses "indignation."

8. MT has the 3ms form of the verb. LXX and multiple other manuscripts have the 3mpl, as here.

9. MT has the singular "cry of the prisoner," as does LXX. MT is probably indicating a collective plural for Israel, but it could also be the king that is intended here.

10. *Bᵉnê tᵉmûṯâ* (lit., "sons of death").

the reproach that they gave to you,[11] *O Lord!*

13 *We are your people, the flock of your pasture;*
We will give praise to you forever;
generation to generation we will recount your praise.

1-4 The opening verses are a description of a catastrophic event, but the description is also meant as a motivation for God to act. Verse 1 opens with a description of what the nations have done to God's home: first, to the *temple* and second, to *Jerusalem,* both of which are God's *inheritance.* Verses 2-3 tell of the fate of the people in the language of *your servants* and *your devoted ones,* further reminding God of their relationship. Verse 4 sums up the overall condition after the fact, and here it changes to *we* language, stressing the state of God's chosen ones.

5-12 This central section consists of petitions to God. These petitions alternate between petitions for God to act for God's people and for God to act against the enemies. This movement from one type of petition to the other is disorienting and dissolves the common patterns in these types of prayers.

Verse 5 begins with the fear that God was and still is angry with the people, and this is the cause of their disaster. This question of *how long* is often followed by a reminder for God to *remember* or *forgive* (see Pss. 80:4 or 89:46). This expected reason for God to restore God's people is in the prayer, but appears in vv. 8 and 9. Verse 6 interrupts the expected flow. This pattern of alternating pleas is the distinguishing mark of this section. The unexpected pattern reflects the state of the people. Their plight is so dire that the pleas come, not in the usual form, but in a jagged fashion indicating the disoriented thinking that comes when disaster hits. Familiar patterns, even of prayer, are disturbed in times of great turmoil.

Verse 5 asks *how long* God will *be angry.* The verse, however, is without a direct object, so the cause of the anger is not specified. Again, an unusual form signals unusual circumstances. Verse 6 asks for God's *wrath* to *pour out* against the other nations, immediately after God is asked to stop being angry in v. 5. The effect is again disorienting. Verse 7 follows and gives the reason why God should be angry with others. Verse 8, as noted above, continues the thought of v. 5. The poem asks God to *forgive,* for the people are *very low.* Verse 9 pleads for God's *help.* Verse 10 continues the theme of vv. 7-8 and reminds God that these other nations do not know God. Verse 11 returns to direct pleas to God for rescue for the prisoners. Verse 12 is a final plea for God to repay the nations sevenfold for the way they have treated God. The pleas are clear and the form

11. Lit., "the reproach that they reproached you." The Hebrew stem system allows for an intensification with the direct object and verb that is difficult to translate into English.

is regular, so that if the psalm's verses were rearranged into a more typical arrangement there would be nine pleas for God to rescue (vv. 5, 8-9, and 11) and eight pleas against the other nations (vv. 6-7, 10, and 12).[12] The effect is to demonstrate the great difficulty that God needs to put right.

13 The final verse is equally disorienting. Pleas for salvation and payback give way without warning not only to *praise,* but praise that continues for generations into the great *forever.* It is the perfect definition of hope. In this moment of suffering, a new situation can barely be imagined. However, Israel's long history with God tells a story that even in the darkest of days, there is a future with God for the people. As Tate notes, in a psalm so filled with the pallor of destruction and pain, the last word of the psalm is *tᵉhillāṯeḵâ, your praise,*[13] making the last twist the most surprising of all.

This psalm returns to the same place as Psalm 74. The people are in dire crisis, and again, God's city and God's people are in ruins. It seems the history lesson in the previous psalm did not have the desired effect. This cycle of psalms reflects the history of God's people. The people cry out to be rescued and at the same time want those that hurt them to be hurt, for a moment forgetting the ways they also grieve God (Psalm 78). It may not be pretty, but it is the human condition.

Unfortunately, most can relate to a psalm of national distress. Wars, terror attacks, and individual acts of mass killings have caused all to cry to God in the midst of national mourning. We all know the dual cries of desire for rescue from our situation mixed with desires for payback. This poem offers a look at the feelings surrounding loss and our very human desire to see those who *gave the corpses of your servants as food for the birds* to receive *sevenfold* what has been done to us. This psalm looks into the depths of our souls and tells it exactly as it is. We might think this is "un-Christian," for it tells of anger and a desire for revenge, but we too have had those feelings. But it also tells in a final quick burst another way of looking beyond fear and desire for retribution. It tells of praise and it encourages us, no matter how long it may take, to make praise the last word to God. It teaches that praise will eventually replace words of hurt and pain.

BETH TANNER

12. Scholars often rearrange the verses and discuss them as groups, as here (Hossfeld and Zenger, *Psalms 2,* p. 307), but this method obscures the very structure of the poem that in and of itself describes distress.

13. Tate, *Psalms 51–100,* p. 301.

Psalm 80: God, Bring Us Back

Psalm 80 continues the same theme of the psalms immediately before it, the faithfulness of God in the midst of great loss. It is another cry of the people to God, yet this time there are no cries against others, only cries for God to restore and bring back the people. The psalm uses a juxtaposition of very formal names for God (LORD and/or God of Hosts, vv. 4, 7, 14 and 19) along with the familial claim of Israel *as the child you, yourself, caused to grow strong* (vv. 15 and 17), demonstrating both the power and the personal nature of God.

The psalm is usually divided into four stanzas. Three of these divisions are almost universally agreed upon, but the third one is debated.[1]

Opening (vv. 1-3)
The current situation (vv. 4-7)
God's involvement then and now (vv. 8-13)[2]
Restore us (vv. 14-19)

Several scholars argue that the psalm was composed in two layers, with the lament sections reflecting an earlier northen kingdom perspective, while the later-added refrain reflects a Jerusalem perspective.[3] This may be the case, but the psalm should be read as a whole message and understood as a reflection on a period when the people realized that their relationship with God had become dangerously strained.

For the leader. On shushan eduth.[4] *An Asaphic psalm.*[5]

1 *O Shepherd of Israel, hear us!*
You who lead Joseph like a flock,
you who dwell on the cherubim,[6] *shine forth.*

1. Vv. 3, 7, and 19 contain a refrain, and although it uses different names for God, it serves as the end of these stanzas.

2. This is the division that is not universally agreed on. Gerstenberger (*Psalms: Part 2,* p. 103) and Kraus (*Psalms 60–150,* pp. 142-43) see the break between vv. 15 and 16. Tate sees it between 16a and 16b (*Psalms 51–100,* p. 308). Zenger divides the psalm between vv. 13 and 14, noting as I have above that each section follows a pattern: appeal to God, lament, and petition (Zenger, *Psalms 2,* p. 309).

3. Zenger, *Psalms 2,* p. 311.

4. Meaning of this Hebrew phrase is unknown. Some translate "On Lilies, a Covenant" (NRSV) or "To the Tune of the Lilies of the Covenant" (NIV).

5. See note 7 on Psalm 73 superscription.

6. Each line begins with a participle which probably is nominative and should be

2 *Before Ephraim and Benjamin and Manasseh,*
awaken your strength!
Come to save us!
3 *O God, bring us back;*
make your face shine and we will be saved.

4 *LORD, God of Hosts,*
how long will your anger be kindled by the prayers of your people?
5 *You have caused them to eat the bread of tears;*
you caused them to drink tears in triple.[7]
6 *You have set us as strife*[8] *to our neighbors;*
and our enemies mock us.
7 *O God of Hosts, return us;*
make your face to shine and we will be saved.

8 *You plucked up a vine from Egypt;*
you drove out the nations and planted it.
9 *You turned its surface,*
the root rooted;[9]
and it filled the land.
10 *The mountains were covered with its shade;*
and its branches, the mighty cedars.
11 *It sent out its branches to the sea;*
and to the river, its shoots.
12 *Why have you broken its walls,*
so all who pass by can plunder it?[10]
13 *Boars from the forest devour it;*
and animals of the field feed on it.

14 *O God of Hosts, return again;*
look from heaven and see;

---

read as a divine epithet. *Shepherd* is the only one that translates smoothly into English as a name for God, but all three should be understood this way.

7. *Šālîš* means both "a third" or "one-third." The expression seems to mean that God is increasing their sorrow.

8. Just as MT reflects. NRSV is reading *mānôd* ("shaking of the head") for *mādôn* ("strife"); Tate, *Psalms 51–100,* p. 306. MT is readable as it is, so a change is not necessary.

9. The more common modern translation of "you cleared the ground for it and it took deep root" is very poetic English, but it removes the physicality of the lines. God literally *turns the surface* of the earth and *the root roots.*

10. NIV adds "grapes" and NRSV and NJPS add "fruit," continuing the metaphor of the vine in this verse, but the direct object is "it" and no addition is needed.

visit this vine!
15 *Support that which your right hand planted;*
the child you, yourself, caused to grow strong.[11]
16 *Burned with fire and cut down,*
from a rebuke of your face they perish![12]
17 *Let your hand rest on the one, your right hand;*
the child of humanity you yourself caused to grow strong.
18 *Then we will not turn from you;*
revive us and on your name we will call.
19 *LORD God of Hosts, return us;*
Make your face to shine and we will be saved.

1-3 The psalm begins with an epithet for God that appears only here: *Shepherd of Israel.* The image of God as shepherd, however, is a recurrent image in the Bible.[13] It is also known as a title meaning king in Israel and the greater ancient Near East.[14] The opening line is in essence a request for an audience with the King God.

The meaning of the next two lines is debated. Tate sees them as additional epithets for God.[15] In their ancient context, this may be the case, but many of the epithets for God developed from God's own acts. Here each of these phrases or names has multiple meanings. First, God is acknowledged for leading Joseph *like a flock,* and this represents first, the lost boy in the wilderness and second, one of the tribes led from Egypt. As the story grew in Hebrew culture, the phrase could also become an epithet for God. In the next phrase, the one *dwelling on the cherubim* represents both the ark that traveled with Israel in the wilderness and the holy of holies later in Jerusalem (Exod. 25:8). But according to Ps. 99:1, it also represents God's eternal throne. These images then cover the entire history of the people and their God. Verse 2 adds

11. NRSV eliminates this line, seeing it as editorial repetition, as do Kraus (*Psalms 60–150,* p. 139) and others. This is possible, but both the LXX and Targum have the line, making it possible it is simply repetition in the ancient poem.

12. Understanding the syntax of this verse presents a challenge. The first line has two passive participles, *burned* and *cut down.* The second line reads as above. The problem is determining the referent or referents. NRSV reads line 1 as referring to Israel's destruction and line 2 as referring to the enemies. NJPS and NIV read both as referring to Israel. The above does not specify who the "they" is, leaving it just as the psalm does as an ambiguous statement.

13. E.g., Ps. 23; 2 Sam. 24:17; Ezek. 34:11-16; Luke 15:1-7; John 10:1-21.

14. Beth Tanner, "King Yahweh as the Good Shepherd: Taking Another Look at the Image of God in Psalm 23," in *David and Zion: Biblical Studies in Honor of J. J. M. Roberts,* ed. Bernard F. Batto and Kathryn L. Roberts (Winona Lake: Eisenbrauns, 2004), pp. 267-84.

15. *Psalms 51–100,* p. 311.

additional tribes to the list with the cry of *Come to save us!*" further expanding the image of God's saving power.

Verse 3 is the refrain that will reappear in similar form in vv. 7 and 19. Most modern translations use "restore us" for *hᵃšîḇēnû,* but the word means, literally, "make us turn around," so the people are literally asking for an about-face, a turning back to God. But a turning back is not quite enough, for God also must *make your face shine.* This is an uncommon phrase, and as Gerstenberger notes, it probably refers to a theophany such as in Deut. 33:2.[16] The people's turning is not enough for restored relationship; God must show up and show favor again for the relationship to be restored. The people must confess, and God must forgive.

4-7 This section opens with another title for God, *ʾᵉlōhîm ṣᵉḇāʾôṯ* ("God of the armies"), which indicates a powerful title for God equivalent to the *Shepherd of Israel* (v. 1). Both titles carry the understanding of king and warrior. What follows is a description of the situation, with a plea for God to set it right. The situation is estrangement between God and the people, so much so that the people ask *how long* God will remain angered by their *prayers* (v. 4). Verses 5 and 6 continue the description of the situation. These verses do not provide the exact details of what has occurred. Instead, they describe how the people perceive God is treating them. Verse 5 may also be a reference to the wilderness, for instead of sweet water and manna, their food and drink are now *tears.* Verse 6 moves to how they are now the laughingstock of the world. The problem here is definitely God and God's anger with the people. Their sorrow is caused by God.

Verse 7 is a duplicate of v. 3, except for the vocative. It is interesting that even if the problem is stated as God's anger, the people ask for God to cause them to *return,* acknowledging they are involved and culpable in the relationship.

8-13 The next section is a poetic history lesson with a question about the present in v. 12. This history begins with God's salvation of the people from bondage in Egypt. Israel here is not portrayed as a flock as in Ps. 79:13, but as a *vine.*[17] This may indicate this section existed as a separate piece before being incorporated into this psalm, but it is also just as likely that there is a free exchange of images in the prayers that come from the general agricultural setting of ancient Israel. The point of the history lesson is all of the care and tending that God has given to the people (vv. 8-9) and the way that God's vine thrived (vv. 10-11). This serves to remind God of all of God's effort poured into these people as a motivation to act, but it can also remind the people exactly

16. *Psalms: Part 2,* p. 104.

17. Israel as a vine is also a common metaphor in the Bible (Isa. 5:1-7; 27:2-6; Jer. 2:21; 12:10; Ezek. 15:1-8; 19:10-14; and John 15:1-6).

what they will be gaining by "returning" to God. This history also recalls the longer lesson of Psalm 78.

Verse 12 is the heart of the matter. The question is as haunting as v. 4. Why have you, God, destroyed what you have worked so hard to build? The remainder gives another shorter version of the situation God's people find themselves in now. Its defenses are destroyed, and any living thing can enter and eat its fill. The people are completely helpless. They are exposed to all of the dangers that the *Shepherd of Israel* protected them from in the past.

14-19 Verse 14 opens with *God of Hosts,* just as each section before it also opened with a powerful title for God. As a whole these titles call on an image of a powerful and kingly God, a God who is truly able to change the current situation. This time it is God who is asked to turn and look and visit the *vine* God had so carefully *planted* and tended. Verse 15 adds to the image as God's *right hand,* a metaphor for power and might, is called forth to again support the vine. Scholars have debated if both vv. 15 and 17 should stand in the current form.[18] But the current form fits the patterns above in the psalm; first God is called on to act (v. 15), then v. 16 tells again of the current situation, and then there is another call for God to act (v. 17) which follows the very same pattern as vv. 4-7.[19]

This section also adds the additional metaphor of the vine as a *child* in v. 15 and a *child of humanity* in v. 17. The vine being equated with a child moves the metaphor forward so that Israel is understood both as vine and as a child.[20] Others have argued that the child refers to the king. This is certainly possible, but I agree with Tate that in this context where v. 18 returns to *we* the referent here is probably Israel as a whole.[21]

The interpretation problems continue with v. 16, where the referent is again in question. Gerstenberger argues this verse should be emended so that the entire verse is a petition against the enemies.[22] Again this is possible, but considering that the remainder of the psalm is about Israel and God, it is more likely to be an echo of the responsibility stated in v. 7.

Verses 17 and 18 finish the call to God. If God will return to the people, then they will return to God and not *turn* again. It may seem as if the people are trying to make a bargain, and this is possible, but another reading is an acknowledgment that Israel cannot restore the relationship alone (as in v. 4). Such is the complexity of the dance. Verse 19 completes the threefold refrain

18. E.g., Kraus, *Psalms 60–150,* p. 138.

19. Zenger also retains the two lines; *Psalms 2,* p. 316.

20. Israel is understood as a child in other texts, such as Hos. 11:1-11.

21. *Psalms 51–100,* p. 315.

22. He thinks the first line should read "they burned it . . . they cut it down," making the referent clearly the others (*Psalms: Part 2,* p. 105), concurring with Kraus (*Psalms 60–150,* 138).

asking God to cause a change in Israel's heart so they can indeed experience God and *be saved.*

This psalm continues the distress of Psalm 79, extending this crisis further than in Psalm 74. Is it a different crisis than the previous psalm? Maybe, and maybe not. Psalms are poetry and thus flexible so they can be applied to later situations. It may be prayed by a community that did not receive the desired rescue in Psalm 79, or it may be that the community finds itself in another difficult place. Either way, the people still know even at the end of the psalm that there is no alternative but to wait and hope for God to act.

Psalm 80 is unique in asking God, not once, but three times to cause Israel to turn around. While Psalm 80 is not one of the penitential psalms, it does approach God in a spirit of brokenness that requires God's *face to shine* for salvation. Here salvation is seen as restored relationship where God tends the *vine* (Israel) and it grows strong. The psalm teaches it is not simply individuals, but also the whole people of God that must honestly repent and seek God's face. Sometimes we might even have to plead and beg God to return to us. We know the truth. Churches and nations and any group of people can and do sin together, sometimes even when we are trying to do the right thing. We often call on individuals to apologize and set the relationship right, but it seems as if we do not hold the same accountability for groups. This psalm tells us clearly that we too need to repent together of our sins and our mistakes and seek reconciliation with God.

Beth Tanner

Psalm 81: God's Side of the Story

Psalm 81 offers a glimpse into the ways Israel worshipped. The first section of the psalm is a call to a festival celebration. It sets the tone for the psalm as exuberant and celebratory (vv. 1-5b). Verses 6-7 give a lesson from history, and vv. 8-16 comprise the word of God to the people. Psalms 79 and 80 reflect the people's cries to God in dire times, and here in Psalm 81 is God's side of the story. God's word begins with what God has done (vv. 5c-7) and continues with how the people refused to respond to these great acts of salvation. It stands as a witness to the ebb and flow of the relationship of the people and God in Book Three. The people want results, and what God desires is a relationship. It is the same dilemma that is also played out again and again in the narrative portions of the Old Testament.

Most scholars agree that the psalm is divided into two main sections. The second section is further subdivided into additional stanzas:[1]

St. 1 The festal announcement (vv. 1-5b)
St. 2 God's answer (vv. 5b-16)
  What God has done (vv. 5c-7)
  God's warning (vv. 8-10)
  The people's response (vv. 11-14)
  What God wishes for the people (vv. 15-16)

The psalm, then, serves as God's response to the people, much like God's response to Jeremiah's lament in Jer. 12:7-13.

The psalm has one difficulty, the change of person in vv. 6 and 7, 11 and 12, 15 and 16. Most modern translations smooth out these difficulties, but there is an important point to be made by leaving the MT as it is. God is involved with the singular "him" (or "her"), the people collectively, whether in either the singular or plural and ending the poem at v. 16 as the personal "you." In other words, the psalm covers all of the bases and possibly indicates that the pronouns incorporated in the matrix should not be seen as set in stone, but flexible so as to address any and all future situations.

1. Tate, *Psalms 51–100,* p. 146; Gerstenberger, *Psalms: Part 2,* p. 107. Kraus uses the same division, but also moves v. 10c to immediately after v. 5; *Psalms 60–150,* p. 146.

For the leader. On the gittîṯ.[2] *Asaphic.*[3]

1 *Sing out to God, our strength;*
shout out to the God of Jacob.
2 *Raise a song, sound the tambourine,*
the sweet lyre with the harp.
3 *Blow a horn at the new moon,*
at the full moon for our festival day;
4 *for it is a statute for Israel,*
an ordinance of the God of Jacob.
5 *He set it as a testimony in Joseph*
when he went out against the land of Egypt.

"I heard speech I did not know;
6 *I took away from his*[4] *shoulder*[5] *his burden;*
his hands[6] *were released from the basket.*
7 *In distress, you called and I delivered you;*
I answered you hidden in thunder;
I tested you at the waters of Meribah." Selah

8 *"Hear my people, and let me warn you;*
O Israel, if you would hear me!
9 *There shall be no strange god among you;*
you shall not bow down to a foreign god.
10 *I am the* LORD *your God,*
who brought you from the land of Egypt.
Open your mouth wide and I will fill it."

11 *"My people did not listen to me;*
Israel did not want me.[7]

2. See note 3 on Psalm 8 superscription.

3. See note 7 on Psalm 73 superscription.

4. Following MT, most modern translations substitute 2ms here, but the change is unnecessary because it is understandable as written.

5. Every attempt is made in this commentary to use inclusive language for humanity. However in this poem, it is an important theological point that the people be understood as a single entity in this section. In English the choice of word is limited to *he.*

6. 11QPs[d] has the singular "his hand" (García Martínez, Tigchelaar, and van der Woude, *Qumran Cave 11: II,* p. 73).

7. Most modern translations use "submit to me," but *'bh* has more of a meaning of "be willing to" or "want to" (*HALOT,* p. 3; also Hossfeld and Zenger, *Psalms 2,* p. 319).

12 *I gave him[8] over to a stubborn heart.*
They followed their own counsel.
13 *Would that my people listen to me;*
Israel would follow in my path.
14 *Quickly I would subdue their enemies;*
I would turn my hand against their foes!"

15 *Those hating the LORD would wither[9] before him;*
their time shall be forever.
16 *I will cause him[10] to eat the finest wheat;*
and (with) honey from the rock I will cause you[11] to be satisfied.

1-5b The psalm begins with shouts of praise that are much like the praises that end the written prayers (Psalm 150). The people are called on to *sing* and *shout* and play their instruments (vv. 1-2). Verse 3 marks the beginning of the festival with the blowing of the *šôp̄ār.*[12] The next verses give the reasons for the festival, for it has been decreed by God. Many scholars have speculated on the use of the three names Israel, Jacob, and especially Joseph here.[13] It may have some ancient meaning, such as a northern Israel tradition, or it may simply be that the group of Asaph psalms reference the events of the exodus and wilderness periods in Israel's history, with the Joseph tribe's name as its primary reference.

While this call to celebrate could represent any of the festivals, scholars have argued that v. 3 represents a fifteen-day festival, making it the Autumn Festival.[14] This is possible, but v. 5 indicates a festival that was *set as a testimony . . . when he (God) went out against the land of Egypt,* making the most probable festival association here the Passover celebration.[15] Also, the first

8. Most modern translations change the 3ms suffix of MT to a plural here. But the *he* probably represents a collective Israel. See commentary.

9. The root *kḥš* is problematic. It means to "grow lean" in the *qal* and "to deceive" in the *piel,* the form here. Only in the *hiphil* does it mean "cringe" (followed by NRSV and NIV). In addition, there is a problem in identifying the "they"; is it the people or is it the enemies of the previous verse? This decision impacts which meaning is selected for the verb (see Commentary).

10. Reading MT's 3ms, most change to a 3 plural here.

11. Reading MT's 2ms.

12. See Lev. 25:9; 2 Sam. 6:15; Pss. 47:5; 98:6.

13. See Kraus, *Psalms 60–150,* p. 150; and Tate, *Psalms 51–100,* p. 323.

14. Kraus, *Psalms 60–150,* p. 148. Mays concurs; *Psalms,* p. 266.

15. Even the date and what combinations of festivals occurred in the ancient period are heavily debated. Julian Morgenstern noted nearly a century ago the problems with multiple calendars and different dates for festivals, and this further complicates the identification of an exact match; "The Three Calendars of Ancient Israel," *HUCA* 1 (1924) 13-78.

appearance of the blowing of the *šôp̄ār* in the story of Israel is in Exod. 19:16, where the blast summons the people to the mountain for God's theophoric giving of the torah. Finally, the only festival in Leviticus associated with the blowing of the *šôp̄ār* is the Day of Atonement (Lev. 25:9). All of this is to say that any of these festivals could have been the setting for Psalm 81.

5c-7 Verse 5c is where many of the difficulties lie in this psalm. At v. 5c, the psalm changes to the first person, but there is no indication of who the speaker is. This issue is compounded by the who of the 3ms object "he" in v. 6 and the 2ms object in v. 7. It is universally agreed that the change of speaker at v. 5c signals the beginning of a divine oracle. We may not be able to prove definitely who delivered the divine oracle, but no matter who it is, it is delivered from God.

The exodus begins with God "hearing their groaning" (Exod. 2:24). It is God's hearing of *speech I did not know* that motivates God to act. Indeed, this pattern of God hearing cries of pain is what the prayers for help are based on. In this way, vv. 5c-6 are, as in Exod. 2:24, God's speech to God. It is what God has done for the people. Verse 7 is God's speech to the people, reminding them of God's gifts to them. The *Selah* at the end of v. 7 indicates a close to this reflection. The next section will also be from God to the people.

8-10 Verses 8-10 are a warning to the people. It is the plea from God for the people to listen and act according to the torah. Using language similar to Exod. 20:2-5, the poem stresses that the people should be devoted only to God because it is God who brought them from the land of Egypt.[16] Several have argued that line 10c is misplaced here, thinking it belongs with line 5c,[17] but no ancient sources support this change. It is just as likely that this line refers to the wilderness events where God did fill the people's mouths with food and drink. All the people had to do was open their mouths like little birds and God would feed them. Just as in Psalm 78, where the history lesson had the purpose of motivating God, here God's history lesson is to remind the people what God had done for them.

11-14 This section tells of God's pain, pain caused by the refusal of the people to *follow.* In v. 11, several modern translations read "Israel would not submit to me," but the word used here is more personal. It is not that Israel would not submit to God's power, but that the people *did not want* God. The people have completely rejected the one who cared so passionately for them. God left them to their own devises, and they took *their own counsel* instead of God's. The people do not know that if they would return, they could live in peace, for God would handle *their enemies* (v. 14).

16. This is very similar to the preamble for the Ten Commandments: "I am the LORD your God, who brought you out of the land of Egypt, out of the house of slavery."

17. See, e.g., Kraus, *Psalms 60–150,* p. 146.

15-16 Verse 15 is another difficult verse to interpret. The verse switches to third person, and it is unclear if *those hating the LORD* are the children of Israel or the *enemies* of v. 14. Add to this the problem of translating the verb, which can mean either "to grow lean or waste" in the *qal* form and "to deceive" in the *piel.* It is also possible that this is an addition to the original poem, since vv. 14 and 16 fit well together. As it is, *those hating the LORD* could be anyone, Israelites or others.[18] The second line is often modified in modern translations,[19] but the above is what appears in the Hebrew. It is possible this is a further reflection of the third commandment mentioned in v. 9. *Those hating the LORD* are singled out as people who not only doom themselves but doom the generations that come after them: *their time shall be forever.*

Verse 16 completes the thought of v. 14. God will remove God's enemies, but those who love God will be fed well and tended. As it is expressed here, it is God's wish to be able to treat the people in this way. The poem ends then without resolution. God is wishing for a different humanity, and there is no indication that the humans have responded in any way to God's plea. God remains at the table without any guests. What began as a great festival, with singing and dancing and joy, ends with God alone.

This psalm turns the prayers of the people in the previous two psalms on their heads. Now it is God who stands alone. The psalm tells of the consequence of our actions in the heart of God. It is a jarring image that reminds us that, just as with that generation in the wilderness, God has also provided us with all we have and has even offered salvation, yet we continue to seek our own counsel and ways instead of the one who gives us all we need. It reminds us that God, too, has a story to tell about this relationship God shares with humanity. Our relationship with God is complex and two-sided, and often as here it gives us pause to contemplate the other side and to see the world, just for a moment, from God's side.

BETH TANNER

18. *Those hating the LORD* also appears in the commandments (Exod. 20:5; Deut. 5:9). It is a sin that is visited on subsequent generations.

19. NRSV "and their doom would last forever."

Psalm 82: King of the Gods

Psalm 82 places the modern reader in a very unfamiliar world. Modern thinking holds to a monotheistic theology, meaning there is only one god and the gods of others simply do not exist. Ancient Israel did not have the same definition of monotheism. Indeed, for them not only did other gods exist, but those gods were active in the world.[1] This psalm gives us a window on the assembly of the gods, a place where the gods are gathered to make decisions about the world.[2] This council is part of the greater ancient Near Eastern mythology and would be a familiar image to ancient Israelites.[3]

Psalm 82 also continues God's side of the story that began in the previous psalm. It shows that humans are not the only entity that occupies God's time. To understand God is to understand some of the mystery that humans do not see clearly. We are central in our own worlds, but the work of God is vast and unending, and this psalm that seems so odd to modern people can remind us of just that reality. God is God in places beyond our grasp.

The psalm itself is straightforward and describes the LORD's judgment on the other gods. In that, it makes the theological claim that Israel's god is the king and chief god of all of the other gods. Its structure is clear, and the only issue of interpretation centers on the identity of the *they* in v. 5. The psalm has three major sections, with additional divisions in the center stanza.[4]

St. 1 Setting (v. 1)
St. 2 God's judgment of the other gods (vv. 2-7)
  God's issue with the others (vv. 2-4)
  Result of the gods' failures (v. 5)
  Sentence on the gods (vv. 6-7)
St. 3 Call for the LORD to judge (v. 8)

1. A multitude of texts demonstrate this belief, e.g., Exod. 20:3-6; Deut. 4:15-20; Josh. 24:14-15. In addition, many prophetic texts extol the people to love God alone and not go after other gods, e.g., Jer. 8:19; Hos. 11:2. In later texts, the theology seems to move more toward an exclusive monotheism; see Isa. 41:21-24.

2. See 1 Kgs. 22:19-23; Job 1:6-12; Zech. 1:7-17.

3. See Cross, *Canaanite Myth and Hebrew Epic,* pp. 177-90.

4. This division of the psalm is agreed on by most scholars; Kraus, *Psalms 60–150,* pp. 156-57; Gerstenberger, *Psalms: Part 2,* p. 113; Tate, *Psalms 51–100,* p. 334.

An Asaphic psalm.[5]

1 *God is standing in the assembly of El;*[6]
in the midst of the gods he is judging.

2 *"How long will you judge unjustly*
and show favor to the wicked?[7] Selah
3 *Give justice to the weak and the orphan!*
Give rights to the poor and oppressed!
4 *Rescue the weak and the needy!*
From the hand of the wicked snatch them away!
5 *They do not know and they do not understand;*
they wander around[8] *in darkness;*
all the foundations of the earth are shaken."
6 *Indeed, I said, "You are gods,*
Children of the Most High, all of you;
7 *Nevertheless, you will all die like a human;*
and like one of the princes, you will fall."

8 *Rise up, O God! Judge the earth!*
For you possess all the nations.

1 Verse 1 serves as an orientation, or an opening for the scene. It transfers the reader to a space rarely seen by humans. The *assembly of El* is often referred to as the divine council. This would be a familiar mythological theme in the ancient near East. *'Ēl* is a known name for the king god of the Canaanite pantheon, and his myths predate the exodus. The God of the Israelites, the LORD, subsumed this title as an epithet, so that El becomes synonymous with YHWH.[9] The function of El was to serve as the creator, parent, king and the head of the council of the gods.[10] God arises and judges the gods as a function of the king of the divine council.

5. See note 7 on Psalm 73 superscription.

6. *Baʿ^a^ḏaṯ 'ēl* or *assembly of El* probably means "divine council," although the phrase appears only here concerning the gods. The term otherwise refers to Israel (Num. 27:17; 31:16; Josh. 22:16-17; Ps. 74:2); see Tate, *Psalms 51–100,* p. 329.

7. Lit., "You lift up the faces of the wicked," meaning "to show favor" (*HALOT,* p. 725).

8. The verb is in the *hithpael* form, meaning "to walk or *wander* to and fro."

9. This psalm does not use the proper name YHWH. Instead, it uses the more generic title of *'^e^lōhîm,* and the use of the same word that means both *God* as an epithet for YHWH and gods is confusing. It is thought this is because this psalm is part of the Elohistic psalter (see Introduction).

10. Cross, *Canaanite Myth and Hebrew Epic,* pp. 15-17.

2-4 God's speech begins with questions. The problem with the other gods is that they are not carrying out the values of God's kingdom. The values they are accused of breaching are much like the job description for the king of Israel in Psalm 72, demonstrating that God's kingdom on earth and that in the heavens share the same values. After the questions comes a series of commands (vv. 3-4) that here are not meant as commands, but according to Tate are points that recall "the commissioning of the gods."[11] The points then tell what the gods were supposed to do but failed. It is the reason for the judgment.

5 The words and grammar in v. 5 are clear. What is not clear is the interpretation. The difficulties are twofold. First, the person changes from second to third, resulting in a possible change of speaker. Second, the referent for the *they* is unclear. Is this a continuation of God's speech? It could be, but it could be that the speech from God moves away from the other gods and is now directed to the rest of the world. Most scholars see the *they* here as the other gods. But the *they* could also be the result of the gods' failure and reflect the impact of their acts on the people. It is certainly possible that the *they* is not one or the other but is both the gods and the people whom the acts of the gods impact. Either way, the result of the acts is quite serious because *the foundations of the earth* are in jeopardy. The situation must be addressed.

6-7 Verses 6-7 place the *gods* on equal footing with the humans. They have lost their immortality, hence their god status.[12] This ability for the God of Israel to demote the others speaks of the power of the king of the council. The king alone can control all of the other gods. This divine trial also demonstrates the fairness of Israel's god. This god is not capricious, but sentences the other gods for their refusal to act in ways that reflect the values of God's kingdom.

8 This final verse is not voiced by God. It is voiced by someone else, possibly the people of the world. Now that the other gods are finished, God is implored to do what they did not, to *rise up* and *judge.* The last line states what was already true: that all the nations, no matter what their god, belong to Israel's great God.

The existence of the other gods in the psalm is puzzling to modern readers, but in our diverse world perhaps this psalm should give us pause and invite us to think of monotheism differently. Others are not necessarily delusional in their belief in their gods, but are simply people from different places with different cultures. Maybe the ancients knew more than we do. We should not assume that others are evil or suspect simply because a group

11. *Psalms 51–100,* p. 336.

12. The Gilgamesh Epic is a story that concerns Gilgamesh's quest for immortality that will make him a god, indicating the importance of immortality in ancient myth.

of people have a different god. This psalm clearly leaves such issues of the gods with God!

Further, the psalm places us in the council reserved for the gods. This is not our usual vision of what goes on in heaven, and in that it invites the readers to stretch their own ideas of what the world of the gods might be. What is clear is that the values of the God of Israel's kingdom have worldwide impact. The other gods are not condemned for deceiving the people or for not worshipping the Chief God, but according to vv. 3-4 for not caring for the ones with the least voice. The values of earth in Psalm 72 are clearly also the values in the heavenly realm. This psalm declares that *the foundations of the earth are shaken,* not by political or theological issues, but by the treatment of those who are homeless and hungry, alone and without justice. We often think of judgment falling on those who do not believe as we do; this psalm declares that the gods judge just as humans, not by what we believe, but by what we choose to do or not to do for the others that God created and loves. In this care of the most vulnerable in the world, we as a world of people of different faiths share a common goal, for each of our beliefs contain this understanding. Maybe this psalm instructs us not to start interfaith dialogue with issues of religion or politics, or even to dialogue at all, but to do for others for the good of the whole earth.

BETH TANNER

Psalm 83: God, Arise Against Our Enemies

Psalm 83 is a community or national prayer for help. The prayer is lifted by a people who are afraid. As with most prayers of help, the exact situation is not reported, although with the list of nations in vv. 6-8, it appears that the threat is grave and that Israel is surrounded by enemies. In addition, both vv. 2 and 5 indicate Israel's enemies are also enemies of God. God is called on to act both on behalf of God's self and on behalf of Israel. What is also clear is that in vv. 9-11 the people call on God to act now because of God's acts in history. These verses serve both to remind God of God's acts in the past and to remind the people praying of the ways God has delivered them in the past as a hope for the current situation.

The two major divisions in the psalm are agreed on by scholars as vv. 1-8 and 9-18. Further stanza divisions in the psalm are not universally agreed. Most scholars set apart v. 1's petitions from the reasons for the petitions in vv. 2-8,[1] but these reasons are central to the plea being lifted. A better arrangement is to attach the petition of v. 1 to all of the reasons since the reasons are directly related to the plea.[2] The second major section consists of cycles of petitions, ending with two final pleas for God to act. The psalm, then, ends without a resolution.

- Plea to God with reasons (vv. 1-8)
  - First set of reasons (vv. 2-5)
  - Second set of reasons (vv. 6-8)
- Petitions for God to act (vv. 9-18)
  - First petitions (vv. 9-12)
  - Second petitions (vv. 13-15)
  - Final wishes (vv. 16-18)

The overall effect of the psalm is singular in its message: God's intervention is desperately needed by the people.

1. McCann, "The Book of Psalms," p. 1010; Tate, *Psalms 51–100*, p. 346; Gerstenberger, *Psalms: Part II*, p. 117.

2. Kraus sets v. 1 apart and makes vv. 2-8 one single section (*Psalms 60–150*, p. 162). Zenger agrees that vv. 1-8 should be a unified whole. He notes there is a *kî* at the beginning of v. 5, but instead of a division, he notes that the description of the enemies and their acts "intensifies the drama" (Hossfeld and Zenger, *Psalms 2*, p. 339).

A song. An Asaphic[3] psalm.

1 *O God! do not be silent!*
Do not be quiet and do not[4] be still, O God.
2 *Behold, your enemies are growling,*
and those hating you have raised their heads.[5]
3 *Against your people they make cunning plans;*
they conspire against those you protect.
4 *They say, "Come, let us destroy them as a nation,*
and the name of Israel will be remembered no more";
5 *for they conspire with one mind together;[6]*
against you they make a covenant.
6 *The tents of Edom and the Ishmaelites,*
Moab and the Hagrites,
7 *Gebal and Ammon and Amalek,*
Philistia with those dwelling in Tyre;
8 *also Assyria is joining with them;*
they have become the strong arm of the children of Lot. Selah

9 *Do to them like Midian;*
like Sisera and Jabin at the Wadi Kishon,
10 *they were destroyed at Endor.*
They became fertilizer[7] for the ground.
11 *Set the nobles like Oreb and Zeeb,*
like Zebah and Zalmunna all their princes,
12 *who said, "Let us possess for ourselves the pastures of God."*
13 *My God, set them as tumbleweed,*
as chaff before the wind;
14 *as fire consumes the forest,*
as flames burn the mountains,
15 *so pursue them with your storm,*
and with your gale dismay them!
16 *Fill their faces with dishonor,*
so they will seek your name, O LORD!

3. See note 7 on Psalm 73 superscription.

4. Many modern translations omit this third *'al,* but its presence is important for emphasis.

5. MT uses the singular "head" as a collective plural.

6. Lit., "they conspire a heart together." In Hebrew, "heart" is the center for thought.

7. The use of the word "dung" is puzzling (NRSV). This word appears only in association with corpses left on the ground in 2 Kgs. 9:37; Jer. 8:2; 9:22; 16:4; 25:33. The idea here seems to be debris or *fertilizer* more than dung.

17 Let them be put to shame and dismayed forever!
Let them be ashamed and perish,
18 so they will know that you,
your name is the LORD,
are alone the Most High over all the earth.

1-8 This section is a disparate cry for God to act on behalf of Israel. It opens with a threefold plea for God to move from silence and inactivity to voice and action (v. 1). This plea confirms that Israel's faith lies in God and not their own power. The situation is dire and God seems silent and still, and this prayer is their call for God to hear and act.

2-5 These pleas are attached to the reasons why God's help is needed. Verses 2-3 remind God that these enemies are not just threatening Israel, but they are God's enemies as well. In v. 2, God's silence of v. 1 is contrasted with the enemies's "growls." The enemies are so confident, they are raising up their heads in triumph[8] and declaring the end of the people (v. 4) even before the battle is fought. Verse 5 is even more frightening, for the enemies have joined together and have made a *covenant* against God *(you)*. This covenant-making would be seen as appalling to God since it indicates a solemn promise to act against God. Tate notes that this is the only place in the whole Old Testament where a covenant is made *against* an entity instead of "with," further pointing out what a shock this image would be to an ancient person.[9] This covenant-making reinforces how serious the threat to God and God's people has become. The enemies, it seems, are all action while the great God is silent.

6-8 The next three verses contain a list of those who are together making this covenant. All of the nations and tribes in the list are known from other biblical sources; however the ten together are not from any known historical event. Zenger has noted that the list is not historical but geographical, with the first nine nations drawing a ring around Israel from southwest to southeast.[10] The last verse deals with a superpower in the region, Assyria, but again the reference is more a theological stereotype than a historical reality.[11] This list not only surrounds Israel but also names a superpower that destroyed the northern kingdom. It describes the peril the people are in: they are surrounded by enemies, trapped on all sides, and in addition there is a powerful and destructive Assyria bearing down as well. The last line of the

8. This could indicate their power as in Judg. 8:28 or victory as noted by Tate (*Psalms 51–100*, p. 346).

9. *Psalms 51–100*, p. 344.

10. Hossfeld and Zenger, *Psalms 2*, p. 342.

11. Assyria is often used as a sign of Israel's oppressor and enemy; see, e.g., the book of Jonah (Assyria here is the Ninevites); Hos. 11:11; Jer. 2:18.

section confirms that Assyria is *the strong arm of the children of Lot,* indicating Assyria's hand in the actions of the smaller nations.[12]

9-18 Description of the threat moves to petitions. Like above, this section is filled with the names of Israel's enemies, but these are enemies that God has dealt with in the past.

9-12 Verses 9-11 contain a series of pleas for God to act based on former action. The enemies listed are from narratives of battles in Judges and 1 Samuel. This section recalls victories from the earliest period of Israel's history.[13] These acts serve both to remind God of what God has done and to remind the people of the same. God will act now because God has acted likewise in the past when Israel was in danger. The images here are fierce, with the bodies of the battle dead becoming *fertilizer.* Yet this is the true picture of war, not romanticized nor sanitized. War is horrible, and the ones preserving these prayers know and speak of that horror. Just in case we might feel for those slaughtered, v. 12 reminds of the words of the enemies. Just as in v. 4, these ones intend nothing less than genocide. We may not like the picture, but the situation told is one of "kill or be killed." These words of the enemies, as in v. 4, are also against God, for they wish to *possess the pastures of God.* This is not just a people and their land; this is God's land, and these are God's sheep (see Psalm 23).

13-15 Verses 13-15 continue the pleas for God to act against those who are threatening Israel. Again to a modern reader, these requests seem offensive and sinful. How can such words of violence be in the Bible? Should they be in the Bible? To an ancient, these questions would not only seem odd but blasphemous. When, they would wonder, did the community cease to cry out to God when the need was grave? When did God's people cease to tell God what they needed? Israel was in a difficult place, and theirs was a true cry of anguish.

16-18 Notice, however, that even as they cry for the enemies' destruction, their fate is not to be one of eternal damnation. Verses 16 and 18 state that one of the reasons for God's acts is so the enemy will *seek* and *know* God. This may seem as offensive as the violence in these verses. How can God's action against the enemy be for their ultimate salvation? This is complex theology, because what it ultimately declares is that what God desires is for all of God's acts to lead humans toward salvation and redemption. The shame of a defeated enemy is an opportunity for the world to be more at peace, for God to settle another human fight.

But this psalm also ends without this resolution. The wishes for God

12. See Gen. 19:30-38.

13. Midian in Judges 6–8; Sisera and Jabin in Judges 4–5; Endor in 1 Samuel 28; Oreb and Zeeb in Judg. 7:25; Zebah and Zalmunna in Judg. 8:5.

to handle the enemy close these Asaph psalms. The nation sits, waiting for God's aid. Their plight is dire, and God remains silent. The full picture of these eleven psalms is not a pretty one. Several things have dominated them. First, this is clearly a serious and chaotic period, as Psalms 74, 79, 80 and 83 declare. In addition, this collection calls for a reassessment of life through questions and reflections. It calls for a reassessment of the relationship between the community and God (Psalms 77 and 78) by means of the psalms that tell God's side of the issues at hand in Psalms 78, 81, and 82. Here is a great deal to digest, and it stresses an important point about this poetry. It takes work and reflection and time to absorb and understand its message.

Violence and vengeance are difficult issues in today's world, and this psalm speaks to the heart of these difficult issues. First is the cry for help in a very fearful time when the nation turns to God for aid. Very few reading this book have known what it is like to be pressed in from all sides. Wars and mass violence happen far from us, and we live in countries protected by massive military power. We do not know what it is to be powerless. This psalm reminds us that our dependence on human power is, in part, folly.

Second, this prayer tells that when God is in charge, the purpose of violence is not retribution or vengeance, but God's gracious will for all. The ultimate purpose of God is so that all will know God and God's name. It may seem like a pipe dream in the world today, but it is the hope to which all Christians cling, that the powers and violence of this world pass away and a new world established by God will come to fruition. Violence and hate are real, if not to us, then to millions of others who live in dangerous places. We need to hear their cries and understand the parts we may play in their oppression, and we need to pray for their lives and ours to be transformed.

BETH TANNER

Psalm 84: A Pilgrim's Prayer

In ancient Israel, a visit to the temple in Jerusalem was a yearly occurrence at best.[1] As a result, it was a special event, one worthy of song and celebration. Psalm 84 is a song believed to have been sung by those traveling to Jerusalem to participate in a great festival. The song is now placed next to the strident cry of Psalm 83 and provides a vision of a nation restored. The songs of Asaph have finished, and it appears that the songs of Korah mark a more positive note.

The song has some problematic lines, with vv. 5b through 7 having multiple issues that result in a variety of translations. Most scholars agree as to the division of the psalm, but several wonder if vv. 8-9 are part of the original composition.[2] The psalm is divided into four sections.

Words of praise (vv. 1-4)
A pilgrim's travel (vv. 5-7)
A prayer for the King (vv. 8-9)
Words of praise (vv. 10-12)

The song is also one that praises Zion, the place of the temple in Jerusalem. The praise of God's house both opens and closes the song.

For the leader. On the gittîṯ.[3] *A Korahite*[4] *psalm.*

1 *How lovely is your dwelling place,*
O LORD of hosts.
2 *My soul longs for and faints*
for the courts of the LORD;
my heart and my flesh sing with joy unto the living God.
3 *Even a bird finds a house,*
and a sparrow a nest for herself,
where she lays her young ones

1. See 1 Sam. 1:3 for Elkanah's yearly visit to the shrine at Shiloh and Luke 2:41 for Joseph's yearly visit to Jerusalem.

2. See, e.g., Hossfeld and Zenger, *Psalms 2,* p. 351.

3. See note 3 on Psalm 8 superscription.

4. There are two collections of the Korahite *(bᵉnê qōraḥ)* psalms. The first is in Book Two: Psalms 42–49, and the second is in Book Three: Psalms 84–85 and 87–88. The name appears in the Hebrew Bible in several different contexts (Exod. 6:21-24; 1 Chr. 6:7; 2 Chr. 20:19). It is impossible to state which or any of these traditions is associated with the psalm. For a more complete explanation, see Tate, *Psalms 51–100,* p. 351. For further information, see note 1 on Psalm 42 superscription.

near[5] your altars,
O Lord of hosts, my king and my God.
4 *Happy are the ones dwelling in your house;*
continually they sing praises to you! Selah

5 *Happy are the ones[6] whose strength[7] is in you,*
paths of pilgrimages in their hearts.[8]
6 *Those passing through the valley of Baca,*[9]
they will make it a spring;
the early rain covers it with blessings.[10]
7 *They go from strength to strength,*
until each one appears[11] before[12] God in Zion.

8 *Lord God of Hosts, hear my prayer!*
Give ear, O God of Jacob! Selah
9 *Behold our shield, O God!*
Look upon the face of your anointed one.

5. Reading *ʾēt* ("beside" or "near") for *ʾet,* marker of accusative, as suggested by the *BHS* critical apparatus, among others.

6. MT has the singular "Happy is *ʾāḏām,*" but it is probably meant in the collective plural sense. The lines before and after it reflect the plural subject.

7. LXX has "help" here in place of the MT's *strength.*

8. Lit., "highways in their hearts." LXX "in his heart, he willed to go up" implies an understanding of ascent or pilgrimage, and thus the *BHS* critical apparatus suggests reading *maʿᵃlôṯ* for *mᵉsillôṯ,* but NRSV "highways to Zion" goes too far. Zenger has recently pointed out that these emendations are unnecessary since the text is understandable in MT (Hossfeld and Zenger, *Psalms 2,* p. 349).

9. MT has *bāḵāʾ,* but other ancient sources (LXX, Vulg, and Syr) read this as coming from the root *bkh,* meaning "tears." Modern translations have returned to the MT and understand *bāḵāʾ* to mean a specific valley instead of the metaphorical "valley of tears."

10. This line is problematic. NRSV and NIV read *bᵉrēḵôṯ* ("pools") for *bᵉrāḵôṯ* ("blessings"), but this change is unsupported. Kraus and the *BHS* critical apparatus note this line is corrupt, and any translation is tentative (*Psalms 60–150,* p. 166).

11. The person of the verb changes here to 3ms and the referent is unclear. Translators are divided between God as the subject (Kraus, *Psalms 60–150,* p. 166; NRSV) and a singular pilgrim as the subject (Tate, *Psalms 51–100,* p. 350; NIV; NJPS). The subject has been the pilgrim(s) since v. 4, and the subject changes to God in v. 8, making this the more likely choice. This entire line is problematic, and any translation is tentative.

12. MT has the unusual *ʾel* ("to" or "toward"), and some change to *ʾēl,* reading "God of Gods" (Hossfeld and Zenger, *Psalms 2,* p. 348). The preposition is unusual but not unreadable, and so the MT can be retained.

10 *For a day in your courts is better than a thousand elsewhere;*
I chose to stand at the threshold[13] *of the house of God,*
instead of dwelling in the tents of the wicked.
11 *For a sun and a shield is the Lord God;*
Favor and honor, the Lord gives.
12 *O Lord of Hosts!*
Happy is the one who trusts in you!

1-4 The opening is a hymn of praise to the *house* of the Lord. It begins with praise for the beauty of Zion (v. 1) and continues to express the longing that pilgrims have for their destination (v. 2). But it is not just God's house, but the place of God's presence that prompts the song. This longing for the *house* is really a longing to be *near* God once again. Verse 3 continues to speak of the peace and safety that birds find in building their nests *near* God. In v. 4, a beatitude tells that, like the birds, those that are fortunate enough to dwell within God's *house* are surely *happy.*[14] This introduction as a whole expresses the longing of pilgrims to stand again within God's temple.

5-7 This section is fraught with difficulties, and any translation is tentative. The section begins with a second beatitude, this time declaring that the pilgrims are *happy* for God gives them *strength,* possibly for the journey. It is in the next line that the difficulties begin, and it is best to look at the rest of this section in its totality, since an exact meaning is impossible to discern. What is clear about vv. 6a and possibly v. 5b is that this section changes the subject from the house of the Lord to the travelers themselves. It is a poetic reading of their trip. The location of the *valley of Baca* is unknown, and it is also unclear if the valley is green at the time of the pilgrimage or if the pilgrims themselves bring blessings to the earth by their travels. Also, some accept the emendation and read "valley of tears." What is clear is that, in the Psalms and other texts, humanity and creation join together in their celebration of the Lord,[15] and here it seems that both humans and creation are celebrating in unison as the parade moves toward Jerusalem, be that through a specific valley or a metaphorical valley of tears.

Verse 7 is also problematic. NJPS translates v. 7a as "they go from rampart to rampart," and this makes good sense; unfortunately, the word *ḥayil* does not refer to "rampart" in any other text. Verse 7 could be referring back

13. This word appears only here, and its meaning is uncertain. A common modern translation is "doorkeeper" (NIV, NRSV), but as Alan Robinson notes, the term for "doorkeeper" in Jer. 35:4 is *šōmēr hassap̱;* since the Korahites were keepers of the temple, they would understand the "doorkeeper" as an important position ("Three Suggested Interpretations in Ps. LXXXIV," *VT* 24 [1974] 380-81). Both Robinson and Tate suggest a meaning of standing on the threshold instead (*Psalms 51–100,* p. 350).

14. See Ps. 1 concerning the centrality of this word to the whole Psalter.

15. See, e.g., Pss. 65, 68, 93, 96, 98, 148; Luke 19:40.

to v. 5 as an *inclusio* for this stanza by using the word *strength* in both verses, conveying that the *strength* of the pilgrims comes from God's gift. Verse 7b adds to the difficulties, for the subject of the sentence is unclear, and it could be either God or "the *one.*" But the change of subject seems unwarranted here, especially since v. 7b indicates the whole purpose of the trip, to *appear before God in Zion.* This whole section then focuses on the traveler and narrates not only the purpose for the trip, but tells of travels (v. 6) and of arrival in the courts of God (v. 7).

8-9 The pilgrim enters the courts and calls upon God (v. 8) and offers prayer for the king. Israel's king is known as a *shield*[16] and also as the *anointed one* or "Messiah."[17] Part of gathering as a community for a festival would entail offering prayers for the king, as Psalm 72 demonstrates. The king is the one responsible for justice and for worship and the right functioning of the kingdom, so prayers are offered on his behalf. The *Selah* at the end of v. 8 either is misplaced or indicates a change of speaker from one pilgrim (*my prayer,* v. 8) to the group (*our shield,* v. 9).

10-12 The psalm concludes with another section of praise. It begins as the psalm did, with praise for the house of God (vv. 10-11). The beginning of the psalm was filled with longing for this place. Now, the longing has turned to wishes made inside the *court* of God. It is as pleasant as the memory told in vv. 1-2. It is better than anywhere else. Verse 10 is problematic because of the uncertainty of the meaning of *histôpēp* as either "doorkeeper" or "standing *at the threshold,*" but if the exact term is unknown the meaning is still clear. Being near God is better than being with *the wicked.*

The last two verses give praise to God, praising God as protector and the giver of good gifts to humans. The last verse is the third and last of the beatitudes. Beginning with the cultic name for God, *LORD of Hosts,*[18] the beatitude declares that those are *happy* who *trust in God (you).*

Psalm 84 is about movement: from outside to inside; from the countryside to Jerusalem and to the temple; from ordinary to extraordinary; from daily concerns to sacred space. In years past, there was a process of preparation for Sunday service. It was a special set-apart time that required a Saturday bath and Sunday-go-to-meeting clothes. Like this pilgrims, this process set Sunday apart from all of the other days around it. In our on-the-go world, our trips to meet God have lost some of that specialness. This psalm reminds us that we should make the effort to celebrate the time we are able to spend in worship and praise.

16. See Ps. 47:9.

17. See, e.g., 1 Sam. 2:10; Pss. 2:2; 89:38, 51.

18. The title is closely associated with the temple and Zion theology; see T. N. D. Mettinger, "Yahweh zebaoth," in *DDD,* p. 920.

Psalm 84

Since the beginning of Book Three at Psalm 73, the prayers have mostly expressed sorrow and pain at the strained relationship between God and the people. There has been little movement, as the people remain stuck and God seems distant. Psalm 84 declares the impasse over. The people sing and travel and celebrate God's presence. Just as in my grandparent's generation, this movement creates anticipation and the feeling that something special is about to happen. It reminds us that we too should seek Zion and look with anticipation to the times when we can move forward and worship the Lord.

Beth Tanner

Psalm 85: God Will Restore Us

Psalm 85 continues the story of Book Three. The Asaph Psalms, 73-83, tell a bigger story than the individual poems. Together they narrate a tumultuous relationship where at times the people are estranged from God and cry out and other times when they gather to praise God. The collection ends, however, first with God's side of the story (Psalms 81 and 82), followed by a cry from the people to God to come to their aid. Then Psalm 84 breaks in, offering the preparation for a festival in Zion. Now Psalm 85 is a song that asks God to restore the relationship and set the world right based on God's great acts in the past.[1] Zenger calls this "a prayerful assurance of YHWH's mighty promises of salvation."[2] Some scholars have argued the psalm was composed as a prayer for the end of the exile.[3] This was certainly a time of estrangement, but it is hardly the only time.[4] The issue in the psalm is the breach that needs to be healed, not the exact event that caused the breach. This is a prayer for anytime the people are in need of restoration. The people come before God in three stanzas:

God's actions of forgiveness in the past (vv. 1-3)
Petitions for God's forgiveness now (vv. 4-7)
Vision of a world restored (vv. 8-13)

The psalm as a whole then is a prayer for God to act now as God has acted in the past to return the people to the vision of God and God's people at peace. The psalm also then functions as a hope for the future completion of the kingdom. It is a prayer that stands as a constant hope for the people to strive for the promises of God.

1. Most see this psalm as a prayer for favor from God based on God's actions in the past. This is a common theme in the prayers for help. Tate argues correctly that the psalm does not contain other elements in prayers for help and should not be considered as such (*Psalms 51–100,* p. 367).

2. *Psalms 2,* p. 363.

3. E.g., Terrien, *The Psalms,* pp. 606-7. Tate (*Psalm 51-100,* p. 367) and Zenger (Hossfeld and Zenger, *Psalms 2,* p. 362) note that the problem with associating it with a historical event, especially the exile, is that the kingdom was not restored to an independent entity at that time.

4. See, e.g., the wilderness period as well as the cyclic turning of the people from God in the book of Judges and the words of the prophets that also indicate the fickle nature of the people.

For the leader. A Korahite[5] psalm.

1 *LORD, you favored your land;*
you returned the fortunes[6] of Jacob.
2 *You lifted the iniquity of your people;*
you covered all their sin. Selah
3 *You withdrew all your fury;*
you turned back from your fierce anger.

4 *Restore us,[7] O God of our salvation!*
Break off your anger toward us!
5 *Will you be angry with us forever?*
Will you stretch your anger from generation to generation?
6 *Will you not turn and give us life,*
so your people will rejoice in you?
7 *Show us your* hesed, *O LORD!*
Give us your salvation!

8 *May I[8] hear God the LORD speak,*
for he speaks peace unto his people, unto his faithful ones;
but let them not return to stupidity.[9]
9 *Truly, his salvation is near to those fearing him,*
for glory is dwelling in our land.

5. See note 1 on Psalm 42 superscription.

6. The exact meaning of the word is unclear. The problem is that the etymology of the word is not certain. It could be from the root *šbh* ("take captive") and so mean "captives," or it could be from the root *šwb* ("to turn back"), meaning "restore back" (BDB, p. 986; *HALOT,* p. 1385).

7. The translation of this word is difficult, as the multitude of translations attests. It could refer to the people as the MT implies, "turn us, O God," or it could refer to God if MT is emended to *šûḇ nāʾ* ("Return, please"), as reflected in NIV and NRSV. The choice is not clear, and as noted by Tate and others, the choice of meaning here ultimately hinges on what the interpreter determines is the psalm's sense (*Psalms 51–100,* p. 365). However, the entire section is a plea addressed to God and asks God to change God's mind about the people; as such, it would seem the subject here should be God.

8. The form here is clearly a cohortative and as such indicates a change in the poem. I read this form as the beginning of the next section; imperatives have given way to the wishes that complete the poem. Interestingly, most do not read the cohortative form here and attach this verse to the ones above (e.g., Tate, *Psalms 51–100,* p. 370).

9. This is another difficult line. LXX reads a different tradition, "and those who turn their hearts to him," and this is followed by NRSV. It is tempting to adopt this reading, since it makes more sense in the context. But MT is readable, and there is no compelling reason to adopt the LXX reading over it. Most scholars do not adopt the LXX reading.

10 Hesed *and faithfulness will meet;*
righteousness and peace will kiss.
11 *Faithfulness will sprout up from the earth,*
and righteousness will look down from heaven.
12 *Indeed, the* LORD *will give what is good,*
and our land will give its produce.
13 *Righteousness will go before him*
and prepare a way for his steps.

1-3 The prayer opens by describing what God has done for Israel. As noted above, the act that caused the estrangement is not specified, only God's reaction to the breach. These three verses are what Westermann calls descriptive praise, for they describe God's acts that are worthy of praise.[10] Interestingly, the prayer connects the people's faithfulness to peaceful possession of the land. This theme appears in the prophets. The land is not a permanent unconditional gift but one that is dependent on the people's fidelity (Isa. 3:1-15; Hos. 10:1-6; Amos 5:18-27). The declaration begins this without introduction, and a hearer struggles to understand the purpose of this unusual opening.

4-7 This next section clarifies the reason for vv. 1-3: they are a history lesson designed both to remind God of God's acts in the past and to offer hope to the people that God will again act as God has before. The center of the section is a fourfold plea for God to forget God's *anger,* given as both imperative statements and questions. The people's only hope is that God will *turn* around *(šûḇ)* and *restore* the people (vv. 4a and 6a). There is no explanation offered or reasons for God to *turn,* except God's own history of doing so in vv. 1-3. The words are direct. The only way back to a relationship is for God to forgive. This section is why several commentators see this psalm as a cry for help.[11] But there is none of the urgency of a critical situation as is the case in prayers for help. It is just as likely that this is a prayer that could be prayed daily, for the relationship always depends on God's forgiveness and God's putting away of anger. God's forgiveness is not for extreme situations. Rather, it is one of the attributes that is a daily staple. It is the reason for life and for rejoicing (v. 6) and *salvation* (v. 7).

8-13 At v. 8, a singular voice is heard. Kraus argues this is a priestly or prophetic oracle given as assurance.[12] It is certainly possible that this is a multivoiced prayer and here another, probably a leader of the congregation, comes to the forefront. But as noted earlier, the more interesting piece is the

10. *Praise and Lament in the Psalms,* p. 117. But interestingly, Westermann sees this prayer as a lament and this section, not as descriptive praise, but a call for God to act (p. 55).

11. E.g., Westermann, *Praise and Lament in the Psalms,* p. 55.

12. *Psalms 60–150,* p. 176.

change in grammar from imperatives and questions in vv. 4-7 to a cohortative form that opens v. 8. To me, this signals a change from pleas to hope for the future based on the past. These wishes take up almost half of the poem. The effect is that by the end of the psalm, the former pleas are forgotten and the words of a peaceful kingdom are the lasting images.

What better word is there for the Lord to speak to the people in answer to their pleading than "shalom" (v. 8)? Shalom, of course, is much more than the absence of war; it is the culmination of God's kingdom, where all have what they need and live in comfort and without fear. But humans being what they are, v. 8c warns the people to remember enough of the past so they do not repeat it.[13] God's anger was the problem in the second section, but here other attributes flood the picture: *salvation* and *glory* (v. 9), *hesed and faithfulness meet* and *righteousness and peace kiss* (v. 10). They greet each other again, it seems, after the estrangement separated them just as the people and God were separated. Verse 11 offers another vision of the reunion, this one with metaphors from creation.

Verses 11-12 affirm that all is now in balance, for the land is producing (v. 12) and righteousness allows for God to walk on the earth. This walking can bring to mind Gen. 3:8, where all is in balance right before God discovered what the humans had done. The design is for all to share the same space, content and peaceful.

This psalm does speak of fearful times when God is angry at the people and the people are pleading for God to change God's mind. Yet its overall message is at the end, where all is again in balance and all is ready for God to walk among the people. The forgiveness of God is what makes this possible. The images of peace and righteousness meeting are just as much a hope today as they were in the ancient past. The psalm also reminds us to hope that God will act now as God is known to have acted in the past. We can depend on the same God that our ancestors did.

Kraus's reading can also be correct as he understands this psalm as a warning or lesson not to repeat the mistakes that caused the breach between God and the people. In this way, the psalm can also serve as a call for us to look at our lives as a people. What acts do we need to confess? Is God angry with us? In a world where others are condemned as evil, how often do we look at our own acts and evaluate them against the values of God's kingdom? This psalm can offer a call to examination and confession in a world that is in desperate need of such confession.

BETH TANNER

13. Much like the warning in Ps. 95:8-11.

Psalm 86: Hear My Prayer

Psalm 86 offers a different perspective from most of the prayers for help in Book Three. It is the prayer of an individual and is the only psalm with a superscription concerning David in Book Three. Its appearance is somewhat surprising after the declaration at the end of Book Two that "The prayers of David, son of Jesse, are completed." In addition, scholars have noted that this psalm reuses phrases from other psalms, and this has often led to a negative perception of this text as unoriginal and secondary.[1] Zenger, however, has noted that this reuse of other materials provides a type of poetic genius of its own that is a summary of the Davidic psalms together with a Sinai theology, providing a new and unique piece.[2] Psalm 86, then, uses older materials to create a new theology for a post-David Israel. David's prayers may be ended, but the dynasty of kings and the nation go on. This prayer of an individual also stands in this book to remind us that individual and community concerns are bound together.

The structure of the psalm is also unique. It both begins (vv. 1-7) and ends (vv. 14-17) with petitions, with a section of hymnic praise and thanksgiving in the center (vv. 8-13).[3] This fluctuation from petition to thanksgiving and back to petition is unusual, but is not unknown, for it appears in Psalm 55 and Jer. 20:7-18. This prayer affirms the cyclic nature of our lives: often praise can come forth in the midst of cries to God as we struggle to deal with our sorrow and fear.

Petitions for God to hear and answer (vv. 1-7)
Praise and thanksgiving (vv. 8-13)
Petitions for God to act (vv. 14-17)

A Davidic prayer.

1 *Incline your ear, O LORD, and answer me,*
for I am poor and needy.
2 *Guard my life,*[4] *for I am loyal;*

1. This was primarily the determination of earlier scholars. E.g., A. F. Kirkpatrick writes, "It claims no poetic originality"; *The Book of Psalms* (Cambridge: Cambridge University Press, 1902), p. 515. Later scholars do not consider originality as the only mark of a good Hebrew poem.

2. *Psalms 2,* p. 369.

3. This structure is seen by some scholars as incorrect, and they rearrange the prayer, placing vv. 8-13 at the end (e.g., Hans Schmidt, *Die Psalmen* [HAT 15; Tübingen: Mohr, 1934], p. 162).

4. Lit., *napšî.* This word has a wide range of meanings: "Soul, living being, self." It is the essence of what makes a sack of bones alive.

Save your servant, the one trusting in you;
you are my God.
3 *Be gracious to me, O Lord;*
unto you I cry all day.
4 *Make glad the soul of your servant,*
for to you I lift up my soul.
5 *For you, Lord, are good and forgiving,*
abounding in hesed *to all calling on you.*
6 *Give ear, O Lord, to my prayer;*
listen to the sound of my pleading.
7 *In the day of my distress, I will call to you,*
for you will answer me.

8 *There is none like you among the gods, Lord;*
and there are no deeds that compare to yours.
9 *All the nations that you made,*
they come and bow down before you, O Lord;
they glorify your name,
10 *for you are great, working wonders.*
You alone are God.
11 *Teach me, O Lord, your way,*
and I will walk in your faithfulness;
unite my heart to fear your name.[5]
12 *I will praise you, O Lord my God, with all my heart;*
I will glorify your name forever,
13 *for great is your* hesed[6] *toward me;*
you snatched me[7] *from the depth of Sheol.*

14 *O God, the insolent rise up against me;*
a violent crowd[8] *is seeking me.*[9]
They do not set you before them.
15 *But you, O Lord, are a God of motherly compassion,*
gracious, slow to anger,

5. *Yaḥēḏ* appears only here as a *piel,* with a meaning of *unite.* LXX reads from a different root, *ḥdh* ("to glorify"). MT is readable, if somewhat awkward.

6. 11QPs[d] has a different word order, but only part of the phrase is preserved: "[for great unto] me is your *hesed*"; García Martínez, Tigchelaar, and van der Woude, *Qumran Cave 11: II,* p. 74.

7. Lit., *nap̱šî.*

8. Modern translations render "band of ruthless ones." However, the word *ʿᵃḏaṯ* is the word used for a congregation. A crowd seems a more appropriate translation.

9. Lit., *nap̱šî.*

and abounding in hesed *and faithfulness.*
16 *Turn to me and be gracious to me!*
Give your strength to your servant!
Save the child of your handmaiden!
17 *Make a sign for me*[10] *of goodness;*
those hating me will see it and be ashamed,
for you are the LORD*;*
you helped me and you comforted me.

1-7 The central image of vv. 1-7 is a desire for God to *listen* and *answer* (vv. 1a, 6a, 6b, 7a, 7b), with various reasons given for the need of God's attention. The pattern inside this frame fluctuates between additional petitions and the reasons for those petitions. The exact problem is not specified, only that the one praying is *poor and needy* (v. 1) and is crying out (v. 3). The other petitions in this section add urgency as this one asks for God to *guard my life* (v. 2), *be gracious* (v. 3), and finally *make glad* (v. 4). This last petition implies that God will not only hear and save but will also cause joy to return, a statement that implies restoration.

A form of the word *nep̱eš* appears three times in vv. 2, 4a, and 4b. This word in Hebrew means much more than the traditional translation of *soul.* The word means, literally, "self" or "life" and indicates here the seriousness of the situation: this one's very *life* is at stake. This one praying is also described as *ʿaḇdeḵā* (vv. 2b and 4a). This word also has an expanded Hebrew meaning of both a *servant* and one who worships. This term then epitomizes one who *trusts* (v. 2b) and one who declares *you are my God* (v. 2c). It is also a term used often of David, which may explain the superscription dedication. This section uses a dual reasoning for why God should hear and answer: first, this one is faithful and second, this one is in distress — a common theme in the individual prayers for help from Book Two that are dedicated to events in David's life.

Finally, this section also offers a description of God in v. 5 which, as Zenger notes, recalls the confession of Exod. 34:6.[11] The attributes this prayer depends on for God's action are the very same attributes that Israel has always depended on. The exodus begins with God hearing the cries of the people (Exod. 2:24) and acting on their behalf, and the one praying now requests the same.

8-13 Without warning, the prayer turns at vv. 8. Cries transform to praise. Verse 8 declares the same as Psalm 82, that the Lord is greater than

10. Lit., "with me" but it can have the meaning of "to" (Waltke and O'Connor, *Biblical Hebrew Syntax,* p. 219).

11. *Psalms 2,* p. 372.

all other gods. Verse 9 echos this by declaring that God *made all the nations* and they all *bow down before* their Creator. Verse 10 again declares that God's deeds are *great* and God is God *alone,* a claim in the ten words given at Sinai. These verses speak of a great and universal God and of the world the way that it should be. The confidence here is disconcerting, for it is such a contrast against vv. 1-7, even if the declarations are common in other biblical contexts.[12] The world does not work this way, then or now. The juxtaposition here causes the hearers to work at how these two sections are related, and from working at the connection, hearers become active participants in doing their own theological work.

Verses 11-13 turn to the state of the one praying. Praise gives way to additional petitions and statements of the transformed life of the one praying. Verse 4 asked for restoration, and so do the petitions of v. 11. The one praying asks to be taught, as in Psalm 51, and for the one's *heart* to be united. This last phrase is unique to this context, but also reflects exactly what the hearers are trying to do in connecting the sections of the psalm — to make connections between the cries of suffering and praise. Verse 12 returns to declaration. Restoration will result in a response of *praise.* Verse 13 ends this section directly opposite of where it began. Verses 8-9 speak of the great Creator God who controls *all the nations,* and here God is praised for God's acts of salvation for the individual. The great God of All is also the personal God of God's servant.

14-17 Again without warning, praise gives way to fear. Verse 14 describes what is troubling the one praying. The description is chilling, with a lone one against *a violent crowd* who are godless — a direct contrast to how the world was described in v. 9. All is not well, and the praise lifted was clearly not in response to a transformed situation. From that fact the prayer reminds all that God and humans do not operate in some automatic universe where God fixes everything that hurts. Belief must stand and praise, even when the world is broken.

The next two verses turn exclusively to God. Verse 15 returns to the attributes of God from Exod. 34:6, and the contrast with the ones of v. 14 is striking. These are the attributes that first appear in the Exodus passage, but are repeated in other forms throughout the Bible: Num. 14:18; Pss. 103:8; 145:8; Joel 2:13; and Jonah 4:2. Verse 16 presents three petitions, and somewhat surprisingly the petitions are not for God to act against the enemies. The petitions are for God to *turn and be gracious, give strength,* and *save* the one praying. In this, the petitions are much like the ones in the first section. The message is that only God can rescue this one from trouble. Verse 17 begins

12. V. 8 is a reflection of Exod. 15:11; Deut. 3:24; 2 Sam. 7:22; 1 Kgs. 8:23; 1 Chr. 17:20. V. 9 is a reflection of Isa. 2:3-4; 66:18-19; Zech. 14:9; Pss. 66:4; 72:11; 148:11. V. 10 reflects Ps. 72:18.

with the last petition, which is a request for God to *make a sign of goodness.* The full meaning of the phrase is uncertain, since it appears only here, but whatever this *sign of goodness is,* it will cause *those hating* to *be ashamed.* It could be a sign of this one's vindication or a sign of God's favor. The prayer ends with another declaration of who God is, based on God's past actions: *you helped me and you comforted me.*

Through the two gaps between the sections, this prayer engages all to contemplate how petition and praise "unite" in this psalm. The one moves into praise and back to petition, so the praise is disinterested praise, for it is not in response to something God provided. The effect then is pedagogical and powerful. Praise is not just given when God fixes our lives. Praise is also offered in the midst of petitions for help. To reinforce this point, the attributes of God are the ones that Israel has always depended on — not for salvation from their enemies but salvation from themselves and their actions. These attributes are the very ones we also depend on: the graciousness and forgiveness of God. Another interesting point is that while the enemies are in full view (v. 14), in the whole scope of the poem it is God that is needed to help and comfort. The enemies, this poem declares, are of little consequence. Ultimately, life depends on God's gracious love and compassion and not on the evil done by humans.

Beth Tanner

Psalm 87: A Song of Zion

While other psalms have sections that are problematic, this short psalm is problematic from start to finish, making it very difficult to translate and interpret. These difficulties result in multiple emendations, and some scholars even rearrange the text, believing this aids in its understanding. In this translation, the MT is followed without the major changes that are adopted by some.[1]

What is clear is that this psalm is a song that celebrates and praises Zion as the city where God resides and as the primeval birthplace of the world. The psalm is divided into two sections by the use of *Selah* at the end of vv. 3 and 6. Verse 7 stands alone and provides a third change of scene.

A Korahite[2] psalm. A song.

1 *His foundation[3] is in the holy mountain.[4]*
2 *The* LORD *loves the gates of Zion,*
more than all the dwellings of Jacob.
3 *Glorious things are spoken of you,*
O city of God. Selah

4 *I will talk of[5] Rahab and Babylon among[6] those knowing me;*
Philistia too, and Tyre with Cush,
"This one was born there."
5 *And of Zion, it is said, "This one and that one were born here.*
The Most High himself establishes it."

1. J. A. Emerton notes that there have been multiple attempts both in rearranging the current text and in emendations of the text. He suggests that the only alternative is to work with MT as it is while understanding there is some corruption of the text; "The Problem of Psalm lxxxvii," *VT* 50 (2000) 183-99.

2. See note 1 on Psalm 42 superscription.

3. This line is probably corrupt. Translation above reflects MT. NRSV follows an emendation that repoints *y^e^sûḏāṯô* as a passive participle, reading "city he founded" as suggested by Dahood, *Psalms II,* p. 299.

4. MT has the plural construct *harrê,* but most read it as an honorific plural; see Waltke and O'Connor, *Biblical Hebrew Syntax,* p. 122.

5. *'Azkîr,* lit., "I will cause to remember." It is problematic, for the causative agent is not clear. Most think it has the force of "I will remember 'x' to 'y,'" which means to speak of one to another. NIV follows Dahood, who argues for "record," relating this to the action in v. 6 of recording in a book (*Psalms II,* pp. 251-52).

6. *L^e^yōḏ'āy* is usually translated as "to" or "for," but the meaning of *those knowing me* is impossible to discern if it is a third party. Most read the preposition with a referent meaning, i.e., Babylon and Rahab know God.

6 *The* LORD *writes in the register of peoples,*
"This one was born there." Selah

7 *Singers as well as dancers say,*[7]
"All my roots[8] *are in her."*

1-3 While there are a few grammatical problems in these verses, the meaning is fairly clear. The section is concerned with giving praise to *Zion,* God's holy abode. Zion is the place where God has placed the *foundation* (v. 1). Zenger notes that the term *mountain* here is more than the area of the actual city of Jerusalem, but also reflects "the cosmic primal mountain that as both world-mountain and mountain of paradise gives the earth stability and life."[9] Verse 2 declares Zion the place of God's heart.[10] Verse 3 reminds that Zion will always be remembered. The section as a whole gives praise to Zion because God chose this city as the place of residence.

4-6 This next section is very problematic, and how one resolves several translation issues will determine the meaning of the entire section. Emerton correctly notes that the central issue is how to understand *zeh yullaḏ-šām* of vv. 4 and 6 along with *ʾîš w*^{e}*ʾîš yullaḏ-bāh* of v. 5.[11] Who is the referent for *zeh* and *ʾîš w*^{e}*ʾîš?* Kraus argues that the referent is the people of the Diaspora,[12] and he further reads v. 5 with the LXX as "But Zion, I call her mother."[13] He sees the meaning as Zion being the mother of both native and foreign-born Jews and all of vv. 4-6 as set in the heavenly council, where the audience can overhear God as God *writes* in a book all of the people and where they were *born.*[14] Thijs Booij argues that the nations represented here are just that — nations — and this section is a mythological one envisioning the primeval event of Zion birthing the nations.[15] His argument is intricate,

7. This line is corrupt. Multiple suggestions have been offered. LXX follows another tradition here, reading "As all rejoicing is your dwelling," which also is very difficult to understand. Most translations add the word "say" or "speak" to aid in interpretation.

8. Lit., *maʿyānay* ("my springs"). Yet as NJPS points out, another meaning for this word is "origin" or "point of origin." so it uses the word *roots,* which seems a better fit within the context.

9. *Psalms 2,* p. 382.

10. See Ps. 78:68 for a similar statement.

11. "The Problem of Psalm lxxxvii," p. 186.

12. *Psalms 60–150,* p. 188.

13. *Psalms 60–150,* p. 184. Reading LXX as preferable to the MT is not accepted by most scholars. Emerton notes that the LXX reading may be "the result of an inner-Greek corruption" and should not be adopted over the Hebrew ("The Problem of Psalm lxxxvii," p. 187).

14. Kraus, *Psalms 60–150,* p. 187.

15. "Some Observations on Psalm lxxxvii," *VT* 37 (1987) 16-25.

using ancient Near Eastern parallels, but is convincing both for its use of the MT text as it is and because it does not require a referent outside of the psalm itself.

If Booij is correct, these verses, then, declare that Zion is not only the favorite of God's heart (v. 2), but that Zion birthed the other nations listed here. So using Booij's cogent reading, v. 4 speaks of nations that were birthed *there,* with *there* referring to *Zion.* The nations covers superpowers, with *Rahab,* another name for Egypt,[16] and *Babylon,* followed by neighbors *Philistia* and *Tyre,* and finally *Cush,* or Ethiopia, as the farthest nation fathomable at the time. The list then is poetic and is not meant as exclusive, but covering the globe. This claim of universal rule from Zion is claimed in several other texts, such as Isa. 2:2 and 19:23-25. Verse 5 confirms the birth of the nations in *Zion* along with the idea that it was the *Most High* that established the city.[17] The final mythological vision is presented in v. 6 as a conclusion to the section where God legalizes this primeval birth by recording it in a *register.* The image is theologically powerful since it declares that these nations, many of whom have fought and conquered Israel, are all wayward children of God. This image of the nations as ungrateful children is similar to Hosea 11, where it is Israel that is the ungrateful child.

7 Here the scene changes, but to exactly what is difficult to say. The verse is corrupt, and to make sense of it at least some other words must be added. What does seem clear here is that the last scene of the prayer is one of celebration of what the psalm has declared, that Zion is the birthplace of the nations. It is certainly possible that this was the first verse of a third section or stanza and this is all that remains.

The psalm as a whole may serve as an introduction for a celebration of Zion. But Zion is not celebrated for any other reason than that God established it and God maintains it by making it a residence, God's home on earth. The people are to celebrate because it is here that they can visit God and be assured of God's presence and protection. There is also a vision of a primeval birthing where all the nations come from the same place, a reminder to all that despite what the world looks like, we are all related; we are one human family. Its placement here signals a preparation for the end of Book Three and the beginning of Book Four, which declares that God is the king and ruler of the world.

In today's world, this psalm seems far removed from our reality. Not only has God gone worldwide in God's presence, but Jerusalem is now a city divided by religious groups that hate each other and often declare that the world will only be safe when all the others are destroyed. We are definitely

16. See Ps. 89:10 or Isa. 30:7.

17. The suffix is 3fs, referring clearly to the city "birthed in her."

removed from the kinship this psalm declares. This is exactly why we may need this little psalm, for it expresses what we often forget: God birthed us all and we all come from the same origin, and eventually all will return to the same source.

Beth Tanner

Psalm 88: I Am As One Dead

Psalm 88 and 89 stand together at the end of Book Three as the darkest place in the whole book of Psalms. Both are prayers for help, and both end without resolution. Psalm 88 is the cry of an individual who sees her problem as God. Its images provide an unflinching view of a human who feels as if God has not only abandoned her, but that God has caused her situation in the first place. The psalm's message is shocking to modern readers who are unaccustomed to the frankness of these ancient prayers for help.

The psalm can be divided into three sections:

Cry to God and Current Situation (vv. 1-9)
Questioning of God (vv. 10-12)
Accusations against God (vv. 13-18)[1]

While these sections can aid in seeing the pattern of the prayer, it is really a monologue thrown against a dark and terrifying void, beginning and ending with unanswered cries to God. The psalm is unusual in that there are none of the gaps that are commonly seen in prayers for help. It offers no change in circumstance or even any hope that there will be a change in the situation.

A song. A Korahite psalm.[2] *For the leader. According to mahalath leannoth.*[3] *A maskil*[4] *of Heman the Ezrahite.*[5]

1 *O LORD, God of my salvation,*
daily, I cry out,
nightly before you.[6]

1. There is a general consensus over the stanza divisions based on the traditional lament divisions of plea (vv. 1-2) and complaint (vv. 3-8, 9-12, and 13-18); see, e.g., Tate, *Psalms 51–100,* p. 398. However, vv. 1-2 and 9 provide an *inclusio* around this large section that suggests this section should not be separated into plea and complaint as individual sections.

2. See note 1 on Psalm 42 superscription.

3. This phrase occurs only here, and its meaning is uncertain. It probably refers to the name of a tune or a musical instrument.

4. See note 2 on Psalm 32 superscription.

5. Heman is mentioned in 1 Kgs. 4:31 as one of a group of wise men during the time of Solomon and in 1 Chr. 6:33 as one of the Kohahites. The Heman here may be one of these two men or another person altogether.

6. The grammar is difficult, reading, lit., "day-I cry out in the night before you," which leads to a plethora of English translations. The issue is whether this verse should be two or three lines long. NRSV and NIV opt for two lines. Most scholars opt for three (Kraus, *Psalms*

2 *May my prayer come into your presence;*
incline your ear to my loud cry,
3 *for my soul is saturated with distress,*[7]
my life draws near to Sheol.
4 *I am thought of as one of those going down to the Pit;*
I am like one without strength.[8]
5 *With the dead, I am set free,*[9]
like the one slain, ones lying in a grave,
whom you do not remember anymore,
who is cut off[10] *from your hand.*
6 *You have put me in the depths of the Pit,*
in a dark place, in the deeps.
7 *Your anger lies heavy upon me;*
with all your waves, you answer (me).[11] Selah
8 *You have caused my companions*[12] *to be far from me;*
You have made me a horror to them;
trapped, I cannot escape.
9 *My eyes*[13] *grow dim from my affliction;*
I cry to you, O LORD, every day;
I spread out my palms to you.

60–150, p. 190; Tate, *Psalms 51–100,* p. 393). Zenger also follows MT as above, with slight variations; *Psalms 2,* p. 389.

7. Hebrew uses the plural here, probably for emphasis (Waltke and O'Connor, *Biblical Hebrew Syntax,* p. 119.

8. The word *ʾeyāl* appears only here. It is listed in BDB (p. 33b) as an Aramaic loanword meaning "help," as reflected in most modern translations (NRSV, NIV). *HALOT,* however, sees it as associated with the Hebrew *ʾayil* ("strength"). *Strength* is probably the better choice, especially with the use of *geḇer* ("man").

9. This word means "to set free," as from slavery in Exod. 21:2. NJPS "abandoned" may go too far. All of the lines refer to one who is dying or dead, so the idea is that the person is clearly moving from the world of the living to the world of the dead. Zenger uses "expelled," which has the same sense; *Psalms 2,* p. 389.

10. Lit., "and they, from your hand, they are cut off." The double use of "they" provides emphasis here, stressing that of all of these terrible things, being *cut off* from God's *hand* is the worst of all.

11. This translation follows the Hebrew literally. The verb has two different meanings: "to answer" and "to be afflicted." Most English translations use a variation of the second meaning to make sense of the line, but if *answer* is used, the line does make sense: not only has God placed the one in a terrible place, but out of God's *anger,* the *answer* given to this one is more turmoil.

12. Lit., *meyuddāʿay* ("the ones knowing me").

13. Hebrew uses the singular here.

10 *Do you do wonders for the dead?*
Or do the Rephaim[14] *rise up to praise you?* Selah
11 *Is your* hesed *declared in the grave?*
Your faithfulness in the place of death?[15]
12 *Are your wonders known in the darkness*
or your righteousness in the land of oblivion?

13 *As for me, O LORD, I cried for help unto you;*
in the morning, my prayer confronts you.[16]
14 *Why, O LORD, do you reject me?*[17]
Why do you hide your face from me?
15 *I have been afflicted and close to death from my youth;*
I suffer your terrors; I am petrified.[18]
16 *Your anger has swept over me;*
your dread assaults destroy me.
17 *They surround me like waters all day;*
they close in on me completely.
18 *You cause the one who loves me*
and my friend to distance themselves from me;
only darkness knows me.[19]

14. The exact meaning of this word is uncertain. It may be from the root *rph* ("to sink"), and this is reflected in the NRSV's "the shades," or dead ones that sink down. It could also be from the root *rp'* ("healers"). *Rᵉpā'îm* also refers to a group of people that predate the Israelites in Canaan (Deut. 2:10-11) and can mean "the dead," as in Isa. 26:14. What seems clear here is that the Rephaim are related to the dead ones in v. 10a and, as noted in several studies in Ugaritic, maybe royal or heroic dead ones; see Tate, *Psalms 51–100*, p. 396.

15. Lit., *'ᵃḇaddôn*, used as parallel to Sheol; see Prov. 15:11.

16. *Qādam* has the sense of "meeting" in the *piel*, but can also mean *confront*, as in Ps. 17:13, where God confronts the enemies. Since God is the problem in this psalm, it is reasonable to assume that the prayer is confronting God.

17. Lit., *napšî*.

18. This word appears only here. LXX has a word meaning "desperate," and most modern translations use some form of "helpless" or "desperate." The *BHS* critical apparatus suggests, based on the LXX, that the word be emended to *'āp̄ûḡâ* ("to be weary"). The reading in 4QPsᵗ appears to be based on the root *pwr* ("I am frustrated"); Ulrich, Cross et al., *Qumran Cave 4: XI*, p. 155. In addition, the cohortative form is puzzling in both MT and the DSS. Zenger, however, takes the word from the root *pwn* ("to grow stiff or paralyzed"), so *petrified;* this is the best solution offered, and MT remains as it is; *Psalms 2*, p. 391.

19. This line is difficult, as various translations indicate. One probable reason for the syntax is so the psalm can end with the word *maḥšāḵ* ("darkness" or "a dark place"). It has traditionally been translated as "my companions are in darkness" (NRSV), which makes little sense. NJPS translates "my companions out of my sight." But there is no compelling reason to make *one who loves me* and *friend* the subject of the *pual* participle with a 1cs suffix. In addition, the conjunction between the two nouns probably indicates a compound subject

1-2 The prayer begins with a salutation, which is somewhat unusual in prayers for help that have an urgency to them. Psalm 22 begins, "My God, my God, why have you forsaken me?" and Psalm 69 begins, "Save me, O God, because the water has come to my neck." Psalm 88 begins instead with *O LORD, God of my salvation,* but this is the first and last line of the psalm that is not one of anguish. Indeed, by the end of the psalm, this one line will scarcely be remembered for all of the pain that pours out. In fact, by the end of the psalm, one may wonder if this epithet for God is an expression of great faith or great irony.

The remainder of the section is pleas to God that also describe the problem. As with most prayers for help, the exact situation is not expressed, but what is clear is that the prayer expresses how one feels when her cries are not being heard. The prayer wishes that these cries would *come into your presence* and that God would turn an *ear* and listen. The problem is with God, and God, it seems, is absent or not listening.

3-9 In one of the most painful pieces of Scripture, suffering is described in terms of abandonment and lostness. Verse 3 describes distress so great that it *saturates* the soul so there is room for nothing else. Verse 4 sets the prayer at the edge of life, and whether that nearness is physical or emotional, the result is the same. This is a prayer spoken in the last moments, when *strength* and hope have faded away.

Verses 5-7 continue the imagery of death, with the first line declaring the deep irony that there may be freedom, but freedom only to be with *the dead.* Verse 5 moves to the heart of the problem, and the problem is God, who does not *remember* and, even worse, has *cut off* this one. Verses 6 and 7 deepen the sorrow as God is accused of placing the person in darkness and God's *anger* is a *heavy* weight. Verse 7 is often translated as "you overwhelm me with your waves"; but this Hebrew word also means "to answer," and so it is possible that the only answer the person receives is the battering of the waves as the person is tossed again and again into the deeps. This psalm certainly presents a contrast with Psalm 139, where God is declared as the one who will be present even at the ends of the earth and in the deepest darkness (139:8-12). Here God appears to cast this one into the darkest places on earth and then turn away. These verses are an expression of what it means to lose all hope and to believe that God has turned against you.

Verse 8 continues the accusations against God, and not only has God withdrawn God's hand, but God has caused human friends to turn away as well. Verses 5-8 describe what it feels like to be totally and completely alone and friendless. In verse 9, *my eyes grow dim from my affliction* refers not to

---

instead of a new line. NIV, probably correctly for the context of the psalm, translates "the darkness is my closest friend." The above translation is a closer translation of the Hebrew, retaining the "knowing" which also appears in v. 8 (see n. 12 above).

eyesight but is a measurement of vitality.[20] The section ends with more cries to God. This provides an *inclusio* with vv. 1 and 2, so the cries to God that go unanswered are the beginning and end of all the other problems. This is a true poetic rendering of a "dark night of the soul."

10-12 The next section presents God with a series of rhetorical questions. The questions are philosophical and inquire what happens after death. These are unusual, for the Hebrew Scriptures rarely ask about the afterlife. These questions are meant to get a rise out of the silent God, to challenge God's power over death, and to stress that with death, the relationship will be broken. This idea of death severing the relationship is seen in other psalms as well, such as 6:5 and 30:9. However, Psalm 139 presents the other side, declaring, "if I make Sheol a bed, behold, there you are!" (v. 8). The one praying feels close to death and can hurl questions at God meant to shock God into action. God should act now before it is too late. This prayer holds nothing back and expresses the pain of a soul lost and seeking a relationship with a silent God.

13-18 The final section moves from questions to accusations. Verse 13 is often translated as "my prayer comes before you," but the verb *qdm* can mean "to confront" as in Ps. 17:13, and this is more of the sense here. This is not a polite Sunday School prayer but a prayer on the edge that is trying to get God to act. This prayer is not meant to wait in the in-box, but is a "howler" of Harry Potter fame. It demands attention. Verse 14 returns to questions, but this time the questions are personal, "why God?" Verses 15-17 set the one praying as an enemy of God who is being attacked. Verse 16 is reminiscent of v. 3, where the one is surrounded and saturated by God's *anger.* The final verse summarizes the aloneness that has saturated the prayer. God has caused all of the humans to turn away, and *darkness* is the only one who now *knows* this one.

Psalm 88 makes people uncomfortable. It confronts the ways we pray and the ways we think prayer must be done. It confronts all of the memories we have of dark and lonely nights in our own lives. It confronts the relationship we have with God. It confronts each of us with its truth stripped bare of any nice platitudes. It shines a bright light on the darkest places where the human soul wallows. Joan Didion has written about her feelings after the sudden loss of her husband of forty years, and her words sound much like this psalm: "I myself felt invisible for a period of time, incorporeal. I seemed to have crossed one of those legendary rivers that divide the living from the dead, entered a place in which I could be seen only by those who were themselves recently bereaved."[21]

20. Tate notes that "eye" has this meaning of vitality in 1 Sam. 14:27, 29; Deut. 34:7; Ps. 19:8; Ezra 9:8 (*Psalms 51–100,* p. 402).

21. *The Year of Magical Thinking* (New York: Knopf, 2005), p. 75.

The psalm also teaches a lesson about the real world, for sometimes there is no happy ending, no gap to jump in a prayer for help that gets us to praise. The hard truth is that people suffer and even die, sometimes in horrible circumstances and crying out to a God that seems silent. For me, this prayer provides legitimacy to all the prayers of praise where the world looks perfect. It speaks to times when there is no reason, theological or otherwise, that can explain the images of violence burned into my brain. It also speaks to those who die feeling as if God is nowhere to be found, for here their words of fear and anger appear as sacred Scripture, showing that God did indeed hear their cries. It also speaks of God, a God who is Creator and King of the Universe and who also does not condemn honest, painful conversation with the humans God created — and in that it may represent better than other texts the love that God has for us, these earthly creatures.

Beth Tanner

Psalm 89: A History Lesson for God

Like Psalm 88, Psalm 89 is a prayer accusing God of not living up to God's promises. In this psalm, the promises are ones made to King David and the Israelites. It has a unique form since it is a prayer for help in reverse. The first thirty-seven verses offer praise to God and tell the story of God's claiming of David and of Israel and the promises God made at the time. Verses 38-51 are the heart of the prayer and state that God has abandoned his anointed and, by extension, the people. The prayer ends like the previous one, without resolution. The final two lines, added by a later editor, stand as the closing words of Book Three and are in sharp contrast to the words that came before, leaving a large gap.

The prayer has two large sections (vv. 1-37 and 38-51) with an editorial ending (v. 52). Each of these sections can be further divided into stanzas.

The relationship of old (vv. 1-4)
Hymns to the Lord (vv. 5-12)
The relationship of the recent past (vv. 13-18)
God's covenant with Israel (vv. 19-37)
The current situation and God's reversal (vv. 38-45)
Seeking relationship with God (vv. 46-51)
Editorial addition (v. 52)

Over the course of scholarship, some have questioned the unity of the psalm and have divided it into three pieces or independent poems (vv. 1-18, 19-37, and 38-51).[1] This may indeed be the case in its early reception history,[2] but the psalm is presented in the biblical text as a whole and stands next to Psalm 88 as a testament to the difficulty of life and relationship, even for God's own chosen one, and to read it as anything other than a whole poetic piece would destroy its unique message. There are also clear connections throughout the psalm in the use of several Hebrew forms of *ḥesed*/"steadfast love" (vv. 1, 2, 14, 24, 28, 33, and 49) and *ʾᵉmônâ*/"faithfulness" (vv. 1, 2, 5, 8, 14, 24, 33, 49). These two key attributes of God (Exod. 34:6) are praised, promised, and then questioned. In like manner, the word for God's promised relationship with

1. See Kraus, *Psalms 60–150,* pp. 202-3.

2. There is also a fragment of Psalm 89 at Qumran (4Q236 = 4QPs89) that poses additional questions, for it is not in the same verse order and appears to contain only some of the verses in MT. The existent text is vv. 20-22, 26, 23, 27-28, and 31. See Peter W. Flint, "A Form of Psalm 89 (4Q236 = 41Ps89)," in *The Dead Sea Scrolls: Hebrew, Aramaic, and Greek Texts with English Translations,* ed. James H. Charlesworth et al., Vol. 4A: *Pseudepigraphic and Non-Masoretic Psalms and Prayers* (Tübingen: Mohr Siebeck and Louisville: Westminster John Knox, 1997), pp. 40-45.

David, *b^erîṯ*/"covenant" (vv. 3, 28, 34, and 39), is also praised, guaranteed, and then challenged. Another connecting poetic device is the dominance of the pronoun *you* in vv. 9-14 and 38-45. The pronoun appears fourteen times in various forms in vv. 9 to 14, and the focus is on the power and supremacy of God. In vv. 38-45, the pronoun appears eighteen times, but the message could not be more different, and the *you* is now not the object of praise, but accusation.[3]

A maskil[4] for Ethan the Ezrahite.[5]

1 *Of the* hesed[6] *of the* LORD[7] *forever I will sing;*
generation to generation I will make known your faithfulness with my mouth;
2 *for I will declare, "Your*[8] hesed *is built to last;*
the heavens, your faithfulness is established in them."[9]
3 *"I cut a covenant with my chosen;*
I have sworn to David, my servant.
4 *I will establish your descendants forever;*
and build your throne for generations." Selah

5 *The heavens praise your wonders, O* LORD,
also your faithfulness in the assembly of holy ones;
6 *for who in the clouds can be compared with the* LORD?
Who is like the LORD *among the divine beings?*
7 *God is feared in the council of the holy ones,*
great and fierce above all surrounding him.
8 *O* LORD, *God of hosts, who is like you?*
O Mighty LORD, *your faithfulness surrounds you.*

3. This includes all uses of the pronoun as the person of the verb, the possessive preposition, and as an independent pronoun. Interestingly, the psalm does have a rough chiastic structure: a = 1-4 and a' 46-51; b = 5-18 and b′ = 38-45 and a center of 19-37. This fits the message as well, for it is God's promises that are the issue in the entire poem.

4. See note 2 on Psalm 32 superscription.

5. Ethan is listed as a Levitical musician in 1 Chr. 15:17, 19 and as a singer in 1 Chr. 6:42. It is not known if this is the same Ethan as in the superscription.

6. MT uses the honorific plural of *ḥeseḏ* here (Waltke and O'Connor, *Biblical Hebrew Syntax*, p. 123).

7. Some translations such as NRSV follow LXX here in adding a 2ms suffix, reading LORD as a vocative, but there is no compelling reason to read this over MT.

8. MT does not have a 2ms suffix. Dahood argues that the 2ms suffix in the second line serves both words (*Psalms II*, p. 312). It is also possible that the text is corrupt.

9. Reading with MT, the *BHS* critical apparatus suggests reading as a comparison; also Kraus, *Psalms 60–150*, p. 200.

9 *You rule over the surging sea;*
when its waves rise, you still them.
10 *YOU crushed Rahab like a corpse;*
with your mighty arm, you scattered your enemies.
11 *The heavens are yours and so is the earth;*
the world and all that is in it, you founded them.
12 *North and south YOU created them;*
Tabor and Hermon joyfully praise your name.

13 *You have a mighty arm;*
your hand is strong, your right hand is lifted.
14 *Righteousness and justice are the foundation of your throne;*
hesed *and faithfulness go before you.*
15 *Happy are the people knowing the festal shout,*[10] *O Lord;*
in the light of your face they walk.
16 *In your name, they rejoice all day;*
in your righteousness, they are raised up,[11]
17 *for the glory of their strength is you,*
and by your favor our horn is exalted;[12]
18 *for our shield belongs to the Lord*
and to the Holy One of Israel, our king.

19 *Then you spoke in a vision to your beloved ones*[13] *and*[14] *you said:*
"I have given help unto a warrior.[15]

10. The word *tᵉrûʿâ* has two meanings. One is a cry of alarm or war cry, and the second is a *shout* to announce a celebration, such as "the day of the Lord" in Zeph. 1:16. Considering the context here, it is possible that the word has the sense both of a shout of celebration and of the great God that controls the world.

11. Most translations turn away from the meaning of the people being lifted up, as indicated in MT, and instead read "they exult." However, it is not out of the question that it is God's *righteousness* that lifts the people up in their celebration, i.e., they are *raised* because of God's righteousness.

12. Reading the Kethib, a *hiphil,* instead of the Qere, a *qal.*

13. Multiple Hebrew manuscripts contain the singular "beloved one," possibly to provide a better connection with 2 Samuel 7, where the oracle is delivered to David. But there is no compelling reason to use the singular, since the MT is readable. 4QPsˣ has *lbḥryk* ("chosen ones"); Ulrich, Cross et al., *Qumran Cave 4: XI,* p. 165.

14. 4QPsˣ lacks the *wāw;* Ulrich, Cross et al., *Qumran Cave 4: XI,* p. 165.

15. Several translations emend *ʿēzer* ("help") to *nēzer* ("crown"), assuming it is a better fit (Kraus, *Psalms 60–150,* p. 200; NRSV). Others, such as Tate, argue based on a Ugaritic word *ǵzr* ("lad") that the line should read, "I have set a boy over warriors" (*Psalms 51–100,* p. 410). Either of these is possible, but the MT is also readable as it is, with God sending *help.*

I have raised up a chosen one from the people.[16]
20 *I found David, my servant;*
with my holy oil[17] *I anointed him,*
21 *whom my hand will sustain continually;*[18]
also my arm will strengthen him.
22 *An enemy will not mistreat him,*[19]
nor a child of unrighteousness humble him.
23 *I will crush his foes in front of his face;*
I will strike down those hating him.
24 *My faithfulness and* hesed *are with him,*
and in my name his horn is exalted.
25 *I will set his*[20] *hand on the sea*
and[21] *on the rivers, his right hand.*
26 *He will declare of me,*
'You are my father, my God, and the rock of my salvation.'[22]
27 *Also*[23] *I will make him the firstborn,*
most high of the kings of the earth.
28 *Forever, I will keep my* hesed *for him;*
my covenant will stand firm with him.
29 *I will establish his offspring forever;*
his throne will be like the days of the heavens.
30 *If his children forsake my torah*
and do not walk with my justice,
31 *if my statutes they profane*
and my commandments they do not keep,
32 *I will punish their transgressions with a rod*

16. 4QPs^x has *mn ʿm.* The preposition is separate and probably reads "from a people"; Ulrich, Cross et al., *Qumran Cave 4: XI,* p. 165.

17. 4QPs^x has *mn smn qdsy* ("from my holy oil"); Ulrich, Cross et al., *Qumran Cave 4: XI,* p. 165.

18. Lit., "whom my hand establishes with him." *Kwn* has the connotation "establish (in an enduring sense)" (1 Sam. 20:31; 1 Kgs. 2:12, etc.), especially when referring to the kingdom, and this is probably the sense here (*HALOT,* p. 464). 4QPs^x reads differently: "whom [ ] his hand sustains you (plural)"; Ulrich, Cross et al., *Qumran Cave 4: XI,* p. 165.

19. The root of the verb is unclear. *HALOT* suggests it is from *nšʾ* ("to treat badly"). It could also be from the root *šʾh* ("to wither or dry out"). 4QPs^x reads "the enemy [ ] will not oppress"; Ulrich, Cross et al., *Qumran Cave 4: XI,* p. 165.

20. 4QPs^x lacks the preposition; Ulrich, Cross et al., *Qumran Cave 4: XI,* p. 165.

21. 4QPs^x is missing the *wāw;* Ulrich, Cross et al., *Qumran Cave 4: XI,* p. 165.

22. 4QPs^x lacks "my God and the rock of my salvation"; Ulrich, Cross et al., *Qumran Cave 4: XI,* p. 165.

23. Missing in 4QPs^x; Ulrich, Cross et al., *Qumran Cave 4: XI,* p. 165.

and their iniquities with plagues.[24]
33 *My* hesed *I will not remove from him,*
nor will I betray my faithfulness.
34 *I will not defile my covenant*
nor alter the words from my lips.
35 *Once and for all, I have sworn by my holiness;*
I will not lie to David.
36 *His descendants will continue forever*
and his throne as the sun before me.
37 *Like the moon, it will be established forever,*
and as a witness in the clouds it is established." Selah

38 *But [now] you have rejected, refused,*
and become very angry with your anointed.
39 *You have renounced your covenant with your servant;*
you have defiled his crown in the land.[25]
40 *You have broken through all his walls;*
you have made his strongholds ruins.
41 *All those passing by plunder him;*
he has become a revulsion to his neighbors.
42 *You have exalted the right hand of his foes;*
you have caused his enemies to rejoice.
43 *Moreover, you have turned back the edge*[26] *of his sword;*
you did not support him in battle.[27]
44 *You have put an end to his splendor;*[28]
you have thrown down his crown on the ground.
45 *You have cut short the days of his youth;*
you have wrapped him in shame. Selah

24. *Nega'* means the onset of an illness or plague (*HALOT,* p. 669), even though the verb means "to hit or strike" (NRSV "with scourges").

25. Most read *lā'āreṣ* as "in the dust." However, there is a Hebrew word for dust, *'āp̱ār,* that is associated with humiliation or the underworld (*HALOT,* p. 862), and it is not used here. It is just as possible that *land* refers to the land of the king's rule, i.e., public humiliation, especially in the context of the verses that follow.

26. *Ṣûr* can mean "Tyre" or "a flint." Some suggest emendations, but these provide no improvement over MT. Tate notes this is probably an idiom for a flint-sharpened edge (*Psalms 51–100,* pp. 411-12).

27. 4QPs^{e} has a *lāmed* in place of the *bêt* of the MT, reading "for battle"; Ulrich, Cross et al., *Qumran Cave 4: XI,* p. 78.

28. The word *miṭṭ^{e}hārô* is found only here. The change above follows NIV, using a correction proposed by Aubrey Johnson, *Sacral Kingship in Ancient Israel* (Cardiff: University of Wales, 1955), p. 103, of *maṭṭēh ṭāhrāw,* "the rod of his splendor"; also Tate, *Psalms 51–100,* p. 412.

46 *How long, O LORD?*
Will you hide forever?
Will your anger burn forever?
47 *Remember how brief my time is;*[29]
for what futility have you created humans?
48 *What human can live and not see death?*
Who can escape[30] *from the hand of Sheol?* Selah
49 *Where is your* hesed[31] *of old, O Lord,*
which by your faithfulness you swore to David?
50 *Remember, O Lord, the reproach of your servant,*[32]
which I am carrying in my bosom, from all the many peoples,[33]
51 *with which your enemies reproach, O LORD,*
with which they taunt every step of your anointed.

52 *Blessed be the LORD forever.*
Amen and Amen.

1-4 This opening section offers praise to God for the promises that offer stability to David and Israel. First, the prayer praises God for the attributes of *hesed* and *faithfulness* as the foundation of the relationship (vv. 1-2), as well as the permanence of those attributes. These attributes appear in Exod. 34:6 as two of the things that Israel has depended on since the exodus and wilderness wandering. Verses 3 and 4 switch from praise to God's own words of promise to David and, by extension, to Israel, as in 2 Samuel 7. The effect of the two together connects the two events of the exodus and the establishment of a covenant with David as the foundational theologies of this people. This intro-

29. This line is corrupt, and the list of emendations is long. Two suggestions are possible, with no easy way to select between them. The first is to emend *ʾănî* to *ʾădōnāy,* so the line reads "Remember, O Lord" (Hossfeld amd Zenger, *Psalms 2,* p. 401). The second is to emend *ʾănî* to *nāʾ* (Tate, *Psalms 51–100,* p. 412). Others, with the support of two manuscripts, also change *ḥāleḏ* to *ḥāḏēl* and read "fleeting." It is difficult to decide which is the better choice. The above is a reflection of the emendation with the least change to MT.

30. Lit., *yᵉmallēṭ napšô.*

31. MT uses an honorific plural; see v. 1.

32. MT and LXX have the plural, while twenty-four other Hebrew manuscripts have the singular. There is slightly more indication that the singular should be used, since it is singular in vv. 3 and 20. The decision is also dependent on how one interprets the next possibly corrupt line.

33. There have been a variety of suggestions for this verse. The above closely reflects MT and reads the second line with its infinitive construct as dependent on the first line. I have emended or assumed a missing particle *from,* which clarifies the sentence. The leader carries (lifts) the people to his *bosom* (Num. 11:12), and the burden is too great; here the *reproach* of the world is too great.

duction establishes the relationship as it should be. The connection to God's promise is further seen with the last line of the section: *I will build your throne for generations.* The use of *bānâ* ("build") is central to the Samuel text, where God promises to "build" David a house instead of David building a house for God. This covenant fidelity of God's is the foundation of royal theology and of the history of political stability in the southern kingdom of Judah.

5-18 The first four verses praised God for the foundations that gave Judah a stable theocracy. In a parallel way, vv. 5-18 praise God as the one who is greater than all other gods (vv. 5-8), the supreme Ruler over chaos (vv. 9-14), and Israel's protector (vv. 15-18). These poetic sections rely heavily on ancient Near Eastern mythology and take an additional step in declaring God as the one who is not only Israel's God, but is also the God who is the creator and controller of the whole world.

Verses 5-8 set the stage in the heavenly council. In vv. 5 and 8, God is praised by *the heavens* for God's *faithfulness,* and this certainly continues the theme of vv. 1-4 while also broadening God's faithfulness to the whole world. The questions in v. 6 are rhetorical, just as in Isa. 40:18 and Pss. 18:31 and 77:13, followed by the declaration of God's clear supremacy among the gods (v. 7). God is not only the God of Israel but is the chief god of *the council,* and all others bow before the LORD.

In vv. 9-14, the scene moves from the heavenly council to images of God as the creator and controller of all of creation. The making and controlling of creation are central elements in all ancient Near Eastern texts that praise the king of the gods.[34] This section declares that God rules over the *sea, Rahab,*[35] and God's *enemies.* Verses 11-13 add the idea of God's ownership of the world, for it is God who created it and thus controls it. Verse 12 uses the images of *north and south* and also *Tabor and Hermon.* The last two are mountains in the northern part of Israel. Tate notes that they may indicate ancient worship sites as part of God's world.[36] However, the mention could also be a parallel with *north and south* of the previous line.[37] Finally, this section ends by declaring that God's attributes found and surround God's *throne* in the council.

34. Kraus, *Psalms 60–150,* p. 207.

35. *Rahab* may have a double meaning here. If read with the lines above, it concerns control of *the sea,* and Rahab could refer to the chaos monster, as in Job 9:13; 26:12. If read with the following line concerning God's enemies, it could refer to Egypt, as it does in Ps. 87:4; Isa. 30:7. But more likely, Rahab is to be read as both the monster and Egypt, as in Isa. 51:9.

36. *Psalms 51–100,* p. 421.

37. While both are in the northern kingdom, Mount Hermon is north of Dan and was land listed as not part of Israel in Joshua (13:5) but claimed as part of the northern region in 1 Chronicles (5:23). Mount Tabor is roughly 40 miles south of Hermon, near Megiddo. It is possible this is a formulaic saying of God's control over this disputed territory.

The same attributes that David and Israel depend on are also the attributes on which the entire universe is founded. God's *hesed* and *faithfulness* have worldwide implications.

Verses 15-18 return to earth and the praise of the people who know this God as their own. This section then returns the focus to the particular way that God has favored Israel. The festal shout *(tᵉrû'â)* has multiple meanings as a cry of both joy and war.[38] Here it may serve as both, for God is praised for "your righteousness" and because the *shields* of the people *belong* to God. Finally, God is praised as *the Holy One of Israel* and as *king* (v. 18).

The praise of vv. 1-4 and 15-18 sets this first major section in a liturgical context. God is praised, the reasons for God's greatness are recited, and God is praised again. This is the relationship that the nation of Israel depended on during their brief time as a unified country. The promises of exodus have merged with the promises of a kingdom and land, and these serve as the foundation of the nation and the people.

19-37 This large center section is a report of an oracle given by God *to your beloved ones.* Its function, however, is not as an oracle delivered to the people on behalf of God, but as the recitation of an oracle given earlier that is now given back to God as a reminder of God's promises in the past.[39] The section first focuses on the choice of David (vv. 19-20), then the promises made to the king (vv. 21-28) and the promises that extend to David's descendants (vv. 29-33), and finally a promise that the covenant will stand with David's line forever (vv. 34-37) as a summary of the whole section. As noted previously, this section has much in common with the oracle given by Nathan in 2 Samuel 7, but it also draws from other images and narratives and also interestingly leaves out some of the warnings given to David in the 2 Samuel oracle.

The first two verses (19-20) focus on the selection of David as God's choice and roughly match the story of David's anointing, which also uses the word *chosen* in the verbal form as a structuring formula (1 Sam. 16:8-13). In addition, the use of *my servant* in v. 20 recalls Nathan's oracle that is to be addressed to "my servant David" (2 Sam. 7:5). These first promises to David (vv. 19-24) focus on strength in battle, and this also corresponds to the early phase of David's rise to power when he is fighting both the Philistines and Saul. What is missing in the psalm account is some of the ways the text portrays David in a more negative light. David here appears as the perfect selection, and the seeds of arrogance seen in 2 Samuel 7 are absent.

38. *Tᵉrû'â* appears as the blowing of horns (Lev. 23:24), as a war cry (Num. 10:7, 9; Josh. 6:10, 16, 20; 1 Sam. 17:52; Amos 1:14; Zeph. 1:16), and as a joyful shout to God (Pss. 27:6; 33:3; 47:6; 150:5).

39. The threefold repetition of *you* in v. 19 makes this clear. God is being addressed with God's own words on behalf of the people.

Verses 25-29 move from military power to David's position as king of Israel. Verse 25 is probably both a metaphor for the far-reaching territory of the kingdom[40] and, as Tate notes, of the "chaotic enemies" that the LORD and the servant king keep in check.[41] Verses 26 and 27 reflect the adoption of the king by God as a son and the elevation of the king to the position of the *most high,* so that the earthly council mirrors the heavenly one of vv. 5-8, as in Psalms 2 and 72. The last two verses, 28-29, restate the promises God made to David that God's *hesed* and *covenant* will be kept *forever,* even to David's *offspring.*

Verses 30-33 are a paraphrase of 2 Sam. 7:12-15 and assure that, even when the human kings do not follow God, their punishment will not result in God's removal of God's *hesed* and *faithfulness.* This promise makes a Davidic dynasty a certainty; just as God chose Israel, now God has chosen David and his family forever. Verse 33 again restates the promise, so each of the sections ends with the promise of God (vv. 24, 28-29, and 33). Here the language is strong, and these promises go beyond 2 Samuel 7 or any other covenant promise in the whole of the biblical text. As McCann notes, vv. 36-37 "suggests that the Davidic dynasty is an enduring structure of God's cosmic rule."[42] This section overall is quite different from the other texts of promise to Judah's king, as the repetition of the promises indicates. It is shaped so that God has no room to change God's mind, even in the face of apostasy by David's human descendants. Indeed, without the next section, the entire psalm to this point is a psalm of praise for God's fidelity to David and by extension to Israel, using the key words *hesed, faithfulness, covenant,* and *forever.* The covenant, it would seem, is set in stone and written in the clouds.

38-45 The first lines tell the real purpose of this psalm. It is not one of praise at all. Without warning, everything has changed. God, it appears, has changed God's mind. The words of vv. 34-37 crash against the verbs of vv. 38 and 39: *you have rejected, refused, become angry,* and *renounced.* One by one, the previous promises are reversed. The *covenant* is *renounced* in v. 39. The king God exalted in v. 27 is humiliated in vv. 39-41. The help in battle of vv. 22 and 23 is given now to the *enemies* in vv. 41-43. The dynasty that was to last forever (vv. 28, 29, 33, 36, and 37) is *cut short* and humiliated (v. 45). What is worse is that God has not just turned God's back and is silent, as in Psalm 88. The eighteenfold appearance of the pronoun *you* in vv. 38-45 makes it clear that God is the cause of the shattered dreams.

46-51 Accusations turn to questions of God. The questions of v. 46,

40. 1 Chronicles 18 claims that David's territory stretches from the sea to the Euphrates River. Likewise, Ps. 80:11 states "It [Israel] sent out its branches to the sea; and to the river, its shoots."

41. *Psalms 51–100,* p. 423.

42. "The Book of Psalms," p. 1036.

unlike the ones in vv. 6 and 8, are cries of disillusionment, hurt, and a desire for restored relationship. Verses 47-48 reflect on the fragility of human life and existence and offer a connection to Psalm 90 that will open Book Four.

The next question is the most chilling of all, for it confronts God with the promises that were repeated throughout the first thirty-seven verses of the psalm: *Where is your steadfast love of old, O Lord, which by your faithfulness you swore to David?* This question takes the hearers to one of the darkest places in all of theology — "Can God, who is ultimate good, not honor the promises God made, and worse yet, how could God break a promise sworn to David (vv. 34-37) which makes it a binding covenantal promise?" Like Psalm 88 before it, there is no answer given to this most troubling question. The psalm ends with a plea for God to *remember* the shame of the current situation, using the very relational words *your servant* and ending with *mᵉšîḥeḵā* ("your messiah" or "anointed one").

52 This last addition contradicts the last verses of this psalm and shares the phrase *blessed be the Lord* with Ps. 41:13, which ends Book One. This is clearly an addition that ends Book Three, just as was seen in Pss. 41:13 and 72:18-20. It also sets the sad story of all of Book Three into a greater context, one in which this was just a small piece of God's history with the people.

Psalm 89 is brutally frank in its questions to God in the face of national disaster. Along with the personal lament of Psalm 88, it brings the questions of theodicy front and center and demands answers from the deity. The last verse, a later addition by an editor, demonstrates that the story did indeed go on and faith did not die here. Psalm 89 is probably a psalm that was shaped by the destruction of Jerusalem and the exile of the officers of the nation in 587 B.C.E., but that is certainly not the only time a nation or group of God's people have cried out in the face of destruction. We, as people of a post–World War 2, post-Holocaust, post-911 world, cannot deny or even ignore the words of this psalm. This psalm speaks of the struggle we undergo as "the suffering and death of innocent children inevitably places the divine will in question and arouses men [sic] to wrath and revolt."[43] This situation, unfortunately, is all too real in our world. Psalm 89 names our deepest fears and asks the most frightening questions. Psalms 88 and 89 together demonstrate that both individuals and the community hang in a space where God seems to have completely disappeared and answers are not to be found. They speak a truth that is an important one, for it is often not voiced. It is not a lack of faith. It is indeed a bold faith that continues to question God and holds God accountable for God's promises, even in the face of unspeakable violence. It is the place where one must go when faced with a world that does not make sense, but it is not a turning away from God into an agnostic existence. Elie

43. Elie Wiesel, *All Rivers Run to the Sea: Memoirs* (New York: Knopf, 1995), p. 84.

Wiesel notes that he has been named as one who lost his faith, but nothing could be further from his own belief: "I have never renounced my faith in God. I have risen against His justice, protested His silence and sometimes His absence, but my anger rises up within faith not outside of it."[44] Likewise, Psalm 89 teaches us to continue the conversation, even when the questions are unspeakably painful and God seems to have disappeared.

BETH TANNER

44. *All Rivers Run to the Sea,* p. 84.

Book Four of the Psalter: Psalms 90–106

INTRODUCTION

Book Four of the Psalter is the shortest of the five books. The book is primarily one of praise, but there are two prayers for help, one that opens the book (see below) and one near the end, Psalm 102. While praise dominates this book, these two psalms remind the reader that cries for help are still part of life and even in the midst of praise do not disappear completely.

Tate, among others, has noted that Book Four begins with a psalm dedicated to Moses and has an overall focus on Moses and the exodus wilderness period.[1] According to Jerome Creach, Moses also appears in the last psalm in the book, at Ps. 106:23, which reports that "Moses, his chosen one, stood in the breach before him, to turn away his destructive anger." This clear reference to Exodus 32 forms an envelope of sorts around the book.[2] Book Three ended with the questions of theodicy in the air, voiced both from an individual (Psalm 88) and a community perspective (Psalm 89). McCann and others argue that in the postexilic shaping of the five books of the Psalter, it was probably the crisis of the destruction and exile in 587 B.C.E. and the subsequent loss of identity as an independent country that precipitated these cries and questions to God. That may be the case, but it is difficult to determine exactly when the psalms were placed in the order that appears in *BHS*. The order of these psalms and the story they tell should not be seen as representing one historical moment, but all of the times that the people stood in a difficult place and questioned God's actions or inaction in the world.

Book Four provides an answer, of sorts, to the questions raised in Psalms 88 and 89. To answer the questions of "why" asked at the end of Book Three,

1. *Psalms 51–100*, p. xxvi.

2. "The Shape of Book Four of the Psalter and the Shape of Second Isaiah," *JSOT* 80 (1998) 65.

this book offers a different theological view focused on God as the God of the people wherever they may now be located. Also, in many of these psalms, God is spoken of as the king of the world. This is a clear change from the focus on David and his descendants so prominent in Books One through Three. In addition, the focus on the exodus and wilderness wandering removes the exclusive focus on the land of promise. Instead, God is praised as king and ruler of the whole world. This transformed theology, then, becomes the answer to the loss of the kingdom and its human king. It calls for a reimagining of Israel's understanding of God for a people scattered and under imperial domination.

Psalm 90 is the first in the book, and the only psalm dedicated to Moses. Its pleas to God are much like the ones Moses made on behalf of the people in Exodus 32. Two individual praise songs follow. Psalm 91 changes the tone, declaring that this time of estrangement between God and the people is finished. Psalm 92, the only psalm dedicated to the Sabbath, is placed immediately before the enthronement psalms. As noted below, there has been a great deal of debate on the function of the enthronement psalms and whether they were part of a great festival to the Lord. This may or may not be the case, but what the placement of this psalm immediately before the enthronement psalms suggests is that, by the time the editors organized Book Four, the enthronement psalms were to be associated with the Sabbath, a point further emphasized by the lack of superscriptions among the psalms that follow Psalm 92.[3] Psalm 92's superscription may be considered the heading for the group of psalms from 92 to 99.

PSALMS 93–99

The enthronement psalms are the center of Book Four. These psalms are not so named because of superscriptional connections, as with other groups, but by their theme, which declares by direct acclamation or by metaphorical flourishes that the Lord is the king of both the universe and Israel. These psalms were named as a collection by Mowinckel, who argued that they were part of an annual enthronement festival of the Lord in preexilic Israel that was patterned from similar festivals in Egypt, Assyria, and Babylon. In the past century, scholars have challenged the theory of an actual festival, but Mowinckel's understanding of the psalms as liturgical is a lasting contribution. Today we understand the psalms, not as history or information, but as poetic, metaphorical, and lyrical. Even without direct proof of a festival, this psalm

3. Ps. 98 does have the superscription "A psalm," but without further information. LXX obviously follows a different tradition, for there the enthronement psalms each have a superscription.

group still comprises an important collection because of its central focus on God as king and ruler.[4]

Most scholars do not include Psalm 94 as part of the enthronement psalms, probably because Mowinckel classified it as a lament.[5] Psalm 94 is an individual prayer for help inserted into the collection by the editors, argues Westermann.[6] The psalm, however, is not so much a prayer for help as a statement of confident trust that God will come and judge the world. So, while it does not use the term "king," its plea for God to judge the world invokes a well-known function of the great king-God. By asking for God to intervene in the world and judge the situation, Psalm 94 requests and even demands what the other psalms praise about God — that God is judge (Psalm 96) and a God-King who listens to and acts on behalf of God's people (Psalm 99).

Although each psalm in this group is unique, they all share a set of metaphors associated with God's kingship: God is king; God is supreme over all the other gods; God is the Creator of all peoples; the earth is created and maintained by God; God protects the righteous and the lowly; God will judge the earth; all the gods and all the peoples of the earth are to give God praise; all the creation — land, sea, and heavens — are to give praise. Each psalm uniquely combines several of these themes. In addition, these psalms recall "God's salvation," perhaps a direct reference to the exodus tradition, but more probably a general statement that recalls all of the times God has delivered both individuals and Israel. Finally, the set of psalms that form the center of this book do not refer to the human king or David or Jerusalem at all. God's throne is described, but in Psalm 93 as existing forever (v. 2); in Psalm 97, it is created in the heavens by the creation itself (vv. 2-5); and Psalm 99 uses the term Zion, but has no corresponding reference to Jerusalem. God's kingship is the focus, and this would fit well with any period of imperial domination of Israel/Judah and/or when there is no longer a definitive physical space where all of God's people reside. God's throne is in the heavens for all people everywhere, removing the singular focus of the preexilic period on the temple.

While most poetic lines in this collection are pure praise, three of the psalms have elements that remind the hearers or readers that life is not just praise. Psalm 94 calls on God to act as judge against the wicked ones who oppress the poor and needy (v. 5). It also states that "happy is the one" the Lord disciplines (v. 12). Part of God's function as king is to judge God's own faithful ones. Psalm 95 contains a warning from the people's history not to act as their ancestors did in the wilderness (vv. 8-11). Finally, Psalm 99 notes

4. For a more in-depth discussion of the scholarly debate concerning these psalms, see Tate, *Psalms 51–100*, pp. 504-9.

5. *The Psalms in Israel's Worship*, p. 227.

6. *Praise and Lament in the Psalms*, p. 257.

that God is both a forgiving and an avenging God. The enthronement psalms, then, do not speak of some idealized world where all of the trials of this one have passed away. Their praise is grounded in the realities of this present world. This makes the fact that God is praised as one who judges the earth all the more amazing. Just as Psalm 94 states "happy is the one" God disciplines, this praise of God as King and Judge is not to be taken lightly. The praise and call is for God to judge all, a weighty proposition indeed.

PSALMS 100–106

Psalm 100 continues many of the themes of Psalms 92–99 and offers pure praise. Psalm 101 is unique in the collection, focusing not on God but on a faithful one, affirming this one's life lived before God. This may explain why it is dedicated to David, as is Psalm 103. These superscriptions are surprising but demonstrate that the David tradition in the psalms did not die with the loss of a monarchy. Indeed, the tradition has been transformed for a new generation as the real David monarchy becomes more of a messianic hope. Psalm 102 is an individual prayer for help, again reminding readers that the real world is still part of life, even if many of the circumstances from the past have been altered. Psalm 104 is a creation hymn that declares God's function as king and creator. Psalms 105 and 106 both tell of God's early history with the people. The first rehearses God's faithfulness through their long sojourn in Egypt, and the second begins with praise but moves to tell of the sins of the people in the deliverance from Egypt and in the wilderness.

The focus of Book Four is on the beginnings of Israel. While not necessarily a Moses book, it does tell of a different time from that in Books One through Three. Why the backward glance? One reason, of course, is that the world changed when they became a small province in a large empire. The old notion of Israel as a nation belonging to God has given way to the idea of a people of God spread among the other peoples of the earth. Second, without a kingdom, the references to the wilderness may possibly make two points. One is that the people were again in the same position, without a home and without the ability to self-govern. The other builds on the fact that, until Psalm 89, the psalms present David not just as king but also as the personification of the people as a whole. Now the people did not have such a leader, so it was up to individuals and communities to pursue that relationship with God that has been so much a part of the psalms. Scholars have referred to this new perspective as the democratizing of the person in the psalms, in that without God-given leaders the people now become the primary "I" of the psalms. I resist that expression simply because it is so tied to American ideology. This democratizing would not have the same meaning in postexilic Judah as it has in the modern-day United States. But I have no better word for this move. The people are definitely the focus here. The examples of wickedness and sin in Book Four come not from the leaders but from the acts of the people. They were responsible. The warning charges them not to begin their new lives as their ancestors did, but to learn from all that has been said and to make better choices. Book Four is a book for a new generation.

Psalm 90: Change Your Mind Regarding Your Servants

Psalm 90 is unique in several ways. As the first psalm of Book Four, it is a new word after the dark and unresolved ending of Book Three (Psalms 88 and 89). Second, it is also the only psalm with a superscription dedicated to Moses. Third, unlike Psalm 89, there is no mention of David or the promises that were the central concern in the preceding Book Three. Psalm 90, then, stands at a crucial place in the psalter and offers a unique message and an answer, of sorts, to the questions posed in the two previous psalms. One might expect that this psalm, like the progression of many of the prayers for help, would open with songs of praise for God and God's salvation. But Psalm 90 is far from a hymn of celebration. In fact, scholars have had a difficult time deciding exactly how to characterize the psalm. For many years, it was viewed as two separate psalms:[1] one of trust followed by a community prayer for help.[2] Gerhard von Rad, on the other hand, saw the psalm as one that "derives from about the same intellectual and theological situation as Ecclesiastes."[3] Since von Rad's assertion, many have characterized this psalm as one of wisdom. Recently however, Richard Clifford has argued convincingly that the poem is a community prayer for help that "asks God to bring an end to a lengthy period marked by divine wrath."[4] Psalm 90, then like Psalms 88 and 89, testifies to the fact that things do not go from cries of abandonment to praise in quick fashion. Book Four will end in praise, but it opens with a cry to God about a situation that feels as if it will never resolve itself. In that, it reflects a historical reality of the exile and of other times of national and personal crisis; the resolution is often one that is delayed for months or even years, and one must wait on the Lord.

The superscription also gives a clue that Book Four is something different, for it is *A prayer of Moses, man of God.* Superscriptions are later additions to the psalms, probably by the editors that shaped the Psalter into a five-book collection.[5] These additions tell a reader about a person or situation that fits with the theme and content of this psalm, But why Moses? Even in Book Three, it was noted that older theologies were part of the theological foundation for Judah. Psalms 86 and 89 both describe God with the same attributes as Exod. 32:6, so this older theology was part of the theology of preexilic Israel. After the destruction of the temple and the loss of their own Davidic

1. Gunkel, *Die Psalmen,* p. 399.

2. Claus Westermann, *The Living Psalms* (trans. J. R. Porter; Grand Rapids: Eerdmans, 1984), p. 158.

3. *God at Work in Israel* (trans. John H. Marks; Nashville: Abingdon, 1980), p. 214.

4. "Psalm 90: Wisdom Meditation or Communal Lament?" in Flint and Miller, *The Book of Psalms,* p. 191.

5. For more information on superscriptions, see the Introduction.

king, the theology had to be reimagined. A dedication to Moses would make sense, for Israel was again enslaved by a foreign power and all of the signs of independence were erased. Israel is back where it started. Moses was the leader who led them out then, so why not call upon their national hero now? In addition, a theme of this psalm is that God is angry at the people and, if Clifford is correct, has been for a long period of time. If this is the case, it is possible that this superscription and connections in the psalm to Exodus and Deuteronomy are an attempt to imagine how Moses might have interceded again for Israel as he did in the wilderness, another time where God was angry with the wayward people.

The psalm has four stanzas and moves from praise to reasons why God should relent to the current situation to a final imagining of life after God has restored Israel:

Praise of the eternal God (vv. 1-2)
Remember how short human life is (vv. 3-6)
God's great anger with us (vv. 7-12)
A relationship restored (vv. 13-17)

The text of the psalm itself presents its own challenges, and the translation of some lines is tentative. In addition, the translation in the LXX either attempts to resolve the multiple textual difficulties or is reading a different version from the one in the MT.[6] Zenger notes that the LXX version of Psalm 90 has a different theme, one of a pedagogical example drawn from history.[7]

A Mosaic prayer. A man of God.

1 *Lord, YOU have been a dwelling place*
for us[8] *in all generations.*
2 *Before the mountains were brought forth,*

6. Gerald Wilson noted, "While the Qumran psalms manuscripts at points yield evidence of considerable variation from the arrangement and contents of the canonical Psalter, variation is practically non-existent in the first three books. By contrast, extensive variations in order and content occur in the last two books"; "Shaping the Psalter: A Consideration of Editorial Linkage in the Book of Psalms," in McCann, *The Shape and Shaping of the Psalter,* p. 73.

7. *Psalms 2,* p. 425.

8. Many translations use "our dwelling place" (NRSV, NIV), but the syntax of the Hebrew is, lit., "Lord, a dwelling place YOU have been to us." The *you* is emphasized by the use of the personal pronoun and the second ms verb. This syntax clearly rules out the possessive "our dwelling place" and instead stresses that God is a dwelling place "to or *for us,*" a seemingly small but theologically significant structure.

or you gave birth[9] *to the earth and the world,*
from eternity to eternity, you are God.

3 *You return humans to pulverized matter,*[10]
saying, "Return, Children of Adam";
4 *for one thousand years in your eyes*
are like yesterday when it is past,
or like a watch in the night.
5 *You sweep them away, they are sleep,*[11]
in the morning, like grass that is renewed.[12]
6 *In the morning, it flourishes and is renewed;*
in the evening it fades and withers.

7 *For we are consumed by your anger,*
and by your wrath we are overwhelmed.
8 *You have set our iniquities before you*
and our secrets in the light of your face,
9 *for all of our days wane away*[13] *under your wrath;*
we finish our years like a sigh.
10 *The number of our years are seventy,*

9. NRSV follows LXX, reading *plassō* ("to mold or form"), but there is no compelling reason for this substitution. The verb *teḥôlēl* is either a *poel* 3fs or 2ms form. The subject could be the feminine *'ereṣ,* with the verb serving both of the nouns *earth* and *world.* The other possibility is that it is the 3ms referring to God. Both readings are possible in the context, but the second is a better fit with the two other lines of the verse; see also Deut. 32:18, a parallel verse: "You were unmindful of the Rock that bore you *(yld);* you forgot the God who gave you birth *(ḥwl).*"

10. This word appears only here. The verb has the meaning of "being crushed" (Ps. 143:3) or "being contrite" (Isa. 57:15). Dahood argues the word may be associated with the underworld (*Psalms 51–100,* p. 323). It is read here as literally from the verbal meaning of crushed or *pulverized.*

11. This line is difficult to understand, as the plethora of translations illustrates. It is translated here as close to the MT as possible. There are many suggestions for emendation, but these are unnecessary. The line before discussed *a watch in the night,* and here the humans are swept away, presumably like *sleep.* See Hossfeld and Zenger, *Psalms 2,* p. 417, for a concurring reading.

12. It is possible this line and v. 6a are corrupt, as argued by Kraus, among others (*Psalms 60–150,* p. 213). *In the morning* may be an addition, possibly via dittography. Without the phrase, the line can be seen as relating to the line before it: both are fleeting. In v. 6a, the second use of the verb of v. 5c is unusual and may indicate further corruption of the text. The above is as close to MT as possible.

13. Lit., *pānû* ("turn"), but as noted by Tate and others, the word should be read here as it is in Jer. 6:4, as "waning" (*Psalms 51–100,* p. 434).

or if strong eighty;
yet their span[14] *is but toil and trouble;*
they are gone quickly and we fly away.
11 *Who knows the strength of your anger?*
Is your wrath like your fearlessness?[15]
12 *So teach us to number our days*
so we gain a wise heart.

13 *Return* L*ORD*! *How long?*
Change your mind,[16] *with regard to your servants.*
14 *Satisfy us in the morning with your* hesed
so we might rejoice and be glad all our days.
15 *Make us glad as many days as you have afflicted us,*
as many years as we have seen evil.
16 *Let your work be shown to your servants*
and your splendor to their children.
17 *Let the splendor of the Lord, our God, be upon us;*
and the work of our hands, establish it for us;
the work of our hands, establish it.

1-2 The opening verses tell of the eternity of God. Verse 1 places the dwelling place of the people in God and stresses that this has been the case for all generations. This verse certainly reflects postexilic theology, where the focus shifts from the land of Israel as a dwelling place of God and the people to a focus on a scattered people who serve a God who is without a physical earthly home. To further stress this point, v. 2 declares that the whole earth was birthed by God, declaring that all of the world, not just Zion, belongs to God.

14. This word appears only here. The word is commonly thought to mean "pride" or "arrogance" from the root *rhb,* but this makes little sense in the context. Tate notes there are other Hebrew manuscripts with *rḥbm* ("breadth/width"); *Psalms 51–100,* p. 435. LXX follows this idea, indicating the Hebrew word *rbm* ("many"). Both then indicate some length or duration of time.

15. The translation of this line is uncertain, as the plethora of translations testifies. Assuming it is a verbless sentence, it may be translated, lit., "and like your fear [is] your wrath," as reflected in NRSV and NIV. Kraus, however, proposes an interesting reading, substituting a *mêm* for the *kāp,* as is suggested by LXX, but then additionally realigning the Hebrew words, reading *mî rō'eh ṯōḵ* ("and who perceives the weight of your wrath"); *Psalms 60–150,* pp. 213, 214. The line above is translated as close to the MT as possible, but any translation is tentative.

16. The *niphal* imperative with the preposition *'al* means "to change one's mind" (see Exod. 13:17; 1 Sam. 15:29; Jer. 4:28; 15:6; Ezek. 24:14; Joel 2:14; Jonah 3:9; Zech. 8:14; Ps. 106:45; 110:4). For further study, see Dale Patrick, "The Translation of Job xli 6," *VT* 26 (1976) 369-71.

3-6 This section contains several textual problems, which makes parts of the translation tentative (vv. 3a, 5, and 6a). The theme of the section is human frailty and the brevity of life, which is heightened by the context of the eternity of God in vv. 1-2. But what is the purpose of this section? Is it a wisdomlike reflection on human life, or is it part of a prayer for help? Many have seen it as a wisdom piece.[17] But Clifford notes, "Verses 3-5 are not a protest against mortality. There are no protests in the Bible against mortality as such, only against premature or shameful death."[18] He goes on to argue that the brevity of life is used here, as in other psalms, to persuade God to stop being angry with the people.[19] This is especially the case considering the contrast set up between these verses and vv. 1-2. God is eternal and the great birth mother of the world, but the humans are transient and frail.

Most commentators note that there are no complaints against the enemies or God in this prayer, and this is why they do not see it as a prayer for help. However, this section could be seen as a complaint. God is named here as the one who sets these rules. Verse 3 in most English translations implies a link with the dust of creation from Gen. 3:19, but this is a different word with an uncertain meaning that indicates a violent, unnatural event that is laid directly at God's feet. Verse 4 contrasts the *thousand years* of God's days to the brief period of the *watch* set up in a city from dusk to dawn. Verses 5-6 have textual difficulties, but if reading correctly here, they compare human life to both the period of *sleep* and the life cycle of desert *grass.* Since the entire section is addressed to God, it would make sense that this is a contrast created for God's benefit, and a contrast that will make God "change God's mind" about the frail humans.

7-12 Zenger sees vv. 7-8 as equivalent to "the wages of sin is death,"[20] but just as Clifford noted with the last section, this understanding of life and death is not seen in the psalms *per se.* The wages of sin is alienation and separation from God, which is sometimes expressed as sickness or death. In other words, sickness and death are causally, but not exclusively, linked with sin.[21] In vv. 7-8, the problem is that God is angry with the people, and vv. 9-10 add that this anger has gone on for a long time. This, then, is a true reflection of the exile, or better yet, the period of Babylonian hegemony that is remembered

17. Von Rad, *God at Work in Israel,* pp. 210-23; Kraus, *Psalms 60–150,* p. 216; Hossfeld and Zenger, *Psalms 2,* p. 418.

18. "Psalm 90," p. 199.

19. "Psalm 90," p. 199, as in Pss. 39, 102, 103.

20. *Psalms 2,* p. 422.

21. This connection of sin and punishment and death is certainly a theme in the book of Job. One could argue it is even the central theme, but this type of reflection rarely appears in other books in a reflective and philosophical way.

as seventy years. The very same period is given in v. 10 as the span of life! It is no wonder then that *our days* are lived *under your wrath.*

Verse 11, then, is a rhetorical question that wonders about how long the *strength* of God's *anger* will hold out against the people.[22] The next line is problematic, so any translation is tentative. However, if the syntax is asking if God's *wrath* will last as long as God's *fearlessness,* then the frightening answer to the second question is "eternity." These two questions are designed just as vv. 3-6 were, to remind God of the contrast between God's eternity and the brevity of human life.

If this is the case, then to what does v. 12 refer? Clifford's research is quite helpful here. He notes that, based on Ugaritic and Akkadian usage of cognates, the phrase "to count the days" does not refer to the span of life, but to a specific preset period of time.[23] Verse 12, then, is not a plea for God to teach the humans wisdom, but a plea for the humans to accurately tally the *days* of God's wrath so that they will understand there is indeed an end to it. This, interestingly, is a parallel to another time of God's anger, that of Exodus 32–34. After the golden calf incident, God was so angry that God refused to be with the Israelites. But after the second intervention of Moses (Exod. 33:12-22), God relented and the second covenant was cut; instead of what happened in 32:1, when the Israelites apparently were not counting days, here Moses is away for forty days and forty nights (34:28) and the apostasy of before is not repeated. The difference seems to be the counting of days that made all the difference.

13-17 The last section is entirely petition. The first twelve verses have been the setup for these petitions, a logical argument to soften up God to hear the petitions of the people. It is here that God is asked to return to the people and to *change* God's *mind.* Interestingly, this is exactly what Moses asks God to do in Exod. 32:12: "turn *(šûḇ)* from your burning anger and change your mind *(hinnāḥēm)* concerning the evil to your people." The superscription to Moses and the parallels in this verse may mean that the superscription is reflecting an intertextual connection within the canonical psalm itself.

Verses 14 through 17 are petitions of God's favor. Verse 14 requests a return of *hesed,* which was so much the question of Psalm 89, and seeks a change from that psalm's haunting question of "where is your *hesed* of old?" Verse 15 asks that the *days* of joy be made equal to the *days* of suffering, a concept that lends further credence to Clifford's argument that God's anger is only for a time. Verse 16 speaks of the return of God's *works* and *splendor* to the people. This again may reflect Exodus 32–34, where God's return to

22. Using different but related reasoning, Clifford concurs; "Psalm 90," p. 202.

23. Clifford, "Psalm 90," p. 203. In both languages, this idiom refers to counting a period for pregnancy, a predetermined period of waiting.

the people resulted in a new set of commandments that are written by God, a tangible product of God's *work* and of their restoration. In vv. 16b and 17a, *splendor* is the request — first, that it be shown to the *children,* who if exile is in sight have never seen it, and then, to let the splendor *be upon us. Splendor* is used of humans in Ps. 8:5 and of the king in Pss. 21:5; 45:4, 6. The restoration of splendor to the humans is a clear sign of God's favor, even if it is now "us" for there is no longer a king. Finally, the last two petitions ask for full restoration, for the work of our hands can be seen as the picture in Isa. 65:17-25 where "they shall build houses and inhabit them; they shall plant vineyards and eat their fruit." The work of the people will no longer be for others, but for their God.

Psalm 90 opens another chapter in the long relationship of God and the people. Yet all is still not well. The questions that ended Book Three still hang in the air unanswered, as this psalm seeks to get God to relent as God has done in the past and restore the people to their former *splendor.* In the struggle reflected here, we see the integrity of the psalms. These ancient folks knew that the answers to theodicy were not instantaneous, or even the answers that we demand to know. Relationship with God can be a struggle, and God can seem absent and angry with individuals, communities, and even a whole people. It is a frightening place to stand. Yet this psalm affirms that stand they did, even in the midst of fear and struggle. In that, we too have hope for our own struggles. We too can learn from them about what to do in those frightening places, be they personal or corporate. The people have taken on the former role of Moses. It is here that the psalms become less about human leaders and followers and more about a community filling the void that the leaders, kings and priests, have left. It is about taking responsibility and voicing our fears to God. It is about creating new ways to speak to and understand God.

BETH TANNER

Psalm 91: God Is Still My Protector

After Psalms 88, 89, and 90, Psalm 91 seems unbelievably naive. It begins with a confession, moves to exhortation, and ends with an oracle that confirms the words spoken in the prayer. In its place in the Psalter, it provides the praise that often ends prayers for help, and it is up to the reader to decide how to finally understand this psalm and its placement by traversing the gap between it and the previous psalms.

The prayer divides into three sections, each with a distinct meaning:

Setting the stage (v. 1)
Encouragement to trust (vv. 2-13)
God's words of confirmation (vv. 14-16)

There is a significant amount of textual and translation difficulties. Nevertheless, the general trajectories of the metaphors can be discerned. There are three voices in the psalm: one of introduction, one of testimony, and one of God. This oracle serves as confirmation, not just of the trust expressed in this prayer, but also serves as God's answer to the crisis seen in all of Book Three and the opening of Book Four. There is no superscription for this psalm in the MT, providing a direct link to Psalm 90.[1] The LXX, however, contains the superscription "A praise song to David."

1 *One living within the hiding place of the Most High,*
in the shadow of the Almighty this one abides.

2 *I say*[2] *to the* L*ORD*, *"My refuge and my stronghold,*
my God[3] *in whom I trust;*
3 *for HE*[4] *will snatch you from the snare,*[5]

1. Wilson has demonstrated that Book Four is an answer to Book Three and that the lack of superscriptions in Book Four is a way to tie several psalms to those that do have superscriptions; *The Editing of the Hebrew Psalter,* p. 215.

2. MT reads "and I say," which separates v. 1 from 2 by a change of person. LXX continues in the 3ms, making v. 2 an extension of v. 1, as does 11QPsAp[a] except it uses the participle with an article; García Martínez, Tigchelaar, and van der Woude, *Qumran Cave 11: II,* p. 202. It is possible these are later attempts to smooth out the text.

3. 11QPsAp[a] adds an additional participle here, *mbṭḥ,* meaning something like "the trusted one, I trust"; García Martínez, Tigchelaar, van der Woude, *Qumran Cave 11: II,* p. 202. This may be a simple expansion by a scribe.

4. MT uses both the pronoun and the 3ms verb, indicating emphasis of the subject.

5. *Paḥ* seems to have a literal meaning of a snare used for hunting birds (Ps. 124:7) but in the Psalms it is used metaphorically as a trap set for humans.

from the thorn of destruction.[6]
4 *With his pinions he will cover you;*
under his wings you will find refuge;[7]
a shield and an encircling protection[8] *is his faithfulness.*[9]
5 *You will not fear terror of the night,*
nor an arrow flying by day,
6 *from destruction that walks in the darkness,*
nor pestilence that destroys at noon.[10]
7 *A thousand may fall at your side,*
ten thousand at your right hand;
but it will not come near you.[11]
8 *Only with your eyes you will look [at it],*[12]
and the reward[13] *of the wicked you will see.*
9 *For you are the* LORD, *my refuge!*[14]

6. *Middeḇer* has a meaning of "plague, pestilence" or "thorn" (as suggested by *HALOT,* p. 212). The term "deadly pestilence" (NRSV, NIV) is possible, but does not fit well in the verse. Zenger notes that a thorn is also an implement used by one hunting birds (*Psalms 2,* p. 427).

7. 11QPsAp[a] has *tskwn* ("you will rest") instead of the MT's "you will find refuge." This is followed by the additional "his *hesed* upon you"; García Martínez, Tigchelaar, van der Woude, *Qumran Cave 11: II,* p. 202.

8. This word appears only here. The root has a meaning of "circle" or "circumference," hence NRSV's "buckler" or NIV's "rampart." The *encircling protection* probably captures the general meaning of the word.

9. 11QPsAp[a] adds an additional *selah* at the end of the verse; García Martínez, Tigchelaar, van der Woude, *Qumran Cave 11: II,* p. 202.

10. 11QPsAp[a] reverses the order of MT: "nor the pestilence that destroys at [no]on; nor destruction that walks in the darkness"; García Martínez, Tigchelaar, van der Woude, *Qumran Cave 11: II,* p. 202. 4QPs[b] is in the same order as the MT; Ulrich, Cross et al., *Qumran Cave 4: XI,* p. 27. LXX has "nor calamity nor demon at noon." There is no reason to emend MT, since it is readable as it is.

11. 11QPsAp[a] has *ygʿ* ("strike") instead of the MT's *ygš* ("come near"); García Martínez, Tigchelaar, and van der Woude, *Qumran Cave 11: II,* p. 202. 4QPs[b] uses the same word as the MT; Ulrich, Cross et al., *Qumran Cave 4: XI,* p. 27.

12. 11QPsAp[a] reverses the word order of MT: "Only you will look with your eyes"; García Martínez, Tigchelaar, van der Woude, *Qumran Cave 11: II,* p. 202. 4QPs[b] follows the MT order; Ulrich, Cross et al., *Qumran Cave 4: XI,* p. 27.

13. This form of the word appears only here, so the meaning is tentative. However, 11QPsAp[a] uses a similar word with the pointed form *šallum* ("compensation"); *HALOT,* p. 1511; García Martínez, Tigchelaar, and van der Woude, *Qumran Cave 11: II,* p. 202.

14. The translation of this line is uncertain. Some move the verb to the first line (NRSV, NIV). Many change the 1cs suffix to 2ms ("your refuge") to retain the person of vv. 3-8, but this change is not necessarily the only possibility. Here I read line 1 as a verbless clause,

the Most High you have set as your dwelling place.[15]
10 *Evil will not meet you;*[16]
destruction will not come near[17] *your tent.*[18]
11 *For his messengers, he will command concerning you,*
to guard you in all your journeys.
12 *Upon their palms, they will carry you,*
so you do not strike your foot against a rock.
13 *Upon a lion and a cobra, you will tread;*
you will trample a young lion and serpent."

14 *"For the one devoted to me, I will set on high;*[19]
I will protect the one knowing my name.
15 *When this one*[20] *calls, I will answer;*
I will be with this one in distress;
I will rescue and I will honor.[21]
16 *With long life, I will satisfy;*
and I will demonstrate my salvation."[22]

---

understanding it as an interjection. This reading is possible and does not alter MT, but is as tentative as the other suggestions offered.

15. 11QPsAp^a has a very broken text, but what exists makes clear it uses a different text: *qr[ ]mḥ[ ]t mḥmdw,* which is reconstructed as "You will announce your shelter . . . his delight"; García Martínez, Tigchelaar, and van der Woude, *Qumran Cave 11: II,* p. 202.

16. 11QPsAp^a is again broken and following a different text, which is reconstructed as "You will see no evil"; García Martínez, Tigchelaar, and van der Woude, *Qumran Cave 11: II,* p. 202.

17. 11QPsAp^a has "see no harm" instead of MT's *ygš* ("come near"); García Martínez, Tigchelaar, and van der Woude, *Qumran Cave 11: II,* p. 202.

18. 11QPsAp^a has the plural "your tents"; García Martínez, Tigchelaar, and van der Woude, *Qumran Cave 11: II,* p. 202.

19. Uncertain grammar leads to a plethora of translations; lit., "for in me he loves and I will set on high." 4QPs^b follows MT with some reconstruction of line 2; Ulrich, Cross et al., *Qumran Cave 4: XI,* p. 27. 11QPsAp^a is very fragmentary. There is a reconstruction, but much of it is tentative and does not yield any more certainty than the MT; García Martínez, Tigchelaar, and van der Woude, *Qumran Cave 11: II,* p. 202.

20. Hebrew "he" here and in vv. 15b and 16.

21. 11QPsAp^a appears to be missing v. 15; García Martínez, Tigchelaar, and van der Woude, *Qumran Cave 11: II,* p. 202. 4QPs^b is fragmentary, but enough is present to show agreement with MT; Ulrich, Cross et al., *Qumran Cave 4: XI,* p. 27.

22. 11QPsAp^a has a different ending, reconstructed as "He will sh[ow you] his victo[ry . . .] and they will ans[wer, "Amen, Amen.] Selah." The text is very broken; García Martínez, Tigchelaar, and van der Woude, *Qumran Cave 11: II,* p. 202.

1 The opening of the psalm is not without its difficulties. The question centers on whether v. 2 should be altered to reflect the same voice as v. 1.[23] This reading makes the opening smoother and solves the problem, but what is not solved is the change of person in v. 9 that forms an envelope around vv. 3-8.[24]

The reading proposed here is more complex but does not require an alteration of the MT. Verse 1 serves as an introduction to the one who will offer the testimony of encouragement. It serves as both an introduction to the subject of the prayer and as the qualifications of the one who will speak.[25] The verse also provides a link with the haunting unanswered questions of Ps. 88:14 ("Why do you *hide* your face from me?") and Ps. 89:46 ("Will you *hide* [your face] forever?") with its declaration, *One living within the* hiding place *of the Most High.* God is not hiding, but is instead providing a *hiding place* for the faithful one.

2 Next, the one speaks of his own *trust* in God. It is this personal testimony that gives the words that follow trustworthiness. He speaks from a position of deep personal faith. The theme is the same as v. 1: God protects. This first person speech also provides a frame for vv. 3-8 and divides this section into two messages.

3-8 The section begins by describing a saving act by God, by *snatching* one from the net which is set by the wicked ones.[26] The *thorn of destruction* implies an additional threat of death. God is rescuing the one that is already trapped with a weapon poised dangerously close (v. 3). Verse 4 provides images of protection, this time tucked under the *wings* of God. What a contrast it is between sure death and the safest place in the world! The last line of v. 4 is problematic, but generally describes that God's *faithfulness* is surrounding the frightened one. The use of the word *faithfulness* is another important link with Psalm 89, where God's faithfulness is questioned (89:49). Nothing can harm or cause *fear* when one is tucked inside the *wings* of God — not *terrors* nor *arrows* nor *destruction* nor *pestilence.* Verses 7 and 8 end this section where it began, with the violent world of humans. Even if v. 8 is textually problematic, the message is clear: even in war, God will surround the faithful one and from a place of safety this one will see the *reward* God gives to the *wicked.*

9 The testimony changes the person addressed to God. This one can make these declarations to others because God has served as refuge in the past. The second line encourages those listening to do the same. As noted, many modern translations alter the person of this line so that there is no break

23. See *BHS* critical apparatus, p. 1174; or Kraus, *Psalms 60–150,* p. 219.

24. Tate, *Psalms 51–100,* p. 452.

25. Tate sees it as an introduction to the psalm, but not as an introduction to the speaker; *Psalms 51–100,* p. 452.

26. See Pss. 119:110; 140:5; 141:9; 142:3.

here. However, a reading of the MT is possible without the change, and like v. 2, it validates the words of the speaker as true confession.

10-13 This section repeats the trust of the first section, using different metaphors. Verse 10 personifies the things we most fear, but only to demonstrate they are already managed by God. Tate notes that the context may be that vv. 3-8 refer to God's protection at home and vv. 10-13 to the dangers when traveling.[27] The overall effect is stressing that God is always with the faithful ones.

14-16 The long silence of Psalms 88, 89, and 90 is over. God speaks a word of deliverance to confirm all that has been said by the faithful one. The next verse further reverses the previous psalms as God declares that God will *answer, be with, rescue,* and *honor.* Finally, the last line tells that God will *demonstrate God's salvation.*

This is the long-awaited answer, but as with all of the biblical texts, it does not deal with the questions of why. It speaks first of trust in God and second of God's confirmation of those words. It does not review or explain the past. It is as if in its place, this prayer hits the reset button on the relationship. It is up to the one hearing these words to decide how these words can serve as a bridge from what came before, to decide what and how things have changed. The gaps here cause us as readers today to work at our own answers. We too know that in times of doubt, with questions of theodicy hanging in the air, the answers that finally come never provide a definitive explanation of why these things happened in the first place. As these ancient people knew, God and our faith in God is a mystery, and for that mystery there are no definitive answers, rational or otherwise, that suffice.

BETH TANNER

27. *Psalms 51–100,* p. 457.

Psalm 92: Sabbath Day Thanksgiving

Psalm 91 confirms the reestablished relationship with God. This psalm that follows is the only song in the psalter dedicated to the Sabbath. It celebrates the restored connection and invites all to come and praise God. Relationship restored, it is now time to return to the regular way to be with God in the celebration of God and God's gifts to God's people.

Psalm 92 is a prayer of thanksgiving that focuses on God's vanquishing of enemies and on God's provision of a safe place for God's people to worship. It continues the theme of recovery after great national losses. Structurally, the psalm has three stanzas:

A call to and the reasons for praise (vv. 1-5)
God's victory over evil ones and the triumph of the one praying (vv. 6-11)
The life lived in God's care (vv. 12-15)[1]

This song moves from call, to praise, to God's acts on behalf of the people, and ends with a description of life without war lived in God's care.

A psalm. A Sabbath-day song.

1 *It is good to give thanks to the LORD,*
to make music to your name, O Most High;
2 *to declare in the morning your* hesed,
and your faithfulness in the night
3 *upon a harp and upon a stringed instrument,*
upon the melody of a harp.
4 *For you, O LORD, cause me to rejoice in your deeds;*
in the works[2] *of your hands I shout for joy!*

5 *How great is your work, O LORD;*
how deep are your thoughts.
6 *A stupid one does not know,*[3]
a fool cannot understand this;

1. Scholars disagree on how to divide the psalm. Several divide the call from the reason (Hossfeld and Zenger, *Psalms 2,* p. 436; Gerstenberger, *Psalms: Part Two,* p. 168; and Tate, *Psalms 51–100,* p. 464, who argues for a chiastic structure with v. 8 as the center), but I believe that the reasons should be directly attached to the call. They are not a new thought; they are a continuation of the call to praise.

2. 4QPs^b has the singular "work"; Ulrich, Cross et al., *Qumran Cave 4: XI,* p. 28.

3. 4QPs^b has an additional *wāw* before the negation-verb complex, resulting in a

7 *though the wicked grow like grass*
and all the evildoers bloom,
they will be destroyed forever.
8 *You are on high forever, O Lord.*
9 *For surely your enemies, O Lord,*
surely your enemies, O Lord, will perish;
all evildoers will be scattered.
10 *You have raised my horn like that of a wild ox;*
you anoint me fresh oil.[4]
11 *My eyes have looked (in triumph)*[5] *on my enemies;*[6]
As evil ones rise against me, my ears hear ———.[7]

12 *The righteous bloom like a palm tree;*
and like a cedar in Lebanon they grow.
13 *They are planted in the house of the Lord;*
in the courts of our God, they vigorously bloom.[8]
14 *They still bear fruit in old age;*[9]
they are[10] *full and green;*
15 *proclaiming that the Lord is upright,*
my Rock, and there is no wrongdoing[11] *in him.*

---

change in sentence structure to "the one who is senseless and does not know"; Ulrich, Cross et al., *Qumran Cave 4: XI,* p. 28.

4. This line is problematic; both Targ and Peshitta read "you have anointed me," while LXX reads, "my old age is in fat oil." Many suggest emending the text from the 1st common singular to a 2ms with a 1cs suffix: "you poured on me." Others read the *qal* verb as passive, but there is no other attestation of this use. The line is emended as suggested in the *BHS* critical apparatus (p. 1175), but the translation is tentative at best.

5. "Looking in triumph" is the full meaning; see Pss. 54:7; 59:10; and Tate, *Psalms 51–100,* p. 45.

6. The root is presumably *šur,* but many emend to *šrr* ("enemy").

7. What is heard is missing from the line. NIV assumes "rout," as in the noise of battle, while NRSV uses "doom." LXX reads "my ears shall hear the wicked that rise up against me." 1QPs[a] has a prefect verb. Unfortunately, the line is broken, so only this verb remains; D. Barthélemy and J. T. Milik, *Qumran Cave I* (DJD 1; Oxford: Clarendon, 1955), p. 69. It would be difficult to select an option for this missing piece, so there is a blank here indicating the fractured line.

8. This is the third appearance of this verb (also vv. 7 and 12). Zenger notes that the use of the *hiphil* here indicates an intensification; *Psalms 2,* p. 453. 4QPs[b] has a *qal* form here also; Ulrich, Cross et al., *Qumran Cave 4: XI,* p. 28.

9. 4QPs[b] adds an additional adjective, *twbh,* meaning "good old age"; Ulrich, Cross et al., *Qumran Cave 4: XI,* p. 28.

10. 4QPs[b] adds an additional *wāw* to begin this line; Ulrich, Cross et al., *Qumran Cave 4: XI,* p. 28.

11. Reading the Qere.

1-5 This psalm begins with the word *ṭôḇ* ("good"), indicating that the reversal in Psalm 91 of the three previous psalms continues here. The people are called to *give thanks* and *make music* to God and to tell of God's *hesed* ("steadfast love") and *faithfulness* (v. 2). These are the attributes Israel has depended on since God's rescue of them from Egypt (Exod. 34:6), the same attributes that were put in question in Ps. 89:49. Life is restored, and instead of questioning the absence of God's love and faithfulness, these attributes are to be lifted up in thanksgiving and song. Verse 3 tells of some of the instruments used in celebration in the liturgical setting. Verses 4 and 5 give the reasons for praise. The first two words, *deeds* (v. 4) and *work* (v. 5), encompass both God's saving acts (Deut. 32:4; Isa. 45:11; Exod. 34:10; Josh. 24:31) and God's creative acts (Pss. 8:6; 19:1). The final line declares the mystery of God in acknowledging the depth of God's *thoughts.* Sabbath is to be characterized by praise and song and celebration.

6-11 The second section opens with a contrast between God's *deep thoughts* and the knowledge of clueless humans (v. 6), who cannot see the long view of life. The people had been through a great deal, and during the events leading up to and the exilic period itself, it was hard to remain faithful. But as in Psalm 1, the foolish way is to give up on God and God's promises. The learned ones declare God's sovereignty (v. 8) and God's eventual triumph over all of the enemies (v. 9). Verses 10-11 are the calm after the long, hard storm. God has lifted up the honor of the ones who remained faithful, and they have seen the downfall of the *enemies* of God (v. 11). The last line of this section appears to be missing a word, but the meaning can be understood without it. *Evil* may *rise* up, but eventually one will *hear* something different.

12-15 The psalm ends with an affirmation of trust in God. Also like Psalm 1, the righteous are described as trees that *bloom* and *grow;* they are securely rooted in God's *house* and are still strong and vigorous, even in *old age* (vv. 12-14). Indeed, the twofold appearance here stands in contrast to the *wicked* who bloomed in v. 7 but were like *grass* instead of powerful trees. These deeply rooted and vital righteous ones proclaim that God is *upright* and that there is no *wrongdoing* in God. This image also stands in contrast to the fleeting nature of humans under God's wrath presented in Psalm 90 as desert grass.

This last stanza then finally provides the answer to the anguished cries of Ps. 89:46-49. Relationship is restored and Sabbath praise is offered for God's great works as the crisis that ended Book Three and Psalm 90 are left behind. There are other things left behind, for this psalm contains praise only of God. The praise of Zion, and Jerusalem, and the Davidic dynasty have also disappeared. Book Four sees the world after events have caused a change in the people's lives, for they are no longer one people in one place, but a people of the world where the Sabbath praise of God is one of the things that unites them still. The theology of the exile exchanges a God of a specific place and a specific people with a global God that is in many places and with many people of different cultures. What unites them now is worship and service to the same God as the one that traveled with Abraham and Sarah and the people in the Egypt and the wilderness.

Another important note is that this is the only "Sabbath" psalm in the whole psalter, and in this particular placement it stands before the enthronement psalms. If these psalms indeed were part of a particular historical festival in a particular place as argued by Mowinckel, the editors of the psalms here gave these psalms a new context, not of a festival of Jerusalem, but of weekly worship of God that is not connected to a festival or a place but to a worshipping people.

We are the heirs to this change in how the people understood God. We, too, as Christians have sometimes tried to reduce God's work to a particular place or a particular people to the exclusion of others. But as this psalm emphasizes, God will not be so confined. God's concern and, indeed, God's kingdom belong to no human or group of humans but are truly a global enterprise.

BETH TANNER

Psalm 93: God Is King on High

Psalm 93 is one of the enthronement psalms (Psalms 47, 93–99), all of which declare that God is king of all. This theme of God as the king is the heart of Book Four and is the answer to the questions of Book Three concerning personal and national defeats and the subsequent questions of theodicy.[1] Mowinckel argued that these psalms are part of an annual enthronement festival, but no concrete evidence exists as to the shape of this festival. What is clear is that whether or not there is a human king on the throne in Jerusalem, the Lord is the supreme king, not only of Israel, but of all of the creation. Indeed, this first of the enthronement psalms concerns only God and God's creation. In that it is a reflection of ancient Near Eastern creation myths where the god not only creates the world, but has control over the chaotic waters.[2] This psalm is brief, but is divided into three stanzas:

God is King and Creator (vv. 1-2)
God is in control of the chaotic waters (vv. 3-4)
God's stable reign (v. 5)

The MT does not have a superscription, but the LXX reads, "For the day before the Sabbath, when the land was inherited, a praise song to David."

1 *The LORD*[3] *is king!*[4]
He is robed in majesty, the LORD is robed;[5]
with strength he has girded himself.[6]

1. Interestingly, while 4QPs[b] has this psalm in the same place as in the MT, 11QPs[s] places this psalm between the *Apostrophe to Zion* and Psalm 141; James A. Sanders, *The Psalms Scroll of Qumrân Cave 11 (11QPs[a])*(DJD 4; Oxford: Clarendon, 1965), p. 43.

2. See, e.g., the *Enuma Elish.*

3. 11QPs[s] omits YHWH and begins with *hllwyh;* Sanders, *The Psalms Scroll of Qumrân Cave 11,* p. 43.

4. This opening line has received a great deal of scholarly attention. Mowinckel argued for a translation of "The LORD has become king!" as part of an enthronement festival (*Psalmenstudien,* 2:6-8). The syntax allows for reading the predicate as a noun or for reading it as a verb, which explains NIV "The LORD reigns" and NRSV "The LORD is king." There are good arguments for either choice, and it should probably be understood as both, reading "the LORD is king and reigns."

5. Retaining the structure in MT contra NRSV, which adds "in majesty" to the MT's "he is robed."

6. 11QPs[s] has a *wāw* suffix on the verb: "he girded himself." This would change the arrangement of these lines to "He is robed with strength. He girded himself"; Sanders, *The Psalms Scroll of Qumrân Cave 11,* p. 43.

Indeed, the world is firmly established;[7] *it will not be shaken.*

2 *Your throne is established from long ago;*
you are from eternity.

3 *The rivers have lifted up, O LORD; the rivers have lifted up their voice;*
the rivers lift up their pounding waves.[8]

4 *Greater than the voice of many waters, mighty ones, breakers of the sea;*
powerful on high is the LORD.[9]

5 *Your decrees are very sure; holiness adorns your house,*[10]
O LORD, for the length of days.

1-2 This first section declares God as *king,* then continues to speak of the attributes of that kingship. The king is *robed* to show the position to all (vv. 1b, 1c). God is *girded* with *strength,* indicating his readiness to battle evil. Finally, the *world* is *firmly* in place because God is in control and has been eternally (v. 2). Chaos and evil are managed because God is king of the world.

3-4 In this section, the *waters* rise up to praise God. The geography of the Middle East places the people in a precarious situation. The wadies were dry except in the period of the fall and winter rains. Israel's literal life was dependent on those rains, for without them they would starve in the dry season. But there is a fine line between enough rain and too much. The waters can *lift up* and roar, bringing with them death and destruction. The waters were seen in ancient Near Eastern mythology to represent chaos because there was no way to control them, and they could bring life or death. Here the waters rise, not to destroy, but to praise their Creator and Controller. Of course, it is also possible to infer the salvation at the Sea (Exodus 14), and that

7. Some scholars and NIV read the *piel* verb as 3ms, "He established the world," but MT is clear with a 3fs niphal verb and a fs noun, indicating that *world* is the subject of the verb.

8. The word *d^{a}ḵî* appears only here, so its meaning is uncertain. It is thought to be from the root *dkh* ("pounding or raging").

9. The grammar of this verse is problematic. It is translated here without additions but reading the first phrase as a comparative, followed by two words describing those waters, with a final phrase that declares the LORD as more powerful than the rising, crashing waters. There are multiple constructions of this verse as indicated by the plethora of translations.

10. 4QPs^{b} has *nwh* instead of MT's *na'^{a}wâ.* Flint believes this is probably a variant of orthography (*The Dead Sea Psalms Scrolls and the Book of Psalms,* p. 95). However, if the word is from the root *nwh,* the line would read "in your house is a dwelling place of holiness" or "in your house is a holy dwelling place," and within the context, this may make more sense. However, since the word is only here in the Dead Sea Scrolls, there is no compelling reason to alter MT.

would not be surprising since it is one and the same message. Pharaoh sent chariots, but God was supreme, and that was demonstrated by God's control of the creation and God's use of the rising waters to destroy the great armies of the powerful Egyptian king.

5 Verse 5 serves as a thematic *inclusio* for the psalm. It returns to the clear theme of God as king, this time praising God's decisions and God's abode and finally declaring again that God's reign is established forever.

This psalm begins and ends with the declaration that God is king of the creation and that kingship has existed from eternity. It is firmly established, and it is that on which we depend. God is in control, and the world is God's servant. The center part of the psalm has the most chaotic part of creation rising up, not in destruction, but in praise of God. God's power is declared as more powerful than the most destructive force that these ancient folks knew.

As much as we often convince ourselves of our power over nature, we have never been completely able to control the rushing water, as floods, tsunamis, and hurricanes readily attest. We may not see the waters as representative of chaos, for we have replaced them with other forces that seem to us the most chaotic and most frightening powers on earth. Unfortunately, our worst fears are now of the destructive power of humans, not of creation. Yet, here the powers of humans are reserved for other psalms. This psalm reminds us of a truth rarely contemplated today, that the earth and its vegetation, its animals, and its water and winds are also part of God's kingdom and ultimately part of the invisible planet that in its own way praises its Creator with dance and song and lifted leaves. The enthronement psalms start without us and serve as a reminder that God's kingship is concerned with much more than humanity. We might be the center of our thoughts, but for God the job is bigger and greater than we are able to fathom. God's great kingdom is not only about us! With this first psalm, we are placed where we belong, as part of God's great created kingdom.

BETH TANNER

Psalm 94: God Will Judge the World

Traditionally, Psalm 94 has not been considered one of the enthronement psalms because it lacks the defining phrase, "the LORD reigns." Indeed, Mowinckel sees this psalm as one of national lament.[1] Dahood, on the other hand, characterizes it as a song of thanksgiving.[2] The psalm certainly opens like a lament, but after the first seven verses moves on to speak of God's teaching of humans and God's protective power. Overall, the psalm does not seem as much a prayer for help as it does a prayer of trust that God will deal with the evil ones by judging the world.[3] Because the psalm is positioned here, dividing the enthronement psalms, its placement has been a frequent topic of discussion. Is it an intrusion into these thematic psalms, or does its placement serve a particular purpose? David Howard has done extensive work on the psalm's placement, in seeking both thematic and lexical connections with the surrounding psalms.[4] He sees the psalm as a lament, but one uniquely suited because its placement bridges the gap between the questions and issues of theodicy before it and the unbridled praise that follows it.[5] It also sets Psalm 93 apart from the rest of the group as one that exclusively focuses on God and creation, reminding the readers that God's kingship is not only in the human realm of the world.

Howard has shown that Psalm 94 can stand among the enthronement psalms and offer a unique message, but should it be considered an enthronement psalm? Enthronement psalms are so characterized because of their theme, not their superscriptions. The word "king" is not used in this psalm. However, the two themes that are present — God as vindicator and judge — both are central to the functions performed by the king god. God as vindicator and protector is a divine warrior function, and this is clearly part of God's kingship (see Psalm 98). Likewise, God's responsibilities as judge are the focus of Psalm 96. The themes, then, certainly are part of the function of kingship, and thus if theme is the only criterion, this qualifies as an enthronement psalm.

But what of the form of the psalm that has so many scholars divided? The psalm certainly is not one of praise as are the other enthronement psalms. It is a call for God to rise up and act as the vindicator and the judge of the

1. *The Psalms in Israel's Worship,* p. 227; also Clifford, *Psalms 73–150,* p. 111.

2. *Psalms II,* p. 346. Because he sees this psalm as one of thanksgiving, he reads the events detailed here in the past tense.

3. Tate concurs with this general direction, arguing this psalm is one of community instruction to strengthen the faith of the people; *Psalms 51–100,* p. 487. Hossfeld sees it as a mixed-type psalm; Hossfeld and Zenger, *Psalms 2,* p. 453.

4. "Psalm 94 among the Kingship-of-Yhwh Psalms," *CBQ* 61 (1999) 667-85.

5. "Psalm 94," p. 685.

world. In the strictest sense then, the psalm is not like the others, yet thematically it is clearly the same. Howard has argued that it is unique among both the prayers for help and the enthronement psalms, and it is. Ultimately, this psalm demonstrates the very things the other psalms praise: God is responsive to and cares about and hears God's creation when it cries out for help. It is a psalm that says the attributes that are being praised here are true and can be trusted. In that way, this psalm too can stand as a psalm that has kingship and the actions of the great King God as its central focus.

The psalm is divided into three sections:

God's work as vindicator (vv. 1-7)
God's work as teacher (vv. 8-15)
God's work can be trusted (vv. 16-23)

These sections work together to affirm God's involvement in human affairs and in human life. Each section also contains a set of questions (vv. 3, 8b-10, 16 and 20).[6] The questions can be seen as rhetorical, but in the context of the enthronement psalms they can also represent the cyclic nature of waiting for God's justice. Doubt is presented in the questions, whereas the answer counters with belief and faith in God's justice. In this way, the psalm is neither a prayer for help nor a prayer of thanksgiving, but is one of testimony[7] about a life lived in anticipation of God's coming to "judge the people with equity" (Ps. 96:10). There are a couple of textual problems that lead to a variety of translations, but these do not hinder the overall meaning of the psalm. The MT has no superscription, but the LXX reads, "A psalm for David for the fourth day of the week."

1 *O God of vindication, O LORD;*
God of vindication, shine forth!
2 *Rise up, O Judge of the Earth,*
turn back on the arrogant what they deserve.
3 *How long will the wicked, O LORD,*
how long will the wicked celebrate?
4 *They gush; they speak arrogance;*
all the evildoers boast.
5 *Your people, O LORD, they crush*

6. Some scholars divide the psalm with the questions as the beginning of each section (Clifford, *Psalms 73–150,* p. 112; Gerstenberger, *Psalms: Part 2,* p. 177), and this division is also possible.

7. Tate concurs: "these verses have the character of communal instruction intended to strengthen faith"; *Psalms 51–100,* p. 487.

and they oppress your heritage.[8]
6 *Widow and sojourner they kill*
and orphans they murder.
7 *And they say, "the Lord does not see;*
the God of Jacob takes no notice."[9]

8 *Understand, you stupid ones among the people!*
Fools, when will you wise up?
9 *Does the one planting the ear not hear,*
or the one who forms the eye not see?[10]
10 *Does the one who disciplines the nations not punish,*
the one teaching knowledge to humans ———.[11]
11 *The* LORD *knows the thoughts of humans,*
that they are but a puff of smoke.
12 *Happy is the one whom you discipline, O Lord,*
and by your instruction, you teach,
13 *providing calm to the one from days of trouble*
until a pit is dug for the wicked one.
14 *For the* LORD *will not forsake his people,*[12]
and his heritage he will not abandon.
15 *Because of righteousness, justice will return in perpetuity;*[13]
and after that, all the upright of heart (will return).[14]

16 *Who will rise up for me against the evil ones?*
Who will stand up for me against workers of woe?
17 *If the* LORD *were not my help,*

8. Lit., "family property," with the understanding that it cannot be sold or taken (Num. 27:5-11), hence the translation of *heritage* or inheritance.

9. Lit., "does not discern."

10. Lit., "does not regard."

11. A final word or phrase is missing (Hossfeld concurs; *Psalms 2,* p. 452). MT suggests "Is the one who teaches without knowledge," and this is very possibly the intended meaning. Tate suggests that "does not he punish" be used for both lines (*Psalms 51–100,* p. 484), but this is less probable because it breaks the pattern where the two lines are related thematically.

12. 4QPs has a direct object marker before *his people;* Ulrich, Cross et al., *Qumran Cave 4: XI,* p. 31.

13. The grammar of this line is problematic, leading to a plethora of translations. The MT notes suggest that the abstract noun *ṣeḏeq* be read as the adjective *ṣaḏîq,* with some textual support; see NRSV. Hossfeld argues that both terms are technical, meaning "law" (*Psalms 2,* p. 452). It is possible to read MT as it is, assuming both *righteousness* and *justice* are abstract personified nouns that come with God's reign (see Ps. 85:8-13).

14. Like most translations, this assumes the verb serves both clauses.

my life[15] *would dwell in silence.*[16]
18 *When I said, "My foot is slipping,"*
your hesed, *O LORD, held me fast.*
19 *When my worries are great,*[17]
your consolations give cheer to me.[18]
20 *Can a throne of destruction be allied with you,*
bringing misery by statute?
21 *They band together against the life of the righteous,*
and they condemn the blood of the innocent.
22 *The LORD has become to me as a stronghold;*
my God is my rock of refuge.
23 *He continuously turns back on them their iniquity;*
and by their wickedness, he will annihilate them;
the LORD our God will annihilate them.

1-7 The opening (vv. 1-2) calls on God to come forth and judge the earth (96:13; 97:2; 98:9; 99:4), to set the world right. It is a brave call of a faithful one who is confident in God's ability to judge a situation and vindicate this one in need. This call has all of the lexical hallmarks of a prayer for help.

Verses 3-7 present the reasons why God's intervention is needed. The *wicked* seem to be winning the day. They have no regard for humans (vv. 5-6), nor for God (v. 7). Indeed, the acts of the wicked are serious, for not only do they *celebrate* and *boast* (vv. 3-4), they also *crush* and *oppress* (v. 5) and *kill* and *murder* (v. 6). They also claim that God either ignores or does not know of their actions (v. 7). Even in the midst of the God-as-king psalms, this stands as a testament to the earthly world. The world needs God as king because such injustice exists. It cannot be brushed aside or ignored. There are still those who oppose God's reign and *oppress* God's own family (*heritage,* v. 5).

8-15 Verses 8-11 are a direct response to vv. 3-7. God is listening, knowing human *thoughts* (v. 11). God knows both the input of the senses *(ear* and *eye)* and the thoughts of humans, and only the *stupid* do not understand this (v. 8)! The *stupid* may be the *wicked* of the last stanza, or people who cannot see that God will eventually set the world right, or both.[19] Either way, they are but *a puff of smoke,* or *hebel,* which reminds us of the lessons of both

15. Lit., *nap̱šî;* this word has a wide range of meaning: "soul, living being, self." It is the essence of what makes a sack of bones alive.

16. Presumably, *silence* means death; see LXX, which uses "in Hades" here.

17. Lit., "many are the disturbed thoughts in my inward part."

18. Lit., *nap̱šî.*

19. Tate concurs that this is probably a double entendre, with the *stupid* referring to both; *Psalms 51–100,* p. 492.

Ecclesiastes and Psalm 90, where the fragile and brief nature of humans is contrasted against the eternity of God.[20]

Verses 12-15 also continue the response, this time in the form of a beatitude that presents a counterimage to the one in vv. 8-11.[21] One who receives the *discipline* and teaching of the Lord is *happy* (v. 12), for that teaching protects in trouble until God sets up God's just kingdom (vv. 13, 15). This one knows what those in the previous verses did not, that God will not *forsake* or *abandon* (v. 14). Unlike the fleeting lives and knowledge of humans, the foundations of God's kingdom are eternal (v. 15).

16-23 But waiting for God's justice is very hard. Questions enter again in v. 16. The *evil ones* are very real, and at times it appears as if there is no help from their vicious attacks. Verses 17-19 affirm that even in those times God was there to *help,* to *hold,* and to *cheer.* It is here that the testimonial character of the psalm comes to the fore. The enthronement psalms speak of God as the great King, Creator, and Controller of the World. God is seen as huge and powerful. Here is the balance, for that great king is also friend and comforter in times of doubt and trouble. God is also a micromanager and cares about our daily struggles.

Until now, the wicked had no identity beyond their acts of oppression and murder. In v. 20, the wicked become those in governmental or systemic power. They are not just citizens, but people with the power to harm by *statute* and law. But even when those in power oppress, God is there as a *stronghold* and *rock of refuge* (v. 22). God is more than a comforter; God has the power to offer protection, even from ones on the throne. The psalm ends as it begins, with the wicked, and answers the question of *How long* asked in v. 3. God will *turn back on them their iniquity* (v. 23). The last two lines seem harsh to a modern audience. But the psalms show forth human emotion, and in the midst of oppression from powers that even escalate to murder, the cry that God *annihilate them* is a true emotion and expresses the belief that God will set the world right, ending the psalm with hope that "justice in perpetuity" will be the way of the new world order.

We too sit and wait, often not patiently, for the culmination of God's kingdom. This psalm confirms our struggles along the way. Even in the midst of psalms that praise God as the great king and controller of all that is, this psalm stands both as a testimony to that belief in God's promises and God's justice and as a confirmation that life lived on this side of that full kingdom is hard. We too see lives of injustice that seem to prosper, and we have seen our share of those in power that oppress those with less. Here on the verge

20. Many scholars see this section as a wisdom piece that complicates discerning the genre of this prayer; see Howard, "Psalm 94," p. 667; or Kraus, *Psalms 60–150,* p. 240.

21. Hossfeld and Zenger, *Psalms 2,* p. 454.

of some of the most extreme praise in the whole psalter, there is real gritty, ugly life. So ultimately, this psalm accomplishes one more purpose: to tell us that this is not artificial or Pollyanna praise, but praise that rises from the realities and struggles of real life.

BETH TANNER

Psalm 95: A History Lesson in the Midst of the Celebration

Psalm 94 asked for God to come and judge the world. Here the people are invited to "move it" and go meet God with celebration. But in the midst of the preparations for worship, the psalm turns to lift a word of caution. The change is abrupt and without explanation. Much of the scholarly discussion has centered on the purpose of the exhortation within a festival celebrating the enthronement of Yahweh, but it is clear that little of the details of such a festival are recoverable. Theologically, however, both Amos 5 and Isaiah 1 speak of the importance of worship with rightness of heart. Words without commitment are an abomination to God. This psalm tells that, even in the midst of a call to worship, there is a reminder that worship is more than words: it involves commitment in all aspects of one's life.

The psalm is clearly divided between vv. 7c and d into two sections. There are no major translation issues. The structure is unusual: three calls to worship (vv. 1, 2-5, 6-7c) in the first section, followed by the warning in vv. 7d-11. The MT has no superscription, but the LXX reads, "A praise song for David."

1 *Move,*[1] *let us shout for joy to the* L*ORD*;
let us shout to the rock of our salvation!
2 *Let us meet his presence*[2] *with thanksgiving;*
with a song, let us shout to him,
3 *for a great God*[3] *is the* L*ORD*,
and a great king over all the gods;
4 *whom*[4] *in his hand are the depths*[5] *of the earth,*
and the peaks[6] *of the mountains are his;*
5 *whom to him is the sea; HE*[7] *made it;*
the dry land his hands formed it.

1. The word here is the imperative of *hālaḵ* ("to walk"), whereas v. 6 begins with the command *bw'* ("to come").

2. Both NRSV and NIV use the familiar phrase "let us come before him," but this is not the same word as in line 1. *Qāḏam* means "to meet or encounter" (*HALOT,* p. 1068), reading lit., "let us meet his face."

3. Lit., *'ēl.*

4. Many modern translations smooth out these verses as "in his hands are the depths . . ." but the Hebrew text begins with the particle *'ăšer,* making vv. 4-5 dependent clauses that refer to the subject God as the focus.

5. This word appears only here. Both LXX and Vulg use "end" or "boundary" (*HALOT,* p. 571).

6. The meaning of this word is uncertain here. *HALOT* (p. 1705) notes it is probably linked with Arabic *yafa'a* ("to tower or stand above").

7. Both the 3ms personal pronoun and the 3ms verb are used for emphasis.

6 *Come, let us bow down and kneel;*
kneel[8] *before the* LORD, *our maker,*
7 *for he is our God,*
and we are the people of his pasture
and the sheep of his hand.

Today if to his voice you would listen!
8 *Do not harden your hearts like at Meribah,*
like the day at Massah in the wilderness,
9 *when your fathers tested me*
and tried me even though they had seen my deeds.
10 *For forty years, I detested that generation, and I said,*
"People with straying hearts are they;
they do not know my ways."
11 *So I swore in my anger, "They will not enter into my rest."*

1-7c The traditional opening of "Come" in English is deceiving. The word is the imperative of "Walk," meaning more like "Move it" or "Let's get going." It implies that it is the beginning of the journey that culminates in v. 2 as one anticipates "encountering the face of God." In addition to movement, the people are also called upon to raise their voices. The NRSV translations of "sing" and "make a joyful noise" are not strong enough here. The two verbs in v. 1 are *rānan* in the intensified *piel* form, meaning to "call loudly," and *rûaʿ*, which is often a war-cry or cry of alarm (also v. 2). This type of song requires great effort and is expressed with as much power as a cry of alarm or war. The effect of a congregation performing in this way would be deafening! The praise is loud and rowdy and would sound threatening and frightening to someone listening. This is praise using all of the force and power that the human body has.

Verses 3-5 give the reasons why the people are to shout and cry out and come before God. God is king over all of the other gods, and the created world belongs to God. The metaphor in v. 1, *rock of our salvation*, and God as *king* and Creator tie these together. The function of Creator is part of God's divine kingship. This was displayed clearly in the exodus, where the Lord defeated the Egyptian god Pharaoh,[9] not with weapons, but with creation. God's function as the creator and controller of creation is what Israel was to see and remember at the crossing of the sea. It is this act that created the kingdom of God with the former slaves.

8. The three verbs here all mean to "bow down" or "kneel." It may not read as well as NRSV, but a trifold repetition places a great deal of emphasis on the center verse of the psalm.

9. In ancient Egypt, human pharaohs were understood to be gods; Henri Frankfort, *Kingship and the Gods* (Chicago: University of Chicago Press, 1948).

The final commands in the section are to offer proper reverence. Three times the congregation is called upon to *bow down and kneel.* The final word for "kneel" is from the root *bārak̲,* which normally means "to bless." This trifold command is not reflected in most English translations, but it is important. It stands as the center of the psalm and calls for the people to show respect for their God as *our maker,* confirming again God's place as the genesis of their very lives. Verse 7 introduces the new images of shepherd and *sheep.* The notion of shepherd here is more than a metaphor. In the ancient Near Eastern context, it is a title that means the same as king.[10] At some point, possibly as a sign of reverence, the loud shouts of the crowd give way to bended knees as the individuals collectively become the *sheep* that God is to lead, just as God led them out with creative force from Egypt into the wilderness.

7d-11 Verse 7c and d serve as a transition to what follows. The verse confesses that the people are God's *sheep,* followed by a wish that the people would listen to God's *voice.* The use of the verb *šāmaʿ* ("listen") recalls Deut. 6:4-9 and also may be what quiets the crowd for the speech to come. The identity of the speaker is unknown. Scholars have suggested it is either a prophet or a priest,[11] but either way, it is the lesson that is preserved, not the one who delivered it.

What follows is a warning that comes from the setting of the wilderness. Indeed, these two events at *Meribah* and *Massah* are used as an example of Israel's sin in several texts (Exod. 17:1-7; Num. 20:13, 24; Deut. 6:16; 9:22; 32:51; 33:8; Pss. 81:7; 106:32). The words here are a warning not to repeat the mistakes of old and not to doubt the power of the Lord as the ancestors did. One key phrase here is they *tried me even though they had seen my deeds.* This generation had been a witness to the power of the Creator God and the leading of the Shepherd King that provided sustenance in the wilderness, and their response was complaint and doubt. The psalm ends here, with God declaring separation from the very people God delivered in the first place. There is no resolution, no assurance of pardon. The people are left on their knees with a stern history lesson. If this is indeed an entry song, one that calls the people into the throne room of the Lord, this psalm does in words what the throne rooms of the ancient Near East do in their structure. Entry into the throne room was a frightening trip, filled with fierce statutes and guards that both protect the king and show forth the king's great power. This entire psalm has stressed the power of the Lord that saved the Israelites through the control of the creation and the anger of the Lord over the actions of the people.

10. See Beth Tanner, "King Yahweh as the Good Shepherd: Taking Another Look at the Image of God in Psalm 23," in *David and Zion,* ed. Bernard F. Batto and Kathryn L. Roberts (Winona Lake: Eisenbrauns, 2004), pp. 267-84.

11. Tate, *Psalms 51–100,* p. 499.

In worship today, God can be seen as too friendly, too nice, too forgiving. We can easily forget the great power of the King God. Our sanctuaries are filled with light and flowers and beauty. We work hard at making them beautiful and calming spaces. Indeed, we make them so much so that the great mysterious God of the Universe may get erased from our minds. Psalm 95 reminds us that worship of this God is serious business. This God is mighty and powerful, and our reverence is due our Great Creator. It also reminds us that worship and the way we live are related. We can make God so angry that worship is an abomination (Amos 5:18-25). This is not a nice word to hear, but it is true. This psalm leaves the people who are anticipating a festival, and indeed whose festival had already begun with the shouts in vv. 1-2, on their knees contemplating the sins of past generations that serve as a warning to them. "Is the praise honest and real?" is the question this psalm asks as the party begins. "Do you really know what you are doing?" "Are you really prepared to encounter God's face?" The questions for these ancient ones should also be ours. Worship, full-voiced praise-filled worship, requires an understanding of the serious nature of that praise, for as one encounters all of these enthronement songs, God is praised for being the Judge and Controller of the creation and all the peoples. The praise of God cannot be taken lightly, and so the congregation is left here on their knees to understand just that.

BETH TANNER

Psalm 96: God Will Judge Us; Let's Celebrate

Psalm 96 makes a fitting follow-up to Psalm 95, which leaves worshippers on their knees before the great God as they are reminded of the serious nature of their praise and worship to God. Psalm 96 begins with *Sing to the LORD a new song.* Many scholars have debated the purpose of this phrase.[1] The phrase opens both Psalms 96 and 98, but here, if the context of following Psalm 95 is taken seriously, this *new song* is one that comes after the history lesson of the last psalm. The new song is praise after great contemplation on the sinful nature of humanity and the often fickle nature of our songs. Tate notes, "The 'new song' is to express a new realization and acknowledgment that the future belongs to Yahweh."[2] Additionally, Psalm 94 called upon God to appear and judge the earth, and Psalm 96 is praise for God's work of judging. These two points demonstrate a connection in these psalms, even if a clear use in an enthronement festival cannot be certain.

The psalm is an extended call to praise and the reasons for that praise (vv. 1-6, 7-9, 11-13). Verse 10 forms the theological center of the psalm as God is declared as king, followed by a third call to praise, this time before the coming King Yahweh. This means the psalm is divided into three unequal sections that each have a call to praise and the reasons for that praise.[3]

Call to sing and recount God's greatness (vv. 1-6)
Call to the peoples of the world (vv. 7-10)
Call to the creation (vv. 11-13)

From a textual standpoint, the psalm is straightforward, with the exception of v. 9. The LXX has a superscription that the MT does not: "When the house was built after the captivity, a song of David."

1 *Sing to the LORD a new song;*
sing to the LORD, all the earth.
2 *Sing to the LORD, bless his name;*
tell from day to day his salvation.
3 *Recount among the nations his glory,*
among all the peoples his wonders;

1. See Tate for a lengthy discussion of the topic; *Psalms 51–100,* p. 513.

2. *Psalms 51–100,* p. 514.

3. Scholars do not agree on the divisions, esp. around v. 10. Clifford sees a break at v. 10 (*Psalms 73–150,* p. 122). Others, such as Tate (*Psalms 51–100,* p. 512) and Hossfeld (*Psalms 2,* p. 464), see two sections with a break after v. 6. Gerstenberger sets v. 10 apart (*Psalms: Part 2,* p. 187).

4 *for great is the* L*ORD*,
to be praised abundantly,
to be feared above all the gods;
5 *for all the gods of the peoples are idols;*[4]
the L*ORD made the heavens.*
6 *Honor and majesty are before him;*
strength and beauty are in his sanctuary.

7 *Ascribe to the* L*ORD*, *families of peoples;*
ascribe to the L*ORD glory and strength.*
8 *Ascribe to the* L*ORD the glory of his name;*
bring an offering and come into his courts.
9 *Bow down to the* L*ORD in the splendor of holiness;*[5]
tremble before his presence all the earth.
10 *Say among the nations, the* L*ORD is king!*[6]
The world is firmly established; it will not be shaken.
He will judge the people with equity.

11 *Let the heavens be glad and the earth rejoice,*
the sea roar and all that fills it.
12 *Let the fields exult and everything in them,*
all the trees in the forest shout
13 *before the* L*ORD for he is coming;*
he is coming to judge the earth;
he will judge the world in righteousness
and the people in his faithfulness.

1-6 The psalm opens with a threefold command to *sing to the* L*ORD* (vv. 1-2). The call is to sing *a new song.* This new song is not reserved for Israel, but is

4. The word *'elîlîm* is often used of pagan gods. Lev. 19:4; 26:1 use this word in parallel with gods of cast metal. The context here is exactly like 1 Chr. 16:26, which places these gods in contrast to the LORD who created the heavens.

5. Lit., "in the splendor of holiness." LXX reads, "in his holy courts," and its origin is unknown. A. F. Kirkpatrick and others note the phrase may indicate holy attire (*The Book of Psalms* [Cambridge: Cambridge University Press, 1901], p. 577). Cross and others argue this means a theophoric appearance (*Canaanite Myth and Hebrew Epic,* p. 153). Here it is left just as it is in MT, so that both God's glory or garments or an appearance are all possible.

6. This line has received a great deal of scholarly attention. Mowinckel argues for a translation of "The Lord has become king!" as part of an enthronement festival (*Psalmenstudien,* 2:6-8). The syntax allows for reading the predicate as a noun or for reading it as a verb, which explains NIV "The Lord reigns" and NRSV "The Lord is king." There are good arguments for either choice, and it should probably be understood as both, reading "The Lord is king and reigns."

a song of *all the earth.* Verses 2-3 give some context, that the song is to tell of God's *salvation day to day.* Mays notes that the Hebrew word *bāśar* in v. 2b "is a verb for the duty of the herald who precedes the victor to bring a report to those who wait for good news of the battle."[7] Each day then adds a stanza to the work of God's salvation for God's people. The telling is also universal, to be sung and recounted to *all the nations* and *all the peoples.* The day-to-day gifts of *salvation* from God are newsworthy worldwide. We are called here to *sing* and *tell* of God's *salvation* and *glory* and *wonders.* Verses 4-6 give the reasons for the songs. First, God is greater than *all* of the other gods (Psalm 82), which anticipates the declaration of God's kingship in v. 10. The other gods are declared as *idols,* because it is the Lord who is the creator, again a mark of kingship in the ancient Near East. The use of the word *idols* should not be equated with the idea that the other gods were not real. In the ancient Near Eastern context, the gods are real, but are unable to act outside of the control of the great Creator God, chief of the pantheon (see Psalm 82). Verse 6 continues to describe the hallmarks of the great God's reign in the splendor of his *sanctuary* or home.[8]

7-10 This section calls on all the people of the world to join in celebration to the Lord. The word translated as *ascribe* in vv. 7-8b is much more complex in Hebrew. It appears only in imperative form as a call to act (Gen. 11:3, 4, 7; Exod. 1:10), as a command to give, spoken in desperation (Gen. 30:1; 47:15), and as an order to choose or select wisely (Deut. 1:13; Josh. 18:4). All three meanings may be intended here. It is certainly a call to act, and by means of its grammar it is a call to give the Lord the praise due God's *glory and strength.* It may also have the understanding of an offering or gift that the people are to bring, as in Psalm 72, where the kings are told to bring tribute to Israel's king for he judges the people with God's justice and righteousness (72:10-14). The world streams to the Lord because of God's great acts toward the world, not as some forced tribute a vassal must give the overlord. Verse 9 is the arrival of these *families* of the earth, literally, before God's face as they bow and tremble at God's feet. Verses 7-8 also have much in common with Ps. 29:1-2. In Psalm 29 it is the "sons of gods" that are called to "Ascribe to the LORD, sons of *Eliym!* Ascribe to the LORD, glory and strength! Ascribe to the LORD the glory of his name! Worship the LORD in holy splendor!" Here it is the *families of peoples* who are to *bring an offering and come into his courts.* The worship here on earth is the same as the praise given to God in the heavens.

Verse 10 brings the acclamation of Israel and the world, declaring "God is king" along with the dual understanding that it is God that secures

7. *Psalms,* p. 308.

8. For a complete explanation of the kingship of God in ancient Near Eastern mythology, see Henri Frankfort, *Kingship and the Gods* (Chicago: University of Chicago Press, 1948).

the world and manages chaos and that God will *judge* all of *the people* fairly. The enthronement psalms are clear. Israel may have been God's chosen as they came trembling out of Egypt, but God's plan is that the whole world be treated equally. God's reign means making a place for all, not just those of a certain heritage or skin color.

11-13 Now the creation is called to join in the celebration. God's kingdom extends beyond humans. The psalm reminds all who hear it that just as we disregard other humans who do not share our immediate communities and culture, we also disregard the relationship that God has with the creation. At the declaration of God's kingship, the earth responds with joyful celebration. Verse 13 tells why the joyful chorus resounds and that God *is coming to judge the earth!* God is celebrated one final time as the one who will come to *judge* with *righteousness* and *faithfulness.*

In some traditions, this good news of God's coming to judge all the peoples with equity has become a threat. God's coming to judge is a reason to be afraid, so afraid that you give your life to Jesus before you die so you do not burn in the fires of hell. Here is a different view of God as judge and jury. We are not to cower in fear before the fierce and punishing God, but we are to bow down in celebration as we tell of God's salvation with a new song each and every day. Brueggemann writes, "The psalm is not only about an event (which most psalms scholarship seems to assume), but is also about the long term process which has been begun here. Such a psalm is always an act of profound hope, for such a realm has clearly not been established simply by the use of the psalm. . . . It is making the future momentarily present now through word, gesture, practice."[9] We are to prepare and come before God and celebrate God's rule as judge of the world. We are to trust that God loves us and loves the world and believe that God's justice will bring about a better world where righteousness and fairness are the ways of the kingdom. We are to pray for the judgment of God. This powerful psalm reminds us of the weighty message that should be the content of our praise.

BETH TANNER

9. *The Message of the Psalms,* p. 145.

Psalm 97: The King Is Coming; Let's Prepare!

Psalm 97 begins with the declaration of God's kingship, complete with a description of God's coming and the earth's response. As part of the enthronement psalms (Psalms 47, 93–99), the psalm moves from God as judge to God who is both the Creator of the world and the great king to be worshipped by creation and humans. Justice, however, is still a theme both in v. 8 and in the last section. The psalm is divided into three sections:[1]

Theophany (vv. 1-5)
Response (vv. 6-9)
God's care of the righteous ones (vv. 10-12)

The text of the psalm is clear and without major difficulties. It presents a very descriptive image of the mystery and majesty of God that is consistent with the images in Isaiah 6 and Exodus 19–20.

1 *The LORD is king!*[2]
Let the earth rejoice; let the many coastlands be glad.
2 *Clouds and thick darkness surround him;*
righteousness and justice are the foundation of his throne.
3 *Fire goes before him*
and consumes his enemies on every side.
4 *His lightning bolts light up the world;*
the earth sees and trembles.
5 *The mountains melt like wax before the LORD,*
before the Lord of all the earth.

6 *The heavens proclaim his righteousness,*
and all the peoples see his glory.
7 *All the servants of images are ashamed,*
the ones boasting in idols.
Worship him, all you gods!
8 *Zion hears and rejoices;*
daughter Judah is glad

1. Most scholars divide the psalm between vv. 5 and 6 (Hossfeld and Zenger, *Psalms 2*, p. 468; Gerstenberger, *Psalms: Part 2*, p. 191). Kraus (*Psalms 61–150*, p. 258) and Terrien (*The Psalms*, p. 680) use these as major divisions but further divide the psalm. They see v. 6 as part of the theophany, but I argue this verse has moved to the response to the theophany of God, first by the heavens and then by the people. Tate is unique in arguing for two divisions, vv. 1-9 and 10-12 (*Psalms 51–100*, p. 518).

2. See note 6 on Psalm 96.

because of your judgments, O LORD.
9 *For you, O LORD,*
are the Most High over all the earth;
you are exalted over all the gods.

10 *The ones loving the LORD hate evil!*[3]
(God is)[4] *guarding the lives*[5] *of the loyal ones;*
from the hand of the wicked, he rescues them.
11 *Light is sown*[6] *upon the righteous,*
and joy to the upright in heart.
12 *Rejoice in the LORD, righteous ones,*
and praise to his holy name![7]

1-5 This opening section tells of the power of God's reign. In language like that of Exodus 19, Isaiah 6, and Habakkuk 3, these verses portray the great mystery of God's inner sanctum. Verse 1 makes the declaration and calls on the earth and the coastlands to sing, expressing the vast expanse of God's land. This is followed by a description of the throne room of God. This throne room is no room; it is creation itself that forms the place for God. Reminiscent of the theophany on Sinai, *clouds* and deep *darkness* form the cover. The throne, the seat of the great God, is founded on *righteousness and justice,* the same attributes God's kingdom on earth is to be founded upon (Psalm 72). The rest of the section demonstrates God's great strength and control of creation. God does not need pyrotechnics. The creation will provide the show as *the earth trembles* at the sheer strength of their God.

6-9 The next section records the response to God's appearance, although there has been a response of the creation since v. 4. Here the psalm turns from description to the response, first of *the heavens* in v. 6a and then

3. Kraus follows Gunkel in emending the text, changing the mpl participle *'ōḥᵃḇê* to ms participle, so the subject remains God, and then changing the mpl imperative *śin'û* to a mpl participle. But the reading of MT is clear and LXX is the same, so there is no reason to make the change as NRSV does, "The LORD loves those who hate evil."

4. The subject returns here to masculine singular, and the implication is that God is the subject. LXX adds "Lord" to this line. Tate (*Psalms 51–100,* p. 516) and Zenger (Hossfeld and Zenger, *Psalms 2,* p. 468) add "he" to the beginning of the sentence. NIV makes it a dependent clause by adding "for" to the beginning of the verse.

5. Lit., *napšôṯ.* This word has a wide range of meaning: "soul, living being, self." It is the essence of what makes a sack of bones alive. Here it is in the plural form.

6. Many suggest emendation to *zāraḥ* ("rise, shine"). But MT is readable and the metaphor used is not a stretch, so it is left here as it is written.

7. Lit., "to his holy memorial," which is sometimes used as a synonym of "name," as in Isa. 26:8; Hos. 12:5 (*HALOT,* p. 271).

the human sphere in the remainder of the section. Verse 7 may seem odd to a modern audience, for we have the attitude that other *gods* do not exist. But that was not the case in ancient times (see Psalm 82). Even if there are other gods, they are under the control of the great King God. All the earth is under the control of the Lord, even the people who think they answer to other gods. For the ones who belong to God, God's coming is the greatest news of all as *Zion* and *Judah* join in the celebration.

10-12 God comes into a real world, and there is much to be set right. God is coming to protect the ones who have followed in God's ways and the ones who are trapped by *the wicked.* Verse 10 is a bit problematic. The subject changes briefly to the people and should be read as an imperative exhortation, as it is in the MT.[8] The verse is certainly awkward in the ancient manuscripts, but that should not be a reason to emend it. This is probably meant as a one-line response to vv. 6-9 and a tie to v. 12, where the people are charged with rejoicing before God. The prayer then returns to descriptive praise of God's acts on behalf of these faithful ones. God will sow *light* and *joy* on God's people (v. 11). Some have changed the text so that light dawns, but if light is not taken literally,[9] God is still here acting as Creator in sowing the seeds of *light* and *joy* to those who have suffered under the evil ones. The final call is one to *rejoice* and sing praises to God for God's great works as king of the universe.

This psalm is set in ancient mythological language. It sees into the very throne room of God and declares the foundations of God's kingdom are righteousness and justice. God's house is made by the creation, a fitting place for the Creator of the World. God's purpose is for the good of the earth and the people. Like Psalm 96, God's judgment is praised as part of God's kingship. One of the costs of a technological world is the loss of imagination. We have learned to believe only what we can see. Psalm 97 invites us to imagine God's throne room that is beyond the physical world. Is this heaven? I am not sure, but it is as close to a portrayal of it as the ancient poets provide. Its images are highly metaphorical and invite imagination into the great mystery of God, and at the same time it calls on us to imagine the scope of God's work as King, Creator, and Judge of all that is.

Beth Tanner

8. Tate (*Psalms 51–100*, p. 516) and Zenger (Hossfeld and Zenger, *Psalms 2*, p. 468) concur.

9. See Kraus, *Psalms 60–150* (p. 257) and NRSV.

Psalm 98: Let Us Sing a New Song!

Psalm 98, like the other enthronement psalms (Psalms 47, 93–99), describes a worldwide party where both heaven and nature sing. The song is pure praise of the great God who is King, Creator, Savior, and Judge. It has much in common with Psalm 96, prompting Westermann to declare, "Psalm 98 almost seems to be a variant of Ps. 96."[1] But in reality, the enthronement psalms all share similar themes of declaring God as the Supreme Creator, King, and Judge, and all call on nature and the humans to give praise. The text of the psalm is clear and without textual problems and has three stanzas:[2]

Call to sing and the reasons God is great (vv. 1-3)
Call to the orchestra (vv. 4-6)
Call to nature (vv. 7-9)

The psalm itself then is an extended call to celebration for humans and the creation.

A psalm.[3]

1 *Sing to the* L*ORD a new song,*
for wonders he has done.
His right hand and his holy arm have saved[4] *for him.*
2 *The* L*ORD has made known his salvation;*
to the eyes of the nations,
his righteousness is uncovered.
3 *He has remembered his* hesed *and faithfulness*
to the house of Israel.
All the ends of the earth have seen
the salvation of our God.

4 *Shout to the* L*ORD, all the earth;*
break forth, shout with joy, make music!
5 *Make music to the* L*ORD with the lyre,*
with the lyre, the sound of song.

1. *Praise and Lament in the Psalms,* p. 148.

2. Most scholars use the same three-stanza division (Hossfeld and Zenger, *Psalms 2,* p. 479; Gerstenberger, *Psalms: Part 2,* p. 195; Terrien, *The Psalms,* p. 681 with a prelude and postlude). Tate sees two stanzas, vv. 1-6 and 7-9 (*Psalms 51–100,* p. 524), as does Kraus but with different divisions of vv. 1-3 and 4-9 (*Psalms 61–150,* p. 264).

3. LXX adds "to David."

4. The *hiphil* verb must have a reflexive meaning here.

6 *With the trumpets and the sound of the horn*
raise a shout before the King, the Lord!

7 *Let the sea roar, and all that fills it,*
the world and those who dwell in it.
8 *Let the rivers clap their hands;*
together let the mountains shout for joy
9 *before the Lord for he is coming*
to judge the earth!
He will judge the world with righteousness
and the peoples with equity.

1-3 The prayer opens with a call to *sing a new song,* and the reason is the *salvation* of the Lord. Certainly, one can see the exodus story here as one possible backdrop with the references to *salvation* before *the nations* and God's remembering of Israel, but this is by no means the only possible reference.[5] Each time God has offered salvation both to the individual and the community is a possible referent here, leaving the past open to be read through the eyes of the reader of the prayer for herself. Brueggemann notes that the praise here is set within the context of Israel's history, both with the broad reference to salvation and reference to "righteousness, steadfast love, faithfulness" that are central to the covenant tradition (Jer. 9:24).[6] It is also clear here that the salvation of God is to be worldwide where *the nations* and *the ends of the earth* know of God and God's great acts.

4-6 The next stanza returns to the call to worship as the orchestra is added. Here no reason for the praise is given, so this stanza is dependent on the first. God is the king and is to be praised with loud and boisterous *music.* Nothing is to be spared in praise of God; every voice and every known instrument are to *raise a shout* of praise. The celebration is to be as over the top as possible, and nothing is too big in the praise of the one who made us and saves us.

7-9 Creation now joins the choir as the seas and the creatures in them join in the song with the world and all of its creatures. The *rivers* and the *mountains* add their *hands* and voice as all the world explodes in noisy praise. The reason at the beginning was a celebration of God's salvation, but here, as in Psalm 96, we are all celebrating, for God is *coming to judge* the world! We *clap* and sing as the judge moves to the place and begins God's work.

Psalm 98 pushes us to think of how much we trust God. Do we today

5. H. C. Leupold has noted the linguistic similarity with parts of Second Isaiah concerning the returning exiles; *Exposition of the Psalms* (Grand Rapids: Baker, 1902), p. 691.

6. *The Message of the Psalms,* p. 148.

celebrate God's judgment? Do we dance and sing when we think of what we now call "judgment day"? Do we trust God to judge with equity all the peoples of the earth? Can we really join in the celebration in loud voices? The celebration here is not trite. We are called to celebrate God's judgment on us and on the world. Ellen Davis reminds us, "Judgment is the positive and passionate assertion of God's will for the world, beginning with the deep foundation of God's rule in the human heart; therefore, it gives no quarter to deception and self-delusion."[7] Praise of God and God's judgment is the ultimate in trust, for it places us squarely in need of salvation.

BETH TANNER

7. "Psalm 98," *Int* 46 (1992) 173.

Psalm 99: The King Listens and Answers

Psalm 99 is the last of the group of enthronement psalms (Psalms 47, 93–99). While it has some of the themes of the group, it also introduces unique aspects. These differences have caused scholars to speculate that the psalm is from a different time period or part of the country than the others.[1] This is possible, but difficult to prove. The focus on Israel then makes it a fitting partner with Psalm 98, which also turns from the whole world to God's acts on behalf of Israel. What is clear is that the psalm's call for the people to praise God is presented in three stanzas:

vv. 1-3 God as king
vv. 4-5 Judge of the world
vv. 6-9 Because God answered the ancestors in faith[2]

The psalm as a whole then speaks of God both as the powerful king and judge over all the world and the one who also heard Moses and Aaron and Samuel when they called out. Textually, the psalm has a few difficult sections that have led to a variety of translations.

1[3] *The LORD is king!*[4]
Let the peoples tremble;

1. Kraus argues it is preexilic, based on its focus on Zion instead of the universal rule of the other enthronement psalms (*Psalms 60–150*, p. 269). Mark Leuchter argues that parts of the psalm originate with eleventh-century Shilonites or possibly even earlier; "The Literary Strata and Narrative Sources of Psalm xcix," *VT* 55 (2005) 37.

2. Gerstenberger notes this text is not easy to analyze because it has shifts in meter and grammatical subjects and repetitions (*Psalms: Part 2*, p. 199). This leads to a difference among scholars concerning the stanza divisions. Tate sees two stanzas, vv. 1-5 and 6-9 (*Psalms 51–100*, p. 528), as does Kraus with different divisions, vv. 1-3 and 4-9 (*Psalms 60–150*, p. 263). Zenger divides the psalm as I have (Hossfeld and Zenger, *Psalms 2*, p. 482), as does Westermann with the exception of v. 9, which he sets apart (*Praise and Lament in the Psalms*, p. 148). Gerstenberger uses a more complex structure of vv. 1-2, 3-4, 5, 6-8, and 9 (*Psalms: Part 2*, p. 199).

3. In 4QPs[k], this psalm is preceded by Ps. 134 and clearly has the superscription "[*ldw*] *d mzmwr*" ("to David, a psalm"); Ulrich, Cross et al., *Qumran Cave 4: XI*, p. 124. In 4QPs[b] however, it is preceded by Ps. 98, and there is no superscription; Ulrich, Cross et al., p. 34.

4. This opening line has received a great deal of scholarly attention. Mowinckel argued for a translation of "The LORD has become king!" as part of an enthronement festival (*Psalmenstudien*, 2:6-8). The syntax allows for reading the predicate as a noun or for reading it as a verb, which explains NIV "The LORD reigns" and NRSV "The LORD is king." There are good arguments for either choice, and it should probably be understood as both, reading "The LORD is king and reigns."

the one who sits upon the cherubim;[5]
let the earth shake.
2 *The* LORD *is great in Zion;*
He is elevated[6] *over all the peoples.*
3 *Let them praise your name;*
great and awesome!
He is holy![7]

4 *The king is strong; he loves justice!*[8]
YOU established equity;
justice and righteousness in Jacob
YOU[9] *formed.*[10]
5 *Exalt*[11] *the* LORD *your God;*
and bow down at[12] *his footstool.*[13]
He is holy!

5. This phrase is unclear. Tate suggests a title "the Cherubim Enthroned One" (*Psalms 51–100,* p. 525, following David M. Howard and A. R. Johnson). However, the phrase appears in several other texts that reflect the meaning of God's throne: "He is sitting on the cherubim," as reflected in NRSV and NIV (1 Sam. 4:4; 2 Sam. 6:2; 2 Kgs. 19:15; Isa. 37:16; 1 Chr. 13:6; Ps. 80:1).

6. The meaning is debated, but *rûm* probably means a lifting or elevating above, as in Ps. 89:13. NRSV and NIV substitute a liturgical term, "exalted," that does not indicate the spacial meaning of the MT.

7. The grammar here is unclear. In MT, the phrase *great and awesome* is clearly set apart from both the first and third phrases, as is represented above. Others such as NRSV and NIV read these words as modifying "your name." Tate (*Psalms 51–100,* p. 525) and Zenger (Hossfeld and Zenger, *Psalms 2,* p. 482) see the terms as names of God, "O Great and Awesome One." Either option is possible, or they may be exclamations of God's attributes, as the spacing in the MT indicates.

8. The grammar of this colon is notoriously difficult, as the plethora of English translations demonstrates. Is the first line, "Mighty King," as NRSV reflects? It is doubtful since all other occurrences of "mighty" as a modifying adjective in the psalms are in the noun-adjective construction (Pss. 61:3; 62:7; 71:7). The second issue is the next phrase. Is it "justice loving," reading "loving" as a participle, or is it "he loves justice," reading it as the 3ms verb as in MT? Finally, the next colon is in the second person. No matter which of the grammar options is chosen, "strength" and "justice loving" are phrases associated with God's kingship (see Pss. 61:3; 62:7; 71:7; 11:7; 33:5; 37:28; Isa 61:8).

9. In both lines are the 2ms personal pronoun and the 2ms verb, indicating emphasis.

10. Lit., "you made or did."

11. This is the same verb as in v. 2, but here it is clearly in a liturgical context, as it is in v. 9.

12. Understanding the *l*ᵉ as one of location (Waltke and O'Connor, *Biblical Hebrew Syntax,* p. 205).

13. The term always appears as *ḥ*ᵃ*d̲ōm ragl̄āyw* ("stool for his feet"). *HALOT* argues that this represents the ark of the covenant, as in 1 Chr. 28:2 (p. 239).

6 *Moses and Aaron were among his priests;*
Samuel was among those who called upon his name.
Calling upon the LORD*; he answered them,*[14]
7 *in the pillar of cloud he spoke to them.*
They kept his decrees and his statutes
he gave to them.
8 *O* LORD *our God, YOU answered them;*
a forgiving[15] *God you were to them;*
And (also) an avenger of their wrongdoings.[16]
9 *Exalt the* LORD*, our God;*
bow down at his holy mountain;
For holy is the LORD*, our God.*

1-3 The psalm opens with the same declaration as Psalms 93 and 97: *The* LORD *reigns/is king.* The declaration is followed by the response of the peoples. The second colon is difficult to translate. It is the participle form of *yšb,* followed by the plural noun form meaning *cherubim.* It may indicate an epithet for God, as argued by Tate, or be a reference to God's throne in the holy of holies in Jerusalem. But in any case, it is a further indication of God's kingship, and the response of the earth is the same as the people's, to *tremble* and *shake* in awe and anticipation of God's appearance. Verse 2 has a reference to *Zion* and a second reference to *the peoples,* indicating that God's center is in Zion but God is still the great God of all the peoples. Verse 3 calls on all to *praise* and declare God *great* and *holy!* Psalm 97 described the celestial throne room, and here is its parallel of God's earthly home of *Zion.*

4-5 This stanza praises God as one who has established *justice* and *equity.* There are several grammatical difficulties in both verses. Verse 4 speaks

14. Again, the grammar here is incertain. Zenger notes two ways. First, the verse is one long thought, with the main verb being "He answered them." Second, the third line begins a new sentence (Hossfeld and Zenger, *Psalms 2,* p. 484). A third option is illustrated above, where the sentence is continued into v. 7. With the reference here to *the pillar of cloud,* it is possible that the second line is a later addition, since this is not part of the Samuel narratives.

15. Lit., "a lifting God," a phrase that appears only here.

16. Some have suggested that God as *an avenger* does not fit the context. Rudolf Kittel added *lō',* reading "and did not visit their wrongdoings"; *Die Psalmen* (KAT 13; 4th ed.; Leipzig: Deichert, 1922), p. 321. R. N. Whybray suggests taking the 3mpl suffix as an objective genitive, reading "on account of the wrongdoings done to them"; "'Their Wrongdoings' in Psalm 99:8," *ZAW* 81 (1969) 238, but this is rejected by most. Zenger notes that this understanding is consistent with Exod. 34:6-7 and should be read as in the MT (Hossfeld and Zenger, *Psalms 2,* p. 484), and this seems the best solution.

of the *king* in the third person in the first colon. The grammar leads to different translations, but it is clear that God's strength is associated with God's justice, and it is God that establishes the important life-giving functions of equality, *justice,* and *righteousness.* This concept, that these are God-given and not human-created attributes, is a common one in the psalms (Pss. 72:1-2; 94:15; 96:10, 13; 97:2; 98:9). God's *justice* and *equity* are also reasons for praise (v. 5). Verse 5 has a spatial quality also, as God is lifted up as the people *bow down.* Scholars have argued that God's *footstool* here refers to the ark of the covenant in the holy of holies, and this is certainly possible. It could also reflect the same understanding as Isa. 6:1, where only the hem of God's garment fills the temple. Whatever the exact reference, the spatial sense is clear: God is high and lofty, and the people *bow down* at God's *footstool.* The stanza ends as the first, with the declaration *He is holy!*

6-9 The first two stanzas began with a focus on God. The first two verses here begin with the ancestors. The section of vv. 6-7a is problematic. Interestingly, Moses and Aaron are referred to as priests, but Samuel is remembered as one calling upon the name of the Lord. It is possible that this line was expanded in the copying process, adding *those who called upon his name* as a conflation of what follows. However, based on the context of the *pillar of cloud,* the keeping of laws, the *forgiving* but still keeping track of sin, and the worship at the *holy mountain,* it is possible that the entire line concerning Samuel is a later addition since none of what follows refers to the Samuel narratives. But whether that is the case or not, the great early leaders[17] of Israel are mentioned here to demonstrate God's long history of listening to and answering God's people. Kraus suggests these three are listed because they "represented prototypes of the transmission of justice."[18] Scholars have also disagreed about v. 8. As noted in the translation, Kittel fixes the problem by adding a negation in the second line, with others suggesting a more complicated formula. Zenger, however, argues, I believe rightly, that this is a reflection of a pivotal verse in the exodus narrative that recalls both God's forgiving and loving nature *and* the fact that sin is not completely erased (Exod. 34:6-7).[19] This is also consistent with Psalm 95, which also contains a reference to God's anger at the wilderness generation. God is forgiving, yes; but there are also consequences to one's actions.

Verse 9 completes the stanza with the same theme as the others end. God's answering, guidance, forgiving, and avenging are to be praised! Again the enthronement psalms remind all that, when we praise God, we praise all

17. An additional issue is that, if early leaders are listed, why is Joshua skipped over in favor of Samuel?

18. *Psalms 60–150,* p. 271.

19. Hossfeld and Zenger, *Psalms 2,* p. 484.

of God's acts, the acts of grace and the acts of punishment. We praise God for holding us accountable. This makes praise a weighty matter, a serious business, an act to be understood and contemplated, instead of mindlessly given.

Beth Tanner

Psalm 100: Praise the One True God

Psalm 100 is a hymn. In fact, for many, it is *the* hymn of the Psalter. "Old Hundredth" is the name given to the tune to which many Western Christians have sung a common paraphrase of Psalm 100:

> All people that on earth do dwell,
> Sing to the Lord with cheerful voice;
> Him serve with mirth, his praise forth tell;
> Come ye before him and rejoice.[1]

Psalm 100 is "old" in many ways — it is ancient, its form and vocabulary are typical, it is familiar, it is comfortable — so familiar and comfortable, in fact, that it can be taken for granted and thus lose its ability to inspire or surprise. Gunkel went so far as to lump it together with other psalms that he considered late, a time in which the "independence and creative power of the singers has ceased" and the poetry has been reduced to "a tired, suppressed tone where expansiveness and accumulation replace powerful brevity." He described these poems, including Psalm 100, as belonging to a "repercussion of hymnic poetry."[2]

The challenge for the reader of Psalm 100, then, is to be like the scribe who is trained for the kingdom — the one who can bring out of the treasury what is old and what is new. Against Gunkel's misguided view of the psalm, Mays offers a more promising summary of the psalm's poetry: the words "are not used casually, but in a careful precision that aims at maximum significance crafted into chiseled brevity."[3] The psalm is an invitation to join in Israel's bold witness and countercultural faith. At the heart of the hymn is the witness that the Lord, and no other, is God. Thus, this old psalm is built around a polemical proclamation that will always seek to break out from underneath the familiar phrases of the text, so that it can be heard again and again.

The setting of the psalm is clearly some sort of public worship service. But it is difficult to know whether one should imagine the psalm solely in the setting of one of Israel's major festivals. Gunkel imagines the hymn sung on the second day of a pilgrimage festival, as the community entered into the sanctuary.[4] But it is interesting to note that Mowinckel never cites the psalm and does not situate it in his New Year's festival. Some scholars have argued that the psalm began as a purely literary composition; the argument goes

1. Text: William Kethe; tune: Louis Bourgeois (*Genevan Psalter,* 1551).
2. *Introduction to Psalms,* p. 64.
3. *The Lord Reigns,* p. 74.
4. *Introduction to Psalms,* pp. 42, 45,

that the poem was composed in an anthological manner, drawing on parts of the previous enthronement psalms, in order to function as the conclusion of those psalms.[5] Gerstenberger offers a strong counterargument that it should be understood as a genuine worship composition.[6] The origin of the text lies hidden behind the veil of history. So, it is more fruitful to focus on the implied theological context of the poem, which is the community entering into God's presence and the witness that community makes about the character of the Lord. Although this context surely had a concrete historical origin, it is a context that transcends the original setting. Indeed, communities of faith across many centuries and in many locales have found themselves in precisely such a "place."

The psalm comprises a single stanza, with two contrasting structures. The first structure is one in which two panels parallel each other. Each panel begins with plural imperative calls to worship, followed by the reasons the imperatives should be obeyed.

Imperative (vv. 1-3a)
    Reasons (v. 3bc)
Imperatives (v. 4)
    Reasons (v. 5)

There is also a centering structure at work in the psalm, which centers the psalm on its middle imperative, *know that the LORD, he is the true God,* meaning to acknowledge that there is but one universal Lord. The centering structure of the whole psalm looks like this:

Triple imperative call to worship (vv. 1-2)
    Central call to *know that the LORD, he is the true God* (v. 3)
Triple imperative call to worship (vv. 4-5)

These contrasting structures do not compete with each other so as to pull the psalm apart, but coexist with each other in such a manner as to hold the psalm together as an elegant, concise composition.

A thanksgiving psalm.[7]

1 *Shout to the LORD, all the earth!*
2   *Serve the LORD with joy!*

5. See Jorg Jeremias, "Ps 100 als Auslegung von Ps 93–100," *SK* 19 (1998) 605-15.
6. *Psalms: Part 2,* p. 205.
7. See note on 3:1.

Come before him with glad singing!
3 *Know that the* LORD, *he is the true God,*
he made us, and we are his[8] *—*
his people and the sheep of his pasture.

4 *Come into his gates with testimony,*
his courts with praise,
testify to him, bless his name.
5 *For the* LORD *is good, his* hesed *endures forever,*
and his faithfulness to each generation.

1-5 This compact psalm has seven plural imperatives: *shout, serve, come, know, come, testify,* and *bless.* It is worth noting that seven is the biblical number of perfection and also that the central imperatival sequence — *come, know, come* — may be a structural signal to their centrality.[9] The psalm, which is an extended summons to worship, can be analyzed under three broad categories: (1) Who is to take action, (2) What actions are to be taken, and (3) Who is the object of that action.

First, who is to take action? The imperatives are directed in v. 1a at *all the earth (kol hā'āreṣ).* The phrase is common in the Psalter, where it parallels terms such as "all those who dwell in the world" (*kol yōšᵉḇê ṯēḇēl;* 33:8), "all peoples" (*kol hā'ammîm;* 96:3; cf. 66:8), "among the nations" (*baggôyim;* 96:10), "all the ends of the earth" (*kol 'apsê 'āreṣ;* 98:3), and "over the heavens" (*'al šāmayim;* 108:5). These parallels indicate that, at least rhetorically, the psalm has a universal audience in mind. The entire earth and all of its inhabitants are poetically summoned to worship the Lord. The universality of the summons is based on Israel's confession that there is only one God, who enjoys a universal reign.

The rhetorical "universal" nature of the call to praise must be balanced by attention to the actual historical worship community that first used Psalm 100 in worship. That community, of course, was Israel — and probably the psalm originated in the postexilic, Second Temple community. The psalm balances the rhetorical call for universal praise with an awareness of its own particularity: *we are his — his people and the sheep of his pasture.* As Clifford notes, " 'sheep of his pasture' is a Hebrew idiom meaning sheep that the Lord personally pastures, not delegating to anyone else (as in Pss 74:1; 79:13; 95:7; Jer 23:1; Ezek 34:31). Every other flock is shepherded by its own divine patron,

8. Reading *wᵉlô* with the Qere. The Kethib, Targ, Jerome, and Aquila *wᵉlō'* ("and not we ourselves"; also LXX and other ancient witnesses) represents an anachronistic view of the human as self-creating that would not have made sense to the ancient community.

9. See esp. Zenger, in Hossfeld and Zenger, *Psalms 2,* p. 493.

whereas Israel is shepherded by the Most High."[10] If the postexilic dating of this psalm is secure, then interpreters might hear in the phrase *we are . . . the sheep of his pasture* a confession of the community's belief that God had kept the promises made by Jeremiah and Ezekiel: "I myself will gather the remnant of my flock out of all the lands where I have driven them, and I will bring them back to their fold" (Jer. 23:3); "I myself will search for my sheep, and will seek them out. . . . I myself will be the shepherd of my sheep, and I will make them lie down, says the Lord God" (Ezek. 34:11, 15). While the call is universal, there is an implicit acknowledgement that not all of the inhabitants of the earth have responded to that call. But for those who have responded, there is a communal vocation to live into — the vocation both to gather other sheep into God's fold and to be God's blessing for the world (cf. Genesis 12). (For more on the metaphor of God as shepherd, see the commentary on Psalm 23.)

Second, what actions are to take place? The first three and last three imperatives describe worship actions: *shout (hārîʿû), serve (ʿiḇḏû), come (bōʾû,* twice), *testify (hôḏû),* and *bless (bārᵃḵû).* Brief interaction with a concordance or a searchable Bible program reveals that all of the terms are common in the Psalter and especially at home in hymns of praise. Clearly this small constellation of terms indicates that the poem assumes a corporate worship setting and that the purpose of the hymn should probably be understood as a call to worship. It is the sort of song that one would expect toward the beginning of worship, its function being to move the worshippers physically and emotionally out of the mundane realm and into the sacred realm. Indeed, the *come into his gates* most likely indicates entry into the temple grounds themselves. But more can said. A closer examination of some of the terms offers deeper insight into the meaning of the psalm. The key term can said to be *serve (ʿāḇaḏ).* The term, similar to the English word "service" or the German *Dienst,* can mean both "work/serve" and "worship." Here the meaning is obviously to worship, but the double sense of the word indicates that an act of worship is part of a deeper relationship that one has with one's God. One serves one's God in the same way that a worker serves an employer, a slave serves a master, or a citizen serves a king or queen. Indeed, in Hebrew to *serve* describes the type of behavior that a human owes both to the king and to God. The Deuteronomistic History repeatedly uses the term precisely to describe Israel's inability to live up the first commandment to have no other gods. Thus Joshua vows, "as for me and my household, we will serve the LORD." Joshua also both exhorts the people to "serve him in sincerity and in faithfulness" but warns them, "You cannot serve the LORD" (Josh. 24:14-15, 19). And indeed, the Deuteronomistic History narrates the story of a people that repeatedly "worshipped *(ʿāḇaḏ)* the baals" rather than the Lord (Judg.

10. *Psalms 1–72,* p. 134.

2:11; cf. Deut. 7:4; 8:19; 11:16, etc.). Thus, the imperative summons to praise is the liturgical translation and version of the first commandment to serve only the Lord (more on this in the Reflections below).

Several of the activities called for in the imperatives are qualified. The people are bid *serve the Lord with joy (bᵉśimḥâ), come before him with glad singing (birnānâ),* and *come into his gates with testimony (bᵉṯôḏâ).* These qualifiers, together with the basic meanings of the words *shout, tesitfy,* and *praise,* describe worship in which the worshippers have abandoned the reserved constraints of civil society and given themselves away to the glad emotion of communion with God. Here, *joy* is not an external plumage required of those who want to come into God's presence, but rather joy wells upward from within. It is the emotion that the Lord draws out of human beings when they are gripped by the divine presence. The thanklessness, negativity, and hopelessness of the world are transformed by the redemptive power of God's presence. These are not requirements of worshippers, but the fruits of the Spirit, so to speak.

As noted above, the (quite literally) central imperative of the psalm is: *Know that the Lord, he is the true God.* The imperative *know (dᵉʿû)* does not imply merely intellectual knowledge. Ancient Hebrew knew no division between theoretical and practical knowledge. As Hos. 4:1-4 shows, to know the Lord is also to follow the Lord's commandments and to do the Lord's will. The term is often translated "acknowledge," which is good as far as it goes, because it captures the polemical edge of the psalm. The psalm is bearing witness to Israel's belief that the Lord is not merely Israel's God, nor is the Lord merely one among many gods, but the Lord alone is God (Deut. 6:4). The Hebrew phrase *kî YHWH hûʾ ʾᵉlōhîm* is emphatic — the Lord is God, and the Lord alone is God. Again, if the postexilic dating of the psalm is accurate, interpreters may be correct to hear in this phrase an echo of promises made to the exilic community. Walther Zimmerli spoke especially of the "recognition formula" that occurs so often throughout the book of Ezekiel: "Then they shall know that I am the Lord."[11] In Ezekiel, the formula is grammatically an indicative and functions as a promise to Israel that the Lord would act on its behalf in the future. Here, the formula is turned into an imperative that is addressed to *all the earth* and functions to call attention to that which God has done in the past. The community is to praise because *he made us, and we are his.* The phrase *he made us* should not be understood as referring to God's act of creation, but to the Lord's action of claiming Israel as God's priestly nation through the election of Abraham (Genesis 12), the redemption of the nation from Egypt (Exodus 19), and the return of the people from exile. The verb translated as *made, ʿāśâ,* is often used for God's redemptive action in history

11. *Erkenntnis Gottes nach dem Buche Ezechiel* (ATANT 27; Zurich: Zwingli, 1954).

(Ps. 118:15-16; 1 Sam. 12:6, etc.). Thus, based on what God has already done, the psalm exhorts: *Know that the LORD, he is the true God.* The exhortation is polemical. It asserts that the Lord, and no other, is truly God. Their historical experiences are the reason Israel should acknowledge God.

Third, who is the object of these actions? Now, obviously according to Psalm 100 the Lord is the object of worship and praise. But carefully observe the text's verbal redundancy that makes the Lord the object of every verb: *shout to the LORD, serve the LORD, come before him, know that the LORD . . . is God, enter his gates, testify to him, bless his name.* The redundant emphasis on the Lord as the object of worship is balanced by the psalm's dual confession of the Lord's actions on behalf of Israel and the world. The first confession occurs in v. 3b: *He made us, and we are his — his people and the sheep of his pasture.* As noted above, the metaphor of the Lord as shepherd and the people as sheep captures Israel's sense of its intimate, communal relationship with God. Because the metaphor of shepherd is always a royal metaphor, it depicts the Lord as the king of Israel. For the community to know itself as God's own possession should, according to the psalm, both motivate it to praise and obey the Lord and also give it the confidence to trust in the Lord's guidance and protection. The second confession occurs in v. 5. It voices the characteristic creed that summarizes the heart of Israel's faith: *For the LORD is good, his* hesed *endures forever, and his faithfulness to each generation.* This confession emphasizes the fidelity of the Lord. It bears witness to the character of God as trustworthy and promises that the actions of God will be consistent with what God has promised, because the Lord's character is trustworthy. It is a character that, as the temporal qualifier *to each generation* implies, has been proven in the past, will be ever renewed in the future, and can be relied upon as long as people exist.

Reflections

Praise and the First Commandment

The psalm is polemical in two ways. First, it does not merely summon the believer to praise the Lord; it summons *all the earth* to praise the Lord. Second, it summons the earth to praise the Lord alone, because, as the text says, *he is the true God.* Thus, praise of the Lord can be understood as the liturgical form of the first commandment. In praise, the believer acknowledges that we humans are not the lords of our own lives, that the good things we have are not solely or even primarily the results of our own strength or effort, and that we are in need of guidance, mercy, grace, and love that can only come from God. The first commandment instructs Israel to serve no other gods. Psalm 100 instructs Israel to serve the Lord and no other, because he is the only *true*

God. The first commandment is the imperative expression of the divine claim that, in Luther's words, we are "to trust and believe him with our whole heart" and "to . . . look for all good and . . . find refuge [in him] in every time of need." Similarly, praise of the Lord responds, "O Lord, you are my Lord." It says, "You are my refuge." "I seek good in you alone." And, above all, it confesses, *the LORD is good, his* hesed *endures forever.* This is the central confession of the psalms. The praise hymns bear witness that the basic character of God is one of fidelity and trustworthiness. Based on that confession, the prayers for help challenge God because the sufferers experience their pain as counter to the expectations that one would assume from a faithful God. As the sufferer in Psalm 77 wonders, "Has his *hesed* ceased forever? Are his promises at an end for all time?" (v. 8). The laments also base their cries for help on God's faithfulness, "Turn, O LORD, deliver my soul; save me for the sake of your *hesed*" (6:4). Similarly, the penitential psalms base the pleas for forgiveness on the Lord's faithfulness (25:7; 51:1); the psalms of trust express confidence in the midst of dire threats because of the assurance of God's fidelity (23:6); the songs of thanksgiving return praise to the Lord in response to a direct experience of God's fidelity (40:9-10); and as already noted, the psalms of praise bear witness to Israel's fundamental conviction that the character of the Lord is the most trustworthy and most defining reality in the universe — and that the character of the Lord is best summed up: *The Lord is good, his* hesed *endures forever.*

ROLF A. JACOBSON

Psalm 101: The Way of Integrity

Psalm 101 is a royal psalm. Some commentators associate the psalm with a particular royal occasion. Mowinckel identifies it with "the great annual [New Year's] feast."[1] Mays writes, "The psalm was composed for use at the inaugural of the king or a celebration of his kingship."[2] Gerstenberger, however, swims upstream against the consensus. Pointing out parallels between the depiction of Job and that of the psalmist, he places the psalm in early Jewish communal life and argues that it paints a "portrait of the ideal believer in Yahweh."[3] Oswald Loretz,[4] similar to Scott Starbuck's[5] treatment of the royal psalms, sees it as a psalm in which the royal tradition has been democratized. Starbuck's general argument is compelling, and this view may hold the most promise for interpreting the "so-called royal psalms," but the term "democratization" is problematic and anachronistic. Similarly, Seybold imagines that an old royal fragment (vv. 2aα, 3-5, 7) was adapted by a later poet, probably of priestly tradition, who refashioned it into a prayer.[6] The royal origin of the text does seem likely, but these latter suggestions point out a more fruitful approach for interpretation than do those approaches that seek to understand the psalm in light of a particular festival or moment in the king's life. The psalm is clearly the prayer of one who has both authority and responsibility for *house, city,* and *land.* Israel had various offices with such responsibility at different times in her history: familial elder, judge, king, priest, governor, and so on. The psalm continued to speak to and for Israel long after the last Davidic king reigned in Jerusalem, as its inclusion in the canonical Psalter indicates. Thus, the approach taken here is that the psalm originated in a royal context. For the sake of the commentary, the speaker of the psalm will be referred to as the king, but note that the psalm's witness should be heard as applying to any vocation to which both authority and responsibility are entrusted.

The structure of the psalm is also debated. The poem employs many repetitions, and depending on how one deciphers these, many and various structures diverge.[7] In addition, whether an interpreter thinks that the speak-

1. *The Psalms in Israel's Worship,* 1:56.

2. *Psalms,* p. 321.

3. *Psalms: Part 2,* p. 209.

4. *Die Königpsalmen* (Münster: Ugarit, 1988).

5. *Court Oracles in the Psalms* (SBLDS 172; Atlanta: Scholars, 1999).

6. *Die Psalmen,* p. 393. See also Michael L. Barré ("The Shifting Focus of Psalm 101," in Flint and Miller, *The Book of Psalms,* pp. 206-23), who sees it as designed for the king's servants, and J. Emmette Weir ("The Perfect Way," *EvQ* 53 [1981] 54-9), who understands it as an instructional psalm.

7. For a summary of the best options, see McCann, "The Book of Psalms," p. 1082. See

ing voice of the psalm changes part way through the psalm will impact how one understands the structure (see below in the commentary). To argue for one structure in this psalm, one must emphasize some data while ignoring other data. While there are many repetitions, they do not shake out cleanly into any discernable pattern. Some have discerned a chiastic structure, with the term *eyes* marking the beginning and end of the two halves of the chiasm — *before my eyes . . . proud eyes* (vv. 3b-5) and *my eyes . . . before my eyes* (vv. 6-7).[8] But note that the repetitions of *the way of integrity* (vv. 2, 6), the verb to *dwell (yāšab̲;* vv. 6, 7), the verb *destroy (ṣāmat̲;* vv. 5, 8), and the noun *land ('ereṣ;* vv. 6, 8) do not fit the supposed chiasm. The approach here is that the four cola of vv. 1-2a introduce the psalm, while the four cola of v. 8 conclude the psalm. In between, there is but one extended stanza.

Introduction: Four cola, marked by 1cs cohortative verbs (vv. 1-2a)
  Stanza (vv. 2b-7)
Conclusion: Four cola, each verse with a common structure
    (l . . . kol . . . // l . . . kol . . .)

A Davidic psalm.

1 *Of* hesed *and of justice, let me sing!*
  To you, O LORD, *let me make music.*
2 *Let me study*[9] *the way of integrity;*
  when will it come to me?[10]

I will ever comport myself with a blameless heart,
  within my house.
3 *I will not set a vile matter before my eyes;*
  I hate deeds[11] *of crookedness;*
  they shall not cleave to me.
4 *A twisted heart shall be far from me;*
  I will not know evil.
5 *The one who slanders*[12] *a neighbor clandestinely*

---

also John S. Kselman, "Psalm 101: Royal Confession and Divine Oracle," *JSOT* 33 (1985) 45-62; Helen A. Kenik, "Code of Conduct for a King: Psalm 101," *JBL* 95 (1976) 391-403.

8. See Kselman, "Psalm 101," p. 47.

9. LXX suggests *wᵉ-*.

10. Kraus supplies *'emet̲* in place of *māt̲ay,* but with no evidence. J. B. Bauer lists other options (" 'Incedam in via immaculata, quando venias ad me?' [Ps. 100 (101):2]," *VD* 30 [1952] 220-21).

11. LXX has *poiountas,* suggesting *'ōśê* ("doers"). MT's infinitive construct is retained; it refers to the action rather than the actor.

12. The Kethib has *mᵉlôšnî;* reading with the Qere, *mᵉlošnî.*

I will destroy.
Proud eyes and a haughty heart
I cannot endure.[13]
6 *My eyes are on the trustworthy of the land,*
that they may dwell with me.
The one who walks in the way of integrity,
that one will serve me.
7 *That one may not dwell within my house*
who practices deceit.
The one who speaks lies
shall not be established before my eyes.

8 *Each morning I shall destroy*
all the wicked in the land,
Cutting off from the city of the LORD
all doers of evil.

1-2a The three opening verbs — *let me sing, let me make music, let me study* — suggest a public setting for the psalm, but a single singer. The king arises before a representative portion of the community, with whose leadership he has been entrusted. A trifold relationship between the king (who sings), the community (in whose presence he sings), and the Lord (to whom he sings) is implied — the king sings *to you, O LORD*. This is the only explicit mention of God in the psalm, but its import should not be missed. The key factor in the relationship between leader and community is neither the leader, nor the community — but God. God has called the king into his role. And the character of the king's reign should match the character of the caller. The reign should be a reign of *hesed* and *justice*. These two terms, a common pair in the Old Testament, describe the very character of the Lord. The terms are ancient and at home in the worship cult (cf. Ps. 36:5-6), and in other royal psalms, such as 72 and 89, they describe both God's commitment to the king and the king's commitment to God's will for his reign. Here, the connection is made between God's character and the character of the king's reign. The king's reign is to share the character of God. The king, to this end, vows to *study the way of integrity*. This is most likely a reference to the law of the king in Deut. 17:18-20, which commands that each king is to write for himself a copy of the scroll of the law and is to study it daily. This interpretation is supported by Ps. 19:7, which says *The instruction (tôrâ) of the LORD is perfect*

13. LXX *toutō ou synēsthion* suggests *'ittô lōʾ ʾōḵēl* ("with him I will not eat"), which may fit better with all of the household imagery in the psalm, but MT is retained as the better parallel to v. 5a.

(tāmîm); tāmîm is translated in Psalm 101 as *integrity*. Thus, the *way of integrity* that the king vows to study is to be equated with the core of the divine instruction *(tôrâ)*. In this law, the Lord has made the divine attributes of *hesed* and *justice* available to those humans who are willing to study it. The term *śāḵal,* translated as *study,* is difficult. Its meaning seems to range from having insight, to achieving success, to teaching, to studying. The majority view is that the term should be translated here as *study.* It is possible here that the meaning should be understood as the king's commitment to teach the way of the Lord, or perhaps that the king is committing himself to make sure that *the way of integrity* prospers (i.e., that it is not neglected). But in context, the most likely sense of the word is "to show good understanding" of the law, as the parallel in 2 Chr. 30:22 suggests. *Hesed* and *justice* are not self-evident virtues. Rather, they are available through *study* of the law. And yet, they are not completely available, as the lamentlike question, *when will (they) come?,* implies (more on this in the Reflection below). The three verbs, *let me sing, let me make music,* and *let me study* are first person singular cohortatives. The forms of the verbs indicate the king's firm commitment to *hesed* and *justice.*

2b-7 As noted above, the body of the psalm is understood here as consisting of one extended stanza, in the voice of the king. The king describes the actions to which he is committing himself. These specific actions may be thought of as the concrete embodiments of the king's understanding of *hesed* and *justice.* These actions concern both his own behavior and the behavior of others. The blanket statement that the king makes is, literally, *I will walk . . . with a blameless heart.* The verb "walk" *(hālaḵ)* is a common metaphor for how to *comport* oneself (cf. Ps. 1:1). The *hithpael* verbal form signifies the enduring, continual nature of the king's vow. The commitment is not merely to *comport* himself blamelessly for a day or a season, but in perpetuity. The *heart* in Hebrew was a metaphor not of emotion, but of will and discernment. The king commits himself to making wise decisions and just rulings in legal disputes. In regard to personal conduct, the king in vv. 3-4 promises that he will have nothing to do with a *vile matter, deeds of crookedness,* or *a twisted heart.* The *vile matter,* literally, "a word of worthlessness" *(dᵉḇar bᵉlîyāʿal),* may refer to the king's role as a judge in legal matters — that he promises not to speak a false verdict. It may also be possible that *dᵉḇar bᵉlîyāʿal* could refer to "false idol," such as the altar that Ahaz and Uriah installed in the temple (2 Kgs. 16:10), which is likely the "defilement" *(niddâ)* that Hezekiah is said to have removed from the temple (2 Chr. 29:5). Either way, the king vows not to set such a thing *before my eyes.* The *eyes* here are a metaphor for desire, rather than merely for perception. Similar to the coveting commandment, there is an awareness here that desire is often the first step on the way to oppression. Similarly, the king also promises to disdain *deeds of crookedness* (the infinitive construct form of *ʿāśâ* should be translated as "deeds" rather than "doers").

What one admires also is often a harbinger of one's future actions — what one admires will have a tendency to *cleave* to a person, as the poignant metaphor acknowledges. The king promises not to honor the deeds of those who oppress, lest such behavior become accepted and cling to him and his office. The king sums up his commitments about his personal conduct with the absolute statement: *I will not know evil.*

The areas over which the king has been entrusted with authority fall into three domains, according to the psalm: his *house,* his *city,* and his *land.* The first of these, the *house* (*bayiṯ,* vv. 2, 7), refers to the entirety of the royal palace. While the term can refer to the king's kin, and specifically to his royal dynasty, here it refers to all of the people that live and move and have their being in and around the king. Because the king's person was the locus of power in the ancient world, the king's *house* was one of the primary locations where corruption could find a nest. The *city* (v. 8) is not simply the urban locale in which the king dwells, but is the heart of the land. In Judah's royal theology, the Lord not only elected David and his line, but also elected Jerusalem as the holy city and chose to dwell in its temple.[14] As part of the covenantal obligation, the Lord promised to dwell in and protect Jerusalem, but the city was expected to be worthy of the Lord's presence (cf. Jer. 7:1-3); the king, in particular, was responsible to make sure that Jerusalem did not become an ethical slum. The king also reigns over the *land* (v. 6), which is not only the nation, but is the place in Jewish tradition where the law is kept. God first gives the law and then gives a *land* in which the law is to be kept (thus, the pentateuchal formula that introduces some laws is "When you enter the land I am giving you"; Lev. 14:34; 23:10, etc.).

In specific, the king promises to curb certain negative behaviors within the city as well as promote others. The king exercises his office both as with a legal authority and with a "convening" or "hosting" authority. In terms of the legal authority, the king prohibits negative actions. In terms of the hosting authority, the king rewards positive actions by making a place in his household, city, and land for those who adhere faithfully to *tôrâ.* The actions that the king promises to limit have analogues in the second table of the Decalogue. On the one hand, the king promises to limit those crimes that stem from falsehood and deception: *the one who slanders a neighbor clandestinely* (*basseṯer,* lit., "in secret," is an adverbial construction meaning something done clandestinely; cf. Deut. 27:15, 24); *the one who speaks lies shall not be established before my eyes; That one may not dwell within my house, who practices deceit* (the term *deceit, remîyâ,* refers here to deception that leads to economic cheating or theft; cf. Micah 6:12). The negative behaviors that the king will punish are summed

14. See J. J. M. Roberts, "The Davidic Origin of the Zion Tradition," in *The Bible and the Ancient Near East* (Winona Lake: Eisenbrauns, 2002), pp. 313-30.

up in the phrase *proud eyes and a haughty heart.* As Clifford has summarized, "'Haughty' and 'arrogant' (v. 5cd) are common attitudes of royalty. Such attitudes interfere with the king's administration of (divine) justice, which has an essential element of respect and care for the poor."[15] On the other hand, the king promises to use his hosting/convening authority to reward those members of the community who embody the divine attributes of being *trustworthy (bᵉne'emnê)* and who, like the king himself, walk in *the way of integrity.* These people shall *dwell (yāšaḇ) with me* and *serve ('āḇaḏ) me.* These two terms are often used in the Old Testament to describe the life of those who serve the Lord — they serve/worship the Lord and dwell with the Lord forever (cf. Ps. 23:6). The king, who is to serve and dwell with the Lord, here serves as the earthly regent of the heavenly king, but in turn allowing the faithful to serve and dwell with him. Thus, the king's role in governing is understood as a vocation in which he is to extend the divine attributes of trustworthiness and *integrity,* so that the land itself is filled with them.

8 The psalm ends with an elegantly composed verse, in which each line shares a parallel structure *(l . . . kol . . . //l . . . kol . . .).* This artistic structure is not apparent in English, because the first *lāmed* carries a distributive, temporal sense (thus translated *each morning*), whereas the second one is part of an infinitive construct, carrying a sense of purpose (thus translated *cutting off*). The artistry of the poetry and the commitment of the king come together with the sense that the king promises himself *every morning* to renew his commitment to forming a *land* and a *city* that embody the characteristics of God.

Reflection

Discipleship as Vocation

As noted above, the king strives to *study the way of integrity* but also offers a lamentlike question, *when will it come to me?* The apposition of the king's promise with his acknowledgement of the illusive nature of the *way of integrity* offers an important insight into the nature of the life of discipleship. To follow what this psalm calls the *way of integrity* and Psalm 1 describes negatively as *not* "the way of the wicked" is the "walk" of a lifetime. The metaphor of way/pathway at once promises both a journey and also a destination to be reached. In terms of the journey, the metaphor is morally normative, in that it prescribes *how* one shall live. Paradoxically, in terms of the destination, the metaphor is aware that in this life the destination will ever be out of reach — thus the king simultaneously commits to renew the striving after the *way of integrity* on a daily basis, but also knows that the way will never fully come.

15. *Psalms 73–150,* p. 137.

Brown has written powerfully about the Psalter's use of the metaphor of "the way": "[T]he metaphor of the pathway 'maps' both God's *tôrâ* and the speaker's response to *tôrâ*." He continues, "In the image of 'pathway,' conduct and destiny are held as an inseparable unity, pointing to a conceptual schema of moral dynamism that binds together act and consequence."[16] The king has a royal calling to follow *the way of integrity* and to extend the embodiment of God's virtues until the whole land is marked by fidelity and integrity. Although this psalm is cast in the persona of the king, as noted above, the king's royal call was later "democratized" (for lack of a better word), so that every believer is called to walk the same *way of integrity* that the king was once called to walk. Anyone who occupies a legitimate vocation — whether that vocation is a job, a family role, a civic status, or a relational commitment — is called by God to *study the way of integrity — When will it come?* As Brown concludes: "The journey of faith is filled with painful wrenchings, yet surprising gifts. The Psalms imagine a world that is at once relentlessly real and stridently hopeful, a journey *within* the fray that is also 'homeward' bound."[17]

ROLF A. JACOBSON

16. *Seeing the Psalms,* pp. 33, 38.
17. *Seeing the Psalms,* p. 53.

Psalm 102: "In-Time" Deliverance

One of the more important features of Psalm 102 is the superscription. It is the only superscription in the Psalter that describes a psalm as intended for a particular instance in a person's life. In this case the composition is *a prayer for an afflicted person, when faint and pouring out one's plea before the LORD*. To note further how unique the superscription is, one should also note that the superscription mentions neither a person or guild with whom the psalm is to be associated (such as David, Korah, Asaph, Solomon, or Moses) nor any liturgical or musical directions (such as to the leader, according to the *gittith*, a maskil, for the dedication of the temple, and so on). Gerstenberger does allow that the superscription has some analogies to the "functional description in Babylonian incantations,"[1] but these analogies should not be pushed too far. And, in any case, the superscription is still unique in the Psalter. The generic nature of the superscription helps us understand the genre of the *t^epillâ* (called a prayer for help in this commentary, but often called a psalm of lament, Kraus calls it a "song of prayer"[2]) — which is a petition for assistance. The generic nature of the superscription also signals something about the interpretation of the psalms in general — namely, that no matter the varied origin of the many psalms of the Psalter, the poems in the Psalter are model psalms. They have been canonized as model prayers for help, songs of praise and thanks, poems of trust, liturgical litanies, and so on. This psalm, in particular, is a model prayer for help for any person in need. In the Western Christian tradition, the psalm is numbered as one of the seven penitential psalms, although like Psalm 6, the psalm lacks a direct confession of sin (however, a tangential reference to penitence can be found in the reference to God's anger in vv. 9-10).[3]

Although discerning the proper division of poetic lines and verses is challenging, the poem seems to have an introductory call to be heard, followed by a long section of complaint (vv. 3-11), a long expression of confidence (vv. 12-22), a brief petition (vv. 23-24), and a concluding section of confidence (vv. 25-28). The various sections betray uneven lengths, so the structure of the poem must be held lightly. However, it should be noted that the psalm does seem to be constructed out of a series of smaller units that are generally six cola in length (see commentary). Here, the structure of the psalm is understood as:

1. *Der bittende Mensch* (WMANT 51; Neukirchen: Neukirchener, 1980), pp. 78-82.

2. Kraus, *Psalms 1–59*, p. 26; see also superscriptions to Pss. 17, 86, 142; and Isa. 1:15; Jer. 7:16; 11:14.

3. See Nasuti, *Defining the Sacred Songs*.

Introduction/Invocation (vv. 1-2)
Complaint (vv. 3-11)
Expression of Confidence (vv. 12-22)
Petition (vv. 23-24)
Renewed Expression of Confidence (vv. 25-28)

A prayer for an afflicted person, when faint and pouring out one's plea before the LORD.

1 *O* LORD, *hear my prayer,*
let my cry come to you!
2 *Do not hide your face from me*
in the day of my distress!
Turn your ear towards me;
in the day when I cry, make haste to answer me!

3 *For my days are spent, like smoke,*
and my bones are scorched, like a hearth.[4]
4 *My heart is crushed and withered — like grass;*
indeed, I sink too low[5] *to eat my food.*
5 *Since the time when my groaning began,*
my bones cling to my skin!
6 *I am like a great owl of the desert;*
I am like an owl of the wastes.
7 *I stay awake;*
I am like a lonely[6] *bird on a roof.*
8 *All day long, my enemies taunt me;*
those who mock me[7] *use my name as a curse.*[8]
9 *Indeed, I eat ash as if it is bread,*
and I have mixed tears as my drink,[9]

4. *BHS,* following the Leningrad Codex, has *k^{e}mô-qēḏ for k^{e}môqēḏ,* with no difference in meaning.

5. For this translation, see *HALOT* entry on *šāḵaḥ* II; cf. J. J. M. Roberts, "*Niškahtî . . . Millēb,* Ps xxxi 13," *VT* 25 (1975) 797-801.

6. Syr and Targ reflect *nôḏēḏ* ("fluttering").

7. LXX *epainountes me* understands the form as *m^{e}ḥal^{e}lay* ("praise me"), which makes no sense in context.

8. For this translation of *bî nišbā'û,* see Kraus, *Psalms 60–150,* pp. 281, 285. The meaning seems to be that because the psalmist has experienced shame and disaster, his *name* is used as a *curse.*

9. Traditional translations usually suggest something such as "mixed tears with my drink," but the verb *māsaḵ* is more along the lines of preparing a drink, i.e. "mixing a drink," than combining two items together. The sense is of preparing one's *tears* as one's only *drink.*

10 *Because of your fury and your wrath,*
for you have lifted me up and flung me aside.
11 *My days are like a lengthening shadow,*
like grass — I wither.

12 *But you, O LORD, are enthroned forever!*
Memory of you endures throughout each generation!
13 *You shall surely rise up and show mercy to Zion;*
indeed the time to be gracious to her,
indeed the appointed time has come!
14 *For your servants delight in its stones,*
and they cherish its dust.
15 *The nations shall fear*[10] *the name of the LORD,*
and all the kings of the earth your glory.[11]
16 *For the LORD will rebuild Zion;*
he shall appear in his glory.[12]
17 *He will regard the prayer*[13] *of the destitute;*
he will not neglect their prayer.
18 *May this be written so that a future generation,*
a created people, may praise the LORD —
19 *"He looks down from his sanctuary on high,*[14]
from heaven, the LORD regards the earth,[15]
20 *To hear the groan of the prisoner,*
to set free those condemned to death" —
21 *So that the name of the LORD will be recounted in Zion,*
his praise in Jerusalem,
22 *When the peoples gather together*
and the kingdoms to worship the LORD.

23 *He*[16] *has humbled my strength, in midcourse,*
he has shortened my days.[17]

10. 4QPs^b lacks the *w^e*-.

11. 4QPs^b reads "his glory" *(kbwdw)*.

12. 4QPs^b lacks the 3ms suffix, reading only *bkbwd*.

13. 11QPs^a has the anomalous *twl't* ("worm") for MT's *t^{e}pillaṯ*. LXX *proseuchēn* supports retaining MT.

14. 4QPs^b has *mm'wn* ("abode"), while 11QPs^a and LXX support MT's *mmrwm*.

15. 4QPs^b supplies *l'rṣ*, while 11QPs^a and LXX support MT's *'l h'rṣ*.

16. 11QPs^a adds *kî*. 4QPs^b and MT, supported by LXX, lack the preposition.

17. In the course of the transmission of the text, the verse has been corrupted. LXX and 11QPs^a support the Kethib, *kōḥô* ("his strength"), while 4QPs^b supports the Qere. LXX has *apekrithē autō*, interpreting *'innâ* as related to *'ānâ* I ("answer") rather than *'ānâ* II ("be wretched"), as most do. LXX also follows a variant verse division, relating the first two words

24 I say, "My God, do not take me away in the midst of my days,
you, whose years endure for generation after generation."

25 Long ago[18] *you founded*[19] *the earth,*
the heavens are the work[20] *of your hands.*
26 They will perish,
but you will endure.
All of them shall wear out, like a garment,
like clothing,[21] *you change them and they are exchanged.*
27 But you are the same;
your years do not end.
28 The children of your servants shall dwell securely;
their seed shall be established in your presence.

1-2 The opening appeal to be heard employs language quite typical of these entreaties — *hear my prayer, let my cry come to you* (39:12), *do not hide your face* (27:9; 143:7), *turn your ear towards me* (31:2; 71:2), *make haste to answer me* (69:17; 143:7). The use of these stock phrases might suggest that the psalm is, as the superscription implies, a liturgical composition designed for generic use by any person in need. The emphasis in this appeal is on the agency of the Lord, as both the emphatic placement of the name YHWH as the first word of the psalm implies and as the verbs suggest — the Lord may choose, if so willing, to *hear* the prayer, *turn* the divine ear toward the petitioner, and *answer* the plea. It has been suggested that the phrase *in the day of my distress* refers to the day in which the petitioner appears at the temple or some other sanctuary to make the appeal,[22] but the more likely interpretation is that it refers to the petitioner's time of crisis or moment of need. At issue is the Lord's presence, both symbolically and spiritually, in the time of crisis. Parallel to those psalms that ask of God, "where are you?" (89:49; 22:1, etc.), the psalmist invokes the divine presence by asking for God not to *hide* the divine *face.*

of the next verse to this verse and pointing them as *ʾemōr ʾēlay* ("say to me"), which is supported by 4QPsᵇ, *qṣr ymy ʾmr ʾly.* This makes sense in terms of equalizing the length of the verses, and in spite of objections that LXX is apologetically motivated (Dominique Barthélemy, *Critique textuelle de l'Ancien Testament,* vol. 4: *Psaumes* [OBO 50/4; Fribourg: Academic and Göttingen: Vandenhoeck and Ruprecht, 2005], p. 689), the redivision seems promising. Here, the Qere, *kōḥî* ("my strength"), is followed and traditional MT verse division is accepted (supported also by 11QPsᵃ). See also Jacobson, *Many Are Saying,* p. 70.

18. LXX adds *kyrie,* implying the addition of *YHWH;* MT is retained.

19. 11QPsᵃ has the *niphal, nwsdh;* 4QPsᵇ and LXX support MT

20. 11QPsᵃ has the plural *wmʿśy.*

21. 11QPsᵃ, supported by LXX, adds the *wāw, wᵉ-,* while 4QPsᵇ supports MT.

22. Clifford, *Psalms 73–150,* p. 140; Kraus, *Psalms 60–150,* p. 284.

3-11 The extended section of complaint that follows the opening invocation features three stanzas, each with six cola. The complaint sections of the prayers for help have famously been categorized as being made up of "I-complaints" in which the psalmist voices personal complaints about his own suffering, "They-complaints" in which the psalmist voices social complaints about the enemies as causing or contributing to the suffering, and "You-complaints" in which the psalmist voices theological complaints about the Lord as a source of the suffering.[23] The three stanzas in this section of complaint correspond to such a categorization: in vv. 3-5 the psalmist complains about his personal, bodily suffering; in vv. 6-8 the psalmist complains about his social isolation and the enemies who *taunt* and *mock;* in vv. 9-11 the psalmist complains about the anger of the Lord.

The first of these sections, the I-complaint, begins with a metaphor for life as depressingly fleeting: *my days are spent, like smoke; ʿāšān* "is a picture of all that is fleeting, transient."[24] Then the psalmist employs a series of metaphors for bodily suffering that are earthy and accessible to any who has suffered or witnessed the suffering of a loved one. *My bones are scorched, like a hearth; my heart is crushed and withered — like grass; my bones cling to my skin.* The pairing of bodily parts with stark images from everyday life (scorched hearth or withered grass) paints a picture of a sufferer whose very body is suffering burning up and drying out from the inside out. As with most of the psalms, the description can be taken literally (this is a prayer of one literally suffering from a raging fever) or metaphorically (the prayer may be prayed by anyone suffering in any way, with the fever serving as a metaphor for any crisis).

The second section of complaint (vv. 6-8) describes the social dimension of the psalmist's suffering (and thus is termed the They-complaint). It contains what might be the most poignant metaphors for social isolation and loneliness in the Old Testament — *I am like a great owl of the desert; I am like an owl of the wastes; I am like a lonely bird on a roof.* The precise identification of the Hebrew *qāʾaṯ* and *kôs* is debated. It is clear that the terms refer to unclean birds (cf. Lev. 11:17-18; Deut. 14:16-17) that inhabit the desert wilderness (Isa. 34:11; Zeph. 2:14). The translations *great owl* and *owl* are preferred to the sometimes used "pelican," primarily because they better fit the lists of scavenger raptors in the pentateuchal law and because the onomapoetic term *kôs* implies the lonely hooting of the *owl.* The bird is a symbol of vulnerability in the Bible (cf. Ps. 11:1; 84:3; 124:7), but note that the unclean status of these birds adds a religiously symbolic dimension to the psalmist's isolation, and thus his vulnerability. The picture of his isolation is hammered home by the adjective *lonely (bôḏēḏ)* and the triple image of the birds in lonely locations:

23. See, e.g., Westermann, *The Psalms,* pp. 54-57.
24. See Kraus, *Psalms 60–150,* p. 285.

desert, the wastes, and *on a roof.* The only break in the psalmist's isolation is the mocking, taunting threat of the enemies. The term *taunt (ḥrp)* regularly refers in the Psalter to a challenge regarding either the power of God or the psalmist's relationship with God; either could be in view here.[25] That the enemies *use my name as a curse* most likely means that the psalmist has sunk so low in suffering that mocking enemies are able to use his name as a synonym for one whom God has abandoned, who is scorned, who is cursed — much as the names Judas or Benedict Arnold are used as synonyms for traitor.

The third section of complaint (vv. 9-11) focuses on theological complaint (the You-complaint). Specifically, the psalmist complains of God's anger. The report of eating *ash as if it is bread* and mixing *tears as my drink* may be a reference to an ordeal-trial by drinking the "water of bitterness" (see Num. 5:11-28), or it may merely be a metaphor for the psalmist's suffering. The psalmist then asserts that her suffering is due to the Lord's anger — *your fury, your wrath.* Again, the psalmist compares her situation to *grass* that withers. She says, *you have lifted me up.* This image is almost always a positive image of God bestowing honor upon a person. But here, the negative force of the image is established by the next word: *and flung me aside.* The psalmist is like *grass* — uprooted, cast aside, withering — or like a thing of little account — picked up and examined for a moment, but judged as worthless and thrown aside. She also complains, *my days are like a lengthening shadow.* The metaphor combines two typical images for death — the shadow and nightfall. It is a dynamic metaphor, conjuring in the imagination a sense of movement — as the sun sinks towards the horizon and night falls, one sees one's shadow lengthen, as it seems to run away with building speed. Such is the psalmist's sense of her life: the end is approaching with a daunting and ever-increasing momentum.

12-22 The second major section of the psalm again seems to unfold in mini-stanzas of three verses. Note that the last couplet in each of the mini-stanzas 12-14, 15-17, and 18-20 has as its subject the people of God *(servants, the destitute, the prisoner).* The entire section is an expansive expression of trust. The confession of confidence is a normal part of the prayer for help (cf. Pss. 13:5; 22:21b-31, etc.). Here, the confession is greatly expanded. In addition, the perspective shifts from that of an individual in crisis to a community hoping in the Lord (i.e., *your servants delight in [Zion's] stones,* v. 14a). It is possible, on the basis of this confusing transition, to question the unity of the psalm, as some scholars have done.[26] Perhaps an earlier *prayer for an afflicted person* was later transposed into a prayer of confidence for the community. But the prayer is understood here as a unified prayer for help, with a lengthy section

25. See Jacobson, *Many Are Saying,* pp. 43-44.

26. For a discussion, see Gerstenberger, *Psalms: Part 2,* pp. 211-14.

of confidence in the middle. One link between the two halves of the poem is the term *tᵉpillâ (prayer)* in the superscription and in v. 17. In addition, as Mays notes, there is a thematic link between the two halves of the poem: "A motif of time runs through the whole."[27] This theme provides the linchpin that connects and holds together the two movements of the psalm. Verse 11 laments the brevity of the psalmist's mortal existence while the latter section praises and expresses confidence in the eternity of the Lord's reign. The confession of confidence, therefore, takes up exactly where the complaint section left off. The last word of the complaint section is *ʾîḇāš*. The first words of the confession of confidence are *wᵉʾāttâ YHWH lᵉʿôlām tēšēḇ*. When modern people read poetry, which was spoken aloud in the ancient world, there is always the possibility that the visual impact of the English line division will overly impact how one interprets a poem. The simple expediency of rearranging the line division makes the point nicely. Without the line break, the poem reads: *I wither, but you, O LORD, are enthroned forever!* The existential crisis of the psalmist leads, at least metaphorically, to that dead end where all human existence ends: mortality. The answer, at least metaphorically, to human finitude and mortality is divine infinitude and immortality. The answer to both the crises of the individual and the crises of the community arises from the same well: The Lord. *Your memorial endures throughout each generation.* A dynamically equivalent translation of *ziḵrᵉḵâ* is difficult to achieve on several levels. The noun *zēḵer,* related to the concept of remember/memory, might here carry the sense of memory, utterance, mention, name, vow, renown, fame, or the like. Further complicating the matter is whether the pronominal suffix should be understood as an objective genitive ("memory about you") or a subjective genitive ("memory caused by you"). *HALOT* understands the term as "the mention and invocation of God in liturgies," while most major translations opt for something like "your fame" or "your renown."[28] Here, surrounded by phrases in which God is the active subject, a subjective genitive is preferred. But note that the line between objective and subjective genitives can be a fine thing. The sense is "a memorial sign of what you have done" (cf. Ps. 111:4). The next phrase suggests that *Zion* herself — understood broadly as the people of God — is the Lord's memorial. In the logic of the psalm, because it is consistent with God's character that there be a permanent memorial sign testifying to the Lord's graciousness, it is time for the Lord to take action: to *rise up,* to *show mercy,* to *be gracious* to the people. The verb *yāšaḇ* ("to sit," here translated as *are enthroned*) implies the potential power that resides in the Lord. The verb *qûm* ("to arise") calls for that potentiality to be transformed into actuality, for the Lord to move to action. The theme

27. *Psalms,* p. 323.
28. *HALOT,* p. 271; cf. NRSV, NIV, NJPS; Goldingay, *Psalms 3,* p. 154.

of time is rung again — the psalm emphasizes that now is the time for God to act, *the appointed time.* The one who reigns from eternity is adjured to enter into the fleeting days of the psalmist and his community in the immediate moment. The image of the people as *servants* is typical language that implies the people are dependent on God's grace. It is a term that also conceives of the people as worshippers (the root *ʿbd* can mean "to serve" as well as "to worship"). Those who worship and are dependent on the Lord treasure the *stones* and very *dust* of *Zion.*

The Lord's election of Zion and its people has global ramifications. As Mays has perceived, the Lord "chooses in sovereign freedom to be king over Israel as a way of bringing in his kingdom over the entire world."[29] Thus, the restoration of *Zion* (v. 16) shall be noticed by *the nations* and by *all the kings of the earth,* who shall *fear the name of the LORD* and his *glory* (v. 15). The restoration of the people, imagined here as the restoration of the city of *Zion,* is understood in an almost incarnational sense. The Lord's *glory* shall be revealed (*nirʾâ, shall appear,* carries the sense of revelation), not alongside of the rebuilding of Zion, but in the very act. This act shall be God's gracious response to the *prayer of the destitute.*

The expression of confidence continues with a return to the theme of time. Similar to the closing prayers of Psalms 19 and 104, in which the psalmists bid that their meditations be acceptable to the Lord, the psalmist understands her poem to have a purpose. Here, its purpose is as a testimony for a future generation. As Allen has commented, *zōʾṯ (this)* "refers to the divine intervention first mentioned in v. 13 and subsequently developed. . . . The purpose of making a 'permanent record' was to preserve the memory of God's work for later generations of worshipers, ensuring that in response adequate praise was given to Yahweh, who was worshiped 'generation after generation.'"[30] The promise of this written record of praise is analogous to the scroll that the author of Psalm 40 deposits in the sanctuary as a testimony of praise (40:7). Such praise is conceived not only as a response to God's grace, but is understood as a witness that in turn has the power to transform the lives of future people — the promised written record will have the power to form *a created people [who] may praise the LORD*. Kraus writes that the term *ʿam nibrāʾ (created people)* "applies to the 'new creation' of the people of God after the exile."[31] In light of the prayer for Jerusalem to be rebuilt (v. 16) and for the prisoners to be *set free* (v. 20), such a historical conclusion is plausible. A similar understanding of *bārāʾ* to refer to the re-creation of the people exists in Second Isaiah (43:7; 48:7), as does a similar understanding of the kings of the

29. *Psalms,* p. 325.
30. *Psalms 101–150,* pp. 21-22.
31. *Psalms 60–150,* p. 286.

earth reacting so strongly to the redemption of the people (52:15–53:11). But it must be noted that the most straightforward way to understand the syntax of the psalm is to understand the psalmist's written testimony as introducing a purpose clause. It is the thing that will create a *people* who *may praise the* LORD *(tikkāṯeḇ zōʾṯ lᵉḏôr ʾaḥᵃrôn . . . ʿam niḇrāʾ yᵉhallel yāh).* In terms of the theology of praise in the Psalter, it should not be lost that a primary purpose of praise is to serve as testimony to the Lord's gracious deeds. And such praise in turn functions as a means of grace, and through such praise God's faithfulness, salvation, steadfast love, and graciousness literally became available to future generations (cf. 40:9-10). Verses 19-20 are a summary statement of praise. The *kî* that introduces vv. 19-20 has been understood as either causal and thus indicating the cause for the future peoples' praise ("For the Lord looked down . . ."; cf NJPS), or, as is more likely, *kî* as recitative, introducing a quotation of the praise that shall be spoken by a future generation: *"For he looks down . . ."* (cf. NIV). The content of this imagined snippet of future praise is generic; it could come from almost any praise psalm (cf. 14:2; 113:6; 33:13-14; 146:5-9, etc.). It is testimony that bears witness to the basic character and nature of God. God is not a remote lord, lacking either agency or concern. God *looks down, regards, hears.* And then God *sets free.* End of quotation. After this quotation from the future, the syntax of the psalm returns to a second purpose clause (the first began in v. 18a). This second purpose clause is introduced by the infinitive construct at the start of v. 21a. *May this be written . . . so that the name of the* LORD *will be recounted in Zion.* The purpose of the written praise-testimony, again, is so that future praise shall again burst forth and so that even the *peoples* and *kingdoms* shall praise the Lord.

23-24 The understanding of this psalm as a unified prayer for help, with a lengthy section of confidence in the middle, is supported by the renewed individual plea in vv. 23-24. The Hebrew is difficult here, with textual corruptions that likely resulted from an originally obscure text (see translation above). But the theme of time returns. The psalmist complains of having been brought up short *in midcourse* (lit., "along the way," *badderek*) and of having had *my days shortened.* Then, again contrasting his own brevity with the Lord's eternity, the psalmist emphatically requests, *do not take me away in the midst of my days, you, whose years endure for generation after generation.* The latter phrase functions as an epithet. The psalmist refers to the Lord first as *my God,* underscoring the covenantal relationship between herself and God, and then as the one *whose years endure for generation after generation,* underscoring the temporally eternal nature of God. The psalmist's plea is to be allowed to live out a full lifespan.

25-28 The psalm closes with another confession of confidence. The poem's established motif of time continues here and is even amplified, as the psalm builds to its concluding crescendo. The initial move of the closing verses is to look back — all the way back to the beginning of time (*l^epānîm* carries a temporal idiom meaning "of old"; cf. Deut. 2:10, 12, 20). In the following verses, the psalm seems to be playing off of the metaphors for creation found in Ps. 104:5-8. The phrase *you founded the earth (hā'āreṣ yāsadtā)* is a common metaphor for creation, which evokes both the idea that the Lord rules over the earth and that the earth is a trustworthy and secure creation. But here the metaphor of the earth founded on ancient foundations is employed to assert that even the universe is not everlasting. That quality belongs to the Lord alone: *they* [the earth and heavens] *will perish, but you will endure.* Psalm 104 also employs the metaphor of the sea as a *garment* that covers the secure foundations of the earth: "Establishing earth upon its foundations — It shall not slip, forever and ever — You spread the deep over it like a garment . . ." (104:5-6a). Here, the *garment* metaphor, too, is turned against creation, as the psalmist reminds God that garments (even garments made of heaven and earth) wear out: *all of them shall wear out, like a garment.* They can be changed into, changed out of, and can be exchanged — the modern metaphor of changing into, out of, and exchanging *clothing* is not too far off of the mark here. Creation is likened to a garment; God is likened to the fickle body who tries creation on but then can discard it, because God alone is eternal: *But you are the same, your years do not end.* The psalm's closing couplet summarizes the trust of the psalmist and her community. Although there are temporal and temporary crises, the future is safe because it has been entrusted to the one being who transcends time itself: *the children of your servants shall dwell securely.*

Reflection

Psalm 102 is unified by the motif of time. The superscription introduces this motif when it labels the psalm as a prayer of help for a person *when faint and pouring out one's plea before the Lord.* That is, it is a prayer specifically designed for times when God's help seems far away. The superscription's inclusion in the canonical Psalter indicates that the editors of the Psalter were aware that the faithful servants of God suffer *specific times* when they need such prayers. The rhetoric of the psalm exploits this theme masterfully. In effect, the psalm takes the present moment of the psalmist's crisis and — through prayer — transforms that moment into a microcosm of the incarnation. In the incarnation, the church confesses, the infinite and immortal person of God was "poured" or "emptied" into a finite and mortal body. In this prayer, the psalmist bids the infinite and immortal Lord of Israel (the one who *founded the earth,* whose *years do not end, whose years endure for generation after generation,* who is *enthroned forever*) to humble himself, not counting these divine qualities as things to be exploited, and so to enter into the present moment and redeem Israel: *Indeed the time to be gracious to her, indeed the appointed time has come!* That is not a bad metaphor for the time of prayer. Prayer is but a moment. It is a moment "in time." But it is a moment in which the pray-er asks for and awaits deliverance. It is a moment in which the infinite God is asked to enter into the finite world, the everlasting Lord to enter the mortal realm — in order to deliver.

The lamenting, complaining nature of the psalm's use of the time motif should not be missed. To be sure, there is faithful confidence in the Lord who sits *enthroned forever.* Yet there is also faithful accusation: *My days are like a lengthening shadow, like grass — I wither; he has humbled my strength, in midcourse; he has shortened my days.* In this regard, Elie Wiesel tells a story from the Hasidic master Israel of Rizhin:

> One day he cried out: "Master of the Universe, how many years do we know each other? How many decades? So please permit me to wonder: is this any way to rule Your world? The time has come for You to have mercy on Your people! And if You refuse to listen to me, then tell me: what am *I* doing here on this earth of Yours?"[32]

Such a story captures well the complaint element of the psalm's use of the time motif. But the psalm ends with confidence. Rebbe Israel could ask, "Does [God] think the next generation will be better? More deserving? I tell him here and now that he is wrong!"[33] But the psalmist understands that she has a connection with the next generation. The psalmist knew that the existence of the next generation meant the fulfillment of the promise that God made to Sarah, that her seed would be so exponentially multiplied that it could not be counted. So she closed with a confession of trust in God's promise: *The children of your servants shall dwell securely; their seed shall be established in your presence.*

ROLF A. JACOBSON

32. *Souls on Fire* (New York: Random House, 1972), p. 158.
33. *Souls on Fire,* p. 158.

Psalm 103: God Is Good!

Psalm 103 is a wide-reaching hymn of praise[1] that reaches out and touches most of the great theological issues of the life of faith — sin and forgiveness, sickness and health, oppression and vindication, God's election of Israel and the gift of the law, God's transcendence and God's mercy, human mortality and divine immortality, and the reign of God. Given the nearly universal scope of the psalm's praise, one might well consider it the most soaring lyric in the Psalter. The poem has a wingspan that nearly seems to outreach the capacity of any one poem. And yet the psalm also manages brevity of expression, being able to sum up the broad scope of its theme in a single, succinct phrase: *all his benefits (kol gᵉmûlāyw).* Philipp Melanchthon famously asserted once that "to know Christ is to know his benefits, and not . . . to reflect upon his natures."[2] The psalm, in similar fashion, describes the Lord, not by naming abstract attributes of the Lord's being, but by describing the Lord in action (i.e., forgiving sins, giving the law, and so on). The psalm, which may be a fairly late composition, draws from Israel's rich theological traditions. Seybold goes so far as to call vv. 7-8 and 15-16 "Scripture citations."[3] This may be too bold of a claim, but Seybold has offered a very helpful structural understanding of the psalm. He has described the psalm as a meditation on the Lord's *hesed* that proceeds in concentric circles. First, the Lord's *hesed* is meditated on from the perspective of the individual, next from the perspective of the community, and finally from the perspective of "the all" (German *der Alle*). Thus, the psalm is a meditation on the character of the Lord (faithfulness is the fundamental attribute of the Lord) as made known through the Lord's *benefits.*

The psalm's beginning and ending phrases (vv. 1a and 22c) form an inclusio: *Praise the LORD, O my soul.* This inclusio structure actually encompasses vv. 1-2 and 20-22, in which the verb *bārak,* translated here as *praise,* occurs a total of six times. The body of the psalm, as indicated above, is understood here as a meditation on the *hesed* of the Lord, from the unfolding perspectives of the individual, the community, and humanity in general. Each of these

1. Some classify the psalm as an individual song of thanksgiving sung by one who has passed through a crisis (likely physical illness, based on the language in vv. 3-5, 15-16); cf. Kraus, *Psalms 60–150,* pp. 289-90 (but Kraus does note that it is "a song of thanksgiving that tends to rise to hymn status"). I follow Gerstenberger (*Psalms: Part 2,* p. 22) and others who see the psalm as a hymn.

2. In *Melanchthon and Bucer,* ed. Wilhelm Pauck (Library of Christian Classics 19; Philadelphia: Westminster, 1969), pp. 21-22.

3. "Schriftzitate" (*Die Psalmen,* p. 402). Seybold maintains that the psalm is built in concentric circles, describing God's *hesed* from the view of the individual, then the community, then "the all." See also Timothy M. Willis, "So Great Is His Steadfast Love": A Rhetorical Analysis of Psalm 103," *Bib* 72 (1991) 525-37.

stanzas culminates with a creedlike confession that is borrowed from Israel's theological tradition.

Introduction	Call to praise (vv. 1-2)
St. 1	The Lord's *hesed* from the perspective of the individual (vv. 3-8)
St. 2	The Lord's *hesed* from the perspective of the community (vv. 9-16)
St. 3	The Lord's *hesed* from the perspective of humanity (vv. 17-19)
Conclusion	Call to praise (vv. 20-22)

Davidic.

1 *Praise the* L*ORD*, *O my soul!*
All that I am — praise his holy name!
2 *Praise the* L*ORD*, *O my soul!*
Do not forget all of his benefits![4]

3 *The one who forgives all your sins,*[5]
who heals[6] *all your diseases,*
4 *Who redeems*[7] *your life from the pit,*
who crowns you with hesed *and mercy,*
5 *Who satisfies your life*[8] *with good,*
so that your youth is renewed like an eagle.
6 *The* L*ORD* *accomplishes vindication*
and justice for all who are oppressed.
7 *He made known his ways to Moses,*
his deeds to the children of Israel.
8 *The* L*ORD* *is merciful and gracious,*
slow of anger, but abounding in hesed.

4. Coptic reads the singular plus 3ms suffix, with no change in meaning.

5. Reading with LXX; the 2fs suffix (referring to *my soul*) here takes the long form *kî,* which is the normal form one expects etymologically. This form is commonly attested at Qumran, although strangely 4QPs[b] has the normal form *(-k)* in vv. 3, 4, 5.

6. 4QPs[b] has *wr-,* reflecting a consecutive form with no change in meaning; MT is retained.

7. 4QPs[b] *hg'l,* with no change in meaning.

8. LXX *epithymia* normally renders Hebrew *t'wh* in the Psalter. MT's *'eḏyēḵ* ("your ornaments") makes little sense here. NIV and NRSV translate the LXX, but as Allen points out, this is a guess (*Psalms 101–150,* p. 26). The emendation to *'dky* is slight and makes the best sense.

9 *He does not always accuse;*
he does not maintain his grievance forever.
10 *He does not deal with us according to our sins;*
he does not repay us according to our iniquities.
11 *For as high as the heavens are above the earth,*
so great is his hesed *toward those who fear him —*
12 *As distant as the rising is from the setting,*
so has he distanced our sins from us.
13 *As a father has mercy upon children,*
the Lord *has mercy on those who fear him —*
14 *For he knows how we were formed;*
he remembers that we are dust.
15 *A human being — like grass are its days,*
like a wildflower, so it flowers.
16 *But a wind blows against it and it is no more,*
and its place acknowledges it no longer.

17 *But the* hesed *of the* Lord *—*
it is from everlasting to everlasting on those who fear him,
and his righteousness is for the children's children,
18 *To those who keep his covenant,*
to those who remember to do his commandments.
19 *The* Lord *has established his throne in the heavens;*
his kingdom rules over all.

20 *Praise the* Lord*, O his angels,*
O mighty ones who do his bidding,
who obey the sound of his word![9]
21 *Praise the* Lord*, all his hosts,*
his ministers who do his will!
22 *Praise the* Lord*, all his works,*
in all the places of his dominion!
Praise the Lord*, O my soul!*

1-2 The hymn begins with one of the most well-known phrases in the entire Psalter. The phrase has traditionally been translated as "Bless the Lord, O my soul, and all that is within me, bless his holy name" (so KJV, RSV, NRSV). But the Hebrew verb *bārak̲* here does not carry the sense of rendering a gift or benefit to another person that the English word "bless" connotes, and so

9. 4QPs[b] has the plural *dbryw* in both cola; LXX reads the plural only in the second cola.

a better translation is necessary. The term here actually carries the sense of declaring God to be the source of blessing, and thus should be translated as *praise* or perhaps "worship." The phrase *kol qᵉrāḇay,* further, should be translated as *all that I am,* or perhaps "all that is me." In parallel with *napšî (my soul),* the opening verse is the psalmist's self-exhortation to hold nothing back in praising God, to commit one's entire being — what Luther called "body and soul; eyes, ears, and all limbs and sense; reason and all faculties"[10] — to the act of praising God. The self-exhortation, in which the psalm speaks to his or her *nep̱eš* (translated here as *soul,* but really meaning one's "total being"), is a strange idiom for English speakers to comprehend. The general concept is that praise is a response. Praise is usually a response to an act of God, such as when Moses and Miriam are described as offering praise in direct response to God's act of deliverance at the sea. Or praise is a response to a call to praise from a liturgical leader, and thus most hymns start out with a call for the congregation to praise of the Lord and the praise that follows is a response to that call to praise. Thus praise is understood as response to God, and therefore one does not generate one's own praise out of nowhere. Here, as well as in Psalm 104 (vv. 1, 35), the psalmist cleverly plays on this tradition by enjoining his or her *nep̱eš* to praise the Lord. The final phrase of v. 2 goes to the purpose of Israel's praise. Praise exists for the purpose of theological witness. To praise is to recall God's past acts and thus to remember those acts (to reactualize them) for the present moment. Here, rather than using the positive formulation "remember" (cf. 22:27; 77:11), the psalmist uses a nearly synonymous negative formulation, *do not forget all of his benefits.* This negative formulation adds the nuance of meaning that if God's people fail to praise the Lord, the Lord's *benefits* will eventually be forgotten.

3-6 After the introductory self-exhortation to praise, the poem meditates on the Lord's *hesed* from the perspective of the individual psalmist (actually, with respect to her *soul;* see below). The character of the Lord is charted by means of a series of five relative clauses in vv. 3-5, each of which begins with a participle that includes the definite article. The Lord is described, in this series of five soaring participles, as the one *who forgives, who heals, who redeems, who crowns,* and *who satisfies.* The identity of the *you* and *your* in these verses is easily missed in English. The second person forms are all feminine singular, referring back to the *soul (nep̱eš).* Thus, the self-exhortatory rhetorical conceit continues in these verses: The psalmist quite literally talks to her "self" about the Lord's benefits. The psalmist reminds her "self": The Lord is the one *who forgives all your sins, who heals all your diseases,* and so on. The objects of the verbs "forgive," "heal," and "redeem" are worth noting.

10. "Small Catechism," in *Martin Luther's Basic Theological Writings* (ed. Timothy F. Lull; 2nd ed.; Minneapolis: Fortress, 2005), p. 322.

They are *all your sins, all your diseases,* and *your life.* The word "sin" *(ʿāwōn)* refers both to action (or inaction) contrary to God's will and also to the guilt that attaches to a person as a result of a sin. The word "diseases" (*taḥᵃlūʾîm,* related to the term for "illness/weakness," *ḥolî*) can refer to physical illnesses, weaknesses, or pains that come from hunger, famine, disease, and perhaps age (cf. Jer. 14:18; 16:4; 2 Chr. 21:19). The reference to saving one's *life from the pit (miššaḥaṯ ḥay)* does not refer to eternal condemnation in the afterlife, but to a rescue from death. Together, these two terms and phrases sum up the broken human condition — we are born into a broken creation and thus we are fallible, frail, and finite. We are sinful, with broken wills that fall short of God's will. We are frail, with bodies that are subject to disease, pain, and weakness. And we are mortal, living lives that can end at any moment — and will end in the grave. But the promise of the psalm is a total promise. The word *all (kol)* should not be missed. It bears the promise that the Lord can forgive all sins and heal all diseases. The verb "redeem" is also an extremely important term, but one which is often misunderstood. It refers to the act of a family member who fulfills familial obligation to a relative in need.[11] The type of obligation fulfilled would have changed, based on the type of need a relative was in. "If a person has been harmed, the vindication may come in the form of taking vengeance (Num 35:19-27). If a woman's husband died before providing her with children, a relative of the deceased husband was required to act as kinsman by conceiving a child with her, a child who would inherit the dead husband's name and provide for the widow (cf. Ruth 3:9-13). If a person was forced to sell property, a kinsman-redeemer was required to buy the property in order to keep it in the clan (cf. Lev 25:25-33; Jer 32:1-15). If a person fell into debt such that he or she was forced to be sold into slavery (particularly to a foreigner), the kinsman-redeemer was to 'redeem' the clan member by paying the debt and purchasing his or her freedom (Lev 25:47-55)."[12] Here, the unqualified description of the Lord as the one *who redeems your life from the pit* translates as the rather global promise that the Lord is able to save one's life, no matter what the nature of the threat or crisis is.

The pattern varies slightly with the fourth and fifth relative clauses. The first three describe God's action of meeting the human creature in our "deficit situation," so to speak — of mending our fallibility, frailty, and finitude. In these clauses, the Lord brings the fallen creation back to a "zero-sum position." The next two clauses describe God's action of blessing, in which the Lord builds the human being up to a surplus position. The Lord is the one

11. See Frank Moore Cross, *From Epic to Canon: History and Literature in Ancient Israel* (Baltimore: Johns Hopkins University Press, 1998), p. 4.

12. Rolf Jacobson, "'The Lord Is a God of Justice' (Isaiah 30:18): The Prophetic Insistence on Justice in Social Context," *WW* 30 (2010) 127-28.

who *crowns* the creature *with good things.* The verb *'āṭar* in the *piel,* translated here as *crown,* is a term borrowed from the semantic field of royalty.[13] It is used metaphorically in Ps. 8:5 to describe the royal-like responsibilities that the Lord has given to human beings in creation, as well as in 65:11 to describe the fall harvest as the "crowning" blessing of the agricultural year. Here, the metaphor paints the blessings that the self has received from God as those befitting a monarch. Rather than crowning the soul with precious metals or jewels, God has crowned the soul with *hesed* and *mercy.* That is, God has reached into God's very own character — "The Lord, the Lord, a God merciful and gracious" (Exod. 34:6) — and transferred God's own attributes onto the psalmist in an act of blessing. In the last relative clause, the Lord is the one *who satisfies.* This verb *(śāḇa')* in its *qal* stem means "to be sated or full," as after a sumptuous meal, as in Exod. 16:8, where the people are promised all the bread they can eat. Here, used in the *hiphil* with the abstract object *good,* it is the confession that the Lord's blessings pile up so much that the psalmist is full up — that there is no other good thing that she is hungry for.

The string of relative clauses culminates with a change in the pattern. The psalmist finishes the string with a result clause: *So that your youth is renewed like an eagle.* More times than not, the simile *like an eagle* is a pejorative expression. It is often used to express the swiftness of an action — especially to express the sad swiftness with which one's mortal life passes (Job 9:26) or the ephemeral allure of earthly wealth (Prov. 23:5). Here, the phrase carries a double entendre. It ironically refers to the swiftness with which God moves to renew and heal. It also depicts the renewed youth of the psalmist as one of soaring and powerful vitality.

Verse 6 is the final verse in this section of the hymn. It also begins with a participle, but it is not a relative clause. Rather, as is fitting of concluding statements, the verse bears witness in a summary fashion to the promise of the psalms: *The Lord accomplishes vindication and justice for all who are oppressed.* The use of *all (kol)* links this promise back to the psalmist's personal confessions about the Lord healing and forgiving *all* her sins and diseases and extends the witness to a universal scope.

7-8 Seybold has described vv. 7-8 as a sort of bridging text, which interrupts liturgical-hymnic development of the psalm with a meditation. This mediation is a reminder that the means and style of divine action — namely the Lord's *hesed* — had already been revealed to Moses.[14] The interlude then quotes from the very heart of Israel's faith, the ancient creedal confession

13. See Rolf Jacobson, "A Rose by Any Other Name: Iconography and the Interpretation of Isaiah 28:1-6," in *Images and Prophecy in the Ancient Eastern Mediterranean,* ed. Martti Nissinen and Charles E. Carter (Göttingen: Vandenhoeck & Ruprecht, 2009), pp. 125-46.

14. Seybold, *Die Psalmen,* p. 404.

that *the Lord is merciful and gracious, slow of anger, but abounding in* hesed (cf. Exod. 34:6; Num. 14:18; Neh. 9:17; Joel 2:13, etc.). By crowning this personal meditation on the Lord's *hesed* with a quotation from the tradition, the psalmist is drawing the link between her own personal experiences and confession and Israel's national experiences and confession. She is saying that her own experience and testimony are a microexample of and faithful to the experience and testimony of the nation. As Mays has written, "Steadfast love *(hesed)* is, of course, the attribute and activity of the Lord celebrated in the psalms as the Lord's essential goodness beyond all others. Steadfast love is both character and act. One can attempt to define it as helpfulness toward those with whom one stands in relationship. To do *hesed* is to do the best in and make the best of a relationship."[15]

9-14 The second major section of the poem meditates on the Lord's *hesed* with respect to the people as a nation, as is evident by the shift to the first person plural *us, our,* and *we.* The organization of the stanza is evident from a brief visual survey of the poem. The first four clauses (vv. 9-10) each begin with the Hebrew word *lōʾ* ("not"). Verses 9-10 announce the good news of God's mercy in terms of the negative — what God will not do — *accuse, deal with us according to our sins,* or *repay us according to our iniquities.* By casting the language in the negative, the psalm implicitly affirms the legitimacy of the Lord's judgment, but also announces the end of judgment. Similar to Isa. 40:1-3, the implication is that the sin of the people is real, that both the judgment and the sentence from God were just, but also that the time for mercy either has come or will come soon (the imperfect verbs in these verses might indicate a future action of God, "he will not," or a habitual action, "he does not"). It is possible that the psalm originally had some particular sin of the community in mind — if so, it refers most likely to the exile, which was broadly interpreted as God's punishment of the people for their inveterate sin. But such precision of interpretation is not possible. And indeed, the long "salvation history" of the people as narrated in the Old Testament is really a long "sin-and-forgiveness history." The confession that God *does not always accuse* is better seen as a summary hymnic witness to the whole history of the people, rather than a liturgical response to any one particular sin. As such, an apt parallel within the psalms is 30:5a: "his anger is for a moment, his favor for a lifetime." Two phrases are difficult to translate. In v. 9b, *w^{e}lōʾ l^{e}ʿôlām yiṭṭôr* might be translated, literally, "and not forever does/will he tend." The words *his grievance* have to be supplied. The sense is that God does not ruminate on Israel's wrongdoings and nurse his grievances. In v. 10b, similarly, the verb *gāmal* is difficult to translate. It has the sense of "having completed" something, such as nursing thus the passive participial form of the verb is used

15. *Psalms,* p. 328.

for a weaned child. The idea here is that God does not end the relationship with Israel just because Israel has sinned. God remains faithful.

The next four verses announce the reason that God does not always *accuse* and does not end the relationship with Israel. The verses are structured chiastically according to an a-b-b′-a′ pattern: vv. 11 and 14 begin with the Hebrew word *kî* "for"), while vv. 12 and 13 begin with the inseparable preposition *k-*. Verses 11-12, the a-b part of the chiasm, form one unit of thought and vv. 13-14, the b′-a′ part of the chiasm, form a second unit of the thought. Both units are as eloquent as they are poignant. The first unit of thought balances on vertical and horizontal metaphors. God's *hesed* (that is, God's faithful love toward Israel) is *as high as the heavens are above the earth,* with the result that God takes away the people's sins, making the distance between people and sin as far *as the rising* [the east] *is from the setting* [the west]. In the second unit of thought, the metaphor changes to that of parenthood and birth. The Lord loves with the parental love of a merciful father to his children *(kᵉraḥēm 'āḇ 'al-bānîm).* The Lord *knows how we were formed* — a reference to creation (Ps. 94:9; 95:5), here especially to the gestational period of human formation (139:16). The Lord *remembers that we are dust* — a reference to both human sin and human mortality. The confession is that because Israel's Lord is also the heavenly father who created humanity and knows human fallibility, frailty, and finitude, he therefore shows the mercy of a loving parent toward imperfect children. The beautiful poetic balance of vv. 12 and 13 should not be missed (I include here only the consonants, so that the parallel structure is more easily seen):

v. 12 *krḥq . . . hrḥq (as distant . . . he distances)*
v. 13 *krḥm . . . rḥm* (as one *has mercy* . . . he is merciful)

All of these benefits are for *those who fear him ('al yᵉrē'āyw,* vv. 11, 13). That is, for those who are so aware of their own inability to author their own stories that they seek the lordship and guidance of God.

15-16 Verses 15-16, again following Seybold, are another sort of interlude or bridging section. These verses interrupt the hymnic development of the psalm and function to link the section in which the psalmist meditates on the *hesed* of the Lord from the perspective of the nation with the final section of the poem, which will meditate on the *hesed* of the Lord from the perspective of humanity as a whole. This interlude meditates on the brevity of human life, that human days are *like grass,* that *a wind blows against it and it is no more.* The formulaic language here is reminiscent of Israel's wisdom tradition, but also is found often in the psalms (cf. 90:3-10; 37:2). The denotative meaning is clear — human beings are mortal. Life is short and when a human's life is over, he or she has likely not left any stamp on the planet that will last. In terms of the structure of the poem, this sapiential reflection opens the door to the broader question of the Lord's *hesed* to all humans, who all are born into an equally mortal condition.

17-19 The final stanza of the hymn meditates on the Lord's *hesed* with respect to God's universal reign: *His kingdom rules over all.* Whereas the previous verses have reflected on the mortal condition of all human life, the final stanza begins with a stark counterconfession: *But the* hesed *of the LORD — it is from everlasting to everlasting on those who fear him.* Thus, the eternal fidelity of the Lord is set as the poetic and theological counter to the ephemeral fate of human finitude. The Lord's faithfulness is promised to *those who fear him (ʿal yᵉrēʾāyw),* the exact phrase mentioned earlier in vv. 11 and 13. Some interpreters regard this as an indication that the psalm still has Israel in view, but in the psalms and elsewhere the concept of God-fearers existing among the nations is prevalent.[16] In fact, many scholars regard "Lord fearers" (*yirʾê YHWH;* cf. Pss. 115:11; 118:4, etc.) as a term that specifically refers to non-Israelites who worship the Lord, but have yet to join themselves completely to Israel. The metaphors of God's universal *kingdom* and heavenly *throne* are employed to lend further gravity to the weight of the psalm's witness to the Lord's *hesed.*

20-22 Having meditated first on the *hesed* of the Lord from the perspective of the self, then on the *hesed* of the Lord from the perspective of the chosen people, and finally from a universal perspective, the psalm fittingly closes with a universal call to *praise.* The Lord's *angels* and *mighty ones* are called to join the psalmist's praise — a reference to the members of the Lord's heavenly, divine council. The fact that the psalm ends with a call to praise that is both universal and eternal is significant. The call to praise form is often misunderstood, or rather is often underappreciated. The call to praise, therefore, does not so much bring the psalm to an end, but rather brings the psalm to a crest — with the idea being that the psalm never really "ends," because the *praise* it has initiated continues wherever and whenever its concluding call to praise finds a receptive ear and voice. The fact that the psalm's last line is a reiteration of the psalmist's opening self-exhortation to praise — *Praise the LORD, O my soul* — suggests that the psalmist imagines his own voice to have a part in that ongoing choir.

Reflections

The Most Important Thing to Know about God

The psalm is a sublime example of what Israel's praise is all about — witness, in song, to the character of the God who elected Israel, guided it through the centuries, and has promised to be faithful. The fundamental character of

16. So, e.g., Kraus, *Psalms 60–150,* p. 293.

God is boiled down to one word — *hesed.* But *hesed* is a concept so rich and so deep that no amount of words can adequately plumb its depths. And yet, the psalm itself is testimony that the *hesed* of the Lord can be communicated through words — through praise. The psalm's praise bubbles up from within the psalmist — from within the psalmist's *soul (nep̄eš),* from the psalmist's inside *(all that is me, kol qᵉrāḇay).* Then the psalm's praise wells out to embrace all of Israel, all of the God-fearers in the world, and even all the heavenly servants and works of the Lord. The message of the psalm is that if one wants to know God's heart, the very center of the Lord's character, one needs to wrap one's mind around the concept of *hesed.* Although the term is often translated as "mercy" or "loving-kindness," or "steadfast love," all of these fail to catch something essential to the concept of *hesed* — namely, that *hesed* includes both "law and gospel" (although not in equal amounts). The psalm testifies that the Lord's *hesed* will include acts of discipline, acts of assigning guilt to the guilty, and of punishing (and thus of limiting) sin. These actions are required by God's character, because only and always to show mercy is to allow injustice to go unchallenged and to allow the oppressor to range unchecked. And yet these acts of condemnation and judgment are not the whole picture. They are fleeting expressions of the Lord's *hesed.* The permanent, enduring expressions of the Lord's *hesed* are those actions of restoration, forgiveness, healing, rescue, and blessing. If you want to know the one thing about the Lord that is worth knowing above all others, says the psalm, know this: *The Lord is merciful and gracious, slow of anger, but abounding in* hesed. Once you truly know that much, you will not be able to stop yourself from wanting to know all of the rest, too.

ROLF A. JACOBSON

Psalm 104: God Is Great!

Psalm 104 is a hymn. In its present place in the canon, it is the twin psalm to Psalm 103. Both begin and end with the self-exhortatory call to praise: *Praise the LORD, O my soul!* They are the only two psalms in the Psalter to begin and end with that formula. While Psalm 103 is a meditation on the *hesed* of the Lord from the perspective of human beings, Psalm 104 is a hymn that celebrates the greatness of God. (The Lord is described as *great, with splendor and majesty. . . .*) As Limburg has put it, "these two psalms complement one another. Psalm 103 speaks of *salvation,* the second article of the Apostles' Creed; the concern of Psalm 104 is *creation* (the first article) and *the Spirit* (the third article)."[1] (For more on the pairing of these psalms, see Reflections, below.)

This psalm is, in Gerstenberger's understated way of putting it, "one of the most debated and used psalms of the Psalter to this very day."[2] In Psalm 103, the rhetorical conceit of the self-exhortatory call to praise extends into the body of the psalm itself, as the psalmist continues to speak, as it were, to her soul (self). Here, that rhetorical posture exists only in the "frame" of the psalm (vv. 1, 35). In the body, the psalmist addresses the implied human congregation (in third person forms) and the Lord (in second person forms). The grammatical shifts back and forth between second and third person forms proceed in a haphazard manner that escapes rational explanation (as evidenced by the textual variants, which at times betray confusion on the part of the ancient scribes). Most likely, the ancient audience would not have been as troubled by the syntactical inconsistency; but since modern readers desire more consistency, this translation generally prefers the second person, at times translating participles with the second person (e.g., v. 10). Gerstenberger has again aptly summed up this approach:

> Six participles . . . describe the majesty and creative power of the cosmic overlord, three with and three without the definite article. The personal address pronoun "you," however is missing. All affirmations are neutral: "who clothes . . . , who stretches . . . , who constructs. . . ." The present context, for want of another reference, lends itself to connect the participles with the preceding colon: "You put on majesty and glory" (v. 1c).[3]

The psalm seems to show evidence of a complex textual history (e.g., v. 26 may be dependent on Job 41:5 and vv. 27-28 may be dependent on Ps. 145:15-16). There are both archaic as well as late lexical forms. The poem as a whole seems to lack semantic and stylistic homogeneity. The lack of unity has suggested

1. *Psalms,* p. 350. See his bibliog., pp. 227-30.
2. *Psalms: Part 2,* p. 221.
3. *Psalms: Part 2,* p. 222.

to some that different sections of the song were sung by different voices, but such speculations are exactly that. Whether the uneven nature of the poem owes itself to a composite authorship and complex textual history or to a complicated liturgical intonation, modern readers are still left with a poem that needs to be read as a whole. Given that there is a clear thematic unity to the psalm, reading it in "final form" is not a complicated matter — the poem is to be read as a poetic meditation on the greatness of the Lord as evidenced in creation. "The psalm is totally concerned with Yhwh's relationship to the world as its creator, in two interwoven aspects, Yhwh's original activity in bringing the world into being, and Yhwh's ongoing activity in making the world work. . . . The different sections move between reference to those initiating acts (vv. 1b-4 and 5-9, 19, 24a-b) and to the ongoing activity (vv. 10-12, 13-18, 20-23, 24c-30)."[4] It should also be noted that the psalm bears striking similarities to other ancient Near Eastern and Egyptian hymns, such as the Egyptian Hymn to the Aton or various Akkadian hymns.[5] While such a comparative analysis does not play a major role in the commentary below, such analysis sheds light both on the distinctive nature of the psalm's witness to the Creator as well as on Israel's view of nature.

The structure of the psalm is:

Introductory call to praise (v. 1a)
St 1 God and the heavens (vv. 1b-4)
St 2 God and the waters (vv. 5-10)
St 3 God and the order of creation (vv. 11-23)
St 4 God and the diversity of creation (vv. 24-30)
St 5 God's glory and the singer's song (vv. 30-35b)
Concluding call to praise (v. 35c-d)

1 [6]*Praise the LORD, O my soul!*

O LORD my God,[7] *you are very great;*
with splendor and majesty you have clothed yourself,[8]
2 *Wrapping on light like a mantle,*
stretching out the heavens like a curtain,

4. Goldingay, *Psalms,* 3:181-82.

5. Cf. *ANET,* pp. 369-71, 385-89.

6. 11QPs^a^ and LXX add *ldwd.*

7. 11QPs^a^ has 1cp suffix, "our God"; 4QPs^d^ is difficult to read, but appears to have no suffix, "God."

8. 4QPs^d^ has *tlbš,* with no apparent change in meaning; 11QPs^a^ and 4QPs^e^ read the same as MT.

3 *The[9] one who secures the rafters of his upper floor on the waters,*
who makes the clouds his chariot,
who moves about[10] on the wings of the wind,
4 *Who makes[11] the winds his messengers,[12]*
burning[13] flames his ministers.[14]

5 *Establishing[15] earth upon its foundations —*
it shall not slip, forever and ever —
6 *You spread[16] the deep over it like a garment.*
waters stood over mountains.
7 *They fled before your rebuke,*
before the sound of your thunder they took flight —
8 *With mountains arising, valleys receding —*
to[17] the place that you had established for them.
9 *You set a boundary that they cannot pass,*
so that they cannot again cover the earth.

10 *You,[18] who release springs to become streams,*
between[19] the hills they run.[20]

11 *They provide water for every[21] living being of the field.[22]*
The wild donkeys satisfy[23] their thirst.

9. 4QPs^d and some LXX mss lack the definite article.

10. 4QPs^d lacks the definite article.

11. Reading *hʿśh* with LXX.

12. 4QPsl reads the singular. 4QPs^d supports MT.

13. 11QPs^a has the feminine participle *lwhṭt,* in order to match the noun; but the correction is unnecessary, since the gender of *ʾēš* is flexible.

14. 4QPsl reads the singular. 4QPs^d and 11QPs^a support MT.

15. Reading *ywsd* with 4QPs^b, the participial form, and thus reading the verse as a continuation of the series of relative clauses. 4QPs^l has *yšd.*

16. LXX has the nominal form *to peribolaion,* reading *kissîṯô* as a noun, something such as *k^{e}sûṯô.*

17. 2QPs has *lkwl* ("to every. . . .").

18. The syntax here, as throughout the psalm, is confusing for English readers, as the address shifts back and forth between second and third person forms. Retaining the MT, with 2QPs and LXX, but 4QPs^d has the third person singular imperfect.

19. 4QPs^d adds the definite article, with no change in meaning.

20. LXX adds *hydata,* implying a second subject, *mayim,* which is unnecessary and unlikely.

21. 4QPs^d omits.

22. 4QPs^d seems to reflect *ʾdwny,* reading "living beings of the Lord"; we retain MT, but note that a *Vorlage* of *YHWH* may be suggested.

23. MT's *yišb^{e}rû* is unlikely, although it is supported by 2QPs; 4QPs^d has *yškyrw* ("to

12 *The birds of the heavens dwell by them;*
they give voice from among the foliage.[24]
13 *You, who provide water for the mountains from his upper floor,*
from the fruit of your works, the earth is satisfied.
14 *You, who make the grass grow for cattle,*
and plants for humanity to till —
In order to bring forth food from the earth,
15 *and wine to bring joy to human hearts;*
In order to make faces shine with oil
and food to sustain human hearts.
16 *The trees of the* LORD[25] *are satisfied;*
the cedars of Lebanon, which he planted,
17 *Where birds make their nests,*
the stork has her home in the juniper trees.
18 *The high mountains are for wild goats.*
The rocks are a refuge for badgers.
19 *He made the moon for appointed times;*
the sun knows its setting time.
20 *You bring on darkness and it becomes night;*
all the living beings of the forest stir.
21 *The lions roar for their prey,*
seeking their food from God.
22 *The sun rises and they gather themselves.*[26]
They lie down in their dens.[27]
23 *Human beings go out to their work,*
to their labor until evening comes.

24 *How diverse are your works, O* LORD*!*
You have made[28] *them all with wisdom.*

---

make drunk"). LXX appears to be confused; its *prosdexontai* would be the only time *prosdexomai* ever renders *šāḇar.* Reading *śāḇa'* ("be sated"), with Syr.

24. Hebrew *'opā'yim* occurs only here. LXX, *petrōn* ("rocks"), apparently did not know the term. Based on Targum *z'zy'* ("foliage") and Akkadian *apū* ("to cover"), the term most likely refers to dense *foliage* or bushes.

25. LXX has *tou pediou,* suggesting *'ᵃṣê śaḏeh* ("trees of the field"; cf. Gen. 4:8). MT is retained, although LXX suggests a *Vorlage* of *'ᵃṣê šadday* ("trees of the almighty").

26. 4QPs[d] has *wy'spw,* leaving off the paragogic *nûn,* while 11QPs[a] adds the *wāw, w'aspyn;* no change in meaning. The *niphal* form is understood as reflexive in meaning. 4QPs[e] supports MT.

27. Reading with 11QPs[a], which has the plural; cf. Jer. 21:13; Job 37:8. 4QPs[d] supports MT; no real change in meaning, the collective singular is implied in the MT form.

28. 4QPs[d] has the first person plural passive form, *n'św,* retaining MT, supported by 11QPs[a] and LXX.

The earth is filled with your possessions.
25 *There*[29] *is the sea, great and wide of measure!*
With things too many to number,[30]
living beings, small and great.
26 *There ships move about,*
Leviathan — this one you have formed to delight in him.
27 *All of them look to you*
to give them their food in due season.
28 *You give it to them and they gather it;*
you open your hand, they are satisfied with good.
29 *You hide your face and they are terrified;*
you withdraw their breath and they die,
and they return to their dust.
30 *You send your spirit and they are created,*
and the face of the earth is renewed.

31 *May the glory of the LORD be forever;*
may the LORD rejoice in his works.
32 *The one who takes notice of the earth and it trembles,*
he touches the mountains and they smoke.
33 *I will sing for the LORD while I live;*
I will make music for my God while I remain.
34 *May my prayer be pleasing to him,*
even as I rejoice in the LORD.
35 *May sinners vanish from the earth,*
and may the wicked be no more.

Praise the LORD, O my soul!
Praise the LORD![31]

1a The psalm begins and ends in an identical fashion with Psalm 103, namely with a self-addressed call to praise: *Praise the LORD, O my soul!* But unlike Psalm 103, the framing call to praise here does not extend into the body of the poem. Rather, it functions to tie this psalm to the preceding hymn and to signal that the psalm is a call to praise. In addition, it signals that the persona

29. 11QPs[a] omits *zeh,* but 4QPs[e] and LXX agree with MT.

30. 11QPs[a] has *rmś hrbh* and *lmspr,* but with little or no change in meaning. 4QPs[d] and LXX support retaining MT.

31. The closing exclamation of praise should most likely be understood as the first line of Psalm 105 (so LXX), rather than the last line of 104, which would then begin and end with the familiar call to praise.

of the psalmist is intended to be heard as a single human being (at least in the final form of the psalm).

1b-4 Whereas the central theological witness of Psalm 103 is that God is good (that is, the Lord is a God of *hesed*), the driving witness of Psalm 104 is that God is great — *O Lord my God, you are very great (gāḏaltā mᵉʾōḏ); with splendor (hôḏ) and majesty (hāḏār) you have clothed yourself.* Some interpreters automatically move to connect this confession with the concept of the Lord's sovereignty: "To say that God is great is to say, in effect, that God reigns supreme, for greatness is frequently associated with sovereignty."[32] But the connection between greatness and sovereignty should not be made too quickly or too naively. The themes of greatness, splendor, and majesty are also associated with God's fidelity, mercy, and passibility (cf. 34:4; 35:27; 40:17; 111:3; 145:5, etc.). Moreover, as the psalm unfolds, it is clear that the Lord's agency is understood not as a completely sovereign agency, but an agency that is mediated — the Lord works through agents, especially when it comes to the Lord's work of creation. That is the case even in these opening verses. The Lord works through agents — securing *clouds, wind* (*rûaḥ,* "spirit"), *flames, waters* as God's *messengers* and *ministers.* At the very least, the psalm (in harmony with the rest of the biblical witness) understands the Lord as a creator who is still involved daily in maintaining and guiding creation, but also as a God who can be moved by the suffering and prayers of the people (cf. vv. 28-30).

The language of the opening stanza is metaphorical and mythological. In terms of being mythological, it draws on ancient myths of a battle against chaos and of the Lord as the one who tames chaos, who *secures the rafters of his upper floor on the waters.*[33] But it should be noted that there is no imagery of violence here — as opposed to Israel's neighbors, the act of creation is not seen as the victory of one God over another, by means of violence. Nor is the substance of creation imagined as the "stuff" of the gods (that is, the universe is not imagined as formed from the corpse of a defeated God). Israel understands God as separate from the created (there is no pantheism here), but not separated from creation (there is also no deism here). In terms of metaphorical language, the stanza speaks of God as wrapped in *light, clothed* in *splendor and majesty.* The image is thus simultaneously one both of revelation and of mystery. The light, glory, and splendor of the creation both reveal God's presence but also conceal God's essence — God is understood as paradoxically revealed and thus knowable and available, yet concealed and thus not fully understandable.

32. McCann, "The Book of Psalms," p. 1097; see also, e.g., Mays, *Psalms,* pp. 332-35; or Goldingay, *Psalms,* 3:183.

33. Cf. Allen, who argues that the mythological language was used polemically (*Psalms 101–150,* p. 45).

5-10 The second major section of the psalm focuses on the taming of the *waters (the deep)*. The mythological language continues here, as many commentators have seen. As Allen notes, these verses "present a version of the ancient Near Eastern myth of the *Chaoskampf* or divine war against chaos, represented by the sea, as in Rev. 21:1. In the OT it is generally reapplied to Yahweh's interventions in Israelite history such as the Exodus, but here it appears in what was probably its primary setting of creation."[34] Fundamental to the witness of the entire psalm is this stanza's first line: [earth] *shall not slip, forever and ever.* This is testimony to the trustworthiness of the creation that the Lord has wrought. Especially when this closing testimony is heard over against the earlier metaphorical language of the Lord establishing creation *on the waters* — that is, on a foundation that is inherently chaotic — the image emerges of the Lord taming the untrustworthy, random elements of chaos. The *thunder* is imagined as God's *rebuke* of the waters, so that they will not run willy-nilly over creation as they are wont to do. Instead, because of the Lord's power, they stay in their place, *that you had established for them.* The Lord's act of creation is thus to bring order out of chaos and thus to fashion, within and among the chaos of the universe, a safe and trustworthy space in which life can flourish. The Lord has *set a boundary that they* [the waters of chaos] *cannot pass.*

11-23 In the third stanza, creation is further described not merely as the taming of chaos, but as the harnessing of chaos so that its waters play a fruitful and productive role in God's order. The waters serve God's *telos,* and the creation that God has fashioned from chaos functions according to discernable patterns — in a word, order.

God has tapped and harnessed the *springs* so that they flow as *streams* and *provide water for every living being of the field.* Thus the waters of chaos have been made to sustain life both directly (for example, by providing the water that satisfies the *thirst* of the *wild donkeys*) and indirectly (for example, by providing the water that makes dense *foliage* grow, which in turn provides habitation for *the birds of the heavens*). Verse 13 offers a summary testimony: *from the fruit of your works, the earth is satisfied.* The term *satisfied (śāḇaʿ)* is a key term for the witness of this psalm (vv. 13, 16, 28; reading it also in v. 11 for *šāḇar;* cf. 103:5; 105:40). The word means to be full or sated, as after a feast. The implication is that God has created an order that can fulfill or satisfy the needs of all life. Again to stress the point, not only is chaos tamed, it is harnessed and its potentially destructive powers are channeled for God's good purposes.

The third stanza goes on to describe how God's waters function within

34. *Psalms 101–150,* p. 45. See Loren R. Fischer, "Creation at Ugarit and in the Old Testament," *VT* (1965) 313-24.

the order of creation, supplying life for vegetation (satisfying the *trees* of *Lebanon*). This vegetation in turn provides the necessities so that animal and human life may thrive. The logic of the psalm is that God has tamed watery chaos and brought it to heel to do God's will, which is that life might thrive and that life might be good. Indirectly, the waters produce vegetation that serves God's will — it is feed *for cattle* and *plants for humanity to till.* The word *till* (*'āḇaḏ*) is the same word used in Gen. 2:5 and 15 for the vocation of the human being, who is placed in God's garden "to till it." God provides for both spirit and body, making *wine to bring joy to human hearts* as well as *food* (literally, "bread") *to sustain human hearts.* Within God's order there are places for the *birds, wild goats,* and *badgers.*

The order of God's creation is seen in the heavenly bodies — *sun* and *moon* — which regulate the rhythms of life both in terms of days (vv. 19b-23) and seasons. The language of the moon being made *for appointed times* is a reference to the monthly religious observations. Similar to Gen. 1:16, which refers to sun and moon as the greater and lesser lights, this may be a polemic against Israel's neighbors, some of whom worshipped the sun and moon as gods. Against this, Psalm 104 says that the moon is not an object of worship, but was made to signal the *appointed times* to worship the Lord.

The following verses describe the discernible order of creation as seen on a daily basis. The Lord brings on *night,* during which times wild *living beings* (cf. v. 11) *stir* from their rest, to hunt and eat. King of the animals is the lion, which receives its food from God as a gift. The Lord then brings on day with the rise of the *sun,* at which time the creatures that rule the night retire to their caves, and *human beings go out to their work, to their labor* (again the word here is from the Hebrew root *'āḇaḏ,* "to till, work, or serve") *until the evening comes.* The emphasis is on the trustworthy and discernible order embedded in creation. For every creature there is a place (in the *trees,* in the *mountains,* in the *rocks*), a *time* (day or night), and for human beings there is also *work* — vocation.

24-30 The next stanza celebrates the wide wonder of God's wild world, the joy that God has fashioned into creation, and the everyday miracle of God's ongoing provision and re-creation of the earth.

Verse 24a boldly declares that manifold diversity (*how diverse are your works, O LORD* — the verb *rabbû* here means not just to be numerous but to be numerous and diverse) is at the very heart of God's creative design. In v. 24b — *you have made them all with wisdom* — it is easy to miss the word *all* (kol). If the first phrase celebrates the wild and wondrous diversity of creation, the second phrase bears witness that each and every one of God's creatures — from the least to the greatest — are reflections of the divine mind. The phrase *with wisdom* here does not so much refer to God's act of creation, but rather to the final result. The psalm is not merely saying that the creator created well, but that the creator embedded a wise and trustworthy order into the very creation and creatures that God made. Each creature holds a place in the created order. The word *possessions (the earth is filled with your possessions)* here mostly likely refers to all living things, which are equally subject to the one Lord who created them all (cf. 105:21).

The psalm then surveys the diversity of creation, starting with the place of chaos *(the sea),* which is filled with living things *too many to number.* The term *living beings (ḥayyôṯ),* usually translated something like "creatures," is a key term for the psalm. The psalm describes the Lord's providential care for the *living beings of the field* who are provided with *water* and eat water-supported vegetation (v. 11), *the living beings of the forest* who are predators that prey on animals who eat the water-supported vegetation (v. 20), and *the living beings* of *the sea* that live directly in the water (v. 25). Thus, the psalm bears an elegant poetic witness to the central place of *water* in creation, upon which all life depends.

On the great, wide water of the sea, *ships move about.* This is the psalm's third use of the verb *hālaḵ,* and the second use of the verb in the relatively rare *hithpiel* stem. In v. 10 the waters *run (yᵉhallēḵûn)* in their stream beds, here the ships *move about (yᵉhallēḵûn)* on the waters of the sea. If the lion is used as the prototypical symbol of the *living beings of the forest* (v. 21), the prototypical symbol of the *living beings* of the sea is *Leviathan* (v. 26). The figure of Leviathan here is much debated. On the one hand, Leviathan is certainly a figure rooted in mythology. At Ugarit, Leviathan is the primordial sea dragon (so also in Ps. 74:14). But commentators are in strong agreement that in Psalm 104, as in Job 41, Leviathan seems to refer to an actual earthly creature.[35] As throughout the psalm, it seems that the poet is drawing on the mythological tradition, but using the language in a "demythologized" fashion to refer to the profane creation. Leviathan is not a fearsome, mythic monster to be conquered, but is just another creature of the Lord — most likely understood here as the whale or the shark. The phrase *lᵉśaḥeq bô* is open to a variety of interpretations. The issue is both in how one translates the infinitive construct form of *śāḥaq* and also what the antecedent of the 3ms pronoun *bô* (most literally, "in him") is. The most common option is to read *śāḥaq* as "to frolic" or "to sport" and take the antecedent as "the sea" — thus "to frolic in it." Another option is take the antecedent as "Leviathan"; thus NJPS renders the phrase "You formed to sport with [him]." But the most common sense of *śāḥaq,* in the *piel,* is "to laugh at," with *to delight in him* as the most dynamically equivalent translation available. A comparison with Job 41:5 is instructive. There, God asks Job regarding Leviathan, "Do you delight in him

35. So Mays, *Psalms,* p. 333; Kraus, *Psalms 60–150,* p. 303; Goldingay, *Psalms,* 3:192; Clifford, *Psalms 72–150,* p. 150; Allen, *Psalms 101–150,* p. 47, etc.

(h^{a}ṯśaḥeq bô) as with a bird?"[36] God's rhetorical question in the book of Job expects the "no" answer — Job does not (or cannot) delight in Leviathan. In Psalm 104 the point scored here goes to the Lord's power (greatness, v. 1) and the Lord's intention for creation. The Lord easily manages what no human can achieve — to laugh at/*delight in* Leviathan, the most fearsome of beasts (a whale, shark, or crocodile). As for God's intention for creation, the point is made that God delights in creation. God has fashioned even the most fearsome creatures of the earth as sources of divine joy and delight.

All of them . . . So begins v. 27. The *all of them* looks back to all of the *living creatures* — of the field, of the forest, of the sea. Thus, these verses are to be understood as the summary and culmination of the poem's meditation. Verses 27-28 have a close parallel in Ps. 145:15-16: "The eyes of all look to you, and you give them their food in its time, opening your hand, and satisfying for every living thing its desire." In Psalm 145, "the eyes of all" refers to all human beings and speaks of the Lord's provision for human sustenance. In Psalm 104, the realm for which the Lord provides extends to the many *living beings, small and great* that populate the fields, the forests, the seas, and also the cities and towns of the human sphere. The polemical nature of the statement here should not be missed. The psalm is asserting that the entirety of creation — including the sea — is ordered by the creator God. Even the sea! Far from being a realm of chaos that falls outside of the Lord's providence, the sea, too, falls within the Lord's orderly creation — it is just another realm in which the Lord has fashioned a trustworthy, discernible order, one in which *food* is provided *in due season (b^{e}ʿittô)*. And yet it is also a realm in which the Lord from time to time exercises judgment and shows anger: *you hide your face and they are terrified.* And all creatures are mortal: *You withdraw their breath and they die.* The term *breath* is the familiar Hebrew word *rûaḥ* — "wind, spirit, breath." As Goldingay has aptly summarized, "The human and animal world has breath . . . and thus life, because Yhwh breathed into it (Gen 2:7; *nešāmâ*) and continues to breathe into it. . . . When we die, Yhwh collects up that breath again."[37] Death is the will of God. It is the Lord's withdrawing of the divine spirit from our bodies. "And where there is no breath, there is no life. Life is not at our disposal."[38]

The poetic play of the psalm can be seen in the chiastic structure of vv. 29-30: *You hide your face (pānêḵā) and they are terrified, you withdraw their breath (rûaḥ) and they die. . . . You send your spirit (rûḥ^{a}ḵā) and they are cre-*

36. My translation. See also Kathryn Schifferdecker, *Out of the Whirlwind: Creation Theology in the Book of Job* (HTS 61; Cambridge: Harvard University Press, 2008), pp. 161, 173.

37. *Psalms,* 3:193.

38. Goldingay, *Psalms,* 3:193.

ated, and the face (p^e^nê) of the earth is renewed. With this lovely poetic play, the psalm bears witness to the promise of ongoing life, perhaps even to the rare idea in the Old Testament that there is the promise of life, breath, and spirit beyond the grave. A larger chiastic structure is evident in vv. 27-30. In vv. 27-28, the psalm describes the Lord's provision for life. In v. 29a, the poem describes the Lord withdrawing provision. In v. 29b, the poem describes the Lord withdrawing *rûaḥ* and thus withdrawing life. Then in v. 30 comes the startling promise that the Lord can send the divine *rûaḥ* to renew life: *you send your spirit (rûaḥ) and they are created.* Again, the witness of the psalm concerns the discernible order of God's creation — in this case, the pattern of life and death. The Lord brings about life and sustains it. The Lord brings life to an end, but also brings about re-creation. The word translated as *they are created* here is the well-known verb *bārā'*, concerning which it is almost a cliché to note that, in the Old Testament, only God is the subject of this verb. But the observation does pertain — the ongoing creation of each generation is understood as the continuing, creative act of the Lord. And only the Lord is capable of this sustaining, creative act: "When live creatures come into being, there is something magically supernatural about the event."[39]

31-35a This resounding hymn concludes with a stanza that touches upon the opening theme of the psalm and includes a dedicatory prayer. The psalm began by declaring God's *greatness, splendor* and *majesty* (v. 1bc). The final stanza begins with a benedictory prayer that the Lord's *glory be forever.* The psalmist's vision is that, just as God's splendid grandeur was revealed in the original creation, so God's enduring glory unfolds with the renewal of the earth in each day, season, and generation. The psalmist even prays that the Lord should continue to delight in each generation of creation: *May the LORD rejoice in his works.* The sense here is really a wish that the Lord should continue to *rejoice* in his creation — just as he formed Leviathan in order to delight in it. The reference in v. 32 may seem out of context to the English reader of the poem. But throughout the psalm, the poet inserts substantive participial clauses that act as epithets that more precisely refine the definition of who the creator God is. The God who is asked to delight in each generation is the very one who has the power to *touch* the earth, to make it *tremble.* For the modern mind, the concepts of delighting in creation and making it tremble may seem antithetical, but not so for the ancient Israelite imagination. The concept here is similar to that in Ps. 130:4: "But there is with you forgiveness, so that you may be revered."

The psalm closes with a dedicatory prayer that is similar to Ps. 19:13-14. Both dedicatory prayers combine the plea that the prayer-song be acceptable or *pleasing* to God with a petition for protection from or elimination of the

39. Goldingay, *Psalms,* 3:194.

threat of the enemies. Here, the psalmist draws again on the poem's key motif of joy. The poet is a singer, who promises to *sing* as long as he lives. His prayer is that the song itself will be *pleasing* to God. The term translated as *pleasing* is *ʿārab̲,* which is a relatively rare word that occurs mainly in later texts. The term refers to an offering that is pleasing to God (Jer. 6:20; Mal. 3:4; cf. also 11QPsᵃ Song of Zion 14). The term translated as *prayer* is often rendered as "meditation," but that English word does not connote the public nature of the Hebrew *śîḥ,* which is usually a prayer for help (cf. 55:2; 64:1, etc.). In fact, the term here may refer specifically to the appeal in v. 35 that *sinners* may *vanish from the earth* and *the wicked be no more,* which is the only lamentlike verse in the poem. Considered in light of the psalm's theme of the ongoing creation of the earth, this petition asks that God would renew the earth in such a way that evil is uncreated. The psalmist uses the emphatic construction *ʾānōk̲î ʾeśmaḥ* (lit., "I, I rejoice") in returning to the theme of joy. The sense is both a wish that the prayer-song be *pleasing* and acceptable to the Lord, but also an emphatic statement that the song itself gives delight to the singer (and thus the translation, *even as I . . .*).

35b The psalm closes in typical, bookend fashion, with a repetition of the opening call to praise. Such a literary *inclusio* functions to bring the poem to a clean conclusion. And this repetition certainly rounds off the poem nicely. But the *inclusio* also has a second function. This second function is to re-sound the opening phrase of the psalm so that it is heard again, but — given the richness of the poem that has unfolded in between — the phrase is heard now with more richness, with a deeper, resounding resonance. Why should the *soul* (self) *praise the LORD*? Because the Lord has imbued joy into creation. Because the Lord renews the face of the earth.

Reflections

1. Joy and the Trustworthiness of Creation

Psalm 104 is a creation hymn.[40] The psalm weaves together several mutually supportive themes — the Lord as once-and-ongoing Creator, the trustworthiness of the Lord's creation, the sufficiency of creation, and joy in creation. One wonders — What if Psalm 104 were placed at the beginning of the Bible instead of Genesis 1-3? Would people of faith place more of an emphasis on the Lord's joyful intention for and design in creation? (The Lord delights in Leviathan, has created wine to gladden the human heart, rejoices in all his works, and the psalmist himself rejoices in the song of praise.) Would people of faith concentrate more on the providential and trustworthy nature of the

40. See Westermann, *The Psalms in Israel's Worship,* pp. 93-96.

creation? (The Lord's work is to create order out of chaos; the waters of chaos are controlled and harnessed towards the Lord's goals; the times of the daily, seasonal, and generational cycles are trustworthy and discernible.) Would people of faith pay more attention to the sufficiency of the Lord's providing and learn to trust in the creator? (The Lord provides enough to satisfy the earth, the trees of the Lord, the wild animals, and indeed satisfies every living being with good.) Would people of faith focus more on the ongoing-and-evolving nature of creation rather than on the once-and-done concept of creation? (The Lord gives *rûaḥ,* withdraws *rûaḥ,* sends his *rûaḥ,* and renews the earth.) Perhaps if Psalm 104 were placed in front of the great congregation of faith, the people of faith might learn to look for the Lord in creation and find God's fingerprints in the trustworthy order, joyful nature, and ongoing wonder of re-creation.

2. A Note on Psalm 103 and 104 as a Pair

For reasons discussed in the introduction to this psalm, Psalms 103 and 104 should be read not only individually, but as a pair. The two psalms inform each other. Psalm 103 focuses on the character of the Lord as a faithful God. Its witness unfolds mainly from a human perspective. Psalm 104 focuses on the power of the Lord as a great, majestic, splendid, glorious God. Its witness is decidedly nonanthropocentric, with its witness unfolding from the perspective of all creation. The two belong together. The one teaches about the character of the Lord, the other about the power that makes that character trustworthy. The one focuses on the special place that human beings have in the Lord's eyes; the other draws our imaginations beyond ourselves so that we can view ourselves as part of a larger ecology. The one sees the self (soul) as part of a vast human family; the other sees the self (soul) as part of an even more vast created order. Both call the reader to join in a simple, joyous song: *Praise the LORD, O my soul!*

ROLF A. JACOBSON

Psalm 105: Chosen for God's Mission

Psalm 105 is a hymn that praises God for the history of God's *wonders* on behalf of Israel. The psalm should be understood as a lengthy praise meditation on the character of the Lord — because the Lord is a God who keeps promises. It would be easy to read the psalm primarily as a recitation of a narrative of God's miracles, since the psalm does indeed offer lengthy testimony to those miracles, especially the miracles related to exodus tradition (the plagues, the guidance and provision in the wilderness, etc.; see vv. 27-44). But to focus primarily on the miracles is to miss the forest for the trees — the miracles are recited as evidence of the character of the God who is faithful and keeps promises: *He has remembered his eternal covenant — a promise he commanded for a thousand generations* (v. 8). The poem draws heavily on two other theological themes — word/promise/command (the Hebrew language does not really distinguish between the concepts) and land (the psalm narrates the people's history from the gift of the land, to the sojourn in the land of Egypt, to the restoration to the land).

The psalm most likely was composed prior to Chronicles (330 B.C.E. is a rather late estimate for the date of Chronicles), which recites vv. 1-15 as part of a composite psalm in 1 Chronicles 16. The psalm most likely was composed after the exile and the completion of the Pentateuch, because the psalm seems to accept the theology of the Priestly Code, which sees the Sinai covenant as the fulfillment of the Abrahamic covenant.[1] In fact, the psalm completely omits the Sinai events in its recitation of the history of God's deeds. The psalm also omits references to Israel's rebellions in the wilderness (cf. 78:17-54). In a creative and insightful study, Karl Jacobson has pointed out that in 1 Chronicles 16 the exodus theme has been consistently and intentionally omitted in favor of a concentration on the eternal covenant with Abraham and ancestors, and David.[2] Psalm 105 was a natural choice to be used by the Chronicler, because with its omission of the Sinai and wilderness-rebellion traditions and its focus on the eternal covenant with Abraham, it was already halfway down the path toward subordinating the Sinaitic covenant to the Abrahamic covenant.

Interpretation of the psalm often focuses on comparing and contrasting the psalm's version of the ancestral and exodus narratives with those in Genesis and Exodus. Although the psalm is probably later than the Pentateuch and dependent at least to some extent on it, the psalm is interpreted here as an independent witness with a poetic testimony of its own.

1. See Kraus, *Psalms 60–150,* p. 309, and further bibliog. cited there.

2. "Mnemohistory and the Chronicler's Re-imagination of Asaph," paper delivered to the 2007 annual meeting of the Society of Biblical Literature, Chronicles-Ezra-Nehemiah Section.

Interpretation of the psalm is also influenced by the citation of 105:1-15 as part of the psalm in 1 Chr. 16:8-36 (portions of Psalms 95 and 106 are also used). The psalm in 1 Chronicles 16 illustrates something of how Psalm 105 was understood in the Second Temple period. The Chronicler recounts that the ark was brought to Jerusalem; Levites were appointed by David "to invoke, to thank, and to praise the LORD, the God of Israel" (16:4); the composite psalm follows; and then the section concludes: "David left Asaph and his kinsfolk there before the ark of the covenant of the LORD to minister regularly before the ark as each day required" (v. 37). Some have used the citation in 1 Chronicles 16 to attempt to reconstruct how Psalm 105 was performed during the Second Temple period, but we cannot know how the psalm was used.[3] More telling about the use of the psalm in 1 Chronicles 16 are the theological conclusions that may be drawn. While narrating the movement of the ark to Jerusalem and the corresponding centralization of Israel's worship that ensued, the Chronicler places the first fifteen verses of this psalm as the first words confessed in the new location. This suggests that the psalm's testimony to the faithfulness of the Lord to the covenant was a message that both spoke from the heart of Israel's faith and also was a timely message for the Chronicler's community. Mark Throntveit has described this community as "insignificant, few in number and regarded as aliens in their own land."[4] Goldingay adds that the psalm "encourages that community to believe that the God who related to and acted on Israel's behalf at the beginning is the same God for them."[5] The promise implicit in the narration of the people's history as they were exiled from their land and then restored to it doubtlessly bore a powerful message to the postexilic community struggling to find their stride back in their land.

The structure of the psalm is fairly straightforward.

St. 1 Introductory call to worship (vv. 1-6)
St. 2 God's faithfulness to Abraham, Isaac, and Jacob (vv. 7-15)
St. 3 God's faithfulness to Joseph (vv. 16-23)
St. 4 God's faithfulness to the people in Egypt (vv. 24-36)
St. 5 God's faithfulness to the people in the wilderness and in the land (vv. 37-45)

3. See Gerstenberger's reconstruction, *Psalms: Part 2*, pp. 233-35.

4. "Songs in a New Key: The Psalmic Structure of the Chronicler's Hymn (1 Chr 16:8-36)," in Strawn and Bowen, *A God So Near*, p. 170.

5. *Psalms*, 3:203.

[Praise the LORD!][6]

1 *Testify to the LORD!*[7] *Call out his name!*
Make his deeds known among the peoples!
2 *Sing of him, make music of him,*
meditate on all his wonders!
3 *Celebrate his holy name!*
Let the heart of those seeking the LORD[8] *rejoice!*
4 *Seek the LORD and his strength;*[9]
seek his face continually.
5 *Remember his wonders that he has achieved,*
his miracles, the judgments of his mouth.
6 *O seed of Abraham, his servant!*[10]
Children of Jacob, his chosen ones![11]

7 *The LORD*[12] *— he is our God;*
throughout the land are his judgments.
8 *He has remembered his eternal covenant —*
a promise he commanded for a thousand generations —
9 *Which he cut with*[13] *Abraham —*
and[14] *his oath to Isaac.*
10 *And he confirmed it for Jacob as a statute,*
to Israel as an eternal covenant,
11 *Saying, "To you*[15] *I give the land of Canaan,*
as the share you shall inherit."

6. The closing exclamation of praise, *halᵉlû yah,* should most likely be understood as the first line of Ps. 105 (so LXX), rather than the last line of 104. The hymn would then begin and end with the familiar call to praise.

7. 11QPsᵃ has *hwdw lYHWH ky ṭwb ky* ("Testify to the LORD *that he is good* [*and his* hesed *endures forever*]"). Presumably this is a harmonization with Pss. 118:1 and 136:1.

8. 11QPsᵃ, after a gap, *rṣwnw,* which appears also to be reflected by the LXX of 1 Chr. 16:10b: *kardia zētousa tēn eudokian autou,* presumably reading *yśmḥ lb mbqšy rṣwnw* ("May the heart of those seeking his favor rejoice").

9. LXX has *krataiōthēte,* presumably reading the verbal form *wᵉʿuzzû* ("and be strong"). The poetic parallelism throughout the stanza supports retaining MT.

10. 11QPsᵃ has *ʿbdyw* ("his servants"); LXX, *douloi autou,* reflects the same. The parallel contrasting between a collective singular and a plural is common, however (cf. Isa. 28:6; 32:1). MT is retained.

11. 11QPsᵃ has the singular, *bḥyrw,* strangely inverting the singular and plural.

12. 11QPsᵃ has *ky hwʾ* ("For he. . . .").

13. 11QPsᵃ has *ʿam* ("people of . . .") in place of *ʾt* ("with").

14. 11QPsᵃ lacks *w-*.

15. 11QPsᵃ has the plural, *lkm,* in place of MT's singular *lk.*

12 *When they were few in number,*
few, and strangers in it,
13 *They were moving about from nation to nation,*
from one kingdom to another people.
14 *He did not allow anyone to oppress them;*
indeed he rebuked kings on their account:
15 *"Do not touch my anointed ones,*
and my prophets do not harm."

16 *Then he called a famine upon the land;*
every staff of bread he broke.
17 *He sent a man before them;*
as a slave he was sold — Joseph.
18 *They inflicted his feet*[16] *with a fetter;*
his neck was placed in iron.
19 *Until his word came to be,*
until the word of the LORD tested him.
20 *A king sent and released him;*
a ruler of the peoples set him free.
21 *He set him as the ruler over his house,*
and lord of all his property,
22 *To instruct*[17] *his princes by means of his life,*
to make wise his elders.
23 *Then Israel came to Egypt;*
Jacob lived as a stranger in the land of Ham.

24 *The LORD made his people very fruitful*
and stronger than their foes.
25 *He turned their heart to hate his people,*
to conspire against his servants.
26 *He sent Moses his servant,*
and Aaron, whom he had chosen,
27 *Who set among them the promises of his signs,*
and wonders in the land of Ham.
28 *He sent darkness, and it grew dark,*[18]

16. The Kethib, which has the plural form *(rglyw),* has been changed in the Qere to the singular *(rglw),* presumably to harmonize the form with the singular *fetter.* But the Kethib should be retained; the number of the two terms need not match.

17. Reading *l^{e}yassēr,* with LXX *(paideusai)* and in parallel with *y^{e}ḥakkēm.*

18. Reading the *hiphil* with the LXX, which takes the syntax as a result clause.

for did they not rebel against his words?[19]
29 *He turned*[20] *their waters to blood,*
and he killed their fish.
30 *Their land swarmed*[21] *with frogs —*
even into the upper floors of their kings!
31 *He spoke and a swarm of gnats came,*
even through all their territory!
32 *He turned their rain into hail,*
flaming fire throughout their land.
33 *He struck down their vines and their fig trees;*
he shattered the trees of their territory.
34 *He spoke and locusts came,*
grasshoppers without number!
35 *They devoured all the foliage in their land,*
and devoured the fruit of their earth.
36 *He struck down every firstborn in their land,*
the first in all of their vigor.

37 *He brought out his people*[22] *with silver and gold,*
and none of their tribes stumbled.
38 *Egypt rejoiced*[23] *when they left,*
because their dread had fallen on them.
39 *He spread out as a covering,*
and a fire to shine at night.
40 *They asked,*[24] *and he brought quail;*
he satisfied them with the bread of heaven.
41 *He opened the rock and water flowed;*

19. The clause is a slight problem. Reading here as a rhetorical question, with most modern versions. LXX's literal rendering of the syntax is in this case no help in translation. Goldingay interprets the meaning of *mārâ* as "defy": "and they did not defy his word" (*Psalms,* 3:202), but the meaning of "rebel against his word/command" is so well attested that this alternative is not likely (cf. Num. 20:24; 27:14; 1 Sam. 12:15, etc.). LXX and Syr omit *lʾ* ("not"). 11QPs[a] seems to have [*db*]*rm* ("their word"). Finally, the Kethib has the plural form, albeit with an unusual form *(dbrww);* this is supported by the LXX and versions. The Qere corrects to the singular form, but this correction is unnecessary.

20. 11QPs[a] has *śm* ("he set") in place of *hpk*. This reading was likely influenced by v. 27.

21. 11QPs[a] has the feminine form, *šrṣh,* matching the gender of the verb with *ʾrṣ* ("land"). But in late texts, such as this, the matching of the genders of verbs and nouns is less consistent.

22. Reading with 11QPs[a] *(wywṣʾ ʿmw)* and 4QPs[e] *(wywṣʾ ʾt ʿmw)*. MT's "he brought them out" *(wywṣyʾm)* carries the same sense.

23. 4QPs[e] has the plural form, *śmḥw,* with no change in meaning.

24. Reading the plural form *šʾlw* with LXX and versions.

it ran like a river in the desert.
42 *For he remembered his holy promise,*
to Abraham his servant.
43 *He brought out his people with rejoicing,*
his chosen ones with shouts of joy.
44 *He gave them the lands of the nations,*
and they inherited the labor of the peoples,
45 *So that they might keep his statutes,*
and keep closely his teachings.
Praise the LORD*!*

1-6 The opening call to praise in Psalm 105 is quite long. The length of the call to praise is a fitting reminder that this is not merely a historical psalm, but is a hymn that praises God for the history of God's faithful actions on Israel's behalf. The hymn offers praise of God as testimony regarding what the Lord has done. That theme is apparent in the psalm's opening word: *Testify!* The term *hôḏû* is often translated as "give thanks," but, as Goldingay has argued, the Hebrew word does not include the sense of being thankful, which the traditional English translation connotes.[25] Rather, as a *hiphil* imperative of the root *yāḏâ,* it more properly means to "make known," as Ps. 32:5 and Prov. 28:13 indicate. The phrase *qir'û bišmô* does not in this case mean "call on his name" in prayer, but rather to cry out *about* his name, to proclaim God's name.[26] Likewise, the prepositions in v. 2 indicate not God as the subject to whom the psalm's music is addressed, but as the subject matter about whom the song is sung (the two *lāmeds* and the *bêt* are used for specification rather than to mark the indirect object).

All of the imperatives are plural, meaning that the entire congregation is to become those who *testify* about God's actions. That is, the congregation is to become a corporate witness to what God has done and to the character of the Lord as a faithful God. The congregation is specified as the *seed of Abraham* and *children of Jacob.* They are further defined as God's *servant* and *chosen ones.* The former term, *servant,* should be understood as referring to the entire people (similar to the servant in much of Isaiah 40–55), rather than as referring only to Abraham. The latter term, *chosen ones,* which in later Judaism became a core title defining the people's identity, emphasizes here that the covenant that God initiated by choosing Abraham had the enduring efficacy of making all of Abraham's descendents similarly *chosen.* Because God elected Abraham, the entire people is elected of God. And the status that Abraham held with respect to God is likewise extended to the entire people (this theme

25. Goldingay, *Psalms,* 3:753.
26. Cf. Allen, *Psalms 101–150,* p. 57.

recurs later, in v. 15). The testimony of the congregation is also for a purpose. The congregation is to testify to *the peoples* — so that among the nations there would be people who serve the Lord and keep his commandments. The idea of the people bearing a mission to the nations (once again consistent with the material found in Isaiah 40-55) is present in the call to praise.

The call to praise is not only for God's mission to the nations, however; it is also for the people themselves. The praise testimony that the congregation is to make known is also aimed at themselves: *Remember his wonders that he has achieved.* When one bears witness to others about the Lord's faithful actions, this witness has the double-effect of reminding one's self about those actions. And to praise God as a way of pointing others to God is simultaneously to reorient one's self to God and to tap again into *the LORD and his strength.* The content of Israel's praise is defined by a series of terms for God's mighty acts — *deeds (ʿᵃlîlôṯāyw), wonders (nip̄lᵉʾôṯāyw), miracles (mōp̄ᵉṯāyw), judgments (mišpᵉṭîm).* But as v. 8 below makes clear, these wondrous deeds are not themselves the point of the psalm, but rather they are germane because they stand as witnesses to the character of the Lord.

7-15 The first main stanza focuses on the Lord's faithful actions toward the ancestors — *Abraham, Isaac,* and *Jacob.* The opening colon expresses the heart of Israel's faith: *The LORD — he is our God.* The syntax of the phrase *(hûʾ YHWH ʾᵉlōhênû)* should not be taken to indicate a new speaker,[27] but rather as an emphatic statement, similar to Ps. 100:3, that the Lord is the true God and the people embrace faith in him. The second colon is usually translated something along the lines of "his laws are in all the earth," with the meaning taken that the laws of God are valid for the entire earth, even among people who do not acknowledge the Lord. But the psalm has a unique concentration on the promised land — the gift of the land (v. 11), the people's alienation from the land (v. 16), the sojourn in the land of Egypt (v. 23), and their eventual return (v. 44). There is an underlying theological current in the psalm that the gifts of the law and of the land go together. To be God's people, the people must *keep* God's law (v. 45). And to keep the law, the people must have a land in which to keep it (vv. 44-45). Interpreted in that broader context, v. 7b should be understood to mean that the laws and statutes of the Lord and the land are mutually related gifts and they belong together. Spoken to a postexilic audience, the phrase is a reminder that, having returned to the land, the people also need to return to a faithful observance of the law.

Verses 8-11 can be seen as the heart of the psalm's proclamation. They describe the relationship that the Lord entered into with Israel as an eternal covenant: *his eternal covenant — a promise he commanded for a thousand generations.* The promise here is that God's choice of *Abraham* and of his

27. Contra Gerstenberger, *Psalms: Part 2,* p. 234.

offspring is a permanent choice. When God chose Abraham, God committed God's self not only to Abraham but to all of Abraham's descendants. The series of verbs emphatically underscores this point. God *remembered (zākar)* the *covenant* — *zākar* here meaning more than intellectual recollection, but active, faithful keeping of the promises that were made to Abraham. God *commanded (ṣiwwâ)* the *promise.* Normally when God is the subject of *ṣiwwâ,* one thinks of laws that God commands humans to keep (i.e., Ps. 78:5). But *ṣiwwâ* is also used to describe God's saving or creative actions (7:6; 33:9; 44:4; 68:28; 71:3). The striking aspect here is that the Lord *commands* the divine self. Thus a divine promise to a human being is simultaneously a self-limiting of divine freedom. God's promise to Abraham entails a divine self-command to be faithful. The ongoing, generation-to-generation nature of this promise unfolds poetically, as the psalm first names God's *oath to Isaac* (an *oath, šᵉḇûʿâ,* is an act of speech in which a speaker binds himself to future actions or inactions), which was confirmed for Jacob as a statute (the *hiphil* of *ʿāmaḏ* means to "establish" and thus here to *confirm). Statute* here does not imply a law for a human to keep, but rather a permanent obligation. The psalm then repeats the promise of the *eternal covenant,* naming *Israel* as the covenant partner — *Israel* here meaning both the individual *Jacob,* whose name was changed to Israel, but also the people who came to bear that name. This section of the psalm culminates with the Lord speaking words in direct address: *"To you I give the land of Canaan, as the share you shall inherit."* By placing the words in direct address, the psalm is emphasizing the promise.[28] With deft poetic touch, the psalmist brings the stanza to a clean close by repeating the word *land ('ereṣ),* which had been used in the first verse of the stanza (vv. 7, 11). The *land* is the inheritance of the people.

Verses 12-15 make up the third subsection of this stanza. This section continues the theme of the Lord's faithfulness to the ancestors and also culminates with divine direct address to the people. The theme of divine faithfulness is advanced in this section by describing Israel's ancestors as a tragically vulnerable group in special need of protection. They were powerless — *few in number.* They were *strangers (gērîm;* often translated as "sojourners" or "aliens," the term refers to those people who lack a kinship group that will provide a place for them in the world). *They were moving about from nation to nation.* This phrase expands on the notion of being *strangers,* describing them as itinerant, placeless people who were constantly on the move (this is the sense of the *hithpiel* of *hālaḵ*). And yet, the psalm testifies, in spite of this tenuous and vulnerable state of the ancestors, the Lord *did not allow anyone to oppress them.* Like the previous subsection, this section culminates with an emphatic section of direct address. Israel is vulnerable, and those likely to *op-*

28. See Jacobson, *Many Are Saying,* pp. 82-130.

press the vulnerable are the most powerful — in this case, *kings* (regarding the ancestors, one thinks specifically of Pharaoh and Abimelech): *Indeed he rebuked kings on their account: "Do not touch my anointed ones, and my prophets do not harm."* It is important to note that the people as a whole are described as God's *anointed ones* and *prophets*. The term *my anointed ones (mᵉšîḥāy)* can refer in the Old Testament to any number of figures who were anointed — specifically kings, prophets, and priests. The psalm may be thinking of Gen. 17:6 here (Abraham is told that "kings shall come from you"), or perhaps it is recalling the tradition of Abraham acting as a priest (Gen. 12:7-8) or prophet (Gen. 20:7). Bur more likely, as in v. 6, the special status of *anointed ones* and *prophets* is extended to the entire people. The psalm is doubtless drawing on the larger biblical themes that the *anointed ones* are protected and may not be harmed (cf. 2 Sam. 1:1-16) and that kings often persecuted prophets (cf. Jer. 26:20-24).

16-23 The third major stanza of the psalm focuses on the Lord's faithfulness to the last of the ancestors of the book of Genesis — *Joseph*. The stanza describes the *famine* that drove the ancestors from *the land*. The phrase *staff of bread* refers to a supply of food (Ezek. 4:16); the metaphor "either refers concretely to a stick on which ring-shaped loaves were hung or figuratively to the bread as the staff of life."[29] The psalm does not discuss God's motivation for calling the famine; it is content to assert that the famine was the divine will (a notion that is not found in Genesis, per se) and to imply that the resulting migration of the ancestral family to *Egypt* was also the result of divine providence. Although the psalm has not yet narrated that migration, the next verse introduces *a man* who was *sent before them* — Joseph: *as a slave he was sold*. In v. 6, Abraham (and by extension the whole people) were referred to as God's *servant ('eḇeḏ)* — one "who belonged to another, was identified, supported, and protected by that other, and did what he did in the context of that belonging."[30] The poetic play on the term goes something like this: Joseph was God's favored *'eḇeḏ (servant)*, and therefore he was forced to become an *'eḇeḏ (slave)* in the rawest sense of the word — one who literally belonged to another, was exploited by another, and did what he did in the context of that belonging. The paradox should not be missed. The psalm, like the book of Genesis, asserts that God's will was being worked out through the suffering and agency of a singular, vulnerable ancestor — Joseph. The sufferings of Joseph are described metaphorically in v. 18: *they inflicted his feet with a fetter; his neck was placed in iron.*

The transition to the story of Joseph comes in v. 19, with the understated phrase: *until his word came to be.* The verse is a reference to the tradition of

29. Allen, *Psalms 101–150*, p. 58.
30. Mays, *Psalms*, 338.

Joseph's gift of interpreting dreams and the story that he languished in prison until the time came when *his word* was fulfilled. The second half of the verse — *until the word of the* LORD *tested him* — is variously interpreted. One view (cf. NIV) is that the *word of the* LORD "proved him true," meaning that the word came true and thus proved Joseph's authenticity (2 Sam. 22:31 provides a possible support for this view, but the passive use of the verb *ṣārap̱* there undermines the interpretation). The preferable interpretation is that Joseph himself was *tested,* with God's word refining him as in a blacksmith's forge. The meaning of *ṣārap̱* is "to be refined, tested" (cf. Ps. 12:6; 26:2 Qere). Not to be missed is the deliberate double entendre. In the first phrase, the *word* is Joseph's and it *comes to be;* in the second phrase the *word* belongs to *the* LORD, and it refines Joseph. There is deliberate ambiguity — the distinction between the prophetic *word* as "divine" and as "prophetic" is always a matter of ambiguity.

The result of the divine word that comes through Joseph is a change in Joseph's circumstances. *A king sent and released him,* the psalm says. The double entendre is hard to miss. On the one hand, Joseph's release was the result of the human *king* (Pharaoh) sending to have him released. But behind the action of this *ruler (mōšēl)* of the peoples was the divine *king,* the true *ruler of the peoples.* The tradition of Joseph being made the steward of all Pharaoh's possessions follows. He was made *lord (ʾāḏôn)* and *ruler (mōšēl)* in Pharaoh's place. Yet again, a double entendre is present — Joseph was accountable to Pharaoh, who had *set him* up as his steward; but Joseph was ultimately responsible to the Lord, who *set him* up as his steward and *lord* and *ruler* in Pharaoh's place. This double entendre continues, as the purpose of Joseph's stewardship is revealed. He was made steward in order *to instruct his princes by means of his life, to make wise his elders.* The tradition of Joseph as an instructor of wisdom for Pharaoh's court is unique. And especially worth paying attention to is the phrase *by means of his life (bᵉnap̱šô,* literally, "in his throat"). Joseph's *life* itself — the story of one who was betrayed by family but was faithful to the Lord, who was sold as a slave and yet became a *lord,* who suffered greatly but was sustained by God's faithfulness — is testimony to God's fidelity, and is a source of wisdom and enlightenment. The stanza ends with the report that *Israel came to Egypt* — meaning both the ancestor of that name and the people who later bore that name. The stanza's last words are: *Jacob lived as a stranger (gār) in the land of Ham* — a *stranger* (often translated as "sojourner" or "alien") was a person who fell outside of the network of kinship responsibilities that ancient people depended on as the social safety net. Jacob and his kin were at risk, having been forced off their land and outside of the human relationships that could protect them. (Egypt is called the *land of Ham* as part of the tradition that Noah's son Ham in turn had four sons, two of whom were *kûš* [*Ethiopia*) and *miṣrayim* [*Egypt*]; cf. Gen. 10:6.)

24-36 The name *the LORD* is not present in the Hebrew text of v. 24, but the Lord is the unmistakable subject of the first phrase of the next stanza: *he made his people very fruitful, and stronger than their foes.* The phrase requires divine agency. And the implied divine subject is the answer to the existential problem posed by v. 23 — although Israel found itself outside of the web of trustworthy human relationships, it still could rely on the Lord, with whom Israel had always been a *stranger (gēr;* cf. Ps. 39:13). And thus, proving faithful to the promises of the ancestors, the Lord made Israel numerous and prosperous (cf. Gen. 12:1-3), hardening the hearts of their enemies (v. 25), and then the Lord *sent Moses his servant and Aaron, whom he had chosen.* The perpetually perplexing tradition of the Lord hardening the hearts of Israel's enemies is here seen as just another example of the Lord's faithful actions on Israel's behalf. The repetition of the terms *servant (ʿeḇeḏ* — here designated as Moses) and *chosen (bāḥar* — here Aaron) is worth noting (cf. v. 6). The Lord works through human agents on behalf of those with whom he is in relationship. These agents (here Moses and Aaron) in turn fulfill God's promises. In the case of Moses and Aaron, they *set among them* (the Egyptians) *the promises of his signs.* The fact that it is Moses and Aaron who *set* God's word *among them* is indicated by the plural form of the verb: *śāmû.* It is also clear that they are performing God's *signs (ʾōtôṯāyw).* The term *dāḇār* (literally, "word") is translated as *promise* here, as is often the case with this term, because it reflects the *telos* in the psalm of the divine word that God uses to keep faith with those with whom he is in relationship (cf. 105:42; 106:24). The *signs and wonders* themselves are neither the objects of faith nor the point of the historical narrative; rather, they are evidence of the faithful character of the Lord.

The next nine verses (28-36) recount the plagues — the means by which the Lord brought about the release of the people from captivity. All of the plagues were the result, according to v. 28b, of Egypt's rebellion against God's word. Those plagues, in order, are *darkness, water into blood, frogs, gnats, hail* and lightening, devastation of the vineyards,[31] *locusts,* and the death of the *firstborn.* Comparing the number and order of plagues here with those recounted in Exodus is a traditional sport for interpreters,[32] but the point that is not to be missed is that the plagues are narrated as examples and evidence of God's faithful actions on behalf of the oppressed, captive people. The poem emphasizes that the plagues reached every corner of the land. Not even the

31. Egypt had no vineyards. Vineyards were one of the primary sources of Israel's later economy, and a source of wine and olive oil that Israel exported to Egypt and Mesopotamia. The poetic description here of Egypt's vineyards having been destroyed by a wasting disease may be a polemical explanation of how Egypt came to lack vineyards. On the other hand, it also may simply be an anachronistic poetic flourish.

32. See, e.g., Allen, *Psalms 101–150,* p. 59; Goldingay, *Psalms,* 3:213.

king's upper chambers were spared from the invasion of *frogs* (v. 30); not even the farthest corners of the land were spared from the swarms of *gnats* or threat of lightening (vv. 31-32). Not even the *vigor* and youth of the firstborn sons was proof against the final plague.

37-45 The final stanza of the poem recounts the departure of the people from Egypt, the Lord's provision and guidance through the wilderness, and the people's restoration to the land. As mentioned in the introduction above, the traditions of the miraculous delivery at the sea, the Sinaitic covenant and the gift of the law, and the rebellions in the wilderness are omitted. The only mention of the people's departure from Egypt has to do with the tradition that as Israel left Egypt, the Egyptians gave them gifts of *silver and gold* as plunder (Exod. 12:35-36). In contrast to the tradition of victory over Pharaoh's army at the Red Sea, the psalm notes that *Egypt rejoiced when they left.* Doubtless the psalmist knew the Red Sea tradition, given how ancient and broadly the tradition is witnessed in the Old Testament. The point scored here is that so thoroughly had the Lord cowed the oppressors of his people *(dread had fallen on them)* that they *rejoiced* to see their former slaves depart. In place of the Sinaitic covenant, the emphasis in this psalm is on the Lord's faithfulness to the ancestral covenant: *For he remembered his holy promise to Abraham his servant* (v. 42). God's initial election of Abraham as God's servant means that the people as a whole are God's *chosen ones (bᵉḥîrāyw).* This emphasis both serves to subordinate the Sinaitic covenant to the Abrahamic covenant and also to emphasize the historical narrative of Israel as a long history testifying to the fidelity of the Lord. In place of the traditions of the wilderness as a place of rebellion (Exod. 16:2-3; Numbers 13–14; 16; 20:2-13; Ps. 78:17-33, 56-66), the psalm sees the wilderness as the marvelous time of the Lord's provision. In this, the psalm's view is more similar to that of Amos and Hosea (Amos 5:25; Hos. 2:14; 13:5), who also conceive of the wilderness as the "honeymoon" phase of Israel's relationship with the Lord — the metaphors that are used are of the Lord courting Israel (Hosea 2) or Israel's childhood (Hosea 11). In Psalm 105, the emphasis is on the Lord's provision for Israel as a sign of God's faithfulness, rather than as a response to Israel's rebellions.

Psalm 105's narrative of Israel's history culminates with the restoration to the land. Although the psalm is clear that the land was the ancient gift to Abraham (v. 11), the entry into the land is simultaneously seen as the gift of *the lands of the nations.* The *nations* here refers not to all of the *gôyīm,* but to the Canaanites and other nations that specifically inhabited the promised land (Exod. 3:8). The land itself is understood as the ultimate sign of the Lord's faithfulness. The gift of the land is paradigmatic of Israel's relationship with God. The history of the people is the history of a folk who were *strangers,* without a place, family, or people. The land is the place that the Lord gave to them in order for them to be in covenant relationship with the Lord. As such, the land is not merely the Lord's gift. It is, at the more profound level, the place that God had set aside for the divine-human relationship. Therefore, the land is also the place for the keeping of the law. God gave the land as the place to be in relationship with the people and thus also as the place *that they might keep his statutes.*

The concluding call to praise not only brings the psalm to a fitting conclusion. It is also a call for the congregation to respond to the psalm's narration of the Lord's faithful, covenantal actions on the people's behalf. The call is an imperative that invites the congregation into the narrative, to respond with a word of praise, and therefore to join the choir of those who *praise the Lord* for the Lord's fidelity to Abraham and his offspring.

Reflections

1. Elected for God's Mission

Three times in the psalm the poetic pair of *servant ('eḇeḏ)* and *chosen (bāḥar/bāḥîr)* occurs (vv. 6, 26, 42-43). The term *'eḇeḏ* further occurs in vv. 17 and 25. The terms are used to describe both Israel's ancestral heroes — Abraham, Isaac, Jacob, Joseph, Moses — as well as the people as a whole. The two terms at once signal Israel's consciousness of election — the identity that the people bear as a result of the Lord's choice of Abraham — as well as Israel's sense of mission — the profound sense that the Lord's choice of Abraham was for the purpose of blessing the world (Gen. 12:1-3). But there is something of what Christians call the theology of the cross in this consciousness. Namely, that the "chosen ones" often look — to the world's sensibility — far from blessed or chosen. Israel, whether represented by their ancestral heroes or by the people as a whole, have wandered as a homeless, alien, *stranger* people. They are those who *were few in number . . . and strangers . . . moving about from nation to nation.* The ancestors were sold as slaves and forced into fetters and chains, those who dwelled in foreign lands as strangers. When Israel tells the history of its election by God, it tells the story of a people who suffered, but who also found God in their suffering — or rather, a people that discovered that God found them in their suffering. Election is not for the elect, but for the purpose of God's mission. And God's blessings are not the sort that the world automatically can recognize. They are the blessings of a God who meets the world in suffering — or, as the Apostle Paul would later say, whose power and fidelity prove perfect in suffering.

2. The Land, the Law, and the Lord's Faithfulness

As is made clear throughout the commentary on Psalm 105, the history of the people is narrated in order to score the point that the Lord has proven faithful to the covenantal promises to Abraham. Again and again, the psalm scores the point that the Lord kept the promises to Abraham. The point is made most clearly in vv. 8-9 and 42:

> He has remembered his eternal covenant —
> A promise he commanded for a thousand generations —
> Which he cut with Abraham —
> And his oath to Isaac.
>
> For he remembered his holy promise
> To Abraham his servant.

The term translated as *promise* throughout the psalm is the Hebrew *dāḇār* — which is also the term used for the "Ten Words" (Ten Commandments) in Hebrew. Hebrew does not have different words for "law" and "promise." The function of a given word in a given context determines whether the word is a word of "law" or "gospel." Even the legal terms *command (ṣiwwâ)* and *statute (ḥōq)* in vv. 8 and 10 function in that context as words of "promise." The point is that God's claim on human beings is absolute, and the part of God's claim that is relational cannot be distinguished from that which is ethical or legal. God claims the chosen ones as his own, which means that they belong to God and the relationship with God cannot be breached. As Paul says, nothing can separate us from the love of God. But God's claim that the chosen ones belong to God also means that God's ethical claims cannot be subordinated to the relational, or ignored. As the end of the psalm makes clear, God has provided a place (the land) for the people both to be in relationship with God and to keep the Lord's statutes and ordinances. The gift of the land is simultaneously the obligation to keep the law in the land.

Even though the people of God are no longer isolated in one distinct land, the spiritual point remains. The God who chose Abraham and proved faithful to him and his offspring also is the God who demands the people that bear his name conform to his law.

ROLF A. JACOBSON

Psalm 106: Chosen by a Faithful Lord

Psalm 106 may be considered the twin psalm to Psalm 105 — but the fraternal, rather than the identical twin. Both are historical psalms and hymns[1] that recount the history of the people as the narrative of the Lord's fidelity to the covenant people. But whereas Psalm 105 *accentuates* the positive (for example, in narrating the exodus, all mention of the rebellions in the wilderness are omitted), Psalm 106 *eliminates* the positive — it narrates the history as the story of one rebellion after another. Psalm 105 concentrates on the third person perils of "the enemy" — recounting how Israel found herself in danger at the hands of oppressors, but that the Lord constantly delivered her from herself. Psalm 106 concentrates on the first person perils of Israel herself — recounting how Israel put herself in danger, and again the Lord constantly delivered her. As such, the two are complementary. Psalm 105 majors in the "God side" of the covenantal relationship, testifying to the Lord as one who initiates the covenant and proves faithful to it — as one who showers blessing after blessing on a sojourning people. Psalm 106, on the other hand, majors in the "human side" of the covenantal relationship, confessing that the humans whom God chose are in bondage to sin, curved in on themselves — one might even say fully depraved. And yet, according to the psalm as well as the rest of the Bible, God *remembered — for their sake — his covenant, and was merciful, according to the multitude of his* hesed (v. 45). That is, the poem is a testimony to the fidelity of the Lord in being forgiving, merciful, and faithful to the covenant in spite of Israel's persistent sin. In this sense, the psalm is similar in genre and theology to the Deuteronomistic History, which narrates the history of Israel from the entry into the land until the fall of Jerusalem. Both stories narrate the history of the Israel-God relationship as one in which the Lord is persistently faithful, in spite of the chronic infidelity of Israel.

As noted above, the psalm is understood here as a hymn that narrates the people's history with God. The form of the psalm is muddled, as Allen notes: "The limitations of the form-critical method are evident from the fact that Ps 106 has features both of a hymn . . . and of a communal lament" psalm.[2] Categorization of the psalm depends on which elements an interpreter emphasizes. Penitential aspects occur, the admission of guilt in v. 6, the call to *remember* in v. 4, and a closing plea for deliverance in v. 47. But in this interpreter's judgment, the hymnic and historical qualities of the psalm prevail — the opening call to praise (v. 1), the closing summation *that we may*

1. Some prefer not to understand the psalm as a hymn, in spite of the opening call to praise. E.g., Goldingay writes: "This is hardly enough to turn Ps. 106 into a hymn" (*Psalms,* 3:223).

2. *Psalms 101–150,* p. 65.

testify to your holy name and celebrate by praising you (v. 47), and most of all the extended narrative recounting of the Lord's faithfulness in Israel's history. There is also an individual aspect to the poem, in vv. 1-5, which consists of the opening call to praise and what Goldingay calls "an individual's plea to be part of the deliverance of the people."[3] These verses should not be understood to turn the psalm into an individual psalm of penitence, but as the voice of a liturgical leader who presides over the communal poem of praise. But it should be noted that the form-critical categories are not as "pure" as most introductions to the psalms suggest. In reality, the elements normally associated within a given genre do occur (and quite often) in psalms of other genres.

The structure of the psalm is as follows:

Introductory call to praise (vv. 1-5)
St. 1 Israel's sin and God's faithfulness in Egypt (vv. 6-12)
St. 2 Israel's sin and God's faithfulness in the desert and at Horeb (vv. 13-23)
St. 3 Israel's sin and God's faithfulness from Horeb to the land (vv. 24-33)
St. 4 Israel's sin and God's faithfulness in the land (vv. 34-46)
Concluding plea and praise (v. 47)

1 *Praise the* LORD*!*[4]
Testify that the LORD *is good,*
for his hesed *endures forever!*
2 *Who can declare the mightiness*[5] *of the* LORD*?*
Or proclaim the entirety of his praiseworthiness?[6]
3 *Fortunate are those who keep justice,*[7]
the one who maintains[8] *righteousness at all times.*
4 *Remember me,*[9] *O* LORD*, when you favor your people;*
attend to me when you deliver,
5 *So that I may see the goodness of your chosen ones,*

3. *Psalms,* 3:65.

4. Syr omits.

5. The plural *g*ᵉ*ḇûrôṯ* functions as the abstract, thus *mightiness* rather than "mighty acts."

6. Reading the plural, with LXX and Versions (no change in the consonantal text is required). The plural again carries the abstract sense.

7. Syr has the plural form plus 3ms suffix.

8. LXX and Versions have the plural *ʿōśê,* but this is unnecessary harmonization; alternating singular and plural is a frequent motif of parallelism.

9. LXX in all Versions have the plural object: "remember us." Apparently the individual of the text was pluralized for communal use.

and join in the rejoicing of your nation,
and in the praising of your inheritance.

6 *We have sinned, like our ancestors;*
we have done wrong and acted wickedly.
7 *Our ancestors in Egypt did not regard your wonders.*
They did not remember the multitude of your faithful actions;[10]
they rebelled at the sea,[11] *at the Sea of Reeds.*
8 *But he delivered them for the sake of his name,*
that they might testify to his mightiness.
9 *He rebuked the Sea of Reeds and it dried up;*
he led them through the depths as through a desert.
10 *He delivered them from the hand of those who hated them;*
he redeemed them from the hand of the enemy.
11 *Water covered their foes;*
not one of them remained.
12 *They trusted in his promises;*
they sang his praises.

13 *They were quick to forget his deeds;*
they did not wait for his plan.
14 *They craved intensely in the desert;*
they tested God in the wilderness.
15 *He gave them their request,*
but then he sent a wasting disease among them.
16 *They were jealous*[12] *of Moses in the camp,*
of Aaron, the holy one of God.
17 *The earth opened*[13] *and swallowed Dathan,*
and covered the company of Abiram.
18 *A fire burned among their company,*
a flame consuming the wicked.
19 *They made a calf at Horeb;*
they worshipped a formed image.

10. Normally in this Commentary the Hebrew *ḥeseḏ* is simply transliterated as *hesed;* but the plural form here, *ḥªsāḏêḵā,* implies repeated events or experiences of God's *hesed.* LXX and Aquila have the singular; the plural is better attested.

11. LXX implies *'ōlîm* ("those going up") for MT's *'al yām.* Other Versions support MT. NRSV accepts the emendation of *'al yām* to *'lywn* ("Most High"), for which there is no manuscript evidence.

12. LXX's *kai parōrgisan* implies *wayyqan'û* ("they provoked").

13. LXX has the passive form, implying the *niphal.* No change in meaning would result.

20 *They exchanged their "Glory"*
for the image of a bull that eats grass.
21 *They forgot God, their deliverer,*
who had done great things in Egypt
22 *and wonders in the land of Ham,*
awesome deeds at the Sea of Reeds.
23 *He intended*[14] *to destroy them,*
except that Moses, his chosen one,
Stood in the breach before him
to turn away his destructive anger.

24 *They rejected the lovely land;*
they did not trust his promise.
25 *They grumbled in their tents;*
they did not listen to the voice of the Lord.
26 *He raised his hand against them,*
to make them fall in the wilderness,
27 *And to make their offspring fall among the nations,*
and to scatter them among the lands.
28 *They joined themselves to the Baal of Peor;*
they ate sacrifices of the dead.
29 *They provoked him*[15] *with their deeds,*
and a plague broke out among them.
30 *Phinehas stood and intervened,*
and the plague was contained.
31 *It is reckoned to him as a righteous deed,*
by every generation, forever.
32 *They provoked him*[16] *at the waters of Meribah,*
and it went ill with Moses on their account.
33 *Because they rebelled against his spirit,*
he lashed out with his mouth.

34 *They did not destroy the peoples,*
as the Lord *had instructed them.*
35 *They mingled with the nations,*
and they learned their ways.
36 *They worshipped their idols,*

14. Lit., "he said to destroy them." The verbs of "speech" can indicate thought, and thus also intention.

15. Reading the 3ms suffix, with LXX.

16. Reading the 3ms suffix, with LXX.

which were a snare to them.
37 *They sacrificed their sons,*
and their daughters to demons.
38 *They shed innocent blood,*
the blood of their sons and daughters,
Whom they sacrificed to the idols of Canaan,
so that the land was polluted with bloodshed.
39 *They became unclean through their customs;*
they prostituted themselves through their actions.
40 *The anger of the LORD burned against his people;*
he loathed his inheritance.
41 *He gave them into the hand of the nations,*
those who hated them ruled over them.
42 *Their enemies oppressed them;*
they were humiliated under their hand.
43 *Many times he delivered them,*
but they, they willfully[17] *rebelled!*
they were brought low by their sin.
44 *But he recognized they were in distress*
when he heard their cry.
45 *He remembered — for their sake — his covenant*
and was merciful, according to the multitude of his hesed.[18]
46 *He gave them over to mercy,*
in front of all their captors.

47 *Deliver us, O LORD our God,*
and gather us from the nations
So that we may testify to your holy name
and celebrate by praising you.
48 *Praised be the LORD God of Israel,*
from everlasting to everlasting,
and let the people say, "Amen."
Praise the LORD!

1-5 The opening call to praise in Psalm 106 includes both plural imperatives typical of hymns *(praise* and *testify)* as well as singular imperatives typical of prayers for help *(remember me* and *attend to me).* The opening call to praise

17. The sense of *ba'ᵃṣāṯām* is that the rebellions of the people were purposeful and intentional.

18. Reading the Kethib (supported by LXX); the Qere *r(ḥᵃsādayw)* is a harmonization with v. 7.

frames the historical narrative and casts everything that follows as praise of the Lord as the God who has been faithful to Israel. The hymn offers praise of God as testimony to *the mightiness of the LORD*. The theme of testimony is apparent in the psalm's opening word: *Testify!* The term *hôḏû* is often translated as "give thanks," but the Hebrew term does not include the sense of being thankful, which the traditional English translation connotes. Rather, as a *hiphil* imperative of the root *yāḏâ,* the term more properly means to "make known," as Ps. 32:6 and Prov. 28:13 indicate.[19] The call-to-praise aspect of the introduction should not be overlooked. This is a call for Israel, paradoxically, to recite the narrative of its own infidelity in order to praise the Lord for the Lord's fidelity. The fact that the psalm is about the Lord's faithfulness is evident because the next line is the most characteristic confession of Israel's faith life: The Lord's *hesed endures forever!* The phrase *g*^{e}*ḇûrôṯ YHWH, the mightiness of the LORD*, usually refers to acts of vindication such as a military victory (cf. Ps. 20:6; 66:7), but in the context of this psalm refers to the Lord's mercy in being forgiving to Israel. The psalm offers an ironic beatitude: *Fortunate are those who keep justice, the one who maintains righteousness at all times. Justice,* as always, refers to the external environment in a society in which all life can thrive. Justice is based in the law; as Mic. 6:8 demonstrates, it is what the Lord "has told you" in the law. *Righteousness* is the disposition of those who keep justice. Because God elected Israel, Israel's vocation is to *keep justice* and *maintain righteousness at all times.* But the beatitude is ironic, as the long narrative that follows shows. Those who do justice and maintain righteousness may be *fortunate,* but Israel as a nation is not among those who have managed to do this.

The individual petitions to *remember me* and *attend to me* are personal requests on behalf of the liturgical leader (most likely a Levitical priest) to be included in the history of reconciliation between the Lord and the people. This is made clear in v. 5, where the psalmist says that the appeal to be heard is so that he may *see the goodness of your chosen ones and join in the rejoicing of the nation.* The term *see (lir'ôṯ)* means "to experience as a reality" (cf. 27:13, etc.). The psalmist's request is thus both an implicit confession of sins that the liturgical leader himself has not been among those who have kept justice and maintained righteousness at all times and thus also an implicit confession of faith that the psalmist is among those who are dependent on the Lord's mercy. The community is referred to here as God's *inheritance (naḥ*^{a}*lâ).* Most commonly, the noun refers to the property that one inherits from a parent. Abstractly, it can refer to the Levites, who did not inherit land but whose "portion" was the Lord (Deut. 10:9; 12:12), and more generally to the whole people (Deut. 32:9). The term here is a powerful metaphor for the relation-

19. *Psalms,* 3:753.

ship between the Lord and the people — the people are God's firstborn, so to speak, those whom the Lord has chosen to "inherit" a unique relationship and mission from God.

6-12 The first main stanza of the psalm's body recounts the story of the Lord's mercy to the nation's ancestors in Egypt. The stanza begins with a confession of sin that frames the entire history recitation that follows — *We have sinned, like our ancestors.* The people's history is a history of sinning against God, with each sin being met by a new display of mercy from the Lord. The sin of the exodus generation, according to the psalm, was that they *did not regard your wonders* and they *did not remember the multitude of your faithful actions.* The terms *regard (hiśkîlû)* and *remember (zaḵrû)* refer to a "sin of omission," but this should be taken to refer to an accidental or incidental neglect. Goldingay interprets the failing as they "did not draw the right implications from their awareness of [God's] wonders."[20] But this interpretation is not strong enough. Israel's failure to *remember* the Lord's *wonders* and *faithful actions* was understood as an aggressive sin — as a failure to trust in God. As such, the sin is at heart a failure to keep the first commandment. The psalm does not explicitly say what the consequence of Israel's sin was, but it implies that the crisis Israel faced at the sea was the result of Israel's distrust of the Lord.

The psalm then confesses the Lord's faithful mercy in the face of Israel's sin: *he delivered them for the sake of his name, that they might testify to his mightiness.* Two aspects of this confession are worth noting. First, the reason for the Lord's fidelity and mercy is described as *for the sake of his name* (cf. Ps. 23:3). That is, the Lord proved faithful because the Lord had given his name in a promise and therefore proved faithful to that promise. Second, as the recipient of the Lord's faithful actions, Israel's vocation is to bear witness to the Lord's fidelity in praise — praise understood as testimony about what the Lord has done. The psalm then recounts the deliverance at the sea (vv. 10-11) and records how Israel faithfully lived up to their vocation — they *trusted in his promises* and *they sang his praises.*

13-23 The second main stanza of the psalm's body focuses on the people's sin during the first stage in the wilderness and at Mount Horeb (Sinai). The theme of forgetting God and God's actions is starkly re-sounded in the stanza's first line: *They were quick to forget his deeds* and *they did not wait for his plan.* The term *plan (ʿēṣâ)* can refer to "counsel" and thus can carry a legal sense similar to "commandment," but in this context the sense is of God's intention for the future (cf. Ps. 33:10-11; Isa. 25:1). Having been led into the wilderness, the people lost faith in God's intention to bring them back to their own land and to provide for their needs until that occurred (cf. Num.

20. *Psalms,* 3:227.

14:26-45). The reference to being *quick to forget* (literally, "they hurried, they forgot"; in the coordination of verbs the first verb functions adverbially) is a commentary on human nature — the innate propensity towards insecurity and fear overwhelms the ability to trust. The psalm then recounts events familiar from the pentateuchal narrative — the people's fear of dying of thirst/hunger and testing God (cf. Exodus 15–17; Numbers 14), the rebellion of Dathan and Abiram (cf. Numbers 16), and the casting of the golden calf at Horeb (cf. Exodus 32). As is the case with interpreting Psalm 105, the point is not to attempt to harmonize the order and description of these sins with the descriptions in the Pentateuch, but to grasp how the recounting of these failings contributes to the witness of the psalm. The history of the people's fragile fidelity is recounted in order to bear witness to the Lord's fidelity in showing mercy.

The psalm introduces a new theme here, the theme of the importance of the agency of the ancestral leaders. On the one hand, the psalm describes how the people were jealous of Moses and Aaron. The rebellion of the people, particularly of Dathan and Abiram, against the Lord's appointed leaders threatened the well-being of the people as a whole. The Lord's vindication of Moses and Aaron was simultaneously a *consuming of the wicked* — the preservation of the people requiring the extreme punishment. Parallel to this, the people *exchanged their "Glory"* for a *formed image.* The term *glory* here is a title for God, as it is in Ps. 3:3. Similar to exchanging obedience to God's servants Moses and Aaron in exchange for trusting in their own choice of leaders was the choice to worship their own image of God (most likely the golden calf was not an image of a false god, but a false image of the true God) in place of the mystery of the Lord's presence. The psalm makes no mention of Aaron's role. Again, the theme of forgetting sums up the sin — *they forgot God, their deliverer.*

The theme of human agency again returns. The psalm recounts God's intention (v. 23; the verb *'āmar,* literally, "say," carries the meaning of God's intention) to destroy the people (cf. Exodus 32). But a human agent — *Moses, his chosen one* — intervened and *stood in the breach before him to turn away his destructive anger.* The latter phrase is a potent metaphor for the priest (a reminder that Moses was of the priestly line of Levi) as intercessor. The *breach (pereṣ)* is a gap in the defenses, through which a threat may pass (cf. 1 Kgs. 11:27; Isa. 58:12; Amos 9:11). The role of Moses, as intercessor for the people, is to turn away the threat through the act of intercession.[21] Although the psalm does not recount the Lord's repentance from the intent to destroy the people, the Lord's act of mercy is assumed by the continuing narrative.

21. See Brueggemann, "Prayer as an Act of Daring Dance: Four Biblical Examples," in *The Psalms and the Life of Faith,* pp. 135-49.

24-33 The psalm continues with a stanza that recounts the people's continuing failings in the desert wanderings — the failure to trust that they could overcome the people of the land (cf. Num. 13:25–14:45), the Lord's renewed intention to abandon the people (cf. Num. 14:11-25), and the people's syncretistic sin of "yoking itself to the Baal of Peor" (Num. 25:3) following their intermarrying with the women of Moab — which led them to the ultimate sin: *they ate sacrifices of the dead.* The meaning of this phrase is debated, but based on v. 37 (see also 1 Kgs. 16:34; 2 Kgs. 16:3) the verse most likely refers to the tradition that Israelites who joined in the worship of false gods often joined in the practice of child sacrifice. This context at least puts in perspective the Lord's violent response of *plague* (cf. Num. 25:9). The rebellion at *the waters of Meribah* is also recounted (cf. Num. 20:1-13).

The theme of the agency of an ancestral "hero" then reoccurs: *Phinehas stood and intervened* (cf. Num. 25:7-13). According to Numbers, the intervention of Phinehas did not take the form of prayerful intercession, but of violent, physical judgment. In vv. 32-33, the Hebrew is difficult to interpret with certainty. The Hebrew clearly says *they provoked him (wayyaqṣîp̱û)* — but to whom does the third person masculine pronoun refer? Goldingay interprets it as referring to Moses, and translated the next phrase "and it was displeasing to Moses because of them."[22] But the majority view holds that the pronoun refers to God and that *wayyēraʿ lᵉmōšeh baʿᵃḇûrām* means *and it went ill with Moses on their account.* This best explains the next verse, which speaks of Moses' rash words in response to the people's sin: *he lashed out with his mouth* (cf. Num. 20:1-13). Again, the theme of the agency of the ancestors is stressed. Because Moses responded poorly when he was provoked by the rebellion of the people, he bore the consequences of his rash actions. Thus, the people's provocation resulted in *ill* for Moses. The psalm does not wonder why the Lord would hold Moses guilty for being provoked by the people's sin, when the Lord was similarly *provoked* twice.

34-46 The psalm's final stanza brings to a culmination both the spatial and spiritual saga of the psalm, as the people entered the land, but *mingled with the nations* that were there and *learned their ways.* Verse 34 is theologically and morally problematic for the post-Enlightenment mind, and with good reason! The verse not only recalls the tradition of the Lord's command to *destroy* utterly the people of the land; it faults the people for failing to fulfill the command.[23] The following verses, which describe the moral and

22. *Psalms,* 3:234.

23. Goldingay seeks to put the verse in some canonical context: "Actually Yhwh did not tell Israel to destroy the peoples. The verb *šāmad* is frequent in Deuteronomy, but there, it is Yhwh who is its subject; destroying the peoples is Yhwh's business. Israel's commission is to 'devote' the peoples by killing them (*ḥāram* hiphil; e.g., Deut. 7:2). This feels the same

spiritual fall that resulted from mingling with the nations, at least put the psalm's perspective in historical context. Those verses describe how Israel mixed with the peoples, began to worship their gods (alongside of the Lord, most likely), and joined in the most objectionable worship practices of the nations — including child sacrifice: *They sacrificed their sons and their daughters to demons. They shed innocent blood, the blood of their sons and daughters.* The term translated as *demons, šēḏîm,* occurs only here and in Deut. 32:17: "They sacrificed to demons, not God, to deities they had never known, to new ones recently arrived, whom your ancestors had not feared."[24] The translation of *demons* is used because of the Septuagint translation *daimoniois,* but the modern concept of a demon is not a perfect fit. The Akkadian cognate *šēdū* can refer to a benevolent spirit, but also to a malevolent deity.[25] Psalm 106 states that sacrificing to such spirits included human sacrifice. When Israel thus intermingled with the nations and adopted such worship practices, the land itself became corrupted — *the land was polluted with bloodshed.* The land, which was intended as the place where the law would be kept, became the place where the law was unkept and thus became defiled. The view here is similar to Hos. 4:1-3, where the land itself bears the consequence of human rebellion.

The Lord's reaction is again severe — *The anger of the LORD burned against his people; he loathed his inheritance.* The reference to Israel as God's *inheritance (naḥᵃlâ)* brings to full circle the story of the psalm. In v. 5, the psalmist had prayed to join in the praise of God's *inheritance* (God's people). Here, the psalm reaches the part of the story where the Lord *loathed* his choice of Israel. Similar to the flood story in Genesis, where the Lord repented of having made humanity, here the Lord has repented of having chosen Jacob as his inheritance. Similar to the theology of the Deuteronomistic History, the psalm says that the Lord *gave them into the hand of the nations.* The psalm does not say that this was a cyclical pattern (à la the book of Judges), but this is implied by v. 43's *many times he delivered them.* The imprint of the Deuteronomistic theology is again apparent in vv. 44-45, which echo the book of Judges' pattern — they cried to the Lord, he heard their cry, and delivered them. Not to be missed is the psalm's emphasis on the Lord's faithful mercy: *He remembered — for their sake — his covenant and was merciful, according to the multitude of his* hesed. This verse can be considered the psalm's capstone.

---

to the peoples but has quite different significance for Israel in its relationship with Yhwh" (*Psalms,* 3:235).

24. NRSV; the translation of Deut. 32:17 is debated, and the debate does not fit here; but the context makes it clear that *šēḏîm* refers to rival objects of worship, in violation of Israel's moral and theological laws.

25. *ši-id lumnin* ("malevolent spirit"); *CAD,* Š.2.

Especially striking is how the verse brings together two earlier elements of the poem. In vv. 7b-8, the psalm says that *at the sea,* the ancestors *did not remember (lōʾ zāḵrû) the multitude of your faithful (rōḇ ḥᵃsāḏêḵā) actions,* yet God *delivered them for the sake of his name (lᵉmaʿan šᵉmô).* Verse 45 borrows the earlier language, with subtle changes. Earlier, the ancestor forgot; here God *remembered (wayyizkōr).* Earlier, the act of mercy was *for the sake of* God's *name;* here is it *for their sake* (literally, "for them"; *lāhem*). Earlier, what the people forgot was the *multitude of your faithful actions* — meaning God's victories over Egypt. Here, the new act of merciful forgiveness is itself a new instance of *the multitude of his* hesed *(kᵉrōḇ ḥᵃsāḏô).* The stanza culminates with a stark statement of God's mercy. In an example of the poetic device of "abstract for concrete," in which the abstract concept stands in metaphorically as a substantive, the poem says, *he gave them over to mercy.* And, as in Psalm 23, where the table is hospitably set in the presence of the enemies, this mercy is shown *in front of all their captors.*

47 The psalm concludes with a plea — *deliver us (hôšîʿēnû;* note the parallel with v. 8a) — that is typical of the communal prayers for help, again showing the way in which the poem exceeds narrowly construed form-critical categories. But the note of praise is also there. The psalm closes with a purpose clause. *Deliver us,* the psalm prays, *so that we may testify to your holy name and celebrate by praising you.*

48 The final verse is not part of Psalm 106 proper. It is the closing doxology to Book Four of the Psalter.

Reflections

The psalm can be considered a lengthy poetic meditation on Israel's history of breaking the first commandment — "You shall have no other gods." According to the pedagogical device employed by generations of catechism teachers, the Ten Commandments are divided into two tables. On the one hand, there is the "vertical table" that governs the people's relationship to God (the commandments to have no other gods, no graven images, not to misuse the Lord's name, and to keep the Sabbath). On the hand, there is the "horizontal table" that governs the people's relationship to each other (the commandments to honor the elderly, not to murder, steal, commit adultery, bear false witness, or covet). But one of the clear messages of Psalm 106 is that this old distinction between "theological" and "ethical" tables is false. Whenever Israel mixed the worship of other gods with the worship of the Lord, the neighbor paid. The psalm cites the most grievous example — human sacrifice (vv. 28, 37-38). But the ethical application is more complex than just one example. Whenever the person of faith puts trust in something other than the true and living

God, the neighbor will suffer. When we worship wealth, we cannot see to our neighbor's needs. When we pursue power, we do so at the expense of the neighbor. When we deify career, or family, or country, concern for the widow, the orphan, and the sojourner will be tragically subordinated.

The first commandment is best known in its negative form: "You shall have no other gods before me" (Exod. 20:3). But the positive form is just as important and relevant: "You shall love the LORD your God with all your heart, and with all your soul, and with all your might" (Deut. 6:5). The positive obligation to keep the commandment includes, according to the language of Deuteronomy, to "remember the LORD your God" (8:18). This remembering does not merely signify intellectual recollection, but means the complete wedding of mind and body, or thinking and acting. To remember God is to know the story of God and to find one's place in the story. It starts with being aware of the narrative, but it is not completed until one's daily life is "taken over" (so to speak) by the awareness of the nearness of God.

And yet, if one credits the witness of the psalm with any sort of accuracy, the human will is so compromised that it is hopeless to think humans are capable of remembering or trusting God. For humans — whether in the individual or collective form — it is "not possible not to sin." Thus, to find one's story in the story of God is to take up one's place in the story of those who have *willfully rebelled* (v. 43). But it is also to take one's place in the story of those who have turned and been delivered and forgiven — again and again — by the Lord. It is to take up one's place in a relationship of dependence upon the gracious forgiveness of God. Perhaps the most important theological message of Psalm 106 is that the history of God's people must never become a glorious narrative of triumph. It must always be the story that admits that *we have sinned, like our ancestors* (v. 6a). The people of God do not celebrate our divine election and the long history of relationship with God as signifying anything positive about ourselves. Rather, it signifies only, as the psalm says, God's fidelity to the covenant and *the multitude of his* hesed (v. 45).

ROLF A. JACOBSON

Book Five of the Psalter: Psalms 107–150

INTRODUCTION

Book Five of the Psalter begins with words of thanks (Ps. 107:1-3) and words of story (Ps. 107:4-32), words that celebrate God's role in delivering the Israelites from captivity in Babylon and returning them as a community to their own land. The reader will recall that in 587 B.C.E., Babylon sacked Jerusalem, destroyed the temple, and took a large number of its inhabitants into exile in Babylon, where they remained for the next fifty years.

In 539, the Persians conquered Babylon and a year later, the Persian king Cyrus allowed the captive Israelites to return to Jerusalem and to resume their lives.[1] The returnees built a new temple and renewed their religious practices, but they remained vassals to the Persian Empire. Ethnic identity and worship practices were restored in Jerusalem, but not a distinct political state with a Davidic king at its head.

Book Four of the Psalter encouraged the Israelites who were in exile in Babylon to think back upon the days of Moses and the wilderness wanderings, days when there was no sovereign over Israel except Yahweh. Book Five continues that encouragement, providing the community of faith with a new way to view their identity as a nation in the complex world in which they found themselves.

Interestingly, the figure of David, who represents kingship and political identity for the Israelites, reappears dramatically in Book Five, after being all but absent in Books Three and Four.[2] And in Book Five, David leads the faithful in a celebration of God as sovereign — protector, provider, and sus-

1. For the text of the so called Cyrus Cylinder, see *ANET,* p. 316.

2. In Book Three of the Psalter, only one Psalm, Ps. 86, is ascribed in its superscription to David. In Book Four, only two psalms, Pss. 101 and 103, have Davidic superscriptions. In Book Five, fourteen of the forty-four psalms are ascribed to David.

tainer — in their new, present life situation. At the heart of the book, Psalm 119 instructs the community of faith in the way in which God will rule over them: through the torah, the instructions that God gave to the Israelites at Sinai (Exodus 19–Numbers 10). If the people acknowledge God as sovereign and keep the torah, then they will survive as the people of Israel.

Psalm 107's opening verses praise God for redeeming the people and gathering them from the east, the west, the north, and the south (vv. 1-3). Its closing words, *whoever is wise will hear these things and the* hesed *ones of the* L*ORD* *will attend* (v. 43), set the scene for the rest of the words of Book Five.

The next three psalms — Psalm 108, a community lament; Psalm 109, an individual lament; and Psalm 110, a community lament — are all identified in their superscriptions as psalms *of David.* The next two psalms in Book Five, Psalms 111 and 112, are concise, compact acrostics. Psalm 111 is an individual hymn of thanksgiving, and Psalm 112 is a wisdom psalm, and for both, the focus is the torah. Together, the two psalms celebrate God's mighty deeds on behalf of the community of faith and instruct them on the proper response to God. Psalms 111 and 112 also begin with the call to praise, "Hallelujah," a characteristic introduction and/or refrain in the following six psalms of Book Five, Psalms 113–18.

Collectively known as "the Egyptian Hallel," Psalms 113–18 are associated with the celebration of Passover. In modern Jewish life, Psalms 113–14 are recited before the Passover meal, and Psalms 115–18 are recited at its conclusion. The massive wisdom acrostic, Psalm 119, occurs after the Egyptian Hallel psalms. Its theme, like that of Psalms 111 and 112, is the torah. Thus, we may view Psalms 111, 112, and 119 as a "torah-oriented frame" around the Egyptian Hallel psalms.

Psalm 119 is followed by a group of fifteen psalms (Psalms 120–34) that share a common superscription, *šîr hammaʿălôṯ* — A Song of the Ascents. Pilgrims on their way to Jerusalem may have sung the Songs of the Ascents, which, except for Psalm 132, are brief and thus easy to memorize. Although these fifteen psalms most likely come from a variety of times and places in the life of ancient Israel, the message of the collection as a whole is that Jerusalem is the place for the people of God to come together for celebrations and commemorations and for acknowledging the goodness and help of the God of Israel. For a full discussion of the Songs of the Ascents, see the Introduction.

James Mays describes Psalms 135–36 as "partners in praise."[3] They are an apt conclusion to the Songs of the Ascents, and some scholars suggest that Psalms 111–18 and Psalms 120–36 form an inclusio around the great torah psalm 119. Psalm 137, an imprecatory community lament, seems out of place in Book Five. Its words stand in stark contrast to the two preceding psalms.

3. *Psalms,* p. 415.

In the midst of the praise to God that dominates Book Five, Psalm 137 is a reminder that the past is always with us as a present reality.

Psalms 138–45 are all ascribed, in their superscriptions, to David. They form a closing chorus for Book Five's words of and about David. The chorus culminates with Psalm 145, an alphabetic acrostic (as are Psalms 111, 112, and 119), identified in its superscription as "a Praise Song of David." The superscription is unique in the Psalter, suggesting that the reader/hearer should pay special attention to its words. In Psalm 145, David celebrates God as *the king* (145:1) and invites the community of faith and all flesh to join in the celebration. Psalms 146–50 form the closing doxological words of Book Five and the entire Psalter. They are called the "Final Hallel" of the book of Psalms, with the word *praise (hālal)* occurring thirteen times in Psalm 150.

Book Five of the Psalter leads readers/hearers from the despair of exile in Babylon to the celebration of a new life in the land of Israel with God as sovereign and the torah as the guide for life. But the celebration is possible only at the end of the story of the Psalter. The postexilic community had to understand where it came from — the failed Davidic kingship — and where it was going — an identifiable entity within the vast Persian, Greek, and Roman empires — in order to participate in the praise of a new life with Yahweh as sovereign. Thus the Psalter is a story of survival in the changed and changing world that confronted the postexilic Israelite community of faith.

Psalm 107: Whoever Is Wise

Psalm 107 opens with the words:

> Give thanks to the LORD, for he is good,
> For his *hesed* is for all time.
> The ones redeemed by the LORD will thus say,
> Those he has redeemed from the hand of the oppressor
> And those from the lands he has gathered in,
> From the east and from the west,
> From the north and from the sea.[1] (vv. 1-3)

These words seem undoubtedly to have been placed at the beginning of Book Five as an answer to the closing words of Book Four:

> Save us, O LORD our God,
> And gather us from among the nations,
> So that we may give thanks to your holy name
> And glory in your praise. (Ps. 106:47)

Psalm 107, a community hymn of praise, was most likely a liturgy of thanks *(tôḏâ)* originally offered by worshippers at a festival at the temple in Jerusalem. Four groups of people appear in its verses, together perhaps representing the *redeemed by the LORD* mentioned in v. 2. Verses 4-9 tell of a group of wanderers, lost in the desert, who finally arrive at their destination. Verses 10-16 tell the story of *prisoners* who are set free. Verses 17-22 tell of *sick* persons who are healed. And vv. 23-32 are about a group of sailors who are saved from shipwreck. Each vignette follows a precise format:

- a description of the distress (vv. 4-5, 10-12, 17-18, 23-27)
- a prayer to the Lord (vv. 6, 13, 19, 28)
- details of the delivery (vv. 7, 14, 19-20, 29)
- an expression of thanks (vv. 8-9, 15-16, 21-22, 30-32)

In each vignette, the "prayer to the Lord" and the "expression of thanks" are identical.

> Then they cried aloud (*ṣāʿaq* in vv. 6, 28; *zāʿaq* in vv. 13, 19) to the LORD
> because of their oppression,
> And from their depths he delivered them. (vv. 6, 13, 19, 28)

1. See the note on this word in the full translation following.

> Let God's *hesed* one give thanks to the LORD
> For his wondrous works for the children of humanity.[2]
> (vv. 8, 15, 21, 31)

The repetition of words in the vignettes provides further evidence that the psalm may have been used in a liturgical setting, in which groups of worshippers recited the words of Psalm 107 antiphonally with presiding priests.

Are the four vignettes actual accounts of deliverance by the Lord sung in celebration at a festival? Or is the psalm purely a literary composition, with the four groups representing, in the words of James L. Mays, "all those who have experienced the redemption of the Lord"?[3] Whatever the original *Sitz im Leben* of Psalm 107, its placement in the Psalter by the shaping community renders it as a hymn celebrating deliverance. And in the story of the Psalter, that deliverance is from the exile in Babylon.

In its original form, Psalm 107 most likely consisted only of vv. 1-32 and was used at the temple in Jerusalem as a liturgy of thanksgiving for deliverance. Verses 33-42, which proclaim that the sovereign Lord can provide the people with all of their needs, may have been a separate composition added to Psalm 107 at some point in its history.[4] In its verses, we read that the Lord makes it possible for the hungry to dwell safely in the land and establish a city; to sow fields, plant vineyards, and gather a harvest; and to have children and increase their cattle (vv. 36-38). In addition, the Lord pours contempt on rulers who oppress the people (vv. 39-40). The future of the upright is secured, and the wicked are left speechless (v. 42). The psalm closes with the words:

> Whoever is wise *(ḥāḵām)* will hear these things,
> And the *hesed* ones of the LORD will attend. (v. 43)

The structure of Psalm 107 may be outlined as follows:

Initial words of thanks to the Lord (vv. 1-3)
Vignette 1: Wanderers lost in a desert (vv. 4-9)
  Description of distress (vv. 4-5)
  Prayer to the Lord (v. 6)
  Details of deliverance (v. 7)
  Expression of thanks (vv. 8-9)

2. The Hebrew word is *b^enê 'āḏām,* a phrase often used to emphasize the absolute difference between humanity and God. E.g., see Ps. 8:4.

3. *Psalms,* p. 345.

4. Gerstenberger argues quite convincingly for the unity of Ps. 107 (*Psalms: Part 2,* pp. 249-50).

Vignette 2: Prisoners who are set free (vv. 10-16)
  Description of distress (vv. 10-12)
  Prayer to the Lord (v. 13)
  Details of deliverance (v. 14)
  Expression of thanks (vv. 15-16)
Vignette 3: Sick persons who are healed (vv. 17-22)
  Description of distress (vv. 17-18)
  Prayer to the Lord (v. 19)
  Details of deliverance (vv. 19-20)
  Expression of thanks (vv. 21-22)
Vignette 4: Sailors who are saved from shipwreck (vv. 23-32)
  Description of distress (vv. 23-27)
  Cry to the Lord (v. 28)
  Details of deliverance (v. 29)
  Expression of thanks (vv. 30-32)
The Lord's ability to provide for the people (vv. 33-42)
Final word of admonition to "the wise" (v. 43)

1 *Give thanks to the LORD, for he is good,*
  For his hesed *is for all time.*
2 *The ones redeemed by the LORD will thus say,*
  Those he has redeemed from the hand of the oppressor
3 *And those from the lands he has gathered in,*
  From the east and from the west,
  From the north and from the sea.[5]

4 *The ones wandering*[6] *in the wilderness, in a wasteland,*[7]
  A pathway to a city of habitation they could not find.
5 *Hungering as well as thirsting,*
  Their inmost being was faint within them.
6 *Then they cried aloud to the LORD because of their oppression,*
  And from their depths he delivered them.

5. The editors of *BHS* suggest emending the word here to *ûmîyāmîn* ("and from the south"), thereby naming all four compass directions and maintaining a parallelism with the first colon of the verse. No Hebrew manuscript, however, attests the emendation, and LXX, Peshitta, and Vulg all translate *sea* here. The Targumim add "southern" to the translation ("the southern sea"). For a full discussion of the issues, see John Jarick, "The Four Corners of Psalm 107," *CBQ* 59 (1997) 270-87.

6. While the verb occurs in the perfect aspect in MT, we will follow the emendation of *BHS* and render it as a participle in agreement with vv. 10, 17, and 23, where the opening verbs are participles.

7. LXX and Syr transpose the *'atnaḥ* from the following word to here.

7 *And he caused their path to be a straight path,*
In order that they might go to a city of habitation.
8 *Let God's* hesed *one*[8] *give thanks to the* LORD
For his wondrous works for the children of humanity.
9 *For he has satisfied the one who was thirsting,*
And the one who was hungering he has filled with good.

10 *The ones dwelling in darkness and the shadow of death,*
Prisoners of suffering and iron,
11 *Because they had rebelled against the sayings of God,*
And the council of God Most High they had scorned,
12 *He subdued their heart*[9] *with toil;*
They stumbled and there was no one to help.
13 *Then they cried aloud to the* LORD *because of their oppression,*
And from their depths he delivered them.
14 *He led them out from the darkness and the shadow of death,*
And their bonds he tore to pieces.
15 *Let God's* hesed *one*[10] *give thanks to the* LORD
For his wondrous works for the children of humanity.
16 *For he has shattered the doors of bronze,*
And the bars of iron he has broken into pieces.

17 *The ones who are sick*[11] *because of their transgression,*
Because of their guilt they are afflicted,
18 *All food their being abhors,*
And they arrive at the gates of death.
19 *Then they cried aloud to the* LORD *because of their oppression,*
And from their depths he delivered them.
20 *He sent his word and he comforted them,*
And he rescued them alive[12] *from their pits.*
21 *Let God's* hesed *one*[13] *give thanks to the* LORD
For his wondrous works for the children of humanity.

8. In LXX and Syr, the word is plural.

9. In MT, the verb occurs in the *hiphil* stem. LXX translates it as *kai etapeinōthē,* rendering the verb in the *niphal* stem, thereby altering the translation to "their heart was subdued."

10. In LXX and Syr, the word is plural.

11. The Hebrew word *(ʾewilîm)* actually means "foolish ones." In the ancient Near East, sickness was often associated with sin or foolishness. See, e.g., Pss. 32:1-5; 38:3, 5. Thus the people here abhor food and arrive at the gates of death.

12. LXX and Syr add a 3 pl suffix to the verb ("and he rescued them").

13. In LXX and Syr, the word is plural.

22 *And they will sacrifice sacrifices of thanks,*
And they will recount his deeds with shouts of joy.

23 *As for the ones going down to the sea in ships,*
Doing business on the great waters,
24 *They saw for themselves the deeds of the* Lord
And his wondrous works in the depth of the sea.
25 *He commanded and he set forth a stormy wind,*
And it lifted up its whirlings.
26 *They went up to the heavens and went down to the depths.*
Their being trembled with suffering.
27 *They reeled and moved to and fro like drunks,*
And all of their wisdom was destroyed.
28 *Then they cried aloud to the* Lord *because of their oppression,*
And from their depths he delivered them.
29 *He made the storm into stillness,*
And their whirlings were quieted.
30 *And they were glad because they had silence,*
and he let them rest in the haven of their pleasure.
31 *Let God's* hesed *one*[14] *give thanks to the* Lord
For his wondrous works for the children of humanity.
32 *And they will exalt him in the assembly of the people,*
And in the dwelling place of the elders they will glorify him.

33 *He turns rivers into a desert*
And springs of water into a thirsty place,
34 *A land of fruit into a barren land*
because of the wickedness of those who dwell in it.
35 *He turns a desert into a pool of water*
And a land of dryness into a spring of water.
36 *And he allows the hungry to dwell there,*
And they establish a city for dwelling.
37 *And they seed fields and they plant vineyards,*
And they reap the fruit of gain.
38 *And he blesses them and they multiply exceedingly,*
And their cattle do not become fewer in number.
39 *And when they become fewer in number and are bowed down,*
Because of oppression, bad things, and sorrow,
40 *Then pouring out contempt on rulers,*
He causes them to wander directionless, with no path.

14. This word is plural in LXX and Syr.

41 *But he raises up the needy out of sufferings,*
And he makes like flocks families.
42 *The upright will see and will be glad.*
And all wickedness will close its mouth.

43 *Whoever is wise will hear these things,*
And the hesed *ones of the* LORD *will attend.*

1-3 In vv. 1-3 the people are instructed to *give thanks* to God because in goodness and *hesed*-ness God has *redeemed* them *from the hand of the oppressor* and *gathered* them in *from the east and from the west, from the north and from the sea.* While the majority of modern English translations render v. 3 as "from the east and from the west and from the north and from the south," the MT clearly has *from the north and from the sea (yām).* Perhaps because of a felt need to have the psalmist refer to the four compass directions, the editors of *BHS* suggest an emendation to *yāmîn* ("right") — "south" when one faces the sunrise. But no Hebrew manuscript reflects the emendation, and the major versions render the word as "sea."[15] Further, the four vignettes that follow in vv. 4-32 can be shown to reflect the directions referred to in v. 3.

4-9 The first vignette recounts the story of a group of wanderers who lose their way in the *wilderness, a wasteland* place where there is no *city.* East of Palestine lies a vast desert that separates it from the eastern side of the Fertile Crescent, Mesopotamia. Few travelers in the ancient Near East dared any attempt to traverse this terrain. They followed the established trade routes: the "Way of the Sea," which led from Egypt to Mesopotamia north along the coast of Palestine, east across the valley of Jezreel, north across Syria, and then south along the Euphrates River; or the "King's Highway," which ran east of the Jordan River, north through Damascus into Syria, and then south along the Euphrates.

The wanderers described in vv. 4-9 hunger and thirst; their *inmost being* is *faint.* They cry out to God, and God causes *their path to be a straight path,* leading them out of the wilderness to a place of *habitation,* an oasis, with wells of water and food to eat.

In v. 8, the common refrain, an expression of thanks, is first sung:

Let God's *hesed* one give thanks to the LORD
For his wondrous works for the children of humanity.

The refrain echoes the opening words of the psalm (v. 1) and maintains the focus of the psalm — thanks to the God who has delivered the people and gathered them together from all the lands.

15. LXX, Peshitta, and Vulg.

Following the refrain of v. 8, the psalmist offers the reason that God's *hesed* one will give praise to the Lord. Verse 9 begins with the Hebrew word *kî,* called by grammarians a causal conjunction. God is worthy of thanks because *(kî)* God has satisfied the thirsting and hungering of the wanderers.

10-16 The second vignette speaks of people *dwelling in darkness and the shadow of death.* Following the four compass directions of v. 3, the west is the location of this group of people. The west is the place where the sun sets, the deathly place of darkness in which the sun dies every night as it makes its journey over the earthly realm. Psalm 19 references the daily journey of the sun through the heavens:

> For the sun, he has set a tent in the heavens,
>   and it goes forth — like a bridegroom from his wedding chamber,
>   it rejoices — like a strong man running a course.
> From the end of the heavens it goes forth,
>   along its circuit to the end.
> There is nothing hidden from its heat. (19:4b-6)

Like the ones wandering lost in the wilderness, *the ones dwelling in darkness* cry out to God, and God leads them *out from the darkness and the shadow of death* and tears to pieces *their bonds* (perhaps prisoners shackled and sent to dwell in places of darkness — caves or underground storerooms). They reemerge in the light with the coming of day, just as the sun reemerges from its deathly place of darkness each morning. They too can offer an expression of thanks (v. 15). Why? The *kî* of v. 16 states that the people can give thanks to God because God *has shattered the doors of bronze* and *broken into pieces* the *bars of iron.*

17-22 The third vignette speaks of *ones who are* sick *because of their transgressions,* [who] *because of their guilt are afflicted.* The word *sick* (from the Hebrew root *'āwal*) actually means "foolish ones." The people of the ancient Near East associated sickness with foolishness or sin and understood it as God's punishment for both foolishness and sin (see Pss. 32:1-5; 38:3, 5). The prophets often depict the north, the third direction mentioned in 107:3, as the direction from which the punishment of God came to the ancient Israelites. The prophet Jeremiah saw "a boiling pot, tilted away from the north," of which God said, "out of the north disaster shall break out on all the inhabitants of the land" (Jer. 1:13-14). In Ezekiel 9, God summons the executioners of Jerusalem, and they "came from the direction of the upper gate, which faces north" (Ezek. 9:2).[16]

In the midst of their oppression, the ones who are *sick* cry out to the

16. See also Jer. 47:2; 50:41-42.

Lord, who sends comforting words and rescues them from the pits. But after the expression of thanks in v. 21, we find no *kî,* no "causal clause." Rather, the ones whom God rescues offer *sacrifices of thanks (tôḏâ)* and *recount* God's *deeds with shouts of joy.*[17] When thank sacrifices were offered to God, the priests and the worshippers shared in a communal meal of gratitude for God's goodness. Thus those who had abhorred food and arrived at the gates of death taste life-giving nourishment once again.

23-32 The last vignette tells the story of *the ones going down to the sea in ships, doing business on the great waters. The sea* is the fourth direction mentioned in v. 3 and represented another real threat in the ancient Near East. Merchant ships sailing out of the Phoenician ports across the Mediterranean Sea often encountered difficulties in its unpredictable waters. Verses 25-29 depict God as the ruler of the sea, able to command its waters to do his bidding.[18] A storm on the waters (vv. 25-27) leads the sailors to cry out to God (v. 28). God then calms the waters and gives the sailors *rest in the haven of their pleasure* (v. 30).

Verse 31 contains the expected expression of thanks that each group has offered in Psalm 107. And as with the ones who were *sick,* the rescued sailors do not state a reason for giving thanks to God (there is no *kî* here). Instead, they *exalt* God *in the assembly of the people,* and *in the dwelling place of the elders they will glorify him* (v. 32).

33-42 The final verses of Psalm 107, which proclaim that the sovereign God can provide the people with all of their needs, appear to be a separate composition added to the psalm at some point in its transmission history. Gerstenberger points out, however, the many ties of this portion of the psalm to vv. 4-9, the story of wanderers in a desert waste. In vv. 33-35, the psalmist proclaims that God has the power to turn habitable land into barrenness and desert into rich farmland. In vv. 36-38, the Lord makes it possible for the hungry to *dwell* safely in the land and establish a city; to sow *fields, plant vineyards,* and gather a harvest; and to have children and increase their *cattle.* The Lord pours *contempt on rulers* who might oppress the people (vv. 39-40). The future of *the upright* is secured, and the wicked are left speechless (v. 42).

Therefore, all those redeemed by the Lord will say, *Give thanks to the* L*ORD*, *for he is good; for his* hesed *is for all time.*

43 Psalm 107 ends with these words:

17. Gerstenberger reminds us, "To offer a sacrifice of gratitude after being saved was an age-old religious obligation in the ancient Near East and in other cultures" (see Pss. 66 and 116); *Psalms: Part 2,* p. 252.

18. For other depictions of God's rule over the waters of the seas, see Pss. 29:3-4; 65:7; 89:9-10; 95:5.

> Whoever is wise will hear these things,
> And the *hesed* ones of the LORD will attend.

These words echo the end of the book of Hosea:

> The one who is wise understands these things;
> the one who is discerning knows them. (Hos. 14:9a)

The singer of Psalm 107 admonishes worshippers to ponder and attend to the words of the psalm. The Israelites returning from exile in Babylon and repopulating the land of Israel had much to learn about being the people of God in a new life situation. They would require a generous helping of God's *hesed* and wisdom.

We may never find ourselves literally wandering in a desert wasteland, forced to dwell in a place of deep darkness, sick to the point of death, or caught in a tumultuous storm at sea. But each of us have or will face those times when we need desperately the redeeming hand of God. Psalm 107 provides a model for how to handle those times: recognize the situation you are in; cry out to God and tell God what you need; accept the deliverance that God brings; and then give thanks to God. And in the end, remember that God — not any earthly strength or power — can provide a "habitable" place for us and allow us to live the good life that God has given to us.

NANCY DECLAISSÉ-WALFORD

Psalm 108: I Will Give Thanks to You among the Peoples

Psalm 108 is constructed of portions of two psalms found in Book Two of the Psalter: Psalms 57:7-11 (vv. 1-5) and 60:5-12 (vv. 6-13). We, therefore, might characterize Psalm 108 as a hybrid, a joining together of two separate psalmic compositions. We further observe that Psalms 57 and 60 are two of the thirteen psalms in the Psalter whose superscriptions recall specific historical events in the life of David. Psalm 57's superscription is:

> To the leader. *Al-tasheth.* A Davidic miktam when he was fleeing from Saul in the cave.

Psalm 60's superscription reads:

> To the leader. On *shushan eduth.* A Davidic miktam for teaching when he fought Aram-naharaim and Aram-ṣobah and Joab returned and killed twelve thousand Edomites in the Valley of Salt.

Scholars disagree about the origin of the composition of Psalm 108. The meaning of its "combination . . . of two completely different pieces" escapes Kraus.[1] So he offers no commentary on Psalm 108, instead referring readers to his analysis of individual verses in Psalms 57 and 60. Allen, on the other hand, explains that

> a new situation prompted the re-use of the second half of Ps 60. . . (and) the second half of Ps 57. . . . The combination of earlier psalms illustrates the vitality of older scriptures as they were appropriated and applied to new situations in the experience of God's people.[2]

We will follow Allen's lead and examine Psalm 108 in its updated context in Book Five of the Psalter.

Psalm 108 is classified as a community lament since it has the usual elements of a lament psalm.[3] We may outline its structure as follows:

> Invocation and prayer of thanks for deliverance (vv. 1-4)
> Petition to God (vv. 5-6)
> Divine assurance of deliverance (vv. 7-9)
> Prayer of inquiry to God (vv. 10-11)
> Petition to God (v. 12)
> Expression of trust and praise to God (v. 13)

1. *Psalms 60–150,* p. 333.
2. *Psalms 101–150,* pp. 69-70. See also Gerstenberger, *Psalms: Part 2,* p. 255.
3. For the structural elements of a lament psalm, see the Introduction.

A song. A Davidic psalm.[4]

1 *Steadfast is my heart, O God;*[5]
I will sing and make music
even more,[6] *my glory!*
2 *Awake, O harp and lyre!*
I will awaken the dawn.
3 *I will give thanks to you among the peoples, O LORD,*
and I will make music to you among the nations.[7]
4 *For great above the heavens is your* hesed,
and as far as the vault of heaven is your faithfulness.

5 *Be exalted above the heavens, O God,*
for over all the earth is your glory.
6 *In order that your beloved ones will be rescued,*
save with your right hand and answer me.

7 *God has spoken in his holiness:*
"I will triumph; I will divide Shechem,
and the valley of Succoth I will measure out.
8 *To me is Gilead, to me is Manasseh;*
Ephraim is the protection of my head;
Judah is my scepter.
9 *Moab is my washing vessel;*
upon Edom I will cast my sandal;
over Philistia I will shout with joy."

10 *Who will lead me to a fortified city?*
Who will guide me[8] *as far as Edom?*
11 *Have you not, O God, rejected us?*
for you do not go forth, O God, with our armies.

4. Many translators and commentators attempt to harmonize Ps. 108 with its parallel verses in Pss. 57 and 60. We will not follow the suggested emendations except in those instances where no sense can be made of the Hebrew of Ps. 108.

5. A few Hebrew manuscripts and LXX and Syr repeat the phrase *steadfast is my heart,* in order to harmonize this verse with Ps. 57:7.

6. LXX renders this word as *en* ("in"). Ps. 57:8 has *ʿûrâ* ("awake").

7. We have followed the emendation of *BHS* and, as with the same phenomenon in Ps. 44:14, removed the *maqqēp̱* from this word, thereby rendering it *balᵉʾummîm (among the nations).*

8. It is best to read this verb as imperfect and explain the missing initial *yôd* as a case of haplography with the previous word.

12 *Come to us as a helper against the oppressor,*
for worthless is the assistance of humanity.

13 *With God we will perform strong deeds,*
and he, he will crush our oppressors.

1-4 The psalm opens with an individual singer addressing God with words of confidence stating that the singer will *give thanks* and *make music* to God in celebration of God's *hesed*-ness and *faithfulness.* The words *yāḏâ (give thanks)* at the beginning of v. 3 and *hesed* in v. 4 echo the introductory words and the refrains of Psalm 107:

> Give thanks to the Lord, for he is good,
> For his *hesed* is for all time. (107:1)
>
> Let God's *hesed* one give thanks to the Lord
> For his wondrous works for the children of humanity.
> (107:8, 15, 21, 31)

The celebration of God's *hesed* now includes *music* and melody-making on the *harp and lyre.* And the words of thanks are sung in such a manner that not only will the redeemed hear them (107:2), but the *nations* and the *peoples* as well.

5-6 In a petition to God, which joins v. 5 (= 57:11) with v. 6 (= 60:5), the psalm-singer admonishes God to *be exalted above the heavens* so that God's *beloved ones will be rescued.* The Hebrew word *yāḏîḏ* ("beloved") in v. 6 occurs only eight times in the Old Testament, and in other ancient Near Eastern contexts it seems to indicate a partner in an intimate love relationship, though not necessarily a sexual one.[9] What is most striking about the use of *yāḏîḏ* here is its phonemic likeness to the verb *yāḏâ (give thanks),* which the reader encounters repeatedly in Psalm 107 and in 108:3. Verse 3 begins with the word *ʾôḏ^{e}ḵā, I will give thanks to you,* and in v. 6 the reader finds *y^{e}ḏîḏêḵā,* your beloved ones. Is the psalmist suggesting that those who give thanks to God for deliverance (Psalm 107) and sing and make melody to God (Psalm 108) are God's *beloved ones?*

7-9 These verses are an oracle of assurance by God in answer to the petition of the psalmist in vv. 5-6. God is God over all *peoples* and all *nations* — *Shechem, Succoth, Gilead, Manasseh, Ephraim, Judah, Moab, Edom,* and *Philistia* — as the psalm-singer proclaims in v. 3.

The inclusion of the nation of *Edom,* which according to Genesis 36 descends from Jacob's twin brother Esau, in this litany of nations and peoples is particularly pertinent. The reader will recall that Book Five of the Psalter

9. LXX translates *yāḏîḏ* as *hoi agapētoi.*

reflects the period in the life of ancient Israel following the Babylonian exile of 587-538 B.C.E., a period of reconstruction and reconstitution, self-reflection and self-realization. The destruction of Jerusalem by the Babylonians in 587 was a watershed event in Israel's history, a dividing line between time past and time future. When the Jewish people were finally allowed by the Babylonians to return to Jerusalem, questions emerged. Who are we? How do we explain what has happened to us? What do we do now? How do we move forward? How do we explain what has happened to us? According to the book of Obadiah, Edom played a role in helping the Babylonians sack the temple and destroy Jerusalem:

> But you should not have gloated over your brother
> on the day of his misfortune;
> you should not have rejoiced over the people of Judah
> on the day of their ruin;
> you should not have boasted
> on the day of distress.
> You should not have entered the gate of my people
> on the day of their calamity;
> you should not have joined in the gloating over Judah's disaster
> on the day of his calamity;
> you should not have looted his goods
> on the day of his calamity. (Obad. 12-13)

Edom — the brother of Jacob! How do we explain what has happened to us? God assures the psalmist that he will *cast his sandal upon* — that is, possess (see Ruth 4:7) — *Edom,* the brother who turned against Israel in its time of distress. God says, *"I will triumph. . . . I will measure out. . . . I will shout with joy"* (108:7, 9). Edom has wronged Israel and will pay the price.

Additionally, the three regions mentioned in v. 9 — *Moab, Edom,* and *Philistia* — are the same places mentioned in the Song of the Sea in Exodus 15:

> The peoples heard, they trembled;
> pangs seized the inhabitants of Philistia.
> Then the chiefs of Edom were dismayed;
> trembling seized the leaders of Moab;
> all the inhabitants of Canaan melted away. (Exod. 15:14-15)

After the Babylonian exile, the people returned to the land and settled in it, just as they had settled in the land at the end of the exodus. In that previous time, God defeated the enemies who could have denied them possession of the land; in this new time, God can and will do the same.

10-11 Verses 10-11 are the complaint portion of the psalm. It begins with the voice of the individual psalmist (v. 10) and ends with the voice of the community of faith (v. 11). The psalmist has voiced an expression of confidence (vv. 1-4), a petition (vv. 5-6), and has received a divine oracle of assurance (vv. 7-9). But what prompted the psalmist to cry out to God in the first place? What event or situation in life led to the words of petition in vv. 5 and 6? The psalmist asks in v. 10:

> Who will lead me to a fortified city?
> Who will guide me as far as Edom?

In v. 11 we hear for the first time the voice of the community of faith suggesting that God has *rejected* the people because God has not gone out before them in battle. What would prompt such words? Recall the historical situation in which the psalm-singers find themselves. Within living memory, Babylon had destroyed Jerusalem and taken the people into exile: *Have you not, O God, rejected us?* (v. 11).

12 A simple petition follows the complaint of vv. 10-11: *Come to us as a helper against the oppressor.* The word *helper* (*ʿezrâ*) derives from the verbal root *ʿāzar* ("to help, to free, to come to help"), the same root behind the similar word in Gen. 2:18:

> Then the LORD God said, "It is not good that the human *(hāʾāḏām)* should be alone; I will make him a helper *(ʿēzer)* as his partner."

The noun *ʿēzer* occurs some sixty-five times in the Old Testament, in most cases refering to the majestic "help" of God in some sort of military situation (Exod. 18:4; Deut. 33:26; Ps. 33:20). In short, *ʿēzer* in the Hebrew Bible conveys the idea of a "help" that is a strong presence, an aid without which humankind would be unprotected and vulnerable to all sorts of unsettling situations.

The end of the petition in v. 12 explains the reason that the community of worshippers cries out to God: *for worthless is the assistance of humanity.* The word translated *humanity* here is *ʾāḏām,* the same word used in the refrains of Psalm 107:

> Let God's *hesed* one give thanks to the LORD
> For his wondrous works for the children of humanity *(ʾādām).*
> (vv. 8, 15, 21, 31)

God alone can perform wondrous works among humanity; therefore the gathered worshippers cry out for God's help against the *oppressor.* The alternative — reliance on human aid — is of no use.

13 The psalm concludes with a two-part expression of trust. First, the worshippers affirm that *with God we will perform strong deeds,* and then they state that God *will crush our oppressors.* The depiction is of people and God in partnership. The people must sing, make music, give thanks, and exalt the Lord (vv. 1, 3, 5). And with God's help *('ezrâ),* they *will perform strong deeds.* God as helper *('ezrâ)* will *triumph, measure out,* and *shout with joy* over the oppressors of Israel (vv. 7, 9). God will provide, in God's own time and in God's own place.

The Israelites who returned to Jerusalem in 538 after the Babylonian exile realized that what had happened to them was wholly dependent on the *hesed* (the covenant love) of their God. Their repatriation was undeserved; it was a gift from God, not earned through the efforts of humanity *('āḏām).* The singers of Psalm 108 could do nothing more than give thanks and learn to rely on their good God. McCann writes, "Psalm 108 teaches us that the people of God never live beyond trouble and the need for God's help."[10] May believers in today's times and places have the insight and the grace to follow in the footsteps of the singers of Psalm 108 by learning to give thanks and by relying on God.

NANCY DECLAISSÉ-WALFORD

10. "The Book of Psalms," p. 1122.

Psalm 109: O God of My Praise, Do Not Be Silent

Psalm 109 is classified as an individual lament, in which the psalmist invokes the wrath of God upon a group of foes. The language and message of the psalm place it within a special category of lament psalms called "imprecatory psalms." "Imprecatory" comes from the Latin word *imprecari,* meaning "to pray to, to invoke." Many psalms of lament contain imprecatory language in the psalmists' petitions to God (see Pss. 17:13; 31:17; 35:4; 59:11-13; 70:2-3). But in a few psalms the imprecatory tone is very apparent: Psalms 12, 58, 83, 137, 139.[1] Psalm 109's imprecatory language is vivid and abundant. In vv. 10-11, we read:

> Let his children continuously roam about and beg;
> let them offer entreaties from their desolate ruins.
> Let a lender lay a snare for all that belongs to him,
> and let strangers treat his possessions with contempt.

Gerstenberger writes, "This clear-cut individual complaint voices overwhelming disgust for and aggression against enemies. There is no other example of individual complaint with an equal share of imprecative and ill-wishing affirmations."[2]

Because of its caustic language, Psalm 109 is virtually ignored by the Christian church. It is not included in lectionary readings; its only reference in the New Testament is in Peter's sermon in Acts 1. There Peter uses the imprecatory words of Ps. 109:8 in speaking about the fate of Judas Iscariot:

> Let another take his position. . . . (Acts 1:20)

How then shall we read and appropriate the harsh words of this psalm? Can we reconcile the language and tone of Psalm 109 with the New Testament's words to love our enemies, turn the other cheek, and pray for those who persecute us? How does the psalm contribute to the "story" of Book Five of the Psalter? Its structure is as follows:

> Complaint against the adversaries (vv. 1-5)
> Petition against the adversaries (vv. 6-19)
> Personal complaint and petition (vv. 20-29)
> Expressions of trust and praise (vv. 30-31)

1. See Erich Zenger, *A God of Vengeance? Understanding the Psalms of Divine Wrath* (trans. Linda M. Maloney; Louisville: Westminster John Knox, 1996).

2. *Psalms: Part 2,* p. 257.

To the leader. A Davidic psalm.

1 *O God of my praise, do not be silent.*
2 *For a wicked mouth and the mouth of the deceiver have opened against me;*
they have spoken to me with a tongue of falsehood.
3 *Words of hatred have surrounded me;*
they fight against me without cause.
4 *In return for my love, they accuse me,*
and I, I prayed for them![3]
5 *They place upon me maliciousness in return for good,*
and hatred in return for my love.

6 *Appoint against him wickedness,*
and let an adversary stand against his right hand.
7 *When he is judged, let wickedness go forth,*
and let his prayer become sin.
8 *Let his days be few;*
let another take his position.
9 *Let his children become orphans,*
and his wives widows.
10 *Let his children continuously roam about and beg;*
let them offer entreaties from their desolate ruins.
11 *Let a lender lay a snare for all that belongs to him,*
and let strangers treat his possessions with contempt.
12 *Let there be for him no one who extends* hesed,
and let there be one who extends favor to his orphans.
13 *Let his posterity be cut off;*
in the next generation, let their names be wiped out.
14 *Let the guilt of his ancestors be remembered to the* Lord,
and let the sin of his mother not be wiped out.
15 *Let them be in the presence of the* Lord *continually,*
and let God cut off their memory from the land.
16 *Because he did not remember acts of* hesed,
and he pursued an oppressed and needy person
and one grieved of heart in order to kill.[4]
17 *He loved condemnation; and it entered him.*
There was no pleasure in blessing; and it was far from him.

3. MT has *waʾ*^{a}*nî ṯ*^{e}*pillâ* ("and I was a pray-er"). LXX (along with Syr and Targ) has *proseuchomēn* ("and I, I prayed"). Syr adds *ʿljhwn* ("for them").

4. MT has *l*^{e}*môṯēṯ (in order to kill).* Syr has *lmwtʾ*, suggesting an emendation to *lammāweṯ* ("to the death").

18 *He clothed himself with condemnation as if it was his coat.*
It entered like water into the midst of his body,
And like oil in his bones.
19 *Let it be to him like a garment that he puts on;*
like a belt continually he will bind it around himself.

20 *This is the doings of my adversaries rather than the* Lord,
the ones speaking maliciously concerning my inmost being.
21 *And so you, O* Lord, *do with me according to your name.*
Because of the goodness of your hesed, *deliver me.*
22 *For I am oppressed and needy,*
and my heart is pierced within my very being.
23 *Like a shadow when it stretches out, I am gone;*
I have been shaken off like the locust.
24 *My knees have stumbled from fasting,*
and my flesh has become lean, without fat.
25 *I, I have become an object of reproach to them;*
they see me; they shake their head.
26 *Assist me, O* Lord *my God.*
Help me according to your hesed.
27 *And they will know that this is your hand.*
You, O Lord, *have done it.*
28 *Let them condemn; but you, you will bless.*
They have risen up, but let them be ashamed,
and let your servant be glad.
29 *Let the ones adverse to me clothe themselves with reproach,*
and let them put on shame as if it were a garment.

30 *I will give thanks to the* Lord *exceedingly with my mouth,*
and in the midst of the multitude I will praise him.
31 *For he stands at the right hand of the needy*
in order to save from the judging ones his inmost being.

1-5 The opening verses of the psalm set the tone for what follows. A *wicked mouth,* a *mouth of a deceiver,* and a *tongue of falsehood* have opened against the psalmist, uttering *words of hatred (śin'â),* accusation *(śāṭān),* and *maliciousness (rā'â),* despite the fact that the psalmist loves and prays for them.

6-19 In the next section of the psalm, words of imprecation are piled one on top of the other. A major issue in the reading of Psalm 109 is that of identifying the voices in the psalm. Are the imprecatory words recited in vv. 6-19 the words of the pray-er against a group of foes, or are they a direct quotation by the pray-er of the words of the foes? Is the psalmist imprecating the judgment of God upon the foes? Or is the psalmist recounting to God the unjust words spoken by the foes?

If we understand vv. 6-19 as the quoted words of the foes, then v. 5's *They place upon me maliciousness in return for good, and hatred in return for my love* is an introduction to their indictment of the psalmist. The NRSV, in fact, adds "They say," to the text at the beginning of v. 6 in order to clearly delineate that the words of vv. 6-19 are the words not of the psalmist, but of the psalmist's foes.

If, on the other hand, we read vv. 6-19 as the words of the psalmist against the foes, then we must understand the psalmist's use of singular nouns and verbs in these verses as a method used to emphasize and personalize the words of indictment. The psalmist, then, is the only speaker in the psalm, and the psalmist formulates the words of vv. 6-19. In this scenario, the imprecatory tone of the psalm seems far more intense.

But is it? Whether the words of vv. 6-19 are those of the foes or those of the psalmist, the imprecation ends with *This is the doings of my adversaries* in v. 20. Are *the doings* the words of the foes or the actions of the foes? The text of Psalm 109 contains no clear answer to the question; it is ambiguous. Perhaps the reader of the psalm should not try to answer the question, but instead simply participate in the ambiguity of the psalm.

The psalmist comes before the community of gathered worshippers and presents a case of injustice before God. Are vv. 6-19 the words of the foes, quoted by the psalmist as hurtful words of condemnation but hurled back at the foes as words of condemnation against them? Or are the foes part of the community of gathered worshippers and present when the one unjustly accused comes before the Lord? Could we picture the psalmist and the foe standing together in the presence of the gathered community, uttering the words in unison?

> Appoint against him wickedness,
>   and let an adversary stand against his right hand.
> When he is judged, let wickedness go forth,
>   and let his prayer become sin. (vv. 6-7)

The Hebrew word translated *adversary* here is *śāṭān*. It is translated by NRSV, NIV, NJPS, and NASB as "an accuser," but NASB adds a note giving alternate readings as "an adversary" or "Satan." The word occurs twenty-seven times in the Old Testament and is used of human adversaries as well as "divine" adversaries. The word almost always has the definite article attached, indicating a descriptive noun rather than a proper name. In 1 Sam. 29:4, the Philistines fear that David might become "an adversary" to them in battle if he is allowed to fight alongside them. In 1 Kgs. 11:14,

Hadad the Edomite is described an "an adversary" whom God raised up against Solomon.

In the prologue to the book of Job and in Zechariah 3, "the adversary" *(haśśāṭān)* is one of the "children of God" *(bᵉnê ʾᵉlōhîm)* who present themselves before the Lord and whose task seems to be to seek out and accuse people who are not faithful to God. The word is not used as a proper name in either of these passages, but rather as a descriptor of one of the divine beings *(bᵉnê ʾᵉlōhîm)*. The only instance in the Old Testament where *śāṭān* could be understood as a proper name is in 1 Chr. 21:1. Here the reader is told, "*śāṭān* stood up against Israel, and incited David to count the people of Israel." Interestingly, the same story in 2 Sam. 24:1 reports that "the LORD incited David to count the people." It is entirely appropriate, then to translate *śāṭān* in 1 Chr. 21:1 as "Satan" or as "an adversary," with the same understanding of the adversary in Job and Zechariah.

Only in the intertestamental and New Testament periods is the term used as a proper name, denoting a being separate from and in absolute opposition to God and the believing community.

Psalm 109 continues with the words of the foe and/or the one being accused. The wish of the speaker is that judgment come swiftly and severely upon the other.

> Let his days be few;
> let another take his position.
> Let his children become orphans,
> and his wives widows. (vv. 8-9)

These verses contain a word familiar to the readers of Book Five of the Psalter — *hesed:*

> Let there be for him no one who extends *hesed* (v. 12)

> Because he did not remember acts of *hesed* (v. 16)

Hesed, the commitment of covenant relationship entered into by God with ancient Israel and a recurring theme of Psalms 107 and 108, is crucial in the indictment of the adversary *(śāṭān)* who is accusing the psalmist in Psalm 109. Rather than reflecting the kindness that is associated with the *hesed* of God, the foe pursues the *oppressed,* the *needy,* and the *grieved of heart in order to kill* them (v. 16). The foe also loves the act of condemnation, clothing the self in it *like a garment* (vv. 17-19).

20-29 *This is the doings of my adversaries,* says the psalmist (v. 20). The psalmist, in a moment of complete capitulation, implores the Lord to *do with me according to your name* (v. 21), followed by:

> Because of the goodness of your *hesed,* deliver me.
> For I am oppressed and needy,
> and my heart is pierced within my very being. (vv. 21b-22)

The words of vv. 21b-22 echo the accusatory words of v. 16:

> Because he did not remember acts of *hesed,*
> and he pursued an oppressed and needy person
> and one grieved of heart in order to kill.

In a subtle literary twist, the imprecatory words of v. 16 are turned squarely upon the foe in vv. 21-22.

In like manner, the condemnation with which the foe *clothed* the self in vv. 17-19 becomes the catalyst for a blessing of God in vv. 28-29. In vv. 18-19, we read:

> He clothed himself with condemnation as if it was his coat.
> It entered like water into the midst of his body,
> And like oil in his bones.
> Let it be to him like a garment that he puts on;
> like a belt continually he will bind it around himself.

But, in vv. 28-29, the psalmist says:

> Let them condemn; but you, you will bless.
> They have risen up, but let them be ashamed,
> and let your servant be glad.
> Let the ones adverse to me clothe themselves with reproach,
> and let them put on shame as if it were a garment.

The accusing words of vv. 6-19 are transformed in vv. 20-29 into words of encouragement for the psalmist.

30-31 The final verses of Psalm 109 are the "expression of trust" (v. 31) and "expression of praise and adoration" (v. 30) that are found in most lament psalms. The psalmist has lived through the dark night of adversity and has emerged on the other side, confident in the God who stands *at the right hand of the needy* (v. 31).

How then, indeed, shall we read and appropriate the harsh words of this psalm? How does the psalm contribute to the "story" of Book Five of the Psalter? This writer reads Psalm 109 as an imprecatory psalm, calling on God to condemn the foe and vindicate the psalmist. Is such language permissible in the context of the biblical text? The overwhelming consensus seems to be "Yes; by all means, yes." People are accused unjustly; goodness is sometimes rewarded with bad; justice is not always served. How should the people of

God respond? With silence? With indifference? With long-suffering? Yes — sometimes. And yet at other times, God calls upon us to speak out, to protest, and to say, "This is not right!"

When the Israelites returned from exile in Babylon in 538 B.C.E., they encountered many adversaries and obstacles in their attempts to rebuild their lives and their community of faith. The prophetic and priestly voices reminded them that they must uphold and honor the covenant relationship *(hesed)* that God had established with their ancestors. And yet they encountered those who did not know and uphold that *hesed* — *He did not remember acts of* hesed, *and he pursued an oppressed and needy person and one grieved of heart in order to kill* (v. 16). Thus the psalmist calls upon God to remember God's *hesed* and help the psalmist against the adversary — according to God's *hesed* (v. 26).

In the act of protesting vehemently to God, the psalmist points out the acts of violence that so often accompany injustice and unexplainable suffering. The psalmist calls out to God to prosecute and condemn the adversary, thereby obviating the need of the psalmist to take matters into his own hands. McCann writes this of Psalm 109:

> It suggests that evil, injustice, and oppression must be confronted, opposed, hated because God hates them. From this perspective, the psalmist's desire for vengeance amounts to a desire for justice and righteousness in self and society. . . . The anger is expressed, but it is expressed in prayer and thereby submitted to God. . . . Thus this vehement, violent sounding prayer is, in fact, an act of non-violence.[5]

We must speak out against injustice, inequality, and acts of violence. But the words of Psalm 109 teach us that anger and action exist in a delicate dance. When and to what extent do we act ourselves, and what do we commit to the safekeeping of the God of all creation? *O God of my praise, do not be silent!*[6]

NANCY DECLAISSÉ-WALFORD

5. "The Book of Psalms," p. 1127.
6. For further discussion, see the commentary for Ps. 129.

Psalm 110: Sit at My Right Hand

The origins of Psalm 110 may most likely be found within the monarchic period of ancient Israel's history (ca. 900-586 B.C.E.). It is classified as a royal psalm, words most likely spoken during an enthronement ceremony for one of ancient Israel's kings.[1] We may outline its brief content as follows:

The first words to the king (vv. 1-3)
  Introductory words (v. 1a)
  The words of the Lord (v. 1b)
  The realization of the words (vv. 2-3)
The second words to the king (vv. 4-7)
  Introductory words (v. 4a)
  The words of the Lord (v. 4b)
  The realization of the words (vv. 5-7)

A Davidic psalm.

1 *An oracle of the LORD to my lord,*
"Sit at my right hand
until I place your enemies
as a footstool for your feet."
2 *The scepter of your power*
the LORD sends forth from Zion.
3 *Your people offer themselves willingly*
on the day of your strength.
In the splendor of holiness[2]
from the womb of the sunrise
to you is the dew of your childhood.[3]

1. The other royal psalms in the Hebrew Psalter are Pss. 2, 18, 20, 21, 45, 72, 89, 101, 132, and 144.

2. In the words of Kraus, "the text is in disarray" (see *Psalms 60–150,* p. 344). This translator has attempted to honor the integrity of MT, although with some very convincing evidence to the contrary. NRSV translates this phrase as "on the holy mountains," a rendering which requires only a minor emendation of MT and for which there is ample attestation. MT reads *bᵉhaḏrê qōḏeš* ("in the splendor of holiness"). NRSV accepts the reading of the text attested in a number of Greek and Hebrew manuscripts: *bᵉharrê qōḏeš* ("in/on the mountains of holiness").

3. For two good discussions of the meaning of the last half of v. 3, see William P. Brown, "A Royal Performance: Critical Notes on Psalm 110:3aγ-b," *JBL* 117 (1998) 93-96; and Gary A. Rendsburg, "Psalm cx 3b," *VT* 49 (1999) 438-553.

4 *The LORD has sworn*
and will not change his mind:
"You are a priest for all time
because of Melchizedek."
5 *My Lord is at your right hand;*
in the day of his anger he will shatter kings.
6 *He will judge between the nations,*
filling them with corpses.
He will shatter the leaders
over the great land.
7 *From the river by the pathway he will drink;*
then he will lift up his head.

1a The words *an oracle of the LORD (nᵉʾum YHWH)* are usually translated "says the LORD." The origin of the word *nᵉʾum* is not certain, but it most likely means "to utter" or "to speak," which accounts for its usual translation. Of the 367 occurrences of the word in the Hebrew Bible, 365 times are in connection with utterances of God, and so *oracle,* which means "divine announcement," may be the most fitting translation. *Nᵉʾum YHWH* — "says the LORD" — is most often placed at the ends of prophetic speeches in the Old Testament.[4] Only in Psalm 110 are the words placed at the speech's beginning. Is the psalm-singer announcing in no uncertain terms that the words to follow are prophetic words and should be heeded as such? The oracle is directed to *my lord (ʾᵃḏōnî),*[5] a term used commonly in the Hebrew Bible to address a human who is superior in some way to oneself.

1b The *oracle of the Lord,* addressed by the prophet/psalmist to *my lord,* contains words most likely used at an enthronement ceremony of an ancient Israelite king. The concept of the monarch sitting at the *right hand* of the deity was common throughout the ancient Near East.[6] The right hand was viewed as a place of privilege and distinction, a place that in Psalm 110 comes with the promise of defeat of enemies.

2-3 In v. 2, the prophet/psalmist assures the new monarch that the Lord has sent the *scepter,* the symbol of reigning power, *from Zion.* Kraus writes,

4. See, e.g., Isa. 3:15; 31:9; 59:20; Jer. 4:17; 22:16; Ezek. 12:25; Amos 3:15; Hag. 1:13.

5. The word *ʾᵃḏōnî* is used in the Hebrew Bible in reference to a superior human being, while the word *ʾᵃḏōnāy* is used when addressing God. Both words are translated with the same English words, but the former word is translated using a lower case letter ("my lord"), while the latter is translated using the upper case ("my Lord").

6. See John W. Hilber, "Psalm CX in the Light of Assyrian Prophecies," *VT* 53 (2003) 353-66.

"Under the outstretched scepter the land becomes the area of the king's authority," even "in the midst of enemies" (v. 1b).[7]

Verse 3 is full of textual difficulties, rendering a number of disputed translations. Its words appear to be an elevated description of the newly-enthroned monarch, obeyed *willingly* by the people and endowed with *strength* and stamina — *the dew of your childhood* — which emanate from *the splendor of holiness.*

4a The introductory words of the second oracle use strong language that demonstrates God's commitment to the new king. *The LORD has sworn (nišbaʿ) and will not change his mind (lōʾ yinnāḥēm).* The verb *šaḇaʿ* ("swear") often is used by God in speeches concerning the promise of land and posterity made to the ancestors of ancient Israel (Gen. 26:3; Exod. 13:5; 32:13; Num. 11:12; Deut. 1:8). References to God "changing God's mind" *(nāḥām)* occur a number of times in the text of the Old Testament. In the Genesis 6 flood narrative, we read: "And God changed his mind about having made humanity upon earth, and he was grieved to his heart" (6:6). In Exodus 32, the story of the golden calf, God resolves to destroy the Israelites whom he had brought out of Egypt. But Moses beseeches God to reconsider, and we read in v. 14, "And the LORD changed his mind about the disaster that he planned to bring on his people." According to Ps. 110:4, God has *sworn,* just as he swore to the ancestors, and God *will not change his mind,* although he has changed his mind in the past.

4b This portion of v. 4 is much discussed and variously interpreted. We will begin with a linguistic/historical analysis. God says to the king, *"You are a priest for all time because of Melchizedek."* The word translated here as *for all time (lᵉʿôlām)* is usually translated "forever." In the context of the Old Testament, however, the word is best understood as present and temporal *(for all time)* rather than as atemporal ("forever"). The words translated here as *because of* are most often translated as "according to/in the order of." The Hebrew phrase consists of the preposition *ʿal,* which means "upon" or "on," and the noun *diḇrāṯî,* which means "cause" or "reason." Therefore, the best translation for the two words is something like "upon the cause of" or "on the reason of." *Because of Melchizedek,* the king who is being enthroned in Jerusalem in Psalm 110 is both king and priest. Mays writes, "The appointment to priestly status is part of the royal installation. In the traditions of kingship observed in Canaan, the king was the principal mediator between God and people."[8]

That brings us to the next question. Who is Melchizedek? Melchizedek is mentioned in only two places in the Old Testament: Gen. 14:18-20 and Ps.

7. *Psalms 60–150,* p. 349.
8. *Psalms,* p. 351.

110:4. In Genesis 14, Melchizedek is described as king of Salem and "priest of the God Most High." Abram (Abraham) appears before Melchizedek after a military confrontation against a coalition of Canaanite kings, and Melchizedek blesses him with these words:

> Blessed be Abram by God Most High,
> maker of heaven and earth;
> and blessed be God Most High,
> who has delivered your enemies into your hand! (Gen. 14:19-20)

"Salem" is most likely the city of Jerusalem, the territory of the Jebusites, which David captured and made his capital in 2 Sam. 5:6-9.[9] Melchizedek recognizes the God of Abraham in Genesis 14. Salem is now the city in which the God of the Israelites dwells. Is the psalmist in Psalm 110 reminding the people — all of the people of the land — that the Israelite king enthroned in Jerusalem is ruler over all? There can be no pretenders to the throne.

5-7 The king enthroned in Jerusalem is absolute ruler. Words of assurance are voiced in vv. 5-7. *My Lord" (*ʾ*ᵃd̲ōnāy) is at your right hand.* The reader will recall that similar words occurred in v. 1: *An oracle of the LORD to my lord (*ʾ*ᵃldōnî), "Sit at my right hand."* Three words are translated with the letters "l-o-r-d" in vv. 1 and 5, but they, in fact, represent three different Hebrew words. In v. 1, the word *LORD* translates the Hebrew *YHWH,* the divine name; *my lord* translates *ʾᵃd̲ōnî,* a term used to address a human being who is in some way superior to the speaker. Verse 5's *my Lord* translates the Hebrew word *ʾᵃd̲ōnāy,* used in the Old Testament only when addressing God. In v. 1, then, *the LORD* (YHWH) assures *my lord (*ʾ*ᵃd̲ōnî),* the king, of a favored position: *"Sit at my right hand."* In vv. 5-6, the psalmist/prophet assures the newly-enthroned king that *my Lord (*ʾ*ᵃd̲ōnāy)* will provide defense against enemies: *my Lord is at your right hand . . . he will judge between the nations . . . he will shatter the leaders.*

As a result, the king *will drink* from *the river* and *lift up his head.* A common method of defeating enemies in ancient Near Eastern warfare was to shut them up in their cities and deprive them of food and water. The promise made in vv. 5 and 6 assures the newly-crowned king that God will defend the king and the people so that life-giving water will not be cut off from Jerusalem.

Psalm 110 is a royal psalm, a psalm celebrating the enthronement of a king of God's choosing in Jerusalem. And its superscription ascribes it to David — David, the king of God's choosing. But the psalm is located in Book Five, that portion of the Psalter which, as we have seen, reflects the postexilic period of ancient Israel's history. In the postexilic period, Israel could not

9. In Ps. 76:2, "Salem" is used in poetic parallelism with "Zion" as a designation for Jerusalem, the dwelling place of God.

have a king, since they were vassals to the Persian, Greek, and then Roman Empires. So why a royal psalm here? Why a royal psalm of David?

In the postexilic period, ancient Israel was seeking a rationale for continued existence as a distinct people within the vast empires of which it found itself a part. The options for the community of faith were to subsume itself under the larger umbrella of Empire or to find a way to remain a separate entity within the empires to which it was subject. The people chose to find a way to remain a separate entity. They rebuilt their temple; they resumed their religious observances; they wrote down their history; and they pledged their loyalty to a leader. But the leader was not the imperial king. The leader — their sovereign — was their God, YHWH — the God of their ancestors: the God of Abraham and Sarah, of Rebekah and Isaac, of Jacob and Leah and Rachel.

David and his descendants had once been kings in Israel. The royal psalms like Psalm 110 recall those halcyon days. But it was not possible to return to those days. So Israel found new leadership, a new way to survive in the vast empire of which it was a part. The book of Psalms recounts that story of survival. And David plays a major role in the story. In Book Five of the Psalter, David, who was conspicuously absent in Books Three and Four,[10] makes a dramatic reappearance. If the people are to pledge allegiance to a new king, a king who is not David, then what better person to lead the acclamation than King David?

The writers of the New Testament quote Psalm 110 some fourteen times, more than any other psalm in the Psalter.[11] For them, the words of Psalm 110 were brought to life in the ministry of Christ — the ultimate priest and king over all people.

NANCY DECLAISSÉ-WALFORD

10. In Book Three, only one psalm is attributed, in its superscription, to David (Ps. 86); in Book Four, only two (Pss. 101, 103).

11. Matt. 22:44; Mark 14:62; 16:19; Luke 22:69; Acts 2:34-35; 7:55-56; Rom. 8:34; Eph. 1:20; Col. 3:1; Heb. 1:3, 13; 8:1; 10:12; 1 Pet. 3:22.

Psalm 111: The Memory of God's Wondrous Acts

Beginning with Psalm 111, the reader encounters a series of psalms that share a common introduction and/or refrain. Psalm 111, along with Psalms 112 and 113, opens with the words *hal*^{e}*lû yāh (yāh* is a shortened form of the divine name *YHWH).* Psalm 113 closes with the same words, as do Psalms 115–17. Only Psalm 114 in this series does not contain the characteristic opening or closing, but some scholars suggest that the closing *hal*^{e}*lû yāh* of Psalm 113 (v. 9) may actually belong to the beginning of Psalm 114.

Psalms 111 and 112 are alphabetic acrostics, as is the massive Psalm 119.[1] In addition, Psalms 111, 112, and 119 share a common theme of reverence for the torah, the instruction given by God to the ancient Israelites at Sinai. Between them lies a collection of psalms (Psalms 113–18) known as the "Egyptian Hallel Psalms," psalms that are recited during the Passover festival celebrated each spring in Jewish life. Passover celebrates the miraculous actions of God in delivering the Israelites from slavery in Egypt. The giving of the torah at Sinai was the centerpiece of the exodus/wilderness wandering experience. In the Psalter, then, a celebration of the torah (Psalms 111, 112, and 119) frames words of praise to God (Psalms 113–18) for deliverance and protection in the defining moment of ancient Israel's history.

Psalm 111 is a succinct and masterful acrostic. It consists of twenty-two cola (excluding v. 1a), each of which begins with a successive letter of the Hebrew alphabet. It is classified as an individual hymn of thanksgiving. In a mere seventy-two words, the psalmist summarizes the history of God's deliverance of ancient Israel in the following structure:

A vow to give thanks (v. 1)
The deeds of the Lord praised (vv. 2-4)
The deeds of the Lord described (vv. 5-9)
An introduction to wisdom (v. 10)

1 *Hallelujah.*
ʾĀlep — *I will give thanks to the* LORD *wholeheartedly*
Bêt — *in the council of the upright and in the assembly.*

Gîmel — 2 *Great are the deeds of the* LORD,
Dālet — *Sought out by all who delight in them.*
Hê — 3 *Majesty and splendor are his work,*
Wāw — *and his righteousness endures for all time.*
Zayin — 4 *A memorial he has made of his wondrous acts;*

1. For a detailed discussion of the acrostic form, see the commentary for Ps. 119.

Ḥêt *showing favor and merciful is the LORD.*

Ṭêt 5 *Food he has given to those who fear him;*
Yôd *He will remember for all time his covenant.*
Kāp 6 *The strength of his deeds he has made known to his people,*
Lāmed *in order to give them the inheritance of the nations.*
Mêm 7 *The deeds of his hands are faithful and just;*
Nûn *trustworthy are all of his precepts.*
Sāmek 8 *They are sustained throughout all time,*
'Ayin *to be done in faithfulness and uprightness.*
Pê 9 *Deliverance he has sent to his people;*
Ṣādê *he has commanded his covenant for all time.*
Qôp *Holy and reverent is his name.*

Rêš 10 *The beginning of wisdom is the reverence of the LORD;*
Śîn *a good understanding comes to all who do it.*[2]
Tāw *His praise endures for all time.*

1 Psalm 111 appears to be the words of an individual worshipper giving thanks to God in a public setting of worship — *the council of the upright* and *the assembly.* While some scholars suggest that these are two different groups of people, the first a small group that gathered around the worshipper and the second the entire congregation of worshippers, most make no distinction between the two.[3]

The words *I will give thanks to the LORD ('ôḏeh YHWH)* tie Psalm 111 to the preceding psalms of Book Five. In Psalm 107, the reader encounters the words "Give thanks to the LORD" in vv. 1, 8, 15, 21, and 31. They occur as well in Pss. 108:3 and 109:30.

2-4 The words of thanks by this individual worshipper are unusual, however, for they recount not an event of God's deliverance of the psalm-singer, but God's deliverance of the entire community. In the opening colon of three successive verses, the psalmist speaks of God's *deeds (ma'ᵃśîm), work (pō'al),* and *wondrous acts (nip̱lā'ôṯ).* Each colon is followed by a response or refrain, culminating in v. 4b's refrain *showing favor (ḥannûn) and merciful (raḥûm) is the LORD.* The words translated *showing favor,* from the Hebrew verbal root *ḥānan,* and *merciful,* from the verbal root *rāḥam,* are two of the self-declarative attributes of God given to Moses in Exod. 34:6, in which God

2. MT has a plural suffix attached to the plural participle, *'ōśêhem* ("all who do them"). LXX and Syr have a third singular suffix, *all who do it.*

3. For the various viewpoints, see Goulder, *The Psalms of the Return,* pp. 153-54; Kraus, *Psalms 60–150,* pp. 357-58; Allen, *Psalms 101–150,* pp. 90-92.

declares, according to the NRSV: "The LORD, the LORD, a God merciful *(raḥûm)* and gracious *(ḥannûn),* slow to anger, and abounding in steadfast love *(ḥesed).*" In Psalm 111, the word order is reversed ("merciful and showing favor" in Exodus 34; "showing favor and merciful" in Psalm 111) because of the constraints of the acrostic structure of the psalm.

5-9 In the verses that follow, the psalmist outlines, in brief descriptive phrases, the deeds, works, and wondrous acts of God. In v. 5, God gives *food (ṭerep̄),* a reference perhaps to the giving of the manna and quail in the wilderness (Exodus 16 and Numbers 11). Verse 6's *the inheritance of the nations (naḥ^a^lat̲ gôyim)* suggests God's giving of the promised land to the Israelites (Deuteronomy 6–7). The *precepts (piqqûd̲)* of vv. 7-8 are part of the torah, the instruction of God given at Sinai (see Ps. 119:27, 104, 173, etc.). And v. 9's reference to *deliverance* summarizes the actions of God in the exodus and wilderness wanderings.

Verse 9 concludes with the words *he has commanded his covenant for all time. Holy and reverent is his name.* God's *covenant (b^e^rît̲)* and God's *name (šēm)* are foundational traditions of ancient Israel. Upon these the community may depend for its future as the people of God.

10 Verse 10 admonishes those who hear Psalm 111 to heed wisdom's call to *reverence of the LORD.* In the summary words of v. 9, the psalmist describes God as *reverent (nôrā').* And the proper response of the worshipper in v. 10 is to "reverence the LORD *(yir'â YHWH),* Most translators and commentators render the Hebrew root *yārē'* in vv. 9 and 10, translated here as *reverent/ reverence,* as "fearsome/fear." "Fear" is a good translation of the word. But in today's culture, the idea of fear is usually connected with the basic human instincts to run, defend, or retaliate. The Hebrew root *yārē'* encompasses a larger meaning of "awe, reverent respect, honor." It appears in the Hebrew Bible as a synonym for "love" (*'āhab̲,* Deut. 10:12); "cling to" (*dāb̲aq,* Deut. 10:20); and "serve" (*'āb̲ad̲,* Deut. 6:13; Josh. 24:14). At its root, the word denotes obedience to the divine will. The result of "reverencing" the Lord is *a good understanding (śēk̲el ṭôb̲).* The wisdom words at the end of Psalm 111 link it incontrovertibly with Psalm 112.

Allen likens the words of Psalm 111 to Rom. 5:1-11. He writes:

> Psalm 111 glories in the present and permanent relevance of the ancient events of salvation. . . . Those events have a once-and-for-all value which the NT in turn attaches to their christological counterparts. . . . They are a window through which God's purposes for each generation of his people can be clearly discerned. They are a signpost pointing to his enduring care and claim.[4]

4. *Psalms 101–150,* p. 93.

Psalm 111

As believing communities recite and reverence the stories of the great deeds and wondrous acts of God performed on their behalf, they maintain and make ever-new their claim of being "the people of God."

Nancy deClaissé-Walford

Psalm 112: Our Response to God's Wondrous Acts

Psalm 112 is the second psalm in a group in Book Five known as the *halᵉlû yāh* psalms (Psalms 111–18). It is, like Psalm 111, a brief alphabetic acrostic, consisting of seventy-nine words (Psalm 111 consists of seventy-two words).[1] In addition, the two psalms share no less than eleven key terms and phrases: *yārēʾ* ("reverence, fear"); *ḥāp̄ēṣ* ("delight in"); *yᵉšārîm* ("upright ones"); *ṭôḇ* ("good"); *ḥannûn wᵉraḥûm* ("showing favor and merciful"); *mišpaṭ* ("just, judgment"); *zaḵār* ("remember"); *sāmûḵ* ("sustained, steady"); *nāṯan* ("give"); *lᵉʿôlām* ("for all time"). While Psalm 111 is classified as an individual hymn of thanksgiving, Psalm 112 is a wisdom psalm. Verse 10 of Psalm 111 acts as the bridge linking them: "The beginning of wisdom is the reverence of the LORD; a good understanding comes to all who do it." The two psalms work together as a celebration of God's mighty deeds on behalf of the people and instruction for the proper response by the people. Seybold observes that Psalm 111 is "theology," while Psalm 112 is "anthropology."[2] Psalm 112's structure is as follows:

A call to praise (v. 1a)
The praise of the one who reverences the Lord (vv. 1b-3)
The fate of the upright ones (v. 4)
The deeds of the one who reverences the Lord (vv. 5-9)
The fate of the wicked ones (v. 10)

	1	*Hallelujah.*
ʾĀlep		*Content is the one who reverences the LORD,*
Bêt		*in the LORD's commandments greatly delighting.*
Gîmel	2	*A mighty one in the land will be that one's descendant;*
Dālet		*a generation of upright ones will be blessed.*
Hê	3	*Riches and wealth are in that person's house,*
Wāw		*and that one's righteousness endures for all time.*
Zayin	4	*A light has shown forth in the darkness for the upright ones,*
Ḥêt		*showing favor and merciful and righteous.*
Ṭêt	5	*Good is the person who shows favor and who lends,*
Yôd		*holding words in judgment.*
Kāp	6	*For all time that one will not stumble;*

1. For a detailed discussion of the acrostic form, see the commentary for Psalm 119.
2. *Die Psalmen,* p. 440.

Lāmed		*as a memorial for all time will be the righteous one.*
Mêm	7	*Of a malicious hearing that person is not afraid;*
Nûn		*having a heart that is established in its inmost part in the* LORD.
Sāmek	8	*The heart is steady; there is no fear*
ʿAyin		*when looking upon oppressors.*
Pê	9	*That person has distributed, has given to the needy;*
Ṣādê		*and that one's righteousness endures for all time;*
Qôp		*having a horn that is exalted with glory.*
Rêš	10	*The wicked one sees and is disturbed;*
Šîn		*the teeth gnash and break in pieces.*
Tāw		*The desire of the wicked ones will perish.*

1a The first words of Psalm 112 mark it as one of the "Hallelujah" psalms of Book Five (see the commentary for Psalm 111).

1b The acrostic body of Psalm 112 opens with the word *ʾašrê (content),* rendered in most English translations as "happy" or "blessed." The verbal root, which most likely is *ʾāšar,* means "go straight, advance, follow the track." *ʾašrê* is used twenty-six times in the Psalter[3] and very often signals that the reader is entering the sphere of Israelite wisdom teachings. The translation "blessed" brings to mind the Hebrew word *bārûḵ,* which carries cultic/sacred connotations. "Happy" does not convey the full depth of the root *ʾāšar.* The translation *content* connotes a sense of peace and feeling settled that seems to come closest to the root meaning of *ʾašrê. Content,* coupled with two other words in the verse, *ʾîš* ("person") and *ḥāp̄ēš* ("delight"), recalls for the hearer the opening words of the Psalter, "Content is the person who does not walk in the path of the wicked . . . but whose delight is in the *tôrâ*" (Ps. 1:1-2).

NRSV translates the word *ʾîš* ("person") in v. 1 as "those," but the noun is singular in Hebrew and is purposely singular to emphasize the importance for each individual hearer to observe the torah and the commandments *(miṣwōṯ).*

For a discussion of the translation *reverence* for *yārēʾ,* see the commentary on Ps. 111:10.

2-4 Verses 2-3a outline the rewards for the one who *reverences the* LORD and *delights in the commandments.* That person will have *mighty, upright,* and *blessed* descendants and a *house* in which are *riches and wealth.* The words of these verses echo in many ways the promises given by God to Abram in Genesis 12, 13, and 15 — descendants, land, house, and blessing.

Verses 3 and 4 evince strong parallels with vv. 3 and 4 of Psalm 111. Yahweh is the subject of 111:3-4's words of thanks:

3. Pss. 1:1; 2:12; 32:1-2; 33:12; 34:8; 40:4; 41:1; 65:4; 84:4, 5, 12; 89:15; 94:12; 106:3; 112:1; 119:1-2; 127:5; 128:1-2; 137:8, 9; 144:15 (twice); 146:5.

Majesty and splendor are his work,
and his righteousness endures for all time.
A memorial he has made of his wondrous acts;
showing favor and merciful is the Lord.

The righteous person is the subject of 112:3-4's wisdom words:

Riches and wealth are in that person's house,
and that one's righteousness endures for all time.
A light has shown forth in the darkness for the upright ones,
showing favor and merciful and righteous.

Just as the *righteousness* of God *endures for all time,* so does the *righteousness* of the "content" person of Psalm 112. Words derived from the Hebrew root *ṣāḏaq,* translated as "righteous, righteousness, be right," occur some 523 times in the Hebrew Bible. The basic meaning of *ṣāḏaq* includes the ideas of "a sense of right," "correct order," "being just," or "being true," and, in the Hebrew Scriptures, has more to do with right actions than with right states of mind. Psalm 119, which celebrates the torah, repeatedly uses words derived from *ṣāḏaq* to describe its ordinances, precepts, and statutes.[4] A striking story of righteousness in the Hebrew Bible is found in Genesis 38. Tamar, Judah's daughter-in-law, in an act of deception conceives twins by him in order to fulfill the Levirate marriage requirements of the torah (Deut. 25:5-10). Though she deceives him, Judah declares at the end of the story, "She is more in the right *(ṣāḏqâ)* than I" (Gen. 38:26). Delighting in the commandments of the Lord renders the "content" person of Psalm 112 righteous.

In v. 4a, the "content" person is promised a *light in the darkness.* While it is not clear to what the *light* refers, nor does v. 4b — *showing favor and merciful and righteous* — have a clear subject, the reader may be permitted to equate the *light* with the Lord, who is described in 111:4b with the same words that describe the *light* in 112:4b — *showing favor and merciful. Upright (yāšār),* found at the end of v. 4a, is often used as a synonym for "righteous." The plural form here *(yᵉšārîm)* parallels the plural form of *wicked (rᵉšāʿîm),* which the hearer will encounter in v. 10.

5-9 Verses 5-9 describe the actions and demeanor of the "content" person of the psalm. In v. 5a, the person *shows favor (ḥônēn)* and *lends (lāwâ)* to others. *Lāwâ* indicates a connectedness to others, as results when one lends to or borrows from another. In v. 5b, we read that the "content" person *holds words in judgment,* being slow to speak words of either praise or condemnation.

Verse 6 acts as an interlude for this portion of the psalm. Here the reader

4. See Pss. 119:7, 138, 144, 160, 164, 172.

learns that the person — now called *the righteous one* with the character traits that have been described in v. 5 and will be described further in vv. 7-9a — *will not stumble* and will be *for all time a memorial (zēḵer).* The verse is strikingly parallel to Ps. 111:4's words, which state that Yahweh is a memorial [*zēḵer*] because of his wondrous acts.

Verses 7-9a continue with a description of the "content/righteous" person. Despite potential danger from *a malicious hearing* and *oppressors,* this one is not afraid, *having a heart that is established* and *steady;* in fact, here is one who reaches out the hand and gives to *the needy.*[5] The final two cola of v. 9 offer a concluding refrain in praise of the "content/righteous" person. The words of v. 9b duplicate those of v. 3b, while v. 9c reiterates the promise of v. 2 concerning the person's might and strength.

10 Verse 10, in true "wisdom" fashion, contrasts the fate of *the wicked one (rāšāʿ)* with the fate of *the righteous one (ṣāddîq,* v. 6b). And in v. 10c, the singular *rāšāʿ* is replaced by the plural *rᵉšāʿîm, the wicked ones,* to parallel the *yᵉšārîm, the upright ones* of v. 4. While a light will shine forth in the darkness for the upright ones (v. 4b), *the desire of the wicked ones will perish* (v. 10c).

Psalm 112 begins with the same word, *ʾašrê (content),* with which Psalm 1 begins. It also ends with the same word, *ʾāḇaḏ (perish),* with which Psalm 1 ends. Wisdom words weave their way through both psalms, words about how to live one's life according to the instructions of God.

Psalms 111 and 112 are a summary statement of what faith is all about: who God is and what humans must do in response to God. In a rich intertwining of language and metaphor, the "content" person of Psalm 112 partners with the God of Psalm 111, and together they work to achieve righteousness — right living, correct order, truth — in the world.

NANCY DECLAISSÉ-WALFORD

5. When the Apostle Paul wants to encourage the church at Corinth to contribute financially to the impoverished church in Jerusalem, he quotes Ps. 112:9 as an example of a cheerful giver (2 Cor. 9:9).

Psalm 113: Praise the Name of the Lord

Psalm 113 is the third psalm in a group of psalms in Book Five known as the *halᵉlû yāh* psalms (Psalms 111–18). It is also the first of a collection of six psalms (Psalms 113–18) known as "the Egyptian Hallel" and which are used in the celebration of Passover. In modern Jewish life, Psalms 113–14 are recited before the Passover meal and Psalms 115–18 are recited at its conclusion. Psalm 113, classified as a community hymn of praise, is sung at the blessing of the first Passover cup of wine. Calling its hearers to praise the name of the Lord for all of the Lord's goodness to the people, it is an apt introduction to the Passover story, which is then recounted in the following psalm, Psalm 114.

Two evenly divided stanzas make up Psalm 113, vv. 1-4 and vv. 5-9, with v. 5a the centerpiece connecting the two parts. Kraus suggests that the psalm may have been used antiphonally, sung by two choirs in a worship setting.[1] In vv. 1-4, the phrase *šēm YHWH (the name of the LORD)* appears three times, and *YHWH* alone occurs twice. The rhetorical question in v. 5a asks, "*Who is like the LORD*?" In vv. 5b-9a, God's activity in the world is described with participial phrases, and v. 9b frames the psalm with a closing *halᵉlû yāh.*

Hallelujah (v. 1a)
The Call to Praise (vv. 1b-4)
"Who is like the LORD?" (v. 5a)
The Praise of the Lord (vv. 5b-9a)
Hallelujah (v. 9b)

1 *Hallelujah.*

Praise, O servants of the LORD,
Praise the name of the LORD.
2 *The name of the LORD is being blessed,*
now and for all time.
3 *From the rising of the sun until its setting,*
the name of the LORD is being praised.
4 *The one who is exalted over all the nations is the LORD;*
over the heavens is his glory.

5 *Who is like the LORD our God,*

the one who dwells on high;
6 *the one who comes down to look*

1. *Psalms 60–150*, p. 367.

upon the heavens and upon the earth?
7 *the one who raises up from the dust the poor;*
from the dunghills he exalts the needy,
8 *to cause them to dwell with princes,*
with the princes of the people;
9 *the one who gives a dwelling place to the barren one of the house,*
a joyous mother of children.

Hallelujah.

1a Psalm 113 opens with the *Hallelujah* that the reader finds at the beginnings of Psalms 111 and 112.

1b-4 The remainder of v. 1 twice repeats the imperative *hal*^{e}*lû* of v. 1a, first naming the subject of the imperative command, *O servants of the Lord*, and then further identifying the object of the praise, *the name of the Lord*. Beginning with v. 2, the poet of Psalm 113 uses an abundance of participles in the call to praise the Lord. In vv. 2 and 3, *the name of the Lord* is being *blessed, now and for all time,* and is being *praised from the rising of the sun until its setting.*

Name was an important concept in the ancient Near East. Names reflected the natures and characters of the persons who bore them and were conceptually equal to the very essence of being. To know someone was to possess some part of that person; to speak a name was to speak into being. The name Jacob means "he usurps," because he grabs Esau's heel at their birth, attempting to be the firstborn twin (Gen. 25:26). He indeed usurps Esau later in life when he coerces Esau into selling to him his birthright and when he tricks Isaac into giving him the blessing. After the incident at the Jabbok, God changes Jacob's name to Israel, which means "he has struggled with God" (Gen. 32:28). In the creation story in Genesis 2, God brings the animals one by one to the first human and we read, "and whatever the human called every living creature, that was its name" (2:19). Here we have a wonderful picture of humanity working together with God as co-creator. Naming brings the animals into being — an ibex becomes an ibex; a hippopotamus becomes a hippopotamus; an eagle becomes an eagle. In Exodus 3, Moses encounters God at the burning bush. In that encounter, Moses replies to God's command to return to Egypt with a seemingly simple request: "If I come to the Israelites and say to them, 'The God of your ancestors has sent me to you,' and they ask me, 'What is his name?' what shall I say to them?" (3:13). Moses asked for God's name. What is the nature and character of the God who is requesting such a thing? God replies with self-naming words of existence, "I am that I am." From the Hebrew words *'ehyeh '*^{a}*šer 'ehyeh,* the ancient Israelites derived the personal name of God, *YHWH.* They possessed an important aspect of the being of God. In Exodus 20, God commanded the Israelites from Mount Sinai that they not "make wrongful use of" God's name. The book of Deuteronomy tells us that God's name will dwell in the place of God's choosing in the land (Deut. 12:5; 14:23-24; 16:2). And Ps. 8:1 states, "O LORD, our lord, how mighty is your name in all the earth." Verse 4 of Psalm 113 echoes Psalm 8. The name of the Lord is being exalted over the nations; God's glory is over the heavens.

5a We may view the beginning of the rhetorical question of v. 5a as the center of Psalm 113, connecting the call to praise of the first verses with the reasons to praise found in the last verses. The question, *Who is like the LORD our God?* needs no answer. The answer is obvious, based on the description of the Lord that follows in vv. 5b-9.

5b-9a Using a series of *hiphil* stem verbs (all but two are participles), the psalm-singer recounts the caring activities of God in the world. The *hiphil* stem emphasizes that God alone is the instigator of the deeds and actions on behalf of the people. God "is seated *on high,*" yet God *comes down.* God *raises up* and *exalts* the *poor* and the *needy* — causing them to *dwell with princes* — and *gives a dwelling place* to the *barren* woman — making her the *joyous mother of children.*

In the context of the Passover story, God who dwells on high looks down upon the earth; sees the needy and the poor Israelites in slavery in Egypt; raises them up from the dunghills and places them in the dwellings of princes; sees barren Israel; and gives her children a place to dwell. The repetition of the verb *to dwell (yāšaḇ)* is striking (vv. 5, 8, 9). When Moses encountered God at the burning bush, God said to him, "I have observed the misery of my people who are in Egypt. . . . Indeed, I know their sufferings, and I have come down to deliver them from the Egyptians, and to bring them up out of that land to a good and broad land" (Exod. 3:7-8). A *dwelling place,* a homeland, was the ultimate promise of God to the children of Israel.

Many commentators connect Ps. 113:5, 7-8, and 9 with vv. 2, 8, and 5b of Hannah's Song in 1 Samuel 2. The story of God's care for Hannah becomes a model for God's care for Israel, memorialized in the Passover celebration.

9b Psalm 113 ends with the same words with which it begins, *halᵉlû yāh.* Since Psalm 114 does not contain the phrase *halᵉlû yāh,* either at its beginning or end (Psalms 111–18 all either begin or end with the phrase), the LXX translators omitted the *halᵉlû yāh* at the end of Psalm 113 and added a *halᵉlû yāh* to the beginning of Psalm 114.

Psalm 113 is a hymn calling a community of believers to praise a transcendent God who cares enough for humankind to look down, reach down, and raise up the poor and needy of the earth. It is sung at the beginning of the Passover celebration in Jewish life. It is read as the Proper Psalm for evening worship on Easter Sunday. In both contexts, the message is clear: "Who is like the LORD our God?" "No one."

NANCY DECLAISSÉ-WALFORD

Psalm 114: Tremble, O Earth

Psalm 114 is the fourth psalm in a group of psalms in Book Five known as the *halᵉlû yāh* psalms (Psalms 111–18). In addition, it is second in the collection of psalms (Psalms 113–18) that are called "the Egyptian Hallel," psalms that are recited at the Passover meal on the eighth day of Passover. Psalms 113 and 114 are read before the meal; Psalms 115–18 are read at its conclusion.

Psalm 114 is somewhat unique in this collection of psalms. First, it does not contain the words *halᵉlû yāh* that are characteristic of this group of psalms. Since Psalm 113 both begins and ends with the words, and Psalms 115–17 end with them, some suggest that the final *halᵉlû yāh* of Psalm 113 should be transposed to the beginning of Psalm 114. The final psalm in this collection, however, Psalm 118, also does not have the expression, either at its beginning or end, so the missing *halᵉlû yāh* in Psalm 114 should not be viewed as problematic.

Second, Psalm 114 is classified as a community hymn, but it lacks the usual words of invitation to worshippers to join in reciting the hymn.[1] Psalm 113 begins with the words of invitation, "Praise, O servants of the LORD, Praise the name of the LORD," while Psalm 114 begins with a narrative, "When Israel went forth from Egypt. . . ." Thus, we may be permitted to read the *halᵉlû yāh* of Psalm 113 as the invitation to worshippers to recite and celebrate the story of Psalm 114.

Four strophes of two bicola each form the structure of Psalm 114. Verses 1 and 2 begin the narration of the story, whose center is the parallel strophes of vv. 3-4 and 5-6. Verses 7 and 8 conclude the psalm.

When Israel went forth from Egypt (vv. 1-2)
The sea, the Jordan, the mountains, and the hills (vv. 3-4)
Why, O sea, O Jordan, O mountains, O hills? (vv. 5-6)
Tremble, O earth (vv. 7-8)

1 *When Israel went forth from Egypt,*
the house of Jacob from a people of a different language,
2 *Judah was his holy place,*
Israel his dominion.

3 *The sea saw and it fled;*
the Jordan turned back;

1. See deClaissé-Walford, *Introduction to the Psalms,* p. 22. She outlines three elements of community hymns in the Hebrew Psalter: 1) an Introduction, in which the psalmist declares the intention of giving thanks and praising God and invites others to join in; 2) a Narrative; and 3) a Conclusion.

4 *the mountains leapt like rams,*
the hills like the young of the flock.

5 *Why is it, O sea, that you flee,*
O Jordan, that you turn back?
6 *O mountains, that you leap like rams,*
O hills, like the young of the flock?

7 *In the presence of the Lord tremble, O earth,*
in the presence of the God of Jacob,
8 *The one who turns the rock into a pool of water,*
the flint into a spring of water.

1-2 The opening words of the psalm place the reciter in the midst of the story of the great saving act of God on behalf of Israel, the exodus from Egypt. The two cola of vv. 1 and 2 are parallel expressions: *Israel* and *house of Jacob, Egypt* and *a people of a different language* in v. 1; *Judah* and *Israel, holy place* and *dominion* in v. 2. The word translated here as *holy place* is *qāḏôš,* from a root which means "to be devoted, set apart." The word translated as *dominion* is from the root *māšal,* meaning "to rule over, to reign." The two cola summarize two important aspects of God's role in the life of ancient Israel: the holy one in the midst of the people (see Hos. 11:9); and the one ruling over the people (see Deut. 33:5). Interestingly, neither of the names for Israel's God, *ʾᵉlōhîm* and *YHWH,* appears in the first verses of Psalm 114, perhaps giving further strength to the idea that Psalm 113 is to be read as a prelude to Psalm 114.

3-4 Verses 3 and 4 introduce the major themes of Psalm 114. They complete the temporal clause begun with v. 1's *When Israel went forth from Egypt.* When . . . then "the sea saw, the Jordan turned back, the mountains and *the hills leapt.* As with vv. 1 and 2, vv. 3 and 4 are parallel expressions: *the sea* and *the Jordan, fled* and *turned back* in v. 3; *mountains* and *hills, rams* and *the young of the flock* in v. 4. *The sea* in v. 3 likely refers to the Reed Sea, which God parted to allow the Israelites to escape from Egypt (Exodus 14); and then God parted the Jordan River to allow the Israelites to enter the land of promise (Joshua 3). In a single verse, an entire historical narrative is encapsulated; the psalmist marks the beginning and the end of the exodus and the wilderness wandering, the single most formative period in the life of ancient Israel.

Not only do *the sea* and *the Jordan* stand in awe of the God of Israel, but *the mountains* and *the hills* leap. *The mountains* may be understood as Mount Sinai, the place where God met the people of Israel and confirmed the covenant promises to them. Perhaps *the hills* are the central hill country of Syria/Palestine, the terrain in which the Israelites first staked out their settlements in the land. Other psalms narrate the leaping of the mountains and hills. In

Ps. 29:6, God causes Lebanon to "skip like a calf, and Sirion like the son of a wild ox."[2]

5-6 Verses 5 and 6 repeat the themes of Psalm 114, but this time in question form. *Why, O sea, O Jordan, O mountains, O hills?* The psalm-singer calls upon nature to explain its behavior, and since vv. 1-4 do not mention God by name, the question leads to the climactic pronouncement of vv. 7 and 8.

7-8 The psalmist knows the answer to the questions of vv. 5 and 6. The singer does not wait for nature, but commands the earth to *tremble* in the presence of *the Lord, the God of Jacob.* The Hebrew verb *ḥûl,* translated here as *tremble,* is a powerful verb with a range of meanings that include "writhe, whirl about, dance, be in labor (as an expectant mother), tremble."

In the presence of the Lord, the Reed Sea parted, the Jordan River stopped flowing, and Mount Sinai quaked and shook. And the psalmist reminds us also that rocks turned into *pools of water* and *flint* became *a spring of water.* Again and again in the narrative of the wilderness wandering, Israel cried out in thirst, and again and again, God provided water for them to drink.[3] The God of Israel has dominion over all the earth, and the God of Israel provides for those who dwell near *his holy place* (see v. 2).

Psalms 113 and 114 are recited on the eighth day of Passover, just before the Passover meal is eaten. Psalm 113 asks, "Who is like the LORD our God, the one who dwells on high; the one who comes down to look upon the heavens and upon the earth?" Psalm 114 asks, "Why is it, O sea, that you flee, O Jordan, that you turn back? O mountains, that you leap like rams, O hills like the young of the flock?" Questions are an important tradition of the Passover celebration. Traditionally, the youngest child at the Passover table asks: (1) Why is this night different from all other nights? (2) Why on all other nights do we eat either leavened bread or *matzah,* but on this night only *matzah?* (3) Why on all other nights do we not dip herbs at all, but on this night we dip them twice? and (4) Why on all other nights do we eat in an ordinary manner, but tonight we dine with special ceremony?

In answer to the questions, the story of the exodus is repeated. And each participant in the Passover celebration becomes a part of the community of Israelites who made their way from slavery to freedom under the powerful leading of the God of Abraham and Sarah, Rebekah and Isaac, and Jacob and Leah and Rachel. Psalms 113 and 114 introduce that story and introduce the importance of asking — and answering — the questions.

NANCY DECLAISSÉ-WALFORD

2. See also Judg. 5:5; Ps. 18:7; Hab. 3:6.

3. See Exod. 15:22-25; 17:1-7; Num. 20:2-13; 21:16-18; Deut. 8:15.

Psalm 115: We Will Praise Yah

Psalm 115 is the fifth psalm in a group of psalms in Book Five known as the *hal^{e}lû yāh* psalms (Psalms 111–18). In addition, it is third in the collection of "Egyptian Hallel" psalms (Psalms 113–18), psalms recited during the Passover meal on the eighth day of Passover. Psalms 113 and 114 are read before the meal; Psalms 115–18 are read at its conclusion.

Psalm 115 does not begin with the words *hal^{e}lû yāh,* leading a number of ancient Hebrew manuscripts of the book of Psalms, along with the Vulgate and the LXX, to join Psalms 114 and 115 into a single unit. In addition, since Psalm 114 neither begins nor ends with *hal^{e}lû yāh,* a number of manuscripts transpose those words at the end of Psalm 113 to the beginning of Psalm 114. Psalms 116 and 117, however, have *hal^{e}lû yāh* only at their ends, not at their beginnings, while Psalm 118 does not contain the words at all. Therefore, we can conclude that the use of *hal^{e}lû yāh* is pervasive but in no way consistent in this collection of psalms, and we are justified in accepting the integrity of the MT, which renders Psalms 114 and 115 as two separate compositions.

Psalm 115 is classified as a community hymn. It is a strong polemic against human-made idols and an affirmation of the sovereignty of God over the heavens and the earth. Some suggest it was recited antiphonally by leaders and congregants in various worship settings in the life of Israel. Thus its words were directed to and meant to be heard by the worshippers as a reminder of the difference between the idols of the peoples and the God of Israel.

Five stanzas make up Psalm 115, which moves from prayer to confession, from calls to trust to assurances of blessings, and from declarations to praise.

Prayer to the Lord (vv. 1-2)
Confession of the uselessness of idols (vv. 3-8)
Calls to trust in the Lord (vv. 9-11)
Assurances of blessings from the Lord (vv. 12-15)
Declarations about and praises of the Lord (vv. 16-18)

1 *Not on account of us, O LORD, not on account of us,*
but on account of your name show forth glory,
because of your hesed, *because of your faithfulness.*
2 *Why do the nations say, "Where is their God?"*

3 *Our God is in the heavens;*
whatever is pleasing, he does.
4 *Their idols are silver and gold,*
the making of the hands of humankind.
5 *There is a mouth to them, but they do not speak;*

eyes to them, but they do not see;
6 *ears to them, but they do not hear;*
a nose to them, but they do not smell.
7 *Their hands do not feel;*
their feet do not walk;
they do not utter any sound in their throats.
8 *Like them are the ones making them,*
all who are trusting in them.

9 *Israel,*[1] *trust in the* LORD,
their help and their shield is he.
10 *House of Aaron, trust in the* LORD,
their help and their shield is he.
11 *The ones who fear the* LORD, *trust in the* LORD,
their help and their shield is he.

12 *The* LORD *has remembered us;*
he blesses us.
He blesses the house of Israel;
he blesses the house of Aaron;
13 *he blesses the ones who fear the* LORD,
the small ones and the great ones.
14 *The* LORD *will give increase to you,*
to you and to your children.
15 *Being blessed are you who belong to the* LORD,
the one who makes heavens and earth.

16 *The heavens are the heavens of the* LORD,
and the earth he has given to humankind.
17 *The dead do not praise* Yāh,
and all who go down to the realm of death.
18 *But we, we will praise* Yāh
from now and for all time.
Hallelujah.

1-2 The usual translation of the opening words of Psalm 115 is "Not *to* us" (NRSV). Should the reader understand that the people of Israel were concerned that the *kāḇôḏ* — glory, honor, weightiness — usually ascribed to the

1. Many Hebrew manuscripts, along with LXX and Syr, place the word *bêṯ* ("house of") at the beginning of the verse in order to harmonize it with v. 12, but the meter of vv. 9, 10, and 11 does not support such an addition.

name of the Lord was being ascribed to them? This seems unlikely. A better translation seems to be *Not on account of us.* In the context of the psalm, the psalm-singer calls God to show forth God's *kāḇôḏ,* not "on account of" the people, but "on account of" God's *name.*[2]

Thus Psalm 115 begins *Not on account of us, O LORD, . . . but on account of your name show forth glory* — on account of the nature and character that your *name* conveys, because of your *hesed* and your *faithfulness.* In v. 2, the psalmist recounts a question with which the nations taunt Israel over and over: *Where is their God?* (see Pss. 42:3, 10; 79:10). Why the question? The remainder of the psalm provides the answer.

3-8 In these verses the psalmist contrasts the God of Israel with the gods of the nations. *Our God is in the heavens* (v. 3). *Their idols are silver and gold, the making of the hands of humankind* (v. 4). In two short phrases, the vast gulf separating the objects of worship of the nations and the object of worship of Israel is delineated. The God of Israel inhabits a realm beyond human existence; the gods of the nations are the crafted product of humanity. In vv. 5-7, the psalm-singer returns the taunt of the nations with statement-questions about their gods: "there is a mouth to them, but they do not speak; eyes . . . but they do not see; ears . . . but they do not hear; a nose . . . but they do not smell; hands and *feet,* but they *do not feel* or *walk; they do not utter any sound in their throats.* The taunt continues in v. 8, as the psalmist compares the crafters and worshippers themselves to these inanimate idols. The God of the Israelites commanded the people in Exodus 20: "You shall not make for yourself an idol, whether in the form of anything that is in heaven above, or that is on the earth beneath, or that is in the water under the earth. You shall not bow down to them or worship them" (Exod. 20:4-5). In the world of the ancient Near East, where the gods of the nations were depicted with human and/or animallike images, a God who had no physical image was difficult to comprehend and embrace.

9-11 Verses 9-11 present two interpretational dilemmas that have spawned much discussion by commentators. First, three groups of people are called upon to *trust in the LORD: Israel,* the *house of Aaron,* and *the ones who fear the LORD.*[3] Should we understand these to be three distinct groups within ancient Israelite life: the Israel community as a whole; the priests and the Levites of the temple; and outsiders who have joined with Israel and adopted

2. For a full discussion of the concept of name in the Old Testament, see the commentary on Ps. 113:1b-4.

3. Ps. 135:19-20 names four groups of worshippers in contrast to Ps 115's three: the house of Israel, the house of Aaron, the house of Levi, and "you that fear the LORD." Commentators suggest that Ps. 135 reflects the strong distinction between the houses of Aaron and Levi that is prevalent in the books of Numbers and Chronicles.

the faith (see, e.g., Exod. 12:38; Josh. 6:25; 9:21)?[4] Should we understand them to be two groups — the Israelites and the priests and Levites, with the phrase *the ones who fear the LORD* as a summary naming of the two?[5] Gerstenberger argues that the identity of the group designated "those who fear the LORD" has been misunderstood as proselytes to the Israelite faith because of the New Testament term "god-fearers" (see Acts 2:5; 13:43; 17:4). He writes, "'To fear Yahweh' is the obligation of all believers (cf. [Pss.] 22:24, 26[23, 25]; 25:12, 14; 34:8, 10[7, 9]; 52:8; 112:1; 145:19; Prov 3:7; 24:21). In most cases, the name 'fearer of Yahweh' indiscriminately means 'Yahweh believer.'"[6] Or should we view the three designations as parallel descriptors for the whole people of ancient Israel?[7] Whatever the identities of the groups may be, the text indicates that *all* are called on to *trust in the LORD*.

Second, why the move in each verse from a second person imperative command to a uniform third person declarative statement? Perhaps the worship leaders recited the command of the first half of each verse: *Israel, trust in the LORD; house of Aaron, trust in the LORD; and the ones who fear the LORD, trust in the LORD,* and each group (whether two or three) responded on behalf of the other(s) with the declarative statement in the second half of each verse: *their help and their shield is he.*[8]

12-15 Many older Hebrew manuscripts of the Psalter begin a new psalm with v. 12 of Psalm 115, but there is no compelling reason to argue for such a divide. In fact, vv. 12 and 13 evince a strong tie to vv. 9-11. Verses 12 and 13 affirm that the Lord, who is the *help* and *shield* of Israel, the house of Aaron, and the ones who fear the Lord, *remembers* and *blesses* them. An additional characterization of the recipients of remembering and blessing — *the small ones and the great ones* — is added at the end of v. 13. If any of the faithful have been omitted from the previous threefold summary, they are included in the concluding cola of v. 13.

In v. 14, the faithful are addressed directly and given a promise that the Lord will give offspring to them and their children and thus assure the ongoing life of the community. How can the faithful be assured of such a promise? Verse 15 reminds the faithful that the Lord, who we are told in v. 3 *is in the heavens,* is also *the one who makes heavens and earth.* The God of Israel is the maker of the very elements — the *silver* and the *gold* (v. 4) — out of which the gods of the nations are fashioned.

4. Kraus, *Psalms 60–150,* p. 381; Gerstenberger, *Psalms: Part 2,* p. 288; Davidson, *The Vitality of Worship,* p. 378; Limburg, *Psalms,* p. 395.

5. Allen, *Psalms 101–150,* p. 110; Terrien, *The Psalms,* p. 773.

6. *Psalms: Part 2,* pp. 301-2.

7. Clifford, *Psalms 73–150,* p. 196.

8. See Goulder, *The Psalms of the Return,* pp. 168-74; Allen, *Psalms 101–150,* pp. 108-9.

16-18 The message of vv. 12-15 continues in vv. 16-18. *The heavens* are the realm of the Lord; *the earth* is a gift to humankind. *The dead* and the ones who *go down to the realm of death* in v. 17 may refer to the idols in vv. 4-7 that human hands have made. Idols fashioned with human hands cannot praise the God of the heavens.

Or the phrases may refer to those who have already gone down to the shadowy death-realm of the ancient Israelite belief system. From there (from Sheol), praising God was not possible; only in the realm of the living could humankind commune with and praise God. The words of praise, then, must be passed on from generation to generation, so that the Israelites might indeed *praise Yāh, from now and for all time.* Thus the Lord will remember and bless those who trust in the Lord and grant them *increase* — they and their children (v. 14).

The lives of believers today are filled with idols that are *the making of the hands of humankind* (v. 4). But, as the psalmist points out, these idols have no voice, no vision, no hearing, no senses of smell or feeling. They cannot walk, and they cannot utter a single sound. They are merely idols — the house, the boat, the car, the fine jewelry, the awards and recognition, the high-paying job, the self-help method. What ultimately matters, what lasts, is the God of the house of Israel, whose blessings extend beyond our own earthly existence to those who come after us. And thus we may declare, along with all the generations of the faithful, *we, we will praise* Yāh *from now and for all time* (v. 18).

Nancy deClaissé-Walford

Psalm 116: I Will Walk in the Land of the Living

Psalm 116 is the sixth psalm in a group of psalms in Book Five known as the *halᵉlû yāh* psalms (Psalms 111–18). And it is the fourth psalm in the collection of the "Egyptian Hallel" psalms (Psalms 113–18), which are recited at the Passover meal on the eighth day of Passover. Psalms 113 and 114 are read before the meal; Psalms 115–18 are read at its conclusion, while drinking the fourth cup of celebratory wine.

While it is categorized as an individual hymn of thanksgiving and possibly was used at a ceremony of thanksgiving during one of the great festivals of ancient Israelite life, Psalm 116 eludes an easy division into discrete sections. Gerstenberger writes that "the structure of the psalm seems haphazard,"[1] and McCann observes that "while the traditional elements of a song of thanksgiving are present, they seem to be presented in no particular order," and adds that "scholars disagree on the structure of the psalm."[2] The three components of an individual hymn of thanksgiving are: (1) the introduction, in which the psalmist expresses the intention to give thanks; (2) the narrative, in which the psalmist describes the events that have taken place; and (3) the conclusion, in which the psalmist praises God for deliverance and protection during the course of events which have taken place. Psalm 116 thus consists of the following elements:

Introduction — intention to give thanks (vv. 1-2)
Narrative — description of the events that have taken place (vv. 3-11)
Conclusion — praise of God for deliverance and protection (vv. 12-19)

1 *I love because the LORD[3] hears*
my voice, my cries for favor.
2 *For he inclines his ear to me,*
and during my lifetime I will cry out.

3 *The cords of death surrounded me,*
and the distresses of Sheol found me;
anguish and sorrow I find.
4 *Then in the name of the LORD I cry out;*
I pray thee, O LORD, deliver my inmost being.
5 *Full of favor is the LORD, and righteous.*

1. *Psalms: Part 2,* p. 291.

2. "The Book of Psalms," p. 1147.

3. Many versions translate *YHWH* as the object of *I love.* In MT, however, *YHWH* is the subject of "hear."

And our God has compassion.
6 *The* Lord *watches over the simple;*
I was brought low but he gave to me help.
7 *Return, O my inmost being, to your restful places,*
for the Lord *has dealt well with you.*
8 *For you have delivered my inmost being from death,*
my eye from tears, my foot from stumbling.
9 *I will walk about in the presence of the* Lord
in the lands[4] *of the living.*
10 *I can stand firm even when I say,*
"I, I am exceedingly bowed down."
11 *I, I say in my oppression,*
"All of humanity deceives."

12 *How shall I give back to the* Lord
all of the good he gives to me?
13 *A cup of helps I will lift up,*
and in the name of the Lord *I will cry out.*
14 *My vows to the* Lord *I will complete*
in the presence of all his people.
15 *Weighty in the eyes of the* Lord
is the death of his hesed *ones.*
16 *O* Lord, *indeed I am your servant,*
I am your servant, the child of your maidservant;
you have unleashed my bonds.
17 *To you I will sacrifice a sacrifice of thanks,*
and in the name of the Lord *I will cry out.*
18 *My vows to the* Lord *I will complete*
in the presence of all his people,
19 *in the courts of the house of the* Lord,
in the midst of you, O Jerusalem.
Hallelujah!

1-2 The introduction (the intention to give thanks) to this individual hymn of thanksgiving is found in vv. 1 and 2. The first verse is filled with interpretational difficulties that have led to a number of textual emendations. The major discussion surrounds the placement of the word *YHWH* in the verse. The MT reads, *I love because the* Lord *hears my voice.* Most modern translations, however, follow the suggested emendation of the editors of *BHS* and place

4. LXX, Syr, and Targ render this word singular, based on the texts of Pss. 27:13 and 52:5.

YHWH as the object of the first verb (perhaps on the models of Pss. 18:1 and 31:23), thus reading, "I love the LORD because he has heard my voice. . . ." Allen points out, though, that the beginning of v. 10 parallels the structure of v. 1, with an initial first singular perfect verb with no direct object followed by the conjunction *kî,*[5] thus lending credence to the MT. Terrien maintains that no textual emendation is necessary. He writes, "The cry 'I love' without a direct object reveals the absolute degree of the psalmist's passion for his God."[6]

God hears the psalmist's *cries for favor (taḥ^{a}nûn)* before God. The word *favor* is derived from the verbal root *ḥānan,* the same root as one of the self-declarative attributes of God given to Moses in Exod. 34:6, in which God declares, according to NRSV: "The LORD, the LORD, a God merciful *(raḥûm)* and gracious *(ḥannûn,* "showing favor"), slow to anger, and abounding in steadfast love *(ḥesed̲)* and faithfulness *('emet̲).*" The Hebrew root *(ḥānan)* carries a basic meaning of "an aesthetically pleasing presentation or aspect of someone or something" or "the pleasing impression made upon one individual by another."[7] The singer of Psalm 116 loves God because God hears the "requests to show favor" from the psalmist.

The psalm-singer begins in vv. 1 and 2 with a statement of "passion" that results from God listening to the cries of the psalmist. In its position in the Egyptian Hallel psalms, might we be permitted to read Psalm 116 as a hymn sung by an ancient Israelite in thanksgiving for deliverance from Egypt? We recall that in Exod. 3:7-8, God says to Moses:

> I have observed the misery of my people who are in Egypt; I have heard their cry on account of their taskmasters. Indeed, I know their sufferings, and I have come down to deliver them from the Egyptians.

3-11 The psalm continues with a narrative describing the events that took place and caused the psalmist to sing a hymn of thanksgiving to the Lord. The psalmist was inflicted with great distress, including the threat of *death,* and cried out in *the name of the LORD.*[8]

Verse 5 opens with the word *ḥannûn* (translated here as *full of favor*). It comes from the same Hebrew verbal root as the closing word of v. 1 *(cries for favor).* There the psalmist loves because God *hears my cries for favor.* God shows favor; thus, the cries for favor of the psalmist do not fall on deaf ears. Three descriptive words are used of God in v. 5: *ḥannûn (full of favor); ṣaddîq (righteous);* and *m^{e}raḥēm (compassionate),* recalling for the psalmist and

5. *Psalms 101–150,* p. 112.

6. *The Psalms,* p. 777.

7. David Noel Freedman and Jack R. Lundbom, "*ḥānan,*" *TDOT* 5:22.

8. For the significance of *name* in the ancient Near East, see the commentary for Psalm 113.

those listening to the psalmist the self-descriptive words of God to Moses in Exodus 34: "The LORD, the LORD, a God compassionate *(raḥûm)* and full of favor *(ḥannûn)*."

The psalm-singer continues in vv. 6 and 7 with words of trust for God's ever-present *help* and words of admonition to the psalmist's *inmost being* to *return to your restful places.* In vv. 8-11, the singer addresses words of thanks directly to God for delivering *my inmost being from death, my eye from tears, my foot from stumbling.* Verse 8 may have been a traditional saying from the life of ancient Israel that was incorporated into the poetry of Psalm 116. As a result, the psalmist is confident of being able to *walk about in the presence of the LORD, in the lands of the living,* and of being able to *stand firm* even when feeling *bowed down,* oppressed, and deceived.

12-19 The conclusion of this hymn of thanksgiving, which contains the psalmist's praise to God for deliverance and protection, may be divided into two sections (vv. 12-14 and 16-19), each with the refrain (vv. 14 and 18): *My vows to the LORD I will complete in the presence of all his people* and a summary statement of the theme of the psalm in v. 15.

In v. 12 the psalmist asks what may be given to the Lord for all the goodness that the Lord bestows. Verses 13 and 14 answer the question: *a cup of helps* and completion of *vows.* The *cup of helps* may refer to some ceremonial function in the cult of ancient Israel (see Exod. 29:40; Num. 28:7).[9] In the context of the "Egyptian Hallel" psalms, the *cup of helps* can refer to the fourth cup of celebratory wine drunk at the Passover meal.

The structure of the psalm, while not always clear-cut in terms of formal elements, may well reflect, according to Gerstenberger, a cultic ceremony for someone fulfilling a vow of thanksgiving to the Lord.[10] Thus v. 14 acts as a concluding statement to the intention to give thanks, the description of the events that have taken place, and the praise of God for deliverance and protection that precede it.

Verse 15 has puzzled commentators for millennia. Most versions follow closely the translation of the 1611 Authorized Version: "Precious in the sight of the LORD is the death of his saints." But as with other portions of this psalm, v. 15 is fraught with interpretational conundrums. The word usually translated as "precious" is from the Hebrew root *yāqār,* which means "be dignified, honorable, heavy, valuable." It occurs nine times in the book of Psalms,[11] and is translated variously in the NRSV as "precious, glory, honor, costly, pomp, and weighty." The use of *yāqār* to describe the death of the LORD's *hesed* ones indicates that God does not happily accept the death of any faithful one,

9. For a detailed treatment of the *cup of helps,* see Kraus, *Psalms 60–150,* p. 116.

10. *Psalms: Part 2,* p. 295.

11. Pss. 36:7; 37:20; 45:9; 49:8, 12, 20; 72:14; 116:15; 139:17.

but considers life the better alternative and counts each death as costly and *weighty.* NJPS translates the first half of v. 15 as "grievous in the LORD's sight."

With v. 16, the psalm-singer returns to praising God for deliverance and protection, in a statement parallel to vv. 12-14. The psalmist states, *Indeed, I am your servant . . . the child of your maidservant; you have unleashed my bonds.* Here there is no question posed, as in v. 12, but nonetheless the psalm-singer responds in vv. 17 and 18 in much the same way as in vv. 13 and 14, with *a sacrifice of thanks* and completion of *vows.* And in this portion of the praise of God, the vow will be completed not only *in the presence of* God's *people,* but *in the courts of the house of the LORD, in the midst of you, O Jerusalem.*

The Passover celebrants raise a cup of wine to God in remembrance of all of God's goodness to their ancestors and to them in the exodus from Egypt. Psalm 116 is recited at each Passover as an individual recounting of God's goodness and deliverance to each celebrant.

Psalm 116 is recited also in Christian tradition during the celebration of communion on Holy Thursday. As in the Passover celebration, so Christians raise a cup of wine in remembrance of all of God's goodness to their ancestors in the faith and to them.

NANCY DECLAISSÉ-WALFORD

Psalm 117: The Lord's *Hesed* Has Become Strong

Psalm 117 is the seventh psalm in a group of psalms in Book Five known as the *halᵉlû yāh* psalms (Psalms 111–18). In addition, it is the fifth psalm of the "Egyptian Hallel" psalms (Psalms 113-18), psalms recited at the Passover meal on the eighth day of Passover. Psalms 113 and 114 are read before the meal; Psalms 115–18 are read at its conclusion, while drinking the fourth cup of celebratory wine.

Only two verses comprise this community hymn of praise, making it the shortest psalm in the Psalter. A number of Hebrew manuscripts and modern scholars connect it to Psalm 116, but the consensus of the textual evidence is that Psalm 117 should be read as a discrete psalm with a simple yet powerful statement about the relationship between a believing community and its God.

> 1 *Praise the* LORD, *all nations;*
> *glorify him, all peoples.*
> 2 *For his* hesed *has become strong over us,*
> *and the faithfulness of the* LORD *is for all times.*
> *Hallelujah.*

1 Psalm 117 follows the basic form of a hymn in the Psalter. It begins with introductory words, in which the psalm-singers declare their intention of giving thanks and praising God. In v. 1, they invite *all nations* and *peoples* to join with them in their *praise* and glorifying of the Lord.

2 The second element of the hymn form is the narrative, which describes what has happened to the psalmists to prompt the words of praise. Verse 2 begins with the conjunction *kî,* a common introduction to a hymnic narrative in the Psalter.[1] The singers call to mind God's *hesed* and *faithfulness ('emeṯ),* two of the characteristics included in God's self-descriptive words to Moses in Exod. 34:6. The third element of the hymn is the conclusion, in which the psalm-singers praise God for all God has done on their behalf. In this short psalm, the final words, *halᵉlû yāh,* make up this third element of the hymn.

Psalm 117 was most likely used as a refrain by the ancient Israelites in a cultic setting of worship. The Apostle Paul wove its essential meaning into his exhortation in Rom. 15:11: "Praise the Lord, all you Gentiles, and let all the peoples praise him." God is the God of all; God is a God of *hesed* and faithfulness; and Psalm 117 is certainly an apt refrain in worship settings today.

NANCY DECLAISSÉ-WALFORD

1. See Pss. 33:4; 135:4, 5, 14; 136:1b, etc.

Psalm 118: The Lord Is for Me; I Will Not Fear

Psalm 118 is the last of the group of psalms in Book Five known as the *halᵉlû yāh* psalms (Psalms 111–18). And it is the last of the "Egyptian Hallel" psalms (Psalms 113–18), psalms which are used at the Passover meal on the eighth day of the Passover celebration. Psalms 113 and 114, both community hymns, are recited before the meal. Psalm 115, a community hymn; Psalm 116, an individual hymn of thanksgiving; Psalm 117, a community hymn; and Psalm 118, an individual hymn of thanksgiving, are recited at the conclusion of the meal while drinking the fourth cup of celebratory wine.

Psalm 118 is an interesting composition, with a long history of transmission and use in Jewish and Christian religious life. Gerstenberger writes that the psalm "abounds in liturgical forms and rhythmic, repetitious, formulaic phrases and shouts."[1] Terrien adds, "The psalm appears to be a conglomeration of independent fragments."[2] The consensus of scholars is that Psalm 118 was most likely used in early Jewish life in liturgical processions, perhaps as an entrance liturgy into the temple in Jerusalem, in much the same way that Psalms 15 and 24 may have been used.[3] According to the Mishnah, the procession around the altar that took place on seven successive days during the Feast of Tabernacles was accompanied by the recitation of Ps. 118:27.[4] And, as stated above, in modern Jewish life, Psalm 118 is recited at the end of the Passover meal.

All four of the New Testament gospel writers use the words of v. 26 — *Blessed is the one who comes in the name of the LORD* — in their Palm Sunday narratives (Matt. 21:9; Mark 11:9-10; Luke 19:38; John 12:13). In Mark 12:10, Jesus quotes v. 22 — *The stone the builders rejected has become a cornerstone* — as the explanation for the so-called parable of the Vineyard. Peter quotes the same verse in Acts 4:11 in reference to Jesus; Paul alludes to it in Eph. 2:20-21; and the words of v. 6 — *The LORD is for me; I will not fear* — echo in Rom. 8:31 and Heb. 13:6. In modern lectionary use, vv. 1-2 and 14-24 is the psalm reading for Easter Sunday in all three years; vv. 1-2 and 19-29 is the reading for Palm Sunday in all three years; and vv. 14-29 is the psalm reading for the second Sunday of Easter in Year C.

As stated above, Psalm 118 is an individual hymn of thanksgiving, but the words of the individual hymn-singer are woven into (Kraus says "anchored in"[5]) the liturgy of the gathered worshipping community. Thus, the psalmic

1. *Psalms: Part 2,* p. 307.
2. *The Psalms,* p. 783.
3. See, esp., the commentary on Psalm 118 in Kraus, *Psalms 60–150,* pp. 392-401.
4. Mishnah *Sukkah* 4:5; 5:1-4. See Clifford, *Psalms 73–150,* p. 208.
5. *Psalms 60–150,* p. 401.

voice moves back and forth between the singular and the plural, as the individual worshipper approaches God in the context of corporate worship with thanks for deliverance from trouble.

Call to Worship (vv. 1-4)
Voice of the Individual (vv. 5-18)
Mingled Voices of the Individual and the Worshipping Community (vv. 19-28)
Conclusion (v. 29)

1 *Give thanks to the* L*ORD*, *for he is good,*
for his hesed *is for all time.*
2 *Let Israel say,*
"His hesed *is for all time."*
3 *Let the house of Aaron say,*
"His hesed *is for all time."*
4 *Let those who fear the* L*ORD say,*
"His hesed *is for all time."*

5 *From narrow straits, I cried out,* "Yah!"[6]
The L*ORD answered*[7] *me with a broad place.*
6 *The* L*ORD is for me; I will not fear.*
What can humanity do to me?
7 *The* L*ORD is for me, helping me;*
and I, I can look upon those who hate me.
8 *It is better to take refuge in the* L*ORD*
than to put confidence in humanity.
9 *It is better to take refuge in the* L*ORD*
than to put confidence in princes.
10 *All the nations have surrounded me.*
In the name of the L*ORD, indeed I will fend them off.*
11 *They have surrounded me, alas they have surrounded me.*
In the name of the L*ORD, indeed I will fend them off.*
12 *They have surrounded me like bees,*
but they were destroyed like the fire of thorn bushes.
In the name of the L*ORD, indeed I will fend them off.*

6. The Hebrew word here, *yāh,* is a shortened form of the tetragrammaton, *YHWH,* which is used frequently in poetic texts.

7. NRSV and NASB add a verb to this phrase ("and set me"), reflecting the ambiguity of the verbal root in the Hebrew text. The verb is *ʿānâ,* which means "to answer," but some have interpreted the root to be *ʿûn* III ("to dwell").

13 *You pushed me hard*[8] *in order to make me fall,*
but the Lord *helped me.*
14 *My strength and song is the* Lord,
and he is to me a deliverer.
15 *There is a sound of rejoicing and deliverance in the tents of the righteous ones.*
The right hand of the Lord *does mighty things.*
16 *The right hand of the* Lord *celebrates (is lifted up),*
the right hand of the Lord *does mighty things.*
17 *I will not die but I will live,*
and I will recount the deeds of the Lord.
18 *The* Lord *has severely punished me,*
but to death he did not give me over.

19 *Open to me the gates of righteousness,*
that I may enter into them.
I will give thanks to the Lord.
20 *This is the gate of the* Lord;
the righteous ones will enter into it.
21 *I give thanks to you because you answered me,*
and you were to me a deliverer.
22 *The stone the builders rejected*
has become a cornerstone.
23 *From the* Lord *is this;*
it is a wonder in our eyes.
24 *This is the day the* Lord *made;*
let us rejoice and be joyful in it.
25 *We beseech you, O* Lord, *please deliver.*
We beseech you, O Lord, *please cause to thrive.*
26 *Blessed is the one who comes in the name of the* Lord.
We will bless you from the house of the Lord.
27 *The* Lord *is God,*
and he fills us with light.
Bind the festal procession with branches
up to the horns of the altar.
28 *You are my God, and I give thanks to you.*
My God, I celebrate you.

29 *Give thanks to the* Lord, *for he is good,*
for his hesed *is for all time.*

8. LXX and Syr render this verb as *niphal* — *niḏḥêṯî,* but this translation maintains the *qal* verb of MT.

1-4 In vv. 1-4, worshippers are called together to *give thanks to the LORD* because of the Lord's goodness and *hesed.*[9] The words of v. 1 are typical gathering words, used in many calls to worship in the Hebrew Bible (see Pss. 106:1; 107:1; 136:1; 1 Chr. 16:34; 2 Chr. 5:13; 7:3; 20:21). In vv. 2-4, three groups of people are called to celebrate the Lord's *hesed: Israel, the house of Aaron, and the ones who fear the LORD* — the same three groups who are called upon to "trust in the LORD" in Ps. 115:9-11.[10] Whatever the identities of the groups may be, we can conclude along with Psalm 115 that the text indicates that "all" are called on to celebrate the Lord's *hesed.* After v. 4 the word *hesed* does not appear again in the psalm until its closing verse, v. 29. Therefore, we may be permitted to understand vv. 5-28 as a description, an example story of *hesed.*

5-7 In v. 5, the individual worshipper recounts the events that prompted this hymn of thanksgiving to God. The psalmist was in *narrow straits,* and God *answered* the cry for help by providing *a broad place* (cf. Pss. 18:19; 31:8). The psalmist thus declares in vv. 6 and 7:

> The LORD is for me; I will not fear.
> What can humanity do to me?
> The LORD is for me, helping me;
> and I, I can look upon those who hate me.

A striking feature of vv. 5-7 is the repetition of the first person pronoun. The words *I* and *me* ring out, emphasizing the individual, intimate care that the psalmist has received from God.

8-9 In vv. 8-9, the reader encounters one of the elements that make Psalm 118 what Terrien calls "a conglomeration of independent fragments." The *it is better . . . than* sayings of vv. 8 and 9 are perhaps best understood as proverbial aphorisms on the model of the *māšāl* sayings of the book of Proverbs (see Prov. 15:16; 16:8; 19:1 and the commentary for Ps. 44:9-14). The individual worshipper has experienced the goodness of God in a deliverance from *narrow straits* to *a broad place* and reflects on the experience with traditional sayings about the Lord.

The word translated *put confidence in* in vv. 8 and 9 comes from the Hebrew verbal root *bāṭaḥ* ("be firmly bound around, feel secure, and rely on"). The psalm-singer suggests that God delivers from the *narrow straits* of the oppressor and provides a more desirable "secure, firmly-bound" place.

10-12 In vv. 10-12, the Hebrew verbal root *sāḇaḇ,* ("surround") occurs three times. In each situation of being surrounded, the psalm-singer cries out, *In the name of the LORD, indeed I will fend them off* (vv. 10, 11, and 12). Therefore, the *narrow straits* of v. 5, which result from the surrounding threat

9. For a full discussion of *hesed,* see the Introduction to the Commentary.

10. For a full discussion of the three groups, see the commentary for Psalm 115.

of the enemy, are avoided when the psalmist cries out to *Yāh* and is thereby able to fend off the enemy.

13-18 In v. 13, the psalmist celebrates having fended off the enemy, but recognizes that someone, somewhere is pushing in order to make the psalmist *fall.* While the Septuagint and Syriac translations render the MT verbal form "you have pushed me" as the passive "I have been pushed," such an emendation is not necessary to grasp the image of this verse. Our psalm-singer is raising a voice in praise and thanks to the Lord within a worldview that acknowledges only one "primal mover" within the created order — God. If an event, a passion, an emotion occurs within humanity, then, if God is the only God, then God must cause such an occurrence.

But regardless of the source of the pushing and resulting *fall,* the Lord responds, and the psalmist celebrates with words of praise in v. 14, affirming that God is *my strength and song, to me a deliverer.* The Hebrew words of v. 14 repeat exactly the words that Moses, Miriam, and the children of Israel sing in Exod. 15:2 after they have crossed the Reed Sea, and the singer of Psalm 118 likens the deliverance rendered in the present situation to the deliverance God gives to the Israelites in the exodus. The psalmist has escaped; the enemy has perished; a new life lies ahead.

Verses 15b and 16 echo the Song of Moses in Exodus 15 (vv. 6, 12) as well, celebrating in a threefold summary the might of *the right hand of the Lord*. And in v. 17, the psalmist affirms, *I will not die but I will live, and I will recount the deeds of the Lord*. Martin Luther inscribed these very words on a wall of Colburg Castle in Bavaria during his 165 days of hiding during the Diet of Augsburg.

19-28 In v. 19, *the gates of righteousness* are opened to the psalm-singer, and the singer enters with *thanks.* These verses in particular mark Psalm 118 as an entrance liturgy, words recited as worshippers enter the gates of Jerusalem and make their way to the temple to worship with sacrifice and celebration. The words of v. 22 are quoted and alluded to in many places in the New Testament, appropriated by its writers as a metaphor for Jesus, the Christ of the early church (see Mark 12:10-11; Acts 4:11; Eph. 2:20-21; 1 Pet. 2:4-8). In the ancient Israelite context of Psalm 118, we may understand the *stone the builders rejected* as the psalm-singer, who has not been cast off, but has become a *cornerstone,* an essential element in the construction of the life of the ancient Israelite faithful.

In v. 24, the voice of the community appears clearly for the first time in the psalm, and the community voice will be mingled with the voice of the individual for the remainder of the psalm. The community declares, *This is the day the Lord made,* and admonishes its hearers, *Let us rejoice and be joyful in it.* It continues with requests in v. 25: *We beseech you, O Lord, please deliver, . . . cause to thrive,* and concludes its celebration in vv. 26 and 27a with words of promise and trust: *We will bless you from the house of the* L*ORD* and *the* L*ORD* *. . . fills us with light.*

The Mishnah, a Jewish commentary on the Scriptures, associates the words of v. 27 with the Feast of Tabernacles, the annual autumn celebration commemorating the wilderness wanderings and the giving of the torah to Moses on Sinai. The words *Bind the festal procession with branches up to the horns of the altar* are explained as follows:

> What was the rite of the willow branch? There was a place below Jerusalem called Motsa. They went down there and collected young willow branches, and they came and set them up right along the sides of the Altar with their tops bent over the top of the Altar. They then sounded a prolonged blast, a quavering note, and a prolonged blast. Each day they walked in procession once around the Altar.[11]

In v. 28, the voice of the individual psalmist returns, mingling individual words of thanks and celebration with the community of worshippers.

29 The final verse of Psalm 118 — *Give thanks to the* L*ORD* — repeats the "gathering words" of v. 1, calling worshippers to praise God because of God's *hesed* and providing a closing envelope structure to this individual hymn of thanksgiving.

The last psalm of the Egyptian Hallels is a rich and powerful psalm in both Jewish and Christian traditions. Each tradition has found within its words an abundance of meaning. In the Jewish tradition, the psalm is recited at the spring festival of Passover, but also is used to commemorate the good provisions of God to the Israelites during the wilderness wandering, celebrated in the autumn festival of the Feast of Tabernacles. For Christians, many of its verses suggest the life and times of Jesus. Psalm 118 is a rich composition, sung first as an individual hymn of thanksgiving in a corporate worship setting; adopted by the ancient Israelites as a song of celebration for the Feast of Tabernacles; and then appropriated by the early Christians as a song about Jesus, the Christ.

NANCY DECLAISSÉ-WALFORD

11. *Sukkah* 4:5.

Psalm 119: Cause Me to Live in Your Instruction

Psalm 119, a massive alphabetic acrostic, follows the "Egyptian Hallel" psalms (Psalms 113–18). It contrasts dramatically with the two alphabetic acrostics that precede the Egyptian Hallels, Psalms 111 and 112. While Psalm 111 consists of only seventy-two words and Psalm 112 of seventy-nine words, Psalm 119 has 176 verses, in which eight verses of the psalmic poem begin with each successive letter of the Hebrew alphabet. The three psalms, however, share a common theme of reverence for the torah, the instruction given by God to the ancient Israelites at Sinai. Psalm 119 begins with the words *Content (ʾašrê) are the ones whose way is sincere, the ones who walk in the instruction (tôrâ)* of the LORD. It is recited at the Feast of Pentecost, the spring festival observed fifty days after Passover, which celebrates the giving of the torah to Moses at Sinai during the wilderness wanderings.

The poet of Psalm 119 employed a common "wisdom" form in composing the psalm — the acrostic. Allen describes it as "the most developed instance [of the acrostic form] in the OT."[1] Kraus writes, "The art of alphabetical organization has produced an unusual opus which in schematism and compulsion of form has no parallel in the OT."[2] Acrostic poems were the works of highly-skilled literary artists and functioned in ancient Israelite literature in a number of ways. Acrostics were most likely memory devices to aid in private and public — individual and corporate — recitation. Literarily, they summarized all that could be said or that needed to be said about a particular subject from *ʾālep* to *tāw,* from A to Z. Adele Berlin comments on the structure of Psalm 145, another alphabetic acrostic:

> The poet praises God with everything from A to Z: his praise is all-inclusive. More than that, the entire alphabet, the source of all words, is marshalled praise of God. One cannot actually use all of the words in a language, but by using the alphabet one uses all potential words.[3]

The acrostic structure of Psalm 119 marks it as a wisdom composition, as do its content and message. Wisdom psalms are defined as those that provide "instruction in right living and right faith in the tradition of the other wisdom writings of the Old Testament — Proverbs, Ecclesiastes, and Job. And in most of these

1. *Psalms 101–150,* p. 139.

2. *Psalms 60–150,* p. 411.

3. "The Rhetoric of Psalm 145," in *Biblical and Related Studies Presented to Samuel Iwry,* ed. Ann Kort and Scott Morschauser (Winona Lake: Eisenbrauns, 1985), p. 18. Kathleen O'Connor, in *Lamentations and the Tears of the World* (Maryknoll: Orbis, 2002), p. 12, adds, "Alphabetic devices embody struggles of survivors to contain and control the chaos of unstructured pain . . . the poems are not spontaneous outbursts but carefully composed works."

psalms the path to wisdom is through adherence to the Torah, the instruction of the Lord."[4] Within the poetic lines of Psalm 119, seven Hebrew words are used in synonymous interchange with the word *tôrâ* (translated below as *instruction*), which itself is used twenty-five times in the psalm. The words are:

- *'ēḏâ,* translated here as "decree" (used 23 times)
- *mišpāṭ,* "ordinance" (23 times)
- *ḥōq,* "statute" (22 times)
- *dāḇār,* "word" (22 times)
- *miṣwâ,* "commandment" (22 times)
- *piqqûḏ,* "precept" (21 times)
- *'imrâ,* "promise" (19 times)

Five of the eight synonyms *(tôrâ, 'ēḏâ, piqqûḏ, miṣwâ, mišpāṭ)* occur in Ps. 19:7-9, leading to the suggestion that Psalm 119 may be dependent upon Psalm 19.[5] While there is no regularity in their use, one of the eight synonymous words occurs in every verse of Psalm 119, except as follows:

- No synonym occurs in vv. 3, 37, 90, 122.
- Two synonyms occur in vv. 16, 48, 160, 168, 172.[6]

Scholars suggest that the literary use of eight synonyms parallels the formal structure of the psalm, in which stanzas of eight verses begin with each letter of the Hebrew alphabet. The distribution of synonyms within each of the eight-verse stanzas is as follows:

vv. 1-8	7 of 8 synonyms
vv. 9-16	7 of 8 synonyms[7]
vv. 17-24	6 of 8 synonyms
vv. 25-32	7 of 8 synonyms
vv. 33-40	8 of 8 synonyms
vv. 41-48	8 of 8 synonyms[8]
vv. 49-56	6 of 8 synonyms[9]

4. deClaissé-Walford, *Introduction to the Psalms,* pp. 25-26. This author includes Pss. 1, 32, 37, 49, 73, 78, 112, 119, 127, 128, 133, and 145 in the *Gattung* "wisdom psalm."

5. Allen, *Psalms 101–150,* p. 139.

6. See David Noel Freedman's intriguing explanation for the omission and doubling of the synonyms in *Psalm 119: The Exaltation of Torah* (Biblical and Judaic Studies 6; Winona Lake: Eisenbrauns, 1999), pp. 25-55

7. This is the only stanza which does not include "instruction" *(tôrâ).*

8. In this stanza, "word" *(dāḇār)* and "commandment" *(mišwôṯ)* occur twice.

9. In this stanza, "instruction" *(tôrâ)* occurs three times.

vv. 57-64	8 of 8 synonyms
vv. 65-72	6 of 8 synonyms
vv. 73-80	8 of 8 synonyms
vv. 81-88	8 of 8 synonyms
vv. 89-96	6 of 8 synonyms
vv. 97-104	7 of 8 synonyms
vv. 105-12	6 of 8 synonyms
vv. 113-20	7 of 8 synonyms
vv. 121-28	7 of 8 synonyms
vv. 129-36	8 of 8 synonyms
vv. 137-44	7 of 8 synonyms
vv. 145-52	7 of 8 synonyms
vv. 153-60	8 of 8 synonyms
vv. 161-68	7 of 8 synonyms
vv. 169-76	7 of 8 synonyms[10]

While each synonym carries a slightly different nuance of meaning, little is gained by attempting to distinguish a separate meaning, theological or otherwise, for each of them. Equally difficult is describing the psalm in any sort of formal structure, other than its alphabetic stanzas.

ʾĀlep

1 *Content are the ones whose way is sincere,*
the ones who walk in the instruction of the L*ORD.*
2 *Content are the ones who keep watch over his decrees;*
with all of their heart they seek him.
3 *They also do not work injustice,*
but in his ways they walk.
4 *You, you have commanded your precepts*
to be guarded[11] *diligently.*
5 *O that my ways were firm,*
in order to guard your statutes.
6 *Then I would not be ashamed*
when I fix my eyes on all of your commandments.
7 *I will give thanks to you with an upright heart,*
when I learn the ordinances of your righteousness.
8 *Your statutes I will guard;*
do not forsake me utterly.

10. In this stanza, "promise" *(ʾimrâ)* occurs twice.

11. While MT has a *qal* infinitive construct, the best sense is found by rendering the translation in the passive voice *(niphal)*, along with NRSV.

Bêt

9 *How can the young person cleanse his path?*
By[12] *guarding your word.*[13]
10 *With all my heart I have sought you;*
do not allow me to stray from your commandments.
11 *In my heart I have hidden your promise*
so that I might not sin against you.
12 *Blessed are you, O LORD;*
Teach me your statutes.
13 *With my lips I have spoken about*
all of the ordinances of your mouth.
14 *In the way of your decrees I find joy*
as in any wealth.
15 *On your precepts I will meditate,*
and I will fix my eyes upon your paths.
16 *In your statutes I will delight;*
I will not forget your way.

Gîmel

17 *Do good to your servant,*
So that I may live and guard your word.
18 *Open my eyes so that I may fix my eyes*
on the wondrous things out of your instruction.
19 *A wanderer am I in the land;*
do not hide from me your commandments.
20 *My inmost being is crushed with longing*
for your ordinances at all times.
21 *You rebuke the stranger, the cursed ones,*
the ones who wander from your commandments.
22 *Roll away from upon me shame and contempt,*
for your decrees I observe.
23 *Though princes sit down and*[14] *concerning me they speak one with another,*
your servant meditates on your statutes.
24 *Even so your decrees are my delight;*
they are my council.

12. In MT, the infinitive construct form has the preposition l^e; LXX emends it to b^e.

13. In numerous places in the psalm, *BHS* suggests emending the MT rendering of one of the eight synonyms from a singular form to a plural form or from a plural form to a singular form. In every instance except v. 98, this translation follows MT.

14. MT has no conjunction here, but LXX and Syr add the *wāw*-conjunction.

Dālet

25 *My inmost being clings to the dust;*
cause me to live according to your word.
26 *My ways I recounted and you answered me;*
teach me your statutes.
27 *The way of your precepts causes me to understand,*
and I will meditate on your wondrous works.
28 *My inmost being trickles away because of sorrow;*
cause me to rise up according to your word.
29 *The way of falsehood put away from me,*
and your instruction bestow upon me.
30 *The way of truth I have chosen;*
your ordinances I have set down.
31 *I cling to your decrees, O LORD;*
do not put me to shame.
32 *The way of your commandments I run after,*
for you enlarge my heart.

Hê

33 *Teach me, O LORD, the way of your statutes,*
and I will observe it to the end.
34 *Cause me to understand and I will keep watch over your instruction,*
and I will guard it with all my heart.
35 *Cause me to walk in the trodden path of your commandments,*
for in it I find pleasure.
36 *Incline my heart to your decrees,*
and not to unjust gain.
37 *Turn my eye away from gazing upon deception;*
in your way cause me to live.
38 *Fulfill for your servant your promise,*
which is for the one who reverences you.
39 *Turn away my reproach which I dread,*
for your ordinances are good.
40 *Behold, I long for your precepts;*
in your righteousness cause me to live.

Wāw

41 *And may your* hesed *come to me, O LORD,*
your help according to your promise.
42 *And I will answer the one who reproaches me with a word,*
for I have trusted in your word.
43 *And do not withdraw from my mouth the word of truth utterly,*
because for your ordinance I wait expectantly.
44 *And I will guard your instruction continually*

for all time and beyond.
45 *And I will walk about in a broad space,*
for your precepts I seek.
46 *And I will speak concerning your decrees in the presence of kings,*
and I will not be ashamed.
47 *And I will delight in your commandments*
that I love.
48 *And I will lift up the palms of my hands to your commandments that I love,*
and I will meditate upon your statutes.

Zayin 49 *Remember the word to your servant,*
concerning which you caused me to wait expectantly.
50 *This is my comfort in my affliction,*
that your promise causes me to live.
51 *The insolent scorn me utterly,*
but from your instruction I have not turned aside.
52 *I have remembered your ordinances from of old, O* L*ORD*,
and I feel comforted.
53 *Hot anger had seized me because of the wicked,*
the ones forsaking your instruction.
54 *Songs will your statutes be to me*
in the house of my dwelling.
55 *I have remembered your name in the night, O* L*ORD*,
and I will guard your instruction.
56 *This has come to me,*
for your precepts I have kept watch over.

Ḥêt 57 *My portion is the* L*ORD*;
I promise to keep your words.
58 *I implore your face with all my heart;*
be gracious to me according to your promise.
59 *I think on my ways;*
I turn my feet toward your decrees.
60 *I hurry and I do not delay*
to keep your commandments.
61 *The snares of the wicked surround me,*
but your instruction I do not forget.
62 *In the midst of the night I rise up to give praise to you*
concerning the ordinances of your righteousness.
63 *A friend am I to all who reverence you*

and to those who keep your precepts.
64 *Your* hesed, *O* L*ORD*, *fills the earth;*
teach me your statutes.

Têt 65 *The good you do with your servant,*
O L*ORD*, *according to your word.*
66 *Good understanding and good knowledge teach me,*
for in your commandments I trust.
67 *Before I was bowed down, I was going astray,*
but now your promise I guard.
68 *Good are you and one who does good;*
teach me your statutes.
69 *The insolent smear me with falsehood,*
but I with all heart will keep watch over your precepts.
70 *As fat as marrow is their heart,*
but I delight in your instruction.
71 *It is good for me that I have been bowed down,*
so that I might learn your statutes.
72 *Good for me is the instruction of your mouth,*
better than thousands of pieces of gold and silver.

Yôd 73 *Your hands made me and fashioned me;*
cause me to understand and I will learn your commandments.
74 *The ones reverencing you will see me and rejoice,*
because for your word I have waited expectantly.
75 *I know, O* L*ORD*, *that righteous are your ordinances*
and in trustworthiness you have bowed me down.
76 *Let your* hesed *be to me a comfort,*
as your promise to your servant.
77 *Your compassions enter into me and I will live,*
for your instruction is my delight.
78 *The insolent will be ashamed, for with falsehood they have seduced me,*
but I will meditate on your precepts.
79 *Those who reverence you will turn to me,*
and those who know your decrees.
80 *My heart is blameless in your statutes,*
so that I am not ashamed.

Kāp 81 *My inmost being wastes away with longing for your help;*
for your word I wait expectantly.

82 *My eyes waste away with longing for your promise,*
saying, "When will you comfort me?"
83 *For you have become like a wineskin in the smoke;*
but your statutes I have not forgotten.
84 *How long are the days of your servant?*
When will you judge those pursuing me?
85 *The insolent have dug for me pits*
that are not according to your instruction.
86 *All of your commandments are trustworthy;*
in falsehood they pursue me. Help me.
87 *Almost they have made me waste away with longing on the earth,*
but I, I have not forsaken your precepts.
88 *In your* hesed *cause me to live,*
and I will guard the decree of your mouth.

Lāmed 89 *For all time, O LORD,*
your word has stood firm in the heavens.
90 *From generation to generation is your trustworthiness;*
you have established the earth and it stands fast.
91 *By your ordinances they stand fast today,*
for all things belong to your servants.
92 *If your instruction were not my delight,*
then I would have perished in my misery.
93 *For all time I will not forget your precepts,*
for by them you have caused me to live.
94 *I am yours; help me,*
for your precepts I have sought.
95 *The wicked lie in wait for me in order to destroy me,*
but your decrees I attend to.
96 *To all perfection I have seen an end,*
but your commandment is exceedingly broad.

Mêm 97 *How I love your instruction;*
all of the day I meditate on it.
98 *Your commandment*[15] *will make me wiser than my enemies,*
because for all time it is with me.
99 *I am more insightful than all of my teachers,*
for your decrees are meditation for me.

15. LXX emends the plural form of *commandment* of MT to the singular form to harmonize with the 3fs independent pronoun *hîʾ* found in the second colon of the verse.

100 *I am more perceptive than the elders,*
for your precepts I attend to.
101 *From every path of the bad I restrain my feet,*
so that I might keep your word.
102 *From your ordinances I do not turn aside,*
for you, you have instructed me.
103 *How your words are pleasant to my palate,*
better than honey to my mouth.
104 *Your precepts I attend to;*
therefore I hate every path of falsehood.

Nûn

105 *A lamp to my foot is your word*
and a light to my trodden path.
106 *I swore an oath and I confirm it,*
to keep the ordinances of your righteousness.
107 *I am bowed down utterly;*
O Lord, cause me to live according to your way.
108 *The gift of my mouth receive graciously, O Lord,*
and your ordinances teach me.
109 *My inmost being is in the palm of my hand continually,*
and your instruction I have not forgotten.
110 *The wicked lay a snare for me,*
but from your precepts I have not gone astray.
111 *I have inherited your decrees for all time,*
for the delight of my heart they are.
112 *I spread out my heart to the doings of your statutes,*
for all time to the end.

Sāmek

113 *Doubters I hate,*
but your instruction I love.
114 *My hiding place and my shield are you;*
for your word I wait expectantly.
115 *Turn aside from me, you doers of wrong things,*
that I may keep watch over the commandments of my God.
116 *Uphold me according to your promise and I will live;*
and do not put me to shame in my hope.
117 *Uphold me and I will be helped,*
and I will look to your statutes continually.
118 *You reject all who go astray from your statutes,*
for falsehood is their deceit.
119 *Like dross, you bring to an end all the wicked ones of the earth;*
therefore I love your decrees.

120 *My flesh trembles because of your awesomeness;*
and your ordinances I reverence.

'Ayin 121 *I have done justice and righteousness;*
do not leave me to my oppressors.
122 *Guarantee to your servant the good;*
do not let the insolent oppress me.
123 *My eyes waste away with longing for your help*
and for the promise of your righteousness.
124 *Do to your servant according to your* hesed,
and your statutes teach me.
125 *Your servant am I; cause me to understand,*
and I will know your decrees.
126 *It is time for the* LORD *to act;*
they have broken your instruction.
127 *Because of this, I love your commandments*
more than gold and more than pure gold.
128 *Because of this all of your precepts*[16] *I declare upright;*
every path of falsehood I hate.

Pê 129 *Wondrous are your decrees;*
because of this my inmost being keeps watch over them.
130 *The insight of your words gives light,*
making perceptive the foolish ones.
131 *My mouth I open wide and pant,*
because your commandments I long for.
132 *Face me and be gracious to me,*
like the justice due to those who love your name.
133 *Make my steps firm in your promise,*
and do not let any iniquity rule over me.
134 *Free me from the oppressor of humanity,*
and I will keep your precepts.
135 *Make your face shine upon your servant*
and teach me your statutes.
136 *Rivers of water my eyes weep,*
because others do not keep your instruction.

Ṣādê 137 *Righteous are you, O* LORD,
and upright are your ordinances.
138 *You have commanded the righteousness of your decrees,*

16. MT's *kol piqqûḏê kōl* is emended to *lᵉḵol piqqûḏêḵā,* following LXX and Jerome.

and they are exceedingly trustworthy.
139 *My zeal consumes me,*
for your words my oppressors have forgotten.
140 *Your promise has been refined exceedingly,*
and your servant loves it.
141 *Small am I and despised,*
but your precepts I have not forgotten.
142 *Your righteousness is righteous for all time,*
and your instruction is trustworthy.
143 *Oppression and distress have found me;*
your commandments are my delight.
144 *Righteous are your decrees for all time;*
cause me to perceive and I will live.

Qôp

145 *I cry out with all my heart. Answer me, O Lord;*
your statutes I will keep watch over.
146 *I cry out to you. Help me,*
and I will guard your decrees.
147 *I have gone out early in the twilight so that I may cry for help;*
for your words I wait expectantly.
148 *My eyes have gone out early in the night watch*
in order to meditate upon your promise.
149 *Hear my voice according to your* hesed, *O Lord,*
according to your ordinance cause me to live.
150 *Those who pursue an evil deed draw near;*
from your instruction they have gone far away.
151 *Near are you, O Lord,*
and all of your commandments are trustworthy.
152 *Long ago I knew your decrees,*[17]
because for all time you have established them.

Rêš

153 *See my affliction and rescue me,*
for your instruction I have not forgotten.
154 *Plead my cause and redeem me;*
on account of your promise cause me to live.
155 *Far from the wicked is help,*
for your statutes they do not seek.
156 *Your compassions are great, O Lord;*

17. Along with Syr, this translation emends the text to omit the preposition *min* from the beginning of *decrees.*

according to your ordinances cause me to live.
157 *Many are those who pursue me and oppress me,*
but from your decrees I have not turned aside.
158 *I have seen deceivers and I loathe them,*
those who do not guard your promise.
159 *See, how I love your precepts;*
O Lord, according to your hesed *cause me to live.*
160 *The essence of your word is trustworthiness,*
and for all time is every ordinance of your righteousness.

Śîn

161 *Princes pursue me without cause,*
but because of your word my heart is in awe.
162 *I leap with joy because of your promise,*
like the finding of great gain.
163 *Falsehood I hate and abhor;*
your instruction I love.
164 *Seven times a day I praise you*
because of the ordinances of your righteousness.
165 *Great well-being is to those who love your instruction,*
and there is not to them a stumbling block.
166 *I wait for your help, O Lord,*
and your commandments I have observed.
167 *My inmost being has kept your decrees,*
and I love them exceedingly.
168 *I have kept your precepts and your decrees,*
for all of my ways are before you.

Tāw

169 *My rejoicing comes into your presence, O Lord;*
according to your word instruct me.
170 *My prayer enters into your presence;*
according to your promise deliver me.
171 *My lips pour forth praise,*
for you teach me your statutes.
172 *My tongue sings your promise,*
for all of your commandments are righteous.
173 *Your hand is my help,*
for your precepts I have chosen.
174 *I long for your help, O Lord,*
and your instruction is my delight.
175 *My inmost being will live and will praise you,*
and your ordinances will help me.

176 *I have gone astray like a perishing*[18] *sheep; seek out your servant,*
for your commandments I have not forgotten.

1-8 The first two verses of Psalm 119 begin with the word *'ašrê,* the same word that begins the Psalter in Ps. 1:1.[19] Contentment in Psalm 119 is traced to the same source as in Psalm 1 — the instruction (torah) of the Lord.

9-16 The second stanza of Psalm 119 begins with a wisdom question — *How can the young person cleanse his path?* — that echoes the wisdom words of Ps. 73:13 and Prov. 20:9. Neither Psalm 73 nor Proverbs 20 provides an answer to the question. According to 119:9, the answer is: "by guarding the word of the LORD." This is the only stanza in Psalm 119 in which the word *tôrâ* does not occur.

17-24 While Psalm 119 is classified as a "wisdom" psalm, lament elements are prominent in many portions of it.[20] Lament elements dominate vv. 17-24. In this stanza, words of petition (vv. 17-18) give way to complaint (v. 19), move on to a description of the oppressors (vv. 21-23), and end with words of trust (v. 24).

25-32 The lament form continues in this stanza, in which the elements of the lament mingle freely. The psalmist's words move between complaint — *My inmost being clings to the dust* (v. 25); petition — *cause me to rise up according to your word* (v. 28); and trust — *I cling to your decrees, O LORD* (v. 31).

33-40 Petition dominates in this stanza. A series of *hiphil*-causative verbs drives the movement of the verses: *teach me* (v. 33); *cause me to understand* (v. 34); *cause me to walk* (v. 35); *incline my heart* (v. 36); *turn my eye away* (v. 37); *fulfill* (v. 38); *turn away* (v. 39).

41-48 In this stanza, the psalmist speaks hopeful words of trust in God, in seeming answer to the petitions of the previous verses. The psalmist *will answer the one who reproaches* (v. 42); *will guard your instruction* (v. 44); *will walk about in a broad space* (v. 45); *will speak concerning your decrees* (v. 46); *will delight in your commandments* (v. 47); and *will lift up the palms of my hands to your commandments* and *meditate upon your statutes* (v. 48).

49-56 This stanza is characterized by the repetition of the verb *remember.* In v. 49, the psalm-singer implores God to *remember,* and in vv. 52 and

18. The usual English translation for *'ōḇēḏ* in v. 176 is "lost" (NRSV, NIV, NASB), but the Hebrew root means "to perish." While the Hebrew root in the *qal* stem is occasionally rendered "to wander off, to stray" in reference to animals, it connotes animals who will perish because they have wandered away from the safety of the herd. See Benedikt Otzen, "*'āḇaḏ,*" *TDOT* 1:19-23.

19. For a full discussion of the meaning of *'ašrê,* see the commentary on Ps. 112:1b.

20. See deClaissé-Walford, *Introduction to the Psalms,* pp. 23-25, for a form-critical analysis of lament psalms.

55, the psalmist says, *I have remembered.* The word *remember* is powerful and pervasive in the Hebrew Bible. In Gen. 9:16, God says to Noah, "When the bow is in the clouds, I will see it and *remember* the everlasting covenant between God and every living creature of all flesh that is on the earth." When the Israelites are in slavery in Egypt, "God heard their groaning, and God *remembered* his covenant with Abraham, Isaac, and Jacob" (Exod. 2:24). In the Decalogue, God calls the Israelites to *remember* the sabbath day, and keep it holy" (Exod. 20:8). The word *remember* occurs nearly two hundred times in the Hebrew Bible and generally conveys the idea of "the presence and acceptance of something in the mind."[21] Interestingly, the word *instruction (tôrâ)* occurs three times in this stanza (vv. 51, 53, and 55).

57-64 This stanza begins with words about God's gift of the land of *promise* to the Israelites. Verse 57's *portion (ḥēleq)* calls to mind the division of land among the Israelites in the book of Joshua (Josh. 15:13; 18:7; 19:9). It ends in v. 64 by declaring that God's *hesed fills the earth. Tôrâ* and all of its synonyms occur in these verses.

65-72 The word *good (ṭôḇ)* occurs six times in this stanza, emphasizing the goodness of God and God's *instruction* even in the midst of the psalmist's despair (vv. 67, 69, 71). In v. 72, it forms a *better than (ṭôḇ . . . min)* structure typical of wisdom literature.[22]

73-80 This stanza affirms that God's *hands made (ʿāśâ)* and *fashioned (kûn)* the psalmist (v. 73), that God's *hesed* is a *comfort* (v. 76), and that God's *compassions (raḥ^{a}mîm)* allow the psalmist to *live* (v. 77). In response, the psalm-singer finds delight in God's instruction (v. 77), *meditates* on God's *precepts* (v. 78) and is not ashamed (v. 80).

81-88 In this stanza, the psalmist complains of *wasting away with longing (kālâ)* (vv. 81, 82, and 87) and states that if God will allow the psalmist to live *in your* hesed, then the psalmist *will guard the decree (ʿēḏûṯ) of your mouth* (v. 88).

89-96 The words of this stanza are an exuberant proclamation by the psalmist that God has *established* the *heavens* and the *earth* and God's *word* stands *firm* in them (vv. 89-90). The words of God's instruction give life to the psalmist (v. 93) and provide hope in times of difficulty (v. 95).

97-104 Here the psalmist expresses *love (ʾāhab)* for the *instruction* of God and employs a number of "wisdom words" to convey the benefits to the psalmist of God's instruction: *wise (ḥāḵam,* v. 98), *insightful (śāḵal,* v. 99), and *perceptive (bîn,* v. 100, 104).

105-12 Just as v. 57's *portion* calls to mind the division of land among the Israelites in the book of Joshua, so does v. 111's *inherit (nāhal,* Josh. 11:23;

21. Hermann Eising, "*zāḵar,*" *TDOT* 4:65.

22. See, e.g., Prov. 12:9; 15:16, 17; 16:8; 17:1, 12; 19:1; 22:1; 25:7, 24; 27:5, 10; 28:6.

14:3). The psalmist celebrates the *decrees (ʿēḏôṯ)* of God as a *delight to the heart* (v. 111).

113-20 Verses 113 and 119 declare the psalmist's *hate (śānēʾ)* for doubters and *love (ʾahab)* for God's instruction and decrees. The psalmist describes God as a *hiding place (sēṯer)* and a *shield (māḡēn)* in v. 114, language found often in the Psalter.

121-28 In this stanza, the psalmist implores God to do *good (ṭôḇ,* v. 122) and *hesed* (v. 124) because of the psalm-singer's *justice (mišpāṭ) and righteousness (ṣeḏeq,* vv. 121) and not leave the psalmist to the devices of *oppressors (ʿōšᵉqāy,* v. 121) and the *insolent (zērîm,* v. 122).

129-36 The stanza begins with the psalmist praising God for God's *wondrous (pālāʾ) decrees* and *insightful (pēṯaḥ) words* (vv. 129-30).[23] The word translated *wondrous (pālāʾ)* occurs in its various forms some thirty-three times in the book of Psalms, often in reference to the deliverance of the Israelites from Egypt (105:2, 5; 106:7, 22; 136:4). The word is used most often in Biblical Hebrew to describe "extraordinary phenomena, transcending the power of human knowledge and imagination."[24] This word finds perhaps its best parallel in the word "miracle." In his 1958 book *Moses,* the Jewish philosopher Martin Buber writes:

> The concept of miracle which is permissible from the historical approach can be defined at its starting point as an abiding astonishment. The philosophizing and the religious person both wonder at the phenomenon, but the one neutralizes his wonder in ideal knowledge, while the other abides in wonder; no knowledge, no cognition, can weaken his astonishment. Any causal explanation only deepens the wonder for him. . . . Miracle is not something "supernatural" or "superhistorical," but an incident, an event which can be fully included in the objective, scientific nexus of nature and history; the vital meaning of which, however, for the person to whom it occurs, destroys the security of the whole nexus of knowledge for him, and explodes the fixity of the fields of experience named "Nature" and "History." Miracle is simply what happens; insofar as it meets people who are capable of receiving it, or prepared to receive it, as miracle.[25]

In response to the *wondrous decrees* and *insightful words* of God, the psalmist *longs for* and *pants* after the *commandments* and implores God to *face me and be gracious to me* (v. 132), *make my steps firm* (v. 133), *free me from the oppressor of humanity* (v. 134), and *make your face shine upon your servant* (v. 135).

23. *pālāʾ* occurs previously in vv. 18 and 27.

24. Joachim Conrad, "*plʾ*," in *TDOT* 11:534.

25. *Moses: The Revelation and the Covenant* (New York: Harper, 1958), pp. 75-76.

The stanza ends with the psalmist weeping because others do not keep the instructions of the Lord (v. 136).

137-44 The psalm-singer repeatedly uses the words *righteous (ṣeḏeq)* and *trustworthy (ʾemeṯ)* in this stanza (vv. 137, 138, 142, 144) to describe God and God's instructions and states that while the oppressors have *forgotten* the *words* of God (v. 139), the psalmist has not (v. 141). Familiar words of petition occur in v. 144: *cause me to perceive (bîn) and I will live (ḥāyâ)* (see vv. 17, 25, 27, 34, 37, 40, 73, 77, 88, 93, 107, 125).

145-52 In this stanza, the psalmist repeatedly cries out to God for an *answer,* for *help,* and for life. *Those who pursue evil* are nearby (v. 150), but the psalm-singer is confident in the God who is *near* (v. 151) and who *long ago established* the *decrees* that the psalmist knows (v. 152). Seven of the eight synonyms occur in this stanza.

153-60 The petition *cause me to live,* which pervades this psalm (see vv. 25, 37, 50, 93, 107, 116, 144, 149), occurs repeatedly in this stanza, in vv. 154, 156, and 159. The psalmist cites God's *promise (ʾimrâ,* v. 154), *ordinances (mišpāṭ,* v. 156), and *hesed* (v. 159) as the basis of the petition. The psalmist has *not forgotten* (v. 153) and has *not turned aside* (v. 157) from God's *instruction* and *decrees,* while *the wicked* (v. 155), the pursuers and oppressors (v. 157), and the *deceivers* (v. 158) *do not seek* (v. 155) and *do not guard* (v. 158) God's *statutes* and *promise.*

161-68 This stanza voices the psalmist's *joy* and sense of *well-being* in the *instruction* of God. Verse 164 states that the psalmist *praises* God *seven times a day.* The verbal root *praise (hālal)* occurs frequently in Book Five (more than sixty times), but its first occurrence in Psalm 119 is in v. 164.

169-76 In the concluding words of Psalm 119, the psalmist rejoices (v. 169), prays (v. 170), *pours forth praise* (v. 171), and *sings* (v. 172) in utter *delight* at the *instruction* of God. Because of this, the *inmost being (nep̄eš)* of the psalmist will *live* and will *praise* God. Just as the first verse of Psalm 119 echoes the first verse of Psalm 1 *(ʾašrê),* so the final verse of Psalm 119 echoes Psalm 1's final verse. In 119:176, the psalmist confesses to having *gone astray like a perishing (ʾōḇēḏ) sheep* and implores God to *seek out your servant, for your commandments I have not forgotten.* Psalm 1:6 states, "for the LORD watches over the way of the righteous, but the way of the wicked will perish *(tōʾḇēḏ).*

The singer of Psalm 119 weaves together words of lament, petition, trust, and exuberant joy in this marvelous ode to the instruction *(tôrâ)* of YHWH. McCann writes, "As a literary artist, the psalmist intended the structure of the poem to reinforce its theological content. In short, *torah* — God's revelatory instruction — is pervasive and all-encompassing."[26] Westermann writes, "If a person succeeds in reading this psalm's 176 verses one after the other at one

26. "The Book of Psalms," p. 1166.

sitting, the effect is overwhelming. In its extent the psalm has the effect of a massive mountain range. One has the feeling that it represents the boundary between the world of the Psalms and a different world, that of law piety."[27]

The instruction (torah) of Yahweh, in its eight synonymous renderings, is the central focus of Psalm 119. But Psalm 119 never actually defines or speaks of the origin of the instruction of Yahweh. Moses, Sinai, the content of the instruction are never mentioned. David Noel Freedman writes, "In Psalm 119 *tôrâ* is a monolithic presence, consisting of individual laws and teachings to be sure, but described in only the most general terms, namely the 8 interchangeable *tôrâ*-words . . . *Tôrâ* has become for the psalmist much more than the laws by which Israel should live, as given in the Pentateuch; *tôrâ* has become a personal way to God."[28] He goes on to suggest, "In short, Psalm 119 gives *tôrâ* virtually the status of a divine hypostasis, like wisdom *(ḥokmâ)* in Proverbs 8."[29]

In Psalm 119, then, the instruction of Yahweh is not presented as a strict set of rules and regulations, but a way of life or approach to being that brings one closer to God. The psalmist repeatedly implores God to *cause me to live* because of the *instruction,* the *decree,* the *precept,* the *ordinance,* the *words,* the *promise,* the *statute,* the *commandment* — because of all of the teachings of God for the good of humankind. In the gospel of Matthew, Jesus says,

> Do not think that I have come to abolish the law or the prophets; I have come not to abolish but to fulfill. For truly I tell you, until heaven and earth pass away, not one iota, not one stroke of a letter, will pass from the law until all is accomplished. Therefore, whoever annuls one of the least of these commandments, and teaches others to do the same, will be called least in the kingdom of heaven; but whoever does them and teaches them will be called great in the kingdom of heaven. (Matt. 5:17-19)

Our God is not a God of arbitrary rules and regulations, although that is what Christianity often feels like in our day and time. God graciously gave the Israelites a means for living as God's people — not in arbitrariness, but in *hesed,* in covenant commitment, loyalty, and love. May we, with the psalmist, be able to sing,

> Your *hesed,* O LORD, fills the earth;
>   teach me your statutes. (119:64)
> See, how I love your precepts;
>   O LORD, according to your *hesed* cause me to live. (119:159)

NANCY DECLAISSÉ-WALFORD

27. *The Psalms,* p. 117.
28. *Psalm 119,* p. 89.
29. *Psalm 119,* p. 89.

The Songs of the Ascents: Psalms 120–134

INTRODUCTION

The superscriptions of Psalms 120–34 identify each of them as "A Song of the Ascents" *(šîr hammaʿ^{a}lôṯ)*.[1] The verbal root of "ascents" is *ʿālâ* ("go up"). The frequent references to Jerusalem and Zion in this collection of psalms (Pss. 122:3, 6; 125:1, 2; 126:1; 128:5; 129:5; 132:13; 133:3; 134:3) may account for their ascriptions. Since Jerusalem sits on a hill, no matter where one comes from, one always "goes up" to Jerusalem.[2] Pilgrims on their way to Jerusalem may have sung the Songs of the Ascents, which, except for Psalm 132, are brief and thus easy to memorize. Although these fifteen psalms most likely come from a variety of times and places in ancient Israel, the message of the collection as a whole is that Jerusalem is the place for the coming together of the people of God for celebrations and commemorations and for acknowledging the goodness and help of the God of the Israelites.

Some speculate that the "ascents" referred to in Psalms 120–34 are the steps of the temple, which Ezekiel calls "ascents" *(maʿ^{a}lôṯ*]. In Ezek. 40:6, the prophet sees a man going into the gateway of the temple, "going up *(ʿālâ)* its steps *(maʿ^{a}lôṯ)*." The *Mishnah* states, "fifteen steps led up within [the Court of the Women] to the Court of the Israelites, corresponding to the fifteen songs of the steps in the Psalms, and upon them the Levites used to sing."[3] And, "The Levites on harps, and on lyres, and with cymbals, and with trumpets and with other instruments of music without number upon the fifteen steps leading down from the Court of the Israelites to the Women's Court, corresponding to 'The Fifteen Songs of Ascent' in the Psalms; upon them the Levites used to stand with musical instruments and sing hymns."[4]

Other scholars suggest that the title "Songs of the Ascents" is a reflection of the very structure of the collection's psalms. Within each psalm, and often as an *inclusio* around the verses of each psalm, the Songs of the Ascents contain verbal "step" connections that move the reciter through the cola and

1. Ps. 121's superscription is slightly different, reading *šîr lammʿ^{a}lôṯ* ("A Song for the Going Up"). Pss. 122, 124, 131, and 133 add *l^{e}dāwiḏ*, and Ps. 127 adds *lišlōmōh*.

2. In 1 Kgs. 12:28, Jeroboam says to the Israelites, "You have gone up *(ʿālâ)* to Jerusalem long enough." Isa. 2:3 and Mic. 4:2 envision a time when "Many peoples shall come and say, 'Come, let us go up *(ʿālâ)* to the mountain of the LORD.'"

3. Herbert Danby, *The Mishnah* (Oxford: Clarendon, 1933), *m. Mid.* 2:5.

4. Danby, *The Mishnah, m. Sukkah* 5:4.

stanzas of the psalm.[5] The "step connections," which were most likely fashioned as mnemonic devices, are as follows:

Psalm 120	
vv. 2 & 3:	"deceitful"
vv. 5 & 6:	"settled"
vv. 6 & 7:	"well-being"
vv. 2 & 6:	"inmost being"
Psalm 121	
vv. 1 & 2:	"my help"
vv. 3 & 4:	"will not slumber"
vv. 4 & 5:	"the one who guards"
vv. 7 & 8:	"guard"
vv. 1 & 8:	"to come" *(bô')*
Psalm 122	
vv. 2 & 3:	"Jerusalem"
vv. 4 & 5:	"there" *(šām)*
v. 5:	"thrones"
vv. 6, 7, & 8:	"well-being"
vv. 8 & 9:	"for the sake of"
vv. 1 & 9:	"house of the LORD"
Psalm 123	
vv. 1 & 2:	"eyes"
vv. 2 & 3:	"show favor"
vv. 3 & 4:	"overwhelmed" and "contempt"
Psalm 124	
vv. 1 & 2:	"if the LORD had not been for us"
vv. 3, 4, & 5:	"then"
vv. 4 & 5:	"waters," "inmost being," and "poured over"
vv. 4, 5, & 7:	"inmost being"
v. 7:	"snare" and "fled"
Psalm 125	
vv. 1 & 2:	"the LORD"
v. 2:	"surround"
v. 3:	"the righteous ones"
vv. 3 & 5:	"wicked"

5. This idea was first proposed in the early nineteenth century by Wilhelm Gesenius (*Thesaurus Philologicus Criticus Linguae Hebraeae et Chaldaeae Veteris Testamenti* [2nd ed.; Leipzig: Vogelius, 1839], 2:1031-32). See the brief discussions in Loren D. Crow, *The Songs of Ascents (Psalms 120–134): Their Place in Israelite History and Religion* (SBLDS 148; Atlanta: Scholars, 1996), pp. 15-18; Clifford, *Psalms 73–150*, pp. 216-17; and Davidson, *The Vitality of Worship*, pp. 404-5.

Psalm 126	
vv. 1 & 4:	"restore"
vv. 2 & 3:	"the Lord has done great things"
vv. 2, 5, & 6:	"rejoicing"
vv. 5 & 6:	"sow"
Psalm 127	
v. 1:	"if," "useless," "keep watch"
vv. 1 & 2:	"useless"
vv. 3 & 4:	"children"
vv. 4 & 5:	"mighty one"
Psalm 128	
vv. 1 & 2:	"content"
vv. 1 & 4:	"reverence" *(yārēʾ)*
vv. 2 & 5:	"good"
vv. 3 & 6:	"children"
Psalm 129	
vv. 1 & 2:	"many times they have oppressed me from my youth"
v. 8:	"bless"
Psalm 130	
vv. 1 & 2:	"voice"
v. 5:	"confident"
vv. 5 & 6:	"inmost being"
v. 6:	"those watching for the morning"
vv. 2 & 6:	"the Lord" *(ʾᵃḏōnāy)*
vv. 5 & 7:	"wait expectantly"
vv. 3 & 8:	"iniquities
vv. 7 & 8:	"deliverance"
Psalm 131	
v. 1:	"not"
v. 2:	"inmost being"; "like a sated child" and "upon"
Psalm 132	
vv. 5, 7, & 13:	"dwelling places"
vv. 10 & 11:	"David" and "turn away"
vv. 11 & 12:	"throne"
v. 12:	"children"
vv. 8 & 14:	"resting place"
vv. 9 & 16:	"priests"
vv. 9, 16, & 18:	"clothe"
Psalm 133	
vv. 1 & 2:	"good"
v. 2:	"beard"
vv. 2 & 3:	"go down"

Psalm 134

vv. 1, 2, & 3: "bless" and "the LORD"

Whatever their origins, these "pilgrim" songs became part of a number of festal celebrations in Jerusalem. The Songs of the Ascents are the psalms traditionally recited at the Feast of Tabernacles (Booths or Sukkoth) in the autumn of the year. The Feast of Tabernacles commemorates God's care of the Israelites during the time of the wilderness wanderings, reinforcing the "pilgrimage" theme of the Songs of the Ascents.

An interesting aspect of the Songs of the Ascents is the wide variety of psalm types included in this relatively small collection — individual and community laments (120, 123, 126, 130), individual and community hymns (121, 122, 124, 125, 129, 131, 134, 135, 136), wisdom psalms (127, 128, 133), and a royal psalm (132). The variety of *Gattungen* represented in the Songs of the Ascents troubles many scholars. They question whether such an eclectic mix could ever have been a collection actually used in the life of ancient Israel. Goulder reminds us, however:

> Why should we think that a collection of psalms is not a unity because it contains pieces from different *Gattungen?* Have such critics never attended a church service that began with a confession, included lessons of instruction, hymns of praise and prayers, and ended perhaps with the General Thanksgiving?[6]

Book Five of the Psalter incorporates a number of psalms that are employed in the festival life of Judaism. Psalms 113–18, the Egyptian Hallel Psalms, are recited during the spring Passover celebration; Psalm 119 is read at the Feast of Pentecost, which occurs on the fiftieth day after Passover; and the Songs of the Ascents are used in the celebration of the Feast of Tabernacles (Booths, Sukkoth) in the autumn of each year. The concentration of festival psalms in the middle of Book Five suggests the intentional shaping of a collection of festal psalms in this portion of the Psalter.

6. *The Psalms of the Return,* p. 24.

Psalm 120: I Am for Well-Being

Psalm 120 is the first of the group of fifteen psalms that are identified in their superscriptions as "Songs of the Ascents" (see the Introduction to the Songs of the Ascents). These psalms were most likely sung by pilgrims as they made their way to Jerusalem to celebrate a number of annual religious festivals, including Passover, the Feast of Weeks, and the Feast of Tabernacles. Psalm 120 is classified as an individual lament, sung by a worshipper who is sojourning in a hostile land outside the security of the land of Israel (v. 5). The psalm-singer longs for *well-being (šālôm),* but is surrounded by lips of falsehood, deceitful tongues, and threats of war (vv. 2, 7). Psalm 120 is a fitting beginning of the pilgrimage Songs of the Ascents. Mays writes that the psalm puts the world from which the pilgrims come "in sharpest contrast to the peace they desire and seek in coming to Zion."[1] The seven verses of this brief psalm may be divided into three stanzas:

Words of trust and petition (vv. 1-2)
Words of vengeance (vv. 3-4)
Words of woe (vv. 5-7)

A Song of the Ascents

1 *To the LORD, concerning the oppression that comes to me,*
I cried out and he answered me.[2]
2 *O LORD, deliver my inmost being from the lip of falsehood,*
from the deceitful tongue.

3 *What will he give to you and what will he add to you,*[3]
O deceitful tongue?
4 *Sharp arrows of a warrior*
with burning coals of broom plants.

5 *Woe to me that I have sojourned in Meshek;*
I have settled among the tents of Kedar.
6 *Too long my inmost being has settled*

1. *Psalms,* p. 388.

2. Although the verbs in v. 1 (perfect followed by imperfect with *wāw*-consecutive) are translated as present tense in NRSV and NIV, a better sense of meaning is achieved by translating them according to their verbal aspects, showing completed action.

3. While NRSV follows LXX and Jerome in rendering these two verbs as passive, the MT forms are active.

among those who hate[4] well-being.
7 *I am for well-being and so I speak;[5]*
but they are for war.

1-2 NRSV translates v. 1 as "In my distress I cry to the LORD, that he may answer me," and NIV as "I call on the LORD in my distress, and he answers me," suggesting that the psalmist is crying out because of a present crisis, which is detailed in the remainder of the psalm. We may follow MT, however, and translate the verbs, which are perfect aspect followed by imperfect aspect with *wāw*-consecutive, as past tense (indicating completed action) by supposing that the psalmist is voicing words of trust in God. God has heard the psalmist's cries of *oppression* in the past and has *answered*, giving the psalmist confidence that God will again hear and answer.[6] In v. 2, the psalmist asks God for deliverance from *the lip of falsehood* and *the deceitful tongue*. Clifford suggests, "Though 'deceitful tongue' may refer to a specific calumny, it may also refer more generally to a society where mutual respect and truthfulness have disappeared (as in Pss 10:7; 12:1-4; 31:18)."[7]

3-4 In v. 3, the psalmist speaks directly to *the deceitful tongue: What will he* [the LORD] *give (nāṯan) to you and what will he add (yāsap̄) to you?* — i.e., "what more will he give you?" The verbal pattern of the question is patterned after oath formulas in other places in the Old Testament, in which parties to an oath swear allegiance at the risk of incurring the wrath of God. The usual formula was, "May the Lord do *(ʿāśâ)* to X and more also *(yāsap̄)* . . . ," in which a main verbal action follows *yāsap̄* ("add, do further or longer"). In 1 Sam. 3:17, after Samuel receives a vision in the house of the Lord, he is afraid to tell Eli the vision. But Eli calls Samuel to him and demands to know what God has said, using oath-taking words: "Do not hide it from me. May God do *(ʿāśâ)* so to you and more also *(yāsap̄)*, if you hide anything from me of all that he told you."[8]

Verse 4 describes the wrath of God that the psalmist wishes on *the deceitful tongue. Sharp arrows* is a metaphor for the tongue in the Psalter (see Pss. 57:4; 64:3). Therefore, the deceitful tongue should have *sharp arrows* and *burning* firebrands hurled against it. The *broom plant* is a hard wood known for its long-burning fires.[9]

4. While MT has a singular participle, a few Hebrew manuscripts, along with LXX, Symmachus, Syr, and Jerome, render it as plural.

5. In MT, the *ʾathnaḥ* occurs at *ʾᵃḏabbēr (so I speak)*, dividing the verse into even cola.

6. For a good summary of the various options for understanding the verbs in v. 1, see Crow, *The Songs of Ascents*, p. 32.

7. *Psalms 73–150*, p. 219.

8. Other examples are 1 Sam. 14:44; 2 Sam. 3:9; 1 Kgs. 2:23.

9. Kraus, *Psalms 60–150*, p. 424; Clifford, *Psalms 73–150*, p. 219. The *broom plant* is also mentioned in 1 Kgs. 19:4-5; Job 30:4.

5-7 In these verses, the psalmist laments sojourning and settling *among those who hate well-being (šālôm)* — in *Meshek* and *among the tents of Kedar.* Meshek and Kedar are geographic locations mentioned in other places in the biblical text. *Meshek* is listed in Gen. 10:2 as one of the descendants of Japheth and is linked with Tubal and Javan. In Ezek. 27:13, Meshek is mentioned as a trading partner with Tyre and in 38:2 and 39:1 as part of the kingdom of Magog. According to Josephus, Meshek was located in eastern Asia, in Cappadocia.[10] Ezekiel 32:26 describes the people of Meshek as "uncircumcised" ones who "spread terror in the land of the living." *Kedar* is, according to Gen. 25:13, the second son of Ishmael, and in other places in the biblical text, his descendants (the Kedarites) are north Arabian Bedouin. Isaiah 21:16-17 describes the Kedarites as warriors with bows, whose glory is about to come to an end.

The psalm-singer may be referring to specific locations or may be using the names as metaphors for places far away from the well-being of the land of Israel. Gerstenberger maintains:

> It is futile to speculate about the historicity and geographical location of such hostile tribes. Arguing from the very nature of psalm texts that were used by many people in succeeding generations, . . . one must admit that any possible reference to a concrete situation must have acquired symbolic value in order to stay meaningful to the users of the text.[11]

The exact location of the psalmist's sojourning and settling is not important; the psalmist's distance from the land of Israel is. Outside the land, the psalmist encounters *those who hate well-being (šālôm)* and *are for war* (v. 7); but the psalmist is *for well-being.* The Hebrew word *šālôm* is usually translated in English as "peace." The deeper meaning of the word has to do with wholeness, wellness, and settledness. Mays writes that *šālôm* is "the hopefulness and wholesomeness of life when living is knit into the fabric of relatedness to God and others and world. It is the at-one-ness that makes for goodness."[12] The psalmist contrasts the tranquility of the *šālôm* found in the land of Israel with the turmoil and strife found in other places.

Lips of falsehood, deceitful tongues, and those who hate *šālôm* are the subject of this first Song of the Ascents. The psalm-singer cries out to God to deliver and to make things right. The organs of speech are cited many times in the Psalter as weapons of oppression and hurtfulness (5:9; 12:4; 50:19; 78:36; 109:2; 140:3). The word *lip (śāp̄â)* occurs some twenty-eight times in the Psalter, and *tongue (lāšôn)* occurs some thirty-five times. In addition, in

10. *Ant.* 1.6.1.
11. Gerstenberger, *Psalms: Part 2,* p. 319.
12. *Psalms,* p. 388.

the book of Proverbs, the word "lip" occurs at least thirty-eight times and "tongue" nineteen times.

Words are a powerful commodity. Humanity has been given the gift of speech by the creator God. We can use it for good or for oppression and hurtfulness. The singer of Psalm 120 longs to be away from the strife of lips of falsehood and deceitful tongues and to find the well-being that comes with being in the presence of God. The psalmist remembers past situations of oppression in which God has answered the psalmist (v. 1). God will be faithful again — the psalmist uses strong words of imprecation in confident expectation that God will respond (vv. 3-4). When lips of falsehood and deceitful tongues overwhelm us with strife, may we recall the words of the psalm-singer and cry out in confident expectation that God will indeed respond.

Nancy deClaissé-Walford

Psalm 121: The Lord Will Guard You

Second in a group of fifteen psalms (Pss 120–34) identified in their superscriptions as "A Song of the Ascents" (see the Introduction to the Songs of the Ascents), Psalm 121 is one of the songs that pilgrims sang as they made their way to Jerusalem to celebrate a number of annual festivals, including Passover, the Feast of Weeks, and the Feast of Tabernacles. The psalm's pervasive theme is God's guarding of the worshipper. Its most quoted phrase is v. 2b's *the maker of heavens and earth,* which was incorporated into the Apostles' Creed: "I believe in God the Father Almighty, Maker of heaven and earth."

Psalm 121 is categorized as an individual hymn of thanksgiving. Two voices are represented in the psalm — an individual singer, who states firm trust in the Lord, and a respondent, who assures the singer that the Lord will indeed guard the singer. The word *guard (šāmar)* occurs six times in the eight verses of Psalm 121 and thus can be considered something of a theme for the psalm. This second Song of the Ascents divides into two sections, corresponding to the two voices in the psalm:

A confession of trust by the individual (vv. 1-2)
A response by the priest or worship officiant (vv. 3-8)

A Song of the Ascents[1]

1 *I lift up my eyes to the mountains;*
from where will come my help?
2 *My help is from the* LORD,
the maker of heavens and earth.

3 *He will not allow*[2] *to stumble your foot;*
the one who guards you will not slumber.
4 *Behold, he will not slumber and he will not be asleep,*
the one who guards Israel.
5 *The* LORD *is the one who guards you;*
the LORD *is your shade, at your right hand.*
6 *By day the sun will not strike you,*
and the moon in the night.

1. Ps. 121 is the only Song of the Ascents in which the preposition *le* is added to *hammaʿalôṯ*.

2. The Hebrew form is *ʾal* + imperfect, which is the usual form of the negative imperative. GKC (107p and 109e) states that it is possible for the form to introduce a negative statement.

7 *The* LORD *will guard you from all malicious things;*
he will guard your inmost being.
8 *The* LORD *will guard your going out and your coming in,*
from now and for all time.

1-2 In its canonical position in the Songs of the Ascents, v. 1's *mountain* seems most likely to be Zion, the mountain of Jerusalem. Mountains and high places were commonly associated with deities in the ancient Near East, and the Old Testament text makes numerous references to high places.[3] We may suggest that the psalm-singer in vv. 1 and 2 asks a rhetorical question while surveying the landscape during the journey to Jerusalem: "From which mountain does my help come?" The answer is obvious: "the mountain of the LORD."

The singer identifies the Lord as *my help ('ēzer)* in vv. 1 and 2 (see the commentary on Ps. 108:12).

The phrase *maker of heavens and earth* appears three times in the Songs of the Ascents (v. 2; 124:8; 134:3) and in Ps. 146:6. Its earliest occurrence in the biblical text is in the blessing of Melchizedek in Gen. 14:19. As stated above, the phrase was incorporated into the Apostles' Creed: "I believe in God the Father Almighty, Maker of heaven and earth."

3-8 After the declaration of trust by the psalm-singer, another voice, the respondent, offers words of assurance to the singer. The Lord will not allow the psalm-singer's *foot* to *stumble;* the Lord, *the one who guards* the psalm-singer, *will not slumber* and will not be found *asleep* (vv. 3-4). In these verses we find the first of six appearances of the word *guard (šāmar),* always used in reference to the Lord. While the psalm-singer refers to the Lord as *my help,* the second voice refers to the Lord as *the one who guards.* Anthony Ceresko points out that the word *šāmar* in v. 5a occurs in the middle of the psalm — an equal number of syllables come before and after the word — and therefore suggests that the Lord's "guarding" of the psalm-singer is the central message of the psalm.[4]

The verbal root *šāmar* means "protect, guard, watch over, take care of." It is attested, with the same meaning, in many ancient Semitic languages — Amorite, Ugaritic, Phoenician, Punic, Old South Arabic, and Old Hebrew.[5] The word is rendered in a number of English translations as "keep" (RSV, NRSV, NASB), but the word conveys a more active concept. The Lord does not just "keep" the psalmist in the sense of providing a space for

3. See, e.g., 1 Sam. 9:11-25; 10:5; 1 Kgs. 3:2-4; 11:4-8; 12:31; 2 Kgs. 12:3; 15:4; 18:4; 23:5; Amos 7:9.

4. "Psalm 121: Prayer of a Warrior?" *Bib* 70 (1989) 499.

5. *HALOT,* pp. 1581-82.

the psalmist. But the Lord "guards, protects, watches over" the psalmist, fending off those who seek out the psalmist or who would do the psalmist harm.

The respondent declares that the Lord *will not slumber* and *will not be asleep* (vv. 3-4). In other places in the book of Psalms, the psalm-singer calls on the Lord to awaken (Pss. 7:6; 35:23; 44:23; 59:4-5). The "sleeping deity" is a literary motif found in numerous texts in the ancient Near East.[6] The words of Psalm 121, which state that God will never slumber, stand in sharp contrast to the texts accusing God of sleeping and thus not paying attention to the cries of the psalm-singer.

In v. 5, the psalm-singer is assured that the Lord is a *shade (ṣēl).* The word occurs ten times in the Psalter, often as part of the phrase "the shadow (*ṣēl)* of your wings" (Pss. 17:8; 36:7; 57:1; 63:7), and connotes the protection provided by a mother bird to her chicks. Isaiah 51:16 says:

> I have put my words in your mouth,
>   and hidden you in the shade *(ṣēl)* of my hand,
> stretching out the heavens
>   and laying the foundations of the earth,
>   and saying to Zion, "You are my people."

In vv. 6-7, the psalm-singer receives further assurance that neither the *sun* in the day nor the *moon* by night will *strike* and harm and that the Lord will protect the *inmost being (nep̄eš)* of the psalmist *from all malicious things (raʿ).* As with v. 2's *maker of heavens and earth,* v. 6's *by day* and by *night* are merisms — word pairs that summarize the total by naming opposite boundaries.

Verse 8 continues with another merism, *your going out and your coming in,* indicating that the Lord will protect the psalm-singer's every movement. Crow suggests that this phrase reflects typical city life in the ancient Near East, in which the worker left the protective confines of the walled city in the morning to carry out field and pasture work and returned in the evening to the shelter of the city walls.[7] Thus the psalmist is guarded *from now and for all time.*

Psalm 121 provides strong words of assurance to worshippers that if they fix their eyes squarely on the source of their *help* (vv. 1-2), then the Lord, *the maker of heavens and earth,* who does not *slumber,* will indeed "guard, keep watch over, protect" and "be a shade." If we take our eyes off of the source of

6. See Bernard F. Batto, "The Sleeping God: an Ancient Near Eastern Motif of Divine Sovereignty," *Bib* 68 (1987) 153-77; and Joel S. Burnett, "The Question of Divine Absence in Israelite and West Semitic Religion," *CBQ* 67 (2005) 215-35.

7. *The Songs of Ascents,* p. 39.

our assuredness, when we look to other "mountains" for help, then the mundane, the ordinary — the sun, the moon, the malicious things — find us and strike us. Thus may we all remember to "lift up our eyes to the mountains."

NANCY DECLAISSÉ-WALFORD

Psalm 122: Let Us Go to the House of the LORD

Psalm 122 is the third of the fifteen Songs of the Ascents (Psalms 120–34; see the Introduction to the Songs of the Ascents). It is classified as an individual hymn of thanksgiving whose theme is "Jerusalem" or "Zion," and can be more specifically classified as a Song of Zion (along with Psalms 46, 48, 76, 84, and 87). In the psalm, we hear the voice of an individual singer who is part of a larger group of pilgrims going up to Jerusalem. The singer rejoices at the prospect of going on pilgrimage to Jerusalem (v. 1) and setting foot inside the city gates (v. 2); celebrates all that the city stands for — security, gathering, and justice (vv. 3-5); and wishes well-being *(šālôm)* for Jerusalem (vv. 6-9).

Three pilgrimage festivals are celebrated each year in Judaism, and all who are able travel to Jerusalem: Passover, the Feast of Weeks, and the Feast of Tabernacles. Any one of these celebrations could have been the occasion for composing the words of Psalm 122. McCann suggests that if we read the Songs of the Ascents as a chronological account of a pilgrim's journey to Jerusalem, then Psalm 120, the first of the fifteen, is the lament of an individual who is far from the holy city and is besieged by falsehood, deceitfulness, and haters of well-being.[1] Psalm 121, the second of the fifteen, is a hymn of thanksgiving sung by the psalm-singer on the approach to Jerusalem; the hills of Jerusalem are in view and God guides the singer's feet. And Psalm 122, the third, is sung in celebration as the pilgrim psalm-singer arrives in Jerusalem and enters the city gates.

The psalm opens and closes, in vv. 1 and 9, with the phrase *the house of the LORD" (bêṯ YHWH),* and its middle verse (v. 5) speaks of *the house of David (bêṯ dāwîḏ).* It may be divided into three stanzas:

> Let us go to Jerusalem, the house of the LORD (vv. 1-2)
> Jerusalem, the thrones of the house of David (vv. 3-5)
> Well-being for Jerusalem, the house of the LORD (vv. 6-9)

A Song of the Ascents, of David[2]

1 *I rejoiced with the ones saying to me,*
"To the house of the LORD let us go."

1. "The Book of Psalms," 1183.

2. Four of the Songs of the Ascents (Pss. 122, 124, 131, 133) are attributed, in their superscriptions, to David. While some suggest that the attributions are a scribal "slip of the pen" because of the prevalence of Davidic superscriptions in the Psalter (see Gerstenberger, *Psalms: Part 2*, p. 326), most manuscripts maintain the superscription of MT. Interestingly, NRSV omits "of David" from the superscription of Ps. 133.

2 *Our feet were standing*
in your gates, O Jerusalem.

3 *O Jerusalem, the one built*
like a city that is bound tightly together.
4 *There the tribes go up, the tribes of Yah.*
A decree for Israel:[3]
to give thanks to the name of the LORD.
5 *For there the thrones of justice dwell,*
the thrones of the house of David.

6 *Ask well-being for Jerusalem.*
May the ones who love you be at ease.
7 *May well-being be in your walls,*
tranquility in your towers.
8 *For the sake of my relatives and my companions*
I will speak well-being within you.
9 *For the sake of the house of the* LORD *our God*
I will seek the good for you.

1-2 The opening word of Psalm 122, *I rejoiced (śāmaḥtî)* sets the tone for the remainder of the psalm. The psalm-singer rejoices at hearing the words *to the house of the* LORD *let us go (nēlēḵ).* These words echo a standard call formula found in the Hebrew Bible, in which the verbs "go" *(hālaḵ)* and "go up" *(ʿālâ)* are used interchangeably (see v. 4). In 1 Sam. 11:14, Samuel speaks to the people, "Come, let us go *(nēlᵉḵâ)* to Gilgal"; Jer. 31:6 says, "Arise, let us go up *(naʿᵃleh)* to Zion."

The singer of Psalm 122 celebrates jubilantly the arrival in Jerusalem and the ascent to *the house of the* LORD. The phrase *the house of the* LORD occurs in vv. 1 and 9, forming an *inclusio* that directs the hearer's attention to the main emphasis of the psalm.

The syntax of v. 2 is difficult, but has a great deal of bearing on the time frame of the psalm. The verse begins with a plural active participle *(ʿōmdôṯ),* which is followed by a third person plural perfect verb from *hāyâ* ("be, become") and the subject of the participle and verb, *our feet.* The question is whether to render the phrase in the past tense, "Our feet were standing," or in the present, "Our feet are standing." Is the psalm sung while the pilgrim is in Jerusalem, in the moment of the jubilation, or sung after the pilgrim returns

3. 11QPsª renders this phrase as *ʿdt yśrʾl* ("the congregation of Israel"), making it parallel to v. 4a: "the tribes, the tribes of Yah." See Thijs Booij, "Psalm cxxii 4: Text and Meaning," *VT* 51 (2001) 262-66.

home, in recollection of the jubilation? NRSV, NIV, and NASB render the verbal structure in the present tense, "Our feet are standing," while the Tanak, Kraus,[4] and this translation opt for the past tense.

3-5 In these verses, the psalm-singer celebrates three characteristics of Jerusalem. In v. 3, the psalmist describes Jerusalem as a *city bound tightly together.* The description conjures up impressions of Jerusalem as a safe place, a place to which people could go in times of trouble and oppression and find security. In the ancient Near East, city walls provided protection and sanctuary for inhabitants and loyal subjects against invading armies.

Verse 4 describes Jerusalem as the place to which *the tribes of Yah go up ('ālâ)* in order to fulfill the *decree ('ēḏûṯ)* that they *give thanks to the name of the LORD.* This verse depicts Jerusalem as the gathering place for the people of Israel. *Yah* is a shortened form of "YHWH," and is used numerous times in the Psalter, particularly in the phrase "hallelujah" *(halᵉlû yāh).*

The thrones of justice (mišpāṭ) . . . the thrones of the house of David in v. 5 refer to the role of the monarchy in ancient Israel as dispenser of justice to the people. In 2 Sam. 8:15, we read, "So David reigned over all Israel; and David administered justice *(mišpāṭ)* and equity *(ṣᵉḏaqâ)* to all his people."[5] The prophet Micah condemns the rulers of Judah and Israel for abhorring justice and perverting equity (Mic. 3:9-12). Mays points out:

> Pilgrimage season was likely a time when conflicts and disputes unsettled in the country courts were brought to the royal officials and their successors. . . . The peace of the community depended on the establishment of justice. Pilgrimage is a journey in search of peace.[6]

6-9 The last stanza of Psalm 122 is masterfully composed. The psalm-singer speaks directly to Jerusalem. Each verse ends with the second feminine singular pronoun suffix *-k* (referring to the city), giving the stanza what Gerstenberger describes as a "homophonous" quality.[7] The theme of the stanza is the *well-being (šālôm)* of Jerusalem. Of the ten Hebrew words that make up vv. 6 and 7, six contain the letters *šîn* and *lāmed: ask (šaʾᵃlû); well-being* (twice) *(šālôm);* Jerusalem *(yᵉrûšālāim);* may they be at ease *(yišᵉlāyû);* and *tranquility (šalwâ)* — acoustically and visually emphasizing the theme of well-being. Verses 8 and 9 begin with *for the sake of (lᵉmaʿan)* and enumerate the reasons for wishing well-being and the good for Jerusalem — the psalm-singer's *relatives and companions* and *the house of the LORD our God.*

Verse 9's *the house of the LORD our God* echoes the words of v. 1, form-

4. *Psalms 60–150,* p. 431.

5. See also 2 Sam. 15:2-6; Deut. 17:8-13.

6. *Psalms,* p. 393.

7. *Psalms: Part 2,* p. 328.

ing an *inclusio* around the words of the psalm. And in v. 5, the middle of the psalm, *the house of David* provides an additional focus of the psalm. *The house of the LORD* symbolized the presence of God among the people of Israel; *the house of David* symbolized justice and equity among the people of Israel. The *well-being* of Jerusalem guaranteed the well-being of the people of God. Allen writes, "Jerusalem was the focus of national unity, a unity which was grounded in worship and issued in the harmonious ordering of life."[8] McCann reminds us, though, that Jerusalem "is not just a place, but a symbol of God's presence in space and time."[9]

Psalm 122 appears in Christian liturgy as the psalm reading for the first Sunday of Advent. The first reading for that Sunday is Isa. 2:1-5, a text that pictures a glorious time when all peoples will "go up" *('ālâ)* to Jerusalem and the Lord will "judge" *(šāp̄aṭ)*. The second and third readings, Rom. 13:11-14 and Matt. 24:36-44, remind the faithful that we do not know when God will decide to act and that we must always live in anticipation and preparedness for the presence of God in space and time.

NANCY DECLAISSÉ-WALFORD

8. Allen, *Psalms 101–150*, p. 159.
9. "The Book of Psalms," p. 1185.

Psalm 123: Show Favor to Us, O Lord

Psalm 123 is the fourth of the fifteen Songs of the Ascents in Book Five of the Psalter (see the Introduction to the Songs of the Ascents), songs that pilgrims sang as they made their way to Jerusalem to celebrate a number of annual religious festivals, including Passover, the Feast of Weeks, and the Feast of Tabernacles. If we read the Songs of the Ascents as a chronological whole, we may understand Psalm 120, the first Song of the Ascents, as the lament of an individual who is far from the holy city and is besieged by falsehood, deceitfulness, and haters of well-being. Psalm 121, the second Song of the Ascents, is a hymn of thanksgiving sung by the psalm-singer on the approach to Jerusalem; the hills of Jerusalem are in view, and God guides the singer's feet. Psalm 122, the third, is a song of thanksgiving sung in celebration as the pilgrim psalm-singer arrives in Jerusalem and enters the city gates. Psalm 123, the fourth Song of the Ascents, is categorized as a community lament, although it begins with the voice of an individual: *To you I lift up my eyes* (v. 1; see Psalm 121). In v. 2, however, the community of pilgrims adds its voice, *thus our eyes (look) to the LORD our God.* Once inside the city gates, the psalm-singers turn their eyes away from the world described in Psalm 120 — "the lip of falsehood" and "the deceitful tongue" (v. 2) — toward God and address God directly, asking the deity to show them *favor.*

The lament begins with an "expression of trust" that includes an invocation — a usual element of a lament psalm: *O the one who dwells in the heavens* (vv. 1-2). It is followed by a "petition" (v. 3) and ends with a "complaint" (v. 4). While the usual format for a lament psalm is: (1) invocation; (2) complaint; (3) petition; (4) expression of trust; and (5) expression of praise and adoration,[1] McCann reminds us that community laments often end with the "complaint" (or "petition") element, and he further suggests that the next psalm, Psalm 124, will provide the trust, praise, and adoration that usually accompany the lament form.[2]

Psalm 123 may be divided into two sections:

Expression of trust (vv. 1-2)
Petition and complaint (vv. 3-4)

A Song of the Ascents

1 *To you I lift up my eyes,*
O the one who dwells in the heavens.

1. See deClaissé-Walford, *Introduction to the Psalms,* pp. 20-25.
2. "The Book of Psalms," p. 1187.

2 *Behold, as the eyes of the servants*
(look) to the hand of their lord,
As the eyes of the maid servant
(look) to the hand of her mistress,
Thus our eyes (look) to the LORD our God,
until he shows favor to us.

3 *Show favor to us, O LORD, show favor to us,*
for we are overwhelmed with contempt.
4 *Our inmost being is overwhelmed with the mockery of the ones who are at ease,*
the contempt of the proud.[3]

1-2 Psalm 123 begins with the voice of the individual (*my eyes,* v. 1) and joins with the voice of the community (*the eyes of the servants,* v. 2). The worshippers lift their eyes to the Lord, just as the psalm-singer in Psalm 121 lifts the eyes to the hills. *The one who dwells in the heavens* is an epithet for the God of the Hebrew Bible (for references in the Psalter, see Pss. 2:4; 11:4; 115:3, 16).

The pilgrims gathered in Jerusalem compare their trust in God to the trust *servants* place in their masters and mistresses. Servants look to their masters and mistresses and stretch out their hands to them in supplication. Masters and mistresses look upon their servants and stretch out their hands to *show favor* in kindness and generosity. In like manner the pilgrims stretch out their hands in supplication to God who must and will stretch out God's hand to *show favor* to the servants. The word translated *show favor,* from the Hebrew verbal root *ḥānan,* is translated commonly as "mercy" (NRSV, NIV) and "graciousness" (NASB).[4]

3-4 The expression of trust in God's *favor* becomes a twice-repeated petition in v. 3, followed by the reason for the petition. As with most laments in the Psalter, the oppressors of the psalm-singers are not named — they are simply identified as those *at ease* and *the proud.* The psalmists feel *overwhelmed* with *contempt* and *mockery.* The word translated *overwhelmed* is from the root *śābaʿ,* which means, literally, "eat one's full, be sated, have enough." And interestingly, the word translated *mockery* is from the root *lāʿag,* which means, literally, "speak with a stammering tongue." The singer of Psalm 73 describes such oppressors:

3. The Qere for this phrase, *ligʾêyônîm* ("the pride of the ones oppressing"), does not significantly change the meaning of the phrase.

4. For a full discussion of *ḥānan,* see the commentary for Ps. 111:2-4.

Therefore their necklace is pride;
 and violence covers them as a garment.
Their eyes bulge out with fatness;
 their hearts overflow with delusions.
They scoff and speak with malice;
 the ones in high station speak of extortion.
They set their mouths in the heavens;
 as their tongues walk in the earth. (73:6-9)

As the pilgrims enter Jerusalem, they turn their eyes toward God and away from those who mock them and hold them in contempt. They begin with words of trust in God (vv. 1-2), recalling times in the past when God showed them favor just as a mistress shows favor to her servants. Because of the past experience, the worshippers can approach God with words of complaint and petition to show favor to them once again in the midst of their oppression. Clifford characterizes Psalm 123 as a "primer on prayer" in which the psalmist "lifts his or her eyes to heaven, symbolically forswearing every other means of support" and "embraces the status of servant and waits, eyes fixed on the hand of the Lord."[5]

Nancy deClaissé-Walford

5. *Psalms 73–150,* p. 229.

Psalm 124: Our Help Is in the Name of the Lord

Fifth in the collection of psalms known as the Songs of the Ascents (see the Introduction to the Songs of the Ascents), Psalm 124 contains words of trust and praise sung by pilgrim worshippers who have entered the city gates of Jerusalem for a festal celebration — Passover, the Feast of Weeks, the Feast of Tabernacles. In the previous psalm, Psalm 123, a community lament, the psalm-singers cry out to God in the midst of overwhelming contempt and mockery and ask God to show *favor (ḥānan)* to them. Though words of trust are voiced in its first two verses, Psalm 123 ends with words of complaint and petition (vv. 3-4).[1] Psalm 124, a community hymn, may be heard as the closing words of trust and praise for the lament-singers of Psalm 123.[2] Psalm 124 uses rich metaphoric images in its three stanzas:

Past deliverance remembered (vv. 1-5)
Praise for past deliverance (vv. 6-7)
Declaration of trust (v. 8)

A Song of the Ascents, of David

1 *If the* L*ORD* *had not been for us,*
let Israel say,
2 *If the* L*ORD* *had not been for us,*
when humanity rose up against us,
3 *Then alive they would have devoured us,*
when their anger kindled against us.
4 *Then the waters would have drowned us,*
a river would have poured over our inmost being.
5 *Then it would have poured over our inmost being,*
the swelling waters.

6 *Blessed is the* L*ORD*
who has not given us as food for their tongues.
7 *Our inmost being like a bird has fled to safety*
from the snare of the fowlers.

1. See the commentary on Ps. 123 for an outline of the five elements of a lament psalm.

2. For another example of a lament psalm whose final words of trust and praise may be located in the following psalm, see Nancy L. deClaissé-Walford, "An Intertextual Reading of Psalms 22, 23, and 24," in Flint and Miller, *The Book of Psalms,* pp. 139-52; and *Introduction to the Psalms,* pp. 35-40.

The snare has been broken in pieces,
and we have fled to safety.

8 *Our help is in the name of the LORD,*
the maker of the heavens and the earth.

1-5 The voice of an individual psalmist speaks the opening phrase of the psalm: *If the LORD had not been for us,* and invites Israel to join in with the words, *Let Israel say.* From that point forward in the psalm, we hear the voice of the community of psalm-singers.

Verses 1 and 2 both begin with *if not (lûlê),* forming the protasis of vv. 1-5. *Lûlê,* however, is only used in Hebrew to express an unreal condition.[3] The psalm-singers are confident that the Lord is on their side. The apodosis occurs in vv. 3-5, introduced by *then (ʾ^{a}zay).* Crow maintains that the statement in vv. 1-5 "is not an 'if . . . then' statement in the tradition of the Greek logicians, but rather a narrative about what might have occurred without YHWH's aid."[4]

In v. 2, the one rising up over the psalmists is identified with the collective noun *humanity (ʾāḏām).* The designation *ʾāḏām* reflects the creation story in Genesis 2, in which humanity *(ʾāḏām)* is formed from the ground *(ʾ^{a}ḏāmâ).* In the structure of vv. 1 and 2, the power of God, without whose support great calamity would befall Israel, is contrasted with the powerlessness of the human community that rises up against the people of Israel.

Beginning with v. 3, the psalm-singers use vivid metaphors — all tied to the theme of water danger — to describe the calamities that might have befallen them if the Lord were not with them. They might have been *devoured alive* (v. 3); *waters would have drowned* them (v. 4); and a *swelling* river *would have poured over* their very *being* (v. 5). Each of these metaphoric images brings to mind the theme of watery chaos that occurs often in the Hebrew Bible and in other literature from the ancient Near East.[5] The sea was a mysterious place with mysterious beasts. In the Mesopotamian creation myth *Enuma Elish,* the god Marduk defeats the sea-goddess Tiamat in a bloody battle and fashions her carcass into the world of human habitation.[6] The myth is reflected in Ps. 89:9-10:

> You rule over the surging sea;
> when its waves rise, you still them.

3. *HALOT,* p. 524; and Waltke and O'Connor, *Biblical Hebrew Syntax,* pp. 637-38.

4. *The Songs of Ascents,* pp. 52-53.

5. For an excellent treatment of water imagery in the book of Psalms, see Brown, *Seeing the Psalms,* pp. 105-34.

6. Bill T. Arnold and Bryan E. Beyer, eds., *Readings from the Ancient Near East* (Grand Rapids: Baker, 2002), pp. 31-50.

> You crushed Rahab like a corpse;
> with your mighty arm, you scattered your enemies.

And the psalmist of Psalm 93, an enthronement psalm,[7] sings:

> The rivers have lifted up, O LORD; the rivers have lifted up their voice;
> the rivers lift up their pounding waves.
> Greater than the voice of many waters; mighty ones, breakers of the sea;
> powerful on high is the LORD. (vv. 3-4)

The remembrance of past deliverance in vv. 1-5 paints a vivid picture of what would have been if God had not been *for* the psalm-singers.

6-7 But the calamity did not occur, because the Lord was with the psalmists. In vv. 6 and 7, the singers praise God for their past deliverance from the "rising up" of *humanity* (v. 2) with more strong metaphoric images. In v. 6, the psalm-singers use a standard introductory formula, *blessed is the LORD*, to reiterate the confident words of v. 3:

> Blessed is the LORD
> who has not given us as food for their tongues *(lāšôn).*

Tongue in v. 6 echoes the individual lament of the pilgrim in Psalm 120, who is on the way to Jerusalem and is traveling through a foreign and hostile land and cries out to the Lord to deliver *from the lip of falsehood, from the deceitful tongue (lāšôn)*" (120:2). The psalmist has now arrived, along with other pilgrims, in Jerusalem, and they join their voices to bless the Lord, who has not *given them as food* for the *tongues* of those rising up against them.

The psalm-singers employ another metaphor in v. 7, likening their safe entry into Jerusalem to a bird's escape *from the snare of the fowlers (paḥ yôqᵉšîm).* A bird caught in a snare is another common metaphor for danger in the Hebrew Bible and the ancient Near East. In the famous Taylor Prism inscription, the seventh-century Assyrian king Sennacherib boasted of King Hezekiah, "He himself I shut up like a caged bird within Jerusalem, his royal city."[8] In Ps. 91:3-4 the psalmist declares: "For he will deliver you from the snare of the fowler *(paḥ yāqûš)* and from the deadly pestilence."

8 The final verse of Psalm 124, a declaration of trust by the psalm-singers, again employs strong imagery along with echoes of phrases already encountered in the Songs of the Ascents and in other places in the Hebrew

7. For a discussion of the *Gattung* "enthronement psalm," see the commentary for Pss. 93 and 95–99.

8. Arnold and Beyer, *Readings from the Ancient Near East,* pp. 146-47.

Psalter. The singers state that their *help (ʿēzer)* is in the *name (šēm)* of the Lord.[9] The phrase *maker of the heavens and the earth* — a merism, indicating all-encompassing totality — occurs three times in the Songs of the Ascents (Pss. 121:2; 124:8; 134:3) and in Ps. 146:6.

Thus the singers of Psalm 124 affirm that God indeed "shows favor to" (see Ps. 123:3) the faithful ones of Israel. Humankind *(ʾāḏām),* who rises up over the faithful (v. 2), is, in the end, mere humanity formed by God from the ground *(ʾᵃḏāmâ).* Psalm 124 has a strong poetic and repetitive quality, suggesting that it was meant to be recited liturgically in a worship setting. The opening words of the first two verses, *if not,* followed by the opening words of the next three verses, *then,* act as strong repetitive devices. The use of vivid images, repeated in successive verses — water, devouring sea monsters, and fowler's traps — adds to the psalm what Clifford characterizes as "swiftness and drama."[10]

In Psalm 124, the power of the Lord on the side of the faithful is set in sharp contrast to the "rising up" of mere humanity. As God defeated the primal chaos of the sea waters and provided escape for the small bird from the fowler's snare, so God can be a help *(ʿēzer)* to the Jerusalem pilgrims (v. 8), show them favor *(ḥānan,* Ps. 123:3), and provide them with well-being *(šālôm,* Ps. 122:6-8). The pilgrimages of our lives require just such actions from God on our behalf.

NANCY DECLAISSÉ-WALFORD

9. For a discussion of the meaning of ʿ*ezer* in the Psalter, see the commentary on Ps. 108:12, and for a discussion of the importance of "name" in the Hebrew Bible, see Ps. 113:1b-4.

10. *Psalms 73–150,* p. 229.

Psalm 125: Do Good to the Upright in Heart

Psalm 125 is the sixth psalm in the collection of fifteen psalms known as the Songs of the Ascents (see the Introduction to the Songs of the Ascents), psalms sung by pilgrims during various festal celebrations in Jerusalem — Passover, the Feast of Weeks, the Feast of Tabernacles. It is a community hymn, and its focus — Jerusalem, Mount Zion — likens it to the group of psalms in the Psalter known as Songs of Zion.[1] Other scholars describe Psalm 125 as a "Song of Confidence" because of its opening words: *Those who trust in the LORD are like Mount Zion, which will not quake; for all time it will remain* (v. 1).[2] The psalm may be divided into three stanzas:

Expression of trust (vv. 1-2)
  Expression of trust moving to petition (v. 3)
Petition moving to a declaration of peace (vv. 4-5)

A Song of the Ascents

1 *Those who trust in the LORD are like Mount Zion,*
which will not quake;
for all time it will remain.
2 *O Jerusalem! The mountains surround it,*
and the LORD surrounds his people
from now and for all time.

3 *Surely the tribe of the wicked ones will not rest*
upon the inheritance of the righteous ones,
in order that the righteous ones will not stretch out
their hands to dishonesty.

4 *Do good, O LORD, to the good ones,*
and to the ones upright in their hearts.
5 *But the ones who turn aside to crookedness,*
the LORD will lead away with the ones who do wickedness.
Well-being be upon Jerusalem!

1-2 Verses 1 and 2 liken *those who trust in the LORD* to *Mount Zion* — Jerusalem. The word translated *trust* is the Hebrew *bāṭaḥ*, the first occurrence of the word in the Songs of the Ascents.[3] Its basic meaning is "be confident in, feel

1. Pss. 46, 48, 76, 84, 87, 122.
2. See Gerstenberger, *Psalms: Part 2,* p. 338.
3. The word is used forty-five other times in the Hebrew Psalter.

secure, be unconcerned." The psalm-singer maintains that those who *trust in* ("rely on, feel secure in") the Lord are like Mount Zion, which will not *quake (yimmôṭ,* from the verbal root *mûṭ).* The same word is translated in Ps. 121:3 as "stumble": "He will not allow to stumble your foot." God grants to those who trust stability, security, and confidence.

The image continues with v. 2's declaration that just as the *mountains surround* Jerusalem, so God *surrounds* God's people *now and for all time.* While Jerusalem itself sits on a hill, it is actually surrounded by higher mountains, particularly to the east. The pilgrim celebrating a festival in Jerusalem looks out at the surrounding mountains and likens them to the way God protectively surrounds God's people.

3 Verse 3's expression of trust and petition begins with an emphatic use of the particle *kî,* here translated as *surely,* and introduces a contrast between *the tribe of the wicked ones* and *the inheritance of the righteous ones.* The words *tribe (šēḇeṭ)* and *inheritance (gôrāl)* appear repeatedly in the account of the settlement and allotting of the land of promise in the book of Joshua. *Tribe (šēḇeṭ)* occurs some thirty times in Joshua, and *inheritance (gôrāl)* occurs twenty-two times. The psalmist speaks words of cautious confidence that the *wicked tribe* will not gain the *inheritance of the righteous ones* and so lead them to *stretch out their hands to dishonesty.* The contrast, the difference, between the *wicked (reša')* and the *righteous (ṣaddîqîm)* is addressed in the opening psalm of the Psalter (Ps. 1:6) and continues as one of the structuring themes of the book of Psalms.[4]

4-5 Verses 4 and 5's petition moving to a declaration of peace continues and expands the contrast between the righteous ones and the wicked ones. The righteous are described as *the good ones (ṭôḇîm)* and *the upright in their hearts (yᵉšārîm bᵉlibbôṯām),* the wicked as those who *turn aside to crookedness ('aqalqal).* In v. 3, the psalmist speaks first of the *wicked* and then the *righteous.* In vv. 4 and 5, the order is reversed, addressing first the righteous and then the wicked. The reversal places the righteous ones in the middle of the literary structure of vv. 3-5, a focal point for the message of the psalm. The psalm ends with the brief petition, *Well-being be upon Jerusalem!* The use of the word *well-being (šālôm)* appears six times in the Songs of the Ascents,[5] a reflection of the pilgrim psalm-singer's wish for *šālôm* upon Jerusalem.

The community of God is made up of those who trust in — are confident in, feel secure in — God. In the Old Testament, Zion was the embodiment of the people of God assembled in the central sanctuary.[6] The sense of trust

4. See, e.g., Pss. 7:9; 11:5; 32:10-11; 37:16; 58:10; 75:10; 92:7, 12; 94:12-15; 112:6-10; 129:4; 140:8-13.

5. Pss. 120:6, 7; 122:6, 7, 8; 125:5.

6. Kraus, *Psalms 60–150,* p. 449.

often comes when we enter our "holy places," and look to our God, who is like a mountain that surrounds us. In holy places, we can call on God to surround us like a mountain and keep us safe from the wicked ones and those who turn aside to crookedness. The Songs of the Ascents remind us that holy places are an important part of our faith, for they provide focal points for our relationship with God.

The vast majority of pilgrims who made their way to Jerusalem for the festival seasons in the postexilic period were not the rich and privileged. They often were the victims of injustices in their daily lives. They most likely felt crushed. As they gathered in Jerusalem, the holy city, and worshipped together at the temple, perhaps some measure of confidence was restored. God *does* do good to those who are good, to those who are *upright in their hearts* (v. 4), despite the circumstances that surround them each day. And at the end of the appointed time, the pilgrims could return home with hope restored and with new energy for the days ahead. May we all find our Jerusalems — those places of gathering in which the upright in heart gain new strength for the days of our journeys.

Nancy deClaissé-Walford

Psalm 126: Restore Our Lives

Psalm 126 is the seventh psalm in the collection of fifteen psalms known as the Songs of the Ascents (see the Introduction to the Songs of the Ascents), psalms sung by pilgrims during various festal celebrations in Jerusalem — Passover, the Feast of Weeks, the Feast of Tabernacles. It is a community lament — one of only two in the Songs of the Ascents.[1] The psalm-singers begin by remembering a time in their past when God restored their lives and did great things among them, and then they petition God to once again restore their lives so that they may rejoice. Mays summarizes Psalm 126 as "joy remembered and joy anticipated."[2] It may be divided into three stanzas:

Expression of trust (vv. 1-3)
Petition (v. 4)
Expression of praise (vv. 5-6)

A Song of the Ascents

1 *When the LORD restored the lives of Zion,*
we were like ones dreaming.[3]
2 *Then our mouth was filled with laughter,*
and our tongue with rejoicing.
Then they said among the nations,
"The LORD had done great things for them."
3 *The LORD has done great things for us;*
we were joyful.

4 *Restore our lives, O LORD,*
like water channels in the Negev.

5 *The ones sowing in tears*
in rejoicing they will reap.
6 *Indeed, the one who goes out weeping,*
carrying the seed for sowing,
Will indeed come in with rejoicing,
carrying the sheaves.

1. The other is Ps. 123.

2. *Psalms,* p. 399.

3. MT is *k^{e}ḥōl^{e}mîm,* whose verbal root *ḥālam* is usually rendered "dream." The LXX translation of v. 1, *hos parakeklemenoi* ("like ones being made strong"), along with the rendering of the same verbal root in Isa. 38:16 as "Restore me to health," suggests that we might also translate the phrase here as "like the healed (or strong) ones."

1-3 The major interpretational issue of Psalm 126 is the rendering of the verbal tense of *restore (šûḇ),* which occurs in vv. 1 and 4. NRSV, NIV, and NASB translate the first occurrence of the verb, in v. 1, as past tense, and the second occurrence, in v. 4, as imperative, part of the petition to God. In vv. 1-3, the people remember a past event of restoration and, in v. 4, call upon God to *restore* them once again. NJPS, however, renders the verb in v. 1 in the future tense: "When the LORD restores the fortunes of Zion. . . ." In this translation, the first three verses of the psalm are not a remembered past, but part of the future restoration that the psalm-singers are calling upon God to enact.

The phrase translated here as *restored the lives (šûḇ šîḇâ)* also causes considerable interpretation difficulty. A few manuscripts of the LXX harmonize *šîḇâ* with v. 4's Kethib, *šᵉḇûṯ,* while others harmonize it with v. 4's Qere, *šᵉḇîṯ.* While *šîḇâ* is most likely formed from the verbal root *šûḇ,* yielding in v. 1 a verb plus its cognate accusative (literally, "return the returning ones"), *šᵉḇûṯ* and *šᵉḇîṯ* are formed from the verbal root "to lead into captivity" *(šāḇâ)* — giving a translation of "return the captives." The phrases are similar enough in morphology and meaning to suggest that the psalmist crafted the first cola of vv. 1 and 4 as parallel statements. Allen suggests that "the stylistic variation of form between [*šᵉḇîṯ*] and [*šᵉḇûṯ*] may have been intended as a pointer to a new beginning at v. 4 and as a means of differentiating the changes of fortune as separate events."[4]

This translation renders the phrases in vv. 1 and 4 as *restore the (our) lives.* NRSV and NJPS translate them as "restore the (our) fortunes"; NASB as "brought back the captive ones" (v. 1) . . . "restore our captivity" (v. 4); and NIV as "brought back the captives" (v. 1) . . . "restore our fortunes" (v. 4). The phrase is used extensively in the Hebrew Bible, particularly in prophetic material to describe the people's change in life circumstances when God's wrath is turned away and God's favor returns (Deut. 30:3; Ezek. 39:25; Jer. 29:14; 30:3; Hos. 6:11; Joel 3:1; Amos 9:14; Zeph. 2:7; 3:20).[5]

The psalm-singers describe themselves in v. 1 as *like ones dreaming.* This plural participle is derived from the verbal root *ḥālam,* which is most often translated as "dream." The verbal root has another underlying meaning, however: "be, become strong." This is the meaning the LXX translators gave to the phrase, and thus they rendered it "like ones being strong" *(hōs parakeklēmenoi).* The LXX translation is credible, based on the translation of *wᵉṯaḥᵃlîmēnî* (a *hithpael* form of the root *ḥālam*) as "make me healthy" in Isa. 38:16.[6]

4. *Psalms 101–150,* p. 174.

5. See also the use of the phrase in Job 42:10; Pss. 14:7; 53:6; 85:1; Lam. 2:14.

6. Hos. 6:11-7:1 speaks of a time when God will "restore the fortunes *(šûḇ šᵉḇûṯ)*" of the people and "heal" (although from a different verbal root, *rāp̱a'*) Israel.

The result of God's actions in v. 1 is that the people's *mouth* is *filled with laughter,* their *tongue* with *rejoicing (rinnâ). Rejoicing* is repeated three times in Psalm 126, in vv. 2, 5, and 6, suggesting it as the unifying theme of the psalm. The result of restoration in the past was rejoicing, just as the result of restoration in the future will be rejoicing. In addition, the nations saw what God had done on behalf of the people and declared among themselves, *The LORD has done great things for them* (v. 3). This declaration is in sharp contrast with the taunting from the nations in other psalms in the Psalter. In Ps. 42:3, the people ask continually, "Where is your God?" In Ps. 3:2, the psalmist laments that many are saying, "There is no deliverance for him in God!" In v. 3, the singers repeat the words of the nations, *The LORD has done great things for us.* And they conclude their words of trust in God in v. 3 with *we were joyful.*

4 The memory of restoration in the past inspires the people to once again petition God: *Restore our lives . . . like water channels in the Negev.* The psalm-singers use a powerful metaphor — water — to concretize their petition. The image of water is used extensively in the Psalter.[7] In Psalm 126, the restorative power of God is likened to the invigorating restoration of dry wadi beds in the *Negev* during the winter rains. The rains came every year; the people could count on them to enliven a parched landscape year after year.

5-6 Using another vivid metaphor, the psalm-singers picture the effects of God's restoration of the people: sowing seeds and reaping the harvest. Gerstenberger suggests that this metaphor evinces wisdom influence as the psalmists employ day-to-day images of human toil to describe God's restorative work.[8] Sowing and reaping also suggest the fertility traditions of the ancient Near East. Sowing the seed in the ground is similar to the burial of the dead; thus the sowers weep as they bury the seed in the ground — as in many ancient Near Eastern fertility rituals. When the seedlings emerge from the ground and the *sheaves* are harvested, then rejoicing ensues. McCann reminds us that while we may read these verses against the background of ancient fertility rituals, "it is just as important to observe that sowing is always an act of anticipation and hope."[9] The repetition of the word *rejoicing (rinnâ)* in vv. 2, 5, and 6 connects the rejoicing of the people at their restoration by God with the rejoicing of the reapers at the harvest. The metaphor is brought full circle — the people are confident they will rejoice in this new event of restoration just as they did in the past event.

Because of the "restoration" language of Psalm 126, most commentators place its origins in the postexilic life of ancient Israel. Clifford suggests that

7. For an excellent treatment of water imagery in the Psalter, see Brown, *Seeing the Psalms.*

8. *Psalms: Part 2,* p. 341.

9. "The Book of Psalms," p. 1195.

the psalm-singers had witnessed one group of returnees from the Babylonian exile and anticipated more to return just as the wadis are returned to flowing streams in the winter and the sown seeds become a bountiful harvest.[10] The result of restoration in the past was rejoicing, just as the result of restoration in the future will be rejoicing. The psalm, however, has meaning for all people who have experienced the restorative work of God in their past, or in the past of someone they know, and who anticipate the restorative work of God in their lives again.

Psalm 126 was the inspiration for the traditional Thanksgiving song, "Bringing in the Sheaves," written by Knowles Shaw in 1874. It is also the lectionary reading for Thanksgiving Day in America and is included as a reading for many Advent and Lenten lections.

NANCY DECLAISSÉ-WALFORD

10. *Psalms 73–150*, pp. 235-38.

Psalm 127: The Inheritance of the Lord Is Children

Eighth in the group of fifteen psalms (Psalms 120–34) identified in their superscriptions as Songs of the Ascents (see the Introduction to the Songs of the Ascents), Psalm 127 is one of the songs which pilgrims sang as they made their way to Jerusalem to celebrate a number of annual religious festivals, including Passover, the Feast of Weeks, and the Feast of Tabernacles. It is classified as a wisdom psalm, the first of three wisdom psalms in the Songs of the Ascents, and one of six in Book Five of the Psalter: Psalms 112, 119, 127, 128, 133, and 145. A wisdom psalm is defined as one that "provides instruction in right living and right faith in the tradition of the other wisdom writings in the Old Testament — Proverbs, Ecclesiastes, and Job."[1] Its theme is found in the first verse of the psalm — *house* — a rich and multivalent word in Biblical Hebrew. Two distinct stanzas make up Psalm 127: vv. 1-2 and vv. 3-5. In the past a number of scholars suggested that the psalm was composed of two distinct proverbial sayings (vv. 1-2 and vv. 3-5); most recent scholars, however, argue for the original integrity of the psalm.[2]

The house (vv. 1-2)
The children (vv. 3-5)

A Song of the Ascents; of Solomon

1 *If the Lord does not build the house,*
uselessly have the building ones labored over it.
If the Lord does not keep watch over the city,
uselessly have the keeping watch ones watched over it.
2 *Useless is it to the ones of you who rise early,*
to the ones of you who are reluctant to sit down,
to the ones of you who eat the bread of anxious labor.
Thus God will give to his beloved sleep.

3 *Behold the inheritance of the Lord is children,*
a reward, a fruit of the womb.
4 *Like arrows in the hand of the mighty one,*
so are the children of youthfulness.
5 *Content is the mighty one who fills the quiver with them;*
they will not be ashamed when they speak with enemies in the gate.

1. deClaissé-Walford, *Introduction to the Psalms,* p. 25.

2. For an excellent treatment of the composition of Ps. 127, see Patrick D. Miller, "Psalm 127 — The House That Yahweh Builds," *JSOT* 22 (1982) 119-32.

1-2 Verses 1 and 2 form the first of what some scholars see as two proverbial sayings of which Psalm 127 is composed. Verse 1 is highly structured, with four parallel units making up each colon: *If the LORD does not ('im YHWH lō')* followed by imperfect verbs with objects (*build the house* and *keep watch over the city*); then, *uselessly (šāwᵉ')* followed by perfect verbs with participles as their subjects *(the building ones have labored* and *the keeping watch ones have watched).*

The word *house (bayiṯ)* has a number of meanings in the Hebrew Bible. It can refer to family dwellings (Gen. 19:2; Judg. 11:31; 2 Kgs. 4:2); to whole households (Gen. 46:27; Josh. 7:18; Ruth 1:8); to the whole people of Israel (Exod. 40:38; 1 Kgs. 20:31; Ezek. 36:22); to ruling dynasties (2 Sam. 3:1; 7:11; 1 Kgs. 16:3); or to the temple in Jerusalem (2 Kgs. 22:3; Ezra 6:15; Jer. 7:2). In its immediate context in Psalm 127, *house* in v. 1 most likely refers to the Jerusalem temple, just as the word *city* in the third colon most likely refers to the city of Jerusalem, since the Songs of the Ascents are pilgrimage songs sung by worshippers on their way to Jerusalem for various festivals, and especially since the superscription of Psalm 127 ascribes it to Solomon, the son of King David.[3] But the polyvalent nature of "house" in the Hebrew Bible allows for a wide-ranging understanding of the words of v. 1.

Verse 2 begins with same word *(šāwᵉ')* that is used in v. 1 to describe the activities of the *building ones* and the *keeping watch ones.* Clifford describes v. 2 as "a beautifully constructed tricolon with a hard-hitting and unexpected final colon."[4] The final colon of the verse begins with the adverb *kēn,* here translated as *thus,* but with a meaning more akin to "in comparison with the above. . . ."[5]

3-5 The word *behold (hinnēh)* at the beginning of v. 3 signals the beginning of a new stanza of Psalm 127, interestingly just as we find in Ps. 128:4. The admonitions given in vv. 1 and 2 move to assurance and declaration in vv. 3-5.[6] The word translated here as *children* is the Hebrew *bānîm,* whose acoustic similarity to the Hebrew words *build (bānâ)* and *house (bayiṯ)* in v. 1, coupled with the polyvalent meaning of the word "house" in the Hebrew Bible, strongly connects the two stanzas of Psalm 127. The word *inheritance (naḥᵃlâ)* is used no less than thirty-seven times in the book of Joshua (as well as extensively in the Pentateuch) in reference to the inheritance of the

3. The only other psalm in the Psalter attributed to Solomon is Ps. 72, the last psalm of Book Two.

4. *Psalms 73–150,* p. 240.

5. See Waltke and O'Connor, *Biblical Hebrew Syntax,* 39.3.4e. For another suggestion on the translation of *kēn,* see J. A. Emerton, "The Meaning of *šēnā'* in Psalm cxxvii 2," *VT* 24 (1974) 15-31.

6. Miller, "Psalm 127," p. 127.

promised land by the Israelites.[7] *Reward (śāḵār)* occurs in Genesis 15, the story of the covenant between God and Abram. God says to Abram, "Do not be afraid, Abram, I am your shield; your reward *(śāḵār)* shall be very great" (15:1). Abram objects because he is childless, but God says to him, "Look toward heaven and count the stars, if you are able to count them . . . so shall your descendants be" (15:5).

The psalmist employs warrior imagery in vv. 4-5 to describe the gift of children — arrows, quivers, and mighty ones. The word translated *mighty one* is *gibbôr,* which means "strong, vigorous, hero, champion," and is often used to describe military figures. In David's lament over the death of Saul and Jonathan in 2 Samuel 1, he describes the shield of Saul as "the shield of the mighty *(gibbôrîm)*" (v. 21); 2 Sam. 23:8 names David's "mighty men" *(gibbôrîm);* and in 2 Kgs. 24:16, the king of Babylon took captive all of the *gibbôrîm* of Jerusalem, 7,000.

Verse 5 begins with the wisdom word *content ('ašrê).*[8] In this verse, the word translated *mighty one is geḇer,* an alternate form of the word that occurs in v. 4, *gibbôr.* The second colon of the verse has some ambiguity in the identification of the antecedent of the pronoun *they.* Since both words translated as *mighty one* are singular in Hebrew, the most reasonable antecedent for *they* is the *children* in vv. 3 and 4.

The *gate (šā'ar)* of a city in the ancient Near East was the gathering place for the elders and judges who settled disputes, rendered judgments, and made important decisions regarding the community. In Amos 5:12, the prophet condemns those "who afflict the righteous, who take a bribe, and push aside the needy in the gate." Boaz goes to the city gate in order to settle the matter of his marriage to Ruth (Ruth 4:1-6). In Deut. 21:18-19, we read that if parents have a rebellious son, they should "bring him out to the elders of his town at the gate of that place." And the husband of the "strong woman" in Proverbs 31 "is known in the city gates" (31:23).

The word translated *enemies ('ôyᵉḇîm)* is used some seventy-five times in the Psalter and can refer to personal enemies and to enemies of the larger community. As in most psalms in the Psalter, the *enemies* in Psalm 127 are not specified, but are unnamed foes. The *children* of the *mighty one,* though, can speak to the enemies and *not be ashamed* — that is, according to the basic meaning of the Hebrew root word *(bôš),* they can "move about with uplifted head"[9] and be able to express themselves freely.

Psalm 127, a wisdom psalm attributed to Solomon, reminds its hearers

7. For a discussion of other words used in Joshua that have to do with "inheritance," see the commentary for Ps. 125:3.

8. For a full discussion of *'ašrê,* see the commentary for Ps. 112:1b.

9. Horst Seebass, "*bôš,*" *TDOT,* 2:51.

that without God, a house is built uselessly, a city is watched over uselessly, and that it is useless to rise early, work late, and worry endlessly. The psalm also celebrates the gift of children who make the mighty one content. Few who read the psalm do not see and hear echoes of the life of King David. In 2 Sam 7:11-13, Nathan speaks these words to David:

> The LORD declares to you that the LORD will make you a house *(bayiṯ)*. When your days are fulfilled and you lie down with your ancestors, I will raise up your offspring after you, who shall come forth from your body, and I will establish his kingdom. He shall build a house *(bayiṯ)* for my name, and I will establish the throne of his kingdom forever.

But the gift and message of Psalm 127 do not stop with David and Solomon. For each pilgrim to Jerusalem, each worshipper, the words ring true. What we build and keep watch over, what we rise early for and stay up late tending in our lives only matters if God is a part of it. Children are indeed a "building project" of life. But the term "children" includes far more than our biological offspring. The fruit of our womb may be a project to end hunger in our community, the hope and encouragement we give to the seniors who wait anxiously every week for our visits, the changed lives of teens who come to our church on Friday evenings instead of cruising with their friends. These children, these "building projects," are the sources of our contentedness in life, the purpose for which God gives us sleep (v. 2).

NANCY DECLAISSÉ-WALFORD

Psalm 128: The Lord Bless You from Zion

Ninth in the group of fifteen psalms (Psalms 120–34) identified in their superscriptions as Songs of the Ascents (see the Introduction to the Songs of the Ascents), Psalm 128 was most likely sung by pilgrims as they made their way to Jerusalem to celebrate a number of annual religious festivals, including Passover, the Feast of Weeks, and the Feast of Tabernacles. It is classified, along with Psalm 127, as a wisdom psalm, the second of three wisdom psalms in the Songs of the Ascents, and one of six in Book Five of the Psalter: Psalms 112, 119, 127, 128, 133, and 145. A wisdom psalm is defined as one that "provides instruction in right living and right faith in the tradition of the other wisdom writings in the Old Testament — Proverbs, Ecclesiastes, and Job."[1]

While commentators offer a variety of structures for Psalm 128,[2] it may be divided into two stanzas, combining wisdom words in vv. 1-4, called by Terrien "sapiential salutations," with benedictory words in vv. 5-6, called by Terrien "priestly blessing."[3]

Wisdom words (vv. 1-4)
Priestly words (vv. 5-6)

A Song of the Ascents

1 *Content is the person who reverences the* LORD,
the one who walks in his paths.
2 *The toil of the palms of your hands surely*[4] *you will eat;*
content you will be and good it will be to you.
3 *Your wife will be like a fruitful vine*
in the inner chambers of your house.
Your children will be like the shoots of olive trees
surrounding your table.
4 *Behold, for thus the mighty one will be blessed,*
the one who reverences the LORD.

5 *May the* LORD *bless you from Zion,*
and may you see[5] *the good of Jerusalem*

1. deClaissé-Walford, *Introduction to the Psalms,* p. 25.

2. See Terrien, *The Psalms,* p. 832; Allen, *Psalms 101–150,* p. 185; and McCann, "The Book of Psalms," p. 1200.

3. Terrien, *The Psalms,* p. 832.

4. The use of *kî* here is emphatic. See *HALOT,* 1:470.

5. The verbs *see (rā'â)* here and in v. 6 are the imperative form. A jussive translation seems most appropriate in the context. Crow, in *The Songs of Ascents,* p. 74, writes, "Probably

all the days of your living.
6 *May you see the children of your children;*
well-being upon Israel!

1-4 The wisdom words of vv. 1-4 contain much of the vocabulary that readers encounter in Psalm 127: *content ('ašrê);*[6] *house (bayîṯ); children (bānîm); behold (hinnēh);* and *mighty one (gibbôr),* suggesting a close link between the two wisdom psalms. The statements in vv. 1 and 4 concerning the one who *reverences (yārē')*[7] *the Lord* form an *inclusio* around the first four verses of Psalm 128.

Grape *vines* and *olive trees* were staples of farm production in ancient Palestine, and the words of v. 3 promise a bounteous harvest for *the one who reverences the Lord.* In contrast to Ps. 127:2, which suggests that human labor is worthless, v. 2 states, *the toil of the palms of your hands you will eat.* The familial words *the inner chambers of your house* and *your table* suggest the intimacy of family relationships.

5-6 Verses 5 and 6 may be characterized as the priestly words of Psalm 128.[8] The stanza begins with v. 5's words of hope: *May the Lord bless you from Zion.* Two imperative verbs *(rᵉ'ēh),* translated here as *may you see,* follow. Psalm 127 does not offer words of blessing in language comparable to Psalm 128. Psalm 128 moves beyond the wisdom admonitions found in Psalm 127 and brings the psalm-singer home to Israel, the place of *goodness (ṭôḇ)* and *well-being (šālôm).*

Psalm 128 moves the reader/hearer from words of wisdom to words of blessing. As observed in the commentary on Psalm 127, a spouse and children are not the only means to blessing by God. Each of our heartfelt endeavors in life can be likened to spouses and children, those in which we invest our lives at the cost of all others. Psalm 128 promises that such endeavors, if they are undertaken with a firm "reverence of the Lord" (vv. 1, 4), will be blessed. And, in due season, they contribute well-being to Jerusalem — that is, the whole body of believers.

Nancy deClaissé-Walford

---

this is to be explained on the basis of the jussive verb *yĕbārĕkkā* (in v. 5), which has YHWH as the subject, so that the imperatives become consequents of that blessing."

6. For a full discussion of *content ('ašrê),* see the commentary for Ps. 112:1b.

7. For a full discussion of *reverence (yārē'),* see the commentary for Ps. 111:10.

8. Many commentators draw parallels between vv. 5-6 and the Priestly Blessing in Num. 6:24-26.

Psalm 129: The Lord Is Righteous

Psalm 129 is the tenth of fifteen psalms in Book Five of the Hebrew Psalter identified in their superscriptions as Songs of the Ascents (Psalms 120–34; see the Introduction to the Songs of the Ascents). These "songs" were most likely sung by pilgrims as they made their way to Jerusalem to celebrate a number of annual religious festivals, including Passover, the Feast of Weeks, and the Feast of Tabernacles. Psalm 129 is broadly categorized as a community hymn, with the individual voice in the psalm representing the collective voice of the whole community of faith. Depending on the translation and interpretation of vv. 5-6, however, the psalm may more specifically be categorized as a song of trust or as an imprecatory psalm. The verbs in vv. 5-6 are Hebrew imperfect, which indicates an incomplete state of action or being (action or being not yet complete or on-going) and can be rendered into English in the future tense, the present tense, or the jussive mood. Thus v. 5 may be translated into English as: "They will be ashamed" (future); "They are ashamed" (present); or "May they be ashamed" (jussive). Although a number of commentators opt to render the verses as future tense,[1] this commentary will follow NIV, NRSV, NASB, and NJPS in translating vv. 5 and 6 as jussive, and thus will read Psalm 129 as an imprecatory psalm.[2] The psalm is composed of three stanzas:

The account of past suffering (vv. 1-3)
The account of divine rescue (v. 4)
Imprecatory words (vv. 5-8)

A Song of the Ascents

1 *Many times have they oppressed me from my youth,*
let Israel say.
2 *Many times have they oppressed me from my youth,*
yet they have not prevailed over me.
3 *Upon my back the plowing ones*[3] *have plowed;*
they have made their furrows long.

4 *The* LORD *is righteous;*
he has cut through the cords of the wicked ones.

1. See Allen, *Psalms 101–150,* p. 186; and Kraus, *Psalms 60–150,* p. 460.
2. For a full discussion of imprecatory psalms, see the commentary for Ps. 109.
3. LXX renders this word, which in MT is $\d{h}\bar{o}r^{e}\check{s}\hat{\imath}m$ and is here translated as *the plowing ones,* as "the wicked ones" ($r^{e}\check{s}\bar{a}{}^{c}\hat{\imath}m$), to harmonize with v. 4.

5 *May they be ashamed and draw back,*
all the ones who hate Zion.
6 *May they be like the grass of the roofs,*
which, before it draws out, it withers;
7 *With which the reaping one does not fill the palm of his hand,*
and his arm, the binding one of the sheaves.
8 *And may the ones passing by not say,*
"The blessing of the LORD to you.
We bless you in the name of the LORD."

1-3 The word translated here as *many times (rabbaṯ)* also appears in Pss. 120:6 and 123:4. In those occurrences the word is translated as "too long" (120:6) and "overwhelmed" (123:4). The singer of Psalm 129, along with the singers of Psalms 120 and 123, expresses a sense of endless and relentless oppression. And for the singer of Psalm 129, the oppression has been present *from my youth (n^{e}ʿûrîm).* This phrase evokes images echoed in the writings of the prophets of Hosea and Jeremiah. The youth of Israel was the time of the exodus from Egypt and the wilderness wandering. In Hos. 2:15b, the prophet says, "There she (Israel) shall respond as in the days of her youth *(n^{e}ʿûrîm),* as at the time when she came out of the land of Egypt." And in Jer. 2:2, we read, "I remember the devotion of your youth *(n^{e}ʿûrîm),* your love as a bride, how you followed me in the wilderness, in a land not sown." The psalmist states that Israel has been oppressed from the time that the Lord chose the people and led them out of Egypt. The phrase in v. 1b, *let Israel say,* suggests, as does the same phrase in Pss. 118:2 and 124:1, a call to worship, an invitation for individual worshippers to join their voices as the one voice of Israel.

Verse 3 employs agricultural imagery to convey the severity of Israel's oppression. The *back* of Israel is likened to a field being plowed, with the plowing ones driving long *furrows* in the soil. In Isa. 51:23, God says to the people, "you have made your back like the ground and like the street for them [your tormentors] to walk on." And the prophet Micah declares, "Zion shall be plowed as a field" (Mic. 3:12).

4 In v. 4, the turning point of the psalm, the singer celebrates the Lord's righteousness[4] and continuous care for the faithful. The Lord *cuts through the cords of the wicked ones.* The word *cord (ʿ^{a}ḇōṯ)* may continue the metaphoric image from v. 3, suggesting the cords which guide the animals in the field. It may also suggest the instruments of punishment used by the Egyptians and others on the backs of subject people (See Ps. 2:3).

5-8 The imprecatory words of Psalm 129 are directed against *all the ones who hate (śānēʾ) Zion. Hate* is a powerful word in the Hebrew Bible,

4. For a discussion of *righteous (ṣaddîq),* see the commentary for Ps. 112:2-4.

used over 170 times with both humankind and God as subjects. God's hate is directed most often toward behaviors and actions rather than specific persons (see Deut. 12:31, Canaanite cultic practices; Deut. 16:22, the erection of sacred pillars; Isa. 1:14, the insincere festivals of the Israelites; Isa. 61:8, unholy offerings). And while "hate" in the Hebrew Bible is an emotionally-charged word, its consequence usually implies a distancing of oneself from another person or thing rather than wishing the other harm. In v. 5, the psalm-singer wishes for *the ones who hate Zion* to *be ashamed and draw back,* echoing the idea of distancing tied to the word's meaning.

The agricultural metaphor begun in v. 3 continues in vv. 6-8 as the psalmist wishes that the "hating ones" *be like the grass* that grows atop sod *roofs,* grass that does not have deep enough roots to produce any crop that the reaper or the binder of sheaves can profitably use. The words of v. 8 seem best understood when they are tied to the agricultural metaphor of vv. 6-7. In Ruth 2:4, Boaz greets the reapers in his field with the words, "The LORD be with you," and they reply, "The LORD bless you." The psalm-singer expresses a wish that *the ones who hate Zion* not gain the *blessing* of the harvest.[5]

Psalm 129 reminds those who have been oppressed that God is righteous and will care for the faithful. That does not mean, however, that the faithful will not suffer. It simply means that when all is said and done, the oppressors will not prevail (v. 2). In our affluent and relatively peaceful Western world, unrelenting oppression is something most of us have never experienced. And imprecatory words (vv. 5-8) seem inappropriate in the Christian era where Jesus taught us to "turn the other cheek." But in the face of absolute injustice and horrid neglect, abuse, and torture, the Christian must cry out. Erich Zenger, in a powerful monograph titled *A God of Vengeance? Understanding the Psalms of Divine Wrath,* writes:

> We have suppressed in our Christian consciousness the idea that judgment is for the sake of justice, especially for those who are the victims of injustice, and that the purpose of this judgment is to restore everything "as it should be" — and even to confront the wicked with their injustice in such a way that they honor justice through their repentance.[6]

NANCY DECLAISSÉ-WALFORD

5. See Clifford, *Psalms 73–150,* p. 246; Kraus, *Psalms 60–150,* p. 462; and Mays, *Psalms,* pp. 404-5.

6. (Trans. Linda M. Maloney; Louisville: Westminster John Knox, 1996), p. 64. For further discussion, see the commentary for Ps. 109.

Psalm 130: From the Depths I Cry to You

Psalm 130 is the eleventh of the fifteen Songs of the Ascents in Book Five of the Psalter (see the Introduction to the Songs of the Ascents), songs that pilgrims sang as they made their way to Jerusalem to celebrate a number of annual religious festivals, including Passover, the Feast of Weeks, and the Feast of Tabernacles. It is classified as an individual lament, in which the traditional elements[1] of a lament are represented as follows:

Invocation	Vv. 1, 2, 3, 5, 7 ("LORD, Lord")
Complaint	V. 1 ("out of the depths")
Petition	V. 1 ("listen to my voice")
Expression of trust	Vv. 4-6 ("for with you is forgiveness")

Its form, however, includes other elements not normally found in an individual lament. Verses 7-8, in particular, in which all of Israel is admonished to *wait expectantly for the LORD*, seem out of place in an individual lament. How then do we describe the form of this psalm?

Psalm 130 reflects the general tone of the Songs of the Ascents, in which the voices of individual worshippers are combined with the voice of the whole community of faith. The individual voice of Psalm 130 may, in fact, be understood as the collective voice of Israel, like the personified voice of the community that the reader encounters in Psalm 129. Thus the oppressed nation acknowledges its culpability for its oppression (129:1-3) and waits expectantly for the deliverance of the Lord (130:7-8).

Psalm 130 may be divided into four two-verse stanzas, based on the occurrences of the personal name of Israel's God, *YHWH or Yah,* in each section.[2]

A cry to the Lord to listen (vv. 1-2)
A statement of trust in the Lord (vv. 3-4)
A statement of hopeful expectation (vv. 5-6)
An invitation for all Israel to join in hopeful expectation (vv. 7-8)

1. See deClaissé-Walford, *Introduction to the Psalms,* p. 24.

2. Some scholars suggest a two-part division for Ps. 130 (see Kraus, *Psalms 60–150,* p. 465; Clifford, *Psalms 73–150,* p. 248; and Gerstenberger, *Psalms: Part 2,* p. 356). Others suggest a three-part division: vv. 1-4, 5-6, and 7-8 (McCann, "The Book of Psalms," p. 1205); and vv. 1-3, 4-6, 7-8 (Terrien, *The Psalms,* pp. 839-40).

A Song of the Ascents

1 *From the depths I cry to you, O* Lord.
Lord, listen to my voice.
2 *Let your ears be attentive*
to the voice of my entreaties.

3 *If iniquities you keep account of, O* Lord,
Lord, who could stand?
4 *But*[3] *there is with you forgiveness*
so that you may be revered.[4]

5 *I am confident in the* Lord, *my inmost being is confident,*
and for his word I wait expectantly.
6 *My inmost being (waits expectantly*[5]*) for the Lord,*
more than those watching for the morning,
those watching for the morning.

7 *Wait expectantly, O Israel, for the* Lord,
for with the Lord *is* hesed,
and abundantly with him is deliverance.
8 *And he will deliver Israel*
from all of its iniquities.

1-2 In each of the four stanzas of Psalm 130, God is addressed or referred to two times. In v. 1, the psalm-singer addresses God by the divine name YHWH; in v. 2, the psalmist uses the more generic *Lord (ʾ^{a}ḏōnāy).* The pattern (divine name followed by generic name) is repeated in vv. 3-4 and in vv. 5-6. Only in vv. 7-8 is the divine name YHWH used twice.

The first word of v. 1, *from the depths (mimmaʿ^{a}maqqîm),* is used elsewhere in the Old Testament in reference to the sea (Isa. 51:10; Ezek. 27:34; Ps. 69:2, 14; cf. Jonah 2:2-6), often considered a place of watery chaos in ancient Israelite thought.[6] Verses 1b and 2 express parallel sentiments. *Listen* (from the root *šāmaʿ*) occurs frequently in an initial position in pleas, both to God and from God (Deut. 6:4; Pss. 4:1; 64:1; 102:1; Mic. 3:9).

3. The Hebrew word *kî* is here translated as *but.* According to Allen, *Psalms 101–150,* p. 192, *kî* introduces "the reason for the negative implication of the condition of v. 3a."

4. MT here is *l^{e}maʿan tiwwārēʾ.* LXX and other Greek Versions translate as if the Hebrew text were *l^{e}maʿan tôrāṯeḵā* [because of your Torah].

5. Not included in MT.

6. For an excellent treatment of water imagery in the Psalter, see Brown, *Seeing the Psalms,* pp. 105-34.

My voice (qôlî) in v. 1b is more fully defined with *the voice of my entreaties (qôl taḥᵃnûnāy)* in v. 2b. *Entreaties* comes from the same verbal root as the word translated in Psalms 111, 112, and 123 as "showing favor" *(ḥānan).* The word is one of the self-declarative attributes of God given to Moses in Exod. 34:6. In Psalm 130, the psalm-singer calls on God to be attentive to the singer's cry "to be shown favor" by God by appealing to a basic characteristic of God.[7] The Latin name for Psalm 130 is *De profundis* ("out of the depths"); the words are used in many countries for invitations to funerals.[8] The mourners cry *De profundis,* and their only request is that God hear and be attentive.

3-4 As in v. 1b, v. 3a includes two addresses to God — Yah and *ʾᵃḏōnāy.* The word *iniquities (ʿᵃwōnôṯ)* occurs over 200 times in the Old Testament and is the primary word used to describe human sin and guilt in the prophetic writings. Rolf Knierim suggests that its root meaning is "to bend, curve, turn aside, or twist,"[9] thus providing a concrete image for a definition of "iniquity" as "an act, or mistake, which is not right or unjust."[10] The question of v. 3, introduced by the particle *if (ʾim),* is a rhetorical question, with the obvious answer, "No one." But God grants *forgiveness* (from the root *sālaḥ).* The word is used only in connection with God's forgiveness in a cultic setting, never in connection with human forgiveness. Psalm 130 describes forgiveness as an entity that is *with* God (*ʿim,* v. 7), perhaps a play on words with v. 3's *if (ʾim),* linking the two verses to contrast human iniquity with God's forgiveness. Forgiveness is with God so that, according to v. 4b, God may be *revered* (from the root *yārēʾ).*[11]

5-6 As in vv. 1 and 3, vv. 5-6 use two words to refer to God — YHWH and *ʾᵃḏōnāy,* although here the words are spoken *about* God, rather than *to* God. Repetition of key words may mark these verses, which contain words of trust, as the focus of Psalm 130. McCann suggests that the repetition "draws out the poetic line; thus it reproduces literarily the effect of waiting."[12] The psalmist *is confident* (from the root *qāwâ*) and *waits expectantly* (from the root *yāḥal*). The two words are similar in semantic range, although *yāḥal* is most often translated as "hope." The word, though, conveys a sense of "patient expecting, anticipating, or waiting." The psalmist is *confident* and *waits expectantly,* more expectantly *than those watching for the morning.* Sentinels often stood guard on city walls, as did soldiers in camps during times of war,

7. For a full discussion of *ḥānan,* see the commentary for Ps. 111:2-4.

8. Terrien, *The Psalms,* p. 839.

9. E. Jenni and C. Westermann, eds., *Theological Lexicon of the Old Testament* (Peabody: Hendrickson, 1997), 2:863.

10. *HALOT,* 2:800.

11. For a full discussion of *revere,* see the commentary for Ps. 111:10.

12. "The Book of Psalms," p. 1205.

watching in the darkness for danger and waiting expectantly for the safety that daylight brought.[13]

7-8 Verses 7-8 refer to God twice, as do the other three stanzas in Psalm 130. But they use only the divine name YHWH, and no other, for God. While vv. 5-6's words of trust may be considered the focus of the psalm, vv. 7-8 are certainly the climax. The voice of Psalm 130 has been first person up to this point; with v. 7 the voice changes. Many scholars suggest that we hear now a priestly exhortation giving assurance of deliverance to the psalm-singer(s).[14] Crow maintains that Psalm 130 combines "fragments of an older [individual lament] psalm that has been taken over by an editor and supplied with an appropriate exhortatory conclusion."[15]

The psalm-singer calls on Israel to *wait expectantly (yāḥal),* tying the words of exhortation to the words of trust in vv. 5-6. The reason that Israel should *wait expectantly* is *that with (kî ʿim)* the Lord is *hesed* and *deliverance* (v. 7), acting to further tie the words of exhortation to the words of v. 4. And, therefore, God *will deliver Israel from all of its iniquities (ʿᵃwōnôṯ,* v. 8), tying the words of exhortation further still to the words of v. 3.

The psalm-singer(s) calls upon God to hear and *be attentive* in vv. 1 and 2 and goes on to express trust and hopeful expectation in the Lord. The response of vv. 7-8 assures the psalm-singer(s), by repeating connective words of the psalmist(s), that God has indeed heard and that God *will deliver.*

Psalm 130 is one of the seven penitential psalms in the Psalter (Psalms 6, 32, 38, 51, 102, 130, and 143), the Lenten liturgy of the medieval church. By order of Pope Innocent III (1198-1216), the psalms were to be prayed while kneeling each day of the Lenten season, or at least every Friday. The penitential psalms remind the reciter of the great divide between the goodness of God and the iniquity of humanity, but they also remind the reciter that "with God" are "forgiveness," *hesed,* and "deliverance." Martin Luther called Psalm 130 "a proper master and doctor of Scripture."

NANCY DECLAISSÉ-WALFORD

13. Clifford, *Psalms 73–150,* p. 249; and Gerstenberger, *Psalms: Part 2,* p. 356.
14. Allen, *Psalms 101–150,* p. 193.
15. *The Songs of Ascents,* p. 90.

Psalm 131: Like a Sated Child

Psalm 131 is the twelfth of the fifteen Songs of the Ascents in Book Five (see the Introduction to the Songs of the Ascents). Pilgrims most likely sang these songs as they made their way to Jerusalem to observe various festivals and celebrations, such as Passover, the Feast of Weeks, and the Feast of Booths. This brief psalm, called by Gerstenberger "a jewel of simplicity,"[1] is broadly classified as an individual psalm of thanksgiving and more narrowly defined as a hymn of trust. It is one of three of the Songs of the Ascents ascribed to David (Psalms 122, 124, and 131), thus giving the psalm a "royal" starting point for interpretation.[2] Three stanzas make up Psalm 131:

Declaration of humility (v. 1)
Declaration of trust in God (v. 2)
Admonition to all Israel to trust in God (v. 3)

A Song of the Ascents. Of David.

1 *O LORD, my heart is not proud*
and my eyes are not haughty.
And I have not occupied myself[3] *with great matters,*
with things too wondrous for me.

2 *Indeed, I have calmed and quieted my inmost being*
like a sated child upon its mother.
Like a sated child upon me is my inmost being.

3 *Wait expectantly, O Israel, for the LORD,*
from now and for all time.

1 The verse begins with a vocative invocation, *O LORD*, usually associated with psalms of lament. The psalmist continues with a threefold negative declaration, *my heart is not (lōʾ) proud; my eyes are not (lōʾ) haughty; I have not (lōʾ) occupied myself with great matters. . . .* The Hebrew word *heart (lēḇ)* refers to the seat of human intelligence, parallel to the English word "mind." The psalm-singer does not think better of self than of others. Nor does the psalm-singer look down upon others haughtily. The reference to mind and *eyes* reflects the inner and outer demeanor of the psalmist.

1. *Psalms: Part 2,* p. 359.

2. See the extensive discussion by Bernard P. Robinson in "Form and Meaning in Psalm 131," *Bib* 79 (1998) 180-97.

3. Lit., "walked about," the *hithpael* form of *hālaḵ*.

In addition, the psalmist has not occupied herself with *great matters (gᵉḏōlôṯ)* or *wondrous things (nip̱lā'ôṯ)*. These two words are used in Pss. 86:10; 136:4; and 145:5-6 to describe the works of God in the world. The psalmist has not sought to do or take credit for Godlike acts in this world. Placing the words of v. 1 on the lips of King David provides the reader/hearer with an added dimension of meaning for Psalm 131. David, the great king of Israel's past, states that he is not *proud, haughty,* or caught up in performing "bigger than life" deeds.

2 Rather than being proud and haughty, the psalmist's *inmost being (nep̱eš)* is *calmed and quieted.* The root of the word *calm (šawâ)* means "to be even, smooth." Verse 2 likens the evenness and quietness of the psalm-singer to a *sated (qal* passive participle of *gāmal) child at its mother's breast.* NRSV, NIV, NASB, and NJPS translate the second colon of v. 2 as "like a weaned child." The Hebrew root of "sated or weaned," *gāmal,* has a basic meaning of "to treat kindly, to be helpful to someone, to complete or perfect." The verbal root came, by analogy, to mean "to wean" in Hebrew. In Gen. 21:8, we read of Isaac, "The child grew and was weaned (*niphal* stem of *gāmal*); and Abraham made a great feast on the day that Isaac was weaned." In 1 Samuel, Hannah tells her husband Elkanah that she will take Samuel to Shiloh "as soon as the child is weaned." Thus in a number of places in the biblical text, the verbal root *gāmal* suggests the completion of the weaning of a child from the mother's breast, an event that usually took place when the child was about three years old. If we understand "weaned" as the meaning of the verb, then the metaphor suggests a child who no longer cries out in hunger for the mother's breast, but who seeks out the mother for her warm embrace and nurturing care. The verb, however, might also describe a suckling child who is well-fed and fully satisfied, resting peacefully in the mother's embrace. Both metaphors are a powerful image of one who finds calmness and quiet in the embrace of God. Did King David, in the midst of conflicts and crises, look to God as a nurturing, life-giving mother? Did David fold himself in God's nurturing embrace? The vivid metaphor of Psalm 131 continues the strong metaphoric imagery of the Songs of the Ascents. From the "sharp arrows" of Psalm 120, the "maid servants" and "mistress" of Psalm 123, the "water channels" of Psalm 126, to the "vines" and "olive trees" of Psalm 128, the Songs of the Ascents are filled with picture examples of God's good provision for the faithful.

3 The words of v. 3 echo those of Ps. 130:5-6, tying the two psalms firmly together and suggesting that they be read together. Verse 3 also joins the words of an individual (in vv. 1 and 2) with the words of the community of all Israel — as in many of the Songs of the Ascents — in what Kraus characterizes as the most tender and intimate of the pilgrimage songs.[4]

4. *Psalms 60–150,* p. 470.

Because of the feminine imagery in Psalm 131, a number of scholars suggest that it was composed by a woman.[5] Assigning authorship to any psalm is problematic, and assuming a feminine voice for Psalm 131 is tenuous at best. Yes, a feminine voice could have been the first to sing the words of the psalm, one whose own life experiences led her to recognize the parallel between a child's need for its mother and every human's need for God in order to live a calm and quiet life. On the other hand, a masculine voice also could have composed the words of Psalm 131, a reflection of one of the most basic interactions of family life in the ancient Near East.[6] The metaphor of God as parent and Israel as child is found elsewhere in the Hebrew Bible. In Hos. 11:3-4, God says of Israel, "Yet it was I who taught Ephraim to walk, I took them up in my arms. . . . I was to them like those who lift infants to their cheeks." And in Deut. 1:31, Moses speaks to the people, "in the wilderness . . . you saw how the LORD your God carried you, just as one carries a child, all the way that you traveled until you reached this place."[7] Regardless of the gender of the voice in Psalm 131, its words reflect a basic trust in God by pilgrims coming to Jerusalem for festivals and celebrations and singing the words of the Songs of the Ascents.

The message of Psalm 131 is simple. Pride, haughtiness, and seeking after great and wondrous things will not provide the calm and quiet that simple reliance on God provides. The psalm-singer stresses the contrast between the two ways of life emphatically in v. 1 with three negative verbal clauses: *my heart is not (lō') proud; my eyes are not (lō') haughty; I have not (lō') occupied myself with great matters* and emphasizes the simplicity of total reliance on God with a repetition of the phrase *like a sated child (k^{e}gāmul)* in v. 2.

In the New Testament, Jesus told the disciples that anyone who did not become like a child would never enter the kingdom of heaven (Matt. 19:13-15; Mark 10:13-16). Psalm 131 teaches us in vivid metaphoric imagery how to be a child in the presence of God.

NANCY DECLAISSÉ-WALFORD

5. See, e.g., Gottfried Quell, "Struktur und Sinn des Psalms 131," in *Das ferne und nahe Wort,* ed. Fritz Maass (BZAW 105; Berlin: Töpelmann, 1967), pp. 181-85; Allen, *Psalms 101–150,* p. 198; McCann, "The Book of Psalms," p. 1208; and Anderson and Bishop, *Out of the Depths,* p. 179.

6. See Gerstenberger, *Psalms: Part 2,* p. 362; and Crow, *The Songs of Ascents,* pp. 97-98.

7. See also Isa. 46:3-4; Jer. 31:20.

Psalm 132: Remember, O Lord, on Account of David

Psalm 132 is the thirteenth of the fifteen Songs of the Ascents (Psalms 120–34). Pilgrims traveling to Jerusalem sang the Songs of the Ascents as they approached, arrived in, and sojourned in Jerusalem to celebrate a number of annual religious festivals, including Passover, the Feast of Weeks, and the Feast of Booths. The length, subject matter, and location within the Songs of the Ascents suggest a special function for Psalm 132. First, this psalm, with eighteen verses, is considerably longer than any of the other Songs of the Ascents. Second, it is classified as a royal psalm and focuses on both the Davidic king and the selection of Zion/Jerusalem as a dwelling place for God. Finally, its position near the end of the Songs of the Ascents suggests that it was recited by festal pilgrims as they stood in the midst of Jerusalem — pausing to wonder at God's great provisions for David and perhaps to find optimism for their own lives and futures.

We may divide Psalm 132 into two major stanzas: vv. 1-10 and vv. 11-18. A number of scholars note a pattern and strong connectedness between the stanzas, as outlined below:[1]

Prayer (vv. 1-10)
  David's vow to God (vv. 1-5)
    The story of the ark (vv. 6-8)
      A prayer for priest and people (v. 9)
        A prayer for David (v. 10)
The response to the prayer (vv. 11-18)
  God's vow to David (vv. 11-12)
    God's response to the story of the ark (vv. 13-15)
      A prayer for priest and people (v. 16)
        The response to David's prayer (vv. 17-18)

A Song of the Ascents

1 *Remember, O LORD, for the sake of David,*
all of his afflictions
2 *that he swore to the LORD,*
that he vowed to the protector of Jacob.

1. See esp. Allen, *Psalms 101–150,* pp. 204-9; McCann, "The Book of Psalms," pp. 1211-12. For an intriguing alternate structure for the psalm, see Limburg, *Psalms,* in which he suggests the following: vv. 1-10, a chosen place; vv. 11-12, a chosen person; vv. 13-18, a chosen place and a chosen person.

3 *I will not*[2] *enter into the tent of my house;*
I will not ascend upon the cushions of my bed;
4 *I will not give sleep to my eyes,*
to my eyelids slumber,
5 *Until I find a place for the* LORD,
dwelling places for the protector of Israel.
6 *Behold, we have heard of it in Ephrathah;*
we found it in the fields of Jaar.
7 *Let us enter his dwelling places;*
let us worship the footstool of his feet.
8 *Arise, O* LORD, *to your resting place,*
you and the ark of your strength.
9 *Your priests will clothe themselves with righteousness,*
and your hesed *ones will rejoice.*
10 *For the sake of your servant David,*
do not turn away the face of your anointed one.

11 *The* LORD *swore to David truth;*
he will not turn away from him.
"From the fruit of your groin
I will establish a throne for you.
12 *If your children keep my covenant*
and my decrees which I will teach them,
Then also their children for all time
will dwell upon your throne."
13 *When the* LORD *chose Zion,*
he coveted it as a dwelling place for himself.
14 *"This is my resting place for all time;*
here I will dwell for I have coveted it.
15 *Its food I have indeed blessed;*
its needy ones I will satisfy.
16 *And its priests I will clothe in deliverance,*
and its hesed *ones indeed they will rejoice.*
17 *There I will cause to sprout a horn for David;*
I have prepared a lamp for my anointed one.
18 *Those who hate him I will clothe with shame,*
and upon him his crown will shine."

2. Here and in the following colon, the word translated *not* is *'im,* usually translated as "if." In a vow formula without an apodosis, *'im* indicates a strong negative; *HALOT,* 1:60.

1-5 The "prayer" portion of this royal psalm begins in vv. 1-5 with the recollection of David's vow to God. The psalm-singer calls on God to *remember (zāḵar) for the sake of David* all that David experienced in his life and all that David promised to do to create a "dwelling place" for God. The words of vv. 1-5 echo the sentiments of David in 2 Samuel 7, when he announced to the prophet Nathan that he planned to build a house for the ark of God (2 Sam. 7:2). The phrase *protector of Jacob (ʾaḇîr yaʿaqōḇ),* which occurs in vv. 2 and 5 and is translated in the NRSV, NIV, and JPS as "mighty one," is an early epithet for God that appears in Gen. 49:24, in Jacob's blessing of his twelve sons (see also Isa. 49:26; 60:16).

The word translated in v. 5 as *dwelling places* comes from the Hebrew root *šāḵan,* which means "to settle down, inhabit, reside." It is reminiscent of God's presence in the tabernacle *(miškān)* during the wilderness wanderings (see Exod. 40:35) and in the temple in Jerusalem (see 1 Kgs. 8:12). The word *miškānôṯ (dwelling places)* is a unifying theme for Psalm 133, occurring in vv. 5 and 7, and used synonymously with *menûḥâ (resting place)* in vv. 8 and 15 and with *môšāḇ (dwelling place)* in v. 13. In 2 Sam. 7:1, the historian writes that "when the king was settled *(yāšaḇ)* in his house, and the LORD had given him rest *(nûaḥ)* from all his enemies," then David determined that he would build a house for the Yahweh. The two words, *dwelling place* and *resting place,* bring to mind for the reciter of Psalm 132 the promise and ultimate fulfillment of God's enduring presence in the midst of the children of Israel.

6-8 In v. 6 the "prayer" continues in the plural voice with the story of the ark of the covenant, which acted as the "throne" or *footstool* of YHWH in the tabernacle and in the temple. A major interpretational issue of these verses is determining the referent for the verbal pronoun suffixes in v. 6. The psalm-singers state that they have "heard of her (3fs)" and "found her (3fs)." None of the possible referent nouns in the previous verses of the psalm are feminine singular. *Place (māqôm*] in v. 5 is masculine, while *dwelling places (miškānôṯ)* in vv. 5 and 7 is feminine plural. The only plausible referents for the 3fs suffixes in v. 6 are the two words used in parallel construction in v. 8, *resting place (menûḥâ)* and *ark (ʾārôn).* The words "arise," "ark" and "rest" are also connected to the song of the ark in Num. 10:35-36. Moses sings when the ark sets out, "Arise, O LORD . . ." and "whenever it came to rest, 'Return, O LORD . . . ,'" strongly suggesting a borrowing of Moses' words in v. 8.

The psalm-singers *have heard of* the *resting place,* the *ark,* in *Ephrathah* and found the *resting place,* the *ark,* in *Jaar.* The place names bring to mind the story of the capture of the ark of the covenant by the Philistines in 1 Samuel 4–6 and the bringing of the ark to Jerusalem by David in 2 Samuel 6. In 1 Samuel 5, the Philistines capture the ark, which the Israelites had taken into battle. The Philistines place it in the temple of Dagon, one of the Philistine gods. After the presence of the ark causes the destruction of the statue of Dagon (1 Sam.

5:1-5) and causes illness to the inhabitants of the cities of the Philistines (vv. 6-12), they send the ark back to the Israelites and, according to 1 Sam. 7:2, "the ark was lodged at Kiraith-jearim." The reference to *Ephrathah* in Ps. 132:6 most likely indicates the area surrounding Bethlehem, the home of David, and *Jaar* most likely refers to Kiriath-jearim, where the ark lodged after its return from the Philistines and until David brought it into Jerusalem (2 Samuel 6).

9-10 The prayer portion of Psalm 132 culminates in words on behalf of the *priests,* of the *hesed ones,* and of *David* — all of the members of the community of ancient Israel.

11-12 Verses 1-5 recollect David's words in 2 Samuel 7 concerning a dwelling place for God. The response portion of Psalm 132 begins with a reiteration of God's promises to David. The words of the sworn *(šāḇaʿ)* vow (v. 11) were an important element of royal enthronement ceremonies in the ancient Near East.[3] David would have royal descendants, and they would rule so long as they kept the covenant and the decrees.

13-15 Verses 13-15 comprise the response of the psalm-singers to vv. 6-8's story of the ark. The Lord chose *Zion* for a *dwelling place (môšāḇ),* as a *resting place (mᵉnûḥâ).* Thus the Lord will dwell in Zion and bless its *food* and *satisfy its needy ones.* Psalm 107:33-42 reminds the people that the sovereign God can provide them with all of their needs — a habitable land, productive fields and vineyards, children, food for the hungry and care for the needy.

16-18 The final verses of Psalm 132 echo vv. 9 and 10. The *priests* will be clothed with *deliverance,* the *hesed ones will indeed rejoice,* a *horn* will *sprout* for David, and *his crown will shine.*

Psalm 132 remembers two important elements of identity for the ancient Israelites: a dwelling place for God and the kingship of David — temple and court. The prayer of vv. 1-10 and its response of assurance in vv. 11-18 give hope to the postexilic pilgrims to Jerusalem that God indeed is dwelling among them. Temple and court may be foreign concepts to Christians today, but McCann suggests that we see in the words of Psalm 132 a reminder that God's presence among us is real and concrete, occupying both time and space.[4] And Elizabeth F. Huwiler, commenting on the "we" voice of the psalm, states, "The 'we,' the voice of the worshipping community, functions both to bring the David story from the historical past into the liturgical present and to transport the congregants from current worship setting into that same historical past."[5]

NANCY DECLAISSÉ-WALFORD

3. See the full treatment of the *Gattung* "royal psalm" in the commentary for Ps. 110.

4. "The Book of Psalms," p. 1213.

5. "Patterns and Problems in Psalm 132," in *The Listening Heart,* ed. Kenneth G. Hogland et al. (JSOTSup 58; Sheffield: JSOT, 1987), p. 207.

Psalm 133: Like Good Oil on the Head

Psalm 133 is the fourteenth of the fifteen Songs of the Ascents in Book Five of the Psalter (Psalms 120–34; see the Introduction to the Songs of the Ascents). These "songs" were most likely sung by pilgrims as they made their way to Jerusalem to celebrate a number of annual religious festivals, including Passover, the Feast of Weeks, and the Feast of Tabernacles. Psalm 133, a celebration of family and community, is one of three wisdom psalms in the Songs of the Ascents — Psalms 127, 128, and 133.[1]

In three short verses, the singer of Psalm 133 summarizes the goodness and pleasantness of kindred living together in unity and likens that goodness and pleasantness to two powerful metaphoric images — oil and dew. A number of scholars suggest that psalm-singers fashioned Psalm 133 for inclusion in the Songs of the Ascents from a traditional proverbial or wisdom saying:[2]

> Behold, how good and how pleasant it is when kindred dwell together in unity. It is like good oil on the head, running down upon the beard. It is like the dew of Hermon.

The two simple images of oil and dew, combined with the images of oil on Aaron's head and dew on Jerusalem, transformed the proverbial saying into a celebration of the goodness and pleasantness of pilgrims dwelling together in Jerusalem, God's dwelling place.

The three verses of Psalm 133 may be structured as follows:

Kindred ones dwell together (v. 1)
Like good oil (v. 2)
Like the dew of Hermon (v. 3a)
The promise to the kindred ones (v. 3b)

A Song of the Ascents; of David

1 *Behold, how good and how pleasant,*
the dwelling together of kindred as one.
2 *It is like the good oil on the head*
that goes down[3] *upon the beard,*

1. The other wisdom psalms in the Psalter are Pss. 1, 32, 37, 49, 73, 79, 112, 119, 145.

2. See, e.g., Allen, *Psalms 101–150,* p. 215; McCann, "The Book of Psalms," p. 1214; Crow, *The Songs of Ascents,* p. 109; Mays, *Psalms,* p. 413.

3. The *qal* active participle *yōrēḏ* in this colon does not have the prefixed relative pronoun *še,* as do the occurrences of the participle in the following two cola (vv. 2b and 3a). Two Hebrew manuscripts add the definite article to the participle in v. 2a, and the editors of *BHS* suggest adding the relative pronoun.

the beard of Aaron,
that goes down upon the edge of his robes.
3 *It is like the dew of Hermon*
that goes down upon the mountains of Zion.
For there the LORD *commanded the blessing,*
life for all time.

1 In its proverbial setting, the wisdom words of v. 1 — *how good and how pleasant* — recall the exclamation of blessing uttered by a traveler or visitor upon entering the home of another in ancient Israel. The word translated *good* is *ṭôḇ,* a word that recalls God's assessment of creation in Genesis 1. In Gen. 1:4, 10, 12, 18, and 21 the creation story tells us that "God saw that it was good." At its conclusion, "God saw everything that God had made, and indeed, it was very good *(ṭôḇ m^{e}ʾōḏ),*" In the Genesis 2 creation story, however, God declares, "It is not good *(lōʾ ṭôḇ)* for the human to be alone; I will make him a helper as his partner" (2:18). The word *good* in Ps. 133:1 reminds the reciter of God's provision of community and relatedness for humanity.[4]

The word translated "pleasant" is *nāʿîm,* from the Hebrew root *nāʿēm.* Its meanings include "lovely, good, attractive, friendly, joyous." It frequently occurs in parallel to *ṭôḇ* (Gen. 49:15; Ps. 147:1; Job 36:11; Prov. 24:25). In ancient Israel, extended families lived together in small communities and shared responsibilities that were common to their communities.[5]

2 *Oil* from the olive was an important commodity in the dry environment of the Near East. Olive oil was mixed with sweet-smelling spices and used for hair and skin care. The oil was poured over the *head,* and, for men, ran down into the *beard.* A basic act of hospitality when visitors entered the homes of others was to wash the visitors' feet and pour soothing and refreshing oil upon their heads.

The oil in Psalm 133 is poured upon the head of *Aaron,* and the oil runs down into his beard and onto the collar of his garments. In Leviticus 8, Moses anoints his brother, Aaron, as high priest of ancient Israel:

> Then Moses took the anointing oil and anointed the tabernacle and all that was in it, and consecrated them. . . . He poured some of the anointing oil on Aaron's head and anointed him, to consecrate him. (Lev. 8:10, 12)

The oil used to anoint the head of the visitor to one's home is used to anoint the head of Aaron, the high priest, celebrating the presence of God in the community of Israel.

4. For a full discussion of the Genesis 2 story, see Nancy L. deClaissé-Walford, "Genesis 2: It Is Not Good for the Human to Be Alone," *RevExp* 103 (2006) 343-58.

5. See Kraus, *Psalms 60–150,* pp. 485-86.

3a Mount *Hermon,* located some 125 miles north of Jerusalem, was known for its abundant *dew.* And in Palestine, which saw little rainfall between the months of April and October, dew was an important commodity. Without the nightly accumulation of dew, the land would be parched and dry for many months out of the year. In Psalm 133, the dew that soothes and refreshes the land comes down on Mount *Zion;* and Jerusalem, the center of worship for ancient Israel, is soothed and refreshed.

3b From Zion, where the God of the ancient Israelites dwelled, the people sought and found *blessing (bᵉrāḵâ).* The word reverberates throughout the pages of the Hebrew Bible — God says to Abram, "In you all the families of the earth shall be blessed" (Gen. 12:3); after Jacob's long night of wrestling, we read, "And there he blessed him" (Gen. 32:29); and Moses says to the Israelites, "Surely the LORD your God has blessed you in all your undertakings" (Deut. 2:7). The oil and the dew are metaphoric symbols of *blessing* that celebrate the goodness and pleasantness of those who dwell together in unity.

The ancient Israelite singers of Psalm 133 would most likely have remembered the proverbial wisdom saying upon which the psalm was based — kindred who dwell together in unity being likened to good oil and dew. They still would have celebrated the joy and goodness of dwelling together as brothers and sisters. But the words of the whole psalm reminded the people that their family relationship was established not by blood, but by their mutual share in the community of God, a community that received blessing from its God. Psalm 133, as one of the Songs of the Ascents, prepared the pilgrims coming to Jerusalem to celebrate together as family, as kindred living in oneness, the festivals of the Lord their God.

In the Christian tradition, Psalm 133 is often used as a text for the observance of the Lord's Supper, which calls the whole people of God to a family table where all are welcome. St. Augustine boldly claimed that Psalm 133 inspired the foundation of monasteries, since its words paint a picture of the ideal of brothers, fellow pilgrims in the faith, dwelling together in unity.

We have our own "kindredness" based on blood ties, but we also share in a covenant community with God in Jesus. We come from kindred families from different places and times, but our ultimate kindredness is assured through our mutual share in the promises of God.

NANCY DECLAISSÉ-WALFORD

Psalm 134: Final Words of Blessing

Psalm 134 is the last of the fifteen Songs of the Ascents in the Hebrew Psalter (Psalms 120–34; see the Introduction to the Songs of the Ascents). These "songs" were most likely sung by pilgrims as they made their way to Jerusalem to celebrate a number of annual religious festivals, including Passover, the Feast of Weeks, and the Feast of Tabernacles. Psalm 134 is a blessing for the pilgrims in Jerusalem, a brief word of departure as they ready themselves to return to their homes in the surrounding countryside. It is classified as a community hymn, and may be divided into two stanzas:

A summons to praise (vv. 1-2)
A blessing (v. 3)

A Song of the Ascents

1 *Behold, bless the LORD,*
all the servants of the LORD,
the ones standing in the house of the LORD
in the nighttime.
2 *Lift your hands to the holy one*
and bless the LORD.

3 *May the LORD bless you from Zion,*
the maker of heaven and earth.

1-2 In these verses, we hear the voice of the worship leader calling the people to a final word of blessing to God. The word translated *bless* comes from the Hebrew root *bārak̲* and occurs more than four hundred times in the Hebrew Bible. The basic meaning of the word is "to kneel," a sign of acquiescence to another. Humans bless other humans (Gen. 27:30; Deut. 33:1; 2 Sam. 6:20); humans bless God (Gen. 24:48; Josh. 22:33; Ps. 66:8); God blesses various God-given entities (animals in Gen. 1:22; the seventh day in Gen. 2:3; bread and water in Exod. 23:25); and God blesses humans (Gen. 12:2; Exod. 20:24; Ps. 115:12).

The *servants of the LORD* is a common designation for the whole of the community of ancient Israel. They, along with *the ones standing in the house of the LORD in the nighttime,* are called on to *lift their hands* and *bless the LORD.* Isaiah 30:29 and Ps. 3:5 suggest that night vigils were held in the temple in Jerusalem for the purpose of prolonged festive celebration or of seeking God's deliverance from life-threatening situations.[1]

1. See Karel van der Toorn, "Ordeal Procedures in the Psalms and the Passover Meal," *VT* 38 (1988) 427-45, for a full discussion.

3 In response to the people's blessing of God, the psalm-singers invoke the blessing of God on the people. Verse 3 tells the people that God is in *Zion* — the sustainer God, who guides the people from the dwelling place in their midst[2] and who is *the maker of heaven and earth* — the creator God, who formed and fashioned them and this world in which they dwell.

In Num. 6:22-26, God gave Moses the words with which the sons of Aaron were to bless the children of Israel:

> The LORD bless *(bārak̲)* you and keep you;
> the LORD make his face to shine upon you, and be gracious to you;
> the LORD lift up his countenance upon you, and give you peace.

The words of Numbers 6 were fitting words for the Israelites as they prepared to enter the promised land; the words of Psalm 134 were fitting for the Israelite pilgrims as they prepared to leave Jerusalem and return to their homes.

The people are called upon to bless the Lord; the Lord is called upon to bless the people. The people acknowledge the presence of God in their lives; God acknowledges the presence of the people in a reciprocal relationship. The pilgrimage is at its end; the acts of worship have been carried out; the words have been spoken; the people ready themselves to return to their lives outside Jerusalem. The words of Psalm 134 are the final words of doxology, of praise to God, and of invocation, calling God to bless the people.

Worship in the sanctuary of God is a wonderfully moving experience, a time of withdrawal and renewal. But we cannot remain in the sanctuary; we must return to the world. At the close of each worship service in the Christian tradition, worship leaders utter words of benediction — concluding words that prepare the congregation to leave the sanctuary and return to the world. Perhaps the most memorable benedictory words are those of Episcopal priest John Rowan Claypool IV, whose benediction was:

> Depart now
> In The Fellowship of God The Father,
> And as You Go, Remember:
> In The *Goodness* of God
> You were Born into This World;
> By The *Grace* of God
> You have Been Kept
> All the Day Long,
> Even Until This Hour;

2. The same words occur in Ps. 128:5.

And By The *Love* of God,
Fully Revealed in the Face of Jesus,
You . . . are Being . . . *Redeemed.*
Amen.[3]

Nancy deClaissé-Walford

3. John R. Claypool IV, by permission.

Psalm 135: Praise the LORD, for Good Is the LORD

Psalm 135, classified as a community hymn, begins with familiar words — *Praise the LORD" (halᵉlû yāh).* Psalms 111–17 contain these familiar words. And, interestingly, Psalms 118 and 136 repeatedly employ the words *for his* (the LORD's) *hesed is for all time.* These two observations lead scholars to suggest that Psalms 111–18 and 135–36 form an *inclusio* around the great torah Psalm 119 and the Songs of the Ascents (Psalms 120–34). Psalm 135 is, indeed, an apt conclusion to the Songs of the Ascents. Its beginning shares a number of words and phrases with the Songs of the Ascents — *the name of the LORD* (Pss. 122:4; 124:8); *servants of the LORD* (Ps. 134:1); and *good* and *pleasant* (Ps. 133:1). And it has extensive ties to Psalm 115, one of the hallelujah psalms that precede the Songs of the Ascents (Ps. 135:6 = 115:3; 135:15-18 = 115:4-8; 135:19-20 = 115:9-10).

Psalm 135's structure may be described in the following way:

Hallelujah (v. 1a)
  A summons to praise (vv. 1b-4)
    A celebration of God's sovereignty over all other gods (vv. 5-7)
      A recounting of God's acts on behalf of Israel (vv. 8-14)
    The gods of the other nations compared with God (vv. 15-18)
  A summons to bless God (vv. 19-21a)
Hallelujah (v. 21b)[1]

1 *Praise the LORD.*

Praise the name of the LORD;
  Praise, O servants of the LORD,
2 *You who are standing in the house of the LORD,*
  in the courts of the house of our God.
3 *Praise the LORD, for good is the LORD.*
  Sing to his name, for it is pleasant.
4 *For Jacob the LORD selected,*
  Israel for his possession.

5 *For I, I know that great is the LORD,*
  our Lord, more than all the gods.
6 *All that the LORD takes pleasure in, he does,*
  in the heavens and in the earth,
  in the waters and all of the deeps.
7 *He causes to go up the clouds from the end of the earth,*

1. Allen suggests this structure in *Psalms 101–150,* p. 226.

lightning for the rain he makes,
the going out of the wind from his storehouse.

8 *He is the one who struck down the firstborn of Egypt,*
from human to beast.
9 *He sent signs and wonders into your midst, O Egypt,*
against Pharaoh and against all of his servants.
10 *He is the one who struck down great nations*
and killed strong kings —
11 *Sihon, king of the Amorites,*
and Og, king of Bashan,
and all of the kingdoms of Canaan.
12 *And he gave their land as an inheritance,*
an inheritance for Israel his people.
13 *O LORD, your name is for all time;*
O LORD, your remembrance is from generation to generation.
14 *For the LORD judges his people,*
and for his servants he feels compassion.

15 *The idols of the nations are silver and gold,*
the making of the hands of humankind.
16 *A mouth to them, but they do not speak;*
eyes to them, but they do not see.
17 *Ears to them, but they do not give ear.*
And there is no breath in their mouths.
18 *Like them are the ones who make them,*
all who trust in them.

19 *O house of Israel, bless the LORD!*
O house of Aaron, bless the LORD!
20 *O house of Levi, bless the LORD!*
O ones who fear the LORD, bless the LORD!
21 *Blessed is the LORD from Zion,*
the one who dwells in Jerusalem.

Praise the LORD!

1a The phrase *Praise the LORD* (and variations of the phrase) occurs some seventy-five times in the Psalter, with no less than fifty-four occurrences in Book Five.[2] The word *praise* is derived from the Hebrew verbal root *hālal,*

2. The phrase is especially prominent in the last five psalms of Book Five, Pss. 146–50, with thirty-four occurrences.

which has a range of basic meanings that include "shout, jubilation, rejoice," and "song of joy." The word may very likely be onomatopoetic, that is, a word formed "by imitation of a sound made by or associated with its referent." So, the word "hallelujah!" may be imitative of the shouted joy of a worshipper in the presence of the holy other.

1b-4 These verses summon the gathered worshippers to *praise the LORD* (vv. 1b-2) and outline the basic reason for giving praise (vv. 3-4). Verse 2's *You who are standing in the house of the LORD* recalls the words of Psalm 134, while v. 3's *good is the LORD* and *for it is pleasant* recall the words of Psalm 133, suggesting a strong tie between Psalm 135 and the Songs of the Ascents.

The worshippers are called to praise the *name* of the Lord; in v. 3, they are admonished to *sing to* the name; and in v. 13 the psalm-singers affirm that the Lord's *name is for all time.*"[3]

5-7 The words of v. 5 echo those of Jethro, Moses' father-in-law, in Exod. 18:11: "Now I know that great is the LORD, more than all the gods." The singer of Psalm 135 continues in vv. 6 and 7 with creation language in celebration of the sovereignty of the God of Israel over all.

8-14 In vv. 8-14, the psalmist recounts God's involvement in the history of ancient Israel, a history that demonstrates that the God of Israel is indeed greater than all the other gods. In the exodus story, referred to in vv. 8-9, God's sovereignty extends over even *Pharaoh,* the god-king of Egypt. During the wilderness wanderings and settlement in the land, recalled in vv. 10-12, God repeatedly delivered the Israelites from oppression. Numbers 21:21-35 tells the stories of *Sihon* and *Og* (v. 11), and the book of Joshua outlines the giving of the land *as an inheritance* (v. 12). God's ultimate care and provision for the people of Israel is celebrated in vv. 12-14.

15-18 Verses 15-18 echo the words of Ps. 115:4-8. Here the psalmist depicts the powerlessness of the idol-gods of the nations. They are *silver and gold,* made by human hands. They have *mouths, eyes,* and *ears,* but they cannot *speak* or *see* or hear.

19-21a Verses 19-20 echo the words of Ps. 115:9-10. In Psalm 115, three groups are called on to bless the Lord — *Israel,* the *house of Aaron,* and the *ones who fear the LORD.*[4] In Psalm 135, an additional group is named: the *house of Levi.* The additional group named in Psalm 135 may suggest a concern by the singer of Psalm 135 to make a distinction between the house of Aaron and the house of Levi.

3. For a discussion of the concept of "name" in the ancient Near East and ancient Israel, see the commentary for Ps. 113:1b-4.

4. For a discussion of these groups of worshippers, see the commentary for Ps. 115:9-11.

The House of Aaron and the House of Levi

According to the books of Ezekiel and Chronicles and the Priestly account in the book of Numbers, the temple personnel were all members of the tribe of Levi, but they were stratified into the Aaronid priests and the Levites. The Levites occupied a subordinate position to the Aaronid priests. In Num. 3:6, 9, we read:

> Bring the tribe of Levi near and set them before Aaron the priest, that they may serve him. And they shall perform the duties for him and for the whole congregation before the tent of meeting, to do the service of the tabernacle. . . . You shall thus give the Levites to Aaron and to his sons; they are wholly given to him from among the children of Israel.

It seems that originally all the members of the tribe of Levi were set aside for special service to the Lord, but those who could show descent directly from Aaron — and from Zadok, according to Ezekiel — occupied higher positions within the cult than the other Levites (see Ezek. 44:10-16; Neh. 7:63-65). Nehemiah reestablished the Levites in the Jerusalem temple during his term as provincial governor (see Neh. 13:10-13), but the Levites performed the more "menial" chores while the Aaronid priests were the ruling elite of the temple.

21b The closing colon of Psalm 135 repeats the opening colon: *Hallelujah.* LXX omits the closing *Hallelujah* here and places it instead at the beginning of Psalm 136. For a discussion of the placement of the "hallelujah" openings and closings, see the introductory words of the commentary for Psalm 115.

Psalm 135 is a hymn of praise to God sung by a gathered community of worshippers. It echoes other words in the Old Testament — Exod. 18:11; Ps. 115:3, 4-8, 9-11, as discussed above; Deut. 7:6 in v. 4; Jer. 10:13 in v. 7; Deut. 32:36 in v. 14, etc.). Allen writes:

> In Ps 135 older materials are unashamedly recycled to create a new composition of praise. The harmony of concerted worship, for which it pleads in vv 19-20, itself finds artistic illustration in the blending of older voices to form a contemporary medley.[5]

The psalms of Book Five tell the story of the postexilic community's quest for and celebration of identity and survival in a world vastly different from the world of their ancestors in the faith. The people were back in their own

5. *Psalms 101–150,* pp. 227-28.

land, the temple was rebuilt, and worship had resumed. But they were not an independent nation with king and court. They were vassals to first the Persians, then the Greeks, then the Romans. According to Sanders, in such situations "only the old, tried, and true has any real authority. . . . A new story will not do; only a story with old, recognizable elements has the power for life required."[6]

In times of transition, in those times when we wonder what our next step in faith should be, it often is helpful to look back over our past. What words have sustained us in the past? On whose shoulders are we standing? What are the very foundations of our faith? The singers of Psalm 135 employed familiar words and ideas to express their faith in God. They felt no need to devise new images and phrases. For, indeed, sometimes "only the old, tried, and true" has any real meaning.

NANCY DECLAISSÉ-WALFORD

6. "Adaptable for Life: The Nature and Function of Canon," in *From Sacred Story to Sacred Text,* p. 18.

Psalm 136: Because for All Time Is the Lord's *Hesed*

Psalm 136, classified as a community hymn, follows and is a companion piece to Psalm 135. Mays describes the two psalms as "partners in praise."[1] They, along with Psalms 111–18, form an *inclusio* around the great torah Psalm 119 and the Songs of the Ascents (Psalms 120–34). The text is unique in the Hebrew Psalter because of its refrain in each verse, which is translated here as *because for all times is the LORD's hesed.* The Talmud calls Psalm 136 "The Great Hallel." The layout of the psalm in the Masoretic Text emphasizes its highly structured format.

136:1	Give thanks to the LORD, for he is good	*kî leʿôlām ḥāsdô*
2	Give thanks to the god of gods	*kî leʿôlām ḥāsdô*
3	Give thanks to the lord of lords	*kî leʿôlām ḥāsdô*

and so forth . . .

In liturgical use in the second temple, a leader most likely recited the first half of each verse, and the gathered worshippers responded with the second half, the refrain. Allen characterizes the psalm as "an imperatival, antiphonal hymn."[2]

Each verse of Psalm 136 follows a format: a call to praise or worship, followed by a refrain which states the reason for praise: *because (kî) for all time is the LORD's* hesed. The same refrain occurs in a number of liturgical passages in the Hebrew Bible (1 Chr. 16:34; 2 Chr. 5:13; 7:3; 20:21; Ezra 3:11) and in other psalms (106:1; 107:1; 118:1-4; 100:5).

The word *hesed* occurs some 245 times in the Hebrew Bible, 127 times in the Psalter.[3] One Jewish scholar defines *hesed* as "a free-flowing love that knows no bounds."[4] *Hesed* is most closely connected in the Hebrew Bible with the covenant relationship between God and the children of Israel. In Genesis 15, God covenants with Abram, saying, "To your descendants I give this land, from the river of Egypt to the great river, the river Euphrates" (Gen. 15:18). Genesis 17 records these words of God to Abram: "I will establish my covenant between me and you, and your offspring after you throughout their generations, for an everlasting covenant, to be God to you and to your offspring after you. And I will give to you, and to your offspring after you,

1. *Psalms,* p. 415.

2. *Psalms 101–150,* p. 231.

3. For recent discussions of *hesed,* see Katharine Doob Sakenfeld, *Faithfulness in Action: Loyalty in Biblical Perspective* (OBT 16; Philadelphia: Fortress, 1985); and Gordon R. Clark, *The Word* Hesed *in the Hebrew Bible* (JSOTSup 157; Sheffield: JSOT, 1993).

4. Arthur Green, *These Are the Words: A Vocabulary of Jewish Spiritual Life* (Woodstock: Jewish Lights, 1999), p. 152.

the land where you are now an alien, all the land of Canaan, for a perpetual holding; and I will be their God" (Gen. 17:7-8). In Exodus 19, God says to the children of Israel, "If you obey my voice and keep my covenant, you shall be my treasured possession out of all the peoples. Indeed, the whole earth is mine, but you shall be for me a priestly kingdom and a holy nation" (Exod. 19:5-6). In each instance, God calls the Israelites into a special relationship centered around a covenant.

Psalm 136 echoes the themes of Psalm 135: God's goodness (135:3; 136:1); God's relationship to other gods (135:5; 136:2-3); God's role in creation (135:6-7; 136:4-9); God's role in the exodus (135:8-9; 136:10-15); God's role in the wilderness wanderings and the settlement in the land (135:10-12; 136:16-22); and God's care and provision for the people of Israel (135:13-14; 136:23-25). We may describe its structure as follows:

> Give thanks to the Lord (vv. 1-3)
> Give thanks to the God who creates (vv. 4-9)
> Give thanks to the God who guides and protects (vv. 10-22)
> Give thanks to the God who provides (vv. 23-25)
> Give thanks to the LORD (v. 26)

1 *Give thanks to the LORD, for he is good,*
  because for all time is the LORD's hesed.
2 *Give thanks to the god of gods,*
  because for all time is the LORD's hesed.
3 *Give thanks to the lord of lords,*
  because for all time is the LORD's hesed;

4 *to*[5] *the one who alone does great wondrous things,*
  because for all time is the LORD's hesed;
5 *to the one who made the heavens by understanding,*
  because for all time is the LORD's hesed;
6 *to the one who spread out the earth upon the waters,*
  because for all time is the LORD's hesed;
7 *to the one who made the great lights,*
  because for all time is the LORD's hesed;
8 *the sun to rule over the day,*
  because for all time is the LORD's hesed;
9 *the moon and the stars to rule over the night,*
  because for all time is the LORD's hesed;

5. The prepositions *l*[e] at the beginnings of vv. 4-7, 13, 16, and 17 mark the direct object of the imperatival verbs *give thanks* in vv. 1-3.

10 *the one who destroyed Egypt through their firstborn,*
because for all time is the LORD*'s* hesed;
11 *and he led Israel out from their midst,*
because for all time is the LORD*'s* hesed;
12 *with a strong hand and with an outstretched arm,*
because for all time is the LORD*'s* hesed;
13 *to the one who divided the Reed Sea in two,*
because for all time is the LORD*'s* hesed;
14 *and he caused Israel to cross over in its midst,*
because for all time is the LORD*'s* hesed;
15 *and he overthrew Pharaoh and his army in the Reed Sea,*
because for all time is the LORD*'s* hesed;
16 *to the one who led his people in the wilderness,*
because for all time is the LORD*'s* hesed;
17 *to the one who destroyed great kings,*
because for all time is the LORD*'s* hesed;
18 *and he killed mighty kings,*
because for all time is the LORD*'s* hesed;
19 *Sihon, king of the Amorites,*
because for all time is the LORD*'s* hesed;
20 *and Og, king of Bashan,*
because for all time is the LORD*'s* hesed;
21 *and he gave their land as an inheritance,*
because for all time is the LORD*'s* hesed;
22 *an inheritance to Israel his servant,*
because for all time is the LORD*'s* hesed;

23 *who in our low estate remembered us,*
because for all time is the LORD*'s* hesed;
24 *and set us free from our oppressors,*
because for all time is the LORD*'s* hesed;
25 *the one who gives bread to all flesh,*
because for all time is the LORD*'s* hesed.

26 *Give thanks to the God of the heavens,*
because for all time is the LORD*'s* hesed.

1-3 Verses 1-3 echo the words of Ps. 135:3-5. The God of Israel is *good (ṭôḇ)* and is above all gods.

4-9 Following the introductory words of vv. 1-3, the psalm-singers begin a lengthy recital of the actions of the God of Israel, often using active participial forms (vv. 4-5 and 7: *ʿōśēh;* v. 6: *rōqaʿ;* vv. 10 and 17: *makkēh;* v. 13:

gōzēr; v. 16: *môlîk̲*). Verse 4 describes God as *the one who alone does great "wondrous things (nipl̲āʾôt̲)"* (see Pss. 78:4; 86:10; 105:2, 5).[6] Verses 4-9 of Psalm 136 echo Ps. 135:6-7. The God of Israel is the creator of the world in which we live.

10-22 In vv. 10-22, using language nearly identical to that found in Ps. 135:8-12, the psalm-singers recount the actions of God on behalf of the Israelites during the exodus, wilderness wanderings, and settlement in the land.

23-25 In the final stanza of Psalm 136, again in an echo of Psalm 135:13-14, the psalmists celebrate the provisions of God for the community of faith. God remembers;[7] God frees from *oppressors (ṣārîm);* and God *gives bread to all flesh.* Limburg reflects on this closing description of God: "Psalm 136 puts the gift of daily food on the same plane as the great acts of creation, exodus, and conquest."[8]

26 Psalm 136 ends as it began: *Give thanks.* This time, though, the Lord is described as *the God (ʾēl) of the heavens.*

Psalm 136 summons the community of faith to respond to a recital of the actions of God on their behalf. The repetition of the response allows gathered worshippers to reflect and ponder on each of the descriptive phrases. Allen writes of "the regular heartbeat of the congregational refrain" in the psalm.[9] A similar liturgical structure can be observed in a form of Psalm 145 included in the Dead Sea scroll 11QPs[a]. Each verse of the psalm is followed by the refrain, "Blessed is God and blessed is his name forever," giving the psalm the following form:

> I will extol you, my god the King; and I will bless your name for all time and beyond.
> *Blessed is God and blessed is his name forever.*
> Every day I will bless you, and I will praise your name for all time and beyond.
> *Blessed is God and blessed is his name forever.*
> Great is the Lord and highly to be praised, and his greatness is unsearchable.
> *Blessed is God and blessed is his name forever.* (vv. 1-3)

Psalm 136 (and Psalm 145 in 11QPs[a]) is a powerful liturgical composition. In *Abiding Astonishment: Psalms, Modernity, and the Making of History,* a study of Psalms 78, 105, 106, and 136, Walter Brueggemann reminds us of the power of liturgy. He maintains that liturgical recitals are "world building" and writes,

6. For a full discussion of *nipl̲āʾôt̲,* see the commentary for Ps. 119:129-36.

7. For a discussion of *remember,* see the commentary for Ps. 119:49-56.

8. *Psalms,* p. 464.

9. *Psalms 101–150,* p. 234.

"They create, evoke, suggest, and propose a network of symbols, metaphors, images, memories and hopes so that 'the world,' in each successive generation, is perceived, experienced, and practiced in a specific way."[10]

As the singers of Psalm 136 enunciated the words of the psalm, they brought the past powerfully into the present. God who created is creating. God who delivered is delivering. God who sustained is sustaining. Our own liturgical acts serve the same purpose. With each recitation of the Lord's Prayer, the Apostles' Creed, the Peace of Christ, we bring the past redemptive acts of God powerfully into the present.

Nancy deClaissé-Walford

10. (Literary Currents in Biblical Interpretation; Louisville: Westminster John Knox, 1991), p. 21.

Psalm 137: Beside the Rivers of Babylon

Psalm 137 is perhaps the most troubling of all the psalms in the Psalter. A community lament in form, its content places it in a group of psalms called "imprecatory."[1] In imprecatory psalms, the psalm-singers invoke the wrath of God upon a foe. In the case of Psalm 137, the foe is clearly Babylon, indicating a setting for the psalm during or just after the Babylonian exile (596-538 B.C.E.).

The placement of Psalm 137 in Book Five of the Psalter is somewhat curious. According to the story of the Psalter, Book Five celebrates the return of the Babylonian exiles to Jerusalem, the rebuilding of the temple, and the continued existence of the Israelites as the people of God. Psalms 135 and 136 praise God's goodness; God's role in creation, in the exodus, the wilderness wanderings and the settlement in the land; and God's care and provision for the people of Israel. The words of Psalm 137 stand in stark contrast to the previous two psalms. It seems that for the Israelites, even in the midst of present rejoicing, the past pain must always be remembered.

This brief psalm may be outlined as follows:

Setting of the lament (vv. 1-3)
Central words of lament (v. 4)
Oath in answer to the lament (vv. 5-6)
Imprecatory words in answer to the lament (vv. 7-9)

1 *Beside the rivers of Babylon,*
there we sat down, also we wept
when we remembered Zion.
2 *Upon*[2] *the willows in her midst,*
we hung up our harps,
3 *Because there our captors asked us for words of a song,*
our tormentors for rejoicing,
"Sing for us from a song of Zion!"

4 *How can we sing a song of the LORD*
upon a foreign land?

5 *If I forget you, O Jerusalem,*
then may my right hand forget.
6 *May my tongue cleave to the roof of my mouth*

1. For a full discussion of imprecatory psalms, see the commentary for Ps. 109.
2. The first words in vv. 1 and 2 are the same Hebrew word, *'al.*

if I do not remember you,
if I do not raise up Jerusalem
as the highest of my rejoicing.

7 *Remember, O LORD, to the children of Edom*
the day of Jerusalem,
the ones who said, "Tear it down! Tear it down!
down to its foundations."
8 *O daughter of Babylon, the one destroyed,*[3]
content will be the one who repays you
for your doings, that which you have done to us.
9 *Content will be the one who seizes and dashes*
your suckling children against the rock.

1-3 Verses 1-3 describe the setting for the words of the psalm. The psalm-singers are sitting and weeping *beside the rivers of Babylon.* The book of 2 Kings tells the story of the capture of Jerusalem by the Babylonians in successive stages beginning in 597. A vast number of Israelites found themselves living in Babylon; Jerusalem and the temple were destroyed; king and court were no more. Verses 1 and 2 begin with the Hebrew word *'al,* a preposition with a range of meanings that carry an idea of being "over, upon, on." The psalm-singers are "*upon* the lands of the rivers of Babylon" (v. 1) and they hang their harps "*upon* the willow trees" (v. 2).

The repetition of *there (šām)* in vv. 1 and 3 emphasizes the location of the psalm's setting. Mays describes the use of the word as "pointing a verbal finger."[4] And the repetition of the first plural pronoun suffix *nû* nine times in vv. 1-3 evokes what Allen describes as a "ring of pathos."[5]

In that foreign setting, the psalm-singers sing no more. Verse 3 uses two words to describe the ones asking the psalm-singers to sing: *captors* and *tormentors.* The word translated *captor* is an active participle derived from the Hebrew verbal root *šāḇâ,* which means "capture in the course of battle." The word translated *tormentors* is also an active participle from the Hebrew root *tālal,* which means "mock" or "trifle with." It is an unusual root in Biblical Hebrew, occurring in the participial form only in Psalm 137, and in other verbal forms in eight places in the Hebrew Bible. LXX translates the word as *hoi apagagontes hēmas* ("the ones leading us away"), while the Aramaic Targum renders the word as "our plunderers."

3. MT has a passive participle here *(haššᵉḏûḏâ).* Symmachus, Syr, and Targ render the verb as an active participle *(haššôḏᵉḏâ).*

4. *Psalms,* p. 422.

5. *Psalms 101–150,* p. 241. See also Isa. 53:4-6.

The psalm-singers report that their *captors* and *tormentors* ask them for *words of a song* and *rejoicing,* specified more exactly in the last colon of v. 3 as *from a song of Zion.*[6] The words of the captors and tormentors in v. 3 may be likened to the words of taunters in other psalms who say to the psalmist "Where is your God?" (Pss. 42:3, 10; 79:10). The psalmists feel the loss of Jerusalem even more because the requests of their captors constantly remind them that they are not in Jerusalem, but in *a foreign land.*

4 Verse 4 contains the central driving words of Psalm 137. The psalm-singers cry out to God, *How can we sing . . . ?* The opening word of the verse, *how ('êḵ),* is a word commonly used to introduce mourning in the Old Testament (see Lam. 1:1; 2:1; 4:1; Hos. 11:8; 2 Sam. 1:25). Interestingly, the psalm-singers transform the words of their captors — *a song of Zion* — to *a song of the LORD*. Zion was the dwelling place of the God of the Israelites; any *song of Zion* was thus a song of YHWH.

5-6 Verses 5 and 6, characterized as an "oath," are the only portion of Psalm 137 sung by an individual voice. The mingling of individual and community voices is not unusual, though, in the community lament psalms. The same phenomenon may be observed in Book Five in Psalms 108 and 123.

In vv. 5a, 6a*b* and 6b, an individual psalm-singer, speaking on behalf of the community of singers, voices three oaths, all formulated with the particle *'im,* which introduces the protasis of a real conditional oath — one that is capable of being fulfilled.[7] The *'im*-clauses of vv. 5a and 6a*b* — *If ('im) I forget you, O Jerusalem* and *if ('im) I do not remember you* — form an *inclusio* around their apodoses in vv. 5b and 6a — *may my right hand forget* and *may my tongue cleave to the roof of my mouth.* If the psalmist forgets (from the verbal root *šāḵaḥ)* the Lord, then the psalmist's right hand will forget *(šāḵaḥ).* The forgetting of Jerusalem will result in the forgetting of the right hand, i.e., the right hand being unable to function as a right hand. The consequence to the tongue is that it will cleave to the roof of the mouth, i.e., be unable to speak. Some suggest that the terms *right hand* and *tongue* are a merism, referring to all human action, thus condemning completely the one who forgets Jerusalem. Others maintain that the reference is to the *right hand* that strums the harp and the *tongue* that sings, meaning that the psalmist vows never to sing again if he or she forgets Zion.[8]

The third oath formula, found in v. 6b, does not contain an apodosis, but rather acts as the closing, summary statement of the psalm-singer's vow.

7-9 In vv. 7-9, the community of psalm-singers reunite with the individual psalmist and voice the imprecatory words of Psalm 137. The imprecation

6. Songs of Zion in the Psalter include Pss. 46, 48, 76, 84, 122.

7. Waltke and O'Connor, *Biblical Hebrew Syntax,* p. 636.

8. For a discussion of the word "remember" in the Hebrew Bible, see the commentary for Ps. 119:49-56.

begins with a cry to the Lord to *remember.* In v. 7, the singers call upon God to *remember the children (bᵉnê) of Edom.* According to the book of Obadiah, Edom played a role in helping the Babylonians sack the temple and destroy Jerusalem in 587.[9]

In verse 8, the psalm-singers address the *daughter (baṯ) of Babylon,* calling her *the one destroyed.* The rendering of the verbal tense of this Hebrew passive participle *(haššᵉḏûḏâ)* determines the dating of Psalm 137. The participle may be translated as "the one being destroyed," "the one having been destroyed," or "the one that will be destroyed."

Verses 8b and 9 are the culmination of the imprecatory words of the psalm. Two phrases are introduced by the word *'ašrê (content),* rendered in most English translations as "happy" or "blessed." The verbal root, which most likely is *'āšar,* means "to go straight, to advance, to follow the track." The translation "blessed" brings to mind the Hebrew word *bārûḵ,* which carries cultic/sacred connotations. "Happy" does not convey the full depth of the root *'āšar. Content* connotes a sense of peace and feeling settled that seems to come closest to the root meaning of *'ašrê.*

Content ('ašrê) occurs twenty-six times in the Psalter, most often as the introductory word of a wisdom psalm. Only in Psalm 137 does it introduce imprecatory words. The word translated *repays* in v. 8 is *yᵉšallem,* which comes from the Hebrew verbal root *šālam* and is most likely used here as a play on words with Jerusalem *(yᵉrûšālaim).*

Clifford states that "Psalm 137 has the distinction of having one of the most beloved opening lines and the most horrifying closing line of any psalm."[10] There is no way to soften the words or alter the sentiment expressed in v. 9. And we should not try to do so. Psalm 137 is a heartfelt lament sung to God, asking for God's justice, in the face of absolute despair and hopelessness. It is a song of revenge sung on behalf of the victims of Babylon's destruction. Erich Zenger writes that Psalm 137

> is an attempt, in the face of the most profound humiliation and helplessness, to suppress the primitive human lust for violence in one's own heart, by surrendering *everything* to God — a God whose word of judgment is presumed to be so universally just that even those who pray the psalm submit themselves to it.[11]

Psalm 137, along with the other imprecatory psalms in the Psalter, reminds us of the basic human desire for revenge when we or those we love have been

9. For a full discussion, see the commentary for Ps. 108:7-9.

10. *Psalms 73–150,* p. 275.

11. *A God of Vengeance?* (trans. Linda M. Maloney; Louisville: Westminster John Knox, 1996), p. 48.

wronged. God does not ask us to suppress those emotions, but rather to speak about them in plain and heartfelt terms. In the speaking out, we give voice to the pain, the feelings of helplessness, and the burning anger. In speaking out to God, we give the pain, the helplessness, and the burning anger to God. And we trust that God's justice will be done.

Nancy deClaissé-Walford

Psalm 138: Because of Your *Hesed* and Your Faithfulness

Psalm 138 is the first of a collection of eight psalms (Pss. 138–45) in Book Five that are attributed, in their superscriptions, to David.[1] The group forms a closing chorus of words of and about David in Book Five of the Psalter. Psalms 138–43 are psalms of an individual (individual hymns of thanksgiving and individual laments); Psalm 144 is a royal psalm; and Psalm 145 is a wisdom acrostic. Psalms 138 and 145 share no less than thirteen terms and verbal roots, forming an envelope structure around the collection: "give thanks" (*yāḏâ,* 138:1, 2, 4; 145:10); "name" (*šēm,* 138:2; 145:1, 2, 21); *ḥeseḏ* (138:2, 8; 145:8, 10, 13, 17); "be faithful" (*'āman,* 138:2; 145:13, 18); "be great" (*gāḏal,* 138:2, 5; 145:3, 6, 8); "cry out" (*qārā',* 138:3; 145:18); "hear" (*šāma',* 138:4; 145:19); "glory" (*kāḇôḏ,* 138:5; 145:5, 11, 12); "exalt" (*rûm,* 138:6; 145:1); "hand" (*yāḏ.* 138:7, 8; 145:16); "for all time" (*lᵉ'ôlām,* 138:8; 145:1, 21); "deliver" (*yāša',* 138:7; 145:19); "make, do" (*'āśâ,* 138:8; 145:4, 9, 10, 13, 17).

In Psalm 138, classified as an individual hymn of thanksgiving, the psalm-singer gives thanks to the Lord for answering when he cries out (v. 3) and doing great things on his behalf (v. 2). Individual hymns of thanksgiving are generally made up of three parts: (1) an introduction, in which the psalmist declares the intention of giving thanks and praising God (138:1, 2, 4, 5); (2) a narrative, in which the psalmist tells what has happened to the psalmist that has prompted the words of praise (v. 3); and (3) a conclusion, in which the psalmist praises God for all that God has done on the psalmist's behalf (vv. 2b, 4b, 5b, 6-8).[2]

The psalm may be divided into three stanzas that reflect not the three parts of an individual hymn of thanksgiving, but rather the groups referred to by the psalmist in the verses of the hymn:

In the presence of the gods (vv. 1-3)
In the presence of the kings of the earth (vv. 4-6)
In the presence of enemies (vv. 7-8)

Davidic.

1 *I give thanks to you*[3] *with all my heart;*
in the presence of the gods I make music to you.

1. The other Davidic collections in the Hebrew Psalter are Pss. 3–41 and 51–76 and 108–10.

2. For a full discussion of the elements of an individual hymn of thanksgiving, see deClaissé-Walford, *Introduction to the Psalms,* pp. 21-23.

3. NRSV, along with a number of translations, adds the vocative "O LORD," reflecting an addition provided in a number of Hebrew manuscripts, including 11QPs[a].

2 *I bow down toward the temple of your holiness,*
and I give thanks to your name
because of your hesed *and your faithfulness.*
For you have made your name and your word great.
3 *In the day that I cried out, you answered me;*
you have made me courageous;
in my inmost being is strength.

4 *All the kings of the earth will give thanks to the* Lord,
for they have heard the words of your mouth.
5 *And they will sing in the paths of the* Lord,
for great is the glory of the Lord.
6 *Though the* Lord *is exalted,*
the lowly he sees
and the haughty from a distance he knows.

7 *If I walk in the midst of oppression,*
you cause me to live in spite of the anger of my enemies.
You send forth your hand and your hand delivers me.
8 *May the* Lord *do favorable things on my behalf.*
O Lord, *your* hesed *is for all time;*
May the doings of your hands not come to an end.

1-3 *In the presence of the gods,* the psalmist gives thanks to God, making music and bowing down *toward the temple.* Second person pronouns abound (eleven occurrences in vv. 1-3), as the psalmist addresses God directly.

Psalms 135 and 136 also talk of *the gods.* In Ps. 135:5, the singer declares "great is the Lord, our Lord, more than all the gods." And in Ps. 136:2-3, we read, "give thanks to the god of gods . . . give thanks to the lord of lords." Such phrases are common in the Old Testament, expressing God's sovereignty over any claimants to the appellation "god." In v. 2 of Psalm 138, the psalm-singer continues the words of thanks, this time to the *name (šēm)* of God, because of God's *hesed* and *faithfulness (ʾemet).*[4]

Hesed is often used in parallel thought construction with the Hebrew word *ʾemet*. Both are self-descriptive words used by God in the revelation to Moses on Mount Sinai (Exod. 34:6-8). The Hebrew verbal root of *ʾemet* is *ʾāman,* meaning "be firm, be reliable, be permanent," and is the root from which the word "amen" is derived.

The psalmist gives thanks to, makes music to, and bows down toward

4. For a discussion of the significance of "name" in the Hebrew Bible, see the commentary for Ps. 113:1b-4. For a discussion of *hesed,* see the commentary for Ps. 136.

God because of God's name, covenant commitment, and firm reliability, then offers a final comment on the thank-worthiness of God in v. 2c: *for you have made your name and your word great.* The Hebrew word translated here as *word* is not the usual term for "word" in the Hebrew Bible *(dāḇār).* Rather, the psalmist speaks of God's *'imrâ,* a word derived from the verbal root *'āmar* ("say"). A more accurate translation for *'imrâ* would be "sayings," which emphasizes the activity of voicing a word rather than the product of the activity — a word.

Verse 3 may be viewed as the "narrative" of the individual hymn of thanksgiving. Here the psalmist states what God has done that has prompted the words of thanks. The phrase *in the day (bᵉyôm)* in English suggests a particular point in time in which the psalmist cried out. In Hebrew, however, the phrase has a broader temporal frame of reference, best understood as "whenever." Thus, the psalm-singer thanks God for answering whenever the psalmist cries out. The two verbal roots *cry out (qārā')* and *answer ('ānâ)* are commonly paired in the Hebrew Psalter (Pss. 3:4; 22:2; 86:7). As a result, the psalmist can be *courageous,* and *strength* is in the *inmost being (nep̄eš).*

4-6 The psalmist shifts the venue of thanks and singing to God from the realm of the gods (v. 1b) to the earthly realm of *kings,* a shift of focus that also occurs in Psalm 2. The psalmist's reference to God also shifts. In vv. 1-3, the singer speaks directly to God, using second person pronouns; in vv. 4-6, God is consistently referred to in the third person.

The reason for thanks and singing by the kings in vv. 4-6 is threefold: (1) The kings have heard the *words* (v. 4b); again, here as in v. 2c, the Hebrew term is derived from the verbal root *'āmar* ("say"); (2) The *glory of the LORD* is *great* (v. 5b); and (3) *the LORD is exalted,* seeing and knowing the states of *the lowly* and *the haughty* (v. 6).

7-8 In the last two verses of Psalm 138, the psalm-singer shifts the focus once again from the earthly realm of kings to the *oppression (ṣārâ)* of *my enemies ('ôyēḇ).* The two words are often used in parallel poetic construction in the Hebrew Psalter (see Psalm 42, for example).

The psalm-singer refers to the *hand* of the Lord three times in the closing cola of Psalm 138. God *sends forth* a hand; God's hand *delivers* the psalmist; and the psalmist requests that the *doings of God's hands* not *come to an end (rāp̄â).* The verbal root *rāp̄â* means "be slack, be loosened, be weak." The psalmist has experienced God's upholding hands over and over in the past and petitions God in v. 8 to continue to uphold and protect.

In the aftermath of the Babylonian exile, the Israelites questioned their very identity and future as the people of God. Book Five of the Psalter celebrates a new realization by the people that they can continue to exist as a specially called people by acknowledging God as their sovereign and worshipping faithfully. Psalms of David dominate the end of the Psalter (Psalms

138–45). David was the great king of ancient Israel, the king with whom God made a lasting covenant. David now leads the people in the acknowledgement of the place of God within their lives. The words of Psalm 138 celebrate the name, the *hesed,* the faithfulness, the words, the glory, and the intimate care of God. The psalm-singer reminds the faithful that their God is a God who remembers and cares and that their God is a God worthy of thanks and worship, a God above all gods.

Nancy deClaissé-Walford

Psalm 139: You Have Searched Me Out and You Know Me

Psalm 139 is the second in a collection of eight psalms of David that occur at the end of Book Five. It, like Psalm 138, is classified as an individual hymn of thanksgiving, a psalm praising God for goodness to or on behalf of the psalm-singer, usually for deliverance from some trying situation.[1] Four verses of Psalm 139, vv. 19-22, stand in stark contrast with the remainder of the psalm. They are often omitted in reading and studying the psalm, but scholars suggest that they may provide a hermeneutical key to understanding the circumstances under which the psalm was composed. In vv. 19-22 the psalm-singer calls on God to *kill the wicked* (v. 19); wishes the bloodthirsty and those *who speak mischief against* God would depart (vv. 19-20); and expresses hatred for those who hate the Lord (vv. 21-22), suggesting that the psalm-singer is someone who has been hurt by others, who feels the wicked, the bloodthirsty, the speakers of maliciousness against God, and those who hate God pressing in. In this context of conflict and hostility, the psalm-singer speaks in trust and thankfulness for God's presence.

Psalm 139 may be divided into four major stanzas, alternating in emphases between God and the psalmist:

God's knowledge of the psalmist (vv. 1-6)
The psalmist cannot hide from God (vv. 7-12)
God's creation of the psalmist (vv. 13-18)
The psalmist's petition to God (vv. 19-24)

To the leader. A Davidic psalm.

1 *O LORD, you have searched me out and you know me.*[2]
2 *You know my resting and my rising up;*
you discern my thought from far off.
3 *My path and my lying down you closely examine,*[3]
and with all my ways you are familiar.
4 *For there is not a word on my tongue;*
Behold, O LORD, you know all of it.
5 *In front and behind you encompass me,*
and you place upon me the palm of your hand.

1. See deClaissé-Walford, *Introduction to the Psalms,* pp. 21-23.

2. The pronoun *me* is not part of MT, but may be implied from the pronoun suffix on the verb *ḥāqar (search)* that directly precedes the verb *yāḏaʿ (know).*

3. The Hebrew verb here is *zārâ* ("winnow, and sift"). It is used metaphorically by the psalm-singer to indicate a close scrutinizing and careful examination.

6 *Too wondrous for me is such knowledge.*
It is high; I am not able to grasp it.

7 *Where can I go from your spirit,*
and where from your face can I flee?
8 *If I ascend to the heavens, there you are!*
And if I make Sheol a bed, behold, there you are!
9 *If I rise up with the wings of sunrise*
and I settle in the remotest region of the sea,
10 *Also, there your hand will guide me,*
and your right hand will take hold of me.
11 *And if I say, "Certainly darkness will cover me,*
and the night will be the light around me."
12 *Also, the darkness is not too dark for you,*
and night, like day, is filled with light;
for darkness is as light.

13 *For you, you formed my inward parts;*
you wove me in the womb of my mother.
14 *I give thanks to you, because reverently and wondrously I was made.*
Wondrous are your doings, my inmost being knows very well.
15 *My bones did not hide themselves from you when I was made in secret,*
when I was shaped in the lowest parts of the earth.
16 *My unshaped form your eyes saw,*
and upon your scroll all of them were written,
the days that were meant to be, when not one of them was.[4]
17 *To me, how weighty are your thoughts, O God,*
how mighty is their sum.
18 *I count them; they are more than the sand,*
and when I awake,[5] *I am still with you.*

19 *If only you would kill, O God, the wicked*
and those who shed blood would turn away from me,
20 *the ones who speak mischief against you*

4. A number of translations accept an emendation of *days (yāmîm)* at the beginning of the third colon to "all of my days" *(kol yāmay),* maintaining that the colon is too short for the structure of the verse (Kraus, *Psalms 60–150,* p. 511). There is no textual evidence for the emendation, however, so this translation has not adopted it.

5. The verb in MT is the *hiphil* perfect form of *qîṣ* ("awaken"). Kraus and Allen, along with a few Hebrew manuscripts, propose reading the verb as *hᵃqiṣṣôṯî,* a denominative of *qēṣ* ("end"). NRSV adopts this reading, rendering the colon as "I come to the end."

and rise up in falsehood against you.[6]
21 *Do not the ones hating you, O LORD, I hate?*
And the ones raising themselves up against you I loathe.
22 *With complete hatred I hate them,*
for enemies they are to me.
23 *Search me out, O God, and know my heart.*
Try me and know my thoughts.
24 *And see if a way of hurtfulness*[7] *is in me,*
and guide me in the way of all time.

1-6 In vv. 1-6, the psalm-singer speaks directly to God, using the divine name twice and pronouns referring to God ten times. In addition, the psalmist refers to self eleven times. The concentration of personal pronouns in the first six verses of Psalm 139 mark the psalm as a reflection of the profound relationship of the "I" and "you" in ancient Israel.[8]

A major theme of Psalm 139 is "knowing." The word *yāḏaʿ* occurs seven times in the psalm (vv. 1, 2, 4, 6, 14, 23 [2x]), four times in vv. 1-6. The Hebrew verbal root covers a whole range of meanings — from simple recognition to intimate sexual relationship. God *knows* all there is about the psalmist, inside and out — every detail of the daily routine and every unspoken thought. For the beleaguered singer of Psalm 139, that thought is comforting.

7-12 In these verses, the psalm-singer muses over the idea that God is all-encompassing and all-present. No matter where the psalmist tries to flee from God — *the heavens, Sheol, the sea,* the *darkness* — God is there. The heavens were the dwelling places of the gods in the ancient Near East — An, Enlil, Utu, Nanna-Suen, Inana, and, later, Marduk. *Sheol* was the shadowy realm where all the dead go.[9]

Darkness, as the antithesis of light, was a realm of uncertainty and fear (see Job 12:22; Pss. 35:6; 88:6, 12; 107:10, 14). At the beginning of the creation story in Genesis 1, the earth is described as "formless and void," with "darkness upon the face of the deep *(tᵉhôm)*" (Gen. 1:2). The creative words of God harnessed the darkness, separating it from the light (Gen. 1:4), and into the

6. V. 20b is problematic. *nāśuʾ* ("being lifted up") is read by most as a corrupted form of *nāśᵉʾû* ("they *rise up*"). The last word of the verse, *ʿārêḵā* ("your cities"), is rendered in a number of Hebrew manuscripts as *ʿāḏêḵā (against you).*

7. LXX translates this Hebrew participle *(ʿōṣeḇ)* as *anomias* ("transgression, evil conduct").

8. See Walter Brueggemann, "The Psalms as Prayer," in *The Psalms and the Life of Faith,* pp. 34-39; and Mays, *Psalms,* p. 427.

9. For a full discussion of Sheol, see the commentary for Ps. 49. For a full discussion of "the sea" in the Psalter, see the commentary for Ps. 46:1-3.

light God created the world. The singer of Psalm 139 marvels that no matter where we go, God is there with us.

13-18 Verses 13-18 describe God's careful creation of the psalmist. The word translated *reverently (nôrāʾôṯ)* in v. 14 is derived from the verbal root *yārēʾ,* often translated as "fear," but better understood as "reverence and awe."[10] The word translated *wondrously (nip̱lêṯî)* in v. 14 comes from the verbal root *pālāʾ,* which means "to be different, striking, remarkable — outside of the power of human comprehension." The word is used repeatedly in the Psalter to describe the acts of God on behalf of the psalm-singers (Pss. 9:1; 40:5; 71:17; 96:3), particularly God's actions in the history of the ancient Israelites (78:4, 11; 105:2, 5; 106:7, 22). Psalm 106:22 employs both of the words used in v. 14:

> wondrous works *(nip̱lāʾôṯ)* in the land of Ham,
> and awesome deeds *(nôrāʾôṯ)* at the Sea of Reeds.[11]

Verse 15's reference to being *shaped in the lowest parts of the earth* echoes the creation story in Genesis 2, where we read, "then the LORD God formed the human *(ʾāḏām)* from the dust of the ground *(ʾᵃdāmâ)*" (Gen. 2:7).

The word translated *unshaped form* in v. 16a is the Hebrew *golmî,* a *hapax legomenon.* In Babylonian Aramaic, the word is used to designate a formless mass or an incomplete vessel. The Syriac word *galmā* means "uncultivated soil."[12] To translate the word as "embryo," as does the Common English Bible translation, is probably overspecific and misleading. And while this verse cannot be used to solve questions such as "When does life begin?", the whole of Psalm 139 affirms the sacredness and God-givenness of life.

The second and third cola of v. 16 are as puzzling as the first. The translation given above is as literal a rendering of the Hebrew as is possible in English. Other references to a *scroll* (book) of God occur in Exod. 32:32-33; Pss. 56:8; 69:28. We read in none of the passages, however, about the numbering of the *days* of an individual life, but rather a description of a scroll in which God has written names (Exodus 32; Psalm 69) and kept account of humanity's troubles (Psalm 56). The psalmist acknowledges that God holds all life in God's hands.

Verses 17 and 18 form a doxological close to the first sixteen verses of Psalm 139. The psalmist marvels at the *thoughts (rēaʿ)* of God, using the same word as in v. 2b, in which the psalmist says to God, *you discern my thoughts from far off.* God's *thoughts* are *weighty, mighty,* and *more* numerous *than the sand.*

19-24 As stated above, vv. 19-24 may provide the setting in life for the composition of Psalm 139. Verse 19 begins with words of imprecation by the psalmist against *the wicked* and *those who shed blood.* In a series of active

10. For a full discussion of the verbal root *yārēʾ,* see the commentary for Ps. 111:10.

11. See also Exod. 34:10; Ps. 145:5, 6.

12. *HALOT,* 1:194.

participles in vv. 20 and 21, the psalmist continues the words of imprecation against those who *speak mischief* and *rise up* deceitfully and affirms hatred for those who *hate* God and *raise themselves up.* The target of the psalmist's enemies appears to be God (vv. 20-21), suggesting that the psalmist is speaking in defense of God and perhaps that the previous verses of the psalm were composed as an "apology" on behalf of God.

In v. 22, the psalmist states emphatically, *With complete hatred (śin'â) I hate (śānē') them.* The verbal root *śānē'* refers to an emotional reaction of aversion to someone or something. But the aversion does not necessarily invoke a desire for harm to come to the other, but rather a desire to distance oneself from the other. In Prov. 19:7, we read, "If the poor are hated even by their kin, how much more are they shunned by their friends!" Isaac says to Abimelech in Gen. 26:27, "Why have you come to me, seeing that you hate me and have sent me away from you?" In the Old Testament, God "hates" particular actions and behaviors rather than particular people. Moses says to the Israelites in Deut. 16:21-22, "You shall not plant any tree as an Asherah beside the altar that you make for the LORD your God; nor shall you set up a stone pillar — things that the LORD your God hates." And in the Psalter, the psalm-singers affirm that God hates "evildoers" (Ps. 5:5), "the lover of violence" (11:5), and "wickedness" (45:7).[13]

Psalm 139 closes with the same words as it opens, *search me out and know me.* In vv. 1-2, however, the words are in the indicative mood, *O LORD, you have searched me out and you know me . . . you discern my thought,* while in v. 23, the words are in the imperative mood, *Search me out, O God, and know my heart . . . know my thoughts.*

Psalm 139 is attributed in its superscription to David, the second in a collection of eight psalms of David at the end of Book Five. Imagining David uttering these words during his tumultuous kingship conjures up a powerful scene in the hearer's imagination. Picturing the returned Babylonian exiles uttering these words in Jerusalem, surrounded by nations and peoples who did not acknowledge YHWH as God, conjures up yet another powerful scene. Each of us was formed and framed by God. God's eyes beheld our unformed substances. Each of us was reverently, wondrously, strikingly, remarkably, differently made — in ways that are beyond human explanation. In any time, in any place where the faithful face wickedness, bloodshed, and deceit, the words of Psalm 139 can provide comforting assurance of God's sovereign creation of and care for each individual.[14]

NANCY DECLAISSÉ-WALFORD

13. Edouard Lipiński, "*śānē'*," *TDOT,* 14:164-74.

14. References to the creation by God of an individual are rare in the Old Testament. See Jer. 1:5; Pss. 22:9; 71:6 for the only other examples.

Psalm 140: Keep Me from the Hands of the Wicked

Psalm 140 is the third in a collection of eight psalms at the end of Book Five that are attributed, in their superscriptions, to David (Psalms 138–45).[1] Psalms 138 and 139 are individual hymns of thanksgiving; the next four psalms (Psalms 140–43) are individual laments. Psalm 140 picks up, in many ways, where Psalm 139 leaves off. In the closing verses of Psalm 139, the psalm-singer declares complete hatred for those who hate God (vv. 21-22) and calls on God to kill the wicked (v. 19). In Psalm 140, the psalmist cries out to God about malicious people and persons of violent ways and calls on God to punish them with burning coals of fire, deep pits, and landlessness. The psalm contains all of the elements of a lament psalm: invocation (vv. 1, 4, 6, 7, 8); complaint (vv. 1-5); petition (vv. 8-11); expression of trust (vv. 6-7, 12); expression of praise (v. 13).[2]

Scholars have suggested a number of structures for Psalm 140. Kraus posits a three-stanza division of the psalm, based on style and contents: vv. 1-5, 6-11, 12-13.[3] Clifford finds a highly structured format for Psalm 140, observing that vv. 1-3 contain twenty-three Hebrew words, ending with *selah;*[4] vv. 4-5 contain twenty-three words, ending with *selah;* vv. 6-8 contain twenty-four words, ending with *selah;* and vv. 9-11 contain twenty-three words. He understands vv. 12-13 as a closing statement of trust.[5] McCann, building on the work of Allen, maintains that Psalm 140 is a chiastic composition whose center, vv. 6-7, proclaims the sovereignty of God:

Persons of violent ways (vv. 1-2)
    Lips (v. 3)
        Wicked, plot (vv. 4-5)
            The sovereignty of God (vv. 6-7)
        Wicked, plot (v. 8)
    Lips (vv. 9-10)
Persons of violent ways (v. 11)
            The acts of the sovereign God (vv. 12-13)[6]

Based on Allen's and McCann's proposition, we may divide Psalm 140 as follows:

1. The other Davidic collections in the Hebrew Psalter are Pss. 3–41, 51–72, and 108–10.
2. For a full discussion of the form individual lament, see the commentary for Ps. 13.
3. *Psalms 60–150,* p. 521.
4. For a discussion of the meaning of *selâ,* see the commentary on Ps. 3:2.
5. *Psalms 73–150,* p. 284.
6. McCann, "The Book of Psalms," pp. 1239-41; Allen, *Psalms 101–150,* p. 267.

Complaint and petition (vv. 1-5)
Expression of trust (vv. 6-7)
Petition (vv. 8-11)
Expressions of trust and praise (vv. 12-13)

To the leader. A Davidic psalm.

1 *Deliver me, O LORD, from malicious*[7] *people;*
from persons of violent ways protect me —
2 *those who plot malicious things in the heart.*
Every day they live among[8] *warfare.*
3 *They sharpen their tongue like a snake,*
the poison of a viper under their lips. Selah
4 *Keep me, O LORD, from the hands of the wicked;*
from persons of violent ways protect me —
those who plot to overthrow my steps.
5 *The proud conceal a trap for me,*
and cords they spread out like a fowler's net.
At the side of the road snares they have set for me. Selah

6 *I say to the LORD, "You are my God;*
lend an ear to the voice of my entreaties.
7 *O LORD, my Lord, my strong help,*
you have sheltered my head on the day of battle.

8 *Do not grant, O LORD, the desires of the wicked;*[9]
their plot do not let succeed,
else they be exalted.[10] Selah
9 *May the heads of those surrounding me*

7. The Hebrew word is *ra'*, most often translated as "evil." The word "evil" in English carries an ethical, moral tone that, while appropriate for Ps. 140, is probably not as appropriate as *malicious,* which means "having, showing, or caused by malice; spiteful; intentionally mischievous or harmful."

8. The Hebrew verbal root is *gûr* ("dwell, sojourn"). LXX translates the verb as *paretassonto* ("organize an army"), suggesting that we might understand the Hebrew verbal root as *gārâ* ("stir up strife"). The meaning of the phrase can be derived, however, without a textual emendation.

9. Vv. 8-10 are fraught with textual and accentual difficulties. This translation will adhere to MT as far as is possible. NRSV incorporates a number of the suggested emendations.

10. This phrase is part of MT. While NRSV omits it, NJPS includes it as an integral part of the verse.

be covered with the mischief of their lips.[11]
10 *May burning coals of fire rain down*[12] *upon them;*
cause them to fall into a deep pit and not rise up.
11 *May persons of the tongue not be established in the land;*
persons of violent ways, may maliciousness hunt them for ruin."

12 *I know*[13] *that the LORD maintains the defense of the oppressed,*
justice for the needy.
13 *Certainly the righteous will give thanks to your name;*
the upright will dwell in your presence.

1-5 The complaint portion of this individual lament is located in vv. 1-5. The psalmist is beset by maliciousness, *violent ways,* sharp *tongues,* and traps and snares. The word translated here as *malicious* is from the Hebrew root *raʿ,* usually translated as "evil." The word "evil" in modern culture often connotes moral and ethical behavior that stems from a depraved consciousness. A dictionary definition is "the force of nature that governs and gives rise to wickedness and sin." In vv. 1 and 2, the "evil" from which the psalmist is seeking deliverance has more to do with conscious actions on the parts of others to harm or act spitefully. *Violent ways* translates the Hebrew word *ḥāmās,* which connotes physical action and attack as well as ill intention.

Using three metaphors — *warfare, snakes,* and hunting, the psalmist cries out to God for deliverance and protection from all who assail in the first petitions of the psalm. The *malicious people,* the *persons of violent ways,* are accustomed to *warfare;* their *tongues* are as poisonous as the tongues of *snakes;* and they have many ways to cause the psalmist to fall into their *traps.*

6-7 In what Allen and McCann maintain is the center of Psalm 140, the psalmist calls on God to listen *(lend an ear)* and reminds God, the psalmist's *strong help,* that God has *sheltered* the psalmist's *head* on past *days of battle.* In the face of *violent ways,* poisonous *tongues,* and endless *snares,* God remains sovereign over any situation, and thus the psalmist can sing this expression of trust in God.

Entreaties (taḥᵃnûnîm) comes from the same verbal root as the word translated in Psalms 111, 112, and 123 as "showing favor," *ḥānan.* The word is one of the self-declarative attributes of God given to Moses in Exod. 34:6. In

11. The verb from the root *kāsâ* and translated here as *be covered by* is in the active voice in MT. The verse reads, lit., "The heads of the one surrounding me, may the mischief of their lips cover them."

12. The verbal root in MT is *mûṭ* (Qere, *niphal, "be made to stagger, totter"). BHS* suggests an emendation of the verbal root to *māṭar* ("let rain fall upon").

13. MT Kethib is 2ms. The Qere is 1cs.

Psalm 143, the psalm-singer calls on God to be attentive to the singer's cry "to be shown favor" by God by appealing to a basic characteristic of God.[14]

8-11 The petition of vv. 8-11 echoes the complaint of vv. 1-5. The psalmist cries out to God to inflict upon the *persons of violent ways* punishments equal to their malicious acts against the psalmist. For those who *plot malicious things* (v. 2), the psalmist asks that God *not grant* their *desires,* not allow *their plot* to *succeed* (v. 8). For those who *sharpen their tongues* and have *poison under their lips* (v. 3), the psalmist asks that God cover their heads *with the mischief of their lips* (v. 9). For those who *conceal a trap, spread out a fowler's net,* and place *snares at the side of the road* (v. 5), the psalmist asks God to *rain down burning coals of fire upon them* and *cause them to fall into a deep pit* (v. 10).

12-13 In the closing verses of Psalm 140, the psalmist sings words of trust and praise to the God who protects and preserves. In v. 12, the psalmist expresses confidence that God will defend and provide *justice* for *the oppressed* and *the needy.* Verses 6 and 7 celebrate God's sovereignty over the world; v. 12 celebrates God's actions as sovereign over the world. In one brief verse, the psalmist summarizes God's role in maintaining "rightness" in the human world.

Verse 13 contains the expression of praise for this individual lament. It proclaims that *the righteous will give thanks* to God's *name* and the *upright will dwell* in God's *presence.* Contrasting the righteous and the wicked is a common theme in the wisdom writings of the Old Testament (see Psalms 1, 32, 37; Prov. 3:33; 10:3; 15:6).

Psalm 140 is a cry from a psalm-singer to God for deliverance and safety. The psalmist remembers God's kind provisions in the past (vv. 1-5) and asks that God once again deliver and provide safety (vv. 8-11). As with the closing verses of Psalm 139 (vv. 19-22), the modern reader may find such words of retribution difficult to voice. But, as McCann reminds us in his commentary on Psalm 109:

> Evil, injustice, and oppression must be confronted, opposed, hated because God hates them. From this perspective, the psalmist's desire for vengeance amounts to a desire for justice and righteousness in self and society. . . . The anger is expressed, but it is expressed in prayer and thereby submitted to God. . . . Thus this vehement, violent sounding prayer is, in fact, an act of non-violence.[15]

The Apostle Paul quotes from the LXX translation of v. 3 of Psalm 140 in his Letter to the Romans:

14. For a full discussion of *ḥānan,* see the commentary for Ps. 111:2-4.
15. "The Book of Psalms," p. 1127.

"Their throats are opened graves;
they use their tongues to deceive."
"The venom of vipers is under their lips."
"Their mouths are full of cursing and bitterness." (Rom. 3:13-14)

Interestingly, Paul is not referring to or condemning the malicious and violent enemies of the faith, but all humanity, both Jews and Greeks (Rom. 3:9). We all are capable of plotting maliciousness and engaging in violent ways. Our faith in a God of goodness and wholeness *(šālôm)* reminds us of our role and responsibility as the children of God in this world.

NANCY DECLAISSÉ-WALFORD

Psalm 141: Watch Over My Mouth, Guard the Door of My Lips

Psalm 141 is fourth in a collection of eight psalms at the end of Book Five that are attributed, in their superscriptions, to David (Psalms 138–45).[1] Psalms 138 and 139 are individual hymns of thanksgiving; the next four psalms (Psalms 140–43) are individual laments. The many verbal links between Psalms 140 and 141 (no less than nine) indicate their connectedness. "Wicked" *(rāšāʿ)* occurs in Pss. 140:4, 8 and 141:4, 10; "righteous" *(ṣaḏîq)* in 140:13 and 141:5; "guard, keep" *(šāmar)* in 140:4 and 141:3, 9; "lip" *(śāp̱â)* in 140:3, 9 and 141:3; "malicious" *(raʿ)* in 140:1, 2, 11 and 141:4; "LORD my Lord" *(YHWH ʾᵃḏōnāy)* in 140:7 and 141:8; "trap" *(paḥ)* in 140:5 and 141:9; "snare" *(môqēš)* in 140:5 and 141:9; and "lend an ear" *(ʾāzan)* in 140:6 and 141:1.

In Psalm 140, the psalmist cries out to God for deliverance from "malicious people, persons of violent ways" (140:1). In Psalm 141, the psalmist asks God for help so that the psalmist's own heart will not be turned toward "malicious things," to *deeds of wickedness* (v. 4). In Psalm 140, the psalmist cries out to God for deliverance from those who "sharpen their tongue like a snake," with "the poison of a viper under their lips" (140:3). But in Psalm 141, the psalmist implores God to *place a guard on* the psalmist's own *mouth,* to *watch over the door of my lips* (v. 3). Allen suggests that the psalm-singer has been associating with "malicious people" and engaging in their deeds and speech and is coming before God asking for protection and guidance.[2] Others, such as Kraus and McCann, maintain that the psalmist is being tempted to join in the deeds and speech of "malicious people," but has not yet done so.[3]

As with Psalm 140, scholars have suggested a number of structures for Psalm 141.[4] This commentary will adopt a threefold division:

Cry for help (vv. 1-2)
Petition (vv. 3-6)
Plea for preservation (vv. 7-10)

Psalm 141 is fraught with textual difficulties, particularly in vv. 5-7. The following translation attempts to follow MT in all instances except where it is simply incomprehensible.

1. The other Davidic collections in the Hebrew Psalter are Pss. 3–41 and 51–72.

2. *Psalms 101–150,* p. 274.

3. Kraus, *Psalms 60–150,* p. 527; McCann, "The Book of Psalms," p. 1243.

4. For a full discussion, see Allen, *Psalms 101–150,* p. 273; McCann, "The Book of Psalms," p. 1243.

A Davidic psalm.

1 *O LORD, I cry out to you; come quickly to me.*
Lend an ear to my voice when I cry out to you.
2 *May my prayer stand firm, an offering of incense in your presence,*
the lifting up of the palms of my hands an evening offering.

3 *Place, O LORD, a guard*[5] *on my mouth;*
watch over the door of my lips.
4 *Do not turn my heart to a malicious*[6] *word,*
so that I do deeds of wickedness
with those who devise deception;
And let me not eat of their delicious food.
5 *Let the righteous strike me with* hesed *and reprove me;*
let my head not refuse such oil.[7]
Indeed[8] *continually my prayer*[9] *is against their maliciousness.*
6 *Let their judges be hurled down into the hands of the rock,*
and then they will hear my sayings, for they are pleasant.

7 *Like the furrowing and breaking up of the earth,*
our bones are scattered to the mouth of Sheol.
8 *Thus toward you, O LORD my lord, are my eyes.*
In you I take refuge;
do not lay bare my inmost being.
9 *Keep me from the hands of the trap they lay for me*
and the snares of those who devise deception.
10 *Let them fall into their own hunter's net,*
while I, I escape!

1-2 The repetition of *I cry out to you (qᵉrāʼṯîḵā)* and the imperative *lend an ear (haʼᵃzînâ)* in v. 1 suggest a sense of urgency on the part of the psalm-singer. The psalmist comes before God with *prayer* and *offerings.* Kraus posits that

5. MT has a 2ms *qal* imperative from the root *šāmar.* LXX translates with a noun — *phylakēn,* as does Syr. Following the imperative *place (šîṯâ)* at the beginning of the verse, a noun form is syntactically more appropriate.

6. For a discussion of the translation of this word *(raʻ),* see note 7 for Ps. 140.

7. V. 5 has many textual difficulties, as can be seen by reviewing various English translations. NJPS comes closest to rendering a literal, understandable translation of the very cryptic Hebrew text.

8. The particle *kî* is understood here as an emphatic.

9. MT *wāw*-conjunction at the beginning of *my prayer (tᵉpillāṯî)* is omitted in the translation.

the prayer takes the place of the *incense* and *evening offerings.*[10] Others, including Mays, point out that in the Hebrew Bible, prayer and sacrifice/offering go hand in hand. Ezra 9:5, for example, says, "At the evening sacrifice I got up from my fasting, with my garments and my mantle torn, and fell on my knees, spread out my hands to the LORD my God, and said. . . ."[11] Mays writes that Psalm 141 does not imply a spiritualization of sacrifice and that "word and sacrament are not at odds here."[12]

3-6 The psalmist begins the petition by asking God to *place a guard* on the psalmist's *mouth* and to *watch over the door of my lips* (v. 3).[13] The psalm-singer then requests that God keep the singer from joining in the words and actions of *those who devise deception,* including eating their *food* (v. 4). The book of Proverbs contains many warnings about whom a person chooses for companionship (see Prov. 22:24; 23:17-18; 24:1, 19-20, for example). The psalm-singer's concerns in vv. 3 and 4 echo the concerns of the singer of Psalm 140. In Ps. 140:1-3, the psalmist asks for deliverance from the lips of malicious and violent people; in 141:3-4, the deliverance sought is from the psalm-singer's own *lips* and own involvement in maliciousness.

Beginning with v. 5, Psalm 141 has numerous textual difficulties that render translation and interpretation difficult. In v. 5, the psalmist asks for reproof from *the righteous,* likening it to *oil* poured on the *head.*[14] The identity of *their judges (šōp̱ᵉṭîm)* in v. 6 is not clear, but perhaps refers to the leaders of v. 4's *those who devise deception.* When they find themselves without leaders, then perhaps they will listen to the psalmist and find that the *sayings* uttered are *pleasant.* The Hebrew word is from the verbal root *nāʿēm,* which means "to be lovely, good, attractive, friendly, joyous" (see Ps. 133:1).

7-10 The psalmist realizes the fleeting nature of all human life and acknowledges that the only safe *refuge* is in the Lord. Verses 9 and 10 return to the hunting imagery of Ps. 140:5. The psalm-singer asks God to deliver and preserve the psalmist, while allowing the wicked to fall into their own traps.

Psalms 140 and 141 contrast wickedness (*rāšāʿ* — 140:4, 8; 141:4) and righteousness (*ṣᵉḏāqâ* — 140:13; 141:5), as do a number of the wisdom psalms in the Psalter. According to Psalm 1, God "watches over the way of the righteous, but the way of the wicked will perish" (v. 6). Psalm 32 encourages the righteous to "be glad in the LORD and rejoice" (v. 11), but states that "many are the torments of the wicked" (v. 10). In Ps. 112:6, the psalmist sings, "For the

10. *Psalms 60–150,* p. 527.

11. For other references to the evening sacrifice, see 2 Kgs. 16:15; Dan. 9:21.

12. *Psalms,* p. 431.

13. For a discussion of references to speech organs in the Psalter, see the commentary for Ps. 120:5-7.

14. For a discussion of the word "righteousness" *(ṣᵉḏāqâ),* see the commentary for Ps. 112:2-4, and for a discussion of oil poured on the head, see the commentary for 133:2.

righteous will never be moved; they will be remembered forever," and in v. 10 proclaims, "The wicked . . . gnash their teeth and melt away; the desire of the wicked comes to nothing." The sapiential tradition of the ancient Near East taught that there was a basic moral governance to the world and consequence followed on action. Thus good things come to those who do good *(ṭôḇ)* and bad things come to those who do bad *(raʿ)*. There is no middle ground.

The singer of Psalm 141 recognizes how seductive wrong paths in life can be. So while in Psalm 140 the psalmist asks for deliverance from the lips and wicked ways of malicious people and persons of violent ways, in Psalm 141 the psalmist asks for deliverance from the psalmist's own lips and own leaning toward malicious speech and deeds of wickedness. The words of Psalm 141 are timely for twenty-first-century Christians. We are surrounded by seductive temptations to follow others in pursuits and lifestyles that are self-centered and harmful to or neglectful of others. May our own prayers for deliverance from such temptations be an ever-present part of our coming before God.

NANCY DECLAISSÉ-WALFORD

Psalm 142: You Are My Refuge and My Portion

Psalm 142 is the fifth psalm in a collection of eight psalms "of David" in Book Five (Psalms 138–45).[1] It, along with Psalms 140, 141, and 143, is an individual lament. But unlike the other three individual laments, it is identified in its superscription as a *Maskil (maśkîl)* rather than a "Psalm" *(mizmôr).*[2] In addition, Psalm 142 is one of thirteen psalms in the Psalter whose superscriptions place them in specific events in the life of David.[3] The superscription of Psalm 142, *A Maskil of David. When he was in the cave. A Prayer,* may be linked to two such events in the life of David. In 1 Samuel 20–22, David escapes from Saul to the cave of Adullam; in 1 Samuel 23–24, David flees to a cave in En-gedi when he learns that Saul is plotting to kill him.[4]

Many scholars choose to ignore the superscriptions of the psalms when offering commentary on them, arguing that the superscriptions were later scribal additions and that placing the psalms in specific historical settings anchors them too securely in the past, rather than allowing them to speak relevantly in the modern context.[5] Others pay close attention to the superscriptions, pointing out that the superscriptions provide an initial context in which to read and interpret the psalms. Sanders summed it up best:

> Does not such editorial work indicate the intense interest of redactors in date lines and historical contexts? They seem to be saying fairly clearly, if the reader wants to understand the full import for his or her (later) situation of what Scripture is saying, he or she had best consider the original historical context in which this passage scored its point.[6]

The superscriptions call readers to go back and review the stories and think about the characters and emotions, the actions and the outcomes. Then, when readers return to the psalms, they are able to ask themselves, "How do the psalms express the emotions and outcomes of the characters and events of those stories?"

1. The other Davidic collections in the Hebrew Psalter are Pss. 3–41, 51–72, and 108–10.

2. For a discussion of the term "Maskil," see the commentary for Ps. 42.

3. The others are Pss. 3, 7, 18, 34, 51, 52, 54, 56, 57, 59, 60, 63.

4. The superscription of Ps. 142 is very similar to the superscription of Ps. 57. For further information on these incidents in David's life, see the commentary for Ps. 57.

5. See, e.g., Brevard Childs, *Introduction to the Old Testament as Scripture* (Philadelphia: Fortress, 1979), pp. 520-22.

6. "Canonical Context and Canonical Criticism," in *From Sacred Story to Sacred Text,* p. 170.

Psalm 142 is the heartfelt cry of an individual to God to deliver. We may divide its verses into the following stanzas, each of which ends with the lament element "expression of trust."[7]

Appeal to be heard and expression of trust (vv. 1-3a)
Complaint and expression of trust (vv. 3b-5)
Petition, complaint, and expression of trust (vv. 6-7)

A Davidic maskil.[8] *When he was in the cave. A prayer.*

1 *With my voice to the* LORD *I cry aloud;*
with my voice to the LORD *I plead.*
2 *I pour out before him my complaint;*
my oppression in his presence I make known.
3 *When my spirit is fainting within me,*
then, you, you know my way.

On the path where I walk,
they have hidden a trap for me.
4 *Look to the right hand and see;*
there is no one regarding me.
A place of escape is lost for me;
there is no one inquiring after my inmost being.
5 *I cry to you, O* LORD*;*
I say, "You are my place of refuge,
my portion in the land of the living."

6 *Attend to my cry,*
for I have become exceedingly weak.
Deliver me from the ones persecuting me,
for they are stronger than I am.
7 *Lead my inmost being out of the prison,*
so that I may give thanks to your name.
Around me the righteous will gather,
for you will deal graciously with me.

1-3a Verses 1 and 2a echo the opening verses of Psalm 141, but are different in two significant ways. While Psalm 141 recounts the psalmist's word to God

7. For a full discussion of the elements of a lament psalm, see deClaissé-Walford, *Introduction to the Psalms,* pp. 23-25.

8. See note 2 on Psalm 32 superscription.

(note the second person pronouns), Psalm 142 describes the psalmist's act of crying aloud to God (note the third person pronouns). Thus, the hearer is the audience of the opening verses of Psalm 142, whereas God is the audience of the opening verses of Psalm 141.

In addition, while English translations of the psalmist's cry to the Lord in Psalms 141 and 142 are for the most part synonymous, two very different Hebrew verbal roots are used. In Psalm 141, the verbal root translated "cry out" in v. 1 is *qārā',* whose range of meanings includes "call, summon, invite, attract attention." The verbal root translated *cry aloud* in Psalm 142:1 is *zā'aq,* which conveys the idea of crying out in acute distress and seeking deliverance. The verbal root occurs only five times in the Psalter, twice in Psalm 142. The other occurrences are in Ps. 22:5 ("To you they [our ancestors] cried [aloud], and were rescued") and in 107:13 and 19 ("Then they cried [aloud] to the LORD because of their oppression, and from their depths he delivered them").

In v. 3a, the psalm-singer shifts from speaking about God to speaking directly to God in an expression of trust that ends the first stanza of Psalm 142. The word translated *spirit* is *rûaḥ,* referring to the very breath of being of the psalmist. When faint from lack of breath because of oppression, the psalmist affirms with an emphatic use of the 2ms pronoun *you ('attâ)* that God indeed knows the psalmist's every move.

3b-5 After expressing trust directly to God, the psalmist enumerates the complaint that prompted the psalm of lament. Those oppressing the psalmist have laid a *trap* (see 140:5; 141:9); *no one* has regard for or inquires after the psalmist. The psalm-singer is left alone to navigate a treacherous *path.* There is, according to v. 4, no *place of escape* (see Job 11:20; Jer. 25:35; Amos 2:14).

In v. 5, the psalmist again *cries aloud (zā'aq)* to God, but this time in an expression of trust: *You are my place of refuge, my portion in the land of the living.* Two Hebrew words are translated as "refuge" in the Psalter, *maḥᵃseh* (used here and eleven other times in the Psalter) and *miśgāḇ* (used eleven times). Both indicate a physical place of safety. *My portion in the land of the living* is most likely a reference to the dividing of the land of promise in the wilderness wandering and settlement narratives. Each tribe was allotted a *portion (ḥēleq)* of the land, except for the Levites. In Deut. 10:8-9, Moses tells the Israelites, "The LORD set apart the tribe of Levi to carry the ark of the covenant of the LORD, to stand before the LORD to minister to him, and to bless in his name, to this day. Therefore Levi has no portion or inheritance with his kindred; the LORD is his inheritance."[9] The singer of Psalm 142 needs no *portion* in this life other than God, just as the Levites needed no other portion.

6-7 In vv. 6 and 7, an *exceedingly weak* psalmist petitions God to *attend to my cry, deliver me,* and *lead my inmost being out of prison.* The word *prison*

9. See also Num. 18:20; Deut. 10:9.

(masgēr) may refer to a physical place of captivity or it may refer to the traps and snares of the ones *persecuting* the psalmist (v. 6). It may also have provided the inspiration for the superscription of the psalm.

The psalm-singer pleads for deliverance by God for one reason: so that the psalmist *may give thanks* to the *name* of God (v. 7; 140:13). In the third and final expression of trust in Psalm 142, the psalmist is confident that after God delivers, *the righteous* will *gather around* and the psalm-singer will no longer feel abandoned and alone.

Psalm 142 voices the lament of a person who has been faithful to God, but who feels oppressed and totally abandoned by the community of faith. Words and phrases such as "complaint," "fainting spirit," "no one regards," "no one inquiring after me," "exceedingly weak," "lead me out of prison" haunt its verses. The psalmist asks God to deliver so that once more the righteous will gather round in community.

The words of Psalm 142 speak volumes to the impersonal world in which we live in the twenty-first century. We work with, go to school with, live next door to, worship with people whom we hardly know. What burdens do they carry? Do they feel that their very breath of life is being sucked away by traps and snares? Do they feel that no one regards them, no one inquires after their well-being? The Christian community has been called to be a place of refuge and a portion in the land of the living.

NANCY DECLAISSÉ-WALFORD

Psalm 143: Cause Me to Know the Way I Should Go

Psalm 142 is the sixth psalm in a collection of eight psalms "of David" in Book Five (Psalms 138–45).[1] It, along with Psalms 140, 141, and 142, is an individual lament, a group of four laments of David framed by Psalms 138 and 139 (individual hymns of thanksgiving) and Psalms 144 and 145 (a royal psalm and a wisdom psalm). Psalm 143 has a number of thematic and verbal links with Psalms 140–42, indicating their integrity as a group. A unique characteristic of Psalm 143 is the psalmist's reference to self in relation to God as *your servant* in vv. 2 and 12. The reference may be in anticipation of the royal psalm that follows.

The psalm divides into two major sections:

The current situation summarized — My life is crushed (vv. 1-6)
Heartfelt petitions and an expression of trust — I am your servant (vv. 7-12)

A Davidic psalm.

1 *O LORD, hear my prayer,*
lend an ear to my entreaties,
in your faithfulness, answer me in your righteousness.
2 *Do not enter into judgment with your servant,*
for no living being is righteous before you.
3 *For the enemy pursues my inmost being,*
crushes my life to the ground,
causes me to sit in dark places
like those dead for all time.
4 *My spirit faints within me;*
in the midst of me my heart despairs.
5 *I remember the days of old;*
I muse over all of your work.
Over the doing of your hands I meditate.
6 *I spread out my hands to you,*
my inmost being[2] *like a parched land for you.*

7 *Hasten, answer me, O LORD;*
my spirit is at an end.

1. The other Davidic collections in the Hebrew Psalter are Pss. 3–41, 51–72, and 108–10.

2. Most English translations add a verb here. NRSV and NIV add "thirsts," while NJPS and NASB add "longs."

Do not hide your face from me,
or I will be like those who go down into the pit.
8 *Let me hear your* hesed *in the morning,*
for in you I trust.
Let me know the way that I should go,
for to you I lift up my inmost being.
9 *Deliver me from my enemies, O Lord;*
in you I have hidden.[3]
10 *Teach me to do your inclination,*
for you are my God.
Let your spirit of goodness lead me on level ground.[4]
11 *On account of your name, O Lord, make me live.*
In your righteousness lead out from oppression my inmost being.
12 *And in your* hesed *destroy my enemies,*
and let perish all those who oppress my inmost being,
for I am your servant.

1-6 Psalm 143 begins with a plea to God for a hearing, as do Psalms 141 and 142.[5] *Entreaties (taḥᵃnûnîm)* comes from the same verbal root as the word translated in Psalms 111, 112, and 123 as "showing favor" *(ḥānan).* The word is one of the self-declarative attributes of God given to Moses in Exod. 34:6. In Psalm 143, the psalm-singer calls on God to be attentive to the singer's cry "to be shown favor" by God by appealing to a basic characteristic of God.[6]

The psalm-singer bases the request for a hearing from God on two other attributes of God — *faithfulness (ʾᵉmet̠)* and *righteousness (ṣᵉd̠āqâ).*[7] Contrasting the *righteousness* of God with the inability of any *living being* to be *righteous before* God, the psalmist asks God not to *enter into judgment.* The phrase *enter into judgment* and the idea that no human is righteous before God occur most frequently in the books of Job and Ecclesiastes,[8] suggesting a sapiential tradition behind Psalm 143. The singer of Psalm 143 does not proclaim innocence, but appeals to the common human condition.

The complaint portion of the psalm begins in v. 3, using words and

3. One Hebrew manuscript, along with LXX, renders the verb *kissit̠î* as *nastî* ("I have fled"); another Hebrew manuscript renders it as *ḥāsît̠î* ("I have fled").

4. Several Hebrew manuscripts render *ʾereṣ* as *ʾōraḥ* ("path, way"), several others as *derek̠* ("path, way").

5. In Ps. 140, the psalmist utters similar words in v. 6.

6. For a full discussion of *ḥānan,* see the commentary for Ps. 111:2-4.

7. For a discussion of the meaning of *ʾᵉmet̠,* see the commentary for Ps. 138:1-3. For a discussion of the meaning of *ṣᵉd̠āqâ,* see the commentary for 112:2-4.

8. For *enter into judgment,* see Job 9:32; 14:3; 22:4; Eccl. 11:9; 12:14); for the idea that no human is *righteous before* God, see Job 9:2; 15:14; 25:4.

phrases common to individual laments. The *enemy ('ôyēḇ) pursues* and *crushes,* leaving the psalmist in *dark places* (see Ps. 107:10; 142:7). Thus the *spirit* of the psalmist *faints* (see 142:3). In the midst of despair, the psalm-singer remembers *the days of old. Remember (zāḵar)* is a powerful word in the Hebrew Scriptures. It occurs nearly 200 times, and generally conveys the idea of "the presence and acceptance of something in the mind."[9] The psalmist *remembers* and then *muses* and *meditates over* all that God has done in the past, spreading out the *hands* (see 141:2) to God with a yearning akin to *parched* ground yearning for water.

The word translated *meditate* in v. 5 is from the same verbal root, *śîaḥ,* as the word translated *complaint* in 142:2. In Psalm 142, the psalmist is agitated by oppression and complains to God; in Psalm 143, the psalmist remembers the works of God in the world and calmly meditates on them.

7-12 Beginning with v. 7, the psalmist embarks on what Allen calls "an urgent, breathless series of appeals":[10] *Hasten, answer me, do not hide your face, let me hear, let me know, deliver me, teach me, let your spirit lead me, make me live, lead out from oppression, destroy my enemies, let perish oppressors.* As with the complaint portion of the psalm, the petitions echo those found in many individual laments, but in Psalm 143 petitions for guidance outnumber petitions for deliverance.

The pit *(bôr)* in v. 7 is a word commonly used in parallel with "Sheol."[11] The petition from the psalm-singer to God to *hear your* hesed *in the morning* echoes other psalms where God's justice appears in the morning, perhaps after a "night vigil" in the temple or at a sanctuary (see Pss. 5:3; 88:13; 90:14).[12] A brief imprecatory tone injects itself into v. 12, but the overall thrust of Psalm 143 is a cry for graciousness in light of the vast gulf between the righteousness of God and the righteousness of humanity.

The ending words of Psalm 143, *for I am your servant,* reinforce the ascription of this group of psalms (Psalms 138–45) to David. To further connect the psalm with David, the LXX and Vulgate add to the superscription the words "when his son [Absalom] pursued him" (see Psalm 3). As with the superscription to Psalm 142, which places it in a particular, turbulent time in the life of David, so Psalm 143's added superscription gives the reader a historical context for reading the psalm.

Psalm 143 is one of the seven penitential psalms of the Psalter (Psalms 6, 32, 38, 51, 102, 130, 143), the Lenten liturgy of the medieval church. By order

9. Herrmann Eising, "*zāḵar,*" in *TDOT,* 4:65.

10. *Psalms 101–150,* p. 285.

11. For a discussion of Sheol, see the commentary for Ps. 49.

12. For an interesting study of "night vigils," see Karel van der Toorn, "Ordeal Procedures in the Psalms and the Passover Meal," *VT* 38 (1988) 427-45.

of Pope Innocent III (1198-1216), the psalms were to be prayed while kneeling each day of the Lenten season, or at least every Friday. The penitential psalms remind the reciter of the great divide between God and humanity and give voice to humanity's entreaties to God to "hasten, answer, and deliver."

The Apostle Paul incorporated the central theme of Psalm 143 into his idea of justification by faith alone, a central tenet of the Christian faith. The psalmist's words, *Do not enter into judgment with your servant, for no living being is righteous before you* (v. 2), become Paul's words in Rom. 3:20: "For 'no human being will be justified in his sight' by deeds prescribed by the law, for through the law comes the knowledge of sin"; and in Gal. 2:16: "yet we know that a person is reckoned as righteous not by the works of the law but through faith in Jesus Christ."

NANCY DECLAISSÉ-WALFORD

Psalm 144: Content Are the People Whose God Is the Lord

The words *Happy (content) are the people whose God is the* L*ORD* form perhaps one of the best-known phrases from the book of Psalms. They occur at the end of Psalm 144, the seventh of eight psalms at the end of Book Five that are attributed, in their superscription, to David. It is classified as a royal psalm, the third in Book Five,[1] but this psalm is an interesting composition. It contain echoes of a number of other psalms in the Psalter, including Pss. 8:4 in 144:3; 39:5-6 in v. 4; 33:2 and 3 in v. 9; and 33:12 in v. 15. But most prevalent in Psalm 144 are connections to Psalm 18, another royal psalm: 18:1, 2, 34, 46, 47 to 144:1, 2; 18:9 to v. 5; 18:14 to v. 6; 18:16, 44, 45 to vv. 7, 11; and Psalm 18's superscription to v. 10.[2]

Many scholars view Psalm 144 as a late composition, from the exilic or postexilic period, in which the psalm-singer appropriates and reworks portions of Psalm 18 and borrows elements from a number of other psalms. Mays writes:

> The composer of Psalm 144 must have found in [Psalm 18] a promise for the psalmist's own time. So the psalmist composed a psalm of praise and prayer to the God who [according to 144:10] "gives salvation to kings and rescues his servant David" as a context for petitions for deliverance from the aliens of the psalmist's time. By re-praying Psalm 18 in a new version, the writer appealed to the LORD to do for the people what the LORD had done for the LORD's servant David.[3]

Gerstenberger cautions, though, that likeness does not necessarily equate with borrowing. He writes:

> The process of composing psalms has to be thought of much more in terms of a broad transmission of sacred texts that to a large extent consisted of traditional vocabulary, stock phrases, and form elements. . . . Conscious use of particular, already existing psalms by late composers would be very difficult to ascertain.[4]

Whatever the origins of Psalm 144, in its canonical context it exhibits remarkable likenesses to a number of other psalms in the Psalter, particularly

1. The other two are Pss. 110 and 132. Royal psalms are so classified because their subject matter is the person of the king. Nine psalms in the Psalter are identified as royal: Pss. 2, 18, 20, 21, 45, 72, 101, 110, 132.

2. Cf. Ps. 108, which juxtaposes whole sections of two psalms (108:1-5 = 57:7-11; 108:6-13 = 60:5-12).

3. *Psalms,* p. 436.

4. *Psalms: Part 2,* p. 427.

Psalm 18, a royal psalm, whose superscription places it in a particular incident in the life of David. Only thirteen psalms in the Hebrew Psalter have such superscriptions — Pss. 3, 7, 18, 34, 51, 52, 54, 56, 57, 59, 60, 63, 142. In addition, Psalm 18 is a duplicate of the song sung by David in 2 Samuel 22. Thus we may say that Psalm 144 (by association) is firmly anchored in the life story of David, the great king of ancient Israel.[5]

The psalm may be divided into two major sections, based on the switch from first person singular language in vv. 1-11 to first person plural language in vv. 12-15, with a further breakdown of vv. 1-11 as follows:

Royal complaint (vv. 1-11)
  Praise of the Lord (vv. 1-2)
  The state of humanity in relation to God (vv. 3-4)
  Petitions to God with refrain (vv. 5-8)
  Reprise with refrain (vv. 9-11)
Community words of trust (vv. 12-15)

Davidic.

1 *Blessed is the LORD, my rock,*
the one who teaches my hands to do battle,
my fingers for warfare.
2 *My* hesed[6] *and my tower,*
my stronghold and the one who delivers me,
my shield in whom I take refuge,
the one who subdues peoples[7] *under me.*

3 *O LORD, what is humanity*[8] *that you regard it,*
children of humans[9] *that you think of them?*
4 *Humanity is like a breath,*
its days like a shadow passing over.

5 *O LORD, bend your heavens and come down;*
touch the mountains and they will smoke.

5. LXX even expands the superscription, which in MT is "of David," to "of David, against Goliath."

6. NRSV emends the text to "my rock" to harmonize with Ps. 18:2 and 2 Sam 22:2.

7. MT reads "my people" *(ʿammî).* Many Hebrew manuscripts, along with Aquila's Greek translation, Syr, and Targ emend to *peoples (ʿammîm,* see Ps. 18:47).

8. The Hebrew word is *ʾāḏam.*

9. The Hebrew is *ben ʾᵉnôš,* singular in Hebrew, but translated as plural to allow the use of gender-neutral language.

6 *Send forth lightning and scatter them;*
send your arrows and confound them.
7 *Send your hands from on high.*
Rescue me and deliver me from the great waters,
from the hand of the children of strangeness,
8 *whose mouth speaks falsehood*
and whose right hand is a right hand of deceit.

9 *O God, a new song I will sing to you;*
upon a harp of ten strings I will make music to you.
10 *The one who gives deliverance to kings,*
the one who rescues David his servant from a malicious sword.[10]
11 *Rescue me and deliver me from the children of strangeness,*
whose mouth speaks falsehood
and whose right hand is a right hand of deceit.

12 *Make content*[11] *our sons like growing plants in their youth;*
our daughters like corner-pillars
sculpted for the building of a temple;
13 *our granaries full,*
producing every kind;
our sheep bringing forth thousands,
ten thousands in our fields;
14 *our cattle pregnant without a breech and without a miscarriage;*
and no shout of sorrow in our streets.
15 *Content is the people for whom it is thus;*
content is the people whose God is the LORD.

1-2 In vv. 1 and 2, the psalm-singer praises God in words similar to Ps. 18:1-2 and 2 Sam. 22:2-3 with a piling up of descriptive phrases and the pronoun *my* (eight times in 18:1-2). In Psalm 18, the psalmist opens with the words, "I love you, O LORD," but in Psalm 144, the psalmist begins *Blessed is the* LORD and goes on to laud God as *the one who teaches my hands to do battle, my fingers for warfare.* David fought many battles in his lifetime, particularly against the Philistines. The word *hand* will figure prominently in Psalm 144 (vv. 1, 7 [two times], 8, 11 [two times]), with a strong distinction made between the divine and human hand.

10. NRSV places the phrase *from a malicious sword* as the object of the first verb of v. 11.

11. MT has the relative particle *ʿaššēr.* Suggested emendations include *ʾašrê* (see v. 15) and *ʿššēr, piel* second person imperative of the denominative verbal root *ʾšr.*

NRSV emends the beginning of v. 2 to "my rock" in order to harmonize the verse with Ps. 18:2 and 2 Sam. 22:2-3. The emendation has no textual precedence, and the other numerous differences between the three texts makes emendation unwarranted. The use of *hesed* in v. 2 connects the psalm with the collection of psalms of David of which it is a part (Psalms 138–45). In Psalm 138, the psalmist proclaims in v. 2, "I give thanks to your name because of your *hesed,*" and the word occurs again in Pss. 141:5; 143:8, 12; 145:8.

3-4 Verse 3 echoes Ps. 8:4 as the psalmist wonders at God's concern for humanity,[12] although it employs different verbs than Psalm 8 (the verbal roots *yāḏaʿ* and *ḥāšaḇ* rather than *zāḵar* and *pāqaḏ*). Verse 4 likens *humanity* to a *breath* and a *shadow,* recalling the words of Pss. 39:5-6; 62:9; 90:9; 109:23, among others. The word translated *breath* is *heḇel,* the same word used by the author of Qoheleth to describe life in this world. The phrase is *hᵃḇēl hᵃḇālîm* (Eccl. 1:2), translated poorly in most English versions as "vanity of vanities," perhaps better translated as "breath of breaths." Gerstenberger maintains that vv. 3 and 4 "lean to sapiential thinking."[13]

5-8 Verses 5-7 employ the language found in Ps. 18:9, 14, 16, 44-45, but McCann points out that the singer of Psalm 144 transforms the affirmations (expressions of trust) of Psalm 18 into petitions.[14] Using cosmic, creation language, the psalmist calls on God to *come down* from the *heavens* and *touch the mountains* with bolts of *lightning,* to *send* forth God's *hands* and scoop the psalmist out of the *great waters.*

The *mountains* and *great waters* are used as metaphors for *the children of strangeness (bᵉnê nēḵār)* in v. 7. NRSV and NASB translate the phrase as "aliens," NIV and NJPS as "foreigners." The phrase is common in the Hebrew Bible, occurring in Gen. 17:12; Exod. 12:43; Lev. 22:25; Isa. 56:3, 6; 60:10; 61:5; 62:8; Ezek. 44:7, 9; Neh. 9:2; Ps. 18:44, 45. In each case, the reference is to those outside the community of ancient Israel. The psalmist asks God to send forth God's *hands* and *deliver* the psalmist from the *hand* of *the children of strangeness,* because their *mouth speaks falsehood (šāwᵉʾ)* and their *right hand* is a *right hand of deceit.* In Ps. 139:20, the psalm-singer cries out against those who "speak mischief . . . and rise up in falsehood" against God.

9-11 The psalmist will sing a *new song* to God upon a *harp of ten strings,* because God *gives deliverance to kings* and *rescues David.* The phrase *new song (šîr ḥāḏāš)* occurs elsewhere in the Psalter in the enthronement psalms 96:1 and 98:1, psalms whose theme is the sovereignty of God over Israel and all creation. In Psalm 145, David will extol and bless God as king (145:1).

12. See also Job 7:17-19; 15:14-16.

13. *Psalms: Part 2,* p. 428.

14. "The Book of Psalms," p. 1254. Or we might say that the singer of Ps. 18 transforms the petitions of Ps. 144 into expressions of trust.

The words of v. 10 recall the superscription of Psalm 18, suggesting another connectedness between Psalm 144 and Psalm 18. The phrase *David his servant* ties Psalm 144 to the end of Psalm 143. The lamenting David of Psalms 140–43 calls on God to deliver because, in the end, he is the servant of God; the royal David of Psalm 144 praises God because God delivers kings and David his servant.

Verse 11 is virtually identical to vv. 7 and 8 and constitutes something of a refrain for the first eleven verses of Psalm 144.

12-15 The tone of Psalm 144 changes abruptly with v. 12. The first person singular voice of the king gives way to the first person plural voice of, presumably, the community of faith. The opening word of v. 12 renders the verbal mood of vv. 12-14 difficult. MT begins v. 12 with the relative particle *ʾ^ašer,* usually translated as "who, which, that." But such a rendering makes no sense in the context. Some suggest emending *ʾ^ašer* to *ʾašrê* ("content"), the word with which v. 15 opens; others suggest *ʾaššēr,* a *piel* imperative of the verbal root *ʾšr* ("make content"). Most English translations virtually ignore the relative particle and translate the verses as either declarative statements ("our sons are like growing plants") or as requests ("may our sons be like growing plants"). This commentary has opted to render the word in question as the *piel* imperative, *Make content our sons like growing plants.*

The items mentioned in vv. 12-14 — *sons, daughters,* grain, *sheep, cattle* — were important assets in ancient Near Eastern families. The list is strikingly similar to the list in Deut. 28:4, part of the blessings for obedience promised to the children of Israel as they prepared to enter the promised land.

The NRSV and NIV translations of v. 14 are very different from the translation in this commentary. The context in MT seems quite clearly to be that of cattle bearing offspring with ease and few complications. As the text note in NRSV indicates, the word "walls" does not occur in MT and is not suggested by any textual variant.

Verse 15 contains two *ʾašrê (content)* statements. The word occurs eleven times in Book Five of the Psalter, almost half of all its occurrences in the Psalter (in which it appears a total of twenty-six times).

Psalm 144 is a masterful example of appropriating traditional phrases, images, and ideas to ever-new situations in life. Whether the psalmist borrowed from Book One of the Psalter in general; from Psalms 8, 18, and 32 in particular; or from a stock of traditions shared by a faith community, the resulting song is a witness to the power of what Sanders calls "the old, tried, and true." He writes:

> In crisis situations, only the old, tried, and true has any real authority. Nothing thought up at the last minute, no matter how clever, can effect the necessary steps of recapitulation and transcendence needed by the

> threatened community, if it is to survive with identity. A new story will not do; only a story with old, recognizable elements has the power for life required.[15]

Book Five of the Psalter tells the story of ancient Israel as it returned from exile in Babylon and attempted to find a way to be God's people in a radically changed world (see the Introduction for a detailed treatment). Psalms sung by David, the great king of ancient Israel, at the end of Book Five remind the people where they have come from, and the words of David help point them in new directions. Old words, words that rang true in the past, are appropriated by David to paint a new picture and give hope to a struggling community.

Our communities of faith today often struggle with identity and place. And when the path doesn't seem clear, we often rely on the "old, tried, and true." We recite Psalm 23; we recall Paul's words in Rom. 8:38-39. With each recital, the "valley of the shadow of death" is different, the "height and depth" is different. Our circumstances change, but the words that sustained us in the past continue to sustain in the present and will continue to sustain us in the future. For that is the nature of Scripture — indeed "old, tried, and true," but ever new in changing circumstances.

NANCY DECLAISSÉ-WALFORD

15. "Adaptable for Life: The Nature and Function of Canon," in *From Sacred Story to Sacred Text,* p. 21.

Psalm 145: My Mouth Will Speak the Praise of the Lord

Psalm 145 is the last of a group of psalms ascribed to David at the end of Book Five of the Psalter. They occur just before the five-psalm doxological closing of the Book (Psalms 146–50). Some scholars suggest that the Hebrew Psalter ended with Psalm 145 at some point in its transmission history and that Psalms 146–50 were added as a concluding expression of the words of Ps. 145:21: *The praise of the LORD my mouth will speak, and all flesh will bless his holy name for all time and beyond.*

Psalm 145 is classified by some as an individual hymn of praise and by others as a wisdom psalm, based mainly on its acrostic structure. It is the fourth acrostic psalm in Book Five, with only three other complete acrostics occurring in the Psalter, all in Book One (Psalms 25, 34, 37).[1] Its superscription, unique to the Hebrew Psalter, reads *Praise (t^ehillâ). Of David.* Within its twenty-one-verse acrostic structure,[2] David, the former great king of Israel, leads the Israelites and all of creation in words of praise and thanksgiving to God as king.

The Babylonian Talmud tractate *Berakot* 4b states that Psalm 145, like the *shema* (Deut. 6:4-5), is to be recited three times a day, and everyone who does so "may be sure that he (or she) is a child of the world to come."[3] Psalm 145 appears in the Jewish prayer book more than any other psalm in the Psalter. The Dead Sea Psalm scroll 11QPs[a] contains a version of Psalm 145 in which the refrain, "Blessed is the LORD and blessed is his name forever and ever," is included after each verse, suggesting some sort of liturgical use. All indications are that the words of this psalm were and are a vital part of the faith of the Jewish people.

The structure of Psalm 145 may be analyzed as follows, as the psalm-singer leads in the celebration of God's sovereignty over all:

The voice of the individual psalmist (vv. 1-2)
Declarative statements by the individual psalmist (vv. 3-9)
The voices of the individual psalmist and the *hesed* ones (v. 10)
Interlude: God's kingdom is for all time (vv. 11-13)
Descriptive statements by the individual psalmist and the *hesed* ones (vv. 14-20)
The voices of the individual psalmist, the *hesed* ones, and all flesh (v. 21)

1. For a full discussion of the acrostic form, see the commentary for Ps. 119.

2. The *nûn* line is missing in MT, but is included in LXX and Syr and in the Dead Sea Psalms scroll 11QPs[a].

3. S. D. Goitein designated Ps. 145 as the "shema" of the book of Psalms; *Biblical Studies* (Tel Aviv: Yavneh, 1957), p. 228.

Davidic praise.

ʾĀlep 1 *I will exalt you, my God the king,*
and I will bless your name for all time and beyond.
Bêt 2 *Every day I will bless you,*
and I will praise your name for all time and beyond.

Gîmel 3 *Great is the* LORD *and exceedingly praiseworthy;*
for his greatness there is no searching out.
Dālet 4 *Generation to generation will glorify your doings,*
and your mighty works they will make known.
Hê 5 *On the splendor of the glory of your majesty,*
and on the words of your wondrous works I will meditate.
Wāw 6 *And the might of your awesome deeds they will tell,*
and your greatness I will recount.
Zayin 7 *The memory of your great goodness they will utter forth,*
and of your righteousness they will sing aloud.
Ḥêt 8 *Showing favor and compassionate is the* LORD,
slow to anger and great of hesed.
Têt 9 *Good is the* LORD *to all,*
and his compassions are over all his works.

Yôd 10 *All of your works will give thanks to you, O* LORD,
and your hesed *ones will bless you.*

Kāp 11 *The glory of your kingdom they will tell,*
and of your mighty works they will speak,
Lāmed 12 *in order to make known to the children of humanity his mighty work*
and the glory and the splendor of his kingdom.
Mêm 13 *Your kingdom is a kingdom for all times,*
and your dominion is for all generations.[4]

Sāmek 14 *The* LORD *supports all who are falling*
and lifts up all who are bent down.
ʿAyin 15 *The eyes of all look to you,*
and you give them their food in its time,
Pê 16 *opening your hand*
and satisfying for every living thing its desire.

4. The missing *nûn* line is inserted here in LXX, Syr, and 11QPs[a] manuscripts and is added to the NRSV and NIV translations.

Ṣādê 17 *Righteous is the* LORD *in all his ways*
and hesed *in all his doings.*
Qôp̄ 18 *Near is the* LORD *to all who cry out to him,*
to all who cry out to him in truth.
Rêš 19 *The desire of the ones who reverence him he fulfills,*
and their cry for help he hears and helps them.
Šîn 20 *The* LORD *watches over all who love him,*
but all the wicked he will destroy.

Tāw 21 *The praise of the* LORD *my mouth will speak,*
and all flesh will bless his holy name for all time and beyond.

1-2 The psalm begins with the psalmist's individual words of praise and blessing for *my God the king.* While the idea of God as king is expressed many times in the Psalter,[5] only here and in Ps. 98:6 does the psalmist refer to God as *the* king. For the significance of *name (šēm)* in the Old Testament, see the commentary for Ps. 113:1b-4.

3-9 In vv. 3-9, the psalm-singer describes a number of attributes of God. The Lord is *great (gāḏôl,* vv. 3, 6), *good (ṭôḇ,* vv. 7, 9), and *compassionate (raḥûm,* vv. 8, 9). Other words, such as *righteousness (ṣ^{e}ḏāqâ), hesed (ḥeseḏ),* and *doings (ma^{ʿa}śeh)* occur repeatedly in the verses. Verses 8-9 echo God's self-descriptive words recorded in Exod. 34:6: "The LORD is compassionate and shows favor, is slow to anger and abounding in *hesed.*"

In vv. 4-6, the psalm-singer uses four different words to describe the acts of God on behalf of humanity. The first, in v. 4, is translated *doings.* Its verbal root, *ʿāśâ,* means simply "do, make, manufacture, prepare." The second word, also in v. 4, translated *mighty works,* is derived from the verbal root *gāḇar* and means "achieve, be strong, increase." In v. 5, the psalmist meditates on God's *wondrous works (nip̱lāʾōṯ),* a word derived from the verbal root *pālāʾ,* "be unusual, wonderful, miraculous."[6]

In v. 6, the psalmist describes the acts of God on behalf of humanity as *awesome deeds,* from the Hebrew root *yārēʾ* ("be awesome, terrible, terrifying").[7] *Wondrous works* and *awesome deeds* are often used in the Old Testament and the Psalter to describe God's actions on behalf of the Israelites during the exodus from Egypt. In Exod. 3:20, God says to Moses, "I will stretch out my hand and strike Egypt with all my wondrous works *(nip̱lāʾōṯ)* that I will perform in it." In Exod. 34:10, God says to Moses, "Behold I make a covenant. Before all your people I will perform awesome deeds *(nip̱lāʾōṯ),*

5. See esp. the collection of enthronement psalms in Book Four, Pss. 93, 95–99.
6. For a full discussion of *nip̱lāʾōṯ,* see the commentary for Ps. 119:129-136.
7. For a full discussion of *yārēʾ,* see the commentary for Ps. 111:10.

such as have not been performed in all the earth or in any nation." In Ps. 86:10, the psalm-singer says, "You are great and do wondrous things *(nip̲lā'ôt̲),*" and the singer of Ps. 136:4 states that God alone "does great wondrous things *(nip̲lā'ôt̲).*"

The psalmist not only describes the attributes of God, but states a firm intention to proclaim to others these attributes. In v. 4, *generation to generation* will *make known* God's *mighty works.* In v. 5 the psalm-singer says *I will meditate,* from the Hebrew verbal root *śîaḥ,* which can mean "muse, speak, talk," even "sing." The generations and the psalmist will *tell* and *recount* in v. 6; will *utter forth* and *sing aloud* in v. 7. The word translated here as *utter forth* is from the verbal root *nāb̲aʿ,* which means "bubble forth, pour out." The psalm-singer and the generations will not only relate a description of their God; they will eagerly and joyously tell others.

10 In v. 10, the voices of the *works* of God *(maʿaśeh)* and God's *hesed ones* join with the psalmist in *thanks* and blessing. *Hesed ones* are those who are part of the covenant community of God. God said to the children of Israel at Sinai,

> You have seen what I did to the Egyptians, and how I bore you on eagles' wings and brought you to myself. Now therefore, if you obey my voice and keep my covenant, you shall be my treasured possession out of all the peoples. Indeed, the whole earth is mine, but you shall be for me a priestly kingdom and a holy nation. (Exod. 19:4-6a)

11-13 The centerpiece, both physically and thematically, of the acrostic Psalm 145 is vv. 11-13. Verse 11 begins with the Hebrew letter *kāp,* v. 12 with *lāmed,* and v. 13 with *mêm.* The letters of these lines, inverted, spell out the Hebrew word for "king" *(melek̲).* And within vv. 11-13, the word *kingdom (malkût̲),* derived from the same consonantal root as "king," occurs four times, at the beginning, the middle, and the end, forming a triangular structure, with its apex at the end of v. 12 and its base at the beginnings of vv. 11 and 13. These verses emphasize the theme of Psalm 145, the kingship of God over Israel and all of God's "works."[8]

14-20 Verses 14-20 are, like vv. 3-9, descriptions of God. But whereas the words of vv. 3-9 declared attributes of God, the words of vv. 14-20 describe actions of God on behalf of humanity. In a series of active participles, the psalm-singer outlines God's generous care for creation: God *supports* (v. 14), *lifts up* (v. 14), *gives food* (v. 15), *opens his hand* (v. 16), *satisfies desires* (v. 16), is *near* (v. 18), *fulfills desires* (v. 19), and *watches over* (v. 20).[9]

8. The enthronement psalms (Pss. 47, 93, 95–99) also celebrate the kingship of God, using much of the same language found in Ps. 145.

9. For similar language about God, see Pss. 107:33-42; 72:1-14.

21 The final words of Psalm 145 begin with the individual voice of the psalm-singer and expand to encompass the voice of all flesh in the praise of God as king. *Praise (t^{e}hillâ), bless (bāraḵ),* name *(šēm),* and *for all time and beyond (l^{e}ʿôlām wāʿeḏ),* words used in the superscription, in v. 1 (the voice of the individual) and v. 10 (the voices of the individual and the *hesed* ones), are repeated in v. 21 (the voices of the individual, the *hesed* ones, and all flesh), bringing to a climax the praise of God as sovereign over all.

Psalms 146–50, the concluding doxology of the Psalter, will continue to voice the praise of God that is initiated in Psalm 145. But Psalm 145's acrostic initiation of praise could well stand on its own. Adele Berlin writes of it:

> The poet praises God with everything from A to Z; his praise is all-inclusive. More than that, the entire alphabet, the source of all words, is marshalled in praise of God. One cannot actually use all of the words in a language, but by using the alphabet one uses all potential words.[10]

Psalm 145 is a masterful composition. It persuades the reader to move from one stage of the psalm to the next, as each successive element builds on the previous. The individual psalm-singer declares an intention to praise and bless the name of God the king (vv. 1-2). The reason for the praise and blessing takes the form of a declaration of the greatness, goodness, and compassion of God. The psalm-singer persuades the generations of the Israelites to join in the act of blessing God (v. 10). And together the individual and the generations describe the great and good and compassionate acts of God the king (vv. 14-20). As a result, not only the individual worshipper, but all flesh (including the generations of the Israelites) will praise and bless the name of the Lord for all time (v. 21).

Might we read Psalm 145 as the summary statement of the theme of the Hebrew Psalter: *The LORD is king over all generations of the Israelites and over all flesh?* And might we hear David, the former earthly king of ancient Israel, leading the Israelites and all flesh in a joyous celebration of that confession? All indications are that the answer to the question is a resounding "yes." In the words of Psalm 145, a new world has been powerfully and decisively spoken into being.

The message for the church today is simple and yet complex. In the midst of turmoil and uncertainty in the world, praising God as sovereign is the solution. But what does that mean? We can speak the words, but how do we put them into action? God is indeed sovereign, but we must be the hands and feet of God in God's world — what some scholars call "a communitization" of kingship. In the ancient Near East, the role of the king was to provide a safe

10. "The Rhetoric of Psalm 145," in *Biblical and Related Studies Presented to Samuel Iwry,* ed. Ann Kort and Scott Morschauser (Winona Lake: Eisenbrauns, 1985), p. 17.

place of habitation for humanity. That safety included dwelling places, farm land, drinking water, abundant harvests, increase of animals, and fertility within the family (see Psalms 72 and 107). In our twenty-first-century world, many people do not have the basic elements of safe habitation — whether as a result of poverty, societal violence, disease, or outright neglect. We must, in God's name, support those who are falling, lift up those who are bent down, give food in its time, open our hands, and hear and respond to cries for help.

NANCY DECLAISSÉ-WALFORD

Psalm 146: The Lord Will Reign for All Time

Psalm 145 ends with the words, "The praise *(t^e^hillâ] of the LORD* my mouth will speak, and all flesh will bless his holy name for all time and beyond" (v. 21). And in the five psalms that follow, Psalms 146–50, that is precisely what takes place. Psalms 146–50 are known as the "Final Hallel" of the book of Psalms. Each opens and closes with "hallelujah" *(hāl^e^lû yāh);* Ps. 146:2 proclaims, *I will praise the LORD with my very life;* and Ps. 150:6 says, "Let every breathing thing praise the LORD."

The opening psalm of the "Final Hallel" is classified as an individual hymn of thanksgiving, in which a psalm-singer praises God (vv. 1-2), offers words of admonition not to trust in earthly rulers (vv. 3-4), celebrates YHWH as creator and sustainer (vv. 5-8b), contrasts the fate of the righteous and the wicked (vv. 8c-9), and celebrates YHWH's sovereignty for all time (v. 10). A number of structures are suggested for the psalm; John Kselman's chiastic arrangement best highlights the major characteristics of Psalm 146.[1]

Opening praise (vv. 1-2)
    Wisdom words (vv. 3-4)
        God as Creator and Redeemer (vv. 5-8b)
    Wisdom words (vv. 8c-9)
Closing praise (v. 10)

1 *Hallelujah!*
O my inmost being, praise the LORD.
2 *I will praise the LORD with my very life;*
I will sing praises to my God for the duration of my being.

3 *Do not trust in earthly rulers,*
in a child of humanity in which there is no help.
4 *Its breath goes out; it returns to its earthen state.*
In that day, its plans will perish.

5 *Content is the one whose help is the God of Jacob,*
whose hope is in the LORD their God,
6 *who makes the heavens and the earth,*
the sea and all that is in them;
who keeps faith for all time;
7 *who provides justice for those being oppressed;*
who gives bread to the hungry;

1. "Psalm 146 in Its Context," *CBQ* 50 (1988) 591-92.

the LORD, *who guides prisoners;*
8 *the* LORD, *who opens the eyes of the blind;*
the LORD, *who lifts up those who are bent down;*
the LORD, *who loves the righteous;*
9 *the* LORD, *who keeps the strangers.*
The orphan and the widow he will make firm,
but the way of the wicked he will make crooked.

10 *The* LORD *will reign for all time,*
your God, O Zion, for all generations.
Hallelujah!

1-2 Psalm 146 opens with an admonishment to the *inmost being (nep̱eš)* to *praise the* LORD (see Ps. 103:1-2; 104:1) and continues with a statement that the psalmist will *praise (hālal)* and *sing praises (zāmar)* to God *for the duration* of the psalmist's *life.* The two verbs used in these verses are found in many individual and community hymns in the Psalter.[2]

3-4 The psalm-singer admonishes those listening to the song of praise not to *trust in earthly rulers (nᵉḏîḇîm),* further identifying the rulers as *a child of humanity (ben 'āḏām),* those who return to their *earthen state ('ᵃḏāmâ)* when their breath leaves them. The words of vv. 3 and 4 recall Genesis 2, in which the first human *('āḏām)* is formed by God from the earth *('ᵃḏāmâ),* reminding us of the transitory nature of human existence.

Commentators have pointed out a number of connections between Psalm 146, the beginning of the end of the Psalter, and Psalms 1 and 2, the beginning of the Psalter. The words of v. 3 echo the sentiments of Psalm 2. In the final colon of v, 4, we read that the plans of the *child of humanity* will *perish ('āḇaḏ),* the same verb used in the final verses of Psalms 1 and 2.

5-8b Verse 5 begins with the wisdom word *content ('ašrê),* the same word with which Psalm 1 opens and Psalm 2 closes. The word *'ašrê* occurs eleven times in Book Five of the Psalter, almost half of all its occurrences in the Psalter (in which it appears a total of twenty-six times). *Content is the one whose help ('ēzer) is the God of Jacob.*[3]

In vv. 6-8b, the singer of Psalm 144 describes the actions and attributes of God in what Gerstenberger calls a "Yahweh hymn,"[4] using language very similar to that we find in Ps. 145:14-20. As in Psalm 145, here in Psalm 144, in a continuous series of participles, the psalm-singer outlines God's generous care for creation and for the *oppressed,* the *hungry, prisoners,* the *blind,* and

2. See Pss. 9, 33, 66, 71, 104, 105, 135.

3. For a full discussion of *'ēzer,* see the commentary for Ps. 108:12.

4. *Psalms: Part 2,* p. 438.

those who are bent down. The passive participle translated as *those who are bent down (kᵉp̄ûp̄îm)* occurs only here and in Ps. 145:14 in the Psalter.

8c-9 Continuing with participles that describe the actions and attributes of God, in vv. 8c-9a, the psalm-singer states that the Lord is the one who *loves the righteous* and *keeps the strangers.* Abruptly the participles cease and the singer switches to imperfect verbs in the remainder of v. 9. Here, the psalmist affirms that God will *make firm* the *orphan and the widow,* but *the way of the wicked (rᵉšāʿîm)* God will *make crooked.* The contrast between the fate of the righteous and the fate of the wicked recalls once again the words of Psalm 1.

10 Verse 10 reiterates the words of Psalm 145:1, 11-13 and the import of Book Four's enthronement psalms: *The LORD will reign for all time.* Thus the beginning of the end of the Psalter states unequivocally the conclusion to which the story of the Psalter has been moving.[5]

Mays calls Psalm 146 a "sung lesson,"[6] one in which those who recite it, along with those who hear it, teach and are taught that God is the eternal sovereign over the world. The words of Psalm 146 have as much to say to those of us who live in the twenty-first-century world as they did to the ancient Israelites. Earthly rulers will return to their earthen states. But God will continue to care and provide for the oppressed, the hungry, the prisoners, the blind, those who are bent down, the strangers, and the orphans and widows. How? With the hands and feet, through the minds and wills, and out of the inmost beings of those who believe that God is indeed sovereign in our world.

NANCY DECLAISSÉ-WALFORD

5. See the Introduction for the story of the shape and shaping of the Psalter.
6. *Psalms,* p. 440.

Psalm 147: Sing to the Lord with Thanks

Psalm 147 is the second of five psalms that form the doxological end of the book of Psalms (Psalms 146–50), known as the "Final Hallel" psalms. As do each of the five psalms, Psalm 147 begins and ends with the word "hallelujah" *(hālᵉlû yāh)*. It is classified as a community hymn and celebrates God's sovereign reign over the community of faith and all of creation. As Psalm 145's words recount the praise of the individual worshipper (David in Psalm 145), the community of faith, and finally all of creation (see the commentary for Psalm 145), so the five psalms that close Book Five move from the praise of an individual in Psalm 146, through the praise of a community of faith in Psalm 147, to the praise of all creation in concert with the community of faith in Psalms 148–50.

Psalm 147 may be divided into three stanzas, each with a call to praise followed by descriptive words about God's sovereignty over the community of faith and the created world.

Invitation to sing praises to God (vv. 1-6)
Invitation to sing and make music to God (vv. 7-11)
Invitation to glorify God (vv. 12-20)

1 *Hallelujah,*
for it is good to sing praises to our God,
for pleasant and fitting is praise.
2 *The one who builds Jerusalem is the Lord;*
the outcast ones of Israel he will gather together;
3 *the one who heals the brokenhearted,*
and the one who binds up their sorrows;
4 *the one who determines the number of the stars,*
to all of them names he gives.
5 *Great is our Lord and abundant is his power;*
of his insight there is no reckoning.
6 *The one who supports the oppressed is the Lord,*
the one who humbles the wicked down to the earth.

7 *Sing to the Lord with thanks;*
make music to our God on a harp;
8 *the one who covers the heavens with darkness,*
the one who attends to the earth with rain,
the one who causes the hills to sprout with grass;
9 *the one who gives the beast its food,*
to the offspring of the ravens what they cry out for.

10 *Not in the strength of the horse does he delight;*
not in the legs of a person does he take pleasure.
11 *The ones who please the* LORD *are the ones who reverence him,*
the ones who wait for his hesed.

12 *Glorify, O Jerusalem, the* LORD;
praise your God, O Zion,
13 *For he has made strong the bars of your gates;*
he has blessed your children in your midst.
14 *The one who lays out your territory in well-being,*
with the best part of the grain he satisfies you.
15 *The one who sends forth his utterance in the earth,*
swiftly his word runs.
16 *The one who gives snow like the wool,*
hoar-frost like the dust he scatters.
17 *The one who casts down his hail like crumbs,*
in the presence of his cold, who can stand?
18 *He will send his word, and it will melt them;*
he will cause his wind to blow; the waters will overflow.
19 *The one who reveals his words*[1] *to Jacob,*
his decrees and his judgments to Israel,
20 *He has not done this for every nation,*
and of such judgments they do not know.
Hallelujah.

1-6 The community of worshippers is invited to participate in singing Psalm 147 with v. 1's imperative *praise the* LORD *(hal^{e}lû yāh).* The two reasons for the invitation follow, each introduced by the particle *for (kî): It is good to sing praises (zāmar) to our God* and *pleasant and fitting is praise (t^{e}hillâ).* The psalmist's use of *t^{e}hillâ* reminds the reader/hearer of the superscription of Psalm 145. In vv. 2-6, a series of participles (see Pss. 145:14-20; 146:6-9) describe God's actions in the history of the community of faith (vv. 2-3, 6) and in all creation (vv. 4-5).

7-11 Verse 7 issues a twofold invitation to participate in singing Psalm 147: *Sing (ʿānâ) to the* LORD *with thanks* and *make music (zāmar) to our God.* The verbal root *ʿānâ* is used only one other place in the Hebrew Psalter, in Ps. 119:172, but it introduces the so-called "Song of Miriam" in Exod. 15:21: "And Miriam sang *(ʿānâ)* to them: 'Sing *(šîr)* to the LORD, for he has triumphed

1. The Kethib is "his word" *(d^{e}ḇārô);* the Qere is "his words" *(d^{e}ḇārāyw).* Qumran, Targ, and many Hebrew manuscripts follow the Qere, while LXX, other Greek translations, and Syr follow the Kethib.

gloriously; horse and rider he has thrown into the sea.'" The particle *for (kî)* does not occur in this stanza; vv. 8-11 continue the participial descriptions of God's actions in history (vv. 10-11) and all creation (vv. 8-9).

12-20 Verse 12 issues the third call to participate in singing Psalm 147: *Glorify (šāḇaḥ),* O Jerusalem, the LORD; praise *(hālal)* your God, O Zion. The particle *kî* at the beginning of v. 13 renders the structure of this stanza parallel to the first stanza of the psalm. Two reasons to participate in glorifying and praising God follow: *he has made strong the bars of your gates* and *he has blessed your children in your midst.* Participles dominate once again, beginning with v. 14, in concluding words of God's actions in history on behalf of the community of faith (vv. 13-14, 19-20) and creation (vv. 15-18). The language used in vv. 15-18 is reminiscent of that found in Job 38, God's speech to Job "out of the whirlwind."

Verses 15 and 18 speak of God *sending forth (šālaḥ)* his *word (dāḇār)* into the world. Psalm 119 uses *dāḇār* twenty-two times as a synonym for torah. The word translated *wind* is *rûaḥ,* which may be translated as "wind, spirit, or breath." In Gen. 1:2, we read in NRSV that a "wind [*rûaḥ*] from God swept over the face of the waters." NIV translates the verse as "the Spirit of God was hovering over the waters."

Psalm 147 is the second of the doxological hymns of the Psalter that were introduced in Ps. 145:21. Psalm 146, the words of an individual psalm-singer, gives way in Psalm 147 to the words of the community of the faithful, indicated by Psalm 147's references to Jerusalem, Zion, Jacob, and Israel (vv. 2, 12, 19). In both Psalms 146 and 147, the psalm-singers celebrate God as sovereign over all creation as well as over the community of faith. Mays sums it up well:

> The history of the community of faith is a small part of reality, but the power that moves its course is the same that governs the stars. On the other hand, the processes of the world are vast, impersonal, and uncaring, but the sovereignty at work in the world is the saving, caring God whom Israel has come to know in its history.[2]

The words of Psalm 147 remind the faithful of the nature and character of the God they worship. It is the lectionary reading for the second Sunday after Christmas Day, along with John 1:10-18 and Eph. 1:3-14. All three texts remind us that God is creator of all and yet God intimately cares for humanity.

NANCY DECLAISSÉ-WALFORD

2. *Psalms,* p. 442.

Psalm 148: Praise the Lord from the Heavens and from the Earth

Psalm 148 is the third of the five "Final Hallel" psalms that close the Hebrew Psalter. Each of the psalms begins and ends with "hallelujah," and the phrase "Praise (the LORD)" occurs twelve times in Psalm 148, perhaps in anticipation of Psalm 150's final unbridled words of praise to God. Psalm 148 is classified as a creation psalm[1] and continues the movement of the final doxological hymns of the Psalter from individual praise (Psalm 146) through the praise of the community of faith (Psalms 147 and 149) to the praise of all creation (Psalms 148 and 150).

Psalm 148 may be divided into two distinct stanzas, each calling upon a particular realm of creation to praise the Lord.

"Praise the LORD from the heavens" (vv. 1-6)
"Praise the LORD from the earth" (vv. 7-14)

1 *Hallelujah.*
Praise the LORD from the heavens;
praise him in the heights.
2 *Praise him, all his messengers;*
praise him, all his hosts.
3 *Praise him, sun and moon;*
praise him, all of the stars of light.[2]
4 *Praise him, the heavens of the heavens*
and the waters which are over the heavens.
5 *Praise the name of the LORD,*
for he commanded and they were created
6 *and he established them for all time;*
a statute he gave and it will not pass away.

7 *Praise the LORD from the earth,*
the sea monsters and all the deep,
8 *fire and hail, snow and smoke,*[3]
the wind of the storm that carries out his word,
9 *the mountains and all the hills,*
the fruit trees and all the cedars,
10 *the wild living beings and all the cattle,*
the creeping thing and the bird of the wing,

1. The other creation psalms in the Hebrew Psalter are Pss. 8, 19, 65, 104.
2. LXX and Syr render this phrase "all of the stars and the light."
3. The Hebrew word *qîṭôr* can mean "fog, mist, smoke." LXX renders it "ice."

11 *kings of the earth and all peoples,*
princes and all of the judges of the earth,
12 *young men as well as young women,*
the elders along with the youth.
13 *Praise the name of the* LORD,
for his name alone is lofty;
his splendor is upon the earth and the heavens.
14 *And he has exalted a horn for his people,*
a hymn of praise for all of his hesed *ones,*
for the children of Israel, the people near to him.
Hallelujah.

1-6 Verses 1-6 call upon the inhabitants of the heavenly realm to praise God — *messengers (malʾāḵîm), hosts (ṣᵉḇāʾôṯ), sun and moon, stars, the heavens of the heavens, and the waters over the heavens.*

The word translated in v. 2 as *messengers* is derived from a verbal root *lāʾaḵ,* which means "send." It is used in the Old Testament to refer both to human messengers (see Gen. 32:6; 1 Sam. 23:27; Ezek. 23:40) and to messengers from God (see Gen. 19:1; Judg. 13:3; 1 Kgs. 13:18). *Hosts* comes from the verbal root *ṣāḇāʾ* meaning "go forth to war." The word occurs extensively in the Old Testament in general and in the Psalter in particular in reference to human armies (see Pss. 44:9; 60:10; 68:12; 108:11) and to "the LORD of hosts" (see Pss. 24:10; 46:11; 69:6; 80:4). The use of *messenger* and *hosts* to describe heavenly beings reflects the ancient Near Eastern idea of a heavenly society that is parallel to earthly societal structures.

The *sun,* the *moon,* and the *stars* were considered by other peoples in the ancient Near East as individual gods. The words of the psalmist in Psalm 148 reflect the creation theology of Genesis 1: the God of the Israelites created the sun and the moon and the stars (in Gen. 1:16, "the two great lights . . . and the stars"). The great lights and the stars are not gods to be worshipped, but objects that worship God (see also Josh. 10:12).

The phrase *the heavens of the heavens (šᵉmê haššāmāyim)* also occurs in Deut. 10:14; 1 Kgs. 8:27. It most likely reflects the ancient Near Eastern concept of the world in which the heavens were separated into the heavens above the dome *(rāqîaʿ)* and the heavens below. The heavens below the dome was the realm of earthly existence (the atmosphere); the heavens above the dome was the realm of the gods. In Psalm 148, the heavens above the dome (the realm of the gods) is called upon to praise the God of Israel.

In like manner, the phrase *the waters which are over the heavens,* which also occurs in Gen. 1:6-8, refers to the ancient Near Eastern concept of the waters above the dome *(rāqîaʿ)* of the earth and the waters below the dome of the earth. The waters below the dome were the source of springs, rivers, and seas. The waters above the dome, which apparently lay between the heavens below and the heavens above, were the source of rainfall.

The singer of Psalm 148 calls on all elements of the heavens to praise the Lord, and in v. 5b provides the reason why, with the characteristic particle *for (kî;* see Psalm 147). Why ought creation to praise God? Because, the psalm-singer says, at God's command all was *created (bārā'),* the same word used in Genesis 1 to describe God's creative activity (Gen. 1:1, 21, 27).

7-14 In vv. 7-14, the focus of the psalm-singer's call to praise moves from the heavenly realm to the earthly realm. Using language reminiscent of both Job 38 (see Ps. 147) and Genesis 1, the singer calls sea monsters, the weather, geological formations, plants, animals, and people from every walk of life to join in the praise. In v. 8, the psalm-singer proclaims that *the wind of the storm carries out* the *word* of God, in language similar to Ps. 147:15, 18.

Verse 13 calls all creation to *praise the name of the LORD* (Ps. 145:21) and once again provides the reason why with *for (kî;* see v. 5).[4] The phrase *the earth and the heavens* in the last colon of the verse occurs elsewhere in the Old Testament only in Gen. 2:4b, the beginning of the so-called second creation account.

Verse 14 focuses again on Israel, the *hesed ones* of God (see Psalm 147) and looks forward to Psalm 149, in which the children of Israel are called upon to "rejoice in their king" (149:2).

Psalm 148 is an invitation for all of creation and its inhabitants — the heavens and the earth — to join in the praise of God. All are included; none are excluded in the call. Clifford observes, "Though moderns tend to think of worship as the response of rational creatures to their God, this psalm rather regards worship as virtually inherent in the world's structure."[5] All creation, animate and inanimate, can participate in celebration of the God of the creation. St. Francis of Assisi (d. 1226) wrote a hymn he titled "The Song of Brother Sun." Its words, adapted to the modern hymn "All Creatures of Our God and King," were inspired by the creation psalms of the Hebrew Psalter: "All creatures of our God and King . . . thou burning sun . . . thou silver moon . . . thou rushing wind . . . ye lights of evening . . . ye folk of tender heart . . . O praise him."

NANCY DECLAISSÉ-WALFORD

4. For a discussion of the significance of "name" in the Old Testament, see the commentary for Ps. 113:1b-4.

5. *Psalms 73–150,* p. 313.

Psalm 149: Sing to the Lord a New Song

Psalm 149 is the fourth of the five "Final Hallel" psalms that form the closing doxology of the Hebrew Psalter. It is a community hymn, as are Psalms 147 and 150. It begins and ends with "hallelujah," as do the other four "Final Hallel" psalms. But it seems out of place in the collection of final doxological psalms, since its focus is on God's vengeance on the nations in defense of the Israelites. Mays writes that Psalm 149 "seems to be a hymn in preparation for holy war."[1] In *The Message of the Psalms,* Brueggemann remarks, "I do not know what to make of this, for it is quite unexpected in the hymns."[2]

Psalm 149 is often viewed as a companion to Psalm 2, a royal psalm whose theme is the sovereignty of God over the king of Israel and all the kings of the earth. In Ps. 2:10-12, the psalmist admonishes:

So now, O kings, be wise!
   Be warned, O rulers of the earth!
Serve the Lord in fear!
   In trembling kiss his feet!
Lest he be angry and you perish in the way,
   for his anger burns quickly.

Kings and rulers are warned of the anger and wrath of God against those who do not serve him. In Psalm 149, God's *hesed ones* (vv. 1, 5, 9) will carry out the vengeance of God on the *nations* and their *kings* and *great ones.* McCann writes that the psalm's "theological thrust is to assert God's universal sovereignty and to invite God's people to join God at God's work in the world."[3] Verse 9 defines "God's work in the world" as *to carry out the justice that is written.*

Psalm 149 may be divided into two stanzas:

A song of praise in the gathering of the *hesed* ones (vv. 1-4)
      High praises with a two-edged sword in their hand (vv. 5-9)

1 *Hallelujah!*
Sing to the LORD *a new song,*
   his praise in the gathering of the hesed *ones.*
2 *Let Israel be glad in his doings;*
   let the children of Zion rejoice in their king.

1. *Psalms,* p. 446.
2. P. 166.
3. "The Book of Psalms," pp. 1276-77.

3 *Let them praise his name with dancing;*
with timbrel and lyre let them make music to him.
4 *For the* LORD *takes pleasure in his people;*
he adorns those who suffer with help.

5 *Let the* hesed *ones rejoice in glory;*
let them shout with joy upon their beds
6 *with the high praises of God in their throat*
and a two-edged sword in their hand;
7 *in order to carry out vengeance on the nations,*
chastisement on the peoples;
8 *in order to bind their kings with chains*
and their great ones with fetters of iron;
9 *in order to carry out on them the justice that is written.*
This is the splendor for all of his hesed *ones.*
Hallelujah!

1-4 The tone of the first four verses of Psalm 149 is much in keeping with the tone of the other Final Hallel psalms. The psalm-singers call on the gathered *hesed ones* to sing *a new song (šîr ḥādāš),* a phrase that occurs in two of the enthronement psalms of the Psalter, Pss. 96:1 and 98:1.[4] Terrien maintains that the phrase "new song" does not indicate a song tune that has never been heard before, but rather refers to the beginning of a new era, a new epoch in history.[5] The "new songs" of Psalms 96, 98, and 149 refer to the reign of God, rather than a king of the line of David, as sovereign over Israel.

Verses 1-4 are filled with images of singing and dancing — a *new song* and a song of *praise* (v. 1); *dancing* and making music *with timbrel and lyre* (v. 3). Singing and dancing were common parts of cultic activity in the ancient Near East. In Exod. 15:20, Miriam "took a tambourine in her hand," and all the women followed, "with tambourines and with dancing." In 2 Sam. 6:14, we read that when the ark of the covenant was being brought into Jerusalem, "David danced before the LORD with all his might." According to 1 Chr. 25:4-6, David appointed temple musicians like the sons and daughters of Heman, who were "under the direction of their father for the music in the house of the LORD with cymbals, harps, and lyres for the service of the house of God."

Verse 4 announces the twofold reason for praise. First, the Lord *takes pleasure (rôṣeh) in his people.* The verbal root of *rôṣeh (rāṣâ)* means "take plea-

4. For a discussion of the *Gattung* "enthronement psalm," see the Introduction to the Commentary.

5. *The Psalms,* p. 924.

sure in, be favorable to, be well disposed toward." Second, the Lord *adorns (pā'ar)* those who suffer with help. The word translated *adorn* is a denominative verb from *p^{e}'ēr,* an Egyptian loanword into Hebrew that means "headdress, head wrap" and is used to describe the head coverings of upperclass women of Jerusalem in Isa. 3:20; of priests in Exod. 39:28; Ezek. 44:18; and of a bridegroom in Isa. 61:10.

5-9 Verses 5 and 6 resume the call to praise of vv. 1-3 and summon the *hesed ones* to *rejoice* and *shout with joy upon their beds* with the *high praises of God in their throat.* And then the reader/hearer encounters a disturbing phrase for this celebratory community hymn: *and a two-edged sword in their hand* (v. 6b). Verse 6 marks a turning point in Psalm 149. Here words of celebration are mixed with words of *vengeance.*

The last three verses of the psalm (vv. 7-9) begin with infinitive construct verbal forms that outline the reasons for the two-edged swords in the hands of the *hesed* ones: *in order to carry out vengeance* and *chastisement, in order to bind their kings* and *their great ones,* and *in order to carry out justice.* The word translated *vengeance* is from the Hebrew root *nāqam,* used frequently in reference to human revenge, but most often in speaking about the vengeance of God upon those who violate the basic order and balance of the created world (see Deut. 32:35; Ps. 58:10; Isa. 34:8).

Verse 9's reason for the two-edged sword of v. 6 is *in order to carry out on them the justice that is written.* The system of righting wrongs outlined in the torah that God gave to Moses at Sinai is one that metes out justice and equity for all who embrace it. In the second colon of v. 9, the *justice* and equity of God is given to the *hesed* ones of God as *splendor.* The word translated as *splendor* is *hādār,* a word used in most of its occurrences in the Psalter to refer to the "splendor" of God and the kings of ancient Israel (see Pss. 29:4; 45:4; 111:3; 145:5, 12), but used in Psalm 149 as it is in 8:5 in reference to all humanity. Psalm 149 continues the impulse of Book Five of the Psalter in suggesting that the responsibilities and benefits of kingship (whether divine or earthly) now belong to the *hesed* ones of God.

Psalm 149's "vengeance" language is difficult for many twenty-first-century Christians to embrace. Mays reminds us that the vengeance called for in Psalm 149 is not "in the emotion of a hate reaction but in the sphere of legal custom. 'Vengeance' was an act to enforce or restore justice where the regular legal processes were not competent or had failed."[6] And the Old Testament tells us over and over that vengeance is not the prerogative of the people, but belongs to God (see Deut. 32:35-36; Jer. 46:10; Pss. 94:1; 99:8). The king, as God's chosen ruler on earth, was the means by which God carried out "the justice that is written"; in Psalm 149, the *hesed ones* become the means.

6. *Psalms,* pp. 302-3.

The author of the book of Hebrews wrote that "the word of God is living and active, sharper than any two-edged sword" (4:12). As Christians today seek God's justice in the world, words can be a powerful weapon against those who cause or allow others to suffer injustice.

Nancy deClaissé-Walford

Psalm 150: Let Every Breathing Thing Praise the Lord

Psalm 150 is the last of the five "Final Hallel" psalms that close the Hebrew Psalter. It, like the collection's other four psalms, begins and ends with "Praise the Lord" *(hal^{e}lû yāh),* but in Psalm 150 the verb "praise" *(hālal)* occurs thirteen times, forming a resounding doxological close to the Psalter.[1] The first two verses of the psalm describe the God to whom the worshippers are called to offer praise; vv. 3-5 describe the method by which the worshippers are to offer praise; and the final verse of the psalm includes all of creation in the praise of God.

Praise him as befits his exceeding greatness (vv. 1-2)
Praise him with loud crashing cymbals (vv. 3-5)
Let every breathing thing praise (v. 6)

1 *Hallelujah!*
Praise God in his sanctuary;
praise him in the firmament of his strength.
2 *Praise him for his mighty deeds;*
praise him as befits his exceeding greatness.

3 *Praise him with the blast of the horn;*
praise him with harp and lyre.
4 *Praise him with timbrel and dance;*
praise him with strings and pipe.
5 *Praise him with clashing cymbals;*
praise him with loud crashing cymbals.

6 *Let every breathing thing praise the Lord!*
Hallelujah!

1-2 The temple in Jerusalem was viewed by the Israelites as the dwelling place of God (or the name of God) on earth.[2] The singers of Psalm 150 refer to the temple as *the sanctuary,* literally, "holy place" *(qōḏeš).* In the act of worship, the sacred and the mundane meet and commune, and for a holy time the boundaries are transcended. Verse 2 offers two reasons for praise — God's *mighty deeds (g^{e}ḇûrâ)* and *exceeding greatness (gōḏel).*

3-5 Verses 3-5 detail the method by which the worshippers are to offer praise to God. Music and dancing were an integral part of worship in

1. The phrase "hallelujah" occurs twelve times in Ps. 148.
2. See Exod. 40:34-35; Deut. 12:10-11; 14:22-23; 1 Kgs. 8:10-13; Pss. 74:2; 135:21.

the ancient Near East.[3] In the other four doxological psalms of Book Five, worshippers announce their intent to sing and make music to God (see Pss. 146:2; 147:1, 7; 149:1, 3), but Psalm 150 details the types of instruments to be used in worship. Clifford describes the array as "a full symphony" in which "every instrument of the orchestra joins the human voice in giving praise."[4]

6 Verse 6's call to *every breathing thing* to praise the Lord echoes and envelops the proclamation by the singer of Psalm 145 that "The praise of the LORD my mouth will speak, and all flesh will bless his holy name" (v. 21). We may speculate about what constitutes *every breathing thing* (v. 6) in contrast to "all flesh" (145:21), but the clear intent of Psalm 150 seems to be that "all creation" will pause and praise the Lord.

The Hebrew Psalter begins with the wisdom words of Psalm 1, calling on the faithful to delight in and meditate on the torah. The story of the Psalter is the story of God's *hesed* care for the Israelites and for all of creation. At the end of the story, the faithful, along with all of creation, offer absolute praise to God.[5]

God calls Christians today to delight in and meditate upon the story of God's dealings with our ancestors in the faith. God also calls us to delight in and meditate upon God's *hesed* care for us and our communities of faith. When we accept the story as our own, accept God as our Lord, the only response is unbridled praise. Hallelujah.

NANCY DECLAISSÉ-WALFORD

3. For a full discussion, see the commentary for Ps. 149:1-4.

4. *Psalms 73–150,* p. 319.

5. For an excellent treatment of these "edges" of the Psalter, see Walter Brueggemann, "Bounded By Obedience and Praise," in *The Psalms and the Life of Faith,* pp. 189-213.

Index of Authors

Index of Names and Subjects

Index of Scripture and Other Ancient Literature